JEPPESEN.
A BOEING COMPANY

GUIDED FLIGHT DISCOVERY
INSTRUMENT
COMMERCIAL

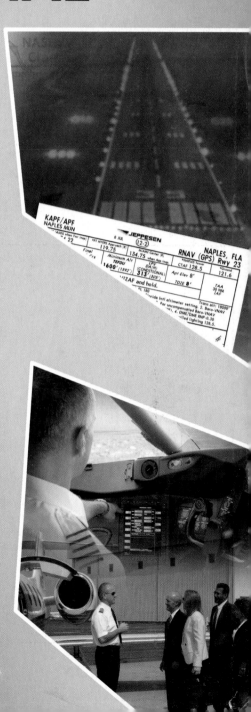

The charts, tables, and graphs used in this publication are for illustration purposes only and cannot be used for navigation or to determine actual aircraft performance.

Cover Photo
Piper Mirage in flight courtesy of Piper Aircraft, Inc.

ISBN - 978-0-88487-130-9

Jeppesen
55 Inverness Drive East
Englewood, CO 80112-5498
Web site: www.jeppesen.com
Email: Captain@jeppesen.com
Copyright © Jeppesen
All Rights Reserved.
Published 1998, 1999, 2000, 2001, 2002, 2003,
2004, 2006, 2012, 2013, 2016

To Paul Sanderson, whose pioneering efforts in aviation training and education inspired generations of pilots and aviation enthusiasts. Since 1956, Paul has made numerous contributions to the development of innovative new products and training courses. His devoted service is greatly appreciated and continues to benefit all of us in aviation.

Acknowledgments

This textbook could not have been produced without the tireless commitment of the Guided Flight Discovery team members listed below.

Writers/Editors

Mike Abbott
Julie (Boatman) Filucci
Dave Chance
Grace Cooke
Jerry Farrell
Michelle Gable
Judi Glenn
Liz Kailey
Jeffrey Marten
George McCray
David Navarro
Jim Mowery
Chad Pomering
James Powell
Matt Ruwe
Dave Schoeman
Ken Shockley
Richard Snyder
Chuck Stout
Anthony Werner
Pat Willits

Graphic Designers

Jennifer Bebernes
Pat Brogan
Jeff Cochran
Paul Gallaway
Richard Hahn
Veronica Mahr
Dean McBournie
Larry Montano
Curtis Osborne
Rick Patterson
Karen Sandenwater
Scott Saunders
Jay Weets

Photographers

Gary Kennedy
Virgil Poleschook
Rick Schoenbeck

Welcome to Guided Flight Discovery

Guided Flight Discovery is a new concept in pilot training designed to make your professional training exciting and enjoyable. This revolutionary system is comprehensive, application-oriented, and it leads you logically through essential aeronautical knowledge areas. The program exposes you to a variety of useful, interesting information which will enhance and expand your understanding of the professional world of aviation.

Although each element of the Guided Flight Discovery Pilot Training System can be used separately, you obtain maximum benefit by using all of the individual components together in a systems approach. To help you organize your studies efficiently and get the most out of your training, Guided Flight Discovery provides cross-references that direct you to related study materials. Here are the main components of the Instrument/Commercial Program.

INSTRUMENT/COMMERCIAL TEXTBOOK

The *Instrument/Commercial* textbook is your primary source for initial study and review. The text contains complete and concise explanations of the advanced concepts and ideas that every professional pilot needs to know. The subjects are logically organized to build upon previously introduced topics. Discovery Insets that are strategically placed throughout the chapters expand upon the core material and add depth and color to your understanding. Periodically, human factors principles are presented in Human Factors Insets to help you understand how your mind and body function while you fly. Throughout the manual, concepts that directly relate to FAA test questions are highlighted by FAA Question Insets. You can evaluate your understanding of material introduced in a particular section by completing the associated review questions. Finally, Chapter 14 — Commercial Maneuvers uses colorful graphics and step-by-step procedure descriptions to help you visualize and understand each maneuver. Performance standards from the Commercial PTS also are included. The Preface offers a more detailed explanation of the text and how to use its unique features.

INSTRUMENT AND COMMERCIAL ONLINE COURSES

Available from JeppDirect.com, the Instrument Pilot and Commercial Pilot online courses work as complete ground schools, providing all academic content with exams, interactive maneuvers lessons in the Commercial course, and outlines for every flight lesson. You can use the online courses together with the textbook and other Jeppesen products to enhance your learning experience.

INSTRUMENT/COMMERCIAL SYLLABUS

The syllabus permits concurrent or separate enrollments in the instrument rating course and the commercial pilot certification course. The instrument segment provides a variety of training options for operators and students including an aviation training device (ATD), a flight training device (FTD), and the airplane. The commercial segment includes single-engine complex and multi-engine airplane training. Ground and flight lessons are coordinated to ensure that your training progresses smoothly and that you are always introduced to topics during ground training before you apply them in the airplane.

SUPPORT MATERIALS

You can use a variety of support materials to increase your understanding of the subject matter for professional pilot training. These resources are described briefly below.

INSTRUMENT RATING AND COMMERCIAL PILOT AIRMEN KNOWLEDGE TEST GUIDES

These valuable study tools provide you with FAA questions that might be included on the Instrument Rating and Commercial Pilot computerized test. The guides provide answers and explanations for each question to allow you to instantly check your understanding of required material.

INSTRUMENT/COMMERCIAL DVD VIDEOS

The Instrument/Commercial DVDs present instrument concepts, airplane systems, and commercial maneuvers. The dynamic videos use state-of-the-art graphics and animation, as well as dramatic aerial photography to help explain complex ideas.

FLIGHT SCHOOL SUPPORT MATERIALS

Flight schools that use the Guided Flight Discovery Pilot Training System may provide a variety of additional resources and instructional support materials. Designed specifically to provide you with a well administered, quality training program, Guided Flight Discovery flight school support materials help foster an environment that maximizes your potential for understanding and comprehension on your way to becoming a professional pilot. Some of these resources are described below.

AVIATION TRAINING DEVICE (ATD)

Many flight schools provide access to an aviation training device. ATDs are designed to facilitate your instrument training and help you to build your skills. They can give you a head start on many instrument maneuvers and procedures.

INSTRUCTOR'S GUIDE

The *Instructor's Guide* is available for use by flight instructors and flight school operators. The Instrument/Commercial portion helps flight training professionals effectively implement the Guided Flight Discovery advanced courses.

Preface

The purpose of the *Instrument/Commercial* textbook is to provide you with the most complete explanations of aeronautical concepts for professional pilots through the use of colorful illustrations, full-color photos, and a variety of innovative design techniques. The *Instrument/Commercial* textbook and other Guided Flight Discovery materials are closely coordinated to make learning fun and effective. To help you organize your study, the *Instrument/Commercial* textbook is divided into four parts:

PART I — DISCOVERING NEW HORIZONS

This part introduces the information you need to begin your professional pilot journey. The first chapter, Building Professional Experience, answers many of your questions about the training process and introduces advanced human factor concepts. Principles of Instrument Flight, Chapter 2, is the foundation for becoming an instrument-rated pilot. Chapter 3 — The Flight Environment introduces air traffic control for instrument flight and emphasizes ATC clearances.

PART II — INSTRUMENT CHARTS AND PROCEDURES

Chapters 4 through 7 of Part II provide a broad introduction to instrument charts in the same sequence you would use them on an instrument flight — departure, enroute, arrival, and approach. Procedural sections follow each chart presentation topic so you can immediately relate operational factors to the interpretation of IFR chart symbology and other features. Chapter 8 — Instrument Approaches combines approach chart formats with an operationally oriented narrative designed to show you how to precisely fly various types of instrument procedures.

PART III — AVIATION WEATHER AND IFR FLIGHT OPERATIONS

In Part III, you become familiar with aviation weather from the perspective of IFR flight operations. In Chapter 9 — Meteorology you will learn how to minimize your exposure to hazardous weather phenomena by using weather reports, forecasts, and charts in the planning phase and in flight. Chapter 10 — IFR Flight Considerations provides a framework for coping with the complex options presented by IFR flight operation, including emergencies.

PART IV — COMMERCIAL PILOT OPERATIONS

Specialized information for commercial pilots characterizes the content of Part IV. Chapter 11 — Advanced Systems provides operational insight for complex and high performance aircraft. Chapter 12 — Aerodynamics and Performance Limitations helps you define the flight envelope and prepares you for predicting performance and controlling weight and balance as you move up to higher performance aircraft. Chapters 13 and 14 — Commercial Flight Considerations and Commercial Maneuvers conclude this part with in-depth analyses of emergency procedures, commercial decision making, and performance of precision flight maneuvers.

Table of Contents

HOW THE TEXTBOOK WORKS

The *Instrument/Commercial* textbook is structured to highlight important topics and concepts and promote an effective and efficient study/review method of learning. To get the most out of your manual, as well as the entire Guided Flight Discovery Pilot Training System, review the major elements in this text.

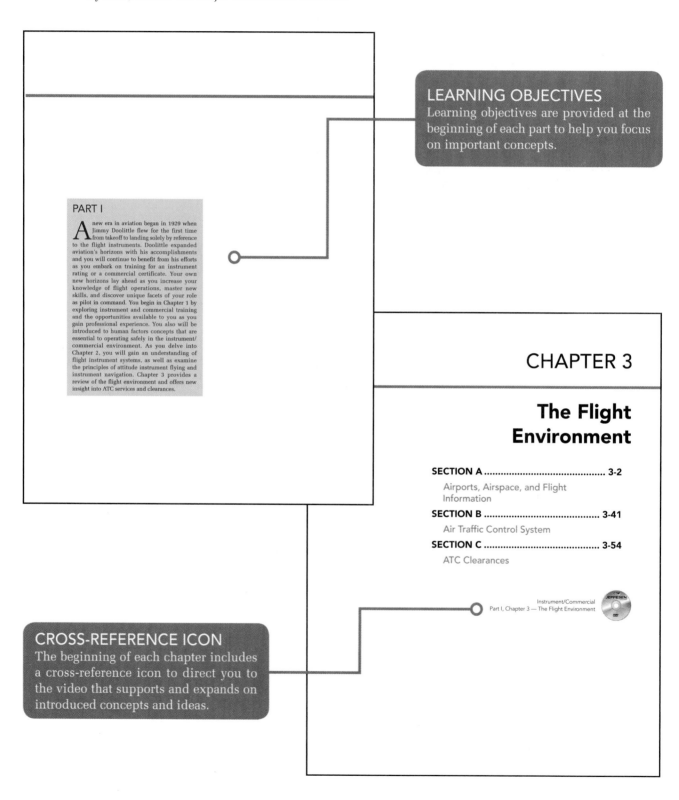

LEARNING OBJECTIVES

Learning objectives are provided at the beginning of each part to help you focus on important concepts.

PART I

A new era in aviation began in 1929 when Jimmy Doolittle flew for the first time from takeoff to landing solely by reference to the flight instruments. Doolittle expanded aviation's horizons with his accomplishments and you will continue to benefit from his efforts as you embark on training for an instrument rating or a commercial certificate. Your own new horizons lay ahead as you increase your knowledge of flight operations, master new skills, and discover unique facets of your role as pilot in command. You begin in Chapter 1 by exploring instrument and commercial training and the opportunities available to you as you gain professional experience. You also will be introduced to human factors concepts that are essential to operating safely in the instrument/ commercial environment. As you delve into Chapter 2, you will gain an understanding of flight instrument systems, as well as examine the principles of attitude instrument flying and instrument navigation. Chapter 3 provides a review of the flight environment and offers new insight into ATC services and clearances.

CHAPTER 3

The Flight Environment

Instrument/Commercial
Part I, Chapter 3 — The Flight Environment

CROSS-REFERENCE ICON

The beginning of each chapter includes a cross-reference icon to direct you to the video that supports and expands on introduced concepts and ideas.

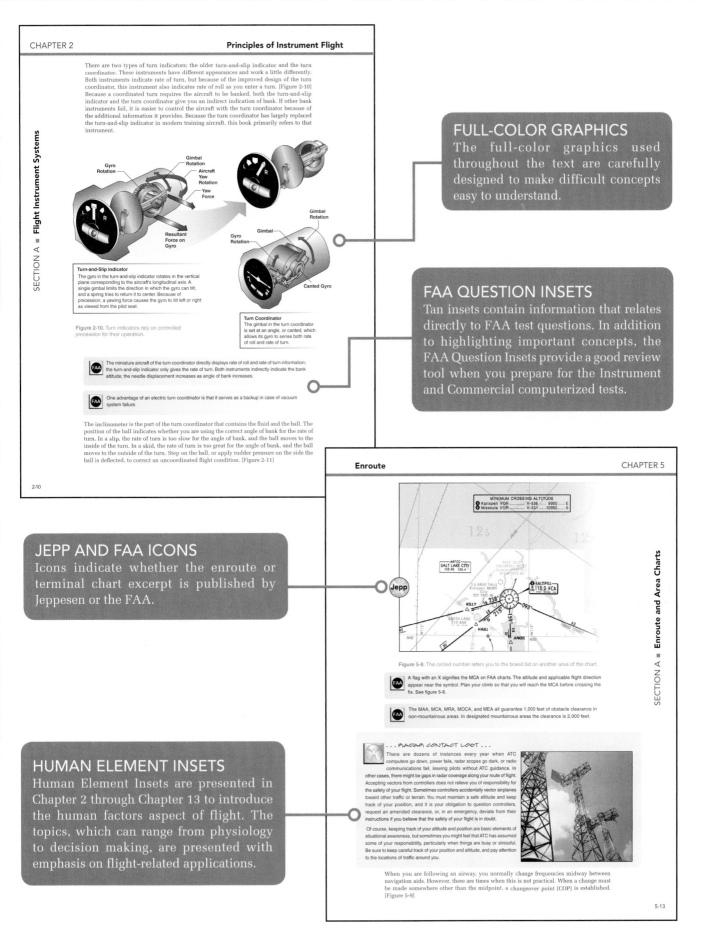

SECTION A ■ Flight Instrument Systems

There are two types of turn indicators; the older turn-and-slip indicator and the turn coordinator. These instruments have different appearances and work a little differently. Both instruments indicate rate of turn, but because of the improved design of the turn coordinator, this instrument also indicates rate of roll as you enter a turn. [Figure 2-10] Because a coordinated turn requires the aircraft to be banked, both the turn-and-slip indicator and the turn coordinator give you an indirect indication of bank. If other bank instruments fail, it is easier to control the aircraft with the turn coordinator because of the additional information it provides. Because the turn coordinator has largely replaced the turn-and-slip indicator in modern training aircraft, this book primarily refers to that instrument.

Turn-and-Slip Indicator
The gyro in the turn-and-slip indicator rotates in the vertical plane corresponding to the aircraft's longitudinal axis. A single gimbal limits the direction in which the gyro can tilt, and a spring tries to return it to center. Because of precession, a yawing force causes the gyro to tilt left or right as viewed from the pilot seat.

Turn Coordinator
The gimbal in the turn coordinator is set at an angle, or canted, which allows its gyro to sense both rate of roll and rate of turn.

Figure 2-10. Turn indicators rely on controlled precession for their operation.

The miniature aircraft of the turn coordinator directly displays rate of roll and rate of turn information; the turn-and-slip indicator only gives the rate of turn. Both instruments indirectly indicate the bank attitude; the needle displacement increases as angle of bank increases.

One advantage of an electric turn coordinator is that it serves as a backup in case of vacuum system failure.

The inclinometer is the part of the turn coordinator that contains the fluid and the ball. The position of the ball indicates whether you are using the correct angle of bank for the rate of turn. In a slip, the rate of turn is too slow for the angle of bank, and the ball moves to the inside of the turn. In a skid, the rate of turn is too great for the angle of bank, and the ball moves to the outside of the turn. Step on the ball, or apply rudder pressure on the side the ball is deflected, to correct an uncoordinated flight condition. [Figure 2-11]

2-10

FULL-COLOR GRAPHICS
The full-color graphics used throughout the text are carefully designed to make difficult concepts easy to understand.

FAA QUESTION INSETS
Tan insets contain information that relates directly to FAA test questions. In addition to highlighting important concepts, the FAA Question Insets provide a good review tool when you prepare for the Instrument and Commercial computerized tests.

JEPP AND FAA ICONS
Icons indicate whether the enroute or terminal chart excerpt is published by Jeppesen or the FAA.

HUMAN ELEMENT INSETS
Human Element Insets are presented in Chapter 2 through Chapter 13 to introduce the human factors aspect of flight. The topics, which can range from physiology to decision making, are presented with emphasis on flight-related applications.

SECTION A ■ Enroute and Area Charts

Figure 5-8. The circled number refers you to the boxed list on another area of the chart.

A flag with an X signifies the MCA on FAA charts. The altitude and applicable flight direction appear near the symbol. Plan your climb so that you will reach the MCA before crossing the fix. See figure 5-6.

The MAA, MCA, MRA, MOCA, and MEA all guarantee 1,000 feet of obstacle clearance in non-mountainous areas. In designated mountainous areas the clearance is 2,000 feet.

. . . RADAR CONTACT LOST . . .
There are dozens of instances every year when ATC computers go down, power fails, radar scopes go dark, or radio communications fail, leaving pilots without ATC guidance. In other cases, there might be gaps in radar coverage along your route of flight. Accepting vectors from controllers does not relieve you of responsibility for the safety of your flight. Sometimes controllers accidentally vector airplanes toward other traffic or terrain. You must maintain a safe altitude and keep track of your position, and it is your obligation to question controllers, request an amended clearance, or, in an emergency, deviate from their instructions if you believe that the safety of your flight is in doubt.

Of course, keeping track of your altitude and position are basic elements of situational awareness, but sometimes you might feel that ATC has assumed some of your responsibility, particularly when things are busy or stressful. Be sure to keep careful track of your position and altitude, and pay attention to the locations of traffic around you.

When you are following an airway, you normally change frequencies midway between navigation aids. However, there are times when this is not practical. When a change must be made somewhere other than the midpoint, a changeover point (COP) is established. [Figure 5-9]

5-13

HOW THE TEXTBOOK WORKS ■ **Instrument/Commercial**

Departure   CHAPTER 4

Like Ships Passing on the Potomac

Development of radio detection and ranging, commonly referred to as radar, began as early as 1922. Researchers at the Naval Aircraft Laboratory in Washington, D.C. observed radio signals reflecting from ships passing in the Potomac River. [Figure A] Reports on radio echo signals from moving objects led to British involvement with radar in 1935. In 1940, MIT Radiation Laboratory, in conjunction with the British Tizard Mission, mounted a crash program to make microwave radar sets for British night fighter airplanes. These efforts led to further developments such as the military Identification of Friend and Foe (IFF) system, and a talk-down blind landing system for aircraft called Ground Controlled Approach (GCA).

The prototype GCA used microwave radar which provided airplane coordinates to a small analog computer called a director. The director compared the coordinates to those of an ideal glide path and developed error signals on meters monitored by the controller. The controller would give the pilot right-left steering instructions and adjustments to rate of descent until the pilot could see the runway and land.

One of the most spectacular successes for GCA occurred when the Soviets blockaded Berlin during the rainy fall and winter of 1948. With all road, rail, and canal links to West Berlin severed, a military GCA set operated around the clock, bringing in a steady stream of planes carrying thousands of tons of food and fuel. Figure B shows one such aircraft, a Douglas C-54, flying a relief mission during the Berlin Airlift. In the end, the GCA was credited with helping to make the airlift successful and breaking the blockade.

SECTION B ■ Departure Procedures

DISCOVERY INSETS

Beginning with Chapter 2, Discovery Insets throughout the text expand on ideas and concepts presented in the accompanying material. The information presented in each Discovery Inset varies, but is designed to enhance your understanding of the world of aviation. Examples include references to National Transportation Safety Board investigations, aviation history, and thought-provoking questions and answers.

COLOR PHOTOGRAPHS

Color photographs are included to enhance learning and improve understanding.

Building Professional Experience   CHAPTER 1

SECTION B
Advanced Human Factors Concepts

As a private pilot, you have experience in managing the physiological factors that affect you in flight. You also have applied **single-pilot resource management (SRM)** techniques to make effective decisions in the VFR environment. Now, you enter a different realm. In the IFR environment, your workload increases and you use additional resources; relying on avionics, instrumentation, charts, and ATC for aircraft guidance. As a commercial pilot, you will typically fly larger, faster airplanes at higher altitudes so you must manage more complex equipment and systems. You also must gain greater skills in coordinating with crew members and dealing with passengers. [Figure 1-18]

Figure 1-18. You must master SRM skills to meet the demands of the IFR and commercial environments.

This section defines SRM concepts and examines aviation physiology that specifically applies to flight in the IFR and commercial environments. The Human Element Insets located throughout this textbook help you to correlate human factors concepts to specific pilot operations and expand upon the fundamental SRM principles introduced in this section. Chapter 10, Section B — IFR Single-Pilot Resource Management describes how to apply SRM in the IFR environment and Chapter 13, Section B — Commercial Pilot SRM specifically examines SRM in the commercial environment.

SECTION B ■ Advanced Human Factors Concepts

1-29

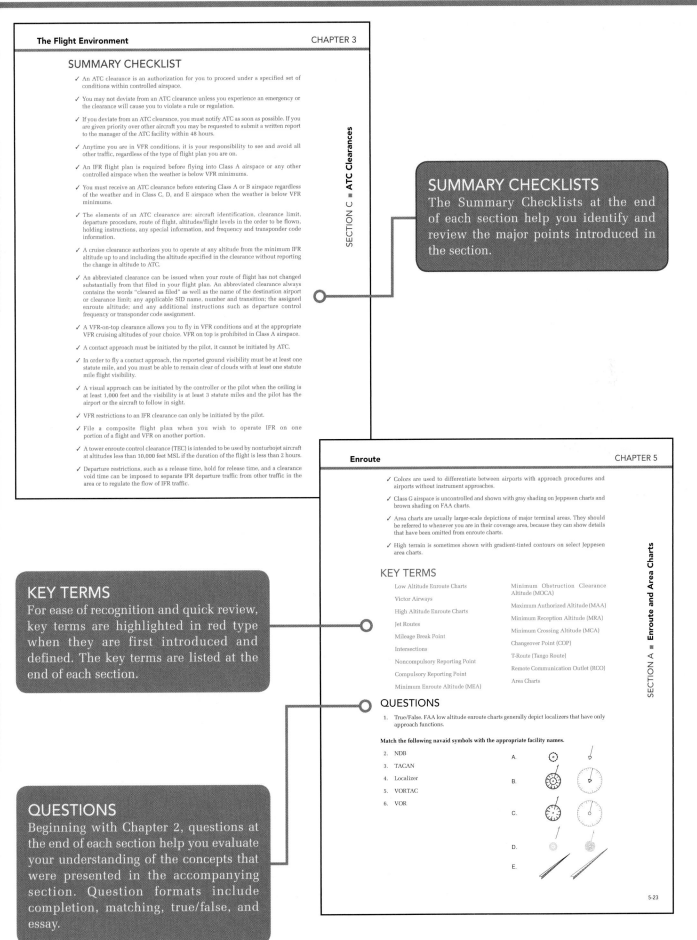

The Flight Environment   CHAPTER 3

SECTION C ■ ATC Clearances

SUMMARY CHECKLIST

✓ An ATC clearance is an authorization for you to proceed under a specified set of conditions within controlled airspace.

✓ You may not deviate from an ATC clearance unless you experience an emergency or the clearance will cause you to violate a rule or regulation.

✓ If you deviate from an ATC clearance, you must notify ATC as soon as possible. If you are given priority over other aircraft you may be requested to submit a written report to the manager of the ATC facility within 48 hours.

✓ Anytime you are in VFR conditions, it is your responsibility to see and avoid all other traffic, regardless of the type of flight plan you are on.

✓ An IFR flight plan is required before flying into Class A airspace or any other controlled airspace when the weather is below VFR minimums.

✓ You must receive an ATC clearance before entering Class A or B airspace regardless of the weather and in Class C, D, and E airspace when the weather is below VFR minimums.

✓ The elements of an ATC clearance are: aircraft identification, clearance limit, departure procedure, route of flight, altitudes/flight levels in the order to be flown, holding instructions, any special information, and frequency and transponder code information.

✓ A cruise clearance authorizes you to operate at any altitude from the minimum IFR altitude up to and including the altitude specified in the clearance without reporting the change in altitude to ATC.

✓ An abbreviated clearance can be issued when your route of flight has not changed substantially from that filed in your flight plan. An abbreviated clearance always contains the words "cleared as filed" as well as the name of the destination airport or clearance limit; any applicable SID name, number and transition; the assigned enroute altitude; and any additional instructions such as departure control frequency or transponder code assignment.

✓ A VFR-on-top clearance allows you to fly in VFR conditions and at the appropriate VFR cruising altitudes of your choice. VFR on top is prohibited in Class A airspace.

✓ A contact approach must be initiated by the pilot, it cannot be initiated by ATC.

✓ In order to fly a contact approach, the reported ground visibility must be at least one statute mile, and you must be able to remain clear of clouds with at least one statute mile flight visibility.

✓ A visual approach can be initiated by the controller or the pilot when the ceiling is at least 1,000 feet and the visibility is at least 3 statute miles and the pilot has the airport or the aircraft to follow in sight.

✓ VFR restrictions to an IFR clearance can only be initiated by the pilot.

✓ File a composite flight plan when you wish to operate IFR on one portion of a flight and VFR on another portion.

✓ A tower enroute control clearance (TEC) is intended to be used by nonturbojet aircraft at altitudes less than 10,000 feet MSL if the duration of the flight is less than 2 hours.

✓ Departure restrictions, such as a release time, hold for release time, and a clearance void time can be imposed to separate IFR departure traffic from other traffic in the area or to regulate the flow of IFR traffic.

SUMMARY CHECKLISTS
The Summary Checklists at the end of each section help you identify and review the major points introduced in the section.

Enroute   CHAPTER 5

✓ Colors are used to differentiate between airports with approach procedures and airports without instrument approaches.

✓ Class G airspace is uncontrolled and shown with gray shading on Jeppesen charts and brown shading on FAA charts.

✓ Area charts are usually larger-scale depictions of major terminal areas. They should be referred to whenever you are in their coverage area, because they can show details that have been omitted from enroute charts.

✓ High terrain is sometimes shown with gradient-tinted contours on select Jeppesen area charts.

KEY TERMS

Low Altitude Enroute Charts

Victor Airways

High Altitude Enroute Charts

Jet Routes

Mileage Break Point

Intersections

Noncompulsory Reporting Point

Compulsory Reporting Point

Minimum Enroute Altitude (MEA)

Minimum Obstruction Clearance Altitude (MOCA)

Maximum Authorized Altitude (MAA)

Minimum Reception Altitude (MRA)

Minimum Crossing Altitude (MCA)

Changeover Point (COP)

T-Route (Tango Route)

Remote Communication Outlet (RCO)

Area Charts

SECTION A ■ Enroute and Area Charts

KEY TERMS
For ease of recognition and quick review, key terms are highlighted in red type when they are first introduced and defined. The key terms are listed at the end of each section.

QUESTIONS

1. True/False. FAA low altitude enroute charts generally depict localizers that have only approach functions.

Match the following navaid symbols with the appropriate facility names.

2. NDB

3. TACAN

4. Localizer

5. VORTAC

6. VOR

A.

B.

C.

D.

E.

5-23

QUESTIONS
Beginning with Chapter 2, questions at the end of each section help you evaluate your understanding of the concepts that were presented in the accompanying section. Question formats include completion, matching, true/false, and essay.

HOW THE TEXTBOOK WORKS ■ **Instrument/Commercial**

Discovering New Horizons

Flying by instruments soon outgrew the early experimental phase. It became a practical reality, and aviation entered a new era. I was grateful for the opportunity to participate in the initial experiments. This work was, I believe, my most significant contribution to aviation.

— James H. "Jimmy" Doolittle

PART I

A new era in aviation began in 1929 when Jimmy Doolittle flew for the first time from takeoff to landing solely by reference to the flight instruments. Doolittle expanded aviation's horizons with his accomplishments and you will continue to benefit from his efforts as you embark on training for an instrument rating or a commercial certificate. Your own new horizons lay ahead as you increase your knowledge of flight operations, master new skills, and discover unique facets of your role as pilot in command. You begin in Chapter 1 by exploring instrument and commercial training and the opportunities available to you as you gain professional experience. You also will be introduced to human factors concepts that are essential to operating safely in the instrument/commercial environment. As you delve into Chapter 2, you will gain an understanding of flight instrument systems, as well as examine the principles of attitude instrument flying and instrument navigation. Chapter 3 provides a review of the flight environment and offers new insight into ATC services and clearances.

CHAPTER 1

Building Professional Experience

SECTION A

Instrument/Commercial Training and Opportunities

If I have seen further it is by standing upon the shoulders of Giants.

— Sir Isaac Newton

I believe that simple flight at least is possible to man and the experiments and investigations of a large number of independent workers will result in the accumulation of information and knowledge and skill which will finally lead to accomplished flight… I wish to avail myself of all that is already known and then if possible add my mite to help on the future worker who will attain final success.

— Wilbur Wright

The future is constructed by pioneers who build upon the knowledge of those who came before. Sir Isaac Newton discovered basic principles of motion. Wilbur and Orville Wright used those principles to construct a flying machine. To design innovative aircraft, create revolutionary technology, and discover new flying techniques each aviation pioneer sees further by standing on the shoulders of such giants as Leonardo daVinci, Otto Lilienthal, the Wright Brothers, and Charles Lindbergh.

As you begin training to earn an instrument rating or commercial pilot certificate, you are poised to take full advantage of the wisdom of those who have blazed the aviation trail. Continue to follow their flight path, and build upon the knowledge and skills that you have already gained as a pilot. Look back into aviation history and then direct your gaze forward to your future. It is time now for *you* to see further.

1914

January 1, 1914 — The first scheduled passenger-service airline in the United States is born. The fare for the trip from Tampa to St. Petersburg, Florida is five dollars.

1918

May 15, 1918 — The first standard airmail route in the United States is established between New York City and Washington, D.C.

1927

July 1, 1927 — Having successfully bid for the transcontinental airmail route from Chicago to San Francisco, the Boeing Airplane Company begins service flying the B-40, a new Boeing-produced airplane powered by the latest air-cooled Pratt and Whitney 400-horsepower Wasp radial engines.

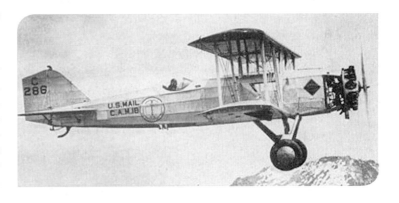

1928

1928 — Edwin A. Link develops the Link Trainer flight simulator as a means of providing affordable flight training to pilots without ever leaving the ground.

SECTION A ■ Instrument/Commercial Training and Opportunities

September 24, 1929 — Jimmy Doolittle makes the first totally blind flight from takeoff to landing in the NY-2 Husky biplane.

1929

Courtesy of the U.S. Air Force

1933

1933 — Boeing develops the Model 247, the first passenger airliner with an autopilot, pneumatically operated de-icing equipment, a variable-pitch propeller, and retractable landing gear.

With 7 stops, the Model 247 completes the trip between New York and Los Angeles in 20 hours, 7 1/2 hours less than the best previous airliner time.

1934 — Elrey B. Jeppesen begins publishing the first airway manuals, which provide pilots with valuable navigation information, airport elevations, heights of obstructions, and runway lengths. Each manual sells for ten dollars.

1934

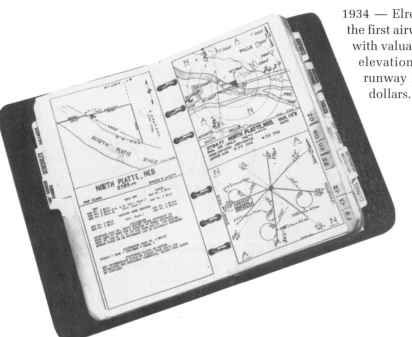

1935

March 15, 1935 — Wiley Post is the first pilot to take advantage of the high winds of the jet stream. Wearing a pressure suit he designed with BF Goodrich, Post covers 2,035 miles in his Lockheed Vega, the *Winnie Mae*, at an average groundspeed of 279 miles per hour, 100 miles per hour faster than the airplane's normal speed.

Courtesy of United Technologies Archive

1935

December 1, 1935 — The first air traffic control center is established at Newark, New Jersey. Initially run by the airlines, less than a year later the Bureau of Air Commerce arranges to take over air traffic control.

1936

1936 — The Douglas DC-3 enters commercial service with American Airlines. The DC-3 dominated airline travel for decades afterward, and the C-47 military cargo version was cited as one of the key factors that led to Allied victory in World War II. More than 10,000 were built, and many are still in everyday cargo service all over the world.

Courtesy of the U.S. Air Force

1949

July, 1949 — Beginning a new era in commercial aviation, the world's first jet airliner, the deHavilland Comet, takes its maiden flight. In 1952, the Comet enters service with the British Overseas Airways Corporation but tragically, in 1954, two Comets are ripped apart in mid-air due to explosive decompression. All of the aircraft were grounded until the problems were corrected.

SECTION A ■ Instrument/Commercial Training and Opportunities

1955

1955 — The Boeing 707, the first jet airliner built in the United States, is purchased by Pan American for passenger service beginning in 1958. The 707 cuts intercontinental travel time almost in half.

People thought we were crazy. — Juan Tripp, Pan American president regarding the first order of B-707s

1958

August 23, 1958 — Prompted by recent midair collisions, the Federal Aviation Act is passed. This action creates the Federal Aviation Agency, an independent government organization that has the sole responsibility for developing and maintaining a common civil-military system of air navigation and air traffic control. In 1966, the agency becomes the Federal Aviation Administration within the Department of Transportation.

Courtesy of Boeing Archives

1969

February 9, 1969 — The first jumbo jet, the Boeing 747, takes to the air for the first time, opening up the world to the traveling masses. The original B-747 is 225 feet long, has a tail as tall as a 6-story building, and can carry 3,400 pieces of baggage in its cargo hold. The airplane contains a ton of air when pressurized.

1976

January 21, 1976 — The Anglo-French Concorde enters commercial airline service, providing the first supersonic travel for paying passengers.

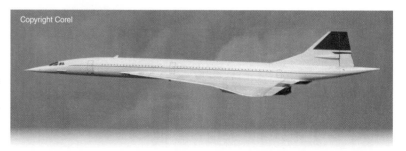

Copyright Corel

1978

1978 — The Airline Deregulation Act frees airlines to compete on routes, pricing, and service. Prices come down and service increases between lucrative hubs, but fares to smaller cities go up, and service to many smaller communities is discontinued.

1993

1993 — The global positioning system (GPS) reaches initial operational capability with a full constellation of 24 satellites.

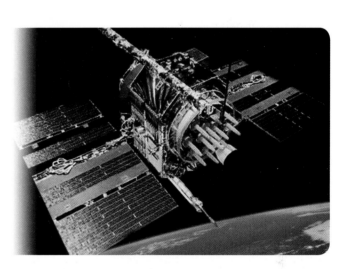

2012

2012 — The SpaceX Dragon becomes the first non-government funded spacecraft to dock with the International Space Station, marking a significant shift from public to commercial development in spaceflight operations.

SECTION A ■ Instrument/Commercial Training and Opportunities

INSTRUMENT FLIGHT

Early airmail planes were not equipped with the proper instruments and navigation equipment to allow pilots to safely fly in clouds or low visibility conditions and weather information often was unavailable. Of the first 40 airmen hired to fly the mail, 31 were killed. A record of this nature was not likely to aid in the development of a reliable, safe air transportation system. As a result, numerous efforts were made to improve the ability of airmail pilots to reach their destinations, day or night, during a wide variety of weather conditions.

> *We had all learned that if we got inside the clouds for any length of time we became confused and fell. We tried things like bobs on the end of a string. I remember one fellow even had a half-full milk bottle that he thought he could use as a level. Of course none of these things worked...we were pretty well convinced that you just couldn't fly blind for any length of time. However, we all learned ways to prolong such flying. We got so that we could climb up through clouds by feel, by bracing our feet and feeling the wind on our cheeks, and things like that. Eventually, even then, we would get confused and the plane would stall and spin down.*

> — Dean Smith, one of the best-known early airmail pilots, as quoted in *The American Heritage History of Flight*

In 1927, the U.S. government began installing the first radio navigation system, the LF/MF four-course radio ranges. This arrangement of multiple radio beacons allowed four courses, called ranges, to be transmitted from one facility To intercept and follow these ranges, pilots listened to the signals on headsets or speakers. The volume of the radio signal and whether it was a constant hum or series of Morse code dots and dashes enabled pilots to determine whether they were approaching or leaving a station and whether they were *on the beam*. [Figure 1-1] However, this system did not allow pilots to fly safely in the clouds. Flying blind with precision required far more sophisticated instruments than any that existed through the 1920s.

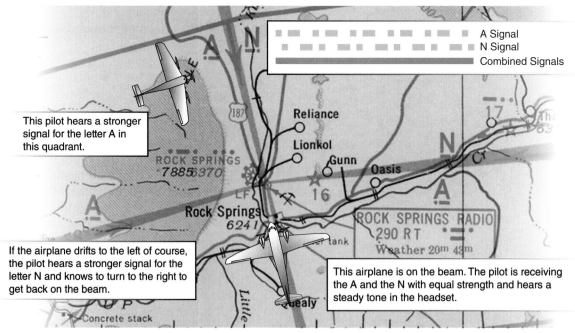

A Signal
N Signal
Combined Signals

This pilot hears a stronger signal for the letter A in this quadrant.

If the airplane drifts to the left of course, the pilot hears a stronger signal for the letter N and knows to turn to the right to get back on the beam.

This airplane is on the beam. The pilot is receiving the A and the N with equal strength and hears a steady tone in the headset.

Figure 1-1. Each station broadcast the Morse code letter A (• —) in two quadrants and the letter N (— •) in the other quadrants. The areas where the signals overlapped formed the four legs of the range.

In 1928, the Daniel Guggenheim Fund for the Promotion of Aeronautics installed a Full Flight Laboratory at Mitchell Field on Long Island, New York. Jimmy Doolittle was assigned to the program and given the task of solving the problems inherent in flying solely by instrument reference, or flying blind. He enlisted the help of Elmer A. Sperry, founder of the Sperry Gyroscope Company, who had harnessed the principles of gyros to build flight instruments. Sperry developed an artificial horizon, which provided a pictorial representation of the airplane's attitude, as well as a directional gyro, which could be set to the magnetic compass.

For a blind landing, an altimeter that was much more precise than any yet available was needed. Doolittle turned to Paul Kollsman who, with the help of a Swiss watch-making firm, developed an altimeter that was accurate to within a few feet.

On September 24, 1929, Jimmy Doolittle, with Ben Kelsey as his safety pilot in the front cockpit of their NY-2 Husky biplane, completed the first flight solely by instrument reference. After a blind takeoff, the flight lasted 15 minutes and included two 180° turns. Doolittle navigated on the beam for part of the exercise prior to setting up for the approach, then successfully made a blind landing. [Figure 1-2]

Courtesy of Honeywell

Courtesy of the U.S. Air Force

Figure 1-2. In the cockpit of Jimmy Doolittle's NY-2, instrument flight was born.

Jimmy has more gifts than any one man has a right to be blessed with. — newspaper man Ernie Pyle, who often accompanied Jimmy Doolittle on stints around the military bases

Courtesy of United Technologies Archive

Jimmy Doolittle in the cockpit of his Laird Super Solution at Newark, New Jersey airport in 1931.

In addition to his instrument flight research, Jimmy Doolittle was a top aeronautical engineer and one of the country's best pursuit and acrobatic pilots. Doolittle won almost every honor in civil aviation including the coveted Mackay Trophy given annually to the most outstanding flier. Flying the Laird Super Solution, he was also the first to win the Bendix Trophy Race from Los Angeles to Cleveland.

In 1940 at age 44, Doolittle was made president of the Institute of Aeronautical Science. Soon after, Major Doolittle became America's first World War II hero as he led 16 planes in a raid that wreaked destruction on Tokyo, Yokohama, Osaka, Kobe, and Nagoya. He was promoted to general and received the Medal of Honor on April 18, 1942.

In addition to improving flight safety by developing instrument systems, the 1920s and 30s realized the genesis of aviation charting. With no aeronautical charts available, many pilots used road maps for navigation. When visibility was limited, early aviators often followed the railroad tracks, which they called *hugging the UP*, or Union Pacific. At times, deteriorating weather conditions forced pilots to land in emergency fields to sit and wait for the skies to improve.

I got the information I needed any place I could — city and county engineers, surveyors, farmers. I drove all the way from Chicago to Oakland, California, and checked out the emergency fields and the obstructions around them, different ways to get in, how far they were from the railroad track and the highway. When the radio ranges came in, I used to take the chief pilot's airplane and go work out a procedure. I guess I devised 80% of the letdown procedures between Oakland and Chicago… I'd come in from a United trip at, say, two or three a.m. and go to the plant where they'd have a stack of letdown procedures, or approach plates, as we started calling them. I'd go all the way through it — I called it dry flying — and check the flight, and initial it. Not one chart went out of there without my initial.

— Elrey B. Jeppesen

In 1930, Elrey B. Jeppesen signed on with Varney Airlines and later with Boeing Air Transport as an airmail pilot to fly the Salt Lake City-Cheyenne/Salt Lake City-Oakland routes. During the winters of 1930 and 1931, Jeppesen experienced the loss of many of his fellow pilots due partly to the lack of published aeronautical information. To improve safety, he began recording pertinent information about flight routes and airports in a 10 cent black notebook. Jeppesen included field lengths, slopes, drainage patterns, information on lights and obstacles, drawings that profiled terrain and airport layouts, as well as phone numbers of local farmers who could provide weather reports. Equipped with an altimeter to record accurate elevations, Jeppesen climbed hills, smokestacks, and water towers on his days off. He flew each leg of the radio ranges and jotted down safe letdown procedures for airports.

Word soon began to circulate that Jeppesen had an amazing record of flight completions and that one of the principal reasons was his secret little black book on airports and landing procedures. Pilots began asking for copies and Jeppesen made them for his friends. However, the demand became so great that he entered the chart publishing business in 1934. [Figure 1-3]

Figure 1-3. Starting in 1934 with his 10 dollar airway manual, the company Elrey B. Jeppesen founded continues to produce charts for airlines and pilots worldwide.

WHY AN INSTRUMENT RATING?

The addition of an instrument rating to your private pilot certificate allows you to fly in a wider range of weather conditions than you can as a VFR pilot. When you are operating under **IFR (instrument flight rules)**, you can fly in the clouds with no reference to the ground or horizon. This is sometimes referred to as flying in **IMC (instrument meteorological conditions)**. The terms IFR, IMC, VFR, and VMC are used frequently in several different ways. Operating under **VFR (visual flight rules)**, you are governed by specific regulations that include minimum cloud clearance and visibility requirements. Instrument flight rules (IFR) govern flight operations in weather conditions below VFR minimums. Instrument and visual flight rules are contained in Title 14 of the United States Code of Federal Regulations (CFR). In this book we refer to these regulations as Federal Aviation Regulations, or FARs. The FARs are divided into numbered parts (Part 61 or Part 91, for example) and each regulation typically is identified by the part number, followed by the specific regulation number, for example: FAR 61.65. [Figure 1-4] When referring to weather conditions, the terms IFR and IMC often are used interchangeably, as are the terms **VMC (visual meteorological conditions)** and VFR. In addition, the terms VFR and IFR can define the type of flight plan under which you are operating. [Figure 1-5]

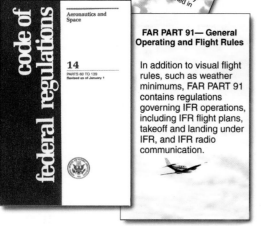

FAR PART 61— Certification: Pilots and Flight Instructors

Instrument rating and currency requirements are contained in FAR PART 61.

Aeronautics and Space

code of federal regulations

14

PARTS 60 TO 139
Revised as of January 1

FAR PART 91— General Operating and Flight Rules

In addition to visual flight rules, such as weather minimums, FAR PART 91 contains regulations governing IFR operations, including IFR flight plans, takeoff and landing under IFR, and IFR radio communication.

Figure 1-4. Instrument and visual flight rules are contained in the Federal Aviation Regulations (FARs).

 FAA You must have an instrument rating to operate under IFR, in weather conditions less than VFR, or in Class A airspace. An instrument rating is required for any flight on an IFR flight plan even if the flight is in VFR conditions.

VFR (Visual Flight Rules) are rules that govern the procedures for conducting flight under visual conditions. The term VFR is also used in the U.S. to indicate weather conditions that are equal to or greater than minimum VFR requirements. In addition, it is used by pilots and controllers to indicate the type of flight plan.

VMC (Visual Meteorological Conditions) are meteorological conditions expressed in terms of visibility, distance from clouds, and ceiling equal to or better than specified minimums.

IFR (Instrument Flight Rules) are rules governing the procedures for conducting instrument flight. This is also a term used by pilots and controllers to indicate the type of flight plan. The International Civil Aviation Organization (ICAO) defines IFR as a set of rules governing the conduct of flight under instrument meteorological conditions.

IMC (Instrument Meteorological Conditions) are meteorological conditions expressed in terms of visibility, distance from clouds, and ceiling less than the minimums specified for visual meteorological conditions.

Figure 1-5. The *Aeronautical Information Manual* (AIM) defines the terms VFR, VMC, IFR, and IMC in the Pilot/Controller Glossary. It is possible for you to be operating on an IFR flight plan in VFR weather conditions.

Although you are provided with more options regarding weather, perhaps the greatest benefit an instrument rating provides is the increase in safety. Instrument training enhances your skill at precisely controlling the aircraft, improves your ability to operate in the complex ATC system, and increases your confidence level. A study of aircraft accidents over an 11-year period showed that continuing, and initiating VFR flight into IMC without an instrument rating were the first and second most prevalent causes of weather-related general aviation accidents. Statistics have shown the risk of a weather-related accident declines as pilots gain instrument flying experience. Pilots with less than 50 hours of instrument time were involved in 58% of all weather accidents, and 47% of fatal weather accidents. As pilots gain more experience (50 to 100 hours of instrument flying time) their risk decreases by more than 80% to a level slightly below 9% of all accidents. [Figure 1-6]

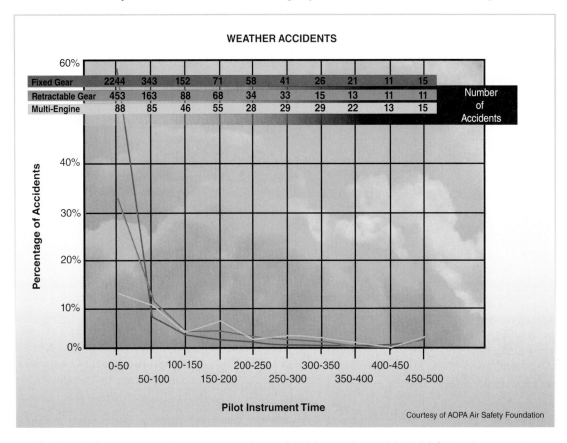

WEATHER ACCIDENTS

	0-50	50-100	100-150	150-200	200-250	250-300	300-350	350-400	400-450	450-500
Fixed Gear	2244	343	152	71	58	41	26	21	11	15
Retractable Gear	453	163	88	68	34	33	15	13	11	11
Multi-Engine	88	85	46	55	28	29	29	22	13	15

Number of Accidents

Pilot Instrument Time

Courtesy of AOPA Air Safety Foundation

Figure 1-6. As instrument time progresses beyond 100 hours, the accident risk factor decreases to a statistically insignificant level.

INSTRUMENT TRAINING

To be eligible for an **instrument rating**, you must have at least a private pilot certificate with an aircraft rating appropriate to the instrument rating sought, be able to read, write, speak, and understand the English language, and complete specific training and flight time requirements described in the FARs. You also must pass a knowledge test and successfully complete a practical test that consists of oral quizzing, performing pilot operations, and executing instrument procedures in the airplane. The FARs require that you receive instruction in specific flight operations and maneuvers, as well as ground instruction in certain knowledge areas. [Figure 1-7]

During instrument training you will

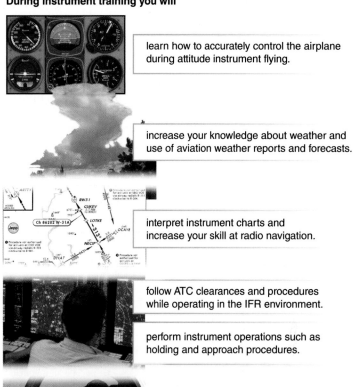

learn how to accurately control the airplane during attitude instrument flying.

increase your knowledge about weather and use of aviation weather reports and forecasts.

interpret instrument charts and increase your skill at radio navigation.

follow ATC clearances and procedures while operating in the IFR environment.

perform instrument operations such as holding and approach procedures.

develop your aeronautical decision-making skills and judgment.

practice emergency procedures.

Figure 1-7. During your instrument training, you will become proficient in controlling the airplane solely with reference to instruments.

You must meet minimum flight hour requirements to apply for an instrument rating. According to FAR Part 61, you must have at least 50 hours of cross-country time as pilot in command (PIC) and 40 hours of actual or simulated instrument time in the areas of operation specified in the regulations. This includes at least 15 hours of instrument flight training from an authorized instructor in the airplane. Some of your instrument time may be conducted with a safety pilot who is appropriately rated for the airplane, enabling you to simulate IMC for practice approaches and other IFR operations. ATC can provide vectors, but no separation service, for procedures that are practiced under VFR. [Figure 1-8]

If your training is accomplished under FAR Part 141, you must have 35 hours of instrument training from an authorized instructor in the areas specified in Appendix C, FAR Part 141 and need not comply with the 50-hour PIC cross-country requirement.

Figure 1-8. Although some of your instrument instruction could occur in actual IFR conditions, you will use a view-limiting device for most of your training in the airplane. This device restricts your view outside the airplane so that you see only the cockpit instruments.

FLYING ON THE GROUND

Part of your instrument training may be accomplished in a **flight simulator**, **flight training device**, or **aviation training device (ATD)**. To count the time toward the instrument rating requirements, an authorized instructor must be present during the simulated flight. The amount of time that may be credited toward your instrument rating depends on the type of device that you are using and on your training curriculum. The FARs specify the maximum hours that can be used in either a flight simulator or flight training device, a flight training device, or an aviation training device (ATD). Advisory Circular (AC) 61-136 provides the requirements that an ATD must meet for FAA certification. An AC-compliant ATD may be used for up to 10 percent of the flight training time required for the instrument rating. [Figure 1-9]

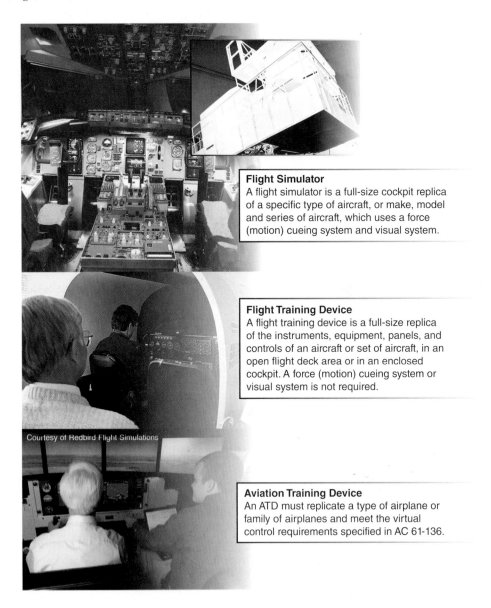

Flight Simulator
A flight simulator is a full-size cockpit replica of a specific type of aircraft, or make, model and series of aircraft, which uses a force (motion) cueing system and visual system.

Flight Training Device
A flight training device is a full-size replica of the instruments, equipment, panels, and controls of an aircraft or set of aircraft, in an open flight deck area or in an enclosed cockpit. A force (motion) cueing system or visual system is not required.

Courtesy of Redbird Flight Simulations

Aviation Training Device
An ATD must replicate a type of airplane or family of airplanes and meet the virtual control requirements specified in AC 61-136.

Figure 1-9. Each type of simulator or training device must have the hardware and software necessary to represent the aircraft in ground and flight operations and must be evaluated, qualified, and approved by the FAA.

Equipment such as a simulator or training device is a very valuable tool for developing your instrument scan and for practicing procedures such as holding and approaches. The simulation can be placed on hold so your position is frozen while you discuss the procedure with your instructor. Exercises can be repeated as many times as necessary and most equipment allows you to position the airplane at any point on a procedure. In addition, a training device provides a lesson opportunity regardless of the weather. Although you should take full advantage of training in actual IFR conditions, at times icing or thunderstorms might prevent practice in the airplane.

It (the Link Trainer) is a box set on a pedestal and cleverly designed to resemble a real airplane. On the inside the deception is quite complete, even to the sound of slip stream and engines. All of the usual controls and instruments are duplicated within the cockpit, and once under way the sensation of actual flight becomes so genuine that it is often a surprise to open the top of the box and discover you are in the same locality.

— Ernest K Gann, *Fate is the Hunter*

The Link Trainer flight simulator, developed in 1928 by Edwin A. Link, was the forerunner of the training devices and flight simulators used today to teach pilots instrument flying procedures. Often referred to as the Blue Box pilot maker, the Link Trainer consisted of a small fuselage with wings and a tail that had movable control surfaces. The trainer cockpit had a full instrument panel, as well as a throttle, a radio, and cockpit lights. Some models of the Link Trainer had a duplicate control console for the instructor, a desktop map plotter, and a full radio beacon/flight path radio simulation system.

To better prepare its pilots and reduce the accident rate, the army purchased nearly 10,000 Blue Box pilot makers which helped qualify more than half a million airmen during and after World War II.

HISTORY NOTE

CURRENCY FOR THE CLOUDS

When you hold an instrument rating, you must also meet certain recency of experience requirements to act as PIC under IFR or in weather conditions that are less than the minimums prescribed for VFR operations. Within the preceding six calendar months, you must have intercepted and tracked courses through the use of navigation systems, performed holding procedures, and flown at least six instrument approaches. These instrument procedures must be accomplished under actual or simulated instrument conditions in flight, in a flight simulator, or in a flight training device.

 Instrument currency is aircraft category-specific. Instrument procedures practiced in a helicopter do not count toward currency requirements in an airplane.

The location and type of each instrument approach and the name of the safety pilot, if required, must be recorded in your logbook. A flight simulator or flight training device may be used to log instrument time provided an authorized instructor is present during the simulated flight. If you do not meet the instrument experience requirements within the six calendar months or within six calendar months after that, you must pass an **instrument proficiency check** consisting of a representative number of tasks required by the instrument rating practical test. [Figure 1-10]

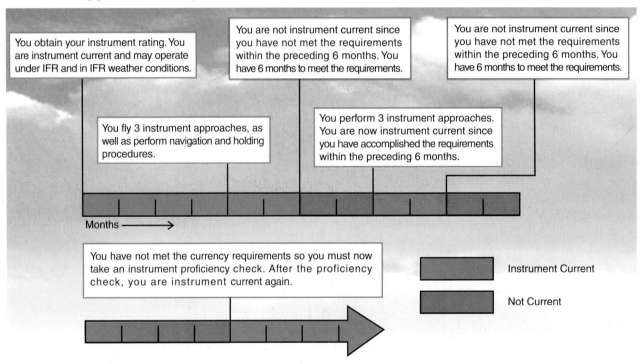

Figure 1-10. You may log instrument time only for that flight time when you operate the airplane solely by reference to instruments under actual or simulated instrument flight conditions.

...flying in heavy rain on one occasion, one of the blades of my wooden propeller started to come apart. The fabric coating, which covered one of these blades, had worn through, and the first thing I knew there was a terrific bang and very heavy vibration. I had to come down on the beach at Le Toquet. We were short of daylight, but my two passengers were very nice. I explained what the problem was, and one of them said. "I've got a penknife on me. I'll have a go at fixing this thing." So he helped me, and we hacked this loose piece of wood and fabric off the blade and got it started up again... In those days the passengers took part in the whole thing in very good spirit.

— Alan Campbell Orde, a British pilot recalling the startup of European commercial airlines in 1919, as quoted in *The American Heritage History of Flight*

THE COMMERCIAL PILOT CERTIFICATE

One of the unique aspects of flying is that you can transform what you have a passion for as a hobby into an exciting and rewarding career. The desire to fly for a living was so strong in the early days of aviation that aviators were willing to pursue dangerous and unstable employment as barnstormers or airmail pilots. You do not have to take the same type of risks today, but you must be willing to face the many challenges that lay ahead on the road to becoming a professional pilot. [Figure 1-11]

 To carry passengers for hire, you must hold at least a commercial pilot certificate.

For you to be eligible for a **commercial pilot certificate**, you must be at least 18 years of age and hold a third-class medical certificate. However, a second-class medical certificate is required for you to exercise the privileges of your commercial pilot certificate. You must be able to read, write, speak, and understand the English language, and meet specific training and flight time requirements described in the FARs. In addition, you must pass an aeronautical knowledge test and a practical test.

You also must possess at least a private pilot certificate and, under FAR Part 141, hold an instrument rating or be concurrently enrolled in an instrument rating course. If you are training under Part 61 regulations and you do not hold an instrument rating in the same aircraft category and class, you will be issued a commercial pilot certificate that contains the limitation, "The carriage of passengers for hire on cross-country flights in excess of 50 nautical miles or at night is prohibited." The experience requirements in Part 61 of the FARs include 250 hours of flight time as a pilot including training from an instructor in various areas of operation specified within that part. Under Part 141 rules, you must receive 120 hours of training that includes at least 55 hours of instruction in operations specified in Appendix D, FAR Part 141. [Figure 1-12]

Figure 1-12. Mastering commercial maneuvers such as the lazy eight requires a high level of proficiency in advanced planning, accuracy, and control coordination.

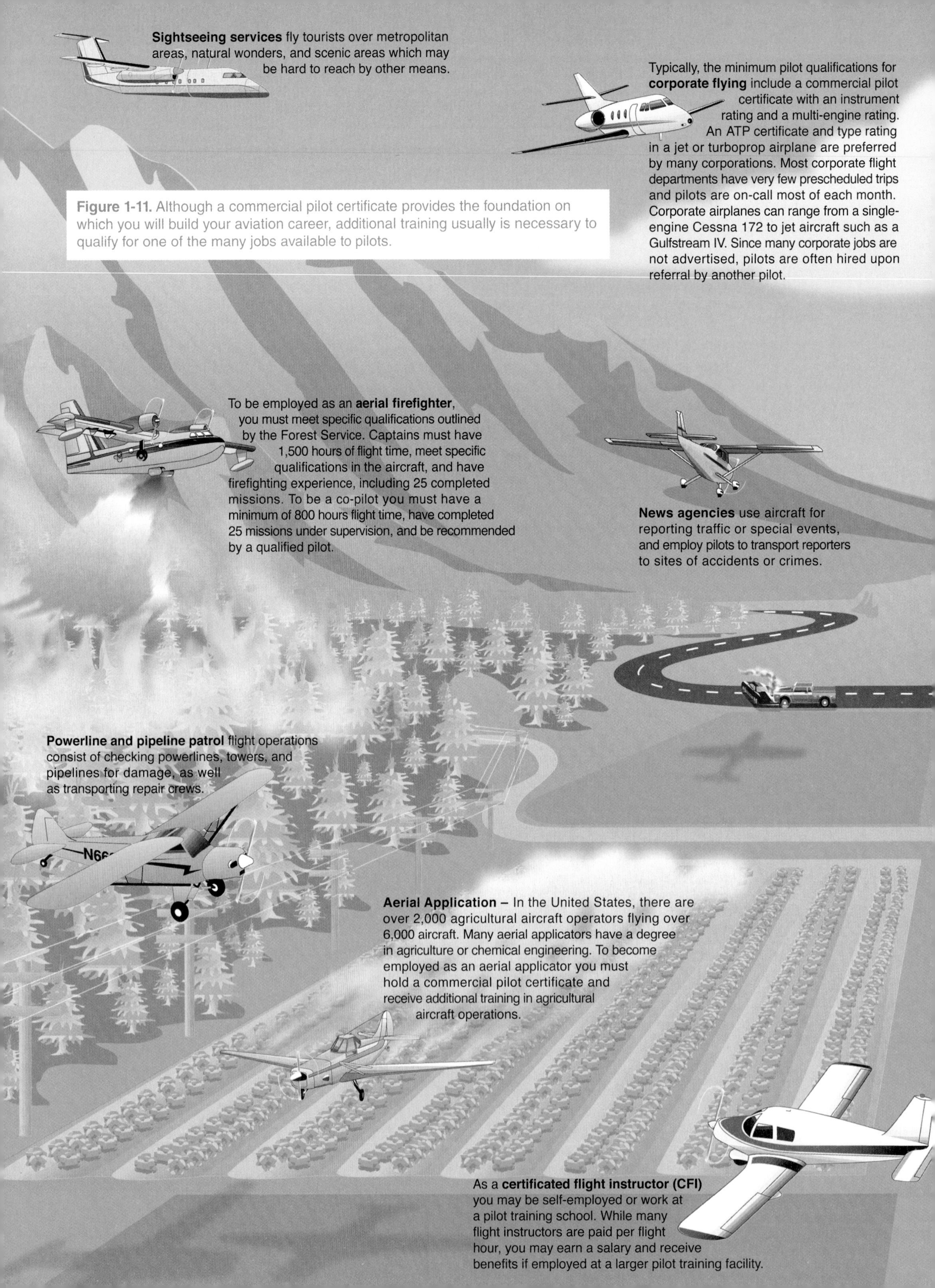

Sightseeing services fly tourists over metropolitan areas, natural wonders, and scenic areas which may be hard to reach by other means.

Typically, the minimum pilot qualifications for **corporate flying** include a commercial pilot certificate with an instrument rating and a multi-engine rating. An ATP certificate and type rating in a jet or turboprop airplane are preferred by many corporations. Most corporate flight departments have very few prescheduled trips and pilots are on-call most of each month. Corporate airplanes can range from a single-engine Cessna 172 to jet aircraft such as a Gulfstream IV. Since many corporate jobs are not advertised, pilots are often hired upon referral by another pilot.

Figure 1-11. Although a commercial pilot certificate provides the foundation on which you will build your aviation career, additional training usually is necessary to qualify for one of the many jobs available to pilots.

To be employed as an **aerial firefighter**, you must meet specific qualifications outlined by the Forest Service. Captains must have 1,500 hours of flight time, meet specific qualifications in the aircraft, and have firefighting experience, including 25 completed missions. To be a co-pilot you must have a minimum of 800 hours flight time, have completed 25 missions under supervision, and be recommended by a qualified pilot.

News agencies use aircraft for reporting traffic or special events, and employ pilots to transport reporters to sites of accidents or crimes.

Powerline and pipeline patrol flight operations consist of checking powerlines, towers, and pipelines for damage, as well as transporting repair crews.

Aerial Application – In the United States, there are over 2,000 agricultural aircraft operators flying over 6,000 aircraft. Many aerial applicators have a degree in agriculture or chemical engineering. To become employed as an aerial applicator you must hold a commercial pilot certificate and receive additional training in agricultural aircraft operations.

As a **certificated flight instructor (CFI)** you may be self-employed or work at a pilot training school. While many flight instructors are paid per flight hour, you may earn a salary and receive benefits if employed at a larger pilot training facility.

As a pilot for a major airline, your typical work schedule includes flying approximately 80 hours (an average of 15 working days) and spending from 10-15 days a month away from home. While each major airline has specific minimum requirements, your qualifications must be competitive for the job market at the time you apply. The qualifications for an airline pilot position can be divided into four categories:

1. Flight experience — Most pilots hired by major airlines have regional airline, corporate, or military flight experience. The average total flight time expected by the airlines varies with the availability of qualified pilots. Multi-engine, turboprop, or jet time accumulated by flying in military or in commercial operations is more impressive to an airline employer than personal flying experience.

2. Certificates and ratings — you must hold an airline transport pilot (ATP) certificate with a multi-engine rating. In addition, you must hold a first-class medical certificate, and you might be required to have a passing score on the flight engineer knowledge test.

3. Education — At a minimum, your credentials should include a four-year college degree. The airlines normally do not require a particular degree or major area of study.

4. Interview skills — During an airline interview you will be evaluated on how well you communicate, your leadership skills, and your ability to perform as a crewmember. Typically, you also have to pass a stringent medical exam and have your flying skills assessed during a simulator flight.

Transporting parachute jumpers, as well as **banner and glider towing,** are services which you can perform as a commercial pilot.

Law enforcement agencies employ pilots for traffic surveys, and search and rescue missions, as well as border and coastline patrol.

As a pilot for a **regional airline**, you will fly advanced turboprop or small jet aircraft during scheduled passenger-carrying flights. You might fly for a regional airline as a way to gain experience for a major airline position. To qualify for a regional airline position, you should accumulate as much total flight time, pilot-in-command time, and multi-engine time as possible. Some regional airlines hire pilots with fairly low flight time and allow them to upgrade as they build experience, while others prefer copilots with sufficient skills to upgrade to captain within a short period of time. However, an ATP certificate is now required, even for a first-officer position.

You may choose to apply to the **FAA** to become a safety inspector, test pilot, or airspace inspection pilot.

Flying for an **air ambulance service** requires transporting patients to health care facilities for specialized treatment.

FBO

You may fly passengers or cargo during scheduled flights or provide on-demand services working for an **air taxi or charter** operation.

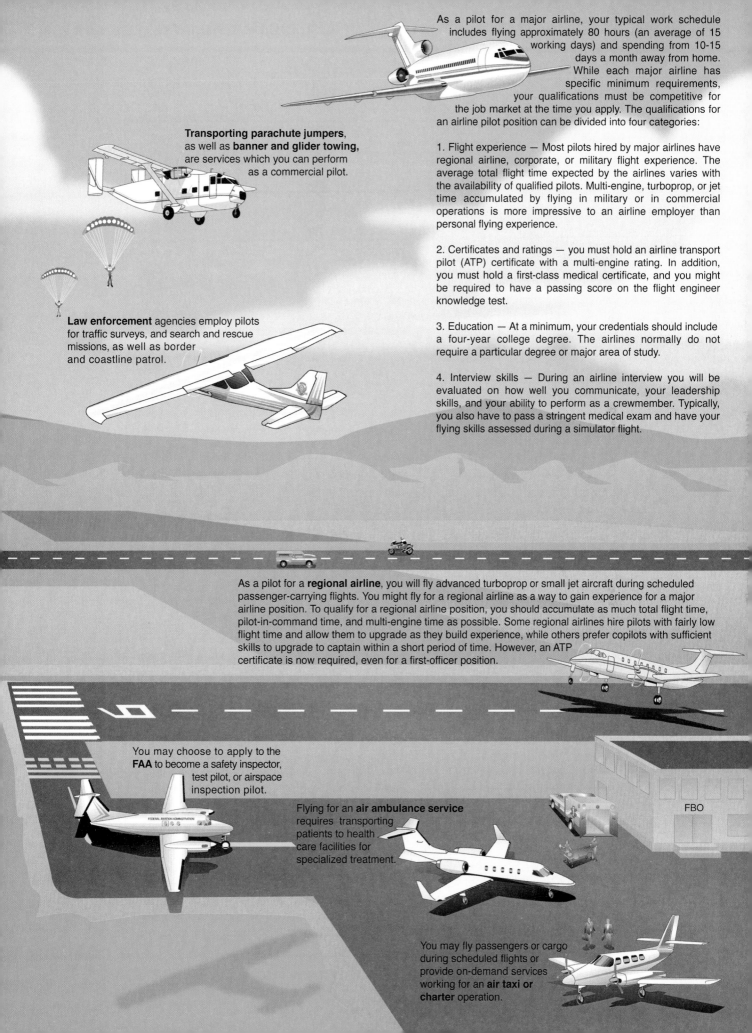

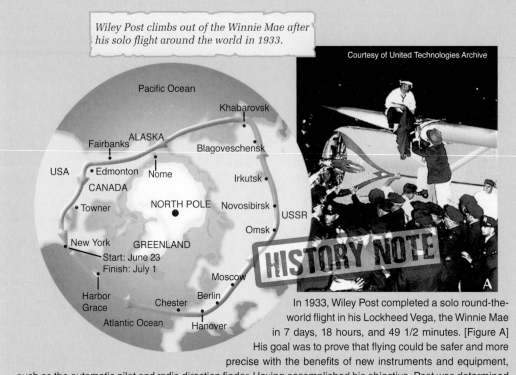

Wiley Post climbs out of the Winnie Mae after his solo flight around the world in 1933.

Pacific Ocean

Khabarovsk

ALASKA

Fairbanks   Blagoveschensk

USA • Edmonton   Nome

CANADA   Irkutsk

• Towner   NORTH POLE   Novosibirsk

                                   USSR

                                   Omsk

New York   GREENLAND

Start: June 23

Finish: July 1

                    Moscow

Harbor   Chester   Berlin

Grace

Atlantic Ocean   Hanover

Courtesy of United Technologies Archive

HISTORY NOTE

A

In 1933, Wiley Post completed a solo round-the-world flight in his Lockheed Vega, the Winnie Mae in 7 days, 18 hours, and 49 1/2 minutes. [Figure A] His goal was to prove that flying could be safer and more precise with the benefits of new instruments and equipment, such as the automatic pilot and radio direction finder. Having accomplished his objective, Post was determined to take aviation technology even further. Upon his return, he announced that if man wanted to fly long distances safely and faster, he would have to fly higher — into the stratosphere, where the powerful jet stream winds blew.

Because Post could not pressurize the Winnie Mae's cabin, he enlisted the help of the BFGoodrich Company to develop a full-pressure suit he could wear while flying the airplane. Post's suit consisted of three layers (long underwear, an inner black rubber air pressure bladder, and an outer cloth contoured suit), and a helmet (containing a special oxygen breathing system and outlets for earphones and a throat microphone). [Figure B]

B

AROU
AROUNE

On February 22, 1935, Post made his first attempt to fly across the country at an altitude of more than 30,000 feet MSL. Only 31 minutes into the flight, he was forced to make an emergency landing in the Mojave Desert after his engine began throwing oil. Post approached a man near the landing sight to ask for assistance in removing his helmet. The man nearly fainted from fright when he saw Post lumbering toward him in his pressure suit.

It was determined that Post's airplane had been sabotaged by a jealous competitor. This did not deter Post from his mission and 3 weeks later, on March 15, 1935, he embarked on a second transcontinental record attempt. Although Post had to turn back when he ran out of oxygen, he had covered 2,035 miles in 7 hours and 9 minutes. This meant that the Winnie Mae's groundspeed averaged 279 miles per hour, over 100 miles per hour faster than the airplane's normal speed. At times the airplane had reached groundspeeds of up to 340 miles per hour. Wiley Post and his Winnie Mae had been in the jet stream.

Within a quarter of a century of Post's high altitude flights, men, women, and children would be hurtling through the stratosphere at almost the speed of sound in the comfortable pressurized cabins of jetliners, wholly ignorant of the frustrating labors of 1934 and 1935, unmindful of the man who met the difficulties in their rudest shapes. Yet every time a contrail runs its white chalkline across the blue, it deserves recollection that it was Wiley Post who pointed the way to putting it there.

— Stanley R. Mohler, M.D. and Bobby H Johnson, Ph.D., written for a National Air and Space Museum Smithsonian Annals of Flight monograph

The FARs specify that you must receive 10 hours of flight training in a **complex airplane** an airplane with retractable landing gear, flaps, and a controllable pitch propeller (a full authority digital engine control [FADEC] system meets the requirement for a controllable pitch propeller). To operate as pilot in command of a complex airplane, you need training and an endorsement from your instructor. It also is possible that you will be introduced to a **high performance airplane** during your flight training. A high performance airplane has an engine with more than 200 horsepower. The training required to receive a high performance or complex airplane endorsement will focus on the operation of advanced airplane systems. [Figure 1-13]

Complex

High Performance and Complex

High Performance

Figure 1-13. To act as pilot in command of a high performance or complex airplane, you must receive specific training outlined in the FARs, as well as an instructor's endorsement in your logbook.

Designers began thinking about retractable landing gear as early as 1911, but the idea was not practical until better technology developed and increasing speed became important. The first fully retractable gear was introduced in 1920. The Dayton Wright R.B. Racer created a sensation as its wheels folded into its fuselage during the Gordon Bennett Cup Race in France. The R.B. Racer was also the first airplane to change the wing camber in flight. As the landing gear extended, a mechanism moved the leading and trailing edges of the wings into a more cambered shape for better lift at low speed.

Two types of airplanes used retractable landing gear during the Pulitzer Trophy Race of 1922. The army flew two Verville-Sperry R-3s, and the Navy competed with the Bee-Line Racer. The Verville-Sperry retracted its gear into its wings, however, the lack of wheel-well covers created unnecessary drag. The landing gear of the Bee-Line had full skirts so that the wheel wells were completely covered with the gear retracted. Pilots operated this early landing gear using hand cranks, but electric and hydraulically retracted gear gradually replaced muscle power, first on the larger designs, then on smaller aircraft.

Bee-Line Racer

HISTORY NOTE

Dayton Wright R.B. Racer

Verville Sperry R-3

COMMERCIAL PILOT PRIVILEGES

FAR 61.133 states that as a commercial pilot, you may act as pilot in command of an aircraft for compensation or hire and you may carry persons or property for compensation or hire provided you meet the qualifications that apply to the specific operation. Although some commercial operations are governed by FAR Part 91, many others must meet additional requirements described in FAR Parts 119, 121, 125, 129, 135, and 137. [Figure 1-14] Terms that help explain various types of commercial operations are defined in FAR Part 119. [Figure 1-15]

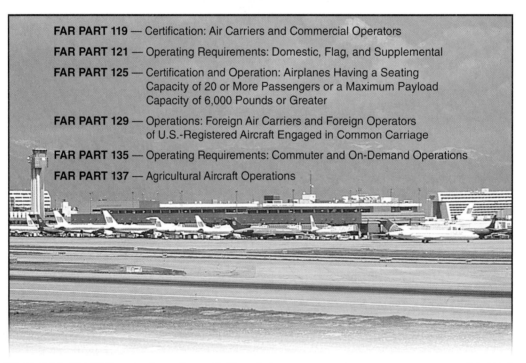

FAR PART 119 — Certification: Air Carriers and Commercial Operators

FAR PART 121 — Operating Requirements: Domestic, Flag, and Supplemental

FAR PART 125 — Certification and Operation: Airplanes Having a Seating Capacity of 20 or More Passengers or a Maximum Payload Capacity of 6,000 Pounds or Greater

FAR PART 129 — Operations: Foreign Air Carriers and Foreign Operators of U.S.-Registered Aircraft Engaged in Common Carriage

FAR PART 135 — Operating Requirements: Commuter and On-Demand Operations

FAR PART 137 — Agricultural Aircraft Operations

Figure 1-14. The FAR parts shown here might apply to you as you pursue a career as a professional pilot, however, you normally will not study these regulations for commercial pilot certification.

Common Carriage is any operation for compensation or hire in which the operator holds itself out, by advertising or any other means, as willing to furnish transportation for any member of the public. Private carriage does not involve holding out.

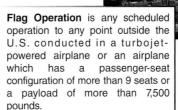

Copyright Corel

Courtesy of Chicago Dept. of Aviation

Figure 1-15. FAR Parts 121, 125, and 135 govern operations ranging from scheduled air carriers to on-demand charters.

On-Demand Operation is any operation for compensation or hire which is one of the following:

• a passenger-carrying public charter where the departure time and location, as well as the arrival location are specifically negotiated with the customer.

• a common-carriage operation using an airplane (including turbojet-powered) having a passenger-seat configuration of 30 seats or less and a payload capacity of 7,500 pounds or less.

• a private carriage operation conducted with an airplane having a passenger-seat configuration of less than 20 seats or a payload capacity of less than 6,000 pounds.

• a scheduled operation with a frequency of less than 5 round trips per week conducted with a nonturbojet-powered airplane with a maximum of 9 passenger seats and a maximum payload capacity of 7,500 pounds.

• a cargo operation conducted with an airplane having a payload capacity of 7,500 pounds or less.

Flag Operation is any scheduled operation to any point outside the U.S. conducted in a turbojet-powered airplane or an airplane which has a passenger-seat configuration of more than 9 seats or a payload of more than 7,500 pounds.

Commuter Operation is any scheduled operation conducted in a nonturbojet-powered airplane having a maximum passenger-seat configuration of 9 seats or less and a maximum payload capacity of 7,500 pounds or less. A commuter operation must be scheduled with a frequency of at least 5 round trips per week on at least 1 route according to published flight schedules.

FARs GOVERNING SPECIFIC COMMERCIAL OPERATIONS						
Airplane Size/Weight	Part 121 Domestic (Scheduled)	Part 121 Flag (Scheduled)	Part 121 Supplemental (Not Scheduled)	Part 135 Commuter (Scheduled)	Part 135 On-Demand (Not Scheduled)	Part 125 (Not Scheduled)
Common Carriage:						
≤9 seats and ≤ 7,500 lbs	No[1]	No[1]	No[2]	Yes[1]	Yes[2]	No
10-30 seats and ≤7,500 lbs	Yes	Yes	No[2]	No	Yes[2]	No
>30 seats or >7,500 lbs	Yes	Yes	Yes	No	No	No
Common Carriage is Not Involved:						
<20 seats or <6,000 lbs	No	No	No	No	Yes	No
≥20 seats or 6,000 lbs	No	No	No	No	No	Yes

[1]Turbojet-powered airplanes used in scheduled passenger-carrying operations must comply with Part 121 regardless of passenger seating or payload capacity.

[2]If turbojet-powered airplanes and other airplanes with 10-30 passenger-seat configurations are used for Part 121 domestic or flag operations, non-scheduled or charter operations with that airplane shall be conducted under Part 121 supplemental rules.

SECTION A ■ **Instrument/Commercial Training and Opportunities**

Under FAR Part 91, you may not engage in **common carriage**, which involves holding out, or advertising your services to furnish transportation for any member of the public. FAR Part 119 lists specific activities not governed by FAR Parts, 121, 125, or 135 for which the holder of a commercial pilot certificate may be paid. [Figure 1-16]

Figure 1-16. Student instruction, certain nonstop sightseeing flights within limited areas, crop dusting, banner towing, aerial photography or survey, firefighting, and some corporate flights are examples of operations that are not governed by FAR Parts 121, 125, and 135.

ADDITIONAL CERTIFICATES AND RATINGS

Although the path to a flying career can vary, many jobs, such as corporate or airline pilot positions, require additional pilot certificates and ratings, as well as flight experience. A multi-engine rating is an essential requirement for most flying jobs, and you must hold an airline transport pilot certificate to operate as an airline captain. In addition, you could choose a rewarding career as a certificated flight instructor, or use flight instruction as a step to gain experience and enhance your professional qualifications.

At first some of the pilots took the whole idea of stewardesses as kind of a joke. Then they realized that they didn't have to hand out box lunches and take care of sick passengers any more... Refueling was sometimes interesting. Sometimes we had to land at an emergency landing field and then we had the gas in two-and-a-half or five-gallon cans. They would form a sort of fire brigade, handing the cans from one to the other, including the stewardess and some of the passengers. Then, if we were some place where there was no crew on the field, somebody had to go out on the left wing to the engine to do something there. The pilot and the copilot were busy inside, so the third member of the crew had to go out on the wing—and that was the stewardess. We did it without a murmur because of the argument that when a third person was needed for something like that the third person should be a man.

— Ellen Church, who became the first airline stewardess when she was hired by Boeing Air Transport in 1930, as quoted in *The American Heritage History of Flight*

MULTI-ENGINE RATING

FAR Part 61 does not specify a minimum number of ground or flight instruction hours required for the addition of a **multi-engine rating** to a pilot certificate, but you will have to pass a practical test. Under FAR Part 141, a multi-engine rating course must include the ground and flight instruction hours in accordance with the applicable Part 141 appendices. Typically, the training can be completed in a short period of time, but most aircraft insurance policies require that you obtain a substantial amount of multi-engine flight time before operating the airplane as pilot in command. To accumulate the necessary experience, you might be able to share flight time and expenses with a qualified pilot who meets the insurance requirements. In general, a multi-engine rating is considered an addition to your private or commercial pilot certificate and the training will be conducted separately. However, it is possible in some curriculums for the multi-engine training to be incorporated within the commercial pilot training requirements. [Figure 1-17]

Figure 1-17. Learning the procedures for flying a multi-engine airplane after an engine failure is perhaps the most challenging aspect of multi-engine training.

CERTIFICATED FLIGHT INSTRUCTOR

Under FAR Part 61, a specific number of ground or flight instruction hours is not required to become a **certificated flight instructor (CFI)**, however, you are required to pass two knowledge exams and a practical test. Under FAR Part 141, a flight instructor course must include the ground and flight instruction hours specified in Appendix F, Part 141. Your CFI training will focus on aspects of teaching that include the learning process, student evaluation, and lesson planning. You can obtain additional ratings for your flight instructor certificate, such as an instrument instructor, or multi-engine instructor rating.

AIRLINE TRANSPORT PILOT CERTIFICATE

To apply for an **airline transport pilot (ATP)** certificate, you must be at least 23 years of age and hold a first-class medical. The flight time requirements to obtain an ATP certificate are demanding: a total of 1,500 hours of flight time including 250 hours of pilot-in-command time, 500 hours of cross-country time, 100 hours of night flight, and 75 hours of instrument experience. Refer to FAR Part 61, Subpart G and Part 141, Appendix E for specific training requirements. The ATP knowledge test emphasizes subjects such as navigation, meteorology, aircraft performance, and air carrier flight procedures. During the practical test, your instrument skills will be evaluated, as well as your ability to correctly perform emergency procedures.

I feel we are on the brink of an era of expansion of knowledge about ourselves and our surroundings that is beyond description or comprehension at this time. Our efforts today and what we've done so far are but small building blocks on a very huge pyramid to come ... Knowledge begets knowledge. The more I see, the more impressed I am not with how much we know but with how tremendous the areas are that are as yet unexplored. — Lieutenant Colonel John H. Glenn Jr. in a speech given to a joint session of congress six days after he orbited the earth in a Mercury space capsule

Whoopee! Man, that may have been a small one for Neil, but that's a long one for me. — Pete Conrad, the third man to walk on the moon after jumping from the last rung of the lunar module ladder to the footpad — the bottom rung was about level with his waist

John Glenn's statement about the future of knowledge is just as true today as it was in 1962. Although aviation and space technology has come a long way since Jimmy Doolittle climbed into the cockpit of his NY-2 Husky biplane for the first blind flight and Wiley Post donned his space suit to cruise the stratosphere, there is still so much more yet to explore. If we approach the future with the same kind of unbridled enthusiasm as Pete Conrad, anything is possible. Conrad is chairman of Universal Space Lines, a venture he hopes will become the first commercial space airline, opening up a new world of discovery and opportunity.

Whether your goal is to earn an instrument rating, embark on a career as a commercial pilot, or reach for the stars as a spacecraft commander carrying passengers to the moon and beyond, you are a part of an industry with unlimited possibilities. You are one of a unique group of people who see further, dare to dream, and then have the passion, courage, and commitment to take the steps, large or small, to see their visions become reality. As you continue your aviation training and set your own dreams in motion, do not forget — you are standing on the shoulders of Giants.

SUMMARY CHECKLIST

✓ The addition of an instrument rating to your private pilot certificate allows you to fly under IFR (instrument flight rules). These regulations govern flight operations in weather conditions below VFR minimums.

✓ When referring to weather conditions, the terms IFR and IMC (instrument meteorological conditions) are often used interchangeably, as are the terms VFR and VMC (visual meteorological conditions). In addition, the terms IFR and VFR can define the type of flight plan under which you are operating.

✓ Statistics have shown the risk of a weather-related accident declines as a pilot gains instrument flying experience.

✓ To be eligible for an instrument rating, you must hold a private pilot certificate, be able to read, write, speak, and understand the English language, and complete specific training and flight time requirements described in the FARs, as well as pass a knowledge and practical test.

✓ Part of your instrument training may be provided by an authorized instructor in a flight simulator, flight training device, or an aviation training device (ATD).

✓ To meet recency of experience requirements for instrument flight, you must have intercepted and tracked courses through the use of navigation systems, performed holding procedures, and flown at least six instrument approaches within the preceding six calendar months.

✓ If you do not meet the instrument currency requirements within six calendar months or within six calendar months after that, you must pass an instrument proficiency check.

✓ For you to be eligible for a commercial pilot certificate, you must be at least 18 years of age, hold a private pilot certificate, be able to read, write, speak, and understand the English language, and meet specific training and flight time requirements described in the FARs, as well as pass a knowledge and practical test. Under FAR Part 141, you must hold an instrument rating or be concurrently enrolled in an instrument rating course.

✓ Although you need at least a third-class medical certificate to be eligible for a commercial pilot certificate, you must have a second-class medical certificate to exercise commercial pilot privileges.

✓ As part of the commercial pilot training requirements, you must receive 10 hours of flight training in a complex airplane—an airplane with retractable landing gear, flaps, and a controllable pitch propeller (or FADEC).

✓ A high performance airplane is defined as an airplane having an engine of more than 200 horsepower.

✓ FAR Parts 119, 121, 125, and 135 govern operations ranging from scheduled air carriers to on-demand charters.

✓ Under FAR Part 91, you may not engage in common carriage, which involves holding out, or advertising your services to furnish transportation for any member of the public.

✓ Student instruction, certain nonstop sightseeing flights within limited areas, crop dusting, banner towing, aerial photography or survey, firefighting, and some types of corporate flights are examples of operations that are not governed by FAR Parts 121, 125, and 135.

SECTION A ■ Instrument/Commercial Training and Opportunities

✓ The addition of a multi-engine rating to your private or commercial certificate does not require a minimum number of ground or flight instruction hours under FAR Part 61. Under FAR Part 141, a multi-engine rating course must include the ground and flight instruction hours in accordance with the applicable Part 141 appendices.

✓ To become a certificated flight instructor (CFI), you must pass two knowledge exams and a practical test. Under FAR Part 61, a specific number of ground or flight instruction hours is not required for CFI training. An FAR Part 141 flight instructor course must include the ground and flight instruction hours specified in Appendix F, Part 141.

✓ To apply for an airline transport pilot (ATP) certificate, you must be at least 23 years of age and hold a first-class medical. A total of 1,500 hours of flight time is required including 250 hours of pilot-in-command time, 500 hours of cross-country time, 100 hours of night flight, and 75 hours of instrument experience.

KEY TERMS

IFR (Instrument Flight Rules)

IMC (Instrument Meteorological Conditions)

VFR (Visual Flight Rules)

VMC (Visual Meteorological Conditions)

Instrument Rating

Flight Simulator

Flight Training Device

Aviation Training Device (ATD)

Instrument Proficiency Check

Commercial Pilot Certificate

Complex Airplane

High Performance Airplane

Common Carriage

Multi-Engine Rating

Certificated Flight Instructor (CFI)

Airline Transport Pilot (ATP)

SECTION B
Advanced Human Factors Concepts

As a private pilot, you have experience in managing the physiological factors that affect you in flight. You also have applied **single-pilot resource management (SRM)** techniques to make effective decisions in the VFR environment. Now, you enter a different realm. In the IFR environment, your workload increases and you use additional resources; relying on avionics, instrumentation, charts, and ATC for aircraft guidance. As a commercial pilot, you will typically fly larger, faster airplanes at higher altitudes so you must manage more complex equipment and systems. You also must gain greater skills in coordinating with crew members and dealing with passengers. [Figure 1-18]

Figure 1-18. You must master SRM skills to meet the demands of the IFR and commercial environments.

This section defines SRM concepts and examines aviation physiology that specifically applies to flight in the IFR and commercial environments. The Human Element Insets located throughout this textbook help you to correlate human factors concepts to specific pilot operations and expand upon the fundamental SRM principles introduced in this section. Chapter 10, Section B — IFR Single-Pilot Resource Management describes how to apply SRM in the IFR environment and Chapter 13, Section B — Commercial Pilot SRM specifically examines SRM in the commercial environment.

SINGLE-PILOT RESOURCE MANAGEMENT

Human factors-related accidents motivated the airline industry to implement **crew resource management (CRM)** training for flight crews. The training helped crews recognize hazards and provided tools for them to eliminate the hazard or minimize its impact. CRM training provided the foundation for SRM training. Applying SRM means using hardware, information, and human resources, such as dispatchers, weather briefers, maintenance personnel, and air traffic controllers, to gather information, analyze your situation, and make effective decisions about the current and future status of your flight. SRM includes these six concepts:

- Aeronautical decision making

- Risk management

- Task management

- Situational awareness

- Controlled flight into terrain awareness

- Automation management

AERONAUTICAL DECISION MAKING

Aeronautical decision making (ADM) is a systematic approach to the mental process used by aircraft pilots to consistently determine the best course of action in response to a given set of circumstances. Your ability to make effective decisions as a pilot depends on a number of factors. Some factors, such as the time available to make a decision, might be beyond your control. However, you can learn to recognize the factors that you can manage, and learn skills to improve your decision-making ability and judgment.

ADM PROCESS

Some situations, such as emergencies, require you to respond immediately using established procedures, with little time for detailed analysis. This reflexive type of decision making—anchored in training and experience—is often referred to as naturalistic or automatic decision making. However, typically during a flight, you have time to recognize changes that occur, gather information, examine options, and assess risk before reaching a decision. Then, after implementing a course of action, you determine how your decision could affect other phases of the flight. To make an analytical decision, you use the **ADM process**. The ADM process consists of the steps that you use to make effective decisions as pilot in command. [Figure 1-19]

The ADM Process

Recognize a change. Identify changes in your situation and be alert for sudden changes that can lead to abnormal and emergency situations.

Define the problem. Use experience and resources to determine the exact nature of the problem.

Choose a course of action. Consider the expected outcome of each possible action and assess the risk involved with each before making a decision.

Implement your decision. Take the necessary action to solve the problem.

Evaluate the outcome. Think ahead and keep track of the situation to ensure that your actions are producing the desired outcome.

Figure 1-19. The ADM process includes defining the problem and monitoring the outcome after you implement a decision.

Although the basic steps are the same, A variety of mnemonics are used by pilots to remember the steps in the decision-making process—you might hear of FOR-DEC, NMATE, DODAR, SAFE, or the FAA's DECIDE model:

1. **D**etect the fact that a change has occurred.

2. **E**stimate the need to counter or react to the change.

3. **C**hoose a desirable outcome for the success of the flight.

4. **I**dentify actions that could successfully control the change.

5. **D**o the necessary action to adapt to the change.

6. **E**valuate the effect of the action.

SELF ASSESSMENT

As pilot in command, you are the ultimate decision maker and your choices determine the outcome of the flight. Just as you must thoroughly check your aircraft to determine if it is airworthy, you must evaluate your own fitness for flight. Your general health, level of stress or fatigue, attitude, knowledge, skill level, and recency of experience are several factors that affect your performance as pilot in command. Establish personal limitations for flight and create a checklist to help you determine if you are prepared for a particular flight. For example, based on your experience, determine your own weather minimums and set limitations for the maximum amount of crosswind that you are comfortable with. After you have reviewed your personal limitations, you can use the **I'M SAFE Checklist** to further evaluate your fitness for flight. [Figure 1-20]

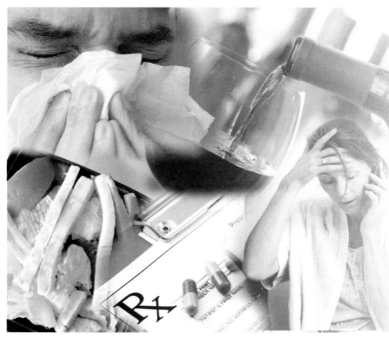

Illness — Do I have any symptoms?

Medication — Have I been taking prescription or over-the-counter drugs?

Stress — Am I under psychological pressure from the job? Worried about financial matters, health problems, or family discord?

Alcohol — Have I been drinking within 8 hours? Within 24 hours?

Fatigue — Am I tired and not adequately rested?

Eating — Am I adequately nourished?

Emotion — Have I experienced any emotionally upsetting event?

Figure 1-20. Using the I'M SAFE checklist is an effective way to determine your physical and mental readiness for flight.

SECTION B ■ **Advanced Human Factors Concepts**

HAZARDOUS ATTITUDES

Whether you are fit to fly depends on more than your experience and physical condition. Your attitude also affects the quality of your decisions. Studies have identified five hazardous attitudes among pilots that can interfere with a pilot's ability to make effective decisions. [Figure 1-21]

Anti-authority — You display this attitude if you resent having someone tell you what to do, or you regard rules and procedures as unnecessary.

Don't tell me.

Antidote — *Follow the rules. They are usually right.*

Impulsivity — If you feel the need to act immediately and do the first thing that comes to mind without considering the best solution to a problem, then you are exhibiting impulsivity.

Do it quickly.

Antidote — *Not so fast. Think first.*

Invulnerability — You are more likely to take chances and increase risk if you think accidents will not happen to you.

It won't happen to me.

Antidote — *It could happen to me.*

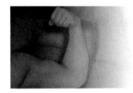

Macho — If you have this attitude, you might take risks trying to prove that you are better than anyone else. Women are just as likely to have this characteristic as men.

I can do it.

Antidote — *Taking chances is foolish.*

Resignation — You are experiencing resignation if you feel that no matter what you do it will have little effect on what happens to you. You may feel that when things go well, it is just good luck and when things go poorly, it is bad luck or someone else is responsible. This feeling can cause you to leave the action to others—for better or worse.

What's the use?

Antidote — *I'm not helpless. I can make a difference.*

Figure 1-21. As pilot in command, you must examine your decisions carefully to ensure that your choices have not been influenced by hazardous attitudes.

SELF-CRITIQUES

In addition to assessing your condition prior to and during flight, perform **self-critiques** after each flight to evaluate your performance, determine the skills that need improvement, and create a plan for increasing your proficiency. If you feel you need to improve your skills, review aircraft manuals, practice procedures using an aviation training device, or obtain refresher training. During flight lessons, both you and your instructor should evaluate your performance and resolve any differences in your assessments before creating a plan for improvement. This is referred to as **learner-centered grading**.

RISK MANAGEMENT

Risk management is critical to making effective decisions. During each flight, you are required to make decisions that involve four fundamental risk elements: the pilot, the aircraft, the environment, and the type of operation. Pilots use a variety of tools to identify, assess, and mitigate risks associated with the risk elements. Two frequently-used tools are **PAVE** and the **5Ps**. [Figure 1-22]

PAVE

Pilot – Evaluate your training, experience, and fitness.
Aircraft – Determine airworthiness, performance, and proper configuration. Check avionics airworthiness.
en**V**ironment – Assess items such as airport conditions, terrain and airspace, and weather.
External Pressures – Evaluate the purpose of the flight and how critical it is to maintain the schedule.

5Ps

Pilot – Evaluate your training, experience, and fitness.
Passengers – Consider your passengers' experience, flexibility, and fitness.
Plane – Determine airworthiness, performance, and proper configuration.
Programming – Check avionics airworthiness, operation, and configuration.
Plan – Assess items such as airport conditions, terrain and airspace, and weather. Evaluate the mission—the purpose of the flight—and how critical it is to maintain the schedule.

Figure 1-22. Both PAVE and the 5Ps remind you of the risk factors that you must manage when planning and implementing flights.

USING THE 5PS DURING FLIGHT PLANNING

Whether you use PAVE or the 5Ps, a risk management tool helps you make an effective Go/No-Go decision during flight planning. For example, 5P checklists provide guidelines on the risk factors to consider as you prepare for a flight. Create your own or make copies of the checklists at the end of this section to use for your flights. [Figure 1-23]

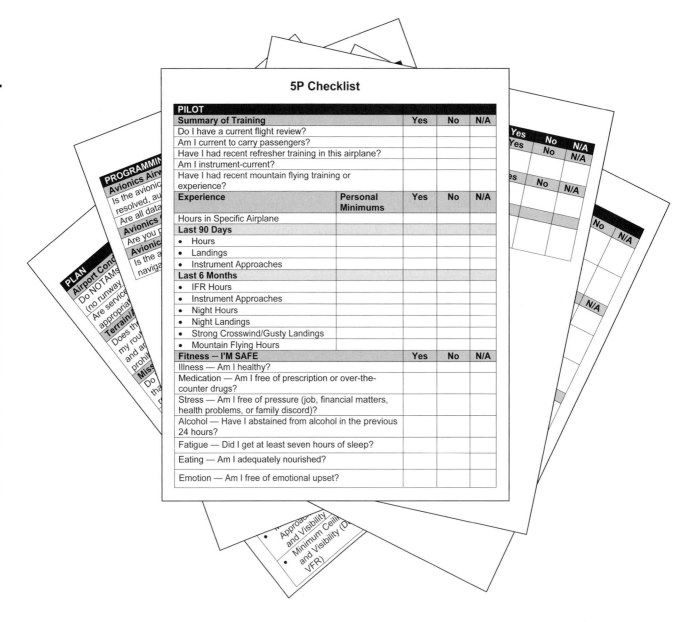

Figure 1-23. Use the 5P checklists to identify and mitigate risks prior to flight. The I'M SAFE checklist is part of the Pilot checklist.

USING THE 5PS IN FLIGHT

Managing risk does not end with a Go decision; you must continue to assess risk to make effective decisions during the flight. The risk management process continues as you evaluate the situation using the 5P check at decision points that correspond to the phases of flight. [Figure 1-24]

At each decision point, consider each of the 5Ps and ask these questions:
- What is the situation?
- What has changed since my Go decision?
- Is the risk associated with a change acceptable?
- What can I do to mitigate risk?

| Before Takeoff | Climb and Initial Cruise | Enroute Cruise | Descent | Before Approach and Landing |

Figure 1-24. You must reevaluate each of the 5Ps during the flight to recognize any changes that might increase your risk.

TASK MANAGEMENT

Task management involves planning and prioritizing tasks to avoid work overload, identifying and using resources to accomplish tasks, and managing distractions. When you are effectively managing tasks, you avoid fixating on one task to the exclusion of others and maintain positive control of the airplane.

PLANNING AND PRIORITIZING

When flying an airplane, your tasks are not evenly distributed over time. By planning ahead and prioritizing tasks, you can prepare for high workload periods during times of low workload. As you gain experience, you realize which tasks you can accomplish ahead of time, and which tasks you need to leave until the moment. Tasks such as organizing charts in the order of use, setting radio frequencies, and planning a descent to an airport help you prepare for what comes next.

RESOURCE USE

Because tools and sources of information are not always readily apparent, you must learn to recognize all the resources available to you and use them effectively. A wide variety of resources both inside and outside the airplane can help you manage tasks and make effective decisions. [Figure 1-25]

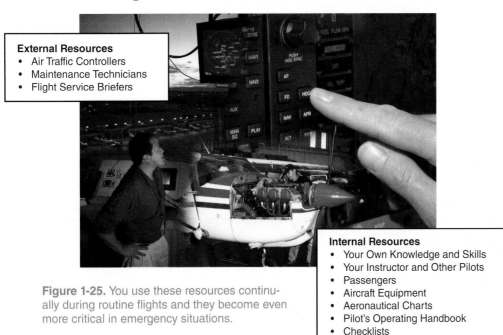

External Resources
- Air Traffic Controllers
- Maintenance Technicians
- Flight Service Briefers

Internal Resources
- Your Own Knowledge and Skills
- Your Instructor and Other Pilots
- Passengers
- Aircraft Equipment
- Aeronautical Charts
- Pilot's Operating Handbook
- Checklists

Figure 1-25. You use these resources continually during routine flights and they become even more critical in emergency situations.

SECTION B ■ **Advanced Human Factors Concepts**

CHECKLISTS

Checklists are valuable resources that help you manage distractions as you perform procedures. You typically use one of two methods for following checklists. With a **do-list**, you read the checklist item and the associated action and then perform the action. Use a do-list when you have time and completing each step in the correct order is critical. A **flow pattern** guides you through the cockpit in a logical order as you perform each step without the written checklist. After completing the flow pattern, refer to the checklist and verify that you have accomplished each item. Use a flow pattern when the checklist item sequence is not critical. Emergency checklists are unique because many have items that you must perform immediately from memory before referring to the checklist. [Figure 1-26]

Do-Lists
Use do-lists for abnormal procedures, such as addressing an electrical malfunction.

Flow Patterns
Use flow patterns to perform normal procedures, such as configuring the airplane and the avionics for specific phases of flight.

Emergency Checklists
Perform critical tasks from memory and then refer to the checklist to manage specific emergencies, such as an engine failure.

Figure 1-26. Use do-lists and flow patterns based on the procedure.

SITUATIONAL AWARENESS

Situational awareness is the accurate perception of all the operational and environmental factors that affect flight safety before, during, and after the flight. At any period of time, you should be able to accurately assess the current and future status of the flight. This includes the status of operational conditions, such as airplane systems, fuel, autopilot, and passengers, as well as the status of environmental conditions, such as your relationship to terrain, traffic, weather, and airspace. Using SRM, including risk management tools such as the 5Ps, task management, and available resources enables you to maintain situational awareness. Resources, such as navigation, traffic, terrain, and weather displays are particularly valuable for maintaining situational awareness if you understand how to use them properly. [Figure 1-27]

Figure 1-27. You are maintaining situational awareness when you have a solid mental picture of the condition of the pilot, passengers, plane, programming, and plan.

BRIEFINGS

Briefings are an effective tool to help you maintain situational awareness by preparing you for critical phases of flight. Standard briefings include a passenger briefing, a takeoff briefing, and a before-landing briefing. Regulations require that you explain to your passengers how to fasten and unfasten the safety belts and shoulder harnesses and when the safety belts must be fastened. The FAA also recommends that you cover certain safety considerations with passengers before flight. You can remember the elements of a passenger briefing by using the acronym SAFETY. [Figure 1-28]

Safety Belts
- How to fasten and unfasten the safety belts and shoulder harnesses.
- When safety belts must be fastened—prior to movement on the surface, takeoff, and landing

Air Vents
- Location and operation
- Operation of heating or air conditioning controls

Fire Extinguisher
Location and operation

Egress and Emergency
- Operation of doors and windows
- Location of the survival kit
- Use of onboard emergency equipment

Traffic and Talking
- Pointing out traffic
- Use of headsets
- Avoiding unnecessary conversation during critical phases of flight

Your Questions
Solicit questions from your passengers.

Figure 1-28. Perform the passenger briefing prior to starting the engine.

The takeoff briefing enables you to mentally rehearse what is about to happen during and after takeoff, and it prepares any other crewmembers or passengers for takeoff. You normally perform the before-landing briefing 15 to 20 miles from the destination airport, after you've obtained airport information. [Figure 1-29]

SECTION B ■ **Advanced Human Factors Concepts**

SECTION B ■ Advanced Human Factors Concepts

Takeoff Briefing
- Wind direction and velocity
- Runway length
- Takeoff distance
- Initial heading
- Initial altitude
- Takeoff and climb speeds
- Departure procedures
- Emergency plan in case of an engine failure after takeoff

Before-Landing Briefing
- Airport information and weather conditions
- Active runway
- Terrain and obstacles
- Airport elevation and pattern altitude
- Traffic pattern entry

Figure 1-29. The takeoff briefing and before-landing briefing help you maintain situational awareness of the airport environment.

OBSTACLES TO MAINTAINING SITUATIONAL AWARENESS

Fatigue, stress, and work overload can cause you to fixate on one aspect of the flight and omit others from your attention. A contributing factor in many accidents is a distraction that diverts the pilot's attention from monitoring the instruments or scanning outside the aircraft. A minor problem, such as a gauge that is not reading correctly, has the potential to become a major problem if you divert your attention to the perceived problem and neglect to properly control the airplane.

Complacency presents another obstacle to maintaining situational awareness. When activities become routine, you can have a tendency to relax and put less effort into your performance. Cockpit automation can lead to complacency—you could assume that the autopilot is doing what you expect, and neglect to cross check the instruments or the airplane's position.

SITUATIONAL AWARENESS DURING GROUND OPERATIONS

In addition to keeping track of your status while in flight, you must maintain situational awareness during ground operations. As you gain pilot experience, you will learn techniques to correctly follow taxi instructions, to know your position on the airport in relation to runways and other aircraft, and to minimize your workload.

CONTROLLED FLIGHT INTO TERRAIN AWARENESS

Controlled flight into terrain (CFIT) occurs when an aircraft is flown into terrain or water with no prior awareness on the part of the crew that the crash is imminent. Air carriers and professional flight departments have significantly reduced the number of CFIT accidents in the United States by implementing extensive training programs and installing specialized aircraft equipment. CFIT is more prevalent in general aviation because pilots do not have the same training and equipment. CFIT normally results from a combination of factors including weather, unfamiliar environment, nonstandard procedures, breakdown or loss of communication, loss of situational awareness, lack of perception of hazards, and lack of sound risk management techniques. Throughout your flight training, you will learn strategies for preventing CFIT during each phase of flight. [Figure 1-30]

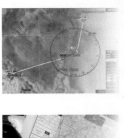

Plan your flight to avoid terrain and obstacles.

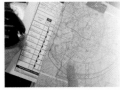

Use current charts and procedures.

Monitor terrain awareness and navigation displays.

Determine your airplane's performance.

Figure 1-30. To prevent a CFIT accident, you must maintain positional awareness.

SECTION B ■ **Advanced Human Factors Concepts**

AUTOMATION MANAGEMENT

Cockpit automation has the potential to increase or decrease the flight safety, depending on how well you use the equipment. Although automation can consist of a simple autopilot that maintains heading and altitude combined with traditional analog instruments and navigation equipment, the concept of **automation management** typically applies to an airplane with an advanced avionics system that includes digital displays, GPS equipment, a moving map, and an integrated autopilot. [Figure 1-31]

Figure 1-31. Advanced avionics airplanes typically have a primary flight display (PFD) with digital instrumentation and a multifunction display (MFD) that depicts a moving map, terrain, traffic, weather, and other flight environment information.

MANAGING WORKLOAD

Cockpit automation can reduce your workload and increase situational awareness. Use of an autopilot can free your attention to handle tasks during high-workload phases of flight and enable you to manage abnormal and emergency situations more effectively. However, if you are unfamiliar with your airplane's equipment, trying to program and interpret advanced avionics and automation systems might be distracting, lead to misinterpretation, and cause programming errors. You must thoroughly understand how to operate your avionics and plan ahead to program equipment during periods of lower workload to avoid falling behind or becoming distracted during high-workload periods.

MODE OF OPERATION

You must be able to correctly interpret your system's annunciations and recognize when the automation is operating in a different mode than you expect. To effectively manage automation, monitor the current mode, anticipate the next mode, and verify that mode changes occur as expected.

AUTOMATION CONSIDERATIONS

Relying too heavily on automation can lead to complacency and a loss of situational awareness. Always monitor aircraft displays, use charts to verify information, and confirm calculations if you use electronic databases for flight planning. Equipment failure can have serious consequences if you become overly dependent on automation. You must maintain your flight skills and your ability to maneuver the airplane manually.

You also need to recognize when automation is increasing your workload and switch to a simpler mode or turn equipment off. For example, if trying to program the GPS equipment or engage the autopilot starts to overwhelm you, flying the procedure manually might be safer. To help you manage automation and other avionics equipment, you can consider using one of three **equipment operating levels** during flight operations. [Figure 1-32]

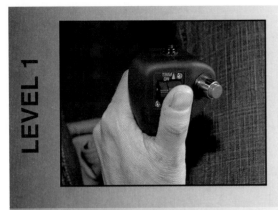

LEVEL 1

Level 1 — Control the airplane manually and use the minimum equipment necessary to perform procedures.

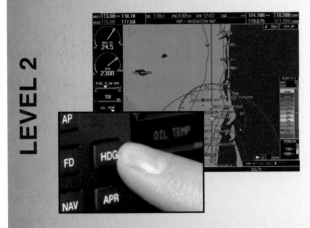

LEVEL 2

Level 2 — Use the autopilot to help manage workload, but manually control the airplane at times. In addition, use the flight environment avionics information to enhance situational awareness and to make effective decisions.

LEVEL 3

Level 3 — Control the airplane primarily by the autopilot. Use a wide variety of avionics tools, including navigation and flight planning information to manage workload and maintain an increased level of situational awareness.

Figure 1-32. As you gain experience with your airplane's specific equipment, you will learn how to determine which equipment operating level to use in specific situations.

AVIATION PHYSIOLOGY

The study of aviation physiology is an important part of human factors training. How you feel physically has a direct impact on how well you fly. As you gain advanced certificates and ratings, you become accustomed to elements of flight, such as motion and pressure differences. However, flying within the instrument and commercial environments also means that you will be exposed to situations you might not have previously encountered. You should be aware of the effects that these situations have on you physically and mentally as you continue your professional training. This information also will help you understand the reactions your passengers could experience, so you can better prepare them for flight.

DISORIENTATION

You sense your body's position in relation to your environment using input from three primary sources: vision, the vestibular system located in your inner ear, and your kinesthetic sense. During flight, you can experience disorientation if your brain receives conflicting messages from your senses. **Kinesthetic sense** is the term used to describe an awareness of position obtained from the nerves in your skin, joints, and muscles. Kinesthetic sense is unreliable, however, because the brain cannot tell the difference between input caused by gravity and that of maneuvering G-loads.

 To prevent or overcome spatial disorientation in IFR conditions, you must rely on and properly interpret the indication of the flight instruments.

 You are more subject to disorientation if you use body signals to interpret flight attitude.

In good weather and daylight, you obtain your orientation primarily through your vision. In IFR conditions or at night, there are fewer visual cues, and your body relies upon the vestibular and kinesthetic senses to supplement your vision. Because these senses can provide false cues about your orientation, the probability of disorientation occurring in IFR weather is quite high. Fatigue, anxiety, heavy pilot workloads, and the intake of alcohol or other drugs increase your susceptibility to disorientation and visual illusions. These factors increase response times, inhibit decision-making abilities, cause a breakdown in scanning techniques, and impair night vision. To alleviate symptoms of disorientation, you must properly interpret and rely on the indications of the flight instruments. Reducing your workload with the use of an autopilot or flight director and improving your cockpit management skills can help prevent overload and reduce the possibility of disorientation.

Common symptoms of disorientation include lightheadedness, dizziness, the feeling of instability, and the sensation of spinning. Spatial or vestibular disorientation can cause you or your passengers to experiencing these sensations during flight. Although the term spatial disorientation often is used to describe vestibular disorientation, the two terms have different meanings.

SPATIAL DISORIENTATION

Spatial disorientation occurs when there is a conflict between the signals relayed by your central vision and information provided by your peripheral vision. Spatial disorientation is more likely when you are in IFR conditions, as your peripheral vision has practically none of the references needed to establish orientation. The movement of rain or snow seen out the window by your peripheral vision can also lead to a misinterpretation of your own movement and position in space. This is similar to the illusion of motion that you experience when an airplane next to yours begins to taxi away from its parking space. Your peripheral vision can misinterpret this visual cue and lead you to believe that your stationary airplane is in motion.

VESTIBULAR DISORIENTATION

When subjected to the different forces of flight during instrument maneuvers, the vestibular system can send misleading signals to the brain resulting in **vestibular disorientation**. The vestibular system, located in your inner ear, consists of the vestibule and three semicircular canals. The utricle and saccule organs within the vestibule are responsible for the perception of gravity and linear acceleration. A gelatinous substance within the utricle and saccule is coated with a layer of tiny grains of limestone called otoliths. Movement of the vestibule causes the otoliths to shift, which in turn causes hair cells to send out nerve impulses to the brain for interpretation.

The semicircular canals are oriented in three planes, each at a 90° angle to the other two. This allows them to sense yaw, pitch, and roll. The canals are filled with fluid, and each has a gelatinous structure called the cupula. When the body changes position, the canals move but the fluid lags behind, causing the cupula to lean away from the movement. Movement of the cupula results in the deflection of hair cells that stimulate the vestibular nerve. This nerve transmits impulses to the brain, which interprets the signals as motion about an axis. [Figures 1-33 and 1-34]

 FAA Without visual reference, changes in centrifugal force can make you feel like you are rising or falling.

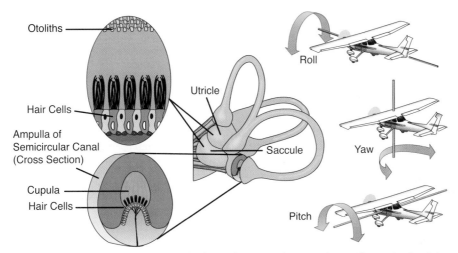

Figure 1-33. The semicircular canals lie in three planes and sense the motions of roll, pitch, and yaw. The vestibular nerve transmits impulses to the brain to interpret the motion.

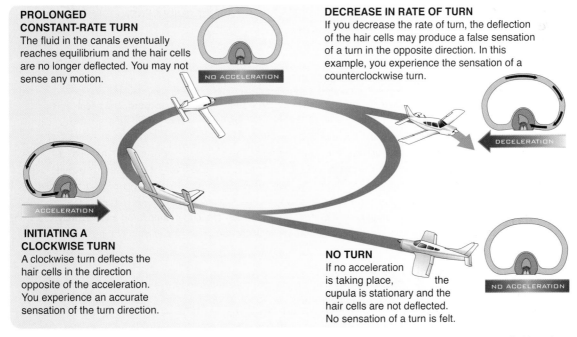

PROLONGED CONSTANT-RATE TURN
The fluid in the canals eventually reaches equilibrium and the hair cells are no longer deflected. You may not sense any motion.

DECREASE IN RATE OF TURN
If you decrease the rate of turn, the deflection of the hair cells may produce a false sensation of a turn in the opposite direction. In this example, you experience the sensation of a counterclockwise turn.

INITIATING A CLOCKWISE TURN
A clockwise turn deflects the hair cells in the direction opposite of the acceleration. You experience an accurate sensation of the turn direction.

NO TURN
If no acceleration is taking place, the cupula is stationary and the hair cells are not deflected. No sensation of a turn is felt.

Figure 1-34. During a prolonged, constant-rate turn, you might not sense any motion because the fluid in the semicircular canals eventually reaches equilibrium and the hair cells are no longer deflected.

The majority of the illusions that lead to vestibular disorientation occur when visibility is restricted. Awareness of these illusions will aid you in coping with them in flight. It takes many hours of training and experience before you are competent to fly an aircraft solely by reference to instruments. [Figure 1-35]

SECTION B ■ Advanced Human Factors Concepts

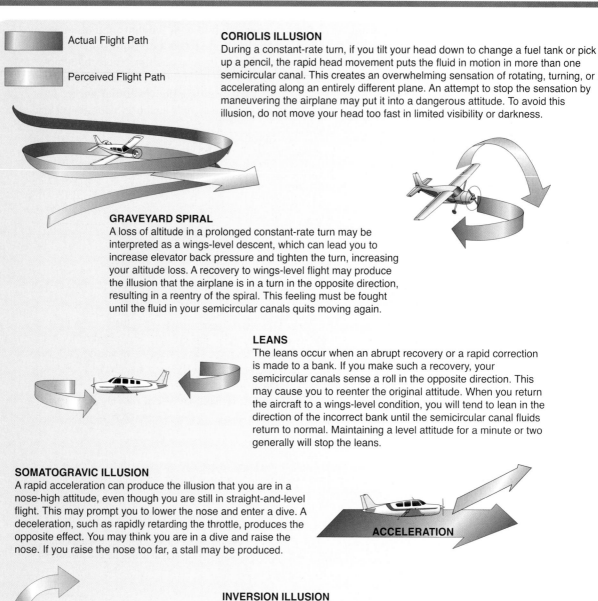

CORIOLIS ILLUSION
During a constant-rate turn, if you tilt your head down to change a fuel tank or pick up a pencil, the rapid head movement puts the fluid in motion in more than one semicircular canal. This creates an overwhelming sensation of rotating, turning, or accelerating along an entirely different plane. An attempt to stop the sensation by maneuvering the airplane may put it into a dangerous attitude. To avoid this illusion, do not move your head too fast in limited visibility or darkness.

GRAVEYARD SPIRAL
A loss of altitude in a prolonged constant-rate turn may be interpreted as a wings-level descent, which can lead you to increase elevator back pressure and tighten the turn, increasing your altitude loss. A recovery to wings-level flight may produce the illusion that the airplane is in a turn in the opposite direction, resulting in a reentry of the spiral. This feeling must be fought until the fluid in your semicircular canals quits moving again.

LEANS
The leans occur when an abrupt recovery or a rapid correction is made to a bank. If you make such a recovery, your semicircular canals sense a roll in the opposite direction. This may cause you to reenter the original attitude. When you return the aircraft to a wings-level condition, you will tend to lean in the direction of the incorrect bank until the semicircular canal fluids return to normal. Maintaining a level attitude for a minute or two generally will stop the leans.

SOMATOGRAVIC ILLUSION
A rapid acceleration can produce the illusion that you are in a nose-high attitude, even though you are still in straight-and-level flight. This may prompt you to lower the nose and enter a dive. A deceleration, such as rapidly retarding the throttle, produces the opposite effect. You may think you are in a dive and raise the nose. If you raise the nose too far, a stall may be produced.

INVERSION ILLUSION
An abrupt change from a climb to straight-and-level flight can create the feeling that you are tumbling backward. The effect may cause you to lower the nose abruptly, which may intensify the illusion.

Figure 1-35. Several illusions associated with the vestibular system can create disorientation.

 A rapid acceleration during takeoff can create the illusion of being in a nose-up attitude, and an abrupt change from climb to straight-and-level flight can create the illusion of tumbling backward. See figure 1-35.

 If you move your head abruptly during a prolonged constant-rate turn in IFR conditions, you might become disoriented. See figure 1-35.

MOTION SICKNESS

Nausea, sweating, dizziness, and vomiting are some of the symptoms of **motion sickness**, which often is caused by vestibular disorientation. During visual flight, you overcome motion sickness by focusing your eyes on the outside horizon. However, in the clouds, precipitation, fog, or haze that constitute IFR conditions, this becomes impossible. To overcome motion sickness without outside visual references, focus on the instrument panel, because it is your only source of accurate position information.

Lost in the Air

A skater executes a jump, and follows an arcing flight path over the ice. Like a pilot, the skater must remain aware of his or her position so that a smooth landing can be made. The skater uses a visual reference during the takeoff portion of the jump to maintain consistency in the rotation and landing. This reference helps the skater balance and know when to open up, stop the rotation, and reach for the ice with the landing foot. If the visual reference is lost, the skater risks becoming lost in the air and unsure of his or her position on the ice.

During flight, much like the skater, you must use a visual reference to maintain orientation. Instrument flight is made more challenging by the lack of an outside visual reference. If you become unsure of your position in space, you must learn to rely on the instruments to avoid becoming lost in the air.

SECTION B ■ Advanced Human Factors Concepts

HYPOXIA

Hypoxia occurs when the tissues in the body do not receive enough oxygen. Hypoxia can be caused by several factors including an insufficient supply of oxygen, inadequate transportation of oxygen, or the inability of the body tissues to use oxygen. An insidious characteristic of hypoxia is that its early symptoms include euphoria, which can prevent you from recognizing a potentially hazardous situation. You should remain alert for the other symptoms of hypoxia such as headache, increased response time, impaired judgment, drowsiness, dizziness, tingling fingers and toes, numbness, blue fingernails and lips (cyanosis), and limp muscles. The forms of hypoxia are divided into four major groups based on their causes: hypoxic hypoxia, hypemic hypoxia, stagnant hypoxia, and histotoxic hypoxia.

FAA Hypoxia is the result of the brain and body tissue not receiving a sufficient supply of oxygen.

HYPOXIC HYPOXIA

As you progress to airplanes that are capable of flying at high altitudes, you must have a good understanding of the adverse physiological effects that can occur due to changes in atmospheric pressure. [Figure 1-36] Although the percentage of oxygen in the atmosphere is constant, its partial pressure decreases proportionately as atmospheric pressure decreases. For example, at 18,000 feet, atmospheric pressure decreases to approximately one-half of sea level pressure. **Hypoxic hypoxia** occurs when there are not enough molecules of oxygen available at sufficient pressure to pass between the membranes in your respiratory system. Hypoxic hypoxia is considered to be the most lethal of all physiological causes of accidents.

As you ascend, the hemoglobin that carries the oxygen molecules throughout your body receives a lower oxygen saturation. For example, at 10,000 feet MSL, the oxygen saturation level of the hemoglobin is approximately 85%. When the saturation value is 85% or lower, your body's functions start to degrade, becoming worse with increased altitude.

Top of the Atmosphere

14.7 Pounds

78% Nitrogen
1% Other Gases
21% Oxygen

Area = 1 Square Inch

Sea Level

Atmosphere

260,000 ft

Figure 1-36. The atmosphere is a mixture of gases that exists in fairly uniform proportions up to approximately 260,000 feet above the earth.

Hypoxia is particularly hazardous during flights with only one pilot because symptoms can be difficult to recognize before your reactions are affected.

Hypoxic hypoxia can occur very suddenly at high altitudes during rapid decompression, or it can occur slowly at lower altitudes when you are exposed to insufficient oxygen over an extended period of time. The **time of useful consciousness** is the maximum time you have to make a rational, life-saving decision and carry it out following a lack of oxygen at a given altitude. [Figure 1-37]

Altitude	Time of Useful Consciousness
45,000 feet MSL	9 to 15 seconds
40,000 feet MSL	15 to 20 seconds
35,000 feet MSL	30 to 60 seconds
30,000 feet MSL	1 to 2 minutes
28,000 feet MSL	2 1/2 to 3 minutes
25,000 feet MSL	3 to 5 minutes
22,000 feet MSL	5 to 10 minutes
20,000 feet MSL	30 minutes or more

Figure 1-37. Beyond the time of useful consciousness, you might not be able to complete even the simplest task, such as putting on your oxygen mask.

OTHER FORMS OF HYPOXIA

Hypemic hypoxia occurs when your blood is not able to carry a sufficient amount of oxygen to your body's cells. This type of hypoxia can be caused by any condition that results in a reduced number of healthy blood cells such as anemia, disease, blood loss, or deformed blood cells. In addition, hypemic hypoxia can be caused by any factor, such as carbon monoxide poisoning, which interferes with the attachment of oxygen to the blood's hemoglobin. Because it attaches itself to the hemoglobin about 200 times more easily than does oxygen, carbon monoxide (CO) prevents the blood from carrying sufficient oxygen. As the hemoglobin becomes progressively saturated with CO, the body tissues are deprived of oxygen, eventually producing physiological symptoms similar to those encountered with hypoxic hypoxia. One difference is that CO poisoning does not produce cyanosis, the blue lips or fingernails symptomatic of some other forms of hypoxia.

Hypemic hypoxia can be encountered at any altitude; however, hypoxia susceptibility due to the inhalation of CO increases as altitude increases. Carbon monoxide can enter an airplane through a faulty cabin heater system. With most single-engine airplanes, ventilation air is heated by flowing through a shroud that surrounds the exterior of the exhaust muffler or manifold. If the exhaust system develops a crack or hole within the cavity, carbon monoxide can combine with the ventilation air and subsequently be delivered to the cabin. During flight, if you suspect that carbon monoxide is entering the cabin, immediately shut off the cabin heat, open the fresh air vents or windows, and land as soon as possible. As an added precaution, if supplemental breathing oxygen is available, you and your passengers should use it until the landing is made. Even after you have eliminated the CO exposure, it can take up to 48 hours for your body to dispose of the carbon monoxide. [Figure 1-38]

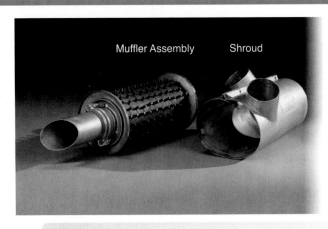

Figure 1-38. To help prevent carbon monoxide poisoning, have the heater shroud and exhaust system inspected regularly for cracks or damage.

 Hypoxia susceptibility due to the inhalation of CO increases as altitude increases.

 Frequent inspections should be made of aircraft exhaust manifold-type heating systems to minimize the possibility of exhaust gases leaking into the cockpit.

If you are a smoker, you most likely contain a certain level of CO in your bloodstream all the time. Approximately 2.5% of the volume of cigarette smoke is carbon monoxide. Inhaling the smoke of 3 cigarettes at sea level can give you a blood saturation of 4% carbon monoxide. This causes a reduction in visual acuity and dark adaptation similar to the mild hypoxia encountered at 8,000 feet MSL. Heavy smokers can have carbon monoxide blood saturation as high as 8%.

Stagnant hypoxia is an oxygen deficiency in the body due to the poor circulation of the blood. During flight, stagnant hypoxia can be the result of pulling excessive positive Gs, or cold temperatures can decrease the blood supply to the extremities. The inability of the cells to effectively use oxygen is defined as **histotoxic hypoxia**. This impairment of cellular respiration can be caused by alcohol and other drugs such as narcotics and poisons. [Figure 1-39]

HYPOXIC HYPOXIA – Inadequate Supply of Oxygen
The more quickly you ascend, the less effective your individual tolerance, and you may be less aware of approaching hypoxia.

HYPEMIC HYPOXIA –Inability of the Blood to Carry Oxygen
Smoking at 10,000 feet MSL produces effects equivalent to those experienced at 14,000 feet MSL without smoking.

STAGNANT HYPOXIA – Inadequate Circulation of Oxygen
A heart problem, a constricted artery, and shock are conditions which can lead to stagnant hypoxia.

HISTOTOXIC HYPOXIA – Inability of the Cells to Effectively Use Oxygen
Research has shown that drinking one ounce of alcohol can equate to about an additional 2,000 feet of physiological altitude.

Figure 1-39. A combination of different types of hypoxia affecting your body can cause you to experience symptoms at much lower altitudes than expected.

SECTION B ■ **Advanced Human Factors Concepts**

PREVENTION OF HYPOXIA

Even if you learn the early symptoms of hypoxia, do not assume that you will be able to take corrective action whenever they occur. Because judgment and rationality deteriorate when you are suffering from hypoxia, prevention is the best approach. Your susceptibility to hypoxia is related to many factors, many of which you can control. You can increase your tolerance to hypoxia by maintaining good physical condition, eating a nutritious diet, and by avoiding alcohol and smoking. If you live at a high altitude and have become acclimated, you normally have an increased tolerance to the conditions that would lead to hypoxia compared to a person living at a lower altitude.

Your body requires more oxygen during physical activity. For example, you risk becoming hypoxic more readily when you are flying the aircraft manually in turbulent IFR conditions than during a smooth VFR flight. In addition, your body uses energy to cope with temperature extremes in the cockpit, which is comparable to increased activity.

SUPPLEMENTAL OXYGEN

If you are planning a flight with a cruise altitude over 12,500 feet MSL, you should review FAR Part 91 for the requirements regarding **supplemental oxygen.** [Figure 1-40] As a general rule, the FAA recommends that you begin using supplemental oxygen whenever you are flying at cabin pressure altitudes greater than 10,000 feet MSL during the day. However, because night vision acuity is highly affected by the partial pressure of oxygen, the FAA recommends the use of supplemental oxygen above a cabin pressure altitude of 5,000 feet while flying at night. Chapter 11, Section B — Environmental and Ice Control Systems describes the various supplemental oxygen systems used in aircraft.

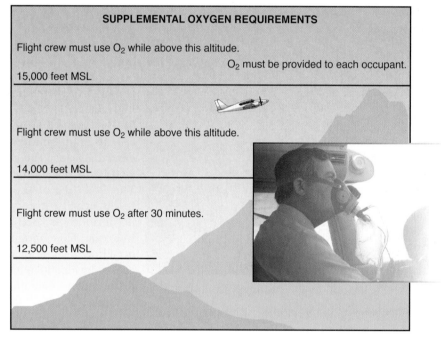

SUPPLEMENTAL OXYGEN REQUIREMENTS

Flight crew must use O₂ while above this altitude.

O₂ must be provided to each occupant.

15,000 feet MSL

Flight crew must use O₂ while above this altitude.

14,000 feet MSL

Flight crew must use O₂ after 30 minutes.

12,500 feet MSL

Figure 1-40. You are required by FAR Part 91 to begin using supplemental oxygen after 30 minutes above 12,500 feet MSL.

HIGH-ALTITUDE TRAINING

Aircraft cabin pressurization is the maintenance of a cabin altitude lower than the actual flight altitude by a system that compresses air. Pressurization systems reduce some of the physiological problems experienced at high altitudes. However, prior to operating a pressurized aircraft, with a service ceiling or maximum operating altitude higher than 25,000 feet MSL, you must complete **high-altitude training.** This training consists of ground instruction on high-altitude aerodynamics and meteorology, respiration, hypoxia,

use of supplemental oxygen, and other physiological aspects of high-altitude flight. More information on high-altitude operations is provided in Chapter 11, Section B — Environmental and Ice Control Systems. [Figure 1-41]

Figure 1-41. Several single-engine and light twin-engine aircraft are pressurized, and you must have a high-altitude logbook endorsement before you can operate them as pilot in command.

DECOMPRESSION SICKNESS

Decompression sickness (DCS) is a condition caused by a rapid reduction in the ambient pressure surrounding the body. When decompression occurs, nitrogen and other inert gases that are normally dissolved in body tissue and fluid expand to form bubbles that rise out of solution, in the same way that dissolved $CO2$ appears as bubbles when you uncap a bottle of soda. These bubbles produce a variety of symptoms, which range from pain in the large joints of the body, such as elbows, shoulders, hips, wrists, knees and ankles, to seizures and unconsciousness. These symptoms tend to increase in severity depending on the rate and amount of pressure change and, if severe enough, can result in death. When DCS develops as a result of the decreased pressure at high altitude, it is commonly referred to as high-altitude sickness or altitude-induced DCS.

Pressure changes resulting from underwater activities such as scuba diving can cause DCS. For example, diving from sea level to a depth of 33 feet subjects your body to twice the sea level air pressure. When combined with breathing high pressure air from diving equipment, there is a significant increase in the amount of nitrogen dissolved in body tissues. If you don't allow the nitrogen level to decrease during your ascent to the water surface, DCS might occur. Even after a dive, it takes some time for the body to completely eliminate the excess nitrogen. If the nitrogen is not removed, a flight at high cabin altitudes can produce severe symptoms of altitude-induced DCS. [Figure 1-42]

The recommended waiting time before ascending to 8,000 feet MSL is at least 12 hours after a dive which has not required a controlled ascent (nondecompression stop diving), and at least 24 hours after a dive which has required a controlled ascent (decompression stop diving). The waiting time before ascending to flight altitudes above 8,000 feet MSL should be at least 24 hours after any scuba dive.

Figure 1-42. If you or a passenger plan to fly after scuba diving, allow enough time for the body to rid itself of excess nitrogen absorbed during diving.

SECTION B ■ Advanced Human Factors Concepts

Normally, people don't experience altitude-induced DCS below 29,000 feet unless the ascent has been extremely rapid or they have been in a high ambient pressure environment before flying. However, DCS can occur if a pressurized airplane rapidly decompresses while at altitude. Rapid decompressions are rare, but if one occurs, be alert for DCS symptoms. Continue to watch for symptoms for a couple of days after the flight. In addition, if the decompression occurred with passengers, brief them on the possible delayed effects so they know to monitor their own condition. If symptoms occur, use supplemental breathing oxygen until proper medical treatment can be obtained, because oxygen helps to flush the nitrogen from the body.

HYPERVENTILATION

Breathing too rapidly or too deeply can cause **hyperventilation**, a physiological disorder that develops when too much carbon dioxide (CO_2) is eliminated from the body. Without a sufficient quantity of CO_2, normal respiration is disturbed, producing symptoms that resemble hypoxia. If you are hyperventilating, you might experience drowsiness, dizziness, shortness of breath, and feelings of suffocation. In addition, hyperventilation can produce a pale, clammy appearance and muscle spasms, in contrast to the cyanosis and limp muscles associated with hypoxia. If you lose too much CO_2 from your body, you might lose unconsciousness as the respiratory system's overriding mechanism takes control of your breathing. After you become unconscious, your breathing rate will be exceedingly low until the CO_2 level in your blood increases enough to stimulate normal respiration.

Hyperventilation can be triggered by tension, fear, or anxiety. Slowing your breathing rate, talking aloud, or breathing into a paper bag normally restores the body's proper carbon dioxide level. Although you might experience hyperventilation in a stressful situation, you should be especially alert to the symptoms of hyperventilation in passengers who might feel anxious about flying.

 Hyperventilation might cause you to experience drowsiness, dizziness, shortness of breath, and feelings of suffocation. The condition is usually caused by an insufficient supply of carbon dioxide, produced by breathing too rapidly or too deeply.

 To overcome the symptoms of hyperventilation, you should slow your breathing rate.

STRESS

Stress is the body's reaction to the physical and psychological demands placed upon it. You might typically think of stress as negative, such as the work- or family-induced stress that confront you in daily living. However, stress can be positive as well. When your body is placed under stress, chemical hormones are released into the blood, and your metabolism speeds up. Heart rate, respiration, blood pressure, and perspiration all increase. A small amount of stress is good because it helps keep you alert and aware. When stress builds, however, it interferes with your ability to focus and cope with a given situation.

For example, a normal flight contains a certain amount of stress, depending on the weather, your familiarity with the route and destination, and the condition of the airplane. Because stress is cumulative, you also bring into the flight varying degrees of stress left over from the other areas of your life. Trouble with a spouse or parent, tension on the job and major life changes can cause large amounts of stress that affect your ability to fly. [Figure 1-43]

Figure 1-43. Stress comes from many different sources, and its cumulative effects can interfere with your capacity to operate an aircraft safely.

FATIGUE

Fatigue deserves special mention when considering the instrument and commercial flight environments. As an instrument pilot, your level of concentration often needs to be highest at the end of a flight, when you are most likely to be tired. If you operate as a commercial pilot for hire, you might be asked to fly many times in one day, several days in a row, and you might feel tired as you adapt to the schedule. Because both realms of flight are typically more demanding than a personal flight in VFR conditions, any residual fatigue you have, from lack of sleep to excess physical work, can significantly affect your ability to operate safely. Many serious accidents attributed to pilot error have occurred at the end of a long duty day, when cockpit crews were tired and pilot performance suffered. Fatigue has been a major factor in many fatal accidents involving very experienced and highly qualified crews.

Noise and vibration in the cockpit environment also add to your fatigue level. If you do not already own one, purchasing a headset can be one of the best investments you can make as a pilot. Make sure the headset fits snugly, and is at least noise-attenuating. Low-cost earplugs are also beneficial, and you should carry some for passenger use during flight.

No amount of training can overcome the effects of fatigue. Getting adequate rest on a regular basis is the only way to perform at your best. Be skeptical of any drug, supplement, or product that claims to provide energy or reduce fatigue. Drugs cannot help you to offset fatigue. There is no substitute for a good night's sleep.

SECTION B ■ **Advanced Human Factors Concepts**

The Key to Success is Knowing When to Quit

On June 4, 1935, two brothers, Fred and Algene Key, took off in a Curtiss Robin named Ole Miss from the airport at Meridian, Mississippi. The Ole Miss did not touch down until July 1 after remaining aloft 653 hours and 34 minutes — a total of 27 days. The airplane was refueled and the brothers received supplies in flight from another airplane 432 times.

A metal catwalk had been constructed around the front of the fuselage to enable the Keys to lubricate the engine and conduct emergency repairs. Because Fred was the smaller of the two brothers, he was tasked with climbing out on the catwalk when necessary. The Key brothers endured thunderstorms, an electrical fire in the cabin, and a close call with turbulence while Fred was on the catwalk, but perhaps their greatest obstacle was fatigue.

By June 30 the stress and fatigue of the grueling flight had taken its toll and it was apparent the brothers would not be able to stay aloft until July 4, their original target date.

The constant vibration was causing two types of fatigue: metal fatigue in which wires and braces were threatening to weaken, and mental fatigue which created disorientation in the pilots. Nerve shock and sheer weariness caused the Key who was resting to have to take as many as five minutes before he could wake and get his bearings. Under such circumstances, emergencies could not be dealt with easily. — The Flying Key Brothers and Their Flight to Remember, by Stephen Owen

Upon landing, a crowd of 35,000 to 40,000 spectators flocked to pay tribute to the exhausted aviation heroes. The mob lifted the weary heroes from the plane after the Ole Miss touched down on the newly-christened Key Field.

ALCOHOL AND DRUGS

Anytime you are ill enough to require medication, you should closely examine your plans to conduct a flight. Many drugs used to alleviate symptoms of illness and disease have side effects that interfere with your ability to fly safely. Prior to flying you should consult an aviation medical examiner about any medication you are using.

Alcohol and other depressants impair the body's functioning in several critical areas, causing decreased mental processing and slow motor and reaction responses. Due to the high level of performance required by instrument and commercial flight operations, using depressants while acting as pilot in command greatly increases your risk of an accident. The FARs specifically state that you must not fly within 8 hours of using alcohol, or when you have a blood alcohol level of .04% or greater. However, the regulations also state that anytime your ability is impaired by alcohol or any drug, you are unfit for flight. Even small amounts of alcohol impair your judgment and decision-making abilities. Most commercial flight departments require pilots to wait 24 hours after consuming alcohol before they fly. Whether your employer requires it or not, you should apply this policy to your own flying in the interest of flight safety.

 Judgment and decision-making abilities can be adversely affected by even small amounts of alcohol.

Commercial airlines and most flight departments conduct random and pre-hire drug tests to reinforce the idea that drugs have no place in the cockpit. Illicit drugs can cause hallucinations and other withdrawal effects that last long after the drugs were taken. [Figure 1-44]

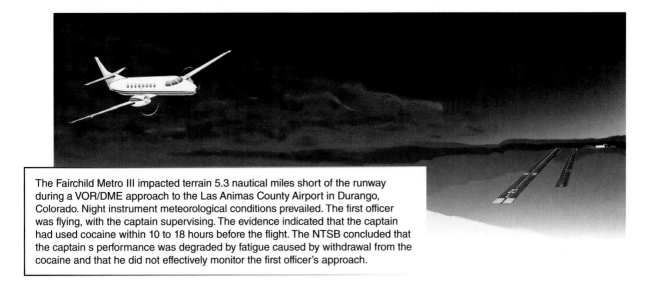

The Fairchild Metro III impacted terrain 5.3 nautical miles short of the runway during a VOR/DME approach to the Las Animas County Airport in Durango, Colorado. Night instrument meteorological conditions prevailed. The first officer was flying, with the captain supervising. The evidence indicated that the captain had used cocaine within 10 to 18 hours before the flight. The NTSB concluded that the captain s performance was degraded by fatigue caused by withdrawal from the cocaine and that he did not effectively monitor the first officer's approach.

Witnesses reported seeing the Grumman American AA-5B flying at tree height when it struck a power line. Following the wire strike, flames erupted from the airplane, and it flew for another mile before hitting a second power line and crashing. A toxicology test revealed that the pilot was under the influence of marijuana at the time of the crash.

Figure 1-44. These accidents graphically illustrate why drugs and flying do not go together.

 FAA When conducting a night flight, avoid the use of regular white light, such as a flashlight, because it will impair night adaptation. In addtion, reduce the interior lighting intensity in the aircraft to a minimum level.

FITNESS FOR FLIGHT

Your overall health has a large impact on how you fly. A general program of exercise and a balanced diet will improve your mental clarity and energy level, and your piloting skills will benefit. [Figure 1-45]

Figure 1-45. An exercise regimen can be as little as 30 minutes of aerobic exercise, such as walking, jogging or cycling, performed at least 3 times a week. Exercise increases your stamina and makes you less prone to a heart attack or stroke.

SECTION B ■ **Advanced Human Factors Concepts**

Before each flight, a run-through of the I'M SAFE checklist will aid you in determining your fitness for flight. In broad terms, ask yourself about any reservations you have concerning the flight. Am I ill, or taking any drugs that might affect my safety as a pilot? Have I had enough rest? Did I eat a good breakfast? Are my issues at work going to interfere with my concentration level in the airplane? If you have any reservations about your ability to make the flight, save the trip for another time. Do not let the pressures of returning home, or impressing friends, or proving your worth as a pilot disrupt your honest evaluation of your fitness to fly. None of these reasons have anything to do with your skill, but they have everything to do with good judgment.

Physiology of the Final Frontier

The International Space Station (ISS) is one of the greatest international scientific and technological endeavors ever undertaken. [Figure A] Thirteen nations around the world worked together to create this permanent laboratory where gravity, temperature, and pressure can be manipulated for a variety of scientific and engineering pursuits in ways that are impossible in ground-based laboratories.

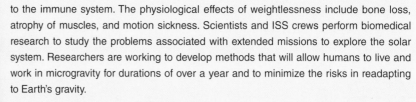

To better prepare crews for missions aboard the ISS, NASA has a wide variety of programs in place to study the physiological effects of living in space. Traveling to the low-gravity environment of Earth orbit affects virtually every system in the body, from bones and muscles to the immune system. The physiological effects of weightlessness include bone loss, atrophy of muscles, and motion sickness. Scientists and ISS crews perform biomedical research to study the problems associated with extended missions to explore the solar system. Researchers are working to develop methods that will allow humans to live and work in microgravity for durations of over a year and to minimize the risks in readapting to Earth's gravity.

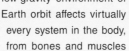

Another research program studies changes in the coordination of head and eye movements associated with adaptation to microgravity, and examines how vestibular and visual information is processed in the absence of a gravitational reference.

Assembly of the ISS required hundreds of hours of space walks, or extravehicular activities (EVAs). The goal of the Neutral Buoyancy Lab (NBL) located at the Johnson Space Center is to prepare for space missions involving EVAs. NASA team members utilize the NBL to develop flight procedures, verify hardware compatibility, train EVA astronauts, and refine EVA operations. [Figure B] The ability to successfully and predictably perform assembly and maintenance operations in orbit is critical to the success of future space endeavors.

The history of aviation has involved not only improvements in aircraft design and equipment, but also an increased understanding of how our minds and bodies function in flight. Both endeavors are crucial to flight safety. Now, as we develop new technology to venture out and investigate the solar system, human factors come to the fore. In order to explore the universe, we must first explore ourselves.

We used to joke about canned men, putting people in a can and seeing how far you can send them and bring them back. That's not the purpose of this program . . . Space is a laboratory, and we go into it to work and learn the new.
— John H. Glenn Jr.

Photos and emblem courtesy of NASA

SUMMARY CHECKLIST

✓ Applying single-pilot resource management (SRM) means using hardware, information, and human resources, such as dispatchers, weather briefers, maintenance personnel, and air traffic controllers, to gather information, analyze your situation, and make effective decisions about the current and future status of your flight.

✓ The airline industry implemented crew resource management (CRM) training to provide tools for flight crews to eliminate hazards or minimize their impact.

✓ Aeronautical decision making (ADM) is a systematic approach to the mental process used by aircraft pilots to consistently determine the best course of action in response to a given set of circumstances.

✓ The ADM process consists of the steps that you use to make effective decisions as pilot in command.

✓ Your general health, stress or fatigue level, attitude, knowledge, skill level, and recency of experience are factors that affect your performance as pilot in command.

✓ Establish personal limitations for flight and use the I'M SAFE checklist to evaluate your fitness for flight.

✓ Five hazardous attitudes that can interfere with a pilot's ability to make effective decisions are: anti-authority, macho, impulsivity, invulnerability, and resignation.

✓ Perform self-critiques after each flight to evaluate your performance, determine the skills that need improvement, and create a plan for increasing your proficiency.

✓ You are using learner-centered grading when both you and your instructor evaluate your performance and resolve any differences in your assessments before creating a plan for improvement.

✓ Risk management involves making decision about four fundamental risk elements: the pilot, the aircraft, the environment, and the type of operation.

✓ PAVE and the 5Ps remind you of the risk factors that you must manage when planning and implementing flights.

✓ 5P checklists provide guidelines on the risk factors to consider during flight planning.

✓ During flight, use the 5P check to evaluate the situation at decision points that correspond to the phases of flight.

✓ Task management involves planning and prioritizing tasks to avoid work overload, identifying and using resources to accomplish tasks, and managing distractions.

✓ When using a do-list, you read the checklist item and the associated action and then perform the action.

✓ A flow pattern guides you through the cockpit in a logical order. Following completion of the flow pattern, refer to the checklist and verify that you have accomplished each item.

✓ Situational awareness is the accurate perception of all the operational and environmental factors that affect flight safety before, during, and after the flight.

✓ Passenger briefings, takeoff briefings, and before-landing briefings are effective tools to help you maintain situational awareness by preparing you for critical phases of flight.

SECTION B ■ Advanced Human Factors Concepts

✓ Fatigue, stress, and work overload can cause you to fixate on one aspect of the flight and omit others from your attention.

✓ Complacency is an obstacle to maintaining situational awareness; when activities are routine, you might relax and put less effort into your performance.

✓ Controlled flight into terrain (CFIT) occurs when an aircraft is flown into terrain or water with no prior awareness on the part of the crew that the crash is imminent.

✓ The concept of automation management typically applies to an airplane with an advanced avionics system that includes digital displays, GPS equipment, a moving map, and an integrated autopilot

✓ To effectively manage automation, monitor the current mode, anticipate the next mode, and verify that mode changes occur as expected.

✓ To help you manage automation and other avionics equipment, consider using one of three equipment operating levels during flight operations.

✓ When there is a conflict between the information relayed by your central vision and your peripheral vision, you might suffer from spatial disorientation.

✓ When subjected to the various forces of flight, the vestibular system can send misleading signals to the brain resulting in vestibular disorientation.

✓ Hypoxia occurs when the tissues in the body do not receive enough oxygen. Hypoxia can be caused by several factors including an insufficient supply of oxygen, inadequate transportation of oxygen, or the inability of the body tissues to use oxygen.

✓ Hypoxic hypoxia occurs when there are not enough molecules of oxygen available at sufficient pressure to pass between the membranes in your respiratory system.

✓ Hypemic hypoxia occurs when your blood is not able to carry a sufficient amount of oxygen to your body's cells.

✓ Because it attaches itself to the hemoglobin about 200 times more easily than does oxygen, carbon monoxide (CO) prevents the blood from carrying sufficient oxygen.

✓ Stagnant hypoxia is an oxygen deficiency in the body due to the poor circulation of the blood. During flight, stagnant hypoxia can be the result of pulling excessive positive Gs.

✓ The inability of the cells to effectively use oxygen is defined as histotoxic hypoxia. This impairment of cellular respiration can be caused by alcohol and other drugs such as narcotics and poisons.

✓ If you are planning a flight with a cruise altitude over 12,500 feet MSL, review FAR Part 91 for the requirements regarding supplemental oxygen.

✓ Prior to operating a pressurized aircraft with a service ceiling or maximum operating altitude higher than 25,000 feet MSL, you must complete high-altitude training.

✓ Hyperventilation is a physiological disorder that develops when too much carbon dioxide (CO_2) has been eliminated from the body, usually caused by breathing too rapidly or too deeply.

✓ Decompression sickness (DCS) is a condition caused by a reduction in the ambient pressure surrounding the body, which causes nitrogen and other gases that are dissolved in body tissue to expand and form bubbles. These bubbles produce a variety of symptoms that range from pain in the large joints of the body to seizures and unconsciousness.

✓ If you or a passenger plan to fly after scuba diving, it is important to allow enough time for the body to rid itself of excess nitrogen absorbed during diving.

✓ Stress is the body's reaction to the physical and psychological demands placed upon it, and it can adversely affect your ability to fly safely.

✓ When you are fatigued, you are more prone to error in the cockpit. No amount of training will allow you to overcome the effects of fatigue. Getting adequate rest on a regular basis is the only way to perform at your best.

✓ Prior to flying you should consult an aviation medical examiner about any medication you are using.

✓ Improving your overall fitness can have a positive effect on your performance as a pilot.

KEY TERMS

Single-Pilot Resource Management (SRM)

Crew Resource Management (CRM)

Aeronautical Decision Making (ADM)

ADM Process

I'M SAFE Checklist

Hazardous Attitudes

Self-Critiques

Learner-Centered Grading

Risk Management

PAVE

5Ps

Task Management

Checklists

Do-List

Flow Pattern

Situational Awareness

Briefings

Controlled Flight Into Terrain (CFIT)

Automation Management

Equipment Operating Levels

Kinesthetic Sense

Spatial Disorientation

Vestibular Disorientation

Motion Sickness

Hypoxia

Hypoxic Hypoxia

Time of Useful Consciousness

Hypemic Hypoxia

Stagnant Hypoxia

Histotoxic Hypoxia

Supplemental Oxygen

High-Altitude Training

Decompression Sickness (DCS)

Hyperventilation

Stress

Fatigue

SECTION B ■ Advanced Human Factors Concepts

5P CHECKLISTS

Use these 5P checklists to identify and manage risks when you plan flights.

Pilot			
Summary of Training	**Yes**	**No**	**N/A**
Do I have a current flight review?			
Am I current to carry passengers?			
Have I had recent refresher training in this airplane?			
Am I instrument-current?			
Have I had recent mountain flying training or experience?			

Experience	**Personal Minimums**	**Yes**	**No**	**N/A**
Hours in Specific Airplane				
Last 90 Days				
• Hours				
• Landings				
• Instrument Approaches				
Last 6 Months				
• IFR Hours				
• Instrument Approaches				
• Night Hours				
• Night Landings				
• Strong Crosswind/Gusty Landings				
• Mountain Flying Hours				

Fitness — I'M SAFE	**Yes**	**No**	**N/A**
Illness — Am I healthy?			
Medication — Am I free of prescription or over-the-counter drugs?			
Stress — Am I free of pressure (job, financial matters, health problems, or family discord)?			
Alcohol — Have I abstained from alcohol in the previous 24 hours?			
Fatigue — Did I get at least seven hours of sleep?			
Eating — Am I adequately nourished?			
Emotion — Am I free of emotional upset?			

Passengers			
Experience	**Yes**	**No**	**N/A**
Are my passengers comfortable flying? (spent time in small aircraft, certificated pilots, etc.)			
Fitness	**Yes**	**No**	**N/A**
Are my passengers feeling well? (sickness, likely to experience airsickness, etc.)			
Flexibility	**Yes**	**No**	**N/A**
Are my passengers flexible and well-informed about the changeable nature of flying? (arriving late, diverting to an alternate, etc.)			

Plane			
Airworthiness	**Yes**	**No**	**N/A**
Are the aircraft inspections current and appropriate to the type of flight? (annual and 100-hour inspections, VOR check, etc.)			
Is the required equipment on board and working for the type of flight? (lights for night flight, onboard oxygen, survival gear, etc.)			
Have all prior maintenance issues been taken care of? (squawks resolved, inoperative equipment placarded, etc.)			
Performance	**Yes**	**No**	**N/A**
Can the aircraft carry the planned load within weight and CG limits?			
Is the aircraft performance (takeoff, climb, enroute, and landing) adequate for the available runways, density altitude, and terrain conditions? — Both engines operating			
Is the aircraft performance (takeoff, climb, enroute, and landing) adequate for the available runways, density altitude, and terrain conditions? — One engine inoperative			
Is the fuel capacity adequate for the proposed flight legs, including to an alternate airport if required?			

Programming			
Avionics Airworthiness	**Yes**	**No**	**N/A**
Is the avionics equipment working properly? (squawks resolved, autopilot functional)			
Are all databases current? (GPS navdata, terrain, etc.)			
Avionics Operation	**Yes**	**No**	**N/A**
Are you proficient at operating the avionics equipment?			
Avionics Configuration	**Yes**	**No**	**N/A**
Is the avionics configuration appropriate for the navigation required?			

SECTION B ■ **Advanced Human Factors Concepts**

Plan				
Airport Conditions		**Yes**	**No**	**N/A**
Do NOTAMs indicate my flight can proceed as planned? (no runway or navaid closures, and so on)				
Are services available at the airport during the appropriate time? (fuel, ATC, Unicom, etc.)				
Terrain/Airspace		**Yes**	**No**	**N/A**
Does the airspace and terrain in the area allow me to fly my route as planned? (Check for mountainous terrain, and areas to avoid, such as TFRs, restricted or prohibited areas).				
Mission		**Yes**	**No**	**N/A**
Do I have alternate plans to manage any commitments that exist at my destination? (reschedule meeting, airline reservations, etc.)				
Did I tell the people whom I'm meeting at my destination that I might be late?				
Do I have an overnight kit containing any necessary prescriptions and toiletries?				

Weather	**Location**	**Yes**	**No**	**N/A**
Are the weather conditions acceptable? (no hazards such as thunderstorms, icing, turbulence, etc.)	departure			
	enroute			
	destination			
Is there a suitable airport that meets the regulatory requirements for an alternate if the forecast at my destination requires an alternate airport?				

Weather Limitations	**Personal Limitations**	**Location**	**Yes**	**No**	**N/A**
Are the weather conditions for my flight within my personal limitations?					
• Minimum IFR Approach Ceiling and Visibility		departure			
		destination			
• Minimum Ceiling and Visibility (Day VFR)		departure			
		enroute			
		destination			
• Minimum Ceiling and Visibility (Night VFR)		departure			
		enroute			
		destination			
• Maximum Surface Wind Speed and Gusts		departure			
		destination			
• Maximum Direct Crosswind		departure			
		destination			

CHAPTER 2

Principles of Instrument Flight

Instrument/Commercial
Part I, Chapter 2—Principles of Instrument Flight

SECTION A
Flight Instrument Systems

To fly under instrument flight rules (IFR), you need to control an aircraft while reading charts, tuning radios, and performing a variety of other complex tasks. During your training, you will study and practice attitude instrument flying until it becomes second nature. One essential skill for successful instrument flying is instrument interpretation. You need a good working knowledge of each of the instruments before you can interpret them consistently and accurately.

The instruments that provide information about the airplane's attitude, direction, altitude, and speed are collectively referred to as the flight instruments. For traditional analog instruments, the operating components and the display are often in a single unit. Digital flight instruments can be incorporated into a single integrated flight display as part of a glass cockpit and are covered later in this section.

The flight instruments are categorized according to their method of operation. Gyroscopic instruments, a convenience for VFR flight, are an absolute necessity for IFR flight. The pitot-static instruments also are essential when flying IFR. In the IFR environment, proper instrument interpretation is the basis for aircraft control. Understanding these instruments and systems helps you quickly interpret the instrument indications so you can translate this information into an appropriate control response to enhance safety under IFR.

The FARs require certain instruments for IFR flight in addition to those required for flight under VFR. [Figure 2-1] The altimeter and static system and the transponder must have been inspected within the preceding 24 calendar months. It is your responsibility as pilot in command to determine that each system has been checked and found to meet FAR requirements for instrument flight.

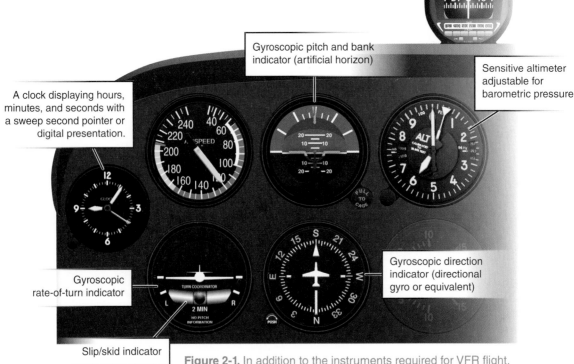

A clock displaying hours, minutes, and seconds with a sweep second pointer or digital presentation.

Gyroscopic pitch and bank indicator (artificial horizon)

Sensitive altimeter adjustable for barometric pressure

Gyroscopic rate-of-turn indicator

Gyroscopic direction indicator (directional gyro or equivalent)

Slip/skid indicator

Figure 2-1. In addition to the instruments required for VFR flight, these six instruments are required for flight under IFR.

You must ensure that the altimeter system test and inspection have been made within the preceding 24 calendar months and that the instruments required for IFR [Figure 2-1] are functioning properly.

GYROSCOPIC FLIGHT INSTRUMENTS

The three gyroscopic instruments in your aircraft are the attitude indicator, heading indicator, and turn coordinator. On most small airplanes, the vacuum system powers the attitude and heading indicators [Figure 2-2]. The electrical system typically powers the turn coordinator. Gyroscopic instrument operation is based on two fundamental concepts that apply to gyroscopes — rigidity in space and precession.

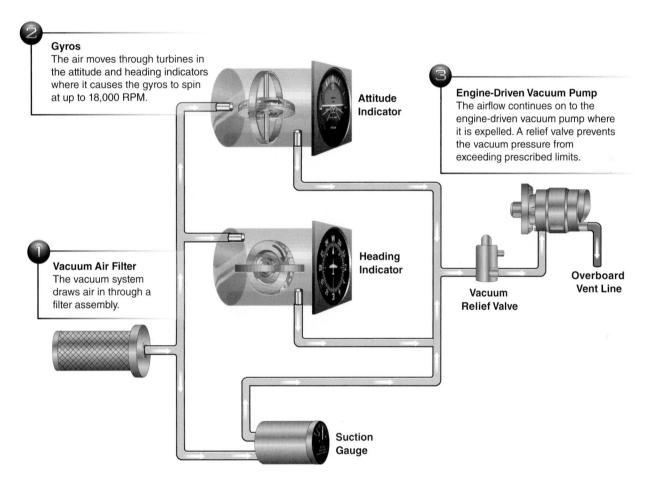

2 Gyros
The air moves through turbines in the attitude and heading indicators where it causes the gyros to spin at up to 18,000 RPM.

Attitude Indicator

3 Engine-Driven Vacuum Pump
The airflow continues on to the engine-driven vacuum pump where it is expelled. A relief valve prevents the vacuum pressure from exceeding prescribed limits.

1 Vacuum Air Filter
The vacuum system draws air in through a filter assembly.

Heading Indicator

Vacuum Relief Valve

Overboard Vent Line

Suction Gauge

Figure 2-2. The vacuum system powers the attitude indicator and heading indicator by using air to spin the gyros.

SECTION A ■ **Flight Instrument Systems**

RIGIDITY IN SPACE

Rigidity in space refers to the principle that a wheel with a heavily weighted rim spun rapidly tends to remain fixed in the plane in which it is spinning. By mounting this wheel, or gyroscope, on a set of **gimbals**, the gyro is able to rotate freely in any plane. If the gimbals' base tilts, twists, or otherwise moves, the gyro remains in the plane in which it was originally spinning. [Figure 2-3] This principle allows a gyroscope to be used to measure changes in the attitude or direction of an airplane.

 A gyro depends upon the resistance to deflection of its internal, spinning disc for proper operation.

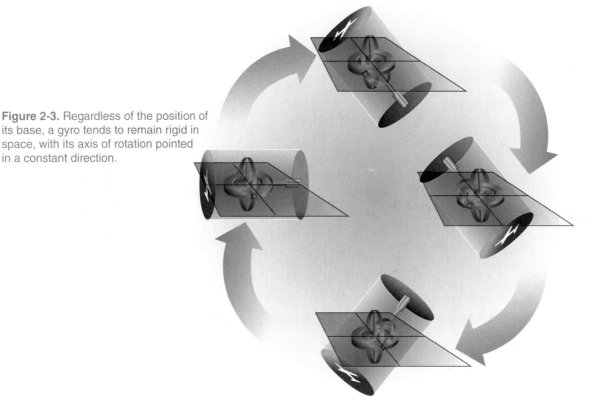

Figure 2-3. Regardless of the position of its base, a gyro tends to remain rigid in space, with its axis of rotation pointed in a constant direction.

Seat of the Pants?

Today we take gyroscopic flight instruments for granted. It was not always apparent that the unique properties of spinning gyros offered the solution to the problem of controlling an aircraft in instrument meteorological conditions.

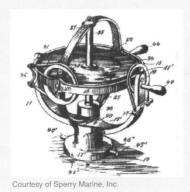
Courtesy of Sperry Marine, Inc.

Some early aviators scoffed at the notion of using delicate flight instruments, preferring to rely on their senses. Their "instruments" consisted of weighted strings hanging from windscreens and silk stockings tied to wing struts. The wiser aviators quickly learned that these tools were inadequate when flying in the clouds, where even the most talented seat-of-the-pants flyers could be in a spin or inverted without even knowing it. An important invention was needed before safe flight in the clouds was possible.

Elmer A. Sperry founded the Sperry Gyroscope Company in 1910, after playing with a child's spinning top and realizing the potential for navigation. Sperry first invented a stabilizer system for ships and then determined gyroscopic principles could be applied to instruments of flight. He invented the bank and turn indicator in 1918, followed by the gyrocompass and the artificial horizon. These three basic gyro instruments are still in use today.

PRECESSION

When an outside force tries to tilt a spinning gyro, the gyro responds as if the force had been applied at a point 90° further around in the direction of rotation. This effect is called **precession**, because the cause precedes the effect by 90°. [Figure 2-4] Unwanted precession is caused by friction in the gimbals and bearings of the instrument, causing a slow drifting in the heading indicator and occasional small errors in the attitude indicator.

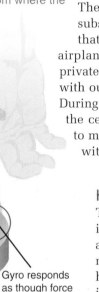

Figure 2-4. When a force (including friction) acts to tilt a spinning gyro, the effect of that force is felt in the direction of rotation 90° from where the force is applied.

Force is applied here.

Gyro responds as though force is applied here.

ATTITUDE INDICATOR

The attitude indicator, or artificial horizon, is a mechanical substitute for the natural horizon. It is the only instrument that gives you an immediate and direct indication of the airplane's pitch and bank attitude. During your integrated private pilot training you learned to use the attitude indicator with outside visual references to control the aircraft precisely. During your instrument training, the attitude indicator becomes the central part of your scan; you use the attitude indicator to make precise adjustments to the aircraft's pitch and bank without outside visual reference.

HOW IT WORKS

The heart of the attitude indicator is a gyro that spins in the horizontal plane, mounted on dual gimbals that allow it to remain in that plane regardless of aircraft movement. [Figure 2-5]. Before the gyro can spin in the horizontal plane, it must erect itself. When the aircraft is taxiing, gravity provides the force to initially level the vacuum driven gyro by use of pendulous vanes. During flight when the airplane is straight and level, these **pendulous vanes** provide the mechanism to erect the gyro if it is not parallel to the ground or horizon. Four air jets spaced at 90-degree angles are placed under the gyro wheel. The outlet for each jet is partly blocked by a tiny hanging door called a

SECTION A ■ Flight Instrument Systems

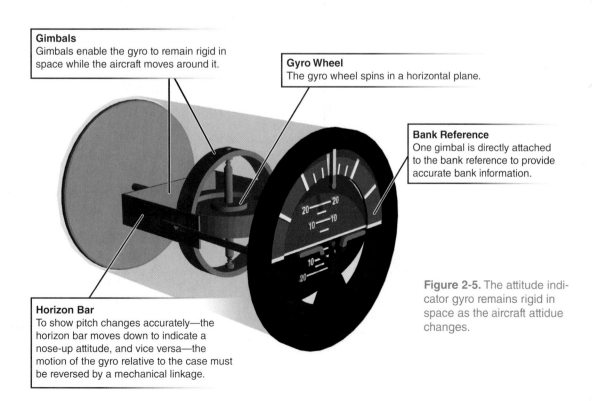

Gimbals
Gimbals enable the gyro to remain rigid in space while the aircraft moves around it.

Gyro Wheel
The gyro wheel spins in a horizontal plane.

Bank Reference
One gimbal is directly attached to the bank reference to provide accurate bank information.

Horizon Bar
To show pitch changes accurately—the horizon bar moves down to indicate a nose-up attitude, and vice versa—the motion of the gyro relative to the case must be reversed by a mechanical linkage.

Figure 2-5. The attitude indicator gyro remains rigid in space as the aircraft attidue changes.

pendulous vane. If the gyro wheel begins to stray from horizontal, gravity opens or closes these doors, releasing jets of air that nudge the gyro back where it belongs. The arrangement of the pendulous vanes takes advantage of precession, applying the force 90 degrees from where the motion is needed. [Figure 2-6]

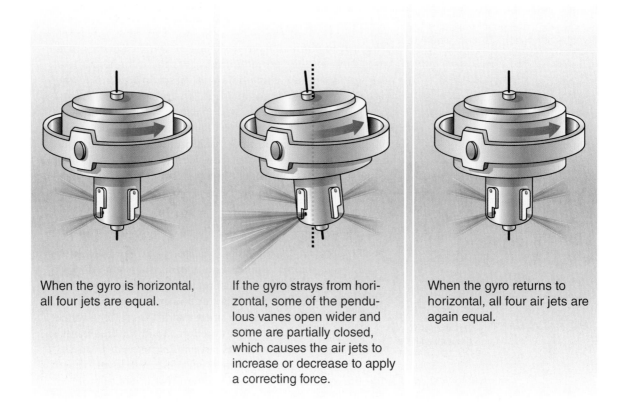

When the gyro is horizontal, all four jets are equal.

If the gyro strays from horizontal, some of the pendulous vanes open wider and some are partially closed, which causes the air jets to increase or decrease to apply a correcting force.

When the gyro returns to horizontal, all four air jets are again equal.

Figure 2-6. Air jets controlled by pendulous vanes cause the gyro to return to horizontal when it is displaced.

ERRORS

Although the basic principle of the attitude indicator is simple, the mechanics of the instrument can cause some errors. These errors are minor, resulting in less than 5° of bank error and less than 1 bar width of pitch error in a 180° turn. Air jets and pendulous vanes continuously work to keep the gyro wheel spinning in the horizontal plane, using gravity as their vertical reference. The forces in a coordinated turn cause this mechanism to try to align the gyro wheel with the apparent force that you feel as load factor. This force is not vertical, but tilted according to the aircraft's angle of bank. This apparent change in the direction of gravity causes the gyro to precess toward the inside of the turn. Errors in both pitch and bank indication are usually at a maximum as the aircraft rolls out of a 180° turn, and cancel after 360° of turn. [Figure 2-7]

 Errors in both pitch and bank indication are usually at a maximum as the aircraft rolls out of a 180° turn. Other errors occur during acceleration and deceleration. See Figure 2-7.

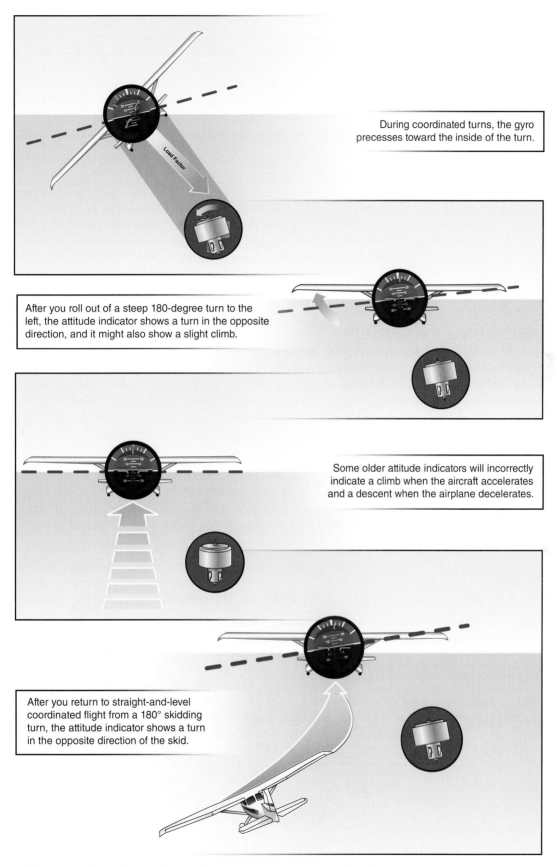

During coordinated turns, the gyro precesses toward the inside of the turn.

After you roll out of a steep 180-degree turn to the left, the attitude indicator shows a turn in the opposite direction, and it might also show a slight climb.

Some older attitude indicators will incorrectly indicate a climb when the aircraft accelerates and a descent when the airplane decelerates.

After you return to straight-and-level coordinated flight from a 180° skidding turn, the attitude indicator shows a turn in the opposite direction of the skid.

Figure 2-7. The attitude indicator displays some minor errors when the airplane is maneuvering. The angles in this figure are exaggerated for illustration purposes.

SECTION A ■ **Flight Instrument Systems**

Acceleration and deceleration also can induce precession errors, depending on the amount and duration of the force applied. During acceleration, the horizon bar moves down, indicating a climb, which, unfortunately reinforces the same illusion you can experience during acceleration. That illusion, called somatogravic illusion (see Chapter 1) falsely makes you feel that the aircraft is in a nose-high attitude. Applying control pressure to correct this indication results in a lower pitch attitude than the instrument shows. The danger is that your angle of climb when accelerating for a missed approach might be too shallow to clear obstacles.

INSTRUMENT TUMBLING

As long as sufficient vacuum is maintained, modern attitude indicators usually are very reliable instruments. Some are designed to function properly during 360° of roll or 85° of pitch. When the gimbals in older indicators hit their limits, the gyros precess rapidly, or tumble, from their plane of rotation. This generally occurs beyond approximately 100° of bank or beyond 60° of pitch. A tumbled instrument is unusable and might take several minutes to re-erect itself. Some of these instruments employ caging devices to prevent the gyro from tumbling or to stabilize the spin axis after it has tumbled.

HEADING INDICATOR

A gyroscopic heading indicator is required for IFR flight. When properly set, this instrument is your primary source of heading information. Because changes in heading during coordinated flight imply the wings are not level, the heading indicator also indirectly indicates bank.

HOW IT WORKS

The heading indicator usually is vacuum powered and senses rotation about the aircraft's vertical axis. In many training airplanes, the heading indicator contains free (as opposed to slaved) gyros. This means they have no automatic, north-seeking system built into them. For the heading indicator to display the correct heading, you must align it with the magnetic compass before flight and recheck it periodically during flight. [Figure 2-8]

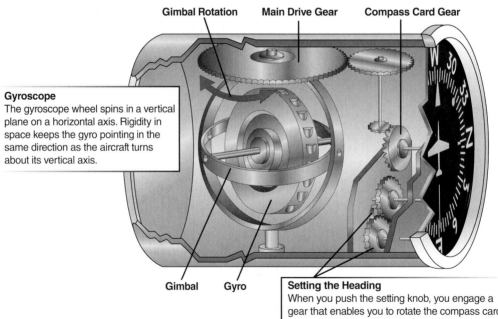

Gimbal Rotation   **Main Drive Gear**   **Compass Card Gear**

Gyroscope
The gyroscope wheel spins in a vertical plane on a horizontal axis. Rigidity in space keeps the gyro pointing in the same direction as the aircraft turns about its vertical axis.

Gimbal   **Gyro**

Setting the Heading
When you push the setting knob, you engage a gear that enables you to rotate the compass card independently of the gyroscope. On many indicators, if the gyro has precessed, pushing in the setting knob mechanically nudges the gyroscope wheel back to the vertical plane.

Figure 2-8. A gyro, gimbals, and gears drive the heading indicator.

ERRORS

If the airplane were never pitched or banked, the heading indicator's gyro could turn freely within a single gimbal with negligible error. Because an airplane does more than yaw, an additional gimbal is needed to allow free rotation of the gyro. Precession can cause the heading to drift from the proper setting, so you must check the heading indicator against the magnetic compass at approximately 15-minute intervals during flight. When you reset the heading indicator, make sure you are in straight-and-level, unaccelerated flight to ensure an accurate magnetic compass indication. Like the attitude indicator, the heading indicator could tumble during excessive pitch and roll conditions. If the indicator has tumbled, you must realign it with a known magnetic heading or with a stabilized indication from the magnetic compass.

TURN INDICATORS

The turn indicator enables you to establish and maintain constant rate turns. A **standard-rate turn** is a turn at a rate of 3° per second. At this rate you complete a 360° turn in 2 minutes. The bank required to maintain a specific rate of turn increases with true airspeed (TAS). You can calculate the approximate required bank for a standard-rate turn in a light training aircraft using the following formula:

$$\text{Angle of Bank} = [\text{True Airspeed in Knots} \div 10] + 5$$

At 100 knots, you must bank the airplane approximately 15° to make a standard-rate turn. To avoid the need for excessive angles of bank, the turn indicators on high-speed airplanes are calibrated for half-standard-rate turns. [Figure 2-9]

 A standard-rate turn is 3° per second. It takes 60 seconds to turn 180°. A half-standard-rate turn is 1-1/2° per second. It takes 4 minutes to turn 360°.

 During a constant-bank level turn, an increase in airspeed results in a decreased rate of turn, and an increased turn radius.

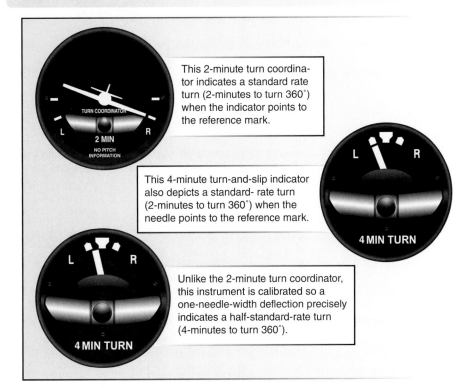

This 2-minute turn coordinator indicates a standard rate turn (2-minutes to turn 360˚) when the indicator points to the reference mark.

This 4-minute turn-and-slip indicator also depicts a standard- rate turn (2-minutes to turn 360˚) when the needle points to the reference mark.

Unlike the 2-minute turn coordinator, this instrument is calibrated so a one-needle-width deflection precisely indicates a half-standard-rate turn (4-minutes to turn 360˚).

Figure 2-9 Turbine aircraft often use 4-minute turn indicators to avoid the steeper banks associated with higher speeds. Your instrument training aircraft probably has a 2-minute turn coordinator.

SECTION A ■ **Flight Instrument Systems**

There are two types of turn indicators; the older **turn-and-slip indicator** and the **turn coordinator**. These instruments have different appearances and work a little differently. Both instruments indicate rate of turn, but because of the improved design of the turn coordinator, this instrument also indicates rate of roll as you enter a turn. [Figure 2-10] Because a coordinated turn requires the aircraft to be banked, both the turn-and-slip indicator and the turn coordinator give you an indirect indication of bank. If other bank instruments fail, it is easier to control the aircraft with the turn coordinator because of the additional information it provides. Because the turn coordinator has largely replaced the turn-and-slip indicator in modern training aircraft, this book primarily refers to that instrument.

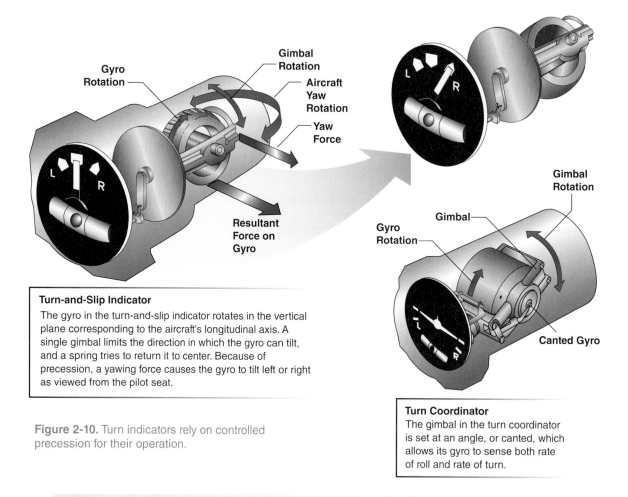

Turn-and-Slip Indicator
The gyro in the turn-and-slip indicator rotates in the vertical plane corresponding to the aircraft's longitudinal axis. A single gimbal limits the direction in which the gyro can tilt, and a spring tries to return it to center. Because of precession, a yawing force causes the gyro to tilt left or right as viewed from the pilot seat.

Figure 2-10. Turn indicators rely on controlled precession for their operation.

Turn Coordinator
The gimbal in the turn coordinator is set at an angle, or canted, which allows its gyro to sense both rate of roll and rate of turn.

 The miniature aircraft of the turn coordinator directly displays rate of roll and rate of turn information; the turn-and-slip indicator only gives the rate of turn. Both instruments indirectly indicate the bank attitude; the needle displacement increases as angle of bank increases.

 One advantage of an electric turn coordinator is that it serves as a backup in case of vacuum system failure.

The **inclinometer** is the part of the turn coordinator that contains the fluid and the ball. The position of the ball indicates whether you are using the correct angle of bank for the rate of turn. In a **slip**, the rate of turn is too slow for the angle of bank, and the ball moves to the inside of the turn. In a **skid**, the rate of turn is too great for the angle of bank, and the ball moves to the outside of the turn. Step on the ball, or apply rudder pressure on the side the ball is deflected, to correct an uncoordinated flight condition. [Figure 2-11]

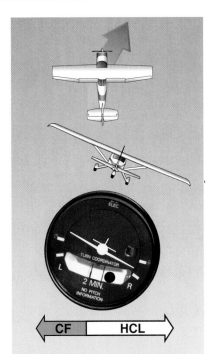

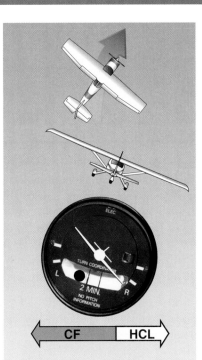

Slip. Because of insufficient right rudder pressure, the air-plane is not turning fast enough for this angle of bank. The horizontal component of lift exceeds the centrifugal force which opposes the turn. As a result, the ball falls to the inside of the turn, and passengers fall against the right side of the aircraft. To balance the forces and coordinate the turn, increase the amount of right rudder and/or decrease the amount of bank.

Skid. Excessive right rudder pressure forces the airplane to turn faster than normal for this angle of bank. The horizontal component of lift is insufficient to overcome the centrifugal force. The ball swings to the outside of the turn, and passengers are pushed against the left side of the aircraft. To balance theforces and coordinate the turn,decrease the amount of rightrudder, and/or increase the amount of bank.

Coordinated Turn. The correct amount of right rudder pressure turns the airplane at the appropriate rate for this angle of bank. The horizontal component of lift exactly balances the centrifugal force. The ball is centered, and passengers feel no side forces.

Figure 2-11. The inclinometer helps you coordinate a turn by measuring the balance between centrifugal force (CF) and horizontal component of lift (HCL).

Slipping or skidding also alters the normal load factor you experience in turns. This happens because the wings must generate enough lift to support the weight of the airplane plus overcome centrifugal force. Because a skid generates a higher-than-normal centrifugal force, load factor is increased. In a slip, load factor decreases because centrifugal force is lower than normal.

FAA The ball of the turn coordinator indicates the quality of the turn. The horizontal lift component causes an airplane to turn. In a skidding turn, the load factor is increased because of the excess centrifugal force. See Figure 2-11.

INSTRUMENT CHECKS

The preflight check of the gyroscopic flight instruments and their power sources is particularly important if departing under IFR. Some instruments display warning flags when they lose their source of vacuum or electric power. Before turning on the master switch or starting the engine, make sure the instruments that have these warning flags are displaying OFF indications. [Figure 2-12]

Figure 2-12. Before turning on the master switch, verify the operation of all instrument failure indicators.

The inclinometer should be full of fluid, with the ball resting at its lowest point. When you turn on the master switch, listen to the electrically driven gyro(s). There should be no abnormal noises, such as grinding sounds, that would indicate an impending failure.

 Prior to engine start, check the turn-and-slip indicator to determine if the needle is approximately centered and the tube is full of fluid. During taxi, the ball should move to the outside of the turn, and the needle should deflect in the direction of the turn.

Check the ammeter immediately after starting the engine for a positive charging rate, or if your aircraft is equipped with a load meter, make sure it indicates a normal value. Listen for the vacuum-driven gyros. If they are malfunctioning, you might hear them over the noise of the engine. If you suspect something abnormal, shut down the engine and listen to the gyros spin down. The gyros should reach full operating speed in approximately five minutes. Until that time, it is common to see some vibration in the instruments. When the gyros stabilize, the miniature airplane in the turn coordinator and the horizon bar in the attitude indicator should be level when the airplane is stopped or taxiing straight ahead.

 Before you start the engine, listen for any unusual mechanical noise. Noise might indicate a problem in the electric gyro instruments.

During turns, the turn coordinator and heading indicator should display a turn in the correct direction. The ball in the inclinometer should swing to the outside of the turn; because you do not bank the airplane on the ground, taxi turns are basically skids. Align the heading indicator with the magnetic compass. Then, recheck it prior to takeoff to ensure it has not precessed significantly. A precession error of 3° or less in 15 minutes is acceptable for normal operations.

 Give the vacuum-driven heading indicator and attitude indicator 5 minutes to spin up. Make sure that the horizon bar on the attitude indicator tilts no more than 5° during taxi turns. After setting the heading indicator to the magnetic heading, verify that it maintains proper alignment with the magnetic compass during taxi turns.

 When making a left taxiing turn, the miniature aircraft on the turn coordinator shows a turn to the left and the ball moves to the right.

Always include the ammeter and suction gauge in your pretakeoff check to ensure the gyro instruments are receiving adequate power. The ammeter should not show a discharge during runup, even with lights and pitot heat turned on. If the vacuum is outside its normal range, the vacuum-driven indicators become unreliable. Some airplanes have vacuum warning lights, as well as low and high voltage warning lights. [Figure 2-13]

Figure 2-13. It is very important to verify the proper operation of your electrical and vacuum systems before departing under IFR.

MAGNETIC COMPASS

The magnetic compass is the only direction-seeking instrument in most light airplanes. It is a self-contained unit not requiring electrical or suction power. To determine direction, the compass uses simple bar magnets suspended in a fluid so they can pivot freely and align themselves with the earth's magnetic field.

ERRORS

Because the magnetic compass is sensitive to in-flight turbulence, FAA regulations require a stable, gyroscopic heading indicator for IFR flight. The heading indicator must be synchronized with the compass regularly to give accurate information, and you need to know how to effectively navigate with the compass if the heading indicator fails during flight. In light turbulence, you might be able to use the compass by averaging the readings. Other errors and limitations you must consider are magnetic variation, compass deviation, and magnetic dip.

VARIATION

As an IFR pilot, you do not concern yourself with variation as much as VFR pilots because all courses on IFR charts are published as magnetic. However, you do need to convert the true winds aloft direction to magnetic before factoring winds into your flight planning. Variation is the angular difference between the true and magnetic north poles. The amount of variation depends on where you are located in relation to these poles. [Figure 2-14]

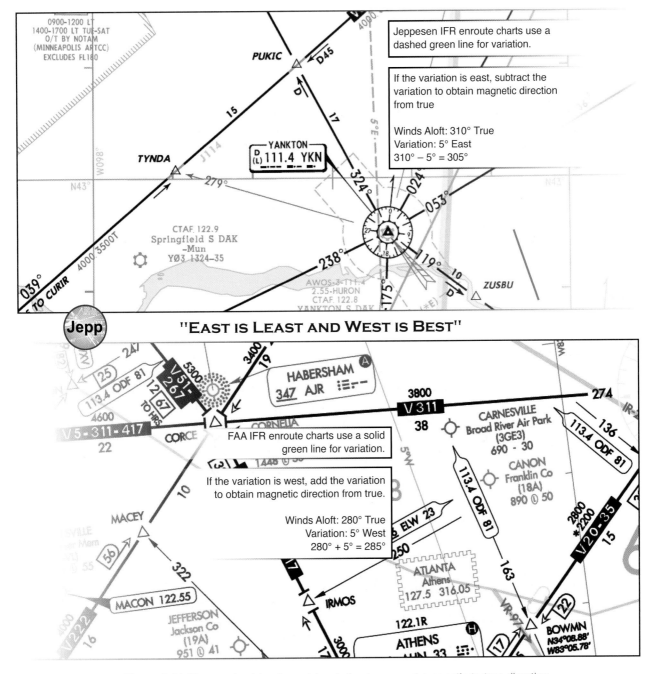

Jeppesen IFR enroute charts use a dashed green line for variation.

If the variation is east, subtract the variation to obtain magnetic direction from true

Winds Aloft: 310° True
Variation: 5° East
310° − 5° = 305°

"EAST IS LEAST AND WEST IS BEST"

FAA IFR enroute charts use a solid green line for variation.

If the variation is west, add the variation to obtain magnetic direction from true.

Winds Aloft: 280° True
Variation: 5° West
280° + 5° = 285°

Figure 2-14. You must subtract or add variation to convert magnetic to true direction.

DEVIATION

Deviation is error due to magnetic interference with metal components in the aircraft, as well as magnetic fields from aircraft electrical equipment. Compensating magnets within the compass housing can reduce, but not eliminate, deviation. These magnets are usually adjusted with the engine and all electrical equipment operating in a procedure called swinging the compass. Any remaining errors are then recorded on a correction card mounted on or near the compass that tells you what direction to steer to get specific headings. [Figure 2-15]

Figure 2-15. If you use this compass to fly a magnetic heading (MH) of 180°, you must steer a compass heading (CH) of 183°.

 Magnetic deviation varies for different headings of the same aircraft.

MAGNETIC DIP

Magnetic dip is responsible for the most significant compass errors. This phenomenon makes it difficult to get an accurate compass indication when maneuvering on a north or south heading. Magnetic dip exists because the magnets in the compass try to point three dimensionally toward the earth's magnetic north pole, which is located deep inside the earth. [Figure 2-16] The internal pivot point that suspends the compass card is designed to minimize the tilting force on the bar magnet caused by magnetic dip. Unfortunately, this system, as well as magnetic dip itself, both contribute to acceleration and turning errors. This section describes the errors that occur in the northern hemisphere due to magnetic dip; in the southern hemisphere, compass errors are opposite of what is described here.

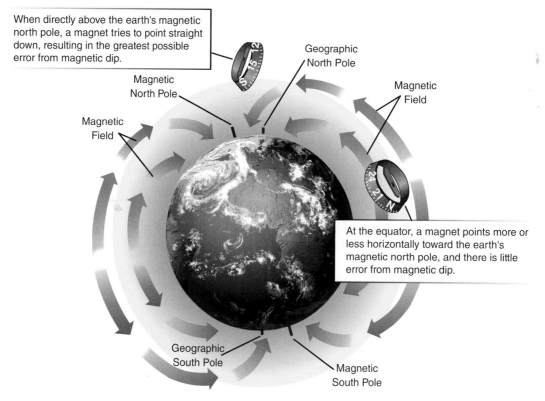

When directly above the earth's magnetic north pole, a magnet tries to point straight down, resulting in the greatest possible error from magnetic dip.

Geographic North Pole

Magnetic North Pole

Magnetic Field

Magnetic Field

At the equator, a magnet points more or less horizontally toward the earth's magnetic north pole, and there is little error from magnetic dip.

Geographic South Pole

Magnetic South Pole

Figure 2-16. Because of the direction of the earth's lines of magnetic force, magnetic dip is most pronounced near the poles and negligible near the equator.

Turning error occurs when you are turning to or from a heading of north or south. This **northerly turning error** is most apparent at the poles and disappears as you approach the Equator. When rolling into a turn from a northerly heading in the northern hemisphere, the compass swings in the opposite direction of the turn. As you proceed with the turn, the compass card reverses and moves in the correct direction, catching up with your actual heading as you reach an east or west heading. When rolling into a turn from a southerly heading, the compass card swings in the correct direction, but leads the actual heading. As you proceed with the turn, the compass card slows down, matching your actual heading as you reach east or west. [Figure 2-17]

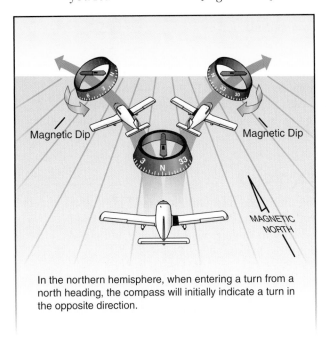

In the northern hemisphere, when entering a turn from a north heading, the compass will initially indicate a turn in the opposite direction.

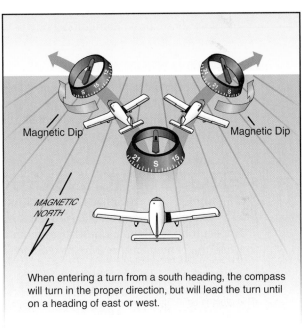

When entering a turn from a south heading, the compass will turn in the proper direction, but will lead the turn until on a heading of east or west.

Figure 2-17. A magnetic compass will indicate correctly entering a turn from an east or west heading, but will experience turning error when entering or completing a turn on a north or south heading.

It is essential you use standard-rate turns if relying on the magnetic compass. When performing a compass turn to a northerly heading, roll out of the turn before the compass reaches the desired heading. When turning to a southerly heading, delay the roll-out until the compass card swings past the desired heading. When determining whether to lag or lead the desired heading on roll-out, remember the acronym, OSUN (Overshoot South, Undershoot North). The amount of correction depends on your latitude and angle of bank. With 15° to 18° bank (a standard-rate turn in a typical piston-powered airplane), the amount of lag or lead approximately matches your latitude, plus the one-half angle of bank you lead the roll-out on any turn. For example, at 35° N latitude and a 16° bank, a right turn to north requires a roll-out point of 317° (360 − 35 − 8). A right turn to south requires a roll-out point of 207° (180 + 35 − 8). When turning left to a north heading the roll-out point is 43° (360 + 35 + 8). When turning left to a south heading it is 153° (180 − 35 + 8).

 Northerly turning error in a magnetic compass is caused by magnetic dip. See Figure 2-17.

The suspension of the compass card and magnetic dip also cause acceleration and deceleration errors. In the northern hemisphere, the compass swings toward the north during acceleration and toward the south during deceleration. When the speed stabilizes, the compass returns to an accurate indication. This error is greatest on east and west headings and decreases to zero on north and south headings. Remember the acronym, ANDS (Accelerate North, Decelerate South) to describe this error in the northern hemisphere. In the southern hemisphere, the error occurs in the opposite direction (Accelerate South, Decelerate North). Because rapid changes in airspeed are infrequent when flying an airplane, acceleration error is not nearly as troublesome as turning error. Nonetheless, you want to be aware of this error if using your compass for navigation when adding power to increase speed, or when reducing power to slow airspeed.

INSTRUMENT CHECK

Because a magnetic compass is required equipment for VFR or IFR flight, you should never take off without verifying its proper operation. Although the compass does have errors, it is predictable and reliable. Simply make sure the compass is full of fluid, and during taxi, verify the compass swings freely and indicates known headings.

PITOT-STATIC INSTRUMENTS

The pitot-static instruments (airspeed indicator, altimeter, and vertical speed indicator) rely on air pressure differences to measure speed and altitude. Pitot pressure, also called impact, ram, or dynamic pressure, is connected only to the airspeed indicator, but static pressure, or ambient pressure, is connected to all three instruments. [Figure 2-18]

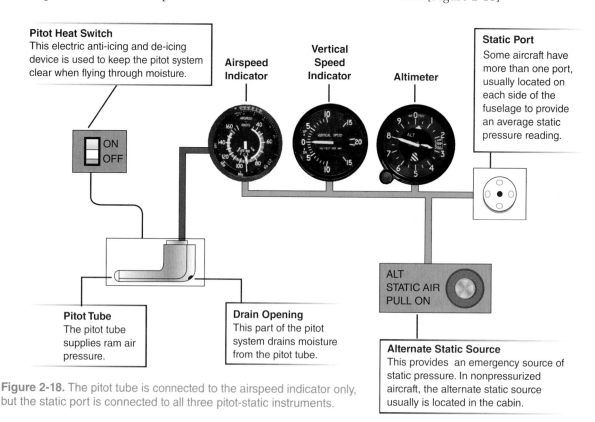

Pitot Heat Switch
This electric anti-icing and de-icing device is used to keep the pitot system clear when flying through moisture.

Airspeed Indicator

Vertical Speed Indicator

Altimeter

Static Port
Some aircraft have more than one port, usually located on each side of the fuselage to provide an average static pressure reading.

ON
OFF

ALT STATIC AIR PULL ON

Pitot Tube
The pitot tube supplies ram air pressure.

Drain Opening
This part of the pitot system drains moisture from the pitot tube.

Alternate Static Source
This provides an emergency source of static pressure. In nonpressurized aircraft, the alternate static source usually is located in the cabin.

Figure 2-18. The pitot tube is connected to the airspeed indicator only, but the static port is connected to all three pitot-static instruments.

AIRSPEED INDICATOR

The airspeed indicator displays the speed of your airplane by comparing ram air pressure with static air pressure — the faster the aircraft moves through the air, the greater the pressure differential measured by this instrument. [Figure 2-19] Manufacturers use **indicated airspeed (IAS)** as the basis for determining aircraft performance. Takeoff, landing, and stall speeds listed in the POH are indicated airspeeds and do not normally vary with altitude or temperature. This is because changes in air density affect the aerodynamics of the airframe and the airspeed indicator equally.

 At higher elevation airports, the indicated airspeed for approach and landing remains unchanged, but the corresponding groundspeed is faster.

Figure 2-19. The airspeed indicator uses a diaphragm to compare ram air pressure with static air pressure.

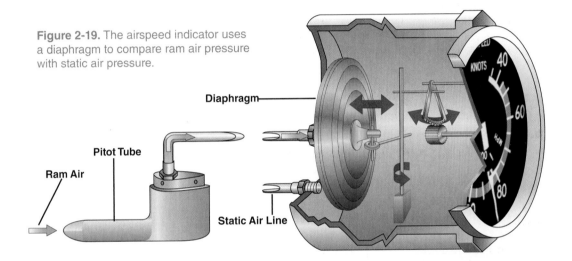

Diaphragm

Pitot Tube

Ram Air

Static Air Line

AIRSPEEDS

As an instrument pilot, you need to understand the different types of airspeed. **Calibrated airspeed (CAS)** is indicated airspeed corrected for installation and instrument errors. Most of the discrepancy occurs because, at high angles of attack, the pitot tube does not point straight into the relative wind. This tends to make the airspeed indicator indicate lower-than-normal at low airspeeds. [Figure 2-20] Manufacturers compensate for this as best they can, but some errors are inevitable. The difference between indicated and calibrated airspeed is minimal at cruise speeds. You can find the corrections in the pilot's operating handbook (POH). As a practical matter, you normally use specific indicated airspeeds for various operations, and only concern yourself with CAS when you need to convert to true airspeed.

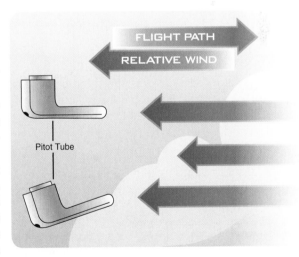

FLIGHT PATH

RELATIVE WIND

Pitot Tube

Figure 2-20. At high angles of attack, the relative wind does not strike the pitot tube straight on. This results in lower-than-normal indicated airspeed.

Equivalent airspeed (EAS) is calibrated airspeed corrected for adiabatic compressible flow at a particular altitude. At airspeeds above 200 KIAS and altitudes above 20,000 feet, air is compressed in front of an aircraft as it passes through the air. Compressibility causes abnormally high airspeed indications, so EAS is lower than CAS. Many electronic and mechanical flight computers are designed to compensate for this error. It is significant to pilots of high speed aircraft, but relatively unimportant to the average light airplane pilot.

Calibrated airspeed (CAS) is indicated airspeed (IAS) corrected for installation and instrument errors. The aircraft's POH contains a chart allowing you to convert IAS to CAS. True airspeed (TAS) is CAS corrected for nonstandard temperature and pressure.

True airspeed (TAS) is the actual speed your airplane moves through undisturbed air. At sea level on a standard day, CAS (or EAS, as appropriate) equals TAS. As density altitude increases, true airspeed increases for a given CAS, or for a given amount of power. You can calculate TAS from CAS (or EAS), pressure altitude and temperature using your flight computer. Assuming conditions close to standard temperature, you can get an approximate true airspeed by adding 2% of the indicated airspeed for each 1,000-foot increase in altitude.

 During a flight at constant power and at a constant indicated altitude, true airspeed increases as outside air temperature increases.

Many high performance aircraft have a Mach indicator incorporated with the airspeed indicator. [Figure 2-21] **Mach** is the ratio of the aircraft's true airspeed to the speed of sound. A speed of Mach 0.85 means the aircraft is flying at 85% of the speed of sound at that temperature. When computing true airspeed from a conventional airspeed indicator, you must factor in air density, which requires a correction for temperature and altitude. These corrections are unnecessary with a Mach indicator because the temperature determines the speed of sound. Thus, Mach is a more valid index to the speed of the aircraft.

Figure 2-21. A Mach Indicator provides a more meaningful speed index for high performance aircraft.

 A Mach meter presents the ratio of the aircraft's true airspeed to the speed of sound.

V-SPEEDS AND COLOR CODES

The color codes on an airspeed indicator provide important information on the operation of the aircraft. These markings actually reflect the airplane's performance envelope. [Figure 2-22]

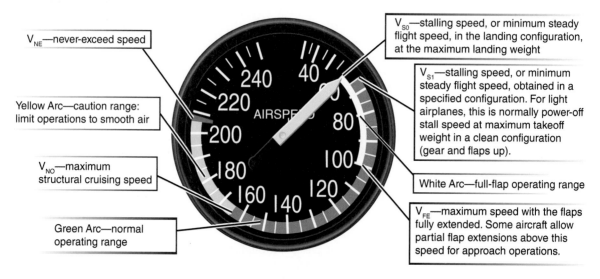

V_{NE}—never-exceed speed

Yellow Arc—caution range: limit operations to smooth air

V_{NO}—maximum structural cruising speed

Green Arc—normal operating range

V_{S0}—stalling speed, or minimum steady flight speed, in the landing configuration, at the maximum landing weight

V_{S1}—stalling speed, or minimum steady flight speed, obtained in a specified configuration. For light airplanes, this is normally power-off stall speed at maximum takeoff weight in a clean configuration (gear and flaps up).

White Arc—full-flap operating range

V_{FE}—maximum speed with the flaps fully extended. Some aircraft allow partial flap extensions above this speed for approach operations.

Figure 2-22. The color-coded arcs on the airspeed indicator define speed ranges. The boundaries of these arcs identify airspeed limitations.

Several important values are not marked on the airspeed indicator. During gusty or turbulent conditions, slow the aircraft below the design maneuvering speed, V_A, to ensure the load factor is within safe limits. At or below V_A, the airplane stalls before excessive G-forces can occur. Design maneuvering speed, which decreases with the total weight of the aircraft, appears in your POH or on a placard. V_{LE}, the maximum speed with the landing gear extended on a retractable gear airplane, and V_{LO}, the maximum speed for extending or retracting the landing gear, also appear in the POH but not on the airspeed indicator.

 Design maneuvering speed is one important value not shown by the color coding of an airspeed indicator. If you encounter severe turbulence during an IFR flight, slow the airplane below this speed. This decreases the amount of excess load that can be imposed on the wing.

INSTRUMENT CHECK

Unless the airplane is facing into a strong wind, the airspeed indicator should read zero before you taxi. If it indicates some value due to wind, verify the indicator drops to zero when you turn the airplane away from the wind. As you accelerate during the takeoff roll, make sure the airspeed indicator comes alive and increases at an appropriate rate. If not, discontinue the takeoff.

ALTIMETER

An altimeter is required for both VFR and IFR flight. For IFR, you need a **sensitive altimeter**, adjustable for barometric pressure—the kind of altimeter you find on most modern aircraft. In addition to helping you maintain terrain clearance, minimum IFR altitudes, and separation from other aircraft, the altimeter helps you maintain aircraft control. An understanding of the operation and limitations of the altimeter enables you to interpret its indications correctly. [Figure 2-23]

Aneroid Wafers
The main component of the altimeter is a stack of sealed aneroid wafers that expand and contract as atmospheric pressure from the static source changes. A mechanical linkage translates these changes into pointer movements on the indicator.

Altitude Indication Scale
The altimeter reads like a clock, with the small hand indicating thousands of feet, and the large hand indicating hundreds of feet.

10,000 Feet Pointer

100 Feet Pointer

Altimeter Setting Window
When the setting on an altimeter is changed, the indication changes in the same direction by approximately 1,000 feet for each inch of pressure.

1,000 Feet Pointer

Cross Hatch Flag
A cross-hatched area appears on some altimeters when displaying an altitude below 10,000 feet MSL.

Static Port

Altimeter Setting Adjustment Knob

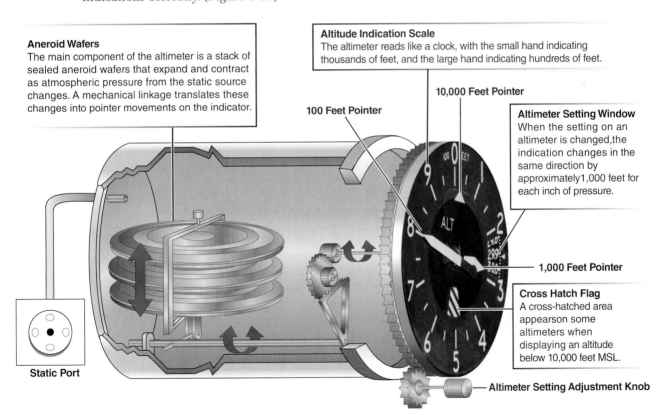

Figure 2-23. This altimeter indicates 2,800 feet MSL. The barometric scale in the window is at 29.92 inches of mercury (in. Hg.).

 Now that you will be flying under IFR, your ability to accurately read and adjust the altimeter is far more important than it was under VFR. See Figure 2-23.

TYPES OF ALTITUDE

The altimeter measures the vertical elevation of an object above a given reference point. The reference can be the surface of the earth, mean sea level (MSL), or some other point. There are several different types of altitude, depending on the reference point used. The altimeter indicates height in feet above the barometric pressure level set in the altimeter window. For example, if the altimeter is set to 30.00, it would indicate the height of the airplane above the pressure level of 30.00 in. Hg. If this is the correct local altimeter setting, then the 30.00 in. Hg. pressure level would be at sea level and the altimeter would indicate the true altitude above sea level (assuming standard temperature).

Indicated altitude is the altitude you read from the altimeter when it is set to the current altimeter setting. When operating below 18,000 feet MSL, you must set the altimeter to the local setting to indicate your approximate height above mean sea level (MSL). **Calibrated altitude** is indicated altitude corrected to compensate for instrument error. **Pressure altitude** is displayed on the altimeter when it is set to the standard sea level pressure of 29.92 in. Hg. It is the vertical distance above a theoretical plane, or **standard datum plane**, where atmospheric pressure is equal to 29.92 in. Hg. Regulations require that you set the altimeter to 29.92 when operating at or above 18,000 feet MSL. These high altitudes are referred to as flight levels (FL); 18,000 feet above the standard datum plane is FL180.

 Set your altimeter to 29.92 in. Hg. when operating at or above 18,000 feet MSL, where all altimeters must be set to display pressure altitude. You can also read pressure altitude below 18,000 feet MSL by setting your altimeter to 29.92 in. Hg.

Density altitude is pressure altitude corrected for nonstandard temperature. It is a theoretical value used to determine airplane performance. When density altitude is high (temperatures are above standard), aircraft performance degrades. Most aircraft documentation gives you performance information based on pressure altitude and temperature, rather than explicitly using density altitude.

 Pressure altitude is the altitude read on the altimeter when the instrument is set to indicate height above the standard datum plane. It is the same as density altitude at standard temperature, and is equal to true altitude under standard atmospheric conditions.

True altitude is the actual height of an object above mean sea level. On aeronautical charts, the elevations of such objects as airports, towers, and TV antennas are true altitudes. Unfortunately, your altimeter displays true altitude in flight only under standard conditions. Nonstandard temperature and pressure cause your indicated altitude to differ from true altitude. The true altitude computations you make with a flight computer assume that pressure and temperature lapse rates match a perfectly standard atmosphere, which is rarely the case. [Figure 2-24]

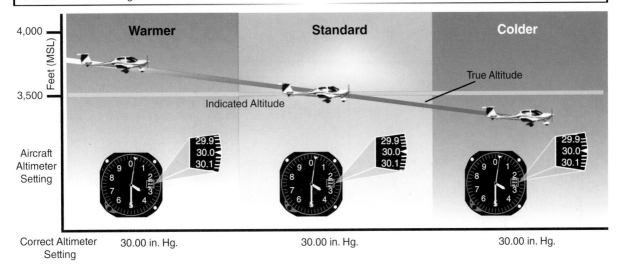

Warmer
When the air temperature is warmer than standard, the altimeter will indicate a lower altitude than that actually flown. True altitude is higher than indicated altitude.

Colder
When the air temperature is colder than standard, the altimeter will indicate a higher altitude than that actually flown. True altitude is lower than indicated altitude.

Figure 2-24. True altitude differs from indicated altitude when the air temperature is warmer or colder than standard.

 When flying from hot to cold, look out below. See Figure 2-24.

True and indicated altitude are only equal when you are flying with the correct altimeter setting and when temperature conditions match **International Standard Atmospheric (ISA)** values—that is, where sea-level temperature is 15°C and the lapse rate is exactly 2°C per 1,000 feet of elevation. However, if the temperature is 10°C colder than standard, true altitude is about 4% lower than indicated altitude. This is an error of 500 feet at 12,000 feet MSL; a significant discrepancy if flying over mountainous terrain on a cold day. True altitude also equals indicated altitude when you are sitting on the airport ramp with the altimeter set to the local altimeter setting where it indicates the field elevation.

Absolute altitude is the actual height of the aircraft above the earth's surface. Some airplanes are equipped with radar altimeters that measure this height above ground level (AGL) directly. During instrument approaches, absolute altitude is used to define the height above the airport (HAA), height above the touchdown zone (HAT), and the threshold crossing height (TCH).

 When you set the altimeter to the local altimeter setting, it indicates true altitude at field elevation. If an altimeter setting is not available, set the altimeter to the field elevation.

SECTION A ■ **Flight Instrument Systems**

ALTIMETER SETTING

The most common altimeter error is also the easiest to correct. It occurs when the altimeter is not kept set to the local altimeter setting. When flying from an area of high pressure to an area of low pressure without resetting your altimeter, the instrument interprets the lower pressure as a higher altitude. When you descend to maintain the same indicated altitude, you will end up at a lower true altitude. This is why, when flying from high to low pressure, look out below. [Figure 2-25]

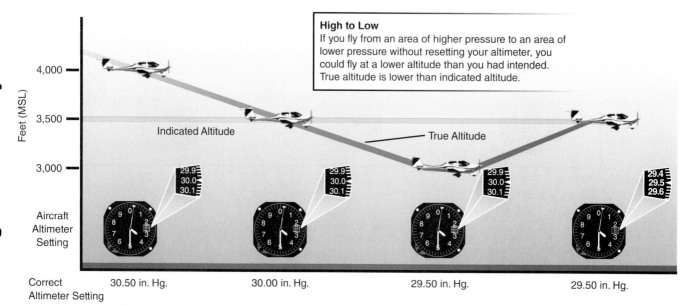

High to Low
If you fly from an area of higher pressure to an area of lower pressure without resetting your altimeter, you could fly at a lower altitude than you had intended. True altitude is lower than indicated altitude.

Figure 2-25. If you reset the altimeter to the correct setting, you can maintain the desired altitude.

If you are departing an airport where you cannot obtain a current altimeter setting, you should set the altimeter to the airport elevation. After departure, obtain the current altimeter setting as soon as possible from the appropriate ATC facility.

 The local altimeter setting should be used by all pilots primarily to provide for better vertical separation of aircraft. ATC periodically advises pilots of the proper altimeter setting.

INSTRUMENT CHECK

In addition to the required static system check, you should make sure the altimeter is indicating accurately during the IFR preflight check. To accomplish this, set the altimeter to the current altimeter setting. If it indicates within 75 feet of the actual elevation of that location, it is acceptable for IFR flight.

 Before an IFR flight, set the altimeter to the current altimeter setting. For acceptable accuracy, the indication should be within 75 feet of the actual elevation.

VERTICAL SPEED INDICATOR

The vertical speed indicator (VSI), sometimes called a vertical velocity indicator (VVI) or rate-of-climb indicator, measures how fast the static (ambient) pressure increases or decreases as the airplane climbs or descends. It then displays this pressure change as a rate of climb or descent in feet per minute. Unlike the altimeter, the VSI is not affected by air temperature because it measures only *changes* in air pressure. [Figure 2-26]

Diaphragm
Any change in static pressure is felt immediately inside the diaphragm but delayed outside the diaphragm, and the diaphragm expands or contracts due to the momentary pressure differential. When the aircraft levels off, the pressure outside the diaphragm equalizes with the pressure inside the diaphragm, and the needle indicates zero.

Mechanical Linkage
A mechanical linkage translates the expansion and contraction of the diaphragm into needle movement.

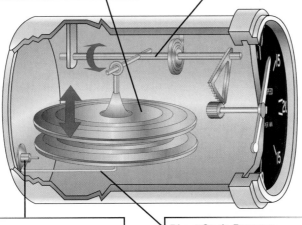

Figure 2-26. The VSI measures changes in static air pressure to determine vertical speed.

Calibrated Leak
Static pressure is indirectly connected to the area outside the diaphragm (the instrument case) via a restricted orifice (calibrated leak) that prevents the pressure outside the diaphragm from changing instantaneously.

Direct Static Pressure
Static pressure is connected directly to the inside of the diaphragm

The VSI displays **rate information** and **trend information**. Although the instrument is designed to display rate of climb or descent, it can take six to nine seconds of lag for the needle to stabilize on an accurate vertical speed indication after you change power or pitch. Even though it takes a few moments to indicate the exact vertical speed, the VSI is valuable because it instantaneously indicates changes in vertical speed, or trend information. When making a steep turn, the VSI usually is the first instrument to tell you a small correction in pitch is needed, because the attitude indicator does not give a precise enough indication of pitch. As you study attitude instrument flying in the next section and practice it in the airplane, you will appreciate the VSI's early warning of deviations from the desired pitch. This instrument provides even more essential pitch information if the gyroscopic attitude indicator fails.

Because the VSI is not designed to instantaneously indicate the rate of climb or descent, it does not give a clear indication during turbulence or when applying abrupt control inputs. You can try to average the erratic readings during turbulence to determine whether you are climbing or descending. Because the VSI uses static air pressure, this instrument does not function if the static port is clogged.

Some aircraft have an instantaneous vertical speed indicator (IVSI). This device incorporates acceleration pumps to compensate for the limitations of the calibrated leak, eliminating the lag found in the typical VSI.

 If you notice that the VSI indicates a descent or climb during taxi, you can use that value as a zero indication.

INSTRUMENT CHECK

The VSI, although not legally required for instrument flight, is an extremely useful instrument. Some pilots will not take off into low IFR conditions unless this instrument is operating properly. Before starting the aircraft engine, check to see that the VSI indicates zero. If you wait until after engine start to check the VSI, you might see needle fluctuations due to the propeller slipstream. Some VSIs have an adjustment screw to zero the instrument. If yours does not, simply make a mental note of where "zero" is, and compensate for that during flight.

PITOT TUBE ICING LEADS TO IN-FLIGHT BREAKUP

From the files of the NTSB...

Aircraft: Piper PA-46-350P

Injuries: *2 Fatal*

Narrative: *Before takeoff, the pilot was advised of IFR conditions along the first part of the route, with flight precautions for occasional moderate turbulence below 15,000 feet, and mixed icing from freezing level (6,000 feet) to 18,000 feet. He filed an IFR flight plan with a cruise altitude of 11,000 feet. During departure, the pilot was cleared to climb to 9,000 feet, and told to expect clearance to 11,000 feet 5 minutes later.*

Radar data showed the aircraft climbed at about 1,500 feet per minute and 100 knots slowing slightly above 8,000 feet. At about 9,000 feet the aircraft started to level and accelerate. It then climbed momentarily, deviated laterally from course, and entered a steep descent. In-flight breakup occurred and wreckage was scattered over a 4,100 foot area. A trajectory study showed breakup occurred between 4,500 and 6,500 feet as the aircraft was in a steep descent in excess of 266 knots. Metallurgical exam of wings and stabilizers revealed features typical of overstress separation; no preexisting cracks or defects were found.

The probable cause, according to the NTSB, was the pilot's failure to activate the pitot heat before flying at and above the freezing level in instrument meteorological conditions (IMC), followed by his improper response to erroneous airspeed indications that resulted from blockage of the pitot tube by atmospheric icing. Spatial disorientation of the pilot was listed as a contributing factor.

The chain of events that led to this accident most likely began with the pilot's lack of experience and training in IFR emergencies, followed by poor judgement regarding the weather conditions. In addition, the pilot failed to effectively manage his workload and was unable to maintain situational awareness during the flight.

SYSTEM ERRORS

The pitot-static instruments usually are very reliable. Gross errors almost always indicate blockage of the pitot tube, the static port, or both. Blockage can be caused by moisture (including ice), dirt, or even insects. During preflight, always check the pitot tube for blockage. If you do this, you also will remember to remove the pitot tube cover. Always check the static port openings as well. If the pitot or static ports are clogged, have them cleaned by a certificated mechanic. It is also possible for the pitot tube to become blocked by visible moisture during flight when temperatures are near the freezing level. If you are flying in visible moisture and your airplane is equipped with pitot heat, turn it on to prevent pitot tube icing.

PITOT BLOCKAGE

The airspeed indicator is the only instrument affected by a pitot tube blockage. There are two types of pitot blockage that can occur. If the ram air inlet clogs but the drain hole remains open, the pressure in the line to the airspeed indicator vents out the drain hole, causing the airspeed indicator to drop to zero. This typically occurs when ice forms over the ram air inlet. [Figure 2-27]

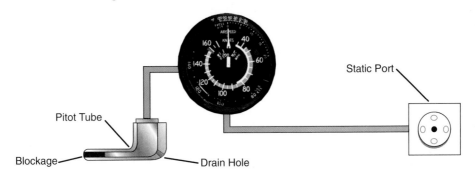

Figure 2-27. A clogged pitot tube, but clear drain hole, will result in an airspeed indication of zero.

The second situation occurs when both the ram air inlet and drain hole become clogged, trapping the air pressure in the line. In level flight, the airspeed indicator typically remains at its present indication, but no longer indicates changes in airspeed. If the static port remains open, the indicator reacts as an altimeter, showing an increase in airspeed when climbing and a decrease in speed when descending. This is opposite the normal way the airspeed indicator behaves, and can result in inappropriate control inputs because you will observe runaway airspeed as you climb and extremely low airspeeds in a descent. In addition, large power changes during level flight will not result in any variations in airspeed. This type of failure can be very hazardous because it is not at all obvious when it occurs. [Figure 2-28]

 If the pitot tube's ram air input and drain hole are blocked, the airspeed indicator will act as an altimeter with indicated airspeed increasing as altitude increases. See figure 2-27.

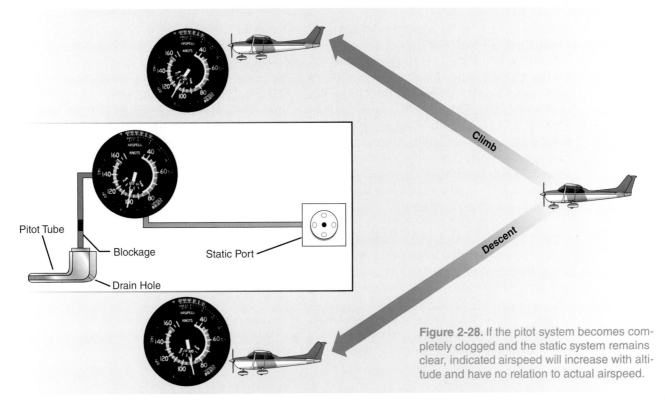

Figure 2-28. If the pitot system becomes completely clogged and the static system remains clear, indicated airspeed will increase with altitude and have no relation to actual airspeed.

STATIC BLOCKAGE

If the static system becomes clogged, the airspeed indicator continues to react to changes in airspeed, because ram air pressure is still being supplied by the pitot tube, but the readings are not be correct. When you are operating above the altitude where the static port became clogged, the airspeed reads lower than it should. Conversely, when you operate at a lower altitude, a faster-than-actual airspeed is displayed due to the relatively low static pressure trapped in the system. The amount of error is proportional to the distance from the altitude where the static system became clogged. The greater the difference, the greater the error. [Figure 2-29]

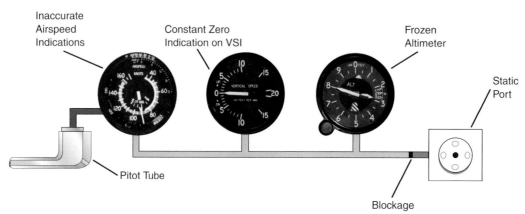

Inaccurate
Airspeed
Indications

Constant Zero
Indication on VSI

Frozen
Altimeter

Static
Port

Pitot Tube

Blockage

Figure 2-29. A blocked static system affects all pitot-static instruments.

 If the static ports are iced over, the VSI pointer will remain at zero, regardless of the actual rate of descent or climb.

Because the altimeter determines altitude by measuring ambient air pressure, any blockage of the static port freezes the altimeter in place and make it unusable. The VSI freezes at zero, because its only source of pressure is from the static port. After verifying a blockage of the static system by cross-checking the other flight instruments, find an alternate source of static pressure.

In many aircraft, an alternate static source is provided as a backup for the main static source. In nonpressurized aircraft, the alternate source usually is located inside the aircraft cabin. Due to the slipstream, the pressure inside the cabin is usually less than that of outside air. Normally, when you select the alternate static source, the altimeter reads a little higher and the airspeed a little faster than normal, and the vertical speed indicator shows a momentary climb. However, this is not always the case. Your airplane's POH might contain information regarding variations in airspeed and altimeter readings due to changes in airplane configuration and use of the alternate static source. In the case of a pressurized aircraft with a static line leak inside the pressurized compartment, the altimeter reads lower than the actual flight altitude, due to the increased static pressure. The airspeed might also read lower than it should, and the vertical speed indicator might indicate a momentary descent.

If the aircraft is not equipped with an alternate static source, you can break the glass of the vertical speed indicator to allow ambient air pressure to enter the static system. Of course, this makes the VSI unusable and does not help in a pressurized airplane; but in an IFR emergency, depressurization is an option to consider.

 If, while in level flight, it becomes necessary to use an alternate source of static pressure vented inside the airplane, the altimeter might read a little higher and the airspeed a little faster than normal, and the vertical speed indicator might show a momentary climb.

INTEGRATED FLIGHT DISPLAYS

Many of today's training airplanes have digital flight instruments that are integrated into a single display, as part of a glass cockpit. Digital flight instruments provide essentially the same information as analog instruments, but in a different format. Because a variety of different **integrated flight display** systems exist, make sure that you are proficient in interpreting and operating the specific system in your airplane. The systems used in smaller general aviation airplanes typically have two screens: a **primary flight display (PFD)** and a **multifunction display (MFD)**. [Figure 2-30]

Primary Flight Display
The PFD contains the primary flight instruments positioned directly in front of you.

Multifunction Display
The MFD contains a variety of information on different pages, such as a moving map display, airport, terrain, and weather data, aircraft systems indications, checklists, and instrument charts.

Backup Instruments
Selected backup analog instruments enable you to control the airplane if digital displays fail.

Figure 2-30. Although some of the features of integrated flight displays vary based on the manufacturer's design, primary and multifunction displays typically contain the same basic information.

PRIMARY FLIGHT DISPLAY

The PFD contains digital versions of traditional analog flight instruments, including the airspeed indicator, altimeter, vertical speed indicator, and attitude indicator. In addition to pitch and bank information, the attitude indicator includes a slip/skid indicator. A horizontal situation indicator (HSI) displays heading and navigation information and includes a turn rate indicator. [Figure 2-31]

SECTION A ■ **Flight Instrument Systems**

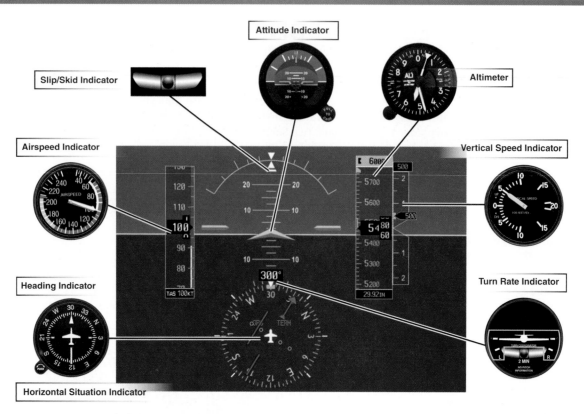

Figure 2-31. The PFD conveys the same information as the six traditional flight instruments.

ATTITUDE AND HEADING REFERENCE SYSTEM

To provide attitude, heading, rate of turn, and slip/skid information, integrated flight displays use an **attitude and heading reference system (AHRS)**. The AHRS uses inertial sensors such as electronic gyroscopes and accelerometers to determine the aircraft's attitude relative to the horizon. An electronic magnetometer provides magnetic heading data. In some systems, GPS equipment also provides data to the AHRS—a general indication of the airplane's attitude is determined by comparing signals received from three antennas located in different parts of the airplane.

MAGNETOMETER

A **magnetometer** used in integrated avionics displays senses the earth's magnetic field to function as a magnetic compass, but without some of the errors associated with a conventional compass. Instead of a suspended bar magnet, the magnetometer uses a flux valve or flux gate, which is an electronic means of sensing magnetic lines of force. The magnetometer is usually located as far as possible from sources of magnetic fields within the aircraft, and connected by a cable to the AHRS. Because the AHRS automatically updates the heading display, you do not have to set the heading to match the compass. The magnetometer does not lead or lag during turns, and does not experience errors due to acceleration.

MEMS GYROS

Some AHRS use MEMS gyros, which are technically not gyroscopes, but angular rate sensors. MEMS gyros take advantage of Coriolis force, which causes a moving object to experience a linear acceleration when it is rotated. In a typical MEMS gyro, tiny quartz fingers or discs move back and forth in one plane, and when the aircraft rotates, that plane is slightly displaced. Sensitive electronic circuitry detects the displacements as small changes in capacitance between the moving and non-moving parts of the sensor, translating the changes into signals that the AHRS uses to determine attitude and rates of rotation.

RING LASER GYROS

The ring laser gyro, which uses light to detect rotation and changes in attitude, is another type of AHRS gyro. Lasers emit light that is all of the same wavelength and moving in the same direction. In a ring laser gyro, a beam of laser light is split in half, and each half is directed by mirrors around a triangular track in opposite directions. If the aircraft changes attitude and the ring laser gyro rotates, changes occur in the wavelengths of the light beams. The AHRS uses this data to determine aircraft attitude. By arranging three ring laser gyros perpendicular to each other, rotation in any direction can be measured. [Figure 2-32]

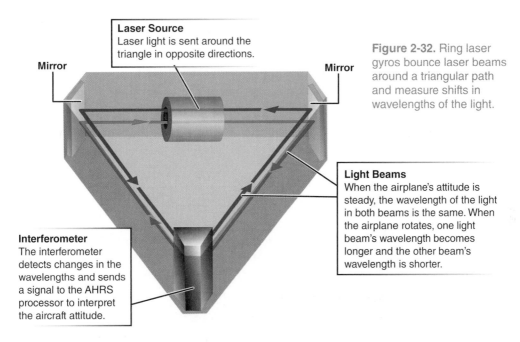

Laser Source
Laser light is sent around the triangle in opposite directions.

Mirror

Mirror

Figure 2-32. Ring laser gyros bounce laser beams around a triangular path and measure shifts in wavelengths of the light.

Light Beams
When the airplane's attitude is steady, the wavelength of the light in both beams is the same. When the airplane rotates, one light beam's wavelength becomes longer and the other beam's wavelength is shorter.

Interferometer
The interferometer detects changes in the wavelengths and sends a signal to the AHRS processor to interpret the aircraft attitude.

ATTITUDE INDICATOR

A digital attitude indicator can have a virtual blue sky and brown ground with a white horizon line or can be displayed over a realistic representation of terrain features. The horizon line can extend the width of the PFD. Near the center of the display, a miniature aircraft symbol shows whether the nose is above or below the horizon and a pitch scale shows pitch angles of 5, 10, 15, and 20 degrees. Bank angle is shown with a roll scale with reference marks at 10, 20, 30, 45, and 60 degrees. Some systems have optional settings to let you choose whether the roll scale moves and the pointer remains stationary, or the pointer moves while the roll scale remains stationary. A **slip/skid indicator** below the roll pointer helps you maintain coordinated flight. [Figure 2-33]

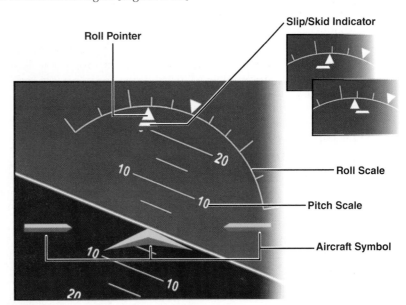

Roll Pointer

Slip/Skid Indicator

Figure 2-33. The digital attitude indicator shows pitch, bank, and slip/skid information.

Roll Scale

Pitch Scale

Aircraft Symbol

SECTION A ■ **Flight Instrument Systems**

HORIZONTAL SITUATION INDICATOR

In addition to a compass card, the digital **horizontal situation indicator (HSI)** displays the current airplane heading in a window. The course indicator arrow and the course deviation indicator (CDI) change color based on the navigation source you select—magenta for a GPS source, and green if the source is a VOR or localizer. Many HSIs have a heading bug to set for navigation systems or autopilot functions or to use as a reference mark when you are hand-flying. A **turn rate indicator** with index marks and a **trend vector** helps you make standard-rate turns. [Figure 2-34]

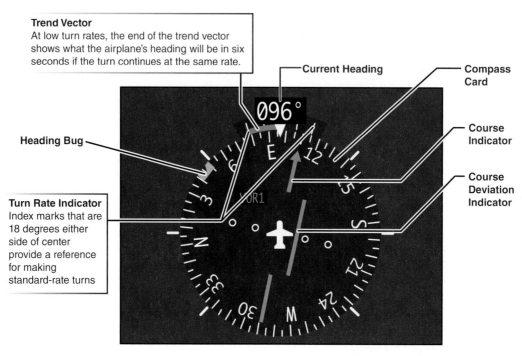

Trend Vector
At low turn rates, the end of the trend vector shows what the airplane's heading will be in six seconds if the turn continues at the same rate.

Current Heading

Compass Card

Heading Bug

Course Indicator

Course Deviation Indicator

Turn Rate Indicator
Index marks that are 18 degrees either side of center provide a reference for making standard-rate turns

Figure 2-34. The digital HSI displays heading, navigation, and turn-rate information.

You might be able to display additional bearing pointers to navaids and GPS waypoints on the HSI for increased situational awareness. Optional windows associated with the HSI can display information such as distance to navaids and their frequencies.

AHRS ERRORS

The AHRS monitors itself constantly, comparing the data from different inputs and checking the integrity of its information. When the system detects a problem, it places a red X over the display of the affected instrument to alert you that the indications are unreliable. As with analog instruments, failures of different sensors affect different combinations of instruments. For example, failure of the magnetometer affects the HSI heading information. Some sensor failures affect multiple instruments—failure of the inertial sensors affects both the attitude indicator and the HSI. [Figure 2-35]

Figure 2-35. A red X on the attitude indicator and heading window and removal of the compass card values means the attitude indicator and HSI are not receiving attitude information from the AHRS.

AHRS INSTRUMENT CHECK

During taxi, check the operation of the attitude and heading instruments. Verify that the heading indicator agrees with the compass. Ensure that the heading indicator and turn indicator show turns in the correct direction and the slip/skid indicator moves to the outside of the turn. In addition, check and set the backup instruments.

AIR DATA COMPUTER

In an integrated flight display system, the pitot tube, static source, and outside air temperature probe provide information to the **air data computer (ADC)**. The ADC uses these pressure and temperature inputs to determine the appropriate readings for the airspeed indicator, altimeter, and vertical speed indicator. In addition, the ADC provides information to display true airspeed and outside air temperature on the PFD.

AIRSPEED INDICATOR

On the digital airspeed indicator, a central window and a pointer on a moving vertical scale show the indicated airspeed. The vertical scale is called the airspeed tape. The tape has colored bars to indicate airspeed operating ranges. Many digital airspeed displays have a trend vector that indicates how much the airplane is accelerating or decelerating. The length of the trend vector is proportional to the rate of change, and the tip of the trend vector shows what the airspeed will be in six seconds if the acceleration or deceleration continues at the same rate. [Figure 2-36]

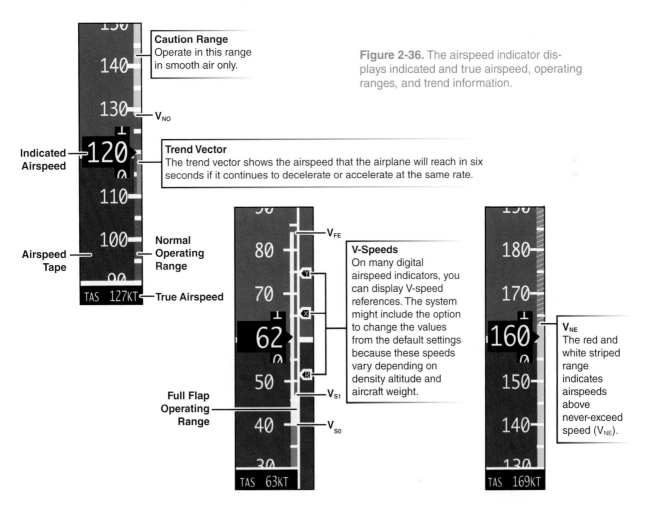

Caution Range
Operate in this range in smooth air only.

V_{NO}

Indicated Airspeed

Trend Vector
The trend vector shows the airspeed that the airplane will reach in six seconds if it continues to decelerate or accelerate at the same rate.

Airspeed Tape

Normal Operating Range

True Airspeed

TAS 127KT

Figure 2-36. The airspeed indicator displays indicated and true airspeed, operating ranges, and trend information.

V_{FE}

V-Speeds
On many digital airspeed indicators, you can display V-speed references. The system might include the option to change the values from the default settings because these speeds vary depending on density altitude and aircraft weight.

V_{S1}

Full Flap Operating Range

V_{S0}

TAS 63KT

V_{NE}
The red and white striped range indicates airspeeds above never-exceed speed (V_{NE}).

TAS 169KT

ALTIMETER

Like the airspeed indicator, the digital altimeter provides a central window and a pointer on a moving tape to display the indicated altitude. The window at the bottom of the display shows the altimeter setting. When the airplane is climbing or descending, the altimeter displays a trend vector. The trend vector shows the altitude that the airplane will reach in six seconds if it continues to climb or descend at the same rate. The altimeter might have a bug to select the reference altitude for the autopilot. You can also set the bug as a reminder to level off at an assigned altitude or at a minimum descent altitude or decision altitude on an instrument approach. The altitude that you select appears in a window above the altimeter tape. [Figure 2-37]

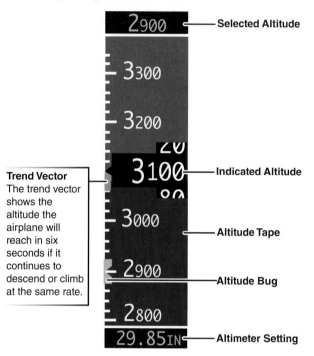

Selected Altitude

Trend Vector
The trend vector shows the altitude the airplane will reach in six seconds if it continues to descend or climb at the same rate.

Indicated Altitude

Altitude Tape

Altitude Bug

Altimeter Setting

Figure 2-37. The digital altimeter includes a trend vector and a bug that you can set as an altitude reference.

VERTICAL SPEED INDICATOR

The vertical speed indicator (VSI) is adjacent to the altimeter. As with the airspeed indicator and altimeter, you read the vertical speed in feet per minute in a window that also serves as a pointer, but on the vertical speed display, the tape remains motionless as the window moves up or down over the scale. [Figure 2-38]

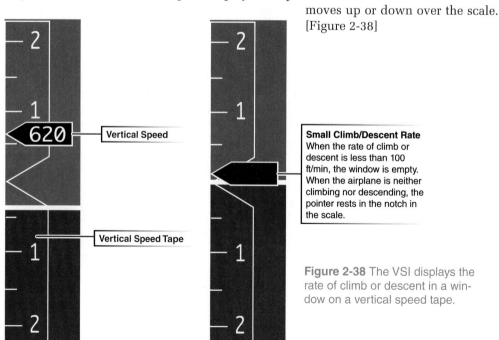

Vertical Speed

Vertical Speed Tape

Small Climb/Descent Rate
When the rate of climb or descent is less than 100 ft/min, the window is empty. When the airplane is neither climbing nor descending, the pointer rests in the notch in the scale.

Figure 2-38 The VSI displays the rate of climb or descent in a window on a vertical speed tape.

ADC SYSTEM ERRORS

The ADC relies on inputs from sensors, such as the pitot tube, static source, and outside air temperature probe, to provide reliable instrument indications. If one or more of these sources stops providing input, or if the computer determines that its own internal operations are not correct, it places a red X over the display of the affected instrument. The failure of a single sensor might affect only one instrument. For example, a blocked pitot tube can disable the airspeed indicator without affecting the other instruments. [Figure 2-39]

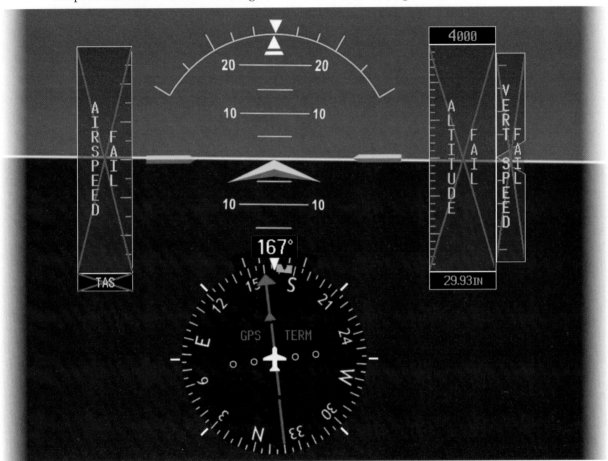

Figure 2-39. A red X on the airspeed indicator, altimeter, and vertical speed indicator means that these instruments are not receiving valid information from the ADC.

ADC INSTRUMENT CHECK

Before takeoff, verify that the airspeed indicator reads zero when the aircraft is at rest and indicates airspeed appropriately during the takeoff roll. Ensure that the altimeter indicates within 75 feet of a known elevation when set to the current altimeter setting. Verify that the VSI reads zero. In addition, check and set the backup instruments.

PFD SCREEN FAILURE

In the most commonly used integrated flight display systems, the screens have a white light source behind an electronic matrix of tiny liquid crystal pixels that can change the white light coming through them into thousands of colors. If the back-light in the display fails, the screen can go black although all the information is still there. The integrated flight display is configured so that the functions of the PFD can be transferred to the MFD screen, and vice versa. If the PFD screen turns black, the PFD instruments should automatically display on the MFD in reversionary mode. In the event that the PFD does not appear on the MFD, most systems enable you to manually switch to reversionary mode. [Figure 2-40]

SECTION A ■ Flight Instrument Systems

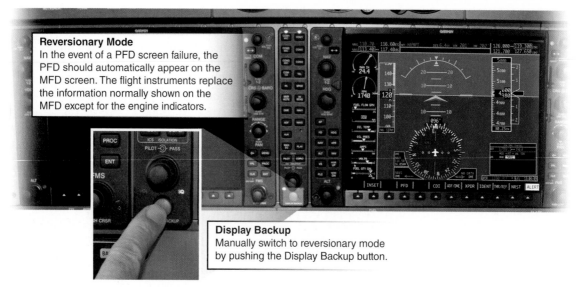

Reversionary Mode
In the event of a PFD screen failure, the PFD should automatically appear on the MFD screen. The flight instruments replace the information normally shown on the MFD except for the engine indicators.

Display Backup
Manually switch to reversionary mode by pushing the Display Backup button.

Figure 2-40. The Garmin G1000 integrated flight display enables you to manually switch to reversionary mode using a Display Backup button.

ELECTRICAL SYSTEM FAILURE

The components of an aircraft electrical system are designed, built, and tested to be extremely reliable, but they can and do occasionally fail. If your aircraft experiences an electrical failure in flight, redundant power sources exist for the instrument systems. Some aircraft have two alternators, and others have a separate battery to power critical systems. Be sure that you understand how your electrical system works, and how to make the best use of your remaining energy resources if an electrical failure occurs.

Even if you have a catastrophic electrical failure and lose all electric power, in many light general aviation aircraft, the backup instruments might not require electric power. The backup attitude indicator can be vacuum-powered and the backup altimeter, airspeed indicator, and magnetic compass usually need no electrical power to function. Other aircraft have electric backup attitude indicators powered by a separate battery that is isolated from the main electrical system. The key to safely handling a failure is knowing your system and practicing for emergency situations. Periodically, practice emergency scenarios with a certificated flight instructor.

MULTIFUNCTION DISPLAY

The primary feature of the MFD is the moving map. The moving map on the MFD can usually display many other kinds of information in the form of overlays, such as terrain, instrument procedures, graphical weather, lightning strikes, and traffic information. In addition to the moving map, the MFD provides separate pages that can include airport information, flight plan data, systems indications, checklists, and instrument charts. [Figure 2-41]

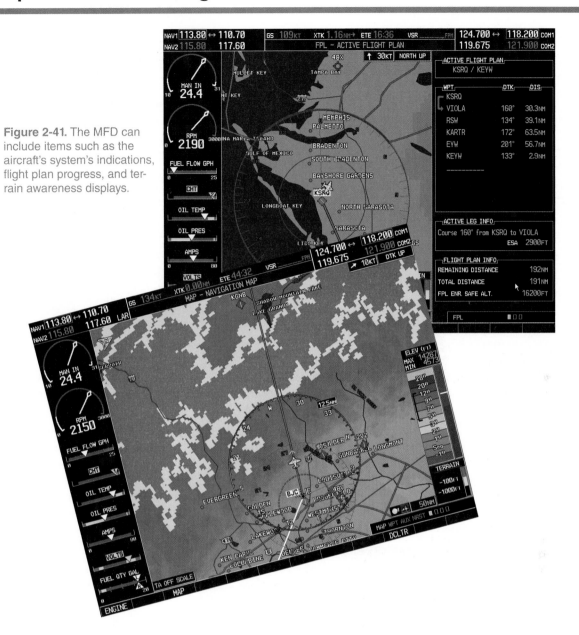

Figure 2-41. The MFD can include items such as the aircraft's system's indications, flight plan progress, and terrain awareness displays.

VISION SYSTEMS

Vision systems technology can improve your situational awareness when flying with an integrated flight display. Vision systems fall under four categories based on their features and how you use them during flight operations. Enhanced vision systems, synthetic vision systems, and combined (enhanced and synthetic) vision systems can be displayed on PFDs and navigation displays. The enhanced flight vision system must be displayed on a conformal head-up display (HUD).

An enhanced vision system (EVS) provides a display of the forward external scene topography through the use of imaging sensors, such as forward looking infrared, millimeter wave radiometry or radar, and low-light-level image intensifying. A synthetic vision system (SVS) is a computer-generated image of the surrounding topography and airport environment created from a database of terrain, obstacles, and cultural features and a navigation source for the aircraft's position, altitude, heading, and track. The image is displayed from the flight crew's perspective or as a plan-view moving map. [Figure 2-42]

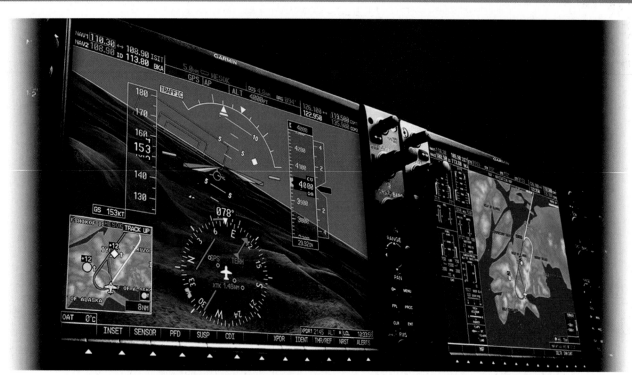

Figure 2-42. SVS real-time, color 3-D imagery of the flight environment enhances situational awareness.

An enhanced flight vision system (EFVS) uses a real-time imaging sensor to provide highly accurate vision performance in low visibility conditions. The EFVS projects an image onto a HUD. Required visual references for instrument approaches become visible in the image before they are visible naturally out the window. In addition, depending on atmospheric conditions and the strength of energy emitted and/or reflected from the scene, you can see these visual references on the display in more detail than you can by looking through the window without enhanced vision. [Figure 2-43]

Figure 2-43. Primarily used in airliners and military aircraft, EFVS displays increase situational awareness during instrument approaches in low visibility conditions.

SUMMARY CHECKLIST

✓ The FARs require these instruments for IFR flight in addition to those required for flight under VFR: gyroscopic pitch and bank indicator, sensitive altimeter, gyroscopic direction indicator, gyroscopic rate-of-turn indicator, slip/skid indicator, and a clock.

✓ The altimeter and static system and the transponder must have been inspected in the preceding 24 calendar months.

✓ The gyroscopic analog instruments are the attitude indicator, heading indicator, and turn coordinator. Gyroscopic instrument operation is based on rigidity in space and precession.

✓ The attitude indicator, or artificial horizon, is the only instrument that gives you an immediate and direct indication of the airplane's pitch and bank attitude.

✓ You must align the heading indicator with the magnetic compass before flight and recheck it periodically during flight.

✓ Turn indicators allow you to establish and maintain standard-rate turns of three degrees per second, or in the case of certain high performance aircraft, half-standard-rate turns.

✓ Both turn coordinators and turn-and-slip indicators indicate rate of turn and the turn coordinator also indicates rate of roll as you enter a turn.

✓ The inclinometer is the part of the turn indicator that indicates whether you are using the correct angle of bank for the rate of turn. Step on the ball to correct a slipping or skidding condition.

✓ The magnetic compass is the only direction-seeking instrument in most light airplanes, but it is susceptible to a number of errors.

✓ The pitot-static instruments are the airspeed indicator, altimeter, and vertical speed indicator (VSI). Blockages in both the pitot and static systems affect the airspeed indicator, and the remaining instruments are affected only by static system blockage.

✓ Calibrated airspeed (CAS) is indicated airspeed corrected for installation and instrument errors.

✓ Equivalent airspeed (EAS) is calibrated airspeed corrected for compressibility.

✓ True airspeed (TAS) is the actual speed your airplane moves through undisturbed air.

✓ Mach is the ratio of the aircraft's true airspeed to the speed of sound at the temperature and altitude in which the aircraft is flying.

✓ The most common altimeter error is failure to keep the current barometric pressure set. The altimeter indicates high when the actual pressure is lower than what is set in the window or when the airplane is in colder-than-standard temperature conditions.

✓ Pressure altitude is displayed on the altimeter when it is set to the standard sea level pressure of 29.92 in. Hg. This also is the altimeter setting when operating at or above 18,000 feet MSL.

✓ Before an IFR flight, verify that the altimeter indicates within 75 feet of the actual field elevation when set to the current altimeter setting.

✓ The VSI instantly displays changes in vertical speed, and gives an accurate indication of the rate of climb or descent a few seconds after a change in vertical speed.

SECTION A ▪ **Flight Instrument Systems**

✓ Complete blockage of the pitot tube can cause the airspeed indicator to react opposite of normal, showing an increase in airspeed as you climb, and a decrease in airspeed in a descent.

✓ The PFD contains digital versions of traditional analog flight instruments, including the attitude indicator, airspeed indicator, altimeter, vertical speed indicator, and HSI.

✓ The AHRS uses inertial sensors such as electronic gyroscopes, accelerometers, and a magnetometer to determine the aircraft's attitude relative to the horizon and heading.

✓ A magnetometer senses the earth's magnetic field to function as a magnetic compass, but without some of the errors associated with a conventional compass.

✓ A slip/skid indicator below the roll pointer of the attitude indicator helps you maintain coordinated flight.

✓ In addition to a compass card, the digital HSI displays the current airplane heading in a window, a course indicator arrow and CDI, and a turn rate indicator with index marks and a trend vector.

✓ When the AHRS system detects a problem, it places a red X over the display of the affected instrument to alert you that the indications are unreliable.

✓ The pitot tube, static source, and outside air temperature probe provide information to the air data computer (ADC), which uses these pressure and temperature inputs to determine the appropriate readings for the airspeed indicator, altimeter, and VSI.

✓ On the digital airspeed indicator, a central window and a pointer on the airspeed tape shows the indicated airspeed.

✓ A trend vector on the digital airspeed indicator shows what the airspeed will be in six seconds if the acceleration or deceleration continues at the same rate.

✓ The trend vector on the digital altimeter shows the altitude that the airplane will reach in six seconds if it continues to climb or descend at the same rate.

✓ The digital altimeter might have a bug that you set to a reference altitude for the autopilot or use as a reminder to level off at a specific altitude.

✓ On the digital VSI, you read vertical speed in feet per minute in a window that also serves as a pointer. The VSI tape remains motionless as the window moves up or down over the scale.

✓ If one or more sensors stops providing input, or if the ADC determines that its own internal operations are not correct, it places a red X over the display of the affected instrument.

✓ If the PFD goes black, integrated flight displays typically enable you to display PFD information on the MFD display in reversionary mode.

✓ If you have a catastrophic electrical failure and lose all electric power, you must use your backup instruments. The backup instruments are not electrically powered or are powered by a separate battery that is isolated from the main electrical system.

✓ The multifunction display (MFD) provides separate pages that can include a moving map, airport information, flight plan data, systems indications, checklists, and instrument charts.

✓ Enhanced vision systems (EVS), synthetic vision systems (SVS), and combined vision systems can improve situational awareness of the flight environment on PFDs.

✓ An enhanced flight vision system (EFVS) displayed on a conformal head-up display (HUD) uses a real-time imaging sensor that provides highly accurate vision performance in low visibility conditions.

KEY TERMS

Rigidity in Space

Gimbals

Precession

Pendulous Vanes

Standard-Rate Turn

Turn-and-Slip Indicator

Turn Coordinator

Inclinometer

Slip

Skid

Magnetic Dip

Northerly Turning Error

Indicated Airspeed (IAS)

Calibrated Airspeed (CAS)

Equivalent Airspeed (EAS)

True Airspeed (TAS)

Mach

Sensitive Altimeter

Indicated Altitude

Calibrated Altitude

Pressure Altitude

Standard Datum Plane

Density Altitude

True Altitude

International Standard Atmosphere (ISA)

Absolute Altitude

Rate Information

Trend Information

Integrated Flight Display

Primary Flight Display (PFD)

Multifunction Display (MFD)

Attitude and Heading Reference System (AHRS)

Magnetometer

Slip/Skid Indicator

Horizontal Situation Indicator (HSI)

Turn Rate indicator

Trend Vector

Air Data Computer (ADC)

SECTION A ■ Flight Instrument Systems

QUESTIONS

1. Which flight instrument is not legally required for flight under IFR?
   A. Slip-skid indicator
   B. Vertical speed indicator
   C. Gyroscopic heading indicator

2. Name the gyroscopic flight instruments. What are two principles that are characteristic of all gyroscopes?

3. Which flight instrument gives you an instantaneous display of both pitch and bank information?

4. True/False. The gyroscopic instruments are the only flight instruments that provide bank information.

5. Why is the turn coordinator a good backup for the attitude and heading indicators in most small airplanes?

6. What is the approximate bank angle required to maintain a standard-rate turn at 90 knots?

7. How long does it take to make a 360° standard-rate turn?
    A. One minute
    B. Two minutes
    C. Four minutes

When referring to the turn coordinators above, assume the pilot is applying rudder pressure in the direction of the turn.

8. Which turn coordinator shows too much rudder pressure being used for the amount of bank?

9. Which turn coordinator shows too little rudder pressure being used for the amount of bank?

10. What condition leads to unreliable operation of the heading indicator and attitude indicator?
    A. Low vacuum pressure
    B. Pitot-static system leak
    C. Short in the electrical system

11. What should you use to correct for magnetic deviation?
    A. Compass correction card
    B. Variation lines on instrument charts
    C. Adjustment knob on the heading indicator

12. During a compass turn, what heading should you use for roll-out if making a right turn to a heading of 360° at a latitude of 45°N? Assume you are using a 16° bank angle.

13. A blocked static source affects which instruments?

For questions 14 through 16, match the V-speed abbreviations with the appropriate definition.

14. V_A A. Maximum landing gear operating speed
                   B. Design maneuvering speed
15. V_{LO} C. Maximum speed with landing gear extended
                   D. Stalling speed in a specified configuration
16. V_{S1} E. Stalling speed in landing configuration

17. How does colder-than-standard temperature affect the relationship between indicated altitude and true altitude?

18. Describe the function of the AHRS.

19. Select the true statement regarding the digital attitude indicator.
     A. The roll scale reference marks are at 10, 25, 45, and 60 degrees.
     B. The turn-rate vector located on the roll scale indicates standard-rate turns.
     C. In a slip, the trapezoid of the slip/skid indicator located beneath the roll pointer moves to the inside of the turn.

20. What information is provided by the trend vector on the HSI?

21. If the AHRS detects a problem with the integrity of the sensor information, what occurs?
     A. A red X is placed over the display of the affected instrument (attitude indicator or HSI).
     B. The system reverts to reversionary mode and PFD information is displayed on the MFD.
     C. After an alert message appears, you must determine the affected instrument by comparing the indications of all instruments.

22. Select the true statement about the ADC.
     A. The ADC determines the readings for the airspeed indicator, attitude indicator, and altimeter.
     B. The failure of a single sensor affects every instrument that receives information from the ADC.
     C. The pitot tube, static source, and outside air temperature probe provide information to the ADC.

23. What is true about the indications on the altimeter?
     A. In six seconds, the airplane will reach an altitude of 8,500 feet MSL if it continues to climb at the same rate.
     B. In ten seconds, the airplane will reach an altitude of 8,460 feet MSL if it continues to climb at the same rate.
     C. In six seconds, the airplane will reach an altitude of 8,460 feet MSL if it continues to climb at the same rate.

24. Describe how the integrated flight display system compensates for a PFD screen failure.

25. True/False. An enhanced flight vision system (EFVS) can be displayed on a PFD.

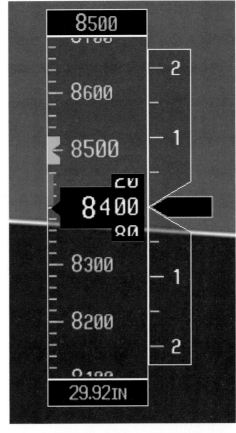

SECTION B
Attitude Instrument Flying

A ttitude instrument flying is controlling an aircraft by reference to flight instruments, rather than outside visual reference. You were introduced to **attitude instrument flying** during your private pilot course. During your instrument training, you will refine this skill so you can maintain precise control of an aircraft by instrument reference while performing the many additional duties of flight under IFR.

FUNDAMENTAL SKILLS

Attitude instrument flying is one of the most important skills you will acquire as a pilot. Before allowing you to move on to other tasks, your instructor will insist you practice attitude flying until it becomes second nature. To achieve positive aircraft control and follow a desired flight path in IFR conditions you must master the fundamental skills of instrument cross-check, instrument interpretation, and aircraft control.

INSTRUMENT CROSS-CHECK

An effective **instrument cross-check**, or scan, requires logical and systematic observation of the instrument panel. It saves time and reduces the workload of instrument flying because you look at the pertinent instruments as you need information. Regardless of your scanning technique, the attitude indicator is essential because it replaces the natural horizon in instrument conditions. You normally cross check the attitude indicator with other instruments that provide information about pitch, bank, and power to verify that the indicated attitude yields the desired results.

The pattern that you use to scan the instruments changes based on the situation and with instruction and practice, you will learn what instruments to cross check in order to maintain a particular flight attitude. The radial cross-check is a scan pattern during which you spend 80 to 90 percent of flight time looking at the attitude indicator and taking only quick glances at the other flight instruments. The radial cross-check works well with a PFD because very little eye movement is required to look at the desired instruments. [Figure 2-44]

Performing the Radial Cross-Check
Your eyes never travel directly between the flight instruments but move by way of the attitude indicator. The maneuver being performed determines which instruments to look at in the pattern.

Radial Cross-Check on the PFD
The extended artificial horizon line enables you to keep the pitch attitude in your peripheral vision at all times and reduces the tendency to fixate on a specific instrument. Return your attention back to the center of the attitude indicator before proceeding to the next instrument and be sure to include the slip/skid indicator.

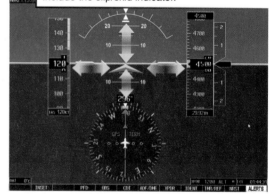

Figure 2-44. Your eyes spend the majority of the time on the attitude indicator during the radial cross-check.

The attitude indicator is the only instrument that provides instant and direct aircraft attitude information, and it is essential to your scan. Loss of the attitude indicator in instrument conditions can result in a distress situation. If this happens, notify ATC immediately, since your ability to comply with clearances is limited.

COMMON CROSS-CHECK ERRORS

As your proficiency increases, you will scan primarily from habit, adjusting your scan rate and sequence to suit the demands of the situation. However, if you do not continue to maintain your proficiency through practice, your scan breaks down. This lapse in instrument cross-checking is usually the result of one or more of the three common cross-check errors — **fixation**, **omission**, and **emphasis**. [Figure 2-45]

Fixation is applying your full concentration on a single instrument and excluding all others. You might have reason to do so, such as when you suspect an instrument is malfunctioning. However, fixation typically causes errors. For example, you notice that you are 200 feet below your assigned altitude. While you fixate on the altimeter as you try to correct your altitude, you drift off of your assigned heading.

Omission is excluding one or more pertinent instruments from your scan. For example, while leveling off from a climb or descent, you might concentrate on pitch control and forget about heading or roll information.

Emphasis is relying on an instrument that you readily understand, even when it provides inadequate information, instead of relying on a combination of instruments. Although you still maintain some scan, control is degraded because you are inappropriately relying on one instrument. For example, you might be able to generally maintain altitude using the attitude indicator, but you cannot hold a precise altitude without including the altimeter in your scan.

Figure 2-45. Fixation, omission, and emphasis dramatically reduce the effectiveness of your scan. These errors also occur when using digital flight instruments.

INSTRUMENT INTERPRETATION

Interpreting the instruments is more effective if you have studied and observed how each instrument operates, and are aware of the instrument indications that represent the desired pitch and bank attitudes for your airplane. Good **instrument interpretation** skills also help your scan. If you understand the limitations of an instrument, you know what other instruments to cross check to get the complete picture. For example, a level pitch indication on the attitude indicator does not necessarily mean the airplane is in a level flight attitude; you need to refer to the altimeter, VSI, and airspeed indicator to confirm that the airplane is in level flight. To confirm bank attitude, refer to the heading indicator and turn coordinator in addition to the attitude indicator.

SECTION B ■ **Attitude Instrument Flying**

"You Got a Bunch of Guys About to Turn Blue."

One of the most watched displays of crew coordination and attitude instrument flying occurred on July 20, 1969 when pilot, Buzz Aldrin, and commander, Neil Armstrong, guided the lunar module, *Eagle*, to a safe landing on the moon's Sea of Tranquility. [Figures A and B] During the landing approach, Aldrin kept his eyes focused on the spacecraft's computer display while Armstrong maneuvered the lunar module into position by following Aldrin's instructions and looking through a window scribed with a vertical scale. (A photo of the lunar module cockpit is shown in figure C.) Armstrong used the scale, which was graduated in degrees, to determine where the computer thought the lunar module would land. The following transcript begins 4 days, 6 hours, 44 minutes, 45 seconds after liftoff and about a minute before the historic landing.

04:06:44:45 — ALDRIN: 100 feet, 3 1/2 down, 9 forward. 5%. [Fuel Remaining]

04:06:44:54 — ALDRIN: Okay. 75 feet. Looking good. Down a half, 6 forward.

04:06:45:02 — DUKE [Charlie Duke, the CapCom (Spacecraft Communicator) for the landing, located in Houston, TX]: 60 seconds. [Fuel Remaining]

04:06:45:04 — ALDRIN: *Light's on.* [Fuel Quantity Light]

04:06:45:08 — ALDRIN: *Down 2 1/2. Forward . . . forward . . . good.*

04:06:45:17 — ALDRIN: *40 feet, down 2 1/2. Kicking up some dust.*

04:06:45:21 — ALDRIN: *30 feet, 2 1/2 down.*

04:06:45:25 — ALDRIN: *4 forward . . . 4 forward. Drifting to the right a little. Okay. Down a half.*

04:06:45:31 — DUKE: *30 seconds.*

04:06:45:32 — ARMSTRONG: *Forward drift?*

04:06:45:33 — ALDRIN: *Yes.*

04:06:45:34 — ALDRIN: *Okay.*

04:06:45:40 — ALDRIN: *Contact Light.* [The 6-foot long probes, which hang from 3 of the lunar module's footpads, have touched the moon's surface.]

04:06:45:43 — ALDRIN: *Okay. Engine stop.*

04:06:45:45 — ALDRIN: *ACA, out of detent.* [The ACA is the Attitude Control Assembly, or control stick.]

04:06:45:46 — ARMSTRONG: *Out of detent.*

04:06:45:47 — ALDRIN: *Mode control, both auto. Descent engine command override, off. Engine arm, off.*

04:06:45:52 — ALDRIN: *413 is in.* [413 is a code which tells the AGS (Abort Guidance System) that the lunar module has landed.]

04:06:45:57 — DUKE: *We copy you down, Eagle.*

04:06:45:59 — ARMSTRONG: *Houston, Tranquility Base here.*

04:06:46:04 — ARMSTRONG: *The Eagle has landed.*

04:06:46:06 — DUKE: *Roger, Tranquility. We copy you on the ground. You got a bunch of guys about to turn blue. We're breathing again. Thanks a lot.*

04:06:46:16 — ARMSTRONG: *Thank you.*

Six and a half hours later, an estimated 600 million people around the world watched as Neil Armstrong became the first person to set foot on the moon. Although Jimmy Doolittle could hardly have envisioned space travel at the time of his first blind flight, the tremendous achievements of Apollo 11 would not have been possible without the application of the basic attitude instrument flight techniques he pioneered nearly 40 years earlier.

Emblem and photos courtesy of NASA

SECTION B ■ Attitude Instrument Flying

AIRCRAFT CONTROL

Aircraft control is the action that you take as a result of cross checking and interpreting the flight instruments. Based on the information you receive from the instruments, adjust the pitch, bank, and power to achieve a desired flight path. Any change in attitude is shown on the attitude indicator and your response should be proportional to the change — small corrections for small deviations, and larger corrections for larger deviations.

During your training, you will develop a feel for how much control pressure achieves a desired change in pitch or bank attitude. Typically, pitch changes are only a few degrees. For example, on an analog attitude indicator, use the width of the bar that forms the wings of the miniature airplane as a reference. For example, a pitch change might involve raising or lowering the nose by half a bar-width.

You achieve precise angles of bank by aligning the index with the markers for 10, 20, and 30 degrees, and you will quickly learn the bank angles to produce a standard-rate turn at each of the airspeeds at which you normally operate. For small course corrections (less than standard rate), a rule of thumb is to use a bank angle that corresponds to the number of degrees you want to turn.

Experience in an airplane teaches you how far to move the throttle to change the power a given amount. Knowledge of approximate power settings for various flight configurations helps you avoid overcontrolling power.

Maintain a light touch on the controls, and keep the airplane properly trimmed. If you are constantly holding control pressure, you cannot apply the precise pressures needed for controlled changes in attitude. An improperly trimmed airplane increases tension, interrupts your cross-check, and can result in abrupt or erratic control. [Figure 2-46]

To properly trim the airplane:

- Do not use the trim alone to establish a change in aircraft attitude. Apply control pressure(s) to establish a desired attitude. Then, adjust the trim so that the aircraft maintains that attitude when you release the flight controls.

- If applicable, adjust the aileron trim to maintain a wings-level attitude and use the rudder trim to maintain coordinated flight by referring to the inclinometer or slip/skid indicator.

- Use balanced power or thrust when possible to help maintain stabilized flight. Changes in attitude, power, or configuration typically require trim adjustments.

Figure 2-46. You can easily adjust the attitude with gentle pressure on the controls if the airplane is properly trimmed.

 The correct sequence in which to apply the three skills used in instrument flying is cross-check, instrument interpretation, and aircraft control.

SECTION B ■ Attitude Instrument Flying

ATTITUDE INSTRUMENT FLYING METHODS

The two generally accepted methods of attitude instrument flying are the control and performance method and the primary and supporting method. Although these techniques differ, they use the same instruments and control inputs to accomplish the same results.

CONTROL AND PERFORMANCE METHOD

The **control and performance method** of attitude instrument flying divides the instruments into three groups: control, performance, and navigation. The control and performance method is based on the idea that if you accurately establish a specific attitude and power setting using the **control instruments**, the airplane will perform as expected. The **performance instruments** indicate how the airplane responds to changes in attitude and power. The navigation instruments indicate the position of the airplane relative to a facility or fix. [Figure 2-47]

CONTROL

PERFORMANCE

NAVIGATION

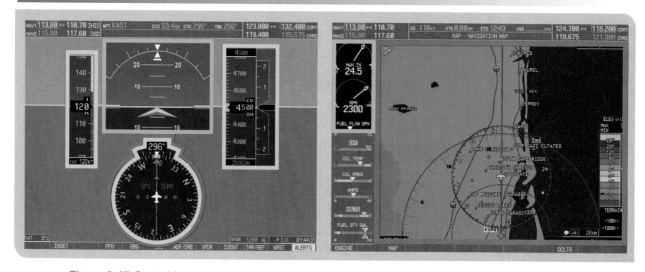

Figure 2-47. Control instruments directly indicate attitude and power and performance instruments provide feedback to confirm and support the control instruments.

SECTION B ■ Attitude Instrument Flying

Knowing the approximate pitch attitude and power settings for your airplane to achieve the desired performance helps reduce your workload. When you cross check the performance instruments you must interpret any deviations and determine the control adjustments necessary to achieve the desired performance. [Figure 2-48]

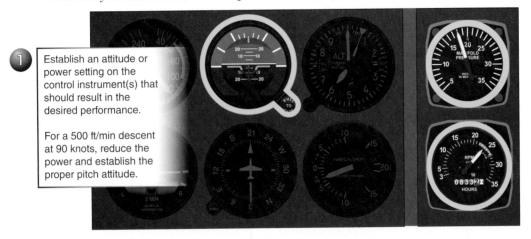

1 Establish an attitude or power setting on the control instrument(s) that should result in the desired performance.

For a 500 ft/min descent at 90 knots, reduce the power and establish the proper pitch attitude.

2 Trim until control pressures are neutralized.

3 Cross check the performance instruments to determine if the established attitude or power setting is providing the desired performance.

Although the airspeed is 90 knots and the altimeter shows a descent, the VSI indicates only a 300 ft/min descent.

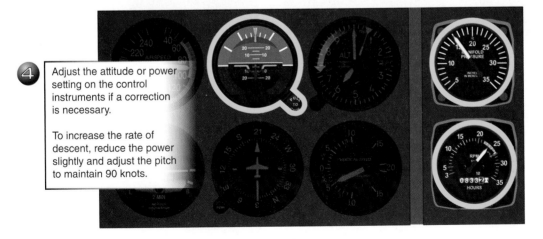

4 Adjust the attitude or power setting on the control instruments if a correction is necessary.

To increase the rate of descent, reduce the power slightly and adjust the pitch to maintain 90 knots.

Figure 2-48. Follow four steps to use the control and performance method of attitude instrument flying.

PRIMARY AND SUPPORTING METHOD

The **primary and supporting method** divides the panel into **pitch instruments, bank instruments,** and **power instruments.** [Figure 2-49] This method further classifies instruments as being primary or supporting depending on the maneuver you are performing and whether you are establishing or maintaining an attitude. Use the primary instruments to provide the most essential information. Supporting instruments reinforce the indications on the primary instruments to help you meet the desired performance. For example, to *establish* a specific airspeed in straight-and-level flight, use the manifold pressure gauge or the tachometer as the primary instrument to adjust power and use the airspeed indicator as the supporting power instrument. To *maintain* the proper airspeed in straight-and-level flight, use the airspeed indicator as the primary power instrument and the manifold pressure gauge or the tachometer as the supporting power instrument.

Pitch Instruments

Bank Instruments

Power Instruments

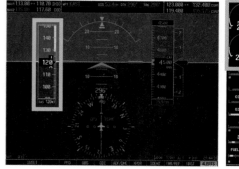

Figure 2-49. The primary and supporting method groups instruments according to their control function.

 The altimeter, airspeed indicator, and vertical speed indicator, in addition to the attitude indicator, are pitch instruments.

BASIC FLIGHT MANEUVERS

The following basic flight maneuvers are presented using the primary and supporting method. The primary and supporting instruments are identified for each situation including which instruments are used to initially establish an attitude and then to maintain the attitude.

STRAIGHT-AND-LEVEL FLIGHT — POWER CONTROL

To make suitable power adjustments, know the approximate power required for a desired airspeed in your airplane. Experiment with various flight configurations, and memorize the required power settings. If you are not achieving the desired airspeed, adjust the power setting by referring to the power instruments (manifold pressure gauge or tachometer). After making a rough power adjustment, continue your scan and then look back to the power instruments to make final adjustments after the indications have stabilized.

After you establish the power setting, check the airspeed indicator for the desired results. Continue monitoring the pitch instruments to verify that you are maintaining altitude; otherwise, the airspeed indications are affected. Monitor the bank instruments closely because changes in power induce turning forces in most propeller-driven airplanes. Remember to trim the airplane after the airspeed stabilizes following a power change. [Figure 2-50]

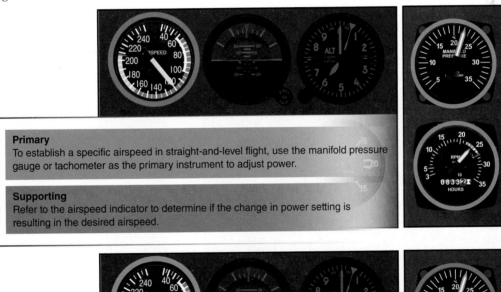

ESTABLISH

Primary
To establish a specific airspeed in straight-and-level flight, use the manifold pressure gauge or tachometer as the primary instrument to adjust power.

Supporting
Refer to the airspeed indicator to determine if the change in power setting is resulting in the desired airspeed.

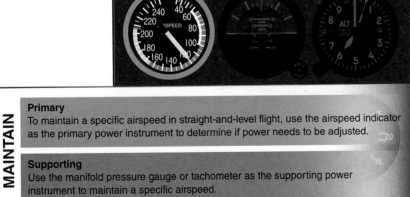

MAINTAIN

Primary
To maintain a specific airspeed in straight-and-level flight, use the airspeed indicator as the primary power instrument to determine if power needs to be adjusted.

Supporting
Use the manifold pressure gauge or tachometer as the supporting power instrument to maintain a specific airspeed.

Figure 2-50. Establishing and maintaining a specific airspeed in straight-and-level flight requires proper power control.

 As you reduce power to change airspeed from high to low cruise in level flight, the instruments that are primary for pitch, bank, and power are the altimeter, heading indicator, and manifold pressure gauge or tachometer. Upon becoming established at the new airspeed, the airspeed indicator becomes the primary instrument for power.

SECTION B ■ **Attitude Instrument Flying**

STRAIGHT-AND-LEVEL FLIGHT — PITCH CONTROL

The attitude indicator provides an instant and direct indication of relative pitch attitude, enabling you to precisely make pitch changes as small as one-half degree. On traditional indicators, align the miniature airplane with the horizon bar prior to takeoff to indicate approximate level flight at cruise speed. Because the required level-flight pitch attitude varies, you might need to adjust the horizon bar in flight. To control pitch during straight-and-level flight, make sure the airplane is trimmed to maintain the desired pitch attitude without any control pressure.

When an altitude deviation occurs, use your judgment and experience in the airplane to determine the rate of correction. Try a couple of degrees of pitch change on the attitude indicator when the airplane is 100 feet or less from your desired altitude, and correct back at twice the rate of your deviation. For example, if you are 100 feet below the desired altitude, climb back at 200 ft/min If you are descending when you discover the deviation, stop the descent first, then pitch up to climb back to the proper altitude. You might need to adjust the power if the altitude is off by more than 200 feet. [Figure 2-51]

ESTABLISH

Primary
Use the attitude indicator as the primary instrument to establish the proper pitch attitude for straight-and-level flight—it provides instant, direct, and corresponding indications of any change in the aircraft's pitch and bank attitude.

Supporting
Scan the other pitch instruments—airspeed indicator, altimeter, and VSI to verify the pitch indications on the attitude indicator.

MAINTAIN

Primary
To maintain altitude, use the altimeter as the primary pitch instrument.

Supporting
Changes in the other pitch instruments can indicate that deviations in altitude will occur.

Figure 2-51. Effectively controlling the pitch attitude enables you to precisely maintain altitude, which is critical in flight under IFR.

FAA Conditions that determine the pitch attitude required to maintain level flight are airspeed, air density, wing design, and angle of attack.

FAA The altimeter provides the most pertinent information (primary) for pitch control for maintaining straight-and level flight. The attitude indicator is the least appropriate pitch instrument for determining the need for a pitch change in level flight at constant thrust.

FAA As a rule of thumb, you should make altitude corrections of less than 100 feet using a half-bar width correction on the attitude indicator, and confirmed on the altimeter and VSI.

STRAIGHT-AND-LEVEL FLIGHT — BANK CONTROL

The heading indicator is primary for bank during straight flight, whether level, climbing, or descending, because this instrument indicates the direction you need to turn to maintain the correct heading. When you see a heading deviation, use the attitude indicator to establish a bank angle equal to the degrees of deviation from the desired heading. For example, if the airplane has drifted 10° off the desired heading, establish a bank of 10°. For larger corrections, you normally limit the bank angle so you do not exceed a standard-rate turn. [Figure 2-52]

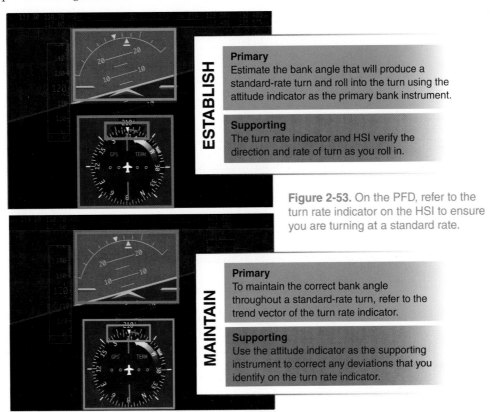

MAINTAIN

Primary
To maintain a particular heading in straight-and-level flight, use the heading indicator as the primary bank instrument.

Supporting
A bank shown on the attitude indicator or turn coordinator will alert you to a deviation from the desired heading.

Figure 2-52. Be alert for deviations in heading—an inadvertent change in heading might not be as noticeable as a change in altitude.

 The heading indicator provides the most pertinent information (primary) for bank control in straight-and-level flight.

STANDARD-RATE TURNS — BANK CONTROL

Under IFR in small airplanes, you normally turn at a standard rate of three degrees per second. To enter a level turn, use the attitude indicator to establish a bank angle that you expect will result in a standard-rate turn. Then refer to the turn rate indicator or turn coordinator, whether you are in a level, climbing, or descending turn, to maintain the proper bank. [Figure 2-53]

ESTABLISH

Primary
Estimate the bank angle that will produce a standard-rate turn and roll into the turn using the attitude indicator as the primary bank instrument.

Supporting
The turn rate indicator and HSI verify the direction and rate of turn as you roll in.

Figure 2-53. On the PFD, refer to the turn rate indicator on the HSI to ensure you are turning at a standard rate.

MAINTAIN

Primary
To maintain the correct bank angle throughout a standard-rate turn, refer to the trend vector of the turn rate indicator.

Supporting
Use the attitude indicator as the supporting instrument to correct any deviations that you identify on the turn rate indicator.

SECTION B ■ Attitude Instrument Flying

SECTION B ■ Attitude Instrument Flying

 The primary bank instrument while establishing a standard-rate turn is the attitude indicator. The turn coordinator or turn rate indicator is a supporting bank instrument during roll-in, and becomes primary after the turn is established.

Rate of turn varies with true airspeed and angle of bank. To estimate the approximate bank angle required for a standard-rate turn, divide the true airspeed in knots by 10 and add 5 to the result. For example, according to this rule of thumb, the angle of bank required for a standard-rate turn at 110 knots is 11 plus 5, or 16°. The rate of turn at any given airspeed depends on the amount of sideward force causing the turn; that is, the horizontal component of lift. This varies directly in proportion to the bank in a coordinated turn, so the rate of turn at a given airspeed increases as the angle of bank increases, and the turn radius decreases. [Figure 2-54]

An increase in bank angle with a constant airspeed increases the rate of turn and decreases the radius of turn.

Constant Airspeed (130 Knots) — Changing Bank Angle			
Bank Angle	10°	20°	36°
Rate of Turn	1.5° /sec	3° /sec	6° /sec
Radius of Turn (approximate)	6,435 ft	3,118 ft	1,562 ft

An increase in airspeed with a constant bank angle decreases the rate of turn and increases the radius of turn.

Constant Bank Angle (20°) — Changing Airspeed			
Airspeed	130 Knots	165 Knots	200 Knots
Rate of Turn	3°/sec	2.4°/sec	2°/sec
Radius of Turn (approximate)	3,118 ft	5,023 ft	7,379 ft

Figure 2-54. Varying either the bank angle or airspeed changes both the rate and radius of turn.

The rate of turn at any airspeed is dependent upon the horizontal component of lift. It can be increased and the radius of turn decreased by increasing the bank and/or decreasing the airspeed. During a constant bank level turn, an increase in airspeed causes the rate of turn to decrease, and the radius of turn to increase.

To stop the turn on the desired heading, lead your roll-out by about one-half the angle of bank. For example, if in a 16° bank, begin your roll-out 8° before you reach the desired heading. With experience, you might choose a different lead point for your rate of roll-out, depending on your technique.

STANDARD-RATE TURNS — PITCH CONTROL

Remember to scan your pitch instruments during roll-in, roll-out, and throughout the turn. It is easy to experience an unintended pitch change because of the loss of vertical lift in a turn. Although the nose tends to pitch down, most pilots automatically apply back pressure, so overcompensation and a nose-up deviation can also occur. [Figure 2-55]

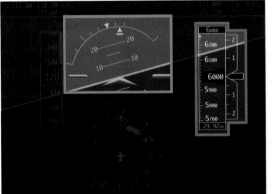

ESTABLISH

Primary
As you roll into a turn, use the attitude indicator to increase the pitch attitude to compensate for the loss of vertical lift.

Supporting
Ensure you do not lose or gain altitude by using the altimeter and the VSI as supporting pitch instruments.

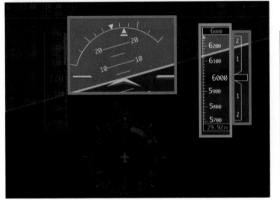

MAINTAIN

Primary
To maintain altitude in the turn, refer to the altimeter as the primary pitch instrument.

Supporting
Continue to use the attitude indicator and the VSI as the supporting pitch instruments.

Figure 2-55. Monitoring the attitude indicator helps you apply precise control adjustments when establishing the turn because this instrument displays both pitch and bank information.

 The primary pitch instrument during a constant altitude turn is the altimeter.

 You must increase the angle of attack to maintain a constant altitude during a coordinated turn because the vertical component of lift has decreased as the result of the bank.

If you reduce power to decrease airspeed in a level turn, the airplane will lose some lift and you must either increase the angle of attack and/or decrease the angle of bank to maintain altitude. Decreasing the bank angle also is necessary to maintain the same rate of turn at a slower airspeed. Conversely, increasing the airspeed results in excess available lift, which requires a decrease in angle of attack and/or an increase in bank angle to avoid climbing. During airspeed changes, as with any maneuver in which your objective is to maintain altitude, the altimeter is primary for pitch, supported by the attitude indicator and VSI. When you roll out of a turn, reduce the back pressure or trim that you used to maintain altitude during the turn. Use the attitude indicator with the VSI to adjust the pitch and monitor the results on the altimeter.

 When airspeed is decreased in a turn, you must decrease the angle of bank and/or increase the angle of attack to maintain level flight. Conversely, when airspeed is increased during a level turn, additional vertical lift is generated. To avoid climbing, you must increase the angle of bank and/or decrease the angle of attack.

STANDARD-RATE TURNS — POWER CONTROL

An airplane tends to lose airspeed in a level turn because the increased angle of attack results in an increase in induced drag. To maintain speed, you need additional power. Although this effect is negligible at cruise speed, it can become significant as you slow to approach speed, where you should increase the power a certain amount while establishing a turn, rather than waiting for the airspeed to bleed off during the turn. [Figure 2-56]

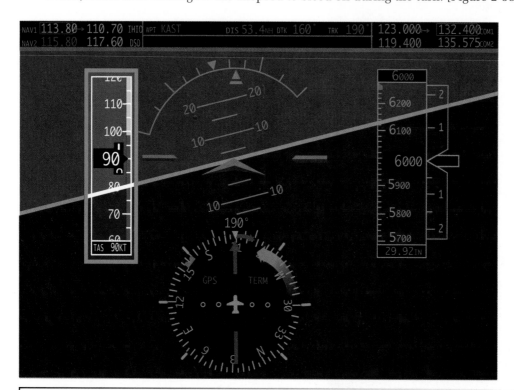

MAINTAIN

Primary
To maintain a specific airspeed in a turn, monitor the airspeed indicator to determine if you need to adjust the power.

Supporting
Use the manifold pressure gauge or the tachometer as the supporting power instruments. If you need to adjust the power to increase or decrease the airspeed, these gauges become primary for power.

Figure 2-56. The airspeed indicator is the primary power instrument for maintaining airspeed in a turn.

 The attitude indicator and VSI are supporting instruments for pitch during a change of airspeed in a level turn. The airspeed indicator is primary for power as the airspeed reaches the desired value.

STEEP TURNS

During instrument training, any turn greater than a standard rate is considered steep. Normally, you practice these turns with a 45° angle of bank. Although you typically do not use this steep of a bank angle in IFR conditions, practicing these turns during your training helps you to react smoothly, quickly, and confidently to unexpected unusual flight attitudes in instrument flight conditions.

The need for a higher angle of attack to compensate for the greatly reduced vertical component of lift magnifies errors in pitch control. You need to speed up your cross-check, interpret the instruments accurately, and apply prompt, smooth control pressures. Because pitch indications on the attitude indicator can be more difficult to interpret in a steep-banked turn, the VSI becomes essential as a supporting pitch instrument. [Figure 2-57]

The airplane usually has a tendency to climb when you roll out of a steep turn because of the nose-up trim applied during the turn. Plan to push forward on the yoke during roll-out and maintain an increased cross-check until the airplane is again trimmed for straight-and-level flight.

Figure 2-57. Steep turns require increased attention to pitch control due to the significant loss of vertical lift.

Primary Bank
The attitude indicator is the primary bank instrument for establishing and maintaining the 45 degrees of bank.

Primary Pitch
Use the altimeter as the primary pitch instrument during the steep turn.

Supporting Pitch
If the VSI starts showing an undesirable trend, use the attitude indicator to make a specific pitch correction, then refer to the VSI and altimeter to verify you have arrested the altitude deviation.

Primary Power
During the steep turn, use the airspeed indicator to determine if you need to adjust the power to maintain the entry airspeed.

CONSTANT AIRSPEED CLIMBS — PITCH CONTROL

Constant airspeed climbs include cruise climbs and climbs at the best rate-of-climb (V_Y) and best angle-of-climb (V_X) speeds. To establish a constant airspeed climb, add power, set the pitch attitude for the desired airspeed, and accept the resulting rate of climb. After you are established in the climb, your objective is to maintain a desired airspeed for a specific power setting. [Figure 2-58]

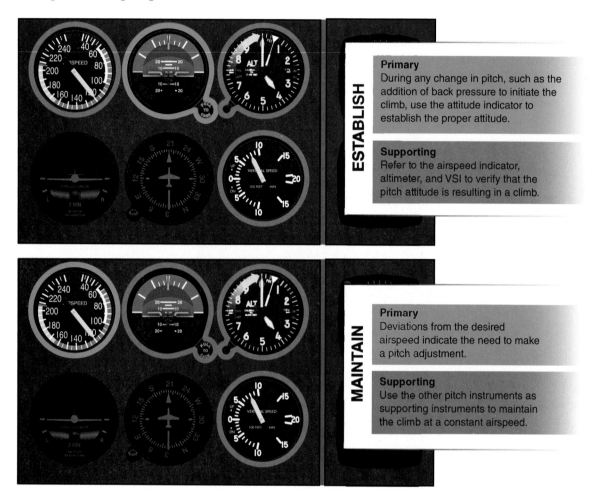

ESTABLISH

Primary
During any change in pitch, such as the addition of back pressure to initiate the climb, use the attitude indicator to establish the proper attitude.

Supporting
Refer to the airspeed indicator, altimeter, and VSI to verify that the pitch attitude is resulting in a climb.

MAINTAIN

Primary
Deviations from the desired airspeed indicate the need to make a pitch adjustment.

Supporting
Use the other pitch instruments as supporting instruments to maintain the climb at a constant airspeed.

Figure 2-58. Whether climbing straight or turning, the airspeed indicator is the primary pitch instrument after the climb is stabilized because its indications tell you whether pitch adjustments are necessary.

 The proper way to transition from cruise flight to a climb at a specific speed is to increase pitch until the attitude indicator shows the approximate pitch attitude for the climb airspeed. The attitude indicator is primary for pitch during a change in pitch and primary for bank during a change in bank. After you are stabilized in a straight or turning climb at cruise-climb airspeed, the primary pitch instrument is the airspeed indicator.

CONSTANT RATE CLIMBS — PITCH CONTROL

In a **constant rate climb** you maintain a specific vertical velocity in addition to controlling airspeed. During IFR flight, you might use a constant rate climb within 1,000 feet of your assigned altitude, where ATC expects you to climb at 500 ft/min. Because of limited horsepower, your training airplane is likely restricted to certain airspeed and climb rate combinations that you will learn with practice.

Although the instrument indications for constant rate climbs are very similar to those for constant airspeed climbs, you emphasize different instruments in your scan. After you are established in the climb, the VSI becomes the primary pitch instrument; if it indicates a lower-than-desired rate of climb, you need to pitch up further. The airspeed indicator is the primary power instrument; if it indicates low, you need to try a higher power setting, if available. [Figure 2-59]

SECTION B ■ Attitude Instrument Flying

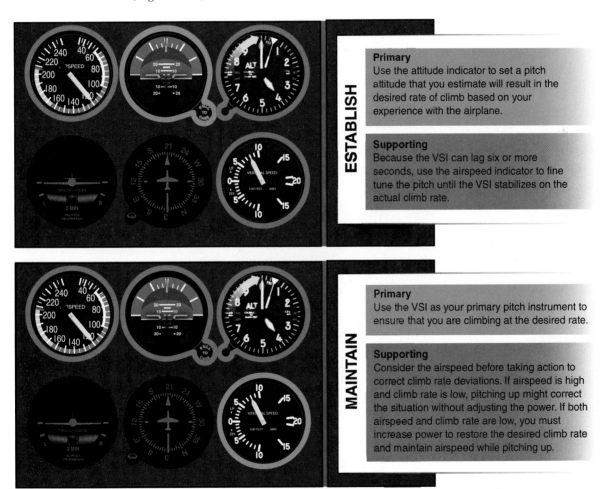

ESTABLISH

Primary
Use the attitude indicator to set a pitch attitude that you estimate will result in the desired rate of climb based on your experience with the airplane.

Supporting
Because the VSI can lag six or more seconds, use the airspeed indicator to fine tune the pitch until the VSI stabilizes on the actual climb rate.

MAINTAIN

Primary
Use the VSI as your primary pitch instrument to ensure that you are climbing at the desired rate.

Supporting
Consider the airspeed before taking action to correct climb rate deviations. If airspeed is high and climb rate is low, pitching up might correct the situation without adjusting the power. If both airspeed and climb rate are low, you must increase power to restore the desired climb rate and maintain airspeed while pitching up.

Figure 2-59. Use the VSI in conjunction with the airspeed indicator to establish and maintain the desired climb rate and airspeed.

FAA The attitude indicator and turn coordinator are supporting bank instruments during a straight, stabilized climb at a constant rate.

CONSTANT AIRSPEED DESCENTS — PITCH CONTROL

Typically, you will perform a **constant airspeed descent**, sometimes called a cruise descent, when you descend from your assigned cruising altitude for arrival at your destination. When you reduce power, the airplane can have a tendency to turn right, so expect to use slight left rudder pressure.

Depending on the airplane, if ATC wants you to maintain maximum forward speed, you might choose little or no power reduction when entering the descent. Even though you do not seek a specific vertical velocity on a constant airspeed descent, establish a pitch and power combination that results in a reasonable rate of descent. If you have a fixed-pitch propeller, make sure you reduce power enough to avoid excessive engine RPM. On high-performance piston engines, reduce power gradually, in accordance with the POH, to avoid damage to the engine from rapid cooling. [Figure 2-60]

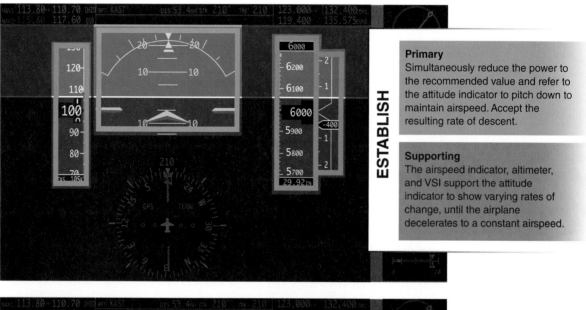

ESTABLISH

Primary
Simultaneously reduce the power to the recommended value and refer to the attitude indicator to pitch down to maintain airspeed. Accept the resulting rate of descent.

Supporting
The airspeed indicator, altimeter, and VSI support the attitude indicator to show varying rates of change, until the airplane decelerates to a constant airspeed.

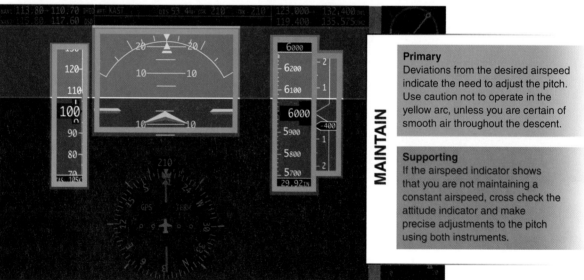

MAINTAIN

Primary
Deviations from the desired airspeed indicate the need to adjust the pitch. Use caution not to operate in the yellow arc, unless you are certain of smooth air throughout the descent.

Supporting
If the airspeed indicator shows that you are not maintaining a constant airspeed, cross check the attitude indicator and make precise adjustments to the pitch using both instruments.

Figure 2-60. A constant airspeed descent is normally used during cruise flight.

 To enter a constant airspeed descent from level cruising flight, and maintain cruising airspeed, simultaneously reduce power and adjust the pitch using the attitude indicator as a reference to maintain the cruising airspeed.

SECTION B ■ Attitude Instrument Flying

CONSTANT RATE DESCENTS — PITCH CONTROL

During the approach phase, where both a constant airspeed and rate of descent is important, use a **constant rate descent**. Although the VSI is the primary instrument to maintain pitch, you must also pay close attention to the airspeed indicator to fly a stabilized approach at a constant rate of descent. [Figure 2-61]

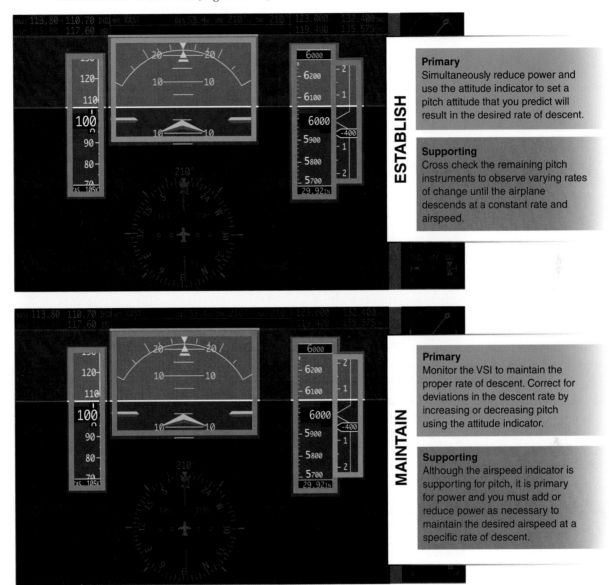

ESTABLISH

Primary
Simultaneously reduce power and use the attitude indicator to set a pitch attitude that you predict will result in the desired rate of descent.

Supporting
Cross check the remaining pitch instruments to observe varying rates of change until the airplane descends at a constant rate and airspeed.

MAINTAIN

Primary
Monitor the VSI to maintain the proper rate of descent. Correct for deviations in the descent rate by increasing or decreasing pitch using the attitude indicator.

Supporting
Although the airspeed indicator is supporting for pitch, it is primary for power and you must add or reduce power as necessary to maintain the desired airspeed at a specific rate of descent.

Figure 2-61. Refer to the VSI and the airspeed indicator to maintain a constant rate of descent at a specific airspeed.

If the airspeed is too slow *and* the rate of descent is too low, simply pitching down might fix both deviations. Conversely, if the airspeed is too fast and the descent rate is too high, you might just need to pitch up slightly. However, you must often use both pitch and power as you correct for descent rate deviations. For example, if you are at the correct airspeed and pitch down to increase the rate of descent according to the VSI, the airspeed increases if you do not reduce power. And, pitching up to decrease the rate of descent causes a corresponding decrease in airspeed so you must add power.

LEVELOFF FROM CLIMBS AND DESCENTS

Leveloff procedures are similar whether climbing or descending. To avoid overshooting the desired altitude, you must lead the leveloff. The amount of lead depends on the airplane, pilot technique, and the desired leveloff speed. As a guide, use 10% of the vertical velocity when you intend to maintain the descent speed during leveloff. For example, if your vertical velocity is 500 ft/min, begin the leveloff 50 feet before you reach the desired altitude. In some situations, you might need to level off at an airspeed higher than your descent airspeed. If descending at 500 ft/min, add power when you are 100 to 150 feet above the desired altitude.

The attitude indicator is the primary pitch instrument during the transition to level flight. The tachometer or manifold pressure gauge is primary for power as you move the throttle to the setting that you estimate will produce the desired airspeed in level flight.

 To level off from a 500 ft/min descent while maintaining airspeed, lead the desired altitude by approximately 50 feet. Use approximately 10% of the vertical velocity to determine how far to lead the leveloff from a climb or descent. To level off at an airspeed higher than the descent speed, add power at approximately 100 to 150 feet above the desired altitude.

CLIMBING AND DESCENDING TURNS

Climbing and descending turns are combinations of the straight climb and descent procedures with turns. As always, expect changes in pitch forces when rolling into and out of turns, and use the attitude indicator to correct any deviations identified on the primary instruments.

COMMON ERRORS

Gaining proficiency in basic attitude instrument flight requires considerable practice. It is not unusual for beginning instrument students to encounter several areas of difficulty. To be proficient at attitude instrument flying, you must be able recognize a recurring problem and learn how to prevent it. [Figure 2-62]

COMMON ERRORS RELATED TO ATTITUDE INSTRUMENT FLYING		
	ERROR	**SOLUTION**
Control Errors	Large deviations from the desired attitude, heading, and airspeed	Do not tolerate small deviations. If you detect an error, initiate a correction immediately.
	Erratic control of airspeed and power	This occurs when you fixate on the airspeed indicator, the manifold pressure gauge, or the tachometer. Be sure to continue a good scan.
	Generally overcontrolling the aircraft	Maintain a light touch on the controls so you can feel the pressures.
	Excessive trim control	Use the trim frequently but in small amounts.
Altitude Errors	Not correcting for pitch deviations during roll-out from a turn	Do not fixate on the heading indicator.
	Consistent loss of altitude during turn entries	During turn entry, apply back pressure to compensate for the loss of vertical lift.
	Consistent gain in altitude when rolling out from a turn	Relax back pressure during roll-out. If you added nose-up trim during the turn, use some forward pressure until you can trim for level flight.
	Chasing the vertical speed indicator	Use a proper cross-check of other pitch instruments, such as the altimeter and attitude indicator. Remember that the VSI has a lag in its indications.
	Applying excessive pitch corrections for the altimeter deviation	Use a proper cross-check of other pitch instruments and increase your understanding of the instrument characteristics.
	Failure to maintain established pitch corrections	Continue to maintain your scan after making a correction and be sure to trim off any control pressures.
Heading Errors	Overshooting the desired roll-out heading	To combat this error, maintain a standard-rate turn by avoiding too much bank angle. Refer to the turn coordinator frequently and begin your rollout with the proper lead.
	Inability to maintain a constant heading	Make sure you continue to cross check the heading indicator and turn coordinator, particularly during changes in power and pitch attitude.
	Failure to keep the heading indicator properly set	Periodically include the magnetic compass in your scan.

Figure 2-62. Control, altitude, and heading errors are common to attitude instrument flying.

INSTRUMENT FAILURES

Although your training gives you some preparation in flying with instrument failures, it is difficult to accurately simulate instrument failure the same way it might occur during flight in actual IFR conditions. Digital instrument failures are easy to recognize because the affected instrument is covered with a red X. Analog instrument failures are not nearly as obvious. For example, an attitude indicator failure can be subtle—the instrument continues to indicate wings level as the airplane gradually drifts off into a diving spiral. Consider practicing instrument failures in a simulator, flight training device, or aviation training device (ATD) for a more realistic experience.

If you suspect an instrument failure, analyze indications from other instruments and systems that provide similar information and accept the indications that agree with each other. You might initiate a small amount of control input to see if the suspected instrument responds. If it does not respond, then assume it is inoperable. [Figure 2-63]

Analog Instrument Failure

Analyze the instrument indications from different instruments and accept the instrument indications that agree with each other. For example, you pitch the nose down to establish a wings-level descent when you notice that the airspeed indicator is slowing down. In place of the airspeed indicator, rely on the altimeter and VSI to give you some sense of airspeed.

OFF Flag

Many analog attitude indicators have flags that indicate an instrument failure.

Digital Instrument Failure

A red X is placed over the display of the affected instrument. The failure of a single sensor might affect only one instrument. For example, a blocked pitot tube can disable the airspeed indicator without affecting the other instruments.

Figure 2-63. A good instrument cross-check can help you identify analog instrument failures.

 To identify an instrument failure, analyze the instrument indications from different instruments and systems and accept the indications of instruments that agree with each other.

PARTIAL-PANEL FLYING

To help prepare for the possibility of instrument failure, you will practice **partial-panel flying** during your training. In an airplane with all analog instruments, you must be prepared to scan and interpret the working instruments for pitch and bank information after the loss of any instruments. In an airplane with digital instruments, you must learn to control the airplane using the appropriate backup instruments if you lose one or more of the instruments on the PFD.

GYROSCOPIC INSTRUMENT FAILURE

The general aviation industry, the NTSB, and the FAA are concerned about the number of fatal aircraft accidents involving spatial disorientation of instrument-rated pilots who have attempted flight in clouds with inoperative primary flight instruments (gyroscopic heading and/or attitude indicators) or loss of the primary electronic flight instruments display. The *Instrument Rating Practical Test Standards* stresses that instrument-rated pilots must be capable of performing instrument flight with the use of the backup systems installed in the aircraft. During your practical test, you will be required to demonstrate a nonprecision instrument approach without the use of the primary flight instruments or electronic flight instrument display.

Aircraft with PFDs are typically equipped with backup flight instruments or an additional electronic flight display that is not located directly in front of the pilot. Many light aircraft with analog instruments are not equipped with dual, independent, gyroscopic heading and/or attitude indicators and in many cases are equipped with only a single vacuum source. If you suspect a problem with the attitude indicator, try a small control input to see if the instrument responds. If it does not reflect the change in control input, do not use if for reference. A recommended practice is to cover the failed instrument with a sticky note or other piece of paper to prevent it from distracting you with conflicting indications. Suspect failure of the heading indicator if the attitude indicator has failed.

When flying in IFR conditions, your first sign of an analog heading indicator failure might be when you experience difficulty tracking a VOR or GPS course. Suspect a failure of the heading indicator if your heading adjustments do not produce the expected results on the navigation instruments. If the CDI indicates an unusual deviation, you can easily make a small correction by using the turn coordinator to make a standard-rate turn for several seconds. Remember to make course corrections a little at a time and give the CDI some time to respond before making additional corrections.

If the gyroscopic attitude indicator and/or heading indicator fails in instrument conditions, immediately inform ATC even if control of the airplane is not an immediate problem. Depending on the conditions, loss of the attitude indicator can be particularly serious, because it can be difficult to comply immediately and accurately with ATC instructions. In many cases, your best option is to divert to a nearby airport with more favorable weather conditions. If you must conduct an approach in IFR conditions without gyroscopic instruments, request a radar approach, if possible. These approaches, during which ATC provides you horizontal, and, in some cases, vertical course guidance, are covered in detail in Chapter 10, Section A, IFR Emergencies.

STRAIGHT-AND-LEVEL FLIGHT

In an airplane without backup instruments, if the attitude indicator fails, you still have the information you need to maintain level flight because the altimeter normally is your primary pitch instrument. However, flying straight-and-level is more difficult because the remaining instruments do not provide you with an instantaneous pitch indication. Apply gentle, precise control inputs, and patiently watch for the results on the instruments. If you inadvertently enter a climb or descent, your first objective is to reestablish level flight, then gently correct back to your intended altitude. Paying attention to how quickly the altimeter is moving up or down can help you determine the amount of deviation from level flight attitude and the approximate correction you need to make.

When using the magnetic compass and turn coordinator to maintain heading, it is important to keep the miniature airplane as level as possible. Even barely visible deviations on the turn coordinator can easily result in heading errors of 30° or more within one minute, and the problem is even worse with the older, less precise, turn-and-slip indicators. Before making adjustments, give the compass time to stabilize in straight-and-level, unaccelerated flight, unless it is obvious that you are significantly off your desired heading. If the compass card bounces or swings, you can average the readings and correct back to your desired heading using timed, standard-rate turns. If you are 10° away from your desired heading, try a three second standard-rate turn. [Figure 2-64]

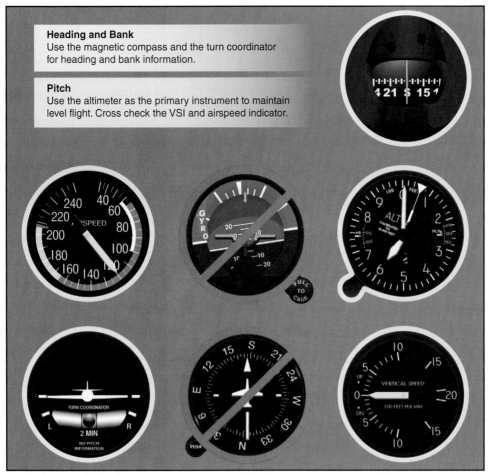

Figure 2-64. Refer to the remaining pitch and bank instrument to maintain straight-level-flight with a partial panel.

FAA If the gyroscopic heading indicator is inoperative, the primary bank instrument in unaccelerated straight-and-level flight is the magnetic compass.

CLIMBS AND DESCENTS

Although you do not have the benefit of an instantaneous attitude indication, you still have instruments to set climb or descent power. Accurately setting power helps the airplane react predictably and makes it easier to control. However, avoid fixating on the power instruments, especially in partial-panel conditions when you need an increased scan rate. Glance at the tachometer or manifold pressure gauge, move the throttle an estimated amount to correct any deviations, and move on with your scan. Check the results of the adjustment in a couple of seconds when your scan returns to the power instrument(s).

Use the altimeter, VSI, and airspeed indicator in place of the attitude indicator to make changes in pitch. Because of the lag of these instruments, make smooth, gradual control inputs and allow a few moments for the change in pitch to be reflected. The rate of movement of the altimeter also gives you indirect pitch information, but requires more interpretation than the VSI.

TURNS

Use the turn coordinator to establish and maintain partial-panel turns. Control of bank is easier than pitch, even with the loss of both the attitude indicator and heading indicator. The turn coordinator, which is the primary instrument for bank, responds quickly enough to adjustments in bank to enable good bank control without the attitude indicator.

COMPASS TURNS

When you perform compass turns to a northerly heading in the northern hemisphere, remember to roll out before the compass reaches the desired heading. When you turn to a southerly heading, wait until the compass passes the desired heading. As you learned in Section A of this chapter, you typically make compass turns at a standard rate, and the amount of lead or lag approximately equals your latitude. Turning error is small when turning to an easterly or westerly heading; no special correction is needed. When you turn to northwest, northeast, southwest and southeast headings, you might have to use some lead or lag to account for turning error.

When performing compass turns, it is common for instrument students to fixate on the compass during rollout. Remember that until the airplane is stabilized in straight-and-level, unaccelerated flight, the indicated heading is not accurate. It is better to concentrate on other instruments to maintain straight-and-level flight before checking the accuracy of the turn.

TIMED TURNS

A timed turn is the most accurate way to turn to a specific heading without the heading indicator. In a timed turn, use the clock instead of the compass card to determine when to roll out. For example, using a standard-rate turn (3 degrees per second), an airplane turns 45 degrees in 15 seconds. You can still use the magnetic compass to back up the clock, when determining the time to roll out of a turn.

Prior to practicing timed turns, you need to determine the accuracy of the turn coordinator. Establish a standard-rate indication on the instrument for 30 seconds and determine whether the airplane turns 90°. If not, keep repeating the turn, adjusting the bank until you find the turn indication that corresponds to an actual standard-rate turn in each direction. Make a mental note of that indication and use it for standard-rate turns.

Divide the degrees of desired heading change by three degrees per second for a standard-rate turn, to get the number of seconds of turn. For example, to turn 180 degrees, using a standard-rate turn: 180 degrees ÷ 3 degrees per second = 60 seconds. Note the time when you start the roll-in, hold the turn at the calibrated standard-rate indication, and begin the roll-out after the computed number of seconds. Do not count the time to roll in and out of the turn, and consider using half-standard-rate turns for small heading changes.

To calculate the time for a standard-rate turn, divide the number of degrees to turn by 3 degrees/second. For example, a 90-degree turn takes 30 seconds.

PITOT-STATIC INSTRUMENT FAILURES

Most of your partial-panel training will focus on failure of the gyroscopic flight instruments. However, you must also practice failures of the airspeed indicator, altimeter, and VSI. For analog instruments, the most insidious of these failures is total blockage of the pitot system. Blockage of both the ram air inlet and the drain hole causes the airspeed indicator to react like an altimeter, moving in the opposite direction from how you would expect the airspeed indicator to move in a climb or descent. [Figure 2-65]

Pitot System Blockage
The airspeed indicator is decreasing, implying a climb, which conflicts with the descent information shown by the attitude indicator, altimeter, and VSI. Trust the attitude indicator, altimeter, and VSI because these instruments agree with each other.

Figure 2-65. Total blockage of the pitot system causes the airspeed indicator to react like an altimeter.

In-flight breakups of aircraft have occurred because the pilot dove the airplane at speeds exceeding red line while the airspeed indication dropped toward stall speed. Use your experience in the airplane when evaluating the indications of the airspeed indicator. If the airplane sounds like it is going fast, and the airspeed indicator decreases even more rapidly when you push forward on the yoke, you should suspect the airspeed is not really decreasing. If you do not hear the stall warning as the airspeed indicator drops to the bottom of the green arc, and the altimeter shows a descent, it is time to revise your thinking about what the airspeed indicator is showing.

Although the altimeter is not immune to failure, it cannot fail in such a way as to show a climb when you are actually descending. When you discover the airspeed indicator is deceiving you and realize you are in a dangerous high-speed dive, immediately reduce power, verify wings level and very slowly adjust pitch to a level flight attitude.

SECTION B ■ **Attitude Instrument Flying**

SECTION B ▪ Attitude Instrument Flying

UNUSUAL ATTITUDE RECOVERY

An unusual flight attitude can occur even with a properly trained instrument pilot, due to failure of the attitude indicator, disorientation, wake turbulence, lapse of attention, or abnormal trim. To become instrument-rated, you must demonstrate recovery from unusual attitudes with or without the attitude indicator.

To practice **unusual attitude recoveries**, your instructor might ask you to pass the controls and close your eyes. Then, your instructor will maneuver the airplane in such a way as to induce disorientation. After opening your eyes, you must take control of the airplane to make a proper recovery. In most cases, you recover from the unusual attitude by performing the appropriate corrective control applications in sequence, but nearly simultaneously. To recover from a nose-high attitude, you must prevent a stall. The objective of a nose-low unusual attitude recovery is to avoid a critically high airspeed and load factor, as well as preventing the loss of altitude. [Figure 2-66]

NOSE-HIGH UNUSUAL ATTITUDE

Instrument Indications
The instrument indications of a nose-high unusual flight attitude are:
- A nose-high pitch of the aircraft symbol on the attitude indicator.
- A rapidly increasing altitude on the altimeter.
- A high rate of climb on the vertical speed indicator.
- A rapidly decreasing airspeed.

Recovery Actions
To recover, perform these actions almost simultaneously but in the following sequence:
- Add power.
- Lower the nose to place the aircraft symbol on the horizon line of the attitude indicator.
- Level the wings using the attitude indicator as a reference to return to the original attitude and heading.

Instrument Indications
The instrument indications of a spiraling nose-low unusual flight attitude are:
- A nose-low pitch of the aircraft symbol on the attitude indicator.
- A rapidly decreasing altitude on the altimeter.
- A high rate of descent on the vertical speed indicator.
- A rapidly increasing airspeed.

Recovery Actions
To recover, perform these actions almost simultaneously but in the following sequence:
1. Reduce power.
2. Level the wings using the attitude indicator as a reference.
3. Raise the nose to place the aircraft symbol on the horizon line of the attitude indicator.

NOSE-LOW UNUSUAL ATTITUDE

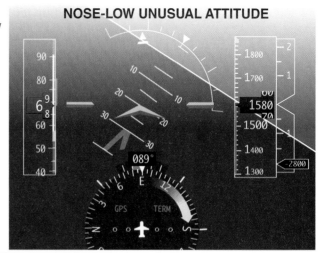

Figure 2-66. You must recognize and perform the proper recovery procedures for nose-high and nose-low unusual attitudes.

 The correct sequence to recover from a nose-high unusual attitude is to add power, lower the nose, level the wings, and return to the original attitude and heading.

The correct sequence to recover from a nose-low unusual attitude is to reduce power, level the wings, and raise the nose to place the aircraft symbol on the horizon line of the attitude indicator.

When recovering from an unusual attitude without the attitude indicator, use the turn coordinator to stop a turn, and the pitot-static instruments to stop an unintended climb or descent. You know you are passing through a level pitch attitude when you stop and reverse the direction of the altimeter and airspeed indicator, and start the VSI moving back toward zero. At this point, use the elevator pressure that maintains this pitch, wait a moment for the instruments to stabilize, then gently correct back to your desired altitude.

 If an airplane is in an unusual flight attitude and the attitude indicator has exceeded its limits, rely on the airspeed and altimeter to determine pitch attitude before starting recovery. The airplane attains approximate level pitch attitude when the airspeed and altimeter stop their movement and the VSI reverses its trend.

STALLS

You might practice stalls during instrument training to demonstrate that the recognition and recovery procedures under instrument conditions are the same as under visual conditions. Recover from a stall by immediately reducing the angle of attack and increasing power to the maximum allowable value. Use the inclinometer or slip/skid indicator to maintain coordinated flight throughout the stall. The wing will drop on the side opposite to the displacement of the ball or slip/skid indicator in an uncoordinated stall and this situation can result in an unusual attitude.

 ### SPIRALING OUT OF CONTROL

From the files of the NTSB. . .

Aircraft: Cessna P210N

Injuries: 5 Fatal

Narrative: The pilot called center while airborne and requested an IFR clearance. About 15 minutes after receiving the clearance, he was given a vector for traffic. The pilot said he needed help and asked if he was on course, then said he was in an unusual attitude and couldn't determine why. About 15 seconds later the pilot indicated he might be in a spin. The controller said he was showing the airplane as level and asked if the pilot was having problems, to which he responded, "yes our vacuum . . . our artificial gyro is showing us at a very unusual attitude." The airplane was observed coming out of the clouds with wings separating from the airplane. The airplane had a vacuum system problem which was recorded as repaired and checked as OK about 2 1/2 months before the accident. The pilot had about 4 hours of actual and about 56 hours simulated instrument time. The vacuum pump was destroyed in the impact.

The NTSB listed the following probable causes of the accident:

1. A partial loss of the airplane's vacuum system which resulted in the total loss of the directional gyro and the attitude indicator.

2. The pilot not maintaining aircraft control due to spatial disorientation.

3. The pilot not correcting for a spiral by using proper recovery techniques which resulted in the overload failure of the wings. A factor in the accident was the pilot's lack of total instrument flight experience.

At the first indication of an instrument failure, concentrate on maintaining control of the airplane using the properly functioning instruments. By flying the airplane first, then navigating, and finally communicating, you provide yourself with the best opportunity to maintain situational awareness and avoid instances where you become spatially disoriented.

If an unusual attitude situation develops despite your best efforts, it is essential that you remain calm and not suddenly pull back on the yoke when the airspeed is running away or the aircraft is in a turn. Reduce power to idle and level the wings before trying to pull out of an unusual diving attitude. You might even consider extending the landing gear to help regain control of the airspeed.

SECTION B ■ Attitude Instrument Flying

SUMMARY CHECKLIST

✓ The fundamental skills of attitude instrument flying are instrument cross-check, instrument interpretation, and aircraft control.

✓ An effective instrument cross-check, or scan, requires logical and systematic observation of the instrument panel.

✓ The radial cross-check is a scan pattern during which you spend 80 to 90 percent of flight time looking at the attitude indicator and taking only quick glances at the other flight instruments.

✓ Fixation is applying your full concentration on a single instrument and excluding all others.

✓ Omission is excluding one or more pertinent instruments from your scan.

✓ Emphasis is relying on an instrument that you readily understand, even when it provides inadequate information, instead of relying on a combination of instruments.

✓ Instrument interpretation is more effective if you have studied and observed how each instrument operates, and are aware of the instrument indications that represent the desired pitch and bank attitudes for your airplane.

✓ Aircraft control is the action you take as a result of cross checking and interpreting the flight instruments.

✓ An improperly trimmed airplane increases tension, interrupts your cross-check, and can result in abrupt or erratic control.

✓ The control and performance method of instrument flying divides the instruments into three groups: control, performance, and navigation.

✓ You accurately establish a specific attitude and power setting using the control instruments, The performance instruments indicate how the airplane responds to changes in attitude and power.

✓ To use the control and performance method: establish an attitude or power setting on the control instrument(s), trim until control pressures are neutralized, cross check the performance instruments, and adjust the attitude or power setting on the control instruments if a correction is necessary.

✓ To establish a specific airspeed in straight-and-level flight, use the manifold pressure gauge or tachometer as the primary instrument to adjust power.

✓ To maintain a specific airspeed in straight-and-level flight, use the airspeed indicator as the primary power instrument to determine if power needs to be adjusted.

✓ Use the attitude indicator as the primary instrument to establish the proper pitch attitude for straight-and-level flight—it provides instant, direct, and corresponding indications of any change in the airplane's pitch and bank attitude.

✓ To maintain altitude, use the altimeter as the primary pitch instrument.

✓ To maintain a particular heading in straight-and-level flight, use the heading indicator as the primary bank instrument.

✓ Estimate the bank angle that will produce a standard-rate turn and roll into the turn using the attitude indicator as the primary bank instrument.

✓ To maintain the correct bank angle throughout a standard-rate turn, refer to the trend vector of the turn rate indicator on the digital HSI.

✓ An increase in bank angle with a constant airspeed increases the rate of turn and decreases the radius of turn.

✓ An increase in airspeed with a constant bank angle decreases the rate of turn and increases the radius of turn.

✓ As you roll into a turn, use the attitude indicator to increase the pitch attitude to compensate for the loss of vertical lift.

✓ To maintain altitude in the turn, refer to the altimeter as the primary pitch instrument.

✓ To maintain a specific airspeed in a turn, monitor the airspeed indicator to determine if you need to adjust the power.

✓ During steep turns, the need for a higher angle of attack to compensate for the greatly reduced vertical component of lift magnifies errors in pitch control.

✓ During any change in pitch, such as the addition of back pressure to initiate a climb, use the attitude indicator to establish the proper attitude.

✓ Deviations from the desired airspeed during a constant airspeed climb or descent indicate the need to make a pitch adjustment.

✓ Use the attitude indicator to set a pitch attitude that you estimate will result in the desired rate of climb or descent based on your experience with the airplane.

✓ Use the VSI as your primary pitch instrument to ensure that you are climbing or descending at the desired rate for constant rate climbs and descents.

✓ Deviations from the desired airspeed indicate the need to adjust the pitch. Use caution not to operate in the yellow arc, unless you are certain of smooth air throughout a descent.

✓ To be proficient at attitude instrument flying, you must be able recognize a recurring problem and learn how to prevent it. Control, altitude, and heading errors are common to attitude instrument flying.

✓ Digital instrument failures are easy to recognize because the affected instrument is covered with a red X.

✓ Analog instrument failures might not be obvious. For example, an attitude indicator failure can be subtle—the instrument continues to indicate wings level as the airplane gradually drifts off into a diving spiral.

✓ If you suspect an instrument failure, analyze indications from other instruments and systems that provide similar information and accept the indications that agree with each other. Initiate a small amount of control input to see if the suspected instrument responds.

✓ To help prepare for the possibility of instrument failure, you will practice partial-panel flying during your training.

✓ The *Instrument Rating Practical Test Standards* stresses that instrument-rated pilots must be capable of performing instrument flight with the use of the backup systems installed in the aircraft.

✓ When you perform compass turns to a northerly heading in the northern hemisphere, remember to roll out before the compass reaches the desired heading. When you turn to a southerly heading, wait until the compass passes the desired heading.

✓ In a timed turn, use the clock instead of the compass card to determine when to roll out. Divide the degrees of desired heading change by three degrees per second for a standard-rate turn, to get the number of seconds of turn.

✓ Blockage of both the ram air inlet and the drain hole causes the airspeed indicator to react like an altimeter, moving in the opposite direction from how you would expect the airspeed indicator to move in a climb or descent.

✓ The correct sequence to recover from a nose-high unusual attitude is to add power, lower the nose, level the wings, and return to the original attitude and heading.

✓ The correct sequence to recover from a nose-low unusual attitude is to reduce power, level the wings, and raise the nose to place the aircraft symbol on the horizon line of the attitude indicator.

KEY TERMS

Attitude Instrument Flying	Pitch Instruments
Instrument Cross-Check	Bank Instruments
Fixation	Power Instruments.
Omission	Constant Airspeed Climb
Emphasis	Constant Rate Climb
Instrument Interpretation	Constant Airspeed Descent
Aircraft Control	Constant Rate Descent
Control and Performance Method	Partial-Panel Flying
Control Instruments	Compass Turn
Performance Instruments	Timed Turn
Primary and Supporting Method	Unusual Attitude Recovery

QUESTIONS

1. Describe the three common instrument cross-check errors.

2. Explain the importance of properly trimming the airplane during attitude instrument flying.

3. Describe the two methods of attitude instrument flying.

4. What is the primary power instrument for establishing a specific airspeed in straight-and-level flight?
    A. Attitude indicator
    B. Airspeed indicator
    C. Manifold pressure gauge or tachometer

5. What is the primary power instrument for maintaining straight-and-level flight at a specific airspeed?
    A. Attitude indicator
    B. Airspeed indicator
    C. Manifold pressure gauge

6. What are the primary and supporting pitch instruments for maintaining straight-and-level flight?
    A. Primary—attitude indicator; supporting—airspeed indicator, altimeter, VSI
    B. Primary—altimeter; supporting—airspeed indicator, attitude indicator, VSI
    C. Primary—VSI; supporting—airspeed indicator, attitude indicator, altimeter

7. What are the primary and supporting bank instruments for establishing a standard-rate turn? For maintaining the standard-rate turn?

8. Select the true statement regarding rate and radius of turn.
    A. An increase in airspeed with a constant bank angle increases the rate of turn and decreases the radius of turn.
    B. An increase in bank angle with a constant airspeed increases the rate of turn and decreases the radius of turn.
    C. A decrease in bank angle with a constant airspeed increases the rate of turn and decreases the radius of turn.

9. What is the primary pitch instrument for establishing a constant airspeed climb or descent?

10. What is the primary pitch instrument for maintaining a constant rate climb or descent?

11. True/False. If leveling off at the descent speed for a 700 ft/min descent, begin the leveloff at approximately 70 feet before you reach the desired altitude.

12. List at least two common errors and their solutions that apply to maintaining altitude during attitude instrument flying.

13. What system has failed and what action should you take to return the airplane to straight-and-level flight.

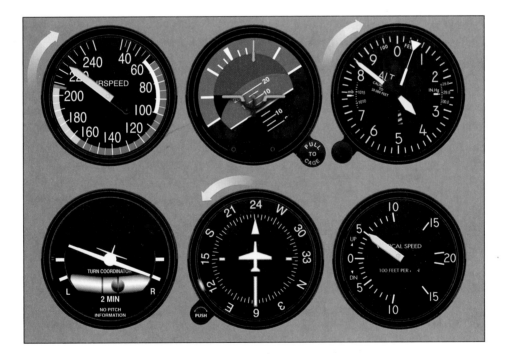

A. The pitot system is blocked; use the attitude indicator to lower the nose and level the wings.
B. The vacuum system has failed; reduce power, roll left to level the wings, and pitch up to reduce airspeed.
C. The electrical system has failed; reduce power, roll left to level the wings, and raise the nose to reduce airspeed.

SECTION B ■ Attitude Instrument Flying

14.   What instrument has malfunctioned and what is the flight attitude?

    A.   Attitude indicator: climbing turn to the left
    B.   Attitude indicator; climbing turn to the right
    C.   Turn coordinator: descending turn to the right.

15.   Describe the proper sequence for recovering from a nose-low, turning, increasing airspeed, unusual flight attitude.

SECTION C
Instrument Navigation

T his section assumes you know how to use VOR, GPS, and ADF equipment for VFR navigation. For IFR operations you must navigate more precisely than you would as a VFR pilot. You also need to refine your instrument navigation skills to the point that you can easily visualize your position without any outside visual reference. In addition, you must become proficient at interpreting a variety of displays, such as horizontal situation indicators, radio magnetic indicators, and integrated GPS displays.

VOR NAVIGATION

In spite of the widespread use of GPS, much of the IFR enroute environment is based on airways defined by VOR facilities. Even if using VOR facilities is eventually replaced as the primary tool of instrument navigation, the displays you use to track a course probably will continue to look and work much like VOR indicators. [Figure 2-67]

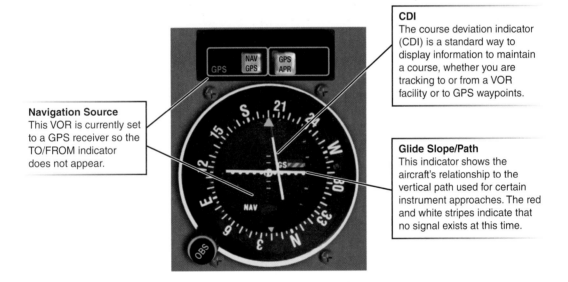

CDI
The course deviation indicator (CDI) is a standard way to display information to maintain a course, whether you are tracking to or from a VOR facility or to GPS waypoints.

Navigation Source
This VOR is currently set to a GPS receiver so the TO/FROM indicator does not appear.

Glide Slope/Path
This indicator shows the aircraft's relationship to the vertical path used for certain instrument approaches. The red and white stripes indicate that no signal exists at this time.

Figure 2-67. You can use VOR indicators to track courses from different navigation sources.

There are various types of indicators for VOR navigation, including the basic VOR indicator, the horizontal situation indicator (HSI), and the radio magnetic indicator (RMI). Although these instruments are somewhat different from a functional standpoint, they all provide a means of orienting to a desired course, tracking that course, and showing your direction of travel to or from a station. This section reviews VOR navigation with an emphasis on an HSI presentation. You also will see how some of these indications appear on a conventional VOR indicator, so you can observe the similarities and differences between the instruments.

HORIZONTAL SITUATION INDICATOR

The name of the **horizontal situation indicator (HSI)** describes its major advantage. The design of this instrument solves nearly all reverse sensing and other visualization problems associated with a conventional VOR indicator. With an HSI, you need not mentally rotate the airplane to a heading that agrees with your selected course to get a clear picture of your situation; the HSI display combines the VOR navigation indicator with a heading indicator, so the display is automatically rotated to the correct position for you. An HSI normally is mounted in the panel in place of the heading indicator. On an HSI, you always can see the course to be intercepted with respect to your airplane, regardless of heading. [Figure 2-68]

 If you know how far you are from a VOR station and the number of dots your CDI is deflected, you can determine your distance from a specific radial. A one-dot deflection indicates a 2° deviation from course, which equals 200 feet off course for each NM away from the VOR. Multiply the number of dots by the distance from the station times 200 feet. For example, 3 dots × 30 NM × 200 feet = 18,000 feet = 3 NM.

The HSI contains a rotating **compass card** which indicates the aircraft's current magnetic heading. In situations where a standard VOR indicator gives you reverse sensing, the HSI compass card turns to provide normal sensing.

The **course indicating arrow** visually shows the orientation of the selected course relative to your current heading. Because of this, left and right indications on the course deviation indicator are always properly oriented.

The **glide slope/path deviation pointer** indicates aircraft position relative to an instrument landing system (ILS) glide slope or to an RNAV approach glide path. When the pointer is below the center position, the aircraft is above the glide slope/glide path and vice versa.

The **symbolic aircraft** shows your position in relation to the selected course as though you are above the aircraft looking down.

The **heading select bug** is used with an autopilot to automatically turn the aircraft to a newly selected heading.

The **course set knob** controls the position of the course indicating arrow.

The airplane's heading is displayed under the **heading index**, also called a lubber line.

The **course deviation indicator** performs the same function as the CDI on a basic VOR indicator, depicting how far you are off course. When you are on course, the course deviation indicator is aligned with the course arrow.

Each dot on an HSI **course deviation scale** is 2°, or 200 feet per nautical mile.

The **TO/FROM indicator** on an HSI points to the head of the course arrow when the selected course is inbound to the navigation facility. When the selected course is outbound from the navaid, the TO/FROM indicator points away from the course arrowhead.

The **heading set knob** is used to position the heading select bug.

Figure 2-68. This HSI shows the airplane on a 070° heading, which is a 30° intercept angle for the 040° course from the station, which is currently 9° to the airplane's right.

On a conventional VOR indicator, left/right and to/from are ambiguous concepts because they must be interpreted in the context of the selected course. When an HSI is tuned to a VOR station, left and right always mean left and right, regardless of the course selected. The TO/FROM indicator is replaced with a simple arrow that always points toward the VOR station or other waypoint. If the arrow points ahead of you, it means TO, and if it points behind you, it means FROM. [Figure 2-69]

There is one situation in which you need to watch out for reverse sensing on an HSI. As you will learn in Chapter 8, Section B, the course indications on a basic VOR indicator are not affected by the OBS setting when tuned to a localizer (a navigation aid for an approach to an airport runway). However, with an HSI tuned to a localizer, the course selector must be set to the inbound front course for both front and back course approaches or the display will be inverted, resulting in reverse sensing.

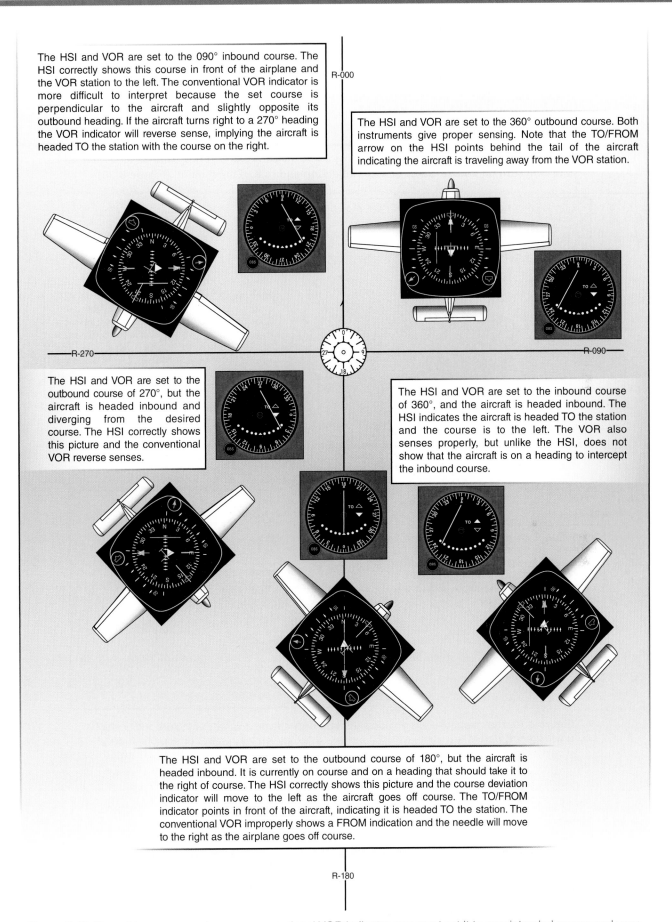

The HSI and VOR are set to the 090° inbound course. The HSI correctly shows this course in front of the airplane and the VOR station to the left. The conventional VOR indicator is more difficult to interpret because the set course is perpendicular to the aircraft and slightly opposite its outbound heading. If the aircraft turns right to a 270° heading the VOR indicator will reverse sense, implying the aircraft is headed TO the station with the course on the right.

The HSI and VOR are set to the 360° outbound course. Both instruments give proper sensing. Note that the TO/FROM arrow on the HSI points behind the tail of the aircraft indicating the aircraft is traveling away from the VOR station.

The HSI and VOR are set to the outbound course of 270°, but the aircraft is headed inbound and diverging from the desired course. The HSI correctly shows this picture and the conventional VOR reverse senses.

The HSI and VOR are set to the inbound course of 360°, and the aircraft is headed inbound. The HSI indicates the aircraft is headed TO the station and the course is to the left. The VOR also senses properly, but unlike the HSI, does not show that the aircraft is on a heading to intercept the inbound course.

The HSI and VOR are set to the outbound course of 180°, but the aircraft is headed inbound. It is currently on course and on a heading that should take it to the right of course. The HSI correctly shows this picture and the course deviation indicator will move to the left as the aircraft goes off course. The TO/FROM indicator points in front of the aircraft, indicating it is headed TO the station. The conventional VOR improperly shows a FROM indication and the needle will move to the right as the airplane goes off course.

Figure 2-69. To avoid reverse sensing on a conventional VOR indicator, you must set it to your intended course and your heading must generally agree with that course. An HSI cannot reverse sense when tuned to a VOR station, even if you set it opposite your intended course or heading.

When using a conventional VOR indicator, flying a heading that is reciprocal to the bearing selected results in reverse sensing. Unlike a conventional VOR indicator, an HSI gives information about your aircraft heading and its relationship to your intended course. See figure 2-69.

INTERCEPTING A COURSE

A successful intercept starts with visualizing your present position and where you want to go. Then, you select a magnetic heading that will intercept the radial or course at a specific angle. During the intercept, scan your navigation instruments carefully and judge when to start your turn on course based on CDI deflection and rate of movement. [Figure 2-70]

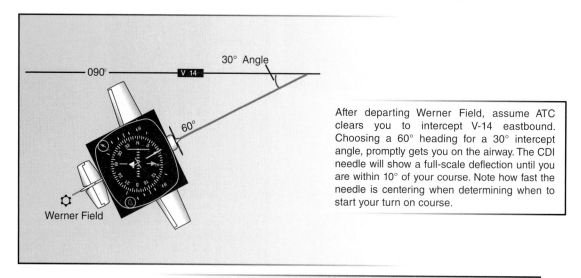

After departing Werner Field, assume ATC clears you to intercept V-14 eastbound. Choosing a 60° heading for a 30° intercept angle, promptly gets you on the airway. The CDI needle will show a full-scale deflection until you are within 10° of your course. Note how fast the needle is centering when determining when to start your turn on course.

Assume ATC gives you a 90° intercept to separate you from traffic ahead. At this angle, be prepared to promptly begin your turn on course when the needle begins to center, or you will overshoot your course before completing the turn.

Figure 2-70. The intercept angle you use normally depends on a variety of factors such as your groundspeed, proximity to the navigation aid, and whether you will track to or from the facility.

TRACKING

As you know, tracking a VOR radial is a trial and error process in which you establish a heading and watch whether it holds the desired course. Your preflight planning and your experience will help you estimate an initial heading. If you do not know the wind direction, simply try your intended course as your heading and watch the CDI needle. If it moves off course, turn 20° toward the needle and hold the heading correction until the needle centers. Reduce the drift correction to 10°, note whether this drift correction angle keeps the CDI centered, and make subsequent smaller corrections as needed. [Figure 2-71]

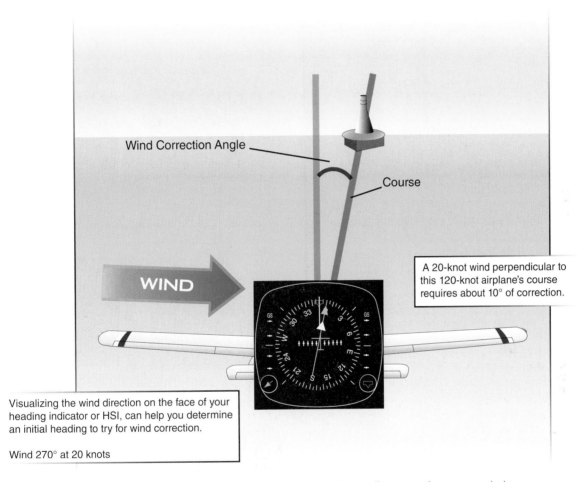

Wind Correction Angle

Course

A 20-knot wind perpendicular to this 120-knot airplane's course requires about 10° of correction.

WIND

Visualizing the wind direction on the face of your heading indicator or HSI, can help you determine an initial heading to try for wind correction.

Wind 270° at 20 knots

Figure 2-71. After making an initial drift correction, make smaller corrections as needed.

 Although it is easier to identify an intersection when you have two VOR receivers, one VOR receiver is the minimum equipment needed. See figure 2-72.

DETERMINING YOUR PROGRESS

In addition to navigating on course, you can use VORs to help you check your progress along your route. If you have two VOR receivers, you can determine your position simply by tuning your second VOR receiver to a station located to the side of your route. This can be especially helpful as you approach navigation fixes that are identified by off-route VORs. If you have only one VOR receiver, then carefully hold the heading that tracks your course from the first VOR while you tune to the second station whose radial intersects your course. [Figure 2-72]

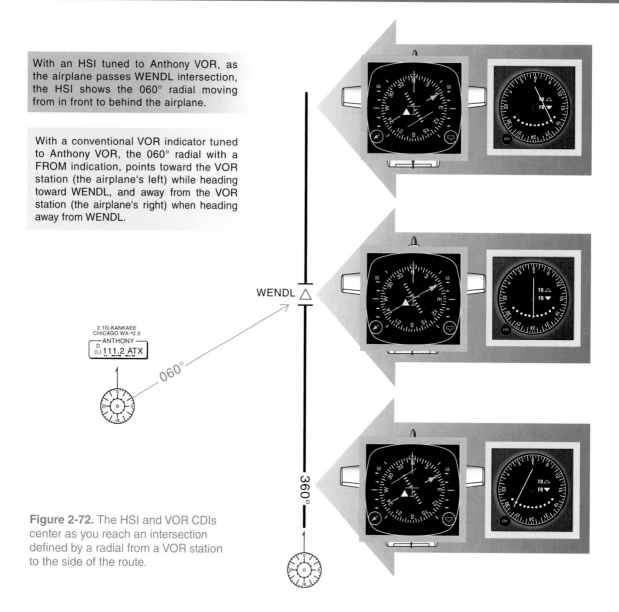

With an HSI tuned to Anthony VOR, as the airplane passes WENDL intersection, the HSI shows the 060° radial moving from in front to behind the airplane.

With a conventional VOR indicator tuned to Anthony VOR, the 060° radial with a FROM indication, points toward the VOR station (the airplane's left) while heading toward WENDL, and away from the VOR station (the airplane's right) when heading away from WENDL.

2.1G-KANKAEE
CHICAGO WX-*2.0
ANTHONY
D
(L) 111.2 ATX

WENDL △

060°

360°

Figure 2-72. The HSI and VOR CDIs center as you reach an intersection defined by a radial from a VOR station to the side of the route.

TIME AND DISTANCE TO A STATION

To gain a greater understanding of VOR operation and provide a foundation for increased situational awareness, you can use formulas or basic geometry to calculate your time and/ or distance to the station. The formula method involves turning to place the station 90° from the aircraft heading and measuring the time it takes to travel to a new radial. The longer it takes to traverse a given number of radials, the farther you are from the station and the longer it will take to get there. Similarly, the smaller number of radials you cross in a given time, the farther you are from the station. After you determine your time to reach a specific radial, you can calculate the time and distance to the station using the formulas shown in figure 2-73.

The isosceles triangle method uses a fundamental geometric principle to determine the time to a station. Procedurally, you turn 10° (or any angle) to the side of your course and twist your course selector the same amount in the opposite direction. Time to station is the same as the time it takes for your CDI to center (assuming no wind). [Figure 2-74]

 For a given course deviation on a conventional (non-RNAV) VOR indicator, the aircraft moves farther away from the radial (in NM) as it travels farther away from the VOR station.

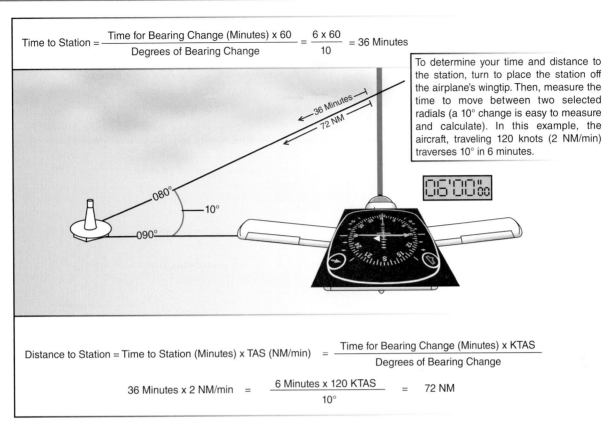

$$\text{Time to Station} = \frac{\text{Time for Bearing Change (Minutes)} \times 60}{\text{Degrees of Bearing Change}} = \frac{6 \times 60}{10} = 36 \text{ Minutes}$$

To determine your time and distance to the station, turn to place the station off the airplane's wingtip. Then, measure the time to move between two selected radials (a 10° change is easy to measure and calculate). In this example, the aircraft, traveling 120 knots (2 NM/min) traverses 10° in 6 minutes.

$$\text{Distance to Station} = \text{Time to Station (Minutes)} \times \text{TAS (NM/min)} = \frac{\text{Time for Bearing Change (Minutes)} \times \text{KTAS}}{\text{Degrees of Bearing Change}}$$

$$36 \text{ Minutes} \times 2 \text{ NM/min} = \frac{6 \text{ Minutes} \times 120 \text{ KTAS}}{10°} = 72 \text{ NM}$$

Figure 2-73. Although it is impractical to use this method on a flight under IFR, the depicted procedure and accompanying formulas provide foundational knowledge regarding time and distance to either a VOR or an NDB.

 You can calculate the time and distance to a station by turning perpendicular to the direct course to the station and measuring the time to move a specific number of degrees to a new radial. See figure 2-73.

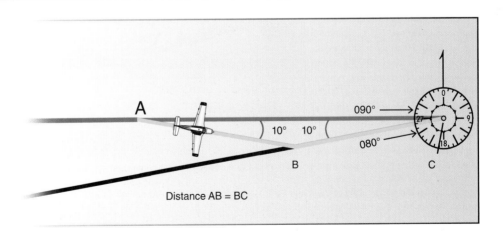

Figure 2-74. The isosceles triangle method enables you to determine the time to a station as you continue generally toward the station.

 You can use the isosceles triangle method to determine time to a station. See figure 2-74.

SECTION C ■ Instrument Navigation

STATION PASSAGE

As you get close to a station, in an area called the **cone of confusion**, the CDI and TO/FROM indicators fluctuate. Station passage is indicated by the first positive, complete reversal of the TO/FROM indicator. If you can determine that you are getting close to a station where you plan a significant course change, consider beginning your turn early to avoid excessive course corrections after station passage. Because the FARs require you operate along the centerline of an airway, turn anticipation can be particularly important in higher performance aircraft. Depending on the amount of course change required, wind direction and velocity, and now quickly you turn, you could stray outside the boundaries of the airway if you are flying faster than 290 knots and wait until after passing the VOR before beginning your turn.

 FAA VOR station passage is the first positive, complete reversal of the TO-FROM indicator.

Precision in Four Dimensions

In the dark days of 1943, the Allies were fighting hard in their war against the Japanese in the Pacific. An intercepted Japanese communication indicated that Admiral Isoroku Yamamoto, the commander in chief of the combined Japanese fleet, would be flying to Ballale in the Solomon Islands on April 18. (Yamamoto had opposed Japan's alliance with Nazi Germany, had opposed attacking the United States, and had even been a student at Harvard before the war.) Besides depriving the Japanese Navy of its leader, killing Yamamoto would be a serious blow to the morale of the Japanese. Yamamoto's airplane would arrive at 9:45 in the morning. The plan was to catch Yamamoto's transports, two twin-engined Mitsubishi G4M bombers, as they descended just before landing. The element of surprise was essential, so to be successful the American airplanes would have to arrive just a few minutes before Yamamoto landed, but late enough to avoid any possibility of the Admiral's airplane being warned. There would be six Japanese fighters escorting the bomber, as well as whole squadrons of Japanese fighters stationed nearby.

To avoid detection on their way to the intercept, the American airplanes would need to take a long and roundabout route to avoid Japanese observers. They would also fly no higher than 50 feet above the sea for most of the way. The U.S. Navy had no airplanes with enough range to fly the indirect route to the interception and return, so Lockheed P-38 Lightnings from the Army Air Force were chosen for the mission. To help them with the hours of dead-reckoning navigation, mechanics added a Navy ship's compass to each P-38. The fighters would need to fly approximately 600 miles at wave-top level, making four precise course changes, with

no visual checkpoints or radio aids en route, arriving at a specific point in space at an exact time. They actually arrived about one minute early, but accomplished their mission, with all but one of the 16 Lightnings returning safely.

Although you have the advantages of VOR and GPS navigation, detailed aeronautical charts, moving maps, and ATC radar, you can learn a lesson from this challenging mission. Plan your routes in detail, navigate precisely, and monitor the progress of your flight carefully.

VOR OPERATIONAL CONSIDERATIONS

A VOR utilizes VHF frequencies like those used by FM radio and broadcast television. Although these signals are limited to line of sight, you can plan on receiving a reliable signal at altitudes published on instrument charts. VOR facilities operate within the 108.0 to 117.95 MHz frequency band and are classified according to their usable range and altitude, or standard service volume (SSV). [Figure 2-75] Terminal VORs (TVOR), which have only 50 watts of power and a usable range of 25 nautical miles, are normally placed in terminal areas to be used primarily for instrument approaches. High altitude VORs (HVORs) and low altitude VORs (LVORs) are used for navigation on most airways, and can also function as approach facilities when located on or near airports. High altitude VORs typically have power outputs of 200 watts and transmit usable signals up to 130 nautical miles. Because a distant station on the same frequency can interfere with the local signal, HVORs on the same frequency are adequately separated to avoid interference up to 45,000 feet, where usable range drops from 130 to 100 nautical miles. You can find the SSV that applies to a particular VOR in the *Chart Supplement.*

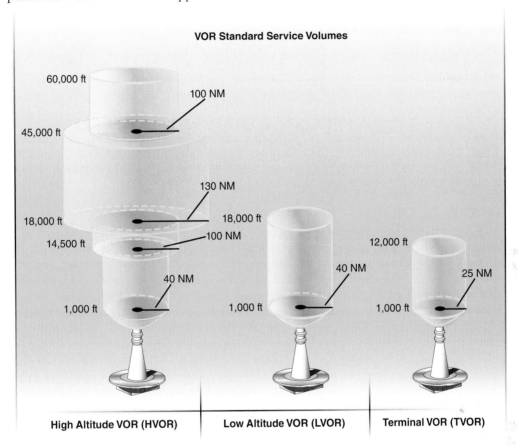

VOR Standard Service Volumes

60,000 ft
100 NM
45,000 ft
130 NM
18,000 ft
18,000 ft
14,500 ft
100 NM
12,000 ft
40 NM
40 NM
25 NM
1,000 ft
1,000 ft
1,000 ft

High Altitude VOR (HVOR)   Low Altitude VOR (LVOR)   Terminal VOR (TVOR)

Figure 2-75. VOR facilities are classified according to standard service volume.

It is extremely important to positively identify a facility before using it for navigation. When you are busy, it can be easy to listen to the identifying tone without making sure you have the correct Morse code identifier. It is essential that you always check the identifier against your chart to make sure you are tuned to the correct facility.

VOR facilities undergoing maintenance might transmit the word, TEST (_ . ... _), or they might transmit no audio at all. The presence of an identifier signal verifies the proper operation of the facility. Do not use a ground station for navigation if it does not transmit an identifier, even if you appear to be receiving valid navigation indications.

 Between 14,500 and 18,000 feet MSL, an (H) Class VORTAC has a usable signal range of 100 NM. Therefore, for direct routes off established airways at these altitudes, the facilities should be no farther apart than 200 NM. An (L) class VOR has a range of 40 NM below 18,000 feet, so they should be no farther apart than 80 NM. Refer to the Chart Supplement to determine what type of VOR facility is shown on a chart and whether the standard service volume applies for that facility.

VOR CHECKS

To use a VOR for flight under IFR, the VOR system must have been tested for accuracy within the preceding 30 days. If it has been more than 30 days, you must perform this check before you may take off under IFR using VOR navigation. There are several ways that you can perform a VOR check, including using a VOR test facility, ground and airborne checkpoints, and a dual system check.

For IFR flight, you are required to have navigation equipment appropriate to the ground facilities to be used. Before using a VOR, you must ensure that a VOR check has been accomplished within the previous 30 days.

VOR TEST FACILITIES

You can make precise VOR accuracy checks from most locations on an airport by using **VOR test facilities (VOTs)**. VOTs transmit only one radial—360°. The airborne use of certain VOTs is also permitted; however, their use is strictly limited to those areas and altitudes specifically authorized in the *Chart Supplement*. Tune your VOR receiver and listen for a series of dots or a continuous tone that identifies the facility as a VOT. Determine that the needle centers, ±4° (ground or airborne), when the course selector is set to 180° with a TO indication, or 360° with a FROM indication. If using an RMI, the bearing pointer should indicate 180°, ±4°.

You can find a VOT frequency for a particular airport in the Chart Supplement or on the A/G Voice Communication Panel of the FAA low altitude enroute chart. When checking your VOR using a VOT, the CDI should be centered and the course selector should indicate that the aircraft is on the 360° radial, ±4°.

VOR CHECKPOINTS

If a VOT is not available, you may determine VOR accuracy using ground or airborne **VOR checkpoints**. On the ground, taxi your aircraft to a specific point on the airport designated in the VOR Receiver Check section of the Chart Supplement. After centering the CDI, compare your VOR course selection to the published radial for that checkpoint. The maximum permissible error is ±4°. Airborne checkpoints, also listed in the Chart Supplement, usually are located over easily identifiable terrain or prominent features on the ground. You also can perform an airborne check by selecting a VOR radial that defines the centerline of an airway. Then, using a sectional chart, locate a prominent terrain feature under the centerline of the airway, preferably 20 miles or more from the VOR station. Maneuver your aircraft directly over the point, twist the course selector to center the CDI needle and note what course is selected. With an airborne checkpoint, the maximum permissible course error is ± 6°.

To make a VOR receiver check when the aircraft is located on a designated checkpoint on the airport surface, set the course selector to center the CDI with a FROM indication. The selected course must be within ±4° of the published radial. The allowable error when using an airborne checkpoint is ±6°.

DUAL SYSTEM CHECK

If a neither a VOT or VOR checkpoint are available, you may conduct a VOR check by comparing the indications of two VOR systems that are independent of each other (except for the antenna). If your aircraft is equipped with two VOR radios, set both to the same VOR facility and note the indications of each. When you check one system against the other, the maximum permissible difference is 4°.

The allowable error when comparing the indications of two VOR receivers, whether in the air or on the ground, is 4° between receivers.

DISTANCE MEASURING EQUIPMENT

Using **distance measuring equipment (DME)** enables you to keep track of your distance to or from a VOR. If your aircraft is equipped with a DME receiver, you can obtain distance information from several types of ground-based navaids including VOR/DME, VORTAC (which obtains distance information from the associated TACAN facility), instrument landing system (ILS)/DME, and localizer (LOC)/DME stations. These facilities provide course and distance information from collocated components under a frequency pairing plan. You tune a DME the same way as a VOR receiver. This is because DME receivers usually display the frequency of the paired VOR rather than the actual DME UHF frequency (962 MHz to 1,213 MHz). Some DME units can be remoted to a VOR receiver so they automatically tune in the DME or TACAN station that is paired with the selected VOR ground facility.

DME receivers work by transmitting paired pulses to a ground station. After measuring the time for the station's reply to return to the receiver, the receiver calculates the distance, and displays the result in nautical miles. Many DME receivers also provide a groundspeed readout that indicates the rate of change of the aircraft's distance from the station. DME groundspeed agrees with actual groundspeed only when you are headed directly toward or away from the station. [Figure 2-76]

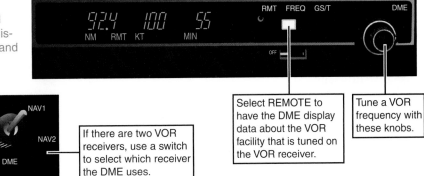

Figure 2-76. A typical DME display shows distance, groundspeed, and time to the station.

If there are two VOR receivers, use a switch to select which receiver the DME uses.

Select REMOTE to have the DME display data about the VOR facility that is tuned on the VOR receiver.

Tune a VOR frequency with these knobs.

DME OPERATIONAL CONSIDERATIONS

Because the DME signal travels in a straight line to and from the ground station, the DME receiver displays slant-range, not horizontal, distance. Slant range error is negligible if the aircraft is 1 mile or more from the ground facility for every 1,000 feet of altitude above the station. [Figure 2-77] Except for this error, DME is accurate to within 1/2 mile or 3%, whichever is greater, and can be received at line-of-sight distances up to 199 nautical miles.

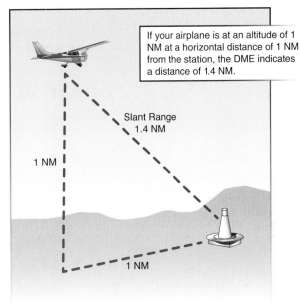

If your airplane is at an altitude of 1 NM at a horizontal distance of 1 NM from the station, the DME indicates a distance of 1.4 NM.

Slant Range 1.4 NM

1 NM

1 NM

Figure 2-77. Slant range error is noticable when the airplane is close to the VOR and decreases at greater distances.

 DME indicates slant-range distance with greatest error at high altitudes close to a VORTAC. The indication should be 1 NM when you are directly over a VORTAC site at approximately 6,000 feet AGL. Generally, you can consider DME accurate when you are at least one horizontal mile from the station for each 1,000 feet above the site elevation.

Because VOR and DME are separate components, each transmits its own identification signal on a time sharing basis. The VOR transmits a 1,020 Hz Morse code identifier and possibly a voice identifier several times for each DME identifier, which is a 1,350 Hz tone at approximately 30 second intervals. If one of these tones is missing, do not use the associated portion of the facility for navigation.

 If, when tuning to a VORTAC, you receive a single coded identification approximately once every 30 seconds, it means the DME component is operative and the VOR component is inoperative. The reverse is true if you hear the 1,020 Hz VOR signal several times and the 1,350 Hz DME tone is missing over a 30-second interval.

 Even if you are receiving navigation indications from a VOR, DME, or NDB facility, the lack of a coded identification indicates the station is undergoing maintenance and is unreliable.

DME ARCS

Many instrument approach procedures incorporate **DME arcs** for transition from the enroute phase of flight to the approach course. This is useful, for example, if you are approaching the airport on an airway from the east, the VOR is on the airport, and you need to fly an approach from the north. A DME arc positions you for the approach so you do not have to fly to the VOR and then fly outbound and reverse course.

It is easiest to fly a DME arc using an RMI. Generally, you intercept the arc while flying to or from a VOR/DME or VORTAC. To join the arc, turn approximately 90° from your inbound or outbound course, making sure you begin your turn early enough so you do not overshoot the arc. For groundspeeds of 150 knots or less, a lead of about 1/2 mile is usually sufficient.

In calm wind conditions, you could theoretically follow the arc by continuously adjusting your heading so that the RMI needle points at the wingtip. In practice, it is easiest to fly slightly inside the arc in a series of straight flight segments, forming a polygon, with course corrections every 10° to 20°. You begin each segment by turning slightly toward the VOR, putting the RMI pointer 5° to 10° ahead of the wingtip. Then, you maintain heading until the bearing pointer moves 5° to 10° behind the wingtip, at which point you repeat the process to fly another segment. [Figure 2-78] As you complete the arc, plan on leading the turn to your inbound or outbound course. The amount of lead you use should be fairly close to the lead you used to turn onto the arc.

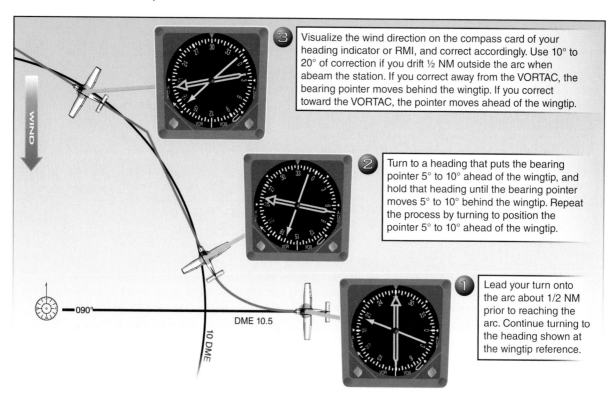

3 Visualize the wind direction on the compass card of your heading indicator or RMI, and correct accordingly. Use 10° to 20° of correction if you drift ½ NM outside the arc when abeam the station. If you correct away from the VORTAC, the bearing pointer moves behind the wingtip. If you correct toward the VORTAC, the pointer moves ahead of the wingtip.

2 Turn to a heading that puts the bearing pointer 5° to 10° ahead of the wingtip, and hold that heading until the bearing pointer moves 5° to 10° behind the wingtip. Repeat the process by turning to position the pointer 5° to 10° ahead of the wingtip.

1 Lead your turn onto the arc about 1/2 NM prior to reaching the arc. Continue turning to the heading shown at the wingtip reference.

WIND

090°

DME 10.5

10 DME

Figure 2-78. In practice, a DME arc is flown using a series of straight segments approximating the arc.

CORRECTING FOR A CROSSWIND

At times, you might find that a crosswind causes you to drift either away from or toward the station. If you are drifting away from the facility, turn to place the bearing pointer ahead of the wingtip; if you are drifting toward the station, turn to place the bearing pointer behind the wingtip. As a general rule, change the relative bearing 10° to 20° for each 1/2 mile you are away from your desired arc when abeam the station. For example, if you are 1/2 mile inside the arc and the RMI needle is pointing to the wingtip, turn 10° to 20° away from the facility to return to the arc.

If you are using a conventional VOR indicator, the recommended procedure is to set the OBS to a radial 20° ahead of your present position. Then turn and maintain a heading 100° from the radial you have just crossed. When your CDI centers or you reach the arc, repeat the process to fly another segment. As with the RMI, this technique will maintain a track slightly inside your desired arc in no-wind conditions. If there is a crosswind, compensate by adjusting your heading toward or away from the station as appropriate.

 As you turn toward the VOR to compensate for a crosswind, the bearing pointer moves ahead of the wingtip reference. Use 10° to 20° of correction if you drift 1/2 nautical mile outside the arc when abeam the station. When correcting away from the VOR, the bearing pointer moves behind the wingtip.

AREA NAVIGATION

Area navigation (RNAV) equipment computes the aircraft position, actual track, and groundspeed and then displays distance and time estimates relative to the selected course or waypoint. RNAV enables you to effectively navigate in the IFR environment using waypoints—predetermined geographical positions for route/instrument approach definition—without the use of ground facilities. Area navigation systems include VOR/DME RNAV and inertial navigation systems (INS), as well as the global positioning system (GPS). RNAV equipment installations must be approved for use under IFR. You must consult the airplane flight manual (AFM) or AFM supplements to determine the specific equipment installed, the approved operations, and the details of using the equipment.

REQUIRED NAVIGATION PERFORMANCE (RNP)

Implemented by the FAA and the International Civil Aviation Organization (ICAO), **required navigation performance (RNP)** is a set of standards that apply to both airspace and navigation equipment. The use of RNP in conjunction with RNAV provides greater flexibility in procedure and airspace design, as well as making it more effective for ATC to offer direct routing.

According to RNP standards, you can use any underlying navigation system, such as GPS, provided that the airplane can achieve the required navigation performance. To comply with RNP standards, your navigation equipment must be able to keep the airplane within a specified distance of the centerline of a route, path, or procedure at least 95% of the time. You must operate within a distance of 2 nautical miles for enroute operations, within 1 nautical mile for terminal operations, and within 0.3 nautical miles for approach operations (the final approach course). [Figure 2-79]

A critical component of RNP is the ability of the aircraft navigation system to monitor its achieved navigation performance, and to identify whether the operational requirement is, or is not being met during an operation. This onboard performance monitoring and alerting capability reduces the need of ATC to intervene to ensure route separation and improves flight safety.

SECTION C ■ Instrument Navigation

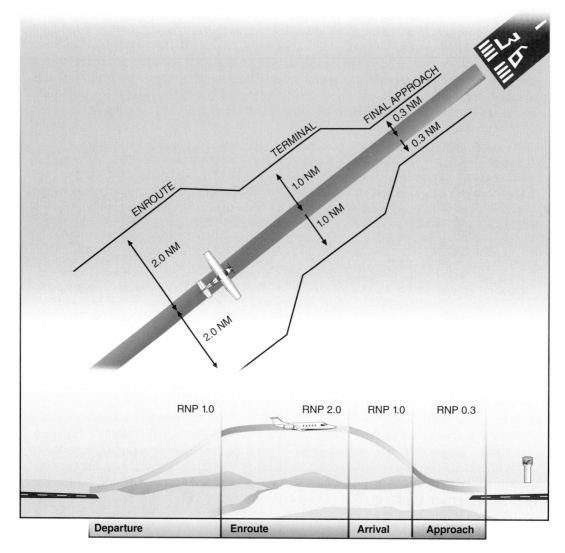

Figure 2-79. The United States recognizes three RNP standards that apply to enroute, terminal, and approach operations. These standards are used during every phase of flight from takeoff to landing.

VOR/DME RNAV

VOR/DME RNAV is a pre-GPS RNAV system that uses an airborne course-line computer (CLC) to create waypoints based on navigation data from VORTAC or VOR/DME facilities. You can still find these systems in older aircraft. These systems create "phantom VORs" at specified radials and distances from actual VORs, enabling more direct navigation. Because VOR/DME RNAV equipment does not extend a VOR's service volume, you must remain within the signal coverage of the physical facilities to navigate to or from phantom VORs. Instrument approaches based on VOR/DME RNAV required manual programming of waypoints in order to fly the approaches, a practice that is prohibited with newer types of RNAV approaches. Although some FMSs use VOR/DME RNAV as part of their navigation solution, manually-programmed VOR/DME RNAV approaches are being phased out.

INERTIAL NAVIGATION SYSTEM

An inertial navigation system (INS) is a self-contained system that uses gyros, accelerometers, and a navigation computer to calculate position. By programming a series of waypoints, the system will navigate along a predetermined track. INS is extremely accurate when set to a known position upon departure. However, without recalibration, INS accuracy degrades one to two nautical miles per hour. To maintain precision, many INS systems automatically update their position by incorporating inputs from VOR, DME, and/or GPS. INS may be approved as a sole means of navigation or used in combination with other systems.

FLIGHT MANAGEMENT SYSTEMS (FMS)

A **flight management system (FMS)** automates the tasks of managing the onboard navigation equipment. An FMS acts as the input/output device for navigational data from navaids, such as VOR/DME and localizer facilities, and from GPS or INS equipment. During flight, the FMS uses this data to indicate airplane position, track, desired heading, and groundspeed and to provide inputs to the airplane's autopilot and navigation displays, such as the HSI, RMI, digital flight deck display, or head-up display. An FMS incorporates a large database of waypoints, airport and navaid information, aircraft performance data, airways, and intersections, as well as instrument departure, arrival, and approach procedures. You can program and store your own waypoints and flight plans in the FMS. In addition, an FMS can create a route from your airplane's current position to any destination, perform the flight planning, including time and fuel calculations, and provide you with an accurate picture of the total flight. [Figure 2-80]

Figure 2-80. You normally control an FMS through a control display unit (CDU), which incorporates a screen and keyboard or touch screen. Many general aviation airplanes have fully integrated systems that use a primary flight display (PFD) and multifunction display (MFD).

GLOBAL POSITIONING SYSTEM

The area navigation system you are most likely to use is the **global positioning system (GPS)**, the satellite-based radio navigation system that broadcasts a signal used by receivers to determine precise position, calculate time, distance, and bearings to waypoints, compute groundspeed, and provide course guidance.

WIDE AREA AUGMENTATION SYSTEM (WAAS)

The accuracy of GPS is enhanced with the use of the **wide area augmentation system (WAAS)**, a series of ground stations that generate a corrective message that is transmitted to the airplane by a geostationary satellite. This corrective message improves navigational accuracy by accounting for positional drift of the satellites and signal delays caused by the ionosphere and other atmospheric factors. In addition, WAAS-certified GPS equipment provides vertical glide path information for GPS instrument approach procedures. [Figure 2-81] More information on using WAAS for GPS approaches is provided in Chapter 8, Section C – RNAV Approaches.

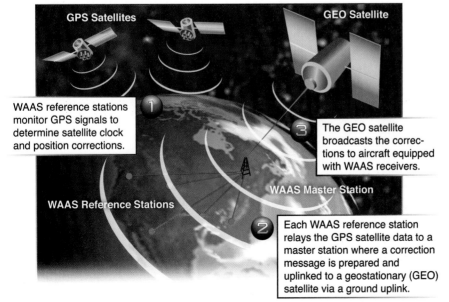

GPS Satellites

GEO Satellite

① WAAS reference stations monitor GPS signals to determine satellite clock and position corrections.

③ The GEO satellite broadcasts the corrections to aircraft equipped with WAAS receivers.

WAAS Master Station

WAAS Reference Stations

② Each WAAS reference station relays the GPS satellite data to a master station where a correction message is prepared and uplinked to a geostationary (GEO) satellite via a ground uplink.

Figure 2-81. WAAS components work with the existing constellation of over 30 GPS satellites.

How GPS Works — Trilateration in Action

The baseline GPS satellite constellation consists of 24 satellites positioned in six earth-centered orbital planes about 20,000 kilometers above the earth. Each satellite transmits a coarse/acquisition (CA) code that contains information on the satellite's position, the GPS system time (from on-board atomic clocks), and the validity and accuracy of the transmitted data. The GPS receiver calculates a distance to the satellite by comparing the reported time the signal left the satellite with the time it arrived at the receiver, based on the receiver's system clock.

When the GPS receiver has distance information from at least three satellites, the GPS equipment can pinpoint your location using a process called trilateration. To improve accuracy and get precise altitude information, a fourth satellite is also included in the position calculation. To understand trilateration, you must visualize three spheres in space.

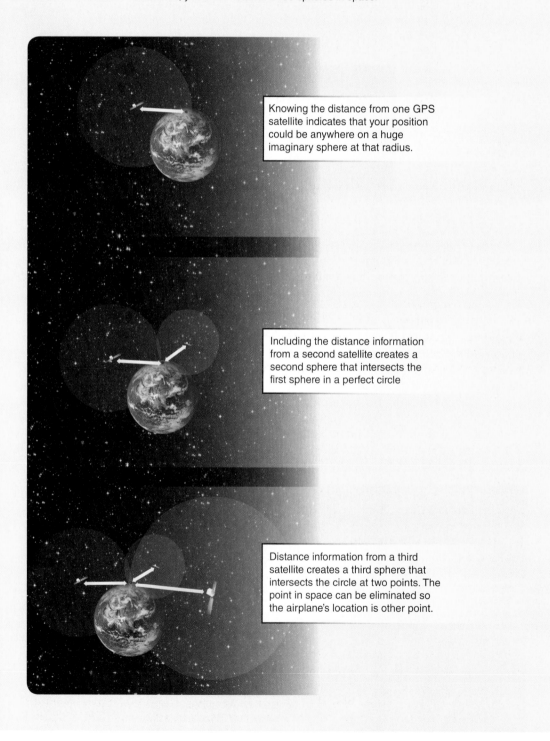

Knowing the distance from one GPS satellite indicates that your position could be anywhere on a huge imaginary sphere at that radius.

Including the distance information from a second satellite creates a second sphere that intersects the first sphere in a perfect circle

Distance information from a third satellite creates a third sphere that intersects the circle at two points. The point in space can be eliminated so the airplane's location is other point.

GROUND-BASED AUGMENTATION SYSTEM

The FAA is working with industry and other service providers to develop the ground-based augmentation system (GBAS), which provides a GPS position correction even more precise than WAAS. Local receivers send corrections to an airport ground facility that transmits the corrections to GBAS-compatible GPS receivers over a VHF radio data link. The aircraft GPS unit uses this information to correct GPS signals. Unlike WAAS correction signals, which are broadcast over a wide area, each GBAS ground facility covers a localized area, generally 20 to 30 miles around an airport. When deployed, GBAS should be able to pinpoint an aircraft's location to within three feet and will provide the required precision and integrity for extremely precise instrument approaches and for airport surface operations, such as low-visibility taxiing.

REQUIREMENTS FOR IFR GPS NAVIGATION

To use GPS equipment for IFR operations, it must be certified according to a technical standard order (TSO). GPS equipment without WAAS capability is approved for IFR operations by the most recent version of TSO-C129. GPS equipment with WAAS capability is certified by the current version of TSO-C145 or TSO-C146. You can determine if your equipment is approved for IFR enroute and approach operations and whether it is WAAS-certified by referring to the airplane flight manual (AFM) or AFM supplements.

 You can determine if a GPS is approved for IFR enroute and approach operations by referring to the airplane flight manual (AFM) or AFM supplements.

IFR-APPROVED GPS EQUIPMENT

You can use GPS equipment certified for IFR operations by TSO-C129 as the sole navigation equipment for short oceanic routes, and it can replace one of the required dual INS systems required for longer transoceanic routes. For domestic enroute and terminal IFR flights, GPS receivers certified according to TSO-C129 are considered supplemental navigation. The airplane must be equipped with the alternate avionics necessary to receive the ground-based facilities that are appropriate for the route to the destination and to any required alternate. In addition, those ground-based facilities must be operational at the time of the flight.

RECEIVER AUTONOMOUS INTEGRITY MONITORING (RAIM)

Another requirement for IFR approval according to TSO-C129 is that the GPS receiver continuously verifies the integrity (usability) of the signals received from the GPS constellation through **receiver autonomous integrity monitoring (RAIM)**. This means that the equipment monitors and compares signals from multiple satellites to ensure an accurate signal. Although basic GPS positioning is almost always available worldwide, the satellite measurement redundancy necessary to ensure integrity of the GPS position is neither worldwide nor continuous. This means you might only find four satellites positioned at the required angle above the horizon (the mask angle) at certain times and locations. Although this is enough to triangulate your position, it does not provide the fifth satellite necessary for integrity monitoring. GPS requires four satellites to provide a three-dimensional solution—latitude, longitude, and altitude. With RAIM, a fifth satellite monitors the position provided by the other four and alerts you of any discrepancy.

Prior to IFR operations, you must confirm that RAIM is available for the intended route and the duration the of flight using current GPS satellite information. If RAIM is predicted to be unavailable, you must use other navigation equipment or delay or cancel your flight. You can verify that RAIM will be available by checking NOTAMs, contacting Flight Service, referring to the FAA RAIM prediction website, or by using your GPS receiver's RAIM prediction function. [Figure 2-82]

During flight, the GPS receiver provides an alert message if RAIM is no longer available. If RAIM capability is lost, you must begin to actively monitor an alternate means of navigation.

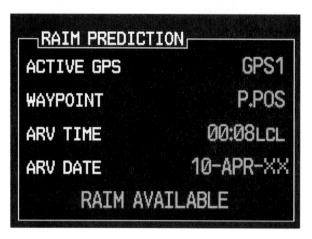

Figure 2-82. Your IFR-approved GPS receiver most likely has a RAIM prediction page that indicates whether RAIM will be available for a specified waypoint, time, and date.

NAVIGATION DATABASE

In addition to ensuring that you have an accurate navigational signal, using GPS for IFR flight requires a current navigational database. Be sure to understand the limitations of the databases for the specific navigation equipment. A database used for a moving map display is not necessarily identical to a printed chart or procedure. [Figure 8-83]

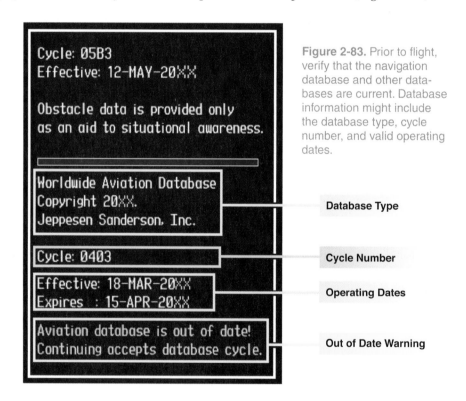

Figure 2-83. Prior to flight, verify that the navigation database and other databases are current. Database information might include the database type, cycle number, and valid operating dates.

WAAS-CERTIFIED GPS

Based on the type of GPS equipment in your airplane, WAAS-certified GPS receivers are approved for IFR operations by either TSO-C145 or TSO-C146. IFR-approved GPS receivers with WAAS capability can be used as the sole navigation equipment for domestic enroute and terminal IFR flights without requiring alternate avionics for navigation and operating ground-based facilities.

Although WAAS coverage is highly dependable—the system is required to be available over 99% of the time—before flying under IFR, you must confirm that WAAS is operational by checking NOTAMs. ATC or ATIS recordings might also alert you to a loss of WAAS. If WAAS loss occurs, the GPS receiver will not display approach procedures that require WAAS capability. If you confirm WAAS coverage along the entire route of flight, you do not need to perform the RAIM prediction check prior to departure.

NAVIGATING WITH GPS

If you fly a variety of airplanes, one of the challenges you face using GPS for IFR operations is dealing with the lack of standardization between different makes and models of GPS receivers. You must become thoroughly familiar with the specific GPS equipment installed in the airplane you are operating. Review the receiver operation manual and the AFM or AFM supplement that covers the equipment installation. In addition, practice navigating with a computer-based flight training device or avionics trainer and use the equipment's simulation mode to become familiar with its operation prior to flying. It is also a good idea to use the equipment in flight under VFR conditions before IFR operation. [Figure 2-84]

Figure 2-84. Although all GPS receivers provide the same basic navigation information, programming steps, available features, and the how the unit displays information can vary.

Although the navigation presentations vary between different GPS manufacturers and models, most GPS receivers provide information about ground track, course, course deviation, groundspeed, and distance and time to waypoints, as well as some type of moving map for situational awareness. The following discussion presents basic GPS functions for IFR navigation using a Garmin G1000 Integrated Flight Deck.

COURSE DEVIATION INDICATOR

For a GPS installation to be approved for IFR operations, it must have a CDI display located in the pilot's primary field of view. Generally, this means the system must be able to display course deviation indications on a conventional VOR or HSI display. You typically have the ability to switch the primary navigation display between a GPS and VOR receiver and an annunciator indicates which equipment is being used as the navigation source. In the case of the G1000, a primary flight display (PFD) incorporates an HSI that provides GPS course deviation information.

The CDI scale on the HSI has different characteristics, depending on the navigation source. When the navigation source is a VOR or localizer, the CDI displays the angular deviation from the course. When the navigation source is the GPS, the CDI displays the lateral distance from the course. The distance off course is called the cross-track error and is normally displayed in nautical miles. For GPS units, the CDI has three different sensitivities, depending on whether you are in the enroute, terminal, or approach phase of flight. The approach sensitivity is similar to that of a localizer on a precision instrument approach. Some GPS navigation systems also use this high sensitivity during portions of the departure phase. [Figure 2-85]

The enroute full-scale deviation normally corresponds to a cross-track error of 2 NM on WAAS-certified GPS systems and 5 NM on non-WAAS systems.

During the terminal phase of flight, which is normally within 30 NM of the departure or destination airports, the full-scale deviation equals a 1 NM cross-track error.

Figure 2-85. As you transition from the enroute and terminal environments to the approach phase of flight, the CDI sensitivity increases. .

During the approach phase–inside the final approach fix–a full scale deflection equals 0.3 NM cross-track error.

WAYPOINTS

One significant benefit of a GPS navigation system is the ability to provide waypoint information from its navigation database. The types of **waypoints** in the database normally include VORs, NDBs, intersections, and airports. Airport information typically includes: airport name, city, elevation, and runway information, as well as communication and ILS frequencies and available instrument procedures. Many GPS receivers also provide access to weather information. With an appropriate satellite weather subscription, you can obtain METARs and TAFs for airports that have weather reporting. As you gain more experience navigating with GPS in the IFR environment, you will also navigate between waypoints specifically designated for departure, arrival, and instrument approach procedures.

GPS equipment provides **auto-sequencing** of waypoints—when you program a departure, arrival, approach, or other route, the receiver senses when the airplane passes a waypoint and automatically cycles to the next waypoint. Some GPS equipment displays a message advising you to set the next course on the VOR indicator or HSI. Integrated systems, such as the G1000, automatically set the course on the HSI.

EQUIPMENT CHALLENGES

As you gain experience, you might fly an increasing variety of airplanes with different avionics equipment. If you do not understand how to properly program and interpret the specific navigation and automation equipment on board your airplane, you increase risk as the following ASRS account clearly illustrates.

I had filed and had been given a direct IFR flight plan route at 5,000 feet. I was having trouble programming the Garmin 650 GPS… is different than the Gamin 430w that I am used to. The GTN 650 is touch screen and menu selections are different. …I activated the GPS approach in the default Vectors mode. I intended to navigate manually and allow the autopilot to intercept and track the approach. After a short period of time I noticed I had descended from 2,500 feet MSL to 1,500 feet MSL and was in a 30-40 degree bank. I turned the autopilot off and leveled the plane and then climbed to 2,000 feet. I called ATC and declared a missed approach. I told the Controller that I would like to go to an airport that was reporting better weather. I also told him that I had about an hour of fuel left. He gave me a couple of options and vectors to other nearby airports. While trying to input the vectors into the GPS and set the autopilot I made at least one 180 turn.

The reason for this event was my total lack of understanding of the newer Garmin GTN650 GPS and allowing that fact to distract me from flying the aircraft safely This aircraft is a rental and I was checked out on it. However, I did not study the GTN650 GPS enough and did not fully understand its interactions with the autopilot. Needless to say I will never let this happen again and consider myself lucky!

Flying as sole pilot in IFR conditions presents one of the most demanding challenges as a pilot because of the high workload. Single-pilot IFR can be accomplished safely if you maintain strict standards for self assessment, which must include ensuring you are proficient in operating all the equipment on the airplane, including programming and interpreting the avionics.

GPS FLIGHT PLANNING

Using a GPS receiver for navigation can be as simple as pressing the Direct-To button, selecting your destination, following the CDI, and monitoring the distance and time to the destination. However, for IFR operations, it is most effective to plan your flight based on existing waypoints, routes, and airways. There are several reasons for this. First, you must fly a flight path that avoids obstacles and enables ATC to properly sequence traffic. It might be necessary to include specific departure and arrival procedures in your flight plan, especially if you are operating to and from busy airports. In addition, if your GPS is not WAAS-certified, your flight plan should correspond to ground-based navaids appropriate for the route to the destination and to any required alternate. To create and use a flight plan in your GPS receiver, you typically open a flight plan window and enter waypoints using a combination of knobs or a keyboard. When you have finished entering all the waypoints and the destination, be sure to activate the flight plan. [Figure 2-86]

Figure 2-86. This flight plan window shows a flight from Centennial Airport (KAPA) in Denver to Las Vegas Airport in New Mexico (KLVS) using a combination of airports, intersections, and VORs as waypoints.

SECTION C ■ **Instrument Navigation**

You might plan a flight strictly following airways and other courses defined by ground-based navaids, or you might combine these routes with random RNAV routes that enable you to fly a more direct course. **Random RNAV routes** that do not correspond with

published courses can only be authorized in a radar environment and route approval depends on ATC's ability to provide radar monitoring and compatibility with traffic volume and flow. Although ATC will monitor your flight, navigation on a random RNAV route is your responsibility, so it is beneficial to create a flight plan with multiple waypoints to enhance situational awareness. Be aware that ATC might not approve direct routing due to traffic flow and other considerations. When planning your flight, comply with the guidelines for using RNAV for IFR flight planning outlined in the AIM. [Figure 2-87]

Most systems display the course—referred to on this system as desired track—and the distance between waypoints. On the active leg, instead of the total distance between waypoints, the system normally displays the distance remaining to the next waypoint.

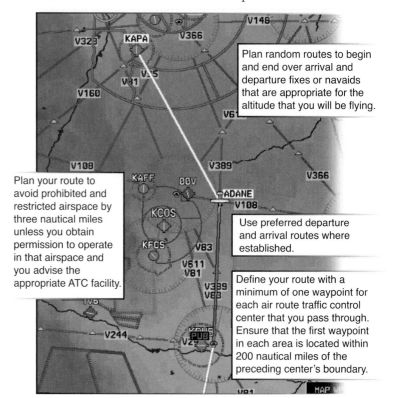

Plan random routes to begin and end over arrival and departure fixes or navaids that are appropriate for the altitude that you will be flying.

Plan your route to avoid prohibited and restricted airspace by three nautical miles unless you obtain permission to operate in that airspace and you advise the appropriate ATC facility.

Use preferred departure and arrival routes where established.

Define your route with a minimum of one waypoint for each air route traffic control center that you pass through. Ensure that the first waypoint in each area is located within 200 nautical miles of the preceding center's boundary.

Figure 2-87. The AIM provides guidelines for planning an RNAV flight under IFR.

An enhanced flight plan view provides cumulative distance (rather than leg distance) fuel remaining at each waypoint, cumulative estimated time enroute, and estimated time of arrival at each waypoint. [Figure 2-88]

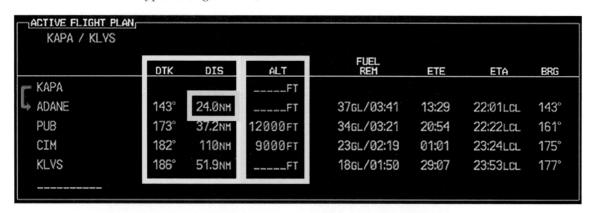

ACTIVE FLIGHT PLAN	DTK	DIS	ALT	FUEL REM	ETE	ETA	BRG
KAPA / KLVS							
KAPA			-----FT				
ADANE	143°	24.0NM	-----FT	37GL/03:41	13:29	22:01LCL	143°
PUB	173°	37.2NM	12000FT	34GL/03:21	20:54	22:22LCL	161°
CIM	182°	110NM	9000FT	23GL/02:19	01:01	23:24LCL	175°
KLVS	186°	51.9NM	-----FT	18GL/01:50	29:07	23:53LCL	177°

Most systems display the course, or desired track, and the distance between waypoints.

On the active leg, instead of the total distance between waypoints, the system normally displays the distance remaining to the next waypoint.

When your flight plan is an IFR departure, arrival, or approach procedure, your GPS might fill in procedural altitudes for some legs to assist you with vertical navigation (VNAV). On enroute legs, you can enter these altitudes manually if you want VNAV guidance.

Figure 2-88. You can refer to the flight plan window to monitor your progress during the flight.

MANUAL COURSE SELECTION

One important difference between GPS and traditional VOR navigation is that the GPS selects your courses for you, based on the waypoints you are flying between. There are situations, however, when you need to manually select a course, as you do with the OBS on your VOR indicator. For example, ATC might clear you to a fix via a different course than what is published and contained in the GPS database. For this reason, IFR-certified GPS equipment allows manual selection of a course. When switching to this mode, you can typically select the course using the OBS on the HSI or VOR indicator that you are using in conjunction with the GPS.

DETERMINING AIRCRAFT POSITION FROM A WAYPOINT

Consider this scenario: you are an instrument-rated pilot flying enroute from Pueblo, Colorado to Phoenix, Arizona using GPS navigation. You began the flight under VFR, but the weather is worse than forecast so you contact ATC to request an IFR clearance. How do you interpret your position so that you can describe it to ATC? Because you have a GPS flight plan programmed, it is easy to report your position relative to the waypoints in your route. In addition, you can interpret the information on the navigation map or use the Nearest function to quickly identify your exact location if your equipment has these features. [Figure 2–89]

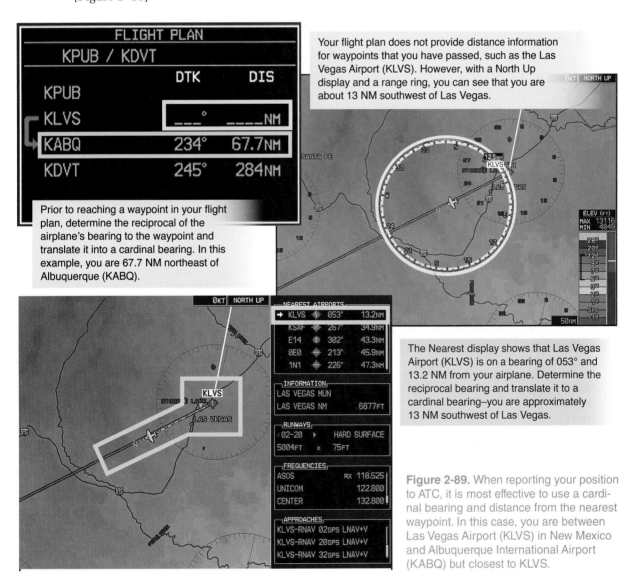

Your flight plan does not provide distance information for waypoints that you have passed, such as the Las Vegas Airport (KLVS). However, with a North Up display and a range ring, you can see that you are about 13 NM southwest of Las Vegas.

Prior to reaching a waypoint in your flight plan, determine the reciprocal of the airplane's bearing to the waypoint and translate it into a cardinal bearing. In this example, you are 67.7 NM northeast of Albuquerque (KABQ).

The Nearest display shows that Las Vegas Airport (KLVS) is on a bearing of 053° and 13.2 NM from your airplane. Determine the reciprocal bearing and translate it to a cardinal bearing—you are approximately 13 NM southwest of Las Vegas.

Figure 2-89. When reporting your position to ATC, it is most effective to use a cardinal bearing and distance from the nearest waypoint. In this case, you are between Las Vegas Airport (KLVS) in New Mexico and Albuquerque International Airport (KABQ) but closest to KLVS.

INTERCEPTING A COURSE

In the VFR environment, you might not have intercepted many courses using your GPS if you primarily flew direct from your airplane's position to a waypoint. In the IFR environment, you must intercept specific courses in a variety of situations: navigating on a departure or arrival procedure, intercepting an airway, resuming your own navigation after flying an assigned heading, and being vectored on to an approach course. Although, you primarily use the CDI for navigation information as you intercept a course, you should include the moving map in your scan (if applicable) to provide increased situational awareness. [Figure 2-90]

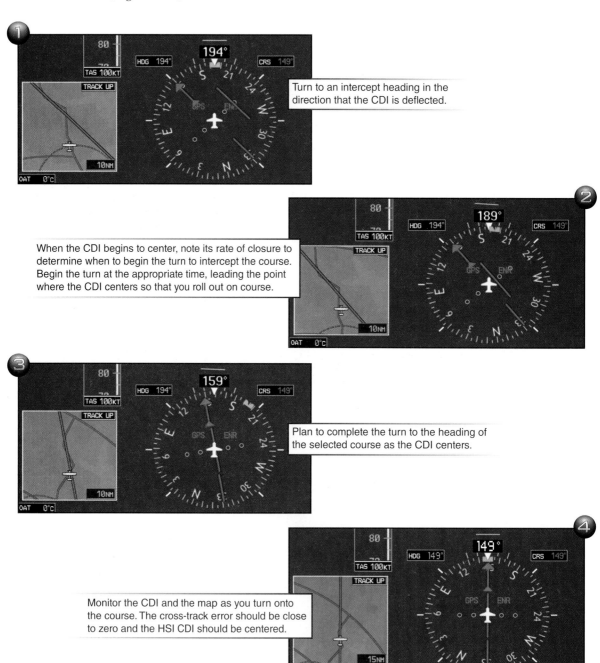

Turn to an intercept heading in the direction that the CDI is deflected.

When the CDI begins to center, note its rate of closure to determine when to begin the turn to intercept the course. Begin the turn at the appropriate time, leading the point where the CDI centers so that you roll out on course.

Plan to complete the turn to the heading of the selected course as the CDI centers.

Monitor the CDI and the map as you turn onto the course. The cross-track error should be close to zero and the HSI CDI should be centered.

Figure 2-90. You have just departed on an IFR flight plan. After flying your initial assigned heading, ATC clears you to intercept your enroute course, V913 on a course of 149°, which is the first leg in your active flight plan.

TRACKING A COURSE

In the IFR environment, it is critical that you track courses precisely to stay within RNP standards, maintain traffic separation, avoid terrain and obstacles, and to ensure you are aligned with the runway when performing instrument approaches. Although the basic concept of establishing a wind correction angle using the CDI applies to GPS tracking, the equipment typically displays a wide variety of additional information that enables you to maintain courses with increased accuracy. [Figure 2-91]

Wind Direction and Speed

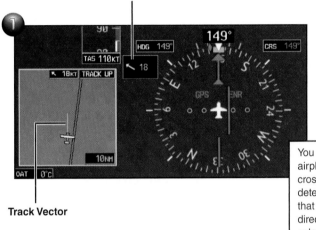

Track Vector

You have intercepted V913 (149° course) but the airplane begins to drift off course due to a strong crosswind from the right. To track any course, you must determine a heading that will compensate for wind so that the airplane remains on the desired track. Use wind direction and speed data to help you anticipate drift and select an appropriate wind correction angle

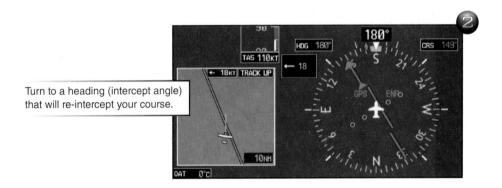

Turn to a heading (intercept angle) that will re-intercept your course.

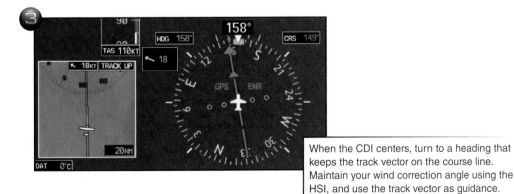

When the CDI centers, turn to a heading that keeps the track vector on the course line. Maintain your wind correction angle using the HSI, and use the track vector as guidance.

Figure 2-91. Your GPS display might include a moving map and wind information to help you track a course effectively.

SECTION C ■ Instrument Navigation

ADF NAVIGATION

The automatic direction finder (ADF) is useful for supplemental navigation information, and as a backup when other aircraft or ground equipment is unavailable. Your ADF can be tuned to any low/medium frequency (L/MF) nondirectional radio beacon (NDB) or commercial broadcast stations of the amplitude modulation (AM) class. Although commercial broadcast stations are not approved for IFR operations, you may use them for VFR navigation. An NDB that is collocated with a marker beacon on a precision instrument approach is called a compass locator. These facilities alert you as you reach specific points on some instrument approaches.

Interpreting ADF indications can be more challenging than VOR indications because you must analyze both heading and bearing information to determine your position. As you know, a fixed-card indicator has zero at the top and directly indicates the angle between the nose of the aircraft and the station, or **relative bearing**. To determine your magnetic bearing (MB) to the station, you add magnetic heading (MH) and relative bearing (RB). [Figure 2-92].

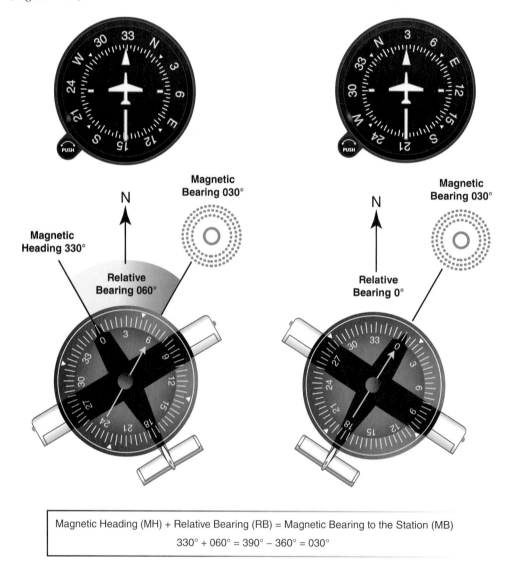

Magnetic Heading (MH) + Relative Bearing (RB) = Magnetic Bearing to the Station (MB)

330° + 060° = 390° − 360° = 030°

Figure 2-92. Using a fixed card indicator, add the magnetic heading to the relative bearing to determine the magnetic bearing to the station.

On a movable-card ADF, you can rotate the scale so your heading appears at the top. This allows you to directly read your magnetic heading to the station under the arrowhead and the bearing from the station under the tail of the arrow. However, when you are frequently changing heading, it might not be practical to keep the ADF card adjusted to your heading. One useful technique is to mentally superimpose the ADF needle over the heading indicator. [Figure 2-93].

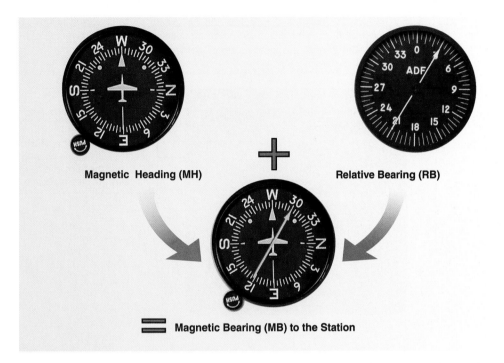

Magnetic Heading (MH)

Relative Bearing (RB)

Magnetic Bearing (MB) to the Station

Figure 2-93. You can quickly visualize the magnetic bearing to a station by mentally superimposing the ADF needle over your heading indicator.

RADIO MAGNETIC INDICATOR

A special instrument, called a **radio magnetic indicator (RMI)**, makes it easy to determine your position in relation to an NDB by combining a slaved compass card and bearing pointer in the same instrument. An RMI is like a movable-card ADF on which the card automatically rotates to reflect the aircraft's magnetic heading.

 Regardless of the type of ADF pointer, the relative bearing is the angle between the needle and the aircraft nose reference. Magnetic heading (MH) plus relative bearing (RB) equals magnetic bearing to the station (MB). On a properly set movable-card ADF, the arrowhead indicates MB to the station and the tail of the arrow indicates MB from the station.

Unlike a standard ADF display, most RMIs have two bearing pointer needles, either one of which can be set to point to an NDB or VOR station. Because the aircraft heading appears at the top of the scale, the instrument always displays the bearing to a station at the head of the arrow, and the bearing from a station at the tail of the arrow. [Figure 2-94]

 An RMI, like an HSI, contains a slaved compass card that receives heading information from a magnetic flux valve mounted at a remote position on the aircraft. On older units, it was occasionally necessary to align the slaved compass card(s) by selecting free gyro mode and pressing buttons to rotate the card clockwise (for a left heading correction) or counterclockwise (to correct to a higher number heading). This is totally automatic on newer systems.

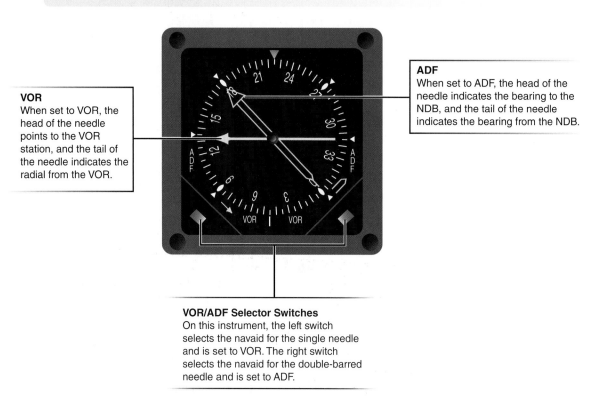

VOR
When set to VOR, the head of the needle points to the VOR station, and the tail of the needle indicates the radial from the VOR.

ADF
When set to ADF, the head of the needle indicates the bearing to the NDB, and the tail of the needle indicates the bearing from the NDB.

VOR/ADF Selector Switches
On this instrument, the left switch selects the navaid for the single needle and is set to VOR. The right switch selects the navaid for the double-barred needle and is set to ADF.

Figure 2-94. An RMI incorporates two bearing pointer needles superimposed over a slaved compass card that indicates heading. One or both of the needles can be set to point to a VOR or an NDB. Some RMIs can also show bearings to GPS waypoints.

 The tail of an RMI needle set to a VOR station indicates the radial you are on FROM the station. The head of an RMI needle set to an ADF shows the bearing TO the station and the tail of the needle indicates the bearing FROM the station.

INTERCEPTING A BEARING

Intercepting a bearing is easiest if you choose an angle, such as 45°, that is easy to read on the compass card. To establish a 45° intercept, turn so that the bearing to be intercepted appears over the 45° reference mark on the RMI to the left or right of the airplane nose. Precisely maintain this heading and look for the ADF needle to also point 45° to the left or right of the airplane's nose. Figure 2-95 shows the steps for intercepting a bearing using a n RMI. When using a fixed-card ADF to intercept a bearing, you must monitor both the ADF indicator and the heading indicator.

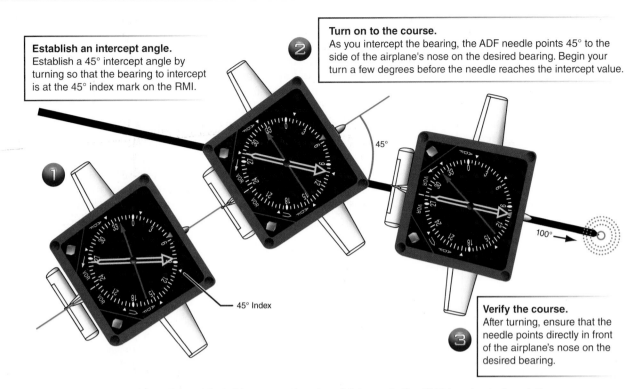

Establish an intercept angle.
Establish a 45° intercept angle by turning so that the bearing to intercept is at the 45° index mark on the RMI.

Turn on to the course.
As you intercept the bearing, the ADF needle points 45° to the side of the airplane's nose on the desired bearing. Begin your turn a few degrees before the needle reaches the intercept value.

45° Index

100°

Verify the course.
After turning, ensure that the needle points directly in front of the airplane's nose on the desired bearing.

Figure 2-95. When flying this 45° intercept, the aircraft intercepts the 100° bearing to the station when the ADF needle indicates a 45° relative bearing.

You can easily see when you have intercepted your bearing if using a 45° intercept or other easy-to-see value such as 30°. If using a 30° intercept, you will have intercepted the bearing to the station when the needle points 30° to the left or right of the airplane's nose.

Sometimes it can be challenging to determine your position when the needle does not exactly indicate the intercept angle. Just remember that the head of the needle is always moving toward the tail of the airplane when intercepting a bearing inbound to the NDB—the head of the needle appears to "fall" toward the desired bearing on the compass card. If the needle is pointing in front of your intercept angle, you have not yet reached the bearing to be intercepted. If it points behind the intercept position, you have passed through your bearing. To intercept a bearing outbound from an NDB, follow the same steps but note that the tail of the needle "rises" toward the bearing. Begin your turn a few degrees before the needle reaches the intercept value. [Figure 2-96]

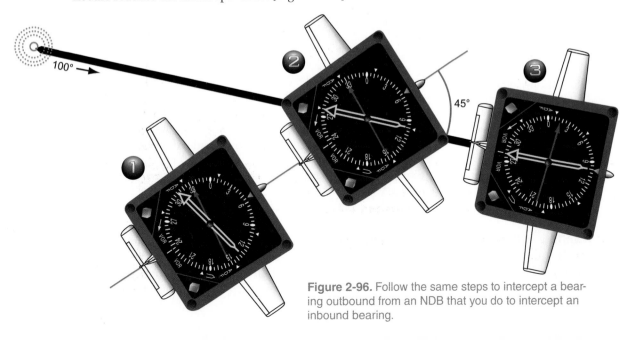

100°

45°

Figure 2-96. Follow the same steps to intercept a bearing outbound from an NDB that you do to intercept an inbound bearing.

TRACKING

For most instrument approaches, you must track a specific path to a station. The basic tracking procedure is to start with a heading you expect will keep you on course. In a no-wind, headwind, tailwind, or unknown wind situation, this heading will be the same as your course. Precisely hold the heading and watch for the needle to drift to the left or right. The ADF needle's indications when tracking inbound tell which way you need to turn to capture your course. Double the ADF relative bearing when turning toward your course. If your heading equals your course and the needle points 10° left, turn 20° left. When holding a heading 20° to the left of your desired course, watch for the ADF needle to move 20° right of the nose. You are on course when the relative bearing equals your course correction. Assuming a wind caused you to drift right of course, you might try a heading 10° left of course to track inbound. This results in a relative bearing of 10° right as long as you maintain course. [Figure 2-97]

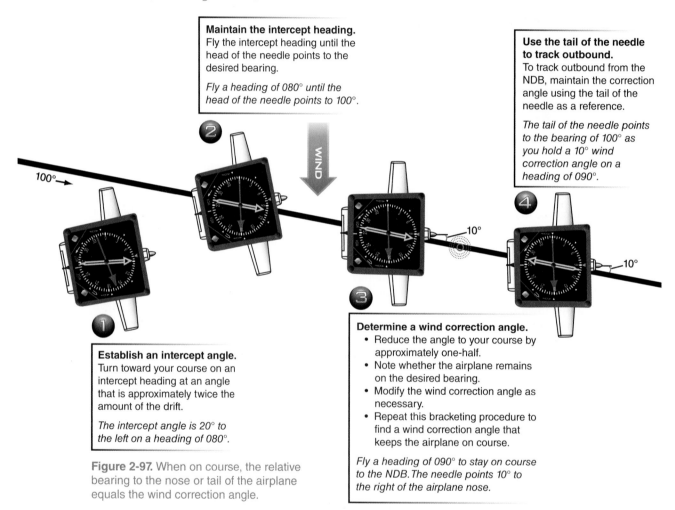

Maintain the intercept heading.
Fly the intercept heading until the head of the needle points to the desired bearing.

Fly a heading of 080° until the head of the needle points to 100°.

Use the tail of the needle to track outbound.
To track outbound from the NDB, maintain the correction angle using the tail of the needle as a reference.

The tail of the needle points to the bearing of 100° as you hold a 10° wind correction angle on a heading of 090°.

Establish an intercept angle.
Turn toward your course on an intercept heading at an angle that is approximately twice the amount of the drift.

The intercept angle is 20° to the left on a heading of 080°.

Determine a wind correction angle.
• Reduce the angle to your course by approximately one-half.
• Note whether the airplane remains on the desired bearing.
• Modify the wind correction angle as necessary.
• Repeat this bracketing procedure to find a wind correction angle that keeps the airplane on course.

Fly a heading of 090° to stay on course to the NDB. The needle points 10° to the right of the airplane nose.

Figure 2-97. When on course, the relative bearing to the nose or tail of the airplane equals the wind correction angle.

If you attempt to correct for a crosswind by continually adjusting your magnetic heading to keep the ADF needled pointed at the airplane's nose (0° relative bearing), you will home to the station instead of tracking to it. This will cause you to fly a curved path over the ground.

 When on the desired track outbound with the proper drift correction established, the ADF pointer will be deflected to the windward side of the tail position.

Unlike VOR navigation, the ADF does not provide accurate position information independent of heading. Unless you are using an RMI with a compass card that automatically aligns itself with magnetic north, you could find yourself substantially off course if you do not check and set your heading indicator against your magnetic compass every 15 minutes.

Homing to a station in a crosswind results in a curved path to the station.

TIME AND DISTANCE TO A STATION

You can calculate your time and distance to a station by turning perpendicular to the inbound course and measuring the time to make a 10° (or any angle) change in bearing. You calculate the time and distance to the station using the same formulas you learned in the VOR discussion earlier in this section. To determine the time to the station, you can also use the double-the-angle-on-the-bow method, which employs the same geometric principle as the isosceles triangle concept discussed earlier. If you hold a constant heading, the time to the station is simply equal to the amount of time it takes for the relative bearing to double. For example, if you hold a constant heading and the ADF needle moves from a relative bearing of 045° to 090° in 5 minutes, the time to the station is 5 minutes.

 If you hold a constant heading, the time to the station is equal to the time it takes for the relative bearing to double.

STATION PASSAGE

As you approach the station, even small deviations from your desired track can result in large needle fluctuations. Therefore, it is important that you do not chase the needle, but use heading corrections no greater than about 5°. As the needle begins to rotate steadily toward a wingtip position, or shows erratic oscillations to the left or right, stay on your last corrected heading. Station passage is considered to have occurred when the needle either points to a wingtip or settles at or near the 180° position. Depending on your altitude, it could take from a few seconds up to 3 minutes from the time that the needle begins to oscillate until you obtain a positive indication of station passage.

ADF OPERATIONAL CONSIDERATIONS

Your ADF uses nondirectional beacons that transmit in the low/medium frequency (L/MF) range between 190 and 535 kHz. The stations normally transmit a simple 400 or 1,020 Hz tone modulated with a Morse code identifier. [Figure 2-98] Radio beacons are subject to disturbances that can result in erroneous bearing information. Such disturbances result from such factors as lightning, precipitation static, etc. At night, radio beacons are vulnerable to interference from distant stations. Nearly all disturbances that affect the ADF bearing also affect the facility's identification.

FACILITY	POWER OUTPUT	USABLE RANGE
Compass Locator	25 Watts	15 NM
MH Radio Beacon	Less Than 50 Watts	25 NM
H Radio Beacon	50 to 1,999 Watts	Up to 50 NM
HH Radio Beacon	2,000 Watts or More	75 NM

Figure 2-98. Although NDBs do not suffer the line-of-sight limitations of VHF and UHF facilities, interference and L/MF wave propagation characteristics can limit their reception range.

Just as you do with a VOR, you should positively identify an NDB before you use it for navigation by listening to the Morse code identifier. In contrast to VOR navigation, however, you should continuously monitor the NDB's identification because ADF receivers do not have a flag to warn you when erroneous bearing information is being displayed.

SECTION C ■ Instrument Navigation

SUMMARY CHECKLIST

✓ The horizontal situation indicator (HSI) display combines a conventional VOR navigation indicator with a heading indicator.

✓ An HSI cannot reverse sense when tuned to a VOR station, even if you set it opposite your intended course or heading.

✓ As you get close to a station, in an area called the cone of confusion, the CDI and TO/FROM indicators fluctuate. VOR station passage is indicated by the first positive, complete reversal of the TO/FROM indicator.

✓ VOR facilities are classified according to their usable range and altitude, or standard service volume (SSV). You can find the SSV that applies to a particular VOR in the Chart Supplement.

✓ When checking your VOR using a VOT, the CDI should be centered and the OBS should indicate that the airplane is on the 360° radial, ±4°. When using a VOR checkpoint, the CDI must center within ±4°. The allowable error using an airborne checkpoint is ±6°. When you conduct a dual system check, the difference between VOR systems should not exceed 4°.

✓ DME is accurate to within 1/2 mile or 3% (whichever is greater), as long as you are at least one mile or more from the DME facility for every 1,000 feet of altitude above the station.

✓ Required navigation performance (RNP) is a set of standards that apply to both airspace and navigation equipment.

✓ To comply with RNP standards, your navigation equipment must be able to keep the airplane within a distance of two nautical miles for enroute operations, within one nautical mile for terminal operations, and within 0.3 nautical miles for approach operations (the final approach course).

✓ VOR/DME RNAV uses an airborne computer to create waypoints based on information from VORTAC or VOR/DME facilities.

✓ A flight management system (FMS) is a system that acts as the input/output device for navigational data to automate the tasks of managing the onboard navigation systems.

✓ The global positioning system (GPS) is a satellite-based radio navigation system that broadcasts a signal used by receivers to determine precise position, calculate time, distance, and bearings to waypoints, compute groundspeed, and provide course guidance.

✓ The wide area augmentation system (WAAS) is a series of ground stations that generate a corrective message that is transmitted to the airplane by a geostationary satellite. This corrective message improves navigational accuracy by accounting for positional drift of the satellites and signal delays caused by the ionosphere and other atmospheric factors.

✓ GPS equipment without WAAS capability is approved for IFR operations by the most recent version of TSO-C129. WAAS-certified GPS receivers are certified by the current version of TSO-C145 or TSO-C146.

✓ You can determine if your equipment is approved for IFR enroute and approach operations and if it is WAAS-certified by referring to the airplane flight manual (AFM) or AFM supplements.

✓ If your GPS receiver is certified according to TSO-C129, your airplane must be equipped with the alternate avionics necessary to receive operational ground-based facilities appropriate for the route to the destination and to any required alternate.

✓ According to TSO-C129, a non-WAAS GPS receiver must continuously monitor and compare signals from multiple satellites to ensure an accurate signal through receiver autonomous integrity monitoring (RAIM).

✓ Prior to the IFR flight, you must confirm RAIM availability for the intended route and duration of the flight by checking NOTAMs, contacting Flight Service, accessing the FAA RAIM prediction website, or by using your GPS receiver's RAIM prediction function.

✓ Using GPS for IFR flight requires a current navigational database.

✓ You can use a WAAS-certified GPS receiver as the sole navigation equipment for domestic enroute and terminal IFR flights without requiring alternate avionics for navigation and operating ground-based facilities.

✓ When the navigation source is the GPS, the CDI displays the lateral distance from course, called the cross-track error.

✓ For GPS units, the CDI has three different sensitivities, one each for enroute, terminal, and approach phase of flight.

✓ Auto-sequencing is when the GPS receiver senses that the airplane is passing a waypoint and automatically cycles to the next waypoint.

✓ For IFR operations, it is most effective to plan your flight based on existing waypoints, routes, and airways to avoid obstacles, enable ATC to properly sequence traffic, and to include specific departure and arrival procedures in your flight plan.

✓ IFR random RNAV routes do not correspond with published courses and can only be authorized in a radar environment and with ATC approval.

✓ Plan any random routes to begin and end over arrival and departure transition fixes or navaids for your altitude, use preferred departure and arrival routes, and avoid prohibited and restricted airspace by three nautical miles.

✓ Define a random RNAV route with a minimum of one waypoint for each air route traffic control center area that you pass through and ensure that the first waypoint in each area is located within 200 nautical miles of the preceding center's boundary.

✓ When reporting your position to ATC, it is most effective to use a cardinal bearing and distance from the nearest waypoint.

✓ In the IFR environment, you must intercept specific courses in a variety of situations: navigating on a departure or arrival procedure, intercepting an airway, resuming your own navigation after flying an assigned heading, and being vectored on to an approach course.

✓ In the IFR environment, it is critical that you track courses precisely to stay within RNP standards, maintain traffic separation, avoid terrain and obstacles, and to ensure you are aligned with the runway during instrument approaches.

✓ The angle between the nose of the airplane and an NDB is the relative bearing.

✓ Magnetic heading (MH) plus relative bearing (RB) equals magnetic bearing to the station (MB).

✓ A radio magnetic indicator (RMI) always displays the bearing to a station at the head of the arrow, and the bearing from a station at the tail of the arrow.

✓ NDB station passage is considered to have occurred when the needle either points to a wingtip or settles at or near the 180° position.

KEY TERMS

Horizontal Situation Indicator (HSI)

Cone of Confusion

VOR Test Facilities (VOTs)

VOR Checkpoints

Distance Measuring Equipment (DME)

DME Arcs

Area Navigation (RNAV)

Required Navigation Performance (RNP)

Flight Management System (FMS)

Global Positioning System (GPS)

Wide Area Augmentation System (WAAS)

Receiver Autonomous Integrity Monitoring (RAIM)

Waypoints

Auto-Sequencing

Random RNAV Routes

Relative Bearing

Radio Magnetic Indicator (RMI)

QUESTIONS

Use the following figure to answer question 1.

1. What displacement from course is indicated by this instrument when used in conjunction with a VOR?
   A. 2-1/2°
   B. 5°
   C. 10°

2. Why is it impossible for a horizontal situation indicator to provide reverse sensing when tuned to a VOR?

3. True/False. Station passage is indicated when the TO/FROM indicator first starts fluctuating.

Use the following figure to answer question 4.

4. Assume that you are 15 nautical miles from the VOR. Using these HSI indications and a 6,000-foot nautical mile, how far off course are you in degrees and nautical miles?

5. Refer to the following figure to match each navigation indicator with the appropriate airplane position.

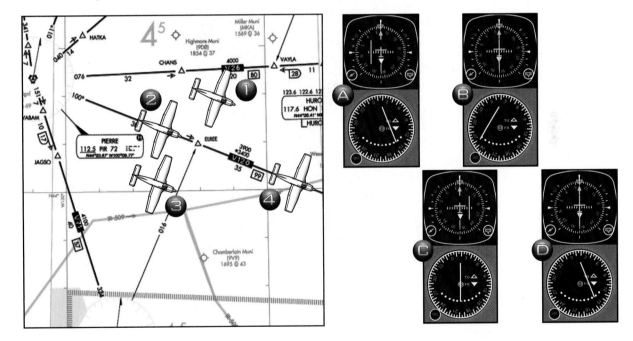

6. True/False. Normally, when flying a DME arc, the bearing pointer reaches the wingtip position when the airplane is slightly outside the arc.

7. What is the maximum distance at which you can expect a reliable signal from a high altitude VOR. At what altitudes does this maximum range occur?

8. True/False. The maximum allowable error on a VOR check using a VOT is 4°.

9. What is the maximum allowable difference when checking two VORs against each other?

10. True/False. When tuning a VOR and hearing the correct 1,020 Hz Morse code identifier signal, you are assured that both the VOR and DME are properly tuned and usable for navigation.

11. What is required navigation performance (RNP)?

12. To comply with RNP standards, you must operate within what distance of the centerline of a route, path, or procedure?
    A. 2 nautical miles for approach operations; 1 nautical mile for terminal operations; 0.3 nautical miles for enroute operations
    B. 2 nautical miles for enroute operations; 1 nautical mile for terminal operations; 0.3 nautical miles for approach operations
    C. 3 nautical miles for enroute operations; 2 nautical miles for terminal operations; 1 nautical mile for approach operations

13. What is a flight management system (FMS)?

14. What is the wide area augmentation system (WAAS)?
    A. WAAS enhances the accuracy of GPS by using a series of ground stations to generate a corrective message that is transmitted to the airplane by a geostationary satellite. This message accounts for positional drift of the satellites and signal delays caused by the ionosphere and other atmospheric factors.
    B. WAAS is a navigation computer in the airplane used in addition to GPS to calculate the position with enhanced accuracy.
    C. WAAS enhances the accuracy of GPS by using receivers to send corrective signals over a localized area, generally 20 to 30 miles.

15. Select the true statement regarding the requirements to use GPS equipment for IFR operations.
    A. WAAS-certified GPS receivers are approved for IFR operations by the current version of TSO-C-129.
    B. You must refer to TSO-C145 or TSO-C146 to determine if your GPS equipment is approved for IFR operations.
    C. You can determine if a GPS is approved for IFR enroute and approach operations by referring to the airplane flight manual (AFM) or AFM supplement.

16. True/False. For domestic enroute and terminal IFR flights with a GPS receiver certified according to TSO-C129, the airplane must be equipped with alternate avionics necessary to receive the ground-based facilities appropriate for the route to the destination and to any required alternate.

17. Prior to using GPS for IFR operations, what actions must you take?
    A. For WAAS-certified GPS equipment, you must verify that RAIM will be available for the intended route and duration of the flight and ensure that your GPS navigational database is current.
    B. For non-WAAS GPS equipment, you must verify that RAIM will be available for the intended route and duration of the flight and ensure that your GPS navigational database is current.
    C. For all GPS equipment, you must you must verify that WAAS will be available for the intended route and duration of the flight and ensure that your GPS navigational database is current.

Use the following figure to answer question 18.

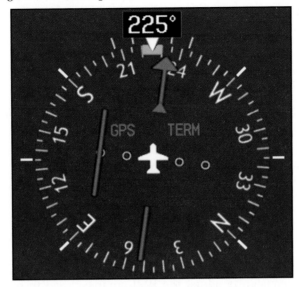

18. A full-scale deviation of the CDI of this HSI equals what cross-track error?
   A. 2.0 nautical miles
   B. 0.3 nautical miles
   C. 1.0 nautical mile

19. What does auto-sequencing mean?

20. True/False. To comply with AIM guidelines, you should plan any random routes to begin and end over arrival and departure transition fixes or navaids that are appropriate for the altitude that you will be flying. You should also define your route with a minimum of one waypoint for each air route traffic control center area that you pass through.

Use the following figure to answer questions 21 through 23.

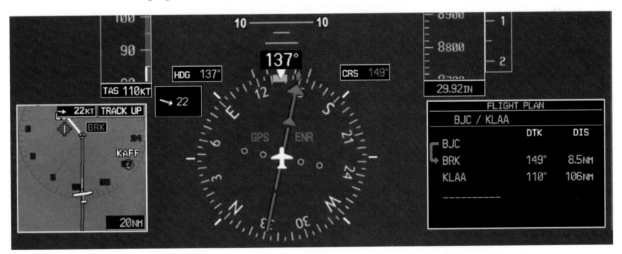

21. ATC asks you to report your position. Which of the following is correct?
   A. You are 8.5 nautical miles northwest of BRK.
   B. You are 8.5 nautical miles southwest of BJC.
   C. You are 8.5 nautical miles southwest of BRK.

22. What is true regarding your flight plan?
   A. You are on the leg from BJC to BRK, which has a total distance of 8.5 nautical miles.
   B. You are on the leg from BJC to BRK and there are 8.5 nautical miles remaining to BRK.
   C. At BRK you will need to program the GPS to turn to a course of 110° to continue your flight to KLAA.

23. What is true regarding the navigation indications shown on this GPS display?
   A. You are off the course 12° to the left and must turn right to intercept the course of 149°
   B. You are on the course of 137° using a wind correction angle to compensate for a 22 knots wind from the east.
   C. You are on the course of 149° using a wind correction angle to compensate for a 22 knot wind from the east.

24. Why is a 45° angle commonly used when intercepting a bearing with an ADF?

25. Select the true statement regarding an RMI?
   A. You must constantly adjust the RMI compass card to match your magnetic heading.
   B. The number under the head of the bearing pointer is the magnetic bearing from the station.
   C. Relative bearing is the angle between the head of the bearing pointer and the aircraft heading index.

26. When you are tracking outbound from an NDB with the proper drift correction established, toward which direction will the head of the ADF bearing pointer be deflected?
   A. To the windward side of the aircraft's tail
   B. To the downwind side of the aircraft's tail
   C. To the downwind side of the aircraft's nose

27. What ADF or RMI indication would you expect when tracking on a bearing toward an NDB with a 10° left wind correction?
   A. 0° relative bearing
   B. 10° left of the aircraft's nose
   C. 10° right of the aircraft's nose

CHAPTER 3

The Flight Environment

Instrument/Commercial
Part I, Chapter 3 — The Flight Environment

SECTION A
Airports, Airspace, and Flight Information

Much of the information in this section is a review of subject areas you studied in your private pilot training. For additional information, refer to your private pilot textbook and the *Aeronautical Information Manual.*

THE AIRPORT ENVIRONMENT

To effectively conduct IFR flight operations you need a sound knowledge of the airport environment, which includes runway markings, airport signs, runway lighting, approach lighting systems, and associated airport lighting. The types of markings, signs, and lighting systems installed might vary from airport to airport, depending on size, traffic volume, and the types of operations and approaches authorized.

RUNWAY MARKINGS

Markings vary between runways used solely for VFR operations and those used for IFR operations. A **visual runway** usually is marked only with the runway number and a centerline, but threshold markings might be included if the runway is used, or intended to be used, for international commercial operations, and aiming point markings might be included on runways 4,000 feet or longer used by jet aircraft. [Figure 3-1]

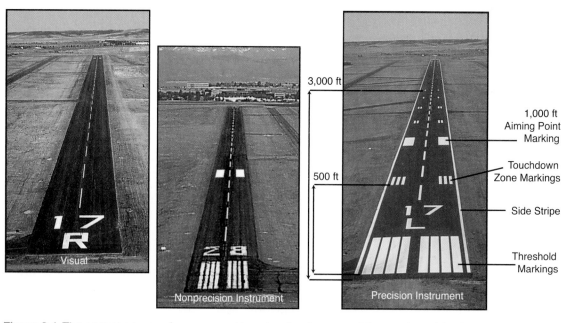

Figure 3-1. The common types of runway markings for visual, nonprecision, and precision instrument runways are shown here.

Runways used for instrument operations have additional markings. A **nonprecision instrument runway** is used with an instrument approach that does not have an electronic glide slope for approach glide path information. This type of runway has the visual runway markings, plus the threshold and aiming point markings.

As shown in figure 3-1, touchdown zone markings are located 500 feet from the beginning of the runway. Aiming point markings are 500 feet beyond the touchdown zone markings.

An Airport Project That Didn't Stay Afloat

In the 1920's, the economic range of a commercial airplane was approximately 500 to 600 miles. To fly farther than that nonstop, an airplane had to carry so much weight as fuel that it was difficult for companies to turn a profit. To make transatlantic air travel successful, Edward Armstrong, an engineer, had an idea to construct seadromes — floating airports strung across the ocean.

Armstrong designed a structure that consisted of a deck, approximately 1,500 feet long and 300 feet wide, placed on 28 steel columns, each 170 feet long. The seadrome was designed to float with the airfield deck 70 feet above the water's surface. A buoyancy chamber would be built into each column 100 feet below the deck, and 60 feet below that would be a ballast chamber filled with iron ore. The sea-drome would be attached to a buoy connected by two 18,000-foot steel cables to a concrete mushroom anchor. This system reduced the great strain that would have been caused by connecting the anchor line directly to the structure, and ensured that the seadrome was free to swing about into the wind. Propellers would allow the seadrome to maneuver while anchored and to navigate in an emergency.

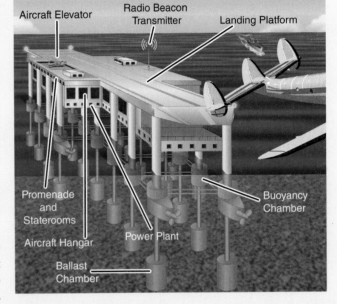

Beneath the deck of the seadrome, Armstrong envisioned hangars, which would use a large elevator to transport airplanes to and from the flight deck. In addition, there were plans for repair shops, a radio station, and a hotel. The 50-room hotel would feature a gymnasium, swimming pool, miniature golf course, billiard room, movie theater, bowling alley, and several tennis courts.

The seadrome project had enthusiastic approval from famous aviators such as Charles Lindbergh. However, it was discontinued by the U.S. government when concern arose about the difficulty of maintaining adequate protection of seadromes built over international waters.

Precision instrument runways are served by nonvisual precision approach aids, such as the instrument landing system (ILS). The ILS uses an electronic glide slope to provide glide path information during the approach. The associated runways are marked so you can receive important visual cues, especially during periods of extremely low visibility. Besides the threshold markings, touchdown zone markings are coded to provide distance information in 500 foot increments. Aiming point markings are located approximately 1,000 feet from the landing threshold.

TAXIWAY MARKINGS

The links between the airport parking areas and the runways are the **taxiways**. They are easily identified by a continuous yellow centerline stripe. At some airports, taxiway edge markings are used to define the edge of the taxiway and are normally used to separate the taxiway from pavement that is not intended for aircraft use. Runway holding position markings, or **hold lines**, are used to keep aircraft clear of runways and, at controlled airports, serve as the point that separates the responsibilities of ground control from those of the tower. Hold lines are usually placed between 125 and 250 feet from the runway centerline. In addition, hold lines can be located at taxiway intersections. At some airports, holding position signs might be used instead of, or in conjunction with, the hold lines painted on the taxiways.

SECTION A ■ **Airports, Airspace, and Flight Information**

At an uncontrolled airport, stop and check for traffic and cross the hold line only after ensuring that no one is on an approach to land. At a towered airport, the controller may ask you to hold short of the runway for landing traffic. In this case, stop before the hold line and proceed only after you are cleared to do so by the controller and you have checked for traffic. [Figure 3-2]

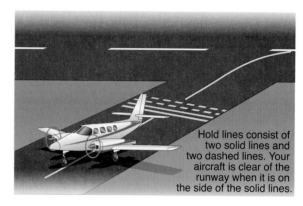

Figure 3-2. When you exit the runway after landing, be sure to cross the hold line before stopping to ensure that you are clear of the runway.

Hold lines consist of two solid lines and two dashed lines. Your aircraft is clear of the runway when it is on the side of the solid lines.

 FAA Hold line markings at the intersection of taxiways and runways consist of four yellow lines (two dashed lines and two solid lines). The dashed lines are nearest the runway.

At airports equipped with an instrument landing system, aircraft near the runway might interfere with the ILS signal. To prevent interference, the hold line might be placed farther from the runway, or you might find two hold lines for a runway. The one closest to the runway is the normal hold line, and the one farthest away is the ILS hold line. At other locations, only an ILS hold line might be used. [Figure 3-3]

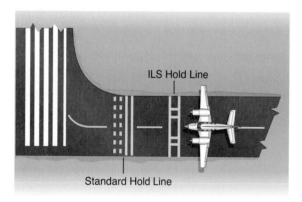

ILS Hold Line

Standard Hold Line

Figure 3-3. When ILS approaches are in progress, you might be asked by the controller to "...hold short of the ILS critical area."

ADDITIONAL MARKINGS

In addition to the markings previously discussed, other markings on runways and taxiways provide information on the permitted use of the surface. [Figure 3-4]

A **displaced threshold** is marked by a solid white line extending across the runway perpendicular to the centerline. It marks the point beyond which all normal takeoff and landing operations are permitted. The operations permitted prior to this point vary. Taxi, takeoff, and rollout areas are marked by white arrows leading to a displaced threshold. When landing, you must touch down beyond the displaced threshold. A taxi-only area is a designated portion of a runway to be used only for taxi operations. It is marked by a yellow taxi line leading to a displaced threshold. When taking off on such a runway, you may use the entire length. However, you must land beyond the displaced threshold marking. When departing from or arriving on the opposite end, you may not consider this area as usable for takeoff or landing, except as an overrun during an aborted takeoff.

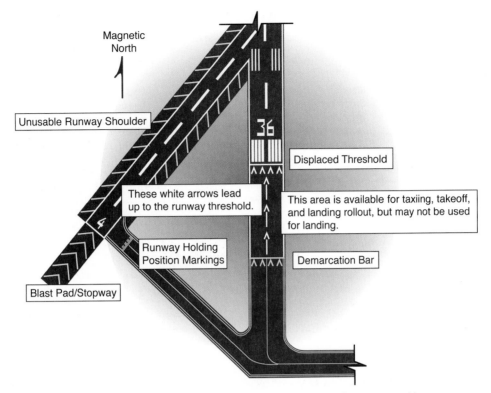

Figure 3-4. This illustration shows some samples of different types of runway markings.

Blast pad/stopway areas are marked by yellow chevrons and are not to be used for taxiing, takeoffs, or landings. The blast pad area allows propeller or jet blast to dissipate without creating a hazard to others. If you must abort a takeoff, the stopway provides additional paved surface for you to decelerate and stop. On some runways with a displaced threshold, a **demarcation bar** separates the displaced threshold area from a blast pad, stopway, or taxiway that precedes the runway.

A closed runway is marked with a large yellow X at each end. Although the closed, or temporarily closed runway may not be used, other runways and taxiways that cross it are not affected unless specifically marked. A closed taxiway might be marked by Xs, or it might simply be blocked off.

 On runways with a displaced threshold, the beginning portion of the landing zone is marked with a solid white line with white arrows leading up to it. Although the pavement leading up to a displaced threshold may not be used for landing, it may be available for taxiing, the landing rollout, and takeoffs.

 When clearing an active runway, you are most likely clear of the ILS critical area when you pass the ILS hold line or sign.

AIRPORT SIGNS

Major airports often have complex taxi routes, multiple runways, and widely dispersed parking areas. In addition, vehicular traffic in certain areas can be quite heavy. As shown in figure 3-5, most airfield signs are standardized to make it easy to identify taxi routes, mandatory holding positions, and boundaries for critical areas. If you fly outside the United States, most of the signs and markings will be familiar because U.S. standards are

FAA As shown in figure 3-5, a mandatory instruction sign has white lettering on a red background.

 Mandatory Instruction Signs denote an entrance to a runway, a critical area, or an area prohibited to aircraft. These signs are red with white letters or numbers. An example of a mandatory instruction sign is a runway holding position sign which is located at the holding position on taxiways that intersect a runway or on runways that intersect other runways.

Location Signs identify either the taxiway or runway where your aircraft is located. These signs are black with yellow inscriptions and a yellow border. Location signs also identify the runway boundary or ILS critical area for aircraft exiting the runway. On some taxiways you may see round pink geographical position signs. These sequentially numbered signs are used to help control taxiing aircraft during low visibility conditions.

 Direction Signs indicate directions of taxiways leading out of an intersection. They have black inscriptions on a yellow background and always contain arrows which show the approximate direction of turn.

 **Destination Signs** indicate the general direction to a location on the airport, such as civil aviation areas, military areas, international areas, or FBOs. They have black inscriptions on a yellow background and always contain an arrow.

Noise Sensitive Area Located Southeast of Runway 9/27

Information Signs advise you of such things as areas that cannot be seen from the control tower, applicable radio frequencies, and noise abatement procedures. These signs use yellow backgrounds with black inscriptions.

Runway Distance Remaining Signs are used to provide distance remaining information to pilots during takeoff and landing operations. The signs are located along the sides of the runway, and the inscription consists of a white numeral on a black background. The signs indicate the distance remaining in thousands of feet.

Figure 3-5. There are six basic types of airport signs — mandatory, location, direction, destination, information, and runway distance remaining.

practically the same as international specifications. Specifications for airport signs include size, height, location, and illumination requirements. [Figure 3-6]

Sometimes the installation of a sign is not practical so a surface-painted sign is used. Surface painted signs can include directional guidance or location information. For example, the runway number might be painted on the taxiway pavement near the taxiway hold line.

RUNWAY INCURSION AVOIDANCE

The official definition of a runway incursion is "any occurrence at an airport involving an aircraft, vehicle, person, or object on the ground that creates a collision hazard or results in loss of separation with an aircraft taking off or intending to take off, landing, or intending to land." Runway incursions are primarily caused by errors associated with clearances, communication, airport surface movement, and positional awareness. There are several procedures that you can follow and precautions that you can take to avoid a runway incursion.

1. During your preflight planning, study the airport layout by reviewing the airport diagram and taxi routes.

2. Complete as many checklist items as possible before taxi or while holding short.

3. Strive for clear and unambiguous pilot-controller communication. Read back (in full) all clearances involving active runway crossing, hold short, or line up and wait instructions.

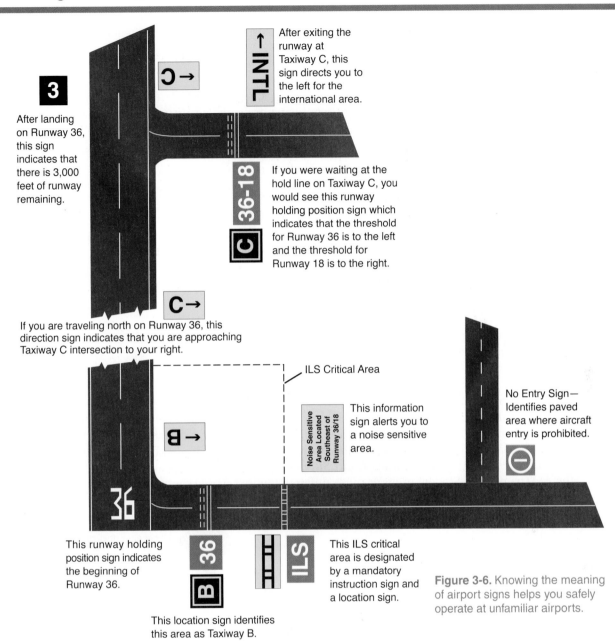

After exiting the runway at Taxiway C, this sign directs you to the left for the international area.

After landing on Runway 36, this sign indicates that there is 3,000 feet of runway remaining.

If you were waiting at the hold line on Taxiway C, you would see this runway holding position sign which indicates that the threshold for Runway 36 is to the left and the threshold for Runway 18 is to the right.

If you are traveling north on Runway 36, this direction sign indicates that you are approaching Taxiway C intersection to your right.

ILS Critical Area

This information sign alerts you to a noise sensitive area.

No Entry Sign— Identifies paved area where aircraft entry is prohibited.

This runway holding position sign indicates the beginning of Runway 36.

This ILS critical area is designated by a mandatory instruction sign and a location sign.

This location sign identifies this area as Taxiway B.

Figure 3-6. Knowing the meaning of airport signs helps you safely operate at unfamiliar airports.

 At controlled airports, runway incursions are often the result of misunderstood clearances, failure to correct an incorrect readback, and incorrect clearances.

 A No Entry sign identifies paved area where aircraft entry is prohibited.

4. While taxiing, know your precise location and concentrate on your primary responsibilities. Don't become absorbed in other tasks or conversation when the aircraft is moving.

5. If unsure of your position on the airport, stop and ask for assistance. At a controlled airport, you can request progressive taxi instructions.

6. If possible, when you are in a run-up area or waiting for a clearance, position your aircraft so you can see landing aircraft.

7. Monitor the appropriate radio frequencies for information or other aircraft cleared onto your runway for takeoff or landing. Be alert for aircraft that might be on other frequencies or without radio communication.

SECTION A ■ Airports, Airspace, and Flight Information

8. After landing, stay on the tower frequency until instructed to change frequencies.

9. To help others see your aircraft during periods of reduced visibility or at night, use your exterior taxi/landing lights, when practical.

10. Report deteriorating or confusing airport markings, signs, and lighting to the airport operator or FAA officials. Also report confusing or erroneous airport diagrams and instructions.

11. Make sure you understand the required procedures if you fly into or out of an airport where land and hold short operations are in effect.

LAND AND HOLD SHORT OPERATIONS (LAHSO)

At controlled airports, **land and hold short operations (LAHSO)** are sometimes used to allow air traffic controllers to make more efficient use of runways and taxiways during periods of heavy traffic. Although takeoffs and landings on intersecting runways might seem risky, LAHSO can be conducted safely provided pilots and controllers know the procedures and understand their responsibilities.

 Pilots should state their position on the airport when calling the tower for takeoff, especially when at an intersection.

PILOT RESPONSIBILITIES

At controlled airports, the tower may clear you to land and hold short of an intersecting runway or taxiway. Accepting the clearance indicates that you have determined that your aircraft can land safely and stop within the available landing distance (ALD). You can find the ALD for specific runways in the *Chart Supplement*, and controllers also will provide the ALD on request. Student pilots or pilots unfamiliar with LAHSO should not participate in the program. [Figure 3-7]

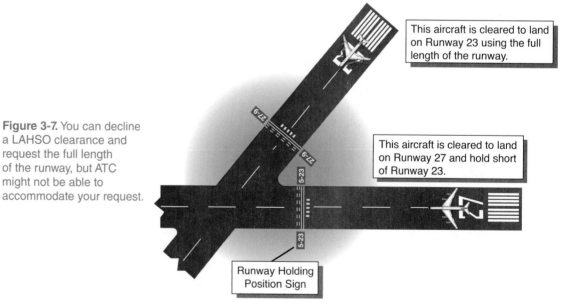

Figure 3-7. You can decline a LAHSO clearance and request the full length of the runway, but ATC might not be able to accommodate your request.

This aircraft is cleared to land on Runway 23 using the full length of the runway.

This aircraft is cleared to land on Runway 27 and hold short of Runway 23.

Runway Holding Position Sign

You have the option of requesting use of the full length of the runway by declining a LAHSO clearance. If you have the slightest doubt that you can land and stop within the ALD, decline a LAHSO clearance. If you decide to decline the clearance, let the controller know as soon as possible. In many situations, you can let ATC know you cannot accept a LAHSO clearance even before it is issued. ATIS broadcasts include LAHSO information,

A pilot has the option to accept or reject any LAHSO clearance regardless of weather conditions.

and good pilot decision making includes knowing in advance whether you can accept a LAHSO clearance if offered. As pilot in command, you are responsible for the safety of the flight, and you have final authority to accept or decline any LAHSO clearance. [Figure 3-8]

ATC: *"Cessna 1293 Golf, cleared to land Runway 6 Right, hold short of Taxiway Bravo for crossing traffic, a Baron."*

Controllers can provide information on the distance you will have available for landing.

Pilot: *"Cessna 1293 Golf, say available landing distance please."*
ATC: *"Cessna 1293 Golf, ALD 2,700 feet."*

If you are sure you can land in the available distance, remember to read back the hold short instructions when you acknowledge the clearance.

Pilot: *"Cessna 1293 Golf, wilco, cleared to land Runway 6 Right, to hold short of Taxiway Bravo."*

Never hesitate to decline a LAHSO clearance if you are at all uncertain of your ability to comply.

Pilot: *"Cessna 1293 Golf, unable to hold short."*

Figure 3-8. Effective pilot-controller communication is crucial when LAHSO procedures are in use.

To prepare for a possible LAHSO clearance, become familiar with all available information on the use of these procedures at your destination airport. You should have available the published ALD and runway combinations, as well as the details of the landing distance for your airplane, given the existing conditions. Be sure to consider the possibility that controllers might ask you to keep your speed up on final, which might cause you to float some distance down the runway before touchdown. Controllers need a full readback of all LAHSO clearances. ATC expects you to do this without prompting. Do not make the controller have to ask for a readback.

You also need to thoroughly understand the airport markings used for LAHSO operations. Review the chapter on Aeronautical Lighting and Other Airport Visual Aids in the *Aeronautical Information Manual* (AIM). LAHSO visual aids include yellow hold-short markings, red and white signage, and in some cases, in-pavement lighting.

After you accept a LAHSO clearance, you must adhere to it like any other ATC clearance, unless you obtain an amended clearance or experience an emergency. A LAHSO clearance does not preclude a rejected landing. However, if you have to go around, maintain safe separation from other aircraft and notify the controller immediately.

If you fly as part of a multi-person crew, effective communication within the cockpit is also critical. In several instances, the pilot operating the radios accepted a LAHSO clearance and forgot to tell the pilot flying the aircraft. As you can imagine, failure to conduct LAHSO properly can result in a fatal collision.

SECTION A ■ Airports, Airspace, and Flight Information

LIGHTING SYSTEMS

Airport lighting systems range from the simple lighting needed for VFR night landings to sophisticated systems that guide you to the runway in IFR conditions. Familiarize yourself with each type of lighting and its significance to VFR and IFR operations.

APPROACH LIGHT SYSTEM

The approach light system (ALS) helps you transition from instrument to visual references during the approach to landing. It makes the runway environment more apparent in low visibility conditions and helps you maintain correct alignment with the runway. Approach light systems use a configuration of lights starting at the landing threshold and extending into the approach area. Normally, they extend outward to a distance of 2,400 to 3,000 feet from precision instrument runways and 1,400 to 1,500 feet from nonprecision instrument runways.

Some approach light systems include **sequenced flashing lights (SFL)** or **runway alignment indicator lights (RAIL)**. SFL and RAIL consist of a series of brilliant blue-white bursts of flashing light. From your viewpoint, these systems give the impression of a ball of light traveling at high speed toward the approach end of the runway. SFL and RAIL usually are incorporated into other approach light systems. Examples of systems with sequenced flashing lights include ALSF (Approach Lighting System with Sequenced Flashing Lights), MALSF (Medium-intensity Approach Lighting System with Sequenced Flashing Lights), and ODALS (Omnidirectional Approach Lighting System). [Figure 3-9]

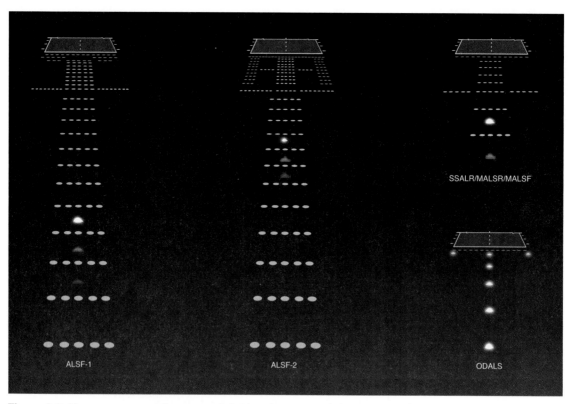

Figure 3-9. Here are some of the approach light systems you might encounter. In these illustrations, the △ symbol represents the sequenced flashing white strobe lights that give the impression of a ball of light racing toward the runway.

At some locations, two synchronized flashing strobe lights are placed at the runway threshold, one on each side of the runway. These high intensity white lights, called **runway end identifier lights (REIL)**, appear with the green threshold lights to help you identify the threshold of a runway surrounded by a preponderance of other lighting, one that lacks contrast with surrounding terrain, or in reduced visibility. They are normally aimed 10° up and 15° away from the runway centerline.

 REIL refers to a pair of synchronized flashing lights that provide rapid identification of the approach end of the runway during low visibility conditions.

VISUAL GLIDE SLOPE INDICATORS

After you have the runway environment in sight, visual glide slope indicators help you establish and maintain a safe descent path to the runway. Their purpose is to provide a clear visual means to determine if you are too high, too low, or on the correct glide path. These indicators are extremely useful during low visibility, or at night, when it might be difficult to judge the descent angle accurately due to a lack of runway contrast. Several different visual glide slope indicator systems are used, but one of the most common is the two-bar **visual approach slope indicator (VASI)**. The two-bar system provides one visual glide path, normally set to 3°. Staying on the VASI glide path assures you of safe obstruction clearance within ±10° of the extended runway centerline and out to 4 nautical miles from the threshold. When using a VASI, fly your approach so the far bars indicate red and the near bars show white. These are the proper light indications for maintaining the glide slope. VASI lights are visible from 3 to 5 miles during the day and up to 20 miles at night.

 If you remain on the proper glide path of a VASI, you are assured safe obstruction clearance in the approach area. Two-bar VASIs normally have an approach angle of three degrees, unless a higher angle is necessary for obstacle clearance. They show red over white when you are on the glide path. See figure 3-10.

Some airports are equipped with three-bar VASI systems consisting of three sets of light sources forming near, middle, and far bars. These systems provide two visual glide paths to the same runway. The first uses the near and middle bars. This glide path is the same as that provided by a standard two-bar VASI installation. The second uses the middle and far bars. This upper glide path is intended for use only by pilots of high-cockpit aircraft and is about one-quarter of a degree steeper than the first. The far bars are located approximately 700 feet beyond the middle bars. When on the upper glide path, the pilot sees red, white, and white. [Figure 3-10]

 The middle and far bars of a three-bar VASI can be used to descend on the upper glide path, which is usually 0.25° steeper than the lower glide path. See figure 3-10.

 When planning a night cross-country flight, be sure to check the availability and status of destination airport lighting systems.

 You are required to turn on anti-collision lights during all operations, day or night, unless you determine that it would improve safety to turn them off.

SECTION A ■ **Airports, Airspace, and Flight Information**

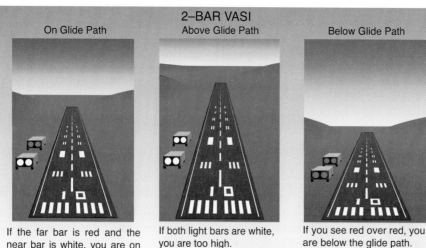

2-BAR VASI

On Glide Path — Above Glide Path — Below Glide Path

If the far bar is red and the near bar is white, you are on the glide path. The memory aid "red over white, you're all right," is helpful in recalling the correct sequence of lights.

If both light bars are white, you are too high.

If you see red over red, you are below the glide path.

Figure 3-10. If you are approaching a runway and all the VASI lights appear to be red, level off momentarily to intercept the proper approach path.

3–BAR VASI

Upper Glide Path	Low	Low	On Glide Path	High
Lower Glide Path	Low	On Glide Path	High	High

FAA If you are conducting an approach to a runway that has a 3-bar VASI and all the VASI lights appear red as you reach the MDA, you should level off momentarily to intercept the proper approach path.

Some airports have a **pulsating visual approach slope indicator (PVASI)** that projects a two-color visual approach path into the final approach area. A pulsating red light indicates you are below the glide path. A steady red light indicates you are slightly below the glide path, and a pulsating white light indicates that you are above the glide path. The on-glide path indication is a steady white light. The useful range is about 4 miles during the day and up to 10 miles at night.

The **precision approach path indicator (PAPI)** uses lights similar to VASI, but the lights are installed in a single row of two- or four-light units. PAPI normally is located on the left side of the runway. [Figure 3-11]

FAA An on-glide path indication from a PAPI is two red lights and two white lights. See figure 3-11.

TRI-COLOR VASI
Another system, which consists of a single light unit projecting a three-color visual glide path into the final approach area of the runway, is referred to as **tri-color VASI**. Depending on visibility conditions, this type of approach slope indicator has a useful range of approximately one-half to one mile during the day and up to five miles at night. [Figure 3-12]

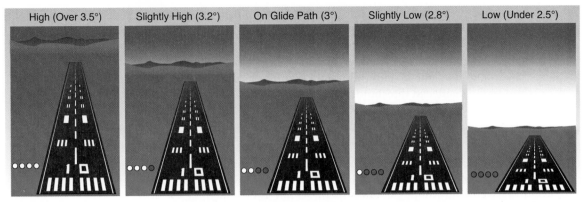

High (Over 3.5°)	Slightly High (3.2°)	On Glide Path (3°)	Slightly Low (2.8°)	Low (Under 2.5°)
If all the PAPI system lights are white, you are too high.	If only the light on the far right is red and the other three are white, you are slightly high.	When you are on the glide path, the two lights on the left are white and the two lights on the right are red.	If you are slightly low, only the light on the far left is white.	If you are below the glide path, all four of the lights are red.

Figure 3-11. The PAPI is normally located on the left side of the runway and can be seen up to 5 miles during the day and 20 miles at night.

 Tri-color VASIs normally consist of one light projector with three colors — amber, green, and red. See figure 3-12.

Figure 3-12. The tri-color VASI uses amber, green, and red lights to show your position with respect to the glide path.

As you descend below the glide path, you may see dark amber during the transition from green light to red, so you should not be deceived into thinking you are too high.

Above Glide Path

On Glide Path

Below Glide Path

RUNWAY LIGHTING

Runway lights outline the landing area by clearly defining its boundaries. Some of these systems have bidirectional features that help you judge your position from the ends of the runway. A thorough understanding of runway lighting is important, particularly during low-visibility, IFR operations.

Runway edge lights are used to outline the runway during periods of darkness or restricted visibility. They are classified according to their brightness — high intensity runway lights (HIRL), medium intensity runway lights (MIRL), and low intensity runway lights (LIRL). The HIRL and MIRL systems have variable intensity controls that may be adjusted from the control tower or by the pilot using the CTAF or UNICOM frequency. The LIRL system normally has only one intensity setting. Runway edge lights are white, except on instrument runways, where amber replaces white on the last 2,000 feet or half the runway length, whichever is less, to indicate a caution zone.

Bidirectional **threshold lights** mark the ends of each runway. As you approach for landing, the lights appear green, indicating the beginning of the landing portion of the runway. As viewed during takeoff in the opposite direction, the threshold lights appear red, marking the departure end of the runway. The threshold lights form a line across the runway perpendicular to the centerline.

SECTION A ■ **Airports, Airspace, and Flight Information**

Lights also help you identify a displaced threshold during low visibility conditions or at night. **Displaced threshold lights** also appear green during approach to a landing, Do not land short of these lights. The absence of runway edge lights prior to the green threshold lights is another cue that no operations are authorized short of the displaced threshold. However, if taxi, takeoff, and rollout are permitted, runway edge lights will mark the area short of the displaced threshold.

You may use the area short of the displaced threshold lights for taxi, takeoff, or rollout purposes when the runway edge lights appear in one of the following combinations:

1. When taxiing for takeoff onto the area of a runway short of the displaced landing threshold, and looking down the runway, the runway edge lights appear red until you get to the threshold and after the threshold, they are white.

2. If the area short of the displaced landing threshold is permissible for landing rollout in the opposite direction, the threshold lights will not be visible from that direction; instead, opposite direction traffic sees red threshold lights at the end of the runway that is usable for them. The edge lights leading to the end of the runway appear yellow for the last 2,000 feet leading to the end of the usable portion of the runway.

 Red runway edge lights signify a displaced threshold, where taxi, takeoff, and rollout operations are permitted.

What's New at Newark?

In 1928, the city of Newark, New Jersey transformed an area of marshland into the Newark Metropolitan Airport, which had the first hard-surfaced runway of any commercial airport in the United States. Designated as the eastern airmail terminal and official airport for the metropolitan area, Newark Metropolitan soon gained the reputation as the busiest airport in the world. Newark became a testing ground for airport control systems, and experiments conducted there aided the development of instrument landing approaches. Initially, Newark's traffic was controlled by an official who stood near the runway and waved aircraft in and out with flags.

At night, the airport was illuminated with floodlights mounted on a platform. Since it was too costly to keep these powerful lights on all night, an invention called Televox was tested in 1929. A pilot approaching the darkened field cranked the handle of a siren in the cockpit and the sound activated a device that switched on the floodlights. The Televox system was adopted at many airports. Newark also experimented with lights embedded in the center of the runway. In addition, wires were installed at right angles to the runway that emitted signals heard as clicks in the pilot's headset. The clicks indicated at what point the airplane was on the approach.

Touchdown zone lighting (TDZL) helps you identify the touchdown zone when visibility is reduced. It consists of a series of white lights flush-mounted in the runway. They begin approximately 100 feet from the landing threshold and extend 3,000 feet down the runway or to the midpoint of the runway, whichever is less. These lights are visible only from the approach end of the runway.

Runway centerline lights (RCLS) are flush-mounted in the runway to help you maintain the centerline during takeoff and landing. They are spaced at intervals of 50 feet, beginning 75 feet from the landing threshold and extending to within 75 feet of the opposite end of the runway. As you approach the runway, the centerline lights first appear white. They change to alternating red and white lights when you have 3,000 feet of remaining runway, then they show all red for the last 1,000 feet of runway. These lights are bidirectional, so you see the correct lighting from either direction.

Land and hold short lights are a row of five flush-mounted flashing white lights installed at the hold short point, perpendicular to the centerline of the runway on which they are installed. Land and hold short lights will normally be on when land and hold short operations are being conducted continuously. Therefore, departing pilots and pilots who are cleared to land using the full length of the runway should ignore the lights.

Taxiway lead-off lights are similar to runway centerline lights. They generally are flush-mounted alternating green and yellow lights spaced at 50-foot intervals. They define the curved path of an aircraft from a point near the runway centerline to the center of the intersecting taxiway. When installed, taxiway centerline lights are green and taxiway edge lights are blue.

Pilot-controlled lighting is designed primarily to conserve energy and is found at some airports that do not have a full-time tower. Typically, you control the lights by keying the aircraft microphone a specified number of times in a given number of seconds. For example, you can key the microphone 7 times in 5 seconds to turn on the lights to maximum intensity. To reduce the lighting level, key the microphone the number of times specified. However, you should be aware that using the lower intensity on some installations might turn the runway end identifier lights completely off. The lights normally turn off automatically 15 minutes after they were last activated. You can find information on pilot-controlled lighting and the airports where they are installed in the *Chart Supplement,* the *Jeppesen Airport Information Directory,* and on applicable instrument approach procedure charts.

AIRPORT BEACON AND OBSTRUCTION LIGHTS

Some of the other lights that are located at or near airports include the airport beacon and obstruction lighting. The beacon helps you to locate the airport at night and during conditions of reduced visibility. Operation of the beacon during daylight hours at an airport within controlled airspace (Class B, C, D, and E surface areas) often indicates that the ground visibility is less than 3 statute miles and/or the ceiling is less than 1,000 feet. However, because beacons are often turned on by photoelectric cells or time clocks, you must not rely on the airport beacon to indicate that the weather is below VFR minimums. An ATC clearance is required if you wish to take off or land when the weather is below VFR minimums.

Obstruction lights are installed on prominent structures such as towers, buildings and sometimes power lines. Flashing red lights or high intensity strobe lights warn you of the obstructions. [Figure 3-13]

AIRCRAFT LIGHTING

As a professional pilot, much of your flying will likely be at night, and the higher workloads and congested airspace associated with busier airports require you to be able to interpret the lights of other aircraft quickly and accurately. If you practice visualizing the patterns that are made by the position lights of other aircraft, recognition will soon become automatic. Your own position lights must be on from sunset to sunrise. To help air traffic controllers and other pilots to see your airplane, regulations require your anti-collision lights to be on for all operations, day and night, unless the pilot in command determines that it would be safer to turn them off. [Figure 3-14]

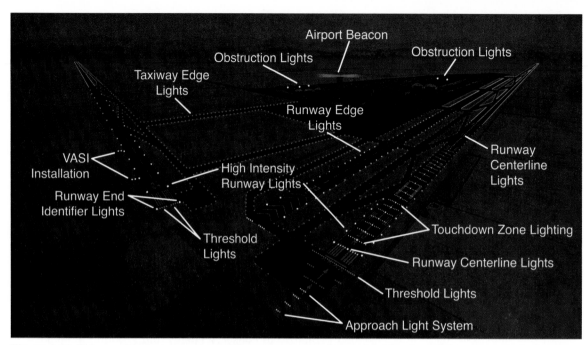

Figure 3-13. This graphic summary shows the various types of airport lighting found at large, controlled airports.

 If the airport is located within controlled airspace, operation of the airport beacon during daylight hours might indicate that the ground visibility is less than 3 statute miles and/or the ceiling is less than 1,000 feet. An ATC clearance is required for takeoffs and landings if the weather conditions are less than VFR.

 Red flashing light beacons indicate obstructions that are hazardous to aircraft.

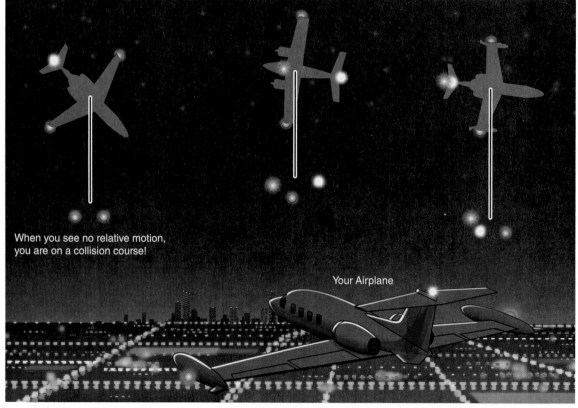

When you see no relative motion, you are on a collision course!

Your Airplane

Figure 3-14. Interpreting the position lights of other aircraft is especially important when there is no relative motion to tell you which way the aircraft is moving.

Anti-collision lights are required to be on during all types of operations, day and night, unless the pilot in command determines that it would be in the interest of safety to turn them off.

 If there is no apparent relative motion between your aircraft and another aircraft, you are probably on a collision course.

 By interpreting the position lights of other aircraft, you can determine which direction the aircraft is heading.

AIRSPACE

Within the United States, airspace is classified as either controlled or uncontrolled. Special use airspace and other airspace areas are additional classifications that can include both controlled and uncontrolled segments. The requirements for aircraft equipment, communication with ATC, flight visibility, and distances from clouds vary with the class of airspace and with altitude. As pilot in command, you must know which requirements apply in each type of airspace.

CONTROLLED AIRSPACE

Controlled airspace means an airspace of defined dimensions within which air traffic control service is provided to IFR flights and to VFR flights in accordance with the airspace classification. Controlled airspace is a generic term that covers Class A, Class B, Class C, Class D, and Class E airspace. As a routine measure, when you are operating under IFR, your flight must conform with ATC clearances from takeoff to touchdown, and your transponder must be on, including Mode C if installed. During this time, ATC provides separation between your aircraft and all other IFR flights. If workload permits, ATC also provides traffic advisories for VFR operations. It is very important to remember that controllers are not required to separate your aircraft from VFR flights and cannot provide separation from aircraft that do not appear on their radar display. [Figure 3-15]

VFR IN CONTROLLED AIRSPACE		
Altitude	**Flight Visibility**	**Distance From Clouds**
Class A	Not Applicable	Not Applicable
Class B	3 Statute Miles	Clear of Clouds
Class C and Class D	3 Statute Miles	500 Feet Below 1,000 Feet Above 2,000 Feet Horizontal
Class E: Less Than 10,000 Feet MSL	3 Statute Miles	500 Feet Below 1,000 Feet Above 2,000 Feet Horizontal
At or Above 10,000 Feet MSL	5 Statute Miles	1,000 Feet Below 1,000 Feet Above 1 Statute Mile Horizontal

Figure 3-15 The basic weather minimums that apply in Class A, B, C, D, and E controlled airspace are listed in FAR 91.155. VFR flight is not permitted in Class A airspace.

 As shown in figure 3-15, VFR requirements for flight visibility and distance from clouds change depending on the class of the controlled airspace.

SECTION A ■ **Airports, Airspace, and Flight Information**

SECTION A ■ Airports, Airspace, and Flight Information

To fly in controlled airspace within the contiguous United States, your aircraft must meet certain equipment requirements. The FARs require that you have an operating transponder with Mode C capability in Class A airspace, Class B airspace, within 30 nautical miles of Class B primary airports, and in and above Class C airspace. In addition, you must have a Mode C transponder when flying at or above 10,000 feet MSL, excluding the airspace at and

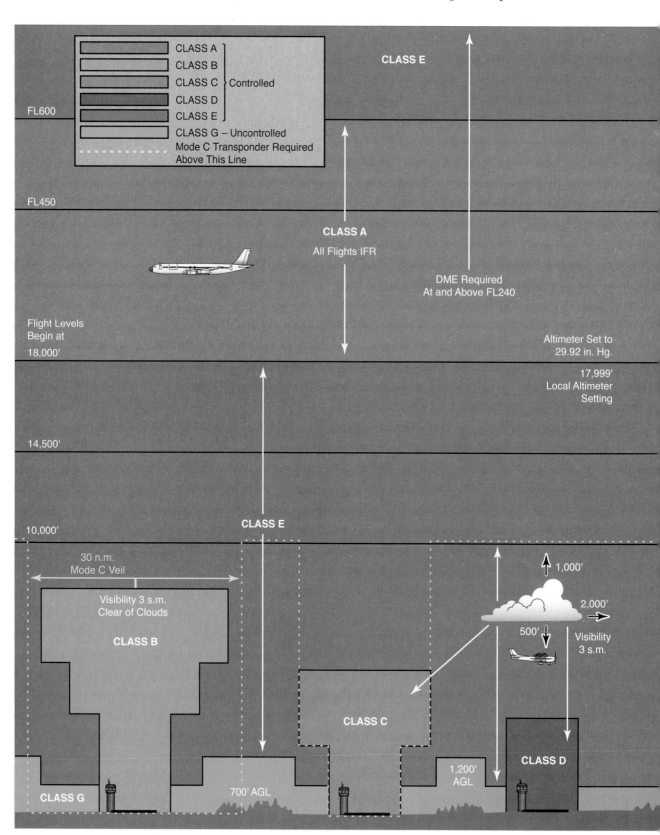

below 2,500 feet AGL. This requirement applies in all airspace (controlled or uncontrolled) within the 48 contiguous states and the District of Columbia. [Figure 3-16]

 A transponder with Mode C capability is required to operate in Class B airspace, within 30 nautical miles of a Class B primary airport, and in and above Class C airspace.

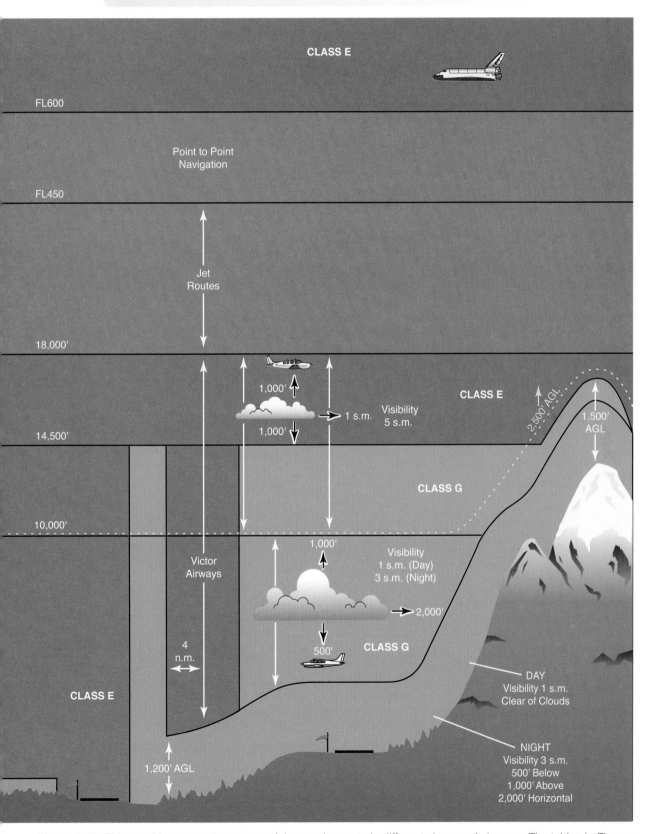

Figure 3-16. This graphic summarizes many of the requirements in different classes of airspace. The tables in Figures 3-15 and 3-22 explain most of the other requirements

CLASS A AIRSPACE

Within the contiguous United States, **Class A airspace** extends from 18,000 feet MSL up to and including FL600. Since VFR flight is not permitted in this area, your instrument training might provide your first opportunity to fly in Class A airspace. Instrument high altitude enroute charts must be used for flights in Class A airspace.

 Over most of the United States , Class A airspace extends from 18,000 feet MSL to FL600.

 A transponder with Mode C is required everywhere in the 48 contiguous states and the District of Columbia at and above 10,000 feet MSL, except at or below 2,500 feet AGL. This means a transponder is also required in Class A airspace.

Because aircraft in Class A airspace typically operate at high speeds, it would be impractical for pilots to reset their altimeters every 100 nautical miles. So, within Class A airspace, you are required to use a standard setting of 29.92 in. Hg. This means that all pilots are maintaining their assigned altitudes using the same altimeter reference. In addition, altitudes are prefaced by the letters FL, meaning flight level, with the last two zeros omitted. For example, 35,000 feet is called FL350.

To fly in Class A airspace, you must adhere to the following guidelines:

1. If acting as pilot in command, you must be rated and current for instrument flight.

2. You must operate under an IFR flight plan and in accordance with an ATC clearance at specified flight levels.

3. Your aircraft must be equipped with instruments and equipment required for IFR operations, including an encoding altimeter and transponder. You are also required to have a radio providing direct pilot/controller communication on the frequency specified by ATC for the area concerned. In addition, you must have navigation equipment appropriate to the ground facilities to be used.

4. When VOR equipment is required for navigation, your aircraft must also be equipped with distance measuring equipment (DME) or a suitable RNAV system if the flight is conducted at or above 24,000 feet MSL. If the DME fails in flight, you must immediately notify ATC. Then, you may continue to operate at or above 24,000 feet MSL and proceed to the next airport of intended landing where repairs can be made.

 To fly in Class A airspace, you must be instrument-rated and current, and on an IFR flight plan. The aircraft must be IFR equipped and, in most cases, DME is required at or above 24,000 feet MSL. If the DME fails, you must notify ATC, but you can continue to the next airport of intended landing and have it repaired.

CLASS B AIRSPACE

At some of the country's busiest airports, **Class B airspace** has been established to separate all arriving and departing traffic. Generally, this airspace is from the surface to 10,000 feet MSL. The airspace consists of a surface area and two or more layers, which are unique for each Class B airspace since they are designed to facilitate traffic separation at a particular terminal. Pilot participation is mandatory, and an ATC clearance must be received before you enter a Class B area. Some of the Class B airspace areas have VFR corridors to allow pilots of VFR aircraft to pass through them without contacting ATC.

 The upper limit for most Class B airspace areas is 10,000 feet MSL. In Denver and Salt Lake City, it is 12,000 feet MSL.

To operate under VFR in Class B airspace, your aircraft must have a two-way radio and a 4096-code or Mode S transponder with Mode C automatic altitude reporting. To operate IFR in Class B airspace, you must also have a VOR receiver or suitable RNAV equipment.

In addition, to take off or land at certain large airports listed in Appendix D of FAR 91, you must hold at least a private pilot certificate. With certain exceptions, a transponder with altitude reporting capability is required anytime you are operating within 30 nautical miles of the primary airport from the surface upward to 10,000 feet MSL.

 To operate in Class B airspace, you must be at least a private pilot, or a student pilot with the appropriate endorsement. However, at certain large airports, student pilot operations are not allowed.

 If your transponder fails within Class B airspace, ATC may authorize you to continue to your destination. If your transponder doesn't have Mode C, ATC may authorize you to enter Class B airspace, but you must ask them while still outside of Class B airspace. If you don't have any transponder, you must call ATC and request approval to operate in Class B airspace at least one hour ahead of time.

CLASS C AIRSPACE

Class C airspace areas are designated at certain airports where ATC can provide radar service for all aircraft. Normally, Class C airspace consists of 2 circular centered on the primary airport. The core area starts at ground level and has a diameter of 10 nautical miles. A larger diameter shelf area normally starts at 1,200 feet AGL and has a diameter of 20 nautical miles. Both typically have upper limits of 4,000 feet above the primary airport. In addition, there is an outer area that is not shown on aeronautical charts. The outer area extends 10 nautical miles beyond the shelf area, and its vertical limits extend from the lower limits of radar/radio coverage up to the ceiling of approach control's delegated airspace Although it is not required, you are strongly encouraged to talk to ATC during flights within the outer area. Before entering the core and shelf areas, you must establish two-way communication with the ATC facility having jurisdiction over the area and maintain radio contact at all times. If you depart a satellite airport located within Class C airspace, you must establish two-way communication with ATC as soon as practicable. [Figure 3-17]

 In the outer area of Class C airspace, ATC provides separation from all IFR aircraft and from participating VFR aircraft.

 You must have two-way radio communication equipment within Class B and C airspace. IFR operations in Class B airspace also require VOR or RNAV equipment.

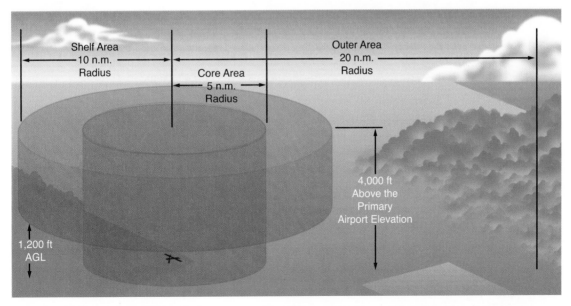

Figure 3-17. The simplest Class C airspace consists of two concentric circles centered on the primary airport. In many locations these areas have irregular boundary shapes or are divided into several sections with different altitude limits. The larger outer area is not depicted on aeronautical charts.

All aircraft operating in Class C airspace, and in all airspace above the ceiling and within the lateral boundaries extending upward to 10,000 feet MSL, must be equipped with an operable transponder with Mode C. Aircraft operating in the airspace beneath Class C airspace will not be required to have a transponder with Mode C.

CLASS D AIRSPACE

Class D airspace areas are designated at airports with operating control towers that are not associated with Class B or C airspace. Before you enter Class D airspace you must establish and maintain two-way radio communication with the control tower. When departing the primary airport within Class D airspace, you must also establish and maintain communication with the tower. At an airport with a part-time control tower, the airspace is Class D only when the control tower is operating.

 You are required to establish communication with the tower before entering Class D airspace.

 If your transponder fails during flight within Class D airspace, no deviation is required because a transponder is not required in Class D airspace.

 At part-time tower locations, Class D airspace normally becomes Class E airspace when the tower is closed. However, if weather observations and reporting are not available, the airspace becomes Class G.

At some locations, there might be a satellite airport within the same Class D airspace designated for the primary airport. If the satellite airport also has a control tower, similar radio communication requirements with that tower prevail for arrivals and departures. If the satellite airport is a nontowered field, arriving aircraft must establish contact with the primary airport's control tower. Departures from a nontowered satellite airport must establish communication with the ATC facility (tower) having jurisdiction over the Class D airspace as soon as practicable after departing. To the maximum extent practical and consistent with safety, satellite airports have been excluded from Class D airspace. [Figure 3-18]

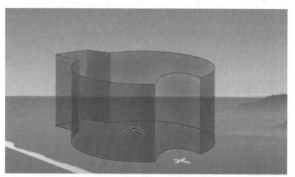

Figure 3-18. At some locations, a satellite airport without an operating control tower might have airspace carved out of the Class D airspace, or it could be placed under a shelf of the Class D airspace.

The ceiling of a Class D airspace area is usually 2,500 feet above the surface of the airport converted to mean sea level, and rounded to the nearest 100-foot increment. If conditions of a particular airspace area warrant, the ceiling might be raised or lowered as appropriate. The ceiling of Class D airspace is shown in hundreds of feet MSL on sectional charts. Laterally, Class D airspace (depicted as blue dashed lines on sectional charts) normally consists of a circular area with a 4 nautical mile radius. However, because the airspace is based on the instrument procedures for which the controlled airspace is established, the lateral dimensions might be larger or smaller and can be irregular in shape.

 Normally, the upper limit of Class D airspace is 2,500 feet AGL and the lateral limits are approximately 4 nautical miles.

CLASS E AIRSPACE

Much of the remaining controlled airspace is designated as **Class E airspace**, which includes several different segments. One portion of Class E consists of the airspace covering the 48 contiguous states, District of Columbia, and Alaska. Also included is the airspace out to 12 nautical miles from the coastlines. Unless designated at a lower altitude, Class E airspace begins at 14,500 feet MSL and extends up to, but not including, the base of the Class A airspace at 18,000 feet MSL. The only exceptions are the Alaska peninsula west of 160° west longitude and airspace within 1,500 feet of the surface.

During flight in Class E airspace between 14,500 and 18,000 feet MSL, you have no additional operating requirements beyond those mentioned previously. For example, you must operate the Mode C feature of your transponder when at or above 10,000 feet MSL, excluding the airspace at or below 2,500 feet AGL, and apply the appropriate cloud clearance and visibility requirements when flying under VFR. Remember that you cannot fly VFR above FL180, which is Class A airspace.

Another segment of Class E airspace is the low altitude airway system connecting one navaid to another. These routes are used by VFR as well as IFR aircraft, and are called Federal airways, or Victor airways. These airways are based on VOR or VORTAC navigation aids and are identified by a V and the airway number. A few airways are based on L/MF (low/medium frequency) navigation aids, or NDBs. The only L/MF airways still in use are in Alaska and coastal North Carolina. Airways are usually 8 nautical miles wide, begin at 1,200 feet AGL, and extend up to, but not including 18,000 feet MSL. Some airway segments, such as those over mountainous terrain, might have a floor greater than 1,200 feet AGL, which is designated on sectional charts. VFR cloud clearance and visibility requirements on an airway depend on your cruising altitude. [Figure 3-19]

SECTION A ■ Airports, Airspace, and Flight Information

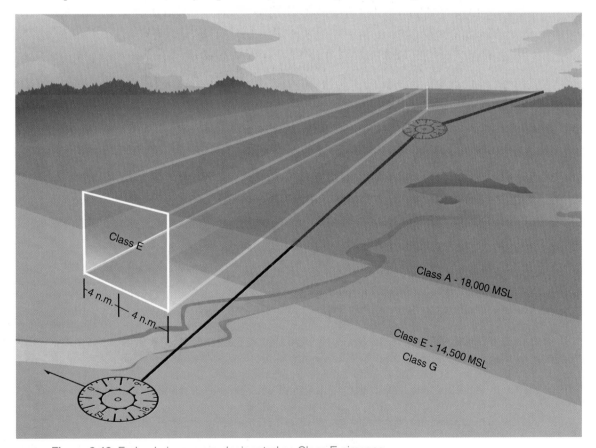

Figure 3-19. Federal airways are designated as Class E airspace.

Federal airways normally begin at 1,200 feet above the surface, extend upward to 18,000 feet MSL, and include the airspace within 4 nautical miles each side of the airway centerline.

Class E airspace transitional areas have also been established between airports and the airway route system to allow IFR traffic to remain in controlled airspace while transitioning between the enroute and airport environments. These segments of Class E airspace usually begin at 1,200 feet AGL if they are associated with an airway. Transitional areas are outlined on sectional charts only if they border uncontrolled airspace.

Some airports located in Class E or Class G airspace areas have operating control towers. You are required by FARs to establish radio communication prior to 4 nautical miles from the airport (up to and including 2,500 feet AGL) and to maintain radio contact with the tower while in the area.

At nontower airports that have an approved instrument approach procedure, Class E transition airspace often begins at 700 feet above the surface. At some nontower airports, Class E airspace extends upward from the surface, and usually encompasses airspace surrounding the airport, in addition to the extensions to accommodate arrivals and departures. Both of these types of Class E airspace are depicted on aeronautical charts. [Figure 3-20]

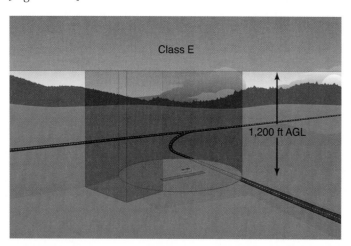

Class E

1,200 ft AGL

Figure 3-20. This nontowered airport is surrounded by Class E airspace that begins at the surface and adjoins Class E airspace, which begins at 1,200 feet AGL.

 The floor of the Class E airspace that is used as a transition area for an airport with an approved instrument approach procedure is 700 feet AGL and extends to the overlying controlled airspace.

SPECIAL VFR

In addition to maintaining the VFR minimums specified in figure 3-14, you may only operate within the areas of Class B, C, D, or E airspace that extend to the surface around an airport, when the ground visibility is at least 3 statute miles and the cloud ceiling is at least 1,000 feet AGL. If ground visibility is not reported, you can use flight visibility. When the weather is below these VFR minimums, and there is no conflicting IFR traffic, a **special VFR clearance** may be obtained from the ATC facility having jurisdiction over the affected airspace. A special VFR clearance can allow you to enter, leave, or operate within most Class D and Class E surface areas and some Class B and Class C surface areas if the flight visibility is at least 1 statute mile and you can remain clear of clouds. At least one statute mile ground visibility is required for takeoff and landing; however, if ground visibility is not reported, you must have at least 1 statute mile flight visibility.

 Special VFR clearances require you to maintain a minimum ground visibility (or flight visibility, if ground visibility is not reported) of one mile and remain clear of clouds.

Special VFR is not permitted between sunset and sunrise unless you have a current instrument rating and the aircraft is equipped for instrument flight. In addition, special VFR clearances are not issued to fixed-wing aircraft (day or night) at the airports that are listed in Section 3 of Appendix D of FAR 91.

 To operate an airplane under special VFR at night within Class D airspace, you must hold an instrument rating and the airplane must be equipped for instrument flight.

CLASS G AIRSPACE (UNCONTROLLED)

Class G airspace is the airspace that has not been designated as Class A, B, C, D, or E airspace and is essentially uncontrolled by ATC. For example, the airspace below a Class E airspace area or below a Victor airway is normally uncontrolled. Most Class G airspace terminates at the base of Class E airspace at 700 or 1,200 feet AGL, or at 14,500 feet MSL. An exception to this rule occurs when 14,500 feet MSL is lower than 1,500 feet AGL. In this situation, Class G airspace continues up to 1,500 feet above the surface. The amount of uncontrolled airspace has steadily declined because of the expanding need to coordinate the movement of aircraft.

 Except for temporary control towers, ATC does not exercise control of air traffic in Class G airspace.

 The maximum altitude for Class G airspace is 14,500 feet MSL, except where that altitude is below 1,500 feet AGL.

Except when associated with a temporary control tower, ATC does not have responsibility for or authority over aircraft in Class G airspace; however, most of the regulations affecting pilots and aircraft still apply. For example, although a flight plan is not required for IFR operations in Class G airspace, both pilot and aircraft must still be fully qualified for IFR flight. In addition, in several cases, the day weather minimums for VFR flight are lower than those in controlled airspace. [Figure 3-21]

VFR CLASS G AIRSPACE (UNCONTROLLED)		
Altitude	**Flight Visibility**	**Distance From Clouds**
1,200 feet or less above the surface (regardless of MSL altitude)	Day: 1 s.m.	Clear of Clouds
	Night: 3 s.m.	500 Feet Below 1,000 Feet Above 2,000 Feet Horizontal
More than 1,200 feet above the surface, but less than 10,000 feet MSL	Day: 1 s.m. Night: 3 s.m.	500 Feet Below 1,000 Feet Above 2,000 Feet Horizontal
More than 1,200 feet above the surface and at or above 10,000 feet MSL	Day and Night: 5 s.m.	1,000 Feet Below 1,000 Feet Above 1 s.m. Horizontal

Figure 3-21. This table shows weather minimums for VFR flight in Class G airspace.

 As shown in figures 3-15 and 3-21, the VFR minimums at or above 10,000 feet MSL (and more than 1,200 feet AGL) are the same in Class G and E airspace.

AIRCRAFT SPEED LIMITS

As you move into faster airplanes, you must also be concerned with speed limits. For example, unless otherwise authorized by air traffic control, you generally may not operate an aircraft below 10,000 feet MSL at a speed greater than 250 knots indicated airspeed (KIAS). Further, unless otherwise authorized or required by ATC, you may not operate an aircraft at or below 2,500 feet above the surface within 4 nautical miles of the primary airport of a Class C or Class D airspace area at a speed greater than 200 KIAS. The 200 KIAS

SECTION A ■ **Airports, Airspace, and Flight Information**

limit also applies to the airspace underlying a Class B airspace area or in a VFR corridor designated through such airspace.

 Normally, the maximum indicated airspeed permitted when at or below 2,500 feet AGL within 4 nautical miles of the primary airport of a Class C or Class D airspace is 200 knots.

SPECIAL USE AIRSPACE

Special use airspace is used to confine certain flight activities and to place limitations on aircraft operations that are not part of these activities. The various types of airspace can be designated as prohibited, restricted, warning, alert, military operations areas, and controlled firing areas. With the exception of controlled firing areas, the dimensions of special use airspace are depicted on aeronautical charts. The information about the hours of operation and effective altitudes might be listed directly on the aeronautical chart, or indexed by area number on a chart panel.

Prohibited areas contain airspace within which the flight of aircraft is prohibited. Such areas are established for security or other reasons associated with the national welfare. **Restricted areas** often have invisible hazards to aircraft such as artillery firing, aerial gunnery, or flight of guided missiles. Permission to fly through a restricted area must be granted by the controlling agency. If ATC issues you an IFR clearance (including a clearance to maintain VFR-on-top) that takes you through restricted airspace, that clearance constitutes authorization to penetrate the airspace. In this case, you need take no further action other than to comply with the clearance, as issued, and maintain normal vigilance.

A **warning area** is airspace of defined dimensions, extending from three nautical miles outward from the coast of the United States, that contains activities that might be hazardous to nonparticipating aircraft. The purpose of such warning areas is to warn nonparticipating pilots of the potential danger. A warning area might be located over domestic or international waters or both. **Alert areas** might contain a high volume of pilot training or an unusual type of aerial activity, such as parachute jumping or glider towing. Flight within alert areas is not restricted, but you are urged to exercise extreme caution. Pilots of participating aircraft, as well as pilots transiting the area, are equally responsible for collision avoidance and compliance with the FARs.

Military operations areas (MOAs) are established to separate certain military training activities from IFR traffic. When you are flying under IFR, you may be cleared through an active MOA if ATC can provide separation. Otherwise, ATC will reroute or restrict your flight operations. Before entering an active MOA under VFR, you should contact the controlling agency for traffic advisories. Information regarding route activity is available from Flight Service.

 MOAs are established to separate certain training activities from IFR traffic.

The distinguishing feature of a **controlled firing area**, compared to other special use airspace, is that its activities are discontinued immediately when a spotter aircraft, radar, or ground lookout personnel determine an aircraft might be approaching the area. Since nonparticipating aircraft are not required to change their flight path, controlled firing areas are not depicted on aeronautical charts.

OTHER AIRSPACE AREAS

Other airspace areas include national security areas, airport advisory areas, military training routes, and areas where temporary restrictions or limitations/prohibitions apply. Recommended procedures for operating in these areas are outlined in the *Aeronautical Information Manual.*

National security areas (NSAs) are established at locations where there is a requirement for increased security and safety of ground facilities. You are requested to voluntarily avoid flying through an NSA. At times, flight through an NSA might be prohibited to provide a greater level of security and safety. A NOTAM is issued to advise you of any changes in an NSA's status.

Local airport advisory areas extend 10 statute miles from airports in Alaska where there is a flight service station (FSS) located on the field and no operating control tower. The FSS provides advisories on wind direction and velocity, favored runway, altimeter setting, and reported traffic within the area. **Military training routes (MTRs)** are established below 10,000 feet MSL for both VFR and IFR operations at speeds in excess of 250 knots. However, some route segments might be at higher altitudes. **Parachute jump aircraft areas** are tabulated in the *Chart Supplement.* Times of operation are local, and MSL altitudes are listed unless otherwise specified.

Temporary flight restrictions (TFRs) are imposed by the FAA to protect persons and property on the surface or in the air. For example, the FAA will normally issue a NOTAM for a TFR to provide a safe environment for rescue/relief operations or to prevent unsafe congestion above an incident or event that could generate high public interest. The restricted airspace for rescue/relief operations is usually limited to within 2,000 feet above the surface within a three nautical mile radius. Incidents near controlled airports are handled through existing procedures and normally do not require issuance of a NOTAM. TFR NOTAMs are issued to restrict flight in the vicinity of space flight operations and in proximity of the President, Vice President, and other public figures. Presidential TFRs can restrict or ground IFR flights that are not conducted by scheduled airlines, but if you do receive an IFR clearance, you don't have to worry about inadvertently violating one if complying with the clearance.

Terminal radar service areas (TRSAs) do not fit into any of the U.S. airspace classes. Originally part of the terminal radar program at selected airports, TRSAs have never been designated as controlled airspace, although they can be collocated with other types of controlled airspace. FAR Part 91 does not contain any specific rules for TRSA operations. Because communication with ATC in a TRSA is voluntary for VFR aircraft, ATC cannot separate IFR traffic from all VFR traffic—only *participating* VFR traffic.

ADIZ

Aircraft entering U.S. domestic airspace from points outside must provide identification prior to entry. **Air defense identification zones (ADIZs)** have been established to facilitate this early identification. You must file a flight plan with an appropriate facility, such as Flight Service, to penetrate or operate within a coastal or domestic ADIZ. If flying VFR, you file a **defense VFR (DVFR)** flight plan. It contains information similar to local flight plans, but helps to identify your aircraft as you enter the country. Unless otherwise authorized by ATC, a Mode A or Mode S transponder with Mode C capability is required, and the transponder must be turned on and operable. You are also required to have a two-way radio and periodically give ATC reports of your location while inbound toward the ADIZ. Figure 3-22 summarizes the features and requirements of the different classes of airspace.

SECTION A ■ **Airports, Airspace, and Flight Information**

SECTION A ■ Airports, Airspace, and Flight Information

Airspace Features	Class A	Class B	Class C	Class D	Class E	Class G
Operations Permitted	IFR	IFR and VFR	IFR and VFR	IFR and VFR	IFR and VFR	IFR and VFR
VFR Entry and Equipment Requirements	IFR Flight Plan and IFR Clearance Required	ATC Clearance Transponder with Mode C	Establish Radio Communication Transponder with Mode C	Establish Radio Communication	None	None
Minimum Pilot Qualifications	Instrument Rating	Private Pilot Certificate Student Pilot Certificate Endorsement	Student Pilot Certificate	Student Pilot Certificate	Student Pilot Certificate	Student Pilot Certificate
Two-way Radio Communications	Yes	Yes	Yes	Yes	Yes for IFR Operations	No
VFR Min. Vis. and Distance from Clouds 1,200 ft AGL or less (Regardless of MSL Altitude)	N/A	N/A	N/A	N/A	N/A	Day 1 s.m. Clear of Clouds Night 3 s.m. 500 ft Below 1,000 ft Above 2,000 ft Horizontal
VFR Minimum Visibility	N/A	3 Statute Miles	3 Statute Miles	3 Statute Miles	**Below 10,000 ft MSL** – 3 s.m. **At or Above 10,000 MSL** – 5 s.m.	**Below 10,000 ft MSL** – Day 1 s.m. Night 3 s.m. **At or Above 10,000 MSL** – 5 s.m. (above 1,200 ft AGL)
VFR Minimum Distance from Clouds	N/A	Clear of Clouds	500 ft Below 1,000 ft Above 2,000 ft Horizontal	500 ft Below 1,000 ft Above 2,000 ft Horizontal	**Below 10,000 ft MSL** – 500 ft Below 1,000 ft Above 2,000 ft Horizontal **At or Above 10,000 ft MSL** – 1,000 ft Below 1,000 ft Above 1 s.m. Horizontal	**Below 10,000 ft MSL** – 500 ft Below 1,000 ft Above 2,000 ft Horizontal (above 1,200 ft AGL) **At or Above 10,000 ft MSL** – 1,000 ft Below 1,000 ft Above 1 s.m. Horizontal (above 1,200 ft AGL)
ATC Services	All Aircraft Separation	All Aircraft Separation	IFR/IFR Separation IFR/VFR Separation VFR Traffic Advisories (workload permitting)	IFR/IFR Separation VFR Traffic Advisories (workload permitting)	IFR/IFR Separation VFR Traffic Advisories on Request (workload permitting)	VFR Traffic Advisories on Request (workload permitting)

Figure 3-22. Use this table as a quick reference to the weather minimums and operating requirements of each class of airspace.

FLIGHT INFORMATION

Regulations require you to familiarize yourself with all available information concerning each flight. The following review of flight information publications is designed to help you fulfill this requirement. The publications in this section include the *Chart Supplement, Aeronautical Information Manual, Notices to Airmen,* advisory circulars, and Jeppesen information services. [Figure 3-23]

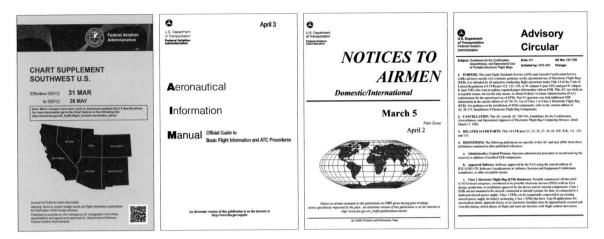

Figure 3-23. These FAA publications help you to familiarize yourself with information concerning your flight, as well as to stay current on recent changes in procedures and regulations.

CHART SUPPLEMENT

The *Chart Supplement* is a series of regional books (also available on the FAA web site) that includes a tabulation of all data on record with the FAA for public-use civil airports, associated terminal control facilities, air route traffic control centers, and radio aids to navigation. A comprehensive legend sample is printed in the first few pages of each book. The legend provides you with a breakdown of all the information in the Chart Supplement . [Figure 3-24]

Figure 3-24. The Chart Supplement provides information in the facility listing that is of special interest to you as an instrument-rated pilot.

Airport Location Information
• This airport is 3 NM southwest of Des Moines.
• To get UTC time, add 6 hours (5 hours from daylight time).
• This airport is on the Omaha sectional chart, H-SC and L-12J enroute charts, and has published instrument approach procedures.
• The elevation is 958 feet MSL.

Services
• Major airframe and powerplant services available.
• 100LL and Jet A fuel plus all types of oxygen.

Runway Information and Sketch
• Includes length and width and composition of runways, lighting aids, approach light systems.
• Includes weight limits for aircraft with various types of landing gear (single, dual, single-tandem, and dual-tandem)
• Includes LAHSO information, including available landing distance for each hold short point.

Weather
You can reach ASOS by telephone or HIWAS on the Des Moines VOR frequency.

Communications
• Includes ATIS frequency as well and phone number on which you can listen to ATIS
• Includes remote communications outlet (RCO) frequency for Fort Dodge flight service station.
• Includes ATC frequencies. The ® indicates that radar approach control is available.

Airspace
This airport is within Class C airspace. If an airport has part-time Class D or E airspace, the times of operation are shown in parenthesis.

Navigation Aids
• The airport is 347° and 5.9 NM from DSM VORTAC, a high altitude facility on 117.5 MHz.
• The airport is 307° and 4.8 NM from FOREM NDB.
• The airport is served by three ILS systems, on RWYs 31, 13, and 05.

SECTION A ■ Airports, Airspace, and Flight Information

The hours of a part-time tower (Zulu time) are shown in parentheses following the tower frequency.

Although airport and facility data make up the bulk of the directory, several other sections also contain essential information. Many of these sections pertain to IFR flight operations. The special notices section furnishes information regarding subjects such as the civil use of military fields, newly certified airports, continuous power facilities, and special flight procedures. Preferred IFR routes, special notices, LAHSO data, and telephone numbers for NWS outlets, as well as numbers for TWEB are provided in the Chart Supplement . You also can find a listing of VOR receiver checkpoints and VOT facilities for each region. If you have not used the Chart Supplement recently, go to faa.gov and look at listings for airports you know to become familiar with the format. Obtain and review the supplemental (back) pages to see what has changed. [Figure 3-25]

AIR ROUTE TRAFFIC CONTROL CENTERS (ARTCCs)

ARTCC NAME	*24 HR RGNL DUTY OFFICE TELEPHONE #	BUSINESS HOURS	BUSINESS TELEPHONE #
Albuquerque	817–222–5006	7:30 a.m.–4:00 p.m.	505–856–4300
Anchorage	907–271–5936	7:30 a.m.–4:00 p.m.	907–269–1137
Atlanta	404–305–5180	7:30 a.m.–5:00 p.m.	770–210–7601
Boston	404–305–5156	7:30 a.m.–4:00 p.m.	603–879–6633
Chicago	847–294–8400	8:00 a.m.–4:00 p.m.	630–906–8221
Cleveland	847–294–8400	8:00 a.m.–4:00 p.m.	440–774–0310
Denver	425–227–1389	7:30 a.m.–4:00 p.m.	303–651–4100
Ft. Worth	817–222–5006	7:30 a.m.–4:00 p.m.	817–858–7300
Houston	817–222–5006	7:30 a.m.–4:00 p.m.	281–230–5300
Indianapolis	847–294–8400	8:00 a.m.–4:00 p.m.	317–247–2231
Jacksonville	404–305–5180	8:00 a.m.–4:30 p.m.	904–549–1501
Kansas City	816–329–3000	7:30 a.m.–4:00 p.m.	913–254–8500
Los Angeles	661–265–8200	7:30 a.m.–4:00 p.m.	661–265–8200

ROUTES   403
LOW ALTITUDE

Terminals	Route	Effective Times (UTC)
SAN FRANCISCO/OAKLAND METRO AREA From SAN FRANCISCO Area: West Bay Airports		
Los Angeles Area..................	(70–90–110–130–150–170) V27 VTU V299 SADDE V107 LAX..............................	1400–0800
From OAKLAND Area: East Bay Airports		
Los Angeles Area..................	(70–90–110–130–150–170) V109 PXN V113 V485 V299 SADDE V107 LAX	1400–0800

Figure 3-25. Areas of the Chart Supplement you might not have used before include the ARTCC sector phone numbers and the low altitude preferred IFR routes.

AERONAUTICAL INFORMATION MANUAL

The *Aeronautical Information Manual* (AIM) contains fundamental information for both VFR and IFR flight operations within the National Airspace System. It is revised twice each year and is an excellent source of operational information that you should review periodically. For example, the AIM describes the capabilities, components, and procedures required for each type of air navigation aid and includes a discussion of radar services, capabilities, and limitations. You can also find a comprehensive description of current airport lighting and runway markings, airspace, and ATC services. Additional coverage addresses altimetry, wake turbulence, and potential flight hazards, as well as safety reporting programs, medical facts for pilots, and aeronautical charts. The Pilot/Controller Glossary promotes a common understanding of the terms used in the ATC system. Some international terms that differ from the FAA definitions are listed after their U.S. equivalents.

NOTICES TO AIRMEN

Notices to Airmen (NOTAMs) contain time-critical, aeronautical information that could affect your decision to make a flight. The information is either temporary in nature or unknown in time for publication on aeronautical charts and/or in other documents. Airport or primary runway closures, changes in the status of navigational aids, radar service availability, and other data essential to enroute, terminal, or landing operations are examples of information that might be included in NOTAMs. NOTAMs are divided into two categories, NOTAM(D) (distant) and Flight Data Center (FDC) NOTAMs.

NOTAM(D) information is disseminated for all navigational facilities that are part of the U.S. airspace system, as well as all public use airports, seaplane bases, and heliports listed in the Chart Supplement. The complete NOTAM(D) file is maintained at the National Weather Message Switching Center in Atlanta, Georgia. Flight Service and most air traffic facilities have access to the entire database of NOTAM(D)s, which remain available for the duration of their validity, or until published. After they are published, you can still obtain them by request during your preflight briefing.

 The *Chart Supplement* together with NOTAMs(D), obtained from the NTAP, online, and Flight Service provide the latest airport status.

FDC NOTAMs are issued by the National Flight Data Center. They contain regulatory information such as temporary flight restrictions or amendments to instrument approach procedures and other current aeronautical charts. FDC NOTAMs are available through ATC and Flight Service.

 FDC NOTAMs alert pilots of new flight restrictions as well as changes to information on instrument approach procedures and aeronautical charts prior to normal publication.

 When FDC NOTAMs are issued too late for the Notices to Airmen publication, you can get them online at FAA.gov; but the FAA still recommends a Flight Service telephone briefing.

The Notices to Airmen publication (NTAP) is issued every 28 days and contains all current NOTAM(D)s and FDC NOTAMs (except FDC NOTAMs for temporary flight restrictions) available for publication. You can also search for current NOTAMs, by area, on the FAA web site. [Figure 3-26]

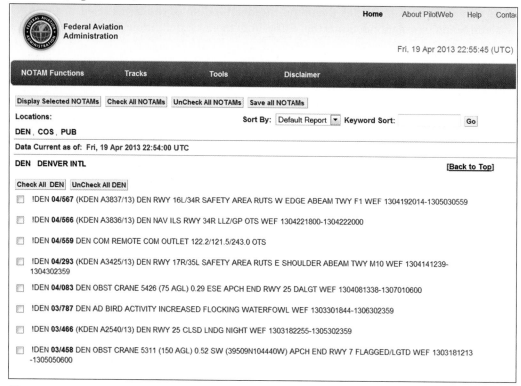

Figure 3-26. You can find NOTAMs, including TFRs, at faa.gov.

Federal airway changes, which are identified as Center Area NOTAMs, are included with the NOTAM(D) listing. Published NOTAM(D) information is not provided during pilot briefings unless requested. Information of a permanent nature is sometimes printed in the NOTAM publication as an interim step prior to publication on the appropriate aeronautical chart or in the *Chart Supplement*.

FAA ADVISORY CIRCULARS AND HANDBOOKS

To provide current aviation information on a recurring basis, the Department of Transportation publishes and distributes **advisory circulars.** These pamphlets provide information and procedures that are necessary for good operating practice, but that are not required unless they are incorporated into a regulation. For ease of reference, advisory circulars use a coded numbering system that corresponds to the subject areas of the FARs. An Advisory Circular Checklist is issued periodically as AC 00-2, and it contains the subjects covered and the availability of each circular. Although there is a charge for many advisory circulars ordered from the U.S. Government Printing Office, you can obtain them free online at FAA.gov, where you can also obtain most FAA handbooks, including the *Instrument Flying Handbook* and *Instrument Procedures Handbook*.

ELECTRONIC FLIGHT BAG

The **electronic flight bag (EFB)** exists either as a mobile device or as equipment that is installed in the aircraft. Depending on the features of the EFB, you can use it during flight planning and during each phase of flight. EFBs can display flight plans, routes, checklists, flight operations manuals, regulations, minimum equipment lists (MELs), moving map and weather displays, approach charts, airport diagrams, logbooks, and operating procedures. You can also use some EFBs to calculate aircraft performance and accomplish many tasks traditionally handled by a dispatcher. [Figure 3-27]

Figure 3-27. You can display charts and a wide variety of flight information on an EFB.

AC 120-76, *Guidelines for the Certification, Airworthiness, and Operational Use of Electronic Flight Bags*, provides information for obtaining certification and approval for EFB use. This AC also describes three types of EFB software applications. Type A applications are primarily intended for use during flight planning, on the ground, or during noncritical phases of flight. Type B applications provide the aeronautical information required to be accessible to you during all phases of flight and Type C applications include communication, navigation, and surveillance functions that require FAA design, production, and installation approval. AC 120-76 also outlines the capabilities and limitations of each of the three classes of EFBs. Classes are primarily based on whether the EFB is portable and the placement of the equipment in the cockpit.

JEPPESEN INFORMATION SERVICES

Many commercial publishers offer information for pilots that is comparable to that found in government sources. For example, Jeppesen publishes both a printed and eBook version of the FAR/AIM, each of which is revised annually. In addition, **Jeppesen Information Services** offers an extensive range of flight information products in both print and electronic formats. These products include:

- Jeppesen VFR+GPS Charts
- JeppView Electronic Charting
- Jeppesen Airport Directories
- Jeppesen Mobile FliteDeck
- Jeppesen Airway Manual

Please visit JeppDirect.com learn more about these pilot information services.

INTERNET RESOURCES

Almost all FAA publications are available at the FAA's web site. It is no longer necessary to order them from the Government Printing Office. You can search and download handbooks and advisory circulars by name or number, as well as practical test standards, airworthiness directives (ADs), and graphic temporary flight restrictions (TFRs). You can also find answers to frequently asked questions. Current Federal Aviation Regulations are available on the Electronic Code of Federal Regulations (eCFR.gov) web site.

SECTION A ■ **Airports, Airspace, and Flight Information**

SUMMARY CHECKLIST

✓ A visual runway normally is marked only with the runway number and a dashed white centerline. It might include additional markings for specific operations. A runway used for instrument approaches has additional markings, such as threshold markings, touchdown zone markings, aiming point markings, and side stripes.

✓ Additional markings for displaced thresholds include taxi, takeoff, and rollout areas, as well as blastpad/stopway areas. Closed runways and taxiways are marked by Xs at some airports.

✓ Hold lines keep aircraft clear of the runways, and at controlled airports, serve as the point that separates the responsibilities of ground control from those of the tower.

✓ There are six basic types of airport signs — mandatory, location, direction, destination, information, and runway distance remaining.

✓ A variety of lighting systems, including approach light systems, sequenced flashing lights, runway alignment indicator lights, and runway end identifier lights are used at airports to aid the pilot in identifying the airport environment, particularly at night or in low visibility conditions.

✓ Various visual glide slope indicators, such as the visual approach slope indicator (VASI), precision approach slope indicator (PAPI), and tri-color VASI help pilots establish and maintain a safe descent path to the runway.

✓ Runway and taxiway lighting are installed at some airports to assist you in landing and taxing at night or during low visibility conditions. This lighting can consist of runway edge lights, threshold lights, displaced threshold lights, touchdown zone lights, runway centerline lights, taxiway lead-off lights, taxiway centerline lights, and taxiway edge lights.

✓ Pilot-controlled lighting is the term used to describe systems that you can activate by keying the aircraft's microphone on a specified radio frequency.

✓ If another aircraft has no apparent relative motion when viewed from your aircraft, you are likely on a collision course.

✓ Unless necessary for safety, you are required to turn on anti-collision lights for all operations, day and night.

✓ When operating in controlled airspace (Class A, Class B, Class C, Class D, and Class E), you are subject to certain operating rules, as well as pilot qualification and aircraft equipment requirements. In addition, specific VFR weather minimums apply to each class of airspace.

✓ The FARs require that you have an operating transponder with Mode C capability when flying at or above 10,000 feet MSL, excluding the airspace at and below 2,500 feet AGL.

✓ To operate within Class A airspace, you must be instrument-rated, your aircraft transponder-equipped, be operating under an IFR flight plan, and controlled by ATC.

✓ Flight levels instead of MSL altitudes are used in Class A airspace.

✓ To operate in Class B airspace, you are required to obtain a clearance from ATC.

✓ Prior to entering Class C airspace, you must establish two-way radio communication with the ATC facility that has jurisdiction and maintain it when you are operating within the airspace.

✓ You must establish two-way radio communication with the tower prior to entering Class D airspace and maintain radio contact during all operations to, from, or on that airport.

✓ Federal airways are normally 8 nautical miles wide, begin at 1,200 feet AGL and extend up to but not including 18,000 feet MSL.

✓ A special VFR clearance must be obtained from ATC to operate within the surface areas of Class B, C, D, or E airspace when the ground visibility is less than 3 statute miles and the cloud ceiling is less than 1,000 feet AGL.

✓ Class G airspace typically extends from the surface to 700 or 1,200 feet AGL. In some areas, Class G extends from the surface to 14,500 feet MSL. ATC normally does not exercise control of air traffic in uncontrolled, or Class G airspace.

✓ Since the airspace at lower altitudes, and especially in the vicinity of airports, tends to be congested, the FAA has established aircraft speed limits.

✓ Prohibited areas are established for security or other reasons associated with the national welfare and contain airspace within which the flight of aircraft is prohibited.

✓ Restricted areas often have invisible hazards to aircraft, such as artillery firing, aerial gunnery, or flight of guided missiles. You must obtain permission from the controlling agency to fly through a restricted area. An IFR clearance that takes you through a restricted area constitutes authorization to penetrate the airspace.

✓ Warning areas extend from three nautical miles outward from the coast of the United States and contain activity that might be hazardous to nonparticipating aircraft.

✓ Alert areas contain a high volume of pilot training or an unusual type of aerial activity.

✓ A military operations area (MOA) is a block of airspace in which military training and other military maneuvers are conducted.

✓ Activities within a controlled firing area are discontinued immediately when a spotter aircraft, radar, or ground lookout personnel determine an aircraft might be approaching the area.

✓ Local airport advisory areas extend 10 statute miles from airports in Alaska where there is an FSS located on the field and no operating control tower.

✓ Generally, military training routes (MTRs) are established below 10,000 feet MSL for operations at speeds in excess of 250 knots.

✓ Temporary flight restrictions are imposed by the FAA to protect persons or property on the surface or in the air from a specific hazard or situation.

✓ Air defense identification zones (ADIZs) are established to facilitate early identification of aircraft in the vicinity of U.S. international airspace boundaries.

✓ The *Chart Supplement* contains a descriptive listing of all airports, heliports, and seaplane bases that are open to the public.

✓ The *Aeronautical Information Manual* (AIM) contains basic flight information, a detailed description of the National Airspace System, ATC procedures, and other items of special interest to pilots, such as medical facts and flight safety information.

✓ NOTAM(D)s are disseminated for all navigational facilities that are part of the National Airspace System, all public use airports, seaplane bases, and heliports listed in the Chart Supplement .

SECTION A ■ **Airports, Airspace, and Flight Information**

✓ FDC NOTAMs contain regulatory information such as temporary flight restrictions, amendments to standard instrument approach procedures, and revisions to aeronautical charts.

✓ Advisory circulars (ACs) provide nonregulatory guidance and information in a variety of subject areas. ACs also explain methods for complying with FARs.

✓ You can use an electronic flight bag (EFB) to display flight information, such as flight plans, routes, checklists, flight operations manuals, regulations, minimum equipment lists (MELs), moving map and weather displays, approach charts, airport diagrams, logbooks, and operating procedures.

✓ Jeppesen Information Services offers an extensive range of flight information products in both print and electronic formats.

KEY TERMS

Visual Runway

Nonprecision Instrument Runway

Precision Instrument Runway

Taxiways

Hold Lines

Displaced Threshold

Blast Pad/Stopway Area

Demarcation Bar

Land and Hold Short Operations (LAHSO)

Sequenced Flashing Lights (SFL)

Runway Alignment Indicator Lights (RAIL)

Runway End Identifier Lights (REIL)

Visual Approach Slope Indicator (VASI)

Pulsating Visual Approach Slope Indicator (PVASI)

Precision Approach Path Indicator (PAPI)

Tri-Color VASI

Runway Edge Lights

Threshold Lights

Displaced Threshold Lights

Touchdown Zone Lighting (TDZL)

Runway Centerline Lights (RCLS)

Land and Hold Short Lights

Taxiway Lead-Off Lights

Taxiway Centerline Lights

Taxiway Edge Lights

Pilot-Controlled Lighting

Class A Airspace

Class B Airspace

Class C Airspace

Class D Airspace

Class E Airspace

Special VFR Clearance

Class G Airspace

Prohibited Area

Restricted Area

Warning Area

Alert Area

Military Operations Area (MOA)

Controlled Firing Area

National Security Area

Local Airport Advisory Area

Military Training Route (MTR)

Parachute Jump Aircraft Area

Temporary Flight Restrictions (TFRs)

Terminal Radar Service Area (TRSA)

Air Defense Identification Zone (ADIZ)

Defense VFR (DVFR)

Chart Supplement

Aeronautical Information Manual (AIM)

Notices to Airmen (NOTAMs)

NOTAM(D)

FDC NOTAM

Advisory Circulars (ACs)

Electronic Flight Bag (EFB)

Jeppesen Information Services

QUESTIONS

For questions 1 through 5, match the lettered callouts in the accompanying illustration to identify the appropriate runway markings.

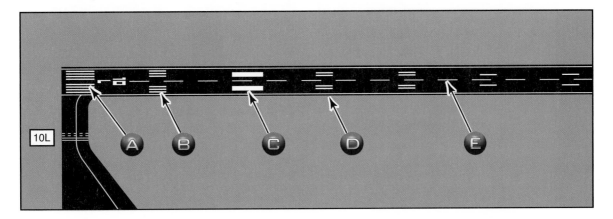

1.   Side stripe

2.   Threshold markings

3.   Runway centerline

4.   Aiming point marking

5.   Touchdown zone marking

6.   True/False. Runway holding position signs are black with yellow inscriptions and yellow borders.

7.   Name the high intensity white strobe lights located laterally, one on each side of the runway threshold.
     A.   Sequenced flashing lights
     B.   Runway alignment indicator lights
     C.   Runway end identifier lights

SECTION A ■ Airports, Airspace, and Flight Information

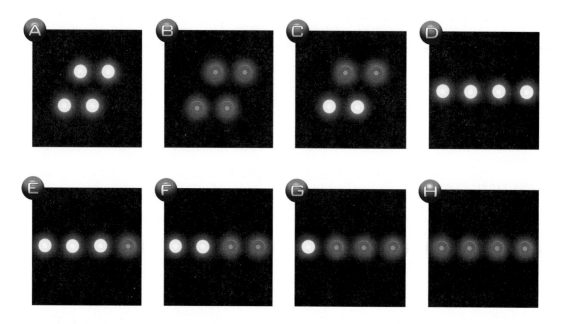

For questions 8 through 11, match each illustration to the correct glide slope description.

8. VASI, on glide path

9. PAPI, slightly low

10. PAPI, on glide path

11. VASI, high

12. As you approach for landing, what color are the runway threshold lights? What color are they when departing the runway?

13. How many feet of runway remain when the centerline lights change from white to alternating red and white lights?

14. What is indicated when the airport beacon is illuminated during daylight hours?

15. There is no apparent relative motion when you see this pattern of lights from your airplane. What is the relationship of the other airplane to yours?
    A. You are following the other airplane.
    B. The other airplane is flying toward you on a collision course.
    C. The other airplane is passing from right to left at a lower airspeed than your own.

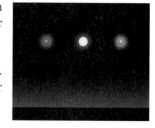

16. When should you turn on your aircraft's anti-collision lights?
    A. Whenever an engine is operating. For all aircraft operations, day and night.
    B. Whenever you, as pilot-in-command, determine that it is in the interest of safety to do so.

17. Excluding the airspace at and below 2,500 feet AGL, transponders with altitude encoding capability are required in all airspace (controlled or uncontrolled) of the contiguous 48 states and the District of Columbia at and above what altitude?
    A. 10,000 feet AGL
    B. 10,000 feet MSL
    C. 14,500 feet MSL

18. What are the dimensions of Class A airspace?

For questions 19 through 25, match the type of airspace with the appropriate description.

    A. Class A
    B. Class B
    C. Class C
    D. Class D
    E. Class E
    F. Federal Airways
    G. Class G

19. That portion of the airspace within which ATC does not control air traffic

20. Airspace at and above 14,500 feet MSL over the 48 contiguous states, District of Columbia, and Alaska east of 160° west longitude, but not including the airspace within 1,500 feet of the surface

21. An airspace segment that is normally 8 nautical miles wide and extends from 1,200 feet AGL (or in some cases higher) up to but not including 18,000 feet MSL

22. Airspace within which the requirements include an operating altitude-encoding transponder, an instrument-rated pilot, an IFR flight plan, and altimeters set to indicate pressure altitude.

23. Airspace within which equipment requirements include an operable VOR (for IFR operations), two-way radio capable of communicating with ATC, an ATC clearance, and a transponder with Mode C automatic altitude reporting

24. Airspace generally consisting of circular areas extending to 4,000 feet above the primary airport where the shelf area has a radius of 10 nautical miles, the core area has a radius of 5 nautical miles, and two-way radio communication is required

25. Airspace outside Class B or Class C airspace that normally extends from the surface up to 2,500 feet above the elevation of the airport and having charted, but possibly irregular, lateral dimensions at which a control tower is operating

26. What is the maximum indicated aircraft speed limit (in knots) below 2,500 feet when within 4 nautical miles of the primary airport of a Class C airspace area?

27. True/False. Military training route flights are generally limited to operations under VFR.

SECTION A ■ Airports, Airspace, and Flight Information

SECTION A ■ Airports, Airspace, and Flight Information

```
NORTH PLATTE REGIONAL AIRPORT LEE BIRD FLD   (LBF)   3 E   UTC-6(-5DT)                OMAHA
         N41°07.56' W100°41.23'                                                       H-1D, L-11A
    2778   B   S4   FUEL 100LL, JET A   OX 4   ARFF Index Ltd.                        IAP
    RWY 12L-30R: H8000X150 (CONC-GRVD)   S-75, D-110, DT-190   HIRL
        RWY 12L: VASI(V4L)—GA 3.0° TCH 55'.       RWY 30R: MALSR. Rgt tfc.
    RWY 12R-30L: H4925X100 (ASPH)   S-42, D-58, DT-106   MIRL
        RWY 12R: Rgt tfc.   RWY 30L: Tree.
    RWY 17-35: H4436X100 (ASPH)   S-28, D-48, DT-86   MIRL
        RWY 17: Road.         RWY 35: REIL. VASI(V4L)—GA 3.0° TCH 41'. Thld dsplcd 234 . Berm.
    AIRPORT REMARKS: Attended 1200-0500Z‡. 5 foot dike 100' from approach end Rwy 35. Waterfowl and deer on and
        in the vicinity of the arpt. PPR 24 hours for unscheduled air carrier ops with more than 30 passenger seats call
        arpt manager 308-532-1900. ACTIVATE HIRL Rwy 12L-30R, MIRL Rwy 17-35, VASI Rwy 12L and Rwy 35,
        MALSR Rwy 30R and REIL Rwy 35—CTAF. For MIRL Rwy 12R-30L ctc arpt manager 308-532-1900.
    WEATHER DATA SOURCES: ASOS 118.425 (308) 534-1617.
    COMMUNICATIONS: CTAF/UNICOM 123.0
        COLUMBUS FSS (OLU) TF 1-800-WX-BRIEF. NOTAM FILE LBF.
        LEE BIRD RCO 122.5 (COLUMBUS FSS)
    Ⓡ DENVER CENTER APP/DEP CON 132.7   CLNC DEL 132.7
    RADIO AIDS TO NAVIGATION: NOTAM FILE LBF.
        (L) VORTACW 117.4   LBF   Chan 121   N41°02.92' W100°44.83'   019° 5 4 NM to fld. 3050/11E.
        PANBE NDB (LOM) 416   LB   N41°04.10' W100°34.35'   295° 6.3 NM to fld. Unmonitored.
        ILS 111.5   I-LBF   Rwy 30R   LOM PANBE NDB. LOM and MM unmonitored.
```

Refer to the *Chart Supplement* excerpt to answer questions 28 through 32.

28. In December, what are the hours (in local time) when the airport is attended?

29. What type of approach lighting system is installed on Runway 30R?

30. How far is the threshold displaced on Runway 35?

31. What is the name of the approach/departure control facility that serves North Platte Regional Airport Lee Bird Field?

32. What is the frequency and identification for the ILS approach?

33. Select the information that you can obtain by referencing the *Aeronautical Information Manual* (AIM).
    A. The official text of regulations issued by the agencies of the Federal government
    B. ATC procedures, a description of the airspace system, and flight safety information
    C. Information regarding specific airports, including runway lengths, communication frequencies, and airport services

34. Explain the differences between NOTAM(D)s and FDC NOTAMs.

SECTION B
Air Traffic Control System

The **air traffic control (ATC)** system, as we know it today, is the result of the Federal Aviation Act in 1958 that created what is now the FAA. Congress passed this act following a midair collision of two airliners over the Grand Canyon. It was clear that for air travel to be viable, this type of risk to the flying public had to be eliminated. So the ATC system was created to *separate air traffic,* specifically IFR traffic. Today, ATC provides a variety of services that help make flying safe, but its main purpose has not changed—providing nationwide traffic separation during all phases of IFR flight using a network of radar and nonradar facilities. These facilities include air route traffic control centers, terminal radar approach control, and control towers.

AIR ROUTE TRAFFIC CONTROL CENTER

The facilities that provide air traffic control service to aircraft operating on IFR flight plans in controlled airspace are the **air route traffic control centers (ARTCCs)**. They are also the central authority for issuing IFR clearances, and they provide nationwide monitoring of each IFR flight, primarily during the enroute phase. Each ARTCC (center), due to its size, is divided into sectors. Each sector is manned by one or more controllers, who maintain lateral and vertical separation of aircraft within its airspace boundaries. In addition, they coordinate traffic arriving and departing their assigned areas. Frequently, sectors are further stratified by altitude. For example, there might be low altitude sectors that extend from the floor of controlled airspace to altitudes of 18,000 to 24,000 feet MSL. Above these levels, one or more high altitude sectors might be established. [Figure 3-28]

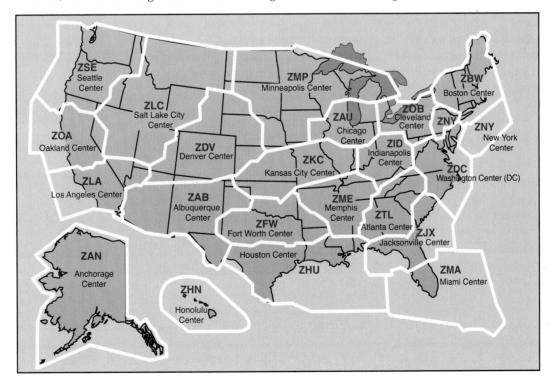

Figure 3-28. Appropriate radar and communication sites are connected to the centers by microwave links and telephone lines.

ARTCC TRAFFIC SEPARATION

In addition to providing for the safe separation of IFR traffic and providing safety alerts, an ARTCC, like any ATC facility, separates IFR traffic from VFR aircraft and provides advisories to VFR aircraft on a workload-permitting basis. The elimination of traffic conflicts begins when you file your IFR flight plan.

PROCESSING THE IFR FLIGHT PLAN

If weather conditions are below VFR minimums, you must submit a flight plan and receive an ATC clearance prior to operating an aircraft within controlled airspace. You can submit an instrument flight plan to Flight Service online or by telephone or to air traffic control tower by radio, if necessary. After your flight plan is filed, it is processed by the center in which the flight originates. The flight plan is entered into the center's computer, where it is scanned for preferred routes. The route is then analyzed by ATC controllers for any restrictions that might be in effect, such as traffic conflicts, inoperable navaids, special use airspace penetration, known or projected delays, and flow control restrictions. Due to the time it takes to check these variables, you should file your IFR flight plan at least 30 minutes prior to your intended departure time.

After your flight plan is processed, your clearance will be ready when you call ATC at your departure airport. In addition, after the route is finalized, it is sent to the various centers covering your flight via the nationwide ARTCC computer system. Your flight data is then reviewed approximately 30 to 45 minutes prior to your entry into that center's airspace. This provides the controller with time to analyze your flight for any restrictions or conflicts and amend your clearance, if necessary.

Flow Control Restrictions

Flow control was originally implemented to help regulate traffic at busy airports during the 1981 air traffic controller's strike. It is now an integral part of the National Airspace System, and is managed by the Air Traffic Control System Command Center (ATCSCC).

Each airport has an arrival rate that is determined by ATC personnel located on the airport. Depending on many factors such as the number of runways, instrument approaches, weather conditions, etc., the rate might be over a hundred aircraft per hour. However, this number could drop to just a few during bad weather conditions. ATCSCC takes a look at the anticipated number of aircraft expected to land during a specific time frame. (This number includes the aircraft enroute and those on the ground awaiting departure.) If the number of arriving aircraft is less than the anticipated number, there is no problem. However,

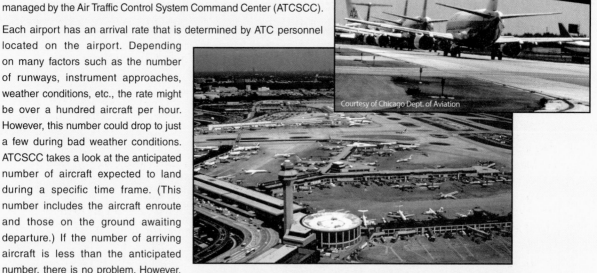

Courtesy of Chicago Dept. of Aviation

if there are more aircraft inbound than the arrival rate allows, the aircraft either have to hold or divert to an alternate. This is not a good thing. Instead, ATCSCC will issue EDCTs (expect departure clearance times). This means that aircraft still on the ground will be held on the ground until they can be worked into the system. So next time you are being held on the ground at an airport where the sun is shining, it is probably due to the fact that your destination is anticipating more arrivals than it can handle.

When departing an airport with an operating control tower, you normally request your clearance through ground control or clearance delivery. If you are departing an airport without a control tower, you may request your clearance by contacting Flight Service by telephone prior to departure. If weather conditions permit, you may obtain the clearance after departing VFR, but use caution to ensure that you can maintain safe terrain clearance prior to receiving your clearance. In this situation, you could contact the ARTCC in the area where your flight originates, or request your clearance from Flight Service.

To prevent computer saturation, most centers delete IFR flight plans a minimum of one hour after the proposed departure time. To ensure your flight plan remains active, advise ATC of your revised departure time if you will be delayed one hour or more.

AIR ROUTE SURVEILLANCE RADAR

The long-range radar equipment used in controlled airspace to manage traffic is **air route surveillance radar (ARSR)**. ARSR facilities relay traffic information to radar controllers at ARTCCs to direct and coordinate IFR traffic. Some of these facilities can detect only transponder-equipped aircraft and are referred to as beacon-only sites. Each ARSR site can monitor aircraft flying within a 200-mile radius of the antenna, although some stations can monitor aircraft as far away as 600 miles through the use of remote sites.

MAINTAINING SEPARATION

During an IFR flight, the controller might need to amend your clearance to maintain adequate separation. Reasons can include deviations due to weather, unplanned pilot requests, flow control restrictions, or aircraft emergencies. The controller has various techniques to ensure adequate separation. Some of the most common include route changes, radar vectoring, altitude crossing restrictions for navaids and intersections, altitude changes, and speed adjustments. Speed adjustments are most commonly used during the arrival phase of a flight. For example, ATC might advise you to *"reduce speed to 100"* as you near your destination. This means that ATC wants you to decrease your indicated airspeed to 100 knots and to maintain that speed within 10 knots. An instruction to *"resume normal speed"* does not change the speed restrictions in a published procedure, unless specifically stated by ATC, nor does it relieve you of speed restrictions in FAR Part 91.117.

 An ATC request for a speed reduction means you should maintain the new indicated airspeed within 10 knots.

PILOT RESPONSIBILITIES

Although ATC has strict requirements for the separation of IFR aircraft, keep in mind there are certain pilot responsibilities as well. For example, you must know the requirements for IFR flight, and you must know when an IFR clearance is required. Regulations state that you may not act as pilot in command of a flight conducted under IFR unless you hold an instrument rating and meet the recency of experience requirements for instrument flight as specified under FAR Part 61. In addition, your aircraft must meet the equipment and inspection requirements of FAR Part 91. If weather conditions are below VFR minimums, you must file an IFR flight plan and obtain an IFR clearance before departing from within, or prior to entering controlled airspace.

ADDITIONAL ARTCC SERVICES

In addition to separation of all IFR traffic, ARTCCs provide other safety-related services. These services include separating IFR aircraft from other traffic known to the controller, and providing weather information, safety alerts, and emergency assistance. ARTCC's radar covers nearly all of the United States, except in areas where mountains can block the signals from the radar sites.

SEPARATION FROM VFR TRAFFIC

ATC's first priority is the separation of all IFR aircraft from one another. However, if workload permits, the controller might advise you of VFR aircraft that could affect your flight. It is important to understand that the controller is not obligated to provide this traffic advisory service. In addition, some aircraft in your area might not appear on the controller's radar display. For this reason, FARs require every pilot to see and avoid other aircraft whenever possible, even when they are operated under positive radar control, as in Class B airspace. When you are operating under IFR in VFR conditions, you must continually search for all other aircraft, regardless of the radar service being provided.

WEATHER AVOIDANCE

There are two types of radar systems available to controllers to assist pilots in avoiding convective weather in flight: airport surveillance radar (ASR) and weather and radar processor (WARP). Approach controllers use ASR and can advise pilots of four levels of precipitation intensity: light, moderate, heavy and extreme. Center controllers use WARP and can advise pilots of three levels of precipitation intensity: moderate, heavy, and extreme. Controllers do not see clouds, thunderstorms or turbulence on their scopes; only precipitation intensity. You must infer the presence of these other hazards based on the precipitation intensity reported to you. It is also important to know that WARP information can be up to six minutes old.

 ATC radar limitations and radio congestion can limit a controller's capability to provide in-flight weather avoidance assistance.

Each controller will provide you with vectors around the displayed precipitation areas, *if requested* on a workload-permitting basis. It is critically important that you communicate your need for weather avoidance assistance to each ATC controller on initial contact. Never assume that any vector will avoid hazardous precipitation unless ATC says that is the purpose of the vector. Advise ATC early if you need a deviation for weather. Their first priority is separation of air traffic, and that becomes more difficult in bad weather.

To ensure that they disseminate timely weather information, each center has a meteorologist who monitors the weather within their airspace and advises pilots of hazardous weather affecting their route of flight. These reports include AIRMETs, SIGMETs, Convective SIGMETs, urgent pilot weather reports (UUA) and center weather advisories (CWAs).

SAFETY ALERTS

A center controller will issue a safety alert when it becomes apparent that your flight is in unsafe proximity to terrain, obstructions, or other aircraft. ATC issues a **terrain or obstruction alert** when your Mode C altitude readout indicates your flight is below the published minimum safe altitude for that area. In general, you will be requested to check your altitude immediately. The controller will then provide the minimum altitude required in your area of flight. [Figure 3-29]

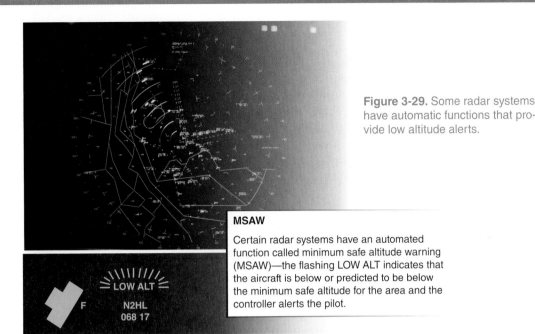

Figure 3-29. Some radar systems have automatic functions that provide low altitude alerts.

MSAW

Certain radar systems have an automated function called minimum safe altitude warning (MSAW)—the flashing LOW ALT indicates that the aircraft is below or predicted to be below the minimum safe altitude for the area and the controller alerts the pilot.

The second type of safety alert is called an **aircraft conflict alert**. This service is provided when the controller determines that the minimum separation between an aircraft being controlled and another aircraft could be compromised. If a conflict alert is issued to you, the controller advises you of the position of the other aircraft and a possible alternate course of action. Keep in mind that for either of these alert services to be available, your aircraft must be under radar control and your Mode C transponder must be fully operational. Terminal radar facilities can also issue both types of safety alerts.

EMERGENCY ASSISTANCE

One advantage of IFR flight is the continual radio contact with ATC. In addition, throughout most of the United States, your flight is continuously in radar contact.

If a problem arises, ATC is immediately available to render a wide variety of services including:

- Clearing conflicting traffic or giving priority to aircraft in emergency situations.

- Providing radar vectors and, if required, a radar approach to the nearest suitable airport.

- Alerting search and rescue (SAR) agencies in the area. [Figure 3-30]

Figure 3-30. If you need to make a forced landing, ATC facilities can notify search and rescue agencies and provide information on your last known position. This narrows the search area, saving valuable time.

TERMINAL FACILITIES

Within the air traffic control system, each terminal facility is closely linked with the associated ARTCC to integrate the flow of IFR departures and arrivals. In busy terminal areas, you contact approach control to coordinate your arrival prior to contacting the control tower and you contact departure control when the tower instructs you to after takeoff. In addition to providing ATIS and taxi, takeoff, and landing coordination, the control tower might have clearance delivery service to provide IFR clearances.

TERMINAL RADAR APPROACH CONTROL

Approach and departure control services are operated by **terminal radar approach control (TRACON)**. TRACON controllers coordinate very closely with the ARTCC to integrate arrival traffic from the enroute state to the terminal area, and transition departure traffic to the enroute phase. TRACON controllers typically monitor an area with a 50-mile radius and up to an altitude of 17,000 feet on radarscopes. This airspace is configured to provide service to a primary airport, but might include other airports that are within 50 miles of the radar service area. In addition to providing IFR separation, TRACON controllers provide vectors to airports, around terrain, and to avoid hazardous weather. Controllers in TRACONs determine the arrival sequence for the control tower's designated airspace.

CONTROL TOWER

Control towers are responsible for the safe, orderly, and expeditious flow of all traffic that is landing, taking off, operating on and in the vicinity of an airport, and when the responsibility has been delegated, towers can also provide for the separation of IFR aircraft in terminal areas.

When arriving IFR at a controlled airport, you are sequenced by approach control for spacing and then advised to contact the tower for landing clearance. The tower controller issues your landing clearance, which might include wind direction, wind velocity, current visibility and, if appropriate, special instructions. This information may be omitted at an airport served by ATIS. If you are arriving under VFR, you should contact the tower approximately 15 miles from the airport.

When a control tower is operational, you are required to obtain a clearance prior to operating in a movement area. This clearance can be from ground control or the tower operator. **Movement areas** are defined as runways, taxiways, and other areas that are used for taxiing, takeoffs, and landings, exclusive of loading ramps and parking areas. Ground control, when available, usually issues clearances for areas other than the active runway. When communicating with ground control or the tower, state your position on the airport surface. One of the position reports that you are required to make is when you are ready for takeoff from a runway intersection.

Aircraft that are departing IFR are integrated into the departure sequence by the tower. Prior to takeoff, the tower controller coordinates with departure control to assure adequate aircraft spacing. After takeoff, you are required to remain on the tower frequency until you are instructed to contact departure control. Within Class D airspace, pilots of VFR aircraft are required to remain on the tower's frequency unless directed otherwise.

 During a takeoff in IFR conditions, contact departure control only after you are advised to do so by the tower controller.

 When departing from a runway intersection, always state your position when calling the tower.

ATIS

At busy airports, airport advisory information is provided by **automatic terminal information service (ATIS)**. This continuous, recorded broadcast of noncontrol information helps to improve controller effectiveness and to reduce frequency congestion. At larger airports, there might be one ATIS frequency for departing aircraft and another one for arriving aircraft. ATIS is updated whenever any official weather is received, regardless of content change. It is also updated whenever airport conditions change. When a new ATIS is broadcast, it is changed to the next letter of the phonetic alphabet, such as Information Bravo or Information Charlie and so on. If the cloud ceiling is above 5,000 feet AGL and the visibility is more than 5 statute miles, inclusion of the ceiling/sky condition, visibility, and obstructions to vision in an ATIS message is optional. [Figure 3-31]

Following the airport name and ATIS phonetic letter identifier, the broadcast will state the time of the current weather report,	*Centennial Airport Information Tango, 1655 Zulu weather,*
magnetic wind direction and velocity,	*wind 070 at 12,*
visibility, obstructions to visibility, and ceiling/sky condition,	*visibility 2 light snow and mist, ceiling 1,200 broken, 2,000 overcast,*
temperature and dewpoint (if available),	*temperature 0, dewpoint 0,*
and altimeter setting.	*altimeter 29.74.*
Next, the instrument approach and runways in use are indicated.	*ILS Runway 35 Right is in use landing and departing Runway 35 Right.*
The ATIS broadcast also contains any other pertinent remarks relating to operations on or near the airport, such as closed runways or temporary obstructions.	*Pilot weather reports; bases 7,200 during approach and departure, light rime icing encountered between 7,000 and 9,000 feet by a King Air and a Learjet. A Boeing 727, 8 miles west of Denver, encountered light rime icing below 9,000 feet. All services, including taxi and IFR clearance available on the tower frequency 118.9.*
The phonetic letter identifier is restated at the end of the broadcast.	*Advise on initial contact you have Information Tango.*

Figure 3-31. ATIS provides information about airport conditions that is especially critical in IFR conditions.

 Regardless of content change, ATIS broadcasts are updated upon receipt of any official weather.

 The absence of the sky condition and visibility on an ATIS broadcast specifically implies the ceiling is more than 5,000 feet AGL and the visibility is more than 5 statute miles.

SECTION B ■ Air Traffic Control System

IT CAN HAPPEN TO ANYONE

Next time you think that you are invincible and that ATC will never allow your aircraft to get close to another, just remember that it can happen to anyone, even Air Force One. Flying west of Washington National Airport, Air Force One was heading west and climbing through 7,500 feet MSL. An MD-88 commercial flight was also west inbound to Washington National on an easterly heading. A 737 commercial flight was southwest of the airport descending from 8,500 feet MSL and circling away from the airport for spacing. Controllers turned Air Force One to the southwest to ensure separation from the MD-88. However, the turn placed Air Force one in the vicinity of the 737. It was determined that Air Force One and the 737 were separated at their closest point by 900 feet and a little over 2 miles.

Although this incident was resolved quickly, the established separation of 3 nautical miles and 1,000 feet in a terminal area was penetrated. Therefore, when flying under IFR conditions, always listen to what is happening with other traffic and visualize where you are in relation to them. If you are concerned that you are being vectored into an area near another aircraft, tell the controller.

CLEARANCE DELIVERY

In order to relieve congestion on the ground control frequency at busier airports, the control tower might provide a discrete **clearance delivery** frequency. This service enables you to receive an IFR clearance prior to contacting ground control for taxi. Additionally, this service can be used by VFR pilots to receive an ATC clearance when departing an airport within Class B or Class C airspace. Clearance delivery can also be used to receive a departure control frequency and transponder code when departing an airport with a radar departure control.

AUTOMATIC DEPENDENT SURVEILLANCE-BROADCAST

The **automatic dependent surveillance-broadcast (ADS-B)** system provides controllers and pilots in both the enroute and terminal environments with specific information about the position and speed of aircraft in the area. The ADS-B system incorporates GPS satellites, aircraft transmitters, and aircraft and ground receivers. Two forms of ADS-B equipment apply to aircraft—ADS-B Out and ADS-B In. ADS-B Out signals travel line-of-sight from transmitting aircraft to ATC ground receivers or aircraft receivers. In order to receive the signal and display traffic information in your aircraft you must also have ADS-B In capability. [Figure 3-32]

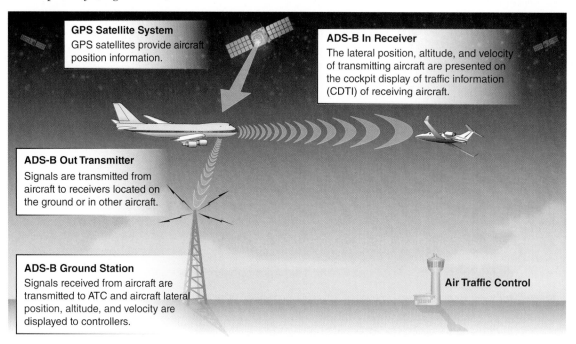

GPS Satellite System
GPS satellites provide aircraft position information.

ADS-B In Receiver
The lateral position, altitude, and velocity of transmitting aircraft are presented on the cockpit display of traffic information (CDTI) of receiving aircraft.

ADS-B Out Transmitter
Signals are transmitted from aircraft to receivers located on the ground or in other aircraft.

ADS-B Ground Station
Signals received from aircraft are transmitted to ATC and aircraft lateral position, altitude, and velocity are displayed to controllers.

Air Traffic Control

Figure 3-32. ADS-B helps you maintain situational awareness regarding your airplane's position in relation to other aircraft.

ADS-B continuously and automatically broadcasts aircraft speed, altitude, position, and other data once per second. Aircraft transmit and receive ADS-B data on one of two frequencies: the 1090 extended squitter (ES) or the 978 MHz universal access transceiver (UAT). [Figure 3-33]

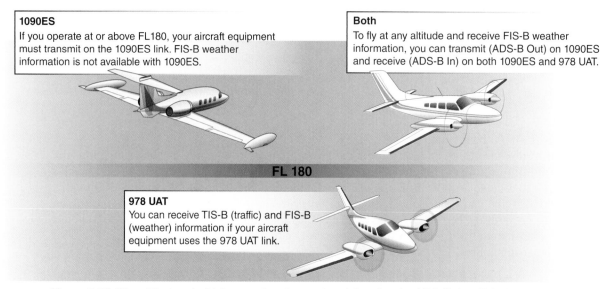

1090ES
If you operate at or above FL180, your aircraft equipment must transmit on the 1090ES link. FIS-B weather information is not available with 1090ES.

Both
To fly at any altitude and receive FIS-B weather information, you can transmit (ADS-B Out) on 1090ES and receive (ADS-B In) on both 1090ES and 978 UAT.

FL 180

978 UAT
You can receive TIS-B (traffic) and FIS-B (weather) information if your aircraft equipment uses the 978 UAT link.

Figure 3-33. The altitudes at which your aircraft operates determine the ADS-B data link that your aircraft requires.

Two additional ADS applications are ADS-Rebroadcast (ADS-R) and ADS-Contract (ADS-C). If you do not have both 1090ES and UAT equipment, your ADS-B equipment cannot see aircraft on the other frequency. ADS-R compensates for this by taking position information received on the ground from UAT-equipped aircraft and rebroadcasting the data on the 1090 frequency and vice versa. ADS-C functions similarly to ADS-B but is primarily used in sparsely trafficked transcontinental areas or oceanic crossings. ADS-C data is transmitted and acknowledged based on a contract between the ground system and an aircraft.

TRAFFIC INFORMATION

ADS-B provides precise shared traffic information so both pilots and controllers have a common operational picture and real-time data when aircraft deviate from their assigned flight paths. It clearly and immediately indicates changes as the conflicting traffic turns, accelerates, climbs, or descends. With an effective range of 100 nautical miles, the system gives controllers a large margin in which to implement conflict detection and resolution. Traffic situational awareness with alerts (TSAA) warns you if your aircraft is too close to another aircraft in flight. You monitor ADS-B traffic data on the cockpit display of traffic information (CDTI). [Figure 3-34]

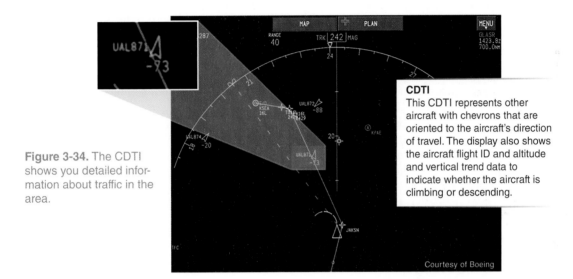

Figure 3-34. The CDTI shows you detailed information about traffic in the area.

CDTI
This CDTI represents other aircraft with chevrons that are oriented to the aircraft's direction of travel. The display also shows the aircraft flight ID and altitude and vertical trend data to indicate whether the aircraft is climbing or descending.

Courtesy of Boeing

Traffic information service-broadcast (TIS-B) is a ground-based, radar-derived service that enables aircraft with ADS-B In and the 978 UAT link to see other transponder-equipped aircraft that are not ADS-B equipped. The cockpit display shows all aircraft in radar contact with controllers—ADS-B equipped or not—within 15 miles, plus or minus 3,500 feet. In addition to in-flight enroute traffic, ADS-B works at low altitudes and on the ground so that it can be used to monitor aircraft surface movement and airport operations. [Figure 3-35]

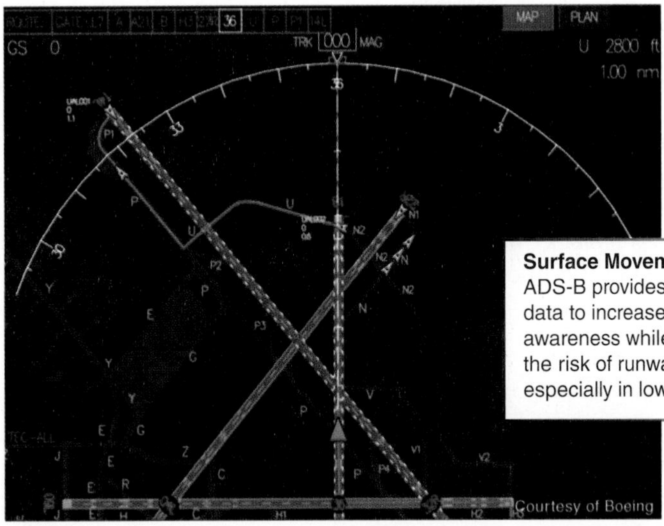

Figure 3-35. ADS-B can provide you with information about aircraft movement on the airport surface.

Surface Movement
ADS-B provides surface movement data to increase your situational awareness while taxiing and reduce the risk of runway incursion, especially in low visibility conditions.

Courtesy of Boeing

SECTION B ■ Air Traffic Control System

RADAR SERVICE FOR VFR AIRCRAFT

Basic radar service provides safety alerts, traffic advisories, limited vectoring, and sequencing for VFR aircraft at certain locations. When you are approaching an airport for landing, contact approach control and state your position, altitude, aircraft call sign, type of aircraft, radar beacon code, and destination. Approach control will issue wind and runway information, except when you state *"have numbers,"* or indicate you have the current ATIS information. For sequencing service, contact approach control when you are approximately 25 miles from the airport. At airports within a terminal radar service area (TRSA), air traffic controllers provide TRSA service, which includes radar vectoring, sequencing, and separation for all IFR and participating VFR aircraft.

Use of basic and TRSA radar service is not mandatory for VFR operations, but pilot participation is strongly urged. Participation does not relieve you of your responsibilities regarding terrain/obstruction clearance, vortex exposure, and to see and avoid other aircraft when operating under VFR. In addition, an ATC instruction to follow a preceding aircraft does not authorize you to comply with any ATC clearance or instruction issued to the preceding aircraft. You must decline a clearance issued by the radar controller that will cause you to violate a rule, such as entering a cloud under VFR. In this situation, tell the controller of your inability to comply with the issued clearance and request a revised clearance or instruction.

CLASS C SERVICE AREAS

Class C airspace areas are established by regulation at locations where traffic conditions warrant. Participation in Class C radar service is mandatory. You are not permitted to operate within Class C airspace unless you have established two-way radio communication with the ATC facility having jurisdiction over the area. In addition, you must maintain radio contact when operating within its limits. You can expect ATC to provide sequencing of all arriving aircraft to the primary airport. ATC also provides separation between IFR and VFR aircraft, traffic advisories, and safety alerts, if appropriate.

 For an IFR flight in Class C airspace, approach and departure control provide separation from all aircraft.

CLASS B SERVICE AREAS

Class B airspace areas are established to accommodate arrivals and departures at the nation's busiest airports. Because you may not operate within Class B airspace unless you obtain a specific ATC clearance, participation in Class B radar service is mandatory. Besides the basic radar services, Class B service provides separation of aircraft based on whether the flight is IFR or VFR, and/or on aircraft weight criteria. More space is required behind heavy aircraft. Sequencing of all arriving aircraft is also provided with Class B service.

TRAFFIC ADVISORIES

No matter what type of ATC radar facility you work with, controllers follow certain conventions when calling traffic to your attention. Normally, you are told the position (azimuth) of the traffic relative to your aircraft, its distance in nautical miles, its direction of movement, the type of aircraft, and its altitude, if known. When calling out traffic, controllers describe the position of the traffic in terms of the 12-hour clock. For example, *"traffic at 3 o'clock"* indicates the aircraft lies off your right wing. Keep in mind that the issuance of traffic information is based on the observation of your ground track and the position of the traffic. [Figure 3-36]

 As shown in figure 3-36, look for traffic based on your ground track, not your heading.

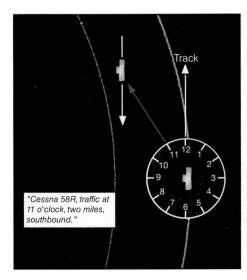

Because the controller is unable to determine your actual heading, you must adjust the traffic callout for any wind correction angle you are using. In this example, the controller advises you about traffic at your 11 o'clock position, but your wind correction angle places it closer to your 10 o'clock position.

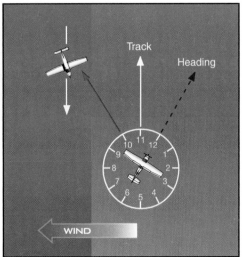

Figure 3-36. A radarscope does not account for the amount of wind correction you use to maintain your track over the ground.

FLIGHT SERVICE STATIONS (ALASKA ONLY)

In Alaska, flight service stations (FSSs) at selected locations provide a number of essential functions for both IFR and VFR aircraft. In addition to conducting weather briefings and handling flight plans, they also provide local airport advisory service. This service is provided by an FSS that is located on an airport that does not have a control tower or where the tower operates on a part-time basis. At these locations, the FSS provides official weather information, and also relays clearances from ATC. When inbound under VFR, you should report when you are approximately 10 miles from the airport and provide your altitude and aircraft type. Also, state your location relative to the airport, whether landing or overflying, and request a local airport advisory. Departing aircraft should state the aircraft type, full identification number, type of flight (VFR or IFR), and the planned destination or direction of flight.

 In Alaska, local airport advisories are provided by flight service stations at certain airports not served by an operating control tower.

SUMMARY CHECKLIST

✓ The main purpose of air traffic control (ATC) is to provide nationwide traffic separation during all phases of IFR flight using a network of radar and nonradar facilities. These facilities include air route traffic control centers, terminal radar approach control, and control towers.

✓ Flight plans are processed by the ARTCC in which the flight originates.

✓ You should file an IFR flight plans at least 30 minutes before departure.

✓ IFR flight plans are usually deleted from the ARTCC computer if they are not activated within one hour of the proposed departure time.

✓ Due to situations, such as weather, unplanned pilot requests, and flow control restrictions, controllers might alter your clearance to maintain proper aircraft separation.

SECTION B ■ Air Traffic Control System

✓ Regardless of whether operating under VFR or IFR, it is the pilot's responsibility to see and avoid other aircraft whenever weather conditions permit.

✓ Approach controllers use airport surveillance radar (ASR) to advise pilots of four levels of precipitation intensity: light, moderate, heavy and extreme.

✓ Center controllers use the weather and radar processor (WARP) to advise pilots of three levels of precipitation intensity: moderate, heavy, and extreme. WARP information can be up to six minutes old.

✓ Controllers will provide you with vectors around the displayed precipitation areas, if requested on a workload-permitting basis.

✓ Center meteorologists monitor the weather within their airspace and issue hazardous weather reports, including AIRMETs, SIGMETs, convective SIGMETs, urgent pilot weather reports (UUA) and center weather advisories (CWAs).

✓ ATC issues a terrain or obstruction alert when your Mode C altitude readout indicates your flight is below the published minimum safe altitude for that area.

✓ ATC issues an aircraft conflict alert when the controller determines that the minimum separation between an aircraft being controlled and another aircraft could be compromised.

✓ ATC provides emergency services, including clearing conflicting traffic or giving priority, providing radar vectors or a radar approach, and alerting search and rescue (SAR) agencies in the area.

✓ TRACON controllers coordinate very closely with the ARTCC to integrate arrival traffic from the enroute state to the terminal area, and transition departure traffic to the enroute phase.

✓ Control towers are responsible for the safe, orderly, and expeditious flow of all traffic that is landing, taking off, operating on and in the vicinity of an airport, and can provide for the separation of IFR aircraft in terminal areas.

✓ Movement areas are defined as runways, taxiways, and other areas that are used for taxiing, takeoffs, and landings, exclusive of loading ramps and parking areas.

✓ Ground control, when available, usually issues clearances for areas other than the active runway.

✓ ATIS is updated whenever any official weather is received, regardless of content change. It is also updated whenever airport conditions change.

✓ If the cloud ceiling is above 5,000 feet AGL and the visibility is more than 5 statute miles, inclusion of the ceiling/sky condition, visibility, and obstructions to vision in an ATIS message is optional.

✓ Clearance delivery service enables you to receive an IFR clearance prior to contacting ground control for taxi.

✓ The automatic dependent surveillance-broadcast (ADS-B) system uses GPS satellites, aircraft transmitters, and aircraft and ground receivers to provide controllers and pilots with specific information about the position and speed of aircraft in the area.

✓ ADS-B Out signals travel line-of-sight from transmitting aircraft to ATC ground receivers or aircraft receivers.

✓ In order to receive the signal and display traffic information in your aircraft you must also have ADS-B In capability.

✓ Aircraft transmit and receive ADS-B data on one of two frequencies: the 1090 extended squitter (ES) or the 978 MHz universal access transceiver (UAT).

✓ You monitor ADS-B traffic data on the cockpit display of traffic information (CDTI).

✓ Traffic information service-broadcast (TIS-B) is a ground-based, radar-derived service that enables aircraft with ADS-B In and the 978 UAT link to see other transponder-equipped aircraft that are not ADS-B equipped.

✓ Basic radar service for VFR aircraft includes safety alerts, traffic advisories, and limited radar vectoring. Sequencing also is available at certain terminal locations.

✓ Basic radar service is located in terminal radar service areas (TRSAs) and in Class C, and Class B airspace.

✓ Traffic advisories from ATC are based on your aircraft's actual ground track, not on your aircraft's heading.

✓ In Alaska, local airport advisory service is provided by flight service stations at certain airports not served by an operating control tower.

KEY TERMS

Air Traffic Control (ATC)

Air Route Traffic Control Center (ARTCC)

Air Route Surveillance Radar (ARSR)

Terrain or Obstruction Alert

Aircraft Conflict Alert

Terminal Radar Approach Control (TRACON)

Control Tower

Movement Area

Automatic Terminal Information Service (ATIS)

Clearance Delivery

Automatic Dependent Surveillance-Broadcast (ADS-B)

Basic Radar Service

QUESTIONS

1. What services do ARTCCs provide for aircraft flying under IFR?

2. Within a given area, what facility is the central authority for processing an IFR flight plan?
   A. Flight Service
   B. Air traffic control tower
   C. Air route traffic control center

3. At least how many minutes prior to your planned departure should you file your IFR flight plan?

4. What requirements do you have to meet to enter controlled airspace when weather conditions are below VFR minimums?

5. IFR flight plans filed in the ARTCC computer are usually deleted if they are not activated within what time period?
   A. 1 hour
   B. 2 hours
   C. 30 minutes

6. When does ATC issue a terrain or obstruction alert?

SECTION B ■ Air Traffic Control System

7. When does ATC issue an aircraft conflict alert?

8. What is the name of the service that enables you to receive an IFR clearance before you contact ground control for taxi?

For questions 9 through 14, match the ATC facility or service with its description.

9. Controls traffic on and in the vicinity of a controlled airport

A. ATIS

10. Transitions aircraft between the control tower and ARTCC

B. ARTCC

11. Controls surface movement on the airport other than on the active runways

C. Control tower

12. Broadcasts a prerecorded message of airport information

D. Ground control

13. Issues IFR clearances at large airports

E. Clearance delivery

14. Controls all enroute IFR air traffic

F. TRACON

15. Select the true statement regarding ADS-B.
    A. Controllers monitor ADS-B traffic data on the CDTI and alert you to conflicts.
    B. ADS-B In signals travel line-of-sight from transmitting aircraft to ATC ground receivers or aircraft receivers.
    C. In order to receive the signal and display traffic information in your aircraft you must have ADS-B In capability.

16. Which services are included in basic radar service for VFR aircraft?
    A. Separation, limited radar vectoring, and traffic advisories
    B. Safety alerts, traffic advisories, sequencing, and separation
    C. Safety alerts, traffic advisories, and limited radar vectoring

17. ATC gives you the following traffic advisory: *"traffic 2 o'clock, 3 miles northbound."* Refer to the accompanying illustration. Which traffic position corresponds to the advisory?

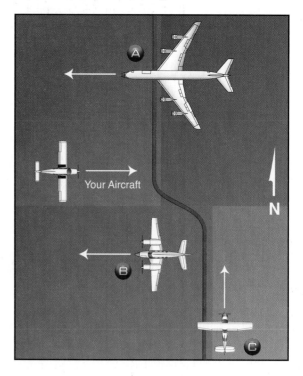

SECTION C
ATC Clearances

An ATC clearance constitutes an authorization for you to proceed under a specified set of conditions within controlled airspace. It is the means by which ATC exercises its responsibility to provide separation between aircraft. It is not, however, an authorization for you to deviate from any regulation or minimum altitude, nor to conduct unsafe operations.

PILOT RESPONSIBILITIES

When ATC issues a clearance, regulations specify that you are not to deviate from it, except in an emergency, unless an amended clearance is received or unless complying with that clearance will cause you to violate a rule or regulation. Therefore, before you accept a clearance, you must determine if you can safely comply with that clearance. Points to consider include whether compliance will cause you to break the rules, such as being vectored into a cloud when you are operating under VFR, or to exceed the performance capabilities of yourself or your aircraft. If, in your opinion, a clearance is unsafe or not appropriate, it is your responsibility to promptly request an amended clearance.

 When operating under VFR, if ATC assigns an altitude or heading that will cause you to enter clouds, you should avoid the clouds and inform ATC that the altitude or heading will not permit VFR.

If you find it necessary to deviate from a clearance due to an emergency, or compliance with the clearance would place your aircraft in jeopardy, you must notify ATC as soon as possible. This also includes a deviation in response to a traffic alert and collision avoidance system (TCAS) resolution advisory (RA). However, if you have to deviate, try not to disrupt the existing traffic flow. In addition, if ATC gives your aircraft priority because of an emergency, you may be requested to submit a written report within 48 hours to the manager of that ATC facility. [Figure 3-37]

Figure 3-37. If you deviate from an ATC clearance, you must notify ATC as soon as possible.

 You may not deviate from a clearance unless you experience an emergency or the clearance will cause you to violate an FAR. If you deviate, you must notify ATC as soon as possible.

 ATC may request a detailed report of an emergency even though a rule has not been violated when priority has been given.

. . . Climb! Climb!

FAR 91.123 authorizes deviations from an ATC clearance when responding to a traffic alert and collision avoidance system resolution advisory (TCAS RA). It also requires pilots to notify ATC as soon as possible if they deviate from a clearance in response to a TCAS RA. TCAS airborne equipment interrogates transponders of other aircraft that have entered monitored airspace. The size of the airspace area being monitored is established by the flight crew using various ranges on the TCAS equipment. By computer analysis of the replies, TCAS equipment determines which transponder-equipped aircraft are potential collision hazards and provides appropriate visual and oral advisory information to the flight crew.

There are two types of TCAS systems. TCAS I is used primarily by corporate and commuter aircraft and TCAS II is used by commercial airliners. TCAS I only provides traffic advisories (TAs), to assist in the visual acquisition of intruder aircraft. There are no recommended avoidance maneuvers provided. TCAS II, on the other hand, provides traffic advisories (TAs) and resolution advisories (RAs). Resolution advisories provide recommended maneuvers in a vertical direction (climbs or descents only) to avoid conflicting traffic. When an RA occurs, the pilot should maneuver as indicated on the RA displays unless doing so would jeopardize the safe operation of the flight or unless the flight crew has definitive visual acquisition of the aircraft causing the RA.

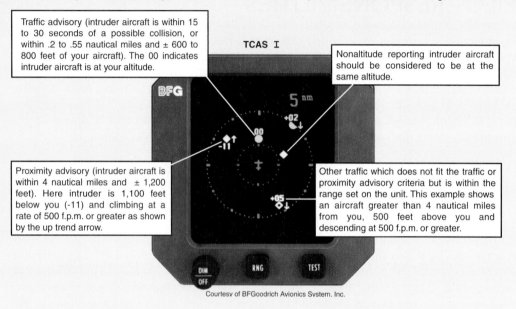

Traffic advisory (intruder aircraft is within 15 to 30 seconds of a possible collision, or within .2 to .55 nautical miles and ± 600 to 800 feet of your aircraft). The 00 indicates intruder aircraft is at your altitude.

Nonaltitude reporting intruder aircraft should be considered to be at the same altitude.

Proximity advisory (intruder aircraft is within 4 nautical miles and ± 1,200 feet). Here intruder is 1,100 feet below you (-11) and climbing at a rate of 500 f.p.m. or greater as shown by the up trend arrow.

Other traffic which does not fit the traffic or proximity advisory criteria but is within the range set on the unit. This example shows an aircraft greater than 4 nautical miles from you, 500 feet above you and descending at 500 f.p.m. or greater.

Courtesy of BFGoodrich Avionics System, Inc.

SEE AND AVOID

When meteorological conditions permit, even whey flying IFR under ATC control, you are responsible to see and avoid other aircraft, terrain, or obstacles. This is a common sense rule for safety. ATC radar cannot detect every aircraft that might pose a hazard to your flight, and ATC's primary responsibility is the separation of *IFR* traffic. Traffic advisories for VFR aircraft are provided only as workload permits. If your airplane is equipped with an autopilot, use it as appropriate to fly the airplane, giving you more time to look for traffic.

 In VFR conditions, you are required to see and avoid all aircraft, even if you are on an IFR flight plan. If there is no apparent relative motion between your aircraft and another aircraft, you are probably on a collision course.

IFR CLIMB CONSIDERATIONS

ATC expects you to maintain a continuous rate of climb of at least 500 ft/min to your assigned cruising altitude. If you are unable to maintain this climb rate, notify ATC of your reduced rate of climb. Unless ATC advises *"At pilot's discretion,"* you are expected to climb at an optimum rate consistent with your airplane's performance to within 1,000 feet of your assigned altitude. Then attempt to climb at a rate of between 500 and 1,500 ft/min for the last 1,000 feet of climb.

FAA You should climb at an optimum rate to within 1,000 feet of your assigned altitude. Then, you should climb at a rate of between 500 and 1,500 feet per minute.

When established on an airway, FAR Part 91 specifies that you must fly the centerline of that airway during climb, cruise, and descent. However, the regulation further provides that you are not prohibited from maneuvering the aircraft to pass well clear of other aircraft in VFR conditions. In addition, the FAA recommends that, when climbing in VFR conditions, you make gentle turns in each direction so you can continuously scan the area around you. As previously discussed, whenever you are operating on an IFR flight plan in VFR conditions, you are responsible for collision avoidance.

 FAA regulations require that you stay on the centerline of an airway except when maneuvering in VFR conditions to detect or avoid other air traffic. When climbing or descending in VFR conditions, ATC expects you to execute gentle banks, left and right, at a frequency that permits continuous visual scanning of the airspace around you.

IFR FLIGHT PLAN AND ATC CLEARANCE

Prior to flying in controlled airspace when the weather is below VFR minimums and in Class A airspace regardless of the weather, you are required to file an IFR flight plan. Keep in mind that you may not file an IFR flight plan unless you hold an instrument rating for the category of aircraft you are flying and you are instrument current as specified in FAR Part 61. In addition, the aircraft to be used must be approved for IFR flight and must have the navigation equipment appropriate to the navigation aids to be used. You may cancel an IFR flight plan anytime you are operating under VFR conditions outside of Class A airspace. However, after you cancel IFR, the flight must be conducted strictly in VFR conditions from that point on. If you encounter IFR weather again, you must remain in VFR conditions while you file a new flight plan and obtain an IFR clearance.

An ATC clearance is required before entering Class A and Class B airspace regardless of the weather conditions. When the weather is below VFR minimums, an ATC clearance is also required in Class C, D, and E airspace.

 You may cancel an IFR flight plan anytime you are operating in VFR conditions outside of Class A airspace.

 You must file an IFR flight plan and receive an ATC clearance before flying in controlled airspace when weather conditions are below VFR minimums, and in Class A airspace regardless of the weather.

ELEMENTS OF AN IFR CLEARANCE

An IFR clearance is made up of one or more instructions. Knowing the order in which ATC issues these instructions makes it easier to understand a clearance. [Figure 3-38]

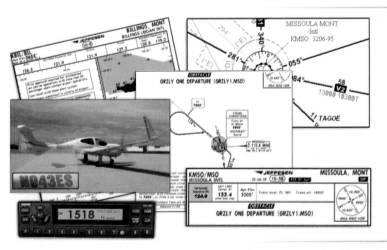

- Aircraft Identification
- Clearance limit
- Departure Procedure
- Route of flight
- Altitudes or flight levels, in order to be flown
- Holding instructions
- Any special information
- Frequency and transponder code information

Figure 3-38. The following items, when appropriate, are contained in an initial IFR clearance in the order shown.

CLEARANCE LIMIT

The clearance issued prior to departure normally authorizes you to fly to your airport of intended landing. However, because of delays at your destination, you might be cleared to a fix short of your destination. If this happens, you will be given an **expect further clearance (EFC)** time. At some locations, you might be given a **short-range clearance**, whereby a clearance is issued to a fix within or just outside of the departure terminal area. A short-range clearance contains the frequency of the air route traffic control center that will issue your long-range clearance. A short-range clearance is often used in a nonradar environment to get you to a location where you can be identified by radar.

DEPARTURE PROCEDURE

ATC can issue specific headings for you to fly and altitude restrictions to separate your aircraft from other traffic in the terminal area. Where the volume of traffic warrants, standard instrument departure procedures (SIDs) have been developed. SIDs and standard terminal arrival routes (STARs) are essentially charted procedures that help simplify the issuance of a clearance. ATC assumes you have all applicable SID and STAR charts and will issue them, as appropriate, without request. If you do not possess SID and STAR charts, or do not wish to use them, include the phrase "No SID No STAR" in the remarks sections of your IFR flight plan. SIDs and STARs are discussed in more detail in Chapters 4 and 6.

ROUTE OF FLIGHT

Clearances are normally issued for the altitude or flight level and route filed by the pilot. However, due to traffic conditions, it is sometimes necessary for ATC to specify an altitude/ flight level or route different from that requested. In addition, flow patterns have been established in certain congested areas, or between congested areas, whereby capacity is increased by routing all traffic on preferred routes. Information on these flow patterns is available in the *Chart Supplement* and in offices where preflight briefings are furnished or where flight plans are accepted.

When required, clearances include data to assist in identifying reporting points. It is your responsibility to notify ATC immediately if your navigation equipment cannot receive the type of signals needed to comply with the clearance.

ALTITUDE DATA

The altitude or flight level instructions in an ATC clearance normally require that you "*maintain*" the altitude or flight level at which the flight will operate when in controlled airspace. Request any change in enroute altitude or flight level well before the time you want to start the altitude change.

When possible, if the altitude assigned is different from the altitude requested, ATC will inform you when to expect a climb or descent clearance or when to request an altitude change from another facility. If a new altitude assignment has not been received prior to leaving the area, and you still desire a different altitude, you should reinitiate the request with the next facility.

ATC may issue a **cruise clearance** in situations where the route segment is relatively short and traffic congestion is not a consideration. In this type of clearance, the controller uses the word "*cruise*" instead of the word "*maintain*" when issuing an altitude assignment. [Figure 3-39]

Figure 3-39. This is an example of a cruise clearance.

"*. . . cleared to Goodland Airport, cruise 8,000.*"

The significance of a cruise clearance is that you may operate at any altitude, from the minimum IFR altitude up to and including, but not above, the altitude specified in the clearance. You may climb, level off, descend, and cruise at an intermediate altitude at any time. Each change in altitude does not require a report to ATC. However, after you begin a descent and report leaving an altitude, you may not climb back to that altitude without obtaining an ATC clearance. Another important aspect of a cruise clearance is that it also authorizes you to proceed to and execute an approach at the destination airport. In other words, you do not need to request, and ATC will not issue, a separate approach clearance at the destination airport when you have been issued a cruise clearance. When you are operating in uncontrolled airspace on a cruise clearance, you are responsible for determining the minimum IFR altitude. In addition, your descent and landing at an airport in uncontrolled airspace is governed by the applicable FARs for flight under VFR.

 A cruise clearance is an authorization to conduct flight at any altitude from the minimum IFR altitude up to and including the assigned altitude without a further clearance. In addition, you may vacate an altitude/flight level within the cruise clearance block of airspace without notifying ATC.

HOLDING INSTRUCTIONS

If you have been cleared to a fix other than the destination airport and a delay is expected, it is the responsibility of ATC to issue complete holding instructions, unless the pattern is charted on the enroute chart or approach procedure. In addition, the controller should issue an EFC time, and a best estimate of any additional enroute or terminal delay. If the holding pattern is charted and the controller does not issue complete holding instructions, you are expected to hold as depicted on the appropriate chart. [Figure 3-40]

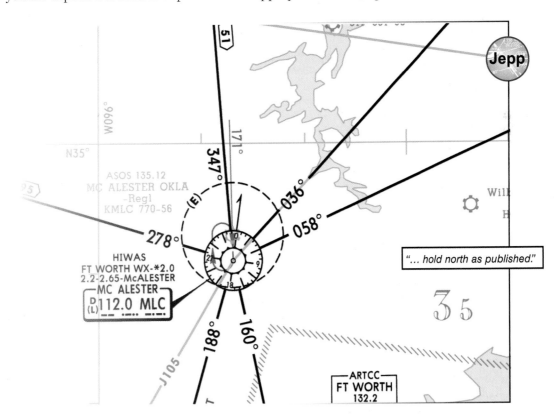

Figure 3-40. When the pattern is charted, the controller might omit all holding instructions except the charted holding direction and the statement "as published." However, controllers will always issue complete holding instructions if you request them.

ABBREVIATED IFR DEPARTURE CLEARANCE

In order to decrease radio congestion and controller workload, ATC issues an **abbreviated IFR departure clearance** whenever possible. This type of clearance uses the phrase *"cleared as filed"* to indicate you have been cleared to fly the route as contained in your IFR flight plan. This technique is particularly useful when numerous navigation fixes and Victor airways are contained in the flight plan, and ATC can accommodate the routing as you filed it with little or no change. However, if ATC finds it necessary to change your requested routing, a full route clearance is issued and the abbreviated clearance procedure is not used.

If you have filed a SID in your flight plan or a SID is in use at the departure airport, the SID or SID transition to be flown is included in the abbreviated clearance. Although SIDs are included in the abbreviated clearance, STARs are considered part of the routing and normally are not stated in the body of the clearance. If, for example, you filed a flight plan that included a STAR, and ATC did not amend it in your clearance, you should plan to fly the entire route, including the STAR, when you are cleared as filed.

An abbreviated clearance only applies to the route segment of the clearance. Besides the statement *"cleared as filed,"* it always contains the name of the destination airport or a clearance limit; any applicable SID name, number, and transition; your assigned enroute altitude, and any additional instructions such as the departure control frequency or transponder code assignment. [Figure 3-41]

 An abbreviated clearance contains the name of your destination airport or clearance limit; the assigned enroute altitude; SID information, if appropriate; and it might include a departure frequency or transponder code assignment.

"*. . . cleared to the Cuyahoga County Airport as filed, maintain 7,000.*"

"*. . . cleared to the Los Angeles International Airport, Rockies 3 Departure, Dove Creek Transition, then as filed. Maintain 10,000, expect flight level 270 within 10 minutes. Departure frequency is 126.1. Squawk 5417.*"

Figure 3-41. Shown are examples of abbreviated IFR departure clearances.

VFR ON TOP

In some situations, it might be to your advantage to request VFR on top during an IFR flight. This type of clearance does not cancel your IFR flight plan. Instead, it allows you more flexibility with regard to altitude assignments. Basically, a **VFR-on-top clearance** allows you to fly in VFR conditions and at appropriate VFR cruising altitudes of your choice. You may only request this clearance if you are in VFR conditions and below Class A airspace, which begins at 18,000 feet. ATC can not initiate a VFR-on-top clearance.

After ATC approves your request, you must maintain VFR flight conditions at all times. Altitude selection must comply with the VFR cruising altitude rules, which are based on the magnetic course of the aircraft. You may not, however, select an altitude that is less than the minimum enroute altitude prescribed for the route segment. [Figure 3-42]

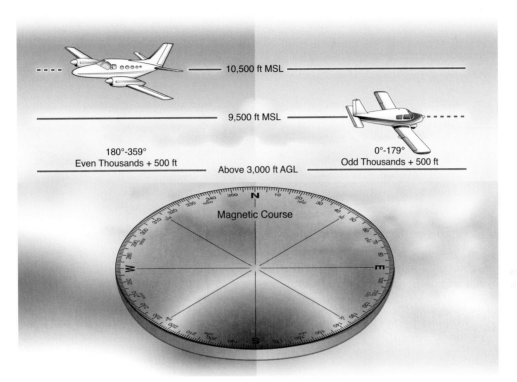

10,500 ft MSL

9,500 ft MSL

180°-359°
Even Thousands + 500 ft

Above 3,000 ft AGL

0°-179°
Odd Thousands + 500 ft

Magnetic Course

Figure 3-42. When operating VFR-on-top, you must choose cruising altitude that both meets VFR rules and is above the minimum IFR altitude.

An ATC authorization to maintain VFR on top does not literally restrict you to on-top operations. You may operate VFR on an IFR flight plan when you are above, below, or between layers, or in the clear. This type of clearance simply allows you to change altitude in VFR conditions after advising ATC of the intended altitude changes. Keep in mind,

 VFR-on-top operations are prohibited in Class A airspace.

 A VFR-on-top clearance can only be assigned by ATC if it has been requested by the pilot and conditions are indicated to be suitable for that type of flight.

 Both VFR and IFR rules apply to a VFR-on-top flight. However, when flying VFR on top, you are required to comply with the VFR cruising altitude rules and the basic VFR weather minimums. See figure 3-39.

however, that all the rules applicable to instrument flight, such as minimum IFR altitudes, position reporting, radio communication, and adherence to ATC clearances, must still be followed. If at any time VFR conditions cannot be maintained, you must inform ATC and receive a new clearance before you enter IFR conditions.

CLIMB TO VFR ON TOP

A variation of the VFR-on-top clearance is a request to **climb to VFR on top**. You would request this type of clearance to climb through a cloud, haze, or smoke layer and then either cancel your IFR flight plan or operate VFR-on-top.

The ATC authorization will contain a top report (or a statement that no top report is available) and a request to report upon reaching VFR-on-top. Additionally, the ATC authorization might contain a clearance limit, routing, and an alternative clearance if VFR-on-top is not reached by a specified altitude. [Figure 3-43]

 A climb-to-VFR-on-top clearance should be requested in order to climb through a cloud layer or an area of reduced visibility and then continue the flight VFR.

"...cleared to RANDI via radar vectors, climb to and report reaching VFR on top, tops reported 3,000, if not on top at 4,000, maintain 4,000 and advise. Maintain VFR on top."

Figure 3-43. This represents a typical climb-to-VFR-on-top clearance.

APPROACH CLEARANCES

You should be aware of a few peculiarities with the issuance of an instrument approach clearance. First, if only one approach procedure exists or if you are authorized by ATC to execute the approach procedure of your choice, you are issued a clearance, such as "... *cleared for approach.*" If more than one approach procedure is available at the destination airport or if ATC restricts you to a specific approach, the controller specifies, "... *cleared for ILS Runway 35 Right approach.*" If you are established on a route or approach segment that has a published minimum altitude, your approach clearance generally will not specify an altitude to maintain. [Figure 3-44]

Figure 3-44. If you are being radar vectored to the final approach course, your approach clearance should always include an altitude to maintain.

"... turn right heading 320°, maintain 2,000 until established on the localizer. Cleared for ILS Runway 36 approach."

When you plan to land on a runway that is not aligned with the approach you are flying, the controller can issue a **circling approach clearance**. In this case, the controller will specify, "... *cleared for VOR Runway 17 approach, circle to land Runway 23.*"

If conditions permit, you can request a **contact approach**, which is then authorized by the controller. A contact approach cannot be initiated by ATC. This procedure might be used instead of the published procedure to expedite your arrival, as long as the airport has a standard or special instrument approach procedure, the reported ground visibility is at least one statute mile, and you are able to remain clear of clouds with at least one mile flight visibility throughout the approach. Some advantages of a contact approach are that it usually requires less time than the published instrument procedure, it allows you to retain your IFR clearance, and provides separation for IFR and special VFR traffic. On the other hand, obstruction clearances and VFR traffic avoidance becomes your responsibility.

When it is operationally beneficial, ATC can authorize you to conduct a **visual approach** to the airport in lieu of the published approach procedure. A visual approach can be initiated by you or the controller. Before issuing a visual approach clearance, the controller must verify that you have the airport, or a preceding aircraft that you are to follow, in sight. If you have the airport in sight but do not see the aircraft you are to follow, ATC might issue the visual approach clearance but will maintain responsibility for aircraft separation. After you report the aircraft in sight, you assume the responsibilities for your own separation and wake turbulence avoidance.

 A contact or visual approach may be used in lieu of conducting a standard instrument approach procedure.

Keep in mind that the visual approach clearance is issued to expedite the flow of traffic to an airport. It is authorized when the ceiling is reported or expected to be at least 1,000 feet AGL and the visibility at least 3 statute miles. You must remain clear of the clouds at all times while conducting a visual approach. At a controlled airport, you might be cleared to fly a visual approach to one runway while others are conducting VFR or IFR approaches to another parallel, intersecting, or converging runway. Also, when radar service is provided, it is automatically terminated when the controller advises you to change to the tower or advisory frequency.

 During a visual approach, radar service is terminated automatically when ATC instructs the pilot to contact the tower.

 The main differences between a visual approach and a contact approach are: a pilot must request a contact approach, but a visual approach may be assigned by ATC or requested by the pilot; and a contact approach may be approved with 1 mile visibility if the flight can remain clear of clouds, but a visual approach requires the pilot to have the airport in sight, or a preceding aircraft to be followed, and the ceiling must be at least 1,000 feet AGL with at least 3 statute miles visibility.

 Without prior pilot request, ATC may issue SIDs, STARs, and visual approach clearances.

VFR RESTRICTIONS TO AN IFR CLEARANCE

During the issuance of an ATC clearance, the controller might direct you to *"maintain VFR conditions."* However, this restriction is only issued when you request it. For example, a VFR restriction is issued when you request a VFR climb or descent. This is the case when you are departing or arriving in VFR conditions and you wish to avoid a complicated, time-consuming departure or arrival procedure. In the case of a VFR departure, for example, you might request a VFR climb, which would allow you to avoid the departure procedure and climb on course. However, you should fully understand that when operating on an IFR flight plan with a VFR restriction, you must remain in VFR conditions and maintain your own traffic separation during the VFR portion of your clearance.

 VFR restrictions to an IFR flight can only be initiated by the pilot.

COMPOSITE FLIGHT PLAN

A **composite flight plan** is a request to operate IFR on one portion of a flight and VFR for another portion. When you file a composite flight plan, include all normal IFR route segments and the clearance limit fix where you anticipate the IFR portion of the flight will terminate. VFR. If the first portion of your flight is VFR, activate your VFR flight plan with Flight Service after departure. As you near the point where you planned to activate your IFR flight plan, contact Flight Service, close your VFR flight plan, and request your IFR clearance. You must remain in VFR conditions until you receive your IFR clearance.

If your flight requires IFR for the first portion and VFR for the latter portion, you are normally cleared IFR to the point where the change is proposed. As you near this point and are operating in VFR conditions, cancel your IFR flight plan and contact Flight Service to activate your VFR flight plan. If you want to continue past your clearance limit on an IFR flight plan, contact ATC five minutes before you reach the limit to request a further clearance. If you reach your clearance limit without receiving a clearance to continue, you are expected to enter a holding pattern and wait for the clearance. [Figure 3-45]

FLIGHT PLAN				
1. TYPE	2. AIRCRAFT IDENTIFICATION	3. AIRCRAFT TYPE/ SPECIAL EQUIPMENT	4. TRUE AIRSPEED	5. DEPARTURE POINT
✔ VFR ✔ IFR ☐ DVFR	N541AJ	DA-40/A	110 KNOTS	KGCC
8. ROUTE OF FLIGHT GCC V536 5HR V8L BIL				
9. DESTINATION (Name of airport and city)		10. EST. TIME ENROUTE		11. REMARKS
KBZN		HOURS 1	MINUTES 25	
12. FUEL ON BOARD	13. ALTERNATE AIRPORT (S)		14. PILOT'S NAME, ADDRES	

Check both the VFR and IFR boxes in block 1.

Include all normal IFR route segments and the clearance limit fix where you expect the IFR portion to end.

Figure 3-45. You may file a composite flight plan any time you plan to fly a portion of the flight under VFR.

 For a composite flight plan, check both the VFR and IFR boxes under type of flight. See figure 3-45.

 You may file a composite flight plan anytime a portion of your flight will be VFR. If the VFR portion is first, contact Flight Service prior to transitioning to the IFR portion, close the VFR portion, and request an ATC clearance.

 When filing a composite flight plan with the first portion of the flight under IFR, include all normal IFR route segments and the clearance limit fix where you anticipate the IFR portion will end.

TOWER ENROUTE CONTROL CLEARANCE

Tower enroute control (TEC) is an alternative IFR procedure that permits you to fly short, low altitude routes between terminal areas. TEC routes are published for certain portions of the United States in the *Chart Supplement* and in the Enroute Section of the *Jeppesen Airway Manual Services*. Essentially, a flight is transferred from departure control at one airport to successive approach control facilities. In most cases, TEC routes are generally intended for nonturbojet aircraft operating below 10,000 feet MSL with a flight duration of normally less than two hours. If you want to fly a TEC route, include the acronym TEC in the remarks section of the flight plan.

DEPARTURE RESTRICTIONS

In order to separate IFR departure traffic from other traffic in the area, or to restrict or regulate the departure flow of traffic, ATC may place time restrictions on your clearance. Some of these restrictions include a release time, a hold for release time, and a clearance void time. A **release time** specifies the earliest time you may depart. This type of restriction is generally a result of traffic saturation, weather, or ATC departure management procedures. Occasionally, you might be advised to *"hold for release."* When ATC issues a hold for release, you may not depart until you receive a release time or you are given additional instructions. Generally, the additional instructions will include the expected release time and the length of the departure delay. When the local conditions and traffic permit, you will be released for departure.

If you are operating at an airport not served by an operating control tower, ATC might find it necessary to issue a **clearance void time** in conjunction with your IFR departure clearance. The wording, *"clearance void if not off by . . . ,"* indicates that ATC expects you to be airborne by a certain time. A common situation for the issuance of a void time is when inbound traffic is expected to arrive at approximately the same time as your departure. In this case, the required traffic separation cannot be achieved without restricting your departure. If you do not depart by the void time, you must advise ATC of your intentions as soon as possible, but no later than 30 minutes after the void time. Your failure to contact ATC within the allotted time after the clearance void time could result in your aircraft being considered overdue, and search and rescue procedures initiated.

 When departing from an airport not served by a control tower, the issuance of a clearance containing a void time indicates that you must advise ATC as soon as possible, but no later than 30 minutes, of your intentions if not off by the void time.

At some non-towered airports, a **ground communication outlet (GCO)** provides a remotely controlled, ground-to-ground communications facility that allows you to obtain an instrument clearance or close a VFR or IFR flight plan. A specific number of microphone clicks connects you to either an ATC facility or Flight Service via a VHF-to-telephone connection. You might also be able to use it to update a weather briefing prior to departure.

CLEARANCE READBACK

Although there is no requirement that an ATC clearance be read back, you are expected to read back those parts of any clearance that contain altitude assignments, radar vectors, or any instructions requiring verification. Additionally, controllers can request that you read back a clearance when the complexity of the clearance or any other factors indicate a need.

 You should read back that portion of a clearance containing altitude assignments, radar vectors, or any instruction requiring clarification.

As the pilot in command, you should read back the clearance if you feel the need for confirmation. Even though it is not specifically stated, it is generally expected that you will read back the initial enroute clearance you receive from clearance delivery, ground control, or Flight Service. When you receive your IFR clearance, the phraseology might be slightly different, depending upon the facility issuing the clearance. The terms *"ATC clears,"* *"ATC advises",* or *"ATC requests"* are used only when a facility other than air traffic control is used to relay information originated by ATC.

CLEARANCE SHORTHAND

To operate efficiently in the IFR environment, you must be able to copy and thoroughly understand clearances. Copying IFR clearances becomes easy with practice. Although numerous changes have been made since the acceptance of the first shorthand used by early instrument pilots, many of the original symbols have been retained. The shorthand symbols in this chapter are considered by the FAA and experienced instrument pilots to be the best. [Figure 3-46]

SHORTHAND SYMBOLS

Words and Phrases	Shorthand	Words and Phrases	Shorthand
Above	ABV	Expect Further Clearance (time or location)	EFC
Above ("*Above six thousand*")	60	Flight Level	FL
Advise	ADV	Flight Planned Route	FPR
After (passing)	< or AFT	For Further Clearance	FFC
Airport	A	From	FR or FRM
(Alternate Instructions)	( )	Heading	HDG
Altitude 6,000 – 17,000	60 – 170	Hold (direction) ("*Hold west*")	H-W
And	&	Holding Pattern	⬭
Approach	AP	Inbound	IB
Final	F	Intercept	⋀ or INT
Instrument Landing System	ILS	Intersection	△ or XN
Localizer Back Course	LBC	Landing	LDG
Localizer Only	LOC	Maintain (or magnetic)	M
Nondirectional Beacon	NDB	Middle Marker	MM
Precision Approach Radar	PAR	Compass Locator at Middle Marker	LMM
Surveillance Radar	ASR	No (or not) Later Than	NLT
VOR	VOR or ⊙	On Course	OC
Approach Control	APC	Outbound	OB
As Filed	AF	Outer Marker	OM
As Published	APUB	Compass Locator at Outer Marker	LOM
At	@	Over (ident over the line)	O̲K̲C̲
(ATC) Advises	CA	Procedure Turn	PT
(ATC) Clears or Cleared	C	Radar Contact	RCT
(ATC) Requests	CR	Radar Vector	RV
Bearing	BRG or BR	Radial (092 radial)	092R
Before (reaching, passing)	>	Report	R
Below	BLO	Report Leaving	RL
Below ("*Below six thousand*")	6̄0̄	Report On Course	R-CRS
Center	CTR	Report Over	RO
Cleared or (ATC) Clears	C	Report Passing	RP
Cleared As Filed	CAF	Report Reaching	RR
Cleared to Land	CL	Report Starting Procedure Turn	RSPT
Climb (to)	↑	Reverse Course	RC
Contact	CT	Runway (number)	RWY 26
Contact Approach	CAP	Squawk	SQ
Course	CRS	Standby	STBY
Cross (crossing)	X	Takeoff	TO
Cruise	→	Tower	Z OR TWR
Depart (departure)	DP	Track	TR
Departure Control	DPC	Turn Left, or Turn Left After Departure	↰ or LT
Descend (to)	↓	Turn Right, or Turn Right After Departure	↱ or RT
Direct	DR or D⇨	Until	til or U
DME Fix (15 DME mile fix)	D or D15	Until Advised (by)	UA
Each	EA	Until Further Advised	UFA
Eastbound	EB	VFR On Top	VFR̲
Established	ESTB	Victor (airway number)	V294
Expect	EX	VOR	⊙
		VORTAC	Ⓣ

Figure 3-46. The purpose of these shorthand symbols is to allow you to copy IFR clearances as fast as they are read. The more clearances you copy, the easier the task becomes.

Proficiency in copying clearances is the result of practice and knowing clearance terminology. Figure 3-47 shows samples of clearances as they might be issued. Each is followed by its appropriate clearance shorthand.

"Commander 480S cleared to the Abilene Municipal Airport as filed. Maintain 12,000. After departure turn right heading 340 for radar vectors. Squawk 2021."

C ABI A AF M120 AFT DP ↱ HDG 340 RV SQ 2021

"Cessna 1351F cleared to the Ardmore Municipal Airport, radar vectors Bonham, Victor 15. Maintain 5,000. Departure control frequency 124.5. Squawk 0412."

C ADM A RV BYP V15 M50 DPC 124.5 SQ 0412

"ATC clears Aztec 103MC to the Addison Airport, Victor 369 Dallas-Ft. Worth, direct. Maintain VFR on top. If not VFR on top at 5,000, maintain 5,000 and advise."

C ADDISON A V369 DFW DR M VFR (or M50 & ADV)

"Cessna 1351F, descend and maintain 8,000. Report reaching 8,000."

↓ M80 RR 80

"Piper 43532, radar contact 15 miles southeast of the Mustang VORTAC. Turn right heading 350. Intercept the Mustang 059 radial. Cleared for the VOR Delta approach to Reno, contact Tower on 118.7 at the VOR inbound."

15 SE FMG ① ↱ HDG 350⊿ FMG 059R C⊙ D AP
RNO CT TWR 118.7 @⊙ IB

Figure 3-47. When using clearance shorthand, the most important consideration is not what symbols you use, but that you can still interpret them after a period of time.

SECTION C ■ ATC Clearances

CAUSES OF COMMUNICATION BREAKDOWN

Controllers are asking, *"what is going on up there?"* as they complain about pilot errors in clearance readbacks, and pilots are asking, *"what is going on down there?"* as they are being informed that they busted the altitudes that they had dutifully read back in their clearance.

Based on studies conducted by the Aviation Safety Reporting System (ASRS), there seem to be four major problem areas causing readback errors.

- **Similar aircraft call signs** — There could be many aircraft with similar call signs operating on the same frequency, at the same time and in the same airspace
- **Only one pilot listening on ATC frequency** — In two-pilot operations, both pilots should be listening to clearances. If one pilot is getting the ATIS report or talking to another facility, backup monitoring is lost.
- **Slips of mind and tongue** — The typical human errors in this category include being advised of traffic at another flight level or altitude and accepting the information as clearance to that altitude; confusing *"one zero"* and *"one one thousand;"* confusing left and right in parallel runways; and the interpretation of *"maintain two five zero"* as an altitude instead of an airspeed limitation.
- **Mind-set, preprogrammed for . . ., and expectancy factors** — The airmen who request *"higher"* or *"lower"* tend to be spring-loaded to hear what they want to hear upon receipt of a blurred call sign transmission.

But why didn't the controller catch the pilot error in the readback?

The main problem here seems to be overload or working too many aircraft. At busy airports, controllers can have a rush of departures/arrivals at the same time they are working land-lines and phones coordinating hand-offs of traffic. This is further complicated by stepped on transmissions where only partial clearances or readbacks are heard.

So what can be done? When pilots read back a clearance, they are asking a question: *"Did we get it right?"* Unfortunately, ASRS reports reveal that ATC is not always listening. Contrary to many pilots' assumptions, controller silence is not confirmation of a readback's correctness, especially during peak traffic periods.

As a pilot, you can take several precautions to reduce the likelihood of readback/hearback failures:

- Ask for verification of any ATC instruction about which there is doubt. Don't read back a best guess at a clearance, expecting ATC to catch any mistakes.
- Be aware that being off ATC frequency while listening to the ATIS or while talking to another facility is a potential communication trap for a two-pilot crew.
- Use standard communication procedures in reading back clearances. *"Okay,"* *"Roger "* and microphone clicks are poor substitutes for readbacks.
- Avoid interpreting altitudes mentioned for purposes other than a clearance as an instruction to proceed to that altitude.
- Be aware of similar sounding call signs, and make sure the clearance is for you.

The preceding discussion was compiled from an ASRS Directline article by Bill Monan.

SUMMARY CHECKLIST

✓ An ATC clearance is an authorization for you to proceed under a specified set of conditions within controlled airspace.

✓ You may not deviate from an ATC clearance unless you experience an emergency or the clearance will cause you to violate a rule or regulation.

✓ If you deviate from an ATC clearance, you must notify ATC as soon as possible. If you are given priority over other aircraft you may be requested to submit a written report to the manager of the ATC facility within 48 hours.

✓ Anytime you are in VFR conditions, it is your responsibility to see and avoid all other traffic, regardless of the type of flight plan you are on.

✓ An IFR flight plan is required before flying into Class A airspace or any other controlled airspace when the weather is below VFR minimums.

✓ You must receive an ATC clearance before entering Class A or B airspace regardless of the weather and in Class C, D, and E airspace when the weather is below VFR minimums.

✓ The elements of an ATC clearance are: aircraft identification, clearance limit, departure procedure, route of flight, altitudes/flight levels in the order to be flown, holding instructions, any special information, and frequency and transponder code information.

✓ A cruise clearance authorizes you to operate at any altitude from the minimum IFR altitude up to and including the altitude specified in the clearance without reporting the change in altitude to ATC.

✓ An abbreviated clearance can be issued when your route of flight has not changed substantially from that filed in your flight plan. An abbreviated clearance always contains the words "cleared as filed" as well as the name of the destination airport or clearance limit; any applicable SID name, number and transition; the assigned enroute altitude; and any additional instructions such as departure control frequency or transponder code assignment.

✓ A VFR-on-top clearance allows you to fly in VFR conditions and at the appropriate VFR cruising altitudes of your choice. VFR on top is prohibited in Class A airspace.

✓ A contact approach must be initiated by the pilot, it cannot be initiated by ATC.

✓ In order to fly a contact approach, the reported ground visibility must be at least one statute mile, and you must be able to remain clear of clouds with at least one statute mile flight visibility.

✓ A visual approach can be initiated by the controller or the pilot when the ceiling is at least 1,000 feet and the visibility is at least 3 statute miles and the pilot has the airport or the aircraft to follow in sight.

✓ VFR restrictions to an IFR clearance can only be initiated by the pilot.

✓ File a composite flight plan when you wish to operate IFR on one portion of a flight and VFR on another portion.

✓ A tower enroute control clearance (TEC) is intended to be used by nonturbojet aircraft at altitudes less than 10,000 feet MSL if the duration of the flight is less than 2 hours.

✓ Departure restrictions, such as a release time, hold for release time, and a clearance void time can be imposed to separate IFR departure traffic from other traffic in the area or to regulate the flow of IFR traffic.

✓ Read back those parts of a clearance that contain altitude assignments, radar vectors, or any instructions requiring verification.

✓ Use shorthand to copy IFR clearances quickly. The type of shorthand you use is not important as long as you can read the clearance accurately later.

KEY TERMS

Expect Further Clearance (EFC)

Short-Range Clearance

Cruise Clearance

Abbreviated IFR Departure Clearance

Cleared As Filed

VFR-On-Top Clearance

Climb To VFR On Top

Circling Approach Clearance

Contact Approach

Visual Approach

Maintain VFR Conditions

Composite Flight Plan

Tower Enroute Control (TEC)

Release Time

Hold For Release

Clearance Void Time

Ground Communication Outlet (GCO)

QUESTIONS

1. An ATC clearance is an authorization to proceed under specified conditions within what type of airspace?

2. If you deviate from a clearance due to an emergency, when must you notify ATC?
   A. As soon as possible
   B. Immediately after landing
   C. Within 24 hours after landing

3. If ATC provides you with priority service because of an emergency, you may be required to submit a written report to the manager of that ATC facility within what time frame?
   A. Immediately after landing
   B. Within 24 hours after landing
   C. Within 48 hours after landing

4. True/False. You are always required to see and avoid other aircraft when operating in VFR conditions, even on an IFR flight plan.

5. True/False. To operate under IFR within controlled airspace, you must file an IFR flight plan and obtain an ATC clearance.

6. Regardless of weather conditions, you are required to file an IFR flight plan before you can legally fly within what class of airspace?
   A. Class A
   B. Class B
   C. All controlled airspace

For questions 7 through 14, use the associated letter of the IFR departure clearance items to arrange them in the correct sequence.

7. _____   A. Aircraft identification

8. _____   B. Altitudes, in the order to be flown

9. _____   C. Any special instructions

10. _____   D. Clearance limit

11. _____   E. Departure procedure

12. _____   F. Frequency and transponder code information

13. _____   G. Holding instructions

14. _____   H. Route of flight

15. True/False. ATC will not issue a standard instrument departure (SID) unless you request it.

16. True/False. When ATC issues a clearance with significant changes to your requested routing, you can expect an abbreviated clearance.

17. What is the significance of the following clearance: "...*cruise 5,000*"?
  A. You can fly at any altitude from 5,000 feet MSL up to the base of Class A airspace.
  B. You can conduct your flight at any altitude from the minimum IFR altitude up to and including 5,000 feet MSL.
  C. You can fly at any altitude from the minimum IFR altitude up to and including 5,000 feet MSL, but you must report leaving each altitude to ATC.

18. Before a contact approach is approved, the reported ground visibility must be at least what?
  A. One statute mile
  B. One nautical mile
  C. Three statute miles

19. Select the true statement when cleared to fly VFR on top on an IFR flight.
  A. Your IFR flight plan is automatically cancelled.
  B. You are required to comply with VFR cruising altitude rules.
  C. You may fly below the minimum enroute altitude prescribed for the route segment you are flying as long as you remain VFR.

20. When you are flying on a composite flight plan, who should you contact to cancel the VFR portion and request a clearance to proceed under IFR?

21. When ATC issues a clearance void time in conjunction with a departure clearance, in what time frame must you depart?
  A. No later than the clearance void time
  B. No later than 30 minutes after the clearance void time
  C. 30 minutes or later after the clearance void time

22. True/False. You should read back all portions of an ATC clearance that contain specific instructions, such as altitude assignments or radar vectors.

23. Decipher the following clearance. (CYS is Cheyenne Airport)

    C CYS A AF ↑M 80 DPC 120.9 SQ5417

24. Rewrite the following clearance using shorthand symbols.

    "Gulfstream 37R, cleared to the Dallas Love Airport (DAL) direct Bonham (BYP) VORTAC. Descend and maintain 12,000, report passing 15,000. Depart Bonham VORTAC heading 210 for vectors to Runway 31 Right ILS final approach course. Landing Runway 31 Right."

SECTION C ■ **ATC Clearances**

PART II

Instrument Charts and Procedures

I didn't develop the charts to get famous. I did it to stay alive.

— Elrey B. Jeppesen

PART II

When Elrey B. Jeppesen began recording aeronautical information in the early 1930s, he did it simply as a means of survival. Although it might not have been his original intention, Captain Jepp also managed to revolutionize air travel by making it a more reliable and safer form of transportation. As an instrument pilot, you will use charts inspired by Captain Jepp's sketches to routinely fly in conditions that ordinarily would keep you on the ground. Of course, reading and understanding the charts is only half of the story. To be a competent instrument pilot, you must also know how to fly the procedures depicted on the charts. To help you interpret the charts and translate the instructions into action, Part II breaks instrument flight into several broad phases. The departure phase, which takes you from the airport to the enroute structure, is covered in Chapter 4. After leaving the departure phase, you begin the enroute portion of your flight, which is discussed in Chapter 5. As you near your destination, you enter the arrival phase, which might begin with a published procedure similar to those shown in Chapter 6. In most cases, your IFR flights will end with an instrument approach to the runway. To prepare you for these operations, Chapter 7 covers approach charts and general approach procedures, and Chapter 8 discusses specific types of approaches and the associated procedures.

CHAPTER 4

Departure

Instrument/Commercial
Part II, Chapter 4 — Departure

SECTION A
Departure Charts

Departure charts are published to help simplify complex clearance delivery procedures, reduce frequency congestion, ensure obstacle clearance, and control the flow of traffic around an airport. In some cases, they help reduce fuel consumption, and may include noise abatement procedures. This section describes instrument departure procedure charts to help you become better acquainted with the symbols and information they contain. The symbols used on both Jeppesen and FAA departure charts are very similar to the symbols found on the respective enroute, area, and approach charts. The practical application of these procedures is covered in the next section.

Prior to any discussion of chart format and published instrument procedures, you should understand that the charts depicted here are examples for teaching purposes only and must not be used for navigation. Use only current charts for navigation.

OBTAINING CHARTS

Instrument charts are produced in electronic and printed formats by Jeppesen and the Federal Aviation Administration (FAA). Although the FAA primarily produces instrument charts for the United States, its territories, and possessions, Jeppesen produces instrument charts for most of the world. FAA printed charts are published in regional volumes called *Terminal Procedures Publications*. [Figure 4-1]

Figure 4-1. You can obtain instrument approach procedure (IAP) charts from Jeppesen or the FAA either by subscription or as a one time purchase. Pilots who regularly fly IFR generally use a chart subscription service to ensure that they always have the most up-to-date charts.

DEPARTURE STANDARDS

IFR departures are designed according to the criteria established in the *U.S. Standard for Terminal Instrument Procedures (TERPs)*. In part, TERPs sets standards for a specific clearance from obstacles at a given distance from the runway based on an aircraft climbing at least 200 feet per nautical mile. [Figure 4-2] If obstacles penetrate a slope of 152 feet per nautical mile, beginning at the elevation of the departure end of the runway, a minimum ceiling and/or climb gradient may be required. In some cases, the aircraft might have to be maneuvered to avoid obstacles. Some departures require a combination of these restrictions to ensure a safe departure.

An obstacle-free departure flight path is based on your aircraft climbing at least 200 feet per nautical mile after it crosses the end of the runway at least 35 feet above the ground. In addition, you must be able to climb to 400 feet above the airport elevation within 2 nautical miles, before reaching a point where a turn is required.

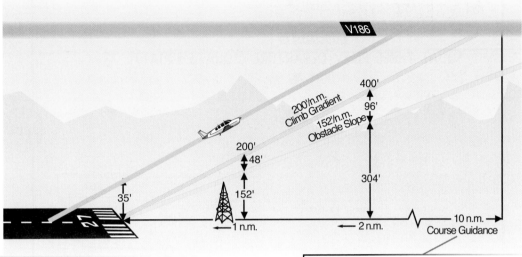

A slope of 152 feet per nautical mile is assessed for obstacles. If none penetrate this slope, the 200 foot per nautical mile climb gradient provides you with a minimum of 48 feet of obstacle clearance for each mile of flight. If obstacles penetrate this slope, special avoidance procedures such as ceiling and visibility minimums, detailed flight maneuvers, and/or greater climb gradients are specified.

Departure routes are based on positive course guidance acquired within 10 nautical miles from the departure end of the runway on straight departures, and 5 nautical miles after completion of turns on departures requiring turns. Surveillance radar, when available, may be used to provide positive course guidance.

Figure 4-2. An obstacle slope of 40:1 is used when analyzing terrain and other obstacles in the airport vicinity.

INSTRUMENT DEPARTURE PROCEDURES

An **instrument departure procedure** is a preplanned IFR procedure published in a graphic or textual format to provide obstruction clearance from the terminal area to the enroute structure. They are used after takeoff to provide a convenient transition from the airport to the enroute environment. There are two types of departure procedures: an **obstacle departure procedure (ODP)** and a **standard instrument departure (SID)**.

Obstacle departure procedures are created by the National Flight Procedures Office (NFPO). They might also be developed for private airports where the FAA is not responsible for developing procedures. ODPs are preplanned IFR departure procedures created when higher-than-standard takeoff minimums or climb gradients are required to ensure specific obstacle clearance. They are published in either textual or graphic form. An ODP is designed solely for obstruction clearance and is easily identified by the word obstacle in the title of the departure. This type of procedure provides a safe route of flight to the enroute structure while maintaining obstacle clearance. You may fly an ODP without ATC clearance unless another departure procedure (SID or radar vector) has been assigned by ATC. The FAA publishes ODPs in the front of the *Terminal Procedures Publication* under the heading Takeoff Minimums and Obstacle Departure Procedures. Jeppesen places ODPs on the airport chart, under the heading Take-off and Obstacle Departure Procedures. In addition, the FAA and Jeppesen publish some ODPs graphically on separate charts. [Figure 4-3]

In contrast, a standard instrument departure procedure (SID) is usually developed at the request of ATC facilities as a means of enhancing operations in the National Airspace System. A SID can increase effective use of the airspace by reducing pilot/controller work load, expediting traffic flow, and reducing environmental impact. SIDs also provide obstacle clearance and are depicted in graphic form. This type of departure terminates at a fix or navaid in the enroute structure and at an altitude where ATC radar services are provided. SIDs may be requested by the pilot or assigned by the controller, but in either situation, you must receive an ATC clearance to fly a SID.

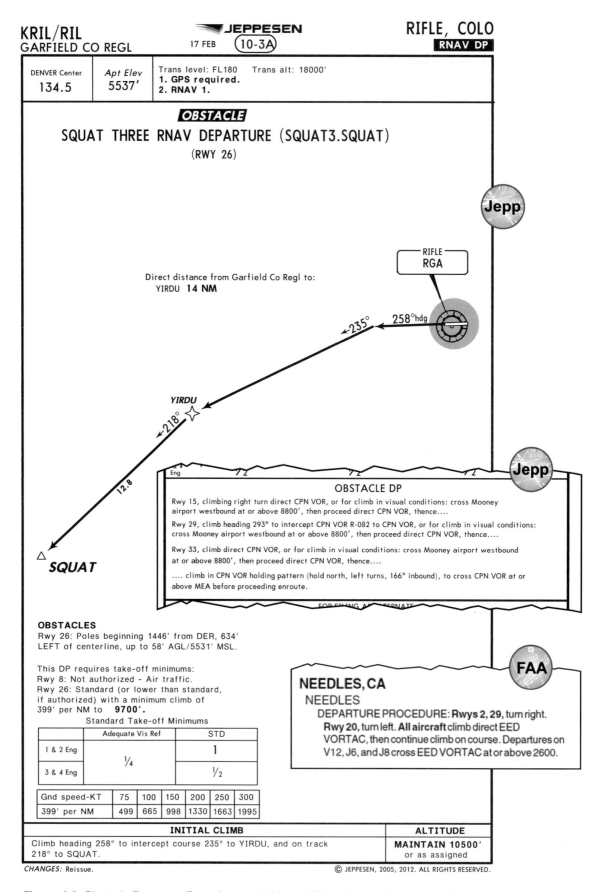

KRIL/RIL
GARFIELD CO REGL

17 FEB 10-3A

RIFLE, COLO
RNAV DP

DENVER Center	*Apt Elev*	Trans level: FL180 Trans alt: 18000'
134.5	5537'	**1. GPS required.**
		2. RNAV 1.

OBSTACLE

SQUAT THREE RNAV DEPARTURE (SQUAT3.SQUAT)
(RWY 26)

Direct distance from Garfield Co Regl to:
YIRDU **14 NM**

RIFLE
RGA

258°hdg

←235°

←218°

YIRDU

12.8

△ *SQUAT*

OBSTACLE DP

Rwy 15, climbing right turn direct CPN VOR, or for climb in visual conditions: cross Mooney airport westbound at or above 8800', then proceed direct CPN VOR, thence....

Rwy 29, climb heading 293° to intercept CPN VOR R-082 to CPN VOR, or for climb in visual conditions: cross Mooney airport westbound at or above 8800', then proceed direct CPN VOR, thence....

Rwy 33, climb direct CPN VOR, or for climb in visual conditions: cross Mooney airport westbound at or above 8800', then proceed direct CPN VOR, thence....

.... climb in CPN VOR holding pattern (hold north, left turns, 166° inbound), to cross CPN VOR at or above MEA before proceeding enroute.

FOR FILING AS ALTERNATE

OBSTACLES
Rwy 26: Poles beginning 1446' from DER, 634'
LEFT of centerline, up to 58' AGL/5531' MSL.

This DP requires take-off minimums:
Rwy 8: Not authorized - Air traffic.
Rwy 26: Standard (or lower than standard,
if authorized) with a minimum climb of
399' per NM to   **9700'**.
Standard Take-off Minimums

NEEDLES, CA
NEEDLES
    DEPARTURE PROCEDURE: **Rwys 2, 29,** turn right.
Rwy 20, turn left. **All aircraft** climb direct EED
VORTAC, then continue climb on course. Departures on
V12, J6, and J8 cross EED VORTAC at or above 2600.

	Adequate Vis Ref	STD
1 & 2 Eng	1/4	1
3 & 4 Eng		1/2

Gnd speed-KT	75	100	150	200	250	300
399' per NM	499	665	998	1330	1663	1995

INITIAL CLIMB	ALTITUDE
Climb heading 258° to intercept course 235° to YIRDU, and on track 218° to SQUAT.	**MAINTAIN 10500'** or as assigned

CHANGES: Reissue.

Figure 4-3. Obstacle Departure Procedures might be published in graphic or textual form.

Whether ODPs or SIDs, all departure procedures require specific aircraft performance to guarantee obstacle clearance. When you are issued a clearance that contains a SID, you are obligated to comply with the provisions listed for the SID and must ensure your aircraft is capable of achieving the performance requirements. For example, when necessary for obstruction clearance, SIDs and ODPs specify a climb gradient in feet per nautical mile. To convert this figure to rate of climb in feet per minute, you can use the table provided on the Jeppesen departure chart or the table provided in the front of the FAA *Terminal Procedures Publication*. [Figure 4-4] Alternatively, you can determine your climb rate mathematically by dividing the groundspeed by 60 and multiplying by the climb gradient. For example, if a procedure requires an altitude gain of 200 feet per nautical mile and your planned groundspeed is 150 knots, the required rate of climb is 500 feet per minute ((150 ÷ 60) × 200 = 500).

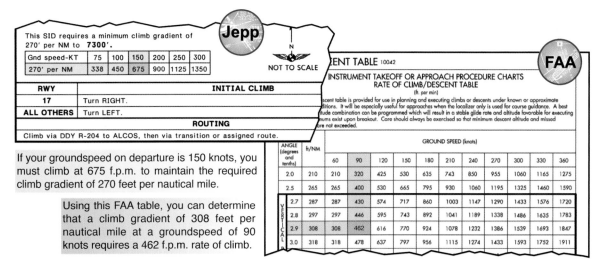

Figure 4-4. Tables are available for converting a minimum climb gradient to a minimum climb rate, based on your groundspeed.

 Minimum climb gradients are given in feet per nautical mile and must be converted to feet per minute for use during departure.

You also should recognize that some departure procedures require you to maintain a climb gradient to altitudes in excess of 10,000 feet. Therefore, the calculated continuous climb performance must be valid to the altitude required in the departure procedure. For example, if the procedure ends along a high altitude, or jet, route most light aircraft will have difficulty complying with it, because jet routes have minimum enroute altitudes (MEAs) of at least 18,000 feet. This could be a significant factor if you encounter adverse weather conditions, such as high density altitude, turbulence, and/or icing during the climb to cruising altitude. Another consideration is the average winds aloft during your departure. Because climb gradient is based on groundspeed, a tailwind requires an even greater rate of climb. Your responsibility as pilot in command is to review each departure procedure, make sure your aircraft can comply with the performance requirements, and refuse any departure procedure that is beyond the limits of your aircraft.

Each departure procedure is identified by an abbreviated name and numeral, then a dot followed by the name of the exit or transition fix. When a significant change in the procedure occurs, the number of the procedure increases by one. After the sequence reaches 9, the next revision is numbered 1. If ATC does not assign a SID or other instructions, you can use an ODP for obstacle clearance to depart the airport, and in some cases, to transition to the enroute structure.

Clearances for instrument departure procedures are issued at the option of ATC. If you do not have the chart for the procedure with you, do not accept the clearance. If you do not want to use a SID, you should indicate "NO SID" in the remarks section of your flight plan.

SIDs can also be categorized as either vector or pilot navigation. ATC develops vector departure SIDs for areas where controllers typically provide radar navigation guidance. A pilot navigation SID procedure allows you to navigate along a specified route with minimal ATC communication. Both charts have many features in common. For example, all departure charts include the name of the primary airport, the name of the departure procedure, the computer code for the procedure that you file on your IFR flight plan, departure control frequencies, navaid or fix information, and any minimum climb gradients or restrictions associated with the procedure. The layout and symbols are similar to the arrival and approach charts produced by their respective publishers.

VECTOR DEPARTURE SID CHART FEATURES

During a **vector departure SID**, ATC provides radar vectors that start just after takeoff and continue until you reach your assigned route or one of the fixes shown on the chart. Vector departure SID charts do not show departure routes or transitions. The chart usually contains an initial set of instructions, such as a heading to fly and an altitude for initial climb. When ATC establishes radar contact, they provide vectors to one of several fixes portrayed on the chart. Because radar vectors depend on radio communication, vector departure SID charts include any nonstandard lost communication procedures.

 When special lost communication procedures are necessary for a SID, they are included on the chart.

When the standard required climb gradient of 200 feet per nautical mile on a vector SID departure procedure cannot guarantee obstacle clearance, the SID might specify a minimum climb gradient. FAA departure procedure charts list the applicable FAA enroute charts below the relevant navaid information box. [Figure 4-5]

 On FAA SIDs, the applicable FAA enroute charts are listed below the navaid information boxes.

Departure Airport
The name of the departure airport is in the heading at the top of the chart.

Procedure Name
The name of the procedure is in the heading.

Computer Code
Use this code when filing your flight plan. Charts with transitions also have computer codes for the transitions.

Airport symbol
The plan view has an airport symbol with the airport's general runway layout.

Restrictions and Notes
Some charts contain restrictions or notes related to the procedure. You must comply with the restrictions. Notes provide advisory information about the departure.

Departure Control Frequency
When the airport has more than one departure control frequency, they might be divided by direction of flight. In this case, the boundaries are indicated by a dashed line.

Initial Departure Instructions
Initial instructions might state a heading and altitude to fly immediately after takeoff, before the controller issues your first vector.

Navaid or Fix Information
Radar vectors direct you to a navaid or fix to join your assigned route.

Enroute Charts
On FAA departure charts, the related FAA enroute charts are listed below the navaid boxes.

Lost Communication Procedures
Because radar vectors depend on radio communication, vector departure charts usually include lost communication procedures.

Minimum Climb Gradient
When the departure requires a climb gradient that is steeper then normal, the chart shows a minimum climb gradient.

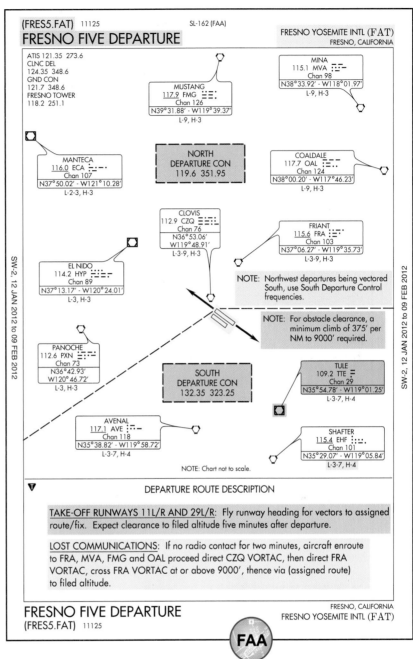

Figure 4-5. During a radar vector SID, ATC will provide vectors to your assigned course via one of the fixes depicted on the departure chart.

PILOT NAVIGATION SID CHART FEATURES

A **pilot navigation SID** usually contains an initial set of instructions that apply to all aircraft, and might also show one or more **transition** routes to navigate to the appropriate fix within the enroute structure. Many pilot navigation SIDs include a radar vector segment that helps you join the SID. Both chart publishers include a textual description of the initial takeoff and transition procedures, and a graphic, or plan view, of the routing. In some cases, textual descriptions are not provided for simple transitions. [Figure 4-6]

 When you file for a SID, be sure to use the appropriate computer identification code in your flight plan.

SECTION A ■ **Departure Charts**

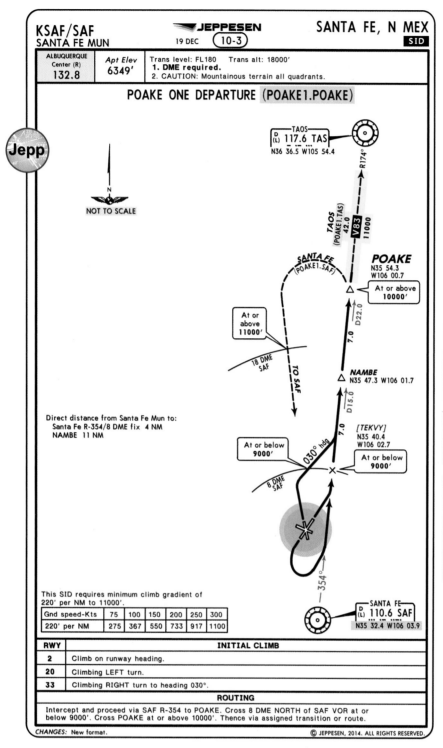

Departure Control Frequencies
Departure control frequencies might be shown for different areas or directions of flight. The (R) indicates radar service.

Departure Code
When filing for the basic portion of this departure, use the code POAKE1.POAKE.

Transition Code
This is the departure code for the POAKE 1 departure with the Taos transition.

Departure Routes
Departure routes and transitions include radials, altitudes, and DME distances. On Jeppesen charts, dashed lines depict transitions. On FAA charts, transitions are shown with light, solid lines.

Scale
Due to the large areas covered, most DP charts are not drawn to scale.

Primary Airport
The primary airport is screened. Other airports might be served by the same DP.

Latitude-Longitude Information
The chart provides the latitude-longitude location of the SAF VOR. In addition to navaids, DP charts also include coordinates of intersections and mileage break points.

Figure 4-6. Charts for pilot navigation SIDs have many features in common with radar vector SIDs. The major difference is the addition of course lines to the exit fix and transitions.

FAA Using the computer identification code for a transition in your flight plan informs ATC you intend to fly both the departure and the appropriate transition.

If you intend to use only the basic portion of the SID shown in figure 4-6 that ends at the POAKE Intersection, you should list the computer identification code, POAKE1.POAKE, as the first part of your route on your IFR flight plan. This code lets ATC know that you intend to use the SID to get from the airport to POAKE Intersection. Following the departure code, list the remainder of the route from POAKE. Your ATC clearance might sound like this: *"Cessna 1732G, cleared to Laramie Regional Airport, Poake One Departure, then as filed. Maintain 12,000."*

If your planned route allows you to follow one of the transitions, it is usually to your benefit to file for the transition. For example, suppose your route of flight takes you over the Taos VORTAC. In this case, you can include the Taos transition in your flight plan. When you file for the Taos transition, the first part of your routing should list the computer identification code, POAKE1.TAS. This tells ATC you plan to fly the POAKE ONE DEPARTURE (POAKE1) and the Taos transition (.TAS). Listing the code exactly as it appears on the chart helps ATC enter it into the computer and reduces the time required to process your flight plan. The remainder of your route, starting at Taos, is entered following this code. Your clearance from ATC might sound like this: *"Cessna 1732G, cleared to Laramie Regional Airport, Poake One Departure, Taos Transition, then as filed. Maintain 12,000."*

RNAV SID CHART FEATURES

You can identify an **RNAV SID** by the inclusion of "RNAV" in the title. AC 90-100, *U.S. Terminal and Enroute Area Navigation (RNAV) Operations* provides guidance for operation on U.S. RNAV routes and IFR departure and arrival procedures. Your aircraft must meet specific equipment and performance standards for you to fly RNAV SIDs.

If your aircraft does not have GPS, you must use DME/DME/IRU updating, which requires two DME units and an inertial reference unit (IRU). In addition, your RNAV equipment must also meet RNAV 1 standards, which require a total system error of no more than one nautical mile for 95% of the total flight time. As you depart, you must engage RNAV equipment no later than 500 feet above airport elevation and you must use a CDI/flight director and/or autopilot in lateral navigation mode. The type of equipment and performance standards are indicated on the SOD chart. Routing on an RNAV SID might be solely pilot navigation, or might be a combination of vectors and pilot navigation. [Figure 4-7]

At times, you might be instructed to maintain runway heading during a departure procedure. In these cases, you are expected to maintain the heading that corresponds with the extended runway centerline, and not apply a drift correction. For example, if the actual magnetic value of Runway 4 centerline is 044°, you should maintain a heading of 044°.

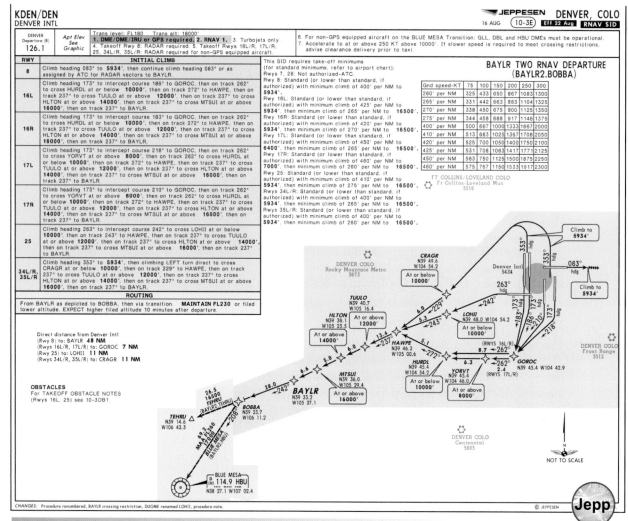

SECTION A ▪ Departure Charts

KDEN/DEN
DENVER INTL

⚓ **JEPPESEN** DENVER, COLO
16 AUG (10-3E) Eff 22 Aug RNAV SID

DENVER Departure (R) 126.1	Apt Elev See Graphic	Trans level: FL180 Trans alt: 18000' 1. DME/DME/IRU or GPS required. 2. RNAV 1. 3. Turbojets only 4. Takeoff Rwy 8: RADAR required. 5. Takeoff Rwys 16L/R, 17L/R, 25, 34L/R, 35L/R: RADAR required for non-GPS equipped aircraft.	6. For non-GPS equipped aircraft on the BLUE MESA Transition: GLL, DBL and HBU DMEs must be operational. 7. Accelerate to at or above 250 KT above 10000'. If slower speed is required to meet crossing restrictions, advise clearance delivery prior to taxi.

INITIAL CLIMB (RWY)

RWY	
8	Climb heading 083° to **5934'**, then continue climb heading 083° or as assigned by ATC for RADAR vectors to BAYLR.
16L	Climb heading 173° to intercept course 186° to GOROC, then on track 262° to cross HURDL at or above **10000'**, then on track 272° to HAWPE, then on track 237° to cross TUULO at or above **12000'**, then on track 237° to cross HLTON at or above **14000'**, then on track 237° to cross MTSUI at or above **16000'**, then on track 237° to BAYLR.
16R	Climb heading 173° to intercept course 183° to GOROC, then on track 262° to cross HURDL at or below **10000'**, then on track 272° to HAWPE, then on track 237° to cross TUULO at or above **12000'**, then on track 237° to cross HLTON at or above **14000'**, then on track 237° to cross MTSUI at or above **16000'**, then on track 237° to BAYLR.
17L	Climb heading 173° to intercept course 218° to GOROC, then on track 262° to cross YORVT at or above **8000'**, then on track 262° to cross HURDL at or below **10000'**, then on track 272° to HAWPE, then on track 237° to cross TUULO at or above **12000'**, then on track 237° to cross HLTON at or above **14000'**, then on track 237° to cross MTSUI at or above **16000'**, then on track 237° to BAYLR
17R	Climb heading 173° to intercept course 210° to GOROC, then on track 262° to cross YORVT at or above **8000'**, then on track 262° to cross HURDL at or below **10000'**, then on track 272° to HAWPE, then on track 237° to cross TUULO at or above **12000'**, then on track 237° to cross HLTON at or above **14000'**, then on track 237° to cross MTSUI at or above **16000'**, then on track 237° to BAYLR.
25	Climb heading 263° to intercept course 242° to cross LOHII at or below **10000'**, then on track 243° to HAWPE, then on track 237° to cross TUULO at or above **12000'**, then on track 237° to cross HLTON at or above **14000'**, then on track 237° to cross MTSUI at or above **16000'**, then on track 237° to BAYLR.
34L/R, 35L/R	Climb heading 353° to **5934'**, then climbing LEFT turn direct to cross CRAGR at or below **10000'**, then on track 229° to HAWPE, then on track 237° to cross TUULO at or above **12000'**, then on track 237° to cross HLTON at or above **14000'**, then on track 237° to cross MTSUI at or above **16000'**, then on track 237° to BAYLR.

ROUTING

From BAYLR as depicted to BOBBA, then via transition.   **MAINTAIN FL230** or filed lower altitude. EXPECT higher filed altitude 10 minutes after departure.

Direct distance from Denver Intl
(Rwy 8) to BAYLR **48 NM**
(Rwys 16L/R, 17L/R) to GOROC **7 NM**
(Rwy 25) to LOHII **11 NM**
(Rwys 34L/R, 35L/R) to CRAGR **11 NM**

OBSTACLES
For TAKEOFF OBSTACLE NOTES
(Rwys 16L, 25) see 10-3OB1.

This SID requires take-off minimums
(for standard minimums, refer to airport chart):
Rwys 7, 26: Not authorized-ATC.
Rwy 8: Standard (or lower than standard, if authorized) with minimum climb of 400' per NM to **5934'**.
Rwy 16L: Standard (or lower than standard, if authorized) with minimum climb of 425' per NM to **5934'** then minimum climb of 265' per NM to **16500'**.
Rwy 16R: Standard (or lower than standard, if authorized) with minimum climb of 420' per NM to **5934'**, then minimum climb of 270' per NM to **16500'**.
Rwy 17L: Standard (or lower than standard, if authorized) with minimum climb of 450' per NM to **6400'**, then minimum climb of 265' per NM to **16500'**.
Rwy 17R: Standard (or lower than standard, if authorized) with minimum climb of 460' per NM to **7000'**, then minimum climb of 260' per NM to **16500'**.
Rwy 25: Standard (or lower than standard, if authorized) with minimum climb of 410' per NM to **16500'**.
Rwys 34L/R: Standard (or lower than standard, if authorized) with minimum climb of 400' per NM to **5934'**, then minimum climb of 265' per NM to **16500'**.
Rwy 35L/R: Standard (or lower than standard, if authorized) with minimum climb of 400' per NM to **5934'**, then minimum climb of 260' per NM to **16500'**.

BAYLR TWO RNAV DEPARTURE
(BAYLR2.BOBBA)

Gnd speed-KT	75	100	150	200	250	300
260' per NM	325	433	650	867	1083	1300
265' per NM	331	442	663	883	1104	1325
270' per NM	338	450	675	900	1125	1350
275' per NM	344	458	688	917	1146	1375
400' per NM	500	667	1000	1333	1667	2000
410' per NM	513	683	1025	1367	1708	2050
420' per NM	525	700	1050	1400	1750	2100
425' per NM	531	708	1063	1417	1771	2125
450' per NM	563	750	1125	1500	1875	2250
460' per NM	575	767	1150	1533	1917	2300

FT COLLINS/LOVELAND COLO
Ft Collins-Loveland Mun
5016

CHANGES: Procedure renumbered, BAYLR crossing restriction, DUGME renamed LOHII, procedure note.

© JEPPESEN   **Jepp**

Equipment Requirement

If your aircraft is not equipped with GPS/GNSS, it must be capable of navigation system updating using DME/DME/IRU.

RNAV 1 Navigation Standard

RNAV 1 requires a total system error of not more than 1 NM for 95% of the total flight time.

Transition

Follow the transition for which you are cleared either to TEHRU waypoint or Blue Mesa (HBU) VORTAC.

Departure Route

Follow the initial climb instructions and depicted routing based on your takeoff runway to BAYLR waypoint and then on a track of 242° to BOBBA waypoint.

Figure 4-7. RNAV SIDs might combine radar vectors and pilot navigation. Prepare for and brief the key points of the RNAV SID prior to departure.

SUMMARY CHECKLIST

✓ Charted departure procedures help simplify clearances, reduce frequency congestion, ensure obstacle clearance, and control traffic flow around an airport. They also help reduce fuel consumption, and might include noise abatement procedures.

✓ Departure procedures require a minimum climb gradient of 200 feet per nautical mile to ensure you can clear departure path obstacles.

✓ Departure procedures are preplanned IFR procedures to provide obstruction clearance during the transition from the terminal area to the enroute environment. The two types of procedures are obstacle departure procedures (ODPs) and standard instrument departures (SIDs).

✓ When you are issued a SID, you must ensure your aircraft is capable of achieving the SID performance requirements.

✓ You must convert climb gradients from feet per nautical mile to feet per minute for use during departure. To perform the conversion, use the table provided on the Jeppesen departure chart or the table in the front of the FAA Terminal Procedures Publication

✓ When you accept a SID in a clearance, or file one in your flight plan, you must possess the SID chart.

✓ To avoid being issued SIDs, enter the phrase "NO SID" in the remarks section of your flight plan.

✓ Jeppesen and FAA list the primary airport served by the procedure and the name of the procedure near the top of the chart.

✓ Vector SIDs exist where ATC provides radar navigation guidance. They usually contain a heading to fly and an altitude for initial climb. When ATC establishes radar contact, they provide vectors to your assigned route or fixes portrayed on the chart.

✓ Pilot navigation SIDs allow you to navigate along a route with minimal ATC communications. They usually contain instructions to all aircraft, and might also show transition routes to navigate to an enroute fix. Some include a radar segment to help you join the SID.

✓ SID transition routes are shown with dashed lines on Jeppesen charts and with light, solid lines on FAA charts.

✓ The computer identification code for a transition in your flight plan informs ATC you intend to fly both the SID and the transition.

✓ RNAV SIDs include "RNAV" in the title. To fly an RNAV SID, your aircraft must meet specific equipment and performance standards.

✓ If you are instructed to maintain runway heading, it means you should maintain the magnetic heading of the runway centerline.

KEY TERMS

Terminal Procedures Publication

U.S. Standard for Terminal Instrument Procedures (TERPs)

Instrument Departure Procedure

Obstacle Departure Procedure (ODP)

Standard Instrument Departure (SID)

Vector SID

Pilot Navigation SID

Transition

RNAV SID

QUESTIONS

1. What is the difference between a SID and an ODP?
   - A. A SID is intended for use only by transport aircraft, but an ODP may be used by all aircraft.
   - B. An ODP is created in situations when high terrain or obstacles necessitate a climb gradient of more than 200 feet per minute, and a SID is often created to meet ATC needs for managing air traffic and reducing frequency congestion.
   - C. SIDs are requested by pilots in IFR flight plans, but ODPs are usually assigned by ATC in clearances.

You will be departing San Diego International — Lindbergh Airport (KSAN) using the BORDER FIVE DEPARTURE. Refer to the accompanying departure procedure chart to answer the following questions.

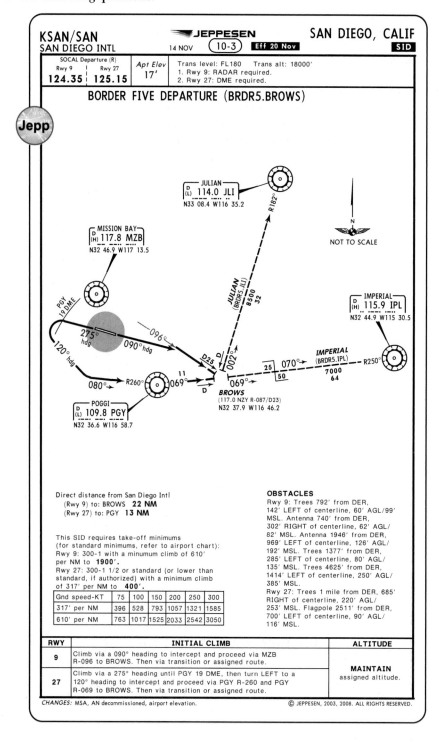

© JEPPESEN, 2003, 2008. ALL RIGHTS RESERVED.

2. When filing your flight plan, what code should you enter on the flight plan for the BORDER FIVE DEPARTURE with Julian Transition?
   A. BRDR5.IPL
   B. BRDR5.JLI
   C. BRDR5.BROWS.JLI

3. If you depart Runway 27, what heading should you use until you reach PGY 19 DME?

4. Where does the basic portion of the BORDER FIVE DEPARTURE procedure end?
   A. At the Poggi VORTAC
   B. At BROWS Intersection
   C. At the Imperial VORTAC

5. What is the departure control frequency for Runway 9 at KSAN?

6. Where does the Imperial Transition begin?
   A. At the Poggi VORTAC
   B. At BROWS Intersection
   C. AT the 19-mile DME fix from the Poggi VORTAC

7. What is the minimum enroute altitude for the Julian Transition?

8. If you plan to take off from Runway 9 and your groundspeed during your initial climb is 100 knots, what rate of climb must you maintain in order to achieve the minimum climb gradient to 1,900 feet MSL?
   A. 317 feet per nautical mile
   B. 528 feet per minute
   C. 1,017 feet per minute

9. If you choose to fly the departure procedure to the BROWS Intersection, what is the appropriate code to enter in your IFR flight plan?
   A. BRDR5.
   B. BRDR5.PGG11
   C. BRDR5.BROWS

10. If you depart Runway 27 on the BORDER FIVE DEPARTURE, Imperial Transition, what initial altitude can you expect?
    A. 7,000 feet at the Poggi VORTAC
    B. 7,000 feet at BROWS Intersection
    C. Your initial altitude will be assigned by the controller

SECTION A ■ **Departure Charts**

SECTION B
Departure Procedures

An IFR departure in a radar environment might be as simple as holding the headings assigned by the departure controller while monitoring your position from local navaids. In other cases, you might be adhering to a detailed instrument departure procedure. At remote locations, you might fly the entire departure without the benefit of radar vectors or a graphic DP. This section covers important considerations for IFR departures, beginning with takeoff minimums.

BRIEFING A DEPARTURE

Whether you are part of a crew or the only pilot aboard, always take enough time to brief the departure thoroughly. Making this a normal part of your routine will help reduce your workload during the busy initial portion of your flight, and can prevent potentially dangerous oversights and omissions. A careful briefing can familiarize you with departures that you have not flown before and keep you from becoming complacent on routes you fly frequently. [Figure 4-8]

TAKEOFF MINIMUMS

Many standard instrument departure charts (SIDs) state that the departure requires takeoff minimums, and if you use Jeppesen charts, you have probably noticed takeoff minimums published on some of your airport charts. As an FAR Part 91 operator, you are not required to comply with published IFR takeoff minimums. These are established for the safe operation of large commercial aircraft flown by experienced professional crews who train regularly for this kind of flying. Your judgment should prevent you from attempting to take off in weather that would ground commercial aircraft. When operating under Part 91, a good rule of thumb is to stay on the ground unless the ceiling and visibility permit you to return and comfortably perform a normal instrument approach and landing in the event you encounter a problem soon after takeoff. Determine the appropriate landing minimums at your departure airport and use them for your takeoff minimums.

Takeoff minimums are typically based on visibility, which is expressed in a variety of ways, including prevailing visibility, runway visibility value, and runway visual range. **Prevailing visibility** is the greatest distance a weather observer or tower personnel can see throughout one-half the horizon. Prevailing visibility is reported in statute miles or fractions of miles.

Runway visibility value (RVV) is the visibility determined for a particular runway by a device located near the runway called a transmissometer. RVV is reported in statute miles or fractions of miles.

Runway Visual Range (RVR), in contrast to prevailing or runway visibility, is a prediction of what a pilot in a moving aircraft should see when looking down the runway from the approach end. It is based on the measurements of a transmissometer near the instrument runway and is reported in hundreds of feet. If you need to convert an RVR value into visibility in statute miles, just recall that a statute mile is 5,280 feet and do the math. Other important aspects of visibility are covered in Chapter 9.

 RVR represents the horizontal distance a pilot sees when looking down the runway from the approach end.

Departure Airport, Procedure Name and Computer Code
Ensure that you have the correct chart and have filed the appropriate computer code with your flight plan based on your intended transition route.

Restrictions and Notes
This departure does not have any restrictions.

Communication Frequencies
Review the published communications frequencies.

Initial Departure Instructions
This procedure includes two sets of initial departure instructions. The departure runway determines which instructions to use.

Departure Route
Review the heading, altitude, and distance for the departure route, which is shown with a bold line and often ends at the point for which the procedure is named—WAGGE in this case.

Transition Route
Make sure you know what to do next after completing the initial departure. The transition routes begin at WAGGE where the departure route ends, and are shown with thinner lines (dashed lines on Jeppesen charts). The MEA on the Lovelock transition is 15,000 feet; on the Mustang transition it is 10,000 feet.

Navaid and Fix Information
Review the navaids and fixes you need for identifying your route during the departure procedure.

Lost Communications Procedures
If you lose radio communications while flying a pilot navigation SID like this one, ATC expects you to fly your clearance. If using a vector SID, like the one in Figure 4-5, review the lost communications procedures published on the chart.

Minimum Climb Gradient
Ensure that your aircraft's performance is sufficient to fly the procedure safely with the current ceiling and visibility. Also calculate the engine-out performance if flying a multi-engine airplane.

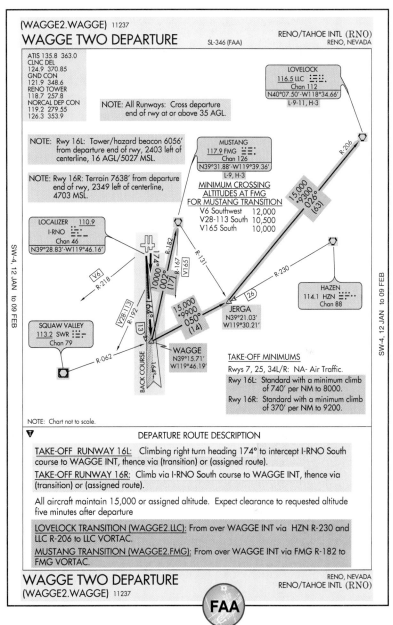

SECTION B ■ Departure Procedures

Figure 4-8 Get in the habit of briefing each of the key points before every IFR departure.

Standard takeoff minimums for commercial operators are one statute mile visibility for airplanes with two engines or less and one-half mile for airplanes with three or more engines. Sometimes the takeoff minimums are higher than standard because of terrain, obstructions, or ATC departure procedures. Jeppesen typically provides nonstandard takeoff minimums on the departure chart, and provides both standard and nonstandard takeoff minimums on the airport chart. The FAA uses a small white "T" enclosed in a black triangle on the approach chart to prompt pilots to look for nonstandard takeoff minimums in the front of the *Terminal Procedures Publication*. [Figure 4-9]

 A ▽ in the minimums section of an FAA approach chart indicates takeoff minimums are not standard and/or IFR departure procedures are published.

The FAA alerts pilots to the existence of nonstandard minimums by including a ▼ on the approach chart for the airport.

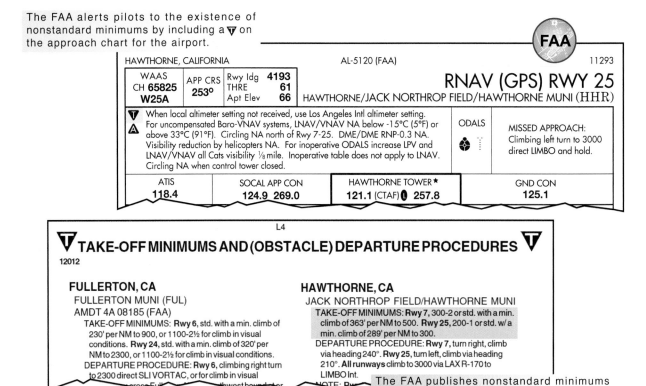

Figure 4-9. This is how the FAA publishes nonstandard minimums that apply to some commercial operators. Jeppesen charts also provide these minimums. Although these limitations do not specifically apply to private aircraft operating IFR under FAR Part 91, good judgment dictates that you not attempt to take off in weather that would ground commercial aircraft.

DEPARTURE OPTIONS

In general, there are four options for departing an airport on an IFR flight. You can use a standard instrument departure (SID), an obstacle departure procedure (ODP), a radar departure, or a VFR departure.

STANDARD INSTRUMENT DEPARTURES

Standard instrument departures (SIDs) are coded departure routes that expedite departures at airports with a large volume of traffic. In general, SIDs simplify clearance delivery and departures for both you and air traffic control, but their purpose might also be to provide obstacle clearance. If you fly from an airport that has a published SID procedure, you can expect to be assigned a SID in your ATC clearance unless you specify "NO SID" in your flight plan. You do not have to accept a SID, but you must advise ATC if you do not want to use one. While it is possible to decline a SID when ATC delivers your clearance, it is much more efficient to file "NO SID" in the remarks section of your flight plan. To fly a SID, you must have the charted procedure or at least the textual description with you. [Figure 4-10]

 To fly a SID, you must have the charted procedure or at least the textual description in your possession; otherwise, you should file "NO SID" in your flight plan.

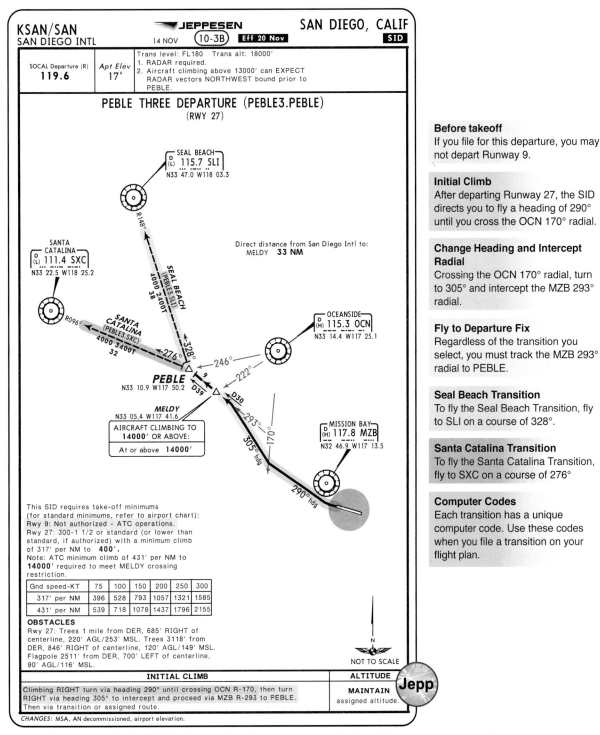

SECTION B ■ **Departure Procedures**

Before takeoff
If you file for this departure, you may not depart Runway 9.

Initial Climb
After departing Runway 27, the SID directs you to fly a heading of 290° until you cross the OCN 170° radial.

Change Heading and Intercept Radial
Crossing the OCN 170° radial, turn to 305° and intercept the MZB 293° radial.

Fly to Departure Fix
Regardless of the transition you select, you must track the MZB 293° radial to PEBLE.

Seal Beach Transition
To fly the Seal Beach Transition, fly to SLI on a course of 328°.

Santa Catalina Transition
To fly the Santa Catalina Transition, fly to SXC on a course of 276°

Computer Codes
Each transition has a unique computer code. Use these codes when you file a transition on your flight plan.

Figure 4-10. Each SID involves performing a sequence of steps. Be sure to set your radios and navigation equipment before takeoff to minimize your inflight workload. To fly this SID, your aircraft must be able to achieve a minimum climb gradient of 317 feet per nautical mile to 400 feet MSL.

OBSTACLE DEPARTURE PROCEDURES

When necessary, **obstacle departure procedures (ODPs)** are established for airports that have high terrain or obstructions near the airport. These procedures might be in graphic or textual form. On FAA charts, you will find the ODPs listed in the front of each *Terminal Procedures Publication*. [Figure 4-11] On Jeppesen charts, the procedure is typically printed as part of the airport chart.

SECTION B ■ Departure Procedures

L1

▼ TAKE-OFF MINIMUMS AND (OBSTACLE) DEPARTURE PROCEDURES ▼

12012   INSTRUMENT APPROACH PROCEDURE CHARTS

▼ IFR TAKE-OFF MINIMUMS AND (OBSTACLE) DEPARTURE PROCEDURES

Civil Airports and Selected Military Airports

ALL USERS: Airports that have Departure Procedures (DPs) designed specifically to assist pilots in avoiding obstacles during the climb to the minimum enroute altitude , and/or airports that have civil IFR take-off minimums other than standard, are listed below. Take-off Minimums and Departure Procedures apply to all runways unless otherwise specified. Altitudes, unless otherwise indicated, are minimum altitudes in MSL.

DPs specifically designed for obstacle avoidance are referred to as Obstacle Departure Procedures (ODPs) and are described below in text, or published separately as a graphic procedure. If the (Obstacle)

CHINO, CA
CHINO
TAKE-OFF MINIMUMS: **Rwy 3,** std. with a min. climb of 270' per NM to 4800. **Rwys 8L/R,** std. with a min. climb of 270' per NM to 4800. **Rwy 21,** Cat A/B std. with a min climb of of 290' per NM 4800, Cat C/D std. with a min. climb of 400' per NM 4800. **Rwys 26L/R,** Cat A/B std. with a min. climb of 270' per NM to 4800, Cat C/D std. with a min. climb of 410' per NM to 4800.
DEPARTURE PROCEDURE: **Rwys 3, 8L/R,** climbing right turn direct PDZ VORTAC. **Rwys 21, 26L/R,** climbing left turn direct PDZ VORTAC. **All aircraft** climb in PDZ VORTAC holding pattern (Hold E, right turns, 258° inbound) to the appropriate MEA.
NOTE: 108' AGL trees 1200' from departure end of runway 3, 600' left of centerline.

EDWARDS AFB (KEDW)
EDWARDS, CA 12012
Rwys 4L/R, Radar Required, Climb 340 ft/NM to 5500, track inbound on EDW R-223 to EDW VORTAC, then out EDW R-043. Climb as instructed, expect radar vectors after passing 4500 or climb on course, cross 15 NM from ARP at or above 4500. **Rwys 22L/R,** Radar and DME Required. CAT ABC track outbound EDW R-223. At 12 DME turn right heading 020°, intercept EDW R-247 to EDW VORTAC. Climb as instructed, expect radar vectors after passing 4500 or climb on course, cross 15 NM from ARP at or above 4500. CAT DE track outbound EDW R-223. At 12 DME turn right, intercept EDW R-247 to EDW VORTAC. Climb as instructed, expect radar vectors after passing 4500 or climb on course, cross 15 NM from ARP at or above 4500.

Figure 4-11. The intent of a textual ODP is to ensure obstacle clearance and a safe transition from takeoff to the IFR enroute structure.

An ODP is seldom assigned as part of your IFR clearance. Except when you are flying a SID, it is your responsibility to determine if an ODP has been established and comply with it. In IFR conditions, the departure procedure is a reliable method of ensuring terrain and obstacle clearance.

RADAR DEPARTURES

A **radar departure** is often assigned at radar-equipped air traffic control facilities and requires close coordination with the tower. If your flight will be radar vectored immediately after takeoff, the tower will provide the heading to be flown, but not necessarily the purpose of the heading. This type of advisory will be issued to you either in your initial IFR routing clearance or by the tower just before takeoff. Once you have received your takeoff clearance, you should understand that coordination of your flight is the responsibility of the tower controller. After you are airborne, you can expect a handoff to the departure controller. [Figure 4-12]

 During the IFR departure, you should not contact departure control until advised to do so by the tower.

 The term *"radar contact"* is used by ATC to advise you that your aircraft has been identified and radar flight following will be provided until radar identification has been terminated.

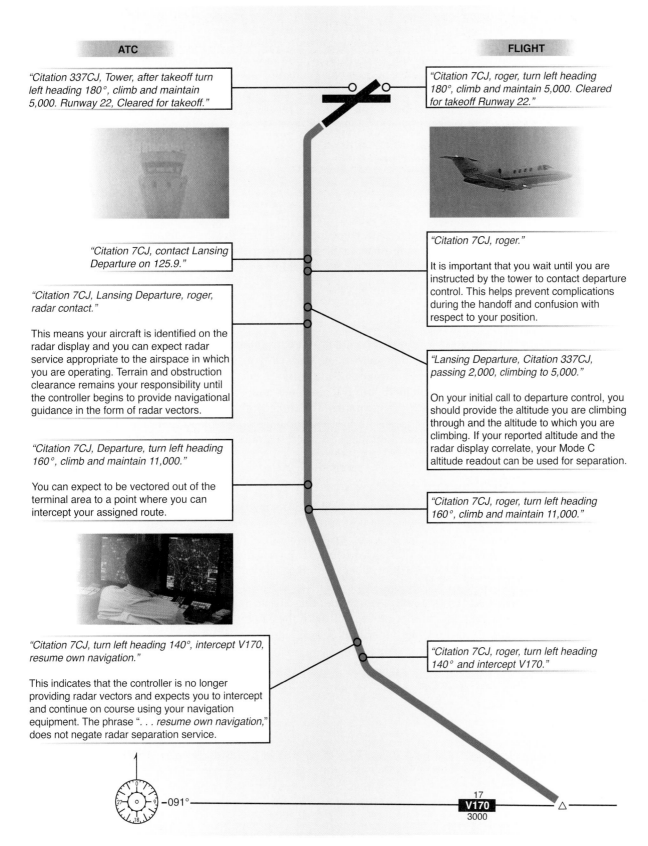

ATC

FLIGHT

"Citation 337CJ, Tower, after takeoff turn left heading 180°, climb and maintain 5,000. Runway 22, Cleared for takeoff."

"Citation 7CJ, roger, turn left heading 180°, climb and maintain 5,000. Cleared for takeoff Runway 22."

"Citation 7CJ, contact Lansing Departure on 125.9."

"Citation 7CJ, roger."

It is important that you wait until you are instructed by the tower to contact departure control. This helps prevent complications during the handoff and confusion with respect to your position.

"Citation 7CJ, Lansing Departure, roger, radar contact."

This means your aircraft is identified on the radar display and you can expect radar service appropriate to the airspace in which you are operating. Terrain and obstruction clearance remains your responsibility until the controller begins to provide navigational guidance in the form of radar vectors.

"Lansing Departure, Citation 337CJ, passing 2,000, climbing to 5,000."

On your initial call to departure control, you should provide the altitude you are climbing through and the altitude to which you are climbing. If your reported altitude and the radar display correlate, your Mode C altitude readout can be used for separation.

"Citation 7CJ, Departure, turn left heading 160°, climb and maintain 11,000."

You can expect to be vectored out of the terminal area to a point where you can intercept your assigned route.

"Citation 7CJ, roger, turn left heading 160°, climb and maintain 11,000."

"Citation 7CJ, turn left heading 140°, intercept V170, resume own navigation."

This indicates that the controller is no longer providing radar vectors and expects you to intercept and continue on course using your navigation equipment. The phrase "... *resume own navigation,*" does not negate radar separation service.

"Citation 7CJ, roger, turn left heading 140° and intercept V170."

—091°

17
V170
3000

Figure 4-12. A radar departure may be a good alternative to a published departure procedure. This can be particularly true when none of the available departure procedures are convenient for your planned route of flight.

In certain circumstances, ATC might issue a vector that takes your flight off a previously assigned route. When this occurs, the controller usually tells you the reason for the vector. Typical reasons include weather avoidance, terrain clearance, or traffic separation. ATC provides radar vectors until your aircraft is back on course and you have been advised of your position. In some cases, you might be handed off to another radar controller with continuing radar surveillance capabilities. If you feel that any vector is given in error, immediately question the controller and verify the purpose of the vector. In addition, you should keep track of your present position at all times so you are prepared to resume your own navigation.

 "Resume own navigation" is a phrase used by ATC to advise you to assume responsibility for your own navigation.

If radar contact is lost for some reason, you can expect the controller to request additional reports from you in order to monitor your flight progress. These requested reports might include crossing a particular navigation fix, reaching an altitude, or intercepting and proceeding on course.

VFR DEPARTURES

When conditions permit, you might be able to depart an airport under VFR and obtain your clearance from ARTCC after takeoff. As always, you must remain aware of your position relative to terrain and obstructions. In addition, you should always maintain VFR conditions until you have obtained your IFR clearance and have ATC approval to proceed on course in accordance with the clearance. If you accept a clearance while below the minimum altitude for IFR operations in the area, you are responsible for your own terrain/obstruction clearance until you reach that altitude.

SELECTING A DEPARTURE METHOD

As you prepare to depart an airport on an IFR flight, you should assess the situation and determine which type of departure is best suited for your circumstances. After analyzing the type of terrain and other obstacles on or in the vicinity of your departure airport, you should determine whether an ODP is available. If one exists, does it allow you to proceed expeditiously on your route? If not, does departure control or ARTCC have the ability to provide you with a radar guided departure? Do the weather and terrain allow you to initially depart VFR? Once you have answered these basic questions, you will be ready to select a course of action, familiarize yourself with the associated procedures, obtain your IFR clearance, and execute your departure.

Like Ships Passing on the Potomac

Development of radio detection and ranging, commonly referred to as radar, began as early as 1922. Researchers at the Naval Aircraft Laboratory in Washington, D.C. observed radio signals reflecting from ships passing in the Potomac River. [Figure A] Reports on radio echo signals from moving objects led to British involvement with radar in 1935. In 1940, MIT Radiation Laboratory, in conjunction with the British Tizard Mission, mounted a crash program to make microwave radar sets for British night fighter airplanes. These efforts led to further developments such as the military Identification of Friend and Foe (IFF) system, and a talk-down blind landing system for aircraft called Ground Controlled Approach (GCA).

The prototype GCA used microwave radar which provided airplane coordinates to a small analog computer called a director. The director compared the coordinates to those of an ideal glide path and developed error signals on meters monitored by the controller. The controller would give the pilot right-left steering instructions and adjustments to rate of descent until the pilot could see the runway and land.

One of the most spectacular successes for GCA occurred when the Soviets blockaded Berlin during the rainy fall and winter of 1948. With all road, rail, and canal links to West Berlin severed, a military GCA set operated around the clock, bringing in a steady stream of planes carrying thousands of tons of food and fuel. Figure B shows one such aircraft, a Douglas C-54, flying a relief mission during the Berlin Airlift. In the end, the GCA was credited with helping to make the airlift successful and breaking the blockade.

A

B

SECTION B ■ **Departure Procedures**

VERTICAL SITUATIONAL AWARENESS

During a recent 26-year period, more than half of the business aircraft accidents that resulted in fatalities occurred when the pilots unknowingly flew their airplanes into the ground. Over two thirds of these controlled flight into terrain (CFIT) accidents resulted from a lack of vertical situational awareness on the part of the crew. As you make a decision about what type of departure to use, you should not only consider the procedures, but also why the procedures exist.

Suppose you plan to depart Reno/Tahoe International Airport's Runway 16R on an IFR flight to the south. If you were to use the textual DP, you would need to fly to the VOR east of the airport and climb in a holding pattern to a safe altitude before proceeding on course. [Figure A] A more viable alternative would be to file for the WAGGE TWO DEPARTURE which allows you to continue southbound as long as you can maintain a minimum climb gradient. [Figure B] Using this departure would not only simplify your clearance, but it would also save you time and fuel. Neither option, however, would provide you with a picture of the surrounding topography. To develop your vertical situational awareness prior to departure, you might consult a variety of sources, including the Jeppesen area chart [Figure C], and the associated sectional chart [Figure D].

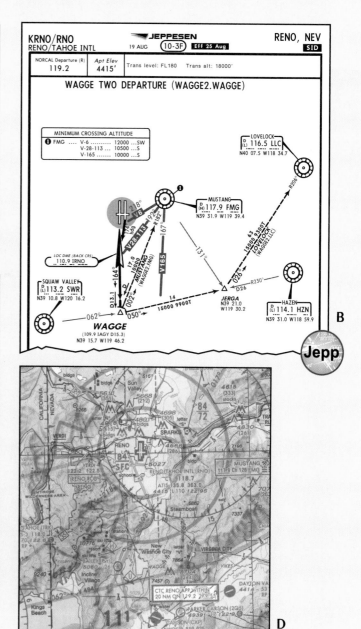

SECTION B ■ Departure Procedures

DEPARTURE PROCEDURE: Rwys 16L/R, climb heading 164° to 6600 then climbing left turn direct FMG VORTAC, thence... or for climb in visual conditions: cross Reno/Tahoe Intl Airport at or above 7000 via heading 054° and FMG R-234 to FMG VORTAC, thence...**Rwy 25,** climb heading 254° to 5000 then climbing right turn direct FMG VORTAC, thence... or for climb in visual conditions: cross Reno/Tahoe Intl Airport at or above 7000 via heading 054° and FMG R-234 to FMG VORTAC, thence... **Rwys 34L/R,** climb heading 344° to 7000 then climbing right turn direct FMG VORTAC, thence... or for climb in visual conditions: cross Reno/Tahoe Intl Airport at or above 7000 via heading 054° and FMG R-234 to FMG VORTAC, thence...

...**All aircraft:** continue climb in FMG VORTAC holding pattern (northeast, left turn, 221° inbound) to cross FMG VORTAC at or above MEA/MCA for route of flight.

A

B

C

D

SUMMARY CHECKLIST

✓ A thorough departure briefing should be a normal part of IFR departure routine.

✓ Published takeoff minimums are developed for commercial operations and do not apply to FAR Part 91 operations.

✓ It is reasonable for a pilot operating under Part 91 to use the applicable approach minimums for the departure airport as takeoff minimums.

✓ Runway visibility value (RVV) is reported in statute miles or fractions of miles.

✓ Runway visual range (RVR) represents the distance you can expect to see down the runway from a moving aircraft.

✓ If you wish to fly a SID or an ODP, you must possess the charted procedure or at least the textual description .

✓ ODPs are not usually assigned as a part of your IFR clearance.

✓ During the IFR departure, you should not contact departure control until told to do so by the tower.

✓ Radar departures are often assigned at radar-equipped air traffic control facilities and require close coordination with the tower.

✓ The term *"radar contact"* means your aircraft has been identified and radar service appropriate to the airspace will be provided until radar identification has been terminated.

✓ During departure, you are responsible for terrain and obstruction clearance until the controller begins to provide navigational guidance in the form of radar vectors.

✓ *"Resume own navigation"* is a phrase used by ATC to advise you to assume responsibility for your own navigation.

KEY TERMS

Prevailing Visibility

Runway Visibility Value (RVV)

Runway Visual Range (RVR)

Standard Instrument Departure (SID)

Obstacle Departure Procedure (ODP)

Radar Departure

SECTION B ■ **Departure Procedures**

QUESTIONS

1. True/False. Runway visibility value (RVV) is normally reported in hundreds of feet.

2. List at least five important items to include in a departure procedure briefing.

3. True/False. IFR takeoff minimums apply to any aircraft operating on an instrument flight plan.

4. What is the recommended procedure if you do not wish to use a standard instrument departure procedure?
   A. Advise departure control upon initial contact.
   B. Enter "NO SID" in the remarks section of the IFR flight plan.
   C. No action is necessary, since ATC will not assign a SID unless you specifically request it.

Refer to the POAKE ONE DEPARTURE to answer questions 5 through 9.

5. If your groundspeed is 150 knots, what rate of climb (in feet per minute) must you maintain to 11,000 feet MSL?

6. If you takeoff on Runway 33, what heading should you fly to intercept the SAF 354° radial?

7. What is the required altitude when crossing the SAF 8 DME arc northbound?

8. When flying the Santa Fe Transition, when must you be at or above 11,000 feet MSL?
   A. At the Santa Fe VORTAC
   B. Crossing the SAF 18 DME arc northbound
   C. Crossing the SAF 18 DME arc southbound

9. When flying the Taos Transition, where do you intercept V83?

10. True/False. When necessary, obstacle departure procedures are established for airports that have high terrain or obstructions near the airport.

11. Where can you find textual obstacle departure procedures published by the FAA?

12. True/False. Textual DPs are seldom assigned as a portion of an IFR clearance.

13. True/False. After the controller advises, "...radar contact," you can assume that terrain and obstruction clearance will be provided.

14. You have been vectored to an airway that is part of your ATC clearance, and departure control advises you to "...resume own navigation." What is meant by this term?
    A. Radar service has been terminated.
    B. You are still in radar contact, but you must make position reports.
    C. You should intercept and maintain the airway centerline by use of your own navigation equipment.

15. Assume that you depart an airport in VFR conditions and obtain your IFR clearance after takeoff. How long are you responsible for your own terrain/obstruction clearance?

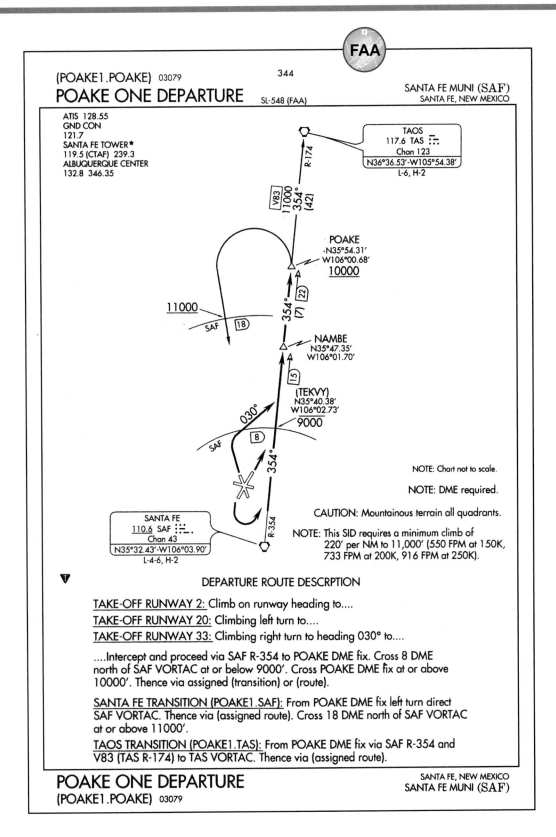

(POAKE1.POAKE) 03079   344

POAKE ONE DEPARTURE

SL-548 (FAA)

SANTA FE MUNI (SAF)
SANTA FE, NEW MEXICO

ATIS 128.55
GND CON
121.7
SANTA FE TOWER★
119.5 (CTAF) 239.3
ALBUQUERQUE CENTER
132.8 346.35

TAOS
117.6 TAS ⠂⠂⠄
Chan 123
N36°36.53'-W105°54.38'
L-6, H-2

R-174

V83
11000
354°
(42)

POAKE
·N35°54.31'
W106°00.68'
10000

354°
(7) 22

11000
SAF 18

354°

NAMBE
N35°47.35'
W106°01.70'

15

030°

(TEKVY)
N35°40.38'
W106°02.73'
9000

SAF 8

354°

SANTA FE
110.6 SAF ⠂⠂⠄
Chan 43
N35°32.43'-W106°03.90'
L-4-6, H-2

R-354

NOTE: Chart not to scale.

NOTE: DME required.

CAUTION: Mountainous terrain all quadrants.

NOTE: This SID requires a minimum climb of
220' per NM to 11,000' (550 FPM at 150K,
733 FPM at 200K, 916 FPM at 250K).

DEPARTURE ROUTE DESCRPTION

TAKE-OFF RUNWAY 2: Climb on runway heading to....

TAKE-OFF RUNWAY 20: Climbing left turn to....

TAKE-OFF RUNWAY 33: Climbing right turn to heading 030° to....

....Intercept and proceed via SAF R-354 to POAKE DME fix. Cross 8 DME
north of SAF VORTAC at or below 9000'. Cross POAKE DME fix at or above
10000'. Thence via assigned (transition) or (route).

SANTA FE TRANSITION (POAKE1.SAF): From POAKE DME fix left turn direct
SAF VORTAC. Thence via (assigned route). Cross 18 DME north of SAF VORTAC
at or above 11000'.

TAOS TRANSITION (POAKE1.TAS): From POAKE DME fix via SAF R-354 and
V83 (TAS R-174) to TAS VORTAC. Thence via (assigned route).

POAKE ONE DEPARTURE
(POAKE1.POAKE) 03079

SANTA FE, NEW MEXICO
SANTA FE MUNI (SAF)

CHAPTER 5

Enroute

Instrument/Commercial
Part II, Segment 1, Chapter 5 — Enroute

SECTION A
Enroute and Area Charts

The increase in the number of navaids and the complexity of the airway and airspace system has made specialized enroute charts a necessity for IFR flight. [Figure 5-1] In addition to helping you keep track of your position, enroute charts provide the information you need to maintain a safe altitude and ensure navigation signal reception. Area charts show major terminal areas in more detail, and are primarily used during the transition to or from the enroute structure. You will see examples of both Jeppesen and FAA charts in this section. Each chart system has its own set of symbols, but you will find them simple to learn and interpret. Although this coverage presents a general description of the symbols, be sure to familiarize yourself thoroughly with the legend for the charts you use, because chart enhancements and symbology improvements are ongoing.

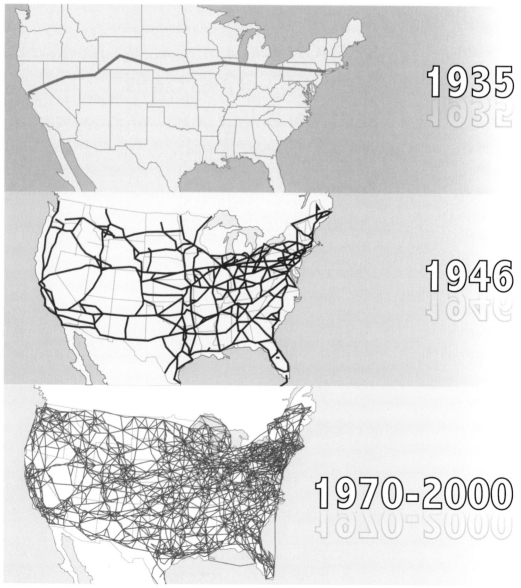

Figure 5-1. The federal airway system has grown in complexity from the days of the four-course radio ranges to the present.

ENROUTE CHARTS

In the United States, 18,000 feet MSL is the lower boundary of Class A airspace, so it is a convenient place to establish the division between the low and high altitude airway structures. Airways below 18,000 feet MSL are depicted on **low altitude enroute charts** and are called **Victor airways**. Those at and above 18,000 feet MSL and up to FL450 are shown on **high altitude enroute charts** and are called **jet routes**. [Figure 5-2]

This section concentrates on low altitude enroute charts, because most of your initial instrument flying will take place below 18,000 feet MSL. High altitude charts use similar symbols, but show only the jet routes. Because aircraft using the jet route system are usually operating at higher speeds, these charts cover larger areas at a smaller scale. [Figure 5-2]

 Because Class A airspace begins at 18,000 feet MSL, it is not shown on low altitude enroute charts. All airways at 18,000 feet MSL and above are jet routes.

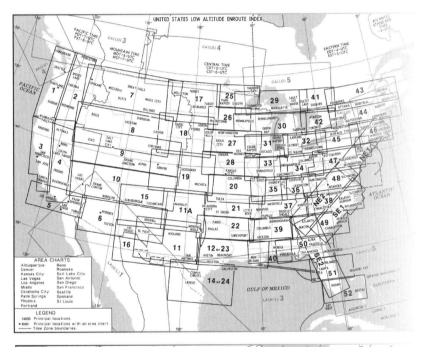

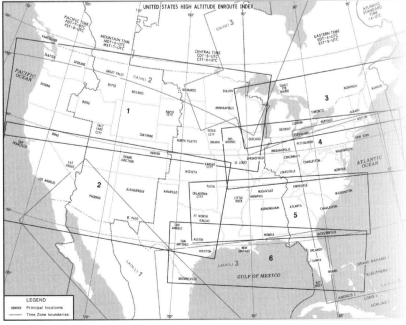

Figure 5-2. Each high altitude chart covers a larger area than a low altitude chart as shown by these Jeppesen chart indexes.

Jeppesen and the FAA publish IFR enroute charts in both paper and electronic form. Jeppesen aeronautical charts are available as a one time purchase or, more commonly, as a subscription that is tailored to meet the needs of all instrument pilots, from individuals to commercial airlines. You might use electronic charts for flight planning and display charts in flight using an electronic flight bag (EFB). [Figure 5-3]

Figure 5-3. You can enter and modify your flight plan on electronic charts and customize the display, such as selecting a night theme for easier readability.

Compared to WAC or sectional charts, the enroute chart is greatly simplified. Some of the symbols are similar, but most of the information depicted on visual navigation charts is missing from enroute charts. The topography features, contour lines, obstruction heights, roads, cities, and towns depicted on visual charts are not included on IFR enroute charts. In fact, the only surface features shown on enroute charts are major bodies of water and airports. Because you will usually follow airways between navaids, and terrain and obstruction clearance is guaranteed by flying minimum IFR altitudes, much of the detail can be omitted to provide space for other information necessary for IFR navigation. [Figure 5-4]

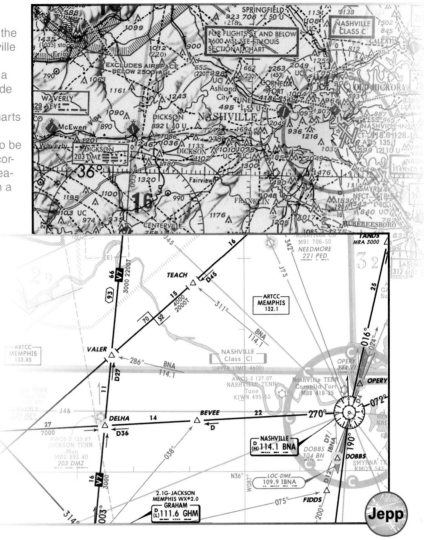

Figure 5-4. This is the area around Nashville as it appears on a WAC chart and on a Jeppesen low altitude enroute chart. The scale of enroute charts can vary from one chart to the next, so be careful to use the correct scale if you measure distances with a plotter.

FRONT PANEL

The front panels of both Jeppesen and FAA show the area covered by that chart. Although both chart systems present similar information, the area covered by individual charts varies. [Figure 5-5]

Figure 5-5. The front panel of this FAA chart shows the whole lower 48 states, while Jeppesen shows an area somewhat larger than the chart.

Although they do not appear on the chart itself, state boundaries and/or major cities are shown on the coverage diagram to help you find the appropriate chart more easily. Jeppesen uses gray shading on the front panel to show where area charts are available. The FAA shows cities that have area charts in black type. Time zone boundaries are included on both charts. The FAA uses a series of dots, while Jeppesen uses a series of Ts.

Both the FAA and Jeppesen furnish legends to help you interpret the symbols on enroute charts. Jeppesen provides a comprehensive legend in a separate introduction section. Most FAA charts have the legend right on the chart. You should maintain a working knowledge of chart symbology and review the appropriate legend periodically for updates and improvements.

NAVIGATION AIDS

Because all airways are defined by electronic navigation aids, you will want to become familiar with the corresponding chart symbols. Note the similarities and differences in how the navaids are depicted on FAA and Jeppesen charts.

VOR — The VOR symbol on enroute charts is a small compass rose. The pointer on the VOR symbol indicates magnetic north, making it easier to measure bearings with a plotter. The center of the FAA symbol is similar to the VOR symbol used on WAC and sectional charts.

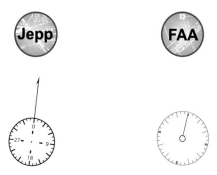

TACAN — Most TACAN stations without a collocated VOR can be used by civilian DME units. Jeppesen's symbol, a serrated circle, represents both TACAN and DME facilities.

VORTAC and VOR/DME — Because these facilities are functionally identical for civilian users, Jeppesen uses a single symbol for both by simply combining the VOR and TACAN/DME symbols. The FAA shows VORTACs and VOR/DMEs by adding the familiar symbols from the WAC and sectional charts to the center of a compass rose.

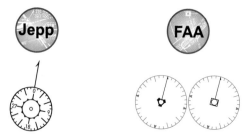

NDB — Nondirectional beacons are also shown with a magnetic north arrow to help you measure magnetic bearings with your plotter. A smaller version of this symbol indicates a compass locator beacon. On Jeppesen charts, compass locators are shown only when the facility provides an enroute function or TWEB information.

ILS Localizer — Localizer symbols are used to show ILS, LDA, and SDF facilities. the FAA uses them only when they serve an enroute ATC function, but Jeppesen shows their availability to assist pilots with flight planning. On Jeppesen charts, when the facility serves an enroute function, the symbol has the frequency and identifier nearby in a round-ended box. The localizer back course is sometimes used to establish a fix, and is labeled as such on the chart.

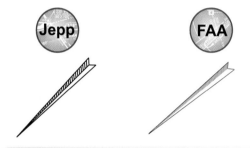

 On FAA enroute charts, localizers and back courses are shown only when they serve an enroute ATC function, such as establishing a fix or intersection.

Remote Communication Outlet (RCO) — This symbol is used for Flight Service remote communication outlets (RCOs) when they are not located adjacent to navaids or airports.

Facility Information — This provides you with the name, frequency, and identifier of navigation aids. Morse code for the identifier is also provided to make recognition easier. On Jeppesen charts, a box indicates that the facility is part of an airway, while off-airway navaid information is not boxed. On FAA charts, information on each navaid is boxed. A variety of other data is shown by letters or symbols near the navaid symbol; a few minutes with the chart legend should acquaint you with the abbreviations.

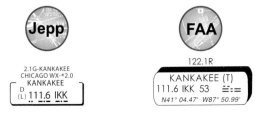

VICTOR AIRWAYS

The V in Victor airways stands for VHF, because these airways connect VOR, VORTAC, and VOR/DME stations. When the first VORs were commissioned, airways between them were given the V designation to distinguish them from the established network of low frequency airways. The number of the airway indicates its general direction. Even-numbered airways usually run more or less east and west, while odd-numbered airways are generally oriented north and south, much like the Interstate highway system. When more than one airway shares a common route segment, all of the airway numbers are shown. Now, of course, Victor airways dominate the domestic airway route structure, but low frequency airways defined by NDBs are still used in Alaska and along the Atlantic coast. In some cases, Victor airways can be categorized under the term air traffic service (ATS) routes, meaning specified routes designed for channeling the flow of traffic. The width of an airway is normally 8 nautical miles, 4 on each side of its centerline. When an airway segment is more than 102 nautical miles long, additional airspace is allocated. [Figure 5-6]

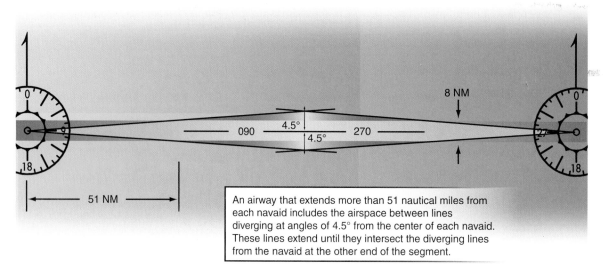

An airway that extends more than 51 nautical miles from each navaid includes the airspace between lines diverging at angles of 4.5° from the center of each navaid. These lines extend until they intersect the diverging lines from the navaid at the other end of the segment.

Figure 5-6. Dimensions of the airway increase when the airway extends more than 51 nautical miles from each navaid.

All distances on enroute charts are in nautical miles. On Jeppesen charts, a number in an outlined hexagonal box indicates total mileage between navaids. The FAA uses the outlined box to show total mileage between navaids and/or compulsory reporting points. A number without an outlined box indicates the mileage between any combination of intersections, navaids, or mileage break points.

A **mileage break point** is shown on a chart by a small x on the airway. Generally, this symbol indicates a point on the airway where the course changes direction and where no intersection is designated. The symbol might also designate a computer navigation fix with no ATC function.

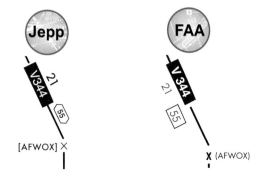

Intersections are checkpoints along an airway that provide a means for you and ATC to check the progress of your flight. They are often located at points where the airway turns or where you need a positive means of establishing your position. Intersections are given five-letter names, and the actual location of an intersection is based on two VOR radials, DME, or other navaids, such as a localizer or a bearing to an NDB. Arrows are placed next to the intersection pointing from the navaids that form the intersection.

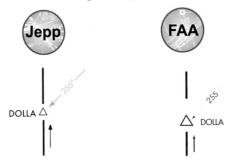

On Jeppesen charts, an intersection that can be defined by DME is indicated by an arrow with the letter D below it, while the FAA uses an open arrow. If it is the first intersection from the navaid, the mileage is found along the airway as a standard mileage number.

When it is not obvious, DME mileage to an intersection follows the letter D on Jeppesen charts. On FAA charts, it is enclosed within a D-shaped outline. This number represents the total distance from the navaid to the fix, as you would see it on your DME.

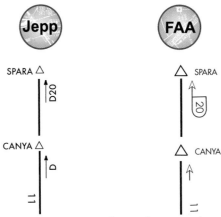

Intersections and navaids are designated as either compulsory or noncompulsory reporting points. **Noncompulsory reporting points** are identified by open triangles, and position reports are not required unless requested by ATC. A **compulsory reporting point** is identified by a solid triangle. In a nonradar environment, you are required to make a position report when you pass over this point. When a navaid is a compulsory reporting point, a black triangle is placed in the center of the navaid symbol.

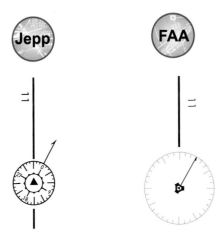

The **minimum enroute altitude (MEA)** is ordinarily the lowest published altitude between radio fixes that guarantees adequate navigation signal reception and obstruction clearance (2,000 feet in mountainous areas and 1,000 feet elsewhere). You can generally expect adequate communication at the MEA, although it is not guaranteed. Although the MEA is defined as providing acceptable navigational signal coverage, under certain circumstances the MEA might have a gap in signal coverage of up to 65 miles. These gaps are noted on Jeppesen charts with a symbol, and with the words MEA GAP on FAA charts.

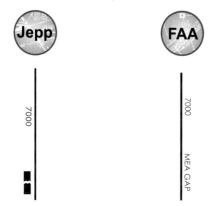

 An MEA is the lowest published altitude which meets obstacle clearance requirements and assures acceptable navigational signal coverage.

A **minimum obstruction clearance altitude (MOCA)** is shown for some route segments. On Jeppesen charts, it is identified by the letter T following the altitude. On FAA charts, an asterisk precedes the altitude. The major difference between an MEA and a MOCA is that the MOCA ensures a reliable navigation signal only within 22 nautical miles of the facility; conversely, the MEA ordinarily provides reliable navigation signals throughout the entire segment. Because you might not be able to receive the facility or navigate along the airway beyond 22 nautical miles, ATC will only issue the MOCA as an assigned altitude when you are close enough to the navaid.

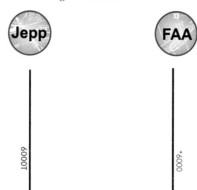

 ATC may assign the MOCA when certain special conditions exist, and when within 22 nautical miles of a VOR. A MOCA does not guarantee you will receive a reliable navigation signal if you are more than 22 nautical miles from the facility. MOCAs are preceded by an asterisk on FAA charts.

When you are not following an airway, such as during a direct segment of an IFR flight, you are responsible for determining your own minimum altitude in accordance with FAR Part 91. Basically, you must remain at least 1,000 feet above the highest obstacle within a horizontal distance of 4 nautical miles from your intended course. In designated mountainous areas, the minimum altitude is increased to 2,000 feet and the distance from the course remains the same. Remember to consider the range limitations of the navigation facilities and your communication requirements when you establish your minimum altitude. Both kinds of charts provide a minimum off-route altitude for each quadrangle of the latitude-longitude grid on the chart. The FAA uses the abbreviation OROCA, for off-route obstruction clearance altitude, and Jeppesen uses MORA, for minimum off-route altitude. The concept is similar to the maximum elevation figures (MEF) shown on sectional charts, except that MEFs show the approximate height of the highest terrain or obstruction in the quadrangle, while MORAs/OROCAs provide 1,000 feet of clearance above the highest terrain or man-made structure within the quadrangle. As with MEAs, the clearance in mountainous areas increases to 2,000 feet.

 In mountainous areas where no other minimum altitude is prescribed, IFR operations must remain 2,000 feet above the highest obstacle within a horizontal distance of 4 nautical miles from the intended course.

Occasionally, it is necessary to establish a **maximum authorized altitude (MAA)** for a route segment. At higher altitudes, you might be able to receive two or more VOR stations simultaneously on the same frequency, making the signals unreliable for navigation. MAA is the highest altitude you can fly based on the line-of-sight transmitting distance of VOR or VORTAC stations using the same frequency. It guarantees that you will only receive one signal at a time on a given frequency. A maximum authorized altitude is shown on the chart with the letters MAA, followed by the altitude, either in feet or as a flight level.

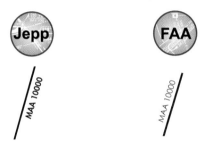

On the other hand, the **minimum reception altitude (MRA)** is the lowest altitude that ensures adequate reception of the navigation signals forming an intersection or other fix. The MEA provides reception for continuous course guidance, but a higher altitude might be necessary to receive signals from the navaids off the airway being flown to enable you to identify a specific position. Operating below an MRA does not mean you will be unable to maintain the airway centerline, only that you might not be able to identify a particular fix or intersection. On both Jeppesen and FAA charts, the letters MRA precede the minimum reception altitude. The FAA also alerts you to an MRA by enclosing the letter R in a flag.

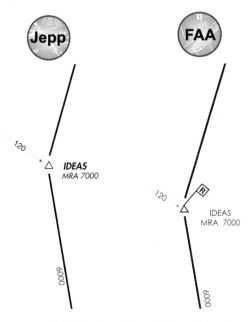

 An MRA is designated where a minimum altitude is needed to receive a navaid away from the airway being flown in order to identify an intersection.

A bar symbol crossing an airway at an intersection indicates a change in MEA. This symbol can also be used to indicate a change in MAA or to show a change in the MOCA when an MEA is not published for the route. When you see this symbol, be sure to compare MEAs and MOCAs along the entire route and look for an MAA to determine the basis for the change.

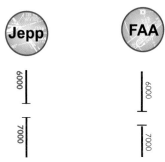

When an MEA changes to a higher altitude, you normally begin your climb upon reaching the fix where the change occurs. If you are able to maintain a climb of at least 150 feet/NM between sea level and 5,000 feet AGL, 120 feet/NM from 5,000 to 10,000 feet AGL, or 100 feet/NM above 10,000 feet, you should have adequate obstruction clearance. In some cases, rising terrain, obstacles, or navigation signal reception might dictate a **minimum crossing altitude (MCA)** at the fix. You must begin climbing prior to reaching the fix in order to arrive over the fix at the MCA. [Figure 5-7] The FAA uses an X enclosed in a flag to alert you to an MCA restriction. Do not confuse this with the flag symbol used to show a minimum reception altitude (MRA).

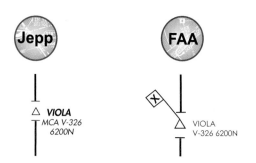

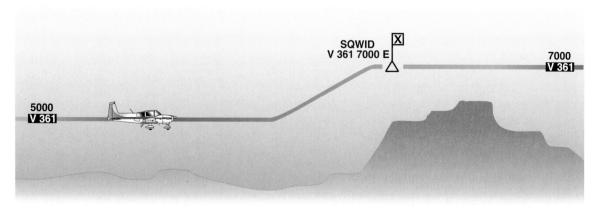

Figure 5-7. In this example, eastbound flights at the lower MEA must climb before reaching the fix (FAA symbols shown).

Jeppesen usually shows an MCA next to the intersection, along with the airway number, altitude, and direction. To reduce clutter around navaids, a reference number in a black circle on the facility box is used to indicate MCAs. The MCAs are listed in a box nearby. [Figure 5-8]

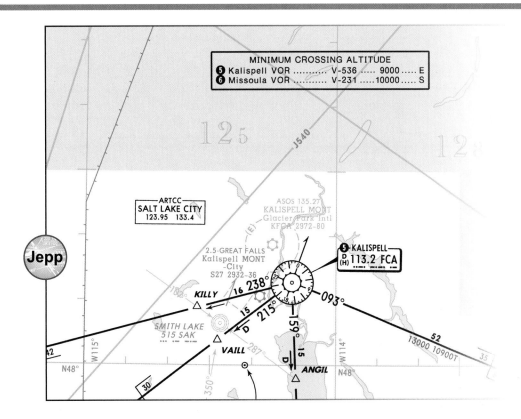

Figure 5-8. The circled number refers you to the boxed list on another area of the chart.

 A flag with an X signifies the MCA on FAA charts. The altitude and applicable flight direction appear near the symbol. Plan your climb so that you will reach the MCA before crossing the fix.

 The MAA, MCA, MRA, MOCA, and MEA all guarantee 1,000 feet of obstacle clearance in non-mountainous areas. In designated mountainous areas the clearance is 2,000 feet.

...RADAR CONTACT LOST...

There are dozens of instances every year when ATC computers go down, power fails, radar scopes go dark, or radio communications fail, leaving pilots without ATC guidance. In other cases, there might be gaps in radar coverage along your route of flight. Accepting vectors from controllers does not relieve you of responsibility for the safety of your flight. Sometimes controllers accidentally vector airplanes toward other traffic or terrain. You must maintain a safe altitude and keep track of your position, and it is your obligation to question controllers, request an amended clearance, or, in an emergency, deviate from their instructions if you believe that the safety of your flight is in doubt.

Of course, keeping track of your altitude and position are basic elements of situational awareness, but sometimes you might feel that ATC has assumed some of your responsibility, particularly when things are busy or stressful. Be sure to keep careful track of your position and altitude, and pay attention to the locations of traffic around you.

When you are following an airway, you normally change frequencies midway between navigation aids. However, there are times when this is not practical. When a change must be made somewhere other than the midpoint, a **changeover point (COP)** is established. [Figure 5-9]

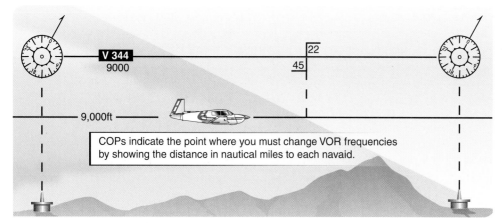

Figure 5-9. During a flight between these VORs, the navigation signals cannot be received from the second VOR at the midpoint of the route, so a changeover point is depicted.

COPs indicate the point where you must change VOR frequencies by showing the distance in nautical miles to each navaid.

FAA You normally change frequencies midway between navaids, unless a changeover point (COP) is designated. The COP symbols are illustrated in figure 5-9.

To help you make the transition between low altitude and high altitude airways, Jeppesen includes the high altitude enroute structure on low altitude charts. These airways are printed in green and include the appropriate jet route number. The MEA for all jet routes is 18,000 feet MSL, unless otherwise specified.

FAA The MEA along jet routes is 18,000 feet MSL, unless otherwise specified.

RNAV ROUTES

If you use GPS for navigation, you might be use RNAV routes published on enroute charts. RNAV routes decrease controller workload by eliminating the need to provide radar vectors. T-routes (Tango routes) are shown on low altitude charts for transition around or through busy terminal areas. [Figure 5-10]

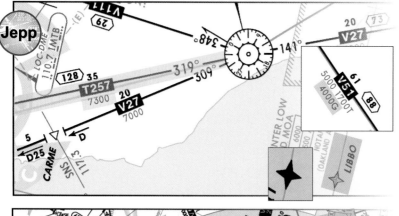

Tango Routes
Tango routes, designated with the letter T are established around or through busy terminal areas. These numbered RNAV routes, shown in blue on FAA charts, have specific MEAs, MOCAs, or MAAs.

Waypoints
Named RNAV waypoints, shown in blue on FAA charts, are open if they are noncompulsory reporting points and solid if they are designated as compulsory reporting points.

GPS/WAAS MEA
On some Victor airways, the MEA might be lower for GPS/WAAS navigation. In this case the MEA is designated with the letter G.

Figure 5-10. The depictions of RNAV routes and waypoints are similar on Jeppesen and FAA charts, except that they are shown in blue on FAA charts.

SECTION A ■ Enroute and Area Charts

COMMUNICATION

Remote communication outlets (RCOs) provide adequate in-flight communication coverage for both Flight Service and air route traffic control centers (ARTCCs). On Jeppesen charts, Flight Service frequencies associated with RCOs are located above navaid facility boxes with airport information, or in a separate box based on the antenna site. Because these frequencies are always in the 120 MHz range, Jeppesen displays only the last two or three digits, thus 122.4 is shown as 2.4. FAA charts show the complete frequency above navaid facility boxes or in separate boxes at the antenna site. The letter G (Jeppesen charts) and the letter R (FAA charts) next to the Flight Service frequency indicates that Flight Service cannot transmit but can receive, or guard, communication on this frequency. In this case, Flight Service transmits over the VOR frequency.

 Most Flight Service facilities are able to use 122.2, as well as the emergency frequency, 121.5. Additional frequencies are shown above navaid boxes.

 FAA charts show the Flight Service RCO frequency above navaid facility boxes or in separate boxes at the antenna site.

Jeppesen charts also indicate the Flight Service facility providing enroute flight advisory service (EFAS). For example, Memphis Flight Watch is listed as MEMPHIS *WX 122.0 with the asterisk represeting part-time service. The standard frequency of 122.2 is sometimes shown on Jeppesen charts with other Flight Service frequencies. FAA charts do not include this frequency. The emergency frequency of 121.5 is not shown on either Jeppesen or FAA charts because it is normally available in all areas.

If HIWAS or TWEB is available at a particular facility, it is indicated above the box on Jeppesen charts. The FAA places a small circled H in the upper right-hand corner of the facility box to indicate HIWAS is available, a circled A to indicate ASOS or AWOS and a circled T in the upper right-hand corner to signify a TWEB at the NAVAID.

 HIWAS is indicated by a small circled H in the upper right-hand corner of the navaid box on FAA charts, while Jeppesen places the acronym itself above the box.

The boundaries between air route traffic control centers (ARTCCs) are designated by distinctive lines on both Jeppesen and FAA charts, with the names of the controlling centers on each side. ARTCC contact information, shown in distinctive lined boxes, includes the center name, remote site name, and the frequency normally used in the area. FAA charts include the UHF frequencies. [Figure 5-11]

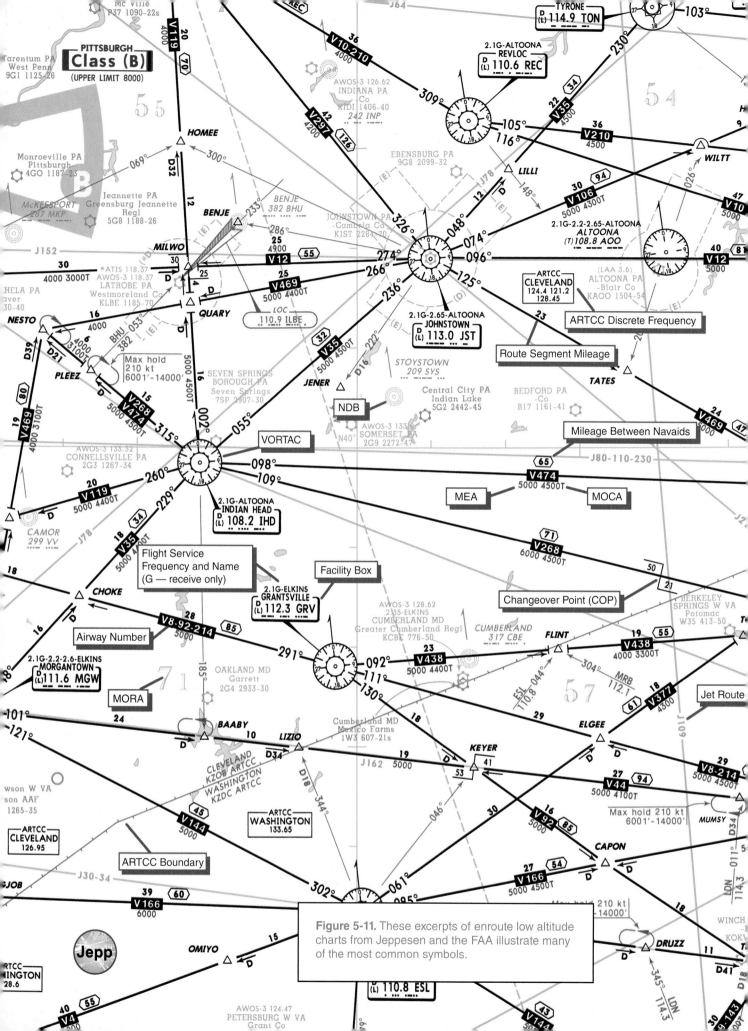

Figure 5-11. These excerpts of enroute low altitude charts from Jeppesen and the FAA illustrate many of the most common symbols.

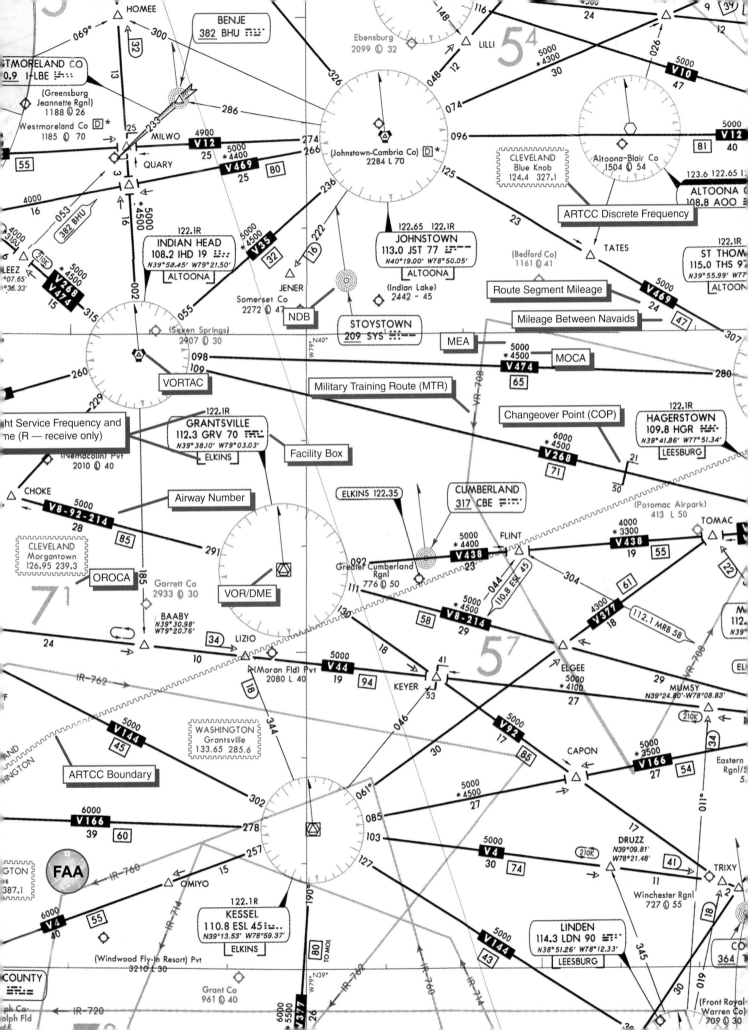

Both charts use distinctive lines to mark the edges of adjacent ARTCCs. Look for ARTCC discrete frequencies in boxes with the name of the controlling center.

SECTION A ■ Enroute and Area Charts

AIRPORTS

Although there are many ways to classify airports, they are divided into two categories on instrument charts — those with a published instrument approach procedure and those without. If an airport has an instrument approach, Jeppesen prints the airport symbol and related information in blue. In addition, the city and state name are in capital letters. Airports without an approach are printed in green, using upper and lower case letters. The FAA also uses color to distinguish between the two types. Airports with an instrument approach are printed in blue or green; airports without an instrument approach are printed in brown. Additional information about airports with instrument approaches can be found on the end panels of both Jeppesen and FAA charts. [Figure 5-12]

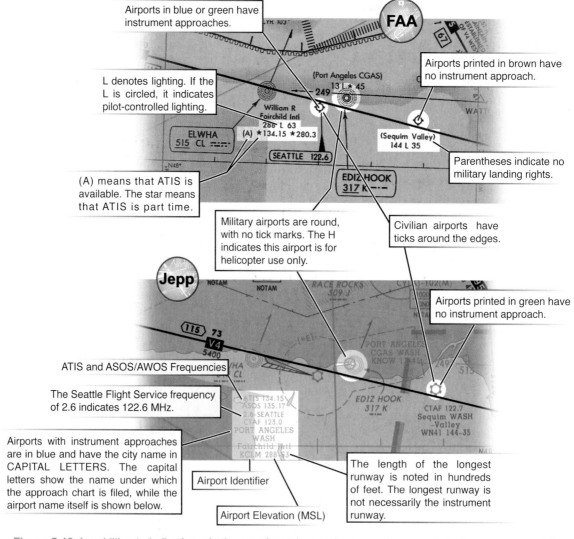

Figure 5-12. In addition to indicating whether an airport has an instrument approach, both Jeppesen and the FAA provide basic information about each airport, such as field elevation and length of the longest runway.

Basic information about each airport is portrayed on enroute charts using symbols from the chart legend. Additional information about airports with instrument approaches is found on the end panels of the chart.

AIRSPACE

Within the contiguous United States, all airspace at and above 14,500 feet MSL, excluding the airspace within 1,500 feet of the ground, is controlled airspace. Below this altitude, the airspace can be either controlled or uncontrolled. Both Jeppesen and the FAA use color to indicate the different types of airspace. Areas in white show controlled airspace, which includes Class B, C, D, and E airspace. Uncontrolled airspace, Class G, is shaded gray on Jeppesen charts and brown on FAA charts.

Class B airspace is outlined on Jeppesen charts by a maroon shaded band with the letter B repeated at intervals around the inside. The altitude limits for the various sectors also are shown. Class C is shown with a blue shaded outline with the letter C. The FAA uses solid blue lines filled with light blue shading to identify Class B, and blue shading with a broken blue outline to denote Class C. In addition, Mode C areas are enclosed with solid blue lines on FAA charts.

 Airspace below 1,200 feet AGL is uncontrolled, unless designated as Class B, C, D, or E.

The letter C or D in a box following the airport name indicates Class C or D airspace on FAA charts. Jeppesen charts show the outlines of Class D and Class E airspace with a dashed blue line and the appropriate letter. An asterisk indicates that the airspace classification is part time, and a tabulation elsewhere on the chart shows the effective hours. Areas where fixed-wing, special VFR clearances are not available are outlined with small squares in either maroon or blue on Jeppesen charts. The FAA follows the convention of sectional charts, placing the notation NO SVFR above the airport name.

On Jeppesen charts, prohibited and restricted areas have maroon hatched outlines, while warning, alert, or military operations areas have green hatching. The FAA uses blue hatching around the edges of all special use airspace except military operations areas and alert areas, which are shown with brown hatched edges. Military training routes (MTRs) also are depicted on FAA low altitude enroute charts. [Figure 5-13] Information concerning each area is listed in or near the airspace, or it can be found in tabular form on a chart panel.

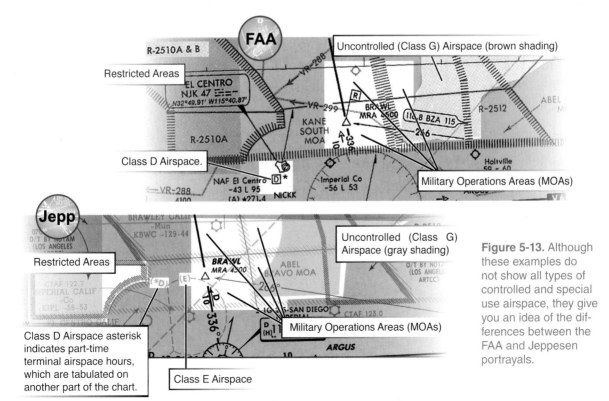

Figure 5-13. Although these examples do not show all types of controlled and special use airspace, they give you an idea of the differences between the FAA and Jeppesen portrayals.

SECTION A ■ Enroute and Area Charts

AREA CHARTS

Near several major air traffic hubs, the density of information on the enroute chart can make it difficult to read and interpret. **Area charts** are created to portray these locations in a larger scale, to improve readability and provide more detail. You might think of these charts as the IFR equivalent of VFR Terminal Area Charts. Area charts do not provide approach or departure information, but can help with the transition from departure to the enroute structure, and from enroute to approach. Even when flying enroute, you should always refer to area charts to navigate through their coverage areas, because they provide important information that might not be shown on the enroute chart. [Figure 5-14]

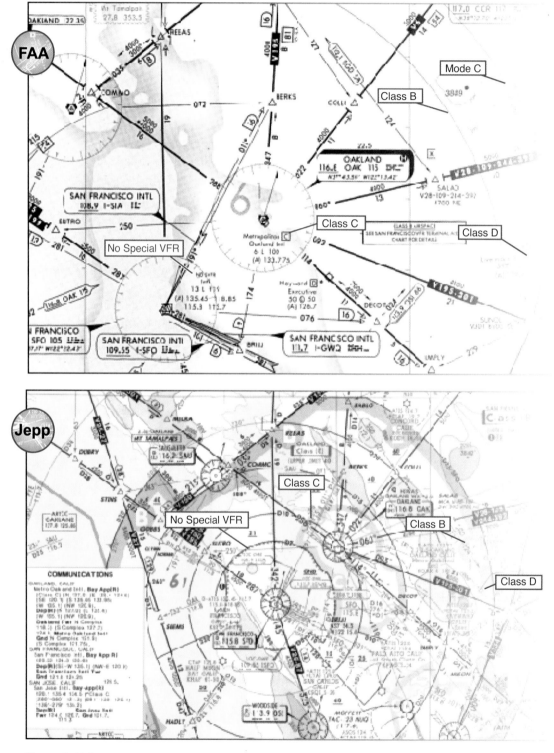

Figure 5-14 Compare these excerpts from the FAA and Jeppesen area charts for San Francisco.

Area chart coverage is shown on both the front panel and the face of enroute charts. On the front panel, Jeppesen uses a gray screen tint to show the actual area covered by area charts, while the FAA prints the names of cities with area charts in black. On the faces of both Jeppesen and FAA enroute charts, a screened gray dashed line shows the area covered by a separate area chart. On the enroute chart, the information within the outlined area might be limited. If your departure or destination airport is within the boundary, you should refer to the area chart for information on arrival and departure routes, speed limit points, and other handy information.

Most of the symbology on area charts is the same as on enroute charts. Jeppesen includes several additional features not found on FAA area charts, for example, select area charts with terrain in excess of 4,000 feet above the main airport elevation can contain generalized contour information. Gradient tints in brown are used to indicate the elevation change between contour intervals, with lighter tints depicting lower elevations. Keep in mind that this contour information does not ensure clearance around either terrain or man-made obstructions. Terrain contours are intended to help you orient yourself and visualize the layout of the terrain in the area. There can be higher uncharted terrain or man-made structures within the same vicinity. You must still comply with all minimum IFR altitudes dictated by the airway and route structure. [Figure 5-15]

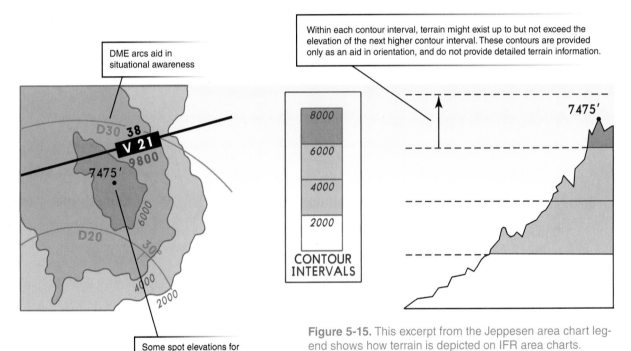

Figure 5-15. This excerpt from the Jeppesen area chart legend shows how terrain is depicted on IFR area charts.

SECTION A ■ Enroute and Area Charts

SUMMARY CHECKLIST

✓ Airways below 18,000 feet MSL are Victor airways. Airways at and above 18,000 feet MSL are jet routes.

✓ Airways are 8 nautical miles wide within 51 nautical miles of a navaid. At distances greater than 51 miles, the airway widens, and is defined by lines diverging at 4.5° from the center of each navaid.

✓ Intersections are defined by two navaids, or by a navaid and a DME distance. All intersections can be used as reporting points. Compulsory reporting points are charted as filled triangles.

✓ The minimum enroute altitude (MEA) generally guarantees both obstruction clearance and navigation signal coverage for the length of the airway segment.

✓ The minimum obstruction clearance altitude (MOCA) has the same terrain and obstruction clearance specifications as MEAs, and OROCAs/MORAs, but only promises reliable navigation signal coverage within 22 nautical miles of the facility.

✓ To provide obstruction clearance when flying outside of established airways, the FAA and Jeppesen provide off-route obstruction clearance altitudes on enroute low altitude charts. The FAA uses the term off-route obstruction clearance altitudes (OROCAs), and Jeppesen calls them minimum off-route altitudes (MORAs).

✓ The maximum authorized altitude (MAA) keeps you from receiving more than one VOR station at a time.

✓ The minimum reception altitude (MRA) ensures reception of both of the navaids that establish a fix. Below the MRA and above the MEA you still have course guidance, but might not be able to receive the off-course navaid that establishes the intersection fix.

✓ The minimum crossing altitude (MCA) reminds you to climb to a higher altitude prior to crossing a fix when rising terrain does not permit a safe climb after passing the fix.

✓ A changeover point (COP) is established where the navigation signal coverage from a navaid is not usable to the midpoint of an airway segment. Instead of changing frequencies at the midpoint of the route segment, you should tune to the next navaid at the COP.

✓ Remote communication outlets (RCOs) provide adequate in-flight communication coverage for both Flight Service and air route traffic control centers (ARTCCs).

✓ On Jeppesen charts, the last two digits of Flight Service frequencies assocatied with RCOs are located above navaid facility boxes, with airport information, or in a separate box based on the antenna site.

✓ FAA charts show the complete Flight Service frequency above navaid facility boxes.

✓ The letter G (Jeppesen charts) and the letter R (FAA charts) next to the Flight Service frequency indicates that Flight Service cannot transmit but can receive, or guard, communication on this frequency.

✓ The boundaries between air route traffic control centers (ARTCCs) are designated by distinctive lines on both Jeppesen and FAA charts, with the names of the controlling centers on each side.

✓ ARTCC contact information, shown in distinctive lined boxes, includes the center name, remote site name, and the frequency normally used in the area.

✓ Colors are used to differentiate between airports with approach procedures and airports without instrument approaches.

✓ Class G airspace is uncontrolled and shown with gray shading on Jeppesen charts and brown shading on FAA charts.

✓ Area charts are usually larger-scale depictions of major terminal areas. They should be referred to whenever you are in their coverage area, because they can show details that have been omitted from enroute charts.

✓ High terrain is sometimes shown with gradient-tinted contours on select Jeppesen area charts.

KEY TERMS

Low Altitude Enroute Charts

Victor Airways

High Altitude Enroute Charts

Jet Routes

Mileage Break Point

Intersections

Noncompulsory Reporting Point

Compulsory Reporting Point

Minimum Enroute Altitude (MEA)

Minimum Obstruction Clearance Altitude (MOCA)

Maximum Authorized Altitude (MAA)

Minimum Reception Altitude (MRA)

Minimum Crossing Altitude (MCA)

Changeover Point (COP)

T-Route (Tango Route)

Remote Communication Outlet (RCO)

Area Charts

QUESTIONS

1. True/False. FAA low altitude enroute charts generally depict localizers that have only approach functions.

Match the following navaid symbols with the appropriate facility names.

2. NDB

3. TACAN

4. Localizer

5. VORTAC

6. VOR

A.

B.

C.

D.

E.

7. What is the symbol for a noncompulsory reporting point on both FAA and Jeppesen charts?
   A. A filled triangle
   B. An open triangle
   C. The letter R in a flag

8. True/False. A small circled H in the upper right-hand corner of a VOR facility box on an FAA chart indicates that the station broadcasts hazardous inflight weather advisory service (HIWAS) information.

Refer to the accompanying low altitude enroute chart excerpt to answer questions 9 through 13.

9. What is the minimum enroute altitude (MEA) for V98 from PIONS Intersection to WOCKY Intersection?
   A. 4,000 feet
   B. 7,000 feet
   C. 10,000 feet

10. What is the minimum crossing altitude (MCA) at PIONS Intersection when flying southbound on V98?
    A. 4,000 feet
    B. 7,000 feet
    C. 10,000 feet

11. True/False. When flying northwestbound on V30 at HIRED Intersection, you must be at 6,000 feet MSL or more to receive LFD.

12. True/False. Williams County airport has no approved instrument approach procedure.

13. What is the MOCA on V221 between Litchfield VORTAC and Jackson VOR/DME?
    A. 1,800 feet
    B. 2,500 feet
    C. 3,000 feet

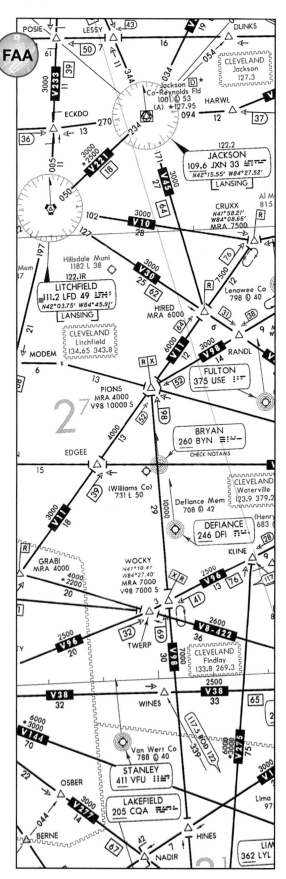

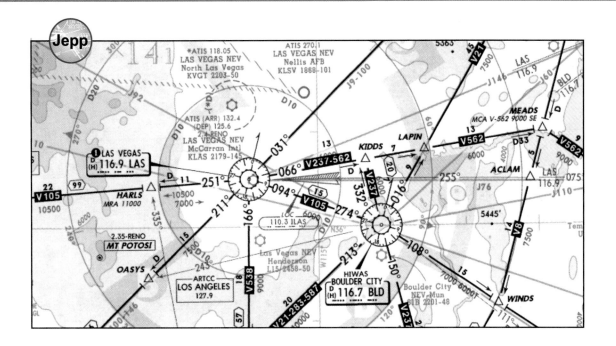

Refer to the accompanying area chart excerpt to answer questions 14 through 16.

14. When flying east from Las Vegas on V562, what is the minimum crossing altitude at MEADS Intersection?
    A. 6,000 feet
    B. 7,500 feet
    C. 9,000 feet

15. True/False. The minimum altitude at which you can expect to receive usable navigation signals from LAS when crossing HARLS Intersection is 11,000 feet.

16. What is the airspace class at the surface on North Las Vegas Airport?
    A. Class B
    B. Class D
    C. Class D (part time)

SECTION B
Enroute Procedures

Before the days of nationwide radar coverage, enroute aircraft were separated from each other primarily by specific altitude assignments and position reporting procedures. Much of the pilot's time was devoted to inflight calculations, revising ETAs, and relaying position reports within the airway structure. Today, pilots have far more information and better tools to make inflight computations easier, and, with the expanded use of ATC, position reports are only necessary as a backup in case of radar failure. Still, the enroute phase of an IFR flight involves more than simply flying the airplane from one point to another. Staying in communication with ATC, making necessary reports, and responding to clearances take up a good portion of your time. The rest should be devoted to monitoring your position and staying abreast of any changes to the airplane's equipment status or weather. [Figure 5-16]

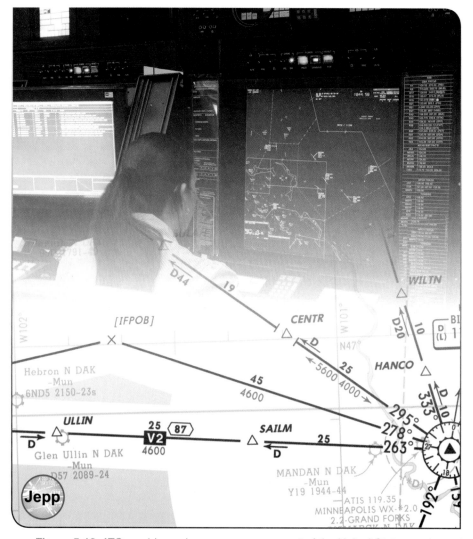

Figure 5-16. ATC provides radar coverage over most of the United States, making the transition between one ARTCC facility and the next relatively seamless.

TO FILE OR NOT TO FILE

"(I) called for a weather briefing. Both San Francisco and Oakland (reported) 1400 feet broken and greater than 6 miles visibility . . . pretty strong winds with a not-so-bad storm blowing through. I didn't file an IFR flight plan when asked by the briefer as the weather sounded OK. The forecast was for improvement, although it had been slow in coming as of that time . . . during preflight (I) noticed mist forming. It was also getting humid. I didn't think it could get foggy or misty with all of that wind. It seemed to be drizzling too. (I) departed Runway 30, and at about 300 feet, (I) started going through wisps of mist . . . (I) looked back and could see some lights along the bay . . . but nothing ahead. This was the last chance I had to stay anything near VFR.

The pilot then flew out over San Francisco Bay, and tried to pick up a clearance.

"They asked me to climb to no greater than 3500 feet in VFR conditions. I told them I was unable, but I could climb to 2000 feet (even though I was nowhere near VFR) . . . I didn't tell them the truth of course — I was so worried about getting in trouble. Within about 5 minutes or so I had the clearance . . . got a vector of 080° for VOR Runway 9R (at) Oakland . . . fumbling with my charts the whole time. What a night! Pilots: don't do this to yourself, just file the IFR flight plan — you can cancel if you don't need it. And thank you, Bay Approach."

The pilot in this ASRS incident report may have felt that he could save time and avoid hassles by going VFR. However, filing IFR when weather conditions are marginal VFR normally is the wisest and safest decision. NTSB reports often show continued flight into marginal VFR conditions as a causal factor in weather-related accidents. The irony is that the pilots involved in these accidents are instrument-rated more times than not.

ENROUTE RADAR PROCEDURES

When you operate as pilot in command under IFR in controlled airspace, the FARs require you to continuously monitor an appropriate center or control frequency. After takeoff, your IFR flight is either in contact with a radar-equipped local departure control or, in some areas, an ARTCC facility. As your flight transitions to the enroute phase, you typically can expect a handoff from departure control to a center frequency if you are not already in contact with center. If you are using the tower enroute control procedure (TEC), you will receive a handoff from departure control to approach control at the next facility. The handoff between two radar facilities normally is a quick and simple procedure, but using the correct technique makes the process easier.

COMMUNICATION

As your flight leaves the departure controller's airspace, either by radar vector or your own navigation, you will be instructed to contact the center. The instructions issued by the controller include the name of the facility, the appropriate frequency, and any pertinent remarks. When you receive instructions to change frequencies, you should acknowledge the change by repeating it back to the controller. This readback also verifies that you understand the instruction and have received the correct frequency. [Figure 5-17]

SECTION B ■ **Enroute Procedures**

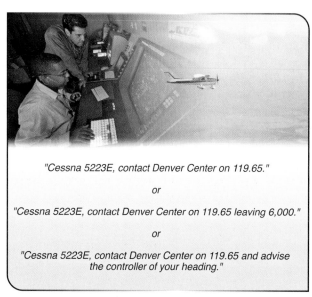

"Cessna 5223E, contact Denver Center on 119.65."

or

"Cessna 5223E, contact Denver Center on 119.65 leaving 6,000."

or

"Cessna 5223E, contact Denver Center on 119.65 and advise the controller of your heading."

Figure 5-17. In addition to stating the facility and frequency, the controller may issue specific instructions during the handoff.

Your initial callup to the center should include the facility identification, your aircraft identification, altitude, and assigned altitude. [Figure 5-18] When your transmission is received, the controller verifies your position and compares your reported altitude to that shown by your Mode C equipment. Once verified, the controller acknowledges your transmission and states," . . . *radar contact.*" You can now expect radar flight following and radar services until you are advised, " . . . *radar contact lost*" or " . . . *radar service terminated.*"

Figure 5-18. Your callup procedure to the center is basically the same as the one used when contacting departure control.

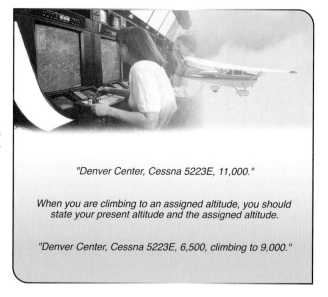

"Denver Center, Cessna 5223E, 11,000."

When you are climbing to an assigned altitude, you should state your present altitude and the assigned altitude.

"Denver Center, Cessna 5223E, 6,500, climbing to 9,000."

If you make a required frequency change and the center does not acknowledge your callup, return to the previously assigned frequency. ARTCC facilities are subject to transmitter/receiver failures, though this is rare, and radio contact may be momentarily lost. Each ARTCC frequency has at least one backup transmitter and receiver which can be put into service quickly, with little or no disruption of service. Technical problems of this type may cause a delay, but the switch-over process rarely takes more than one minute. Therefore, you should wait at least that long before deciding that the center's radio has failed. If you cannot establish contact using the newly assigned frequency, return to the one previously assigned and request an alternate frequency. If you are still unable to establish radio contact, try again on any ARTCC frequency. Failing that, contact the nearest FSS in the area for further instructions.

REPORTING PROCEDURES

In addition to acknowledging a handoff to another controller, there are reports that you should make without a specific request from ATC. Certain reports should be made at all times regardless of whether you are in radar contact with ATC, while others are necessary only if radar contact has been lost or terminated.

RADAR/NONRADAR REPORTS

Whether or not you are in radar contact, when you are cleared from an altitude to one newly assigned, you should report leaving the previous altitude. However, when you reach the newly assigned altitude, you are not required to report unless ATC requests you to do so. If you are operating on a VFR-on-top clearance, you should advise ATC of an altitude change. You should report your time and altitude upon reaching a holding fix or clearance limit and report when you are leaving a holding fix or clearance limit. If you cannot continue your instrument approach to a landing, you must report missed approach and request a clearance for a specific action. You may request to proceed to an alternate airport or try another approach. Changes in your aircraft's performance also warrant a report. For example, you should notify ATC if you are unable to climb or descend at a rate of at least 500 feet per minute, or if your average true airspeed at cruising altitude varies by 5% or 10 knots (whichever is greater) from that filed in your flight plan.

 You should advise ATC when your airspeed changes by 5% or 10 knots, whichever is greater. You should also inform ATC if your DME fails.

If you experience any loss of VOR, TACAN, ADF, low frequency navigation receiver capability, complete or partial loss of ILS receiver capability or impairment of air/ground communication capability, you are required by the FARs to advise ATC. This report should include your aircraft identification, the equipment affected, the degree to which your capability to operate under IFR in the ATC system is impaired, and the nature and extent of assistance you desire. ATC uses these reports to help regulate traffic and to avoid any conflicts which might develop. For example, if you lose your DME equipment, the controller will know that you cannot accept a hold or approach that requires DME at your destination. You also are required by regulation to advise ATC if you encounter weather conditions which have not been forecast or hazardous weather, as well as any information relating to the safety of flight.

NONRADAR REPORTS

If radar contact has been lost or radar service terminated, the FARs require you to provide ATC with **position reports** over designated VORs and intersections along your route of flight. These **compulsory reporting points** are depicted on IFR enroute charts by solid triangles. Position reports over fixes indicated by open triangles are only necessary when requested by ATC. If you are on a direct course that is not on an established airway, report over the fixes used in your flight plan that define the route. Compulsory reporting points also apply when you conduct your IFR flight in accordance with a VFR-on-top clearance.

 When ATC advises *"...radar service terminated"* during the enroute portion of the flight, you should begin position reporting.

 When flying on a VFR-on-top clearance, you should make the same position reports as on any IFR flight.

SECTION B ■ **Enroute Procedures**

Whether your route is on airways or direct, position reports are mandatory in a nonradar environment, and they must include specific information. A typical position report includes information pertaining to your position, expected route, and ETAs. You may state time in minutes only when no misunderstanding is likely to occur. [Figure 5-19]

Figure 5-19. Position reports must include specific information.

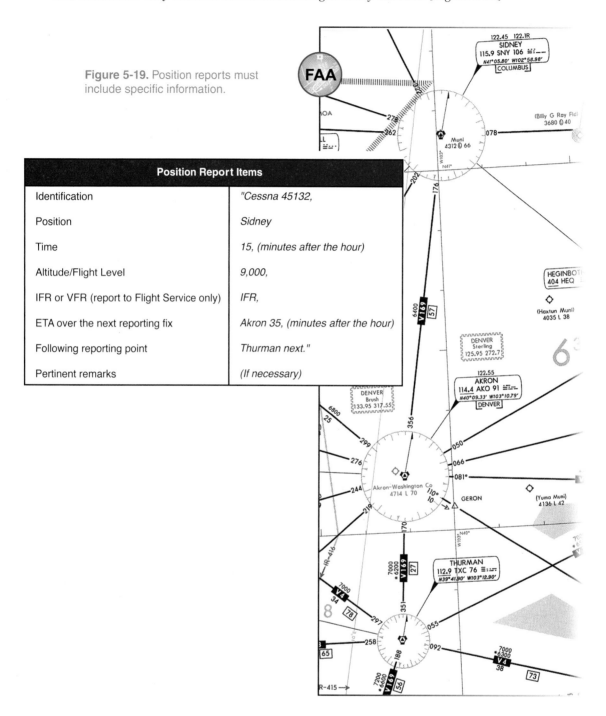

Position Report Items	
Identification	"Cessna 45132,
Position	Sidney
Time	15, (minutes after the hour)
Altitude/Flight Level	9,000,
IFR or VFR (report to Flight Service only)	IFR,
ETA over the next reporting fix	Akron 35, (minutes after the hour)
Following reporting point	Thurman next."
Pertinent remarks	(If necessary)

There are several additional reports that you should make if you are not in radar contact with ATC. When it becomes apparent that an estimated time that you previously submitted to ATC will be in error in excess of 3 minutes, you should notify the controller. In addition, you should report the final approach fix (FAF) inbound on a nonprecision approach, and when you leave the outer marker (OM), or fix used in lieu of it, on a precision approach. FAFs and other approach terms are covered in more detail in Chapter 7. [Figure 5-20]

While flying on a direct route, the fixes that define the route become compulsory reporting points.

RADAR/NONRADAR REPORTS	
These reports should be made at all times without a specific ATC request.	
Leaving one assigned flight altitude or flight level for another	*"Cessna 45132, leaving 8,000, climb to 10,000."*
VFR-on-top change in altitude	*"Cessna 45132, VFR-on-top, climbing to 10,500."*
Leaving any assigned holding fix or point	*"Cessna 45132, leaving FARGO Intersection."*
Missed approach	*"Cessna 45132, missed approach, request clearance to Chicago."*
Unable to climb or descend at least 500 feet per minute	*"Cessna 45132, maximum climb rate 400 feet per minute."*
TAS variation from filed speed of 5% or 10 knots, whichever is greater	*"Cessna 45132, advises TAS decrease to 140 knots."*
Time and altitude or flight level upon reaching a holding fix or clearance limit	*"Cessna 45132, FARGO Intersection at 05, 10,000, holding east."*
Loss of nav/comm capability (required by FAR 91.187)	*"Cessna 45132, ILS receiver inoperative."*
Unforecast weather conditions or other information relating to the safety of flight (required by FAR 91.183)	*"Cessna 45132, experiencing moderate turbulence at 10,000."*

NONRADAR REPORTS	
When you are not in radar contact, these reports should be made without a specific request from ATC.	
Leaving FAF or OM inbound on final approach	*"Cessna 45132, outer marker inbound, leaving 2,000."*
Revised ETA of more than three minutes	*"Cessna 45132, revising SCURRY estimate to 55."*
Position reporting at compulsory reporting points (required by FAR 91.183)	*See figure 5-17 for position report items.*

Figure 5-20. You are assisting ATC in maintaining aircraft separation by reporting changes in altitude, aircraft performance, and navigation equipment status, as well as by making position reports in the nonradar environment.

 When not in radar contact on a nonprecision approach, report to ATC any time you leave a final approach fix inbound on final approach.

ENROUTE NAVIGATION USING GPS

If you have a panel-mounted, IFR enroute-approved GPS, you may use it as your primary means of point-to-point navigation. However, unless the IFR GPS is equipped to receive a wide area augmentation system (WAAS) correction signal, your aircraft must be equipped with an alternate means of navigation, such as VOR, appropriate to the flight. Active monitoring of the alternate navigation equipment is not required if the GPS receiver uses receiver autonomous integrity monitoring (RAIM).

 GPS systems certified for only VFR operation, including hand-held GPS devices, may be used during IFR operations as an aid to situational awareness.

Due to the traffic saturation in crowded airspace, such as in the northeast United States, you most likely will use the GPS to fly on published airways. In less congested areas, you may opt to file a direct route between published waypoints or those you program yourself.

RANDOM RNAV ROUTES

The ability to go direct to your destination is a core advantage of RNAV. If you can remain in radar contact over the entire route, ATC may clear you for a **random RNAV route.** If your route takes you from one center facility to another, you should file the waypoint latitude/longitude coordinates on your flight plan along with the departure point and destination. Center facilities possess maps of the airspace they control, but only portions of the surrounding airspace, making location of a point in another center's area difficult unless coordinates are provided. When flying direct, you should program an airway route into your GPS unit as a backup, since ATC can request a switch to traditional airways at any time. [Figure 5-21]

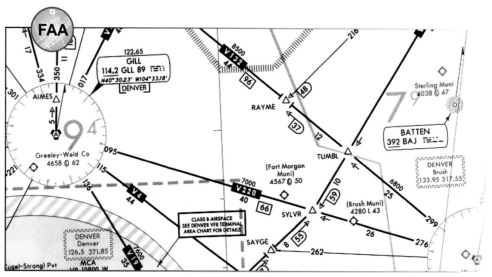

Figure 5-21. A flight between Greeley and Sterling, Colorado would be awkward if flown on VOR radials. Area navigation, such as GPS, makes a direct route feasible.

GPS operation must be conducted in accordance with the FAA-approved aircraft flight manual (AFM) or flight manual supplement. Prior to using a GPS for IFR enroute flights, you must be thoroughly familiar with the particular GPS equipment installed in your aircraft, the receiver operation manual, and the AFM. Unlike traditional navigation equipment, such as the VOR receiver, basic operation, receiver presentation, and capabilities of GPS units can vary greatly. Most receivers have a simulator mode which allows you to become familiar with the equipment's operation prior to using it in the aircraft. In addition, you should use the equipment in flight under VFR conditions prior to attempting IFR operation. Reviewing appropriate GPS NOTAMs prior to a flight should alert you to any satellite outages. Many GPS-equipped airplanes also have autopilots. When coupled with a GPS, an autopilot can compensate for wind and keep the airplane on course and at the assigned altitude. Be sure you fully understand how to operate the autopilot before using it, and continue to monitor your position carefully when the system is flying the airplane.

T-ROUTES AND Q-ROUTES

Tango routes or **T-routes,** enable RNAV-equipped aircraft to more efficiently fly around or through terminal areas with Class B and Class C airspace. These routes also reduce controller workload by providing a published route instead of controllers having to radar vector aircraft along those flight paths. Because the minimum enroute altitude (MEA) for GPS navigation is not affected by NAVAID limitations, MEAs for T-routes are frequently lower than MEAs for conventional airways.

The routes between some points in the high altitude environment are very popular, so these paths are given route designators and published on charts. The U.S. and Canada use "Q" as a designator for RNAV routes on high altitude enroute charts. **Q-routes** facilitate high-altitude. long-range direct flights and closely-spaced Q-routes can accommodate increased operations within congested airspace areas, such as the east and west coasts of the U.S.

Q-routes 1 through 499 are allocated to the U.S., while Canada is allocated Q-routes numbered from 500 through 999. One benefit of this system is that aircraft with RNAV or RNP capability can fly safely along closely spaced parallel flight paths on high-density routes, which eases airspace congestion. [Figure 5-22]

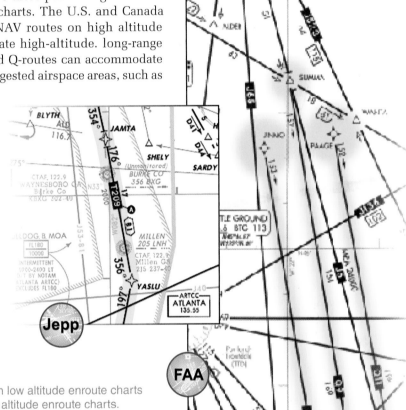

Figure 5-22. T-routes are shown on low altitude enroute charts and Q-routes are depicted on high altitude enroute charts.

ENROUTE RNP

For enroute operations, the U.S. standard RNP values or levels are for routes that support RNAV operations based on GPS or earth-referenced navigation systems such as the inertial navigation system (INS) and the inertial reference system (IRS). RNP levels are depicted on affected aeronautical charts and procedures, and these references can include notations that refer to eligible aircraft by specific navigation sensors.

ICAO defines required navigation performance as a statement of required navigation accuracy in the horizontal plane (lateral and longitudinal position fixing) necessary for operation in a defined airspace. For federal airways that extend four nautical miles either side of the airway centerline, the airway has an equivalent RNP of 2, which refers to a required navigational performance accuracy of two nautical miles of the desired flight path at least 95 percent of the time flying. [Figure 5-23]

SECTION B ■ **Enroute Procedures**

SECTION B ■ Enroute Procedures

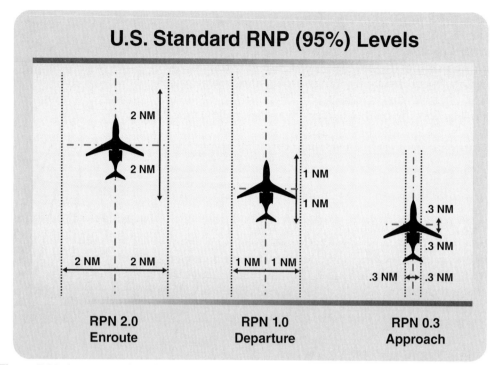

Figure 5-23. As you transition from the enroute to the terminal environment, your navigation equipment must keep the airplane within a specified distance when performing RNP procedures.

SPECIAL USE AIRSPACE

The flexibility that you gain by flying random RNAV routes requires additional care during preflight planning. In contrast to IFR flight on airways, which mostly circumvent special use airspace, direct routes are more likely to go through this airspace. An advantage of operating IFR is that your ATC clearance provides automatic authorization to penetrate special use airspace; however, if you plan your flight through special use airspace that is active at the time of your flight, ATC will not clear you for the route you planned when you request your clearance. Your enroute chart can help you plan around special use airspace. With the exception of controlled firing areas, special use airspace areas are depicted, and their times of operation are shown on the communications panel. Refer to the AIM for additional information regarding IFR operations in special use airspace. [Figure 5-24]

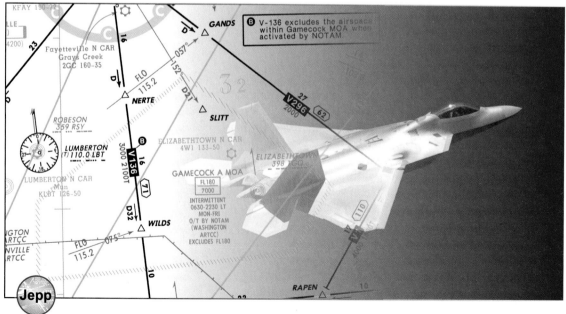

Figure 5-24. In contrast to the ATC procedures regarding restricted areas, civilian IFR traffic may be cleared through an active MOA if ATC can provide separation.

IFR CRUISING ALTITUDES

FAR 91.179 provides information on **IFR cruising altitudes**. When operating under IFR in controlled airspace in level cruising flight, you must fly at the altitude or flight level assigned by ATC. For IFR flight in uncontrolled airspace, FAR 91.179 specifies altitudes which you must maintain based on your magnetic course. This hemispheric rule states that when operating below 18,000 feet MSL on a magnetic course of zero through 179°, you must fly an odd thousand foot MSL altitude, and for courses of 180° through 359°, an even thousand foot altitude must be maintained. Out of common practice, pilots normally file, and ATC usually assigns, IFR altitudes which agree with the hemispheric rule. However, in controlled airspace, you may request and receive altitude assignments that do not comply with east/west rules. [Figure 5-25]

 You normally will file, and receive a clearance for, a cruising altitude which agrees with the hemispheric rule. See figure 5-25.

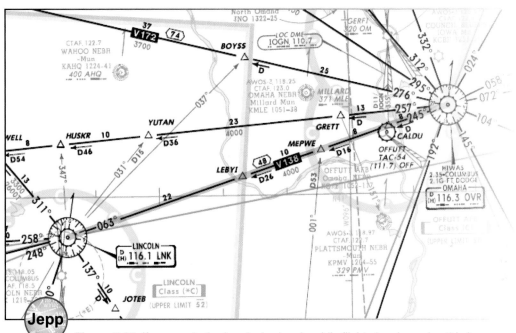

Figure 5-25. If you apply the hemispheric rule while flight planning using this low altitude enroute chart, the highest usable altitude for a southwest-bound IFR flight on V138 from the Omaha VORTAC to the Lincoln VORTAC is 16,000 feet MSL.

If you are on an IFR flight plan below 18,000 feet MSL, and operating on a VFR-on-top clearance, you may select any VFR cruising altitude appropriate to your direction of flight between the MEA and 18,000 feet MSL, that allows you to remain in VFR conditions. Of course, you must still report any change in altitude to ATC and comply with all other IFR reporting procedures. VFR-on-top is not authorized in Class A airspace.

 Although you are on an IFR flight plan when assigned a VFR-on-top clearance, you should fly at an appropriate VFR cruising altitude.

When you cruise below 18,000 feet MSL, keep your altimeter adjusted to the current setting, as reported by a station within 100 nautical miles of your position. In areas where weather reporting stations are more than 100 nautical miles from your route, you may use the altimeter setting of a station that is closest to you. During IFR flight, ATC advises you periodically of the current altimeter setting, but it remains your responsibility to update your altimeter in a timely manner.

SECTION B ■ **Enroute Procedures**

At or above 18,000 feet MSL, you will be operating at **flight levels**, and the FARs require you to set your altimeter to 29.92. A flight level is defined as a level of constant atmospheric pressure related to a reference datum of 29.92 in. Hg. Each flight level is stated in three digits which represent hundreds of feet. For example, FL250 represents an altimeter indication of 25,000 feet. Conflicts with traffic operating below 18,000 feet MSL may arise when actual altimeter settings along the route of flight are lower than 29.92. Therefore, FAR 91.121 specifies the **lowest usable flight levels** for a given altimeter setting range. [Figure 5-26]

Table of Usable Altitudes	
Current Altimeter Setting	**Lowest Usable Flight Level**
29.92 (or higher)	180
29.91 — 29.42	185
29.41 — 28.92	190
28.91 — 28.42	195
28.41 — 27.92	200
27.91 — 27.42	205
27.41 — 26.92	210

Figure 5-26. As local altimeter settings fall below 29.92, a pilot operating in Class A airspace must cruise at progressively higher indicated altitudes to ensure separation from aircraft operating in the low altitude structure.

REDUCED VERTICAL SEPARATION MINIMUMS

Vertical separation minimums of 2,000 feet for high altitudes were created more than 40 years ago when altimeters were not very accurate above FL 290. With better flight and navigation instruments, vertical separation has been safely reduced to 1,000 feet in many parts of the world. **Reduced Vertical Separation Minimums (RVSM)** airspace is any airspace between FL 290 and FL 410, inclusive, where airplanes are separated by 1,000 feet vertically. This increases airspace capacity and saves fuel by allowing aircraft to fly a more optimal profile. RVSM adds six additional usable altitudes between FL 290 and FL 410.

ATC separates aircraft by 1,000 feet vertically when flying within the U.S. Domestic Reduced Vertical Separation Minimum (DRVSM) airspace. In order to operate an aircraft utilizing RVSM, Part 91.706 requires that both you and your aircraft comply with Appendix G — Operations in Reduced Vertical Separation Minimum (RVSM) Airspace. Typically, you do not experience RVSM when flying light general aviation aircraft; however, if you pursue a career as a professional pilot, you may use RVSM on a regular basis.

DESCENDING FROM THE ENROUTE SEGMENT

As you near your destination, ATC will issue a **descent clearance** so that you arrive in the approach control's airspace at an appropriate altitude. There are two basic descent clearances that ATC issues. ATC may ask you to descend to and maintain a specific altitude. Generally, this clearance is for enroute traffic separation purposes, and you need to respond to it promptly. Descend at the optimum rate for your aircraft, until you are 1,000 feet above the assigned altitude. You should report vacating any previous altitude for a newly assigned altitude, and your last 1,000 feet of descent should be made at a rate of 500 to 1,500 f.p.m. The second type of descent clearance allows you to descend *"...at pilot's discretion."* When ATC issues you a clearance **at pilot's discretion**, you may begin the descent whenever you choose. You also are authorized to level off, temporarily, at any intermediate altitude during the descent. However, once you leave an altitude, you may not return to it.

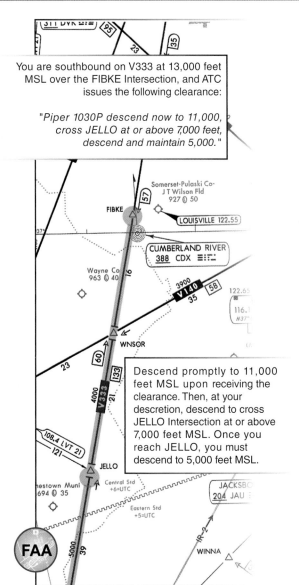

You are southbound on V333 at 13,000 feet MSL over the FIBKE Intersection, and ATC issues the following clearance:

"Piper 1030P descend now to 11,000, cross JELLO at or above 7,000 feet, descend and maintain 5,000."

Descend promptly to 11,000 feet MSL upon receiving the clearance. Then, at your descretion, descend to cross JELLO Intersection at or above 7,000 feet MSL. Once you reach JELLO, you must descend to 5,000 feet MSL.

A descent clearance also may include a segment where the descent is at your discretion, such as *" . . . cross the Joliet VOR at or above 12,000, descend and maintain 5,000."* This clearance authorizes you to descend from the assigned altitude whenever you choose, so long as you cross the Joliet VOR at or above 12,000 feet MSL. After that, you should descend at a normal rate until you reach the assigned altitude of 5,000 feet MSL. [Figure 5-27]

Clearances to descend at pilot's discretion are not just an option for ATC. You may also request this type of clearance so that you can operate more efficiently. If you are enroute above an overcast layer, you may ask for a descent at your discretion, which would allow you to remain above the clouds for as long as possible. You may find this particularly important, for example, if the outside air temperature is conducive to icing conditions. Your request permits you to stay at your cruising altitude longer, in order to conserve fuel and avoid prolonged periods of IFR flight in icing conditions. This type of descent also minimizes your exposure to turbulence, by allowing you to level off at an altitude where the air is smoother.

Figure 5-27. A descent clearance which specifies a crossing altitude allows you to descend at your discretion, but only for that flight segment to which the altitude restriction applies.

SECTION B ■ **Enroute Procedures**

SUMMARY CHECKLIST

✓ During a radar handoff, the controller may advise you to give the next controller certain information, such as a heading or altitude.

✓ If you cannot establish contact using a newly assigned frequency, return to the one previously assigned and request an alternate frequency.

✓ You should make the following reports to ATC at all times: leaving an altitude, an altitude change if VFR-on-top, time and altitude upon reaching a holding fix or clearance limit, leaving a holding fix or clearance limit, missed approach, inability to climb or descend at a rate of at least 500 feet per minute, and change in true airspeed by 5% or 10 knots (whichever is greater).

✓ You are required by regulation to report a loss of airplane navigational capability, unforecast or hazardous weather conditions, and any other information relating to the safety of flight.

✓ If radar contact has been lost or radar service terminated, the FARs require you to provide ATC with position reports over compulsory reporting points.

✓ The compulsory reporting points on a direct route include those fixes that define the route.

✓ The standard position report includes your identification, current position, time, altitude, ETA over the next reporting fix, the following reporting point, and any pertinent remarks.

✓ In a nonradar environment, you should report when you reach the final approach fix inbound on a nonprecision approach, and when you leave the outer marker inbound on a precision approach. In addition, a report is necessary when it becomes apparent that an estimated time that you previously submitted to ATC will be in error in excess of 3 minutes.

✓ To use panel-mounted, IFR enroute-approved GPS as your primary means of navigation, your aircraft must be equipped with an alternate means of navigation, such as VOR-based equipment, appropriate to the flight. The alternate navigation system is not required for WAAS-equipped IFR-approved GPS systems.

✓ Active monitoring of alternate navigation equipment is not required if the GPS receiver uses receiver autonomous integrity monitoring (RAIM).

✓ T-routes reduce controller workload by providing a published route around or through Class B and Class C airspace for RNAV-equipped aircraft.

✓ Q-routes are RNAV routes depicted on high altitude charts that facilitate high-altitude, long-range direct flights and can accommodate increased operations within congested airspace areas, such as the east and west coasts of the U.S.

✓ Reduced Vertical Separation Minimums (RVSM) airspace is any airspace between FL 290 and FL 410, inclusive, where airplanes are separated by 1,000 feet vertically.

✓ ATC usually does not issue an IFR route clearance that crosses an active restricted area, but inactive areas are often released for use.

✓ Though you may request and be assigned any altitude in controlled airspace, most pilots file flight plan altitudes that correspond to the hemispheric rule.

✓ Lowest usable altitudes are specified for use above 18,000 feet MSL when the barometric pressure is below certain values.

✓ When you are given a descent clearance "…*at pilot's discretion*," you are authorized to begin the descent whenever you choose, and level off temporarily during the descent, but you cannot return to an altitude once you vacate it.

KEY TERMS

Position Report	Flight Level
Compulsory Reporting Point	Lowest Usable Flight Level
Random RNAV Route	Reduced Vertical Separation Minimums (RVSM)
T-Route	
Q-Route	Descent Clearance
IFR Cruising Altitude	At Pilot's Discretion

QUESTIONS

1. What does it mean when ATC advises you that your aircraft is in *"...radar contact?"*
   A. You can expect radar flight following.
   B. You no longer need to watch for other traffic, even if you are in VFR conditions.
   C. The controller no longer needs you to advise of any change in airspeed or performance.

2. If you attempt to contact the center after a handoff from departure control, and you get no response, what action should you take?

3. You filed a true airspeed of 130 knots. While enroute, you calculate your true airspeed to be 135 knots. Do you need to advise ATC?

4. True/False. You do not need to report a malfunction of your ADF receiver to ATC if you are in radar contact.

5. True/False. When you are operating VFR-on-top, you should report to ATC when you are leaving an altitude.

6. You are on an IFR flight plan and ATC tells you that radar contact is lost. What additional reports are you required to make in a nonradar environment?

7. You are operating in a nonradar environment on a direct course that is not an established airway. Select the true statement regarding position reports in this situation.
   A. You should report over the fixes used to define your route.
   B. You should report your position to ATC every 30 minutes until radar contact has been reestablished.
   C. You do not need to report your position until you are established on a Victor airway over a compulsory reporting point.

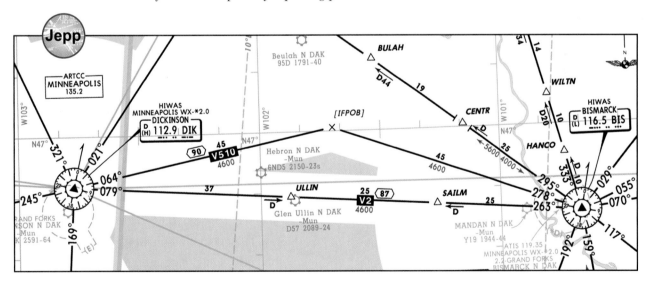

8. You are on an IFR flight in Aztec 3490R, heading east on V2. Prior to reaching Dickinson, ATC advises you that radar contact has been lost. You are instructed to report ULLIN Intersection. Assuming the time is 1330, your groundspeed is 150 knots, and you are cruising level at 9,000 feet MSL, give a position report to Minneapolis Center over Dickinson VOR.

9. If you apply the hemispheric rule, what is the highest usable altitude on an eastbound IFR flight on V2 between Dickinson VOR and Bismarck VOR?

10. What is the purpose of a Tango route?

11. True/False. If the route filed on your IFR flight plan requires you to penetrate a restricted area, you must request a special clearance from the restricted area's controlling agency.

12. True/False. An RNP enroute level of 2.0 means the navigation equipment must be capable of maintaining the aircraft within 2 NM either side of the centerline of the route 95 percent of the time during flight.

13. True/False. RVSM provides six additional usable altitudes between FL 290 and FL 410.

SECTION C
Holding Procedures

Holding patterns are a method of delaying airborne aircraft to help maintain separation and provide a smooth flow of traffic. When the volume of traffic becomes overwhelming, or in the event of a radar failure, the need for holding patterns increases. There are a few areas that do not have ATC radar coverage, and holding patterns routinely help controllers manage the traffic in those areas. Holding patterns also are used when you reach a clearance limit, or may be required following a missed approach. There might be times when you will want to request a hold, for instance, when you need to climb to reach an assigned altitude, or when weather at your destination is improving and a few more minutes might make the difference between diverting to an alternate and a successful landing at your destination. Thus, it is important that you know what is expected of you and how to properly execute this classic instrument maneuver.

CAN HOLDING PATTERNS MAKE YOU DIZZY?

Disorientation can occur at any time, but is more likely in low visibility or instrument conditions. In some cases, disorientation can be so severe that the pilot cannot control the aircraft. Instrument-rated pilots are just as susceptible as noninstrument-rated pilots. The frequent turns and continuous workload of flying a holding pattern in turbulent, windy conditions can create a prime environment for both vestibular and spatial disorientation. To minimize the risk in such situations, avoid rapid head movements, which can precipitate an attack of vestibular disorientation. This is where good cockpit management really helps. Arrange to have necessary charts and pilot supplies easily available. Think before you reach for the next chart, lean over to switch fuel tanks, or look for a dropped pencil.

THE STANDARD HOLDING PATTERN

Holding patterns are shaped like the oval racetracks you see on sectionals. In a **standard holding pattern**, the turns are to the right, while a **nonstandard holding pattern** uses left turns. Below 14,000 feet MSL, a holding pattern is usually two standard-rate 180° turns separated by 1 minute straight segments. Thus, with no wind, each circuit takes 4 minutes. Above 14,000 feet MSL, the straight legs are flown for 1 and 1/2 minutes, so each trip around takes 5 minutes with no wind. For simplicity in this section, assume holding patterns below 14,000 feet. The physical size of the holding pattern varies with your speed. Discounting the effects of wind, each circuit takes the same amount of time whether you fly fast or slow. [Figure 5-28] Each holding pattern has a fix, a direction from the fix, and a line of position (NDB bearing or VOR

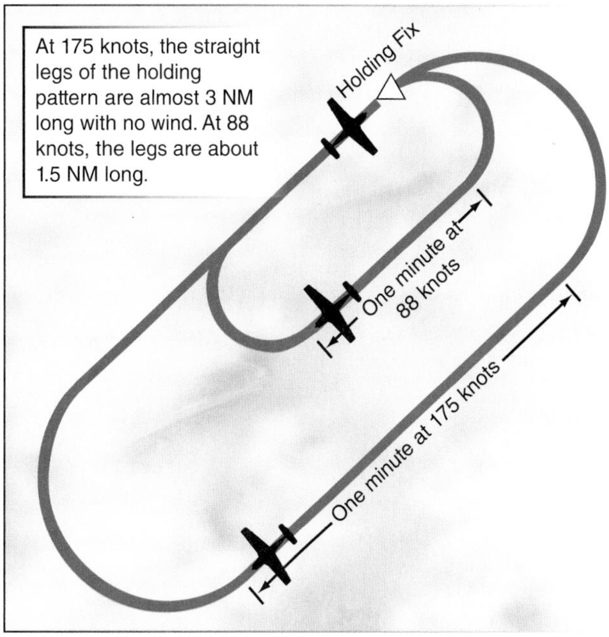

At 175 knots, the straight legs of the holding pattern are almost 3 NM long with no wind. At 88 knots, the legs are about 1.5 NM long.

Holding Fix

One minute at 88 knots

One minute at 175 knots

Figure 5-28. There is no advantage to flying any faster than necessary. Slowing down saves fuel and uses less airspace.

radial) on which to fly one leg of the pattern. These elements, along with the direction of the turns, define the holding pattern. Each circuit of the holding pattern begins and ends at the **holding fix**. The holding fix may be an intersection, a navaid, a GPS waypoint, or a certain DME distance from a navaid. The **inbound leg** of the pattern is flown toward the fix on the **holding course**. The holding course can be a VOR radial, GPS course, or NDB bearing. As you would expect, the side of the holding course where the pattern is flown is called the **holding side**. [Figure 5-29]

> Turns are made to the right in a standard holding pattern, and to the left in a nonstandard holding pattern.

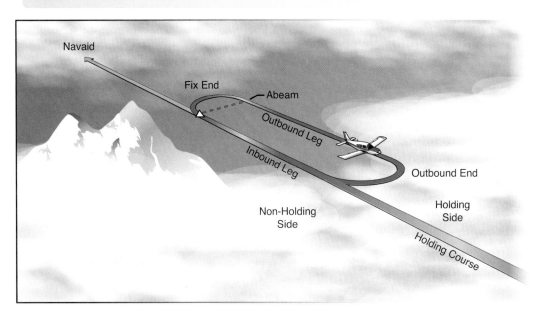

Figure 5-29. The airspace is protected on the holding side. If the holding pattern is flown correctly, you are guaranteed obstacle clearance and separation from other air traffic.

So Many Planes, So Little Time

As air commerce expanded in the early 1930s, the rapid increase in the number of commercial, military, and private flights began to create traffic conflicts and congestion problems, so in July of 1936, the federal government took over control of air traffic. Just as traffic lights delay some ground traffic in order to allow other traffic to move, pilots were often instructed to circle over a designated spot so that another airplane could complete its approach. By the early 1940s, part of the standard holding procedure called for pilots to fly along the right edge of the on-course signal to a radio range station so that departing traffic could fly out on the other side of the same on-course signal. The holding pattern itself was flown between the holding fix and a point four minutes flying time away.

Although different navaids have replaced the low frequency radio ranges and now radar covers most of the country, holding patterns are still used as backup procedures today.

OUTBOUND AND INBOUND TIMING

The challenge during holding is to make your inbound legs one minute long. Since it is difficult to predict the effects of wind, use the first trip around to find some approximate correction factors for subsequent circuits. Begin timing the outbound leg when you are abeam the holding fix. If you cannot identify the abeam position, you should start timing when you complete the turn outbound. After turning inbound, time your inbound leg to gauge the effect of the wind, and adjust the timing for subsequent outbound legs to achieve an inbound time of one minute. A longer inbound leg indicates that you should shorten the outbound leg, and vice versa. [Figure 5-30]

 Timing for the outbound leg of either a standard or nonstandard holding pattern should begin abeam the holding fix. If the abeam position cannot be identified, start timing the outbound leg at the completion of the turn outbound.

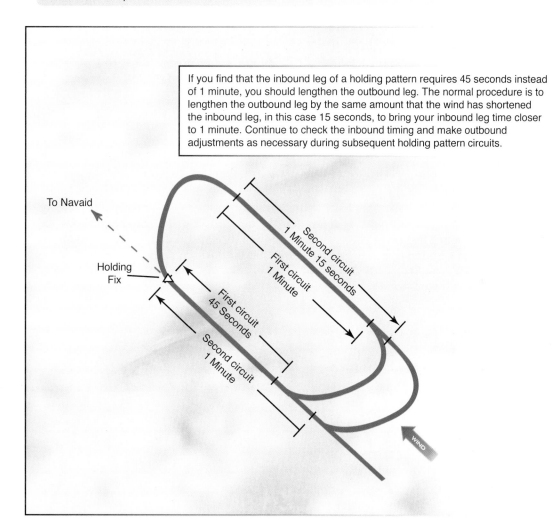

If you find that the inbound leg of a holding pattern requires 45 seconds instead of 1 minute, you should lengthen the outbound leg. The normal procedure is to lengthen the outbound leg by the same amount that the wind has shortened the inbound leg, in this case 15 seconds, to bring your inbound leg time closer to 1 minute. Continue to check the inbound timing and make outbound adjustments as necessary during subsequent holding pattern circuits.

To Navaid

Holding Fix

Second circuit 1 Minute 15 seconds

First circuit 1 Minute

First circuit 45 Seconds

Second circuit 1 Minute

WIND

Figure 5-30. If you have a tailwind blowing you directly toward the navaid, you will need a longer outbound leg to make your inbound leg come out to one minute.

Sometimes DME distances are used instead of timing the inbound and outbound legs. When DME is used, the same holding procedures apply, but the turns are initiated at specified DME distances from the station. The holding fix is on a radial at a designated distance. If you are asked to hold at a DME fix and the holding pattern lies between the DME fix and the navaid, remember that you are holding at the fix, not the navaid. Your inbound leg to the holding fix will be outbound from the navaid. [Figure 5-31]

SECTION C ■ Holding Procedures

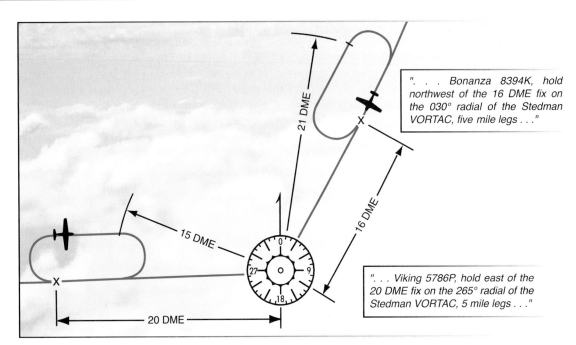

". . . Bonanza 8394K, hold northwest of the 16 DME fix on the 030° radial of the Stedman VORTAC, five mile legs . . ."

". . . Viking 5786P, hold east of the 20 DME fix on the 265° radial of the Stedman VORTAC, 5 mile legs . . ."

Figure 5-31. When holding at a DME or RNAV fix, the leg length will be specified by ATC.

CROSSWIND CORRECTION

If you fly your holding pattern without correcting for crosswind drift, you could inadvertently stray from the protected airspace area or have difficulty coming back to the inbound course before passing the fix. To avoid these problems, use your normal bracketing and drift correction techniques to determine the amount of drift correction necessary during the inbound leg. Once you determine the wind correction angle (WCA) required to maintain the inbound course, triple the correction for the outbound leg. [Figure 5-32]

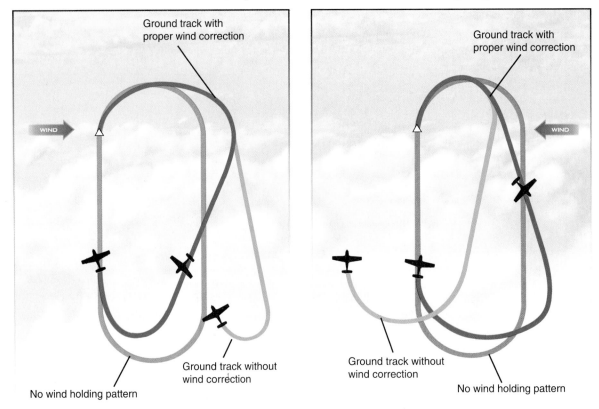

Figure 5-32. Using insufficient wind correction on the outbound leg causes the aircraft to over- or undershoot the course during the turn inbound. Tripling the inbound correction on the outbound heading should give you room to intercept the inbound course again while remaining on the holding side of the course.

MAXIMUM HOLDING SPEED

As you have seen, the size of the holding pattern is directly proportional to the speed of the airplane. In order to limit the amount of airspace that must be protected by ATC, **maximum holding speeds** have been designated for specific altitude ranges. [Figure 5-33] Even so, some holding patterns may have additional speed restrictions to keep faster airplanes from flying out of the protected area. If a holding pattern has a nonstandard speed restriction, it will be depicted by an icon with the limiting airspeed. If the holding speed limit is less than you feel is necessary, you should advise ATC of your revised holding speed. Also, if your indicated airspeed exceeds the applicable maximum holding speed, ATC expects you to slow to the speed limit within three minutes of your ETA at the holding fix. Often pilots can avoid flying a holding pattern, or reduce the length of time spent in the holding pattern, by slowing down on the way to the holding fix.

 The maximum holding airspeeds for civil aircraft are: 200 KIAS at 6,000 feet MSL and below; 230 KIAS from 6,001 feet MSL through 14,000 feet MSL; and 265 KIAS above 14,001 feet MSL.

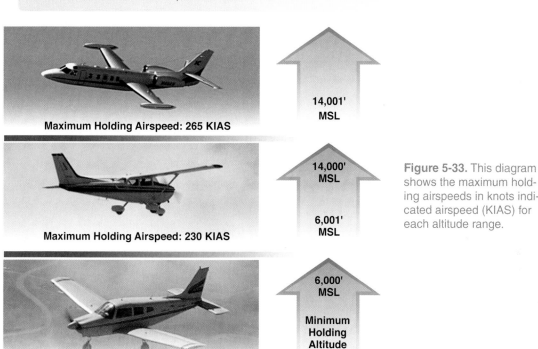

Maximum Holding Airspeed: 265 KIAS

14,001' MSL

Maximum Holding Airspeed: 230 KIAS

14,000' MSL

6,001' MSL

Maximum Holding Airspeed: 200 KIAS

6,000' MSL

Minimum Holding Altitude (MHA)

Figure 5-33. This diagram shows the maximum holding airspeeds in knots indicated airspeed (KIAS) for each altitude range.

High Performance Holding

The maximum holding airspeeds in figure 5-30 may be above the red line airspeed for the airplane you use for instrument training, but in time your instrument flying may involve higher performance aircraft. Certain limitations come into play when you operate at higher speeds; for instance, aircraft do not make standard rate turns in holding patterns if their bank angle will exceed 30°. If the aircraft is using a flight director system, the bank angle is limited to 25°. Since any aircraft must be traveling at over 210 knots TAS for the bank angle in a standard rate turn to exceed 30°, this limit applies to relatively fast airplanes. An aircraft using a flight director

Courtesy of the U.S. Air Force

would have to be holding at more than 170 knots TAS to come up against the 25° limit. These true airspeeds correspond to indicated airspeeds of about 183 and 156 knots, respectively, at 6,000 feet in a standard atmosphere.

Since some military aircraft need to hold at higher speeds than the civilian limits, the maximum at military airfields is higher. For example, the maximum holding airspeed at USAF airfields is 310 KIAS.

SECTION C ■ Holding Procedures

HOLDING PATTERN ENTRIES

Three holding pattern entry procedures have been developed to get you headed in the right direction on the holding course without excessive maneuvering. The entry you use depends on your magnetic heading relative to the holding course when you arrive at the fix. [Figure 5-34] The entries for standard holding patterns are shown. Entries to nonstandard patterns are mirror images of those illustrated.

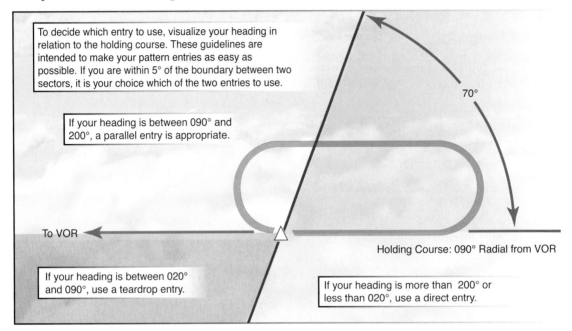

To decide which entry to use, visualize your heading in relation to the holding course. These guidelines are intended to make your pattern entries as easy as possible. If you are within 5° of the boundary between two sectors, it is your choice which of the two entries to use.

70°

If your heading is between 090° and 200°, a parallel entry is appropriate.

To VOR

Holding Course: 090° Radial from VOR

If your heading is between 020° and 090°, use a teardrop entry.

If your heading is more than 200° or less than 020°, use a direct entry.

Figure 5-34. Entry sectors are established by imagining a line at 70° across the holding course. For example, if the holding course is the 090° radial from a VOR, the entry sectors are defined by a line through the fix coinciding with headings of 020° and 200°.

 FAA The entry procedure for a holding pattern depends on your heading relative to the holding course. The recommended entries are shown in figure 5-31.

DIRECT ENTRY

The **direct entry** procedure is the most often used, because it can be applied throughout 180°. When you use the direct entry, you simply fly across the fix, turn right to the outbound heading, and fly the pattern. [Figure 5-35]

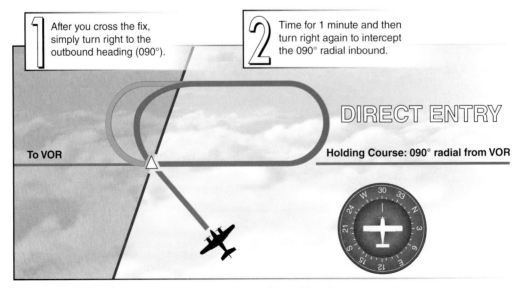

1 After you cross the fix, simply turn right to the outbound heading (090°).

2 Time for 1 minute and then turn right again to intercept the 090° radial inbound.

DIRECT ENTRY

To VOR

Holding Course: 090° radial from VOR

Figure 5-35. Direct entry—at the fix, turn to the outbound heading.

Things to Think About While Holding

The first radio stations for aviation use were operated by the Post Office, and went into service in the early 1920s. DeHaviland mail planes could home on these beacons with primitive battery-powered direction finding receivers.

In 1923, the lighted airway beacon system was begun, using electric or acetylene lamps. By 1941 there were 2,274 airway light beacons over 32,679 airway miles.

The first four-course radio ranges began transmitting in 1929. These provided a specific on-course signal about 3° wide to define the airways. Terms like *"radio beams"* and *"flying on the beam"* entered the common vocabulary. Low powered marker beacons along the routes gave position fixes. That is why the white marker beacon indicator light in many older airplanes is labeled AIRWAY.

Adcock 4 course range station

Runway numbering was not standardized until the late 1930s. Before that, each airport would number its runways as Number 1, Number 2, etc., usually according to the order in which they were built. Many pilots felt that the new system based on magnetic headings was confusing, since the same runway now had two numbers, depending on which direction was being used.

The first VOR airway was created in 1950, and within a few years there were more than 500 VOR stations. DME stations multiplied at a slower rate. As the new Victor airways were created, the radio ranges and lighted airways were dismantled.

TEARDROP ENTRY

The **teardrop entry**, is similar to the direct entry, with the exception that after crossing the fix, you turn to a heading which is approximately 30° away from the holding course outbound on the holding side of the pattern. Once you are established on this heading, fly outbound for approximately 1 minute; then, turn right to intercept the holding course inbound, and return to the fix. This procedure is necessary to give you some maneuvering room for your turn inbound onto the holding course. [Figure 5-36]

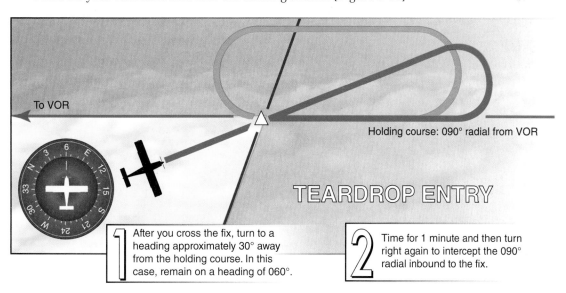

To VOR

Holding course: 090° radial from VOR

TEARDROP ENTRY

1 After you cross the fix, turn to a heading approximately 30° away from the holding course. In this case, remain on a heading of 060°.

2 Time for 1 minute and then turn right again to intercept the 090° radial inbound to the fix.

Figure 5-36. Teardrop entry—at the fix, turn to a heading which is approximately 30° away from the holding course.

PARALLEL ENTRY

The **parallel entry** involves paralleling the holding course outbound on the nonholding side. After crossing the holding fix, turn the airplane to a heading that parallels the holding course and begin timing for one minute. Then, begin a left turn and return to the fix or reintercept the course from the holding side and proceed to the holding fix. [Figure 5-37]

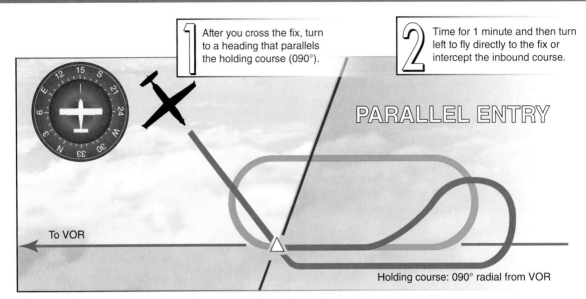

Figure 5-37. Parallel entry—at the fix, turn parallel to the outbound course.

VISUALIZING ENTRY PROCEDURES

The key to easy holding pattern entries is to accurately visualize your position relative to the holding pattern before you arrive over the fix. Many methods have been invented to make this easier, including sketching the holding pattern on your aeronautical chart, using the wind side of a flight computer, employing the aircraft heading indicator, referring to a holding pattern inscription on a plotter, or using specially designed pattern entry computers. Different pilots prefer different methods, but the value of any technique depends on how well it helps you visualize the holding pattern and the appropriate entry. Figure 5-38 depicts a general rule of thumb for determining the correct entry.

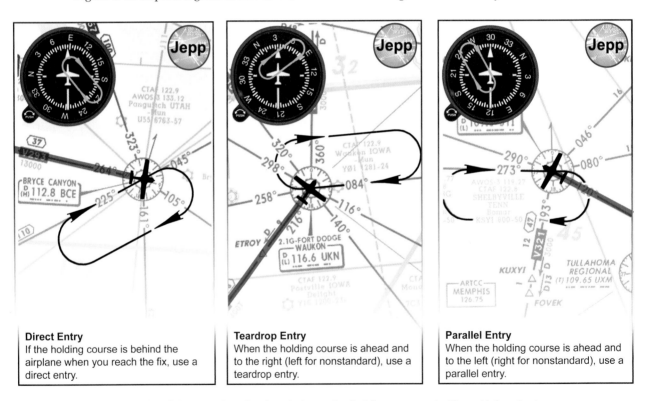

Direct Entry
If the holding course is behind the airplane when you reach the fix, use a direct entry.

Teardrop Entry
When the holding course is ahead and to the right (left for nonstandard), use a teardrop entry.

Parallel Entry
When the holding course is ahead and to the left (right for nonstandard), use a parallel entry.

Figure 5-38. Visualizing your heading in relation to the holding course clarifies which entry to use.

ATC HOLDING INSTRUCTIONS

When controllers anticipate a delay at a clearance limit or fix, you will usually be issued a **holding clearance** at least five minutes before your ETA at the clearance limit or fix. If the holding pattern assigned by ATC is depicted on the appropriate aeronautical chart, you are expected to hold as published, unless advised otherwise by ATC. In this situation, the controller will issue a holding clearance which includes the name of the fix, directs you to hold as published, and includes an **expect further clearance (EFC) time**. An example of such a clearance is: *"Cessna 1124R, hold east of MIKEY Intersection as published, expect further clearance at 1521."* When ATC issues a clearance requiring you to hold at a fix where a holding pattern is not charted, you will be issued complete holding instructions. This information includes the direction from the fix, name of the fix, course, leg length, if appropriate, direction of turns (if left turns are required), and the EFC time. You are required to maintain your last assigned altitude unless a new altitude is specifically included in the holding clearance, and you should fly right turns unless left turns are assigned. Note that all holding instructions should include an expect further clearance time. If you lose two-way radio communication, the EFC allows you to depart the holding fix at a definite time. Plan the last lap of your holding pattern to leave the fix as close as possible to the exact time. [Figure 5-39]

There are at least three items in a clearance for a charted holding pattern:

• Direction to hold from the holding fix	*"...Hold southeast*
• Holding fix	*of PINNE Intersection as published.*
• Expect further clearance time	*Expect further clearance at 1645."*

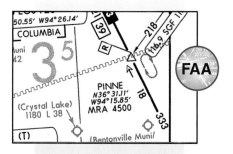

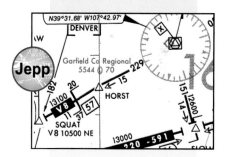

A clearance for an uncharted holding pattern contains additional information:

• Direction to hold from holding fix	*"...Hold west*
• Holding fix	*of Horst Intersection*
• The holding course (a specified radial, magnetic bearing, airway or route number)	*on Victor 8*
• The outbound leg length in minutes or nautical miles when DME is used	*5 mile legs*
• Nonstandard pattern, if used	*left turns*
• Expect further clearance time	*expect further clearance at 1430."*

Figure 5-39. Some elements of the holding clearance depend on whether the holding pattern is published on the chart.

If you are approaching your clearance limit and have not received holding instructions from ATC, you are expected to follow certain procedures. First, call ATC and request further clearance before you reach the fix. If you cannot obtain further clearance, you are expected to hold at the fix in compliance with the published holding pattern. If a holding pattern is not charted at the fix, you are expected to hold on the inbound course using right turns. This procedure ensures that ATC will provide adequate separation. [Figure 5-40]

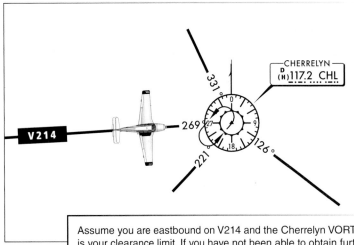

Figure 5-40. If you are approaching your clearance limit and cannot obtain further clearance before you reach the fix, you are expected to enter the published holding pattern.

Assume you are eastbound on V214 and the Cherrelyn VORTAC is your clearance limit. If you have not been able to obtain further clearance and have not received holding instructions, you should plan to hold southwest on the 221° radial using left-hand turns, as depicted. If this holding pattern was not charted, you would hold west of the VOR on V214 using right-hand turns.

SUMMARY CHECKLIST

✓ A holding pattern is a time delay used by ATC to help maintain separation and smooth out the traffic flow.

✓ You may request a hold, for example, to wait for weather conditions to improve.

✓ Holding pattern size is directly proportional to aircraft speed; doubling your speed doubles the size of your holding pattern.

✓ Turns are to the right in standard holding patterns, and to the left in nonstandard holding patterns.

✓ Each circuit of the holding pattern begins and ends at the holding fix.

✓ Adjust the timing of your outbound leg to make your inbound leg one minute long.

✓ To correct for crosswind drift in the holding pattern, triple your inbound wind correction angle on the outbound leg.

✓ To keep the volume of the protected airspace for a holding pattern within reasonable limits, maximum holding airspeeds are designated according to altitude.

✓ The entry procedure for a holding pattern depends on your heading relative to the holding course. The three recommended procedures are direct, teardrop, and parallel.

✓ A holding clearance should always contain the holding direction, the holding fix, and an expect further clearance (EFC) time. If the holding pattern is not published, the clearance also contains the holding course. For nonstandard patterns, left turns are specified. For patterns using DME, the clearance gives the outbound leg length in nautical miles.

KEY TERMS

Standard Holding Pattern

Nonstandard Holding Pattern

Holding Fix

Inbound Leg

Holding Course

Holding Side

Maximum Holding Speeds

Direct Entry

Teardrop Entry

Parallel Entry

Holding Clearance

Expect Further Clearance (EFC) Time

SECTION C ■ **Holding Procedures**

QUESTIONS

1. True/False. Turns are made to the left in nonstandard holding patterns.

2. Above what altitude are the straight legs for a standard holding pattern one and a half minutes?
   A. 10,000 feet MSL
   B. 12,000 feet MSL
   C. 14,000 feet MSL

3. What is the speed limit in holding patterns below 6,000 feet MSL?

4. The first complete circuit of your standard holding pattern at 10,000 feet MSL takes a total of 3 minutes and 52 seconds. To achieve an inbound leg time of 1 minute on your next circuit, assuming there is no crosswind, approximately how many seconds should you fly outbound before turning?
   A. 52 seconds
   B. 60 seconds
   C. 68 seconds

5. Assume you are flying toward the Kelly VOR on a magnetic heading of 015°. What kind of holding pattern entry would be appropriate for the following clearance? "*. . . cleared to the Kelly VOR. Hold southwest on the 215 radial . . .*"
   A. Direct
   B. Parallel
   C. Teardrop

6. If you are flying west on V345 toward the ENNUI Intersection, and are instructed to ". . . *hold west of ENNUI on Victor 345, left turns,*" which holding pattern entry is recommended?
   A. Direct only
   B. Parallel or Teardrop
   C. Teardrop or Direct

SECTION C ■ Holding Procedures

7. Inbound to the PJG VORTAC on a magnetic heading of 060°, you receive the following clearance: "... *cleared to the PJG VORTAC, hold south of the VOR on the 160 radial, left turns ...*" Which holding pattern entry should you use?
    A. Direct
    B. Parallel
    C. Teardrop

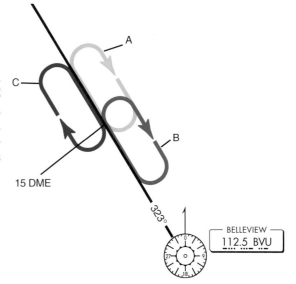

8. If you were cleared to hold northwest of the 15 DME fix on the 323° radial from Belleview VORTAC, which illustration in the accompanying figure correctly depicts your holding pattern?
    A. A
    B. B
    C. C

9. True/False. All holding clearances must contain an expect further clearance time.

CHAPTER 6

Arrival

Instrument/Commercial
Part II, Segment 1, Chapter 6 — Arrival

SECTION A
Arrival Charts

The ability to file IFR gives you easier access to large airports that you might not venture into under visual flight rules. As traffic into an airport increases, procedures for sequencing aircraft to an instrument approach must be established. Arrival charts provide a smooth transition between the enroute structure and busy terminal areas, simplifying complex clearances and providing an expected plan of action for both pilots and controllers. Knowing how to integrate standard arrival procedures into your flight plan enables you to fly IFR into the most congested airspace with more confidence. Arrival charts have many features and symbols in common with other IFR charts, but there are significant differences. [Figure 6-1]

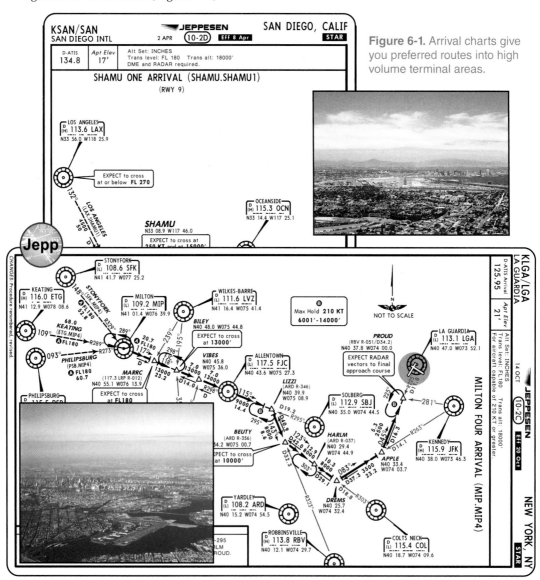

Figure 6-1. Arrival charts give you preferred routes into high volume terminal areas.

STANDARD TERMINAL ARRIVAL ROUTE

The **standard terminal arrival route (STAR)** is a bridge between the enroute structure and your destination. STARs are established to simplify clearance delivery procedures. STARs usually terminate with an instrument or visual approach procedure. Often they are simply called arrivals. A **transition** is one of several routes that bring traffic from different directions into one STAR.

 STARs are established to simplify clearance delivery procedures.

Both Jeppesen and the FAA publish STARs in print and electronic format. Jeppesen includes the applicable arrival charts in the basic terminal chart subscription. If you use paper Jeppesen charts, you file STAR charts with the airport's approach charts. The FAA includes STARs at the front of the *Terminal Procedures Publication* for each region.

INTERPRETING THE STAR

STARs use many of the same symbols as departure and approach charts. In fact, a STAR looks much like a graphic SID, except that the direction of flight is reversed and the procedure ends at an approach fix. The STAR officially begins at the navaid or intersection where all the transitions to the arrival converge. This way, the same chart can accommodate incoming flights from several directions, and traffic flow is routed appropriately within the congested airspace.

A STAR is usually named for the navaid or fix where its associated transitions converge and the arrival procedure begins. The name also includes a number. When a significant change in the procedure occurs, such as a change to an altitude, a route, or data concerning a fix, the number of the procedure increases by one. After the sequence reaches nine, the next revision is numbered one again. For example, when a significant portion of the SHAMU ONE ARRIVAL is revised, the arrival becomes the SHAMU TWO ARRIVAL. The computer code for an arrival is similar to a standard instrument departure (SID).

Transitions are usually named for the fix or navaid where they begin, and you use that identifier in the computer code when filing your IFR flight plan. When filing for a transition and a STAR, the computer code for the transition comes before the dot and the name of the STAR. Although this might seem to be the opposite of the convention for filing departures, it is logical and easy to remember. In both cases, the segments are listed in the order that you fly them. For example, the Los Angeles transition and the SHAMU arrival would be written LAX.SHAMU1.

 A STAR begins at a navaid or intersection where all arrival transitions converge.

To ease your transition from enroute to terminal navigation, initial fixes on the STAR chart correspond to fixes on the enroute chart. Routes between fixes contain courses, distances, and minimum altitudes. Although FAA charts and Jeppesen charts contain most of the same information, they organize and display the information somewhat differently. [Figures 6-2 and 6-3]

SECTION A ■ **Arrival Charts**

Location
The top of the chart identifies the city and the primary airport served by the STAR.

Top Strip
The top strip provides the ATIS frequency, primary airport elevation, and other information.

Identification
The STAR is named for the navaid or fix where the arrival begins.

Transition Route
Transition routes include courses, altitudes, and distances. This chart has only one transition. On Jeppesen charts, transitions are shown as dashed lines.

Arrival Route
The arrival route begins at the navaid or fix where all of the transitions converge and leads to an approach fix.

Navaids
Identification information and frequencies are provided for relevant navaids.

Primary Airport
A gray circle indicates the primary airport on Jeppesen charts. The same STAR might serve other airports in the same area.

Scale
In general, STAR charts are not drawn to scale.

Computer Codes
File the correct computer code on your flight plan. For the SHAMU arrival, you would use SHAMU.SHAMU1. For the SHAMU arrival with the Los Angeles transition, you would file LAX.SHAMU1. The segments are listed in the order that you fly them.

Lost Communications Procedure
Nonstandard procedures for lost communications are stated on the chart.

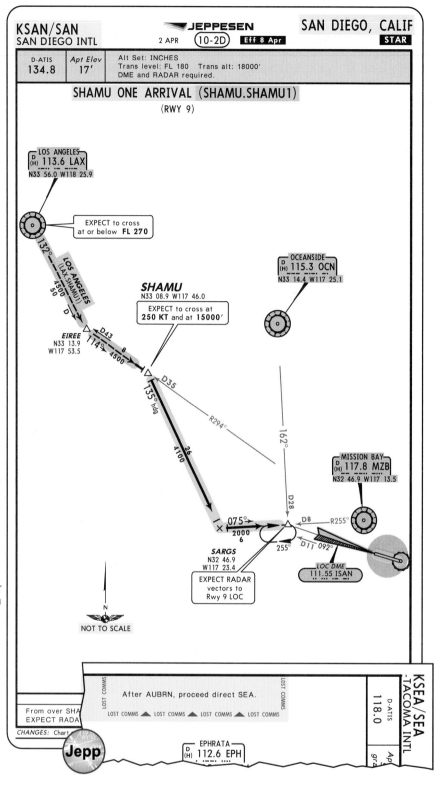

Figure 6-2. This is the Jeppesen chart for the SHAMU ONE ARRIVAL at San Diego, California. The legend found in the front of the Jeppesen Airway Manual will help answer any questions you have regarding STAR symbology.

Units of Measure
On both FAA and Jeppesen charts, all altitudes are feet MSL, courses are magnetic, airspeeds are in knots, and distances are in nautical miles.

Transition Route
On FAA charts, transitions are shown with lighter, solid lines.

Vertical Navigation Planning
Many arrival charts provide expected altitudes for key fixes along the route to assist descent planning in turbine-powered airplanes.

Radar Vectors
Many arrivals include a radar vector segment.

Restrictions and Notes
Be sure to check for restrictions or notes related to the procedure.

Textual Description
Some charts provide a textual description of the procedure.

Lost Communications Procedure
Nonstandard procedures for lost communications are stated on the chart.

Approach Control Frequency
The frequency for approach control is in a corner on most FAA charts.

Figure 6-3. This is the same arrival depicted in Figure 6-2 as it appears on an FAA chart. The symbology on this chart is described in the legend at the beginning of the FAA *Terminal Procedures Publication.*

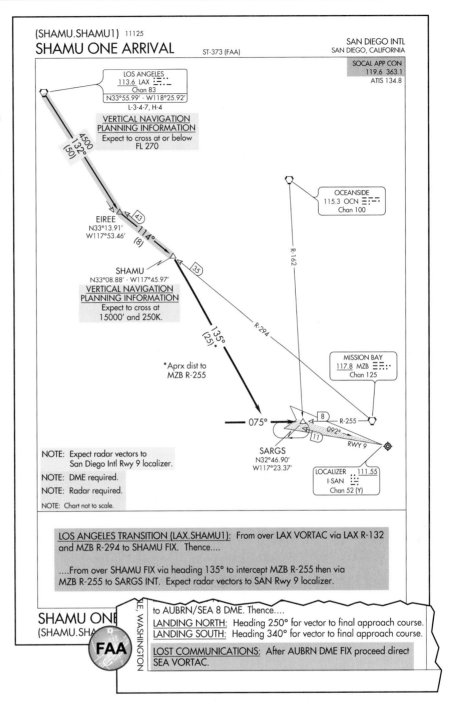

SECTION A ■ **Arrival Charts**

Arrival routes on an FAA STAR are depicted by large numerals and a heavyweight line.

The frequency for approach control is in a corner of the FAA chart. See figure 6-3.

REDUCING PILOT/CONTROLLER WORKLOAD

Safety is enhanced when both pilots and controllers know what to expect. Being able to rehearse a proposed route or clearance in advance means that the pilot can pay more attention to situational awareness during the corresponding portion of flight. Eliminating repetitive clearances reduces congestion on busy control frequencies.

To accomplish this, STARs are developed according to the following criteria:

- STARs must be simple, easily understood and, if possible, limited to one page.
- A STAR transition should be able to accommodate as many different types of aircraft as possible. That way, both turbojets and slower aircraft can use the same chart for arrival.
- Navaids and waypoints used by both military and civilian aircraft are used wherever possible, so that both can use the same arrivals.
- The FAA avoids creating DME arcs within a STAR.
- When ATC frequently assigns altitude crossing and airspeed restrictions, they are included in the STAR.

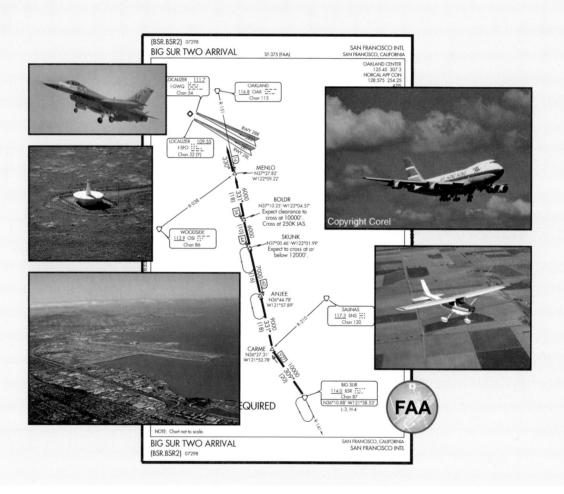

You can identify an **RNAV STAR** by the inclusion of "RNAV" in the title. RNAV STARs require specific equipment and performance standards. The type of equipment and performance standards are indicated on the STAR chart.

RNAV STARs might be designed with vertical profiles optimized to facilitate a continuous descent from the top of descent (TOD) to touchdown. Optimized profile descents (OPDs) are designed to reduce fuel consumption, emissions, and noise by enabling you to set the engines near idle throttle to descend. OPDs use the capabilities of the FMS to fly a continuous descending path without level segments. [Figure 6-4.]

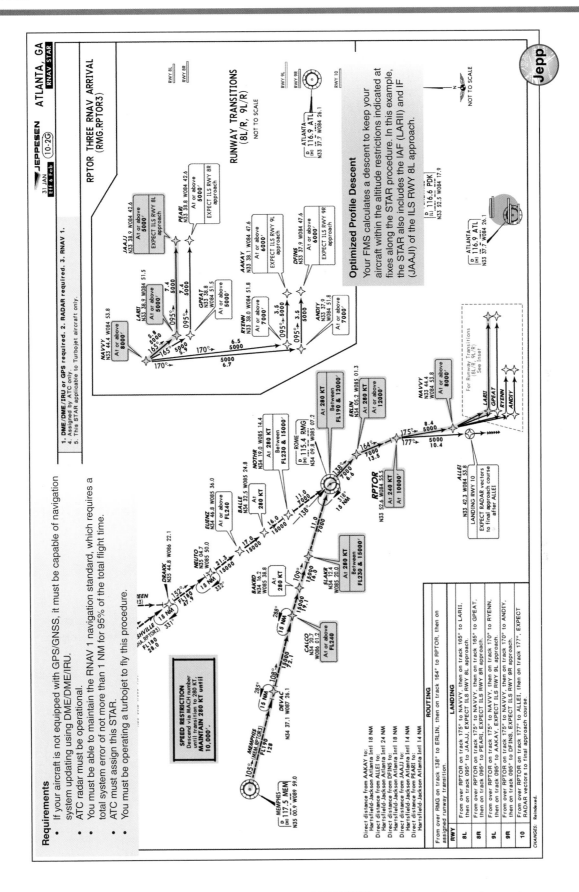

Figure 6-4. When cleared to "descend via," select the RNAV STAR transition and procedure codes (MEM.RMG.RPTOR3) from your onboard navigation database and conform to altitude and speed restrictions on the charted procedure.

VERTICAL NAVIGATION PLANNING

Many STARs include information on **vertical navigation planning** to help crews of jets and turboprops save fuel by reducing the amount of time they fly at lower altitudes. The charts provide expected altitudes for key fixes along the route. Knowing these expected altitudes in advance allows the pilots of high-performance aircraft to plan the power settings and aircraft configurations that will result in the most efficient descent, in terms of time, fuel requirements, and engine wear.

Whether you are flying a STAR, an instrument approach procedure, or just planning a descent for a destination airport under VFR, you need to be able to calculate the required rate of descent (vertical speed) to reach a specific altitude at a specific point. Or, if you are planning a certain rate of descent, you might need to calculate the point at which to begin your descent to reach the crossing altitude.

The following calculations assume that you will maintain your present groundspeed during the descent. If your groundspeed increases during descent, you should use the new groundspeed to calculate your descent.

CALCULATING A REQUIRED RATE OF DESCENT

Suppose that you are flying at 11,000 feet MSL, and ATC tells you to cross an intersection at 5,000 feet MSL. The intersection is 20 NM away, and your groundspeed is 150 knots. What rate of descent must you use to meet the crossing restriction?

1. You need to descend 6,000 feet in 20 NM.

2. The time to reach the intersection:
    20 NM ÷ 150 knots × 60 minutes/hour = 8 minutes

3. The required rate of descent to meet the crossing restriction:
    6,000 feet ÷ 8 minutes = 750 feet/minute
Or, you can use the formula:

> Rate of Descent = Altitude to Descend ÷ Distance (NM) × Groundspeed (Knots) ÷ 60

In this example:
> 6,000 feet ÷ 20 NM × 150 knots ÷ 60 = 750 feet/minute

 On an instrument approach at 90 knots groundspeed, you cross the FAF at 2,500 feet MSL and descend to the MDA of 500 feet MSL. To calculate the rate of descent to reach the MDA over the next 5 NM:

> 2,000 feet ÷ 5 NM × 90 knots ÷ 60 = 600 feet/minute

CALCULATING WHERE TO BEGIN A DESCENT

Suppose that you have the same crossing restriction (5,000 feet MSL), but you are farther away and at 12,000 feet MSL. You are in an unpressurized airplane, and you want to descend at 500 feet/minute. How far away from the intersection should you begin your descent?

1. You need to descend 7,000 feet at 500 feet/minute.

2. The time to complete the descent:
    7,000 feet ÷ 500 feet/minute = 14 minutes

3. The distance you will travel during the descent:
    14 minutes × 150 knots ÷ 60 minutes/hour = 35 NM
Or, you can use the formula:
> Distance = Altitude to Descend ÷ Rate of Descent × Groundspeed (Knots) ÷ 60

In this example:
> 7,000 feet ÷ 500 feet/minute × 150 knots ÷ 60 = 35 NM

SUMMARY CHECKLIST

✓ Standard terminal arrival routes (STARs) provide a standard method for leaving the enroute structure and entering a busy terminal area. STARs are established to simplify clearance delivery procedures.

✓ STARs are grouped along with other airport charts in a Jeppesen subscription, and appear in the front of FAA terminal procedures publications. The charts are available in both electronic and printed form.

✓ If you accept a STAR, you must have the chart that describes it. The chart may be graphic or textual.

✓ When filing for a transition and a STAR, the computer code for the transition comes before the dot and the name of the STAR.

✓ STARs use symbology similar to departure and approach charts. Altitudes are given in reference to mean sea level, courses are magnetic, airspeeds are in knots, and distances are in nautical miles.

✓ A STAR begins at a navaid or intersection where all arrival transitions join.

✓ STARs are usually named for the point where the procedure begins. They are revised in numerical sequence.

✓ Jeppesen and FAA charts contain most of the same information, but the layout and symbols are different.

✓ RNAV STARs include "RNAV" in the title, and require specific equipment and performance standards.

✓ RNAV STARs might be designed with optimized profile descents (OPDs) to enable you to fly a continuous descending path without level segments.

✓ Vertical navigation planning information is given to aid pilots of turbine powered airplanes in making more efficient descents from the enroute structure to approach fixes.

KEY TERMS

Standard Terminal Arrival Route (STAR)

Transition

RNAV STAR

Vertical Navigation Planning

SECTION A ■ **Arrival Charts**

QUESTIONS

Refer to the WISKE THREE ARRIVAL chart to answer questions 1 through 6.

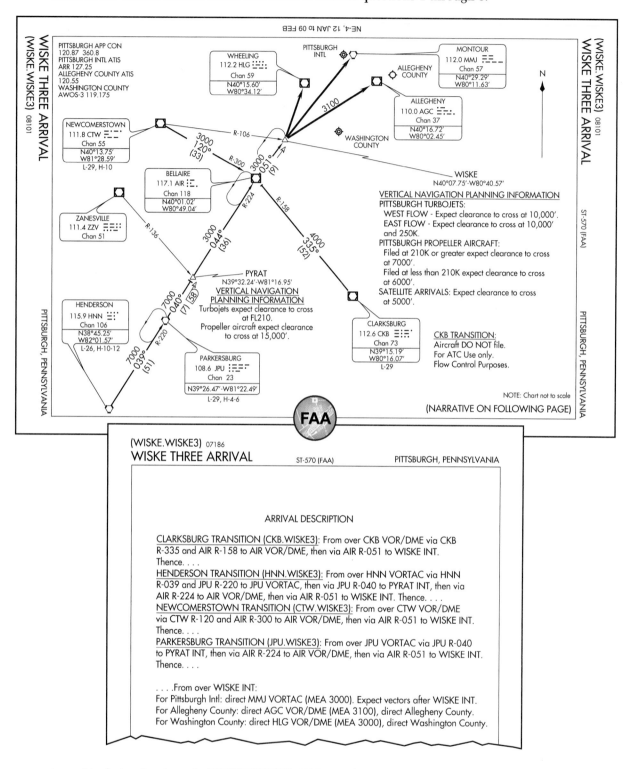

SECTION A ■ Arrival Charts

1. At what point does the WISKE THREE ARRIVAL begin?

2. Which airports are served by this STAR?
   A. Only Pittsburgh International
   B. Pittsburgh International, Allegheny, Montour, and Wheeling
   C. Pittsburgh International, Allegheny County, and Washington County

3. What is the minimum altitude for the STAR segment from Henderson VORTAC to PYRAT Intersection within the Henderson Transition?

4. How would you indicate that you wanted to use the WISKE THREE ARRIVAL, Newcomerstown Transition on an IFR flight plan?

5. If you are flying the WISKE THREE ARRIVAL into Pittsburgh in a propeller-driven aircraft, at what altitude should you expect to cross the WISKE Intersection, if you filed for a TAS of less than 210 knots?

6. What frequency would you use to contact approach control if you were flying into Washington County Airport?

7. True/False. ATC can include a STAR in your clearance even if you have not requested one.

SECTION A ■ Arrival Charts

Section B
Arrival Procedures

Preparation for a well-executed arrival and approach begins long before you descend from the enroute phase of the flight. Planning your approach in advance, while there are fewer demands on your attention, leaves you free to concentrate on precise control of the airplane during the approach. The ability to use the autopilot effectively can also reduce your workload. You also will be better equipped to deal with any problems that might arise during the last segment of the flight.

PREPARING FOR THE ARRIVAL

With the appropriate charts, you may accept a STAR within a clearance, or you may file for one in your flight plan. As you near your destination airport, ATC may add a STAR procedure to your original clearance. Keep in mind that ATC can assign a STAR even if you have not requested one. To accept the clearance, you must have a chart with at least a textual description of the procedure in your possession. If you do not want to use a STAR, you must specify "No STAR" in the remarks section of your flight plan. Although you can refuse the STAR when it is given to you in your clearance, the system works much better if you advise ATC when you file your flight plan.

STARs typically provide a smooth transition from the enroute structure to the final approach course, but some lead to a fix where radar vectors will be provided to the final approach course. When ATC assigns **minimum crossing altitudes** or airspeed restrictions at least 75 percent of the time, the restrictions are added to the procedure and shown on the charts. These expected altitudes and airspeeds are not part of your clearance until ATC includes them verbally. A STAR is simply a published routing, and it does not have the force of a clearance until issued specifically by ATC.

 ATC will issue a STAR when they deem one appropriate, unless you request "No STAR."

As early as practical, listen to ATIS to obtain current weather information, runways in use, and NOTAMs involving the destination airport. You may also monitor AWOS or ASOS, or to contact the UNICOM on the field for updated weather and airport information when no ATIS is available. If you are landing at an airport with approach control services that has two or more published instrument approach procedures, you will receive advance notice of the instrument approaches in use. This information will be broadcast by either ATIS or a controller, however, it might not be provided when the visibility is three miles or better and the ceiling is at or above the highest initial approach altitude established for any instrument approach procedure for the airport.

BRIEFING THE STAR PROCEDURE

If ATC issues a STAR clearance, review and brief the procedure so you understand what you are expected to perform. Whether you are part of a crew or the only pilot aboard, always take enough time to brief the arrival procedure thoroughly. Your workload typically increases throughout the arrival and approach, and without advance preparation, it is easy to become overloaded, make mistakes, and lag behind the airplane. The briefing becomes even more important when you are flying into an unfamiliar airport. [Figure 6-5]

Identification
Verify that you have the correct STAR chart for your clearance and destination.

Restrictions
Verify that the procedure is appropriate for your aircraft, the airport equipment, the route of flight, and the runway. Brief other potential restrictions that might exist for you, such as the weather, time of day, or other conditions.

Transition Routes
Review the details of your transition route. A STAR might have only one transition route.

Routing
Review your arrival route. The plan view of a STAR chart is a graphic depiction of the arrival route. A textual description of the procedure is often included as well.

Holding
Review any holding patterns that apply to your route. Some holding patterns are indicated on charts, but others might be assigned by ATC controllers. A holding pattern symbol calls attention to what you should expect.

Altitude
Altitudes on STARs are always in feet MSL. When flying a STAR into a terminal area, ATC will either clear you with specific altitude information or give you a *descend via* clearance, directing you to follow the altitudes published on the STAR. The expected altitudes printed on STARs don't apply to you unless assigned by ATC or in cases of lost communications.

Distance
Arrival charts are not usually drawn to scale. The chart displays segment mileage between fixes in nautical miles.

Final Approach Clearance
Determine where you can expect to receive a clearance for your final approach and review any published instructions so that you know what to expect.

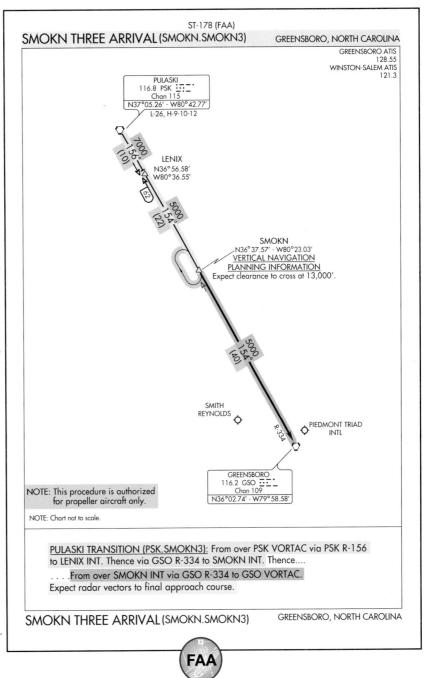

Figure 6-5. When your IFR flight plan includes a STAR arrival, there are a number of items you should cover specifically in the briefing.

FLYING THE ARRIVAL

With the arrival procedure clear in your mind, set your radios and navigation equipment to minimize the number of changes you have to make during the procedure. Set up as many of the available autopilot functions as you can to reduce your workload. Cockpit automation can be very helpful, but be sure you thoroughly understand its operation; an IFR arrival in congested airspace is not the time to make assumptions or explore unfamiliar features in your equipment. While STARs simplify ATC clearances, the procedures themselves might involve several turns and altitude changes. Listen to the other traffic around you to help maintain situational awareness, and be ready for ATC to assign a holding pattern or radar vectors. [Figure 6-6]

SECTION B ■ Arrival Procedures

Establish a descent that puts you at 7,000 feet as you cross the Pulaski VOR.

Begin the transition at the Pulaski VOR and fly outbound on the 156° radial for 10 miles to the LENIX fix.

After crossing LENIX fix, navigate to the Greensboro VOR with a heading of 154°, inbound on the 334° radial. Begin a gradual descent to 5,000 feet.

ATC might request a hold at the SMOKN fix.

The arrival begins at SMOKN inbound on the 334° radial to Greensboro VOR.

After crossing the Greensboro VOR, expect radar vectors for the final approach course to Greensboro Piedmont Triad International airport.

Figure 6-6. You have finished briefing the STAR and ATC has issued a *descend via* clearance for the SMOKN THREE ARRIVAL to Greensboro Piedmont Triad International airport via the Pulaski transition. For this example, you are starting approximately 15 nautical miles north of the Pulaski VOR at 9,000 feet.

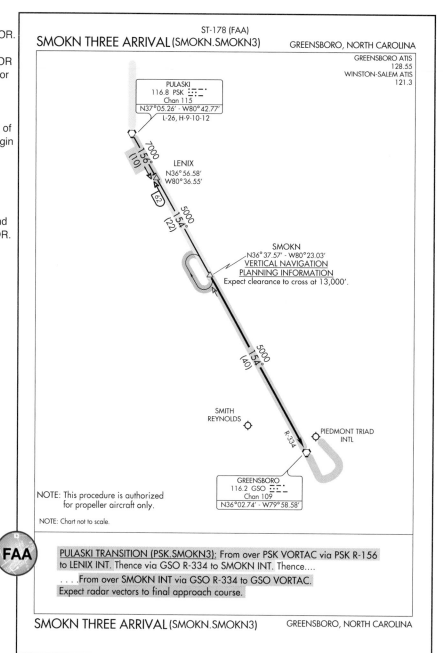

ST-178 (FAA)

SMOKN THREE ARRIVAL (SMOKN.SMOKN3)

GREENSBORO, NORTH CAROLINA

GREENSBORO ATIS
128.55
WINSTON-SALEM ATIS
121.3

PULASKI
116.8 PSK
Chan 115
N37°05.26' - W80°42.77'
L-26, H-9-10-12

7000
156°
(10)

LENIX
N36°56.58'
W80°36.55'

62

5000
154°
(22)

SMOKN
N36°37.57' - W80°23.03'
VERTICAL NAVIGATION
PLANNING INFORMATION
Expect clearance to cross at 13,000'.

5000
154°
(40)

SMITH
REYNOLDS

PIEDMONT TRIAD
INTL

R-334

GREENSBORO
116.2 GSO
Chan 109
N36°02.74' - W79°58.58'

NOTE: This procedure is authorized for propeller aircraft only.

NOTE: Chart not to scale.

FAA

PULASKI TRANSITION (PSK.SMOKN3): From over PSK VORTAC via PSK R-156 to LENIX INT. Thence via GSO R-334 to SMOKN INT. Thence....

....From over SMOKN INT via GSO R-334 to GSO VORTAC. Expect radar vectors to final approach course.

SMOKN THREE ARRIVAL (SMOKN.SMOKN3)   GREENSBORO, NORTH CAROLINA

CONFLICTING SIGNALS

On April 10, 1989, a Fairchild FH-227 crashed into a fog-shrouded mountainside in southeastern France. The twin-engine turboprop was on a published arrival route into Valence, flying in light rain and a stratified cloud layer. The crew had both an NDB and a VOR tuned in, but only the ADF receiver was tuned to the proper frequency. The VOR receiver was tuned to a VOR located 13 miles to the northeast, putting the FH-227 off of the intended course by 10 miles. Ninety seconds before impact, the captain noted on the cockpit voice recorder that there was a 30° difference between the ADF and VOR indications. His fatal assumption? That "the ADF (was) no good." The crew and 19 passengers perished in the crash.

One of the most critical safety concerns on board any instrument flight is instrument cross-check. If two navigation receivers give you conflicting messages, one of them may be incorrect. However, do not assume that you know which one is incorrectly tuned, or inoperative, until you double check all frequencies, volumes, and warning lights. A thorough look at the chart also may reveal the true problem. Use all your resources to maintain situational awareness and avoid the trap of a mind-set regarding your position. You may be in a completely different position than you think.

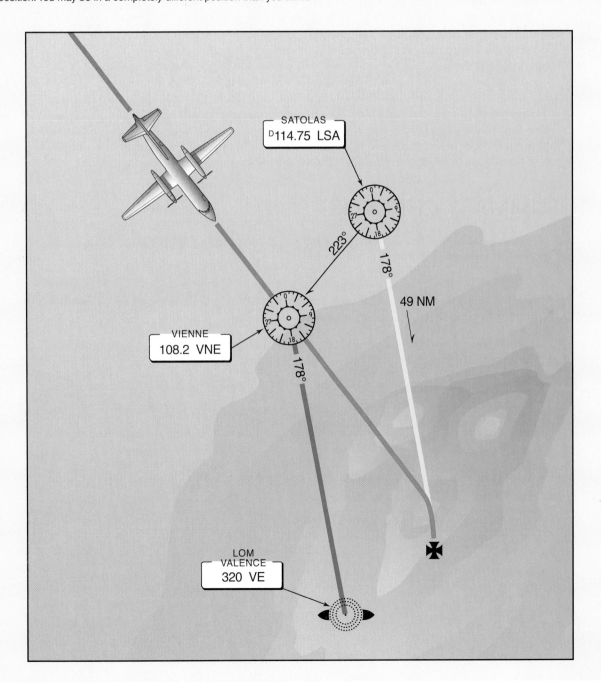

ALTITUDE

During your arrival in the terminal area ATC will either clear you to a specific altitude, or they will give you a **descend via** clearance, which instructs you to follow the altitudes published on the STAR. On receiving a *descend via* clearance, you can begin to descend at your discretion from your previously assigned altitude to the altitude published for the next waypoint or fix on the STAR.

AIRSPEED

During the arrival, expect to make adjustments in indicated airspeed at the controller's request. ATC may ask you to change your airspeed to help with traffic sequencing and separation and to reduce the amount of vectoring required in the terminal area. When you operate a reciprocating-engine or turboprop within 20 miles of your destination airport, 150 knots is usually the lowest speed you will be assigned. If your aircraft cannot maintain the assigned airspeed, you must advise ATC. In this case, the controller might ask you to maintain the same airspeed as those aircraft ahead of you or behind you on the approach. ATC expects you to maintain an assigned airspeed plus or minus 10 knots. At other times, ATC may ask you to increase or decrease your speed by 10, 20, or 30 knots. When ATC no longer requires the speed adjustment, they will advise you to "*...resume normal speed.*"

Keep in mind that the maximum speeds specified in FAR 91.117 still apply during speed adjustments. It is your responsibility, as pilot in command, to advise ATC if an assigned speed adjustment would cause you to exceed these limits. However, for operations in Class C or D airspace at or below 2,500 feet AGL, within 4 nautical miles of the primary airport, ATC has the authority to request or approve a higher speed than those prescribed in FAR 91.117.

SUMMARY CHECKLIST

✓ ATC may assign a STAR at any time, and it is your responsibility to accept or refuse the procedure.

✓ Writing "No STAR" in the remarks section of your flight plan will alert ATC that you do not wish to use these procedures during your flight. You also may refuse a clearance containing a STAR, but avoid this practice if possible.

✓ When cleared for a STAR, brief the procedure thoroughly to reduce your workload later in the arrival.

✓ A descend via clearance instructs you to follow the altitudes published on the STAR, with descent at your discretion.

✓ ATC may issue a descent clearance which includes a crossing altitude. Comply by using distance and groundspeed to calculate the rate of descent required.

✓ Expect to make airspeed adjustments as required by ATC. As PIC, you are responsible for complying with FAR 91.117.

KEY TERMS

Minimum Crossing Altitudes

Descend Via

QUESTIONS

1. When should you plan to obtain weather information for your approach during an IFR flight?

2. What does a descend via clearance authorize you to do?

3. True/False. ATC is responsible for ensuring you are not cleared for an airspeed that violates FAR 91.117.

4. Assume you are cruising at 12,000 feet MSL. You are cleared to cross the FREDY Intersection at 8,000 feet MSL, which is 30 nautical miles ahead of you. If your current groundspeed is 180 knots and you expect a descent rate of 500 feet per minute, where should you begin your descent?

5. Select the appropriate phrase to enter in the Remarks section of your flight plan if you do not wish to use a STAR during your flight.
    A. Use no STARs
    B. No STAR
    C. No STARs approved

CHAPTER 7

Approach

Instrument/Commercial
Part II, Segment 2, Chapter 7 — Approach

SECTION A
Approach Charts

You use a standard **instrument approach procedure (IAP)** published on an instrument approach chart to descend safely by reference to instruments from the enroute altitude to a point near the destination runway from which you can make a landing visually. This section is designed to help you become proficient at interpreting approach chart information. There are many different types of instrument approaches using a variety of navigation systems. However, some general considerations apply to the majority of instrument approach procedures that are a foundation for interpreting chart symbology, understanding approach procedures, and performing specific approaches.

APPROACH PROCEDURE TYPES

There are three types of instrument approach procedures: precision approach, approach with vertical guidance, and nonprecision approach. These types are based on the final approach course guidance provided and are further classified according to the primary navigation system. A **precision approach (PA)** provides lateral guidance to align the airplane with the runway and vertical guidance in the form of a glide slope indication to enable you to maintain the airplane in a stabilized vertical descent to the runway. A precision approach provides the most accurate guidance and must meet specific standards of precision and integrity limits. An **approach with vertical guidance (APV)** provides lateral guidance to align the airplane with the runway and vertical guidance in the form of a glide path display. Although an APV provides vertical guidance, it does not meet the criteria to be classified as a precision approach. A **nonprecision approach (NPA)** provides only lateral guidance to align the airplane with the runway. You must determine the appropriate rate of descent to maintain the airplane at or above minimum altitudes shown on the approach chart. [Figure 7-1]

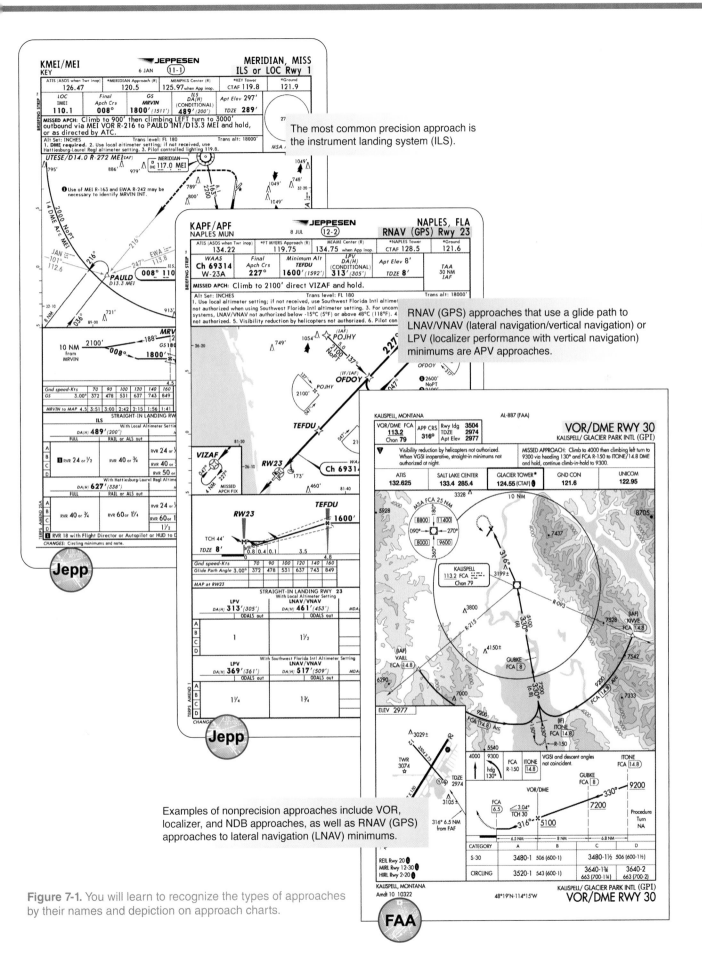

The most common precision approach is the instrument landing system (ILS).

RNAV (GPS) approaches that use a glide path to LNAV/VNAV (lateral navigation/vertical navigation) or LPV (localizer performance with vertical navigation) minimums are APV approaches.

Examples of nonprecision approaches include VOR, localizer, and NDB approaches, as well as RNAV (GPS) approaches to lateral navigation (LNAV) minimums.

Figure 7-1. You will learn to recognize the types of approaches by their names and depiction on approach charts.

SECTION A ■ **Approach Charts**

APPROACH SEGMENTS

An instrument approach might be divided into as many as four approach segments: initial, intermediate, final, and missed approach. In addition, there are several different methods that enable you to transition from the enroute structure to the initial approach segment to begin the approach procedure, including standard terminal arrival procedures, feeder routes, terminal arrival areas, and radar vectors. An approach chart indicates distance, course, and minimum altitudes for approach segment. [Figure 7-2]

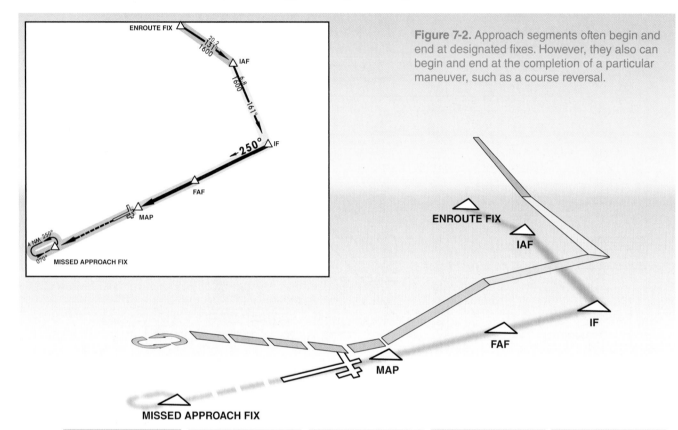

Figure 7-2. Approach segments often begin and end at designated fixes. However, they also can begin and end at the completion of a particular maneuver, such as a course reversal.

Enroute Transition	Initial Approach Segment	Intermediate Approach Segment	Final Approach Segment	Missed Approach Segment
Fly a route and altitude designated by a STAR procedure, feeder route, terminal arrival area, or radar vectors to transition from the enroute structure to the initial approach fix (IAF).	Follow an initial approach segment from the initial approach fix (IAF) to an intermediate fix (IF).	From the IF, follow the intermediate approach segment to the final approach fix (FAF).	You begin a descent to the runway. The final approach segment ends with a landing or at the missed approach point (MAP) or decision altitude.	At the missed approach point (MAP) or a decision altitude, if you cannot continue the approach to land, follow the missed approach segment, which often includes a holding pattern.

TRANSITION FROM ENROUTE TO APPROACH

In some cases, the navaid that defines the end of the enroute phase of flight is also the initial approach fix. However, in many situations you must fly a route to transition from the enroute structure to the approach structure. The route that you use depends on the airplane equipment and the type of approach.

Feeder routes are shown on instrument approach charts to provide a link between an enroute fix or navaid and the initial approach fix. Some RNAV (GPS) approaches include a terminal arrival area (TAA) that enables you to navigate directly to an approach fix, and ensures that you have adequate obstacle clearance, provided that you stay at or above the published minimum altitude. For any instrument approach with radar coverage, ATC can provide radar vectors as the transition to an initial approach fix. In addition, a standard terminal arrival route (STAR) might be published for a busy terminal area to provide common transitions for all aircraft to navigate from the enroute structure to an approach fix. [Figure 7-3]

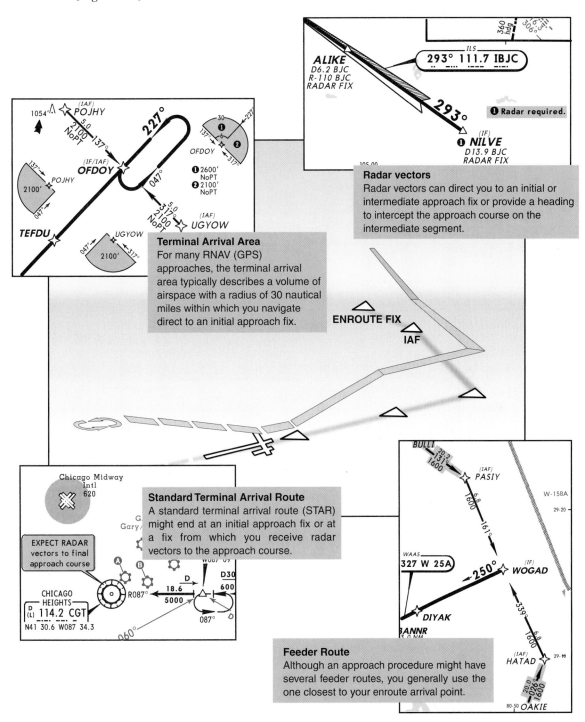

SECTION A ■ Approach Charts

Radar vectors
Radar vectors can direct you to an initial or intermediate approach fix or provide a heading to intercept the approach course on the intermediate segment.

Terminal Arrival Area
For many RNAV (GPS) approaches, the terminal arrival area typically describes a volume of airspace with a radius of 30 nautical miles within which you navigate direct to an initial approach fix.

Standard Terminal Arrival Route
A standard terminal arrival route (STAR) might end at an initial approach fix or at a fix from which you receive radar vectors to the approach course.

Feeder Route
Although an approach procedure might have several feeder routes, you generally use the one closest to your enroute arrival point.

Figure 7-3. The route you fly from the enroute portion of the flight to begin the approach procedure depends on your navigation equipment, your position, and your ATC clearance. These approach excerpts show different transitions from the enroute to approach structure. You will learn how to interpret the chart information to fly these routes.

INITIAL APPROACH SEGMENT

The purpose of the initial approach segment is to provide a method for aligning the airplane with the approach course. The initial approach segment begins at an **initial approach fix (IAF)** and usually ends where it joins the intermediate approach segment. The letters IAF on an approach chart indicate the location of an initial approach fix. [Figure 7-4]

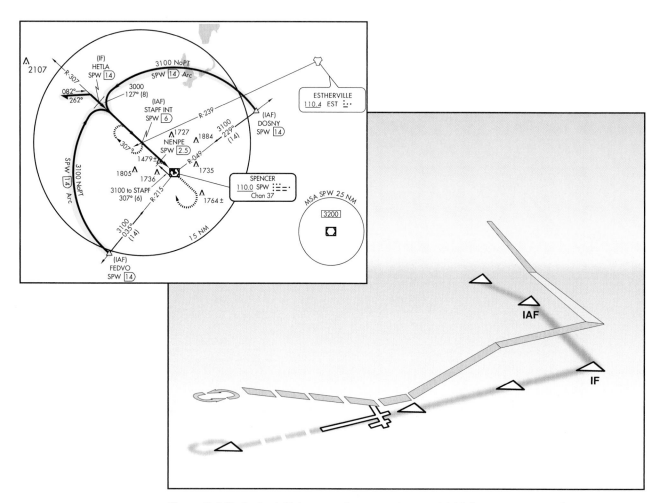

Figure 7-4. To fly the initial approach segment, you might follow an arc procedure, a course reversal, or a straight route that intersects the final approach course.

INTERMEDIATE APPROACH SEGMENT

The intermediate segment is designed primarily to position the airplane for the final descent to the airport. The intermediate segment, normally aligned within 30° of the final approach course, begins at the **intermediate fix (IF)**, or intermediate point, and ends at the beginning of the final approach segment. In some cases, an intermediate fix is not shown on an approach chart. In this situation, the intermediate segment begins at a point where you are proceeding inbound to the final approach fix, are properly aligned with the final approach course, and are located within the prescribed distance from the final approach fix. [Figure 7-5]

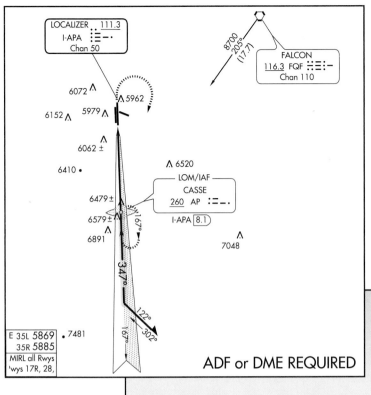

Figure 7-5. The most common example of an approach that does not have a charted intermediate approach fix is one in which you can reverse your course to be able to intercept the inbound course to the runway. The intermediate segment begins when you intercept the inbound course after completing the course reversal.

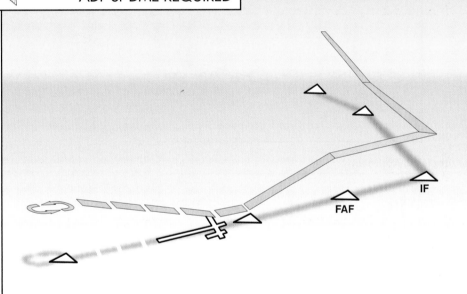

FINAL APPROACH SEGMENT

The final approach segment allows you to navigate safely to a point from which, if you have the required visual references in sight, you can continue the approach to a landing. Depending on the approach procedure, the final approach segment begins at a **final approach fix (FAF)**, **final approach point (FAP)**, or where you begin the descent when referring to vertical descent indications. [Figure 7-6]

Precision Approach and APV

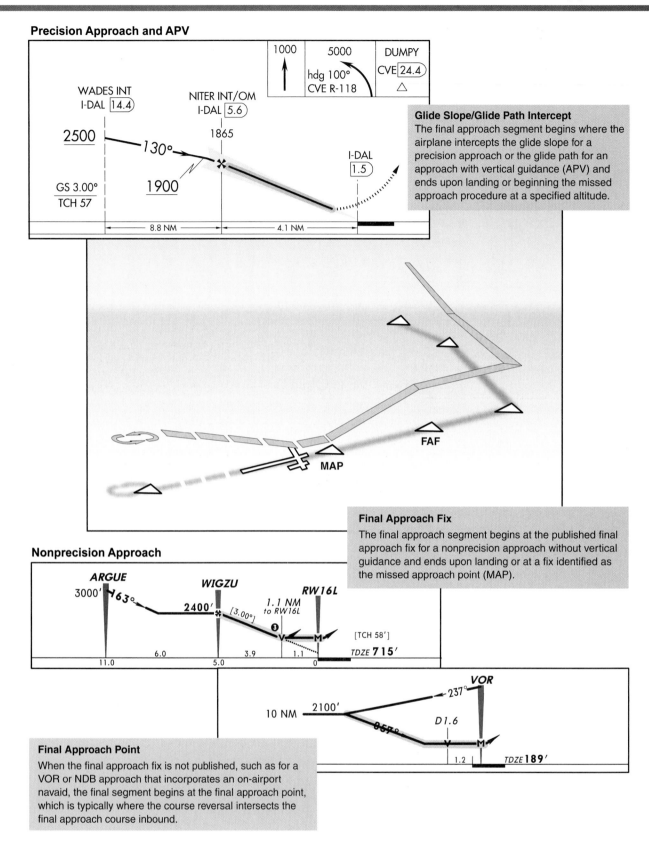

Glide Slope/Glide Path Intercept
The final approach segment begins where the airplane intercepts the glide slope for a precision approach or the glide path for an approach with vertical guidance (APV) and ends upon landing or beginning the missed approach procedure at a specified altitude.

Final Approach Fix
The final approach segment begins at the published final approach fix for a nonprecision approach without vertical guidance and ends upon landing or at a fix identified as the missed approach point (MAP).

Nonprecision Approach

Final Approach Point
When the final approach fix is not published, such as for a VOR or NDB approach that incorporates an on-airport navaid, the final segment begins at the final approach point, which is typically where the course reversal intersects the final approach course inbound.

Figure 7-6. The characteristics of the final approach are what distinguish a precision approach, an approach with vertical guidance, and a nonprecision approach from each other.

ELEVATION AND HEIGHT REFERENCES

Approach procedures use a variety of elevation and height references that apply to the altitudes you use during the final approach segment. [Figure 7-7]

FAA The threshold crossing height (TCH) is the AGL height at which you cross the threshold if you continue the approach to a landing while maintaining the glide slope/path or vertical descent angle.

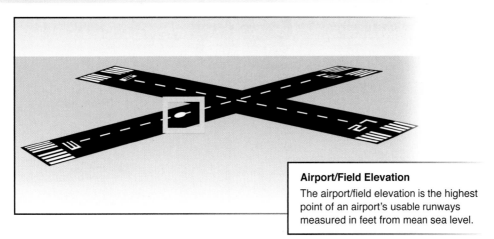

Airport/Field Elevation

The airport/field elevation is the highest point of an airport's usable runways measured in feet from mean sea level.

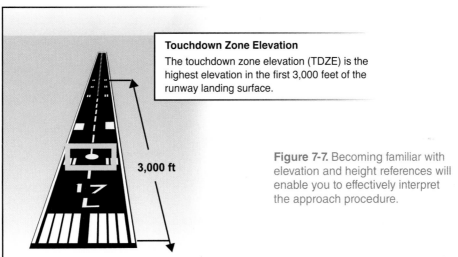

Touchdown Zone Elevation

The touchdown zone elevation (TDZE) is the highest elevation in the first 3,000 feet of the runway landing surface.

3,000 ft

Figure 7-7. Becoming familiar with elevation and height references will enable you to effectively interpret the approach procedure.

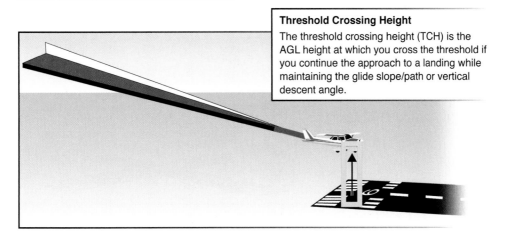

Threshold Crossing Height

The threshold crossing height (TCH) is the AGL height at which you cross the threshold if you continue the approach to a landing while maintaining the glide slope/path or vertical descent angle.

FAA The touchdown zone elevation (TDZE) is the highest elevation in the first 3,000 feet of the landing surface.

SECTION A ■ **Approach Charts**

MINIMUM DESCENT REQUIREMENTS

Each instrument approach procedure has a minimum altitude to which you may to descend before you must have any required visual references of the runway environment in sight. The terms that describe this altitude depend on whether the approach procedure provides lateral guidance only or both lateral and vertical guidance. [Figure 7-8]

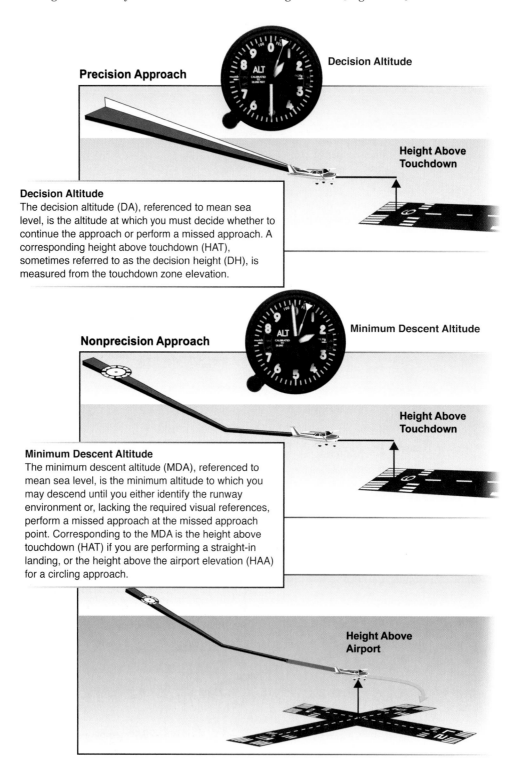

Precision Approach

Decision Altitude

Height Above Touchdown

Decision Altitude
The decision altitude (DA), referenced to mean sea level, is the altitude at which you must decide whether to continue the approach or perform a missed approach. A corresponding height above touchdown (HAT), sometimes referred to as the decision height (DH), is measured from the touchdown zone elevation.

Nonprecision Approach

Minimum Descent Altitude

Height Above Touchdown

Minimum Descent Altitude
The minimum descent altitude (MDA), referenced to mean sea level, is the minimum altitude to which you may descend until you either identify the runway environment or, lacking the required visual references, perform a missed approach at the missed approach point. Corresponding to the MDA is the height above touchdown (HAT) if you are performing a straight-in landing, or the height above the airport elevation (HAA) for a circling approach.

Height Above Airport

Figure 7-8. Minimum descent requirements are stated as altitudes referenced to mean sea level and heights referenced to ground level.

MISSED APPROACH SEGMENT

You perform the missed approach segment to navigate from the missed approach point to a point where you can attempt another approach or continue to another airport. The missed approach segment begins at the decision altitude for precision approaches and for approaches with vertical guidance. For nonprecision approaches, with lateral guidance only, this segment begins at a **missed approach point (MAP)**, which is identified as a fix, navaid, or an elapsed time after you cross the final approach fix. The missed approach segment often includes a holding pattern and ends at a designated point, such as an initial approach fix or enroute fix. [Figure 7-9].

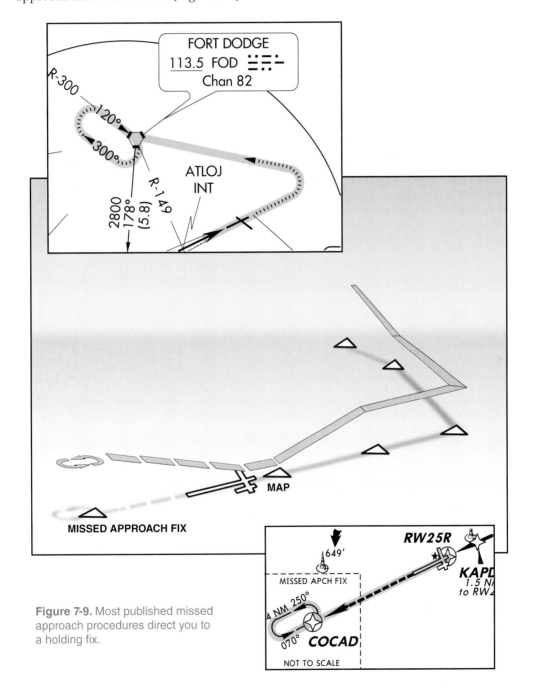

Figure 7-9. Most published missed approach procedures direct you to a holding fix.

RUNWAY AND APPROACH LIGHTING

Runway and approach lighting systems facilitate the transition from instrument to visual flight as you approach the airport. There are a number of different approach lighting configurations, but all approach lighting systems start at the landing threshold and extend into the approach area. For a precision approach, these lights typically extend 2,400 to 3,000 feet. Nonprecision approach lighting configurations might only extend 1,400 to 1,500 feet. Certain lighting configurations allow lower minimum visibilities and altitudes for approaches. [Figure 7-10]

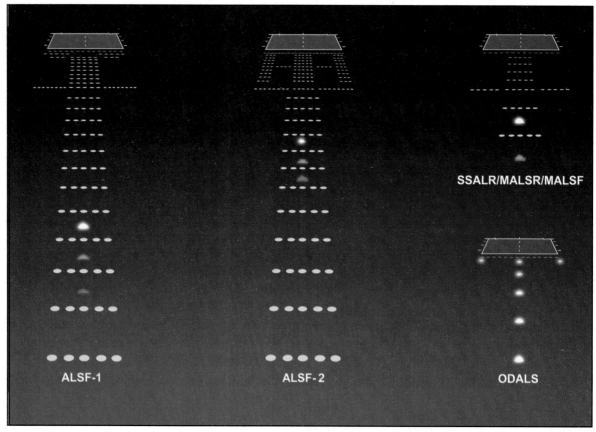

Figure 7-10. You will become familiar with these approach light configurations and approach charts will specify the types of approach lights installed for a particular runway.

INTERPRETING APPROACH CHARTS

Although there are many different types of approaches, most incorporate common procedures and chart symbology. Therefore, your ability to interpret one approach chart generally means you will be able to interpret others. However, due to the dynamic nature of charting, you must familiarize yourself with the chart legend and review chart symbology on a continuing basis to stay abreast of any changes. The most common approaches you will fly are the ILS, localizer, VOR, VOR/DME, RNAV (GPS), and NDB approaches. Specific approach types and procedures are examined in more detail in Section B of this chapter and Chapter 8 — Instrument Approaches.

CHART LAYOUT

Both Jeppesen and FAA charts portray the instrument approaches available at a given airport. Generally, both chart formats present the same information, however, the symbology and chart layout vary. The arrangement of information on Jeppesen Briefing Strip™ charts is based on studies of how charts are reviewed and used in the cockpit. FAA charts use the Pilot Briefing Information chart format. Both Jeppesen and FAA approach

...

Charting Evolution

The nature of instrument flight cartography involves continuous chart enhancement. Captain Elrey B. Jeppesen's original little black book from the 1930s depicts slopes, drainage patterns, terrain, and airport layouts, as well as provides information on field lengths, lights, and obstacles. [Figure A]

As instrument approach procedures improved, a standard format was developed and evolved into an identifiable instrument approach chart look. Shown here is the Buffalo Municipal Airport instrument approach chart, revised August 2, 1945. Note that the approach chart depicts the old range airway system, using the Morse code letters A and N. [Figure B]

Enhancements in today's highly refined standard instrument approach procedures (SIAPs) and instrument chart formats are driven by complex changes in airspace, air traffic control, advanced technology, human factors, and many other issues. Jeppesen's briefing strip charts represent many instrument approach chart advancements. [Figure C]

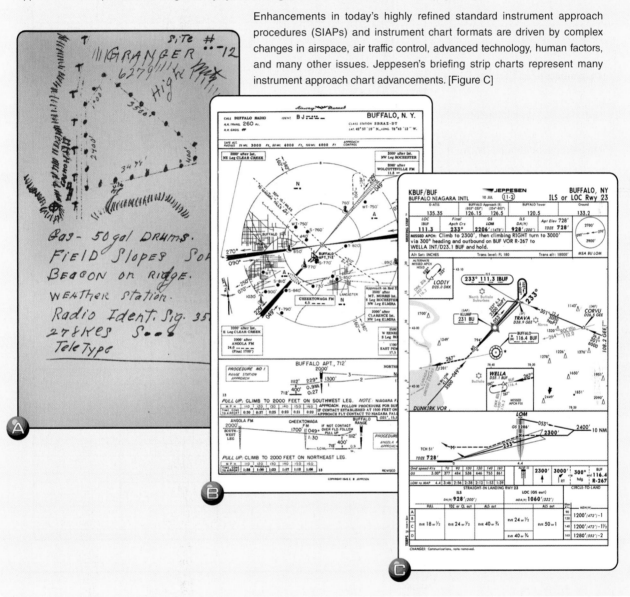

and airport charts are available in paper and electronic versions. Jeppesen paper charts are filed in a loose-leaf format by state, then by city within each state. FAA paper charts are published in regional volumes referred to as *Terminal Procedures Publications*, with each airport filed alphabetically by the name of the associated city. The following discussion employs a standard format to explain the features of approach charts. First, each section of the chart is introduced. Then, examples of the chart section are shown in Jeppesen and FAA formats, and specific features and symbology are described in text boxes. The chart used throughout the following discussion is the ILS Runway 1 approach to Key Field at Meridian, Mississippi. [Figures 7-11 and Figure 7-12]

SECTION A ■ **Approach Charts**

Heading Section

Communications Section

Approach Briefing Information

Minimum Safe Altitude (MSA)

Plan View

Profile View

Descent/Timing Conversion Table

Lighting Box

Missed Approach Icons

Landing Minimums Section

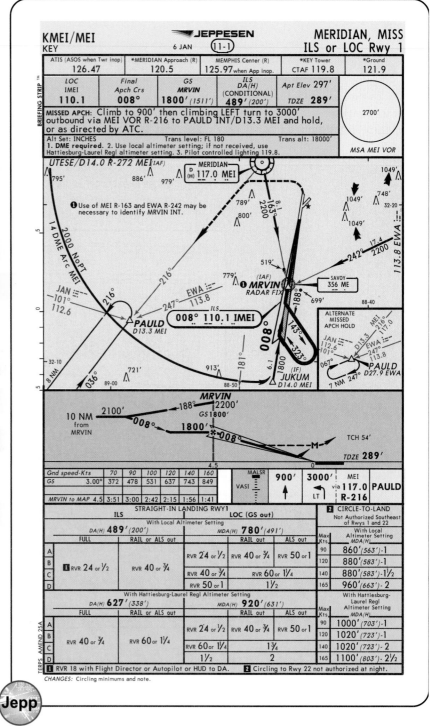

Figure 7-11. Jeppesen Approach Chart Layout

Heading Section

Pilot Briefing Information

Communications Section

Minimum Safe Altitude (MSA)

Plan View

Profile View

Missed Approach Icons

Airport Sketch

Time and Speed Table

Landing Minimums Section

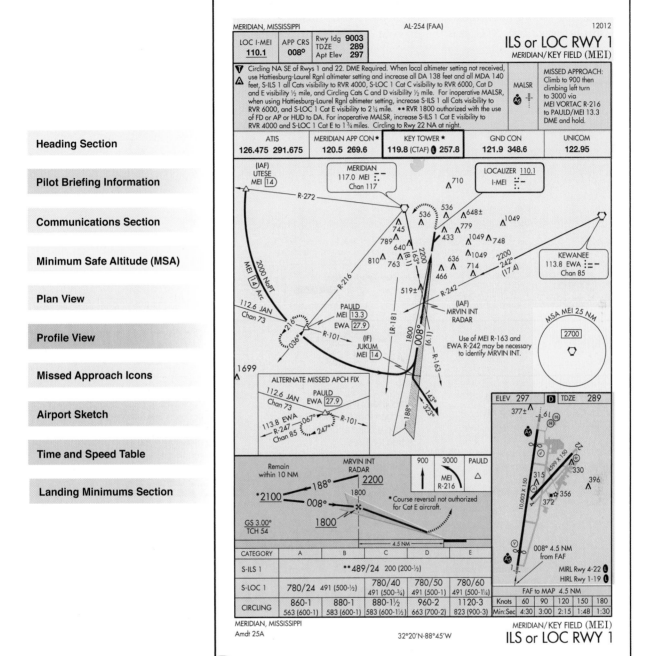

Figure 7-12. FAA Approach Chart Layout

SECTION A ■ Approach Charts

HEADING SECTION

The heading section provides the information to quickly locate a particular approach chart and to determine whether the chart is current. On both Jeppesen and FAA charts, the heading section identifies the city, airport, instrument approach procedure title, and the airport identifier. ATC uses the procedure title when clearing you for the approach. The procedure title indicates the type of approach system used and the equipment required to fly the final approach segment. Because additional equipment, such as DME, might be required to fly other approach segments, you should study the entire instrument procedure to determine all the equipment necessary to fly the approach. [Figures 7-13 and 7-14]

FAA The procedure title indicates the type of approach system used and the equipment required to fly the final approach segment.

Chart Dates
All Jeppesen charts have a revision date, but if the chart is issued before you can use it, there is also an effective date. In that case, use the previous version of the chart until the effective date.

Airport Location
The location consists of the applicable city and state.

Jepp

JEPPESEN
25 JUL (11-1) Eff 31 Jul

KMEI/MEI
KEY

JEPPESEN
6 JAN (11-1)

MERIDIAN, MISS
ILS or LOC Rwy 1

Airport Identifier and Name
The airport name is below the ICAO identifier.

Chart Index Number
The chart index number helps you file a chart and distinguish certain features.

Procedure Title
The procedure title indicates:
- The type of approach.
- The runway served for straight-in landing procedures.
- The equipment required to perform the final approach segment.

Figure 7-13. Jeppesen Heading Section

Procedure Title
The procedure title indicates:
- The type of approach.
- The runway served for straight-in landing procedures.
- The equipment required to perform the final approach segment.

FAA

Chart Index Number
This number is used to identify and categorize the chart.

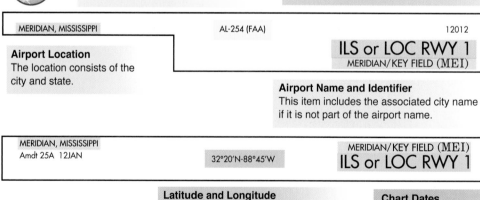

MERIDIAN, MISSISSIPPI   AL-254 (FAA)   12012

ILS or LOC RWY 1
MERIDIAN/KEY FIELD (MEI)

Airport Location
The location consists of the city and state.

Airport Name and Identifier
This item includes the associated city name if it is not part of the airport name.

MERIDIAN, MISSISSIPPI
Amdt 25A 12JAN   32°20'N-88°45'W

MERIDIAN/KEY FIELD (MEI)
ILS or LOC RWY 1

SC-4, 27 AUG to 24 SEP

Latitude and Longitude
Coordinates are for the official airport reference point.

Chart Dates
The terminal procedures publication volume and the chart effective dates are on the sides of the chart.

Figure 7-14. FAA Heading Section

Approach

When a procedure title has an alphabetical suffix, such as VOR-A, it means the procedure does not meet the criteria for a straight-in landing. In this case, a turning maneuver, called a circling approach, may be required to complete the landing. If two or more approaches use the same primary navigation source for a particular runway, a letter (starting with Z and working back through the alphabet) appears in the procedure title, such as RNAV (GPS) Z RWY 6 and RNAV (GPS) Y RWY 6.

Both Jeppesen and the FAA use chart index numbers to identify the chart. On a Jeppesen chart, the first digit of the chart index number is the airport number. When more than one airport shares the same city and state name, the first airport is given the number 1, the second the number 2, and so on. The second digit identifies the chart procedure type. [Figure 7-15] The third digit is used to index charts with the same approach types. For example, the first ILS approach at the second airport is given an index number of 21-1. The second ILS at the same airport receives the number 21-2. The first VOR approach at this airport receives the number 23-1.

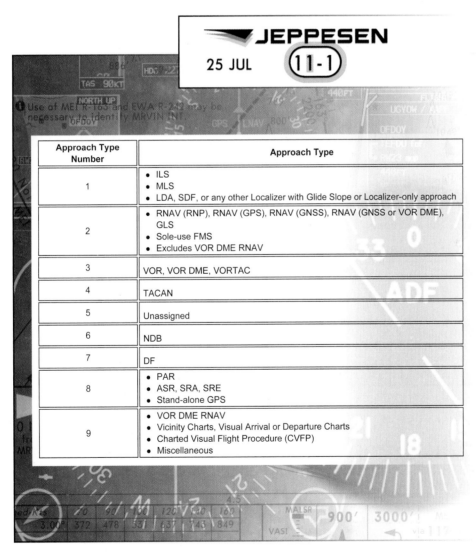

Approach Type Number	Approach Type
1	• ILS • MLS • LDA, SDF, or any other Localizer with Glide Slope or Localizer-only approach
2	• RNAV (RNP), RNAV (GPS), RNAV (GNSS), RNAV (GNSS or VOR DME), GLS • Sole-use FMS • Excludes VOR DME RNAV
3	VOR, VOR DME, VORTAC
4	TACAN
5	Unassigned
6	NDB
7	DF
8	• PAR • ASR, SRA, SRE • Stand-alone GPS
9	• VOR DME RNAV • Vicinity Charts, Visual Arrival or Departure Charts • Charted Visual Flight Procedure (CVFP) • Miscellaneous

Figure 7-15 The second digit of the Jeppesen chart index number is used to identify the chart procedure type.

The chart dates in the heading section indicate when a change to the chart information has occurred. However, these dates refer to a change in *any* information. If a procedural update has been made, a procedural amendment reference date is located on the lower left of approach charts. [Figure 7-16]

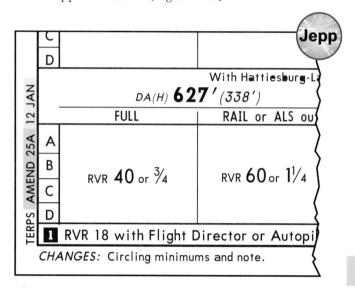

Amendment Number

Procedure Amendment Reference Date

Figure 7-16. Jeppesen and FAA procedure amendment reference dates help you keep track of procedural changes to approaches.

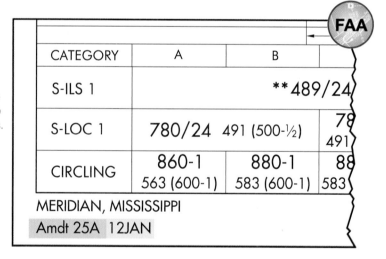

COMMUNICATIONS SECTION

Jeppesen and the FAA place their communication frequencies in a row of boxes near the top of the approach chart. While the specific communication facilities vary from airport to airport, the frequencies are always listed in the order in which you normally use them when approaching the airport. Part-time facilities are indicated by an asterisk. You should refer to the *Airport Facility Directory (AFD)* or other flight supplement to determine the hours of operation for part-time facilities. [Figures 7-17 and 7-18]

 Communication frequencies are listed on approach charts in the normal sequence used by arriving aircraft. See figures 7-17 and 7-18.

ATIS (ASOS when Twr inop)	*MERIDIAN Approach (R)	MEMPHIS Center (R)	*KEY Tower	*Ground
126.47	120.5	125.97 when App inop.	CTAF 119.8	121.9

Airport and Weather Information
Use these frequencies to obtain airport and weather information from facilities such as ATIS, ASOS, and AWOS.

Primary Contact Frequencies
Use these frequencies to contact approach, tower, ground control, and UNICOM, as applicable.

Radar Equipped
A parenthetical R indicates that the airport is equipped with radar and that the approach or center is the controlling facility.

Part-Time Operation
An asterisk next to a frequency indicates part-time operation. An alternate contact and frequency might be included. You can find hours of operation in the *Chart Supplement.*

Figure 7-17. Jeppesen Communications Section

ATIS	MERIDIAN APP CON ★	KEY TOWER ★	GND CON	UNICOM
126.475 291.675	120.5 269.6	119.8 (CTAF) ⓛ 257.8	121.9 348.6	122.95

Airport and Weather Information
Use these frequences to obtain airport and weather information from facilities such as ATIS, ASOS, and AWOS.

Primary Contact Frequencies
Use these frequencies to contact approach, tower, ground control, and UNICOM frequencies, as applicable. A heavy-lined box indicates the tower frequency.

Part-Time Operation
An asterisk next to a frequency indicates part-time operation. You can find the hours of operation in the *or Chart Supplement.*

Pilot-Controlled Lighting
An L symbol indicates that when the tower is closed, you activate pilot-controlled lighting on the CTAF.

Figure 7-18. FAA Communications Section

BRIEFING INFORMATION

Prior to flying an instrument approach, you should perform an approach briefing to ensure you are thoroughly familiar with the approach procedure. The briefing section found at the top of the chart presents information to help you prepare for the approach. [Figures 7-19 and 7-20]

SECTION A ■ Approach Charts

WAAS CH **69314** **W23A**	LOC IMEI **110.1**	Final Apch Crs **008°**	GS MRVIN **1800'** *(1511')*	ILS DA(H) (CONDITIONAL) **489'** *(200')*	Apt Elev **297'** TDZE **289'**

MISSED APCH: Climb to 900' then climbing LEFT turn to 3000' outbound via MEI VOR R-216 to PAULD INT/D13.3 MEI and hold, or as directed by ATC.

Alt Set: INCHES   Trans level: FL 180   Trans alt: 18000'
1. DME required. 2. Use local altimeter setting; if not received, use Hattiesburg-Laurel Regl altimeter setting. 3. Pilot controlled lighting 119.8.

Primary Navigation Information
This includes the navaid type, identifier, and frequency.
Example: This approach uses a localizer with the identifier IMEI on a frequency of 110.1.

In the case of an RNAV (GPS) approach, the chart shows the space-based augmentation system (i.e. WAAS), the facility channel number, and the approach identifier.

Final Approach Course
This box shows the course you use when flying the final segment of the approach procedure.
Example: After intercepting the localizer, you fly a final approach course of 008° to the runway.

Altitude at Glide Slope/Path Intercept or FAF
This box shows the MSL altitude and the height above touchdown altitude as you pass over the fix at which you normally intercept the glide slope for a precision approach or glide path for an approach with vertical guidance (APV). For a nonprecision approach, it shows the minimum altitude at the final approach fix.
Example: At MARVIN intersection, you should be at 1,800 feet MSL, or 1,511 feet above touchdown, if you are on the glide slope.

DA(H) or MDA(H)
Depending on the approach procedure, this box contains either the decision altitude (DA) or minimum descent altitude (MDA).
For a precision approach or APV, the box contains the lowest DA and DH based on a straight-in landing with all equipment operating.
For a nonprecision approach, the box contains the lowest MDA and HAT for a straight-in landing. An HAA is shown if a touchdown zone elevation (TDZE) is not given for the approach.
For approaches without a straight-in landing or those that apply to more than one runway, a note refers to the landing minimums section of the chart.
Example: The decision altitude is 489 feet MSL with a decision height of 200 feet. The conditional note indicates that the decision altitude is based on certain conditions. You should refer to the landing minimums section of the chart for details.

Elevations
This box includes the airport elevation and the runway touchdown zone elevation (TDZE).
Example: The airport elevation is 297 feet MSL, and the Runway 1 touchdown zone elevation is 289 feet MSL.

Missed Approach Instructions
These instructions are a full textual description of the missed approach procedure.
Example: If you must perform a missed approach, first climb to 900 feet MSL and then begin a climbing left turn to 3,000 feet MSL to intercept the 216° radial from the Meridian VOR/DME to PAULD intersection at 13.3 DME and hold, or as ATC directs you.

Notes and Limitations
This box contains general equipment and procedural limitations associated with the approach, if applicable. If there are no notes associated with the approach, this row is omitted.
Example: Procedural notes indicate that DME is required for this approach and instruct you to use the Hattiesburg-Laurel Regional Airport altimeter setting if the local altimeter setting is unavailable. In addition, pilot-controlled lighting is available on the tower frequency of 119. 8.

Figure 7-19. Jeppesen Approach Briefing Information

 The available landing distance for a given approach procedure is shown with the TDZE and airport elevation at the top of an FAA chart.

WAAS CH **69314** **W23A**	LOC I-MEI **110.1**	APP CRS **008°**	Rwy ldg **9003** TDZE **289** Apt Elev **297**		

▼ ⚠ Circling NA SE of Rwys 1 and 22. DME Required. When local altimeter setting not received, use Hattiesburg-Laurel Rgnl altimeter setting and increase all DA 138 feet and all MDA 140 feet, S-ILS 1 all Cats visibility to RVR 4000, S-LOC 1 Cat C visibility to RVR 6000, Cat D and E visibility ½ mile, and Circling Cats C and D visibility ½ mile. For inoperative MALSR, when using Hattiesburg-Laurel Rgnl altimeter setting, increase S-ILS 1 all Cats visibility to RVR 6000, and S-LOC 1 Cat E visibility to 2¼ mile. **RVR 1800 authorized with the use of FD or AP or HUD to DA. For inoperative MALSR, increase S-ILS 1 Cat E visibility to RVR 4000 and S-LOC 1 Cat E to 1¾ miles. Circling to Rwy 22 NA at night.

MALSR

MISSED APPROACH: Climb to 900 then climbing left turn to 3000 via MEI VORTAC R-216 to PAULD/MEI 13.3 DME and hold.

Primary Navigation Information
This includes the navaid type, identifier, and frequency. The underline indicates that no voice is transmitted on this frequency.
Example: This approach uses a localizer with the identifier of I-MEI on a frequency of 110.1.

In the case of an RNAV (GPS) approach, the chart shows the space-based augmentation system (i.e. WAAS), the facility channel number, and the approach identifier.

Approach Course
This box shows the course you use when flying the final segment of the approach procedure.
Example: After intercepting the localizer, fly a final approach course of 008° to the runway.

Runway Information
This box includes the available landing distance, touchdown zone elevation (TDZE), and airport elevation.
Example: Runway 1, which is the straight-in landing runway for the approach, is 9,003 feet long with a touchdown zone elevation of 289 feet MSL. The airport elevation is 297 feet MSL.

Notes and Limitations
This box shows icons that indicate nonstandard takeoff minimums or obstacle departure procedures and nonstandard alternate minimums and other procedure limitations associated with the approach.
Example: You must refer to the front of the Terminal Procedures Publication to locate the nonstandard takeoff minimums and nonstandard alternate minimums, indicated by the T and A symbols. Other notes specify increased landing minimums that apply when the local altimeter setting is unavailable or when certain approach lighting systems are inoperative.

Approach Lighting
This symbology depicts approach lighting systems that you can reference in the legend of the *Terminal Procedures Publication.*
Example: Runway 1 has a medium intensity approach lighting system with runway alignment indicator lights (MALSR).

Missed Approach Instructions
These instructions are a full textual description of the missed approach procedure.
Example: If you must perform a missed approach, first climb to 900 feet MSL and then begin a climbing left turn to 3,000 feet MSL to intercept the 216° radial from the Meridian VOR/DME to PAULD intersection at 13.3 DME and hold.

Figure 7-20. FAA Pilot Briefing Information

The approach lighting information is shown in the briefing area prior to the missed approach instructions, and on the airport sketch at the bottom of an FAA chart. The airport sketch also includes locations of VASIs or PAPIs, plus other airport lighting information.

MINIMUM SAFE/SECTOR ALTITUDE

The **minimum safe/sector altitude (MSA)**, shown on approach charts, provides 1,000 feet of obstruction clearance within 25 nautical miles of the indicated facility, unless some other distance is specified. The 1,000-foot criterion applies over both mountainous and non-mountainous terrain. Each MSA applies only to the approach on which it is displayed, and it may not be used for any other approach.

There are three important considerations regarding the MSA. First, it only provides obstruction clearance within the sector. Neither navigation nor communication coverage is guaranteed. Second, the MSA is designed only for use in an emergency or during VFR flight, such as during a VFR approach at night. And third, an MSA is not listed for every approach. Its omission may be due to the lack of an easily identifiable facility upon which to orient the MSA circle. [Figures 7-21]

> **FAA** The MSA provides 1,000 feet of obstruction clearance within a specified distance, usually 25 nautical miles, from the facility. However, neither navigation nor communication coverage is guaranteed within this distance.

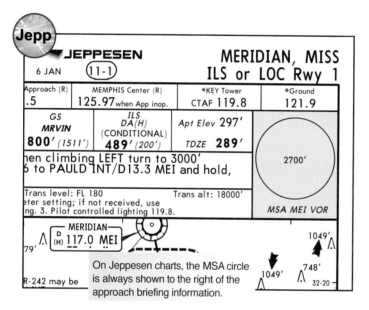

On Jeppesen charts, the MSA circle is always shown to the right of the approach briefing information.

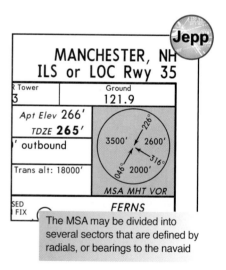

The MSA may be divided into several sectors that are defined by radials, or bearings to the navaid

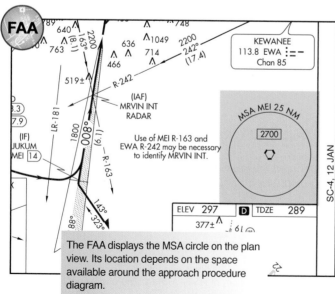

The FAA displays the MSA circle on the plan view. Its location depends on the space available around the approach procedure diagram.

Figure 7-21. Jeppesen and FAA MSA Circles

Some RNAV procedures use a terminal arrival area (TAA). An MSA does not apply to these approaches because minimum altitudes for areas that extend 30 nautical miles from initial approach fix waypoints are depicted on the chart plan view. [Figure 7-22]

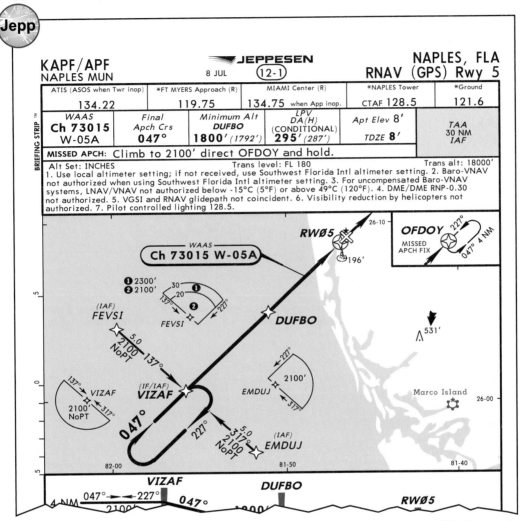

Figure 7-22. For RNAV (GPS) approaches with TAAs, FAA charts do not depict an MSA circle and on Jeppesen charts, it is replaced with a reference to the TAA 30 NM boundary within which you proceed to an initial approach fix.

PLAN VIEW

When you prepare to perform an approach procedure, it is important to maintain positional awareness in relation to the approach course, navaids, and the airport. The plan view is an overhead presentation of the entire approach procedure.

NAVAID AND FLIGHT PATH DEPICTION

The plan view provides the navaid facility information and flight path depiction that enable you to transition from the enroute environment and navigate on each segment of the approach procedure. The chart prominently displays the courses to navigate on the approach procedure and missed approach tracks. Navaids and fixes along these routes enable you to maintain awareness of your position on the approach. [Figures 7-23 and 7-24]

 Approach chart symbology provides information about navaids, such as the availability of DME or voice capability. See figures 7-23 and 7-24.

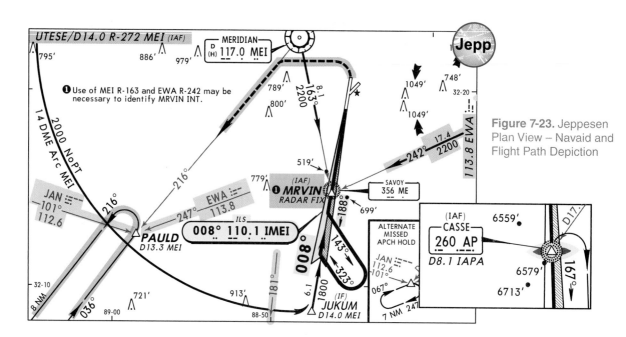

Figure 7-23. Jeppesen Plan View – Navaid and Flight Path Depiction

Navaid Facility Information

These boxes indicate the navaid name or type (in the case of an ILS approach), and the frequency, identifier, and identifier Morse code. The final approach course is also shown for an ILS approach. A heavy outline and shadow indicate the primary facility upon which the approach is based.

Example: This approach is based on the Meridian (IMEI) localizer. The ILS localizer frequency is 110.1. The letter I precedes the identifier to indicate an ILS localizer.

Initial Approach Fixes

The letters IAF indicate initial approach fixes. There might be several initial approach fixes for the approach procedure.

Example: UTESE intersection is the initial approach fix if you are performing the DME arc, and the MRVIN radar fix/intersection is the initial approach fix if you are performing the course reversal.

Approach Procedure Track

The approach procedure track is a heavy line with an arrow indicating the direction to the runway. The final approach magnetic course is in large text, and the outbound course is in smaller text. The localizer arrow symbol is depicted along the course, if applicable.

Example: Depending on your position and ATC clearance, you can perform a DME arc or a procedure turn to intercept the final approach course of 008°. The outbound course is 188°.

Nonflyable Radials

These radials, which identify fixes, are depicted as gray lines without minimum altitudes.

Example: You can use the 247° radial from Kewanee VOR/DME (EWA), the 216° from Meridian VOR/DME (MEI) and the 101° radial from Jackson VOR/DME (JAN) to define PAULD Intersection.

Feeder Routes

A feeder route that enables you to transition from the enroute environment, is depicted as a heavy line arrow with the magnetic course, minimum altitude, and DME mileage from the navaid shown along the route.

Example: The feeder route on the 242° radial from Kewanee VOR/DME (EWA) has a minimum altitude of 2,200 feet MSL. The DME mileage from Kewanee VOR/DME to MRVIN intersection is 17.4 nautical miles.

Lead-In Radial

For some DME arcs, a lead-in radial assists you in leading the turn to the final approach course by at least 2 NM. To indicate that this is a nonflyable radial, the chart depicts it as a thin line with no minimum altitude.

Example: Start your turn from the DME arc to the final approach course of 008° as you cross the 181° radial from Meridian VOR/DME (MEI).

Missed Approach Track

This dashed line shows the initial missed approach flight path. If the missed approach procedure requires holding, the holding pattern is also shown.

Example: The initial missed approach path is a left turn after climbing to 900 feet MSL, and the missed approach hold is at PAULD intersection.

Outer Marker (OM)

Some ILS approaches have an outer marker beacon to provide range information. The chart shows the marker beacon as a lens-shaped symbol.

Example: This approach has an outer marker collocated with Casse NDB.

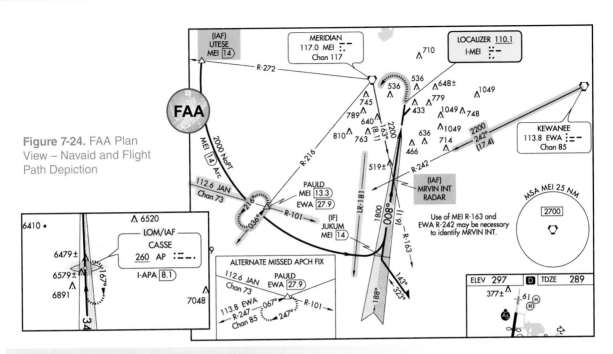

Figure 7-24. FAA Plan View – Navaid and Flight Path Depiction

Navaid Facility Information
These boxes indicate the navaid name or type (in the case of a localizer), and the frequency, identifier, and identifier Morse code.
Example: This approach is based on the Meridian (IMEI) localizer. The ILS localizer frequency is 110.1. The letter I precedes the identifier to indicate an ILS localizer.

Initial Approach Fixes
The letters IAF indicate initial approach fixes. There might be several initial approach fixes for the approach procedure.
Example: UTESE intersection is the initial approach fix if you are performing the DME arc, and the MRVIN radar fix/intersection is the initial approach fix if you are performing the course reversal.

Approach Procedure Track
The approach course is a heavy line with an arrow indicating the direction to the runway. The final approach magnetic course is in large text, and the outbound course is in smaller text. The localizer arrow symbol is depicted along the course, if applicable.
Example: Depending on your position and ATC clearance, you can perform a DME arc or a procedure turn to intercept the final approach course of 008°. The outbound course is 188°.

Nonflyable Radials
These radials, which identify fixes, are depicted as thin lines without minimum altitudes.
Example: You can use the 247° radial from Kewanee VORTAC (EWA), the 216° from Meridian VORTAC (MEI) and the 101° radial from Jackson VORTAC (JAN) define PAULD Intersection.

Feeder Routes
A feeder route that enables you to transition from the enroute environment, is depicted as a heavy line arrow with the magnetic course, minimum altitude, and DME mileage from the navaid shown along the route.
Example: The feeder route on the 242° radial from Kewanee VORTAC (EWA) has a minimum altitude of 2,200 feet MSL. The DME mileage from Kewanee VOR/DME to MRVIN intersection is 17.4 nautical miles.

Lead-In Radial
For some DME arcs, a lead-in radial assists you in leading the turn to the final approach course by at least 2 NM. To indicate that this is a nonflyable radial, the chart depicts it as a thin line with no minimum altitude.
Example: Start your turn from the DME arc to the final approach course of 008° as you cross the 181° radial from Meridian VOR/DME (MEI).

Missed Approach Track
This dashed line shows the initial missed approach flight path. If the missed approach procedure requires holding, the holding pattern is also shown.
Example: The initial missed approach path is a left turn after climbing to 900 feet MSL, and the missed approach hold is at PAULD intersection.

Outer Marker (OM)
Some ILS approaches have an outer marker beacon to provide range information. The chart shows the marker beacon as a lens-shaped symbol.
Example: This approach has an outer marker collocated with Casse NDB, indicated as a locator outer marker (LOM).

COURSE REVERSAL DEPICTION

Depending on how you approach the airport, you might have to reverse your course to intercept the final approach course. Several types of **course reversals** are shown on approach charts. A **procedure turn** is a standard method of reversing your course. When the procedure turn is depicted on the plan view, it means you may reverse course any way you desire as long as the turn is made on the same side of the approach course as the symbol, the turn is completed within the distance specified in the profile view, and you remain within protected airspace. If a holding or teardrop pattern is shown instead of a procedure turn, it is the only approved method of course reversal. If no procedure turn, holding pattern, or teardrop pattern is shown, a course reversal is not authorized. [Figures 7-25 and 7-26]

Course Reversal Not Authorized

If a procedure turn, holding pattern, or teardrop pattern is not shown, a course reversal is not authorized.

Example: To intercept the localizer course, you can track the 232° radial from Red Table VOR/DME. Because no procedure turn, holding pattern or teardrop pattern is depicted, do not perform a course reversal.

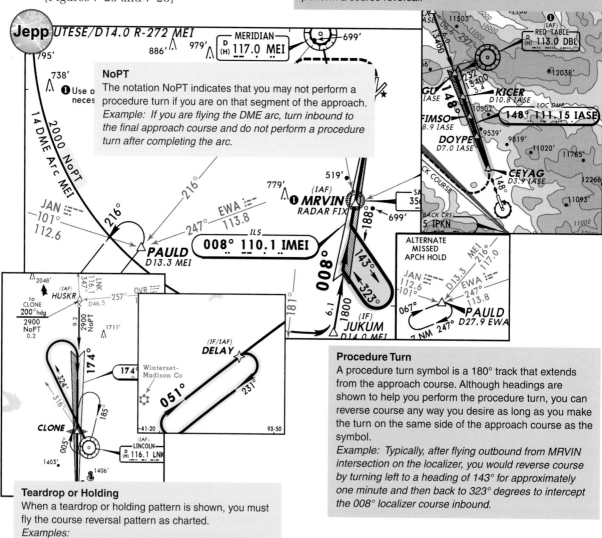

NoPT

The notation NoPT indicates that you may not perform a procedure turn if you are on that segment of the approach.
Example: If you are flying the DME arc, turn inbound to the final approach course and do not perform a procedure turn after completing the arc.

Procedure Turn

A procedure turn symbol is a 180° track that extends from the approach course. Although headings are shown to help you perform the procedure turn, you can reverse course any way you desire as long as you make the turn on the same side of the approach course as the symbol.
Example: Typically, after flying outbound from MRVIN intersection on the localizer, you would reverse course by turning left to a heading of 143° for approximately one minute and then back to 323° degrees to intercept the 008° localizer course inbound.

Teardrop or Holding

When a teardrop or holding pattern is shown, you must fly the course reversal pattern as charted.
Examples:
• To perform the teardrop pattern course reversal as depicted, after you reach Lincoln VOR/DME, track outbound on the 324° radial and then make a right turn to intercept the localizer course of 174°.
• To perform the holding pattern course reversal as depicted, after reaching DELAY intersection, enter the hold to intercept the localizer course of 051°.

Figure 7-25. Jeppesen Plan View – Course Reversal Depiction

 Absence of a procedure turn or holding pattern indicates that a course reversal is not authorized. See figures 7-25 and 7-26.

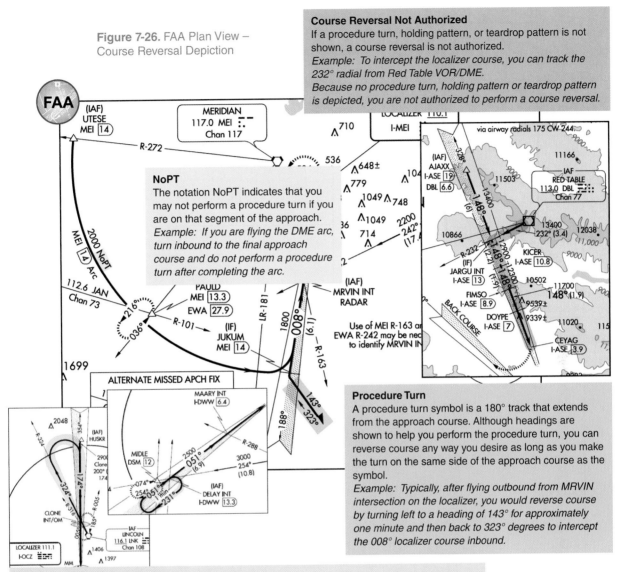

Figure 7-26. FAA Plan View – Course Reversal Depiction

Course Reversal Not Authorized

If a procedure turn, holding pattern, or teardrop pattern is not shown, a course reversal is not authorized.

Example: To intercept the localizer course, you can track the 232° radial from Red Table VOR/DME.

Because no procedure turn, holding pattern or teardrop pattern is depicted, you are not authorized to perform a course reversal.

NoPT

The notation NoPT indicates that you may not perform a procedure turn if you are on that segment of the approach.

Example: If you are flying the DME arc, turn inbound to the final approach course and do not perform a procedure turn after completing the arc.

Procedure Turn

A procedure turn symbol is a 180° track that extends from the approach course. Although headings are shown to help you perform the procedure turn, you can reverse course any way you desire as long as you make the turn on the same side of the approach course as the symbol.

Example: Typically, after flying outbound from MRVIN intersection on the localizer, you would reverse course by turning left to a heading of 143° for approximately one minute and then back to 323° degrees to intercept the 008° localizer course inbound.

Teardrop or Holding

When a teardrop or holding pattern is shown, you must fly the course reversal pattern as charted.

Examples:

• *To perform the teardrop pattern course reversal as depicted, after you reach Lincoln VORTAC, track outbound on the 324° radial and then make a right turn to intercept the localizer course of 174°.*

• *To perform the holding pattern course reversal as depicted, after reaching DELAY intersection, enter the hold to intercept the localizer course of 051°.*

SECTION A ■ Approach Charts

TERRAIN AND OBSTACLE DEPICTION

Because approach charts are intended for use during instrument weather conditions, they show only limited terrain and obstruction information. However, obstruction clearance is provided throughout the approach when the procedure is flown as depicted. On both Jeppesen and FAA charts, some, but not all, terrain high points and man-made structures are depicted with their elevations. These references cannot be relied on for terrain or obstruction avoidance since there might be higher uncharted terrain or obstructions within the same vicinity. Generally, terrain or structures less than 400 feet above the airport elevation are not depicted on Jeppesen charts. [Figure 7-27]

 Adherence to the minimum altitudes depicted on approach charts provides terrain and obstacle clearance.

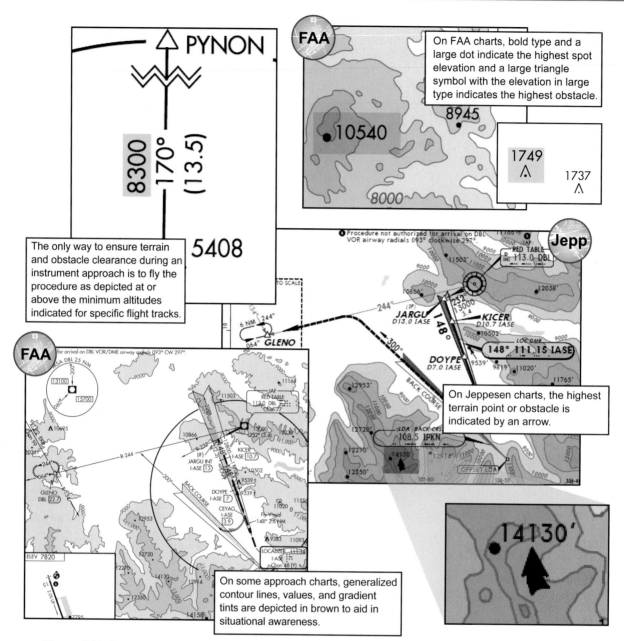

Figure 7-27. Jeppesen and FAA Plan View – Terrain and Obstacle Depiction.

PROFILE VIEW

You review the profile view to orient yourself to the vertical flight path that you fly during the approach procedure. The profile view shows the approach from the side and displays the flight path and facilities, as well as minimum altitudes in feet MSL. In addition, several different altitudes that are referenced to the runway or airport elevation are included on the profile view.

FLIGHT PATH DEPICTION

The profile view displays the segments of the approach, including the course reversal and final approach path and course reversal. Flight paths are depicted differently for precision and nonprecision approaches. Jeppesen charts also show unique flight path depictions for approaches with vertical guidance and for nonprecision approaches with a vertical descent angle. [Figures 7-28 and 7-29]

 The procedure turn must be completed within the prescribed distance from the facility. See figures 7-28 and 7-29.

Approach

Approach Path
- The chart shows the inbound magnetic course and the altitude to which you may descend after intercepting the inbound course in bold type.
- An arrow with a solid outline represents the ILS glide slope.
- A solid line depicts the approach path. An additional dashed line depicts the nonprecision approach path for a localizer-only approach without the use of the glide slope.

Example: You intercept the localizer inbound on a course of 008° and descend to 1,800 feet MSL.
On the final approach segment, the precision approach path continues on the glide slope to the decision altitude while the nonprecision approach path shows a level flight path after the airplane reaches the minimum descent altitude.

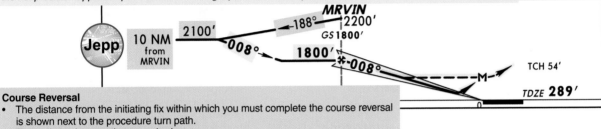

Course Reversal
- The distance from the initiating fix within which you must complete the course reversal is shown next to the procedure turn path.
- The outbound magnetic course is shown.
- The minimum altitude to complete the course reversal is shown along the path.

Example: After tracking an outbound course of 188°, you must complete the procedure turn within 10 N.M. of MRVIN intersection at an altitude no lower than 2,100 feet MSL.

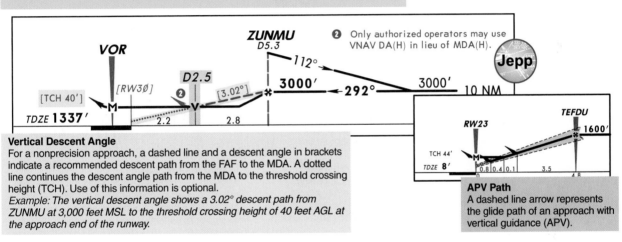

Vertical Descent Angle
For a nonprecision approach, a dashed line and a descent angle in brackets indicate a recommended descent path from the FAF to the MDA. A dotted line continues the descent angle path from the MDA to the threshold crossing height (TCH). Use of this information is optional.
Example: The vertical descent angle shows a 3.02° descent path from ZUNMU at 3,000 feet MSL to the threshold crossing height of 40 feet AGL at the approach end of the runway.

APV Path
A dashed line arrow represents the glide path of an approach with vertical guidance (APV).

Figure 7-28. Jeppesen Profile View — Flight Path

Course Reversal
- A notation indicates the distance from the initiating fix within which you must complete the course reversal.
- The outbound magnetic course is shown.
- A line below the number indicates the minimum altitude to complete the course reversal.

Example: After tracking an outbound course of 188°, you must complete the procedure turn within 10 NM. of MRVIN intersection at an altitude no lower than 2,100 feet MSL.

Approach Path
- The chart shows the inbound magnetic course and the altitude to which you may descent after intercepting the inbound course.
- A shaded arrow represents the ILS glide slope.

Example: You intercept the localizer inbound on a course of 008° and descend to 1,800 feet MSL to intercept the glide slope and fly the final approach segment.

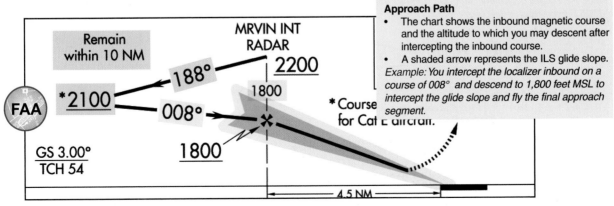

Figure 7-29. FAA Profile View — Flight Path Depiction

SECTION A ■ Approach Charts

MISSED APPROACH INSTRUCTIONS

If you fly the approach procedure and you do not see the runway environment, you will need to perform a missed approach. The profile view and the missed approach icons contain the necessary instructions. Missed approach icons represent initial pilot actions in the event of a missed approach. They provide symbolic information about the initial up-and-out maneuvers, and improve the connection between the profile view graphic and the initiation of a missed approach procedure. You should always refer to the missed approach instructions in the heading section and the plan view graphic for complete information about the missed approach procedure. If using an autopilot, you must understand how it operates during a missed approach, and ensure it is programmed correctly as you plan the approach. [Figures 7-30 and 7-31]

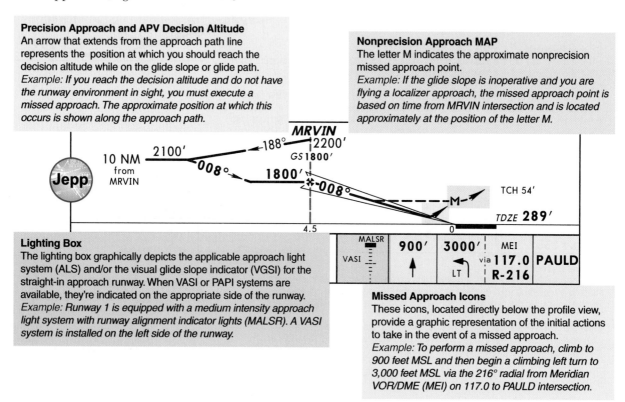

Precision Approach and APV Decision Altitude
An arrow that extends from the approach path line represents the position at which you should reach the decision altitude while on the glide slope or glide path.
Example: If you reach the decision altitude and do not have the runway environment in sight, you must execute a missed approach. The approximate position at which this occurs is shown along the approach path.

Nonprecision Approach MAP
The letter M indicates the approximate nonprecision missed approach point.
Example: If the glide slope is inoperative and you are flying a localizer approach, the missed approach point is based on time from MRVIN intersection and is located approximately at the position of the letter M.

Lighting Box
The lighting box graphically depicts the applicable approach light system (ALS) and/or the visual glide slope indicator (VGSI) for the straight-in approach runway. When VASI or PAPI systems are available, they're indicated on the appropriate side of the runway.
Example: Runway 1 is equipped with a medium intensity approach light system with runway alignment indicator lights (MALSR). A VASI system is installed on the left side of the runway.

Missed Approach Icons
These icons, located directly below the profile view, provide a graphic representation of the initial actions to take in the event of a missed approach.
Example: To perform a missed approach, climb to 900 feet MSL and then begin a climbing left turn to 3,000 feet MSL via the 216° radial from Meridian VOR/DME (MEI) on 117.0 to PAULD intersection.

Figure 7-30. Jeppesen Missed Approach Instructions

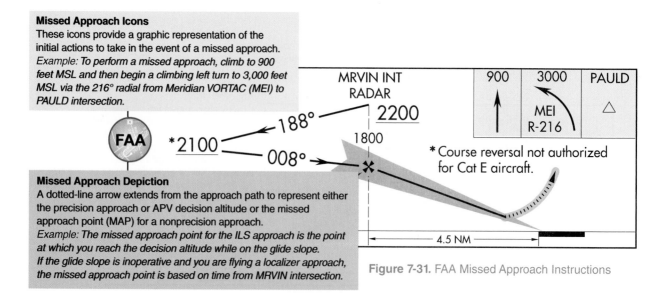

Missed Approach Icons
These icons provide a graphic representation of the initial actions to take in the event of a missed approach.
Example: To perform a missed approach, climb to 900 feet MSL and then begin a climbing left turn to 3,000 feet MSL via the 216° radial from Meridian VORTAC (MEI) to PAULD intersection.

Missed Approach Depiction
A dotted-line arrow extends from the approach path to represent either the precision approach or APV decision altitude or the missed approach point (MAP) for a nonprecision approach.
Example: The missed approach point for the ILS approach is the point at which you reach the decision altitude while on the glide slope. If the glide slope is inoperative and you are flying a localizer approach, the missed approach point is based on time from MRVIN intersection.

Figure 7-31. FAA Missed Approach Instructions

POSITION INFORMATION

The profile view depicts the fixes, altitudes, and distances that enable you to maintain the proper position as you perform the approach procedures. [Figures 7-32 and 7-33]

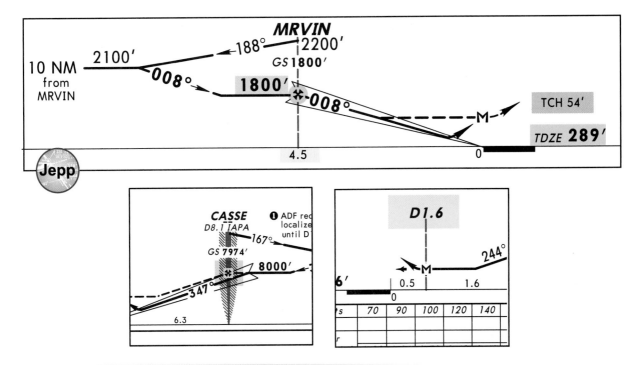

Minimum Glide Slope Intercept Altitude and Glide Slope Intercept Point
A bend in the solid approach path line indicates the point at which you intercept the glide slope when operating at the minimum glide slope intercept altitude shown along the approach path.
This point may or may not coincide with the localizer final approach fix on an ILS approach.
Example: When flying at 1,800 feet MSL having intercepted the localizer flying inbound on the ILS approach, you should intercept the glide slope at the point indicated by the bend in the solid approach path line, in this case at MRVIN intersection.

Nonprecision Approach FAF
A cross indicates the nonprecision approach final approach fix (FAF), which is an outer marker, navaid, or other fix.
Example: If you are flying a nonprecision localizer approach because of an inoperative glide slope, the final approach fix is at MRVIN intersection.

Threshold Crossing Height (TCH)
The TCH is the height above ground level at which you cross the threshold if you continue the approach to a landing while on the glide slope.
Example: You will cross the runway threshold at 54 feet AGL.

Approach Distances
Distances along the approach path and between fixes are shown below the flight path.
Example: The distance from MRVIN intersection to the threshold of the runway is 4.5 NM.

Touchdown Zone Elevation (TDZE)
The TDZE is the highest elevation in the first 3,000 feet of the landing surface.
Example: The TDZE is 289 feet MSL.

DME Fix
DME fixes are shown with the letter D next to the DME mileage.
Example: For this nonprecision approach, the missed approach point (MAP) is at 1.6 DME from the VOR/DME.

Figure 7-32. Jeppesen Profile View — Position Information

SECTION A ■ **Approach Charts**

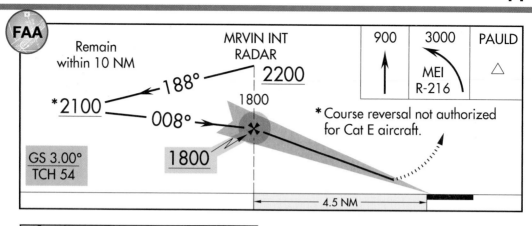

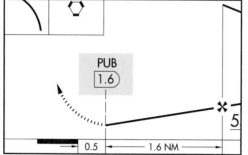

Minimum Glide Slope Intercept Altitude and Glide Slope Intercept Point
A lightning bolt indicates the point at which you intercept the glide slope when operating at the minimum glide slope intercept altitude, shown next to the symbol.
Example: When flying at 1,800 feet MSL after intercepting the localizer inbound on the ILS approach, you should intercept the glide slope at the point indicated by the lightning bolt symbol, in this case at MRVIN intersection.

Nonprecision Approach FAF
A cross indicates the nonprecision approach final approach fix (FAF), which is an outer marker, naviad, or other fix.
Example: If you are flying a nonprecision localizer approach because of an inoperative glide slope, the final approach fix is at MRVIN intersection.

Glide Slope Angle and Threshold Crossing Height (TCH)
The threshold crossing height is the AGL height at which you cross the threshold if you continue the approach to a landing while on the glide slope.
Example: If you maintain the glide slope, your approach path to the runway is at an angle of 3.00° and you will cross the runway threshold at 54 feet AGL.

Approach Distances
Distances between the approach path fixes are shown in a row below the flight path.
Example: The distance between MRVIN intersection and the runway threshold is 4.5 N.M.

DME Fix
DME fixes consist of the navaid identifier on top of a D-shaped box enclosing the DME mileage.
Example: For this nonprecision approach, the missed approach point (MAP) is at 1.6 DME from the VORTAC (PUB).

Figure 7-33. FAA Profile View — Position Information

 The precision approach FAF is located at the glide slope intercept point, marked by a lightning bolt on FAA charts.

 Distances along the approach path and between fixes are shown on the profile view. See figures 7-32 and 7-33.

Approach

CHAPTER 7

STEPDOWN FIXES

Many approaches incorporate one or more **stepdown fixes**, which are commonly used along approach segments to enable you to descend to a lower altitude after you overfly obstacles, or in conjunction with the design of local ATC procedures. Only one stepdown fix normally is located between the final approach fix and the missed approach point. If you cannot identify this stepdown fix, typically the altitude just prior to the fix becomes your MDA for the approach. [Figure 7-34]

 Some approaches incorporate a stepdown fix that can be identified using equipment beyond the minimum required for an approach—such as DME when flying a VOR approach. If you are equipped to identify the stepdown fix, you might have lower minimums; otherwise your MDA is the minimum altitude prior to the fix. See figure 7-34.

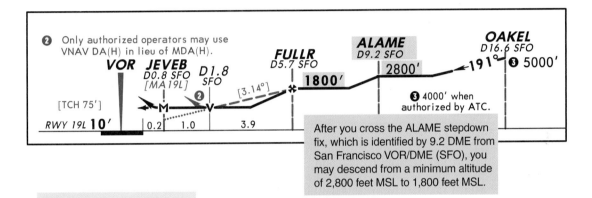

After you cross the ALAME stepdown fix, which is identified by 9.2 DME from San Francisco VOR/DME (SFO), you may descend from a minimum altitude of 2,800 feet MSL to 1,800 feet MSL.

If you cannot identify RICOL, your MDA is 1,240 feet MSL, which is shown in the profile view and landing minimums section of the approach chart.

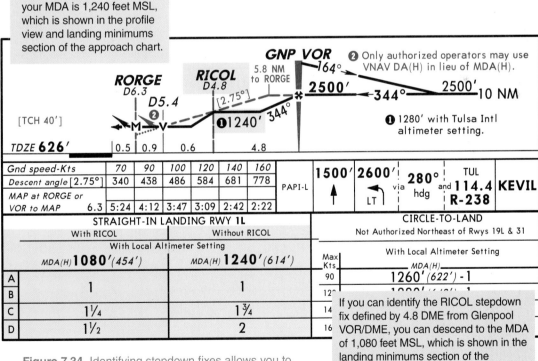

If you can identify the RICOL stepdown fix defined by 4.8 DME from Glenpool VOR/DME, you can descend to the MDA of 1,080 feet MSL, which is shown in the landing minimums section of the approach chart.

Figure 7-34. Identifying stepdown fixes allows you to descend to lower altitudes along the approach path, and, in some cases, allows a lower MDA.

SECTION A ■ Approach Charts

7-33

VISUAL DESCENT POINT

You have broken out of the clouds at the minimum descent altitude while flying a nonprecision approach. To ensure that you clear terrain and obstacles prior to descending from the MDA to land, some nonprecision approaches provide a **visual descent point (VDP)**, depicted in the profile view by the letter V. A VDP is the point from which you can make a normal descent to a landing if you have the required visual references in sight and you are starting from the MDA. At the VDP, you should be able to continue your descent to the runway threshold while maintaining the angle of the visual glide slope indicator (VGSI), or if there is no VGSI, then an angle of 3.00° or the vertical descent angle (VDA), whichever is greater. If you are not equipped to receive the VDP, you should fly the approach procedure as though no VDP had been provided. [Figure 7-35]

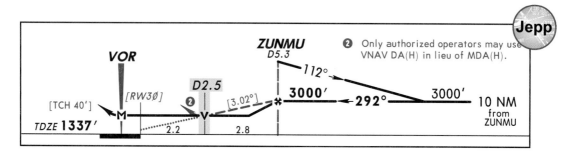

After you pass the final approach fix of ZUNMU intersection, you descend to the MDA. If you have the runway in sight, remain at the MDA until you reach 2.5 DME from Spencer VOR/DME (SPW) before descending below the MDA to land.

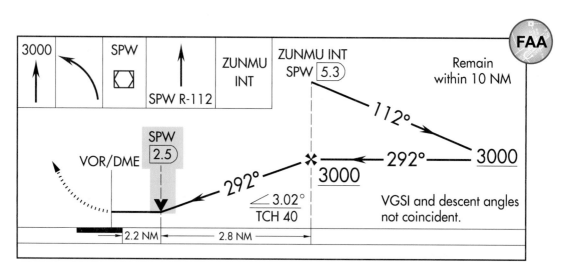

Figure 7-35. A visual descent point is depicted by the letter V on both Jeppesen and FAA charts.

DESCENT/TIMING CONVERSION TABLE

The **descent/timing conversion table** on Jeppesen charts provides information that helps you complete the final approach descent. Many times the missed approach point in a nonprecision approach is not a fix but an elapsed time. The table indicates the distance from the final approach fix to the missed approach point and the elapsed times to the missed approach point based on groundspeed. In addition, the table indicates the angle of the glide slope, glide path, or vertical descent, and a recommended rate of descent. [Figure 7-36]

FAF to MAP Time
Some nonprecision approaches show the elapsed time based on groundspeed from the final approach fix to the missed approach point. If timing is not shown, then you cannot determine the missed approach point by time, and a timed approach is not authorized.
Example: If you are flying the localizer approach to Runway 1 at Meridian and maintaining a groundspeed of 90 knots, your time from the final approach fix to the missed approach point is three minutes.

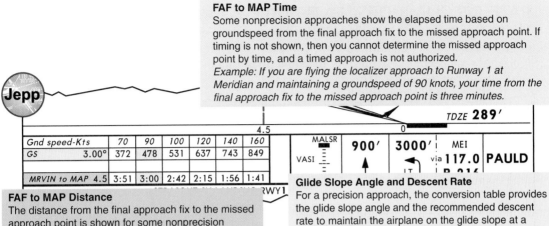

Gnd speed-Kts	70	90	100	120	140	160
GS 3.00°	372	478	531	637	743	849
MRVIN to MAP 4.5	3:51	3:00	2:42	2:15	1:56	1:41

FAF to MAP Distance
The distance from the final approach fix to the missed approach point is shown for some nonprecision approaches depending on the approach procedure.
Example: The distance between the final approach fix of MRVIN intersection and the missed approach point is 4.5 NM.

Glide Slope Angle and Descent Rate
For a precision approach, the conversion table provides the glide slope angle and the recommended descent rate to maintain the airplane on the glide slope at a particular groundspeed.
Example: If your groundspeed is 90 knots, your rate of descent should be 478 feet per minute to maintain the airplane on a 3.00° glide slope angle.

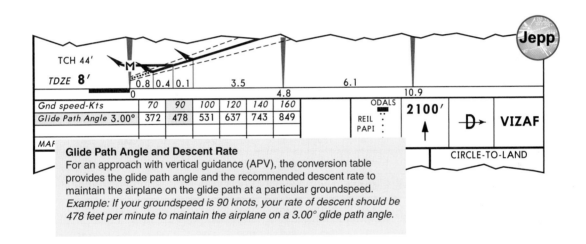

Gnd speed-Kts	70	90	100	120	140	160
Glide Path Angle 3.00°	372	478	531	637	743	849

Glide Path Angle and Descent Rate
For an approach with vertical guidance (APV), the conversion table provides the glide path angle and the recommended descent rate to maintain the airplane on the glide path at a particular groundspeed.
Example: If your groundspeed is 90 knots, your rate of descent should be 478 feet per minute to maintain the airplane on a 3.00° glide path angle.

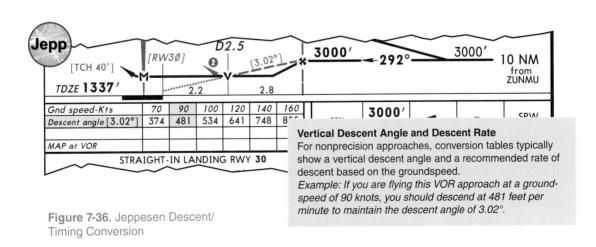

Gnd speed-Kts	70	90	100	120	140	160
Descent angle [3.02°]	374	481	534	641	748	8⁻⁻
MAP at VOR						

STRAIGHT-IN LANDING RWY 30

Vertical Descent Angle and Descent Rate
For nonprecision approaches, conversion tables typically show a vertical descent angle and a recommended rate of descent based on the groundspeed.
Example: If you are flying this VOR approach at a groundspeed of 90 knots, you should descend at 481 feet per minute to maintain the descent angle of 3.02°.

Figure 7-36. Jeppesen Descent/Timing Conversion

TIME AND SPEED TABLE AND RATE OF CLIMB/DESCENT TABLE

The FAA provides a **time and speed table** that indicates elapsed times to the MAP based on groundspeed. A separate Rate of Climb/Descent table contained in each *Terminal Procedures Publication* provides the recommended rate of descent to maintain a specific angle of descent. [Figure 7-37]

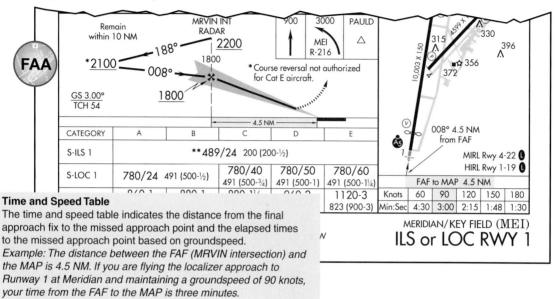

Time and Speed Table
The time and speed table indicates the distance from the final approach fix to the missed approach point and the elapsed times to the missed approach point based on groundspeed.
Example: The distance between the FAF (MRVIN intersection) and the MAP is 4.5 NM. If you are flying the localizer approach to Runway 1 at Meridian and maintaining a groundspeed of 90 knots, your time from the FAF to the MAP is three minutes.

CLIMB/DESCENT ANGLE (degrees and tenths)	ft/NM	GROUND SPEED (knots)										
		60	90	120	150	180	210	240	270	300	330	3
2.0	210	210	320	425	530	635	743	850	955	1060	1165	1275
2.5	265	265	400	530	665	795	930	1060	1195	1325	1460	1590
2.7	287	287	430	574	717	860	1003	1147	1290	1433	1576	1720
2.8	297	297	446	595	743	892	1041	1189	1338	1486	1635	1783
2.9	308	308	462	616	770	924	1078	1232	1386	1539	1693	1847
3.0	318	318	478	637	797	956	1115	1274	1433	1593	1752	1911
3.1	329	329	494	659								

(VERTICAL PATH)

Descent Table
For a precision approach or an approach with vertical guidance (APV), a descent table contained in the *Terminal Procedures Publication* provides the recommended descent rate to establish the airplane on the glide slope or glide path at a particular groundspeed.
Example: If your groundspeed is 90 knots, your rate of descent should be 480 feet per minute to establish the airplane on a 3.0° glide slope angle.

Figure 7-37. FAA Time and Speed Table and Rate of Climb/Descent Table

LANDING MINIMUMS

Landing minimums, which contain both minimum visibility and minimum altitude requirements, have been established for each approach at a given airport. Factors that affect these minimums include the type of approach, type of approach lights installed, and obstructions in the approach or missed approach paths. The landing minimums you use are also affected by the equipment on board your aircraft, your approach speed, and whether you are executing a straight-in landing or flying a circling approach.

 Landing minimums published on instrument approach charts consist of both minimum visibility and minimum altitude requirements.

AIRCRAFT APPROACH CATEGORIES

Each aircraft is placed into an **approach category** based on its reference landing speed (V_{REF}). If V_{REF} is not specified, you must use a computed approach speed of $1.3V_{S0}$ (the stalling speed or minimums steady flight speed in the landing configuration) at the maximum certificated landing weight. For example, a V_{S0} of 50 knots times 1.3 equals a computed approach speed of 65 knots. This speed places your aircraft in approach category A. If you operate at a faster airspeed than the upper limit of the airspeed range of an aircraft category, you must use the minimums for the category that you your airspeed falls in. Although you must use higher category minimums if you are using a faster approach speed than that of your aircraft's category, you may not use the minimums of a slower approach category. These requirements ensure your airplane is contained within the area of protection of the approach design. For example, based on speed, your airplane is allowed a certain height loss at decision altitude and must be contained within a specific area during the missed approach turn or while circling to land. [Figure 7-38].

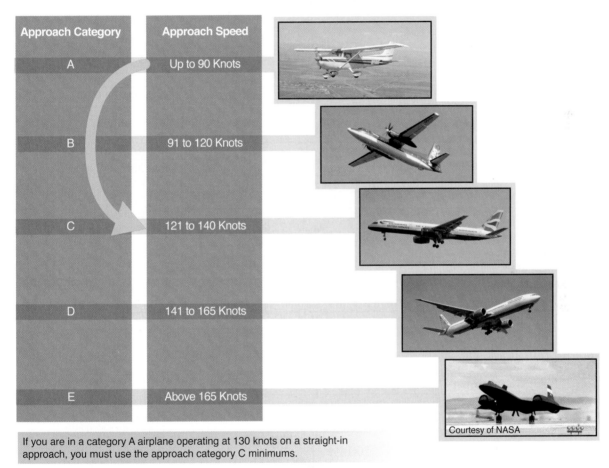

SECTION A ■ **Approach Charts**

CATEGORY	A	B	C	D	E
S-ILS 1	**489/24 200 (200-½)				
S-LOC 1	780/24 491 (500-½)		780/40 491 (500-¾)	780/50 491 (500-1)	780/60 491 (500-1¼)
CIRCLING	860-1 563 (600-1)	880-1 583 (600-1)	880-1½ 583 (600-1½)	960-2 663 (700-2)	1120-3 823 (900-3)

Figure 7-38. When you have determined your aircraft's approach category, you can use the landing minimums section of the approach chart to determine your visibility and descent minimums for that procedure. Although Category E is shown, it usually is not included on approach charts, because it applies only to certain military aircraft. If it is not shown, Category D applies to all civil aircraft with a computed approach speed of 141 knots or more.

VISIBILITY REQUIREMENTS

According to FAR 91.175, you may descend below the approach minimums only if the flight visibility is not less than the visibility prescribed in the approach procedure. Visibility is listed on approach charts in either statute miles or hundreds of feet. When it is expressed in miles or fractions of miles, it is usually a prevailing visibility that is reported by an accredited observer such as tower or weather personnel. When the visibility is expressed in hundreds of feet, it is determined through the use of runway visual range (RVR) equipment. RVR figures represent the horizontal distance a pilot should see when looking down the runway from a moving airplane. If RVR minimums for landing are prescribed for an instrument approach procedure, but RVR is inoperative and cannot be reported for the intended runway at the time, RVR minimums should be converted and applied as ground visibility. [Figure 7-39]

> **FAA** If RVR minimums for landing are prescribed for an instrument approach procedure, but RVR is inoperative and cannot be reported for the intended runway at the time, RVR minimums should be converted and applied as ground visibility. For example, RVR 24 translates to 1/2 statute mile visibility. See figure 7-39.

Jepp

	STRAIGHT-IN LANDING RWY1					**2** CIRCLE-TO-LAND	
	ILS			LOC (GS out)		Not Authorized Southeast of Rwys 1 and 22	
	With Local Altimeter Setting					With Local Altimeter Setting	
	DA(H) **489'** (200')			MDA(H) **780'** (491')		Max Kts	Altimeter Setting MDA(H)
	FULL	RAIL or ALS out		RAIL out	ALS out		
A	**1** RVR 24 or ½	RVR 40 or ¾	RVR 24 or ½	RVR 40 or ¾	RVR 50 or 1	90	860' (563')-1
B						120	880' (583')-1
C			RVR 40 or ¾	RVR 60 or 1¼		140	880' (583')-1½
D			RVR 50 or 1	1½			

RVR
The visibility minimum for the full ILS Runway 1 approach is RVR 24 or 2,400 feet. If RVR is not reported, ½ statute mile applies.

Prevailing Ground Visibility
The ground visibility for the circling approach for category A and B aircraft is 1 statute mile.

	With Hattiesburg-Laurel Regl Altimeter Setting						
			MDA(H) **920'** (631')				
				RAIL out	ALS out		
			RVR 24 or ½	RVR 40 or ¾	RVR 50 or 1	90	1000' (703')-1
						120	1020' (723')-1
C	RVR 40 or ¾	RVR 60 or 1¼	RVR 60 or 1¼	1¾		140	1020' (723')- 2
D			1½	2		165	1100' (803')- 2½

1 RVR 18 with Flight Director or Autopilot or HUD to DA.　　**2** Circling to Rwy 22 not authorized at night.

FAA

CATEGORY	A	B	C	D	E
S-ILS 1	** 489/24 200 (200-½)		780/40 491 (500-¾)	780/50 491 (500-1)	491 (500-1¼)
CIRCLING	860-1 563 (600-1)	880-1 583 (600-1)	880- 583 (600		

Prevailing Ground Visibility
The ground visibility for the circling approach for category A and B aircraft is 1 statute mile.

RVR
The visibility minimum for the full ILS Runway 1 approach is RVR 24 or 2,400 feet.

Converting RVR to Ground Visibility
To convert an RVR minimum to ground visibility if RVR is not reported, use the table found in the front of the *Terminal Procedures Publication* or in FAR 91.175.
Do not interpolate when you convert RVR values that fall between listed values; use the next higher RVR value.

RVR (feet)	Visibility (statute miles)
1,600	1/4
2,400	**1/2**
3,200	5/8
4,000	3/4
4,500	7/8
5,000	1
6,000	1 1/4

Figure 7-39. Jeppesen and FAA Landing Minimums Section – Visbility Requirements

MINIMUM DESCENT REQUIREMENTS

The landing minimums section includes the minimum altitude to which you are permitted to descend while performing the approach. The terms used to describe this altitude depend on the type of approach. Precision approaches and approaches with vertical guidance (APV) have a decision altitude in feet above MSL and a decision height in feet above touchdown. Jeppesen charts show a DA(H), as an MSL altitude followed by the height above touchdown (HAT) in parentheses. FAA charts show the MSL altitude with the HAT listed after the visibility requirement.

For nonprecision approaches, Jeppesen charts show an MDA(H) as a minimum descent altitude in feet MSL with the HAT, in the case of a straight-in landing, or HAA, in the case of a circling approach, shown in parentheses following it. The FAA shows the MDA and includes the HAT after the visibility requirement. [Figures 7-40 and 7-41]

 If the glide slope becomes inoperative during an ILS procedure, localizer minimums are used. See figures 7-40 and 7-41.

SECTION A ■ Approach Charts

Jepp	STRAIGHT-IN LANDING RWY1					**2** CIRCLE-TO-LAND	
	ILS		LOC (GS out)			Not Authorized Southeast of Rwys 1 and 22	
	With Local Altimeter Setting					With Local Altimeter Setting	
	DA(H) **489'** *(200')*		MDA(H) **780'** *(491')*		Max Kts	MDA(H)	
	FULL	RAIL or ALS out		RAIL out	ALS out		
A			RVR 24 or ½	RVR 40 or ¾	RVR 50 or 1	90	860' *(563')*-1
B	**1** RVR 24 or ½	RVR 40 or ¾				120	880' *(583')*-1
C			RVR 40 or ¾	RVR 60 or 1¼		140	880' *(583')*-1½
D			RVR 50 or 1	1½		165	960' *(663')*- 2
	With Hattiesburg-Laurel Regl Altimeter Setting					With Hattiesburg-Laurel Regl Altimeter Setting	
	DA(H) **627'** *(338')*		MDA(H) **920'** *(631')*		Max Kts	MDA(H)	
	FULL	RAIL or ALS out		RAIL out	ALS out		
A			RVR 24 or ½	RVR 40 or ¾	RVR 50 or 1	90	1000' *(703')*-1
B	RVR 40 or ¾	RVR 60 or 1¼				120	1020' *(723')*-1
C			RVR 60 or 1¼	1¾		140	1020' *(723')*- 2
D			1½	2		165	1100' *(803')*- 2½
1 RVR 18 with Flight Director or Autopilot or HUD to DA.				**2** Circling to Rwy 22 not authorized at night.			

Decision Altitude (DA) in Feet MSL
When flying the ILS approach to Runway 1, you must either continue the approach or execute a missed approach at the decision altitude of 489 feet MSL.

Decision Height (DH) in Feet Above Touchdown
At the decision altitude of 489 feet MSL, your decision height above touchdown measured from the touchdown zone elevation is 200 feet.

Minimum Descent Altitude (MDA) in Feet MSL
When flying the localizer-only approach to Runway 1, you must have the runway environment in sight to descend lower than the MDA of 780 feet MSL.

Height Above Touchdown (HAT)
At the MDA of 780 feet MSL, your height above touchdown, measured from the touchdown zone elevation, is 491 feet.

Conditions that Apply to Minimums
If you cannot obtain the local altimeter setting, you must use the Hattiesburg-Laurel Regional Airport altimeter setting, and higher minimums apply.

Minimum Descent Altitude (MDA) in Feet MSL
To descend lower than the MDA of 860 feet MSL when flying a circling approach to another runway, you must be continuously in a position from which you can make a descent to a landing on the intended runway using a normal rate of descent and normal maneuvering.

Height Above Airport (HAA)
At the MDA of 860 feet MSL, your height above the airport, which is measured above the highest point of an airport's usable runways, is 563 feet.

Figure 7-40. Jeppesen Landing Minimums Section — Minimum Descent Requirements.

SECTION A ■ Approach Charts

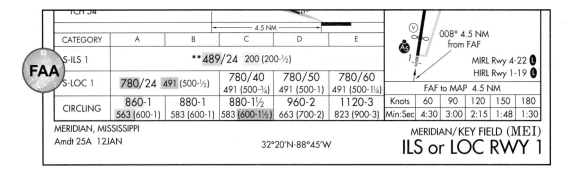

CATEGORY	A	B	C	D	E
S-ILS 1	**489/24** 200 (200-½)				
S-LOC 1	780/24 491 (500-½)		780/40 491 (500-¾)	780/50 491 (500-1)	780/60 491 (500-1¼)
CIRCLING	860-1 563 (600-1)	880-1 583 (600-1)	880-1½ 583 (600-1½)	960-2 663 (700-2)	1120-3 823 (900-3)

008° 4.5 NM from FAF

MIRL Rwy 4-22 **L**
HIRL Rwy 1-19 **L**

FAF to MAP 4.5 NM

Knots	60	90	120	150	180
Min:Sec	4:30	3:00	2:15	1:48	1:30

MERIDIAN, MISSISSIPPI
Amdt 25A 12JAN

32°20'N-88°45'W

MERIDIAN/KEY FIELD (MEI)
ILS or LOC RWY 1

Decision Altitude (DA) in Feet MSL
When flying the ILS approach to Runway 1, you must either continue the approach or execute a missed approach at the decision altitude of 489 feet MSL.

Decision Height (DH) in Feet Above Touchdown
When flying the ILS approach, at the decision altitude of 489 feet MSL, your decision height above touchdown measured from the touchdown zone is 200 feet.

Minimum Descent Altitude (MDA) in Feet MSL
When flying the localizer-only approach to Runway 1, you must have the runway environment in sight to descend lower than the MDA of 780 feet MSL.

Height Above Touchdown (HAT)
When flying the localizer-only approach, at the MDA of 780 feet MSL, your height above touchdown, measured from the touchdown zone elevation, is 491 feet.

Conditions that Apply to Minimums
If you cannot obtain the local altimeter setting, you must use the Hattiesburg-Laurel Regional Airport altimeter setting, and higher minimums apply.

Minimum Descent Altitude (MDA) in Feet MSL
To descend lower than the MDA of 860 feet MSL when flying a circling approach to another runway, you must be continuously in a position from which you can make a descent to a landing on the intended runway using a normal rate of descent and normal maneuvering.

Height Above Airport (HAA)
At the MDA of 860 feet MSL, your height above the airport, which is measured above the highest point of an airport's usable runways, is 563 feet.

The ceiling and visibility figures in parenthesis on FAA charts are used for planning purposes by the military.

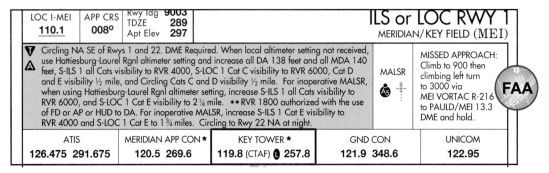

LOC I-MEI 110.1	APP CRS 008°	Rwy Idg 9003 TDZE 289 Apt Elev 297	ILS or LOC RWY 1 MERIDIAN/KEY FIELD (MEI)

Circling NA SE of Rwys 1 and 22. DME Required. When local altimeter setting not received, use Hattiesburg-Laurel Rgnl altimeter setting and increase all DA 138 feet and all MDA 140 feet, S-ILS 1 all Cats visibility to RVR 4000, S-LOC 1 Cat C visibility to RVR 6000, Cat D and E visibility ½ mile, and Circling Cats C and D visibility ½ mile. For inoperative MALSR, when using Hattiesburg-Laurel Rgnl altimeter setting, increase S-ILS 1 all Cats visibility to RVR 6000, and S-LOC 1 Cat E visibility to 2¼ mile. **RVR 1800 authorized with the use of FD or AP or HUD to DA. For inoperative MALSR, increase S-ILS 1 Cat E visibility to RVR 4000 and S-LOC 1 Cat E to 1¾ miles. Circling to Rwy 22 NA at night.

MALSR
A5

MISSED APPROACH: Climb to 900 then climbing left turn to 3000 via MEI VORTAC R-216 to PAULD/MEI 13.3 DME and hold.

FAA

ATIS	MERIDIAN APP CON ★	KEY TOWER ★	GND CON	UNICOM
126.475 291.675	120.5 269.6	119.8 (CTAF) **L** 257.8	121.9 348.6	122.95

Figure 7-41. FAA Landing Minimums Section – Minimum Descent Requirements

INOPERATIVE COMPONENTS

Landing minimums usually increase when a required component or visual aid becomes inoperative. If more than one component is inoperative, each minimum is raised to the highest minimum required by any single inoperative component. ILS glide slope inoperative minimums are published on instrument approach charts as localizer minimums. Jeppesen depicts inoperative component minimums in the landing minimums section. [Figure 7-42] For FAA charts, to determine the appropriate corrections to the landing minimums when an approach component is inoperative, consult the Inoperative Components or Visual Aids Table in the *Terminal Procedures Publication*. [Figures 7-43]

 If more than one component of an approach is unusable, use the highest minimum required by any single component that is unusable.

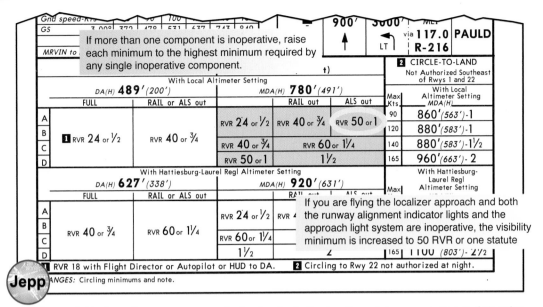

Figure 7-42. On a Jeppesen approach chart, refer to the landing minimums section to determine the appropriate corrections to your minimums.

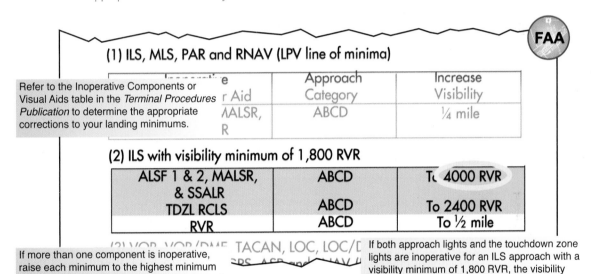

Figure 7-43. Using an FAA approach chart and the *Terminal Procedures Publication*, take these actions to determine your landing minimums with inoperative components.

FAA If an ILS visual aid is inoperative, the visibility requirements are raised on approaches where 1,800 RVR is authorized.

AIRPORT SKETCH

The FAA places an **airport sketch** in the lower left or right corner of each approach chart. The airport sketch enhances situational awareness by providing runway and airport environment information including identifying approach and lighting systems. The airport sketch uses a coded symbol placed adjacent to the runway to indicate the type of lighting system. [Figure 7-44]

Runway Information

- Runway numbers
- Runway length and width
- Displaced threshold
- Approach runway touchdown zone elevation

Airport Environment Information

- Airport elevation
- Position and elevation of the control tower
- Location of the airport beacon
- Position and elevation of selected reference points

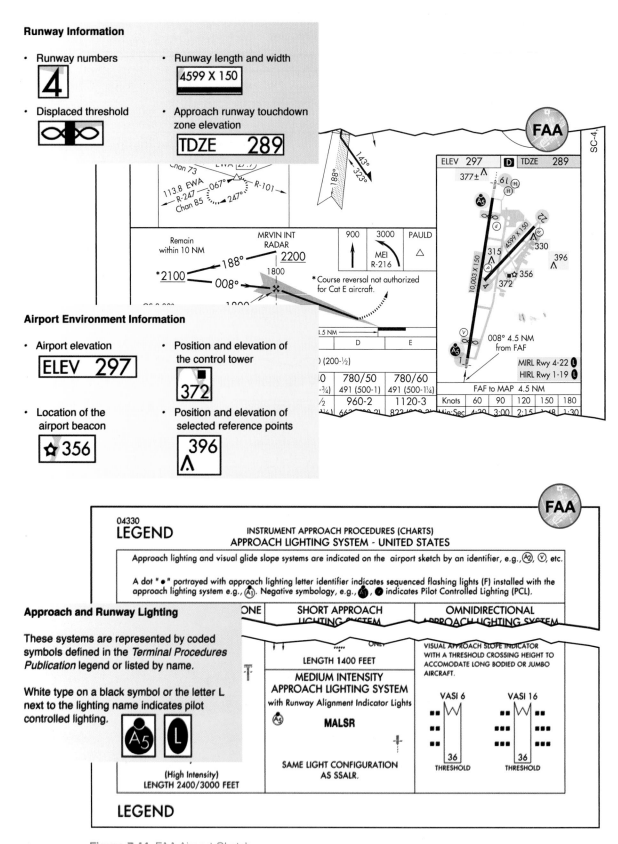

Approach and Runway Lighting

These systems are represented by coded symbols defined in the *Terminal Procedures Publication* legend or listed by name.

White type on a black symbol or the letter L next to the lighting name indicates pilot controlled lighting.

Figure 7-44. FAA Airport Sketch

AIRPORT CHART AND AIRPORT DIAGRAM

Instead of an airport sketch on the approach chart, Jeppesen uses a separate airport chart for each airport. This chart is usually located on the reverse side of the first approach chart for a given airport. At larger airports, Jeppesen may provide additional airport charts to cover more detailed information. Like Jeppesen's approach chart, the airport chart is divided into several sections. [Figure 7-45]

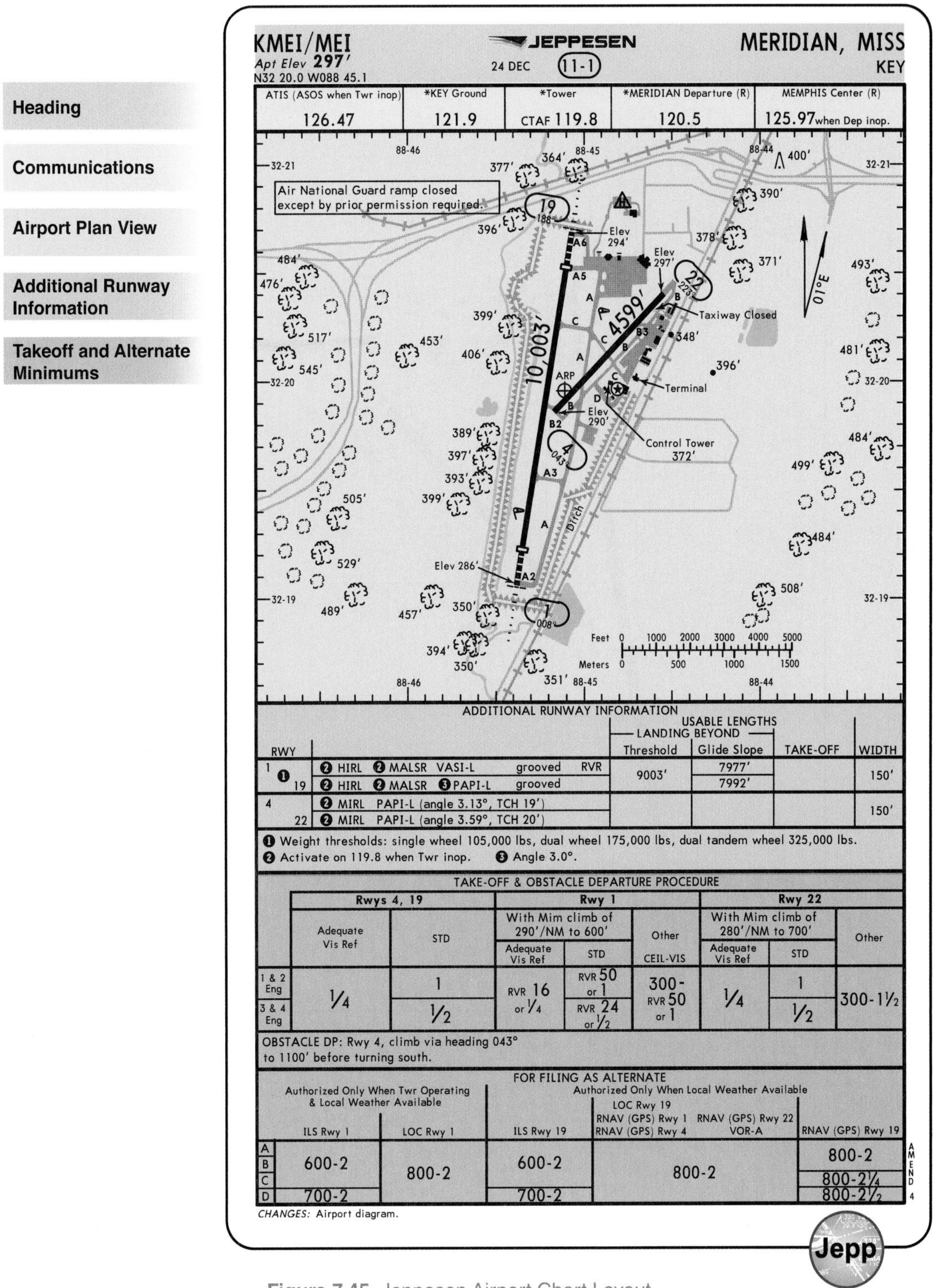

Heading

Communications

Airport Plan View

Additional Runway Information

Takeoff and Alternate Minimums

Figure 7-45. Jeppesen Airport Chart Layout

SECTION A ■ **Approach Charts**

SECTION A ■ **Approach Charts**

The FAA provides a full-page airport diagram for selected airports to assist the movement of ground traffic where complex runway and taxiway configurations exist. The airport diagram provides communication frequencies and more detailed runway and airport environment information than is shown on the airport sketch but is not divided into separate sections like the approach chart. [Figure 7-46]

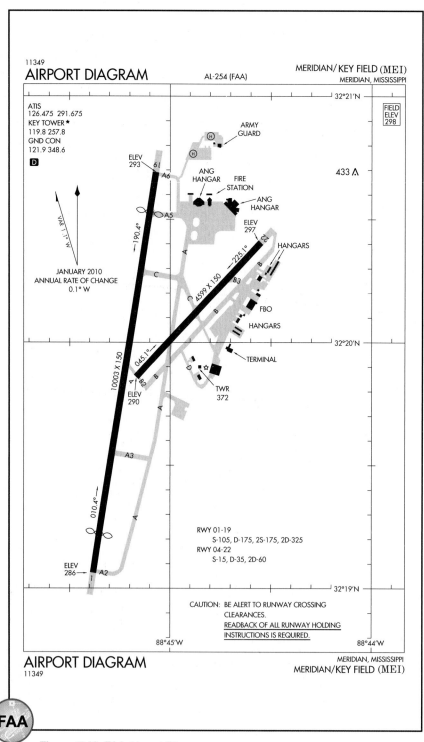

Figure 7-46. FAA Airport Diagram

HEADING AND COMMUNICATIONS

Both the Jeppesen airport chart and the FAA airport diagram show the airport name, identifier and location, as well as a chat index number and effective dates. On Jeppesen airport charts, communication frequencies are listed in the order in which they are normally used during departure. [Figures 7-47 and 7-48]

Airport Identification
Airport identification information includes the city, state, and airport name as well as the airport ICAO identifier.

Chart Dates
The chart shows a revision date and lists an effective date if the chart is issued before you can use it. You should continue to use the previous chart until the effective date.

Chart Index Number
The chart index number helps you file a chart and distinguish certain features.

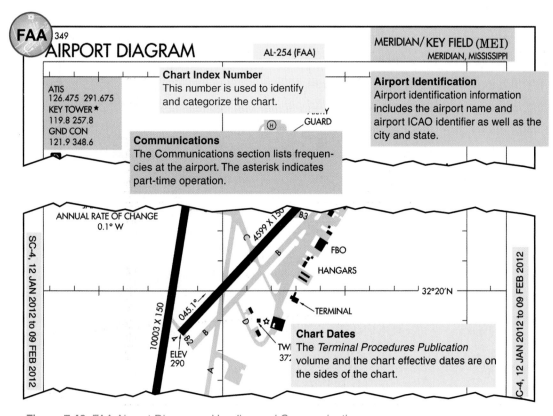

Elevation and Latitude/Longitude
This section includes the airport elevation and the latitude and longitude of the official airport location.

Communications
The Communications section lists frequencies in the order in which you normally use them when departing the airport.

Figure 7-47. Jeppesen Airport Chart – Heading and Communications Sections

Chart Index Number
This number is used to identify and categorize the chart.

Airport Identification
Airport identification information includes the airport name and airport ICAO identifier as well as the city and state.

Communications
The Communications section lists frequencies at the airport. The asterisk indicates part-time operation.

Chart Dates
The *Terminal Procedures Publication* volume and the chart effective dates are on the sides of the chart.

Figure 7-48. FAA Airport Diagram – Heading and Communications

SECTION A ■ **Approach Charts**

AIRPORT ENVIRONMENT

A plan view of the airport provides airport environment information, such as runway data and lighting systems. The **airport reference point (ARP)**, shown on Jeppesen charts, is the approximate geometric center of all usable runway surfaces. The official latitude and longitude coordinates are derived from the ARP. [Figures 7-49 and 7-50]

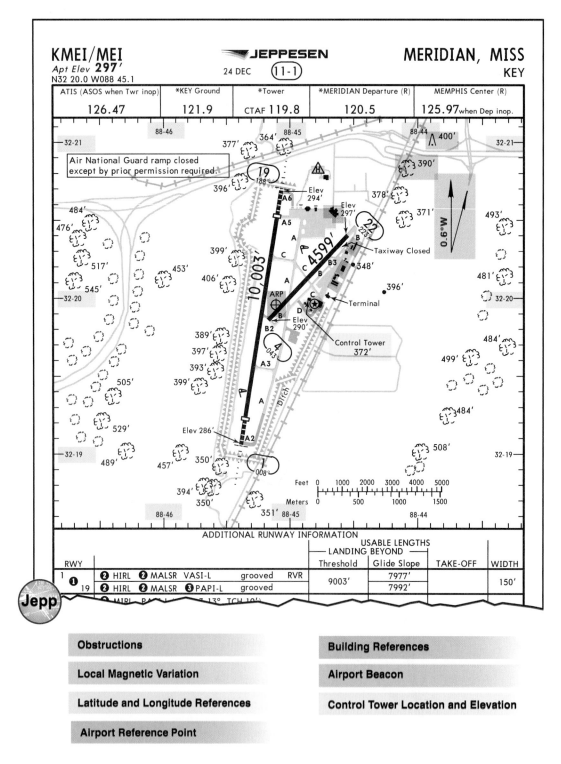

SECTION A ▪ Approach Charts

Figure 7-49. Jeppesen Airport Chart – Plan View; Airport Environment

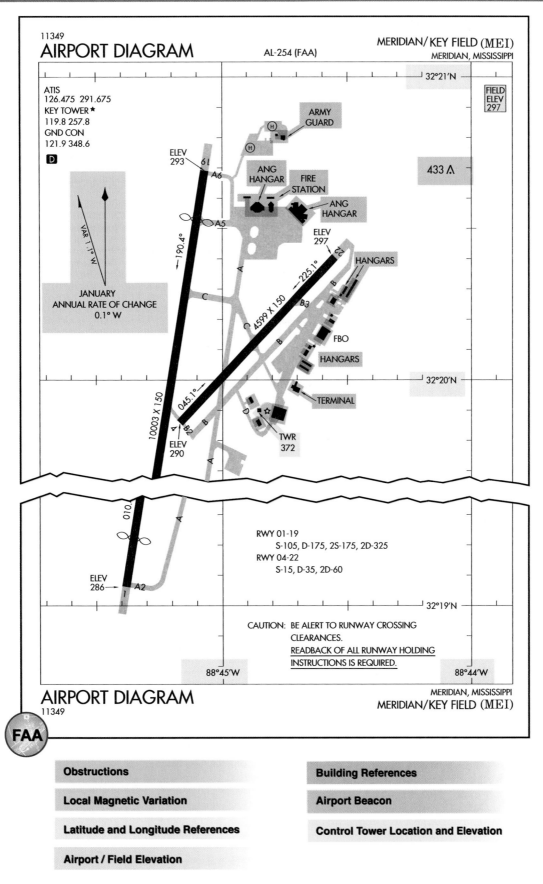

Figure 7-50. FAA Airport Diagram – Plan View; Airport Environment

RUNWAY INFORMATION

The Jeppesen airport chart shows runway and lighting data on the plan view as well as in the additional runway information section. Jeppesen and the FAA both provide information regarding runway incursion hotspots, if applicable. Jeppesen shows detailed hotspot information below the additional runway information, and the FAA lists this information under Hotspots in the *Terminal Procedures Publication*. [Figures 7-51 and 7-52]

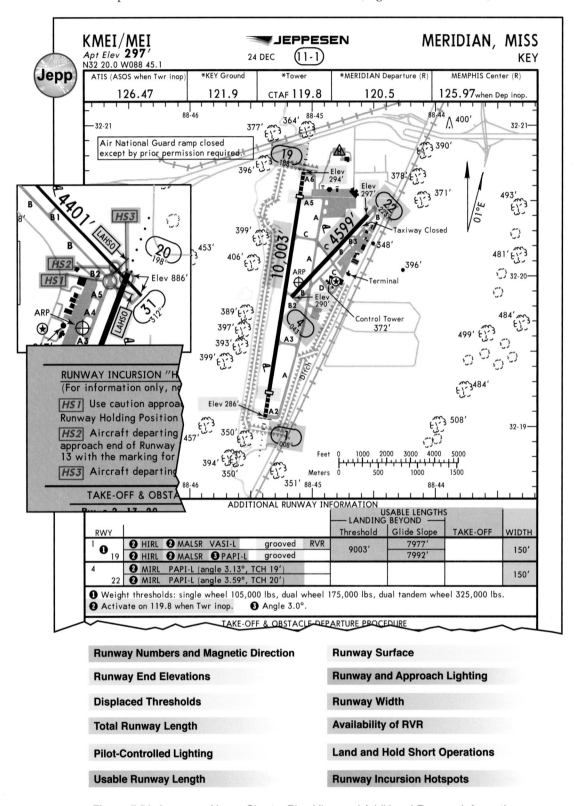

Runway Numbers and Magnetic Direction

Runway Surface

Runway End Elevations

Runway and Approach Lighting

Displaced Thresholds

Runway Width

Total Runway Length

Availability of RVR

Pilot-Controlled Lighting

Land and Hold Short Operations

Usable Runway Length

Runway Incursion Hotspots

Figure 7-51. Jeppesen Airport Chart – Plan View and Additional Runway Information.

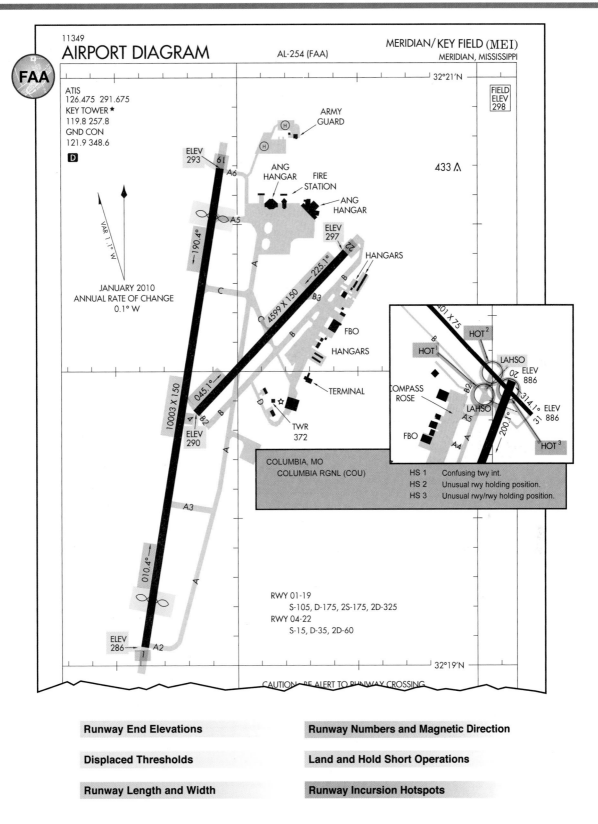

Figure 7-52. FAA Airport Diagram – Plan View and Additional Runway Information.

Runway End Elevations

Displaced Thresholds

Runway Length and Width

Runway Numbers and Magnetic Direction

Land and Hold Short Operations

Runway Incursion Hotspots

ALTERNATE AIRPORTS

When you obtain a weather briefing as you prepare for an IFR cross-country flight, you must determine whether you need to list an alternate airport in your flight plan. Both Jeppesen and FAA charts provide information regarding nonstandard takeoff and alternate minimums. You must plan for and include an alternate airport in your flight plan if the destination weather forecast for your estimated time of arrival (plus or minus one hour) indicates a ceiling of less than 2,000 feet or a visibility of less than three statute miles. To use an airport as an alternate, you must determine if the forecast weather at the estimated time of arrival at the alternate, plus or minus one hour, meets or exceeds specific alternate minimums. The following standard alternate minimums apply:

- For a precision approach procedure — a 600-foot ceiling and two statute miles visibility.
- For a nonprecision approach procedure — an 800-foot ceiling and two statute miles visibility.
- For an airport with no instrument approach procedure — a ceiling and visibility that allow for descent from the MEA, approach, and landing under basic VFR conditions.

The Jeppesen airport chart includes both standard and nonstandard alternate minimums as well as restrictions to alternate minimums for specific approaches. [Figure 7-53] When you use an FAA approach chart, you must refer to the approach chart and then the *Terminal Procedures Publication* to determine whether you may use the airport as an alternate and to determine the nonstandard alternate minimums specified for the procedure. [Figure 7-54]

	Authorized Only When Twr Operating & Local Weather Available		FOR FILING AS ALTERNATE			**Jepp**
			Authorized Only When Local Weather Available			
	ILS Rwy 1	LOC Rwy 1	ILS Rwy 19	LOC Rwy 19 RNAV (GPS) Rwy 1 RNAV (GPS) Rwy 22 RNAV (GPS) Rwy 4 VOR-A		RNAV (GPS) Rwy 19
A	600-2	800-2	600-2	800-2		800-2
B						
C						800-2¼
D	700-2		700-2			800-2½

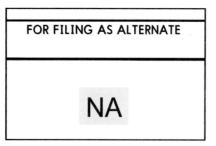

FOR FILING AS ALTERNATE

NA

Figure 7-53. Jeppesen Airport Chart – Takeoff and Alternate Minimums; Alternate Minimums

Restrictions to Alternate Minimums
Notes indicate restrictions to alternate minimums. These restrictions are specific conditions under which you can use the listed minimums.

Standard and Nonstandard Alternate Minimums
These include visibility and ceiling minimums that apply to the specific aircraft category and type of approach.

Alternate Not Authorized
The letters NA indicate that using this airport as an alternate is not authorized.

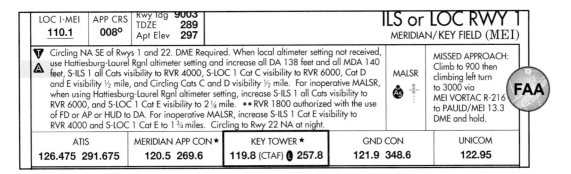

LOC I-MEI	APP CRS	Rwy Idg **9003**	ILS or LOC RWY 1
110.1	**008°**	TDZE **289** Apt Elev **297**	MERIDIAN/KEY FIELD (MEI)

Circling NA SE of Rwys 1 and 22. DME Required. When local altimeter setting not received, use Hattiesburg-Laurel Rgnl altimeter setting and increase all DA 138 feet and all MDA 140 feet, S-ILS 1 all Cats visibility to RVR 4000, S-LOC 1 Cat C visibility to RVR 6000, Cat D and E visibility ½ mile, and Circling Cats C and D visibility ½ mile. For inoperative MALSR, when using Hattiesburg-Laurel Rgnl altimeter setting, increase S-ILS 1 all Cats visibility to RVR 6000, and S-LOC 1 Cat E visibility to 2¼ mile. **RVR 1800 authorized with the use of FD or AP or HUD to DA. For inoperative MALSR, increase S-ILS 1 Cat E visibility to RVR 4000 and S-LOC 1 Cat E to 1¾ miles. Circling to Rwy 22 NA at night.

MALSR

MISSED APPROACH: Climb to 900 then climbing left turn to 3000 via MEI VORTAC R-216 to PAULD/MEI 13.3 DME and hold.

FAA

ATIS	MERIDIAN APP CON ★	KEY TOWER ★	GND CON	UNICOM
126.475 291.675	120.5 269.6	119.8 (CTAF) 🔊 257.8	121.9 348.6	122.95

 NA

NAME	ALTERNATE MINIMUMS

MERIDIAN, MS

KEY FIELD .... ILS or LOC Rwy 1[1][2][3]
ILS or LOC Rwy 19[2][3]
RNAV (GPS) Rwy 1[3][4]
RNAV (GPS) Rwy 4[3][4]
RNAV (GPS) Rwy 19[3][5]
RNAV (GPS) Rwy 22[3][4]
VOR-A[3][4]

[1]NA when control tower closed.
[2]ILS, Category D, 700-2; Category E, 900-3. LOC, Category E, 900-3.
[3]NA when local weather not available.
[4]Category E, 900-3.
[5]Category C, 800-2¼; Category D, 800-2½; Category E, 1100-3.

The A Symbol
You should look in the Notes and Limitations box in the pilot briefing information section for an A symbol, which means that the airport has nonstandard alternate minimums.

Alternate Not Authorized
The letters "NA next to the A symbol mean that this airport is not authorized as an alternate. The reason might be that the airport navaid is unmonitored, or there is no weather reporting available.

Alternate Minimums Section
If you see the A symbol, refer to the specific airport in the Alternate Minimums section of the *Terminal Procedures Publication* to find the alternate minimums that apply to your aircraft category for the approach procedure.
Example: The nonstandard alternate minimum of a 700-foot ceiling applies for the ILS approach for category D aircraft.

Restrictions to Alternate Minimums
Refer to the additional notes that indicate restrictions to alternate minimums for specific conditions under which you can use the listed minimums.
Examples:
- If you are planning to use the ILS or localizer approaches for Runway 1, the tower must be operating and local weather available for you to file a flight plan with this airport as an alternate.
- Local weather must be available if you are planning to use any other approach.

Figure 7-54. On FAA approach charts, the A symbol in the pilot briefing information means the airport has nonstandard alternate minimums and you must refer to the Terminal Procedures Publication for additional information.

SUMMARY CHECKLIST

✓ A precision approach (PA) provides lateral guidance to align the airplane with the runway and vertical guidance in the form of a glide slope indication.

✓ An approach with vertical guidance (APV) provides lateral guidance to align the airplane with the runway and vertical guidance in the form of a glide path display, but does not meet the criteria to be a precision approach.

✓ A nonprecision approach provides only lateral guidance.

✓ To transition from the enroute structure to the approach structure, an approach might use a feeder route, terminal arrival area (TAA), radar vectors, or a standard terminal arrival route (STAR).

✓ The initial approach segment, used to align the airplane with the approach course, begins at an initial approach fix (IAF) and usually ends where it joins the intermediate approach segment.

✓ The intermediate segment, designed to position the airplane for the final descent to the airport, begins at the intermediate fix (IF), or intermediate point, and ends at the beginning of the final approach segment.

✓ The final approach segment allows you to navigate safely to a point at which, if the required visual references are in sight, you can continue the approach to a landing.

✓ The final approach segment begins at a final approach fix (FAF), final approach point (FAP), or where you begin the descent when referring to vertical descent indications.

✓ The touchdown zone elevation (TDZE) is the highest elevation in the first 3,000 feet of the runway landing surface.

✓ The airport/field elevation is the highest point of an airport's usable runways measured in feet from mean sea level.

✓ The threshold crossing height (TCH) is the AGL height at which you cross the threshold if you continue the approach to a landing while remaining on the glide slope/path.

✓ The decision altitude (DA), referenced to mean sea level, is the altitude at which you must decide whether to continue the approach or initiate a missed approach. The decision height (DH) is the corresponding height above touchdown (HAT) measured from the touchdown zone elevation.

✓ The minimum descent altitude (MDA), referenced to mean sea level, is the minimum altitude to which you may descend and remain until you either identify the runway environment or, lacking the required visual references, perform a missed approach. Corresponding to the MDA is the height above touchdown (HAT) for a straight-in landing, or the height above the airport elevation (HAA) for a circling approach.

✓ The missed approach segment is used to navigate to a point where you can attempt another approach or continue to another airport.

✓ The missed approach segment begins at the decision altitude for precision approaches and approaches with vertical guidance or at a missed approach point (MAP), which is identified as a fix, navaid, or an elapsed time after you cross the final approach fix for nonprecision approaches.

✓ Approach lighting systems start at the runway threshold and extend 2,400 feet to 3,000 feet into the approach area for a precision approach and 1,400 to 1,500 feet for a nonprecision approach.

✓ The procedure title in the heading section on an approach chart indicates the type of approach system used and the equipment required to perform the final approach segment.

✓ When a procedure title has an alphabetical suffix, such as VOR-A, it means the procedure does not meet the criteria for a straight-in landing.

✓ The chart dates in the heading section indicate a change to any chart information. If a procedural update has been made, a procedural amendment reference date is located on the lower left of the chart.

✓ Communication frequencies are listed in the order in which they are normally used when approaching the airport. Part-time facilities are indicated by an asterisk.

✓ Jeppesen approach briefing information includes the primary navigation information, final approach course, altitude at OM or FAF, DA(H) or MDA(H), airport and touchdown zone elevations, missed approach instructions, and notes and limitations.

✓ FAA pilot briefing information includes primary navigation information, the approach course, runway information, notes and limitations, approach lighting, and missed approach instructions.

✓ The minimum safe/sector altitude (MSA) provides 1,000 feet of obstruction clearance within 25 nautical miles of the indicated facility, unless some other distance is specified.

✓ Operating at or above the MSA does not guarantee navigation nor communication coverage, and the MSA is designed only for use in an emergency or during VFR flight, such as during a VFR approach at night

✓ The plan view is an overhead presentation of the entire approach procedure, including navaid facility information, feeder routes, and the approach procedure track, including course reversals and the missed approach track, approach fixes, minimum altitudes, and terrain and obstacles.

✓ When the procedure turn is depicted on the plan view, you may reverse course any way you desire as long as you make the turn on the same side of the approach course as the symbol and the complete the turn within the distance specified in the profile view.

✓ If a holding or teardrop pattern is shown instead of a procedure turn, it is the only approved method of course reversal. If a procedure turn, holding pattern, or teardrop pattern is not shown, a course reversal is not authorized.

✓ There may be higher uncharted terrain or man-made structures than those depicted on the approach charts. Adherence to the minimum altitudes depicted on approach charts provides terrain and obstacle clearance.

✓ Generalized terrain contour lines, values, and gradient tints depicted in brown do not ensure clearance above or around the terrain and you must not rely on them for descent below the minimum altitudes specified on the approach procedure.

✓ The profile view shows the approach from the side and displays the flight path and facilities, as well as minimum altitudes in feet MSL.

✓ Missed approach icons provide symbols depicting the initial up-and-out maneuvers. Refer to the missed approach instructions in the heading section, plan view, and profile view for complete information about the missed approach procedure.

✓ Stepdown fixes are used along approach segments to allow you to descend to a lower altitude, and identifying specific stepdown fixes may permit lower landing minimums.

✓ A visual descent point (VDP) represents the point from which you can make a normal descent to a landing, assuming you have the runway in sight and you are starting from the minimum descent altitude.

✓ The descent/timing conversion table on Jeppesen charts provides the time and distance from the FAF to the MAP, the glide slope, glide path, or vertical descent angle, and the applicable descent rates.

SECTION A ■ Approach Charts

SECTION A ■ **Approach Charts**

✓ The FAA time and speed table indicates elapsed times to the MAP based on groundspeed. A separate Rate of Climb/Descent table contained in each *Terminal Procedures Publication* provides the recommended rate of descent for specific descent angles.

✓ The lighting box graphically depicts the applicable approach light system (ALS) and/or the visual glide slope indicator (VGSI) for the straight-in approach runway. VASI or PAPI systems are indicated on the appropriate side of the runway.

✓ Landing minimums (visibility and minimum altitude requirements) are based on the type of approach, approach lights, and obstructions. The landing minimums you use depend on the equipment onboard your airplane, your approach speed, and whether you are performing a straight-in landing or flying a circling approach.

✓ Each aircraft is placed into an approach category based on its reference landing speed (V_{REF}), if specified. If V_{REF} is not specified, you must use a computed approach speed of $1.3V_{S0}$ (the stalling speed or minimums steady flight speed in the landing configuration) at the maximum certificated landing weight.

✓ If you operate at an airspeed in excess of the upper limit of the airspeed range of an aircraft category, you must use the minimums for the higher category.

✓ According to FAR 91.175, you can descend below the approach minimums only if the flight visibility is not less than the visibility prescribed in the approach procedure.

✓ Visibility is listed on approach charts in either statute miles or hundreds of feet (RVR).

✓ If RVR minimums are prescribed for an instrument approach procedure, but RVR is not reported for the intended runway, convert RVR minimums to ground visibility.

✓ In the landing minimums section, precision approaches and APV have a DA in feet MSL and a DH in feet above touchdown. For nonprecision approaches, the charts show an MDA in feet MSL with the HAT, for straight-in landings, or HAA, for circling approaches, shown in parentheses following it.

✓ If more than one approach component is inoperative, each minimum is raised to the highest minimum required by any single inoperative component.

✓ ILS glide slope inoperative minimums are published on instrument approach charts as localizer minimums.

✓ Jeppesen depicts inoperative component minimums in the Landing Minimums section. For FAA charts, consult the Inoperative Components or Visual Aids Table in the *Terminal Procedures Publication.*

✓ The airport sketch on the FAA approach chart provides runway and airport environment information, including approach and lighting systems.

✓ The FAA provides a full-page airport diagram with communication frequencies and detailed runway and airport information for selected airports.

✓ Jeppesen uses a separate airport chart for each airport. The chart is normally located on the reverse side of the first approach chart for a given airport.

✓ The heading section of the Jeppesen airport chart shows the airport name, identifier, elevation, location, chart date, and index number.

✓ Communication frequencies are listed in the order in which they are normally used during departure on Jeppesen airport charts.

✓ The plan view of a Jeppesen airport chart is an overhead view of the airport that provides information about runways, lighting systems, latitude and longitude coordinates, and the airport reference point (ARP).

✓ Additional runway and lighting and runway incursion hotspot information is shown below the plan view of Jeppesen airport charts.

✓ You must plan for and include an alternate airport in your flight plan if the destination forecast weather at your estimated time of arrival (plus or minus one hour) indicates a ceiling of less than 2,000 feet or a visibility of less than three statute miles.

✓ To use an airport as an alternate, determine if the forecast weather at the estimated time of arrival at the alternate, plus or minus one hour, meets or exceeds the alternate minimums specified for the approach procedure (non-standard alternate minimums).

✓ If you see the A symbol on FAA charts, refer to the Alternate Minimums section of the *Terminal Procedures Publication* to find the nonstandard alternate minimums.

✓ The standard alternate minimums for precision approaches are a 600-foot ceiling and two statute miles visibility. For nonprecision approaches, an 800-foot ceiling and two statute miles apply. For an airport with no instrument approach procedure, the alternate minimums are a ceiling and visibility that allow for descent from the MEA, approach, and landing under basic VFR conditions.

KEY TERMS

Instrument Approach Procedure (IAP)

Precision Approach (PA)

Approach with Vertical Guidance (APV)

Nonprecision Approach (NPA)

Feeder Routes

Initial Approach Fix (IAF)

Intermediate Fix (IF)

Final Approach Fix (FAF)

Final Approach Point (FAP)

Touchdown Zone Elevation (TDZE)

Airport/Field Elevation

Threshold Crossing Height (TCH)

Decision Altitude (DA)

Minimum Descent Altitude (MDA)

Height Above Touchdown (HAT)

Height Above Airport (HAA)

Missed Approach Point (MAP)

Minimum Safe/Sector Altitude (MSA)

Course Reversal

Procedure Turn

Stepdown Fix

Visual Descent Point (VDP)

Descent/Timing Conversion Table

Time and Speed Table

Landing Minimums

Approach Category

Airport Sketch

Airport Reference Point (ARP)

QUESTIONS

1. Name the four segments of instrument approach procedures.

2. Select the true statement regarding the transition from the enroute structure to the approach structure.
   A. You will only receive radar vectors to transition to the approach structure if you have a navigation equipment failure.
   B. Feeder routes provide a link between an enroute fix and the initial approach fix.
   C. RNAV (GPS) approach design requires feeder routes to navigate from an enroute fix to the initial approach fix.

3. At what points do the final approach segment for a precision approach or an approach with vertical guidance begins and end?
   A. Begins at the final approach fix and ends upon landing or performing the missed approach at the minimum descent altitude.
   B. Begins at the final approach point and ends upon landing or performing the missed approach after crossing a fix identified as the missed approach point.
   C. Begins where the airplane intercepts the glide slope/glide path and ends upon landing or performing the missed approach at the decision altitude.

Refer to the Jeppesen Twin Falls, Idaho ILS or LOC Rwy 25 approach chart to answer questions 4 through 18.

4. When Twin Falls Approach is not operating, what facility can you use as an alternate contact?
   A. Salt Lake Center
   B. Twin Falls Tower
   C. An alternate facility is not necessary because Twin Falls Approach operates full time.

5. What defines the sectors of the MSA circle?
   A. Radials from Twin Falls VOR
   B. Bearings to the TW locator outer marker
   C. Radii emanating from the airport reference point (ARP)

6. On what frequency can you activate pilot controlled lighting?
   A. 135.02
   B. 118.05
   C. 118.2

7. Identify the ILS localizer frequency and final approach course.

8. True/False. PAPI is available on the left side of Runway 25.

9. On the LOC (GS out) approach, how can the MAP be identified?
   A. When crossing the middle marker
   B. At 0.8 DME from the Twin Falls VORTAC only
   C. At 0.8 DME from the Twin Falls VORTAC, or timing from STRIK

10. Explain the purpose of the missed approach icons.

11. What is the minimum visibility requirement for a Category A aircraft flying the ILS approach with RAIL or ALS inoperative?

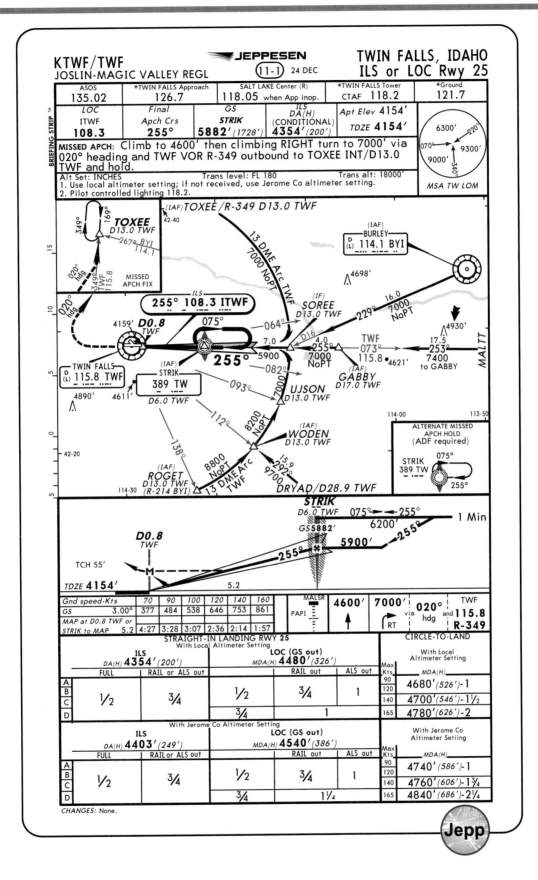

Match the following descriptions to the appropriate altitudes.

12. Touchdown zone elevation

13. Initial altitude to which you climb when executing the missed approach procedure

14. Decision altitude

15. Glide slope intercept altitude

16. Circle to land MDA for Category A aircraft

17. Minimum altitude at which you should perform the holding pattern course reversal

18. MDA for the localizer approach

A. 4,354 feet MSL

B. 5,900 feet MSL

C. 4,154 feet MSL

D. 6,200 feet MSL

E. 4,480 feet MSL

F. 4,680 feet MSL

G. 4,600 feet MSL

Refer to the FAA Dallas Love Field ILS or LOC RWY 31L approach chart to answer
questions 19 through 30.

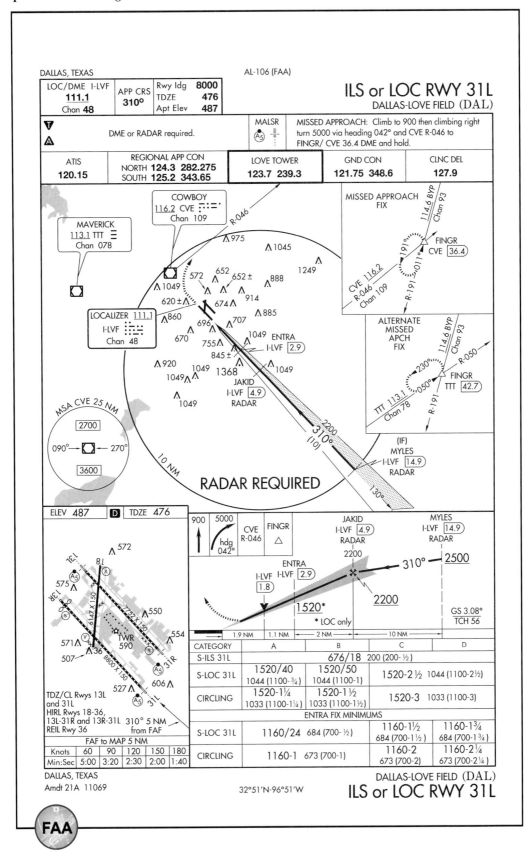

SECTION A ■ Approach Charts

19. What is the appropriate frequency to receive airport information at Dallas Love Field?

20. What is the elevation of Dallas Love Field?
     A. 485 feet MSL
     B. 487 feet MSL
     C. 685 feet MSL

21. Identify the ILS localizer frequency and final approach course.

22. What is the minimum glide slope intercept altitude when you are inbound on the intermediate approach segment?
     A. 1,520 feet MSL
     B. 2,200 feet MSL
     C. 2,500 feet MSL

23. If the glide slope becomes inoperative, resulting in a localizer approach, where is the final approach fix located?
     A. At ENTRA, identified by 2.9 DME on the localizer (I-LVF)
     B. At JAKID, identified by radar or 4.9 DME on the localizer (I-LVF)
     C. At MYLES, identified by radar or 4.9 DME on the localizer (I-LVF)

24. At what height will you cross the runway threshold if you remain on the glide slope/ glide path and continue the approach to a landing?
     A. 50 feet
     B. 56 feet
     C. 200 feet

25. What is the difference in feet between the touchdown zone elevation and airport elevation?
     A. 2 feet
     B. 5 feet
     C. 11 feet

26. According to straight-in landing minimums, what is the decision altitude for a Category A aircraft?
     A. 676 feet MSL
     B. 200 feet MSL
     C. 1,160 feet MSL

27. If the glide slope is not operational, what is the straight-in MDA?
     A. 1,520 feet MSL if you can identify ENTRA
     B. 1,160 if you can identify ENTRA
     C. 676 feet MSL

28. If you maintain a groundspeed of 90 knots while flying a localizer approach, what is the elapsed time from JAKID to the MAP?

29. What is the MDA for a Category C aircraft performing a circling approach?

30. Which runways are equipped with MALSR installations?
     A. 18 and 36 only
     B. 18, 36, 31R, 13R
     C. 13L, 31L, and 31R only

31. True/False. When you are filing Dallas Love Field as an alternate airport, standard alternate minimums apply for all aircraft categories and all runways.

SECTION B
Approach Procedures

Under VFR, you fly the traffic pattern to prepare for landing and align your airplane with the final approach course. In IFR conditions, you perform an instrument approach procedure (IAP) to accomplish the same goal. While a standard rectangular traffic pattern is used at most airports, the direction and placement of the pattern, the altitude at which it is flown, and the procedures for entering and exiting the pattern might vary. A similar situation exists for instrument approaches. While IAPs have many basic features in common, each approach procedure is unique. [Figure 7-55]

Figure 7-55. When you understand the fundamental elements of instrument approaches, you will be able to apply this knowledge to interpret and execute specific procedures depicted on approach charts.

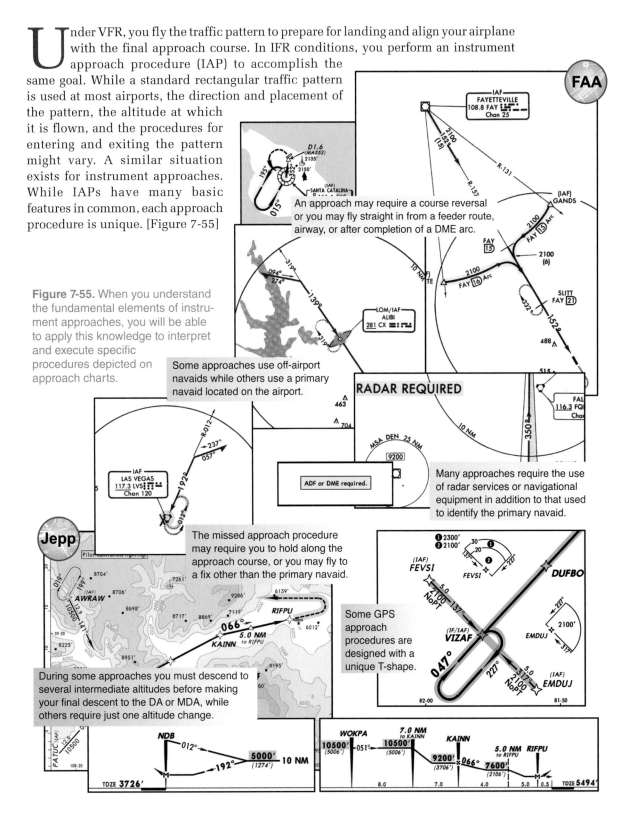

An approach may require a course reversal or you may fly straight in from a feeder route, airway, or after completion of a DME arc.

Some approaches use off-airport navaids while others use a primary navaid located on the airport.

Many approaches require the use of radar services or navigational equipment in addition to that used to identify the primary navaid.

The missed approach procedure may require you to hold along the approach course, or you may fly to a fix other than the primary navaid.

Some GPS approach procedures are designed with a unique T-shape.

During some approaches you must descend to several intermediate altitudes before making your final descent to the DA or MDA, while others require just one altitude change.

PREPARING FOR THE APPROACH

During your IFR flight planning, you should examine the approach charts for your destination to review procedures and symbology. As you approach your destination, ATC or ATIS will advise you of the type of approach to expect to help you plan your arrival actions. This information is not an ATC clearance or commitment and is subject to change. For example, a shift in wind direction, fluctuations in weather conditions, and a blocked runway are conditions that might result in changes to approach information that you previously received.

APPROACH OVERVIEW

As you near your destination, you should perform an **approach overview**. This is an initial review of the chart for the expected approach procedure so you can form a general picture of the procedure and to determine if there are any factors that might affect your ability to perform the approach. Landing minimums, terrain and obstacles, unique procedure features, and airport information are elements you should include in an approach overview. [Figure 7-56]

APPROACH BRIEFING

After ATC advises you as to which approach to expect, you should familiarize yourself and your copilot, if applicable, with the specific approach procedure by performing an **approach briefing**. It can be effective to verbalize the primary elements of the approach even if you are flying alone. You can brief these items in any order based on your preference and the chart layout. [Figure 7-57]

APPROACH CLEARANCE

Because several instrument approach procedures, using a variety of navaids, might be authorized for an airport, ATC might clear you for a specific approach procedure just to expedite traffic. You should notify the controller immediately if you want a different approach; however, it might be necessary for ATC to withhold clearance for the approach until such time as traffic conditions permit. If ATC does not specify an approach but states, *"cleared approach,"* you may perform any one of the authorized IAPs for that airport. This clearance does not permit you to fly a contact or visual approach. Except when you are being radar vectored to the final approach course, you must execute the entire procedure commencing at an IAF or an associated feeder route unless you receive an appropriate new or revised ATC clearance is received, or the IFR flight plan is canceled.

PERFORMING THE APPROACH

As you transition from the enroute to the terminal environment, your workload increases. During an instrument approach procedure, you must accomplish an extensive sequence of tasks and normally more precise flying and navigation skills are required than during enroute operations. On many approaches, an autopilot can fly a very accurate approach path and relieve you of some of the work. If your aircraft has an autopilot, be sure that you understand its operation and especially its limitations for use in an instrument approach.

This section introduces some general procedures for performing approaches, while more detailed descriptions of specific nonprecision and precision approach procedures are presented in Chapter 8.

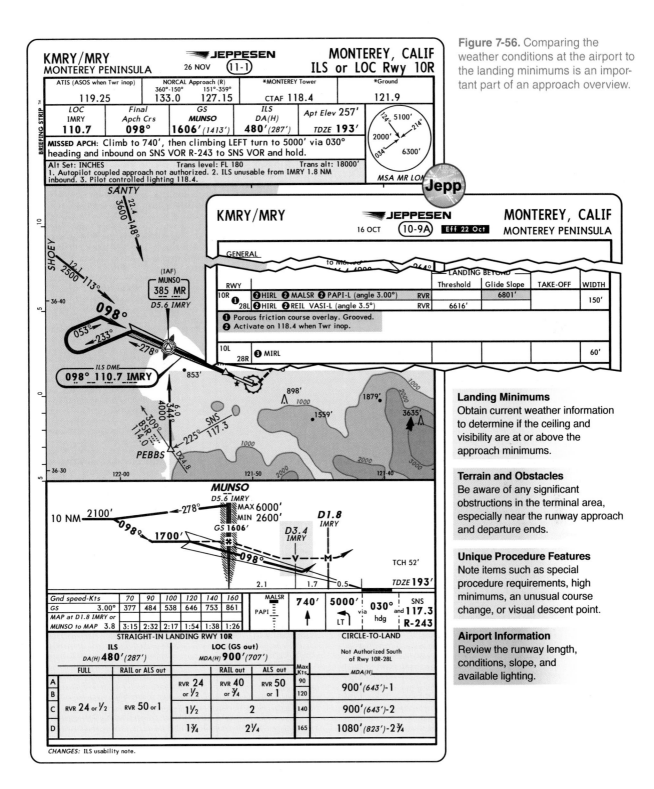

Figure 7-56. Comparing the weather conditions at the airport to the landing minimums is an important part of an approach overview.

SECTION B ■ **Approach Procedures**

Landing Minimums
Obtain current weather information to determine if the ceiling and visibility are at or above the approach minimums.

Terrain and Obstacles
Be aware of any significant obstructions in the terminal area, especially near the runway approach and departure ends.

Unique Procedure Features
Note items such as special procedure requirements, high minimums, an unusual course change, or visual descent point.

Airport Information
Review the runway length, conditions, slope, and available lighting.

SECTION B ■ Approach Procedures

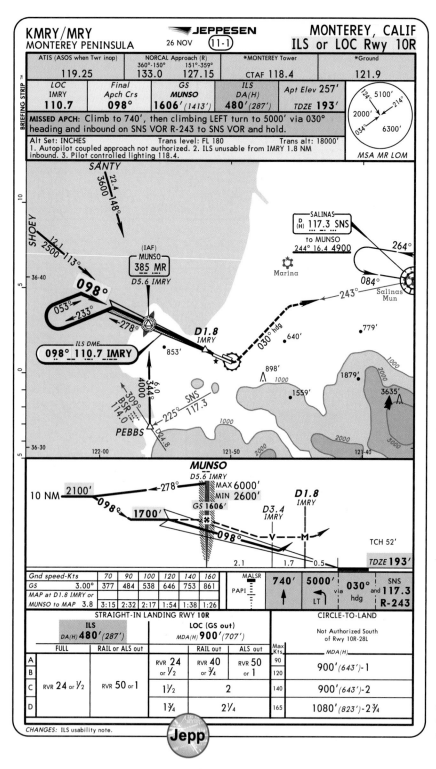

Procedure Title
State the type of approach and runway.

Communication Frequencies
Set the frequencies in the active and standby radio fields as appropriate.

Primary Navaid Frequency or Approach Selected
Tune and identify the frequency or load the approach procedure into the GPS receiver.

Final Approach Course
Specify the course to fly inbound on the approach.

Approach Altitudes
State the altitude at the IAF, at any stepdown fixes, and at the FAF or glide slope/path intercept point.

DA (Precision Approach or APV) or MDA (Nonprecision Approach)
Specify the appropriate altitude based on a straight-in landing or circling approach.

Airport Information
Include items such as the airport elevation and touchdown zone elevation.

Missed Approach Instructions
Emphasize the initial actions to take in the event of a missed approach.

Procedural Notes
Describe actions that affect approach operations.

Figure 7-57. The briefing information at the top of the chart contains the items that should be included in an approach briefing.

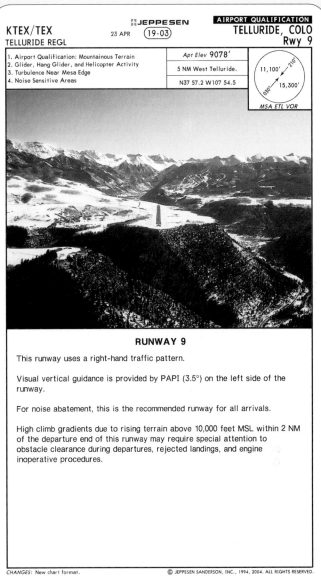

ᏕᎢᎯᎢᎬ ᏉᎾᏌᎡ ᏧᏌᎯᏞᏆᎦᏆᏟᎯᎢᏆᎾᏁᏕ

The airport is located on a 1,000-foot mesa. Strong vertical turbulence and variable crosswinds may exist in the area of the mesa's edge.

The high landing minimums and special missed approach procedures are designed to allow for clearance of high terrain near the airport.

These advisories are included on an airport qualification chart for Telluride Regional Airport. Airport qualification charts were developed to help pilots meet the requirements of FAR 121.445, Pilot in Command Airport Qualification: Special Areas and Airports. This regulation requires that pilots in command of Part 121 carriers meet special qualifications to operate at selected airports due to surrounding terrain, obstructions, or complex approach or departure procedures.

One way to meet these qualifications is for the pilot in command or second in command to have performed a takeoff and landing at the applicable airport as a flight crewmember within the preceding 12 calendar months. Another way is through the use of acceptable pictorial means and that is where airport qualification charts come in.

Airport qualification charts are valuable tools to help pilots maintain situational awareness during approaches to challenging airports. These charts provide photos of the airport, graphic and textual descriptions of the surrounding terrain and obstacles, as well as typical weather conditions and other unique airport information of concern to pilots. While they were originally developed for Part 121 airlines, airport qualification charts are an effective resource used by pilots in a wide variety of operating environments, including corporate and general aviation flights.

SECTION B ■ Approach Procedures

STRAIGHT-IN LANDING VS. CIRCLING APPROACH

When you fly an instrument approach, you complete the procedure with either a straight-in landing or circling approach and you use the applicable landing minimums on the approach chart. **Straight-in landing** minimums normally are specified when the final approach course is positioned within 30° of the runway and a minimum of maneuvering is required to align the airplane with the runway. If the final approach course is not properly aligned, or if it is desirable to land on a different runway, a circling approach may be executed and circling minimums apply. [Figure 7-58] While most approach procedures provide landing minimums for both straight-in and circling maneuvers, some only have circling minimums. [Figure 7-59]

SECTION B ■ Approach Procedures

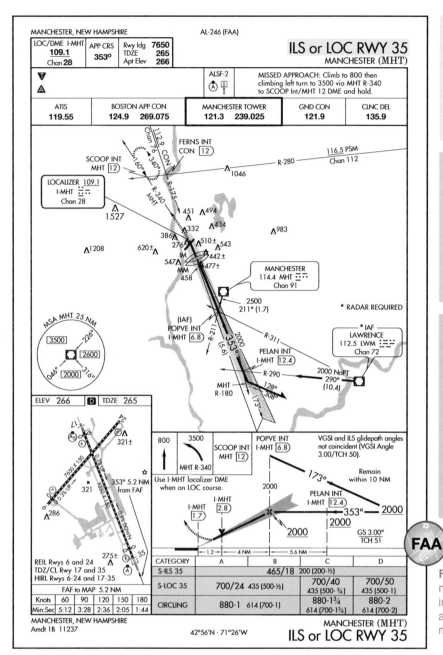

Straight-In Landing Procedure Name
An approach that provides straight-in landing minimums is named to identify the type of navaid which provides final course guidance and the specific runway aligned with the final approach course.
Example: This approach is a precision ILS or nonprecision localizer approach to Runway 35.

Straight-In Landing Minimums
When the final approach course is positioned within 30° of the runway, normally straight-in landing minimums apply.
Example: The localizer course of 353° is aligned with Runway 35. The straight-in landing minimums for the ILS approach for all aircraft categories is a decision altitude of 465 feet MSL and a visibility of 18 RVR.

Circling Approach Minimums
Circling approach minimums are used when the final approach course is not aligned within 30° of the runway, such as when you fly an approach to one runway but must circle to land to another runway due to traffic, wind, or runway conditions.
Example: If a strong wind favored Runway 17, you might request and receive a clearance to perform a circling approach to Runway 17. In this case, the circling MDA of 880 feet and visibility of either 1 mile, 1¾ mile or 2 miles applies depending on aircraft category.

Figure 7-58. You perform an instrument approach with either a straight-in landing or a circling approach, and you use the applicable landing minimums on the approach chart.

Procedure Title
A procedure that provides only circling approach minimums is identified by a letter following the primary approach navaid.
Example: The VOR/DME-A approach title does not include a runway number.

Circling Approach Minimums Only
Because the final approach course is not aligned within 30° of the runway, only circling minimums are published for this procedure.
Example: When you reach the MDA of 1,440 feet MSL (category A,B, and C aircraft), you perform a circling approach to land on either Runway 18 or Runway 36.

VOR/DME-A
HALEYVILLE/ POSEY FIELD (1M4)

CATEGORY	A	B	C	D
CIRCLING	1440-1 510 (600-1)	1440-1¼ 510 (600-1¼)	1440-1¾ 510 (600-1¾)	1480-2 550 (600-2)

Figure 7-59. An example of an approach with only circling minimums uses a VOR/DME facility not closely aligned with the runway.

STRAIGHT-IN APPROACH

In contrast to a straight-in landing, the controller terminology, *"cleared for straight-in approach . . ."* means that you should not perform any published procedure to reverse your course, but does not reference landing minimums. For example, you could be *"cleared for straight-in ILS Runway 25 approach, circle to land Runway 34."* A **straight-in approach** may be initiated from a fix closely aligned with the final approach course, may commence from the completion of a DME arc, or you may receive vectors to the final approach course. [Figure 7-60]

 A straight-in approach does not require nor authorize a procedure turn or course reversal.

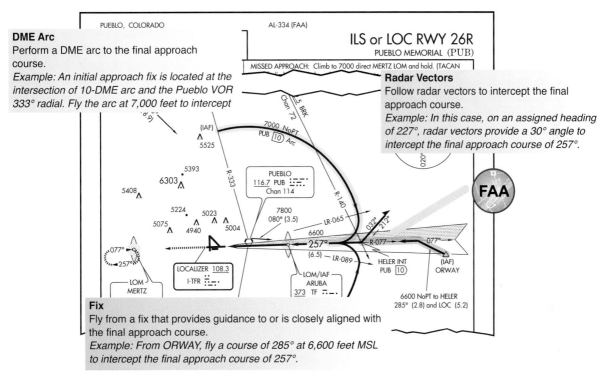

DME Arc
Perform a DME arc to the final approach course.
Example: An initial approach fix is located at the intersection of 10-DME arc and the Pueblo VOR 333° radial. Fly the arc at 7,000 feet to intercept

Radar Vectors
Follow radar vectors to intercept the final approach course.
Example: In this case, on an assigned heading of 227°, radar vectors provide a 30° angle to intercept the final approach course of 257°.

Fix
Fly from a fix that provides guidance to or is closely aligned with the final approach course.
Example: From ORWAY, fly a course of 285° at 6,600 feet MSL to intercept the final approach course of 257°.

Figure 7-60. Depending on the approach procedure and your position as you near the airport, actions you take to initiate a straight-in approach vary.

You also make a straight-in approach if an airway leads directly to the final approach course. The approach chart might show a NoPT (no procedure turn) arrival sector formed by airways leading to an enroute navaid that also serves as an initial approach fix. [Figure 7-61]

USE OF ATC RADAR FOR APPROACHES

In locations where radar is approved for approach control service, ATC may also use it in conjunction with published instrument approach procedures to provide guidance to the final approach course or to the traffic pattern for a visual approach. In addition, approach control radar is used for airport surveillance radar (ASR) and precision approach radar (PAR) approaches and to monitor nonradar approaches. ATC provides azimuth guidance and range information during an ASR approach and navigational guidance in azimuth, range, and elevation during a PAR approach. You might use these approach procedures in an emergency situation, such as a loss of gyroscopic instruments. ASR and PAR approaches are discussed in greater detail in Chapter 10, Section A — IFR Emergencies.

 ATC radar approved for approach control service is used for course guidance to the final approach course, ASR and PAR approaches, and to monitor nonradar approaches.

SECTION B ■ Approach Procedures

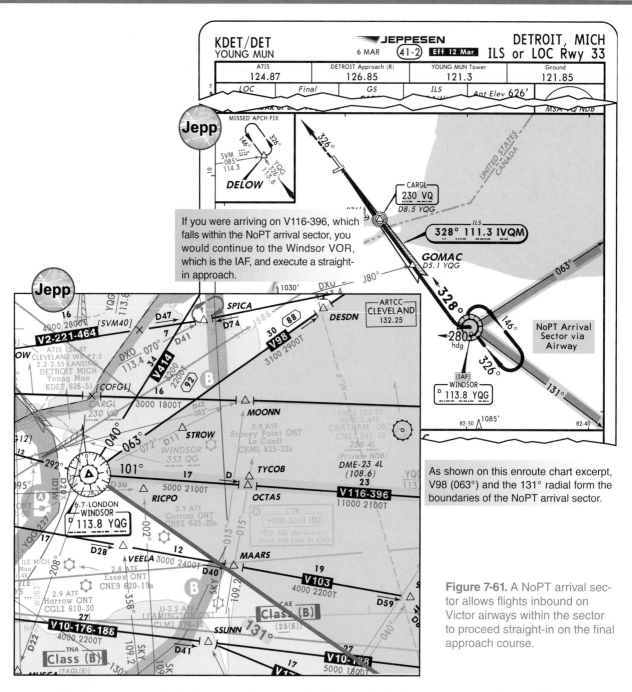

As shown on this enroute chart excerpt, V98 (063°) and the 131° radial form the boundaries of the NoPT arrival sector.

Figure 7-61. A NoPT arrival sector allows flights inbound on Victor airways within the sector to proceed straight-in on the final approach course.

Radar vectors to the final approach course provide a method of intercepting and proceeding inbound on the published instrument approach procedure. During an arrival, you normally are cleared to the airport or an outer fix that is appropriate to your arrival route. After you have been handed off to approach control, you continue inbound to the airport or to the fix in accordance with your last route clearance. ATC will advise you to expect radar vectors to the final approach course for a specific approach procedure unless that information is included in ATIS. When ATC provides radar vectors, a published course reversal is not required. [Figure 7-62]

 When you are cleared for an approach while being radar vectored, you must maintain your last assigned altitude until established on a segment of the published approach. See figure 7-62.

 If you are conducting a practice instrument approach and approach control assigns an altitude or heading that will cause you to enter the clouds, you must inform ATC that that altitude or heading will not permit VFR.

1 ATC issues a radar vector and altitude assignment for spacing and aircraft separation, typically providing a heading to position you outside the FAF.
Example: ATC provides this clearance, "Piper 8450B, turn left heading 190, descend and maintain 3,000, vectors to the ILS Runway 35 final approach course."

2 After you are outside the FAF, ATC typically provides a heading approximately perpendicular to the final approach course.
Example: ATC directs, "Piper 50B, turn right heading 270."

If it becomes apparent the assigned heading will cause you to pass through the final approach course, maintain that heading and question the controller.

3 ATC provides an intercept angle for the final approach course of no greater than 30° and issues the approach clearance including a minimum altitude to maintain until you are established on a segment of the published approach procedure.
Example: ATC clears you for the approach, "Piper 50B, 6 miles southeast of NITTE, turn right heading 320 maintain 3,000 until established on the localizer. Cleared for ILS Runway 35 approach, contact tower 120.77 at NITTE."

4 Maintain the last assigned heading and altitude until you turn inbound and intercept the final approach course.
Example: You fly a heading of 320° and 3,000 feet MSL until you intercept the localizer course of 354° inbound.

5 After you are on the approach course, descend according to the minimum altitudes published on the final approach chart, if appropriate.
Example: Now that you are established on the localizer, you descend to 2,500 feet to intercept the glide slope just prior to NITTE.

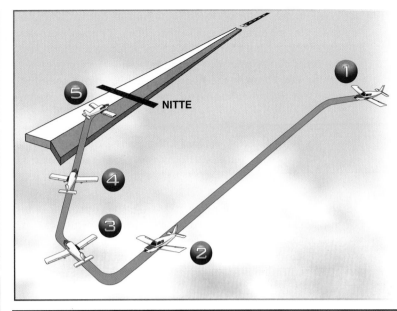

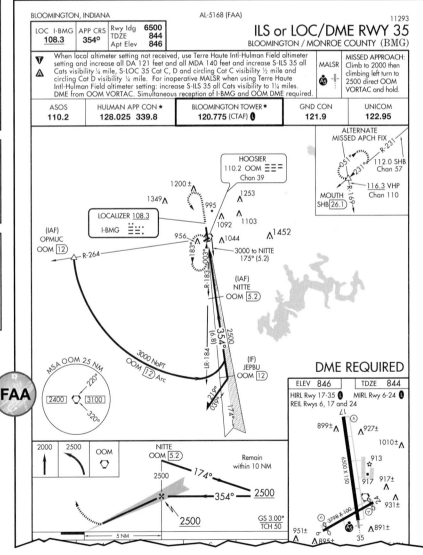

SECTION B ■ Approach Procedures

 Figure 7-62. Although radar vectors are frequently used in conjunction with ILS approaches, they also can be used with nonprecision approaches.

 During an instrument approach procedure, a published course reversal is not required when radar vectors are provided.

While being radar vectored, you should not turn inbound on the final approach course until you are cleared for the approach. If it appears imminent that an assigned heading will cause you to cross through the final approach course and you have not been advised that you will be vectored through it, question the controller. The controller may intentionally vector you through the final approach course to achieve traffic separation. If this is the case, the controller should advise you and state the reason such as, *". . . expect vector across final approach course for spacing."*

 If it becomes apparent an assigned heading will cause you to pass through the final approach course, you should maintain that heading and question the controller.

During the process of radar vectoring, the controller is responsible for assigning altitudes that are at or above the **minimum vectoring altitude (MVA)**. These altitudes are established in terminal areas to provide terrain and obstruction clearance. The MVA in a given sector is not shown on approach charts and may be lower than the nonradar MEA, MOCA, or other minimum altitude on instrument charts. [Figure 7-63]

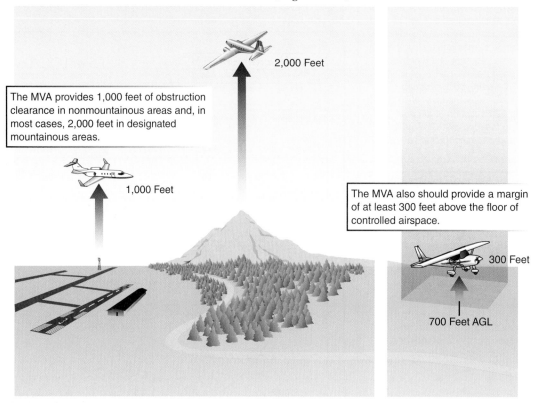

2,000 Feet

The MVA provides 1,000 feet of obstruction clearance in nonmountainous areas and, in most cases, 2,000 feet in designated mountainous areas.

1,000 Feet

The MVA also should provide a margin of at least 300 feet above the floor of controlled airspace.

300 Feet

700 Feet AGL

Figure 7-63. The altitudes ATC assigns when providing radar vectors ensure terrain and obstruction clearance, as well as keep your airplane within controlled airspace.

COURSE REVERSALS

Some approach procedures do not provide for straight-in approaches unless you are being radar vectored. In these situations, you are required to complete a **course reversal**, generally within 10 nautical miles of the primary navaid or fix designated on the approach chart, to establish the airplane inbound on the intermediate or final approach segments. The maximum speed in a course reversal is 200 knots IAS. A course reversal is depicted on a chart as a procedure turn, a holding pattern, or a teardrop procedure. [Figure 7-64] When a holding pattern is published as a course reversal, you must make the proper entry and follow the depicted pattern to establish the airplane on the inbound course. [Figure 7-65]

Often the terms procedure turn and course reversal are used interchangeably. For example, if you are flying an approach segment shown on the chart with the notation, NoPT (no procedure turn) you may not execute the course reversal depicted whether it is indicated by the procedure turn symbol, holding pattern course reversal, or teardrop pattern.

The maximum speed in a procedure turn is 200 knots IAS.

 If you are above the altitude designated for the course reversal, you may begin descent as soon as you cross the IAF. See figure 7-64.

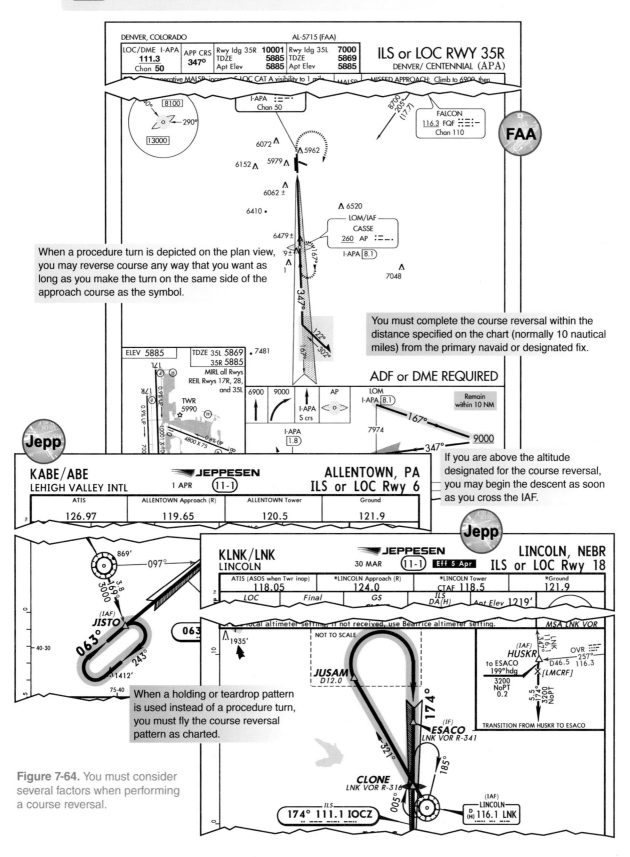

SECTION B ■ Approach Procedures

When a procedure turn is depicted on the plan view, you may reverse course any way that you want as long as you make the turn on the same side of the approach course as the symbol.

You must complete the course reversal within the distance specified on the chart (normally 10 nautical miles) from the primary navaid or designated fix.

If you are above the altitude designated for the course reversal, you may begin the descent as soon as you cross the IAF.

When a holding or teardrop pattern is used instead of a procedure turn, you must fly the course reversal pattern as charted.

Figure 7-64. You must consider several factors when performing a course reversal.

Course reversals must be completed within the distance specified on the chart which is typically 10 nautical miles from the primary navaid or fix indicated on the approach chart. See figure 7-64.

 If a chart depicts a course reversal with a lower altitude inbound (see Figure 7-56 for example), and if you are cleared for the approach, you may begin descent to the inbound altitude for the final approach course after intercepting the inbound course.

 When more than one circuit of the holding pattern is needed to lose altitude or become better established on course, the additional circuits can be made only if you advise ATC and ATC approves.

 If a teardrop or holding pattern is shown on an approach chart, you must execute the course reversal as depicted. See figure 7-64.

Use the appropriate entry procedure – teardrop, parallel, or direct – depending on the airplane's position.

Continue inbound on the approach course if you are cleared for the approach prior to returning to the fix. Additional circuits are not necessary or expected by ATC.

When you need more than one circuit to lose altitude or become better established on course, you must advise ATC and receive clearance.

Fly the holding pattern with one-minute legs or the published leg length.

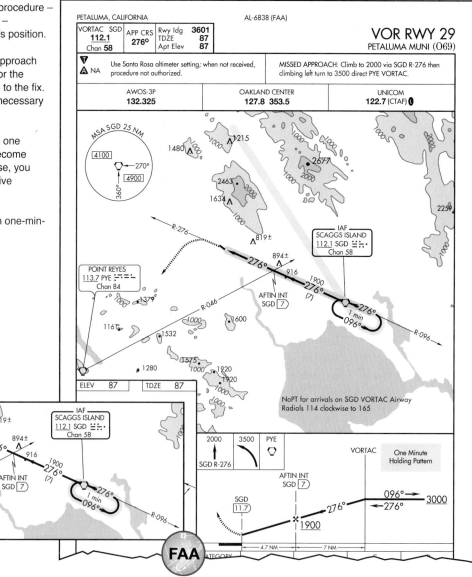

Figure 7-65. Combine your knowledge of performing holding patterns with interpreting the approach procedure to master the holding pattern course reversal.

TIMED APPROACHES FROM A HOLDING FIX

Timed approaches from a holding fix are generally conducted at airports where the radar system for traffic sequencing is out of service or is not available and numerous aircraft are waiting for approach clearance. [Figure 7-66] ATC may not specifically state that timed approaches are in progress. However, if you are issued a time to depart the holding fix inbound, it means that timed approaches are being used. The holding fix may be the FAF on a nonprecision approach, while a precision approach might use the outer marker or a fix used in lieu of the outer marker for holding. [Figure 7-67]

Timed approaches from a holding fix may be conducted if the following conditions are met.

- A control tower is operating at the airport where the approaches are conducted.

- After you are cleared for the approach, you must not perform a procedure turn.

- You maintain direct communication with the center or approach controller until you are instructed to contact the tower.

- If more than one missed approach procedure is available, none require a course reversal.

- If only one missed approach procedure is available, a course reversal is not required, and the reported ceiling and visibility are equal to or greater than the highest circling approach minimums for the approach procedure.

Figure 7-66. Timed approaches from a holding fix are not performed at all airports. ATC initiates timed approaches only if certain conditions are met.

If more than one missed approach procedure is available, a timed approach from a holding fix may be conducted if none require a course reversal.

Timed approaches from a holding fix are only conducted at airports which have operating control towers.

If only one missed approach procedure is available, a timed approach from a holding fix may be conducted if the reported ceiling and visibility minimums are equal to or greater than the highest prescribed circling minimums for the IAP.

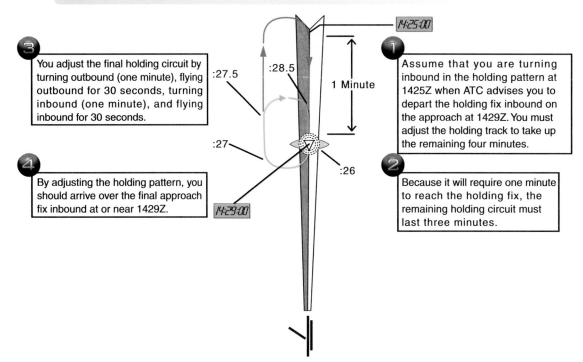

3 You adjust the final holding circuit by turning outbound (one minute), flying outbound for 30 seconds, turning inbound (one minute), and flying inbound for 30 seconds.

4 By adjusting the holding pattern, you should arrive over the final approach fix inbound at or near 1429Z.

1 Assume that you are turning inbound in the holding pattern at 1425Z when ATC advises you to depart the holding fix inbound on the approach at 1429Z. You must adjust the holding track to take up the remaining four minutes.

2 Because it will require one minute to reach the holding fix, the remaining holding circuit must last three minutes.

14:25:00
14:29:00
:27.5   :28.5   1 Minute   :27   :26

Figure 7-67. When timed approaches are in progress, ATC gives you advance notice of the time you should leave the holding fix.

When making a timed approach from a holding pattern at the outer marker, adjust the holding pattern so you will leave the outer marker inbound at the assigned time. See figure 7-67.

FINAL APPROACH

The procedure for flying the final approach segment depends upon whether you are performing an approach with lateral guidance only or with both lateral and vertical guidance. You must understand how procedures differ based on the use of an DA or MDA and when you can descend below these minimum altitudes to land.

OPERATING BELOW THE DA OR MDA

While the published approach procedure guides your descent to the DA or MDA, one of the most important elements of the final approach is knowing when you can safely continue below the minimum altitude designated for the approach. The regulations list the requirements that you must meet to descend below the DA or MDA. You must be able to identify specific visual references of the runway environment and comply with visibility and operating requirements. [Figure 7-68]

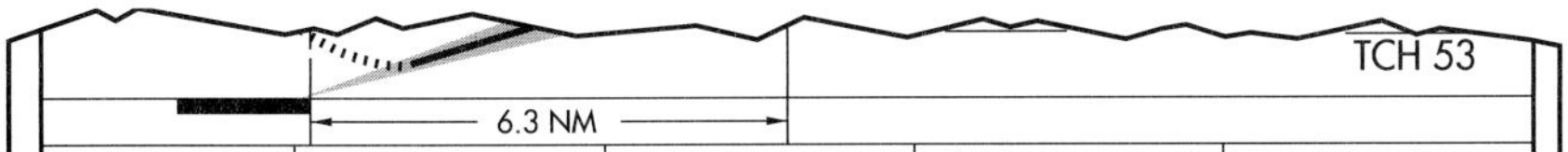

				TCH 53

			6.3 NM		
CATEGORY	A	B	C	D
S-ILS 35R	6085-½ 200 (200-½)			
S-LOC 35R	6760-¾ 875 (900-¾)		6760-2 875 (900-2)	6760-2¼ 875 (900-2¼)
SIDESTEP RWY 35L	6760-1¼ 891 (900-1¼)		6760-2¾ 891 (900-2¾)	6760-3 891 (900-3)
CIRCLING	6760-1 875 (900-1)	6760-1¼ 875 (900-1¼)	6760-2½ 875 (900-2½)	6760-2¾ 875 (900-2¾)

FAA   39°34'N-104°51'W

DENVER/ CENTENNIAL (APA)
ILS or LOC RWY 35R

You must have flight visibility at or greater than that required for the approach.

You must be continuously in a position to descend at a normal rate to land on the intended runway by using normal maneuvers.

You must establish the runway environment in sight, which includes at least one of these visual references:
- Approach light system, but you must see the red terminating bars (ALSF-1) or side row bars (ALSF-2) to descend below 100 feet above the touchdown zone elevation
- Runway end identifier lights
- Visual approach slope indicator
- Threshold, threshold markings, or threshold lights
- Touchdown zone, touchdown zone markings, or, touchdown zone lights
- Runway, runway markings, or runway lights

Figure 7-68. To descend below the MDA or DA to land, you must meet several regulatory requirements.

Enhanced Vision System

Imagine if you could meet the visual requirements for descending below the DA or MDA by enhancing your vision electronically. An enhanced flight vision system (EFVS) uses radar-imaging sensors to display the natural and man-made features ahead of your airplane, including the terrain and runway environment. FAR 91.175 includes specific requirements for descending below the DA or MDA using an enhanced flight vision system.

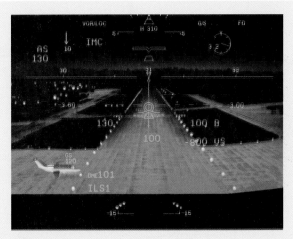

DESCENDING TO THE DA OR MDA

When performing an approach with a decision altitude as a landing minimum, you descend on the electronic glide slope or glide path to the DA, and at that point, you make a decision to land if you meet the visual requirements or to perform a missed approach if you do not have the runway environment in sight. In contrast to a decision altitude, when you reach the MDA, you must remain at or above the MDA until you have the required visual references in sight and you are in a position where you can establish a normal rate of descent from the MDA to the runway using normal maneuvers. If these requirements are not met, you must perform the missed approach at the missed approach point (MAP), which is often at the runway threshold. [Figure 7-69]

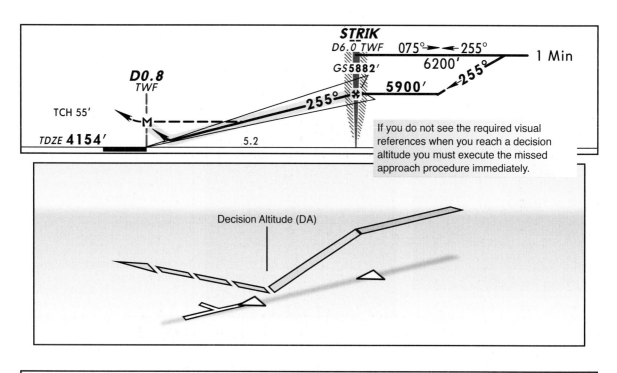

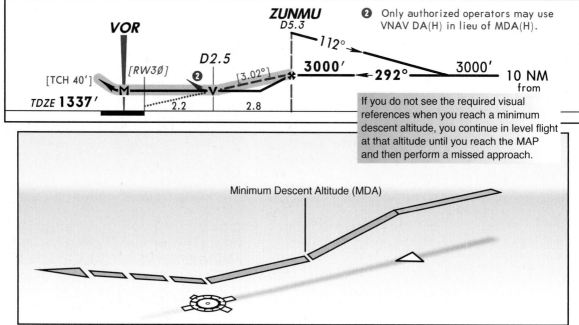

Figure 7-69. You perform different procedures when operating with a decision altitude or minimum descent altitude.

A Perfect Approach Plus a Bounced Landing Equals Success

Some of the most successful landings on Mars resulted from a series of bounces. The Mars Pathfinder landing in 1997, and the Spirit and Opportunity landings in 2004 used a system of airbags to cushion the impact with the Martian surface.

All of the spacecraft used the same four methods to slow down from orbital speed to a reasonably gentle stop on the Martian surface.

As each spacecraft entered the Martian atmosphere, its heatshield decelerated the lander from around 12,000 mph to about 1,000 mph. This aerodynamic braking took the high kinetic energy of the spacecraft and turned it into heat. While the surface of the heatshield reached temperatures as hot as the surface of the Sun, the lander remained at a comfortable room temperature.

At an altitude of 30,000 feet, the spacecraft deployed a supersonic parachute. This type of parachute was used successfully in 1976 as the two Viking landers entered Mars' atmosphere.

At a speed of about 150 mph and an altitude of about 300 feet above the surface, retro rockets fired to reduce the vertical speed of the spacecraft to zero, and, in the case of Spirit and Opportunity, to reduce lateral motion as well.

Each lander then cut the cord holding it to the parachute and retro rocket assembly, dropping the remaining 40 feet to the surface. Cushioned by airbags all around, the landers bounced, and bounced, and bounced before coming to rest. Each lander may have bounced 15-30 times before rolling to a stop.

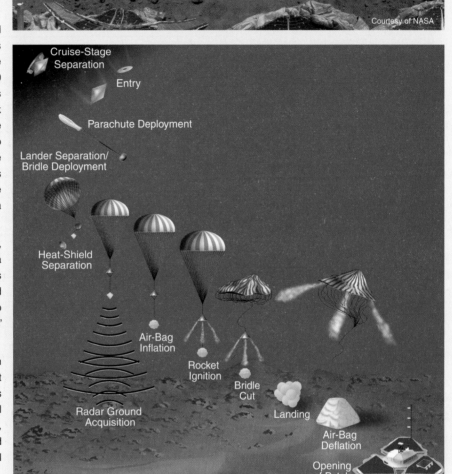

Courtesy of NASA

Cruise-Stage Separation
Entry
Parachute Deployment
Lander Separation/ Bridle Deployment
Heat-Shield Separation
Radar Ground Acquisition
Air-Bag Inflation
Rocket Ignition
Bridle Cut
Landing
Air-Bag Deflation
Opening of Petals

Courtesy of NASA

Whether on the cratered plains of Mars or at the local airport, every landing has similar objectives — to bring vertical and horizontal speed to zero without damaging the craft or its occupants. Each time you land, you use aerodynamic drag to slow the airplane before touchdown, and the friction of the wheel brakes and tires to turn your remaining kinetic energy into heat as you bring the airplane to a stop. Some airplanes also use reverse thrust to shorten the landing roll. Perhaps someday airplanes will approach, flare, and land on Mars, and Earth craft will tumble and bounce to a stop on airbags.

SECTION B ■ Approach Procedures

If you are flying a nonprecision approach, you must plan the descent from the final approach fix to the MDA so the airplane is in a position to land prior to the missed approach point. To accomplish this, you must establish a sufficient rate of descent while maintaining an appropriate airspeed to ensure that you reach the MDA prior to the MAP and to provide plenty of time to establish the required visual cues and perform an approach to landing. For nonprecision approaches, Jeppesen charts indicate a vertical descent angle (VDA) and an associated descent rate as a guideline for performing a stabilized descent to arrive at the MDA prior to the missed approach point. The vertical descent angle should keep you above the minimum altitudes designated for stepdown fixes; however, it is still your responsibility to monitor your descent and ensure you comply with stepdown fix minimum altitudes. [Figure 7-70]

The vertical descent angle to maintain a stabilized descent from 3,000 feet MSL at WOLFY final approach fix to the threshold crossing height of 40 feet is 3.14°.

At 90 knots, you must descend at approximately 500 feet per minute to maintain the vertical descent angle of 3.14°.

The vertical descent angle path is depicted as a gray dashed line to the MDA and as a dotted line to the threshold crossing height. You may not continue to descend below the MDA along this path unless you have the required visual cues in site.

Some navigation equipment enables input of the vertical descent angle to display an advisory glide path. Certain authorized operators can follow the advisory glide path and use the MDA as a DA. These operators must make a decision upon reaching the MDA to continue the approach to landing or perform a missed approach.

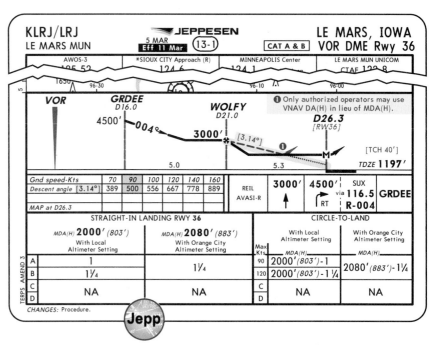

Figure 7-70. Jeppesen charts indicate the vertical descent angle in the profile view and in the descent/timing conversion table.

VASI

At airports with operating control towers, you must maintain a glide path at or above the VASI while approaching a runway served by a VASI installation. If a glide slope malfunction occurs when you are in IFR conditions during an ILS approach, you must apply the localizer-only minimums (MDA) and report the malfunction to ATC. When you have established visual references, you may continue the descent at or above the VASI glide path for the remainder of the approach. [Figure 7-71]

Figure 7-71. VASI lights can help you maintain the proper descent angle to the runway after you have established visual contact with the runway environment

You are executing an ILS approach and are past the OM to a runway which has VASI. If the glide slope malfunctions, and you have the VASI in sight, you may continue the approach using the VASI glide slope in place of the electronic glide slope.

LANDING ILLUSIONS

When you have the runway in sight on the approach, you should be alert for **landing illusions**. These visual illusions are the product of various runway conditions, terrain features, and atmospheric phenomena which can create the appearance of incorrect height above the runway or incorrect distance from the runway threshold. [Figure 7-72]

Situation	Illusion	Result
Upsloping Runway or Terrain	Greater Height	Lower Approaches
Narrower-Than-Usual Runway	Greater Height	Lower Approaches
Featureless Terrain	Greater Height	Lower Approaches
Rain on Windscreen	Greater Height	Lower Approaches
Haze	Greater Height	Lower Approaches
Downsloping Runway or Terrain	Less Height	Higher Approaches
Wider-Than-Usual Runway	Less Height	Higher Approaches
Bright Runway and Approach Lights	Less Distance	Higher Approaches
Penetration of Fog	Pitching Up	Steeper Approaches

Figure 7-72. You should pay particular attention to illusions that lead to a lower-than-normal final approach profile.

 Due to a visual illusion, when landing on a narrower-than-usual runway, the aircraft will appear to be higher than it actually is, leading to a lower-than-normal approach.

 An upsloping runway creates the same effect as a narrower-than-usual runway.

 A sloping cloud formation, an obscured horizon, and a dark scene spread with ground lights and stars can create an illusion known as false horizons.

CIRCLING APPROACHES

Several situations may require you to execute a **circling approach**. For example, you need to perform a circling approach if the instrument approach course is not aligned within 30° of the runway. Unfavorable winds or a runway closure might make a straight-in landing impractical. Circling minimums appropriate to each aircraft approach category are established in accordance with TERPs criteria. Each circling approach is confined to a protected area that is defined by TERPs and also published in the AIM. The size of this area varies with aircraft approach category. You are assured obstacle clearance at the MDA during circling maneuvers only if you remain within the protected area. In addition, you must remain at or above the circling MDA unless the airplane is continuously in a position from which you can descend to a landing on the intended runway, using a normal rate of descent and normal maneuvering. [Figure 7-73]

In simple terms, the circling approach procedure involves flying the approach, establishing visual contact with the airport, and positioning the aircraft on final approach to the runway of intended landing. However, the circling approach is not a simple maneuver, because you are required to fly at a low altitude at a fairly slow airspeed while remaining within a specifically defined area. Remember that you fly the circling approach at or above the MDA, and you cannot descend from the MDA until the airplane is properly positioned to make a normal descent to the landing runway. [Figure 7-74]

SECTION B ■ **Approach Procedures**

The circling approach protected area is established by the connection of arcs drawn from each runway end. The radii (r) which define the size of the areas vary with the approach category. As the approach speeds increase, the turn radii increase which often results in higher circling MDAs.

Approach Category	Radii (n.m.)
A	1.3
B	1.5
C	1.7
D	2.3
E	4.5

Jepp CIRCLE-TO-LAND

Max Kts.	MDA(H)
90	**6260'**(501')-1
120	**6280'**(521')-1
140	**6700'**(941')-2¾
165	**6740'**(981')-3

If obstacles are present within the protected area, a procedural note may be added which prohibits circling within a portion of that area.

CIRCLE-TO-LAND
Not Authorized
North of Rwy 10-28

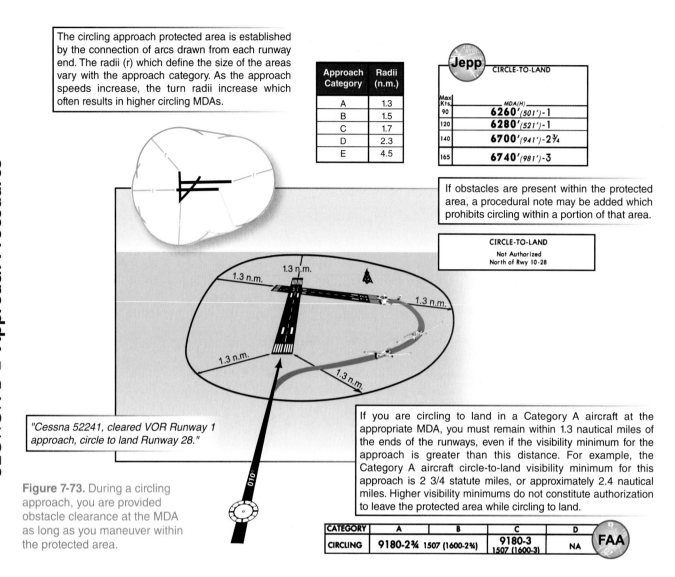

"Cessna 52241, cleared VOR Runway 1 approach, circle to land Runway 28."

Figure 7-73. During a circling approach, you are provided obstacle clearance at the MDA as long as you maneuver within the protected area.

If you are circling to land in a Category A aircraft at the appropriate MDA, you must remain within 1.3 nautical miles of the ends of the runways, even if the visibility minimum for the approach is greater than this distance. For example, the Category A aircraft circle-to-land visibility minimum for this approach is 2 3/4 statute miles, or approximately 2.4 nautical miles. Higher visibility minimums do not constitute authorization to leave the protected area while circling to land.

CATEGORY	A	B	C	D	
CIRCLING	9180-2¾ 1507 (1600-2¾)		9180-3 1507 (1600-3)	NA	**FAA**

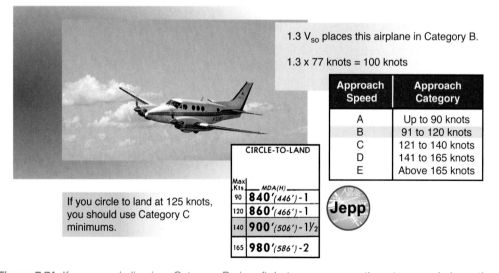

1.3 V_{so} places this airplane in Category B.

1.3 x 77 knots = 100 knots

Approach Speed	Approach Category
A	Up to 90 knots
B	91 to 120 knots
C	121 to 140 knots
D	141 to 165 knots
E	Above 165 knots

CIRCLE-TO-LAND

Max Kts	MDA(H)
90	**840'**(446')-1
120	**860'**(466')-1
140	**900'**(506')-1½
165	**980'**(586')-2

Jepp

If you circle to land at 125 knots, you should use Category C minimums.

Figure 7-74. If you are circling in a Category B aircraft, but you are operating at a speed above the Category B speed limit, you should use the MDA and visibility requirement appropriate to Category C.

You may execute a straight-in landing if the IAP has only circling minimums if you have the runway in sight in sufficient time to make a normal approach for landing and you have been cleared to land.

Circling approaches can be extremely hazardous when combined with such factors as low visibility, hilly or mountainous terrain, and/or night operations. You must remain within the protected area for your aircraft approach category while circling, and after you descend below the MDA, obstacle clearance is your responsibility. If conditions prevent you from seeing well enough to guarantee obstruction clearance during the final descent, do not continue the approach. Many accidents have occurred during circling approaches because the pilot saw lights in the vicinity but did not see hilly or mountainous terrain between the aircraft and the airport. As a general rule when performing a circling approach, plan on a traffic pattern entry that requires the least amount of maneuvering. [Figure 7-75]

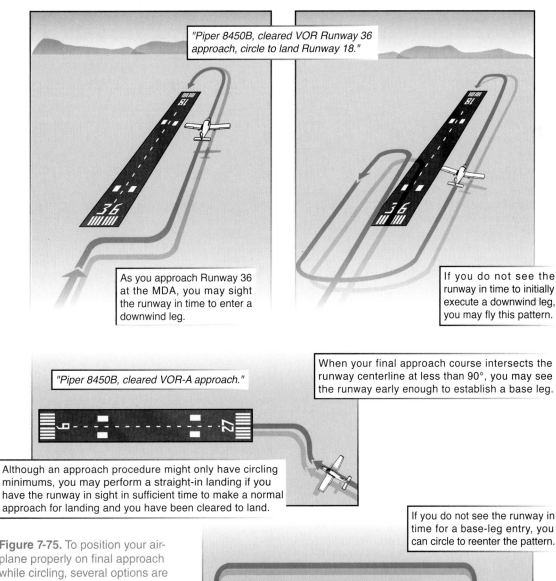

"Piper 8450B, cleared VOR Runway 36 approach, circle to land Runway 18."

As you approach Runway 36 at the MDA, you may sight the runway in time to enter a downwind leg.

If you do not see the runway in time to initially execute a downwind leg, you may fly this pattern.

"Piper 8450B, cleared VOR-A approach."

When your final approach course intersects the runway centerline at less than 90°, you may see the runway early enough to establish a base leg.

Although an approach procedure might only have circling minimums, you may perform a straight-in landing if you have the runway in sight in sufficient time to make a normal approach for landing and you have been cleared to land.

If you do not see the runway in time for a base-leg entry, you can circle to reenter the pattern.

Figure 7-75. To position your airplane properly on final approach while circling, several options are available to you as you enter the traffic pattern, including an upwind, base, or downwind entry

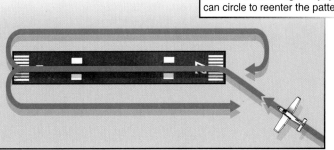

SIDESTEP MANEUVER

Under certain conditions, your approach clearance might include a **sidestep maneuver**. At some airports where there are two parallel runways that are 1,200 feet or less apart, you might be cleared to execute an approach to one runway followed by a straight-in landing on the adjacent runway. When cleared to perform a sidestep maneuver, you are expected to fly the approach to the primary runway and begin the approach to a landing on the parallel runway as soon as possible after you have it in sight. [Figure 7-76]

 When cleared to execute a published sidestep maneuver for a landing on a parallel runway, you should commence the maneuver as soon as possible after the runway or runway environment is in sight.

ATC: *Diamond Star 505JF, cleared ILS Runway 28 Left approach, sidestep to Runway 28 Right.*

Parallel Runways
The runway layout shows the parallel runway configuration of Runways 28L and 28R. The ILS approach is aligned with Runway 28L.

Sidestep Landing Minimums
In this case, the sidestep MDA of 460 feet for all aircraft categories is significantly lower than the MDA for a circling approach.

Beginning the Maneuver
Because the runway thresholds for 28L and 28R are aligned, it is critical to reach the MDA and establish the runway environment in sight in plenty of time to perform the sidestep maneuver.

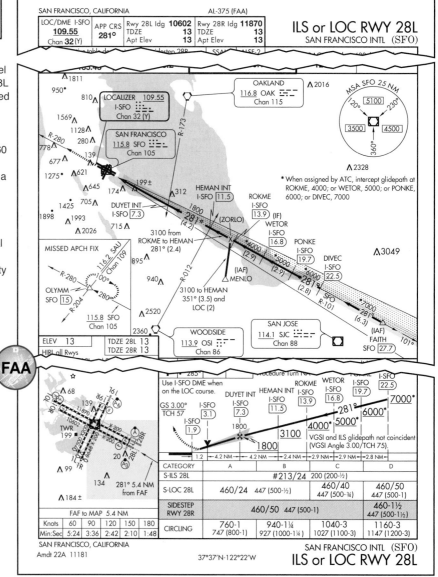

Figure 7-76. Sidestep landing minimums are normally higher than those for a straight-in landing to the runway.

MISSED APPROACH PROCEDURES

The most common reason for a **missed approach** is low visibility conditions that do not permit you to establish required visual cues. However, there are several situations that require you to perform a missed approach. [Figure 7-77] A published missed approach procedure is carefully designed and flight tested so you will have adequate obstacle clearance throughout the missed approach segment. Each procedure is unique to the airport and to the particular approach. Depending on obstacles and surrounding terrain, a missed approach segment may designate a straight climb, a climbing turn, or a climb to a specified altitude, followed by a turn to a specified heading, navaid, or navigation fix. [Figure 7-78]

You cannot establish the runway environment in sight at the MAP due to low visibility.

The airplane is not properly aligned on the final approach course.

You encounter wind shear that causes you to deviate from your desired airspeed.

ATC requests that you perform a missed approach because of inadequate aircraft separation.

The runway is suddenly closed because of a disabled aircraft.

Ground or airborne navigation components become inoperative.

Figure 7-77. You might make the decision to perform a missed approach procedure for a variety of reasons.

Regardless of the reason for a missed approach, it is very important that you can maneuver the aircraft safely throughout the missed approach segment. This is generally not difficult when you begin the missed approach at the missed approach point. In this situation, you simply fly the procedure as described and depicted on the approach chart. On occasion, however, you will be required to initiate a missed approach from a position that is not at the missed approach point and might not be on the missed approach segment. If the missed approach procedure requires a turn, an early turn is not considered in the approach design. To ensure obstacle clearance if you must initiate a missed approach prior to the missed approach point, you must remain at or above the MDA. You should fly the lateral navigation path of the instrument procedure to the missed approach point while climbing to the altitude specified in the missed approach procedure, except when a maximum altitude is specified between the final approach fix (FAF) and the MAP. In that case, comply with the maximum altitude restriction.

SECTION B ■ Approach Procedures

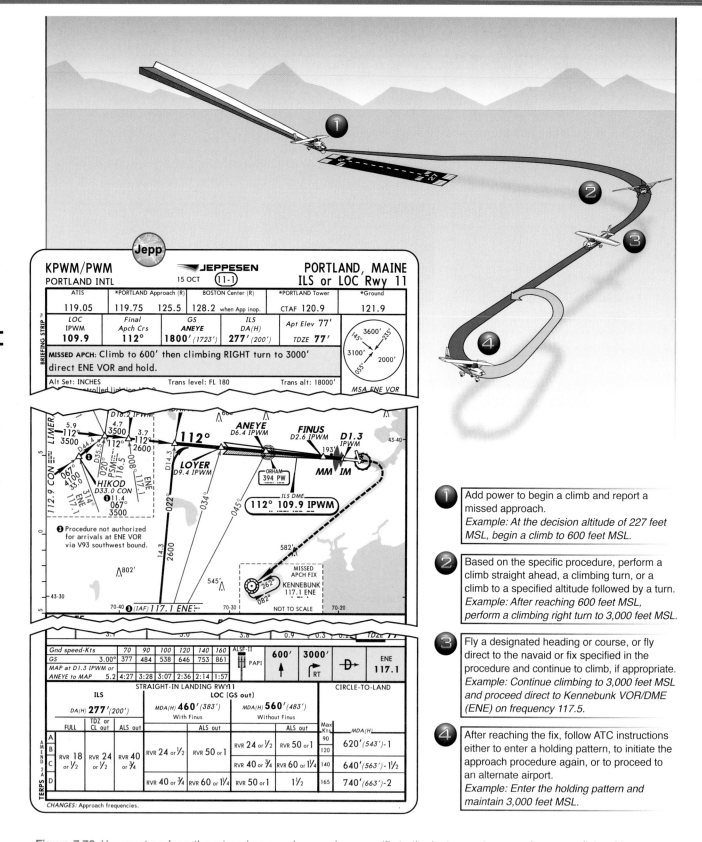

Figure 7-78. You must perform the missed approach procedure specific to the instrument approach you are flying. However, most missed approach procedures have some general steps in common. You should always review the missed approach procedure before beginning the approach.

Another good example is when you are executing a circling maneuver and suddenly lose sight of the runway. According to the AIM, you should make an initial climbing turn toward the landing runway to become established on the missed approach course. The airspace over the airport affords you the greatest obstacle clearance protection. Because the missed approach point for a nonprecision approach usually is the runway threshold, a turn toward the runway will keep you over the airport and may position you very close to the actual missed approach point. Because you may accomplish a circling maneuver in more than one direction, different patterns are required to become established on the missed approach course. The one to use depends on the position of the aircraft at the time visual reference is lost. [Figure 7-79]

 If an early missed approach is initiated before reaching the MAP, you should proceed to the missed approach point at or above the MDA or DA before executing a turning maneuver.

 If you lose visual reference while circling to land from an instrument approach and ATC radar service is not available, you should initiate a missed approach by making a climbing turn toward the landing runway and continue the turn until established on the missed approach course.

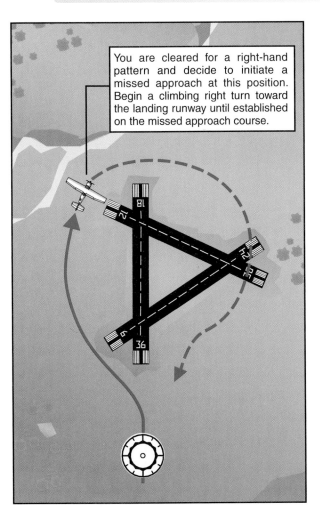

You are cleared for a right-hand pattern and decide to initiate a missed approach at this position. Begin a climbing right turn toward the landing runway until established on the missed approach course.

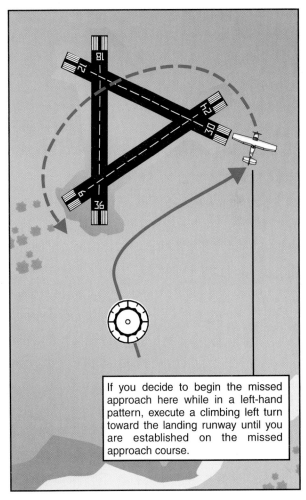

If you decide to begin the missed approach here while in a left-hand pattern, execute a climbing left turn toward the landing runway until you are established on the missed approach course.

Figure 7-79. These patterns are shown in the AIM and are intended to ensure that an aircraft will remain within the circling and missed approach obstruction clearance areas.

SECTION B ■ Approach Procedures

VISUAL AND CONTACT APPROACHES

To expedite traffic, ATC may clear you for a **visual approach** in lieu of the published approach procedure if flight conditions permit. Requesting a **contact approach** may be to your advantage because it requires less time than the published instrument procedure, allows you to retain your IFR clearance, and provides separation from IFR and special VFR traffic. Visual and contact approaches were introduced in Chapter 3, Section C — ATC Clearances. [Figure 7-80]

SECTION B ■ Approach Procedures

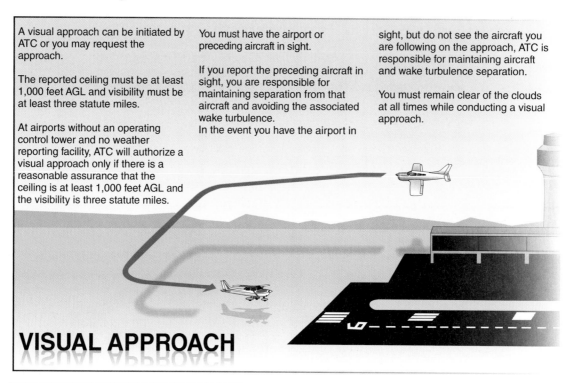

A visual approach can be initiated by ATC or you may request the approach.

The reported ceiling must be at least 1,000 feet AGL and visibility must be at least three statute miles.

At airports without an operating control tower and no weather reporting facility, ATC will authorize a visual approach only if there is a reasonable assurance that the ceiling is at least 1,000 feet AGL and the visibility is three statute miles.

You must have the airport or preceding aircraft in sight.

If you report the preceding aircraft in sight, you are responsible for maintaining separation from that aircraft and avoiding the associated wake turbulence.
In the event you have the airport in sight, but do not see the aircraft you are following on the approach, ATC is responsible for maintaining aircraft and wake turbulence separation.

You must remain clear of the clouds at all times while conducting a visual approach.

VISUAL APPROACH

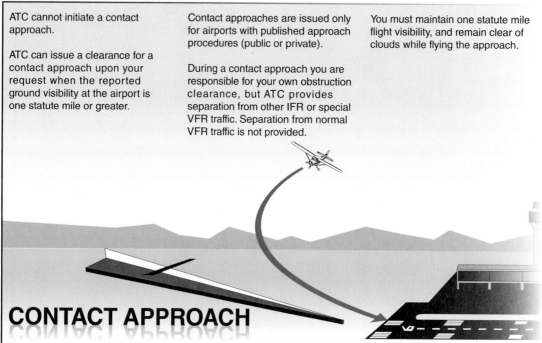

ATC cannot initiate a contact approach.

ATC can issue a clearance for a contact approach upon your request when the reported ground visibility at the airport is one statute mile or greater.

Contact approaches are issued only for airports with published approach procedures (public or private).

During a contact approach you are responsible for your own obstruction clearance, but ATC provides separation from other IFR or special VFR traffic. Separation from normal VFR traffic is not provided.

You must maintain one statute mile flight visibility, and remain clear of clouds while flying the approach.

CONTACT APPROACH

Figure 7-80. Pilot and controller responsibilities differ significantly between visual and contact approaches.

Charted visual flight procedures (CVFPs) might be established at some controlled airports for environmental or noise considerations or when necessary for the safety and efficiency of air traffic operations. Designed primarily for turbojet aircraft, CVFPs depict prominent landmarks, courses, and recommended altitudes to specific runways.

You must have a charted visual landmark or a preceding aircraft in sight, and weather must be at or above the published minimums before ATC will clear you for a CVFP. When instructed to follow a preceding aircraft, you are responsible for maintaining a safe approach interval and wake turbulence separation. You should advise ATC if at any point you are unable to continue a charted visual approach or lose sight of a preceding aircraft. [Figure 7-81]

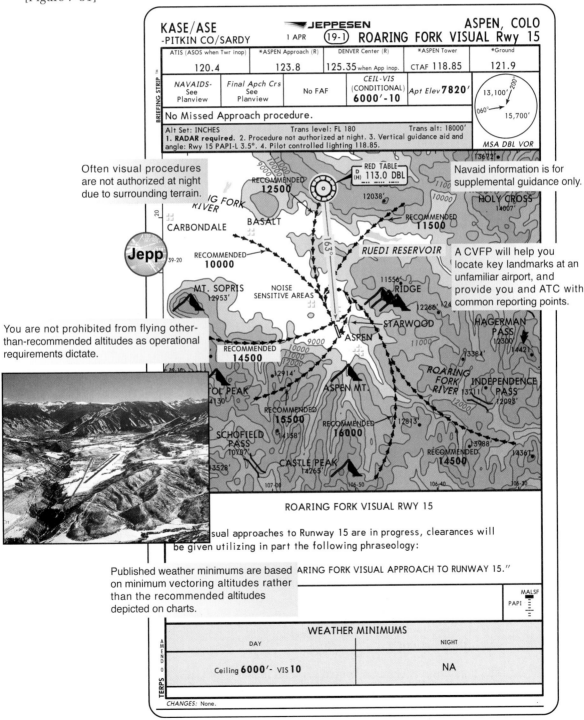

Often visual procedures are not authorized at night due to surrounding terrain.

Navaid information is for supplemental guidance only.

A CVFP will help you locate key landmarks at an unfamiliar airport, and provide you and ATC with common reporting points.

You are not prohibited from flying other-than-recommended altitudes as operational requirements dictate.

Published weather minimums are based on minimum vectoring altitudes rather than the recommended altitudes depicted on charts.

Figure 7-81. When you are flying the Roaring Fork Visual Approach, mountains, rivers, and towns guide you to Aspen Colorado's Sardy Field instead of VORs, NDBs, and DME fixes.

SUMMARY CHECKLIST

✓ As you near your destination, you should perform an approach overview including a review of landing minimums, terrain and obstacles, unique procedure features, and airport information, to form a general picture of the procedure and to determine if there are any factors that might affect your ability to perform the approach.

✓ After ATC advises which approach to expect, you should perform an approach briefing to include the procedure title, communication frequencies, primary navigation frequency or approach selected, final approach course, approach altitudes, DA or MDA, airport information, missed approach instructions, and procedural notes.

✓ If ATC does not specify a particular approach but states, *"cleared approach,"* you may execute any one of the authorized IAPs for that airport.

✓ Straight-in landing minimums normally are used when the final approach course is positioned within 30° of the runway and a minimum of maneuvering is required to align the airplane with the runway.

✓ If the final approach course is not properly aligned, or if it is desirable to land on a different runway, a circling approach may be executed and circle-to-land minimums apply.

✓ You might initiate a straight-in approach from a fix closely aligned with the final approach course or from the completion of a DME arc, or you might receive vectors to the final approach course.

✓ A straight-in approach does not require nor authorize a procedure turn or course reversal.

✓ A NoPT arrival sector allows flights inbound on Victor airways within the sector to proceed straight in on the final approach course.

✓ ATC radar approved for approach control service is used for course guidance to the final approach course, ASR and PAR approaches, and to monitor nonradar approaches.

✓ Radar vectors to the final approach course provide a method of intercepting and proceeding inbound on the published instrument approach procedure.

✓ During the process of radar vectoring, the controller is responsible for assigning altitudes that are at or above the minimum vectoring altitude (MVA), which provides terrain and obstruction clearance in a given sector.

✓ An MVA might be lower than the nonradar MEA, MOCA, or other minimum altitude shown on instrument charts.

✓ During an instrument approach procedure, a published course reversal is not required when radar vectors are provided.

✓ If it becomes apparent that the heading assigned by ATC will cause you to pass through the final approach course, you should maintain that heading and question the controller.

✓ A course reversal might be depicted on a chart as a procedure turn, holding pattern, or teardrop pattern.

✓ The maximum speed in a course reversal is 200 knots IAS.

✓ When more than one circuit of a holding pattern is needed to lose altitude or become better established on course, the additional circuits can be made only if you advise ATC and ATC approves.

✓ Timed approaches from a holding fix are generally conducted at airports where the radar system for traffic sequencing is out of service or is not available and numerous aircraft are waiting for approach clearance.

✓ When timed approaches are in progress, you will be given advance notice of the time you should leave the holding fix.

✓ To descend below the MDA or DA, you must be able to identify specific visual references, as well as comply with the visibility and operating requirements that are listed in the regulations.

✓ When performing an approach with a decision altitude as a landing minimum, you descend on the electronic glide slope or glide path to the DA, and at that point, you make a decision to land if you meet the visual requirements or to perform a missed approach.

✓ When performing a nonprecision approach, when you reach the minimum descent altitude, you must remain at or above the MDA until you have the required visual references in sight and you are in a position where you can establish a normal rate of descent from the MDA to the runway using normal maneuvers. If these requirements are not met, you must perform the missed approach at the missed approach point (MAP).

✓ For nonprecision approaches, Jeppesen charts indicate a vertical descent angle (VDA) and an associated descent rate as a guideline for performing a stabilized descent to arrive at the MDA prior to the missed approach point.

✓ VASI lights can help you maintain the proper descent angle to the runway after you have established visual contact with the runway environment.

✓ Visual illusions are the product of various runway conditions, terrain features, and atmospheric phenomena which can create the appearance of incorrect height above the runway or incorrect distance from the runway threshold.

✓ A circling approach is necessary if the instrument approach course is not aligned within 30° of the runway, or if an unfavorable wind or a runway closure makes a straight-in landing impractical.

✓ Each circling approach is confined to a protected area which varies with aircraft approach category.

✓ When executing a circling approach, if you operate at a higher speed than is designated for your aircraft approach category, you should use the minimums of the next higher category.

✓ When cleared to perform a sidestep maneuver, fly the approach to the primary runway and begin the approach to a landing on the parallel runway as soon as possible after you have it in sight.

✓ Low visibility conditions that do not permit you to establish required visual cues, wind shear, an ATC request, a disabled aircraft on the runway, inoperative navigation components, or not being properly aligned with the final approach course are reasons for a missed approach.

✓ If an early missed approach is initiated before reaching the MAP, you should proceed to the missed approach point at or above the MDA or DA before performing a turning maneuver.

✓ If you lose visual reference while circling to land from an instrument approach and ATC radar service is not available, you should initiate a missed approach by making a climbing turn toward the landing runway and continue the turn until established on the missed approach course.

SECTION B ■ Approach Procedures

✓ If the ceiling is at least 1,000 feet AGL and visibility is at least three statute miles, ATC may clear you for a visual approach in lieu of the published approach procedure.

✓ ATC can issue a clearance for a contact approach upon your request when the reported ground visibility at the airport is one statute mile or greater. ATC cannot initiate a contact approach.

✓ Charted Visual Flight Procedures (CVFPs) might be established at some controlled airports for environmental or noise considerations, as well as when necessary for the safety and efficiency of air traffic operations.

KEY TERMS

Approach Overview	Landing Illusions
Approach Briefing	Circling Approach
Straight-In Landing	Sidestep Maneuver
Straight-In Approach	Missed Approach
Radar Vectors	Visual Approach
Minimum Vectoring Altitude (MVA)	Contact Approach
Course Reversal	Charted Visual Flight Procedure (CVFP)
Timed Approaches From a Holding Fix	

QUESTIONS

1. What actions should you take when performing an approach chart overview?
    A. Obtain current weather information to determine if the ceiling and visibility are at or above the approach landing minimums.
    B. Memorize the minimum altitudes for each segment of the approach procedure.
    C. Request runway length, conditions, slope, and available lighting from ATC.

2. What are the elements that you normally include in an approach briefing
    A. Procedure title, communication frequencies, primary navaid frequency or approach selected, initial approach course, vertical descent angle, DA or MDA, airport information, missed approach instructions, procedural notes
    B. Procedure title, communication frequencies, primary navaid frequency or approach selected, final approach course, approach altitudes, DA or MDA, highest obstruction elevation, minimum safe altitude, procedural notes
    C. Procedure title, communication frequencies, primary navaid frequency or approach selected, final approach course, approach altitudes, DA or MDA, airport information, missed approach instructions, procedural notes

3. Explain the difference between the terms straight-in landing, circling approach and straight-in approach.

Refer to the ILS or LOC Rwy 34 approach chart for Easterwood Airport to answer questions 4 through 9.

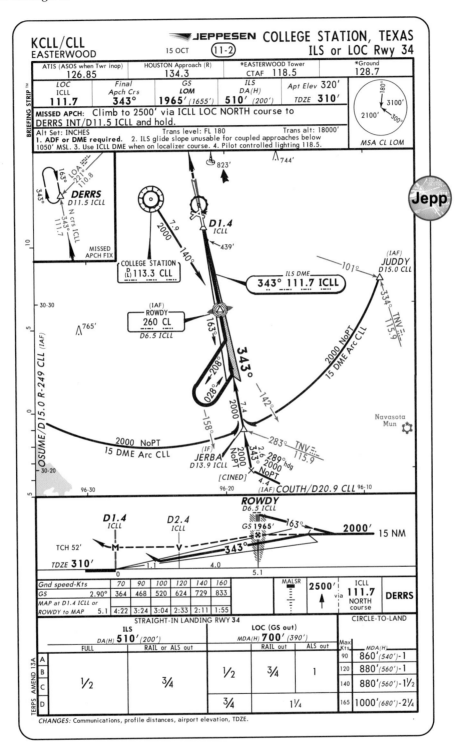

4. What magnetic course and minimum altitude applies to the feeder route depicted on this approach chart?

5. A straight-in approach can be executed from which initial approach fix?
   A. Rowdy LOM
   B. COUTH Intersection
   C. The intersection of the 15 DME arc and the 142° radial from College Station VOR/DME

6. Select the true statement regarding the course reversal for this approach procedure.
   A. You may reverse course any way that you want as long as you make the turn on the same side of the course as the symbol.
   B. You must execute the procedure turn exactly as it is depicted on the chart.
   C. You must complete the procedure turn within 10 nautical miles of ROWDY.

7. To remain in protected airspace during the procedure turn, you must not fly beyond how many nautical miles from Rowdy LOM?
   A. 7.4 nautical miles
   B. 10 nautical miles
   C. 15 nautical miles

8. If you are circling to land at 100 knots in a Category A aircraft, what is your MDA(H) and visibility requirement?

9. What is the maximum airspeed you can use when executing a course reversal?

10. What conditions must be met for timed approaches from a holding fix to be conducted at an airport?
    A. A control tower must be in operation.
    B. Course reversal is required for the missed approach procedure.
    C. The ceiling must be at least 1,000 feet AGL and visibility must be at least three statute miles.

11. The flight visibility is greater than the visibility prescribed in the standard instrument approach procedure being used; however, at the MDA you cannot identify any of the runway references described in FAR 91.175. Can you descend below the MDA for landing?

12. What is the true about descending to a DA versus an MDA?
    A. You descend on the electronic glide slope or glide path to the DA, and at that point, you maintain the DA until you meet the visual requirements to land or perform the missed approach at the MAP.
    B. After reaching the DA, you must remain at or above the DA until you have the required visual references in sight and you are in a position where you can establish a normal rate of descent from the DA to the runway using normal maneuvers. If these requirements are not met, you must perform the missed approach at the MAP.
    C. You descend on the electronic glide slope or glide path to the DA, and at that point, you make a decision to land if you meet the visual requirements or to perform a missed approach if you do not have the runway environment in sight.

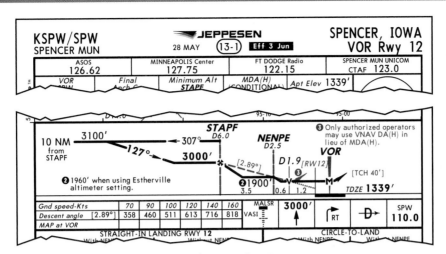

13. What is true regarding this approach procedure?
    A. The vertical descent angle of 2.89° is shown as a reference for maintaining the glide slope on a precision approach.
    B. Descending at a rate of 460 feet per minute at 90 knots is a guideline for maintaining the vertical descent angle of 2.89°.
    C. If you fly the path that corresponds to the vertical descent angle you will reach the MDA at the runway threshold.

14. True/False. When landing on a narrower-than-usual runway, the tendency is to fly an approach that is too high.

15. If you made a decision to perform a missed approach prior to the MAP and the procedure specifies a climbing right turn to 5,000 feet, what action should you take?
    A. Immediately initiate a climbing right turn.
    B. Climb straight ahead to 5,000 feet, then initiate a climbing right turn.
    C. Proceed to the MAP while climbing to 5,000 feet MSL, then initiate a turn.

16. Explain the difference between a visual approach and a contact approach.

SECTION B ■ **Approach Procedures**

CHAPTER 8

Instrument Approaches

Instrument/Commercial
Part II, Segment 2, Chapter 8 — Instrument Approaches

SECTION A
VOR and NDB Approaches

In Chapter 7, you learned about instrument approach charts and procedures. Now you will become oriented to different types of approach procedures beginning with nonprecision approaches. To fly VOR and NDB approaches, you use basic navigation procedures to track lateral courses and maintain the altitudes indicated on the approach procedure for vertical guidance to the runway. There are two basic types of VOR or NDB approaches—those that use a navaid located beyond the airport boundaries and those with the navaid located on the airport. You can easily determine whether the procedure uses an off-airport facility or on-airport facility by looking at the approach chart profile view. [Figure 8-1]

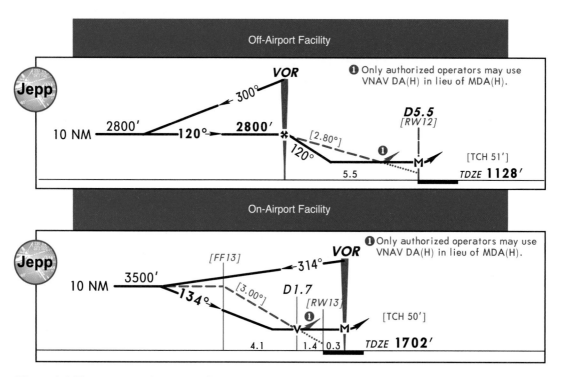

Figure 8-1. These approach chart profiles show the basic differences in approaches with off-airport and on-airport facilities. When the navaid is not located on the airport, it often serves as both the IAF and FAF.

FLYING A VOR/DME APPROACH

Many VOR approaches incorporate DME fixes as an essential part of the approach procedure. To fly a **VOR/DME approach**, you track specific radials to and from VORs, use DME to identify fixes along the approach course, and, at times, fly a DME arc to intercept the final approach course.

Your destination is Kalispell, Montana's Glacier Park International Airport (KGPI). Assume you are approaching from the southwest on V536. Your route will take you to VAILL intersection, an initial approach fix from which you plan to fly the DME arc of the VOR/DME Runway 30 approach. Prior to reaching VAILL, you listen to ATIS. [Figure 8-2]

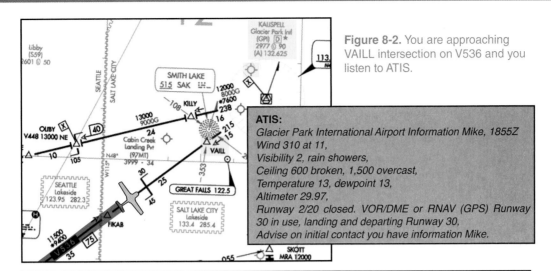

Figure 8-2. You are approaching VAILL intersection on V536 and you listen to ATIS.

ATIS:
Glacier Park International Airport Information Mike, 1855Z
Wind 310 at 11,
Visibility 2, rain showers,
Ceiling 600 broken, 1,500 overcast,
Temperature 13, dewpoint 13,
Altimeter 29.97,
Runway 2/20 closed. VOR/DME or RNAV (GPS) Runway
30 in use, landing and departing Runway 30,
Advise on initial contact you have information Mike.

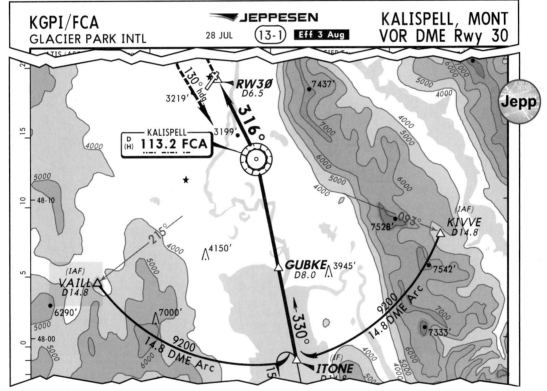

PREPARING FOR THE APPROACH

Preparation to fly an approach should begin well before flying the procedure. During the **approach overview**, determine which approaches are in use or likely to be in use at the destination airport, and review those procedures as early as possible. Use the weather information for the destination airport to analyze whether a successful approach is likely. After you select an approach, perform an **approach briefing**, in which you focus on specific details of the final and missed approach segments.

APPROACH OVERVIEW

After you listen to ATIS, you perform an approach overview for the VOR/DME Runway 30 approach. Compare the landing minimums for a category A airplane operating at 90 knots with the reported ceiling and visibility, look for significant terrain and obstacles, determine if there are unique features that you need to take into consideration, and review the airport information using the airport chart. [Figure 8-3]

SECTION A ■ VOR and NDB Approaches

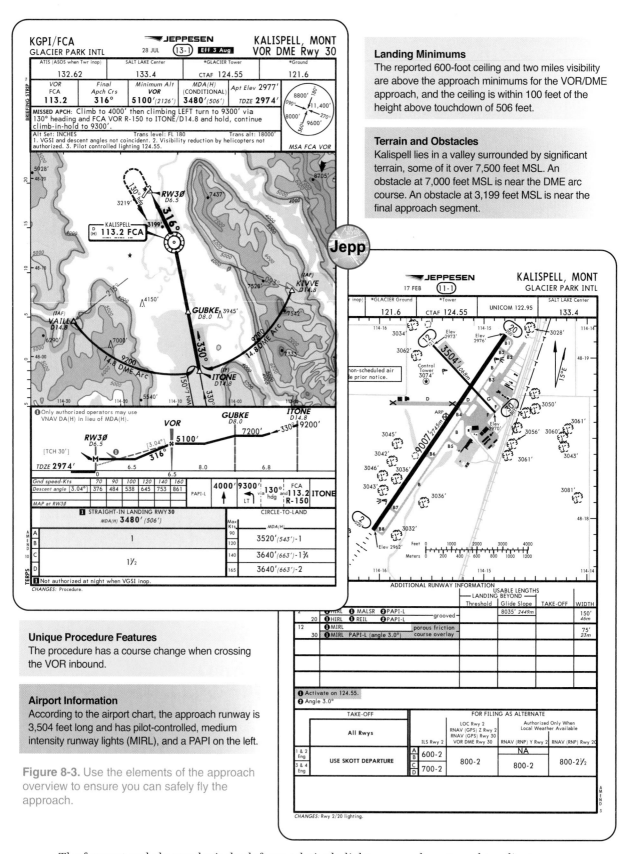

Landing Minimums

The reported 600-foot ceiling and two miles visibility are above the approach minimums for the VOR/DME approach, and the ceiling is within 100 feet of the height above touchdown of 506 feet.

Terrain and Obstacles

Kalispell lies in a valley surrounded by significant terrain, some of it over 7,500 feet MSL. An obstacle at 7,000 feet MSL is near the DME arc course. An obstacle at 3,199 feet MSL is near the final approach segment.

Unique Procedure Features

The procedure has a course change when crossing the VOR inbound.

Airport Information

According to the airport chart, the approach runway is 3,504 feet long and has pilot-controlled, medium intensity runway lights (MIRL), and a PAPI on the left.

Figure 8-3. Use the elements of the approach overview to ensure you can safely fly the approach.

The forecast and observed winds aloft are relatively light, so you do not need to adjust your approach speed or rate of descent to maintain the correct groundspeed for the approach. With a 600-foot ceiling, you can expect to reach the MDA just after breaking out of the clouds. Because the ceiling is close to the MDA, you must be prepared for the possibility that you will not see the runway environment and will need to perform a missed approach.

APPROACH BRIEFING

As you continue toward VAILL intersection, you receive the following transmission from Salt Lake Center: *"Cessna 20JA, descend and maintain 11,000, expect VOR/DME Runway 30 approach at Kalispell."* This is the time to brief the approach so you can memorize the important details of the procedure. [Figure 8-4]

Procedure Title
The procedure is the VOR/DME approach for Runway 30 at Glacier Park International in Kalispell, Montana.

Communication Frequencies
Listen to ATIS or ASOS on 132.62. Talk to Salt Lake Center on 133.4. set the frequency for Glacier Tower to 124.55 and Ground Control to 121.6.

Primary Navaid Frequency
Ensure that you have the Kalispell VOR (FCA) frequency of 113.2 set and identified and that the DME is set to that VOR receiver.

Final Approach Course
The final approach course is 316°.

Approach Altitudes
At VAILL, intercept the DME arc and descend to 9,200 feet MSL. After intercepting the course of 330°, descend to 7,200 feet MSL. At GUBKE—8 DME from Kalispell VOR—descend to 5,100 feet MSL.

MDA (Nonprecision Approach)
The MDA is 3,480 feet MSL.

Airport Information
The airport elevation is 2,977 feet MSL. The touchdown zone elevation (TDZE) is 2,974 feet MSL.

Missed Approach Instructions
Climb straight ahead to 4,000 feet MSL, and then enter a climbing left turn to 9,300 feet MSL to a heading of 130° to intercept the FCA 150° radial to ITONE intersection at 14.8 DME. Enter the holding pattern while continuing to climb to 9,300 feet MSL in the hold.

Procedural Notes
The visual glide slope indicator angle does not coincide with the 3.04° degree descent angle. Pilot-controlled lighting is on 124.55.

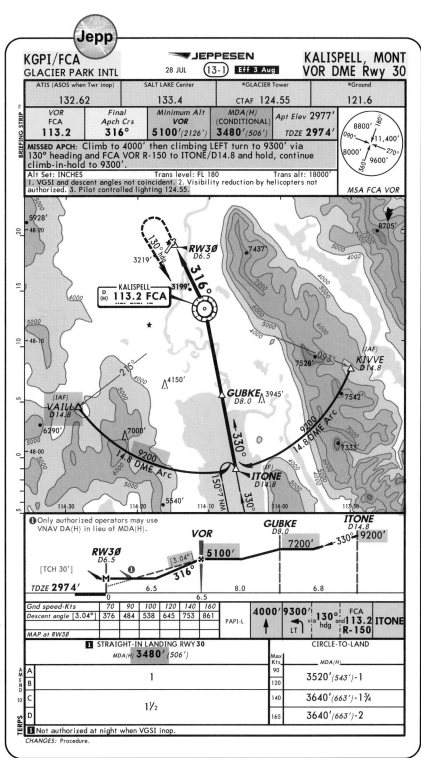

SECTION A ■ VOR and NDB Approaches

Figure 8-4. During the approach briefing, make sure you understand the approach procedure details and verify that your navigation equipment is set.

PERFORMING THE APPROACH

You have set the altimeter, briefed the approach, and set and identified the Kalispell VOR frequency. The DME display is decreasing toward 14.8, the distance for the arc that identifies the VAILL intersection, the initial approach fix. You put away the enroute chart and focus on the approach chart.

APPROACH CLEARANCE

As you near the VAILL intersection, you receive your approach clearance from Salt Lake Center: *"Cessna 20JA, cleared for the VOR/DME Runway 30 approach at Glacier Park. Maintain 11,000 until established on the approach. Contact Glacier Tower at Kalispell inbound."*

INITIAL APPROACH SEGMENT

Monitor the DME as you get closer to the arc. About one mile prior to reaching the arc, turn right to the heading shown at the wingtip reference, which is approximately 90 degrees to the inbound course of 035°. Your initial approach segment begins when you intercept the 14.8 DME arc. [Figure 8-5]

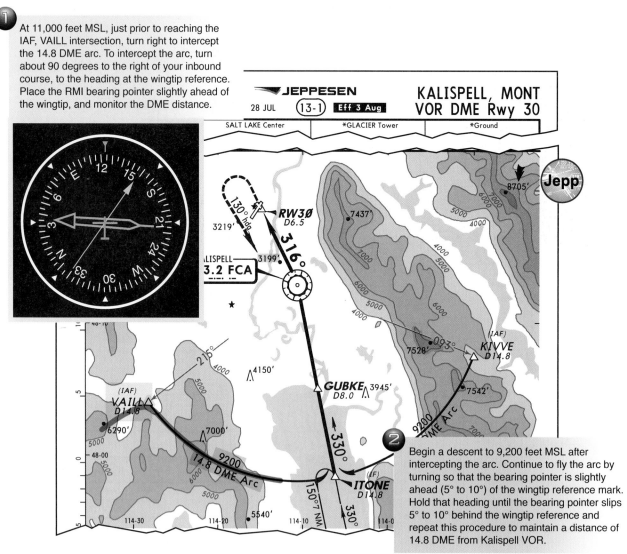

1 At 11,000 feet MSL, just prior to reaching the IAF, VAILL intersection, turn right to intercept the 14.8 DME arc. To intercept the arc, turn about 90 degrees to the right of your inbound course, to the heading at the wingtip reference. Place the RMI bearing pointer slightly ahead of the wingtip, and monitor the DME distance.

2 Begin a descent to 9,200 feet MSL after intercepting the arc. Continue to fly the arc by turning so that the bearing pointer is slightly ahead (5° to 10°) of the wingtip reference mark. Hold that heading until the bearing pointer slips 5° to 10° behind the wingtip reference and repeat this procedure to maintain a distance of 14.8 DME from Kalispell VOR.

Figure 8-5. Initial Approach Segment

SECTION A ■ **VOR and NDB Approaches**

INTERMEDIATE APPROACH SEGMENT

The intermediate approach segment begins at ITONE where you turn to intercept a course of 330°. [Figure 8-6] On the intermediate segment, ensure the before-landing checklist is complete with the possible exception of the extending the flaps and landing gear, if applicable. When you are established on the course of 330°, begin a descent to 7,200 feet MSL to the final approach fix. Make sure you know the rate of descent required to reach stepdown altitudes and the MDA by the appropriate time. For example, at 90 knots (1½ NM/min), it will take a little over four minutes to travel the 6.8 miles to the FAF GUBKE, and you need to descend 2,000 feet. Therefore, 500 feet per minute should be a sufficient rate of descent.

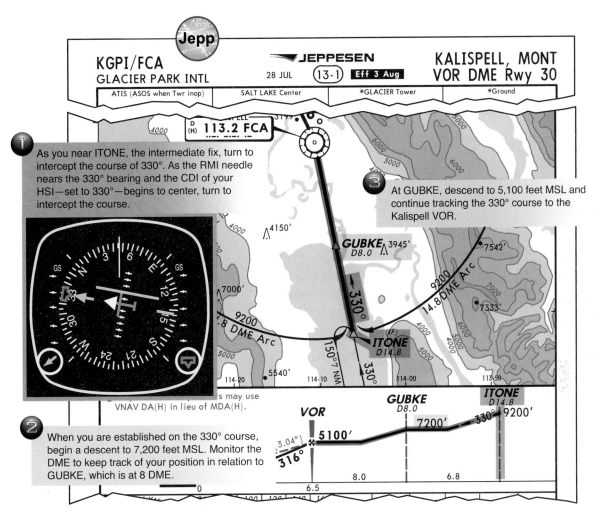

Figure 8-6. Intermediate Approach Segment

FINAL APPROACH SEGMENT

Begin the final approach segment at Kalispell VOR. On most approaches, it is not necessary to change course when crossing the VOR, but for this approach procedure, you must turn left to track the final approach course. Report your position to the tower on 124.55: *"Glacier Tower, Cessna 20JA, Kalispell VOR, inbound on the VOR/DME Runway 30 approach."* Periodically scan ahead for the runway environment and the required visual cues and keep track of your altitude so that you know when you reach the MDA of 3,480 feet MSL. It is critical that you do not descend below the MDA until you are in a position to make a normal landing approach to Runway 30 with adequate visual reference. [Figure 8-7]

SECTION A ■ VOR and NDB Approaches

SECTION A ■ VOR and NDB Approaches

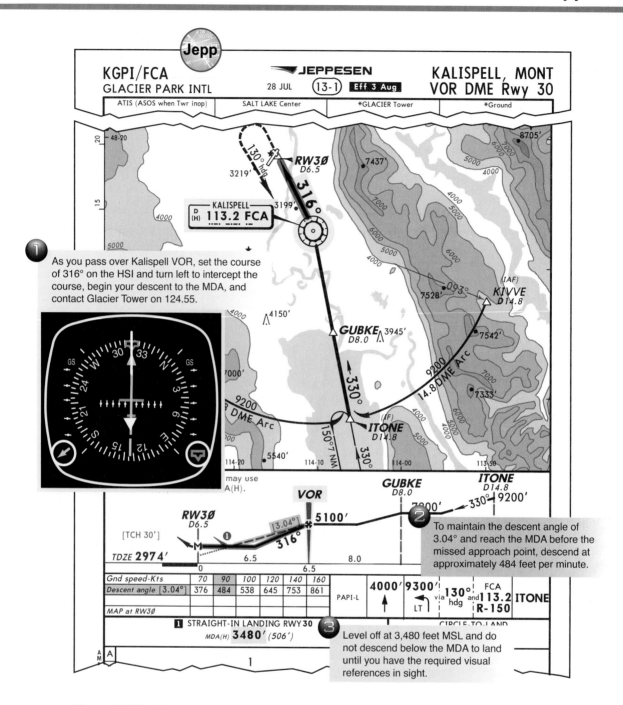

Figure 8-7. Final Approach Segment

MISSED APPROACH SEGMENT

At the missed approach point, you do not have the required visual references in sight, so add power to start climbing and begin the missed approach. It is important to remain focused and vigilant during the missed approach procedure so that you do not make errors in navigation that could lead to controlled flight into terrain. Report the missed approach to Glacier Tower and, upon the controller's direction, contact Salt Lake Center to request clearance for another approach or routing to your alternate. In this case, the controller clears you to fly the published missed approach procedure. [Figure 8-8]

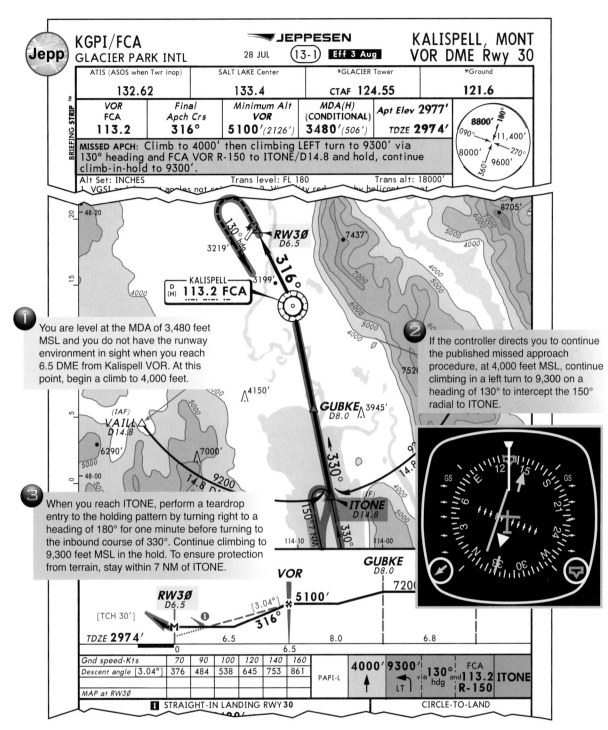

Figure 8-8. Missed Approach Segment

FLYING AN NDB APPROACH

Many of the first radio navaids were nondirectional beacons, so some of the first instrument approaches were NDB approaches and many airports still have these approach procedures. To fly an NDB approach, you must know how to track specific bearings using an ADF display and heading indicator to fly a course to the runway.

Your destination is South Big Horn County Airport in Greybull, Wyoming. You are planning to perform the NDB Runway 34 approach. Your route will take you from the Cody VOR to the Greybull NDB, the initial approach fix. As you near Cody, you listen to ASOS. [Figure 8-9]

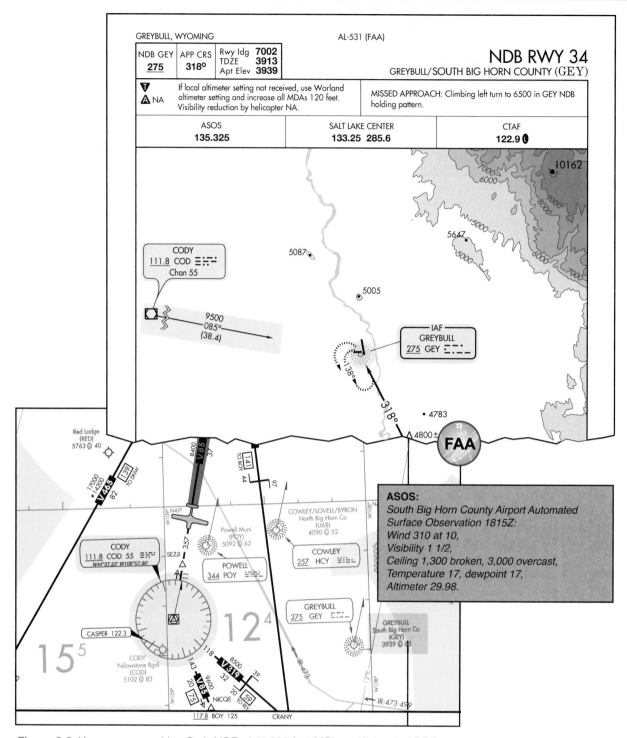

Figure 8-9. You are approaching Cody VOR at 11,000 feet MSL and listen to ASOS.

PREPARING FOR THE APPROACH

To prepare for the approach, you should perform an approach overview. After you have determined that you can perform the procedure, a thorough approach briefing will help familiarize you with the details of the approach.

APPROACH OVERVIEW

To perform an approach overview, compare the reported ceiling and visibility with the landing minimums for a category A airplane operating at 90 knots, look for significant terrain and obstacles, determine if there are unique features that you need to take into consideration, and review the airport information using the airport diagram. [Figure 8-10]

Landing Minimums
The reported 1,300-foot ceiling and 1½ miles visibility are only slightly above the approach minimums. You can use the lowest landing minimums because you are performing a straight-in landing and you have the local altimeter setting.

Terrain and Obstacles
The only significant obstacle near the approach path is at 4,800 feet MSL.

Unique Procedure Features
Because the NDB facility is at the airport, there is no designated final approach fix. The final approach segment begins at the final approach point (FAP) when you have intercepted the final approach course after completing the procedure turn. The missed approach point is at the NDB.

Airport Information
The approach runway is 7,002 feet long and has pilot-controlled lighting for medium-intensity runway lights and runway end identifier lights. The NDB is located to the left of the runway.

SECTION A ■ VOR and NDB Approaches

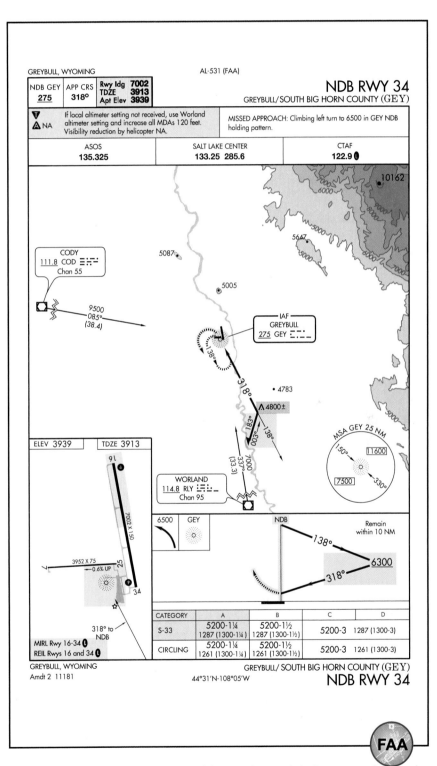

Figure 8-10. One element of the approach overview is to check the landing minimums that apply to the approach procedure If the ASOS had been inoperative, you would need to use the Worland Municipal altimeter setting, which changes the straight-in landing minimums to 5,320 feet MSL.

APPROACH BRIEFING

After listening to ASOS, you receive this transmission from ATC: *"Diamond Star 505JF, descend and maintain 10,000, expect NDB approach Runway 34, Greybull."* As you review the approach altitudes during the approach briefing, it is important to plan your descent rate. In this example, you need to lose 3,200 feet during the procedure turn and remain within 10 nautical miles of the NDB at an approach speed of 90 knots. With no wind, you will cover 1.5 nautical miles per minute. Unless there are strong winds, a three-minute outbound leg will keep you within 10 nautical miles of the NDB. A descent rate of 750 feet per minute will ensure that you reach 6,300 feet MSL prior to intercepting the final approach course. [Figure 8-11]

Procedure Title
The procedure is the NDB approach for Runway 34 at South Big Horn County Airport in Greybull, Wyoming.

Communication Frequencies
Listen to ASOS on 135.325. Talk to Salt Lake Center on 133.25. Set the CTAF on 122.9.

Primary Navaid Frequency
Set the ADF to 275 and identify the GEY NDB.

Final Approach Course
The final approach course is 318°.

Approach Altitudes
Outbound from Greybull, descend and maintain 6,300 feet MSL in the procedure turn. Begin the final descent after completing the procedure turn and intercepting the final approach course.

MDA
The MDA is 5,200 feet MSL.

Airport Information
The runway length is 7,002 feet. The touchdown zone elevation is 3,913 feet MSL and the airport elevation is 3,939 feet MSL.

Missed Approach Instructions
Perform a climbing left turn to 6,500 feet MSL in a holding pattern at Greybull (GEY) NDB.

Procedural Notes
You have the local altimeter setting.

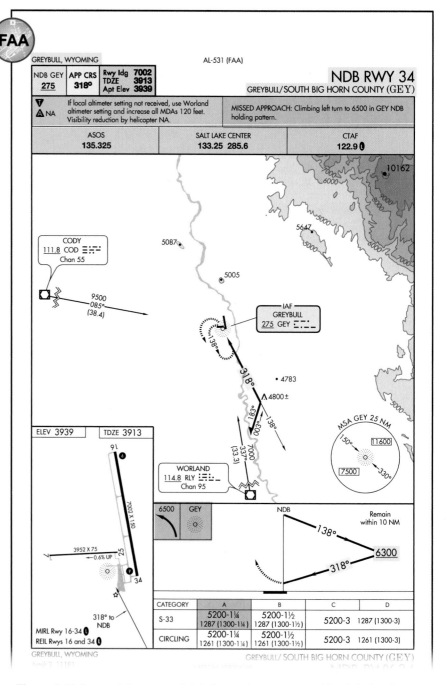

Figure 8-11 A complete approach briefing reduces your workload during the approach and can prevent potentially dangerous oversights and omissions.

PERFORMING THE APPROACH

As you perform the approach, the primary navigation instruments are the ADF display and heading indicator. The altimeter provides your primary vertical references.

APPROACH CLEARANCE

Before you reach Greybull NDB, you receive this transmission from Salt Lake City Center: *"Diamond Star 505JF, cleared for the NDB Runway 34 approach to South Big Horn County. Descend and maintain 9,500 until established on the approach. Contact local traffic advisory when procedure turn inbound."* While flying from Cody VOR to Greybull NDB, descend to 9,500 feet MSL. After you are level at 9,500, perform the before landing checklist with the possible exceptions of extending the landing gear and flaps.

12 MILES, CLEARED FOR THE APPROACH?

A light aircraft was just passing 12 DME inbound to Runway 26, when the approach controller cleared the flight crew for a 12 DME arc approach to Runway 26 instead of the straight-in approach that the crew had planned. Because the aircraft was already inside the 12 DME arc, and because of unclear phraseology from the controller, the crew proceeded with a straight-in approach. Fortunately, the discrepancy was discovered without incident; the crew obtained an amended clearance and completed the approach. The following excerpt was taken from the ASRS report which was filed subsequent to the incident.

"While tuned to approach control we were just passing 12 DME on the inbound radial upon being told "12 miles, cleared VOR Runway 26 approach, descend to 3,000 feet." The first officer read back "cleared VOR Runway 26, descend to 3,000 feet," to which approach rogered. I then briefed the VOR Runway 26 approach. At approximately 6 DME the controller inquired as to our DME, which we replied. Controller said that we were cleared for the 12 mile arc VOR Runway 26 approach. We informed him that we never heard arc or DME approach and would execute the VOR Runway 26 approach due to our proximity. The approach was then uneventful. It has been my experience that when you are to fly an arc approach you are given clearance at least 2 miles prior to the arc to commence your turn."

"Communication is the culprit here. Precise terminology should be used and the approach should be renamed (or referred to by the controller as) 12 DME Arc Runway 26 approach."

The ASRS contains frequent reports of controllers using nonstandard terminology in clearances. In some cases, the controller made modifications to published departure procedures which confused the flight crew. Unfortunately, pilot requests for clarification were not always satisfactorily handled, at least according to the pilots filing these reports.

It is not only your right as a pilot to get clarification for a confusing clearance—it is your duty. There are times when you may need to be assertive. Refuse a clearance if necessary, and ensure the controller provides a clearance that makes sense to you.

INITIAL APPROACH SEGMENT

As you pass over Greybull NDB (the IAF) the reversal of the ADF pointer prompts you to begin a turn to intercept the outbound bearing of 138°. Because you are established on the initial approach segment, descend to 6,300 feet MSL at the approach speed of 90 knots. Use the ADF to navigate on course and use the clock or stopwatch to time your outbound leg. Proceed outbound for three minutes to give yourself time to descend, but stay within 10 nautical miles of the NDB. [Figure 8-12]

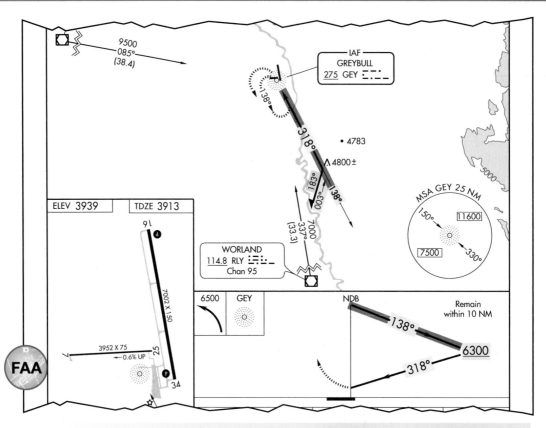

To intercept the 138° bearing outbound from the NDB, turn to a heading of 158° to set up a 20° intercept angle. When the tail of the ADF needle approaches the 20° intercept angle, turn back to a heading of 138° and verify that the ADF needle is centered. Begin a descent to 6,300 feet MSL.

After three minutes, begin the procedure turn by turning right to a heading of 183°.

Fly for one minute, then turn left to a heading of 003°. Level off at 6,300 feet.

Monitor the ADF indicator to determine when you are nearing the 318° bearing, which is when the pointer reaches the 45° relative bearing mark.

Figure 8-12. Initial Approach Segment

FINAL APPROACH SEGMENT

The final approach segment begins when you intercept the inbound course. This approach does not have an intermediate segment. After completing the procedure turn, monitor the ADF so you can turn on to the final approach course when the ADF pointer approaches the 45° relative bearing mark. After you are established on the course, reduce power and lower flaps and landing gear as appropriate to begin your descent to the MDA. [Figure 8-13]

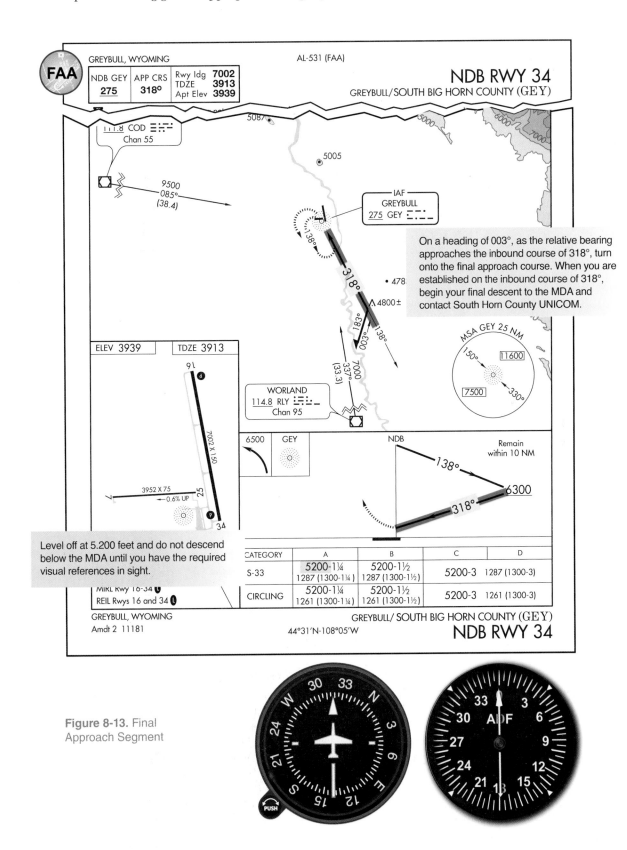

Figure 8-13. Final Approach Segment

MISSED APPROACH SEGMENT

At the MDA, level off, look for the runway environment, and monitor the ADF indicator. If you do not have the runway environment in sight when the ADF pointer indicates that you are passing the NDB, add power to start a climbing turn to the left to begin the missed approach. [Figure 8-14]

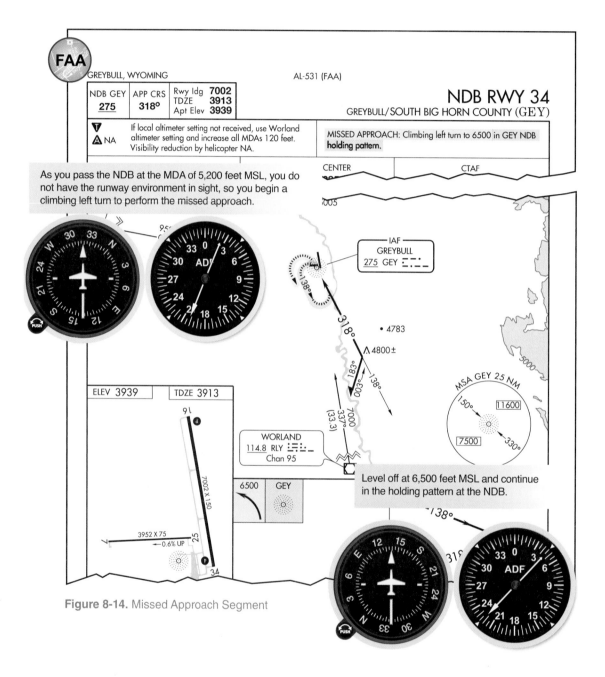

Figure 8-14. Missed Approach Segment

SECTION A ■ VOR and NDB Approaches

FAA

GREYBULL, WYOMING   AL-531 (FAA)

NDB GEY	APP CRS	Rwy Idg	**7002**
275	**318°**	TDZE	**3913**
		Apt Elev	**3939**

NDB RWY 34
GREYBULL/SOUTH BIG HORN COUNTY (GEY)

▽ NA   If local altimeter setting not received, use Worland altimeter setting and increase all MDAs 120 feet. Visibility reduction by helicopter NA.

MISSED APPROACH: Climbing left turn to 6500 in GEY NDB **holding pattern.**

As you pass the NDB at the MDA of 5,200 feet MSL, you do not have the runway environment in sight, so you begin a climbing left turn to perform the missed approach.

Level off at 6,500 feet MSL and continue in the holding pattern at the NDB.

CENTER   CTAF

IAF
GREYBULL
275 GEY

• 4783
∆ 4800±

MSA GEY 25 NM

318°   183°   003°   138°

WORLAND
114.8 RLY
Chan 95

7000
337°
(33.3)

ELEV 3939   TDZE 3913

6500   GEY

7002 X 150
3952 X 75
0.6% UP

8-16

SUMMARY CHECKLIST

✓ VOR and NDB approaches primarily fall into two categories—those that use an on-airport facility and those with an off-airport facility. When the navaid is not located on the airport, it often serves as both the IAF and FAF.

✓ Listen to ATIS, AWOS, or ASOS for the visibility and ceiling at the airport and, during the approach overview, refer to the landing minimums to determine whether a successful approach is likely.

✓ You should always brief the missed approach procedure and be prepared to fly it, especially if the weather conditions are close to the minimums for the approach.

✓ If using an RMI to fly a DME arc, turn so that the bearing pointer is slightly ahead (5° to 10°) of the wingtip reference mark. Hold that heading until the bearing pointer slips 5° to 10° behind the wingtip reference. Repeat this procedure as you maintain a specified distance from the VOR.

✓ Upon intercepting the approach course, make sure you know what rate of descent is required to reach stepdown altitudes or the MDA by the appropriate time.

✓ Complete your before-landing checklist prior to the FAF.

✓ During an off-airport VOR approach, course changes can occur at the VOR, so be sure to set your course selector to the new course.

✓ When reaching the MDA, add power to level off until you have the runway environment in sight and are in a position from which you can descend safely for landing.

✓ You must perform a missed approach if you reach the missed approach point (MAP) and you do not have the required visual references in sight or if you lose sight of the runway at any time while maneuvering to land.

✓ When executing a missed approach, report it to ATC, and request a clearance for another approach or routing to your alternate airport.

✓ For an approach that uses an on-airport NDB, you must time your outbound leg appropriately to give yourself time to descend, but stay within the specified distance of the NDB.

✓ The final approach segment begins when you intercept the inbound course after completing the procedure turn when flying an NDB approach with an on-airport facility.

✓ If the MAP is the NDB and you do not have the runway environment in sight when the ADF pointer indicates that you are passing the NDB, you must perform a missed approach.

KEY TERMS

Off-Airport Facility

On-Airport Facility

VOR/DME Approach

NDB Approach

QUESTIONS

Refer to the Baker City VOR/DME RWY 13 approach chart to answer questions 1 through 6.

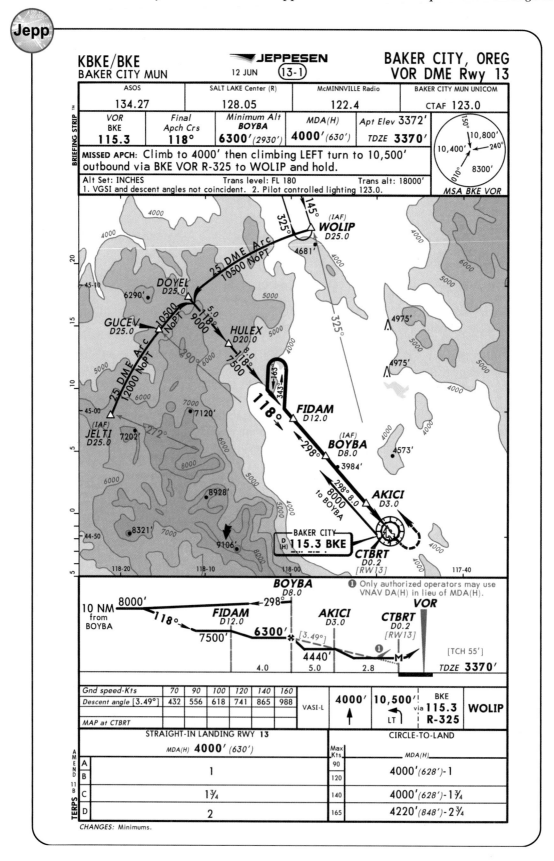

1. You are planning to fly the VOR/DME Runway 13 approach at Baker City Municipal Airport. You are in a category A airplane flying the approach at 90 knots, and ASOS indicates a 700-foot ceiling and 1¼ mile visibility. What element might you include in an approach overview for this approach?
   A. There is terrain near the missed approach holding fix that rises above 8,000 feet MSL.
   B. The missed approach point is at the VOR.
   C. The reported weather conditions are just above the ceiling and visibility minimums required for the approach.

2. As you near your destination, Salt Lake Center advises you to expect the VOR/DME Runway 13 approach. What elements should you include in your approach briefing?
   A. Contact Baker City Tower on 122.4.
   B. The final approach course is 118°.
   C. The DA is 4,000 feet MSL.

3. When you are approaching WOLIP intersection, Salt Lake Center transmits this clearance: *"Maintain 11,000 until established on the approach, cleared for VOR/DME Runway 13."* What actions should you take?
   A. Descend to 10,500 feet MSL prior to reaching WOLIP.
   B. After you are established on the 25 DME arc, descend to 10,500 feet MSL.
   C. After you are established on the 25 DME arc, descend to 8,000 feet MSL.

4. You are approaching DOYEL on the 25 DME arc. What is your next step?
   A. Intercept the final approach course, and then descend to 9,000 feet MSL.
   B. Descend to 9,000 feet MSL, and then turn to intercept the final approach course.
   C. Remain at 10,500 feet MSL until reaching FIDAM, and then descend to 6,300 feet MSL.

5. What is the correct procedure for flying the final approach segment of VOR/DME RWY 13 approach?
   A. At BOYBA, descend to 4,440 feet MSL. At AKICI, descend to the MDA of 4,000 feet MSL. If you do not have the required visual references in sight at CTBRT, perform a missed approach.
   B. At BOYBA, descend to 4,440 feet MSL. At AKICI, descend to the MDA of 4,000 feet MSL. If you do not have the required visual references in sight when you reach BKE VOR, perform a missed approach.
   C. At BOYBA, descend at approximately 556 feet per minute to 4,000 feet MSL. If you do not have the required visual references in sight when reaching 4,000 feet MSL, perform a missed approach.

6. You are level at the MDA after reaching the MAP, and you do not have the required visual references in sight. What is the correct missed approach procedure?
   A. Perform a climbing left turn to 10,500 feet MSL on the 325° radial from Baker City VOR to WOLIP intersection. Enter the holding pattern at SHEDD.
   B. Climb to 4,000 feet MSL and then perform a climbing left turn to intercept the 325° radial from Baker City VOR to WOLIP intersection. Enter the holding pattern at WOLIP.
   C. Intercept the 325° radial from Baker City VOR, and then climb to 4,000 feet MSL. Proceed to WOLIP intersection and continue to climb to 10,500 feet MSL in the hold at WOLIP.

SECTION A ■ VOR and NDB Approaches

SECTION A ■ VOR and NDB Approaches

Refer to the Deer Park NDB-A approach chart to answer questions 7 through 11.

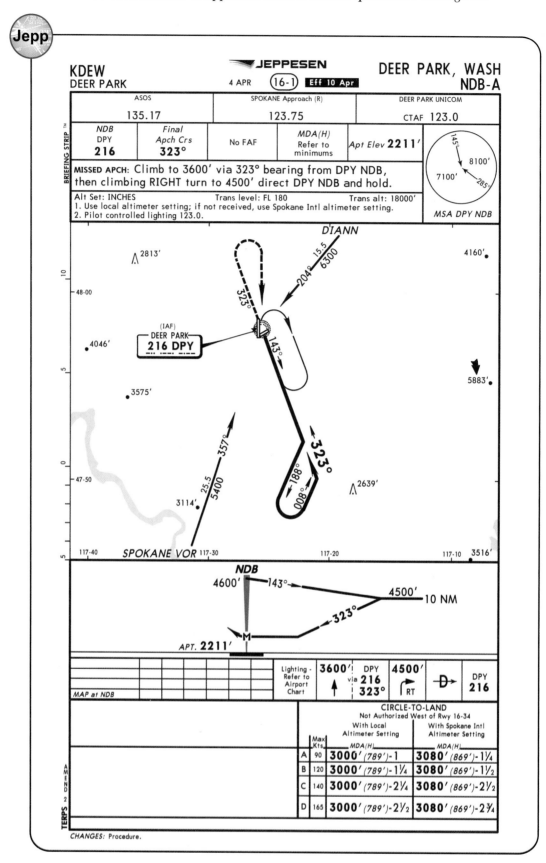

7. You are planning to fly the NDB-A approach at Deer Park Airport. You are in a category A airplane flying the approach at 90 knots, and ASOS indicates an 800-foot ceiling and 1¼ mile visibility. What element might you include in an approach overview for this approach?
   A. There is terrain over 5,000 feet MSL near the NDB.
   B. There are different minimums for Runway 4.
   C. The reported weather conditions are just above the ceiling and visibility minimums required for the approach.

8. As you near your destination, Spokane Approach advises you to expect the NDB-A approach. What elements should you include in your approach briefing?
   A. Contact Deer Park Radio on 123.0.
   B. The final approach course is 323°.
   C. The DA is 3,000 feet MSL.

9. When you are approaching DIANN intersection, Spokane Approach transmits this clearance: *"Maintain 7,000 until established on the approach, cleared for NDB-A approach at Deer Park Airport."* What actions should you take?
   A. After DPY, enter the holding pattern course reversal and maintain 7,000 feet MSL.
   B. After you pass over DPY, intercept the 143° bearing outbound and descend to 4,500 feet MSL.
   C. After you pass DIANN, descend to 4,500 feet MSL.

10. What is the correct procedure for flying the final approach segment of the NDB-A approach with a fixed-card ADF indicator and the local altimeter setting?
    A. On a heading of 008° in the procedure turn, intercept the final approach course of 323° when the ADF pointer approaches the 45° relative bearing mark. When established on the final approach course, descend to the MDA of 3,000 feet MSL. If you do not see the required visual references at DPY, perform a missed approach.
    B. On a heading of 008° in the procedure turn, intercept the final approach course of 323° when the ADF pointer approaches the 20° relative bearing mark. When established on the final approach course, descend to the MDA of 3,000 feet MSL. If you do not see the required visual references at DPY, perform a missed approach.
    C. After completing the procedure turn on a heading of 008°, intercept the final approach course of 323° when the ADF pointer approaches the 45° relative bearing mark. When established on the final approach course, descend to the MDA of 3,080 feet MSL. If you do not see the required visual references upon reaching the MDA, perform a missed approach.

11. Flying inbound after the procedure turn, you have the airport in sight as you near the NDB. The airport's ASOS is reporting winds from 250° at 15 knots. You circle to land on Runway 22. On short final you lose sight of the airport. What is the correct missed approach procedure?
    A. Climb straight ahead to 3,600 feet MSL. Then, turn right to a heading of 323° and climb to 4,500 feet MSL. After reaching 4,500 feet MSL, proceed direct to the NDB and hold.
    B. Climb straight ahead until passing the NDB, then turn right and intercept the 323° bearing from the NDB. Climb straight ahead to 3,600 feet MSL, then make a climbing right turn to 4,500 feet MSL direct to the NDB and hold.
    C. Climb straight ahead until passing the NDB, then turn right and intercept the 323° bearing from the NDB. Climb straight ahead to 3,600 feet MSL, then make a climbing right turn to 4,500 feet. Return to the NDB and enter a holding pattern with an outbound heading of 143°.

SECTION B
ILS Approaches

The instrument landing system (ILS) is a precision approach navigational aid that provides highly accurate course, glide slope, and distance guidance to a given runway. The ILS can be the best approach alternative in poor weather conditions for several reasons. First, the ILS is a more accurate approach aid than any other widely available system. Secondly, the increased accuracy generally allows for lower approach minimums. Third, the lower minimums make it possible to perform an ILS approach and land at an airport when it otherwise would not have been possible using a nonprecision approach.

ILS CATEGORIES AND MINIMUMS

There are three general classifications of ILS approaches—Category I, Category II, and Category III. The basic ILS approach is a Category (CAT) I approach and requires only that you be instrument rated and current and that your airplane be equipped appropriately. CAT II and CAT III ILS approaches typically have lower minimums and require special certification for operators, pilots, aircraft, and air/ground equipment. [Figure 8-15]

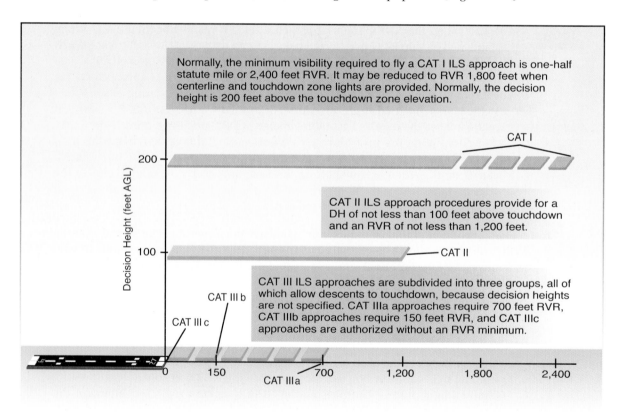

Normally, the minimum visibility required to fly a CAT I ILS approach is one-half statute mile or 2,400 feet RVR. It may be reduced to RVR 1,800 feet when centerline and touchdown zone lights are provided. Normally, the decision height is 200 feet above the touchdown zone elevation.

CAT II ILS approach procedures provide for a DH of not less than 100 feet above touchdown and an RVR of not less than 1,200 feet.

CAT III ILS approaches are subdivided into three groups, all of which allow descents to touchdown, because decision heights are not specified. CAT IIIa approaches require 700 feet RVR, CAT IIIb approaches require 150 feet RVR, and CAT IIIc approaches are authorized without an RVR minimum.

Figure 8-15. Because of the complexity and high cost of the equipment required, CAT III ILS approaches are used primarily in air carrier and military operations.

Even if an ILS runway is equipped with a capable lighting system like MALSR, the published visibility for an ILS approach can be 3/4 SM or higher if obstacles penetrate the obstacle identification surfaces (OIS), and you must be careful in the visual segment to avoid any obstacles.

ILS COMPONENTS

The basic components of an ILS approach are the localizer, glide slope, and the outer marker, compass locator, or fix identified in the approach procedure used to provide range information. An inner marker may be installed for Category II and III approaches. You receive guidance information from ground-based localizer and glide slope transmitters. To help you determine your distance from the runway, the ILS procedure design might provide a marker beacon or fixes located along the ILS approach path. In addition, to facilitate the transition from instrument to visual flight as you approach the airport, runway and approach lighting systems are installed. [Figure 8-16]

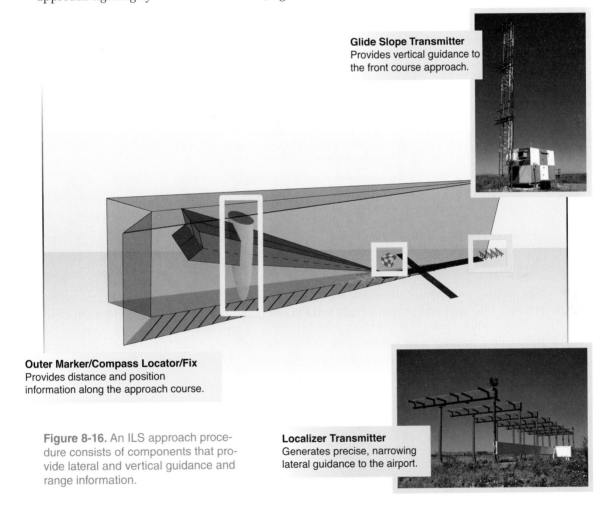

Glide Slope Transmitter
Provides vertical guidance to the front course approach.

Outer Marker/Compass Locator/Fix
Provides distance and position information along the approach course.

Figure 8-16. An ILS approach procedure consists of components that provide lateral and vertical guidance and range information.

Localizer Transmitter
Generates precise, narrowing lateral guidance to the airport.

LOCALIZER

The ILS uses a localizer transmitter to provide information regarding the airplane's alignment with the runway centerline. A localizer transmitter antenna at the departure end of the runway sends a navigational array in two directions. The front course signal covers the runway and extends forward to provide the approach course. A back course signal extends in the opposite direction. You should not use the back course signals for navigation unless a back course approach is established and ATC has authorized you to perform the procedure. [Figure 8-17]

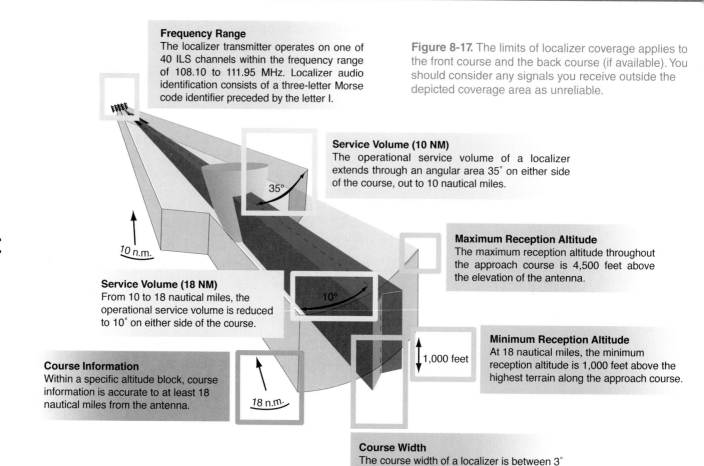

Frequency Range
The localizer transmitter operates on one of 40 ILS channels within the frequency range of 108.10 to 111.95 MHz. Localizer audio identification consists of a three-letter Morse code identifier preceded by the letter I.

Figure 8-17. The limits of localizer coverage applies to the front course and the back course (if available). You should consider any signals you receive outside the depicted coverage area as unreliable.

Service Volume (10 NM)
The operational service volume of a localizer extends through an angular area 35° on either side of the course, out to 10 nautical miles.

35°

10 n.m.

Maximum Reception Altitude
The maximum reception altitude throughout the approach course is 4,500 feet above the elevation of the antenna.

Service Volume (18 NM)
From 10 to 18 nautical miles, the operational service volume is reduced to 10° on either side of the course.

10°

Minimum Reception Altitude
At 18 nautical miles, the minimum reception altitude is 1,000 feet above the highest terrain along the approach course.

1,000 feet

Course Information
Within a specific altitude block, course information is accurate to at least 18 nautical miles from the antenna.

18 n.m.

Course Width
The course width of a localizer is between 3° and 6° in order to provide a signal width of approximately 700 feet at the runway threshold.

The signal from the localizer transmitter represents only one magnetic course to the runway. Therefore, the course selected on the OBS of a basic VOR indicator does not affect deviation indications. However, you might find it helpful to set the published course of the ILS on the course selector as a reminder of the inbound course during tracking and heading corrections. Regardless of what course you select, the CDI senses off-course position only with respect to the localizer course.

If you are using an HSI for the approach, you normally must set it to the ILS front course for guidance. When you are tracking the front course of an ILS toward the runway using a basic VOR indicator, CDI sensing is normal; that is, you turn right when the CDI is deflected to the right. Reverse CDI sensing occurs whenever the aircraft travels on the reciprocal heading of the localizer course. When using a basic VOR indicator, normal sensing occurs inbound on the localizer front course and outbound on the back course. Reverse sensing occurs inbound on the back course and outbound on the front course. With an HSI, you can avoid reverse sensing by setting the published front course on the course selector. This applies regardless of your direction of travel, whether inbound or outbound on either the front or back course. Each dot of displacement on your CDI equates to a specific distance from the localizer centerline, depending on your distance from the runway. [Figure 8-18]

When using a basic VOR indicator, normal sensing occurs inbound on the front course and outbound on the back course. Reverse sensing occurs inbound on the back course and outbound on the front course. With an HSI, you can avoid reverse sensing by setting the published front course under the course index. This applies regardless of your direction of travel, whether inbound or outbound on either the front or back course. See figure 8-15.

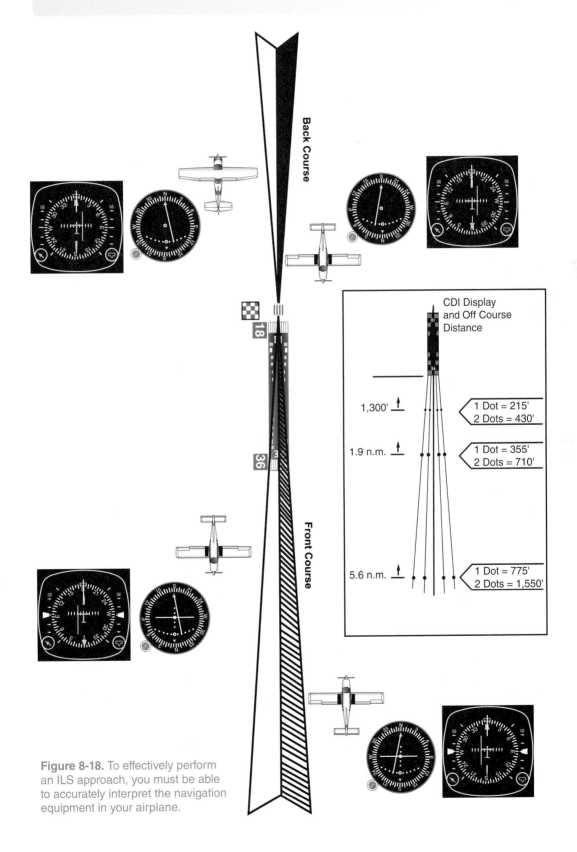

Figure 8-18. To effectively perform an ILS approach, you must be able to accurately interpret the navigation equipment in your airplane.

Depending on your distance from the runway, each dot of displacement on the CDI and on the glide slope indicator equates to a specific distance from the localizer centerline and glide slope centerline, respectively. For example, if the airplane is 1.9 nautical miles from the runway threshold and is two dots to the right of the localizer and two dots above the glide slope, the airplane is 710 feet to the right of the localizer centerline and 140 feet above the glide slope.

As you fly on a localizer course you will notice that the CDI is more sensitive than during VOR navigation. For instance, when navigating using a VOR, full-scale deflection of the CDI represents a 20° radial span, or 10° to each side of course. However, when using localizer signals, the total span of the CDI is 5°, or 2.5° each side of the course. The advantage of greater CDI sensitivity is that you can track a localizer course with a theoretical accuracy four times that of a VOR radial. However, the resulting CDI movement is more rapid during localizer tracking which requires timely corrections for off-course indications. Make relatively small corrections to help prevent overshooting the desired course.

GLIDE SLOPE

A **glide slope** transmitter broadcasts a navigational signal to provide accurate, narrowing vertical guidance on a front course ILS approach. You refer to the glide slope indicator to maintain a glide path to the runway. Glide slope transmitters operate on a UHF frequency paired to the associated localizer frequency so that you automatically select the correct glide slope channel when you setting the localizer frequency. [Figure 8-19]

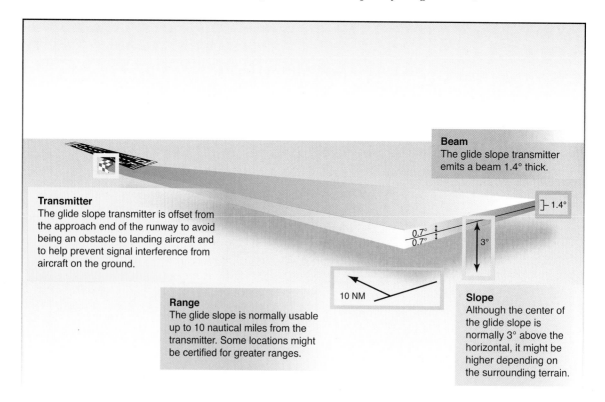

Figure 8-19. The glide slope transmitter emits a signal that provides accurate vertical guidance during an ILS approach.

The glide slope signal provides vertical navigation information for descent to the lowest authorized decision altitude for the associated approach procedure. If you receive glide slope guidance below the decision altitude you should consider it unreliable. You might also receive other erroneous navigation information, such as false signals and reverse sensing, at high angles above the normal 3° glide slope projection. To avoid navigation errors, rely only on glide slope indications from the time you approach the glide slope intercept altitude shown on the approach chart until you reach decision altitude.

Because full-scale deviation of the glide slope needle is 0.7° above or below the center of the glide slope beam, a position only slightly off the glide slope centerline produces large deflections on the navigation indicator. To fly a precise approach, you must respond immediately to glide slope indications with pitch and/or power changes. [Figure 8-20]

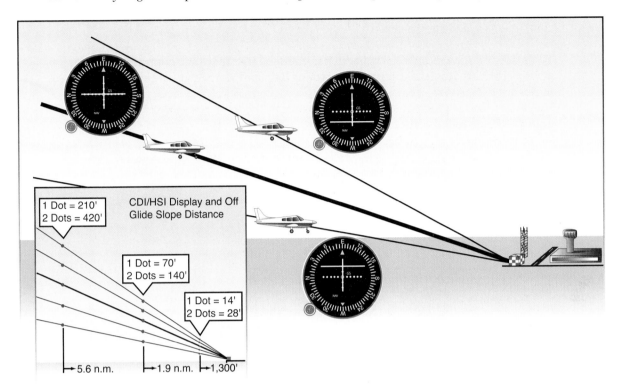

1 Dot = 210'
2 Dots = 420'

CDI/HSI Display and Off Glide Slope Distance

1 Dot = 70'
2 Dots = 140'

1 Dot = 14'
2 Dots = 28'

5.6 n.m.   1.9 n.m.   1,300'

Figure 8-20. To ensure obstacle clearance, do not fly below the glide path. Depending on your distance from the runway, each dot of displacement on your glide slope indicator equates to a specific distance from the glide slope centerline.

RANGE INFORMATION

ILS approach procedures use a variety of methods to provide range to the runway during the approach. A standard feature of an ILS procedure is a means to identify the final approach fix for the localizer-only approach and the location at which you can expect to intercept the glide slope at the glide slope intercept altitude. An outer marker, compass locator, NDB, published DME or VOR fixes, precision approach radar (PAR), and airport surveillance radar (ASR) may be used for range information on an ILS approach. You can also use an IFR-approved RNAV system to identify fixes in the ILS approach procedure.

 An outer marker, compass locator, NDB, published DME or VOR fixes, precision approach radar (PAR), and airport surveillance radar (ASR) may be used for range information on an ILS approach.

OUTER MARKER AND COMPASS LOCATOR

The ILS **outer marker (OM)** beacon projects an elliptical signal upward from the antenna site. At about 1,000 feet above the antenna, the signal is 2,400 feet thick and 4,200 feet wide. The placement of the outer marker varies from four to seven miles from the runway, depending on the installation. It usually is placed just inside the point where an airplane flying the ILS intercepts the glide slope.

At some locations with Category II and III ILS operations, an inner marker (IM) is installed to indicate approximately 100 feet above the touchdown zone elevation, which is typically the decision height for a Category II approach. Occasionally, a marker beacon is located on a localizer back course as a final approach fix. In the past, middle markers were installed approximately 3,500 feet from the runway threshold, but they are no longer primary components of ILS approaches.

The marker beacon receiver is typically incorporated into the audio control console for the avionics. Marker beacon receivers use a flashing light and Morse code audio identification to indicate when the airplane has passed the beacon. Controls enable you to select high or low receiver sensitivity and to mute the audio identification. [Figure 8-21]

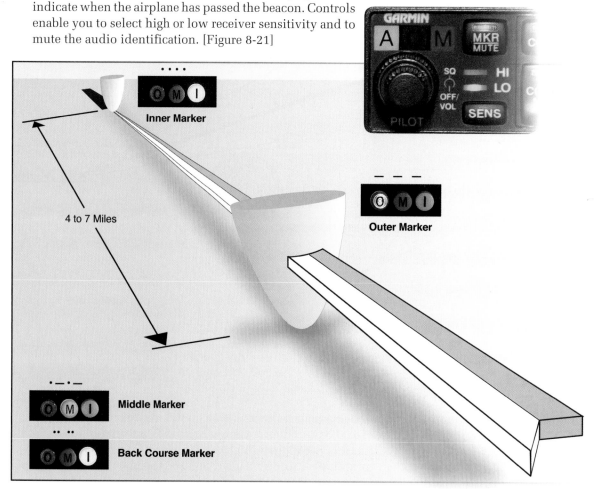

Figure 8-21. When your airplane passes through the signal array of a marker beacon, the associated light flashes and the Morse code identification sounds.

 As you pass over a marker beacon, the appropriate visual display and audio identification is activated. See figure 8-21.

Some ILS approaches use a low power, low or medium frequency (L/MF) radio beacon, called a **compass locator** collocated with the outer marker and referred to as a locator outer marker (LOM). Compass locators usually have a power output of less than 25 watts, resulting in a reception range of at least 15 miles. At some locations, high powered NDBs of up to 400 watts are used in combination with the outer marker. The frequency range for compass locators is 190 to 535 kHz. A compass locator at the outer marker transmits a two-letter Morse code identifier. Localizer identifiers begin with the letter I and the first two letters of the localizer identifier that follow the letter I designate the LOM. For example, the LOM associated with the localizer IAPA would transmit the letters (AP). [Figure 8-22]

> **FAA** Localizer identifiers begin with the letter I and the first two letters of the localizer identifier that follow the letter I designate the LOM.

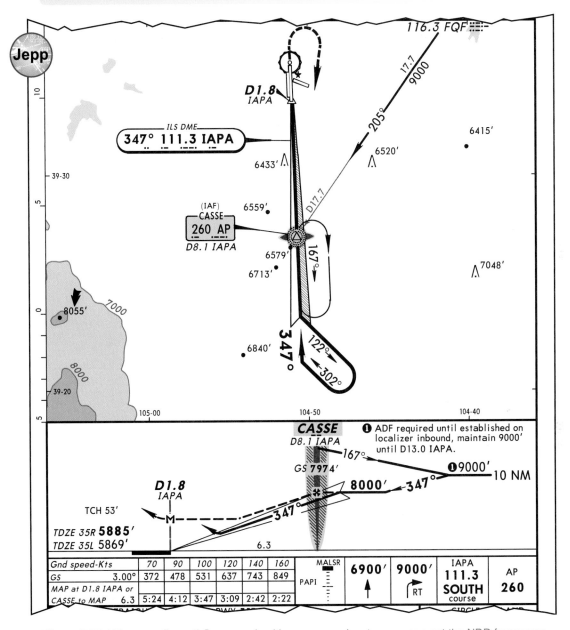

Figure 8-22. When you fly an ILS approach with a compass locator, you can set the NDB frequency for greater situational awareness. CASSE transmits the first two letters of the localizer identifier "AP."

DME AND VOR FIXES

On many ILS procedures, a DME transmitter is placed at or near the localizer or glide slope transmitter to provide runway distance information. In some cases, you also might use DME information from a separate facility, such as a VORTAC. VOR radials that intersect the localizer course are also used in combination with DME fixes. On Jeppesen charts you can determine if DME is associated with the localizer frequency by looking for the ILS/DME notation on top of the facility box. FAA charts include the DME/TACAN channel in the localizer frequency box. [Figure 8-23]

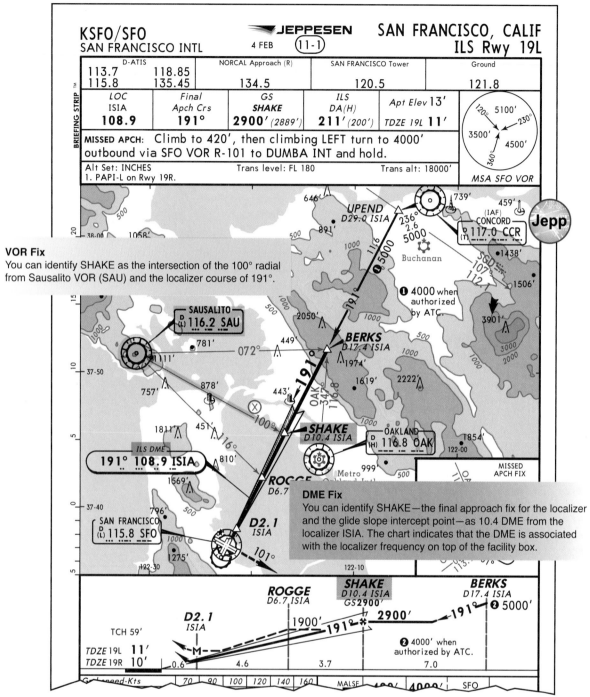

VOR Fix
You can identify SHAKE as the intersection of the 100° radial from Sausalito VOR (SAU) and the localizer course of 191°.

DME Fix
You can identify SHAKE—the final approach fix for the localizer and the glide slope intercept point—as 10.4 DME from the localizer ISIA. The chart indicates that the DME is associated with the localizer frequency on top of the facility box.

Figure 8-23. Many ILS approach procedures use VOR radials or DME fixes from the localizer or from a VOR to provide range information.

 When DME is available through the localizer frequency, Jeppesen charts publish the notation, ILS/DME on the top of the facility box. On FAA charts, a DME/TACAN channel is shown in the facility box.

RADAR FIXES

If the approach procedure uses radar to identify fixes on the ILS approach, ATC will provide you with position information in relation to the fixes, and radar services must be available for you to perform the approach. The approach procedure might provide several fixes as options for ATC to direct you to intercept the glide slope, depending on your altitude. [Figure 8-24]

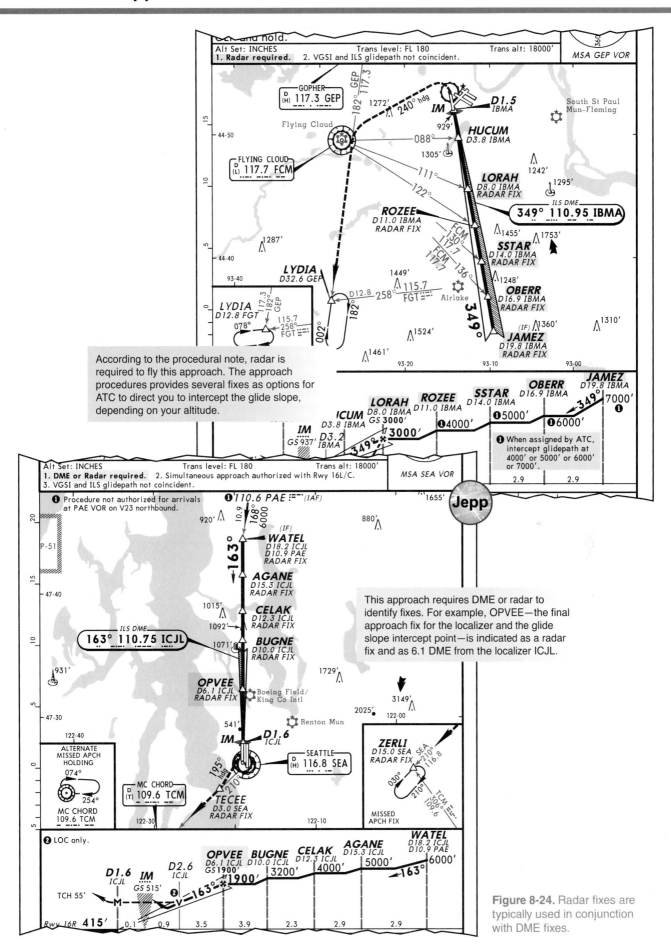

According to the procedural note, radar is required to fly this approach. The approach procedures provides several fixes as options for ATC to direct you to intercept the glide slope, depending on your altitude.

This approach requires DME or radar to identify fixes. For example, OPVEE—the final approach fix for the localizer and the glide slope intercept point—is indicated as a radar fix and as 6.1 DME from the localizer ICJL.

Figure 8-24. Radar fixes are typically used in conjunction with DME fixes.

FLYING THE ILS

While tracking the localizer, the CDI senses horizontal movement of the aircraft away from the course. Simultaneously, a glide slope display provides a precise descent path to the runway. [Figure 8-25]

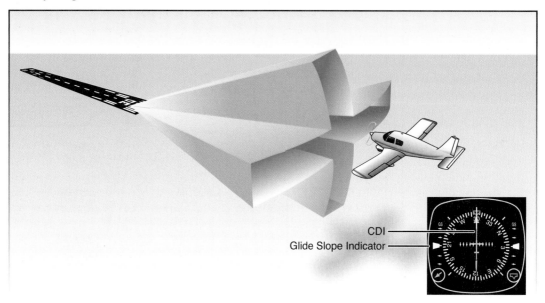

Figure 8-25. When flying an ILS, you track the line formed by the intersection of the glide slope and localizer courses.

Prior to intercepting the ILS glide slope, you should concentrate on stabilizing your airspeed and altitude while establishing a magnetic heading that keeps the airplane on the localizer centerline. Flying at a constant airspeed is not only desirable, but essential for smooth, accurate descents to the decision altitude. At glide slope interception, initiate a descent to stay on the glide slope by reducing power, or by extending flaps or landing gear, if appropriate. [Figure 8-26]

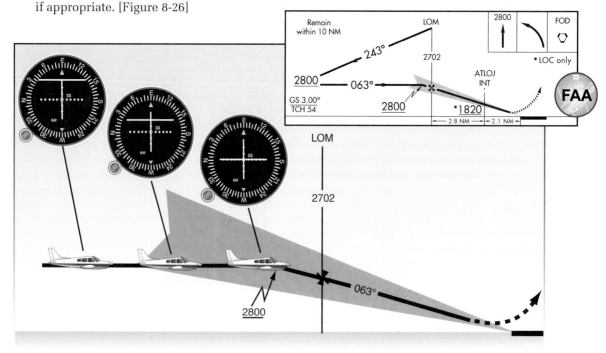

Figure 8-26. Because your airplane is usually below the glide slope during the intermediate approach segment, the glide slope indicator displays a full-up deflection. Observe the initial downward movement of the indicator so you can begin your descent as the glide slope indcator centers.

Intercepting the glide slope at the proper speed makes the descent more stable. However, if your airspeed is too high after glide slope interception, you need to make a further power reduction. As the airspeed decreases, you should make a pitch adjustment to keep the airplane from going below the glide slope. After the descent rate stabilizes, use power as necessary to maintain a constant approach speed. You can use small pitch changes to maintain the glide slope. However, if the glide slope indicator approaches full scale deflection, respond immediately with pitch and power adjustments to re-intercept the glide slope.

 If the glide slope and localizer are centered but your airspeed is too fast, your initial adjustment should be to reduce power.

The rate of descent you should maintain primarily depends on your groundspeed. For the same glide slope angle, you need a lower rate of descent as your groundspeed decreases, and vice versa. For example, in no-wind conditions, a 555-foot per minute rate of descent keeps the airplane on a 3° glide slope if you maintain 105 KIAS. However, with a 15-knot headwind (90-knot groundspeed), you have to reduce the rate of descent to 480 feet per minute to stay on a 3° glide slope.

 If your groundspeed decreases, the rate of descent required to stay on glide slope must also decrease, and vice versa.

While inbound on the localizer, as the course narrows, make small drift corrections and reduce them proportionately. Establish drift correction accurately enough to permit you to complete the approach with heading corrections no greater than 2° in calm wind conditions.

 Localizer and glide slope indications become more sensitive as you get closer to the runway. You should not need heading corrections greater than 2° in calm wind conditions.

During actual IFR weather conditions, it is usually apparent when you can continue the approach visually. However, prior to the DA or MDA (GS out), you should continue your instrument cross-check with only brief glances outside until you are sure that you have established positive visual contact with the runway environment. It is not unusual on an ILS approach to establish visual contact at 500 to 600 feet AGL and then lose outside visual references as the descent continues. This may be due to a very low fog layer that allows visual contact from above but causes loss of visual cues on a horizontal plane within the layer. For this reason, you should avoid descents below the glide slope before you reach the DA, even though you have visual contact with the runway. If you have not established the required visual references at the DA on an ILS approach, you must perform the missed approach. A missed approach also is required if you cannot maintain the required visual references all the way to touchdown. During a missed approach, you must comply with the published procedure unless ATC specifies otherwise.

 If you have not established the required visual references at the DA on an ILS approach, you must perform the missed approach.

FLYING A STRAIGHT-IN ILS APPROACH

If radar is available, normally you receive radar vectors to the final approach course of an ILS approach. In addition, many ILS procedures have straight-in (NoPT) initial approach segments to enable you to fly the approach without performing a course reversal. The following discussion assumes you are inbound from the north for landing at Lebanon Municipal Airport, Lebanon, New Hampshire. [Figure 8-27]

SECTION B ■ ILS Approaches

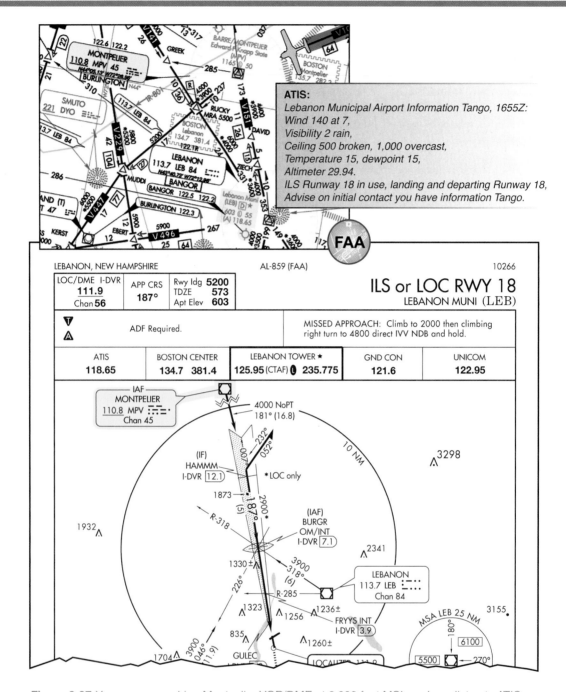

Figure 8-27. You are approaching Montpelier VOR/DME at 6,000 feet MSL and you listen to ATIS.

PREPARING FOR THE APPROACH

To prepare for the approach, perform an approach overview to ensure you can safely perform the approach. After ATC tells you which approach to expect, brief the details of the approach procedure.

APPROACH OVERVIEW

After listening to ATIS, perform an approach overview of the ILS Runway 18 approach to ensure that landing minimums for a category A airplane operating at 90 knots are higher than the reported ceiling and visibility. In addition, to increase your situational awareness, look for significant terrain and obstacles, determine if there are unique approach features that you need to consider, and review the airport information. [Figure 8-28]

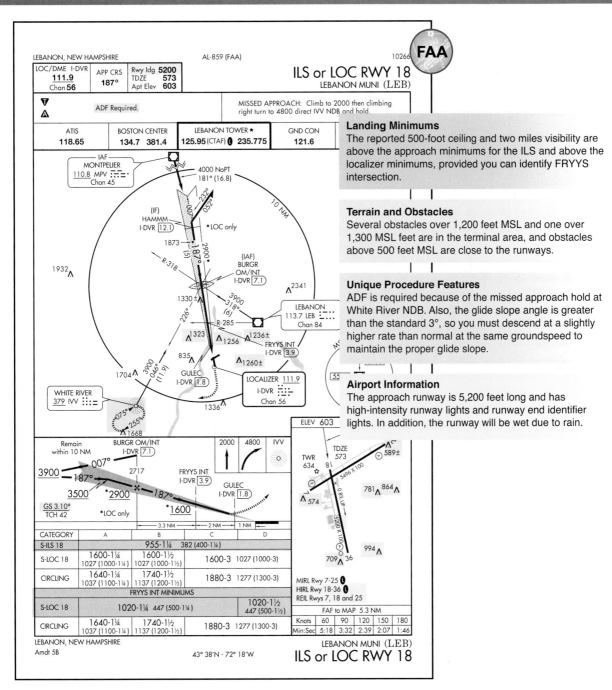

Landing Minimums
The reported 500-foot ceiling and two miles visibility are above the approach minimums for the ILS and above the localizer minimums, provided you can identify FRYYS intersection.

Terrain and Obstacles
Several obstacles over 1,200 feet MSL and one over 1,300 MSL feet are in the terminal area, and obstacles above 500 feet MSL are close to the runways.

Unique Procedure Features
ADF is required because of the missed approach hold at White River NDB. Also, the glide slope angle is greater than the standard 3°, so you must descend at a slightly higher rate than normal at the same groundspeed to maintain the proper glide slope.

Airport Information
The approach runway is 5,200 feet long and has high-intensity runway lights and runway end identifier lights. In addition, the runway will be wet due to rain.

Figure 8-28. The approach overview includes items that increase your situational awareness.

APPROACH BRIEFING

As you continue to the airport, you receive this ATC transmission: *"Diamond Star 505JF, maintain 6,000, to Montpelier, expect ILS Runway 18 approach, Lebanon."* During the approach briefing, set and identify the localizer frequency in your primary VOR receiver to display course information on the HSI. Leave the other VOR receiver tuned to Montpelier VOR/DME. Set the ADF to White River NDB for the missed approach. Verify that the frequencies are correct and the navaids are operating by listening to the identification feature. Then, turn on the marker beacon receiver and test it for proper operation. [Figure 8-29]

SECTION B ■ ILS Approaches

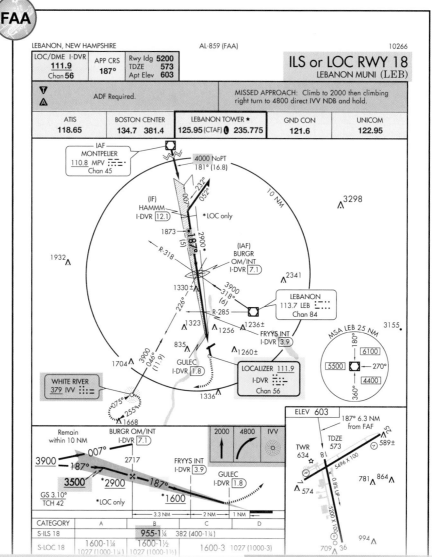

LEBANON, NEW HAMPSHIRE   AL-859 (FAA)   10266

| LOC/DME I-DVR **111.9** Chan **56** | APP CRS **187°** | Rwy ldg **5200** TDZE **573** Apt Elev **603** | **ILS or LOC RWY 18** LEBANON MUNI (LEB) |

ADF Required.

MISSED APPROACH: Climb to 2000 then climbing right turn to 4800 direct IVV NDB and hold.

ATIS	BOSTON CENTER	LEBANON TOWER ★	GND CON	UNICOM
118.65	134.7 381.4	125.95 (CTAF) 235.775	121.6	122.95

CATEGORY	A	B	C	D
S-ILS 18		955-1¼ 382 (400-1¼)		
S-LOC 18	1600-1¼ 1027 (1000-1¼)	1600-1½ 1027 (1000-1½)	1600-3 1027 (1000-3)	

Procedure Title
The procedure is the ILS or localizer approach for Runway 18 at Lebanon Municipal Airport.

Communication Frequencies
Listen to ATIS on 118.65. Talk to Boston Center on 134.7. Set Lebanon Tower on 125.95 and Ground Control on 121.6.

Primary Navaid Frequency
Set and identify the localizer frequency of 111.9.

Final Approach Course
The localizer course is 187°.

Approach Altitudes
From Montpelier VOR/DME to HAMMM intersection, maintain 4,000 feet MSL. When established on the localizer, descend to 3,500 feet MSL to intercept the glide slope.

DA (Precision Approach)
The decision altitude is 955 feet MSL for a straight-in landing on the ILS approach.

Airport Information
The runway length is 5,200 feet. The touchdown zone elevation is 573 feet MSL and the airport elevation is 603 feet MSL.

Missed Approach Instructions
Climb to 2,000 feet MSL and then perform a climbing right turn to 4,800 feet MSL direct to White River (IVV) NDB and hold.

Procedural Notes
Tune and identify White River NDB on frequency 379° in preparation for the missed approach.

Figure 8-29. Set the navigation equipment that you are using for every segment of the approach.

PERFORMING THE APPROACH

Although you will begin this approach by tracking from the VOR/DME, your primary navigation instrument is the HSI set to the localizer after you are established on the final approach course. You track the localizer course using the CDI and follow the glide slope indications for your vertical descent on final approach.

APPROACH CLEARANCE

Prior to reaching Montpelier VOR/DME, Boston Center advises, *"Diamond Star 505JF, you are cleared for the ILS Runway 18 approach to Lebanon. Maintain 6,000 until established on the approach. Contact Lebanon Tower at BURGR."* With this clearance, you begin the approach when you arrive at the IAF.

INITIAL APPROACH SEGMENT

Because Montpelier VOR/DME is an IAF, you can begin a descent to 4,000 feet MSL after you are established on the 181° radial from Montpelier VOR/DME. Using a 500-foot per minute rate of descent at 120 knots, you should reach 4,000 feet in two minutes and level off about 12 miles prior to reaching HAMMM. This is a good time to complete your before landing checklist, with the possible exception of the landing gear and flaps. As you approach HAMMM, scan the HSI for localizer indications. As the CDI begins to center, you should time your turn to roll out on the final approach course. [Figure 8-30]

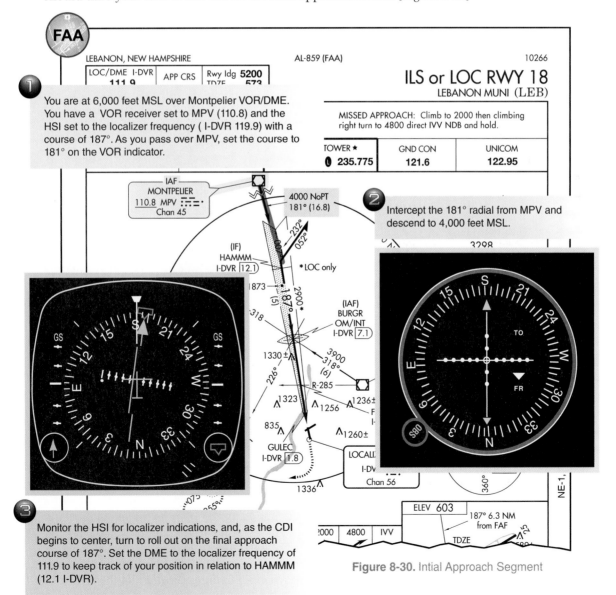

Figure 8-30. Intial Approach Segment

INTERMEDIATE APPROACH SEGMENT

After you are established on the localizer, descend to 3,500 feet MSL, as shown on the chart profile view. Continue to scan the HSI because you might need to use a wind correction angle to stay on course. As you level off prior to the outer marker, make sure you are at approach speed and monitor the HSI for glide slope indications. [Figure 8-31]

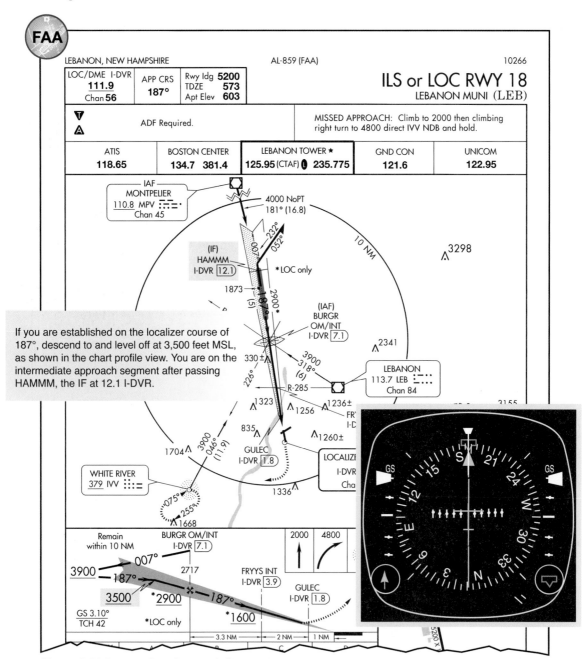

Figure 8-31. Intermediate Approach Segment

FINAL APPROACH SEGMENT

When the glide slope indicators center, reduce power and, depending on the airplane, lower the landing gear and extend partial flaps to begin a stabilized descent to remain on the glide slope while simultaneously tracking the localizer. You can monitor your progress toward the outer marker using DME as well as scanning for the outer marker on-glide-slope altitude of 2,721 feet MSL. You know you have arrived at the OM when the marker beacon receiver flashes a blue light and emits a series of dash tones. As directed earlier, contact Lebanon tower: *"Lebanon Tower, Diamond Star 505JF at BURGR inbound on the ILS Runway 18 approach."* Depending on traffic, you might receive a landing clearance at this time. As you continue the approach, make corrections as necessary to stay on the localizer and glide slope. Remember to use pitch attitude to control your position relative to the glide slope and adjust the throttle to maintain airspeed. [Figure 8-32] While descending toward the runway, systematically monitor the altimeter so you know precisely when you reach the DA of 955 feet MSL. If you establish visual contact with the runway environment prior to, or at, the DA, continue for a straight-in landing.

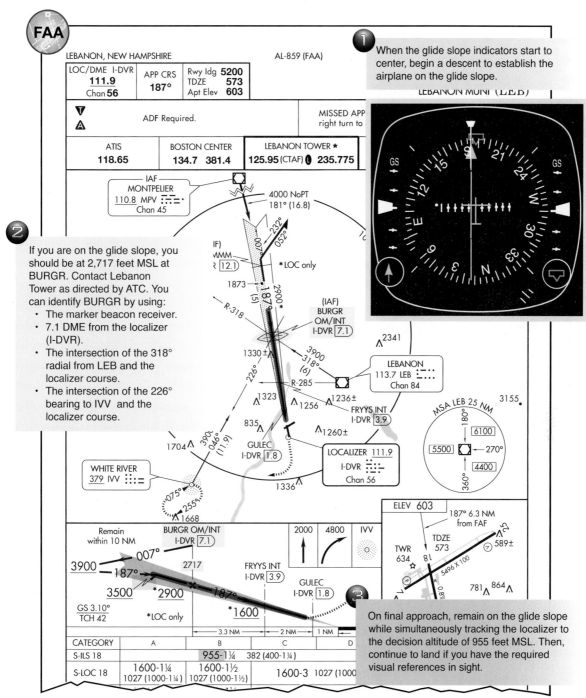

Figure 8-32. Final Approach Segment.

If the glide slope fails on the final approach segment, you must be prepared to continue the approach to the localizer MDA. In this case, if you can identify FRYYS intersection, you can descend to 1,020 feet MSL. Your missed approach point is at GULEC (1.8 I-DVR or 3:32 minutes from BURGR at 90 knots.)

MISSED APPROACH SEGMENT

If you reach the decision altitude and determine that you must perform a missed approach, add power, disengage autopilot, increase pitch attitude, and raise the gear and flaps, as appropriate. In this example, when you report the missed approach to the tower you will probably be told to contact Boston Center to request clearance for another approach or routing to your alternate. However, you might be directed to continue on the published missed approach procedure. [Figure 8-33]

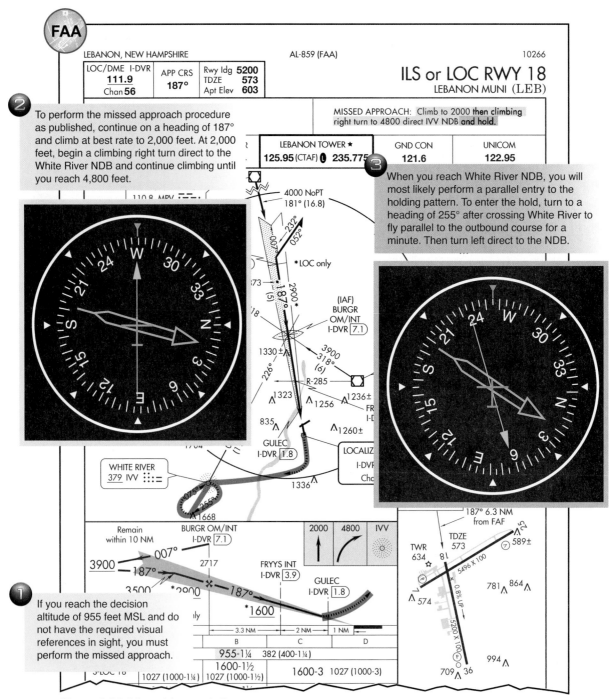

2 To perform the missed approach procedure as published, continue on a heading of 187° and climb at best rate to 2,000 feet. At 2,000 feet, begin a climbing right turn direct to the White River NDB and continue climbing until you reach 4,800 feet.

3 When you reach White River NDB, you will most likely perform a parallel entry to the holding pattern. To enter the hold, turn to a heading of 255° after crossing White River to fly parallel to the outbound course for a minute. Then turn left direct to the NDB.

1 If you reach the decision altitude of 955 feet MSL and do not have the required visual references in sight, you must perform the missed approach.

LEBANON, NEW HAMPSHIRE — AL-859 (FAA) — 10266

LOC/DME I-DVR **111.9** Chan **56**	APP CRS **187°**	Rwy ldg **5200** TDZE **573** Apt Elev **603**

ILS or LOC RWY 18
LEBANON MUNI (LEB)

MISSED APPROACH: Climb to 2000 then climbing right turn to 4800 direct IVV NDB and hold.

LEBANON TOWER ★ 125.95 (CTAF) ● 235.775	GND CON 121.6	UNICOM 122.95

Figure 8-33. Missed Approach Segment.

ILS APPROACH WITH A COURSE REVERSAL

Radar vectors to the approach course are not always available. Some ILS procedures, particularly those serving airports without radar coverage, require a course reversal depending upon your direction of flight as you approach the airport. [Figure 8-34].

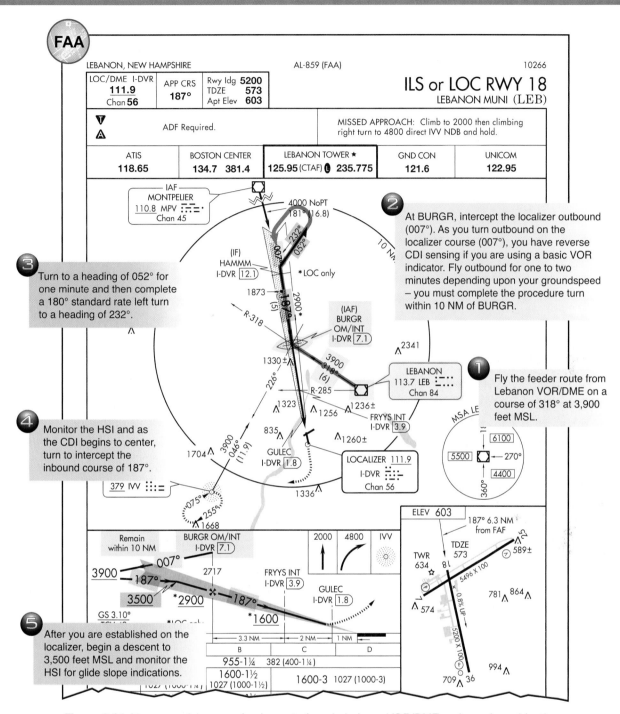

Figure 8-34. You are arriving on a feeder route from Lebabnon VOR/DME and are cleared for the ILS approach, so you must perform the procedure turn to reverse course.

ILS APPROACHES TO PARALLEL RUNWAYS

At airports that have two or three parallel runway configurations, approach operations may be authorized on each runway. ILS approaches to parallel runways are divided into three classes depending on runway centerline separation and ATC procedures and capabilities. [Figure 8-35]

Due to the close proximity of aircraft during some parallel procedures, it is imperative that you maintain situational awareness and strict radio discipline. During the approach, you should avoid lengthy and/or unnecessary radio transmissions to allow final approach controllers time to issue critical instructions as needed. In addition, to help eliminate any confusion among aircraft, you should always use your full call sign when responding to ATC.

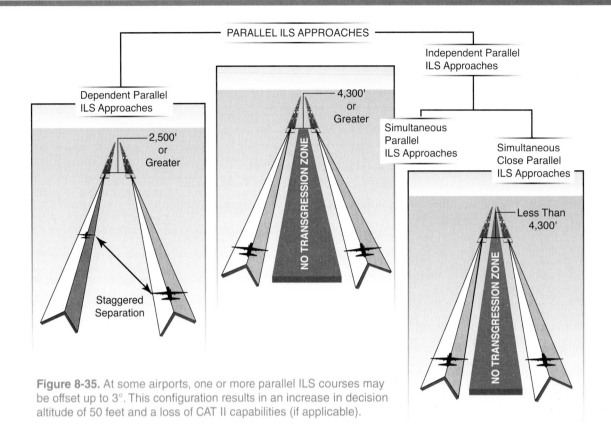

Figure 8-35. At some airports, one or more parallel ILS courses may be offset up to 3°. This configuration results in an increase in decision altitude of 50 feet and a loss of CAT II capabilities (if applicable).

PARALLEL (DEPENDENT) ILS APPROACH

Parallel (dependent) ILS approach operations may be conducted to parallel runways with centerlines at least 2,500 feet apart. [Figure 8-36] However, due to the close proximity of the final approach courses, aircraft are separated by a minimum of 1.5 miles diagonally. If the runway centerlines are more than 4,300 feet but no more than 9,000 feet apart, ATC must maintain a diagonal separation between aircraft of at least two miles. The procedures you use to fly the approach are the same as a standard (nonparallel) ILS approach.

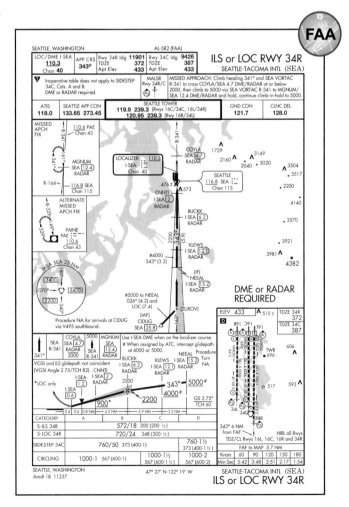

Figure 8-36. While the approach chart is not required to indicate that parallel approaches may be conducted, you will be informed by ATC or through the ATIS broadcast if parallel approaches are in progress.

A parallel ILS approach provides aircraft with a minimum of two miles separation between successive aircraft on the adjacent localizer course.

Flying the Ball

You have just completed your assigned mission. You are hundreds of miles from land but only have enough fuel to fly for about another 45 minutes. Your job is to make an approach and land on a 400-foot runway which is moving away from you and pitching up and down as much as 30 feet. If you are a carrier-based Naval Aviator, this is probably just another day at the office. [Figure A]

U S Navy photo by Mass Communication Specialist 2nd Class Scott Taylor

Day or night, Navy pilots rely heavily on an alignment device, called a fresnel lens optical landing system (FLOLS), to provide approach guidance. The stabilized system consists of a yellow light, commonly referred to as the meatball (or simply the ball), which appears to move vertically, depending on the aircraft's position relative to the ideal glide slope. When on the proper approach angle, the ball is centered between two rows of fixed green lights. The FLOLS, which is the Navy's primary landing guidance system, is located on the port (left) side of the deck edge. [Figure B]

Courtesy of U.S. Navy

The glide slope coverage of the FLOLS is 1.7° high by 40° wide. If flown correctly, the aircraft will cross over the ramp of the carrier through a window 5 feet high and 20 feet wide. By keeping the ball in the center, the pilot flies the aircraft to a point which results in the aircraft's tailhook catching the 3rd of 4 arresting wires. To accomplish this feat, every pilot on approach must scan 3 critical items—the aircraft's angle of attack, lineup on the flight deck marking and/or lighting, and the ball. The pilot receives additional guidance from a Landing Signal Officer (LSO) stationed on the flight deck. [Figure C] While you may not have the same tools available to you as a carrier pilot, you also don't have to land on a pitching, rolling, heaving runway.

Courtesy of U.S. Navy

SIMULTANEOUS (INDEPENDENT) PARALLEL ILS APPROACH

A **simultaneous (independent) parallel ILS approach** differs from a parallel (dependent) approach in that the runway centerlines are separated by 4,300 to 9,000 feet and the approaches, which do not require staggered separation, are monitored by dedicated final controllers. [Figure 8-37] The final monitor controllers track aircraft position and issue instructions to pilots of aircraft observed deviating from the localizer course.

During the approach, ATC is not required to maintain staggered aircraft separation. You are instructed to monitor the tower frequency for advisories while on final approach. The final monitor controller has the ability to override the tower controller if needed to issue instructions to aircraft deviating from the localizer course. If an aircraft does not respond correctly or enters the no transgression zone (NTZ) between runways, the final monitor controller may issue breakout or missed approach instructions. If necessary, the controller may also instruct the aircraft on the adjacent approach to alter course.

SECTION B ■ ILS Approaches

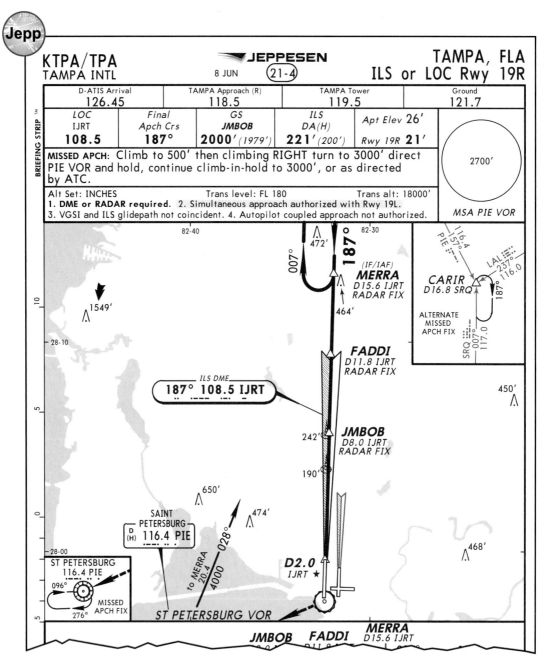

Figure 8-37. A note is included on the approach chart of an ILS approach that is certified for simultaneous operations. In addition, ATC or the ATIS broadcast will advise you if simultaneous parallel approaches are in progress. If you do not want to fly this type of approach, you should advise ATC immediately.

You fly a simultaneous parallel ILS approach as you would any other ILS approach. You are radar monitored during the approach; however radar monitoring is terminated when you report the runway environment in sight, or you are one mile or less from the threshold, or when visual separation is applied. In any case, do not expect that the final monitor controller will advise you when radar monitoring is terminated.

 When simultaneous approaches are in progress, each pilot may receive radar advisories on tower frequency.

SIMULTANEOUS CLOSE PARALLEL ILS APPROACH

Typically, a single-runway approach procedure can support 29 arrivals per hour. Two simultaneous independent flows of approach traffic can double an airport's capacity on two parallel runways. Historically, the parallel runways had to be at least 4,300 feet apart for ATC to authorize simultaneous parallel ILS approaches; however, this is no longer the case with the advent of a system called the **precision runway monitor (PRM)**.

The PRM uses a radar offering one second (or faster) updates on targets, a high-resolution color ATC display, audio and visual alert systems for controllers, and software for projecting aircraft track vectors. This system, which can display turns as they occur, does not require any extra equipment on the aircraft or sensors on the airport other than the PRM electronically guided antenna. [Figure 8-38]

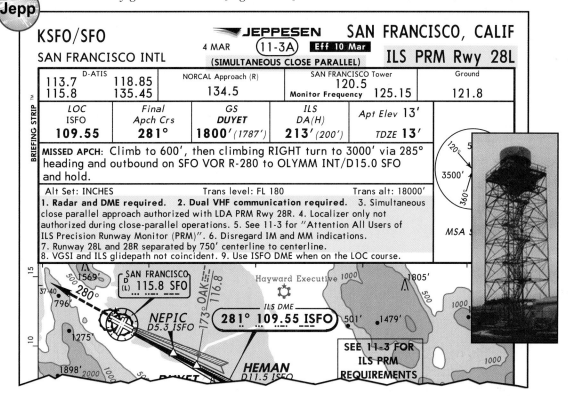

SECTION B ■ ILS Approaches

Figure 8-38. Although you must meet many requirements to perform a simultaneous close parallel ILS approach, you fly it using normal ILS procedures. The photo shows a PRM mounted on a tower.

Aircraft on **simultaneous close parallel ILS approaches** are monitored by a radar controller to ensure that neither aircraft enters, or "blunders," into the NTZ which lies between the runways. If the 10-second projected track indicates that an aircraft is going to enter the NTZ, the system alerts the controller. If the aircraft's displayed position enters the NTZ, the controller immediately issues breakout instructions to the pilots. Breakout instructions involve discontinuing the approach, turning outward, climbing to minimum safe altitude, and executing a missed approach.

The PRM has been able to provide a solution to increased air traffic around busy airports with closely spaced parallel runways. The system is not only safe and efficient, but it is also a much more cost effective and practical alternative to building new runways.

SIMULTANEOUS CONVERGING INSTRUMENT APPROACH

Airports which have runways situated at an angle of 15° to 100° to each other may have approval for conducting simultaneous instrument approaches to the converging runways. [Figure 8-39] The development criteria for **simultaneous converging instrument approaches** requires that the approaches have missed approach points at least three miles apart and missed approach procedures that do not overlap. Other requirements vary somewhat depending on whether or not the runways intersect. Although you fly the converging approach as you would any other similar approach, converging approaches all terminate with a straight-in landing.

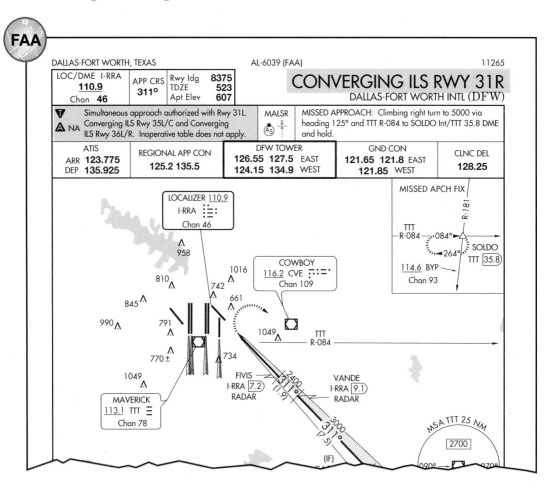

Figure 8-39. As with other simultaneous approaches, you are informed of converging simultaneous operations on initial contact with the controller or via ATIS. Authorization for converging simultaneous approaches is noted on the associated approach charts.

SIMULTANEOUS OFFSET INSTRUMENT APPROACHES

Simultaneous offset instrument approaches (SOIAs) are classified as simultaneous close parallel PRM approaches. SOIAs allow simultaneous approaches to two parallel runways spaced apart by at least 750 feet but less than 3,000 feet. The SOIA procedure uses an ILS PRM, RNAV PRM or GLS PRM approach to one runway and an offset localizer-type directional aid (LDA) PRM approach with glide slope to the adjacent runway. The procedures and system requirements for SOIA approaches are identical to those used for a typical simultaneous close parallel PRM approach until you near the MAP if you are flying the LDA PRM approach. At the MAP, you must visually acquire the aircraft on the adjacent approach path to then fly a visual segment to landing.

The approach charts used in SOIA operations are identical to other PRM approach charts but show a note that provides the separation between the two runways for simultaneous approaches. The LDA PRM approach chart displays the required notations for closely spaced approaches as well as depicting the visual segment of the approach. Pilots must complete special pilot training, as outlined in the AIM, before accepting a clearance for a simultaneous close parallel ILS/PRM or LDA/PRM approach.

LOCALIZER APPROACH

There are two situations when you might perform a **localizer approach**. First, if it is authorized, you can fly the localizer portion of an ILS approach if you cannot, or choose not, to use glide slope guidance. The second instance occurs on approaches designed specifically as nonprecision procedures using a localizer transmitter. [Figure 8-40] Since the characteristics of the localizer are the same as those associated with an ILS approach, you fly a localizer approach using the same procedures to maintain course as you would for an ILS.

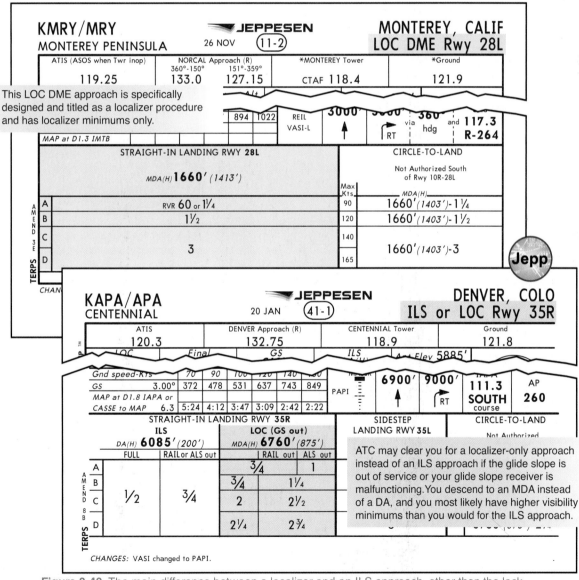

Figure 8-40. The main difference between a localizer and an ILS approach, other than the lack of a glide slope, is that since the localizer is a nonprecision approach, you descend to a minimum descent altitude instead of a decision altitude.

LOCALIZER BACK COURSE APPROACH

At an airport where ILS equipment is installed, a **localizer back course approach** might be published. Although a localizer back course approach does not have an associated glide slope, you might receive false glide slope signals from the front course ILS equipment. It is important that you disregard any glide slope information while performing a back course approach. Another important consideration is the type of equipment you have onboard your airplane. Reverse sensing occurs on a back course localizer inbound when you are using a basic VOR indicator. With an HSI, you can avoid reverse sensing if you set the front course on the course selector. Except for these considerations, flying a back course localizer is very much like performing any other localizer approach. [Figure 8-41]

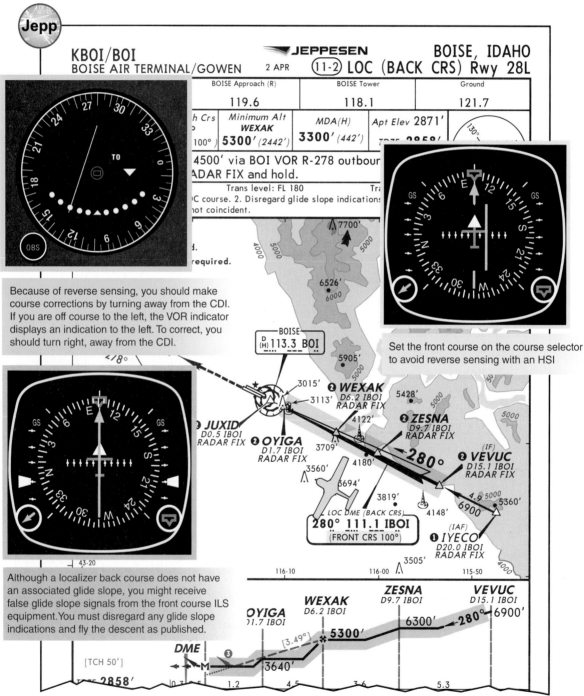

Because of reverse sensing, you should make course corrections by turning away from the CDI. If you are off course to the left, the VOR indicator displays an indication to the left. To correct, you should turn right, away from the CDI.

Set the front course on the course selector to avoid reverse sensing with an HSI

Although a localizer back course does not have an associated glide slope, you might receive false glide slope signals from the front course ILS equipment. You must disregard any glide slope indications and fly the descent as published.

Figure 8-41. Assume you are inbound to Boise Air Terminal and are cleared for the LOC (BACK CRS) Rwy 28L approach.

LDA AND SDF APPROACHES

Approaches that are similar to localizer or ILS procedures include the nonprecision localizer-type directional aid (LDA) and simplified directional facility (SDF) approaches. You can fly an LDA or SDF approach if your airplane is equipped to track a localizer.

LDA APPROACH

A **localizer-type directional aid (LDA)** can be thought of as a localizer approach system that is not aligned with the runway centerline. In fact, the identifier for an LDA begins with an I followed by a 3-letter group, just like a localizer. The LDA course width is the same as a localizer associated with an ILS—between 3° and 6° wide. Some LDA approaches have an electronic glide slope, although this is not a requirement for the system. If the final approach course is aligned to within 30° of the runway centerline, straight-in landing minimums also might be available. [Figure 8-42]

SECTION B ■ ILS Approaches

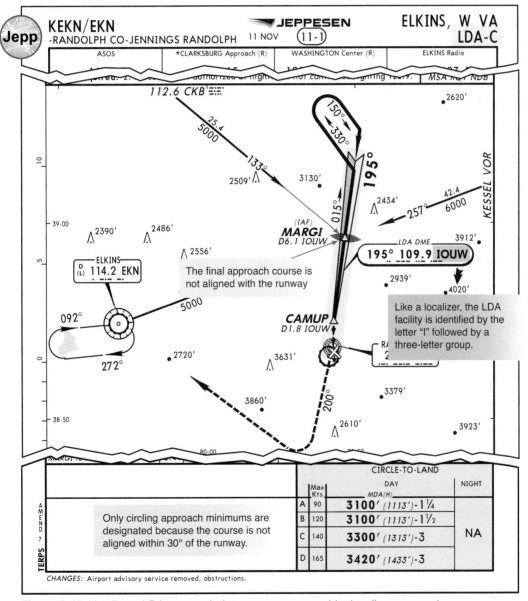

Figure 8-42. You fly an LDA approach the same as you would a localizer approach.

 An LDA approach is comparable to a localizer, but it is not aligned with the runway. The LDA course width is between 3° and 6°. When performing an LDA approach with a glideslope, you must initiate the missed approach at the decision altitude if you do not have the required visual references in sight.

SDF APPROACH

The **simplified directional facility (SDF)** approach system does not incorporate an electronic glide slope and offers less accuracy than the LDA. While the typical ILS or LDA localizer is between 3° and 6° wide, an SDF localizer course is fixed at either 6° or 12° wide. The lateral limits of SDF course guidance are 35° either side of centerline; you should disregard any SDF navigation information you receive beyond 35°. As with any other navaid, you should tune and identify the facility prior to using it for navigation. While similar to a localizer or LDA, an SDF 3-letter identifier is not preceded by an I. [Figure 8-43]

 An SDF course (which is either 6° or 12° wide) may be offset from the runway centerline.

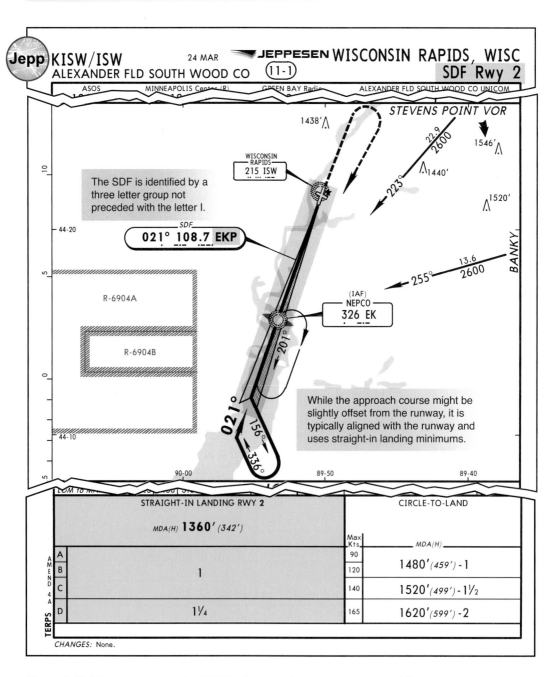

Figure 8-43. When you are on the SDF final approach course, use essentially the same procedures that you use when flying a localizer or LDA approach; however, you might experience reduced CDI sensitivity during the approach.

SUMMARY CHECKLIST

✓ ILS approaches are classified as Category I, Category II, or Category III.

✓ The ILS localizer transmitter emits a navigational signal from the far end of the runway to provide you with information regarding your airplane's alignment with the runway centerline.

✓ When using a basic VOR indicator, normal sensing occurs inbound on the front course and outbound on the back course. Reverse sensing occurs inbound on the back course and outbound on the front course.

✓ You can avoid reverse sensing when using an HSI by setting the published inbound course on the course selector. This applies regardless of your direction of travel, whether inbound or outbound on either the front or back course.

✓ Full-scale deflection of the CDI when set to a localizer is 2.5° each side of the course.

✓ The glide slope signal provides vertical navigation information for descent to the lowest authorized decision altitude for the associated approach procedure. The glide slope may not be reliable below decision altitude.

✓ An outer marker, compass locator, NDB, published DME or VOR fixes, precision approach radar (PAR), and airport surveillance radar (ASR) may be used for range information on an ILS approach. A standard feature of an ILS procedure is a means to identify the final approach fix for the localizer-only approach and the location at which you can expect to intercept the glide slope at the glide slope intercept altitude.

✓ A compass locator is a low power, low or medium frequency (L/MF) radio beacon collocated with the outer marker, referred to as a locator outer marker (LOM).

✓ When the airplane passes through the signal of a marker beacon, a colored light flashes on the marker beacon receiver and a Morse code identification sounds.

✓ Prior to intercepting the ILS glide slope, you should concentrate on stabilizing airspeed and altitude while establishing a magnetic heading that keeps the airplane on the localizer centerline.

✓ The rate of descent you must maintain to stay on the glide slope must decrease if your groundspeed decreases, and vice versa.

✓ Establish drift correction accurately enough to permit you to complete the approach with heading corrections no greater than 2° in calm wind conditions.

✓ On an ILS approach, you must perform a missed approach if you have not established the required visual references at the DA or if you lose sight of the required references after the DA.

✓ When you perform the approach briefing, in addition to the localizer, you must verify that all other navaids used for the approach, such as a VOR/DME or NDB, are set and identified.

✓ Parallel (dependent) ILS approach operations may be conducted on parallel runways with centerlines at least 2,500 feet apart.

✓ Simultaneous (independent) parallel ILS approaches may be conducted to airports with parallel runway centerlines separated by 4,300 to 9,000 feet.

✓ When certain requirements are met, including the installation of a precision runway monitor, simultaneous close parallel ILS approach procedures may be established at airports with parallel runway centerlines less than 4,300 feet apart.

SECTION B ■ ILS Approaches

✓ ATC or the ATIS broadcast will inform you if parallel approaches are in progress.

✓ A localizer-type directional aid (LDA) is an approach system that uses a localizer course that is typically not aligned with the runway centerline. If the final approach course is aligned to within 30° of the runway centerline, straight-in landing minimums might be available.

✓ A simplified directional facility (SDF) course is fixed at either 6° or 12° wide. Because most SDF courses are aligned within 3° of the runway, SDF approaches are typically published with straight-in minimums.

KEY TERMS

Instrument Landing System (ILS)

Localizer

Glide Slope

Outer Marker (OM)

Compass Locator

Parallel (Dependent) ILS Approach

Simultaneous (Independent) Parallel ILS Approach

Precision Runway Monitor (PRM)

Simultaneous Close Parallel ILS Approach

Simultaneous Converging Instrument Approach

Simultaneous Offset Instrument Approach (SOIA)

Localizer Approach

Localizer Back Course Approach

Localizer-Type Directional Aid (LDA)

Simplified Directional Facility (SDF)

QUESTIONS

1. What are the typical landing minimums for a CAT I ILS approach with all components operative?
   A. Visibility – 2400 RVR or ½ statute mile; DH – 200 feet MSL
   B. Visibility – 1200 RVR or ½ statute mile; DH – 200 feet above the touchdown zone elevation
   C. Visibility – 2400 RVR or ½ statute mile; DH – 200 feet above the touchdown zone elevation

2. What is the full-scale deflection of a CDI when tuned to a localizer?
   A. 10°
   B. 5°
   C. 2.5°

3. Refer to the accompanying illustration to match each navigation indicator with the appropriate aircraft positions. More than one aircraft position may apply to each CDI.

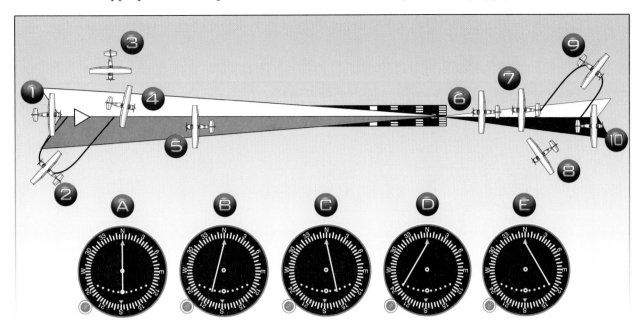

4. Refer to the accompanying illustration to match each navigation indicator with the appropriate aircraft positions. More than one aircraft position may apply to each HSI.

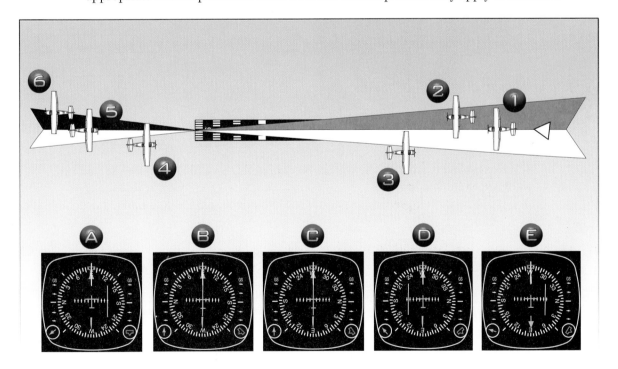

SECTION B ■ ILS Approaches

Refer to the following illustration to answer question 5.

5. If you are 1.9 nautical miles from the runway and your VOR indicator matches the display shown, how many feet are you displaced from the localizer centerline and the glide slope?

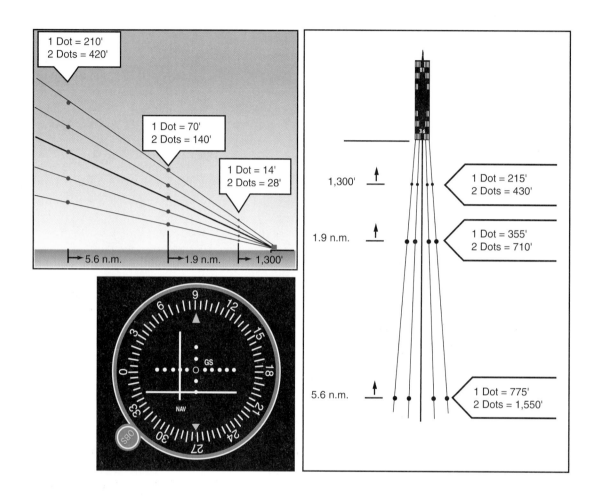

6. If your airspeed is too high but you are on course and on glide slope, should you initially adjust pitch or power?

Refer to the ILS RWY 17R approach to Will Rogers World Airport, Oklahoma City to answer questions 7 through 12.

7. You are planning to fly the ILS RWY 17R at Will Rogers World Airport, Oklahoma City. You are in a category A airplane flying the approach at 90 knots, and ATIS indicates a 600-foot ceiling and one mile visibility. What element might you include in an approach overview for this approach?
    A. There is an obstacle 1,577 feet MSL near the missed approach path.
    B. The reported weather conditions are above the ILS minimums but below the minimums for the localizer approach.
    C. DME is required for this approach and simultaneous approaches with 17L are authorized.

8. As you near your destination, ATC advises you to expect the ILS RWY 17R approach. What elements should you include in your approach briefing?
    A. You should intercept the glide slope at 3,000 feet MSL.
    B. The localizer frequency is 113.4.
    C. The DA is 3,000 feet MSL.

9. You are at 4,000 feet MSL tracking the 354° radial from Will Rogers VOR to FILUM intersection. You have been cleared for the approach with the course reversal. What is true regarding the actions you should take to fly the initial approach segment?
    A. At FILUM, descend to 3,000 feet MSL. Use a teardrop entry to the hold. After one minute, turn right to intercept the localizer course of 175° to FILUM.
    B. At FILUM, use a teardrop entry to the hold. After one minute, turn right to intercept the localizer course of 175° to FILUM. Maintain 4,000 feet MSL until crossing FILUM inbound.
    C. At FILUM, use a teardrop entry to the hold. Continue in the hold for several turns as you descend to 3,000 feet MSL. Contact the tower when you are ready to proceed inbound on the approach.

10. You are at 4,000 feet MSL on the localizer course inbound at FILUM, what is your next step?
    A. Maintain 4,000 feet MSL. Descend to 3,000 feet MSL at IVEYI.
    B. Descend to 1,800 feet MSL and monitor your HSI for glide slope indications as you approach IVEYI.
    C. Descend to 3,000 feet MSL and monitor your HSI for glide slope indications as you approach IVEYI.

11. What is the correct procedure for flying the final approach segment of ILS RWY 17 approach?
    A. At IVEYI, descend to 1,800 feet MSL. Maintain this altitude until passing COTOX and then descend to the MDA of 1,640 feet MSL. If you do not have the required visual references in sight when you reach 1.8 DME, perform a missed approach.
    B. At IVEYI, descend on the glide slope to the DA of 1,482 feet MSL. If you do not have the required visual references in sight when you reach the DA, perform a missed approach.
    C. At IVEYI, descend on the glide slope to the DA of 1,800 feet MSL until passing the VDP at 2.8 DME. Then, continue the descent to the DA of 1,482 feet MSL. If you do not have the required visual references in sight when you reach the DA, perform a missed approach.

12. When reaching the DA, you do not have the required visual references in sight. What is the correct procedure for performing the published missed approach procedure?

SECTION B ■ ILS Approaches

SECTION B ■ ILS Approaches

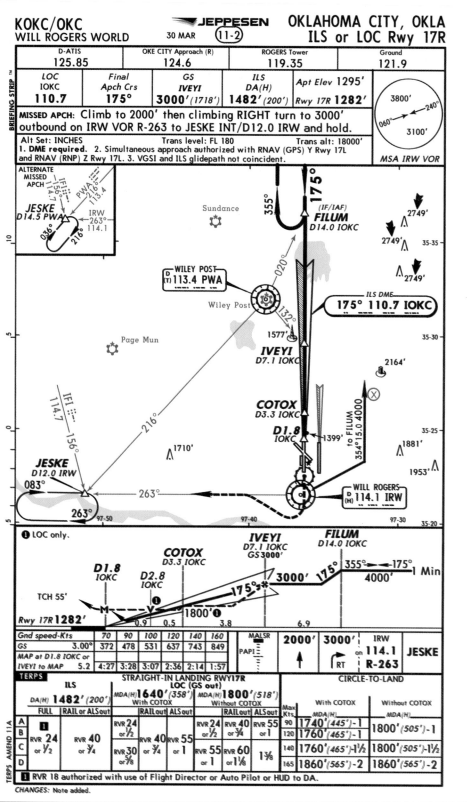

13. If the glide slope fails after passing IVEYI, what is the minimum altitude to which you can descend? How can you identify the MAP?

14. What is true regarding flying a localizer back course approach?
    A. If you set the HSI course selector to the front course, you will experience reverse sensing of the CDI.
    B. If you receive glide slope indications, use them to fly a stabilized descent to the MDA.
    C. When using a basic VOR indicator to fly the approach, you should make course corrections by turning away from the CDI.

15. Select the true statement regarding ILS approaches to parallel runways.
    A. Parallel (dependent) ILS approaches require staggered separation, and approach charts are not required to indicate that these approaches are conducted.
    B. Simultaneous (independent) ILS approaches require staggered separation, and approach charts are not required to indicate that these approaches are conducted.
    C. A PRM is used for parallel (dependent) ILS approaches.

16. What are the course widths associated with an LDA and SDF, respectively?

SECTION C
RNAV Approaches

The most common type of RNAV approach procedure uses GPS navigation and is indicated on the chart procedure title as an **RNAV (GPS) approach.** Most likely, you already understand GPS operating principles and have used GPS equipment for navigation. Now, you will learn how to apply that knowledge to perform GPS approach procedures. GPS approach procedures are very versatile. Because they do not rely on ground-based navaids, approaches can easily be designed to avoid terrain and obstacles and accommodate ATC operational considerations at almost any airport. In addition to being able to effectively interpret the charted procedure, you must have a thorough knowledge of the specific GPS equipment installed in your airplane to safely and effectively perform RNAV (GPS) approach procedures.

APPROACH DESIGN

RNAV (GPS) approaches have a variety of designs. Some GPS approach procedures include one or more feeder routes that lead to one or more initial approach fixes for straight-in approaches. Other designs incorporate a holding pattern course reversal. Some designs do not publish an initial approach fix and require radar service to fly to the intermediate approach fix to begin the published approach. [Figure 8-44]

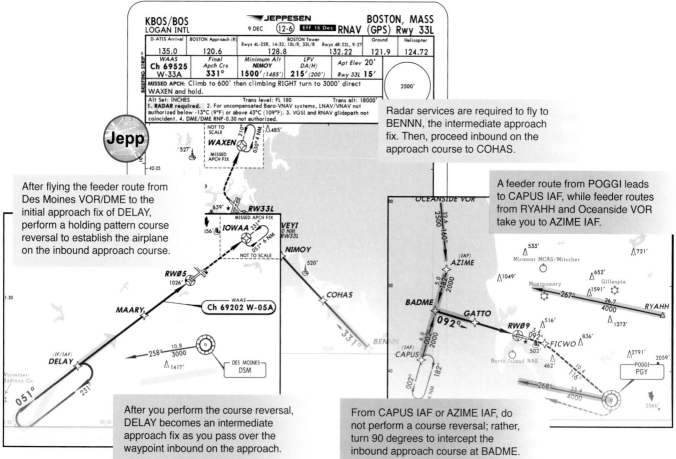

Figure 8-44. Like other approach procedures, these approach designs incorporate the minimum safe altitude (MSA) for use in emergencies that extends 25 nautical miles from the waypoint at the runway threshold.

TERMINAL ARRIVAL AREA

In some cases, RNAV (GPS) approaches are designed with a **terminal arrival area (TAA)**. This design has some unique features indicated on the approach chart. Icons on the plan view indicate minimum altitudes that you must maintain as you arrive from the enroute structure to a specific initial approach fix, therefore, no MSA is published. In addition, the chart shows a **Basic T approach segment configuration**, which is optimum for transition from the enroute to the terminal environment within a TAA. [Figure 8-45]

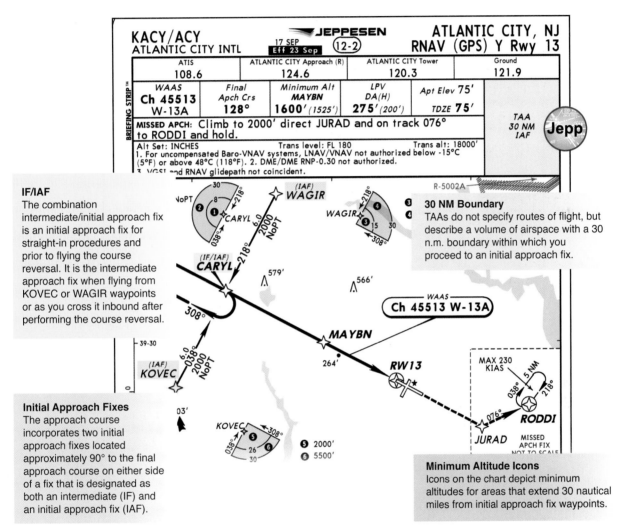

IF/IAF
The combination intermediate/initial approach fix is an initial approach fix for straight-in procedures and prior to flying the course reversal. It is the intermediate approach fix when flying from KOVEC or WAGIR waypoints or as you cross it inbound after performing the course reversal.

30 NM Boundary
TAAs do not specify routes of flight, but describe a volume of airspace with a 30 n.m. boundary within which you proceed to an initial approach fix.

Initial Approach Fixes
The approach course incorporates two initial approach fixes located approximately 90° to the final approach course on either side of a fix that is designated as both an intermediate (IF) and an initial approach fix (IAF).

Minimum Altitude Icons
Icons on the chart depict minimum altitudes for areas that extend 30 nautical miles from initial approach fix waypoints.

Figure 8-45. The Basic T approach segment configuration consists of three areas: the straight-in area, the left base area, and the right base area. Modifications to this configuration might be necessary to accommodate operational requirements.

WAYPOINTS

When you perform GPS approach procedures, GPS equipment provides waypoint sequencing for each approach segment. Database coding indicates whether waypoints are fly-over or fly-by, and your GPS receiver provides appropriate guidance for each. For a **fly-by waypoint**, the GPS receiver anticipates the turn and displays navigation indications to begin the turn so that you do not overshoot the next flight segment.

For a **fly-over waypoint** (depicted by the waypoint symbol enclosed in a circle), navigation indications will not provide guidance for a turn until you pass over the waypoint, followed either by an intercept maneuver to the next flight segment or by direct flight to the next waypoint. [Figure 8-46]

SECTION C ■ RNAV Approaches

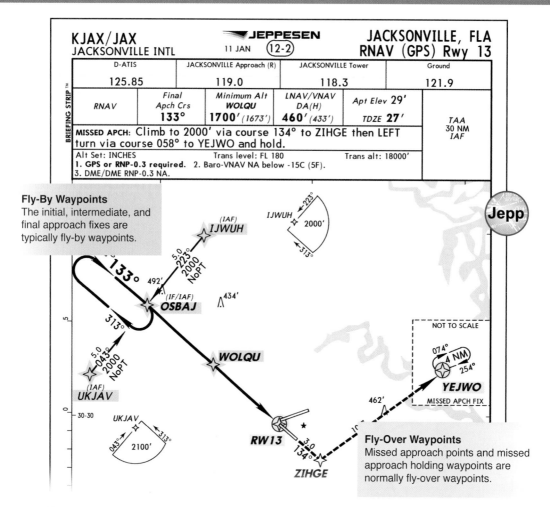

Figure 8-46. Approach charts depict fly-by waypoints with the waypoint symbol only. Fly-over waypoints are shown as the waypoint symbol enclosed in a circle.

GPS APPROACH EQUIPMENT

To fly RNAV (GPS) approach procedures with lateral navigation, GPS equipment must be certified not just for IFR enroute and terminal navigation but must also be approved for IFR approaches according to the current version of technical standard order (TSO) C129. Additional equipment requirements must be met to fly GPS approaches that incorporate vertical navigation. The primary types of equipment used to perform GPS approaches with vertical navigation are barometric vertical navigation (baro-VNAV) systems or WAAS-certified GPS equipment that is approved according to the most recent version of TSO-C145 or TSO-C146. In addition, AC 20-138 provides guidance for the airworthiness approval of installed GPS and RNAV equipment. You must determine the allowable uses for the specific GPS installation by referring to the airplane flight manual (AFM) or AFM supplement.

 You can determine if a GPS is approved for IFR enroute and approach operations by referring to the airplane flight manual(AFM) or AFM supplement.

BARO-VNAV

Used primarily in larger airplanes, **baro-VNAV equipment** builds a glide path by sensing and then comparing the airplane's altitude with a calculated altitude for the airplane's position on the glide path. You must enter the current local altimeter setting on the GPS equipment to ensure an accurate calculated glide path. In addition, there are high and low temperature limitations for the use of baro-VNAV equipment. [Figure 8-47]

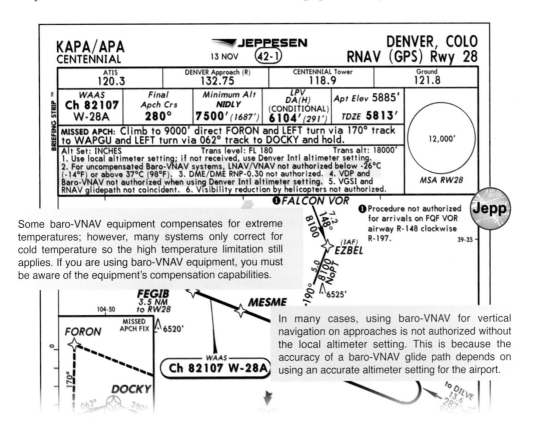

Some baro-VNAV equipment compensates for extreme temperatures; however, many systems only correct for cold temperature so the high temperature limitation still applies. If you are using baro-VNAV equipment, you must be aware of the equipment's compensation capabilities.

In many cases, using baro-VNAV for vertical navigation on approaches is not authorized without the local altimeter setting. This is because the accuracy of a baro-VNAV glide path depends on using an accurate altimeter setting for the airport.

Figure 8-47. Approach chart notes indicate baro-VNAV limitations.

WAAS-CERTIFIED GPS

WAAS-certified GPS equipment determines a glide path by its vertical and horizontal GPS position and eliminates the errors caused by barometric altimetry. This equipment computes a glide path independent of the altimeter setting, and its operation is not limited by temperature. [Figure 8-48]

When you plan an IFR flight, there are several requirements regarding GPS approach procedures that you must consider depending on whether your GPS equipment is WAAS-certified. For example, airplanes with non-WAAS GPS receivers must be equipped with alternate avionics necessary to receive the ground-based facilities appropriate for enroute navigation to the destination and to any required alternate, but this requirement does not extend to the destination approach procedure. You are not required to monitor or have ground-based navigation equipment to perform an RNAV (GPS) approach at the destination. However, although you may perform an approach at an alternate airport using GPS equipment, any required alternate airport must have an approved instrument approach procedure other than GPS that is anticipated to be operational and available at the estimated time of arrival, and that the airplane is equipped to fly.

SECTION C ■ RNAV Approaches

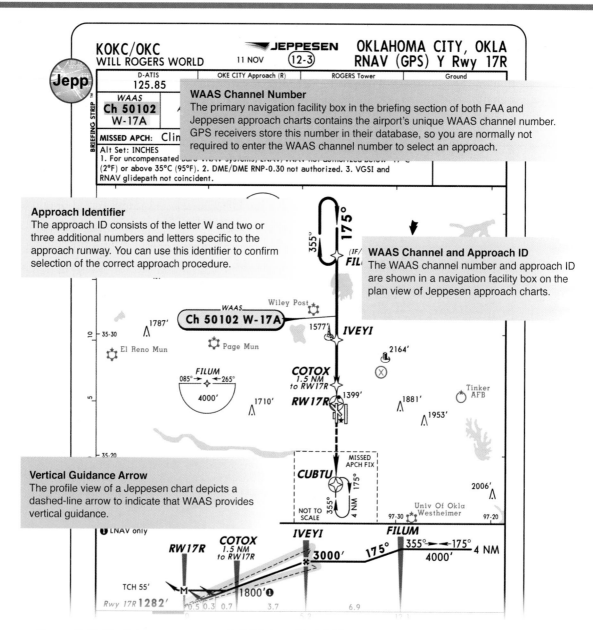

Figure 8-48. For flying approaches with WAAS-certified GPS equipment, WAAS information is displayed on several sections of RNAV (GPS) approach charts.

 When using non-WAAS GPS for navigation and instrument approaches, any required alternate airport must have an approved operational instrument approach procedure other than GPS.

If you have WAAS-certified GPS equipment, the requirement for the non-GPS approach procedure does not apply and you can use an airport as an alternate that only has a GPS approach available. However, for flight planning purposes for a destination or an alternate, you must consider the lateral navigation (LNAV) landing minimums only, even if the approach procedure has minimums associated with vertical navigation. [Figure 8-49]

GPS Approach Equipment	Certified By	Approved For	Destination Airport	Alternate Airport
Basic IFR Enroute and Approach Certified Equipment	TSO-C129	Lateral Navigation	May perform an RNAV (GPS) approach Not required to monitor or have ground-based navigation equipment	May perform an RNAV (GPS) approach Instrument approach procedure other than GPS and appropriate navigation equipment required
WAAS-Certified Equipment	TSO-C145 or TSO-C146	Vertical and Lateral Navigation	May perform an RNAV (GPS) approach Not required to monitor or have ground-based navigation equipment Must use lateral navigation (LNAV) minimums for flight planning	May perform an RNAV (GPS) approach Not required to have available instrument approach procedure other than GPS Must use lateral navigation (LNAV) minimums for flight planning

Figure 8-49. To effectively plan an IFR flight, you must know whether the airplane's GPS equipment is WAAS certified and how this affects approach procedures at the destination airport and any required alternate airport.

LANDING MINIMUMS

An RNAV (GPS) approach chart might indicate several different landing minimums for the approach based on whether the procedure uses vertical guidance. The GPS receiver only displays the approach procedures available for the particular equipment capabilities. For example, if your GPS equipment is not WAAS-certified, approach procedures that incorporate landing minimums based on vertical guidance are not available for you to select and activate. You use the appropriate minimums for the approach based on the GPS equipment capabilities.

LNAV

An approach chart that just depicts lateral navigation (LNAV) minimums means that the procedure is based on lateral guidance only. You can fly LNAV approaches with GPS equipment certified for IFR approach procedures by TSO-C129. LNAV course guidance has larger integrity limits than those of a localizer. You fly the LNAV approach to a minimum descent altitude (MDA). [Figure 8-50]

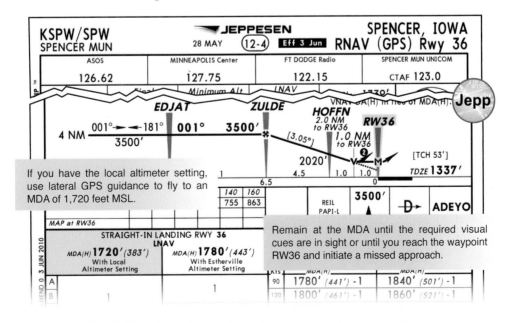

Figure 8-50. An LNAV landing minimum is a minimum descent altitude (MDA).

LNAV+V

If you have a WAAS-certified GPS unit, it most likely will provide advisory vertical guidance for an LNAV approach indicated as **LNAV+V** on the GPS display. In this case, the landing minimum is still an MDA even though the GPS receiver shows a vertical path that provides a stabilized descent. Although following the glide path should keep the airplane above any step-down minimum altitudes, you must pay close attention to these altitudes and ensure the airplane does not descend below them. Most LNAV approaches provide vertical guidance, but some do not, For example, approaches that are not aligned with the runway, such as an RNAV (GPS)-A approach, do not have an advisory glide path. [Figure 8-51]

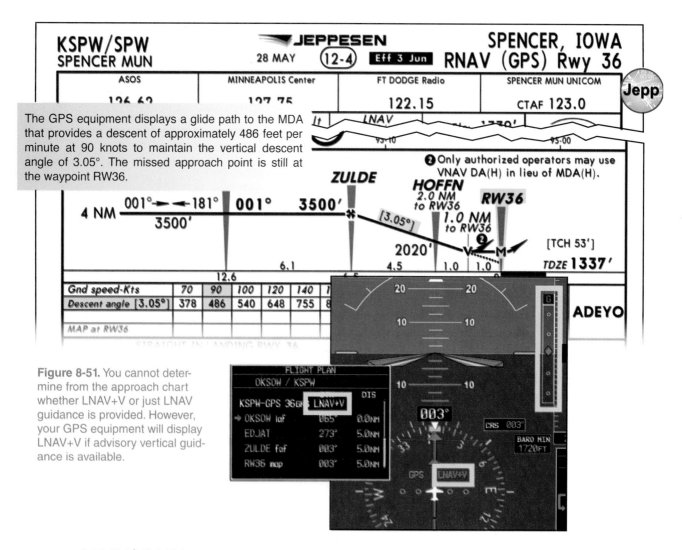

The GPS equipment displays a glide path to the MDA that provides a descent of approximately 486 feet per minute at 90 knots to maintain the vertical descent angle of 3.05°. The missed approach point is still at the waypoint RW36.

Figure 8-51. You cannot determine from the approach chart whether LNAV+V or just LNAV guidance is provided. However, your GPS equipment will display LNAV+V if advisory vertical guidance is available.

LNAV/VNAV

Many RNAV (GPS) approaches provide vertical guidance that enables you to descend to a minimum altitude that is typically lower than that provided for lateral navigation only. **Lateral navigation/vertical navigation (LNAV/VNAV)** landing minimums apply to approaches that provide lateral and vertical guidance that is displayed using baro-VNAV or WAAS-certified equipment. The integrity limits for LNAV/VNAV approaches are larger than those of a precision approach. However, the LNAV/VNAV landing minimum is a decision altitude (DA), not an MDA.

LPV

Localizer performance with vertical guidance (LPV) minimums are also provided for RNAV (GPS) approach procedures that have vertical guidance capability. These minimums apply to approaches that provide lateral and vertical guidance with integrity limits that are close to an ILS precision approach. The LPV landing minimum is a decision altitude. Your

GPS equipment must be WAAS-certified to fly approaches to LPV minimums; baro-VNAV equipment does not provide the required precision. If WAAS is not available, you must fly the approach to LNAV minimums; WAAS capability does not downgrade from LPV precision to LNAV/VNAV integrity. [Figure 8-52]

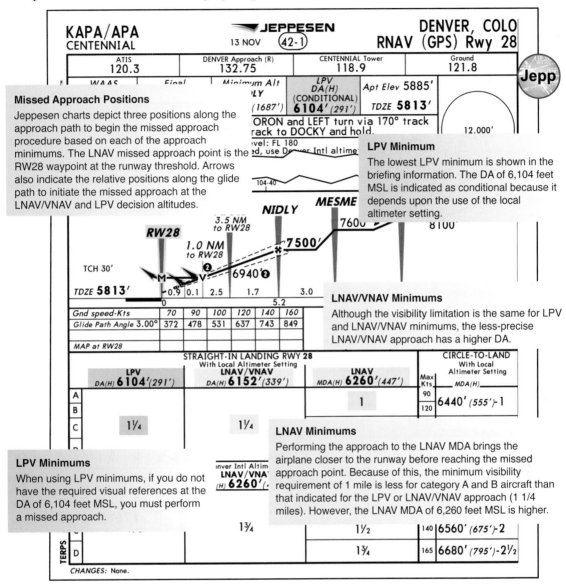

Missed Approach Positions

Jeppesen charts depict three positions along the approach path to begin the missed approach procedure based on each of the approach minimums. The LNAV missed approach point is the RW28 waypoint at the runway threshold. Arrows also indicate the relative positions along the glide path to initiate the missed approach at the LNAV/VNAV and LPV decision altitudes.

LPV Minimum

The lowest LPV minimum is shown in the briefing information. The DA of 6,104 feet MSL is indicated as conditional because it depends upon the use of the local altimeter setting.

LNAV/VNAV Minimums

Although the visibility limitation is the same for LPV and LNAV/VNAV minimums, the less-precise LNAV/VNAV approach has a higher DA.

LPV Minimums

When using LPV minimums, if you do not have the required visual references at the DA of 6,104 feet MSL, you must perform a missed approach.

LNAV Minimums

Performing the approach to the LNAV MDA brings the airplane closer to the runway before reaching the missed approach point. Because of this, the minimum visibility requirement of 1 mile is less for category A and B aircraft than that indicated for the LPV or LNAV/VNAV approach (1 1/4 miles). However, the LNAV MDA of 6,260 feet MSL is higher.

Figure 8-52. You must select the appropriate landing minimums for the approach based on your airplane's equipment capabilities. If your GPS receiver is not WAAS certified, or WAAS is not available, the LPV approach will not be displayed in the list of available approaches.

LP

Approaches to **localizer performance (LP)** minimums are commonly referred to as WAAS procedures without vertical guidance. Baro-VNAV equipment cannot be used to fly approaches to LP minimums. These approaches have integrity limits close to a localizer and have smaller lateral protected areas than approaches to LNAV minimums. LP and LPV minimums are not published as part of the same instrument approach—each procedure has a different WAAS channel. This means that you cannot perform an LPV approach with vertical guidance and, upon losing WAAS capability, switch to an LP approach.

Although an LP approach has an MDA, this altitude is often lower than an MDA associated with a similar nonprecision approach procedure. Some MDAs for LP approaches can be as low as 300 feet above the runway. LP approach procedures are published in locations where vertical guidance is not feasible due to terrain, obstacles, or other operational limitations. [Figure 8-53]

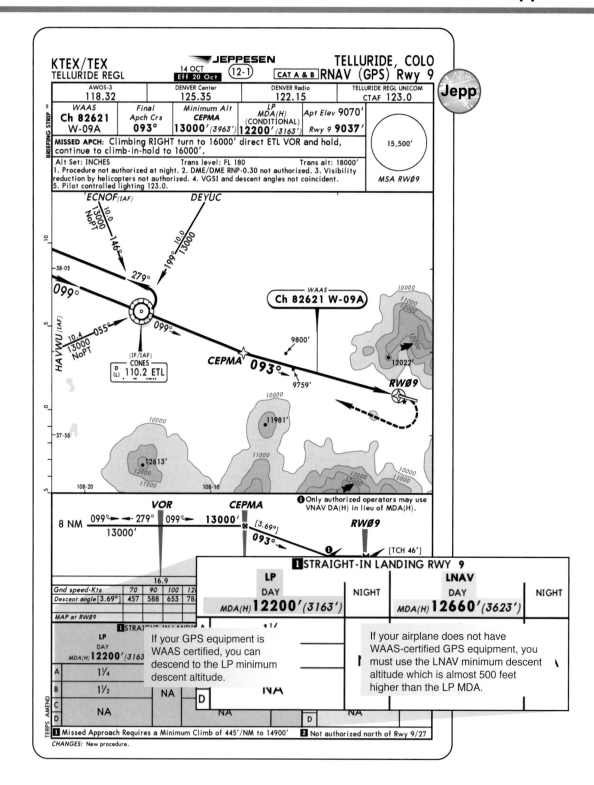

Figure 8-53. Due to the extremely high terrain surrounding Telluride Regional Airport, the RNAV (GPS) approach provides no vertical guidance and the LP minimum is over 3,000 above the runway.

DETERMINING LANDING MINIMUMS

To determine the landing minimums to use for an RNAV (GPS) approach procedure, you must have a complete understanding of the procedure, know the capabilities of the airplane's GPS equipment, and be able to accurately interpret the GPS receiver displays. [Figure 8-54]

RNAV (GPS) Approach Minimums	Type of Minimum	Type of Equipment Required	Guidance	Integrity Limits
LNAV	MDA	GPS certified for IFR approaches	Lateral only	Larger than a localizer
LNAV+V	MDA	WAAS or baro-VNAV (for advisory vertical guidance)	Lateral Advisory vertical guidance	Larger than a localizer
LNAV/VNAV	DA	WAAS or baro-VNAV	Lateral Vertical	Larger than an ILS approach
LPV	DA	WAAS	Lateral Vertical	Close to an ILS approach
LP	MDA	WAAS	Lateral only	Close to a localizer

Figure 8-54. To safely perform RNAV (GPS) approaches, you must not only know how to precisely navigate using GPS equipment, but you must also understand the different landing minimums associated with GPS approaches.

Custom Charts

Some companies request charts that are tailored to their airplane equipment. For example, although the RNAV (GPS) Runway 22L approach to Boston can be flown to LPV minimums with WAAS-certified GPS equipment, (Figure A) the customized approach chart shows only LNAV/VNAV and LNAV minimums (Figure B). This is because the company's airplanes only have baro-VNAV equipment and no WAAS capabilities.

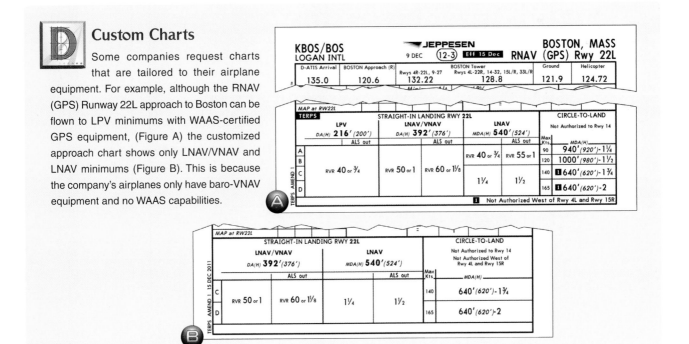

RNP APPROACH

RNP (required navigation performance) approaches are designed to be flown with any type of equipment that meets the RNP integrity requirements specified for the approach procedure. However, to perform RNP approaches, you and your aircraft must meet authorization required (AR) performance criteria that is outlined in AC 90-101, *Approval Guidance for RNP Procedures with AR*. [Figure 8-55]

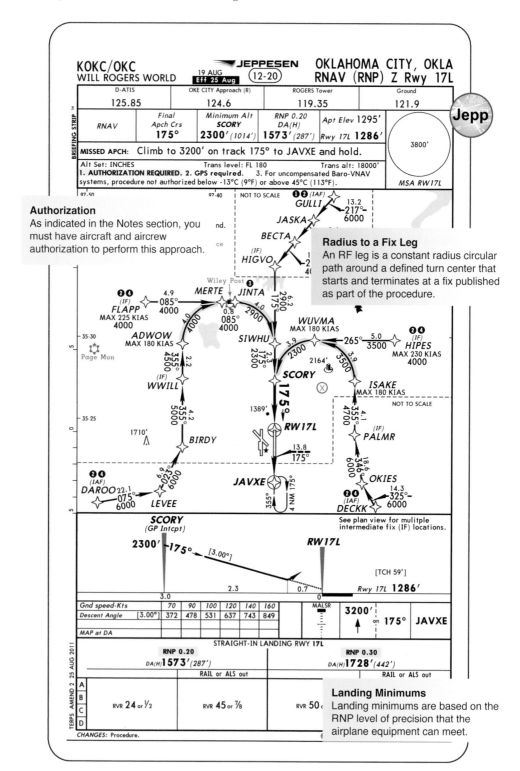

Figure 8-55. One of the unique features of an RNP approach is the use of radius to a fix (RF) legs.

RAIM FAILURE DURING AN APPROACH

When you are performing a GPS approach procedure with non-WAAS GPS equipment, the receiver performs a RAIM prediction at least two nautical miles prior to the final approach fix to ensure RAIM availability before it enters approach mode. You should verify that the receiver has sequenced from "Armed" to "Approach" mode prior to the final approach fix.

If the GPS receiver detects an integrity problem, it displays an alert message. In this case, there might not be enough satellites available to provide RAIM, or RAIM has detected a potential error that exceeds tolerances for the current phase of flight. If RAIM is not available when you set up a GPS approach, you should use another type of navigation and approach system. If the receiver does not sequence into the approach mode or indicates RAIM failure prior to the final approach fix, do not descend to the DA or MDA. Proceed to the missed approach point, perform the missed approach procedure, and contact ATC as soon as possible. If a RAIM failure occurs after the final approach fix, the GPS receiver continues to operate without a failure indication for up to five minutes so you can complete the approach. However, if you do notice a RAIM failure indication after the final approach fix, perform a missed approach immediately and contact ATC.

 If RAIM is not available when you set up a GPS approach, you should select another type of navigation and approach system.

FLYING AN RNAV (GPS) APPROACH TO LPV MINIMUMS

There are some unique aspects to consider as you prepare for and perform an RNAV (GPS) approach, such as determining the appropriate minimums, correctly programming your equipment, and interpreting the approach design. A benefit to using GPS equipment to navigate on the approach course is the increased situational awareness gained by receiving course guidance from a CDI and being able to see time and distance information to each waypoint and the airplane's position on the approach with a moving map display. In the following example, you are flying a category A airplane with an IFR-approved Garmin G1000 that is WAAS-certified. Your destination is Naples Municipal Airport in Naples, Florida. [Figures 8-56 and 8-57]

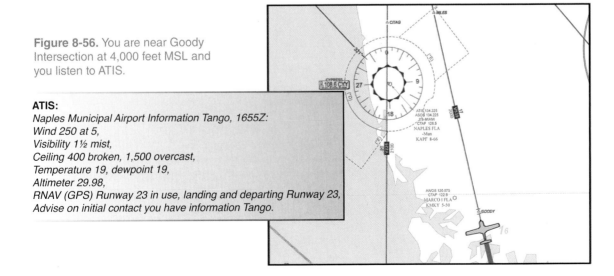

Figure 8-56. You are near Goody Intersection at 4,000 feet MSL and you listen to ATIS.

ATIS:
Naples Municipal Airport Information Tango, 1655Z:
Wind 250 at 5,
Visibility 1½ mist,
Ceiling 400 broken, 1,500 overcast,
Temperature 19, dewpoint 19,
Altimeter 29.98,
RNAV (GPS) Runway 23 in use, landing and departing Runway 23,
Advise on initial contact you have information Tango.

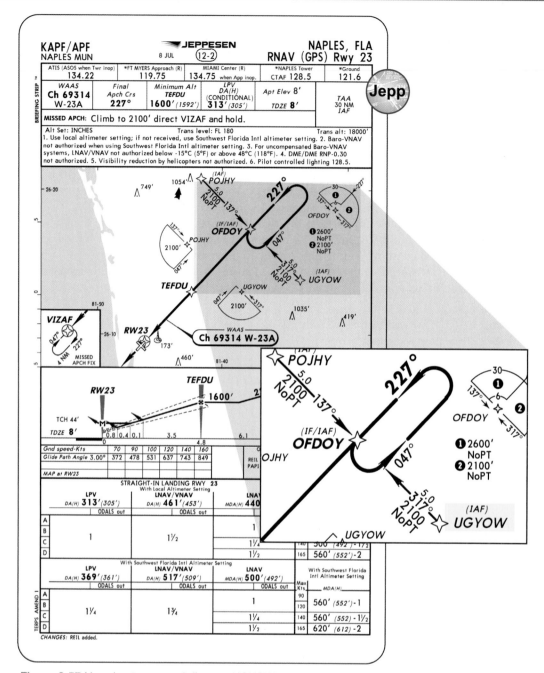

Figure 8-57. You plan to proceed direct to UGYOW waypoint, the initial approach fix for the RNAV (GPS) Runway 23 approach.

PREPARING FOR THE APPROACH

To prepare for the approach, perform an approach overview to ensure you can safely perform the approach. After ATC tells you which approach to expect, brief the details of the approach procedure.

APPROACH OVERVIEW

After listening to ATIS, you perform an approach overview. Compare the landing minimums for a category A airplane operating at 90 knots with the reported ceiling and visibility, look for significant terrain and obstacles, determine if there are unique features that you need to take into consideration, and review the airport information using the airport chart. [Figure 8-58]

Unique Procedure Features

The approach uses a terminal arrival area (TAA) to enable you to transition from the enroute environment direct to the initial approach fix. In addition, higher minimums apply if you cannot obtain the local altimeter setting and must use Southwest Florida International Airport's altimeter setting.

Terrain and Obstacles

A tower at 1,035 feet MSL is just south of UGYOW waypoint, the initial approach fix. There is also a tower at 173 feet MSL to the left of the final approach course near the runway.

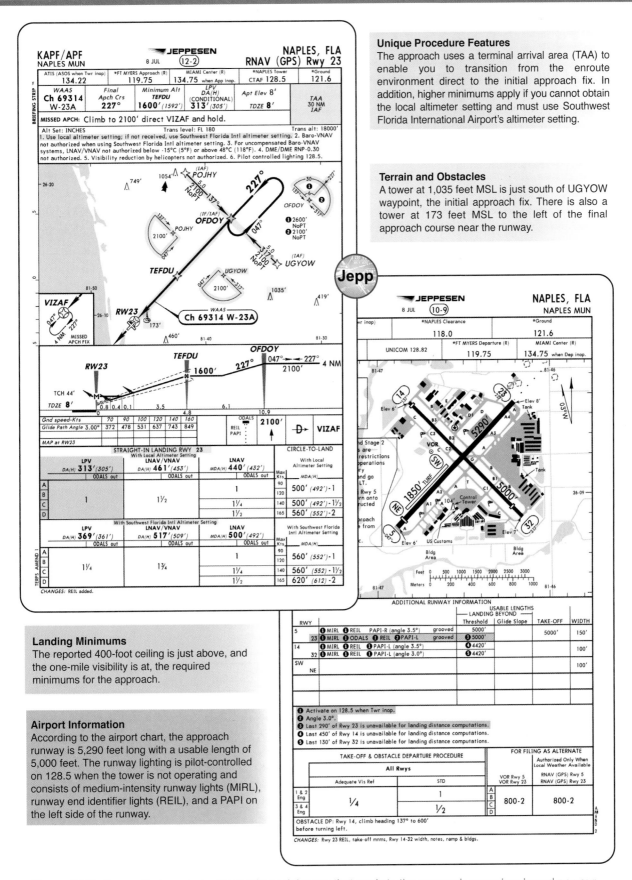

Landing Minimums

The reported 400-foot ceiling is just above, and the one-mile visibility is at, the required minimums for the approach.

Airport Information

According to the airport chart, the approach runway is 5,290 feet long with a usable length of 5,000 feet. The runway lighting is pilot-controlled on 128.5 when the tower is not operating and consists of medium-intensity runway lights (MIRL), runway end identifier lights (REIL), and a PAPI on the left side of the runway.

SECTION C ■ RNAV Approaches

Figure 8-58. Ensure that you know the landing minimums that apply to the approach procedure based on your specific GPS equipment. In this case, with a WAAS-certified GPS receiver, you intend to fly the approach with vertical guidance to LPV minimums.

APPROACH BRIEFING

As you continue inbound to the airport, you receive this transmission from ATC: *"Cessna 20JA, descend and maintain 3,000, direct to UGYOW, expect RNAV Runway 23 approach, Naples."* During the approach briefing, load the approach procedure on the GPS receiver and verify that the waypoints and transition names coincide with names on the approach chart and are spelled the same. If your check indicates a potential error, do not use the procedure or waypoint until you have verified that the latitude and longitude, waypoint type, and altitude restrictions match the published data. [Figure 8-59]

Procedure Title
The procedure is the RNAV (GPS) approach for Runway 23 at Naples Municipal Airport at Naples.

Communication Frequencies
Listen to ATIS on 134.22. Talk to Fort Myers Approach on 119.75 or Miami Center on 134.75. Set Naples Tower on 128.5. Ground Control is on 121. 6.

Primary Navaid Frequency or Approach Selected
Before loading the approach, ensure the GPS display shows the RNAV 23GPS LPV, channel 69314, with an ID of W23A, which matches the chart.

Final Approach Course
The final approach course is 227°.

Approach Altitudes
From UGYOW to OFDOY, maintain 2,100 feet MSL. After intercepting the approach course at OFDOY, descend to 1,600 feet to TEFDU, the FAF.

DA (Precision Approach)
The LPV DA is 313 feet MSL for a straight-in landing.

Airport Information
The airport elevation and the touchdown zone elevation is 8 feet MSL.

Missed Approach Instructions
Climb to 2,100 feet MSL while proceeding direct to VIZAF and hold.

Procedural Notes
You have the local altimeter setting, so use the applicable minimums.

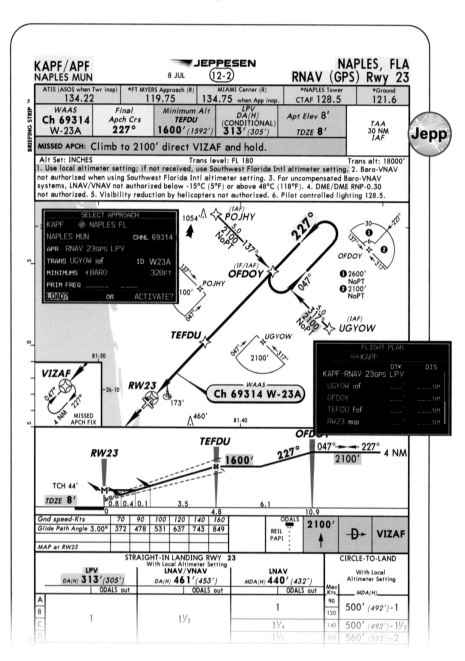

Figure 8-59. Ensure that you brief the approach minimums that apply to the type of procedure you will fly based on the airplane's GPS equipment. In this case, you have a WAAS-certified GPS receiver, so you are flying the approach to the LPV decision altitude.

PERFORMING THE APPROACH

As you perform the approach, the primary navigation instrument is the HSI (or a traditional VOR display set to GPS). If you are using a separate GPS unit, you can display a backup CDI on the GPS receiver or display the moving map for situational awareness.

APPROACH CLEARANCE

As you near UGYOW waypoint, Ft. Meyers Approach advises: *"Cessna 20JA, cleared for the RNAV (GPS) Runway 23 approach to Naples Municipal. Maintain 3,000 until established on the approach. Contact Naples Tower on 128.5 at TEFDU."* With clearance for the approach, activate the approach on the GPS receiver. [Figure 8-60]

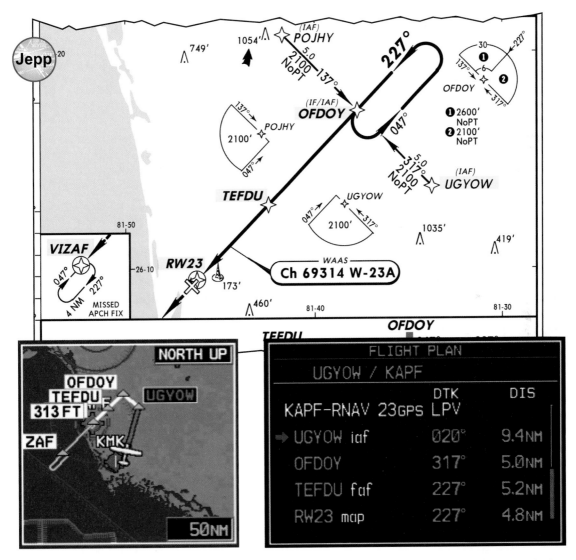

Figure 8-60. After activating the approach, ensure that the waypoints are generally logical in location, in the correct order, and that their orientation to each other matches the approach chart.

While flying to UGYOW, descend to 3,000 feet MSL. After you are level at 3,000, perform the before-landing checklist with the possible exceptions of the landing gear and flaps. Throughout the approach, use the autopilot as appropriate to ease your workload.

INITIAL APPROACH SEGMENT

Immediately before you reach UGYOW, the GPS receiver prompts you to begin a turn to 317°. When you are established on the initial approach segment, descend to 2,100 feet MSL at the approach speed of 90 knots. Use the HSI to navigate on course and keep track of your position by monitoring the GPS display. [Figure 8-61]

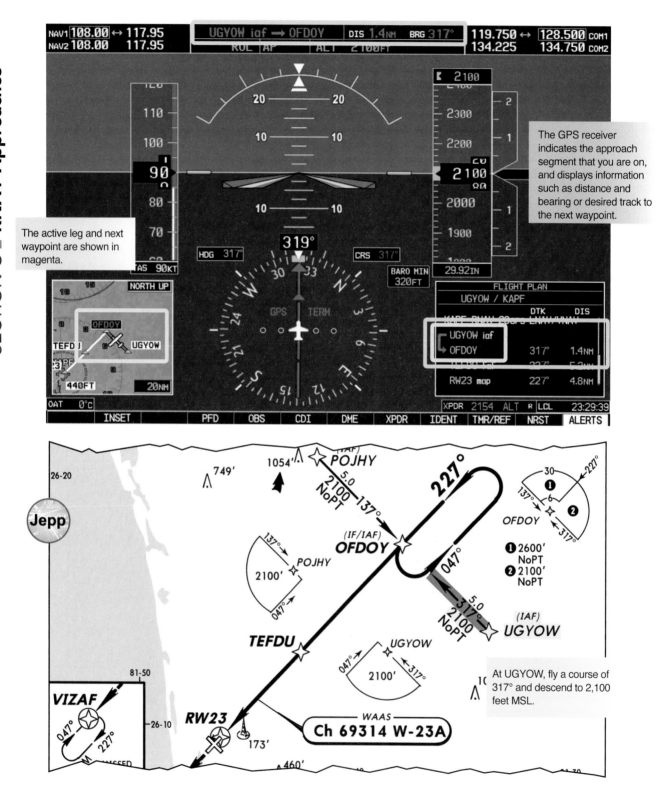

Figure 8-61. Initial Approach Segment

INTERMEDIATE APPROACH SEGMENT

Just prior to the intermediate fix at OFDOY, the GPS receiver prompts you to begin a turn to the inbound course of 227°. After turning left, descend to 1,600 feet MSL at your approach speed of 90 knots. Use the HSI to track the inbound course. [Figure 8-62]

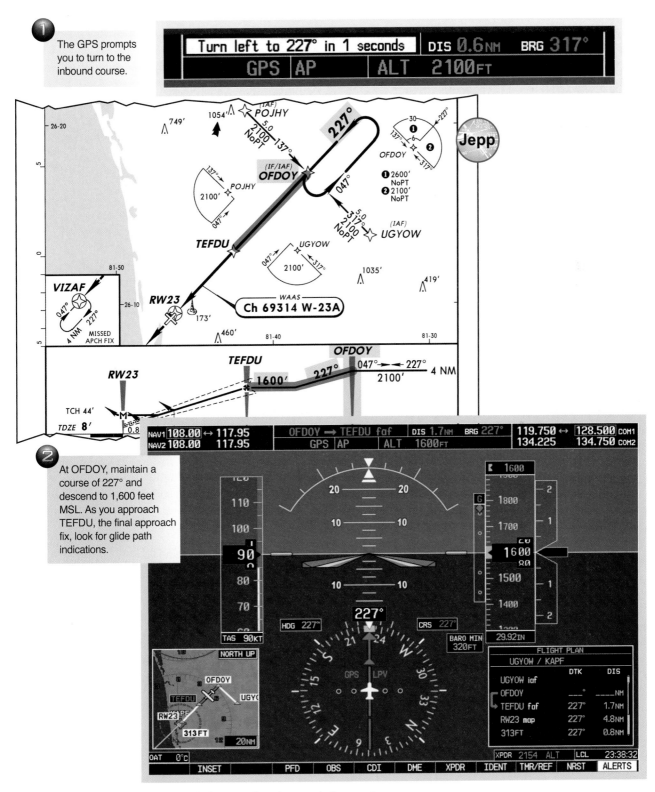

Figure 8-62. Intermediate Approach Segment.

FINAL APPROACH SEGMENT

At TEFDU, begin a descent at 90 knots following the glide path. Contact Naples Tower: *"Naples Tower, Cessna 20JA at TEFDU inbound on the RNAV Runway 23 approach."* The tower clears you to land on Runway 23. Continue inbound descending to the decision altitude (DA) of 313 feet MSL. Periodically scan ahead for the runway environment and required visual cues and keep track of your altitude so that know when you reach the DA. [Figure 8-63]

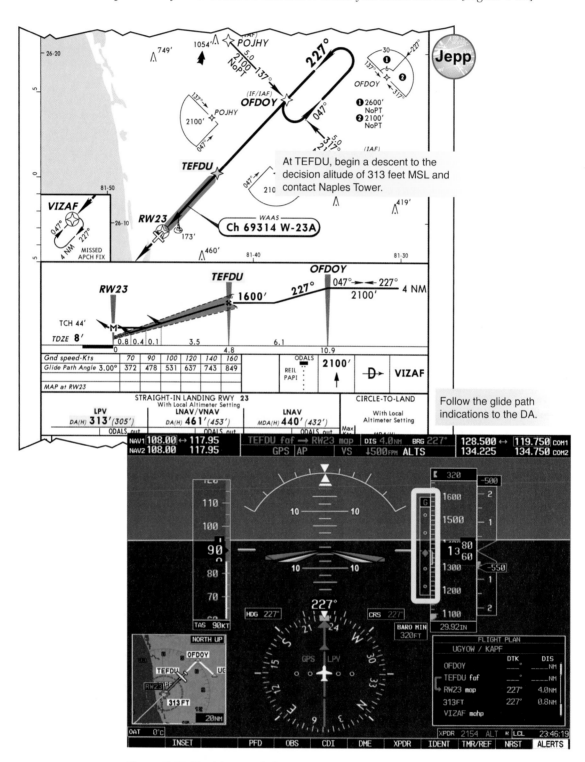

Figure 8-63. Final Approach Segment

MISSED APPROACH SEGMENT

At the DA, you do not have the runway environment in sight, so add power to start climbing and begin the missed approach. As the airplane crosses the missed approach point, the GPS receiver suspends automatic approach waypoint sequencing. [Figure 8-64]

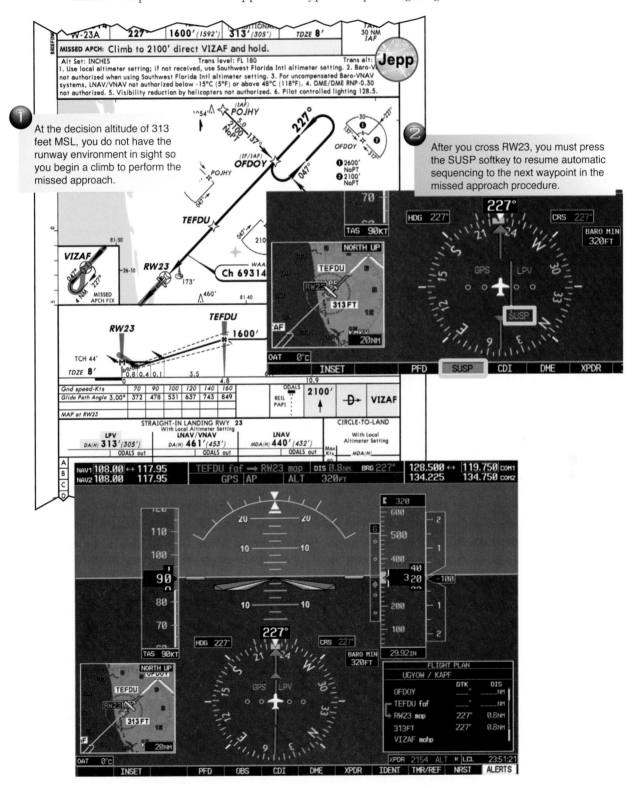

① At the decision altitude of 313 feet MSL, you do not have the runway environment in sight so you begin a climb to perform the missed approach.

② After you cross RW23, you must press the SUSP softkey to resume automatic sequencing to the next waypoint in the missed approach procedure.

Figure 8-64. Missed Approach Segment – Initiating the Missed Approach.

Take the GPS receiver out of suspend mode so it will sequence to VIZAF—the missed approach holding point (MAHP). Report the missed approach to Naples Tower and, upon the controller's direction, contact Fort Myers approach to request clearance for another approach or routing to your alternate. If the approach controller clears you to fly the published missed approach procedure, continue climbing to 2,100 feet and enter the holding pattern at VIZAF. [Figure 8-65]

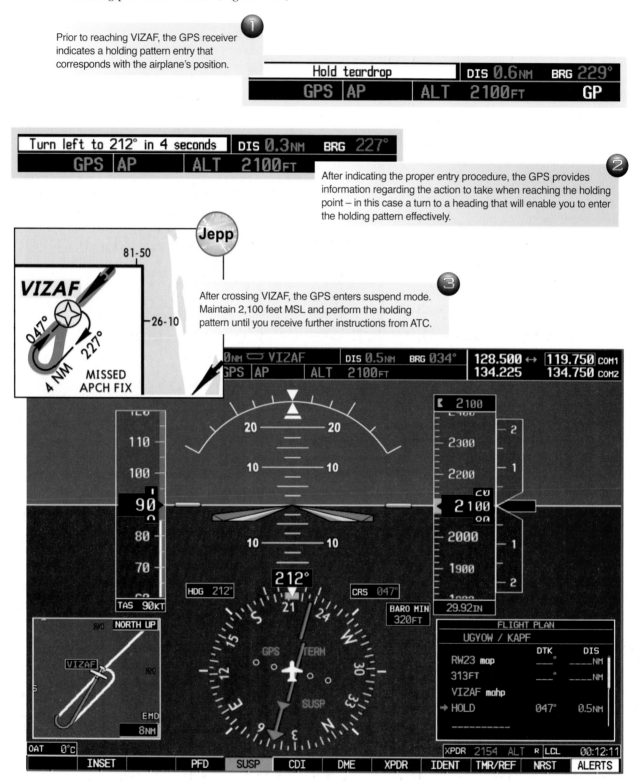

1 Prior to reaching VIZAF, the GPS receiver indicates a holding pattern entry that corresponds with the airplane's position.

2 After indicating the proper entry procedure, the GPS provides information regarding the action to take when reaching the holding point – in this case a turn to a heading that will enable you to enter the holding pattern effectively.

3 After crossing VIZAF, the GPS enters suspend mode. Maintain 2,100 feet MSL and perform the holding pattern until you receive further instructions from ATC.

Figure 8-65 Missed Approach Segment – Entering the Holding Pattern

FLYING A GPS APPROACH TO LNAV MINIMUMS

If the GPS approach procedure does not have LNAV/VNAV or LPV minimums or you do not have baro-VNAV equipment or a WAAS-certified GPS, you must fly the approach to LNAV minimums without vertical guidance. In this case, if you were to fly the RNAV (GPS) Runway 23 approach at Naples, the GPS receiver displays LNAV guidance as your only option. [Figure 8-66]

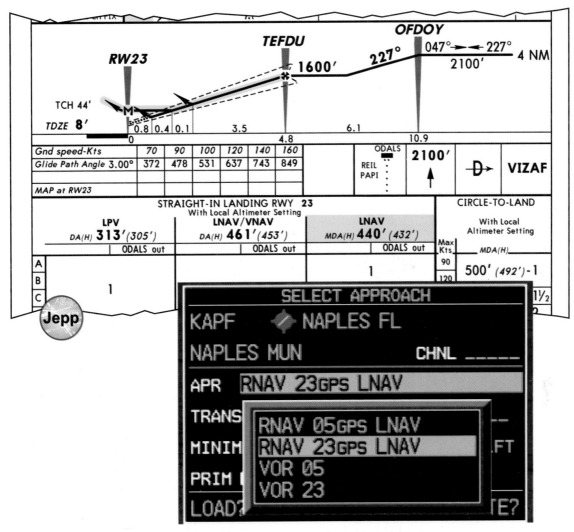

Figure 8-66. The menu to select an approach at Naples only displays the LNAV procedures.

PERFORMING THE APPROACH

The steps to perform the initial and intermediate segments of the GPS Runway 23 approach to LNAV minimums are no different than those used to fly the LPV approach. You fly the altitudes and courses indicated on the approach chart from the initial approach fix to the intermediate approach fix and then to the final approach fix. However, at the final approach fix, the procedure changes. You are now flying an approach to an MDA without vertical guidance as part of the published approach procedure. [Figure 8-67]

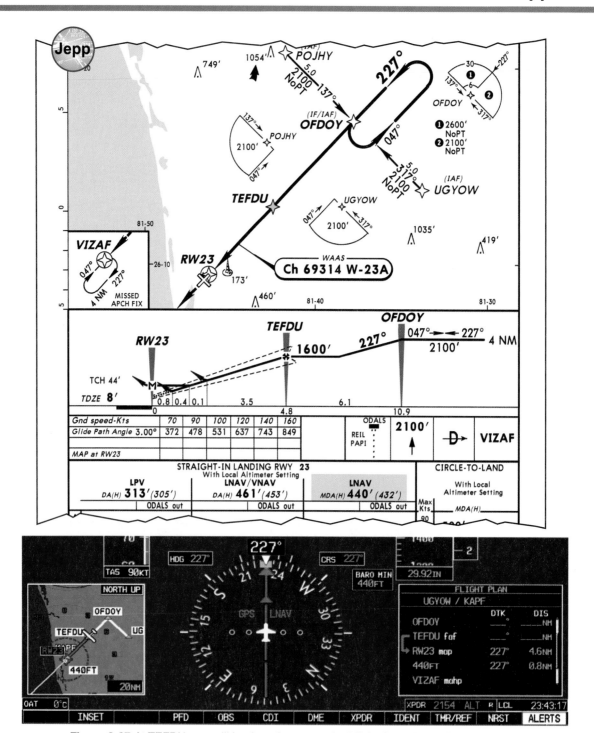

Figure 8-67. At TEFDU, you will begin a descent to the MDA of 440 feet MSL. After reaching 440 feet MSL, you must remain at this altitude until you have the runway environment in sight or you reach the missed approach point of RW23.

SECTION C ▪ RNAV Approaches

GPS Satellite Anatomy 101

Have you ever wondered what GPS satellites look like? How big are they? How they work? Well, there have been several different types of GPS spacecraft since the original NAVSTAR (Navigation System with Timing and Ranging) launch in 1978. The first 10 satellites in orbit were the Block 1 spacecraft, built by Rockwell Space Systems and weighing 945 pounds each. These satellites averaged nearly eight years in service before they wore out and were replaced by Rockwell's Block 2 and Block 2A spacecraft, which were launched from 1989 through 1996. The next series of satellites, the Block 2R model produced by Lockheed Martin, provided dramatic improvements over previous blocks [see figure]. They could determine their own position by performing inter-satellite ranging with other Block 2R satellites. The follow-on generation of GPS satellites, Block 2F, is built by Boeing. Improvements on these satellites include a design life of 12 years and a civil signal on a third frequency.

Each spacecraft is basically a box-shaped central structure with large solar panels on each side to provide electrical power. On Block 2R spacecraft, the solar panels span more than 30 feet and provide about 1,136 watts of electrical power. The satellite is stabilized in all 3 axes so it always points straight down. Attitude is maintained by electrically-actuated reaction wheels. Driving the reaction wheel in one direction causes the spacecraft to rotate in the opposite direction. By arranging three reaction wheels to correspond to the 3 axes of rotation, the spacecraft can be kept in any desired attitude. A system of hydrazine propulsion thrusters makes changes in the orbital position of the spacecraft.

As you know, timing is at the heart of the GPS concept, so each satellite has four atomic clocks on board, two rubidium clocks and two cesium clocks. The accurate time signals are of no use if they are not broadcast to your receiver, so each spacecraft has an array of 12 L-band antennas for the downlink transmitters. The spacecraft use S-band radios to communicate with ground controllers and UHF to communicate with each other. The satellites also carry nuclear detonation detectors, and are protected from laser and nuclear radiation. They are military spacecraft, after all.

SECTION C ■ RNAV Approaches

SUMMARY CHECKLIST

✓ The terminal arrival area (TAA) approach design has icons on the plan view to indicate minimum altitudes that you must maintain as you arrive from the enroute structure to a specific initial approach fix, therefore, no MSA is published.

✓ The basic T approach segment configuration is optimum for transition from the enroute to the terminal environment within a TAA.

✓ For fly-by waypoints (depicted with the waypoint symbol), the GPS receiver anticipates the turn and displays navigation indications that prevent you from overshooting the next flight segment.

✓ For fly-over waypoints (depicted by the waypoint symbol enclosed in a circle), navigation indications will not provide guidance for a turn until you pass over the waypoint, followed either by an intercept maneuver to the next flight segment or by direct flight to the next waypoint.

✓ Missed approach points and missed approach holding waypoints are normally fly-over waypoints and the initial, intermediate, and final approach fixes are typically fly-by waypoints.

✓ To fly RNAV (GPS) approach procedures with lateral navigation, your GPS equipment must be certified according to TSO-C129.

✓ To fly GPS approaches that incorporate vertical navigation using WAAS, your GPS equipment must be certified according to TSO-C145 or TSO-C146.

✓ You can determine the allowable uses for the specific GPS installation by referring to the airplane flight manual (AFM) or AFM supplement.

✓ Baro-VNAV systems calculate a glide path based on an altimeter setting and are subject to high and low temperature limitations.

✓ A WAAS-certified GPS unit determines a glide path by its vertical and horizontal GPS position independent of the altimeter setting, and its operation is not limited by temperature.

✓ If your airplane is equipped with a GPS receiver certified for instrument approaches, you are not required to monitor or have ground-based navigation equipment to perform an RNAV (GPS) approach at the destination.

✓ If your GPS equipment is not WAAS-certified, you may use GPS to perform an approach at an alternate airport only if the alternate airport has an approved instrument approach procedure other than GPS.

✓ If your GPS equipment is WAAS-certified, you can use an airport that only has a GPS approach available as an alternate.

✓ Lateral navigation (LNAV) course guidance has larger integrity limits than those of a localizer, and the approach is flown to a minimum descent altitude (MDA).

✓ A WAAS-certified GPS receiver typically displays advisory vertical guidance to provide a stabilized descent to the MDA for an LNAV approach, indicated as LNAV+V on the GPS display.

✓ Lateral navigation/vertical navigation (LNAV/VNAV) minimums apply to approaches that provide lateral and vertical guidance using baro-VNAV or WAAS-certified equipment.

✓ Although the integrity limits for LNAV/VNAV approaches are larger than those for a precision approach, the landing minimum is a decision altitude (DA).

✓ LPV (localizer performance with vertical guidance) minimums apply to approaches that provide lateral and vertical guidance to a decision altitude with integrity limits that are close to an ILS precision approach.

✓ Your GPS equipment must be WAAS-certified before you can fly approaches to LPV minimums; baro-VNAV equipment does not provide the required precision.

✓ Approaches to localizer performance (LP) minimums are published in locations where vertical guidance is not feasible due to terrain, obstacles, or other operational limitations. These approaches have integrity limits close to a localizer and have an MDA for a landing minimum.

✓ Required navigation performance (RNP) approaches can be flown with any type of equipment that meets specified RNP integrity requirements as long as the airplane and pilot meet SAAR criteria.

✓ A radius to a fix (RF) leg is a constant radius circular path around a defined turn center that starts and terminates at a fix published as part of an RNP approach procedure.

✓ Non-WAAS GPS receivers perform a RAIM prediction by two nautical miles prior to the FAF to ensure that RAIM is available as a condition for entering the approach mode.

✓ If RAIM is not available when you set up a GPS approach, you should use another type of navigation and approach system.

✓ If the GPS receiver does not sequence into the approach mode or indicates RAIM failure prior to the final approach fix, do not descend to the DA or MDA. Proceed to the missed approach point, perform the missed approach procedure, and contact ATC as soon as possible.

✓ If a RAIM failure occurs after the final approach fix, the GPS receiver continues to operate without a failure indication for up to five minutes so you can complete the approach.

SECTION C ▪ RNAV Approaches

KEY TERMS

RNAV (GPS) Approach

Terminal Arrival Area (TAA)

Basic T Approach Segment Configuration

Fly-By Waypoint

Fly-Over Waypoint

Baro-VNAV Equipment

WAAS-Certified GPS Equipment

Lateral Navigation (LNAV)

LNAV+V

Lateral Navigation/Vertical Navigation (LNAV/VNAV)

Localizer Performance with Vertical Guidance (LPV)

Localizer Performance (LP)

Required Navigation Performance (RNP) Approach

QUESTIONS

1. What are at least two characteristics of an RNAV (GPS) approach procedure that is designed with a terminal arrival area (TAA)?

2. Select the correct statement regarding fly-by and fly-over waypoints depicted on this chart.

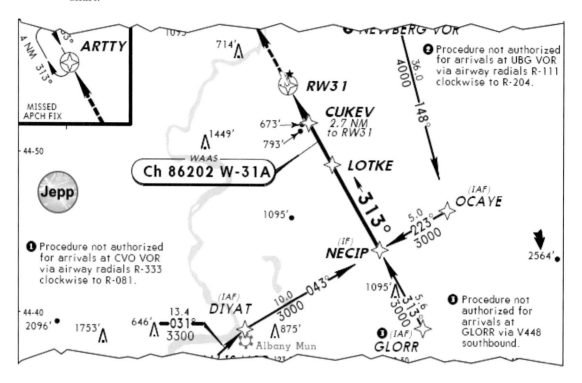

   A. Prior to reaching NECIP, a fly-by waypoint, the GPS receiver anticipates the turn and displays navigation indications to begin the turn so that you do not overshoot the next flight segment.
   B. Prior to reaching RW31, a fly-over waypoint, the GPS receiver anticipates the turn and displays navigation indications to begin the turn so that you do not overshoot the next flight segment.
   C. Navigation indications as you approach OCAYE, a fly-over waypoint, will not provide guidance for a turn until you pass over the waypoint.

3. How can you determine the allowable uses for the specific GPS installation in your airplane?

4. WAAS-certified GPS equipment is approved for IFR approach operations by the current version of which document?
   A. TSO-C129
   B. TSO-C145 or TSO-C146
   C. The airplane flight manual

5. Select the true statement regarding baro-VNAV equipment.
   A. It builds a glide path by sensing and then comparing the airplane's altitude with a calculated altitude for the airplane's position on the glide path.
   B. It can be used to perform approaches to LPV minimums.
   C. It determines a glide path by its vertical and horizontal GPS position to eliminate the errors caused by barometric altimetry.

6. Select the true statement regarding WAAS-certified equipment for RNAV (GPS) approaches when planning an instrument flight.
   A. Any required alternate airport must have an approved instrument approach procedure other than GPS.
   B. If RAIM is not available, you must monitor traditional ground-based navaids while flying an RNAV (GPS) approach.
   C. The destination or alternate airport is not required to have an approved instrument approach other than an RNAV (GPS) approach.

For questions 7 through 11, match the following RNAV (GPS) approach minimums to the appropriate descriptions.

   A. LPV
   B. LNAV/VNAV
   C. LNAV
   D. LNAV+V
   E. LP

7. Uses a DA; requires WAAS-certified or baro-VNAV equipment; provides lateral and vertical guidance; has integrity limits larger than an ILS approach

8. Uses an MDA; requires WAAS-certified equipment; provides lateral guidance only; has integrity limits close to a localizer

9. Uses an MDA; requires WAAS-certified or baro-VNAV equipment; provides lateral guidance and advisory vertical guidance; has integrity limits larger than a localizer

10. Uses a DA; requires WAAS-certified equipment; provides lateral and vertical guidance; has integrity limits close to an ILS approach

11. Uses an MDA; requires GPS equipment certified for IFR approaches; provides lateral guidance only; has integrity limits larger than a localizer

12. Select the true statement regarding an RNP approach procedure.
    A. As long you have WAAS-certified GPS equipment, you may fly an RNP approach.
    B. You and your airplane equipment must meet SAAR (Special Aircraft and Aircrew Authorization Required) criteria to fly an RNP approach.
    C. RNP approaches provide lateral guidance only and are flown to an MDA.

13. How does RAIM apply to performing RNAV (GPS) approach procedures if your GPS equipment is not WAAS-certified?
    A. If RAIM is not available when you set up a GPS approach, you should use another type of navigation and approach system.
    B. If the receiver does not sequence into the approach mode or indicates RAIM failure prior to the final approach fix, continue the approach to the DA or MDA and then perform a missed approach.
    C. To ensure that RAIM is available as a condition for entering the approach mode, the GPS receiver performs a RAIM prediction at the final approach fix.

SECTION C ■ RNAV Approaches

Refer to the RNAV (GPS) RWY 31 approach chart to answer questions 14-19.

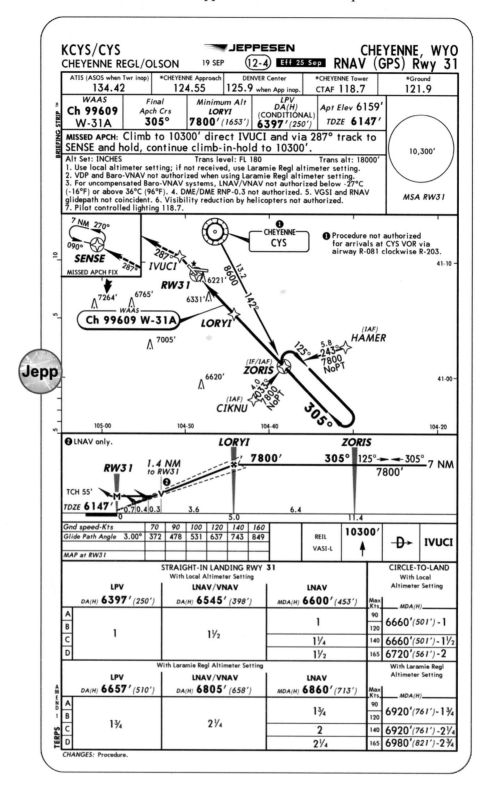

You are in a category A airplane, planning to fly the RNAV (GPS) Runway 31 approach to Cheyenne Regional/Jerry Olson Airport, Cheyenne, Wyoming. Your approach speed will be 90 knots. You have WAAS-certified GPS equipment and intend to use LPV minimums. ATIS reports a 300-foot ceiling and one mile visibility.

SECTION C ■ RNAV Approaches

14. What element might you include in an approach overview for this approach?
    A. The approach uses a terminal arrival area (TAA) design to enable you to transition from the enroute environment direct to the initial approach fix.
    B. The reported weather conditions are just above the ceiling and visibility minimums required for the LNAV approach.
    C. Towers at 6,331 feet and 6,221 feet are located close to the airport along the final approach path.

15. As you near your destination, Cheyenne Approach advises you to expect the RNAV (GPS) Runway 31 approach. What elements should you include in your approach briefing?
    A. Verify that the waypoints and transition names on the GPS display match those on the procedure chart.
    B. State that final approach course is 125°.
    C. Select the LPV DA of 6,600 feet MSL for a straight-in landing.

16. What is the correct procedure for flying the initial and intermediate approach segments?
    A. Track the 142° radial from CYS VOR/DME at 8,600 feet MSL to ZORIS waypoint. At ZORIS, turn right to track inbound on the approach course of 305° to LORYI and descend to 7,800 feet MSL.
    B. At CIKNU, fly a course of 033° to ZORIS at 7,800 feet MSL. At ZORIS, turn right for a direct entry into the holding pattern. After flying outbound for one minute in the holding pattern, turn inbound on the approach course of 305°. Maintain 7,800 feet MSL to LORYI.
    C. At HAMER, fly a course of 243° at 7,800 feet MSL to ZORIS. At ZORIS, turn right to intercept the approach course of 305° to LORYI. Maintain 7,800 feet MSL.

17. What is the correct procedure for flying the final approach segment from LORYI?
    A. Descend to 6,600 feet MSL on the glide path on a course of 305°. Maintain 6,600 MSL until reaching the visual descent point. If you do not have the runway environment in sight at the VDP, perform the missed approach procedure.
    B. Track a course of 305° and begin a descent on the glide path. If you do not have the runway environment in sight by the time you reach the DA of 6,397 feet MSL, perform the missed approach procedure.
    C. Track a course of 305° and descend to 6,397 feet MSL. Maintain 6,397 feet MSL until reaching the missed approach point of RW31. If you do not have the runway environment in sight at RW31, perform the missed approach procedure.

18. Describe how to perform the missed approach procedure.

19. Select the true statement regarding performing the RNAV (GPS) Runway 31 approach in an airplane without baro-VNAV or WAAS-certified GPS equipment.
    A. If you do not have the runway environment in sight at 1.4 nautical miles from the runway threshold, you must perform the missed approach procedure.
    B. You can fly the approach to either the LNAV/VNAV DA of 6,545 feet MSL or to the LNAV MDA of 6,600 feet MSL.
    C. You must fly the approach to the LNAV MDA of 6,600 feet MSL.

SECTION C ■ RNAV Approaches

PART III

Aviation Weather and IFR Flight Operations

Weather bothers a pilot only in a few basic ways. It prevents him from seeing; it bounces him around to the extent that it may be difficult to keep the airplane under control and in one piece; and by ice, wind, or large temperature variations, it may reduce the airplane's performance to a serious degree.

— Robert N. Buck

PART III

Decision making for VFR pilots is relatively easy; if there is any chance of getting caught in IFR weather conditions, you cancel your flight. Although you have more options as an instrument-rated pilot, your ability to fly IFR does not mean you can operate in any weather conditions. You must exercise better judgment because you have the opportunity to experience weather hazards that do not affect VFR pilots. Chapter 9 reviews basic weather theory, discusses hazards that affect IFR operations, and reviews weather reports, forecasts, graphic weather products, and sources of weather information. Chapter 10 looks at emergencies unique to instrument flight, explores single-pilot resource management in the IFR environment and gives you the tools you need to effectively plan flights under IFR.

CHAPTER 9

Meteorology

Instrument/Commercial
Part III, Chapter 9 — Meteorology

SECTION A
Weather Factors

The reports and forecasts you obtain in a weather briefing do not always give you the complete picture of the weather conditions along your entire route of flight. For example, the conditions between reporting points might be difficult to determine, especially in areas with dramatically changing topography. In situations like these, you need to have a solid understanding of basic weather theory, because the determination of whether the flight can be made will most likely be based on your own observations.

THE ATMOSPHERE

The atmosphere is a remarkable mixture of life-giving gases surrounding our planet. Without the atmosphere there would be no protection from X rays, ultraviolet rays, and other harmful radiation from the sun. Though this protective blanket is essential to life on earth, it is extraordinarily thin — almost all of the earth's atmospheric mass is within 30 miles (50 km) of the surface. As a comparison, if the Earth were the size of a beach ball, 99.9% of the atmosphere would be within 1/16 of an inch of the surface. The atmosphere does not have a clearly defined upper limit, but simply fades away with increasing altitude. [Figure 9-1]

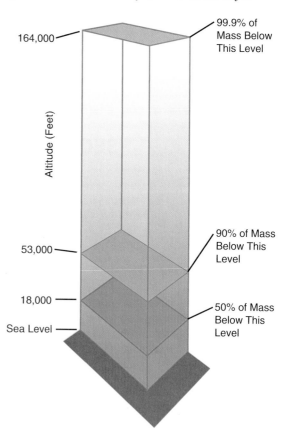

Figure 9-1. Almost all of the earth's atmosphere exists within 50 km (164,000 feet) of the surface. 90% of the atmospheric mass exists below 16 km (53,000 feet).

The most common way of classifying the atmosphere is according to its thermal characteristics. The **troposphere** is the layer from the surface to an altitude that varies between 24,000 and 50,000 feet. It is characterized by a decrease in temperature with altitude. The top of the troposphere is called the **tropopause**. The height of the tropopause varies with the season and latitude. It tends to be higher where it is warmer. The abrupt change in temperature lapse rate at the tropopause acts as a lid that confines most water vapor, and the associated weather, to the troposphere. Severe thunderstorms are one of the few phenomena that extend into the next layer, the **stratosphere**. The uppermost layers, which contain almost no atmospheric gases, are the mesosphere and thermosphere. [Figure 9-2]

In the troposphere, temperatures decrease with altitude up to the tropopause, where an abrupt change in the temperature lapse rate occurs. The average height of the troposphere in the middle latitudes is 36,000 to 37,000 feet. As shown in figure 9-2, the temperature in the lower part of the stratosphere (up to approximately 66,000 feet) experiences relatively small changes in temperature with an increase in altitude.

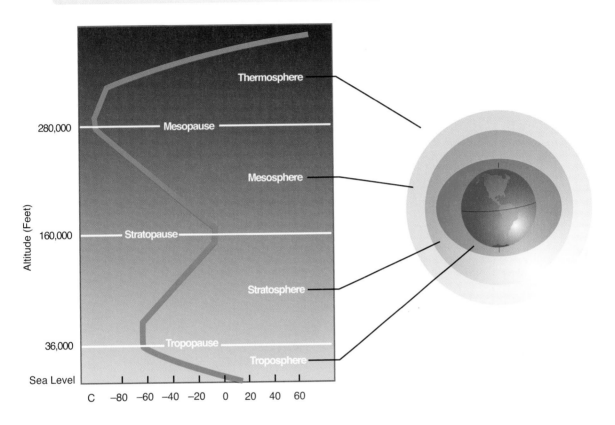

Figure 9-2. The thickness of the atmospheric layers is exaggerated for clarity. Notice that the temperature remains constant in the lower part of the stratosphere before it begins to increase with an increase in altitude.

Additional layer designations help identify the vertical structure of the atmosphere. The ozone layer is characterized by a high concentration of O_3, with maximum concentration at about 80,000 feet MSL. This special type of oxygen molecule absorbs harmful solar radiation and accounts for the increase in temperature with altitude in that part of the atmosphere. The ionosphere is a deep layer of charged particles beginning about 30 miles above the surface. The electrical characteristics of the ionosphere can affect radio communications around sunrise and sunset, and during periods of increased solar activity.

ATMOSPHERIC CIRCULATION

Solar radiation strikes the earth at different angles at different locations, depending on the latitude, the time of day, and the time of year. Cloud cover can also block solar radiation. The variables cause the earth's surface to heat unevenly. This uneven heating is the driving force behind all weather. Because of the tilt of the earth's axis, the northern hemisphere receives more solar radiation than the southern hemisphere from March through September, and the southern hemisphere receives more from September through March. In general, the most direct rays of the sun strike the earth at latitudes near the equator. At higher latitudes the sunlight is less concentrated, and the poles receive the least direct light and energy from the sun. [Figure 9-3]

The sun's energy is more concentrated near the equator. At higher latitudes the solar radiation spreads over a much greater surface area.

Courtesy of NASA

Figure 9-3. Solar heat is most concentrated in areas where the sun's rays strike the earth most nearly perpendicular to the surface.

 Every physical process of weather is accompanied by or is the result of a heat exchange. The primary cause of all changes in the earth's weather is the variation of solar energy received by the earth's regions.

PRESSURE AND WIND PATTERNS

The unequal heating of the surface modifies air density, causing differences in pressure. Meteorologists plot pressure readings from weather reporting stations on charts and connect points of equal pressure with lines called **isobars**. These lines are normally labeled in millibars. The resulting pattern reveals the **pressure gradient**, or change in pressure over distance. When isobars are spread widely apart, the gradient is considered to be weak, and closely spaced isobars indicate a strong gradient.

Isobars help identify pressure systems, which are classified as highs, lows, ridges, troughs, and cols. A **high** is a center of high pressure surrounded on all sides by lower pressure. A **low** is an area of low pressure surrounded by higher pressure. A **ridge** is an elongated area of high pressure and a **trough** is an elongated area of low pressure. A **col** can designate either a neutral area between two highs or two lows, or the intersection of a ridge and a trough. [Figure 9-4] Low pressure areas are areas of rising air, which can encourage bad weather, but high pressure areas consist of descending air that encourages good weather. [Figure 9-5]

A low pressure area or trough is an area of rising air, and a high pressure area or ridge is characterized by descending air. See figure 9-5.

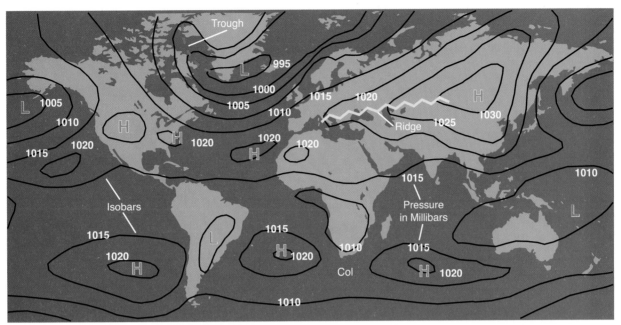

Figure 9-4. You can identify highs, lows, ridges, troughs, and cols when isobars are plotted on a weather chart.

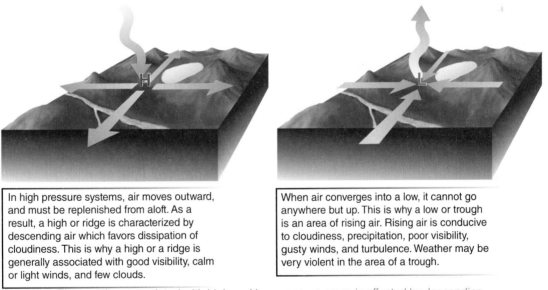

In high pressure systems, air moves outward, and must be replenished from aloft. As a result, a high or ridge is characterized by descending air which favors dissipation of cloudiness. This is why a high or a ridge is generally associated with good visibility, calm or light winds, and few clouds.

When air converges into a low, it cannot go anywhere but up. This is why a low or trough is an area of rising air. Rising air is conducive to cloudiness, precipitation, poor visibility, gusty winds, and turbulence. Weather may be very violent in the area of a trough.

Figure 9-5. The weather associated with high and low pressure areas is affected by descending and rising air.

Wind is caused by airflow from cool, dense high pressure areas into warm, less dense, low pressure areas. The speed of this wind depends on the pressure gradient force. The stronger the gradient force, the stronger the wind. As the earth rotates beneath this airflow, **Coriolis force** counterbalances the pressure gradient force and deflects airflow to the right as it flows out of a high pressure area in the northern hemisphere. This results in clockwise circulation leaving a high and counterclockwise, or **cyclonic**, circulation entering a low.

 Wind is caused by pressure differences as air flows outward from a high pressure area to a low pressure area. However, the wind does not flow directly from a high to a low because of Coriolis force, which deflects air to the right in the northern hemisphere. The result is a wind that flows in a clockwise direction leaving a high and in a counterclockwise, or cyclonic, direction when entering a low.

Coriolis force affects air that flows independent of the earth's surface. Although this force deflects winds aloft parallel to the isobars, airflow near the surface is influenced by friction with the surface, which weakens the effects of Coriolis force. As a result, pressure gradient force causes surface winds to cross the isobars at an angle. For this reason, wind direction tends to shift when you descend to within 2,000 feet of the surface. [Figure 9-6]

 Coriolis force:
- Is caused by the rotation of the earth.
- Acts at a right angle to the wind.
- Deflects winds into a curved path moving from high-to low-pressure area, until parallel to the isobars:
- To the right in the Northern Hemisphere
- To the left in the Southern Hemisphere

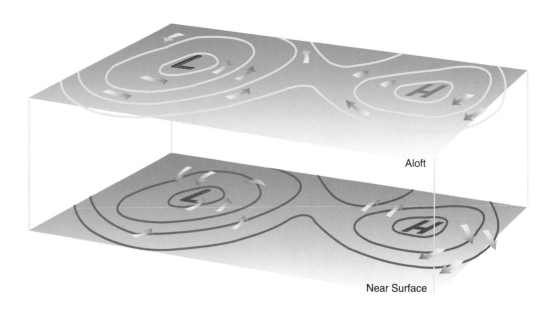

Aloft

Near Surface

Figure 9-6. Near the surface, friction retards the airflow and weakens the effects of Coriolis force, so air flows more directly from a high to a low. When flying from a high to a low, the wind is typically from your left in the northern hemisphere. This general rule applies at any altitude.

 Winds aloft parallel the isobars because Coriolis force tends to counterbalance the pressure gradient force. Surface winds, however, cross isobars at an angle and are weaker because of surface friction.

 As shown in figure 9-6, when flying to an area of low pressure, which is generally an area of unfavorable weather conditions, you will most likely experience a crosswind from the left. As pressure gradient gets stronger toward the center of the low, the winds increase.

LOCAL CONVECTIVE CIRCULATION

Winds near bodies of water are caused by differences in temperature between the land and water surfaces. Because land surfaces warm or cool more rapidly than water surfaces, land usually is warmer than water during the day. This creates a sea breeze, which is a wind that blows from cool water to warmer land. As afternoon heating increases, the sea breeze can reach speeds of 10 to 20 knots. At night, land cools faster than water, and a land breeze blows from the cooler land to the warmer water. Because the temperature contrasts are smaller at night, the land breeze is generally weaker than the sea breeze. [Figure 9-7]

Convective circulation patterns associated with sea breezes are caused by land absorbing and radiating heat faster than water. Cool air must sink to force warm air upward. See figure 9-7.

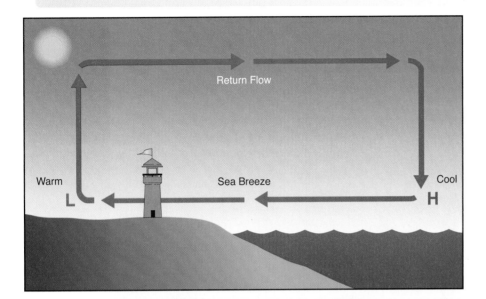

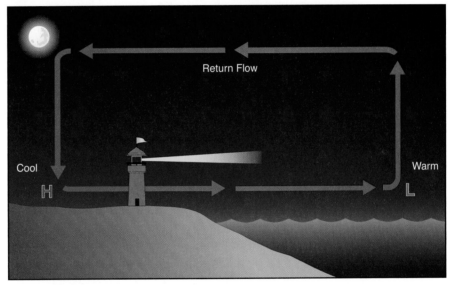

Figure 9-7. During the warm part of the day, air rises over the relatively warm land mass and sinks over the cooler water. This circulation pattern results in an onshore flow. At night, when the land cools more than the water, the circulation pattern reverses.

MOISTURE, PRECIPITATION, AND STABILITY

Although the sun provides the energy that drives the earth's weather, water with its special thermal properties, stores and releases this energy in ways that dramatically affect the weather. Water can exist in a solid (ice), liquid, or gaseous (vapor) state. Water vapor is added to the atmosphere through evaporation and sublimation. **Evaporation** occurs when heat is added to liquid water, changing it to a gas. **Sublimation** is the changing of ice directly to water vapor, bypassing the liquid state. Water vapor is removed from the atmosphere by condensation and deposition. **Condensation** occurs when the air becomes saturated, and water vapor in the air becomes liquid. **Deposition** is when water vapor freezes directly to ice. Of course, liquid water can also freeze, and ice can melt into liquid water.

 Moisture is added to a parcel of air by evaporation and sublimation.

The Ultimate Instrument Airplane

The Research Aviation Facility (RAF) of the National Center for Atmospheric Research (NCAR) operates two National Science Foundation (NSF) aircraft used for weather research.

The Lockheed EC-130Q Hercules and the L-188 Electra are four-engine turboprops that can carry up to 16 researchers in addition to the 3 flight crewmembers. The Hercules offers nearly 90 kilowatts (kw) of electric power for research equipment and can stay aloft for 10 hours. The Electra powers up to 50 kw of equipment and can stay aloft 8-1/2 hours.

NASA's Dryden Flight Research Center is currently using the L-188 in a study on detecting and forecasting clear air turbulence (CAT), discussed in the next section. Other typical research applications include oceanographic investigations, air-sea interaction studies, cloud physics studies, tropospheric profiling, atmospheric chemistry, and aerosol studies. Qualified researchers interested in utilizing these aircraft can submit a formal application to NCAR and the National Science Foundation.

Courtesy of NCAR/Research Aviation Facility

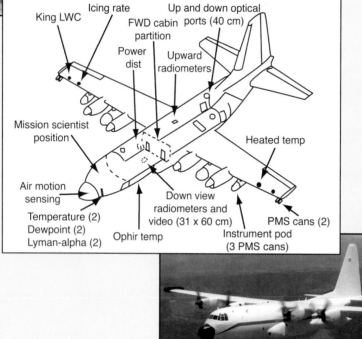

Courtesy of NCAR/
Research Aviation Facility

DEWPOINT

The amount of water vapor the air can hold decreases with the air's temperature. When the air cools to the dewpoint, it contains all the moisture it can hold at that temperature, and is said to be saturated. Relative humidity increases as the temperature/dewpoint spread decreases. When the air is saturated, the relative humidity is 100%. On cool, still nights, surface features and objects might cool to a temperature below the dewpoint of the surrounding air. When this happens, dew condenses on the cold surfaces. Frost forms when water vapor changes directly to ice on a surface that is below freezing.

FAA The amount of water vapor that air can hold largely depends on air temperature. Dewpoint is the temperature to which air must be cooled to become saturated. The temperature and dewpoint spread decreases as the relative humidity increases. At 100% humidity, water vapor condenses, forming clouds, fog or dew. Frost forms when the temperature of the collecting surface is below the dewpoint and the dewpoint is below freezing.

Clouds are composed of very small droplets of water or ice crystals. When they form near the surface, clouds are referred to as fog. You can anticipate the formation of fog or very low clouds when the temperature/dewpoint spread is decreasing below 2°C, or about 4°F.

PRECIPITATION

When condensed water droplets grow to a size where the atmosphere can no longer support their weight, they fall as precipitation. Water droplets that remain liquid fall as drizzle or rain. With low relative humidity, rain might evaporate before it reaches the surface. When this occurs, it is called virga. [Figure 9-8]

 Virga is best described as streamers of precipitation trailing beneath clouds that evaporate before reaching the ground.

Figure 9-8. Virga appears as streamers of precipitation trailing from clouds.

Sometimes water droplets can remain in liquid form even though they are cooled below freezing. When this **supercooled water** strikes an object, such as an airplane in flight or the earth's surface, it immediately turns to ice, or freezing rain. Ice pellets, by contrast, freeze as they fall through cold air and are more likely to bounce off your aircraft rather than freeze to it. The presence of ice pellets generally indicates the existence of freezing rain and warmer air at higher altitudes.

 The presence of ice pellets normally indicates freezing rain at higher altitudes.

Unlike ice pellets, which fall directly to the ground, hail forms in clouds with strong vertical currents. The freezing water droplets are carried up and down increasing in size as they collide and freeze with other water droplets. When they become too large for the air currents to support, they finally fall as hail. [Figure 9-9] If the air currents are particularly strong, hailstones can grow as large as 5 inches in diameter and weigh up to 1-1/2 pounds. Obviously, large hailstones are very dangerous and can cause tremendous damage.

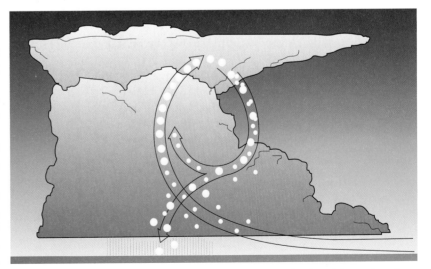

Figure 9-9. One way hail can grow large is by being recirculated through a storm.

 Upward currents enhance the growth rate of precipitation.

Snow forms through the process of deposition, rather than condensation. It differs from ice pellets and hail in that it does not start as liquid water and then freeze. Snow grains are the solid equivalent of drizzle. They are very small, white, opaque particles of ice different from ice pellets in that they are flatter and they neither shatter nor bounce when they strike the ground. If the temperature of the air remains below freezing, the snow falls to the ground as snow; otherwise, it melts and turns to rain.

 The presence of wet snow indicates the temperature is above freezing at your flight altitude.

LATENT HEAT OF WATER

The difference between the latent heat of water vapor and liquid water results in significant temperature differences that dramatically influence weather. It takes 540 calories (2,260 joules) of heat to vaporize one gram of water. This is referred to as the latent heat of evaporation. That is why on hot days it is cooler near lakes and rivers, and why you feel cold when getting out of the shower. In more familiar terms, about 5/8 kilowatt hour (kwh) is needed to vaporize one liter (1 kg) of water. Conversely, when one liter of water condenses, it gives back 5/8 kwh of heat. This latent heat of condensation is the reason such violent energy is released when thousands of tons of moisture condense into a thunderstorm cloud.

The latent heat of water also changes between freezing and liquid states. However, the heat exchange between melting and freezing is small, only 80 calories/gram. Although this is enough to keep a soft drink cold, it has relatively little effect on weather.

STABILITY

Stability is the atmosphere's resistance to vertical motion. The stability of a parcel of air determines whether it rises or sinks in relation to the air around it. Stable air resists vertical movement, but unstable air has a tendency to rise. The combined effects of temperature and moisture determine the stability of the air and, to a large extent, the type of weather produced. The greatest instability occurs when the air is both warm and moist. Tropical weather, with its almost daily thunderstorm activity, is a perfect example of weather that occurs in unstable air. Air that is both cool and dry resists vertical movement and is very stable. A good example of this can be found in the polar regions during winter.

Air that is lifted expands due to lower atmospheric pressure. Lifting can occur orographically, as when air is forced up a mountain slope, or it can be caused by frontal activity. Lifting is also caused by convective currents that are generated by uneven heating of the earth's surface. As the air expands, it cools through a process known as adiabatic cooling. Conversely, air compresses and its temperature increases as it sinks. [Figure 9-10]

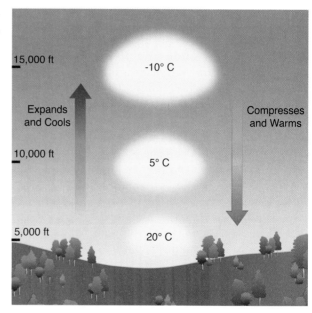

Figure 9-10. When any gas, such as air, expands, the temperature decreases because of decreased molecular density.

The **dry adiabatic lapse rate (DALR)** is 3°C (5.4°F) per 1,000 feet that a parcel of unsaturated air is lifted. To find out whether a parcel of air is unstable, you must determine whether it will be warmer than the surrounding air after it is lifted. Because of the latent heat contained in water vapor, stability is strongly related to the moisture of the lifted air.

 When unsaturated air is forced to ascend a mountain slope, it cools at the rate of approximately 3°C per 1,000 feet.

When condensation occurs in a parcel of rising air, adiabatic cooling is partially offset by warming due to the release of latent heat. Keep in mind that latent heat never completely offsets adiabatic cooling. A saturated parcel continues to cool as it rises, but at a slower rate than if it were dry. The rate of cooling of a rising, saturated parcel is called the moist, or **saturated adiabatic lapse rate (SALR)**. Although DALR is a constant 3°C per 1,000 feet, SALR is variable. It is about the same as DALR at extremely cold temperatures (−40°F), but is only a third of the DALR value at very hot temperatures (100°F). This is because saturated air holds much more water vapor at high temperatures, so there is much more latent heat to release when condensation occurs. [Figure 9-11]

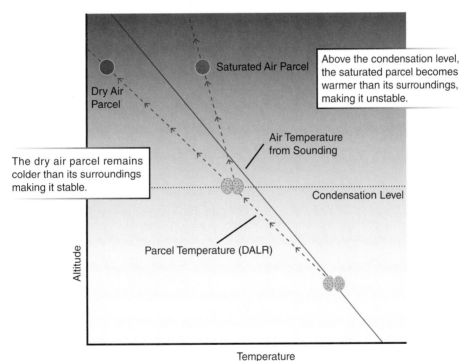

Figure 9-11. If two parcels of air are lifted the same distance, starting from the same level and the same initial temperature, the parcel of air that becomes saturated is warmer than the unsaturated parcel.

Air is unstable when its adiabatic lapse rate is less than the ambient air lapse rate. The standard temperature at sea level is 15°C and decreases at an average rate of 2°C (3.5°F) per 1,000 feet, but this can vary. When the lapse rate causes the ambient, or surrounding, air to be colder than a lifted parcel of air, lifted air tends to rise and be unstable. When there is an **inversion** in the lapse rate, causing the air above to be warm, it discourages a parcel of air from rising, contributing to stability.

 Because the standard temperature at sea level is 15°C, and it decreases at an average rate of 2°C per 1,000 feet, the standard temperature at 10,000 feet is −5°C (15°C − 20°C = −5°C).

SECTION A ■ **Weather Factors**

Measuring the Lapse Rate

Radiosondes are instruments, often encased in Styrofoam, that measure pressure, temperature and humidity when launched into the upper atmosphere on a weather balloon. Wind speed and direction are measured by monitoring the balloon's progress from ground level to altitudes that often exceed 20 miles. The observed data is transmitted to ground equipment that processes the data into weather information. Less than half of the radiosondes launched by the National Weather Service are recovered and reused.

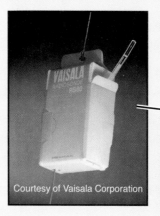

Courtesy of Vaisala Corporation

Courtesy of Vaisala Corporation

FAA   The ambient lapse rate allows you to determine atmospheric stability.

Inversions usually are confined to fairly shallow layers and might occur near the surface or at higher altitudes. They act as a lid for weather and pollutants. When the humidity is high, visibility often is restricted by fog, haze, smoke, and low clouds. Temperature inversions normally occur in stable air with little or no wind and turbulence. One of the most familiar types of ground- or surface-based inversions forms from radiation cooling just above the ground on clear, cool nights. A frontal inversion occurs when cool air is forced under warm air, or when warm air spreads over cold air.

FAA   A common type of ground- or surface-based temperature inversion is that which is produced by ground radiation on clear, cool nights with calm or light winds. An inversion normally forms only in stable air. When humidity is high, you can expect poor visibility due to fog, haze, or low clouds.

The **condensation level** is the level at which the temperature and dewpoint converge, and a cloud forms in rising air. Below the condensation level, the rising air parcel cools at the DALR; above that level, it cools at the SALR. With dewpoint decreasing at 1°F per 1,000 feet, and a DALR of 5.4°F per 1,000 feet, the temperature and dewpoint converge at about 4.4°F (2.5°C) per 1,000 feet.

To estimate cloud bases, divide the surface temperature/dewpoint spread by the rate that the temperature approaches the dewpoint. For example, if the surface temperature is 25°C and the surface dewpoint is 0°C, you would divide the 25°C spread by 2.5°C to get the approximate height of the cloud base in thousands of feet. In this case, 10,000 feet AGL.

FAA   To estimate the bases of cumulus clouds, in thousands of feet, divide the temperature/ dewpoint spread at the surface by 2.5°C (4.4°F). If using the quick estimate method, divide the temperature/dewpoint spread by 4°F (2.2°C).

If you know the stability of an airmass, you can predict its characteristics. Stable air is associated with stratus clouds, poorer visibility and lack of turbulence. Unstable air supports cumulus clouds, good visibility outside the clouds, and generally more extreme weather such as icing, heavy rain, hail, and turbulence. [Figure 9-12]

 When air is forced to ascend, the cloud structure, whether stratiform or cumuliform, is dependent upon the stability of the air being lifted.

	Stable Air	**Unstable Air**
Clouds	Wide areas of layered or stratiform clouds or fog; gray at low altitude, thin white at high altitude	Cumuliform with extensive vertical development; bright white to black; billowy
Precipitation	Small droplets in fog and low-level clouds; large droplets in thick stratified clouds; widespread and lengthy periods of rain or snow	Large drops in heavy rain showers; showers usually brief; hail possible
Visibility	Restricted for long periods	Poor in showers or thundershowers, good otherwise
Turbulence	Usually light or nonexistent	Moderate to severe
Icing	Moderate in mid-altitudes; freezing rain, rime, or clear ice	Moderate to severe clear ice
Other	Frost, dew, temperature inversions	High or gusty surface winds, lightning, tornadoes

Figure 9-12. The stability of an airmass can tell you a lot about the clouds and weather.

 As shown in figure 9-12, when moist, stable air is forced upwards through convection, frontal activity, or by orographic lifting, the result is stratiform clouds, with continuous precipitation and little or no turbulence. Stability contributes to smoke, dust, and haze concentrated at the lower levels with resulting poor visibility. Lifting of unstable, moist air results in cumuliform type clouds (those with extensive vertical development), good visibility outside the cloud, showery precipitation, turbulence, and possible clear icing in clouds.

CLOUDS

As air cools to its saturation point, condensation changes invisible water vapor to a visible state. Most commonly, this visible moisture takes the form of clouds or fog. Clouds are composed of very small droplets of water or, if the temperature is low enough, ice crystals. Condensation is facilitated by **condensation nuclei**, which can be dust, salt from evaporating sea spray, or products of combustion.

TYPES OF CLOUDS

Clouds are divided into four basic groups, or families, depending upon their characteristics and the altitudes where they occur. The groups are low, middle, high, and clouds with vertical development.

 The four families of clouds are high, middle, low, and those with extensive vertical development.

SECTION A ■ **Weather Factors**

SECTION A ■ **Weather Factors**

Cloud names are based on the terms, cumulus (heap), stratus (layer), nimbus (rain), and cirrus (ringlet). The prefixes alto and cirro denote cumulus and stratus clouds from the middle and high families, respectively. The prefix nimbo and the suffix nimbus denote clouds that produce rain.

 The suffix nimbus, used in naming clouds, means a rain cloud.

Cumulus clouds form when moist air is lifted and condenses. They usually have flat bottoms and dome-shaped tops. Widely spaced cumulus clouds that form in otherwise clear skies are called fair weather cumulus. These clouds generally form in unstable air, but are capped at the top by stable air. At and below the cloud level, you can expect turbulence, but little icing or precipitation. If you can fly above a fair weather cumulus cloud, you can expect smooth air at that altitude.

 Fair weather cumulus clouds indicate turbulence at and below the cloud level.

Stratus clouds are associated with stable air. They frequently produce low ceilings and visibilities, but usually have little turbulence. Icing is possible if temperatures are at or near freezing. Stratus clouds can form when air is cooled from below, or when stable air is lifted up sloping terrain. They also might form along with fog when rain falls through cooler air and raises the humidity to the saturation point. Nimbostratus clouds are stratus clouds that produce rain. They can be several thousand feet thick and contain large quantities of moisture. If temperatures are near or below freezing, they can create heavy icing.

LOW CLOUDS

Low clouds extend from near the surface to about 6,500 feet AGL. Low clouds usually consist almost entirely of water but sometimes contain supercooled water that can create an icing hazard for aircraft. Types of low clouds include stratus, stratocumulus, and nimbostratus. [Figure 9-13]

Low Clouds

Stratus Clouds
Stratus clouds are layered clouds that form in stable air near the surface due to cooling from below. They have a gray, uniform appearance and generally cover a wide area.

Nimbostratus Clouds
Nimbostratus clouds can be several thousand feet thick and contain large quantities of moisture. These clouds vary from gray to black, depending on thickness and moisture content.

Stratocumulus Clouds
Stratocumulus clouds are white, puffy clouds that form as stable air is lifted. They often form as a stratus layer breaks up or as cumulus clouds spread out.

Figure 9-13. Low clouds are found at altitudes extending from the surface to about 6,500 feet AGL.

Fog is a low cloud that has its base within 50 feet of the ground. [Figure 9-14] If the fog is less than 20 feet deep, it is called ground fog. Having an instrument rating does not eliminate fog as a flight hazard. Aside from its ability to reduce visibility even below safe IFR minimums, fog can contain icing hazards. Fog is covered in detail in the next section.

Figure 9-14. Fog is a cloud that forms next to the ground.

MIDDLE CLOUDS

Middle clouds have bases that range from about 6,500 to 20,000 feet AGL. They are composed of water, ice crystals, or supercooled water, and can contain moderate turbulence and potentially severe icing. Altostratus and altocumulus are classified as middle clouds. [Figure 9-15]

HIGH CLOUDS

High clouds have bases beginning above 20,000 feet AGL. They are generally white to light gray in color and form in stable air. They are composed mainly of ice crystals and seldom pose a serious turbulence or icing hazard. The three basic types of high clouds are called cirrus, cirrostratus, and cirrocumulus. [Figure 9-16]

Middle Clouds

Altostratus Clouds
Altostratus clouds are flat, dense clouds that cover a wide area. They are a uniform gray or gray-white in color. Although they produce minimal turbulence, they can contain moderate icing.

Altocumulus Clouds
Altocumulus clouds are gray or white, patchy clouds of uniform appearance that often form when altostratus clouds start to break up. They may produce light turbulence and icing.

Figure 9-15. Middle clouds are found at altitudes extending from 6,500 feet to 20,000 feet AGL.

High Clouds

Cirrus Clouds
Cirrus clouds are composed mostly of ice crystals that usually form above 30,000 feet.

Figure 9-16. High clouds are found at altitudes above 20,000 feet AGL.

Cirrostratus Clouds
Cirrostratus clouds also are thin, white clouds that often form in long bands or sheets against a deep blue background. Although they may be several thousands of feet thick, moisture content is low and they pose no icing hazard.

Cirrocumulus Clouds
Cirrocumulus clouds are white patchy clouds that look like cotton. They form as a result of shallow convective currents at high altitude and may produce light turbulence.

Cirrus clouds are thin, wispy clouds composed mostly of ice crystals that usually form above 30,000 feet. White or light gray in color, they often exist in patches or narrow bands across the sky. Because they are sometimes blown from the tops of thunderstorms they can be an advance warning of approaching bad weather.

SECTION A ■ **Weather Factors**

SECTION A ■ Weather Factors

 A high cloud is composed mostly of ice crystals.

CLOUDS WITH VERTICAL DEVELOPMENT

When lifting and instability are present, cumulus clouds can build vertically into **towering cumulus** or cumulonimbus clouds. The bases are typically at 1,000 to 10,000 feet MSL, and their tops sometimes exceed 60,000 feet MSL. [Figure 9-17] Towering cumulus clouds indicate a fairly deep layer of unstable air. They contain moderate to heavy convective turbulence with icing and often develop into thunderstorms.

 Towering cumulus clouds indicate convective turbulence.

**Clouds with
Vertical Development**

Cumulus Clouds
These puffy white clouds usually have flat bottoms and dome-shaped tops.

Cumulonimbus Clouds
Cumulonimbus clouds, or thunderstorms, are large, vertically developed clouds ranging from gray-white to black in color. They contain large amounts of moisture, turbulence, icing, and lightning.

Figure 9-17. Clouds with vertical development, or cumuliform clouds, indicate instability.

Towering Cumulus
Towering cumulus clouds are similar to cumulus clouds, except they have more vertical development.

Cumulonimbus clouds, or thunderstorms, are large, vertically developed clouds that form in moist, unstable air. They are gray-white to black in color and contain large amounts of moisture, turbulence, icing, and lightning. You can think of them as severe versions of towering cumulus. Thunderstorms are discussed in more detail in the next section.

AIRMASS

An airmass is a large body of air with fairly uniform temperature and moisture content. It usually forms where air remains stationary or nearly stationary for at least several days. During this time, the airmass takes on the temperature and moisture properties of the underlying surface. The area where an airmass acquires the properties of temperature and moisture that determine its stability is called its source region. [Figure 9-18]

 An airmass is a body of air that covers an extensive area and has fairly uniform properties of temperature and moisture.

As an airmass moves over a warmer surface, its lower layers are heated, and vertical movement of the air develops. Depending on temperature and moisture levels, this can result in extreme instability, characterized by cumuliform clouds, turbulence, and good visibility outside the clouds. When an airmass flows over a cooler surface, its lower

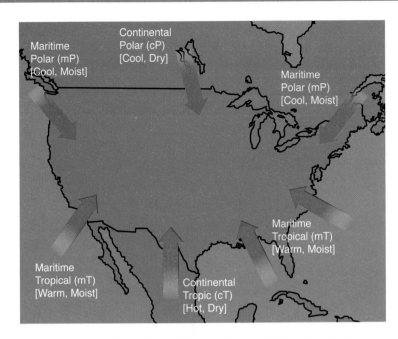

Maritime Polar (mP) [Cool, Moist]

Continental Polar (cP) [Cool, Dry]

Maritime Polar (mP) [Cool, Moist]

Maritime Tropical (mT) [Warm, Moist]

Maritime Tropical (mT) [Warm, Moist]

Continental Tropic (cT) [Hot, Dry]

layers are cooled and vertical movement is inhibited. As a result, the stability of the air is increased. If the air is cooled to its dewpoint, low clouds or fog can form. This cooling from below creates a temperature inversion and might result in low ceilings and restricted visibility for long periods of time.

Figure 9-18. Airmass source regions surround North America. As airmasses move out of those regions, they often converge to form the continent's major weather systems.

 Cooling from below increases the stability of an airmass and warming from below decreases it.

 When a cold airmass moves over, or is heated by, a warm surface, the result is cumuliform clouds, turbulence, and good visibility. When the air is moist and unstable, the updrafts are particularly strong, resulting in cumulonimbus clouds.

 ## Safe From Lightning?

Some bolts of lightning are powerful enough to light a small city. With this much electricity hitting one spot, it is easy to see why lightning is so dangerous.

One common myth is that the rubber tires of a car act as an insulator to lightning. Although rubber is considered an electrical insulator, it is ineffective against a 300,000 volt per foot electrical charge that can jump up to two miles through air. In fact, when lightning strikes a car, it usually destroys the tires as it punches through them on the way to the ground.

Because it is nearly impossible to insulate against an electrical charge as powerful as lightning, the key to effective lightning protection is to conduct the electricity along a path in which it can do no harm. An enclosed metal vehicle can provide effective protection, because the vehicle frame conducts the electricity around, rather than letting it go through, the occupants. Motorcycles and convertibles provide no such protection.

Courtesy of NOAA, Cmdr. John Bortniak

Metal aircraft also protect their occupants from lightning. As you will learn in the next section, the primary aviation hazards from thunderstorms are not from lightning, but from icing and turbulence.

FRONTS

When an airmass moves out of its source region, it comes in contact with other airmasses that have different moisture and temperature characteristics. The boundary between airmasses is called a front and often contains hazardous weather.

When you cross a front, you move from one airmass into another with different properties. The changes between the two might be very abrupt, indicating a narrow frontal zone. On the other hand, changes might occur gradually, indicating a wide and, perhaps, diffused frontal zone. These changes can give you important cues to the location and intensity of the front.

A change in the temperature is one of the easiest ways to recognize the passage of a front. At the surface, the temperature change usually is very noticeable and can be quite abrupt in a fast-moving front. With a slow-moving front, it is less pronounced. When you are flying through a front, you can observe the temperature change on the outside air temperature gauge. However, the change could be less abrupt at middle and high altitudes than it is at the surface.

The most reliable indications that you are crossing a front are a change in wind direction and, less frequently, wind speed. The new direction of the wind is difficult to predict, but the wind always shifts to the right in the northern hemisphere as the front passes.

 A change in the wind is always associated with the passage of a frontal system.

As a front approaches, atmospheric pressure usually decreases, with the area of lowest pressure lying directly over the front. Pressure changes on the warm side of the front generally occur more slowly than on the cold side. The important thing to remember is that you should promptly update your altimeter setting after crossing a front.

The type and intensity of frontal weather depend on several factors, including the availability of moisture, the stability of the air being lifted, and the speed of the frontal movement. Other factors include the slope of the front and the moisture and temperature variations between the two fronts. Although some frontal weather can be severe and hazardous, other fronts produce relatively calm weather.

 CAN ARTHRITIS SUFFERERS PREDICT THE WEATHER?

Many of those with arthritis are convinced that their pain and stiffness increase with deteriorating weather. In a 1960 study, Dr. Joseph Hollander at the University of Pennsylvania found that 11 of his 12 subjects reported worsened symptoms 73 percent of the time they were simultaneously exposed to high humidity and falling barometric pressure. More recent studies have showed no such correlation.

According to the Arthritis Society, living in a cold, damp climate might make you feel your arthritis more than living in a hot, dry one. They go on to state that a rise in humidity and a fall in barometric pressure might also make the joints feel worse temporarily, but not everyone with arthritis can predict weather change.

It seems there is no consensus on this issue. Many researchers feel arthritis victims notice their pain more when the weather is bad because people feel worse anyway when it is dreary outside. On the other hand, if the joints ache, yet the weather stays nice, a person might feel better and forget that their joints predicted a bad day.

COLD FRONTS

A **cold front** separates an advancing mass of cold, dense, and stable air from an area of warm, lighter, and unstable air. Because of its greater density, the cold air moves along the surface and forces the less dense, warm air upward. In the northern hemisphere, cold fronts are usually oriented in a northeast to southwest line and can be several hundred miles long. Movement is usually in an easterly direction. A depiction of the typical cold front and a summary of its associated weather is shown in figure 9-19.

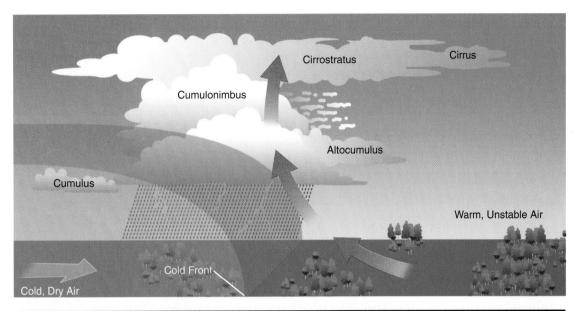

TYPICAL COLD FRONT WEATHER			
	Prior to Passage	**During Passage**	**After Passage**
Clouds	• Cirriform • Towering cumulus and/or cumulonimbus	• Towering cumulus and/or cumulonimbus	• Cumulus
Precipitation	• Showers	• Heavy showers • Possible hail, lightning, and thunder	• Slowly decreasing showers
Visibility	• Fair in haze	• Poor	• Good
Wind	• SSW	• Variable and gusty	• WNW
Temperature	• Warm	• Suddenly cooler	• Continued cooler
Dewpoint	• High	• Rapidly dropping	• Continued drop
Pressure	• Falling	• Bottoms out, then rises rapidly	• Rising

Figure 9-19. Cumuliform clouds and showers are common in the vicinity of cold fronts.

FAST-MOVING COLD FRONTS

Fast-moving cold fronts are pushed along by intense high pressure systems located well behind the front. Friction slows the movement at the surface, causing the front's leading edge to bulge out and steepen its slope. Because of the steep slope and wide differences in moisture and temperature between the two airmasses, fast-moving cold fronts are particularly hazardous.

Fast-moving cold fronts rapidly force warmer air to rise, which can cause widespread vertical cloud development along a narrow frontal zone. If sufficient moisture is present, an area of severe weather forms well ahead of the front, and usually clears quickly as the front passes. You often notice reduced cloud cover, improved visibility, lower temperatures, and gusty surface winds following the passage of a fast-moving cold front.

SLOW-MOVING COLD FRONTS

The leading edge of a slow-moving cold front is much shallower than that of a fast-moving front. This produces clouds extending far behind the surface front. A slow-moving cold front meeting stable air usually causes a broad area of stratus clouds to form behind the front. A slow-moving cold front meeting unstable air usually causes large numbers of vertical clouds to form at and just behind the front, creating hazards from icing and turbulence. Fair weather cumulus clouds can extend well behind the surface front.

SECTION A ■ **Weather Factors**

WARM FRONTS

Warm fronts occur when warm air moves over the top of cooler air at the surface. They usually move at much slower speeds than cold fronts. The slope of a warm front is very gradual, and the warm air could extend over the cool air for several hundred miles ahead of the front. A depiction of the typical warm front and a summary of its associated weather is shown in figure 9-20.

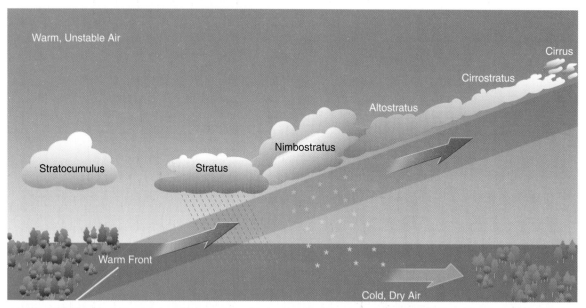

TYPICAL WARM FRONT WEATHER			
	Prior to Passage	**During Passage**	**After Passage**
Clouds	• Cirriform • Stratiform • Fog • Possible cumulonimbus in the summer	• Stratiform	• Stratocumulus • Possible cumulonimbus in the summer
Precipitation	• Light-to-moderate rain, drizzle, sleet, or snow	• Drizzle, if any	• Rain or showers, if any
Visibility	• Poor	• Poor, but improving	• Fair in haze
Wind	• SSE	• Variable	• SSW
Temperature	• Cold to cool	• Rising steadily	• Warming, then steady
Dewpoint	• Rising steadily	• Steady	• Rising, then steady
Pressure	• Falling	• Becoming steady	• Slight rise, then falling

Figure 9-20. Although stratus clouds usually extend out ahead of a slow-moving warm front, cumulus clouds sometimes develop along and ahead of the surface front if the air is unstable.

The stability and moisture content of the air in a warm front determines what type of clouds will form. If the air is warm, moist, and stable, stratus clouds and steady precipitation can develop. If the air is warm, moist, and unstable, cumulus clouds and showery precipitation can develop.

 Steady precipitation, in contrast to showers, preceding a front is an indication of stratiform clouds with little or no turbulence.

STATIONARY FRONTS

When the opposing forces of two airmasses are balanced, the front that separates them might remain stationary and influence local flying conditions for several days. The weather in a **stationary front** usually is a mixture of that found in both warm and cold fronts.

OCCLUDED FRONTS

A **frontal occlusion** occurs when a fast-moving cold front catches up to a slow-moving warm front. The difference in temperature within each frontal system strongly influences which type of front and weather are created. A cold front occlusion develops when the fast-moving cold front is colder than the air ahead of the slow-moving warm front. In this case, the cold air replaces the cool air at the surface and forces the warm front aloft. A warm front occlusion occurs when the fast-moving cold front is warmer than the air ahead of the slow-moving warm front. In this case, the cold front rides up over the warm front, forcing the cold front aloft. A depiction of the typical cold and warm front occlusions and a summary of their associated weather is shown in figure 9-21.

 In a cold front occlusion, the air ahead of the warm front is warmer than the air behind the overtaking cold front.

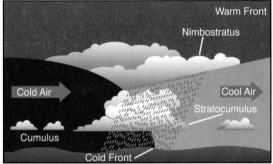
COLD FRONT OCCLUSION

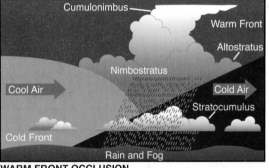
WARM FRONT OCCLUSION

TYPICAL OCCLUDED FRONT WEATHER			
	Prior to Passage	**During Passage**	**After Passage**
Clouds	• Cirriform • Stratiform	• Nimbostratus • Possible towering cumulus and/or cumulonimbus	• Nimbostratus • Altostratus • Possible cumulus
Precipitation	• Light-to-heavy precipitation	• Light-to-heavy precipitation	• Light-to-moderate precipitation, then clearing
Visibility	• Poor	• Poor	• Improving
Wind	• SE to S	• Variable	• W to NW
Temperature	• Cold Occlusion: Cold to Cool • Warm Occlusion: Cold	• Cold Occlusion: Falling • Warm Occlusion: Rising	• Cold Occlusion: Colder • Warm Occlusion: Milder
Dewpoint	• Steady	• Slight drop	• Rising, then steady
Pressure	• Falling	• Becoming steady	• Slight drop; however, may rise after passage of warm occlusion

Figure 9-21. When the air being lifted by a cold front occlusion is moist and stable, the weather will be a mixture of that found in both a warm and a cold front. When the air being lifted by a warm front occlusion is moist and unstable, the weather will be more severe than that found in a cold front occlusion.

THE FRONTAL CYCLONE

One important process by which fronts are set in motion is the **frontal cyclone**, sometimes referred to as an extratropical cyclone or a frontal low. As you might recall, cyclonic circulation is counterclockwise in the northern hemisphere. Because there is an excess of solar energy received at the equator and a deficit at the poles, a temperature gradient occurs and is concentrated in an area called the polar front. If that temperature gradient becomes excessive at some point along the polar front, a disturbance occurs to equalize the pressure. The circulation patterns that result from this activity act to transport the warm air toward the pole and cold air toward the equator and reduce the temperature gradient.

In addition to the polar fronts, other areas are conducive to the formation of frontal cyclones. For example, in winter, locally strong temperature gradients are found along some coastlines where cold continents are next to very warm oceans. This is the case for the U.S. just off the Gulf of Mexico and along the East Coast. When fronts move into these areas, the development of a low pressure area around which these fronts can circulate is common. [Figure 9-22]

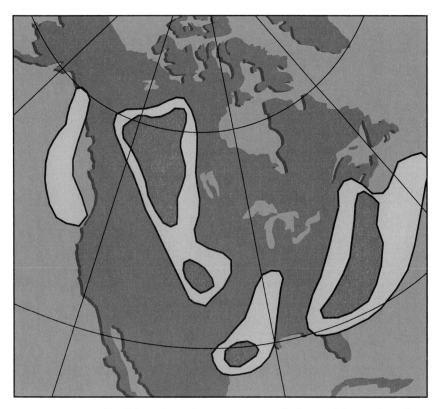

Figure 9-22. Frontal cyclones develop in areas with strong temperature gradients. Regions with the highest frequency of cyclone development are shown in red.

Orographic lifting from large mountain chains and latent heat from condensation of moist air also can enhance cyclone development (cyclogenesis). These two processes frequently work together to produce lows on the east slopes of the Rocky Mountains.

STRUCTURE AND DEVELOPMENT

The surface development of a frontal cyclone in the northern hemisphere follows a distinctive life cycle. Before the **frontal wave** development begins, a stationary or slow-moving cold front is present in the area. The frontal zone is characterized by a change in wind speed and/or direction (wind shear) from the warm side to the cold side. As the cyclone development begins, pressure falls at some point along the original front, and counterclockwise circulation is generated. At this point, the cyclone is in the incipient, or wave cyclone, stage because the original front has been distorted into a wave shape in response to the developing circulation. [Figure 9-23]

 Frontal waves normally form on slow-moving cold fronts or stationary fronts.

SECTION A ■ **Weather Factors**

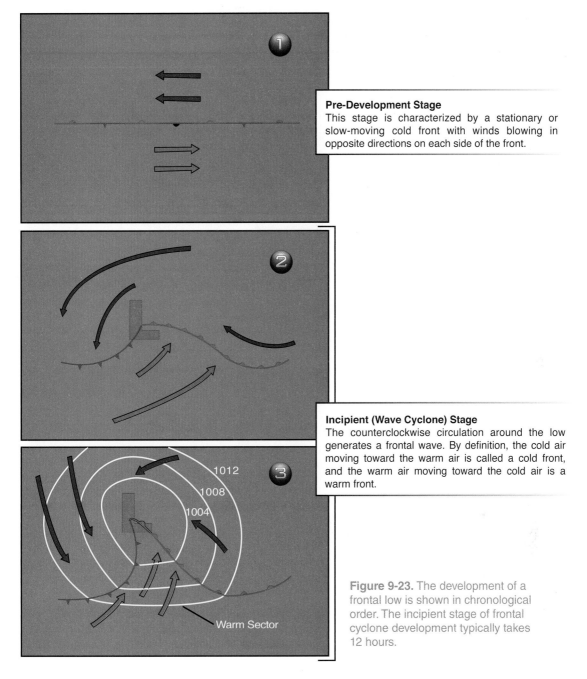

Pre-Development Stage
This stage is characterized by a stationary or slow-moving cold front with winds blowing in opposite directions on each side of the front.

Incipient (Wave Cyclone) Stage
The counterclockwise circulation around the low generates a frontal wave. By definition, the cold air moving toward the warm air is called a cold front, and the warm air moving toward the cold air is a warm front.

Warm Sector

Figure 9-23. The development of a frontal low is shown in chronological order. The incipient stage of frontal cyclone development typically takes 12 hours.

Frontal cyclones do not necessarily develop beyond the incipient stage. These stable waves can simply move rapidly along the polar front, and finally dissipate. However, a cyclone that continues to develop moves northeastward at 15 to 25 knots, pushing warm air northward ahead of it, and bringing cold air to the south into the wake of the cyclone. As it progresses eastward, the central pressure continues to fall; the cyclone deepens, and the winds around it increase in response to the greater pressure gradient. About 12 hours after the initial appearance of the frontal low, the cold airmass trailing the cyclone is swept around the low and overtakes the retreating cold air ahead of the cyclone. This process pushes the warm sector air aloft and the cyclone enters the occluded stage. [Figure 9-24]

As the cyclone enters the dissipating stage of its life cycle, the central pressure begins to rise. The weakening of the cyclone begins 24 to 36 hours after the initial formation of the disturbance and lasts for another few days. The weakening occurs because the temperature gradient, from which the cyclone draws its energy, has been diminished by the mixing of warm and cold air.

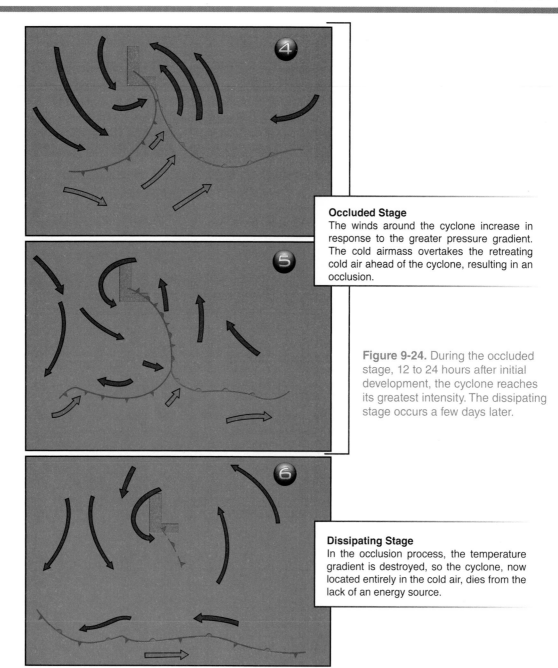

Occluded Stage
The winds around the cyclone increase in response to the greater pressure gradient. The cold airmass overtakes the retreating cold air ahead of the cyclone, resulting in an occlusion.

Figure 9-24. During the occluded stage, 12 to 24 hours after initial development, the cyclone reaches its greatest intensity. The dissipating stage occurs a few days later.

Dissipating Stage
In the occlusion process, the temperature gradient is destroyed, so the cyclone, now located entirely in the cold air, dies from the lack of an energy source.

HIGH ALTITUDE WEATHER

If you transition into jet or turboprop aircraft, it will become important to understand weather patterns at and above the tropopause. The height of the tropopause varies between 24,000 feet MSL near the poles and 50,000 feet MSL near the equator. The tropopause, which is the boundary between the troposphere and the stratosphere, is characterized by an abrupt change in the temperature lapse rate. In International Standard Atmospheric (ISA) conditions, the height of the tropopause is approximately 36,000 feet. From this altitude up to 66,000 feet in the standard atmosphere, the temperature remains constant at −57°C. The tropopause acts like a lid, because it resists the exchange of air between the troposphere and the stratosphere above. However, in the northern hemisphere, there are generally two breaks in the tropopause. One is between the polar and subtropical airmass and the other is between the subtropical and tropical airmass.

 A jet stream is defined as wind of 50 knots or greater.

Jet streams often are embedded in the zone of strong westerlies at these breaks in the tropopause. [Figure 9-25] A **jet stream** is a narrow band of high speed winds that reaches its greatest speed near the tropopause. Typical jet stream speeds range between 60 knots and about 240 knots. Jet streams normally are several thousand miles long, several hundred miles wide, and a few miles thick.

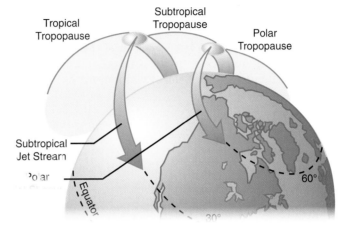

Figure 9-25. The jet stream occurs at breaks in the tropopause, which vary with the seasonal migration of airmass boundaries.

The polar front jet stream occurs at about 30°N to 60°N latitude. Although it exists year round, the polar front tends to be higher, weaker, and farther north in the summer. The subtropical jet stream is found near 25°N latitude. It reaches its greatest strength in the wintertime and is nonexistent in the summer.

 The strength and location of the jet stream is normally weaker and farther north in the summer. During the winter months in the middle latitudes, the jet stream shifts toward the south and speed increases.

The tropopause slopes upward from polar to tropical regions. If you could stand at the breaks in the tropopause with the wind at your back, a distinctly higher tropopause would occur on the right side of each jet stream and a separate, lower tropopause on the left. This structure is reversed in the Southern Hemisphere.

SUMMARY CHECKLIST

✓ The atmosphere is commonly divided into a number of layers according to its thermal characteristics. The lowest layer, the troposphere, is where most weather occurs.

✓ Uneven heating of the earth's surface is the driving force behind all weather. The special characteristics of water also affect the release of heat into the atmosphere, and dramatically affect the weather.

✓ Atmospheric circulation patterns are caused by differences in pressure. Above the friction layer, Coriolis force diverts wind to the right as it flows out of a high pressure area in the northern hemisphere. Near the surface, wind flows more directly from a high to low pressure area, or across the isobars.

✓ The amount of water vapor that air can hold decreases with temperature. At the dewpoint, the air is saturated.

✓ Precipitation occurs when water vapor condenses out of the air and becomes heavy enough to fall to earth. The type of precipitation is influenced by the temperature and other conditions under which condensation occurs.

✓ Stability is the atmosphere's resistance to vertical motion. Air is stable when a lifted parcel of air is cooler than the ambient air. Dry air tends to cool more when lifted and tends to be more stable. Ambient air with a low or inverted lapse rate also contributes to stability.

✓ Clouds occur when water vapor condenses. They are divided into four basic families: low, middle, high, and clouds with vertical development.

✓ Cumulus clouds form when unstable air is lifted. Stratiform clouds form when stable air is lifted. The lifting of moist, unstable air results in good visibility outside the cloud, showery precipitation, and turbulence. However, the lifting of moist, stable air results in continuous precipitation, little or no turbulence, and poor visibility.

✓ An airmass is a large body of air that has fairly uniform temperature and moisture characteristics. A front is a discontinuity between two airmasses. A cold front occurs when cold air displaces warmer air. A warm front occurs when warm air overruns colder air.

✓ A frontal cyclone starts as a slow-moving cold front or stationary front and can end as a cold front occlusion with potentially severe weather.

✓ Jet streams are bands of strong westerly winds that occur at breaks in the tropopause in the northern hemisphere. Although they can provide beneficial winds when flying west to east, they also can be associated with strong turbulence.

KEY TERMS

Troposphere

Tropopause

Stratosphere

Isobars

Pressure Gradient

High

Low

Ridge

Trough

Col

Coriolis Force

Cyclonic

Evaporation

Sublimation

Condensation

Deposition

Dewpoint

Supercooled Water

Latent Heat

Stability

Dry Adiabatic Lapse Rate (DALR)

Saturated Adiabatic Lapse Rate (SALR)

Inversion

Condensation Level

Condensation Nuclei

Low Clouds

Middle Clouds

High Clouds

Towering Cumulus

Cumulonimbus Clouds

Cold Front

Warm Front

Stationary Front

Frontal Occlusion

Frontal Cyclone

Frontal Wave

Jet Stream

QUESTIONS

1. In which level of the atmosphere does most of the earth's weather occur? Why?

2. What is the major driving force behind the weather?
    A. Variations in moisture content
    B. Uneven heating of the earth's surface
    C. Rotation of the earth and its effect on the movement of high and low pressure areas

3. What is indicated by close spacing of isobars on a weather map?
    A. Weak pressure gradient and weak winds
    B. Weak pressure gradient and strong winds
    C. Strong pressure gradient and strong winds

4. Select the true statement regarding Coriolis force.
    A. Coriolis force is strongest within 2,000 feet of the surface.
    B. Coriolis force causes cyclonic circulation around high pressure areas.
    C. In the northern hemisphere, Coriolis force deflects wind to the right as it flows out of a high pressure area.

Match the following items with the associated weather characteristics.

5. Instability

6. Stability

7. Stratus

8. SALR

9. Supercooled water

10. Nimbus

11. Towering cumulus

12. DALR

A. Resistance to vertical motion

B. Layered clouds with little turbulence

C. Clouds with vertical development

D. Rain clouds

E. The result of a high ambient lapse rate combined with a low adiabatic lapse rate

F. 2°C per 1,000 feet

G. Liquid water that is colder than 0°C

H. 3°C per 1,000 feet

I. As low as 1°C per 1,000 feet

13. Select the characteristic(s) associated with the cloud shown in the accompanying photo. More than one might apply.
    A. Hail
    B. Drizzle
    C. Lightning
    D. Stable air
    E. Turbulence
    F. Restricted visibility for long periods

14. True/False. When an airmass is warmed from below, it becomes more stable.

Courtesy of Ralph Kresge NOAA/NWS

15. True/False. Passage of a fast-moving cold front creates a narrow frontal zone with less severe weather than the passage of a slow-moving cold front.

16. Steady precipitation with little turbulence precedes what type of front?
    A. Cold front
    B. Warm front
    C. Occluded front

17. What is the most reliable indication that you have flown through a front?
    A. Change in pressure
    B. Change in temperature
    C. Change in wind direction

18. What conditions favor the formation of a frontal wave?
    A. A fast-moving warm front overtaking a cold front
    B. A deep low pressure area located northeast of a ridge
    C. A stationary front or slow moving cold front with a strong temperature gradient

19. Jet stream winds occur at which location?
    A. South of highs
    B. Parallel to troughs
    C. Breaks in the tropopause

SECTION B
WEATHER HAZARDS

This section covers some of the weather hazards that you need to understand to safely fly under both VFR and IFR. Instrument operations require a sound knowledge of hazardous weather phenomena. When flying in instrument meteorological conditions, you are often unable to see weather hazards directly. Knowledge of the conditions that produce hazardous weather increases your ability to recognize and avoid dangerous conditions.

THUNDERSTORMS

Thunderstorms produce some of the most dangerous weather in aviation and should be avoided. Remember, there are three conditions necessary to create a thunderstorm — air that has a tendency toward instability, some type of lifting action, and relatively high moisture content. [Figure 9-26]

 Thunderstorm formation requires an unstable lapse rate, a lifting force, and a relatively high moisture level.

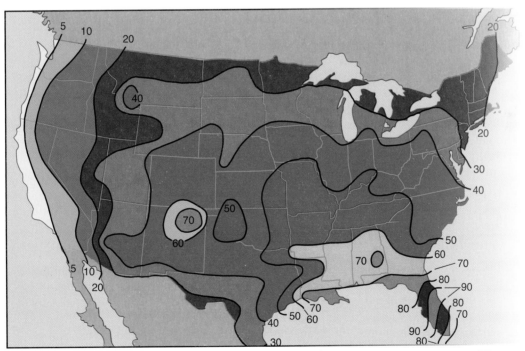

Figure 9-26. This map shows the average number of thunderstorms that occur each year in different parts of the United States.

Several factors can provide the lifting action, such as rising terrain (orographic lifting), fronts, or the heating of the earth's surface (convection). Thunderstorms progress through three distinct stages — cumulus, mature, and dissipating. [Figure 9-27]. You can anticipate the development of thunderstorms and the associated hazards by becoming familiar with the characteristics of each stage. Other weather phenomena might prevent you from seeing their characteristic shapes. For example, a cumulonimbus cloud might be embedded, or contained within, other cloud layers making it impossible to see. At night, darkness makes hazardous cloud formations more difficult to see.

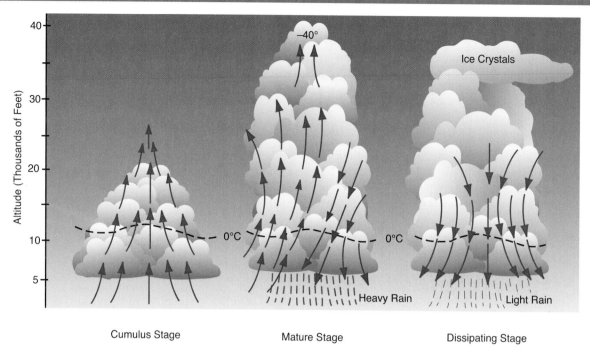

Cumulus Stage   Mature Stage   Dissipating Stage

Figure 9-27. A typical airmass thunderstorm consists of three states — cumulus, mature, and dissipating.

 An embedded thunderstorm is one that is obscured by massive cloud layers and cannot be seen.

In the **cumulus stage**, a lifting action initiates the vertical movement of air. As the air rises and cools to its dewpoint, water vapor condenses into small water droplets or ice crystals. If sufficient moisture is present, heat released by the condensing vapor provides energy for the continued vertical growth of the cloud. Because of strong updrafts, precipitation usually does not fall. Instead, the water drops or ice crystals rise and fall within the cloud, growing larger with each cycle. Updrafts as great as 3,000 ft/min might begin near the surface and extend well above the cloud top. During the cumulus stage, the convective circulation causes the cloud to grow rapidly into a towering cumulus (TCU) cloud that typically grows to 20,000 feet in height and 3 to 5 miles in diameter. The cloud reaches the mature stage in about 15 minutes.

 The cumulus stage is characterized by continuous updrafts.

As the water drops in the cloud grow too large to be supported by the updrafts, precipitation begins to fall to the surface. This creates a downward motion in the surrounding air and signals the beginning of the **mature stage**. The resulting downdraft can reach a velocity of 2,500 ft/min The down-rushing air spreads outward at the surface, producing a sharp drop in temperature, a rise in pressure, strong gusty surface winds, and turbulent conditions.

 Thunderstorms reach the greatest intensity during the mature stage, which is signaled by the beginning of precipitation at the surface.

Turbulence develops when air currents change direction or velocity rapidly over a short distance. The magnitude of the turbulence depends on the differences between the two air currents. Within the thunderstorm cloud, the strongest turbulence occurs in the shear between the updrafts and downdrafts. Early in the mature stage, the updrafts continue to increase up to speeds of 6,000 ft/min The adjacent updrafts and downdrafts cause severe turbulence. Near the surface, an area of low-level turbulence develops as the downdrafts spread out across the surface. The difference in speed and direction between the surrounding air and the cooler air of the downdraft creates a **shear zone**. The gusty winds and turbulence of this shear zone are not confined to the thunderstorm itself, but can extend outward for many miles from the center of the storm. The leading edge of the downdraft is referred to as a **gust front**. As the thunderstorm advances, a rolling, turbulent, circular-shaped cloud might form at the lower leading edge of the cloud. This is called the **roll cloud**. [Figure 9-28]

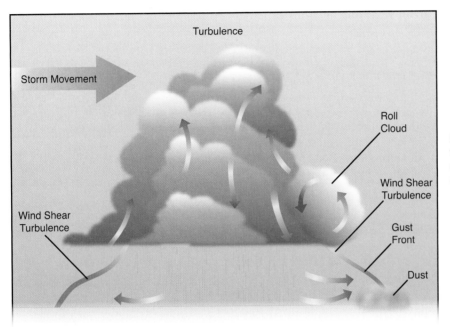

Figure 9-28. The most violent weather occurs during the mature phase of the life cycle.

SECTION B ■ **Weather Hazards**

 Wind shear areas can be found on all sides of a thunderstorm, as well as directly under it.

As the mature stage progresses, more and more air aloft is disturbed by the falling drops. Eventually, the downdrafts begin to spread out within the cell, taking the place of the weakening updrafts. Because upward movement is necessary for condensation and the release of the latent heat energy, the entire thunderstorm begins to weaken. When downdrafts become the dominant air movement within the cell, it is in the **dissipating stage**. During this stage, the upper level winds often blow the top of the cloud downwind, creating the familiar anvil shape. [Figure 9-29]

Figure 9-29. An anvil shape might form at the top of a thunderstorm during the dissipating stage, but severe weather can still occur well after the anvil appears.

Thunderstorms usually have similar physical features, but their intensity, degree of development, and associated weather differ significantly. Thunderstorms are generally classified as airmass or severe storms. **Airmass thunderstorms** generally form in a warm, moist airmass and are isolated or scattered over a large area. They are usually caused by solar heating of the land, which results in convection currents that lift unstable air. These thunderstorms are most common during hot summer afternoons when winds are light. They are also common along coastal areas at night. Airmass storms can also be caused by orographic lifting. Although they are usually scattered along individual mountain peaks, they can cover large areas. They also might be embedded in other clouds, making them difficult to identify when approached from the windward side of a mountain. Nocturnal thunderstorms can occur in late spring and summer during the late night or early morning hours when there is relatively moist air aloft. Usually found from the Mississippi Valley westward, nocturnal storms cover many square miles, and their effects might continue for hours at a given location. **Severe thunderstorms** are usually associated with weather patterns like fronts, converging winds, and troughs aloft. They are more intense than airmass thunderstorms, and have wind gusts of 50 knots or more, hail 3/4 of an inch or more in diameter, and might produce strong tornadoes.

 A dissipating thunderstorm is characterized by predominant downdrafts.

A **single cell** airmass storm typically lasts an hour or less. A **supercell** severe thunderstorm might last two hours or more. A **multicell** storm is usually a cluster of airmass thunderstorms in various stages of development. Because of the interaction of the various stages, a multicell storm can last much longer than a single cell storm. [Figure 9-30]

 Convective currents are most active on warm summer afternoons when the winds are light.

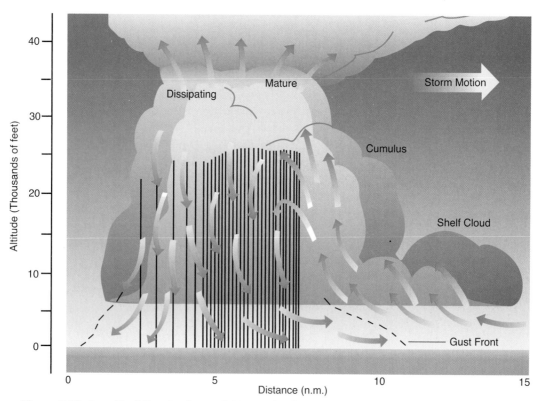

Figure 9-30. A multicell thunderstorm might contain all stages of a thunderstorm as individual cells combine or interact with each other. A shelf cloud often indicates the rising air over the gust front.

The term **frontal thunderstorm** is sometimes used to refer to storms that are associated with frontal activity. Those storms that occur with a warm front are often obscured by stratiform clouds. Expect thunderstorms when there is showery precipitation near a warm front. In a cold front, the cumulonimbus clouds are often visible in a continuous line parallel to the frontal surface. Occlusions can also spawn storms. A **squall line** is a narrow band of active thunderstorms that normally contains very severe weather. Although it often forms 50 to 200 miles ahead of a fast-moving cold front, the existence of a front is not necessary for a squall line to form.

A squall line is a band of thunderstorms that often forms several miles in front of a fast-moving cold front and contains some of the most severe types of weather-related hazards.

Thunderstorms typically contain many severe weather hazards, such as lightning, hail, turbulence, gusty surface winds, and even tornadoes. These hazards are not confined to the cloud itself. For example, you can encounter turbulence in VFR conditions as far as 20 miles from the storm. You can think of a cumulonimbus cloud as the visible part of a widespread system of turbulence and other weather hazards. In fact, the cumulonimbus cloud is the most turbulent of all clouds. Indications of severe turbulence within the storm system include the cumulonimbus cloud itself, very frequent lightning, and roll clouds.

 Cumulonimbus clouds by themselves indicate severe turbulence. Other indications of turbulence are very frequent lightning and roll clouds. Turbulence can be encountered as far as 20 miles from the cumulonimbus cloud.

Lightning is one of the hazards that is always associated with thunderstorms and is found throughout the cloud. Although it rarely causes personal injury or substantial damage to the aircraft structure in flight, it can cause temporary loss of vision, puncture the aircraft skin, or damage electronic navigation and communications equipment. Your aircraft can also be struck by lightning when you are clear of the thunderstorm, but still in the vicinity.

 Lightning is always associated with thunderstorms.

Hail is another thunderstorm hazard. You can encounter it in flight, even when no hail is reaching the surface. In addition, large hailstones have been encountered in clear air several miles from a thunderstorm. Hail can cause extensive damage to your aircraft in a very short period of time.

 Hail is most likely associated with a cumulonimbus cloud but it can be encountered several miles from the cloud.

Funnel clouds are violent, spinning columns of air that descend from the base of a cloud. A funnel cloud that reaches the earth's surface is called a **tornado**. If it touches down over water, it is a **waterspout**. Wind speeds within tornadoes can exceed 200 knots. In rare cases, wind speeds exceed 250 knots. The diameter of most tornadoes is between 300 and 2,000 feet, although there have been tornadoes a mile in diameter. [Figure 9-31]

Courtesy of Sean Waugh NOAA/NSSL

Figure 9-31. Wind speeds within a tornado can exceed 250 knots.

SECTION B ■ Weather Hazards

How Lightning Forms

As a towering cumulus develops, a large electrical charge separation builds up within the cloud. Lightning results when this electrical charge becomes strong enough to jump from the cloud to the ground, to another cloud, or to an opposite electrical charge within the same cloud.

Although the process that creates lightning is not fully understood, it is enhanced substantially when the cloud grows above the freezing level. As the outer boundaries of water droplets start to freeze, positive ions, or particles with a positive electrical charge, flow to the area of ice formation. This creates an outer shell that is positively charged and a center that is negatively charged.

When the interior freezes and expands, it shatters the outer shell. The droplets can also be broken up by colliding with other particles. In either case, the lighter pieces are then carried in the updrafts to the top of the cloud. The heavier, negatively charged particles fall to the bottom of the cloud. This makes the top of the cloud have a net positive charge and the lower part has a net negative charge.

As the negative charge builds at the bottom of the cloud, it repels the negative charge on the earth's surface. This leaves the area below the cloud with a positive charge. This positive charged area acts like a shadow that follows the cloud as it moves.

When the cloud has a very intense negative charge at its base, it seeks to neutralize itself by discharging to a positive area. This discharge is what we see as lightning. When it discharges it goes to the most accessible opposite charge. This is usually within the cloud itself, or between clouds. At times, however, it goes from the cloud to the ground.

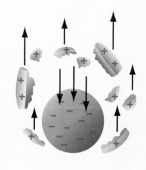

Lightning begins when a negatively charged pilot leader descends from the cloud. This leader forms a conductive path approximately eight inches in diameter and from thirty-five to one hundred fifty feet long. At this point, the electrons in the cloud begin to descend down the path. This recharges the path and causes additional leaders to extend earthward. These leaders are called stepped leaders because they seek the most conductive path to the ground and might try several branches before the best is located. As the path is extended the electrons from the cloud extend further downward.

The final stepped leader takes place a few feet above the earth where it is met by a rising positive flow from the surface. With the path completed, the positive ions on the earth can now flow to the cloud and neutralize the lower portion of the cloud . This upward flow is referred to as the return stroke and because it energizes the air molecules and illuminates the path, you see it as lightning.

Before the path dissipates, the first stroke is followed by additional strokes that further neutralize the negative charges in the cloud. What appears to be a single lightning flash can actually be three or four strokes. The actual stroke of lightning takes less than a half second to occur and that includes the leaders and three or four return strokes.

The peak current in the channel can reach ten thousand amps and the air in the channel can be heated to a temperature hotter than the surface of the sun. This causes the air in the path to expand violently, producing the sound waves we hear as thunder.

THUNDERSTORM AVOIDANCE

Avoid thunderstorms by at least 20 miles. This general guideline applies even to jet fighters and large airliners. Hail and severe turbulence can exist well outside the storm cloud. If you plan to deviate around a thunderstorm, fly on the upwind side so that your path does not converge with the path of the storm. Also, hail often falls from the anvil-shaped top of the storm, and wind can carry it for a considerable distance ahead of the visible cloud.

Don't be tempted to try to fly under a thunderstorm, even if you can see through the rain to the other side. Besides rain, hail, and lightning, the area under a thunderstorm typically contains severe turbulence, including microbursts, wind shear, and downdrafts that can exceed your aircraft's climb capability. Trying to fly over a developing storm is also dangerous, as the rising clouds can usually outclimb your airplane.

During night operations, lightning can help you to locate a storm, but lightning might not yet have developed in younger storms and might have ceased in older ones. Even without visible lightning, storms can still contain destructive turbulence or hail. The best approach during night operations or during flight under instrument conditions is to avoid areas where thunderstorms exist or are likely to develop.

If the aircraft you are flying is equipped with a weather avoidance system, such as weather radar, you can use it to avoid thunderstorms. With radar, you should avoid intense thunderstorm echoes by at least 20 miles. [Figure 9-32]

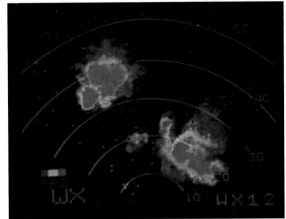

Figure 9-32. A general recommendation is that you should not fly between intense radar echoes unless they are at least 40 miles apart.

 Avoid intense radar echoes by at least 20 miles and do not fly between them if they are less than 40 miles apart.

Airborne weather radar is designed for avoiding severe weather, not for penetrating it. Weather radar detects drops of precipitation; it does not detect the minute droplets that make up clouds. Therefore, do not try to use it to avoid instrument weather associated with clouds and fog. Also, be sure you are familiar with the operation of the systems and the manufacturer's recommendations appropriate to your system.

 Airborne weather radar provides no assurance of avoiding IFR weather conditions.

Although you cannot expect ATC to keep you out of thunderstorms, controllers can often advise you of where their radar displays indicate precipitation. When ATC tells you that precipitation is in your path, the controller does not provide advice on how you should manage your flight. You are responsible for requesting vectors around pricipitation, or a deviation from an assigned course, or additional information. As PIC, you are responsible for the safety of your flight, so be ready to ask ATC for help. If it appears to you that a clearance or vector will take you too close to a thunderstorm, inform ATC and request a heading change.

TURBULENCE

In addition to turbulence in and near thunderstorms, three other categories of turbulence affect aviation operations: low-level turbulence, clear air turbulence, and mountain wave turbulence. The effects of turbulence can vary from occasional light bumps to severe jolts that cause injuries to occupants and/or structural damage to the airplane. If you enter turbulence unexpectedly, or if you expect to encounter it during flight, or if you unintentionally enter a thunderstorm, slow the airplane to maneuvering speed (V_A) or less, or the recommended rough air penetration speed. Then, attempt to maintain a level flight attitude and accept variations in airspeed and altitude. This helps avoid the high structural loads that can be imposed on the airplane if you try to maintain a specific airspeed and

 If you encounter turbulence during flight, establish maneuvering or penetration speed, maintain a level flight attitude, and accept variations in airspeed and altitude.

SECTION B ■ **Weather Hazards**

altitude. If you encounter turbulent or gusty conditions during an approach to a landing, consider flying a power-on approach and landing at an airspeed slightly above the normal approach speed. This helps to stabilize the airplane, giving you more control.

 When turbulence is encountered during the approach to a landing, it is recommended that you increase the airspeed slightly above normal approach speed to attain more positive control.

LOW-LEVEL TURBULENCE

Although **low-level turbulence (LLT)** is often defined as turbulence below 15,000 feet MSL, most low-level turbulence originates due to surface heating or friction within a few thousand feet of the ground. LLT includes mechanical turbulence, convective turbulence, frontal turbulence, and wake turbulence.

MECHANICAL TURBULENCE

When obstacles such as buildings or rough terrain interfere with the normal wind flow, turbulence develops. This phenomenon, referred to as **mechanical turbulence**, is often experienced in the traffic pattern when the wind forms eddies as it blows around hangars, stands of trees, or other obstructions. As the winds grow stronger, mechanical turbulence extends to greater heights. For example, when surface winds are 50 knots or greater, significant turbulence due to surface effects can reach altitudes in excess of 3,000 feet AGL. [Figure 9-33]

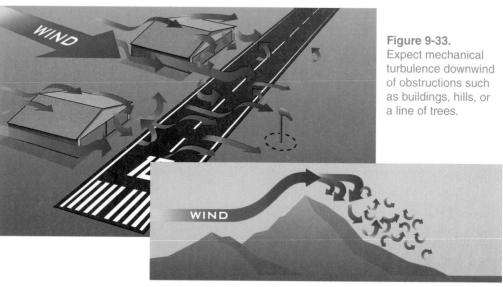

Figure 9-33.
Expect mechanical turbulence downwind of obstructions such as buildings, hills, or a line of trees.

Mechanical turbulence also occurs when strong winds flow nearly perpendicular to steep hills or mountain ridges. In comparison with turbulence over flat ground, the relatively larger size of the hills produce greater turbulence. In addition, steep hillsides generally produce stronger turbulence because the sharp slope encourages the wind flow to separate from the surface. Steep slopes on either side of a valley can produce particularly dangerous turbulence for aircraft operations.

CONVECTIVE TURBULENCE

Convective turbulence, which is also referred to as thermal turbulence, is typically a daytime phenomena that occurs over land in fair weather. It is caused by vertical air currents, or thermals, that develop in air heated by contact with the warm surface below. This heating typically occurs when cold air is moved horizontally over a warmer surface or when the ground is heated by the sun. When the air is moist, the currents might be marked by build-ups of cumulus cloud formations. In some cases, you can find relief from this turbulence by climbing into the **capping stable layer** that begins at the top of the convective layer. This can sometimes be identified by a layer of cumulus clouds, haze, or dust. The height of the capping layer is typically a few thousand feet above the ground, although it can exceed 10,000 feet AGL over the desert in the summer. [Figure 9-34]

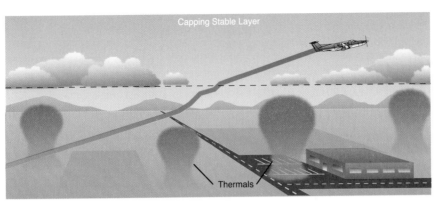

Figure 9-34. Your flight might be smoother in the capping stable layer above the bases of the cumulus clouds.

FRONTAL TURBULENCE

Frontal turbulence occurs in the narrow zone just ahead of a fast-moving cold front where updrafts can reach 1,000 ft/min When combined with convection and strong winds across the front, these updrafts can produce significant turbulence. Over flat ground, any front moving at a speed of 30 knots or more generates at least a moderate amount of turbulence. A front moving over rough terrain produces moderate or greater turbulence, regardless of its speed.

WAKE TURBULENCE

Whenever an airplane generates lift, air spills over the wingtips from the high pressure areas below the wings to the low pressure areas above them. This flow causes rapidly rotating whirlpools of air called **wingtip vortices**, or **wake turbulence**. The intensity of the turbulence depends on aircraft weight, speed, and configuration. [Figure 9-35]

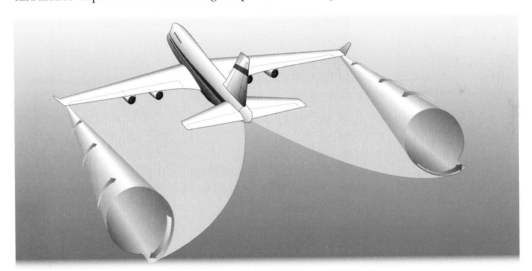

Figure 9-35. Wake vortices are created when lift is generated by the wing of an aircraft.

 Wingtip vortices can exceed the roll rate of an aircraft, especially when flying in the same direction as the generating aircraft.

The greatest wake turbulence danger is produced by large, heavy airplanes operating at low speeds, high angles of attack, and in a clean configuration. These conditions are most common during takeoff and landing, so be alert for wake turbulence near airports used by large airplanes. Wingtip vortices from large commercial jets can induce uncontrollable roll rates in smaller airplanes. Although wake turbulence settles, it persists in the air for several minutes, depending on wind conditions. In light winds of three to seven knots, the vortices can stay in the touchdown area, sink into your takeoff or landing path, or drift over a parallel runway. The most dangerous condition for landing is a light, quartering tailwind, because the wind can move the upwind vortex of a landing airplane over the runway and forward into the touchdown zone.

SECTION B ■ **Weather Hazards**

 The greatest vortex strength occurs when the generating aircraft is heavy, slow, in a clean configuration, and operating at a high angle of attack.

 A light crosswind of about 7 knots can cause the upwind vortex to remain over the runway.

 Wingtip vortices tend to sink below the flight path of the aircraft that generated them. They are most hazardous during light, quartering tailwind conditions.

If you are in a small airplane approaching to land behind a large airplane, controllers must ensure adequate separation. However, if you accept a clearance to follow an aircraft you have in sight, the responsibility for wake turbulence avoidance is transferred from the controller to you. On takeoff, controllers provide a two-minute interval behind departing heavy jets (three minutes for intersection takeoffs or takeoffs in the opposite direction on the same runway). You may waive these time intervals if you wish, but this is not a wise procedure. If a heavy aircraft crosses your course near your altitude, try to stay slightly above its path. [Figure 9-36]

To avoid turbulence when landing behind a large aircraft, stay above the large airplane's glide path and land beyond its touchdown point.

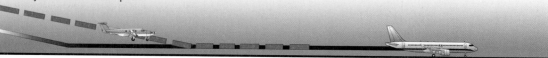

If a large airplane has just taken off as you approach to land, touch down well before the large aircraft's liftoff point.

When departing after a large aircraft has landed, lift off beyond its touchdown location.

When taking off behind a large aircraft, lift off before the large airplane's rotation point and climb out above or upwind of its flight path.

Figure 9-36. Maintaining a safe distance from a large aircraft can be critical.

 As shown in figure 9-36, you should avoid the area below and behind an aircraft generating wake turbulence, especially at low altitude where even a momentary wake encounter could be hazardous.

Jet engine blast is a related hazard. It can damage or even overturn a small airplane if it is encountered at close range. To avoid excessive jet blast, you must stay several hundred feet behind a jet with its engines operating, even when it is at idle thrust.

In a slow hover-taxi or stationary hover near the surface, helicopter main rotor(s) generate downwash producing high velocity outwash vortices to a distance approximately three times the diameter of the rotor. When rotor downwash hits the surface, the resulting outwash vortices have behavioral characteristics similar to wingtip vortices produced by fixed wing airplanes. However, the vortex circulation is outward, upward, around, and away from

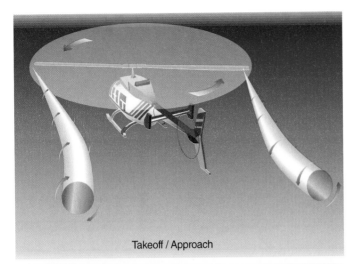

Takeoff / Approach

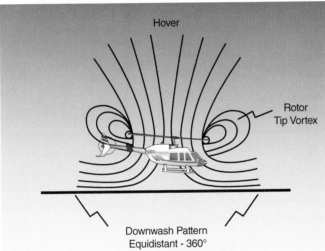

Hover

Rotor
Tip Vortex

Downwash Pattern
Equidistant - 360°

the main rotor(s) in all directions. If piloting a small airplane, avoid operating within three rotor diameters of any helicopter in a slow hover-taxi or stationary hover. For a large helicopter, this distance might be 200-250 feet, and for a small helicopter, 75-100 feet. In forward flight, departing or landing helicopters produce a pair of strong, high-speed trailing vortices similar to the wingtip vortices of large fixed wing airplanes. As with large airplanes, use caution when operating behind or crossing behind landing or departing helicopters. [Figure 9-37]

Figure 9-37. Moving helicopters produce vortex circulation similar to a large airplane. Avoid hovering or slow moving helicopters by at least a distance equal to three rotor diameters.

CLEAR AIR TURBULENCE

Clear air turbulence (CAT) is commonly thought of as a high altitude phenomenon. It usually is encountered above 15,000 feet, however, it can take place at any altitude and is often present with no visual warning. Although its name suggests that it cannot occur except in clear skies, CAT can also be present in nonconvective clouds. Clear air turbulence can be caused by the interaction of layers of air with differing wind speeds, convective currents, or obstructions to normal wind flow. It often develops in or near the jet stream, which is a narrow band of high altitude winds near the tropopause. CAT tends to occur in thin layers, typically less than 2,000 feet deep, less than 20 miles wide and more than 50 miles long. CAT often occurs in sudden bursts as the airplane intersects thin, sloping turbulent layers. [Figure 9-38]

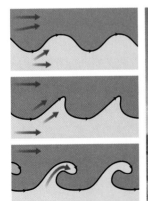

Figure 9-38. Clear air turbulence can form when a layer of air slides over the top of another, relatively slower moving layer. Eventually, the difference in speed might cause waves and, in some cases, distinctive clouds to form.

Turbulence that is encountered above 15,000 feet AGL that is not associated with cumuliform cloudiness, including thunderstorms, are reported as clear air turbulence.

SECTION B ■ **Weather Hazards**

Jet streams can sometimes be identified by long streams of cirrus cloud formations or high, windswept-looking cirrus clouds. The turbulence associated with a jet stream can be very strong, and because it often occurs in clear air, it is difficult to forecast accurately. As a rule of thumb, clear air turbulence can be expected when a curving jet is found north of a deep low pressure system. It can be particularly violent on the low pressure side of the jet stream when the wind speed at the core is 110 knots or greater. [Figure 9-39]

 The jet stream and associated clear air turbulence can sometimes be visually identified in flight by long streaks of cirrus clouds.

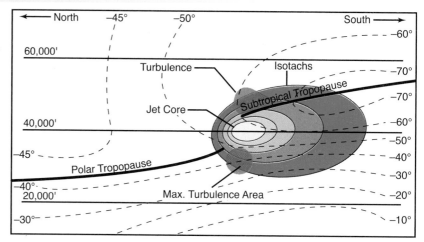

Figure 9-39. This is a cross section of a polar jet stream core. Note the wind speed gradient, shown by the spacing of the isotachs, or lines of equal wind velocity, is much stronger on the polar side of the jet. For this reason, wind shear or CAT is usually greater in an upper trough on the polar side. Precise analysis of the jet stream core is not possible, so you should anticipate CAT whenever you are near a jet stream.

Clear air turbulence has become a very serious operational factor to flight operations at all levels and especially to aircraft flying in above 15,000 feet. The best available information on this phenomena comes from pilots via the PIREP reporting procedures. All pilots encountering CAT conditions are urgently requested to report the time, location and intensity of the CAT to the FAA facility with which they are maintaining radio contact.

 A curving jet stream associated with a deep low-pressure trough can be expected to cause great turbulence. In addition, a strong wind shear can be expected on the low-pressure side of a jet stream core when the speed at the core is stronger than 110 knots.

 As shown in figure 9-39, a common location of clear air turbulence is in an upper trough on the polar side of a jet stream.

MOUNTAIN WAVE TURBULENCE

When stable air crosses a mountain barrier, the airflow is smooth on the windward side. Wind flow across the barrier is laminar — that is, it tends to flow in layers. The barrier can set up waves, called **mountain waves**. In order for mountain waves to form, the wind speed at the summit must be at least 20 knots. In addition, the wind direction should be roughly perpendicular to the range. Winds flowing more nearly parallel to the range produce weaker mountain waves. Wind speeds in excess of 40 knots can create very strong turbulence. The wave pattern can extend 100 miles or more downwind, and the wave crests might extend well above the highest peaks. Below the crest of each wave is an area of rotary circulation, or a rotor, which forms below the mountain peaks. Both the rotor and the waves can create violent turbulence.

 The greatest turbulence normally occurs as you approach the lee side of mountain ranges, ridges, or hilly terrain in strong headwinds.

 Mountain wave formation can be anticipated when the winds across a ridge are 20 knots or more, and the air is stable. Winds in excess of 40 knots can create strong turbulence.

If sufficient moisture is present, characteristic clouds warn you of the mountain wave. A rotor cloud (sometimes called a roll cloud) might form in the rotors. The crests of the waves might be marked by lens-shaped, or lenticular, clouds. Although the winds within the clouds might be 50 knots or greater, the clouds often appear stationary because they form in updrafts and dissipate in downdrafts. Because of this, they are sometimes called standing lenticulars. Another cloud that can signal the presence of mountain wave turbulence is called a cap cloud. In some instances, cap clouds might obscure the mountain peaks. [Figure 9-40]

 The presence of standing lenticular clouds and rotor clouds indicates the possibility of strong turbulence.

When conditions indicate a possible mountain wave, try to fly at least 3,000 to 5,000 feet above the peaks. Climb to this altitude approximately 100 miles before you get to the mountain range, depending on wind and aircraft performance. Also, try to approach the ridge from a 45° angle to permit a safer retreat if turbulence becomes too severe. If winds exceed 30 knots at your planned flight altitude, the FAA recommends against flight over mountainous areas in small aircraft. If you plan to fly over mountainous terrain, consider a

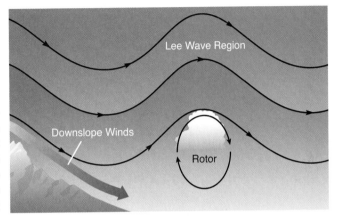

Figure 9-40. Mountain waves can create significant turbulence particularly along the lee slopes downwind from the mountains.

mountain flying course or at least a thorough checkout by a qualified flight instructor. Because local conditions can vary widely, consult pilots with experience in the area before you go. Remember that aircraft performance decreases with altitude, and allow a safety margin when applying the numbers from your POH for the altitudes you expect to fly. Mountain downdrafts can exceed the climb capabilities of even high performance aircraft.

REPORTING TURBULENCE

You are encouraged to report encounters with turbulence, including the frequency and intensity. Your reports help other pilots to avoid turbulence or to reduce its effects. Turbulence is considered to be **occasional** when it occurs less than one-third of a given time span, **intermediate** when it covers one-third to two-thirds of the time, and **continuous** when it occurs more than two-thirds of the time. You can classify the intensity using the following guidelines:

Light — Slight erratic changes in altitude or attitude; slight strain against seat belts. **Light chop** is slight, rapid bumpiness without appreciable changes in altitude or attitude.

 Light turbulence momentarily causes slight, erratic changes in altitude and/or attitude.

Moderate — Changes in altitude or attitude, but the aircraft remains in positive control at all times; usually causes variations in indicated airspeed; occupants feel definite strains against seat belts. **Moderate chop** is rapid bumps or jolts without appreciable changes in altitude or attitude.

 Moderate turbulence causes changes in altitude and/or attitude, but aircraft control remains positive.

SECTION B ■ **Weather Hazards**

SECTION B ■ Weather Hazards

Severe — Large abrupt changes in altitude or attitude; usually causes large variations in indicated airspeed; aircraft might be momentarily out of control; occupants forced violently against seat belts.

Extreme — Aircraft practically impossible to control; might cause structural damage.

Where's the CAT?

On flights conducted under FAR Part 121, passengers are only required to have their seat belts fastened during takeoff and landing, and when the pilot in command instructs them to buckle up. However, there are compelling reasons to keep your seat belt fastened throughout any flight. One important reason is the potential for sudden and severe CAT. To further increase airline safety, researchers are looking for ways to detect and predict the presence of CAT far enough ahead so that pilots can avoid the worst areas.

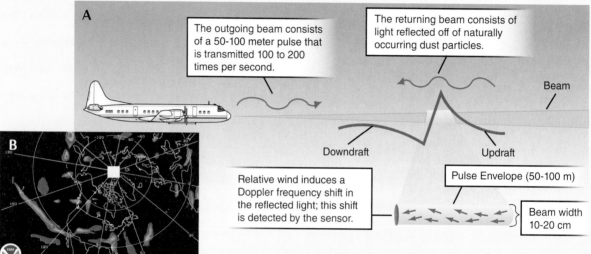

The National Center for Atmospheric Research (NCAR), with the National Oceanic and Atmospheric Administration (NOAA), NASA and other researchers, has developed a system that can detect the wind patterns that are associated with CAT before the airplane on which it is installed reaches the turbulent area. Airborne Coherent LiDAR (for Light Detection and Ranging) uses a form of laser technology to measure changes in the velocity of particles in the air up to 10 miles ahead, giving pilots up to 45 seconds to plan for the encounter, or to steer around it, if possible. [Figure A] You can gain access to CAT forecasts at NOAA.gov by searching the site for Clear Air Turbulence. These forecasts are issued for 12 and 24 hours and are valid for altitudes from FL 300 to 350. [Figure B]

As a general aviation pilot, you can find comfort in the fact that severe CAT is most often found at altitudes above FL 300. However, you can take a cue from the airlines and ask that your passengers keep their seat belts fastened throughout the flight. Until more is known, it is hard to tell where the CAT might lurk.

WIND SHEAR

Wind shear is a sudden, drastic shift in wind speed and/or direction that occurs over a short distance at any altitude in a vertical or horizontal plane. It can subject your airplane to sudden updrafts, downdrafts, or extreme horizontal wind components, causing loss of lift or violent changes in vertical speeds or altitudes. Wind shear can be associated with convective precipitation, a jet stream, or a frontal zone. Wind shear also can materialize during a low-level temperature inversion when cold, still surface air is covered by warmer air that contains winds of 25 knots or more at 2,000 to 4,000 feet above the surface.

 Wind shear is a sudden, drastic change in wind speed and/or direction and can exist at any altitude and can occur in all directions.

Wind shear is an atmospheric condition that might be associated with a strong low-level temperature inversion with strong winds above the inversion, a jet stream, a thunderstorm, or a frontal zone.

Generally, wind shear is most often associated with convective precipitation. Although not all precipitation-induced downdrafts are associated with critical wind shears, one such downdraft, known as a **microburst**, is one of the most dangerous sources of wind shear. Microbursts are small-scale intense downdrafts that, on reaching the surface, spread outward in all directions from the downdraft center. This causes both vertical and horizontal wind shear that can be extremely hazardous to all types and categories of aircraft, especially when within 1,000 feet of the ground. Never attempt an approach into known microburst or strong wind shear conditions.

 Microbursts are intense, localized downdrafts seldom lasting longer than 15 minutes from the time the burst first strikes the ground until dissipation. The maximum downdrafts encountered in a microburst can be as strong as 6,000 feet per minute.

A microburst downdraft is typically less than 1 mile in diameter as it descends from the cloud base to about 1,000 to 3,000 feet above the ground. In the transition zone near the ground, the downdraft changes to a horizontal outflow that can extend to approximately 2-1/2 miles in diameter. The downdrafts can be as strong as 6,000 feet per minute. Horizontal winds near the surface can be as strong as 45 knots resulting in a 90 knot shear as the wind changes from a headwind to a tailwind across the microburst. These strong horizontal winds occur within a few hundred feet of the ground.

A typical microburst intensifies for about 5 minutes after it first strikes the ground, with the maximum intensity winds lasting approximately 2 to 4 minutes. An individual microburst seldom lasts longer than 15 minutes from the time it strikes the ground until dissipation. Sometimes microbursts are concentrated into a line structure, and under these conditions activity might continue for as long as an hour. Once microburst activity starts, you can expect multiple microbursts in the same general area. [Figure 9-41]

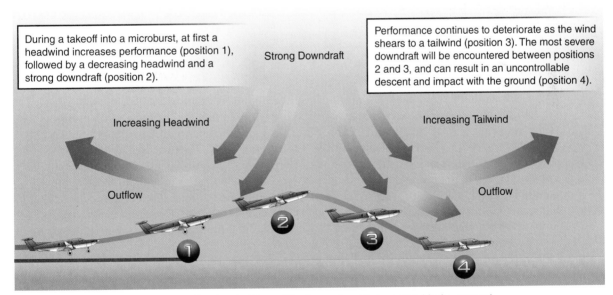

During a takeoff into a microburst, at first a headwind increases performance (position 1), followed by a decreasing headwind and a strong downdraft (position 2).

Strong Downdraft

Performance continues to deteriorate as the wind shears to a tailwind (position 3). The most severe downdraft will be encountered between positions 2 and 3, and can result in an uncontrollable descent and impact with the ground (position 4).

Increasing Headwind

Increasing Tailwind

Outflow

Outflow

Figure 9-41. An encounter with a microburst at low altitude can lead to impact with the ground.

 An aircraft that encounters a headwind of 45 knots within a microburst can expect a total shear across the microburst of 90 knots.

 The performance of an aircraft changes drastically as it flies through a microburst. See figure 9-41.

SECTION B ■ **Weather Hazards**

SECTION B ■ **Weather Hazards**

On an approach, monitor the power and vertical velocity required to maintain your glide path. If you encounter an unexpected wind shear during an approach, it might be difficult to stay on the glide path at normal power and descent rates. If there is ever any doubt that you can regain a reasonable rate of descent and land without abnormal maneuvers, apply full power and make a go-around or missed approach. [Figure 9-42]

 During an approach, monitoring the power and vertical velocity required to remain on the proper glideslope is the most important and most easily recognized means of being alerted to possible wind shear.

	WIND SHEAR			
	From	**To**	**From**	**To**
	Headwind	Calm or Tailwind	Tailwind	Calm or Headwind
Indications				
Indicated Airspeed	Decreases		Increases	
Pitch Attitude	Decreases		Increases	
Aircraft	Tends to Sink		Balloons	
Groundspeed	Increases		Decreases	
Actions				
Power	Increase		Decrease	
Fly	Up to Glideslope		Down to Glideslope	
Be Prepared to	Reduce Power		Increase Power	
To Stay on Glide Path	Increase Rate of Descent (Due to faster groundspeed)		Decrease Rate of Descent (Due to slower groundspeed)	

Figure 9-42. if you encounter wind shear during a stabilized landing approach, the FAA recommends specific actions shown in the lower portion of this table.

 See figure 9-42 for recommended actions if you encounter a wind shear during a stabilized approach.

If you encounter a wind shear on an approach or departure, you are urged to promptly report it to the controller. A warning can assist other pilots to avoid or cope with a wind shear on approach or departure. When describing conditions, avoid using the terms "*negative*" or "*positive*" wind shear. PIREPS of "*negative wind shear on final*" intended to describe loss of airspeed and lift, have been interpreted to mean that no wind shear was encountered. The recommended method for wind shear reporting is to state the loss or gain of airspeed and the altitudes at which it was encountered. "*Tulsa Tower, American 721 encountered wind shear on final, gained 25 knots between 600 and 400 feet, followed by a loss of 40 knots between 400 feet and surface.*" If you are unable to report wind shear in these specific terms, you are encouraged to make reports in terms of the effect upon your aircraft. "*Miami Tower, Gulfstream 403 Charlie encountered an abrupt wind shear at 800 feet on final, max thrust required.*"

With frontal activity, the most critical period for wind shear is either just before or just after frontal passage. The onset of LLWS follows a cold frontal passage and precedes a warm frontal passage. Typical periods for critical LLWS with frontal passages are one to three hours after a cold front and up to six hours before a warm front. Wind shear with a warm front causes the most problems because it lasts longer and frequently occurs with low ceilings and poor visibilities.

 Look for wind shear before a warm front passes and after a cold front passes.

WIND SHEAR WARNING SYSTEMS

To help detect hazardous wind shear associated with microbursts, **low-level wind shear alert systems (LLWAS)** have been installed at many airports. The LLWAS uses a system of anemometers placed at strategic locations around the airport to detect differences in the wind readings. Many systems operate by sending individual anemometer readings every 10 seconds to a central computer that evaluates the wind differences across the airport. A wind shear alert is usually issued if one reading differs from the average by at least 15 knots. If you are arriving or departing from an airport equipped with LLWAS, air traffic controllers issue wind shear alerts. They will provide the wind velocities at two or more of the sensors. Consult the *Chart Supplement* listings to determine if an airport has LLWAS.

In addition to LLWAS, **terminal doppler weather radar (TDWR)** systems have been installed at many airports with high wind shear potential. These radar systems use a more powerful and narrower radar beam than conventional radar. The TDWR can provide a clearer, more detailed picture of thunderstorms that allows better wind shear prediction.

The **weather systems processor (WSP)** enhances selected airport surveillance radar (ASR-9) facilities, providing air traffic with warnings of hazardous wind shear and microbursts similar to TDWR. The WSP also provides terminal area weather involving extreme precipitation, storm cell locations and movement, as well as the location and predicted future position and intensity of wind shifts that can affect airport operations.

IN-FLIGHT VISUAL INDICATIONS

In areas not covered by LLWAS or TDWR, you might only be able to predict the presence of wind shear using visual indications. In humid climates where the bases of convective clouds tend to be low, wet microbursts usually have a visible rain shaft. In the drier climates of the deserts and mountains of the western United States, the higher thunderstorm cloud bases result in the evaporation of the rain shaft producing a dry microburst. The only visible indications under these conditions might be virga at the cloud base and a dust ring on the ground. It's important to note that because downdrafts spread horizontally across the ground, you can encounter low-level wind shear beyond the boundaries of the visible rain shaft. Avoid any area that you suspect could contain a wind shear hazard. [Figure 9-43]

Figure 9-43. A visible rainshaft or virga indicates the possibility of a microburst. A dry downburst might create a dust ring on the ground.

LOW VISIBILITY

One of the most common aviation weather hazards is low visibility. As a pilot, you usually are concerned with two types of visibility — prevailing visibility and flight visibility. As you already know, prevailing visibility represents the greatest horizontal surface distance an observer can see and identify objects through at least half of the horizon. This is the visibility you find in aviation routine weather reports (METARs). Flight visibility is defined as the average forward horizontal distance, from the cockpit of an aircraft in flight, at which prominent unlighted objects may be seen and identified by day and prominent lighted objects may be seen and identified by night. However, your most practical concern in flight operations often is slant-range visibility. The slant-range visibility might be greater or less than the surface horizontal visibility, depending on the depth of the surface condition. Slant-range visibility is important when you are performing an instrument approach. Horizontal visibility at the surface is most important during IFR takeoff operations. Poor visibility creates the greatest hazard when combined with a low cloud ceiling.

RESTRICTIONS TO VISIBILITY

Particles that can absorb, scatter, and reflect light are always present in the atmosphere. The amount of particles in the air varies considerably, and explains why visibility is better on some days than on others. Restrictions to visibility can include fog, haze, smoke, smog, and dust. Fog requires both sufficient moisture and condensation nuclei on which the water vapor can condense. It is more prevalent in industrial areas, due to an abundance of condensation nuclei. One of the most hazardous characteristics of fog is its ability to form rapidly. It can completely obscure a runway in a matter of minutes.

Fog is classified according to the way it forms. **Radiation fog**, also known as **ground fog**, is very common. It forms over fairly level land areas on clear, calm, humid nights. As the surface cools by radiation, the adjacent air is also cooled to its dewpoint. Radiation

 Industrial areas typically produce more fog because they have more condensation nuclei.

Figure 9-44. Radiation fog usually burns off by mid-morning.

fog usually occurs in stable air associated with a high pressure system. As early morning temperatures increase, the fog begins to lift and usually burns off by mid-morning. If higher cloud layers form over the fog, visibility will improve more slowly. [Figure 9-44]

Advection fog is caused when a low layer of warm, moist air moves over a cooler surface, which could be either land or water. It is most common under cloudy skies along coastlines, where sea breezes transport air

 Radiation fog forms over fairly flat land on clear, calm nights when the air is moist and there is a small temperature/dewpoint spread.

from the warm water to cooler land. Winds up to 15 knots can increase the fog. Above 15 knots, turbulence creates a mixing of the air, and the fog usually lifts enough to form low stratus clouds. Advection fog is usually more persistent and extensive than radiation fog and can form rapidly during day or night. It commonly forms in winter when airmasses move inland from the coasts. **Upslope fog** forms when moist, stable air is forced up a sloping land mass. Like advection fog, upslope fog can form in moderate to strong winds and under cloudy skies.

 Advection fog can appear suddenly during the day or night and is more persistent than radiation fog.

 Advection fog is most likely to form in coastal areas when moist air moves over colder ground or water.

 Surface winds stronger than 15 knots tend to dissipate or lift advection fog into low stratus clouds.

 Advection fog and upslope fog are both dependent upon wind for their formation.

Precipitation-induced fog can form when warm rain or drizzle falls through a layer of cooler air near the surface. Evaporation from the falling precipitation saturates the cool air, causing fog to form. This fog can be very dense, and usually does not clear until the rain moves out of the area. This type of fog might extend over large areas, completely suspending most air operations. It is most commonly associated with warm fronts, but can occur with slow moving cold fronts and stationary fronts.

 Precipitation-induced fog is usually associated with warm fronts and is a result of saturation due to evaporation of precipitation.

Steam fog occurs as cool air moves over warmer water. It rises upward from the water's surface and resembles rising smoke. [Figure 9-45] Ice fog occurs in cold weather when the temperature is much below freezing and water vapor sublimates directly as ice crystals. Conditions favorable for its formation are the same as for radiation fog except for cold temperatures, usually −32°C (−25°F) or colder. It occurs mostly in the Arctic regions, but can occur in the middle latitudes during the cold season. Ice fog can be quite blinding to pilots flying into the sun.

Figure 9-45. As warm water evaporates and saturates a thin layer of cold air above the water, steam fog can form.

 Different types of fog form in different locations. For example, radiation fog forms over land areas, advection fog is most common along coastal areas, and steam fog forms over water.

Haze, smoke, smog, and blowing dust or snow can also restrict your visibility. Haze is caused by a concentration of very fine dry particles. Individually, they are invisible to the naked eye, but in sufficient numbers, can restrict your visibility. Haze particles might be composed of a variety of substances, such as salt or dust particles. It occurs in stable atmospheric conditions with relatively light winds. Haze is usually no more than a few thousand feet thick, but it can occasionally extend to 15,000 feet. Visibility above the haze layer is usually good; however, visibility through the haze can be very poor. Dark objects tend to be bluish, and bright objects, like the sun or distant lights, have a dirty yellow or reddish hue. Haze can also create the illusion of being at a greater distance than actual from a runway, causing you to fly a lower approach.

 ## FIDO Saves the Day

Suppose that after flying for several hours on a dangerous bombing mission you arrived back over friendly territory to find all of the available airfields covered with fog. Wouldn't it be wonderful if there were a system that could simply disperse the fog over a runway, improving visibility so that you could land?

The British developed and used just such a system during World War II. The system, called Fog Investigation and Dispersal Operations (FIDO), consisted of a pair of long fuel pipes that ran along each side of a runway. Burners spaced along the pipes sprayed fuel into the air, which was ignited to form a wall of flame on each side of the runway. Heat from the flames evaporated the fog, and the flames themselves served as a helpful visual aid for landing aircraft. Before FIDO, the primary option for crews returning to foggy British airfields was to bail out over the English countryside, sending their aircraft to crash in the Channel.

The system was operational at sixteen British airfields, as well as four in the United States. The photo shows an Avro Lincoln ready to touch down between the flaming runway edges. The enormous amount of fuel consumed (125,000-250,000 gallons or 450,000-900,000 liters per hour) made the system prohibitively expensive for routine use, but saved hundreds of Allied bombers and their crews during the war.

Because ATC cannot disperse the fog at your destination, it is up to you to use forecasts and weather tools to plan carefully so that visibility is adequate when you are ready to land.

SECTION B ■ **Weather Hazards**

Smoke is the suspension of combustion particles in the air. The impact of smoke on visibility is determined by the amount of smoke produced, wind velocity, diffusion by turbulence, and distance from the source. You can often identify smoke by a reddish sky as the sun rises or sets, and an orange-colored sky when the sun is well above the horizon. When smoke travels distances of 25 miles or more, large particles fall out and the smoke tends to become more evenly distributed, giving the sky a grayish or bluish appearance, similar to haze.

Smog is a combination of fog and smoke, and it can create very poor visibility over a large area. In some geographical areas, stable air and topographical barriers, such as mountains, can trap pollutants. This causes smog to build up, further reducing visibility.

Dust refers to fine particles of soil suspended in the air. When the soil is loose, the winds are strong, and the atmosphere is unstable, dust might be blown for hundreds of miles. Dust gives a tan or gray tinge to distant objects, and the sun can appear colorless, or with a yellow hue. Blowing dust is common in areas where dry land farming is extensive, such as the Texas panhandle.

 Restrictions to visibility, such as haze, make objects appear farther away. When approaching to land, haze creates the illusion of being higher above the runway, causing pilots to fly a lower approach.

VOLCANIC ASH

Although lava from volcanoes generally threatens areas only in the immediate vicinity of the volcano, the ash cloud can affect a much more widespread area. Volcanic ash consists of gases, dust, and ash from a volcanic eruption. It can spread around the world and remain in the stratosphere for months or longer. Due to its highly abrasive characteristics, volcanic ash can pit the aircraft windscreens and landing lights to the point they are rendered useless. Under severe conditions, the ash can clog pitot-static and ventilation systems as well as damage aircraft control surfaces. Piston aircraft are less likely than jet aircraft to lose power due to ingestion of volcanic ash, but severe damage is possible, especially if the volcanic cloud is only a few hours old. If you suspect that you are in the vicinity of an ash cloud, try to stay upwind. If you inadvertently enter a volcanic ash cloud you should not attempt to fly straight through or climb out of the cloud because an ash cloud might be hundreds of miles wide and extend to great heights. Reduce power to a minimum, altitude permitting, and reverse course to escape the cloud. [Figure 9-46]

Courtesy of USGS

Figure 9-46. A volcanic ash cloud might not be easy to distinguish from ordinary clouds when approached from a distance.

ICING

Icing can be divided into two general types based on whether it affects power production or aerodynamics. Induction icing affects engine power, and includes carburetor icing as well as air intake icing. Carburetor icing forms in the carburetor venturi. It is most likely to occur when the outside air temperature is between approximately −7°C (20°F) and 21°C (70°F) and relative humidity is above 80%. Some aircraft have a carburetor air temperature gauge to help detect potential carburetor icing conditions. A typical gauge is marked with a yellow arc between −15° and +5° Celsius. The yellow arc indicates the carburetor temperature range where carburetor icing can occur. However, it is dangerous for the indicator to be in the yellow arc only if the moisture content of the air, as well as the air temperature, is conducive to ice formation. Carburetor heat should be used as recommended in the pilot's operating handbook.

Air intake icing, like airframe icing, usually requires the aircraft surface temperature to be 0°C (32°F) or colder with visible moisture present. However, it also can form in clear air when relative humidity is high and temperatures are 10°C (50°F) or colder.

Structural icing builds up on any exposed surface of an aircraft, causing a loss of lift, an increase in weight, and control problems. There are two general types of structural ice: rime and clear. Mixed icing is a combination of the two. **Rime ice** normally is encountered in stratus clouds and results from instantaneous freezing of tiny water droplets striking the aircraft surface. It has an opaque appearance caused by air being trapped in the water droplets as they freeze. The major hazard of rime ice is its ability to change the shape of an airfoil and destroy lift. Because rime ice freezes instantly, it builds up on the leading edge of airfoils, but it does not flow back over the wing and tail surfaces. [Figure 9-46A]

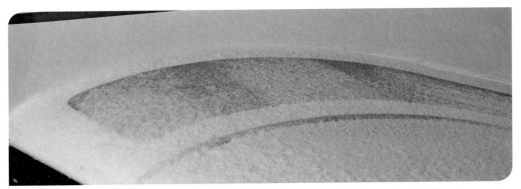

Figure 9-46A. Rime ice, like frost, roughens the surface of an airfoil, destroying its lift.

 Ice, snow, or frost having the thickness and roughness of sandpaper can reduce lift by 30% and increase drag by 40%.

Clear ice can develop in areas of large water droplets that are found in cumulus clouds or in freezing rain beneath a warm front inversion. Freezing rain means there is warmer air at higher altitudes. When the droplets flow over the aircraft structure and slowly freeze, they can glaze the aircraft's surfaces. Clear ice is the most serious of the various forms of ice because it has the fastest rate of accumulation, adheres tenaciously to the aircraft, and is more difficult to remove than rime ice.

 If you encounter rain that freezes on impact, the temperatures are above freezing at some higher altitude.

The effects of ice buildup on aircraft are cumulative. Ice increases drag and weight, and decreases lift and thrust. Tests have shown that ice, snow, or frost with a thickness and roughness similar to medium or coarse sandpaper on the leading edge and upper surface of a wing can reduce lift by as much as 30% and increase drag by 40%. These changes in lift and drag significantly increase the stalling speed and reduce the angle of attack at which the airplane stalls. If you encounter icing, you must quickly alter your course or altitude to maintain safe flight. In extreme cases, two to three inches of ice can form on the leading edge of an airplane wing in less than five minutes.

 Freezing rain is most likely to have the highest rate of accumulation of structural icing.

Two conditions are necessary for a substantial accumulation of ice on an aircraft. First, the aircraft must be flying through visible moisture, such as rain or clouds. Second, the temperature of the water or of the aircraft must be 0°C (32°F) or lower. Keep in mind that aerodynamic cooling can lower the temperature of an airfoil to 0°C, even though the ambient temperature is a few degrees warmer.

SECTION B ■ **Weather Hazards**

When water droplets are cooled below the freezing temperature, they are in a **supercooled state**. They turn to ice quickly when disturbed by an aircraft passing through them. Clear icing is most heavily concentrated in cumuliform clouds in the range of temperature from 0°C to –10°C, (32°F to 14°F) usually from altitudes near the freezing level to 5,000 feet above the freezing level. However, you can encounter clear icing in cumulonimbus clouds with temperatures as low as –25°C (–13°F). In addition, supercooled water and icing have been encountered in thunderstorms as high as 40,000 feet, with temperatures of –40°C (–40°F). Small supercooled water droplets also can cause rime icing in stratiform clouds, although rime does not usually accumulate as fast as clear ice. Continuous icing can be expected in stratiform clouds in the temperature range from 0°C to –20°C (32°F to –4°F). You are least likely to encounter icing in high clouds, because these clouds consist of ice crystals and this already-frozen moisture will not adhere to your airframe. Icing might also occur as a mixture of both rime and clear. This commonly is the case with frontal systems, which can produce a wide variety of icing conditions. [Figure 9-47]

FAA — High clouds are least likely to contribute to aircraft structural icing.

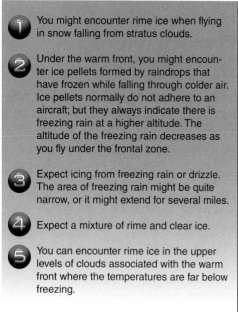

1. You might encounter rime ice when flying in snow falling from stratus clouds.

2. Under the warm front, you might encounter ice pellets formed by raindrops that have frozen while falling through colder air. Ice pellets normally do not adhere to an aircraft; but they always indicate there is freezing rain at a higher altitude. The altitude of the freezing rain decreases as you fly under the frontal zone.

3. Expect icing from freezing rain or drizzle. The area of freezing rain might be quite narrow, or it might extend for several miles.

4. Expect a mixture of rime and clear ice.

5. You can encounter rime ice in the upper levels of clouds associated with the warm front where the temperatures are far below freezing.

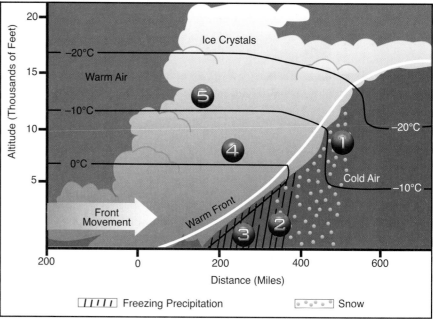

Figure 9-47. This profile of a warm front shows the typical icing areas..

FAA — The presence of ice pellets indicates a warm front is about to pass and that freezing rain probably exists at a higher altitude. See figure 9-47.

ESTIMATING FREEZING LEVEL

Knowing the location of the freezing level is important when you select a cruising altitude for an IFR flight. You can estimate the freezing level by using temperature lapse rates. The standard, or average, temperature lapse rate is approximately 2°C (3.5°F) per 1,000 feet. If the surface temperature is 60°F, subtract 32°F and divide by 3.5°F to determine the freezing level (60 – 32 = 28 ÷ 3.5 = 8). This means the freezing level is approximately 8,000 feet AGL, assuming the actual lapse rate is close to 3.5°F.

FAA — Assuming a standard lapse rate, if the temperature is +8°C at an elevation of 1,350 feet, the approximate freezing level is 5,350 feet. (8 ÷ 2 = 4 or 4,000 + 1,350 = 5,350 feet).

AVOIDING ICE ENCOUNTERS

Obviously, you should avoid areas where icing is forecast or expected. If you unintentionally get into an icing situation without ice removal equipment, there usually are only limited courses of action available. Also, remember that you must obtain approval from ATC if you need to make a diversion while operating on an IFR flight plan. When you encounter icing while flying in stratiform clouds, you can climb or descend out of the visible moisture or to an altitude where the temperature is above freezing or lower than −10°C (14°F).

If you encounter cumuliform clouds and suspect icing conditions, a simple change of course might be the best action. If this is impractical, descend to a lower altitude to avoid the ice. Overflying developed cumuliform clouds might be beyond the performance capability of your aircraft. Your remaining option is a 180° turn, which in some cases is the best choice.

If you encounter freezing rain, you must take immediate action. One option is to climb into the warmer air above. If you choose to do this, start the climb at the earliest possible moment. Otherwise, you might not have enough power to reach a higher altitude, because ice buildup quickly degrades your aircraft's performance. Also, if the frontal surface slopes up in the direction of your flight, you might not be able to climb fast enough to reach the warm air. Other options include making a 180° turn and reversing course or descending to a lower altitude. You might choose to make a descent if the free air temperature at lower altitudes is above freezing or cold enough to change the precipitation into ice pellets (sleet). A 180° turn or a descent is probably the best course of action if the altitude of warmer air aloft is unknown and your aircraft's performance will not permit a rapid and extended climb. If enough ice accumulates to make level flight impossible, descent is inevitable, so trade altitude for airspeed to maintain control.

In weather forecasts or pilot reports, aircraft structural icing is normally classified as trace, light, moderate, or severe depending on the accumulation rate. A **trace** means ice is perceptible, but accumulation is nearly balanced by its rate of sublimation. De-icing equipment is unnecessary, unless icing is encountered for an extended period of time. **Light ice** accumulation can be a problem during prolonged exposure (over one hour) if you do not have adequate de-icing/anti-icing equipment. In **moderate icing** conditions, even short encounters become potentially hazardous unless you use de-icing/anti-icing equipment. **Severe icing** produces a rate of accumulation greater than the reduction or control capabilities of the de-icing/anti-icing equipment.

Most small general aviation airplanes are not approved for flight into icing conditions. Those that are have special de-ice and anti-ice equipment to protect airframe surfaces, as well as the induction system, and have been flight tested to demonstrate their ability to fly in icing conditions. However, even these airplanes cannot fly in severe icing, and prolonged flight in moderate icing can become hazardous due to ice accumulation on unprotected surfaces. Because ice protection systems vary widely in both operation and effectiveness, be sure to consult the POH for detailed information on system operation. A general discussion of de-ice and anti-ice systems is included in Chapter 11, Section B.

Frost is a related element that poses a serious hazard during takeoff. It interferes with smooth airflow over the wings and can cause early airflow separation, resulting in a loss of lift. This means the wing stalls at a lower-than-normal angle of attack. Although frost increases drag, the airplane can probably reach takeoff speed. The danger is that it might stall shortly after liftoff. Always remove all frost from the aircraft surfaces before flight.

 If frost is not removed from the wings before flight, it can cause an early airflow separation that decreases lift and increases drag. This causes the airplane to stall at a lower-than-normal angle of attack.

SECTION B ■ **Weather Hazards**

HYDROPLANING

Hydroplaning is caused by a thin layer of standing water that separates the tires from the runway. It causes a substantial reduction in friction between the airplane tires and the runway surface and results in poor or nil braking action at high speeds. Severe hydroplaning can cause your airplane to skid off the side or the end of the runway. Hydroplaning is most likely at high speeds on wet, slushy, or snow-covered runways that have smooth textures.

 High aircraft speed, standing water, slush, and a smooth runway texture are factors conducive to hydroplaning.

The best remedy for hydroplaning is to prevent its occurrence. You should study hydroplaning speeds and recommended procedures for your airplane. When selecting a runway, pick one that is longer than required and allows you to use only light braking pressures to stop the airplane safely. Because it can take several seconds for the wheels to reach their rotational speed after landing, do not apply the brakes too quickly. More detailed information on hydroplaning is available in Chapter 12, Section B.

COLD WEATHER OPERATIONS

Prior to a flight in cold weather, you must observe additional precautions. As mentioned above, you must remove any frost, snow, or ice on the airplane. Also inspect all control surfaces and their associated hinges, control rods, and cables for snow or ice that could interfere with their operation. Be sure to check the crankcase breather lines, because vapor from the engine can condense and freeze, preventing the release of air from the crankcase. [Figure 9-48]

 During preflight in cold weather, crankcase breather lines should receive special attention because they are susceptible to being clogged by ice from crankcase vapors that have condensed and subsequently frozen.

Figure 9-48. If ice or snow is removed by melting, be sure the water does not run into the control surface hinges and refreeze.

Another important consideration is whether or not to preheat the airplane prior to flight. If temperatures are so low that you will experience difficulty starting the engine, you should preheat it. Many instruments are adversely affected by cold temperatures, so consider preheating the cabin as well as the engine compartment.

 During cold weather operations, you should preheat the cabin as well as the engine.

Follow the manufacturer's recommended procedures for priming before you try to start the engine. Overpriming can result in poor compression and difficulty in starting the engine. If the engine fires for only a few revolutions and then quits, ice can form on the sparkplug electrodes. If this happens, you can heat the engine or have a mechanic remove the sparkplugs from the engine and heat them separately.

SUMMARY CHECKLIST

✓ The life of a thunderstorm passes through three distinct stages. The cumulus stage is characterized by continuous updrafts. When precipitation begins to fall, the thunderstorm has reached the mature stage. As the storm dies during the dissipating stage, updrafts weaken and downdrafts become predominant.

✓ Airmass thunderstorms are relatively short-lived storms and are usually isolated or scattered over a large area. Severe thunderstorms contain wind gusts of 50 knots or more, hail 3/4 inch in diameter or larger, and/or tornadoes.

✓ A squall line is a narrow band of active thunderstorms that often forms 50 to 200 miles ahead of a fast moving cold front. It often contains very severe weather.

✓ Weather hazards associated with thunderstorms, such as lightning, hail, and turbulence, are not confined to the cloud itself.

✓ Avoid thunderstorms by at least 20 miles. When using airborne weather radar, avoid intense radar echoes by at least 20 miles.

✓ If you encounter turbulence during flight, establish maneuvering or penetration speed and try to maintain a level flight attitude.

✓ Mechanical turbulence is created as wind blows over hangars, stands of trees, or other obstructions.

✓ When sufficient moisture is present, cumulus cloud build-ups indicate the presence of convective turbulence.

✓ Any front traveling at a speed of 30 knots or more produces at least a moderate amount of turbulence.

✓ Wake turbulence is created when an aircraft generates lift. The greatest vortex strength occurs when the generating aircraft is heavy, slow, in a clean configuration, and at a high angle of attack.

✓ Helicopters produce vortices similar to wingtip vortices of a large fixed-wing airplane.

✓ Clear air turbulence often develops in or near the jet stream, which is a narrow band of high altitude winds near the tropopause.

✓ Strong mountain wave turbulence can be anticipated when the winds across a ridge are 40 knots or more, and the air is stable. The crests of mountain waves might be marked by lens-shaped, or lenticular, clouds.

✓ Wind shear can exist at any altitude and can occur in a vertical or horizontal direction. A microburst is one of the most dangerous sources of wind shear.

✓ Restrictions to visibility can include fog, haze, smoke, smog, and dust.

✓ Volcanic ash clouds are highly abrasive to aircraft and engines, andthey also restrict flight visibility.

✓ The three types of structural ice are rime, clear, and mixed.

✓ The accumulation of ice on an aircraft increases drag and weight and decreases lift and thrust.

✓ Ice pellets usually indicate the presence of freezing rain at a higher altitude.

SECTION B ■ **Weather Hazards**

KEY TERMS

Cumulus Stage	Intermediate Turbulence
Mature Stage	Continuous Turbulence
Shear Zone	Light Turbulence
Gust Front	Light Chop
Roll Cloud	Moderate Turbulence
Dissipating Stage	Moderate Chop
Airmass Thunderstorm	Severe Turbulence
Severe Thunderstorm	Extreme Turbulence
Single Cell Thunderstorm	Wind Shear
Supercell Thunderstorm	Microburst
Multicell Thunderstorm	Low-Level Wind Shear Alert System (LLWAS)
Frontal Thunderstorm	Terminal Doppler Weather Radar (TDWR)
Squall Line	
Lightning	Weather Systems Processor (WSP)
Hail	Radiation Fog
Funnel Clouds	Ground Fog
Tornado	Advection Fog
Waterspout	Upslope Fog
Low-Level Turbulence (LLT)	Precipitation-Induced Fog
Mechanical Turbulence	Steam Fog
Convective Turbulence	Ice Fog
Capping Stable Layer	Haze
Frontal Turbulence	Smoke
Wingtip Vortices	Smog
Wake Turbulence	Dust
Jet Engine Blast	Volcanic Ash
Clear Air Turbulence (CAT)	Induction Icing
Jet Stream	Structural Icing
Mountain Waves	Rime Ice
Occasional Turbulence	Clear Ice

Supercooled State

Severe Icing

Trace Ice

Frost

Light Icing

Hydroplaning

Moderate Icing

QUESTIONS

1. What are the three basic ingredients needed for the formation of a thunderstorm?

2. Continuous updrafts occur in a thunderstorm during what stage?
    A. Cumulus stage
    B. Mature stage
    C. Dissipating stage

3. Thunderstorms reach their greatest intensity during which stage?
    A. Cumulus stage
    B. Mature stage
    C. Dissipating stage

4. What is the term used to describe a narrow band of thunderstorms that normally contains the most severe types of weather-related hazards?
    A. Airmass thunderstorms
    B. Frontal boundary thunderstorms
    C. Squall line thunderstorms

5. What type of cloud is associated with the most severe turbulence?
    A. Cumulonimbus
    B. Cumulus
    C. Standing lenticular altocumulus

6. What hazard is always associated with a thunderstorm?
    A. Heavy rain
    B. Lightning
    C. Severe icing

7. True/False. You can encounter hail in clear air several miles from a thunderstorm.

8. When using on-board weather radar to avoid thunderstorms, you should avoid intense echoes by at least how many miles?
    A. 10 miles
    B. 20 miles
    C. 30 miles

9. What should you do if you unexpectedly encounter turbulence?

10. Wake turbulence is greatest from a large, heavy airplane that is operating in what configuration?
    A. Low speeds and low angles of attack
    B. Low speeds and high angles of attack
    C. High speeds and high angles of attack

SECTION B ■ Weather Hazards

11. Should you plan to land before or after the touchdown point of a large, heavy airplane?

12. True/False. There is no correlation between clear air turbulence and the jet stream.

13. What type of turbulence is indicated by the presence of rotor, cap and lenticular clouds?
     A. Convective
     B. Wake
     C. Mountain wave

14. Turbulence that causes changes in altitude or attitude resulting in definite strains against seatbelts is classified as what?
     A. Light
     B. Moderate
     C. Severe

15. During a stabilized landing approach, what happens if the wind unexpectedly shifts from a headwind to a tailwind?
     A. Pitch attitude decreases, IAS decreases, and the airplane tends to sink below the glide path
     B. Pitch attitude decreases, IAS increases, and the airplane tends to sink below the glide path
     C. Pitch attitude increases, IAS increases, and the airplane tends to rise above the glide path

16. Discuss the in-flight visual indications of possible wind shear.

17. What is the name of the fog that typically forms over fairly level land on clear, calm, humid nights?
     A. Steam fog
     B. Radiation fog
     C. Advection fog

18. Haze can create the illusion that you are
     A. closer to the runway than you actually are.
     B. at a greater distance from the runway than you actually are.
     C. lower on the approach than you actually are.

19. What is the recommended course of action if you inadvertently enter a volcanic ash cloud?
     A. Reverse course
     B. Attempt to climb up and out of the cloud
     C. Continue straight ahead to exit on the opposite side

20. Carburetor icing is most likely when the relative humidity is above 80% and the outside air temperature is between
     A. -18°C (0°F) and 1°C (34°F).
     B. -15°C (5°F) and 5°C (41°F).
     C. -7°C (20°F) and 21°C (70°F).

21. True/False. Airframe icing increases drag and weight and decreases lift and thrust.

22. True/False. Airframe icing cannot occur when the outside air temperature is above 0°C.

23. When the surface temperature is 53°F at sea level, the estimated freezing level is
    A. 4,700 feet AGL.
    B. 6,000 feet AGL.
    C. 10,500 feet AGL.

24. To avoid hydroplaning after landing on a wet runway, you should
    A. apply the brakes immediately.
    B. delay the application of brakes.
    C. carry a higher-than-normal power setting after touchdown.

SECTION C
Printed Reports and Forecasts

Weather information is available through a vast network of government agencies and commercial sources. Electronic media can provide an enormous selection of weather information. Although some sites have information that is accurate, relevant, and current, few online sources are tailored specifically to your needs as a pilot, and much of the information can be outdated, unreliable, or inaccurate. The best practice is to obtain your weather information from recognized sources such as the National Weather Service (NWS) or Aviation Digital Data Service (ADDS). You might not always have easy access to Flight Service weather briefers or NWS meteorologists to interpret the textual data for you, so you need to be able to gather and decipher the appropriate reports and forecasts on your own.

PRINTED WEATHER REPORTS

In general, a weather report records measurements and observations of existing conditions at a particular time and place. It differs from a forecast, which is a prediction of conditions expected sometime in the future. A variety of reports disseminate information gathered by trained observers, automated systems, radar, and pilots. Some of the reports you might encounter include aviation routine weather reports, radar weather reports, and pilot weather reports.

AVIATION ROUTINE WEATHER REPORT

An **aviation routine weather report** (METAR) is an observation of surface weather that is reported in a standard format. Although the METAR code has been adopted worldwide, each country is allowed to make modifications or exceptions to the code. Such modifications usually accommodate local procedures or particular units of measure. The following discussion covers the elements in a METAR originating in the United States. [Figure 9-49]

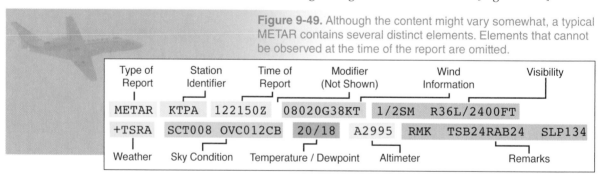

Figure 9-49. Although the content might vary somewhat, a typical METAR contains several distinct elements. Elements that cannot be observed at the time of the report are omitted.

TYPE OF REPORT
METAR KTPA...

The two types of reports are the METAR, which is taken every hour, and the **non-routine (special) aviation weather report (SPECI)**. The SPECI weather observation is an unscheduled report indicating a significant change in one or more elements.

STATION IDENTIFIER
METAR **KTPA** 122150Z...

Each reporting station has a four-letter International Civil Aviation Organization (ICAO) identifier. In the contiguous 48 states, station identifiers begin with the letter K, which precedes the three-letter domestic location identifier. For example, the domestic identifier for Tampa International Airport is TPA, and the ICAO identifier is KTPA. In other areas of the world, the first two letters indicate the region, country, or state. Alaska identifiers begin with PA, Hawaii identifiers begin with PH, and the Canadian prefixes are CU, CW, CY, and CZ. You can find the identifiers for specific reporting stations or decode unfamiliar identifiers using the *Chart Supplement* or the NOAA/NWS website.

TIME OF REPORT
...KTPA **122150Z** 08020G38KT...

The date (day of the month) and time of the observation follows the station identifier. The time is given in UTC, or Zulu, as indicated by a Z following the time. The report in the example was issued on the 12th of the month at 2150Z.

MODIFIER
When a METAR is created by a totally automated weather observation station, the modifier AUTO follows the date/time element (e.g., ...251955Z AUTO 30008KT...). Automated stations are classified by the type of sensor equipment they use, and AO1 or AO2 will be noted in the remarks section of the report. AO2 in the remarks indicates that the station has a precipitation discriminator (which can determine the difference between liquid and frozen/freezing precipitation). AO1 indicates that the automated station did not use a precipitation discriminator.

The modifier COR is used to indicate a corrected METAR, which replaces a previously disseminated report. There is no station type designator in the remarks section of a corrected report from an automated station. A METAR with no modifier (as in this example), means that the observation was taken at a manual station or that an automated station had manual input.

WIND INFORMATION
...122150Z **08020G38KT** 1/2SM R36L/2400FT...

The wind direction and speed are reported in a five digit group, or six digits if the speed is over 99 knots. The first three digits represent the direction from which the wind is blowing, in reference to true north.

The next two (or three) digits show the speed in knots (KT). Calm winds are reported as 00000KT. Gusty winds are reported with a G, followed by the highest gust. In the example, wind was reported to be from 080° true at 20 knots with gusts to 38 knots.

If the wind direction varies 60 degrees or more and the speed is more than six knots, a variable group follows the wind group. The extremes of wind direction are shown separated by a V. For example, if the wind is blowing from 020°, varying to 090°, it is reported as 020V090. A wind of 6 knots or less that is varying in direction is indicated with the contraction VRB. [Figure 9-50]

CODED METAR DATA	EXPLANATIONS
00000KT	Wind calm
20014KT	Wind from 200° at 14 knots
15010G25KT	Wind from 150° at 10 knots, gusts to 25 knots
VRB04KT	Wind variable in direction at 4 knots
210103G130KT	Wind from 210° at 103 knots with gusts to 130 knots

Figure 9-50. These examples help you to become familiar with the METAR formats for wind direction and speed.

VISIBILITY
...08020G38KT **1/2SM R36L/2400FT** +TSRA...

Prevailing visibility is the greatest distance an observer can see and identify objects. To determine prevailing visibility, an observer looks at distinctive objects, such as towers or smokestacks, that are a known distance from the observation site. At night, observers use lighted objects to determine visibility. When the prevailing visibility is greater in one direction than in another, the visibility in

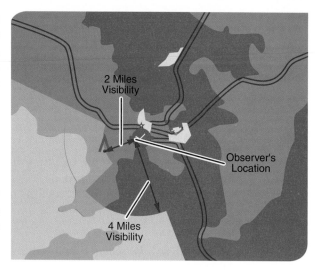

Figure 9-51. In this example, the visibility element says P6SM because more than half of the horizon has visibility greater than six miles. The Remarks section might say VIS W 2SM, VIS S, SW 4SM.

the majority of the sky is reported. If visibility varies significantly, the observer can report the visibility in individual sectors in the remarks section of the METAR. [Figure 9-51]

Visibility is reported in statute miles (SM) in the United States and in meters elsewhere in the world. For example, 1/2SM indicates one-half statute mile and 4SM indicates 4 statute miles. Sometimes **runway visual range (RVR)** is reported following prevailing visibility. RVR is based on what a pilot in a moving aircraft should see when looking down the runway. RVR is designated with an R, followed by the runway number, a slant (/), and the visual range in feet (FT). In the example, R36L/2400FT

 The runway visual range (RVR) value represents the horizontal distance a pilot should see down the runway from the approach end of a runway.

means Runway 36 Left visual range is 2,400 feet. Variable RVR is shown as the lowest and highest visual range values separated by a V. Outside the United States, RVR is normally reported in meters.

WEATHER

Weather or obstructions to vision that are present at the time of the observation are reported immediately after the visibility in the following order: intensity or proximity, descriptor, precipitation, obstruction to visibility, and any other weather phenomena. The intensity or proximity and/or descriptor are used to qualify the precipitation, obscuration, or other weather phenomena.

QUALIFIER AND DESCRIPTOR
...1/2SM R36L/2400FT +**TS**RA SCT008 OVC012CB 20/18...

Intensity or proximity of precipitation is shown just before the precipitation codes. The indicated intensity applies only to the first type of precipitation reported. Intensity levels are shown as light (–), moderate (no sign), or heavy (+). In the example, the precipitation was reported as heavy.

DESCRIPTOR CODES	
TS – Thunderstorm	DR – Low Drifting
SH – Shower(s)	MI – Shallow
FZ – Freezing	BC – Patches
BL – Blowing	PR – Partial

Weather occurring near, but not at, the airport is prefixed with VC, for "in the vicinity" of the airport. The vicinity is typically between five and 10 statute miles of the observation point. VC is not used when an intensity qualifier is reported.

The type of precipitation or obscuration is described by a two-letter code. In the example, a thunderstorm (TS) was reported.

Taking the Guesswork Out of Visibility

Without a frame of reference, determining how far you can see down a runway is just a guess. To determine ground visibility at some airports, weather observers have several selected objects at known distances from a specific location. When visibility is restricted, the farthest visible object determines the reported visibility.

A much better way of determining visibility is with an optical instrument called a transmissometer. A transmissometer measures runway visual range (RVR) down a specific runway. It is made up of two components. The first is a projector that sends a beam of light, at a known intensity, down the length of the runway. The second component, the receiver, contains a photoelectric cell that measures the amount of light penetrating the obscuring phenomena. A computer then converts the amount of light received into runway visual range.

SECTION C ■ Printed Reports and Forecasts

WEATHER PHENOMENA
...1/2SM R36L/2400FT +TS**RA** SCT008 OVC012CB...

The weather phenomena section can include codes for nine types of precipitation, eight kinds of obscurations, and six rather uncommon weather events. Up to three types of precipitation can be coded in a single grouping of present weather conditions. When more than one is reported, they are shown in order of predominance. In the example, rain (RA) was observed in connection with the thunderstorm.

Obscurations are factors that limit visibility, and are shown after any reported precipitation. Fog (FG) is listed when the visibility is less than 5/8 statute mile. If the visibility is between 5/8 and 6 statute miles, the code for mist (BR) is used. Shallow fog (MIFG), patches of fog (BCFG), or partial fog (PRFG) might be coded if the prevailing visibility is seven statute miles or greater. Other weather phenomena might be listed following the obscurations.

WEATHER PHENOMENA CODES

Precipitation

RA — Rain	GR — Hail (> 1/4")
DZ — Drizzle	GS — Small Hail/Snow Pellets
SN — Snow	SG — Snow Grains
IC — Ice Crystals	PL — Ice Pellets
UP — Unknown Precipitation	

Obstructions to Visibility

FG — Fog	PY — Spray
BR — Mist	SA — Sand
FU — Smoke	DU — Dust
HZ — Haze	VA — Volcanic Ash

Other Weather Phenomena

SQ — Squall	SS — Sandstorm
DS — Duststorm	PO — Dust/Sand Whirls
FC — Funnel Cloud	
+FC — Tornado or Waterspout	

SKY CONDITION

The sky condition groups describe the amount of clouds, if any, their heights and, in some cases, their type. In addition, a vertical visibility might be reported if the height of the clouds cannot be determined due to an obscuration.

When a squall (SQ) is reported, you can expect a sudden increase in wind speed of at least 16 knots to a sustained wind speed of 22 knots or more for at least 1 minute.

AMOUNT
...+TSRA **SCT**008 **OVC**012CB 20/18...

The amount of clouds covering the sky is reported in eighths, or octas, of sky cover. Each layer of clouds is described using a code that corresponds to the octas of sky coverage. If the sky is clear, it is designated by SKC in a manual report and CLR in an automated report. Because an automated station cannot detect clouds above 12,000 feet, a report of clear indicates there were no clouds detected below 12,000 feet. FEW is used when cloud coverage is greater than zero to 2/8 of the sky. Scattered clouds, which cover 3/8 to 4/8 of the sky, are shown by SCT. Broken clouds, covering 5/8 to 7/8 of the sky, are designated by BKN, and an overcast sky is reported as OVC. In the example, there is a layer of scattered clouds (SCT) and an overcast layer (OVC).

The sky cover condition for a cloud layer represents total sky coverage, which includes any lower layers of clouds. Whether human or automated, the observer can only report conditions that are visible from a point on the ground. The observer cannot determine the extent of an upper layer that is partly hidden by a lower layer, so the the observer must add the amount of sky covered by the lower layers to the amount of sky covered the upper layer. [Figure 9-52]

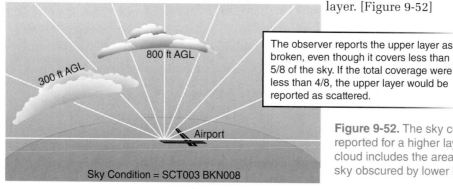

The observer reports the upper layer as broken, even though it covers less than 5/8 of the sky. If the total coverage were less than 4/8, the upper layer would be reported as scattered.

Figure 9-52. The sky coverage reported for a higher layer of cloud includes the area of the sky obscured by lower layers.

HEIGHT, TYPE, AND VERTICAL VISIBILITY
...+TSRA SCT**008** OVC**012CB** 20/18...

The height of clouds or the vertical visibility into obscuring phenomena is reported with three digits in hundreds of feet above ground level (AGL). To determine the cloud height, add two zeros to the number given in the report. When more than one layer is present, the layers are reported in ascending order. Automated stations can only report a maximum of three layers at 12,000 feet AGL and below. Human observers can report up to six layers of clouds at any altitude. In the example, the scattered layer was at 800 feet AGL and the overcast layer was at 1,200 feet AGL.

 If the MSL height of the top of a cloud layer is known, you can easily determine the layer's thickness by adding the airport elevation (MSL) to the height of the cloud base (AGL), and then subtracting this number from the height of the cloud tops.

METAR KMDW 121856Z AUTO 32005KT 1 1/2SM +RA BR OVC007 17/16 A2980

For example, in this METAR, the overcast begins at 700 feet AGL. If the field elevation is 620 feet MSL, and the tops of the overcast layer are reported at 6,500 feet MSL, then the cloud layer is 5,180 feet thick.

    620 feet (MSL field elevation)

    + 700 feet (AGL height of cloud base)
    ―――――――――――――――――――――
    1,320 feet (MSL height of cloud base)

    6,500 feet (MSL top of overcast)

    -1,320 feet (MSL height of cloud base)
    ―――――――――――――――――――――
    5,180 feet (thickness of cloud layer)

In a manual report, a cloud type can be included if towering cumulus clouds (TCU) or cumulonimbus clouds (CB) are present. The code follows the height of their reported base. In the example, the base of the reported cumulonimbus clouds was at 1,200 feet AGL.

When more than half of the sky is covered by clouds, a ceiling exists. By definition, a **ceiling** is the AGL height of the lowest layer of clouds that is reported as broken or overcast, or the vertical visibility into an obscuration, such as fog or haze. Human observers may rely simply on their experience and knowledge of cloud formations to determine ceiling heights, or they can combine their experience with the help of reports from pilots, balloons, or other instruments. The ceiling and visibility determine if flight conditions are VFR. To depart under VFR from a controlled airport (without a special VFR clearance), the ceiling must be at least 1,000 feet and the visibility at least 3 statute miles.

 A ceiling is defined as the height of the lowest layer of clouds or obscuring phenomena aloft that is reported as broken or overcast.

Unlike clouds, an obscuration does not have a definite base. Obscuration is caused by phenomena such as fog, haze, or smoke that extend from the surface to an indeterminable height. In METAR reports, a total obscuration is shown with a VV followed by three digits indicating the vertical visibility in hundreds of feet. For example, VV006 describes an indefinite ceiling at 600 feet AGL. Obscurations that do not cover the entire sky might be reported in the remarks section of the METAR.

 In a METAR observation VV008 indicates that the sky is obscured with a vertical visibility of 800 feet.

TEMPERATURE AND DEWPOINT
...SCT008 OVC012CB **20/18** A2995...

METARs list the observed air temperature and dewpoint in degrees Celsius immediately following the sky condition. In the example, the temperature and dewpoint are reported as 20°C and 18°C, respectively. Temperatures below 0° Celsius are prefixed with an M to indicate minus. For instance, M10 indicates a temperature of 10°C below zero. Temperature and dewpoint readings to the nearest 1/10°C can be included in the remarks section of the METAR.

ALTIMETER
...20/18 **A2995** RMK TSB24RAB24 SLP134

The letter A followed by a four-digit group reports the altimeter setting in inches of mercury with the decimal omitted. In the example, the altimeter setting was 29.95 in. Hg.

REMARKS
...A2995 **RMK TSB24RAB24 SLP134**

The remarks section can include other significant weather, such as wind data, variable visibility, beginning and ending times of a particular weather phenomena, pressure information, and precise temperature/dewpoint readings. The start of the remarks section is identified by the code RMK. The beginning of an event is shown by a B, followed by the time in minutes after the hour. If the event ended before the observation, the ending time in minutes past the hour is noted by an E. In the example, a thunderstorm began at 24 minutes past the hour (TSB24). Rain also began at 24 minutes past the hour (RAB24). Additionally, the sea level pressure (SLP) was 1013.4 millibars, or hectoPascals (hPa). A hectopascal is the metric equivalent of a millibar (1 mb = 1 hPa). Examples of other coded remarks are shown in figure 9-53.

 The beginning of the remarks section is indicated by the code RMK. The remarks section reports weather considered significant to aircraft operations that are not covered in the previous sections of the METAR. See figure 9-53.

SECTION C ■ **Printed Reports and Forecasts**

CODED DATA	EXPLANATIONS
A02	Automated station with precipitation discriminator
PK WND 20032/25	Peak wind from 200° at 32 knots, 25 minutes past the hour
VIS 3/4V1 1/2	Prevailing visibility variable 3/4 to 1 and 1/2 miles
FRQ LTG NE	Frequent lightning to the northeast
FZDZB45	Freezing drizzle began at 45 minutes past the hour
RAE42SNB42	Rain ended and snow began at 42 minutes past the hour
PRESFR	Pressure falling rapidly
SLP045	Sea level pressure in millibars (hPa), 1004.5 mb (hPa)
WSHFT 30 FROPA	Wind shift occurred at 30 minutes past the hour due to frontal passage
T00081016	Temperature/dewpoint in tenths °C, .8 °C/–1.6 °C (Since the first digit after the T is a 0, it indicates that the temperature is positive; the dewpoint in this example is negative since the fifth digit is a 1.)

Figure 9-53. Examples of coded remarks are shown in the left column, with the corresponding explanations on the right.

RADAR WEATHER REPORTS

NEXRAD weather radar detects general areas of precipitation, which can help you to avoid thunderstorm areas. The **radar weather report** (SD/ROB) is a textual product derived automatically from weather radar data without human intervention. The reports can be up to 80 minutes old, and they provide only a general idea of the location of precipitation, however, these reports can be a good resource in the absence of other radar information.

Radar does not show clouds, so radar weather reports do not help you to avoid IFR conditions, but they can define areas of precipitation that are associated with clouds. They provide information on the type, intensity, and location of the echo top of the precipitation. The reports normally include movement (direction and speed) of cells. Altitudes are in hundreds of feet MSL. [Figure 9-54]

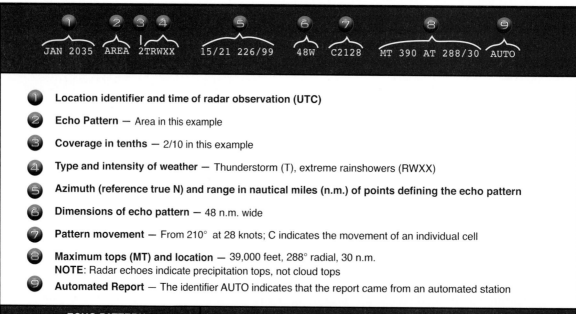

Figure 9-54. Radar weather reports are useful in determining areas of severe weather. Tops at high levels can indicate thunderstorms.

As shown in figure 9-54, the abbreviation MT is used to denote maximum tops of the precipitation in the clouds. Heights are reported in hundreds of feet MSL followed by the radial and distance in nautical miles from the reporting location.

Workload Management Through Cockpit Automation

As early as the 1970s there has been an effort by the world airlines to reduce the workload imposed on flight deck crews. ACARS is one of the answers. This technology provides bi-directional, non-verbal communications from the cockpit of an airborne aircraft to a dispatcher on the ground. Not only can the crew send and receive discrete company messages, but the system also provides many automated functions timed to support the crew in the different phases of flight. The automatic functions include weather updates, weight and balance information, runway data, and enroute engine performance. ACARS also sends block times, wheels-off, and wheels-on times, as well as present position automatically so the airline dispatcher knows the location of the aircraft at all times.

A manual input feature allows the crew to request weather reports and landing data. When there is a problem, maintenance information can be transmitted directly to the cockpit. When using the ACARS print capability, the crew can save time and reduce the possibility of copy errors from voice communications. By reducing the communications workload, pilots can more fully concentrate on their jobs.

The data communications (data comm) program moves some communication off the voice channel using data link technology. This capability provides a verifiable record to reduce communication errors and increases air traffic efficiency by decreasing the time spent on routine tasks, such as communication transfers. Using systems, such as the future air navigation system (FANS), enables flight crews and air traffic controllers to communicate information through data links established on satellite-based networks and GPS. In the terminal environment, data comm enables you to digitally receive and confirm departure clearances and revisions and taxi instructions. During enroute operations, controllers and flight crews send ATC clearances, requests, instructions, notifications, voice frequency communication transfers, and aircraft position reports as a supplement to voice communications.

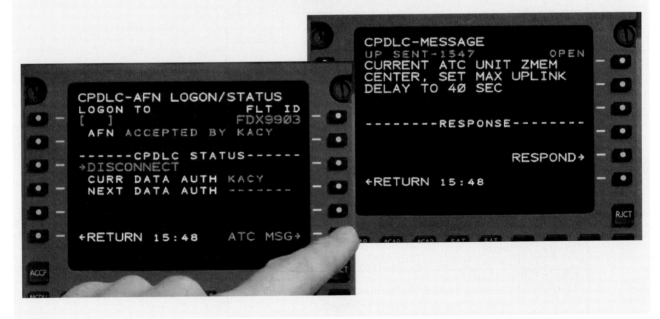

SECTION C ■ **Printed Reports and Forecasts**

PILOT WEATHER REPORTS

Pilot weather reports (PIREPs) are often your best source to confirm such information as the bases and tops of cloud layers, in-flight visibility, icing conditions, wind shear, and turbulence. When significant conditions are reported or forecast, ATC facilities are required to solicit PIREPs. Anytime you encounter unexpected weather conditions, you are encouraged to make a pilot report. When you make a PIREP, the ATC facility or Flight Service adds your report to the distribution system so it can be used to brief other pilots or provide in-flight advisories. [Figure 9-55]

```
UA/OV MRB 065046/TM 1600/FL100/TP AC68/SK 024
BKN   032/042   BKN-OVC/TA   -12/IC   LGT-MDT
RIME 055-080/RM WIND COMP HEAD 020 MH310
TAS 180
```

This PIREP decodes as follows: Pilot report, 46 n.m. on the 065° radial from Martinsburg at 1600UTC at 10,000 feet. Type of aircraft is an Aero Commander. First cloud layer has a base at 2,400 feet broken with tops at 3,200 feet. The second cloud layer has a base at 4,200 broken occasionally overcast with no tops reported. Outside air temperature is -12 degrees Celsius. Light to moderate rime icing is reported between 5,500 and 8,000 feet. The headwind component is 20 knots. Magnetic heading is 310 degrees and the true airspeed is 180 knots.

PIREP FORM		
Pilot Weather Report		
3-Letter SA Identifier	1. UA Routine Report	UUA Urgent Report
— — —		
2. /OV	Location: In relation to a NAVAID	
3. /TM	Time: Coordinated Universal Time	
4. /FL	Altitude/Flight Level: Essential for turbulence and icing reports	
5. /TP	Aircraft Type: Essential for turbulence and icing reports	
Items 1 through 5 are mandatory for all PIREPs		
6. /SK	Sky Cover: Cloud height and coverage (scattered, broken, or overcast)	
7. /WX	Flight Visibility and Weather: Flight visibility, precipitation, restrictions to visibility, etc.	
8. /TA	Temperature (Celsius): Essential for icing reports	
9. /WV	Wind: Direction in degrees and speed in knots	
10. /TB	Turbulence: Turbulence intensity, whether the turbulence occurred in or near clouds, and duration of turbulence	
11. /IC	Icing: Intensity and Type	
12. /RM	Remarks: For reporting elements not included or to clarify previously reported items	

Figure 9-55. PIREPs can contain up to 12 elements. The first five are required, but you need not report all of the others.

 PIREPs are the best source for current weather, such as icing and turbulence, between reporting stations.

 PIREPs use a standard format, as shown in figure 9-55. Note that altitudes are given in hundreds of feet above mean sea level (MSL).

Make your PIREP concise and as complete as possible, but do not be overly concerned with strict format or terminology. The important thing is to make the report so that other pilots can benefit from your observation. The Aeronautical Information Manual contains detailed information on the interpretation of PIREPs.

Another type of PIREP is called an AIREP or air report. Disseminated electronically, these reports are used almost exclusively by commercial airlines. However, when accessing the internet for current weather you might see the abbreviation ARP followed by a weather report that was captured from an Aeronautical Radio Incorporated (ARINC) communications addressing and reporting system (ACARS) transmission.

PRINTED WEATHER FORECASTS

Many of the reports of observed weather conditions are used to develop forecasts of future conditions. Every day, Weather Forecast Offices (WFOs) prepare over 2,000 forecasts for specific airports, over 900 route forecasts, and a variety of other forecasts for flight planning purposes. The printed forecasts that pilots use most often include the terminal aerodrome forecast, aviation area forecast, and the winds and temperatures aloft forecast.

TERMINAL AERODROME FORECAST

One of your best sources for an estimate of what the weather will be in the future at a specific airport is the **terminal aerodrome forecast (TAF)**. TAFs normally are valid for a 24-hour period and scheduled four times a day at 0000Z, 0600Z, 1200Z, and 1800Z. Each TAF contains these elements: type, ICAO station identifier, issuance date and time, valid period, and the forecast. [Figure 9-56]

 A terminal aerodrome forecast (TAF) is valid for a 24-hour period and is issued four times a day. A TAF covers a geographical proximity within a 5-mile radius from the center of an airport runway complex, and should be your primary source of weather information for your destination.

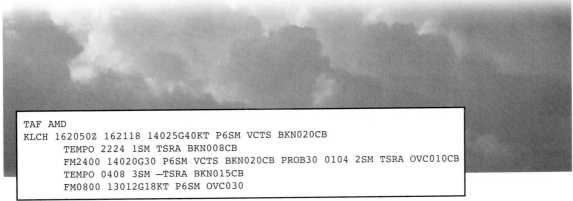

```
TAF AMD
KLCH 162050Z 162118 14025G40KT P6SM VCTS BKN020CB
      TEMPO 2224 1SM TSRA BKN008CB
      FM2400 14020G30 P6SM VCTS BKN020CB PROB30 0104 2SM TSRA OVC010CB
      TEMPO 0408 3SM —TSRA BKN015CB
      FM0800 13012G18KT P6SM OVC030
```

Figure 9-56. With a few exceptions, the codes used in the TAF are similar to those used in the METAR.

TYPE OF FORECAST
TAF AMD

KLCH...

The TAF normally is a routine forecast. However, an amended TAF (TAF AMD) might be issued when the current TAF no longer represents the expected weather. TAF or TAF AMD appears in a header line prior to the text of the forecast. The abbreviations COR and RTD indicate a corrected or a delayed TAF, respectively. The example depicts an amended TAF.

STATION IDENTIFIER AND ISSUANCE DATE/TIME
TAF AMD

KLCH 162050Z 162118...

The four letter ICAO location identifier code is the same as that used for the METAR/SPECI. The first two numbers of the date/time group represent the day of the month, and the next four digits are the Zulu time that the forecast was issued. The example TAF is a forecast for Lake Charles Regional Airport (KLCH) that was issued on the 16th day of the month at 2050Z.

VALID PERIOD
...162050Z **162118** 14025G40KT...

Normally, the forecast is valid for 24 hours. The first two digits represent the valid date. Next is the beginning hour of the valid time in Zulu, and the last two digits are the ending hour. The forecast for Lake Charles Regional Airport is valid from 2100Z on the 16th of the month to 1800Z the next day. Because the TAF in this example was amended, the valid period is less than 24 hours. At an airport that is open part time, the TAFs issued for that location will have the abbreviated statement AMD NOT SKED AFT (closing time)Z added to the end of the forecast text. For TAFs issued when these airports are closed, the word NIL appears in place of the forecast text.

FORECAST
...162050Z 162118 **14025G40KT P6SM VCTS BKN020CB**...

The body of the TAF contains codes for forecast wind, visibility, weather, and sky condition. Weather, including obstructions to visibility, is added to the forecast when it is significant to aviation.

The forecast wind is depicted by a five digit group with the first three digits representing the wind direction and the last two digits the wind speed. If the wind speed is 100 knots or more, there will be three digits. The contraction KT follows to denote that the wind speed is in knots. Wind gusts are noted by the letter G appended to the wind speed followed by the highest expected gust. A variable wind direction is noted by VRB, which indicates the wind is 3 knots or less. A calm wind is forecast as 00000KT. In this example, the winds are predicted to be from 140°at 25 knots with gusts to 40 knots.

In a TAF, variable winds are noted with the contraction VRB and indicates the wind speed is 3 knots or less. A calm wind is indicated by 00000KT.

The next area is the expected prevailing visibility in miles, including fractions of miles. The SM indicates the measurement is in statute miles. Expected visibilities greater than 6 miles are forecast as a P6SM, which means plus 6 statute miles.

P6SM in terminal aerodrome forecast implies that the prevailing visibility is expected to be greater than 6 statute miles.

The weather phenomena and sky conditions are given next using the same format, qualifiers, and contractions as the METAR reports. If no significant weather is expected to occur during a specific time period in the forecast, the weather group is omitted for that time period. CLR is never used in the TAF. In this example, thunderstorms are forecast to be in the vicinity (VC) and a broken cloud layer, made up of cumulonimbus clouds, is forecast at 2,000 feet AGL.

The letters SKC are used in a terminal aerodrome forecast to indicate a clear sky.

Low-level wind shear that is not associated with convective activity might be included using the code WS followed by a three digit height (up to and including 2,000 feet AGL), a forward slash (/) and the winds at the height indicated. For example, WS010/18040KT indicates low-level wind shear at 1,000 feet AGL, wind 180° at 40 knots.

 The letters WS indicates that low-level wind shear that is not associated with convective activity might be present during the valid time of the forecast. WS005/27050KT indicates that the wind at 500 feet AGL is 270° at 50 knots.

FORECAST CHANGE GROUPS

When a significant change to the weather conditions is expected during the valid time, a change group is used. The changes can be temporary, rapid, or gradual. Each change indicator marks a time group within the TAF.

TEMPORARY FORECAST

...TEMPO 2224 1SM TSRA BKN008CB

FM2400 14020G30 P6SM VCTS BKN020CB PROB30 0104 2SM TSRA OVC010CB

TEMPO 0408 3SM -TSRA BKN015CB

FM0800 13012G18KT P6SM OVC030

Wind, visibility, weather, or sky conditions that are expected to last less than an hour are described in a temporary (TEMPO) group, followed by beginning and ending times. The first temporary group in the example predicts that between 2200Z and 2400Z, visibility is expected to be reduced to 1 statute mile in moderate rain associated with a thunderstorm. A broken layer of cumulonimbus clouds with bases at 800 feet is also predicted to occur. It's important to remember that these conditions only modify the previous forecast and are expected to last for periods of less than one hour. The second temporary group predicts that between 0400Z and 0800Z, the visibility is likely to be 3 statute miles in light rain associated with a thunderstorm. The ceiling is expected to be a broken layer of cumulonimbus clouds with the bases at 1,500 feet.

FROM OR BECOMING FORECAST

...TEMPO 2224 1SM TSRA BKN008CB

FM2400 14020G30 P6SM VCTS BKN020CB PROB30 0104 2SM TSRA OVC010CB

TEMPO 0408 3SM -TSRA BKN015CB

FM0800 13012G18KT P6SM OVC030

If a rapid change, usually within one hour, is expected, the code for from (FM) is used with the time of change. The conditions listed following the FM will continue until the next change group or the end of the valid time of the TAF. In the example, the first forecast change group indicates from 2400Z, the wind will be from 140° at 20 knots with gusts to 30 knots, the visibility will be greater than 6 statute miles, with thunderstorms in the vicinity and a cloud layer, made up of cumulonimbus clouds, is expected to be broken at 2,000 feet AGL. From 0800Z, the wind is forecast to be from 130° at 12 knots gusting to 18 knots, visibility will improve to greater than 6 statute miles and the sky will be overcast at 3,000 feet AGL.

A more gradual change in the weather, taking about two hours, is coded as BECMG, followed by beginning and ending times of the change period. The gradual change is expected to occur at an unspecified time within this time period. All items, except for the changing conditions shown in the BECMG group, are carried over from the previous time group. For instance, BECMG 2310 24007KT P6SM NSW indicates a gradual change in conditions is expected to occur between 2300Z and 1000Z. Sometime during this period, the wind will be from 240° at 7 knots, visibility is predicted to improve to greater than 6 miles with no significant weather (NSW). The NSW code is used only after a time period in which significant weather was forecast. NSW only appears in BECMG or TEMPO groups.

PROBABILITY FORECAST
...FM2400 14020G30 P6SM VCTS BKN020CB **PROB30 0104 2SM TSRA OVC010CB**

TEMPO 0408 3SM -TSRA BKN0015CB...

TAFs can include the probability of thunderstorms or precipitation events with the associated wind, visibility, and sky conditions. A PROB group is used when the probability of occurrence is between 30 and 49%. The percentage is followed by the beginning and ending time of the period during which the thunderstorm or precipitation is expected. In the example, there is a 30% chance of a thunderstorm with moderate rain and 2 statute miles visibility between 0100Z and 0400Z. In addition, there is a 30% probability of an overcast layer of cumulonimbus clouds with bases at 1,000 feet AGL during the four hour time period.

 The term PROB40 2102 +TSRA in a terminal aerodrome forecast indicates that there is approximately a 40% probability of thunderstorms with heavy rain between 2100Z and 0200Z.

AVIATION AREA FORECAST
An **aviation area forecast (FA)** covers general weather conditions over several states or a known geographical area and is a good source of information for enroute weather. It also helps you determine the conditions at airports that do not have Terminal Aerodrome Forecasts. FAs are issued three times a day for six regions in the 48 contiguous states, and amended as required. FAs are issued by the National Aviation Weather Advisory Unit in Kansas City, Missouri. A specialized Gulf of Mexico FA is issued by the National Hurricane Center in Miami, Florida. The NWS offices issue FAs for Hawaii and Alaska, however, the Alaska FA uses a different format. [Figure 9-57]

 Aviation area forecasts are issued three times each day and generally include a total forecast period of 18 hours. They cover a geographical group of states or well known areas.

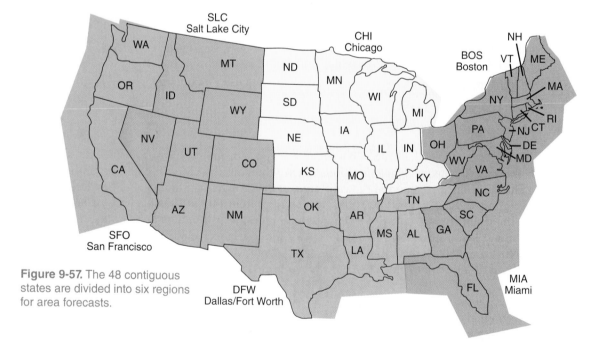

Figure 9-57. The 48 contiguous states are divided into six regions for area forecasts.

The FA consists of four sections: a communications and product header section, a precautionary statement section, and two weather sections (synopsis and VFR clouds and weather). Each area forecast covers an 18-hour period. They are written using standard abbreviations and word contractions. The sample forecast in Figure 9-58 is interpreted in the accompanying paragraphs.

COMMUNICATIONS AND PRODUCT HEADERS

In the heading SLCC FA 141045, the SLC identifies the Salt Lake City forecast area, C indicates the product contains a clouds and weather forecast, FA means area forecast, and 141045 tells you this forecast was issued on the 14th day of the month at 1045Z. Because these forecasts are rounded to the nearest full hour, the valid time for the report begins at 1100Z. The synopsis is valid until 18 hours later, which is shown as the 15th at 0500Z. The clouds and weather section forecast is valid for a 12-hour period, until 2300Z on the 14th. The outlook portion is valid for six hours following the forecast, from 2300Z on the 14th to 0500 on the 15th. The last line of the header lists the states that are included in the Salt Lake City forecast area. [Figure 9-58]

Heading Section

```
SLCC FA 141045
SYNOPSIS AND CLDS/WX
SYNOPSIS VALID UNTIL 150500
CLDS/WX VALID UNTIL 142300... OUTLK VALID 142300-150500
ID MT NV UT WY CO AZ NM
```

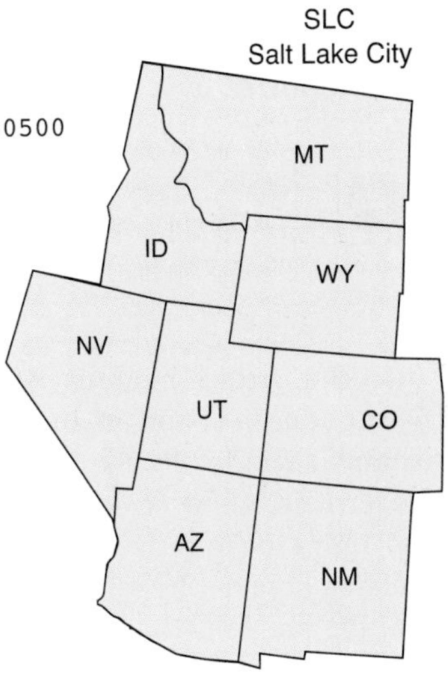

Precautionary Statements

```
SEE AIRMET SIERRA FOR IFR CONDS AND MTN OBSCN.
TSTMS IMPLY PSBL SVR OR GTR TURBC SVR ICG LLWS
AND IFR CONDS.

NON MSL HGTS ARE DENOTED BY AGL OR CIG.
```

Synopsis

```
SYNOPSIS...HIGH PRES OVER NERN MT CONTG EWD
GRDLY. LOW PRES OVR AZ NM AND WRN TX RMNG
GENLY STNRY. ALF...TROF EXTDS FROM WRN MT INTO
SRN AZ RMNG STNRY.
```

VFR Clouds and Weather

```
.
ID MT
FROM YXH TO SHR TO 30SE BZN TO 60SE PIH TO LKT TO
YXC TO YXH.
70-90 SCT-BKN 120-150. WDLY SCT RW-. TOPS SHWRS 180.
OTLK...VFR
RMNDR AREA...100-120. ISOLD RW- MNLY ERN PTNS AREA.
OTLK...VFR
.
UT NV NM AZ
80 SCT-BKN 150-200. WDLY SCT RW-/TRW-. CB TOPS 450.
OTLK...VFR
.
WY CO
FROM BZN TO GCC TO LBL TO DVC TO RKS TO BZN.
70-90 BKN-OVC 200. OCNL VSBY 3R-F. AFT 20Z WDLY SCT
TRW-. CB TOPS 450. OTLK...MVFR CIG RW.
```

SLC
Salt Lake City

Figure 9-58. Area forecasts are easier to interpret when you understand the order and content of the four sections.

Amendments to FAs are issued whenever the weather significantly improves or deteriorates based on the judgment of the forecaster. An amended FA is identified by the contraction AMD in the header along with the time of the amended forecast. When an FA is corrected, the contraction COR appears in the heading, along with the time of the correction.

PRECAUTIONARY STATEMENTS

Following the headers are three precautionary statements that are part of all FAs. The first statement alerts you to check the latest AIRMET Sierra, which describes areas of mountain obscuration forecast for the area. The next statement is a reminder that thunderstorms imply possible severe or greater turbulence, severe icing, low-level wind shear, and instrument conditions. Therefore, when thunderstorms are forecast, these hazards are not included in the body of the FA. The third statement points out that heights that are not MSL are noted by the letters AGL (above ground level) or CIG (ceiling). All heights are expressed in hundreds of feet.

SYNOPSIS

The synopsis is a brief description of the location and movement of fronts, pressure systems, and circulation patterns in the FA area over an 18-hour period. When appropriate, forecasters use terms describing ceilings and visibility, strong winds, or other phenomena. In the example, high pressure over northeastern Montana will continue moving gradually eastward. A low pressure system over Arizona, New Mexico, and western Texas will remain generally stationary. Aloft (ALF), a trough of low pressure extending from western Montana into southern Arizona is expected to remain stationary.

VFR CLOUDS AND WEATHER

The VFR clouds and weather portion is usually several paragraphs long and broken down by states or geographical regions. It describes clouds and weather that could affect VFR operations over an area of 3,000 square miles or more. The forecast is valid for 12 hours, and is followed by a 6-hour categorical outlook.

 The VFR clouds and weather section of an aviation area forecast summarizes sky conditions, cloud heights, visibility, obstructions to vision, precipitation, and sustained surface winds of 20 knots or greater.

When the surface visibility is expected to be six statute miles or less, the visibility and obstructions to vision are included in the forecast. When precipitation, thunderstorms, and sustained winds of 20 knots or greater are forecast, they will be included in this section. The term OCNL (occasional) is used when there is a 50% or greater probability, but for less than 1/2 of the forecast period, of cloud or visibility conditions that could affect VFR flight. The area covered by showers or thunderstorms is indicated by the terms ISOL (isolated, meaning single cells), WDLY SCT (widely scattered, less than 25% of the area), SCT or AREAS (25% to 54% of the area), ad NMRS or WDSPRD (numerous or widespread, 55% or more of the area). In addition, the term ISOL is sometimes used to describe areas of ceilings or visibility that are less than 3,000 square miles.

The outlook follows the main body of the forecast, and gives a general description of the expected weather, using the terms VFR, IFR, or MVFR (marginal VFR). A ceiling less than 1,000 feet and/or visibility less than 3 miles is considered IFR. Marginal VFR areas are those with ceilings from 1,000 to 3,000 feet and/or visibility between 3 and 5 miles. Abbreviations are used to describe causes of IFR or MVFR weather.

In the example shown in figure 9-58, the area of coverage in the specific forecast for Wyoming and Colorado is identified using three-letter designators. This area extends from Bozeman, Montana, to Gillette, Wyoming, to Liberal, Kansas, to Dove Creek, Wyoming, to Rock Springs, Wyoming, and back to Bozeman. As mentioned previously under the header, the valid time begins on the 14th day of the month at 1100Z for a 12-hour period. A broken to overcast cloud layer begins between 7,000 to 9,000 feet MSL, with tops extending to 20,000 feet. Because visibility and wind information is omitted, the visibility is expected to be greater than six statute miles, and the wind less than 20 knots. However, the visibility (VSBY) is forecast to be occasionally 3 miles in light rain and fog (3R-F). After 2000Z, widely scattered thunderstorms with light rain showers are expected, with cumulonimbus (CB) cloud tops to 45,000 feet. The 6-hour categorical outlook covers the period from 2300Z on the 14th to 0500 on the 15th. The forecast is for marginal VFR weather due to ceilings (CIG) and rain showers (RW).

 When the wind is forecast to be 20 knots or greater the categorical outlook in the aviation area forecast includes the contraction WND.

WINDS AND TEMPERATURES ALOFT FORECAST

A **winds and temperatures aloft forecast (FD)** provides an estimate of wind direction in relation to true north, wind speed in knots, and the temperature in degrees Celsius for selected altitudes. Depending on the station elevation, winds and temperatures are usually forecast for nine levels between 3,000 and 39,000 feet. You may request information for two additional levels (45,000 foot and 53,000 foot) from a Flight Service briefer or NWS meteorologist, but they are not included on an FD. [Figure 9-59]

Heading Information
The heading includes the type of forecast, the day of the month, and the time of transmission.

Time
The second line tells you the forecast is based on observations at 1200Z and is valid at 1800Z on the 15th. It is intended for use between 1700Z and 2100Z on the same day.

```
FD KWBC 151640

BASED ON 151200Z DATA

VALID 151800Z FOR USE 1700-2100Z  TEMPS NEG ABV 24000
```

FD	3000	6000	9000	12000	18000	24000	30000
ALA			2420	2635-08	2535-18	2444-30	245945
AMA		2714	2725+00	2625-04	2531-15	2542-27	265842
DEN			2321-04	2532-08	2434-19	2441-31	235347
HLC		1707-01	2113-03	2219-07	2330-17	2435-30	244145

Winds and Temperatures
Since temperatures above 24,000 feet are always negative, a note indicates that the minus sign is omitted for 30,000 feet and above. The column on the left lists the FD location identifiers. The columns to the right show forecast information for each level appropriate to that location.

Figure 9-59. This excerpt from an FD shows winds only to the 30,000-foot level. As stated on the report, all temperatures above 24,000 feet are negative.

 In a winds and temperatures aloft forecast, winds are given in true direction and speed is shown in knots.

It is important to note that temperatures are not forecast for the 3,000-foot level or for any level within 2,500 feet of the station elevation. Likewise wind groups are omitted when the level is within 1,500 feet of the station elevation. At Denver (DEN), for example, the forecast for the lower two levels is omitted, because the station elevation at Denver is over 5,000 feet.

 A winds and temperatures aloft forecast (FD) does not include winds within 1,500 feet of the station elevation. Likewise temperatures for the 3,000-foot level or for a level within 2,500 feet of the station elevation are omitted.

The presentation of wind information in the body of the FD is similar to other reports and forecasts. The first two numbers indicate the true direction from which the wind is blowing. For example, 2635-08 indicates the wind is from 260° at 35 knots and the temperature is –8°C. Quite often you must interpolate between two levels. For instance, if you plan to fly near Hill City (HLC) at 7,500 feet, you must interpolate. Refer to figure 9-59. Because your planned flight altitude is midway between 6,000 and 9,000 feet, a good estimate of the wind at 7,500 feet is 190° at 10 knots with a temperature of –2°C.

 Wind direction and speed information on an FD are shown by a four-digit code. The first two digits are the wind direction in tens of degrees. Wind speed is shown by the second two digits. The last two digits indicate the temperature in degrees Celsius. All temperatures above 24,000 feet are negative and the minus sign is omitted.

Wind speeds between 100 and 199 knots are encoded so direction and speed can be represented by four digits. This is done by adding 50 to the two-digit wind direction and subtracting 100 from the velocity. For example, a wind of 270° at 101 knots is encoded as 7701 (27 + 50 = 77 for wind direction, and 101 − 100 = 01 for wind speed). A code of 9900 indicates light and variable winds (less than five knots). However, wind speeds of 200 knots or more are encoded as 199.

To decode a forecast of winds between 100 and 199 knots, subtract 50 from the two-digit direction code and multiply by ten. Then add 100 to the two-digit wind speed code. The code 9900 indicates the winds are light and variable.

AIRMETS AND SIGMETS

AIRMETs, SIGMETs, and convective SIGMETs are textual forecasts that advise enroute aircraft of the development of potentially hazardous weather. You can get them from Flight Watch or FIS-B during flight and in some cases ATC will broadcast the alert. You also can get these advisories during your preflight weather briefing to learn of the latest adverse conditions affecting your flight. These advisories use the same location identifiers (VORs, airports, and well-known geographic areas) to describe the location of the hazardous weather. If obtaining your briefing over the Internet, you can view the affected areas on an interactive map, either from Flight Services (1800WxBrief.com) or from the Aviation Weather Center (AviationWeather.gov). The depictions of the affected areas are easier to visualize on these graphs than from the boundary descriptions read to you over the radio or telephone. [Figure 9-60]

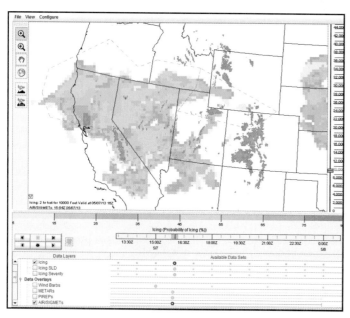

Figure 9-60. SIGMETs and AIRMETs can be presented graphically on ADDS maps that are available in the Aviation Weather Center. Some of this information is also available on glass cockpit weather displays.

AIRMET

AIRMET is an acronym for airman's meteorological information. **AIRMETs (WAs)** are issued every six hours, with amendments issued as necessary, for weather phenomena that are of operational interest to all aircraft, but hazardous mainly to light aircraft. There are three types of AIRMETs: Sierra, Tango, and Zulu. AIRMET Sierra describes IFR conditions (ceilings less than 1,000 feet or visibility less than three miles) and/or extensive mountain obscurations. AIRMET Tango describes moderate turbulence, sustained surface winds of 30 knots or greater, or nonconvective low-level wind shear. AIRMET Zulu describes moderate icing and provides freezing level heights. AIRMETs are numbered sequentially for easier identification.

The maximum forecast period for an AIRMET is 6 hours.

SIGMET

SIGMETs (WSs) are issued for hazardous weather (other than convective activity) that is considered significant to all aircraft. SIGMET stands for significant meteorological information, and includes severe icing, severe and extreme turbulence, clear air turbulence (CAT), duststorms and sandstorms lowering visibility to less than three miles, and volcanic ash. [Figure 9-61]

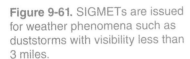

Figure 9-61. SIGMETs are issued for weather phenomena such as duststorms with visibility less than 3 miles.

Courtesy of NASA

 When used in combination with the information from PIREPs and AIRMETs, SIGMETs are your best source for information on icing conditions whether current or forecast.

 SIGMETs warn of hazardous weather conditions that concern all aircraft; such as severe icing, volcanic ash, severe turbulence, or sandstorms and duststorms lowering visibility to less than 3 miles.

SIGMETs are unscheduled forecasts that are valid for four hours, but if the SIGMET relates to hurricanes, it is valid for six hours. SIGMETs use alphanumeric designators November through Yankee, excluding Sierra and Tango. [Figure 9-62]

```
DFWP UWS 051710
SIGMET PAPA 1 VALID UNTIL
052110
AR LA MS
FROM MEM TO 30N MEI TO BTR
TO MLU TO MEM
OCNL SVR ICING ABV FRZLVL
EXPCD.
FRZLVL 080 E TO 120 W.
CONDS CONTG BYD 2100Z.
```

```
MIAT WA 151900 AMD
AIRMET TANGO UPDT 2 FOR TURBC
VALID UNTIL 160100
AIRMET TURBC...GA FL
FROM SAV TO JAX TO CTY TO TLH
TO SAV
MDT TURBC BLO 100 EXPCD
COND IPVG
AFT 160000Z
```

Figure 9-62. The first issuance of a SIGMET, as shown on the left, is labeled UWS (Urgent Weather SIGMET). PAPA 1 means it is the first issuance for a SIGMET phenomenon; PAPA 2 would be the second issuance for the same phenomenon. In the example on the right, AMD means this is an amended AIRMET of the phenomenon (moderate turbulence) identified as TANGO. The alphanumeric designator stays with the phenomenon even when it moves across the country.

CONVECTIVE SIGMET

Convective SIGMETs (WSTs) are issued for hazardous weather related to thunderstorms that is significant to the safety of all aircraft. They always imply severe or greater turbulence, severe icing, and low-level wind shear, so these items are not specified in the advisory. WSTs include any of the following phenomena: tornadoes, lines of thunderstorms, thunderstorms over a wide area, embedded thunderstorms, hail ¾ inch in diameter or more, or wind gusts to 50 knots or greater. A WST consists of either an observation and a forecast or simply a forecast. [Figure 9-63]

Figure 9-63. Convective SIGMETs are issued for clusters of thunderstorms. This photograph, taken from the Space Shuttle Orbiter, displays a variety of weather elements including overshooting thunderstorm tops, squall lines, and areas of probable high-speed downdrafts or microbursts.

Courtesy of NASA

 Convective SIGMETs contain either an observation and a forecast, or just a forecast, for tornadoes, significant thunderstorm activity, or hail 3/4 inch or greater in diameter.

 In-flight aviation weather advisories include forecasts of potentially hazardous flying conditions for enroute aircraft, including information on volcanic eruptions that are occurring or expected to occur.

Convective SIGMETs are issued for the Eastern, Central, or Western United States. Convective SIGMETs are not issued for Alaska or Hawaii, where convective SIGMET conditions are included in (non-convective) SIGMETs. Convective SIGMETs are issued at 55 minutes past each hour, and numbered sequentially for each area each day. Special bulletins are issued as required. SIGMET forecasts are valid for 2 hours or until superseded by the next hourly issuance. When convective SIGMETs are not necessary, the message CONVECTIVE SIGMET...NONE is issued at 55 minutes after each hour. [Figure 9-64]

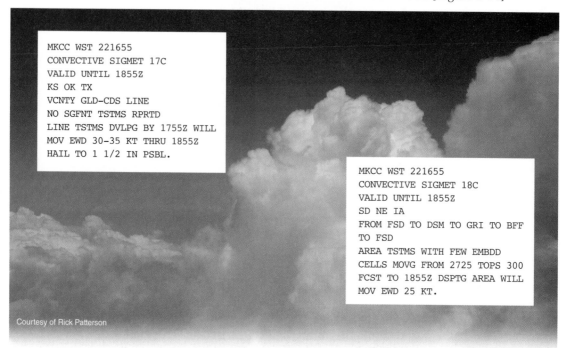

```
MKCC WST 221655
CONVECTIVE SIGMET 17C
VALID UNTIL 1855Z
KS OK TX
VCNTY GLD-CDS LINE
NO SGFNT TSTMS RPRTD
LINE TSTMS DVLPG BY 1755Z WILL
MOV EWD 30-35 KT THRU 1855Z
HAIL TO 1 1/2 IN PSBL.
```

```
MKCC WST 221655
CONVECTIVE SIGMET 18C
VALID UNTIL 1855Z
SD NE IA
FROM FSD TO DSM TO GRI TO BFF
TO FSD
AREA TSTMS WITH FEW EMBDD
CELLS MOVG FROM 2725 TOPS 300
FCST TO 1855Z DSPTG AREA WILL
MOV EWD 25 KT.
```

Courtesy of Rick Patterson

Figure 9-64. WST in the header identifies these reports as convective SIGMETs. The designators 17C and 18C indicate they are consecutive issuances for the central U.S. One forecasts a line of thunderstorms with possible hail, and the other forecasts embedded thunderstorms over a large area.

SEVERE WEATHER REPORTS AND FORECASTS

Although much weather gathering activity is concerned with routine reports and forecasts, considerable effort is also devoted to monitoring and reporting severe weather conditions. The National Hurricane Center in Miami, Florida issues hurricane advisories, and the National Severe Storms Forecast Center in Kansas City, Missouri issues special reports and forecasts for other severe weather conditions. These include convective outlooks, and severe weather watch bulletins, AIRMETs, SIGMETs, and convective SIGMETs.

HURRICANE ADVISORY

When a hurricane is located at least 300 nautical miles offshore, but threatens a coast line, a **hurricane advisory (WH)** is issued. The WH gives the location of the storm center, its expected movement, and the maximum winds in and near the storm center. It does not contain specific ceilings, visibility, and weather hazards. As needed, those details will be reported in Area Forecasts, Terminal Aerodrome Forecasts, and in-flight advisories. [Figure 9-65]

Figure 9-65. Hurricane Bonnie, shown in this Space Shuttle photograph, never reached landfall. Even as a category 1 hurricane, Bonnie likely would have been reported in a WH and its effects would have been evident on the eastern seaboard.

Courtesy of NASA

CONVECTIVE OUTLOOK

The **convective outlook (AC)** is a national forecast of thunderstorm activity covering two 24-hour periods: Day 1 and Day 2. AC's describe areas in which there is a slight, moderate, or high risk of severe thunderstorms, as well as areas of general thunderstorm activity. Severe thunderstorm criteria include surface winds of 50 knots or higher, hail $3/4$ inch in diameter or greater, and tornadoes. The textual AC forecast is part of the Convective Outlook chart, which is a graphic depiction of forecast convective activity.

 A convective outlook describes prospects for an area coverage of both severe and general thunderstorms during the following 48-hour period.

SEVERE WEATHER WATCH BULLETIN

A **severe weather watch bulletin (WW)** defines areas of possible severe thunderstorms or tornadoes. WWs are issued on an unscheduled basis and are updated as required. Because severe weather forecasts and reports might affect the general public as well as pilots, they are widely disseminated through all available media. When it becomes evident that no severe weather will develop or that storms have subsided, cancellation bulletins are issued.

In order to alert forecasters and weather briefers that a severe weather watch bulletin is being issued, a preliminary message, called an **alert severe weather watch (AWW)** is sent. Each AWW is numbered sequentially beginning with the first of January each year. [Figure 9-66]

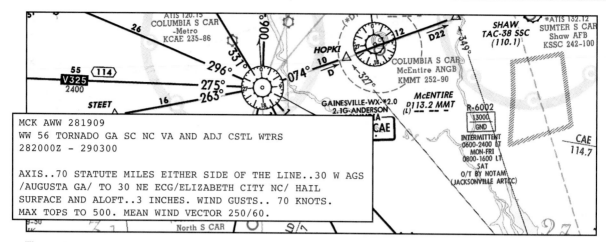

```
MCK AWW 281909
WW 56 TORNADO GA SC NC VA AND ADJ CSTL WTRS
282000Z - 290300

AXIS..70 STATUTE MILES EITHER SIDE OF THE LINE..30 W AGS
/AUGUSTA GA/ TO 30 NE ECG/ELIZABETH CITY NC/ HAIL
SURFACE AND ALOFT..3 INCHES. WIND GUSTS.. 70 KNOTS.
MAX TOPS TO 500. MEAN WIND VECTOR 250/60.
```

Figure 9-66. AWW in the header identifies this report as a severe weather forecast alert. This message warns of possible tornado activity, large hail, and winds in excess of 60 miles per hour. The watch area is defined by a line from a point 30 miles west of Augusta, Georgia to a point 30 miles northeast of Elizabeth City, North Carolina. A detailed severe weather watch bulletin (WW) immediately follows the alert message.

FAA Severe weather watch bulletins are issued only when required.

Tornado Myths

Many myths about tornadoes have been promoted as fact. One such misconception is that you should open the windows in your house to equalize the pressure difference as the storm approaches. In fact, your windows will probably get broken anyway because the winds in the walls of the vortex can reach 100 to 200 miles per hour. In addition, inside the tornado is a barrage of boards, stones, tree limbs, and anything else that the winds can move through the air.

Given the aerodynamics of a house, it is unlikely that open windows would allow the strong winds of a tornado to pass through the house and leave it undamaged. In reality the open windows allow the air to exert pressures on the structure from the inside, blowing it up like a balloon. The best thing for you to do is to leave the windows alone and move to the basement or other shelter as quickly as possible.

SUMMARY CHECKLIST

✓ An aviation routine weather report (METAR) is an observation of surface weather written in a standard format that typically contains 10 or more separate elements.

✓ A non-routine aviation weather report (SPECI) is issued when a significant change in one or more of the elements of a METAR has occurred.

✓ Prevailing visibility is the greatest distance an observer can see and identify objects through at least half of the horizon.

✓ Runway visual range (RVR) is based on what a pilot in a moving aircraft should see when looking down the runway. If included in a METAR, RVR is reported following prevailing visibility.

✓ A ceiling is the height above ground level of the lowest layer of clouds aloft that is reported as broken (BKN) or overcast (OVC), or the vertical visibility (VV) into an obscuration.

✓ A radar weather report (SD/ROB) defines general areas of precipitation, particularly thunderstorms. Because their information can be up to 80 minutes old and lacks detail, they should only be used when you cannot obtain other radar information.

✓ The bases and tops of cloud layers, in-flight visibility, icing conditions, wind shear, and turbulence can be included in a pilot weather report (PIREP).

✓ Terminal aerodrome forecasts (TAFs) predict the weather at a specific airport for a 24-hour period of time.

✓ An aviation area forecast (FA) is a good source of information for weather at airports that do not have terminal aerodrome forecasts, as well as for enroute weather.

✓ You can find an estimate of wind direction in relation to true north, wind speed in knots, and the temperature in degrees Celsius for selected altitudes in the winds and temperatures aloft forecast (FD).

✓ AIRMETs, SIGMETs, and convective SIGMETs are textual forecasts that predict the development of potentially hazardous weather. Although these are text products, you can view the affected areas on an interactive map when online.

✓ AIRMETs are issued every six hours for weather phenomena that are of operational interest to all aircraft, but hazardous mainly to light aircraft.

✓ SIGMETs are issued for hazardous weather that affects all aircraft, including severe icing, severe and extreme turbulence, clear air turbulence (CAT), duststorms, sandstorms and volcanic ash.

✓ Convective SIGMETs are issued for hazardous thunderstorm-related weather that affects the safety of all aircraft. They include tornadoes, thunderstorms in lines or over a wide area, embedded thunderstorms, large hail, and 50-knot wind gusts.

✓ A convective outlook (AC) forecasts general thunderstorm activity for the next 48-hour period.

✓ Areas of possible severe thunderstorms or tornadoes are defined by a severe weather watch bulletin (WW).

SECTION C ■ **Printed Reports and Forecasts**

KEY TERMS

Aviation Routine Weather Report (METAR)

Non-Routine (Special) Aviation Weather Report (SPECI)

Prevailing Visibility

Runway Visual Range (RVR)

Ceiling

Radar Weather Report (SD/ROB)

Pilot Weather Report (PIREP)

Terminal Aerodrome Forecast (TAF)

Aviation Area Forecast (FA)

Winds And Temperatures Aloft Forecast (FD)

AIRMET (WA)

SIGMET (WS)

Convective SIGMET (WST)

Hurricane Advisory (WH)

Convective Outlook (AC)

Severe Weather Watch Bulletin (WW)

Alert Severe Weather Watch (AWW)

QUESTIONS

Use the following METAR for Ponca City Municipal Airport (KPNC), to answer questions 1 through 5.

METAR KPNC 161954Z 03015G27KT 2SM -RA BR BKN007 BKN017 OVC030 07/06 A2978 RMK PK WND 06030/51 SLP086 T00670061

1. What are the reported winds?
   A. 03° at 015 knots with gusts from 220° at 7 knots
   B. 300° at 15 knots with gusts at 27 knots
   C. 030° at 15 knots with gusts to 27 knots

2. What is the reported intensity of the rain in Ponca City, Oklahoma?
   A. Moderate
   B. Light
   C. Heavy

3. What is the height of the lowest ceiling at Ponca City Municipal?
   A. 700 feet
   B. 1,700 feet
   C. 3,000 feet

4. What is the actual temperature/dewpoint at Ponca City Municipal Airport?

5. What is the sea level pressure in millibars?

6. True/False. Altitudes given in PIREPs are in hundreds of feet MSL.

7. In a TAF what does the code TEMPO indicate?

Use the following TAF for Dallas Fort Worth International Airport (KDFW), to answer questions 8 through 11.

```
TAF

KDFW AMD 161849Z161918 14015G20KT P6SM VCTS BKN015CB OVC040

    FM2100 17015G20KT P6SM VCTS BKN020CB OVC050

    FM0200 20008KT P6SM BKN012 OVC030

    TEMPO 0206 2SM -RA OVC008

    FM0600 24012KT P6SM BKN012 OVC030 PROB30 0612 -RA

    FM1400 24010KT P6SM SCT020 BKN060
```

8. What is the valid period for the KDFW TAF?
    A. 1900Z to 1800Z the following day
    B. 1600Z to 1900Z the following day
    C. 1600Z to 1800Z the following day

9. What weather conditions are forecast to exist between 0200Z and 0600Z?

10. What does the statement **PROB30 0612 -RA** indicate?
    A. There is a probability of light rain over 30% of the vicinity
    B. There is a 30% probability of light rain during the forecast
    C. There is a 30% probability of light rain occurring between 0600Z and 1200Z

11. True/False. After 1400Z the visibility at KDFW will be less than 6 statute miles.

Use the following area forecast excerpt to answer questions 12 through 15.

```
. . .

SLCC FA 191145

SYNOPSIS AND VFR CLDS/WX

SYNOPSIS VALID UNTIL 200600

CLDS/WX VALID UNTIL 200000 . . . OTLK VALID 200000-200600

ID MT    NV    WY    CO    AZ    NM.

.

SEE AIRMET SIERRA FOR IFR CONDITIONS AND MTN OBSCN.

TSTMS IMPLY PSBL SVRE OR GTR TURBC SVR ICG LLWS

AND IFR CONDS.

NON MSL HTS ARE DENOTED BY AGL OR CIG.

.

ID WY    MT

ERN WY 30 BKNV OVC. SCT SW-. OTLK . . . VFR.

RMDR AREA . . . 60-80 BKN. OCNL SW IN MTNS.

.

CO

WRN PTN 80-120 SCT. 18Z 60-100 BKN. VSBY 4-6 SW-.

OTLK . . . MVFR CIG SW. E OF DVD . . . 15-25 OVC WITH OCNL
CIGS BLO 20 OVC VSBYS BLO 5 R-S-. OTLK . . . MVFR CIG BCMG
VFR BY 02Z.
```

12. What is the outlook for Wyoming?
    A. VFR
    B. IFR
    C. MVFR

13. True/False. In Colorado, the sky condition after 1800Z is forecast to be 6,000 feet to 10,000 feet broken.

14. What are the forecast ceilings east of the divide?

15. What is the outlook for Colorado by 0200Z?
    A. VFR
    B. IFR
    C. MVFR

16. In the winds and temperature aloft forecast at 30,000 feet, how is 751015 decoded?

17. True/False. Weather phenomena that are of operational interest to all aircraft are reported in an AIRMET.

18. Select the weather phenomena that can initiate the issuance of a SIGMET.
    A. Severe icing
    B. Embedded thunderstorms
    C. Hazardous convective weather

19. Convective SIGMETs include information on
    A. thunderstorms, super cells, and tornadoes.
    B. tornadoes, embedded thunderstorms, and lines of thunderstorms.
    C. embedded thunderstorms, severe thunderstorms with hail greater than or equal to 1/2 inch in diameter, and/or wind gusts 50 knots or greater.

SECTION D
Graphic Weather Products

When flight service stations were located at airports, pilots could visit them and view large printouts of weather maps. Now, Lockheed Martin Flight Services provides most aviation weather briefings, and graphic weather products are delivered online to pilots' computers and mobile devices.

A challenge with graphic weather products that are meant for electronic distribution is adapting them to smaller pages and various size screens. The quality of many of these graphics is not sufficient to fully utilize the high-definition displays of current computers and mobile devices. On some fixed-size versions of these graphics, small station symbols are difficult to read, even when they are enlarged to fill the screen. [Figure 9-67].

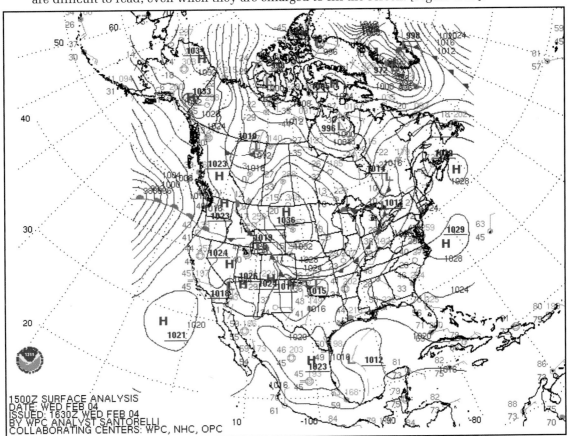

Figure 9-67. Raster-based graphic weather products delivered over the Internet can be small and low-resolution, making it difficult to read the station symbols.

New vector-based charts from the **Aviation Digital Data Service (ADDS)** dramatically improve the usability of these products. To display the information on different size screens and printouts, the amount of chart detail changes according to the zoom level (sometimes referred to as *decluttering*). The charts also use color to communicate information effectively. [Figure 9-68]

ADDS products are delivered side by side with older graphic products. You can find both in the Aviation Weather Center (AWC) at <u>AviationWeather.gov</u>. Some of the newer generation products are labeled with restrictions until proven and accepted. FAA policy regarding which weather products are acceptable for pilot briefings is evolving. As pilot in command, you must decide which weather graphics meet your preflight requirements and comply

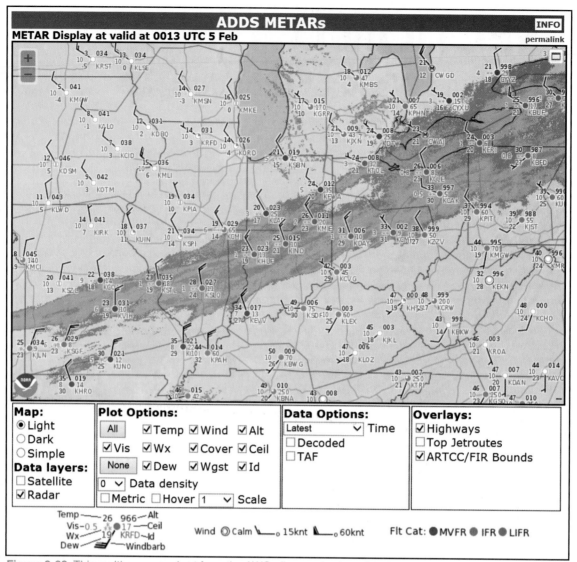

Figure 9-68. This multi-purpose chart from the AWC allows selection of multiple layers of information, showing at a glance storm activity with areas of VFR and IFR conditions

with any restrictions displayed on government-sourced charts. To let the FAA choose weather products for you, obtain your briefing from Flight Service (1800wxBriefing.com).

This section covers the primary graphic weather products that you can expect when obtaining a briefing from either Lockheed Martin Flight Service or from the National Weather Service Aviation Weather Center. "Classic" versions of these charts are typically presented to help you learn the basic weather symbols. However, as the ADDS continues to develop new and improved weather products, and as the FAA approves these products for their required weather briefings, you can expect the appearance and functionality of these weather charts to vary significantly, even within the AWC. You also can expect more products to be updated in real time instead of only at standard issuance intervals. Interactive weather maps can include information typically found on multiple charts covered in this section. You can select chart layers to display the symbols and areas of the weather phenomenon that apply to a specific flight.

GRAPHIC ANALYSES

An analysis is an enhanced depiction of observed data—a map or chart—that can also include interpretation by a weather specialist. Analysis charts show weather that is observed or measured and then plotted graphically for easy interpretation. The most commonly used graphic analyses are the surface analysis chart, weather depiction chart, radar summary chart, and satellite weather pictures.

SURFACE ANALYSIS CHART

The **surface analysis chart**, sometimes referred to as a surface weather map, shows weather conditions as of the valid time shown on the chart. By reviewing this chart, you obtain a picture of atmospheric pressure patterns at the earth's surface. [Figure 9-69] You also can see the locations of high and low pressure systems and associated fronts. [Figure 9-70] This chart is transmitted every three hours.

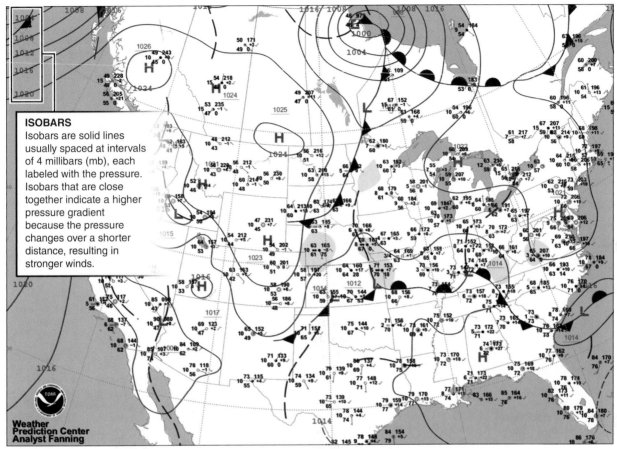

ISOBARS

Isobars are solid lines usually spaced at intervals of 4 millibars (mb), each labeled with the pressure. Isobars that are close together indicate a higher pressure gradient because the pressure changes over a shorter distance, resulting in stronger winds.

Figure 9-69. The surface analysis chart covers the contiguous 48 states and adjacent areas. The next two figures show some common chart symbols. ADDS versions of these charts use standard colors to improve readability.

Figure 9-70. The front symbols used on surface charts are standardized symbols used on other charts as well. When charts are rendered in color, the symbols normally appear in the colors shown here.

SYMBOL	DESCRIPTION
H	High Pressure Center
L	Low Pressure Center
▼▼▼	Cold Front
●●●	Warm Front
●▼●	Stationary Front
●●▼	Occluded Front
—●●—●●—	Squall Line
— — —	Trough
ᘯᘯᘯᘯ	Ridge
ᴖᴖᴖᴖ	Dry Line

FAA When solid lines, called isobars, are close together on the chart, the pressure gradient is greater and wind velocities are stronger.

As shown in figure 9-69, a dashed line on a surface analysis chart indicates a weak pressure gradient.

 A surface analysis chart is a good source for general weather information over a wide area, depicting the actual positions of fronts, pressure patterns, temperatures, dewpoint, wind, weather, and obstructions to vision at the valid time of the chart.

As space permits, surface analysis charts provide **station models** that depict observations collected at airports. Models that appear over water display information gathered by ships, buoys, and offshore oil platforms. [Figure 9-71]

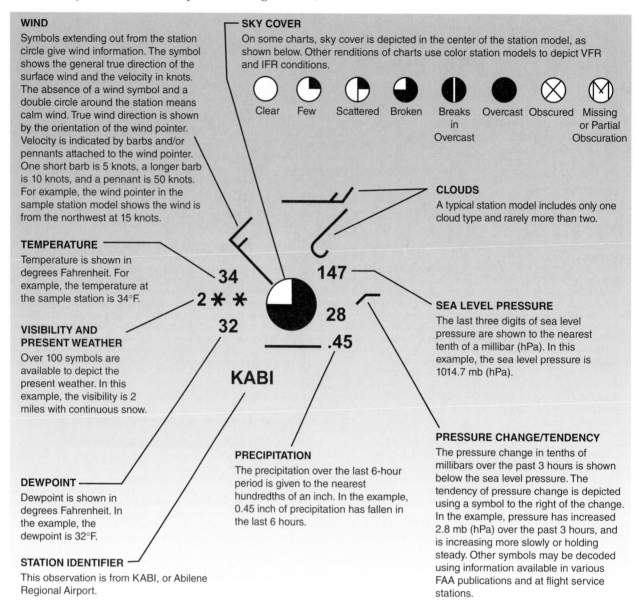

WIND

Symbols extending out from the station circle give wind information. The symbol shows the general true direction of the surface wind and the velocity in knots. The absence of a wind symbol and a double circle around the station means calm wind. True wind direction is shown by the orientation of the wind pointer. Velocity is indicated by barbs and/or pennants attached to the wind pointer. One short barb is 5 knots, a longer barb is 10 knots, and a pennant is 50 knots. For example, the wind pointer in the sample station model shows the wind is from the northwest at 15 knots.

TEMPERATURE

Temperature is shown in degrees Fahrenheit. For example, the temperature at the sample station is 34°F.

VISIBILITY AND PRESENT WEATHER

Over 100 symbols are available to depict the present weather. In this example, the visibility is 2 miles with continuous snow.

DEWPOINT

Dewpoint is shown in degrees Fahrenheit. In the example, the dewpoint is 32°F.

STATION IDENTIFIER

This observation is from KABI, or Abilene Regional Airport.

SKY COVER

On some charts, sky cover is depicted in the center of the station model, as shown below. Other renditions of charts use color station models to depict VFR and IFR conditions.

Clear   Few   Scattered   Broken   Breaks in Overcast   Overcast   Obscured   Missing or Partial Obscuration

CLOUDS

A typical station model includes only one cloud type and rarely more than two.

SEA LEVEL PRESSURE

The last three digits of sea level pressure are shown to the nearest tenth of a millibar (hPa). In this example, the sea level pressure is 1014.7 mb (hPa).

PRECIPITATION

The precipitation over the last 6-hour period is given to the nearest hundredths of an inch. In the example, 0.45 inch of precipitation has fallen in the last 6 hours.

PRESSURE CHANGE/TENDENCY

The pressure change in tenths of millibars over the past 3 hours is shown below the sea level pressure. The tendency of pressure change is depicted using a symbol to the right of the change. In the example, pressure has increased 2.8 mb (hPa) over the past 3 hours, and is increasing more slowly or holding steady. Other symbols may be decoded using information available in various FAA publications and at flight service stations.

Figure 9-71. This sample station model shows information that can be depicted on various weather charts. Refer to the Aviation Weather Center for legends that show the possible cloud and weather symbols.

WEATHER DEPICTION CHART

The **weather depiction chart** provides an overview of VFR and IFR weather conditions. It is an excellent resource to determine general weather conditions during flight planning. Information plotted on the weather depiction chart is derived from aviation routine weather reports (METARs). Like the surface chart, the weather depiction chart is prepared and transmitted by computer every three hours, and is valid at the time of the plotted data. Although you will see some of the same symbols as the surface analysis chart, the station symbols mainly show visibility and ceiling, with other information as space permits. [Figure 9-72]

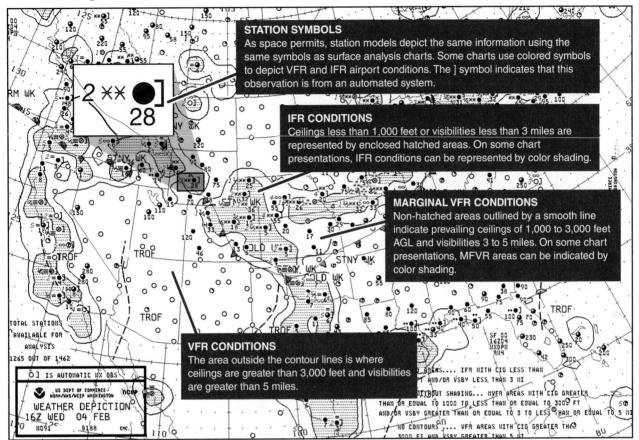

STATION SYMBOLS
As space permits, station models depict the same information using the same symbols as surface analysis charts. Some charts use colored symbols to depict VFR and IFR airport conditions. The] symbol indicates that this observation is from an automated system.

IFR CONDITIONS
Ceilings less than 1,000 feet or visibilities less than 3 miles are represented by enclosed hatched areas. On some chart presentations, IFR conditions can be represented by color shading.

MARGINAL VFR CONDITIONS
Non-hatched areas outlined by a smooth line indicate prevailing ceilings of 1,000 to 3,000 feet AGL and visibilities 3 to 5 miles. On some chart presentations, MFVR areas can be indicated by color shading.

VFR CONDITIONS
The area outside the contour lines is where ceilings are greater than 3,000 feet and visibilities are greater than 5 miles.

Figure 9-72. The weather depiction chart provides a big picture view of areas of non-VFR weather. However, enroute conditions might vary from the depicted conditions because of variations in terrain or weather between reporting stations.

 A ( ]) plotted to the right of a station circle on the weather depiction chart means the station is an automated observation location.

 As shown in figure 9-72, when total sky cover is FEW or scattered, the height shown on the weather depiction chart is the base of the lowest layer.

 The weather depiction chart provides a graphic display of VFR and IFR weather, as well as the type of precipitation. See figure 9-72.

RADAR SUMMARY CHART

The **radar summary chart** is a computer-generated mosaic of radar echo intensity contours issued hourly and based on radar weather reports. Radar weather information is gathered by special weather radar systems that transmit pulses of radar energy from a rotating antenna. Precipitation reflects the pulses back to the antenna, producing "echoes" that are presented on a radar display that shows the strength and location of the radar return. The radar summary chart uses this data to depict the location, size, shape, and intensity of precipitation, as well as the direction of cell movement. In addition, the chart shows lines and cells of hazardous thunderstorms as well as heights of the tops and bases of precipitation areas. [Figure 9-73]

Although the radar summary chart is a valuable preflight planning tool, it has certain limitations. Because radar only detects precipitation, either in frozen or liquid form, it does not detect all cloud formations. For instance, fog is not displayed, and actual cloud tops might

SECTION D ■ **Graphic Weather Products**

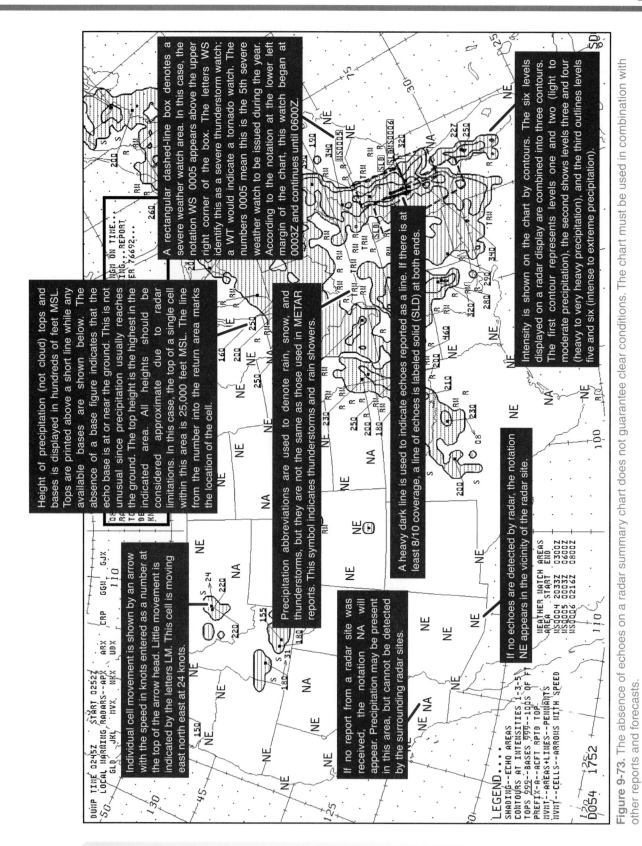

A rectangular dashed-line box denotes a severe weather watch area. In this case, the notation WS 0005 appears above the upper right corner of the box. The letters WS identify this as a severe thunderstorm watch; a WT would indicate a tornado watch. The numbers 0005 mean this is the 5th severe weather watch to be issued during the year. According to the notation at the lower left margin of the chart, this watch began at 0003Z and continues until 0600Z.

Height of precipitation (not cloud) tops and bases is displayed in hundreds of feet MSL. Tops are printed above a short line while any available bases are shown below. The absence of a base figure indicates that the echo base is at or near the ground. This is not unusual since precipitation usually reaches the ground. The top height is the highest in the indicated area. All heights should be considered approximate due to radar limitations. In this case, the top of a single cell within this area is 25,000 feet MSL. The line from the number into the return area marks the location of the cell.

Intensity is shown on the chart by contours. The six levels displayed on a radar display are combined into three contours. The first contour represents levels one and two (light to moderate precipitation), the second shows levels three and four (heavy to very heavy precipitation), and the third outlines levels five and six (intense to extreme precipitation).

A heavy dark line is used to indicate echoes reported as a line. If there is at least 8/10 coverage, a line of echoes is labeled solid (SLD) at both ends.

Precipitation abbreviations are used to denote rain, snow, and thunderstorms, but they are not the same as those used in METAR reports. This symbol indicates thunderstorms and rain showers.

Individual cell movement is shown by an arrow with the speed in knots entered as a number at the top of the arrow head. Little movement is indicated by the letters LM. This cell is moving east north east at 24 knots.

If no report from a radar site was received, the notation NA will appear. Precipitation may be present in this area, but cannot be detected by the surrounding radar sites.

If no echoes are detected by radar, the notation NE appears in the vicinity of the radar site.

The absence of echoes on a radar summary chart does not guarantee clear conditions. The chart must be used in combination with other reports and forecasts.

Figure 9-73. The absence of echoes on a radar summary chart does not guarantee clear conditions. The chart must be used in combination with other reports and forecasts.

 Radar summary charts are the only weather charts that show lines and cells of thunderstorms. You can also determine the tops and bases of the echoes, the intensity of the precipitation, and the echo movement. See figure 9-73.

 A radar summary chart is most effective when used in combination with other charts, reports, and forecasts.

be higher than the precipitation returns indicate. Also, keep in mind that the radar summary chart is an observation of conditions that existed at the valid time. Because thunderstorms develop rapidly, examine other weather sources for current and forecast conditions that might affect your flight. [Figure 9-74]

Figure 9-74. Thunderstorms can develop quickly, and therefore might not be depicted on a radar summary chart.

Courtesy of George McCray Jr.

Radar data is typically presented in a **composite radar image**, a computer-generated presentation that combines the echoes from multiple radar sites. The composite image overcomes limitations of single sites, which cannot see through mountains or storms.

SATELLITE WEATHER PICTURES

Some of the most recognizable weather products come from satellites. Specialized weather satellites not only generate photos, but also record temperatures, humidities, wind speeds, and water vapor locations. Two types of images are available from weather satellites — visible and infrared (IR). Visible pictures are used primarily to determine the presence of clouds as well as the cloud shape and texture. IR photos depict the heat radiation emitted by the various cloud tops and the earth's surface. The difference in temperature between clouds can be used to determine cloud height. For example, because cold temperatures show up as light gray or white, the brightest white areas on an IR satellite photo depict the highest clouds. Both types of photos are retransmitted every 30 minutes except for nighttime when photos using visible light are not available. [Figure 9-75]

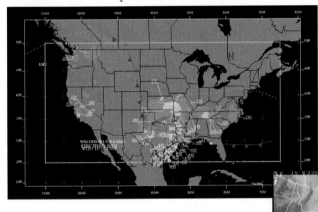

Figure 9-75. When a composite radar image and an infrared photo of the same area are viewed together they show the extent of the cloud cover that you can expect.

SECTION D ■ **Graphic Weather Products**

What's going on out there?

Satellite imaging is changing the way we look at the world. The photographs from the earliest weather satellites were rarely seen by the public, but now the weather segment of your local evening news would not be complete without a loop of the day's satellite pictures. A number of internet resources allow you to zoom in to your neighborhood or get a birds-eye view of your local airport.

If you need photos for a specific date or time, there are commercial services that offer low-cost, high-resolution satellite images that can be delivered directly to your personal computer or mobile device. Commercial satellite images typically have a resolution of a meter or less, which means that each pixel of the image represents about 39 inches or less on the surface of the earth.

Though this type of surface imaging will not completely replace aerial photography, in many situations it can be of great value for planning or research. In the past, the primary use of detailed satellite imagery was to gather military intelligence, but wide-ranging applications have developed in meteorology, agriculture, water use, geology, archaeology, urban planning, oceanography, forestry, environmental conservation, and education. In addition to visible light, images are collected in other wavelengths to provide a more detailed understanding of surface conditions and processes.

Even though sending images of our planet from spacecraft is not a new technology, continuing advancements will improve the quality and availability of images, prompting additional new uses and applications.

CONSTANT PRESSURE ANALYSIS CHART

The **constant pressure analysis chart** is an upper air weather map that is referenced to a specific pressure level. The use of pressure levels is suitable for high-altitude weather analysis because pilots use pressure altitude rather than true altitude when operating above 18,000 feet MSL. In addition, the radiosonde balloons that collect this data report pressure instead of altitude. The metric equivalent of a millibar is a hectoPascal (1 mb = 1 hPa), so the abbreviation mb/hPa is commonly used to label the pressure levels.

 For flight planning purposes, constant pressure analysis charts provide a very good resource for observed winds, temperatures, and temperature/dewpoint spread along a route of flight.

The chart is issued twice daily, with data from 1200Z and 0000Z for each of six pressure altitude levels. These pressure levels correspond to approximate altitudes of 5,000, 10,000, 18,000, 30,000, 34,000, and 39,000 feet:

- 850-millibar (5,000 feet MSL)—The general level of clouds associated with bad weather. Use this chart for forecasting thunderstorms, rain, snow, overcast, and heavy cloudiness.

- 700-millibar (10,000 feet MSL)—Shows wind conditions associated with heavy clouds and rain, but only well-developed fronts extend to this level.

- 500-millibar (18,000 feet MSL)—Represents average troposphere conditions. This chart is useful in determining average wind and temperature conditions for long-range flights at or near FL180.

- 300-millibar (30,000 feet MSL), 250-millibar (34,000 feet MSL), and 200-millibar (39,000 feet MSL)—The charts for these pressure levels show conditions in the upper atmosphere that are significant to high-altitude flight.

Constant pressure charts depict highs, lows, troughs, and ridges aloft with height contour patterns that resemble isobars on a surface map. They provide important information on humidity and stability and indications of general flying conditions. Fronts are depicted at the pressure levels to which they extend—mostly on the 850-millibar and 700-millibar charts. **Isotherms**—lines of equal temperature—show the horizontal temperature variations at the chart's level. **Isotachs**—lines of equal wind velocity—are drawn only for the 300-, 250-, and 200-millibar charts. Regions of high wind speeds are highlighted by alternate bands of shading and no-shading at 40-knot intervals beginning at 70 knots. [Figure 9-76]

FAA Shaded bands on a constant pressure analysis chart indicate wind speeds above 70 knots.

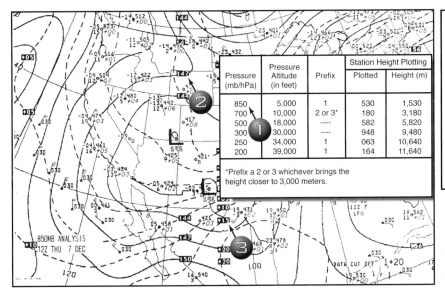

Pressure (mb/hPa)	Pressure Altitude (in feet)	Prefix	Station Height Plotting	
			Plotted	Height (m)
850	5,000	1	530	1,530
700	10,000	2 or 3*	180	3,180
500	18,000	----	582	5,820
300	30,000	----	948	9,480
250	34,000	1	063	10,640
200	39,000	1	164	11,640

*Prefix a 2 or 3 whichever brings the height closer to 3,000 meters.

1. The 850-mb/hPa chart represents a pressure altitude of 5,000 feet.
2. The solid line with the notation 147 means the height of the 850-millibar level at all points along this line is 1,470 meters (4,823 feet).
3. An isotherm labeled +15 indicates a line of equal temperature at +15°C.

Figure 9-76. Constant pressure charts help meteorologists and pilots understand weather patterns at higher altitudes.

The Profiler

What is a wind profiler? A wind profiler is a ground-based, remote sensing Doppler radar that is used to observe winds aloft. The system is designed to operate in nearly all weather conditions and without human intervention, providing nearly continuous measurements of vertical wind structure up to 53,000 feet in the atmosphere.

Starting in the early 1930s upper air measurements were taken with remote telemetry equipment that was carried aloft by a helium balloon. Radiosondes are still in use today. Even though wind profilers are being used on a limited basis at select locations, they represent the first major advance in quantitative upper air measurements since the radiosonde was introduced.

Unlike the twice per day labor intensive radio soundings, wind profilers provide continuous measurements automatically. The information gathered by the profiler aids in the forecast of severe storms, tornadoes, downbursts, and flash floods. For the weather researcher, the data is increasing the understanding of the origin and evolution of regional weather events. With the increase in weather knowledge and computer modeling of the atmosphere aloft, forecasters are able to make accurate weather forecasts at the surface. When used with other existing observational systems, wind profilers help provide the essential information needed to improve weather services.

Constant pressure charts allow for deeper analysis by pilots trained to interpret high-altitude weather. They can include station symbols that provide specific information for various points along a route. [Figure 9-77]

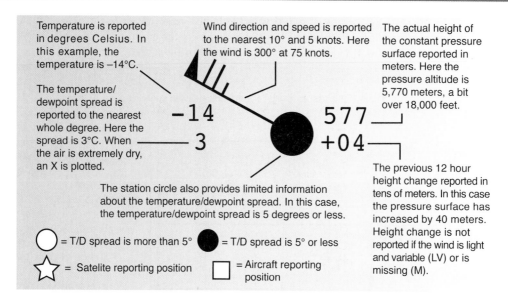

Temperature is reported in degrees Celsius. In this example, the temperature is −14°C.

The temperature/dewpoint spread is reported to the nearest whole degree. Here the spread is 3°C. When the air is extremely dry, an X is plotted.

Wind direction and speed is reported to the nearest 10° and 5 knots. Here the wind is 300° at 75 knots.

The actual height of the constant pressure surface reported in meters. Here the pressure altitude is 5,770 meters, a bit over 18,000 feet.

The station circle also provides limited information about the temperature/dewpoint spread. In this case, the temperature/dewpoint spread is 5 degrees or less.

The previous 12 hour height change reported in tens of meters. In this case the pressure surface has increased by 40 meters. Height change is not reported if the wind is light and variable (LV) or is missing (M).

○ = T/D spread is more than 5°   ● = T/D spread is 5° or less

☆ = Satellite reporting position   ☐ = Aircraft reporting position

Fiigure 9-77. This is a sample station model with information from a radiosonde as it could be plotted on a constant pressure analysis chart.

 The station model as depicted in figure 9-77 provides wind direction and speed, temperature, and dewpoint information in a graphic format.

GRAPHIC FORECASTS

A forecast is a prediction of the development and movement of weather phenomena based on meteorological observations and mathematical models. Some of the charts that present forecasts graphically are U.S. significant weather (SigWx) prognostic charts, severe weather outlook charts, and forecast winds and temperatures aloft charts.

SIGNIFICANT WEATHER (SIGWX) PROGNOSTIC CHARTS

Prognostic (prog) charts are a primary U.S. Government graphic aviation forecast product. They are available in the Aviation Weather Center (AWC) for surface, low-level, mid-level, and high-level forecasts in time frames from 6 to 48 hours, as well as surface extended forecasts up to 7 days.

Surface prog charts forecast surface pressure systems, fronts and precipitation. Short range surface progs cover a two day period, but you can obtain charts that provide up to 7 days of outlook forecasts. To gain access to surface progs, go to the AWC website and look under Forecasts for Prog Charts. Select *Surface* and then select the time frame. [Figure 9-78]

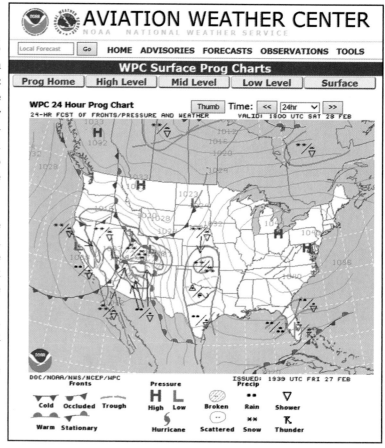

Figure 9-78. You can obtain various prog charts in the Aviation Weather Center under Forecasts.

You can also view low, mid, and high level progs for the next 24 hours. You can choose from among the four issuance times to compare the forecasts for various time periods.

U.S. LOW-LEVEL SIGNIFICANT WEATHER PROGNOSTIC CHART

The four panel presentation of the **U.S. low-level significant weather prognostic chart** enables easy comparison of different times—the 12-hour forecasts are on the left and the 24-hour forecasts are on the right. The bottom two charts forecast surface weather and the top two charts forecast the low-level weather up to the 400-millibar pressure level (24,000 feet). Prog charts are designed to help you plan flights to avoid areas of low visibilities and ceilings as well as areas where turbulence and icing might exist. [Figure 9-79]

 A low-level significant weather prognostic chart depicts weather conditions forecast to exist at the specific valid time, in the future.

 The upper limit of the low-level significant weather prognostic chart is 400-millibars, which is about 24,000 feet MSL.

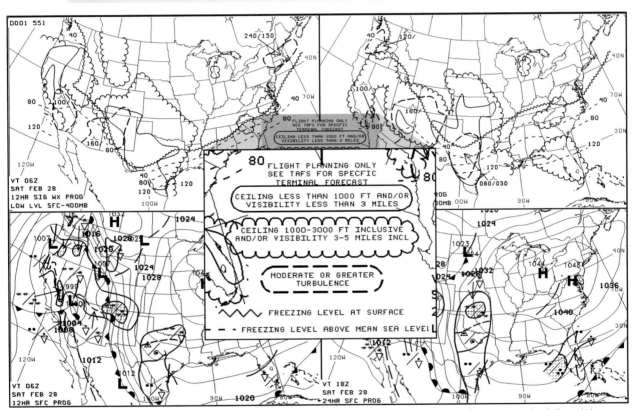

Figure 9-79. The four-panel low-level prog chart enables easy comparison of the 12-hour forecast on the left and the 24-hour forecast on the right. Legend information is included on the chart.

 As shown in figure 9-79, symbols used to define areas of IFR, MVFR, VFR, and moderate or greater turbulence, as well as the forecast altitude of the freezing level, are depicted in the legend between the two upper panels of the low-level significant weather prog chart.

SIGNIFICANT WEATHER (SIGWX) PANELS

The upper panels show areas of nonconvective turbulence and freezing levels as well as IFR and marginal VFR (MVFR) weather. Areas of forecast nonconvective moderate or greater turbulence are shown using a heavy dashed contour line. Numbers within these areas give the height of the turbulence in hundreds of feet MSL. Figures below a line show the expected base, and figures above a line represent the top of the turbulence. Because moderate or greater turbulence is assumed to exist near thunderstorms, turbulence symbols are not plotted in thunderstorm areas.

Forecast **freezing levels** are also depicted on the SigWx panels. Freezing level height contours for the highest freezing level are drawn at 4,000-foot intervals with dashed lines. These contours are labeled in hundreds of feet MSL. A zigzag line labeled SFC shows where the freezing level is at the surface.

SURFACE PROG PANELS

The two lower panels are the surface prog panels. They contain standard symbols for fronts and pressure centers. In addition, areas of precipitation, as well as thunderstorms, are surrounded by a solid line. The area inside the line is unshaded if the forecast precipitation is intermittent (periodic and patchy), and shaded if precipitation is expected to be continuous (a dominant and widespread event). Symbols within or adjacent to the outlined area indicate the types of precipitation. A mixture of two precipitation types is shown as two symbols separated by a slash. [Figure 9-80]

Symbol	Meaning	Symbol	Meaning	Symbol	Meaning
(snow symbols)	Intermittent snow covering half or less of the area.	(rain shower symbol)	Rain Shower	(severe turbulence symbol)	Severe Turbulence
(rain shower symbol)	Intermittent rain showers covering half or less of the area.	(snow shower symbol)	Snow Shower	(moderate icing symbol)	Moderate Icing
(continuous rain symbol)	Continuous rain covering more than half of the area.	(thunderstorm symbol)	Thunderstorms	(severe icing symbol)	Severe Icing
(rain showers/thunderstorms symbol)	Continuous rain showers and thunderstorms covering more than half of the area.	(freezing rain symbol)	Freezing Rain	(rain symbol)	Rain
		(tropical storm symbol)	Tropical Storm	(snow symbol)	Snow
		(hurricane symbol)	Hurricane (Typhoon)	(drizzle symbol)	Drizzle
		(moderate turbulence symbol)	Moderate Turbulence		

Figure 9-80. An area that is expected to have precipitation is enclosed by a solid line, with shading inside the line if the precipitation is expected to be continuous. Some of the symbols that show the forms and types of precipitation are shown here—a complete listing is available in the Aviation Weather Center.

 Low-level significant weather prog charts graphically depict showery precipitation, thunderstorms, rain showers, and when appropriate, tropical storms. Turbulence is depicted on the low-level significant weather prog chart with a peaked symbol. Underneath the symbol, figures indicate the top and base of the turbulence. See figure 9-80.

MID AND HIGH-LEVEL SIGWX PROG CHARTS

The mid and high level SigWx charts cover similar weather phenomena using similar symbology. The mid SigWx chart covers altitudes from 10,000 feet MSL to FL 450. The **high-level significant weather prog chart** covers altitudes from FL 250 to FL 630. It presents a forecast of thunderstorms, tropical cyclones, squall lines, moderate or greater turbulence, widespread duststorms and sandstorms, tropopause heights, the location of the jet streams, and volcanic activity. [Figure 9-81]

 In figure 9-81, the areas enclosed in scalloped lines indicate that you can expect cumulonimbus clouds (CBs), icing, and moderate or greater turbulence.

 A high-level significant weather prognostic chart forecasts clear air turbulence, tropopause height, sky coverage, embedded thunderstorms, and jet stream velocities between 24,000 feet MSL and 63,000 feet MSL. See figure 9-81.

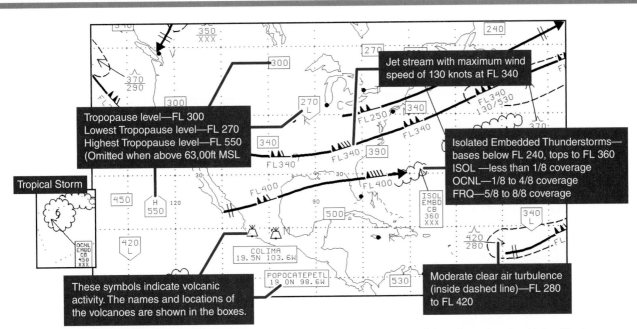

Jet stream with maximum wind speed of 130 knots at FL 340

Tropopause level—FL 300
Lowest Tropopause level—FL 270
Highest Tropopause level—FL 550
(Omitted when above 63,00ft MSL

Isolated Embedded Thunderstorms—
bases below FL 240, tops to FL 360
ISOL —less than 1/8 coverage
OCNL—1/8 to 4/8 coverage
FRQ—5/8 to 8/8 coverage

Tropical Storm

These symbols indicate volcanic activity. The names and locations of the volcanoes are shown in the boxes.

Moderate clear air turbulence (inside dashed line)—FL 280 to FL 420

Figure 9-81. The mid- and high-level significant prog charts are useful to pilots planning high-altitude flights over long distances.

CONVECTIVE OUTLOOK CHART

The **convective outlook chart** forecasts thunderstorm activity. The Day 1 panel depicts the outlook for general and severe thunderstorm activity. It is issued five times daily, with the first issuance valid beginning at 1200Z and all five issuances valid until 1200Z the following day. [Figure 9-82] The Day 2 panel also outlines areas of general and severe storms and the Day 3 panel outlines only the areas of severe thunderstorms. Lines with arrowheads depict the locations of forecast thunderstorm activity. When facing in the direction of the arrow, thunderstorms are to the right of the line. Abbreviations within the outlined area indicate the probability of well-organized severe thunderstorms. The abbreviations SLGT and MRGL indicate low coverage during the forecast period. Higher risk categories are moderate (MDT), enhanced (ENH), and high (HIGH).

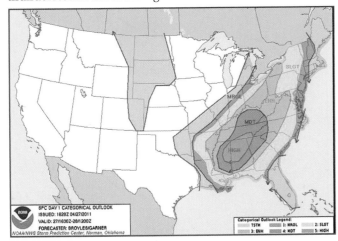

Figure 9-82. This convective outlook chart displays all six levels of forecast thunderstorm activity from general (light green) to high probability of severe storms (magenta).

 The convective outlook chart is used primarily for advance planning and provides a three day outlook for general and severe thunderstorm activity.

 A line with an arrowhead on the convective outlook chart depicts forecast general thunderstorm activity. When facing in the direction of the arrow, thunderstorm activity is expected to the right of the line. SLGT is used to denote slight risk and MDT is used to denote moderate risk on the outlook.

NATIONAL CONVECTIVE WEATHER FORECAST

The **national convective weather forecast (NCWF)** is a near real-time, high resolution display of current and one-hour extrapolated forecasts of selected hazardous convective conditions for the contiguous United States. Based on WSR-88D weather radar, the NCWF

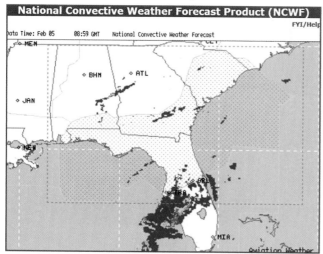

also provides echo intensity (four levels), cloud tops, lightning frequency, and direction of cell movement. You can use the NCWF together with convective SIGMETs to gain situational awareness about current and upcoming convective weather hazards. The NCWF is intended for general aviation, aircraft dispatchers, and traffic management units, and is updated every five minutes. [Figure 9-83]

Figure 9-83. The national convective weather forecast (NCWF), which provides nearly real-time and predictive thunderstorm conditions, is available in the Aviation Weather Center.

FORECAST WINDS AND TEMPERATURES ALOFT

Graphic winds and temperatures aloft are presented on an interactive map in the Aviation Weather Center (AviationWeather.gov) and through chart overlays in the Lockheed Martin Flight Services Portal (1800WxBrief.com). You select the altitude and time frame for your forecast (6, 12, or 24 hours) and the system draws wind direction arrows that depict the direction at each station. Pennants and barbs at the end of each arrow depict the forecast

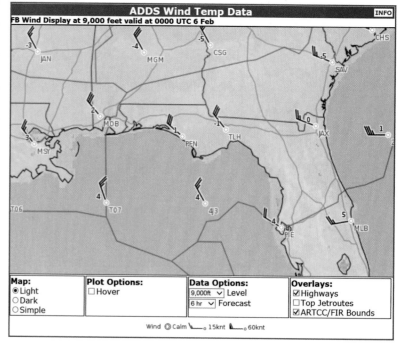

wind speed as on the other charts, and the temperature in degrees Celsius. [Figure 9-84] When calm winds are expected, the station circle has no arrow. If the altitude you have selected is less than 1,500 feet above the station, the station circle is not shown. Forecast temperatures for altitudes more than 2,500 feet above the station elevation are shown as degrees Celsius near each station circle.

Figure 9-84. The ADDS winds and temperatures aloft presentation allows the pilot to choose the altitude and forecast period on an interactive chart.

CURRENT AND FORECAST ICING PRODUCTS

The **current icing product (CIP)** combines sensor and numerical weather prediction (NWP) model data to provide an hourly three-dimensional picture of icing risks. The **forecast icing product (FIP)**, using the same graphic depiction, uses an NWP model to predict the probability of icing in the future in a given area. The icing severity product depicts the expected severity of ice if it does occur. [Figure 9-85]

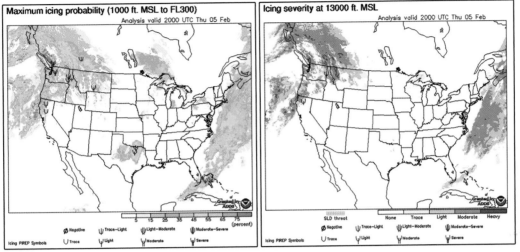

Figure 9-85. Although the AWC icing products do not detect the actual presence of ice, they use numerical models to predict the probability and severity of icing.

CEILING AND VISIBILITY ANALYSIS

The ceiling and visibility analysis (CVA) provides a real-time display of current observed and estimated ceiling and visibility across the continental United States. The CVA can help VFR-only pilots avoid IFR conditions, and is updated every 5 minutes. [Figure 9-86]

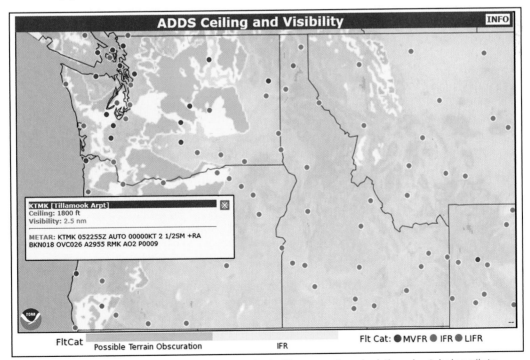

Figure 9-86. The AWC ceiling and visibility analysis, like a weather depiction chart, helps pilots avoid areas of IFR conditions.

SECTION D ■ **Graphic Weather Products**

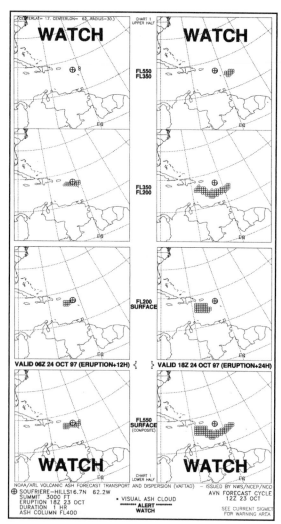

VOLCANIC ASH FORECAST AND DISPERSION CHART

As volcanic eruptions are reported, a **volcanic ash forecast transport and dispersion chart (VAFTAD)** is created. The chart is developed, with input from National Centers for Environmental Prediction (NCEP), using a model that focuses on hazards to aircraft flight operations with emphasis on the ash cloud location. The concentration of volcanic ash is forecast over 6- and 12-hour time intervals, beginning 6 hours following the eruption. The VAFTAD uses four panels in a column for each valid time period. The top three panels in a column reflect the ash location and relative concentrations for an atmospheric layer. The bottom panel in a column shows the total ash concentrations from the surface up to 55,000 feet (FL 550). [Figure 9-87] The VAFTAD chart is designed specifically for flight planning purposes only; it is not intended to take the place of SIGMETs regarding volcanic eruptions and ash.

Figure 9-87. This VAFTAD shows the panels associated with the 12- and 24-hour valid times.

SUMMARY CHECKLIST

✓ With new-generation chart products from the Aviation Digital Data Service (ADDS) that pilots can view in the Aviation Weather Center (AWC), graphic weather products are evolving, becoming more interactive, and changing in appearance.

✓ ADDS products are being delivered side-by-side with older raster graphic products. You must choose your products carefully from the AWC or obtain your briefing from Flight Service.

✓ To get a picture of atmospheric pressure patterns at the earth's surface, you can refer to the surface analysis chart.

✓ The surface analysis chart provides information obtained from surface weather observations from a large number of reporting points throughout the United States and over coastal waters.

✓ The weather depiction chart is very useful during the preflight planning process for determining general weather conditions and areas of IFR and MVFR weather.

✓ The radar summary chart shows the location, size, shape, and intensity of areas of precipitation, as well as the direction of individual cell movement. Although the chart plots the location of lines and cells of hazardous thunderstorms, it does not show cloud formations.

✓ Constant pressure analysis charts are upper air weather maps referenced to various pressure levels—850, 700, 500, 300, 250, and 200 millibars. They are useful for quickly determining winds and temperatures aloft at your approximate altitude over your route.

✓ Both visible and infrared (IR) imagery are available from weather satellites. The visible picture is used generally to indicate the presence of clouds as well as the cloud shape and texture. IR photos, which depict the heat radiation emitted by the various cloud tops and the earth's surface, can be used to determine cloud height.

✓ Significant weather prognostic (prog) charts are available in the Aviation Weather Center (AWC) for surface, low-level, mid-level, and high-level forecasts.

✓ The surface prog charts forecast surface pressure systems, fronts and precipitation. They use standard symbols for fronts and pressure centers.

✓ The SigWx low, mid, and high-level prog charts show areas of nonconvective turbulence, freezing levels, and areas of IFR, MVFR, and VFR weather.

✓ The convective outlook charts forecast thunderstorm activity over the next 72 hours. The day 1 chart depicts the outlook for general thunderstorm activity and severe thunderstorms for the first 24-hour period beginning at 1200Z, and the day 2 chart provides a forecast for the second 24-hour period. The day 3 chart covers the third 24-hour period, but only predicts severe thunderstorm activity.

✓ The national convective weather forecast (NCWF) is a near real-time, high resolution display of current and one-hour extrapolated forecasts of selected hazardous convective conditions for the contiguous United States.

✓ Graphic winds and temperatures aloft are presented on an interactive map and through chart overlays. You select the altitude and time frame for your forecast and the system draws wind direction arrows that depict the direction and velocity at each station, and the temperature in degrees Celsius.

✓ The current and forecast icing products combine sensor and numerical weather prediction (NWP) model data to provide an hourly three-dimensional picture of icing risks, and to predict the probability of icing in the future in a given area.

✓ The ceiling and visibility analysis is an interactive graphic weather map that provides a real-time analysis of current observed and estimated ceiling and visibility across the continental United States to help VFR-only pilots avoid IFR conditions.

✓ The volcanic ash forecast transport and dispersion chart (VAFTAD) forecasts the concentration of volcanic ash over 6- and 12-hour time intervals, beginning 6 hours following a volcanic eruption. The VAFTAD chart is not intended to take the place of SIGMETs regarding volcanic eruptions; it is designed specifically for flight planning purposes.

SECTION D ■ **Graphic Weather Products**

SECTION D ■ Graphic Weather Products

KEY TERMS

Aviation Digital Data Service (ADDS)

Surface Analysis Chart

Station Model

Weather Depiction Chart

Radar Summary Chart

Composite Radar Image

Constant Pressure Analysis Chart

Isotherms

Isotachs

U.S. Low-Level Significant Weather Prognostic Chart

Freezing Levels

High-Level Significant Weather Prog Chart

Convective Outlook Chart

National Convective Weather Forecast (NCWF)

Graphic Winds and Temperatures Aloft

Current Icing Product (CIP) and Forecast Icing Product (FIP)

Volcanic Ash Forecast Transport And Dispersion Chart (VAFTAD)

QUESTIONS

1. A surface analysis chart shows
    A. Forecast surface winds and temperatures at selected reporting stations.
    B. Fronts and pressure systems.
    C. Areas of VFR, IFR, and MVFR.

2. What ceiling and visibility can you expect to encounter in the shaded areas of a weather depiction chart?

3. Primarily, what can be ascertained by examining visible and infrared satellite weather pictures?

4. On the following excerpt from the low-level surface prog chart, what does the symbol in southern California indicate?

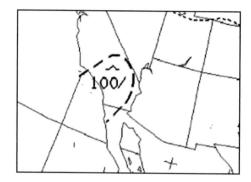

5. What information does the ceiling and visibility analysis (CVA) product provide?
    A. A display of current observed and estimated ceiling and visibility across the continental United States that is updated every five minutes.
    B. A forecast of ceiling, visibility, and areas of moderate or severe turbulence over the next three hours for VFR pilots.
    C. A computer-generated real-time display with color-coded outlines for areas of VFR, IFR, and MVFR based on automated observations from the past hour.

Use the station model to answer questions 6 through 9.

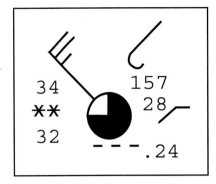

6. What is the wind direction and speed?

7. True/False. This station is reporting overcast skies.

8. What is the present weather?
   A. Light snow
   B. Continuous snow
   C. Snow mixed with fog

9. What is the sea level pressure for this station?

10. What is the significance of a bracket shown with a station model on a weather depiction chart?

Use the following weather depiction chart excerpt to answer question 11 through 13.

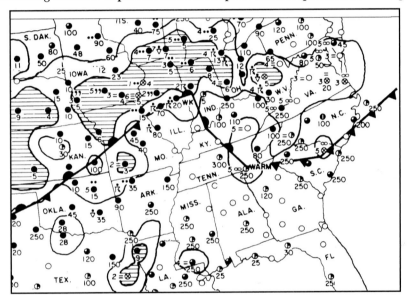

11. What type of weather condition exists over southern Iowa?
    A. IFR
    B. VFR
    C. MVFR

12. A flight from North Carolina to Georgia passes through what type of front?
    A. Cold front
    B. Warm front
    C. Stationary front

13. True/False. Thunderstorms and rain are being reported over northwestern Arkansas.

SECTION D ■ **Graphic Weather Products**

Use the radar summary chart excerpt to answer questions 14 through 16.

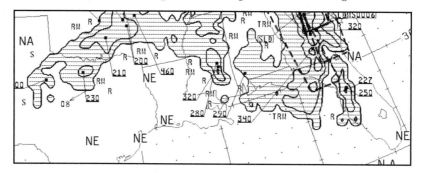

14. What is the direction of movement and speed of the thunderstorm cell in north central Texas?
    A.   The cell is moving west south west at 8 knots.
    B.   The cell is forecast to move to the west at 8 knots.
    C.   The cell is moving south at 230 knots.

15. What is indicated by the 250 in central Florida?

16. What is the meaning of the NE in southwest Louisiana and NA in south central Texas?

17. Although constant pressure charts depict observed temperature, temperature/dew-point spread, wind direction and speed, and the height of a particular pressure surface, the most useful information for general aviation pilots is what?
    A.   Height of the tropopause
    B.   Winds and temperatures aloft
    C.   Location of fronts at the 500 millibar level

18. What is an isotherm?
    A.   A line of equal wind speed
    B.   A line of equal temperature
    C.   International Standard Thermal Unit

Use the accompanying low-level significant weather prognostic chart to answer questions 19 through 21.

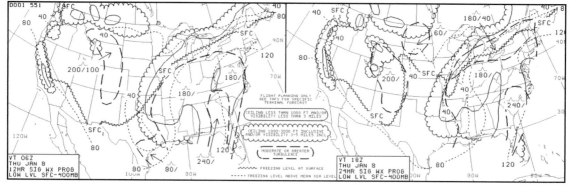

19. The low-level significant weather prognostic chart is for use from the surface up to what altitude?
    A.   10,000 feet
    B.   18,000 feet
    C.   24,000 feet

20. What is the forecast weather over northern Idaho and eastern Washington?
    A.   VFR at 0600Z and IFR at 1800Z
    B.   IFR at 0600Z and IFR at 1800Z
    C.   MVFR at 0600Z and VFR at 1800Z

21. What does the symbol 200/100 in Utah indicate?

Use the following high-level significant prognostic chart to answer question 22 through 25.

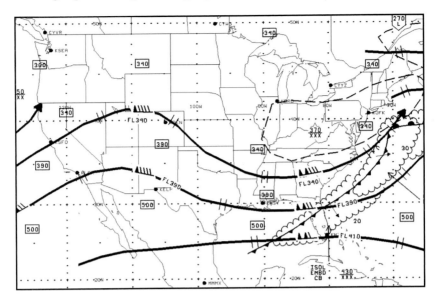

22. What does the symbol over southern Montana indicate?

23. What is the height and speed of the jet stream over New Mexico?
    A. 39,000 feet AGL at 90 knots
    B. 39,000 feet MSL at 90 knots
    C. 39,000 feet MSL at 90 mph

24. True/False. The area in the scalloped line over Florida indicates isolated, embedded thunderstorms with tops at 43,000 feet and bases below 24,000 feet.

25. What conditions are forecast for the area contained within the dashed line over the northeastern states?

26. What chart can you refer to for a forecast of general thunderstorm activity?
    A. Weather depiction chart
    B. Surface analysis chart
    C. Convective outlook chart

SECTION E
Sources of Weather Information

Part of being a safe pilot is keeping up to date on the latest weather developments, and maintaining the ability to adjust your plans. The weather briefing process usually begins several days before your flight, when you look at mass-disseminated weather information and form an initial opinion regarding the feasibility of your flight. As the flight gets closer, you should gather more detailed information about the weather along your route. Then, during your flight, you update your weather information using the various in-flight sources to determine what lies ahead.

PREFLIGHT WEATHER SOURCES

Federal regulations require that a pilot obtain weather reports and forecasts when operating IFR or when operating VFR away from an airport. The FAA's primary preflight weather information source is a centralized facility that replaces its previous network of flight service stations—**Flight Service** provides live telephone briefers, a pilot Internet portal, and a recorded telephone information briefing service. Other preflight weather sources are the Direct User Access Terminal System, the NOAA/NWS Aviation Weather Center, and a variety of commercial vendors.

FLIGHT SERVICE

Flight Service is your primary FAA source of preflight weather information. In Alaska, the FAA maintains and staffs their own flight service stations, but in the Continental United States (CONUS), Hawaii, and Puerto Rico, Lockheed Martin Flight Services provides weather services under an FAA contract. You can obtain a **preflight weather briefing** from Flight Service 24 hours a day by calling the toll free number, 1-800-WX BRIEF.

PREFLIGHT WEATHER BRIEFING

When you call for a briefing in the CONUS, an automated telephone system asks which state you are departing from and then routes your call, workload permitting, to a briefer who specializes in the weather for that area. When you reach the briefer, identify yourself as a pilot and supply the following information: type of flight planned (VFR or IFR), aircraft number or your name, aircraft type, departure airport, route of flight, destination, flight altitude(s), estimated time of departure (ETD), and estimated time enroute (ETE). The briefer can then concentrate on the weather affecting your flight. It helps to save your questions until the end of the briefing, so that the briefer can present the information in a predetermined order and not miss essential information.

Although Flight Service weather briefers do not actually predict the weather, they are specially qualified to translate and interpret reports and forecasts into terms that describe the weather conditions you can expect along your route of flight and at your destination. You can request one of three types of preflight weather briefings — standard, abbreviated, or outlook.

STANDARD BRIEFING

Request a **standard briefing** when you are planning a trip and have not obtained preliminary weather or a previous briefing. This is the most complete weather briefing, and assumes you have no familiarity with the overall weather picture. When you request a standard briefing, the briefer provides information that applies to your proposed flight in a specific sequence. [Figure 9-88]

1. **ADVERSE CONDITIONS** — This includes the type of information that might influence you to alter your proposed route or cancel the flight altogether. Examples include such things as hazardous weather or airport closures.

2. **VFR FLIGHT NOT RECOMMENDED** — If the flight service briefer indicates that VFR flight is not recommended, it means that, in the briefer's judgment, it is doubtful that you can complete the flight under VFR. Although the final decision to conduct the flight rests with you, this advisory should be taken seriously.

3. **SYNOPSIS** — The briefer will provide you with a broad overview of the major weather systems or airmasses that affect the proposed flight.

4. **CURRENT CONDITIONS** — This information is a rundown of existing conditions, including pertinent hourly, pilot, and radar weather reports. Unless you request otherwise, this item is omitted if your proposed departure time is more than two hours in the future.

5. **ENROUTE FORECAST** — The briefer will summarize the forecast conditions along your proposed route in a logical order from departure through descent for landing.

6. **DESTINATION FORECAST** — The briefer will provide the forecast for your destination at your estimated time of arrival (ETA). In addition, any significant changes predicted for an hour before or after your ETA will be included.

7. **WINDS AND TEMPERATURES ALOFT**—You will be given a summary of forecast winds for your route. If necessary, the briefer will interpolate wind direction and speed between levels and stations for your planned cruising altitude(s). Temperature information will be provided on request.

8. **NOTICES TO AIRMEN** — The briefer will supply NOTAM information pertinent to your proposed route of flight. However, information which has already been published in the *Notices to Airmen* publication will only be provided on request.

9. **ATC DELAYS**— You will be advised of any known air traffic control delays that might affect your proposed flight.

10. **REQUEST FOR PIREPS** — The briefer may ask you to file a PIREP if the current conditions would benefit from additional inflight weather reports.

11. **EFAS** — You will be notified of the availability and appropriate frequency for Flight Watch for enroute weather updates.

12. **OTHER INFORMATION** — Upon request, the briefer will provide you with other information such as MOA and MTR activity within 100 n.m. of the flight plan area, ATC services and rules, as well as customs and immigration procedures.

Figure 9-88. The briefer may present the first three items of a standard briefing in any order if the briefer believes it will help describe the conditions more clearly.

ABBREVIATED BRIEFING

When you need only one or two specific items or would like to update weather information from a previous briefing or other weather sources, request an **abbreviated briefing**. Provide the briefer with the source of the prior information including the time you received it, as well as any other pertinent background information. This allows the briefer to limit the conversation to information you did not receive, plus any significant changes in weather conditions. Usually, the sequence of information will follow that of the standard briefing. If you request only one or two items, you still will be advised if adverse conditions are present or forecast.

OUTLOOK BRIEFING

If your proposed departure time is six or more hours in the future, you can request an **outlook briefing**. An outlook briefing provides forecast information that can help you make an initial judgment about the feasibility of your flight. The outlook briefing is designed for planning purposes only; as your departure time draws near, you should request either a standard or abbreviated briefing to obtain current conditions and the latest forecasts.

SECTION E ■ **Sources of Weather Information**

TELEPHONE INFORMATION BRIEFING SERVICE

When calling Flight Service, you can gain access to recorded weather information by selecting from a menu a weather forecast area that covers your route. The system that disseminates this recorded information is called the **telephone information briefing service (TIBS).** It provides continuous recordings of area and route meteorological briefings, airspace procedures, and special aviation-oriented announcements, and can include selected METARs and TAFs. TIBS is a preliminary briefing tool to determine the overall feasibility of a proposed flight, and is not intended to replace a complete briefing from a Flight Service specialist. After you listen to the recorded TIBS information, you can connect with a live briefer if needed.

 The telephone information briefing service (TIBS) provided by Flight Service includes continuous recordings of meteorological and aeronautical information available by telephone.

LOCKHEED MARTIN FLIGHT SERVICES WEB PORTAL

You can obtain a weather briefing online using the web portal at 1800wxBrief.com, or search for *Lockheed Martin Flight Services.* You must register and create a user account to gain access to pilot briefing and flight planning tools. Just like telephone briefings, these web portal briefings are FAA-sanctioned briefings for which official records are kept. You can file and save flight plans and aircraft data, as well as obtain NOTAMs, including TFRs and GPS RAIM data. These briefings are organized to present the forecast weather along your route of flight at your ETA over each weather reporting station, and at your destination. The portal also depicts SIGMETs and AIRMETs and other weather conditions graphically over a map of your route.

The pilot web portal can also send you updates by text or email. By registering for the Adverse Conditions Alerting Service (ACAS), you are notified when a new adverse condition arises after you obtain a briefing or file a flight plan in the web portal. The alerts are specific to your flight, and can include TFRs, NOTAMs for closed airports or runways, AIRMETs, SIGMETs, convective SIGMETs, center weather advisories (CWAs), severe weather watches and warnings, and urgent PIREPs. [Figure 9-89]

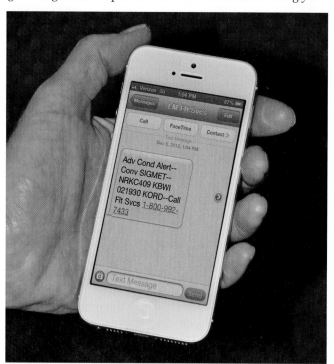

Figure 9-89. ACAS will send you alerts for adverse conditions within 25 NM of your flight plan route corridor.

DIRECT USER ACCESS TERMINAL SYSTEM

The FAA-funded Direct User Access Terminal System (DUAT/DUATS) pioneered the use of a computer as an alternative to calling for a weather briefing and filing a flight plan orally. DUAT and DUATS began operation by providing simple text briefings. Services evolved to include Internet-based graphic weather products. Many of the functions of DUAT/DUATS are also available through the Lockheed Martin Flight Services Web Portal. To learn the current availability of DUAT/DUATS with phone numbers and websites, search the *Aeronautical Information Manual.*

NATIONAL WEATHER SERVICE

Flight Service does not forecast weather, it just disseminates the information to pilots in an FAA-approved briefing. Many pilots prefer obtaining preliminary and supplemental weather information directly from the National Weather Service (NWS). The NWS is an essential part of a number of interrelated agencies that collect, analyze, and distribute weather information. The National Oceanic and Atmospheric Administration (NOAA), part of the Department of Commerce, coordinates U.S. government weather-related activities. Under NOAA, the National Weather Service and National Centers for Environmental Prediction (NCEP), provide weather information directly to pilots through NCEP's Aviation Weather Center (AWC), or indirectly through Flight Service and private vendors.

AVIATION DIGITAL DATA SERVICE

The **Aviation Digital Data Service (ADDS)** is a joint effort of NWS and several other agencies to meet an FAA mandate "to provide better information to pilots on the location and severity of weather hazard areas, and better methods of using weather information to make safe decisions on how and when to make a flight." ADDS provides its next-generation interactive weather products to pilots through the Aviation Weather Center.

THE AVIATION WEATHER CENTER

The **Aviation Weather Center (AWC)** is the part of the NWS that is designed to provide direct services to pilots. Although many organizations work together to provide pilot weather information, you can find the information you need in one place—just go to AviationWeather.gov or search for *Aviation Weather Center.* [Figure 9-90].

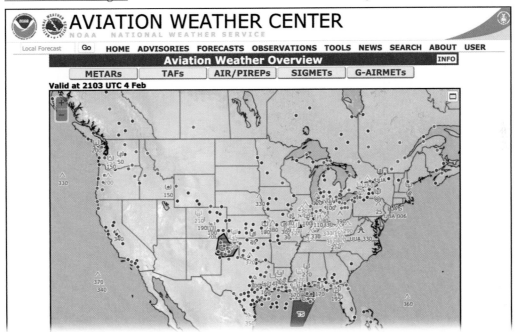

Figure 9-90. The Aviation Weather Center is the preferred method for pilots to gain access to National Weather Service reports and forecasts.

PRIVATE INDUSTRY SOURCES

Prior to World War II, the U.S. Weather Bureau (the predecessor of today's National Weather Service) was the lone disseminator of weather data. Now, in addition to government sources, more than 100 companies provide weather information to the aviation industry. Some of these services are integrated into flight planning software, apps, or in services delivered directly to aircraft avionics. You can find dozens of websites that provide weather information and many of these sites are directed towards aviation. However, it is important to understand that weather information received from non-FAA or non-NWS sites might not be current, accurate, or relevant. Therefore, you must ensure that you are using weather information from reliable and trusted sources.

Many private industry sources, such as Jeppesen, meet FAA and EASA requirements for weather information and conform to ICAO requirements. Others do not. It is essential to ensure that a nongovernment weather source meets FAA requirements before using it for an FAA-required preflight briefing.

IN-FLIGHT WEATHER SOURCES

Because forecasting is an inexact science, weather conditions can change rapidly and unexpectedly over a few hours. This uncertainty requires updating weather information while in flight. You can obtain weather updates from transcribed weather broadcasts (in Alaska), the hazardous in-flight weather advisory service, Flight Service or enroute flight advisory service, air route traffic control centers, flight information services-broadcast, and automated weather observing systems.

FLIGHT SERVICE

Although some pilots might think of it primarily as a preflight planning tool, Flight Service can also provide valuable information during your flight. Typically, you should contact Flight Service when you need to update a previous briefing. After establishing contact, specify the type of briefing you want as well as information about your flight similar to what you supply to a preflight briefer. If conditions along your route warrant, the specialist might direct you to Flight Watch or other sources of in-flight information.

ENROUTE FLIGHT ADVISORY SERVICE

You can obtain updated weather information and report the weather conditions you are flying through for the benefit of other pilots by using the **enroute flight advisory service (EFAS)**, also known as **Flight Watch.** EFAS provides weather advisories tailored to your

Enroute flight advisory service (EFAS) provides enroute aircraft with timely and meaningful weather advisories pertinent to the type of flight intended, route, and altitude.

Times of operation for EFAS facilities, as well as the high altitude EFAS frequencies can be found in the Chart Supplement.

EFAS is obtained by contacting flight watch, using the name of the ARTCC facility identification in your area, your aircraft identification, and name of the nearest VOR, on 122.0 MHz below FL180.

type of flight, route, and cruising altitude. EFAS can be the best source of current weather information along your route of flight because it is a central collection and distribution point for PIREPs. EFAS is also equipped with weather radar displays that can be particularly valuable in helping you avoid areas of thunderstorm activity.

You can usually reach EFAS from 6 a.m. to 10 p.m. anywhere in the contiguous U.S. and Puerto Rico between 5,000 feet AGL and 17,500 feet MSL on the common EFAS frequency, 122.0 MHz. Because EFAS facilities can serve large geographic areas through remote communications outlets (RCOs), make your initial callup using the name of the air route traffic control center (ARTCC) serving the area. This allows the briefer to reply over the nearest RCO that will provide the best communications coverage. After the ARTCC identifier, use the EFAS call sign, *Flight Watch*, followed by your aircraft identification and the name of the VOR nearest your position. For example, *"Denver Flight Watch, Cherokee 141FS, Casper VOR."* Because sectional charts do not show EFAS outlets or parent facilities, you sometimes will not know your EFAS area. In that case, just say: *"Flight Watch, Cherokee 141FS, Casper VOR."* The briefer will then respond with the name of the controlling facility.

Although EFAS is part of the Flight Service system, you should confine your EFAS requests to weather information along your route of flight. EFAS is not intended for flight plans, position reports, preflight briefings, or obtaining weather reports or forecasts unrelated to your flight. For these items, contact Flight Service on the published frequencies.

TRANSCRIBED WEATHER BROADCAST (ALASKA ONLY)

Transcribed weather broadcasts (TWEB) are transmitted continuously over selected low frequency NDBs and/or VORs in Alaska. On a sectional chart, a circled T in the upper right corner of a communication box indicates TWEB capability. The information in a TWEB varies with the type of recording equipment that is available. Generally, a broadcast includes route-oriented data with specially prepared National Weather Service forecasts, in-flight advisories, winds aloft, and preselected information such as weather reports, NOTAMs, and special notices.

At some locations, telephone access to the recording is available, providing an additional source of preflight information. Telephone numbers for this service, called TEL-TWEB, are listed in the *Chart Supplement*.

HAZARDOUS IN-FLIGHT WEATHER ADVISORY SERVICE

A program for broadcasting hazardous weather information on a continuous basis over selected VORs is called **hazardous in-flight weather advisory service (HIWAS)**. The broadcasts include advisories such as AIRMETs, SIGMETs, convective SIGMETs, and urgent PIREPs. When a HIWAS is updated, ARTCC and terminal facilities will broadcast an alert on all but emergency frequencies. The alert

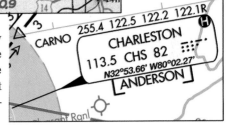

Figure 9-91. HIWAS availability is indicated by an H in the upper right corner of the associated navaid box.

will provide the type and number of the updated advisory and the frequencies to which you can tune for complete information. Chart notations depict the VORs that have HIWAS capability. In addition, a note in the Chart Supplement indicates if a particular VOR is HIWAS-equipped. [Figure 9-91]

 The Hazardous In-flight Weather Advisory Service (HIWAS) is a continuous broadcast of in-flight weather advisories over selected VORs of SIGMETs, convective SIGMETs, AIRMETs, severe weather forecast alerts (AWW), and center weather advisories (CWA).

CENTER WEATHER ADVISORIES

A **center weather advisory (CWA)** is an unscheduled weather advisory issued by an ARTCC to alert pilots of existing or anticipated adverse weather conditions within the next two hours. A CWA can be initiated when a SIGMET has not been issued but, based on current PIREPs, conditions meet those criteria. Additionally, a CWA can be issued to supplement an existing in-flight advisory as well as any conditions that currently or will soon adversely affect the safe flow of traffic within the ARTCC area of responsibility.

 AIRMETs and center weather advisories (CWA) provide an enroute pilot with information about moderate icing, moderate turbulence, winds of 30 knots or more at the surface, and extensive mountain obscurement.

Weather advisory broadcasts, including severe weather forecast alerts (AWW), convective SIGMETs, and SIGMETs, are provided by ARTCCs on all frequencies, except emergency, when any part of the area described is within 150 miles of the airspace under their jurisdiction.

Air route traffic control centers broadcast CWAs as well as SIGMETs, convective SIGMETs, and AWWs once on all but emergency frequencies when any part of the area described is within 150 miles of the airspace under the ARTCC jurisdiction. In terminal areas, local control and approach control might limit these broadcasts to weather occurring within 50 miles of the airspace under their jurisdiction. These broadcasts contain the advisory identification and a brief description of the weather activity and general area affected.

WEATHER RADAR SERVICES

The NWS operates a nationwide network of weather radar sites that provides real-time information for textual and graphic weather products, and that also furnishes EFAS and FSS specialists with data for in-flight advisories. Because weather radar can detect coverage, intensity, and movement of precipitation, an EFAS or Flight Service specialist might be able to provide you with suggested routing around areas of hazardous weather. It is important to remember, however, that simply avoiding areas highlighted by weather radar does not guarantee clear weather conditions.

Going in Circles Really Fast

Tornadoes carry some of the most devastating forces available in nature. The amount of energy in an F5 tornado's 250 m.p.h. wind is four times that of a 125 m.p.h. wind encountered in a hurricane. It is little wonder that tornadoes pick up houses, buildings, and large trucks and scatter them like toothpicks.

How do they measure such wind speeds? Even if a tornado should pass directly over traditional measuring equipment, it is unlikely the equipment could survive such an encounter. Professor T. Fujita of the University of Chicago, who developed the widely-used Fujita scale for measuring tornado intensity, originally determined wind speeds by analyzing film of tornadoes and calculating the velocity of the flying debris.

Now, doppler radar accurately measures wind speed inside tornadoes. Forecasters not only can determine the location, speed and direction of movement of a tornado, but also can predict how devastating it is likely to be, and warn people accordingly. The National Weather Service's WSR-88D, or NEXRAD, radar system, together with new geostationary operational environmental satellites (GOES) and the automated surface observation system (ASOS) network, is expected to save many lives by pinpointing the time and place where severe weather is likely to strike.

Courtesy NOAA

AUTOMATED WEATHER REPORTING SYSTEMS

Although human weather observers contribute to weather reports at larger airports, many surface weather observation tasks are automated. The FAA operates the automated weather observing systems and automated weather sensor systems, and the NWS operates the automated surface observing systems. Although their complexity and capabilities vary, these systems are primarily designed to provide weather information for aviation.

AUTOMATED WEATHER OBSERVING SYSTEM

The **automated weather observing system (AWOS)** was developed for the FAA and was the first widely installed automated weather data gathering system at U.S. airports. The AWOS uses various sensors, a voice synthesizer, and a radio transmitter to provide real-time weather data. There are four types of AWOS—AWOS-A reports only altimeter setting; AWOS-1 also measures and reports wind speed, direction and gusts, temperature, and dew point; AWOS-2 provides visibility information in addition to everything reported by an AWOS-1; and the most capable system, the AWOS-3, also includes cloud and ceiling data.

AUTOMATED SURFACE OBSERVING SYSTEM

The **automated surface observing system (ASOS)** was a joint effort between the FAA and the NWS to deploy a network of high-grade weather monitoring stations across the United States. ASOS has more advanced capabilities than basic AWOS systems and is the primary surface weather observing system in the United States, with about 1,000 stations installed at airports across the U.S. [Figure 9-92]

Using an array of sensors, computers, and digitized voice communications, ASOS provides continuous minute-by-minute observations. The ASOS measures and reports the same elements as an AWOS-3 as well as variable cloud height, variable visibility, rapid pressure changes, precipitation type, intensity, accumulation, and beginning and ending times. The ASOS is also capable of measuring wind shifts and peak winds. Some ASOS stations can determine the difference between liquid precipitation and frozen or freezing precipitation. If the station has this capability, it is designated as an AO2. Otherwise, it carries an AO1 designation.

Figure 9-92. ASOS stations like this one are the primary source of U.S. weather observations.

AUTOMATED WEATHER SENSOR SYSTEM

The **automated weather sensor system (AWSS)** is a newer system with the same capabilities as ASOS, but is operated by the FAA rather than the NWS. There are a handful of installations at airports not served by ASOS, and AWSS is likely to replace some FAA AWOS systems. From a pilot perspective, the system is the same as ASOS and the more advanced AWOS systems.

DOES A HUMAN PERFORM BETTER WEATHER OBSERVATIONS THAN A MACHINE?

Both human observers and automated systems have limitations when it comes to determining the complete weather picture. The measurements from AWOS/ASOS systems are completely objective, and in the strictest sense, error free. However, the AWOS/ASOS systems are limited in their ability to deduce an overall view of the weather at various locations in the airport vicinity. A human observer is able to look around the sky and quickly make a subjective judgment as to sky condition, visibility and present weather. However, depending on the complexity of the weather, and on other duties, a human observer can only make one or two observations per hour. An automated system looks at a single part of the sky over a period of time, and averages this data.

According to the FAA, the fixed time, spatial averaging technique used by human observers, and the automated system's fixed location, time averaging technique, yield remarkably similar results. Keep in mind, it is possible for an automated system to report inaccurately if there is a localized condition near the reporting equipment and little or no cloud movement.

OBTAINING AUTOMATED WEATHER INFORMATION

ASOS/AWSS/AWOS information is broadcast over discrete VHF frequencies or the voice portions a local navaids. You can normally receive these weather report transmissions within 25 miles of the site and up to 10,000 feet AGL. Locations and frequencies are shown on aeronautical charts and listed in the *Chart Supplement*. You can also listen to ASOS/AWSS/AWOS by telephone using the telephone numbers listed in the *Chart Supplement*.

At many airports around the U.S. that have both a part-time tower and an automated weather system, the automated weather information is automatically broadcast over the ATIS frequency when the tower is closed.

AIRBORNE WEATHER EQUIPMENT

Thunderstorms present hazards to all aircraft, regardless of size or performance. Ground-based radar cannot identify all dangerous areas with certainty, because the signal can be reflected back by nearer weather phenomena. To find the cells hidden from ground based weather radar, it is necessary to utilize equipment onboard the aircraft. That is why most jet aircraft and many turboprop aircraft have airborne equipment for avoiding severe weather. Certain light twin and high-performance single engine aircraft also offer this type of equipment. Although having weather avoidance equipment does not necessarily make it safe to operate near embedded thunderstorms, it does offer properly trained pilots some help in avoiding the most hazardous weather.

AIRBORNE WEATHER RADAR

Airborne weather radar operates under the same principle as ground-based radar. The directional antenna, normally behind the airplane's fiberglass nose cone, transmits pulses of energy out ahead of the aircraft. The signal is reflected by water and ice, and is picked up by the antenna from which it was transmitted. The bearing and distance of the weather is plotted, normally on a color display. These displays are useful for indicating different degrees of precipitation severity. A radar unit might use green to indicate light precipitation, yellow for moderate rain, and red to depict heavy storms. [Figure 9-93]

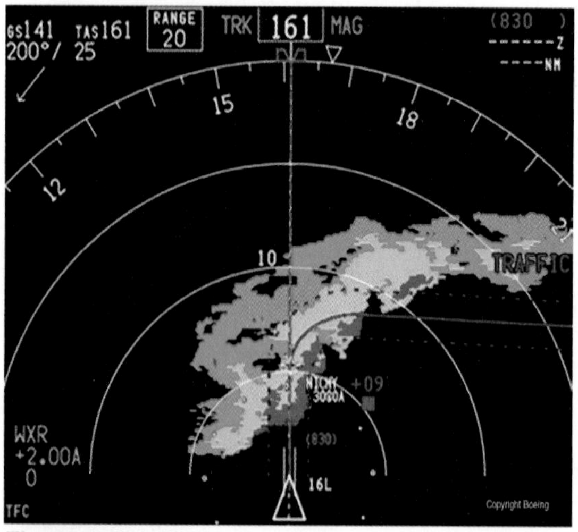

Figure 9-93. Airborne weather radar allows pilots to see and avoid many thunderstorms which do not appear on ground-based radar.

Aircraft radar generally use one of two frequency ranges — X-band and C-band. X-band systems, which are more common in general aviation aircraft, transmit on a frequency of 9,333 gigahertz (gHz), which has a wavelength of only 0.03 mm. This extremely short wave is reflected by very small amounts of precipitation. Due to the high amount of reflected energy, X-band systems provide a higher resolution and "see" farther than C-band radars. A disadvantage is that very little energy can pass through one storm to detect another that might be behind the first. The C-band frequency (5.44 gHz) can penetrate farther into a storm, providing a more complete picture of the storm system. This capability makes C-band weather radar systems better for penetration into known areas of precipitation. Consequently, C-band radars are more likely to be found on large commercial aircraft.

Aircraft radar is prone to many of the same limitations as ground-based systems. It cannot detect water vapor, lightning, or wind shear. Training and experience as well as other on-board equipment and ATC radar are important tools for enhancing your mental picture of the weather ahead.

LIGHTNING DETECTION EQUIPMENT

Because lightning is always associated with severe thunderstorms, systems that detect lightning can reliably indicate the active parts of these storms. [Figure 9-94] **Lightning detection equipment** is more compact, uses substantially less power than radar, and requires less interpretation by the pilot. The equipment is designed to help a pilot completely avoid storm cells. However, lightning detection equipment does not directly indicate areas of heavy precipitation, hail, and wind shear and might not provide as accurate information as radar about these hazards.

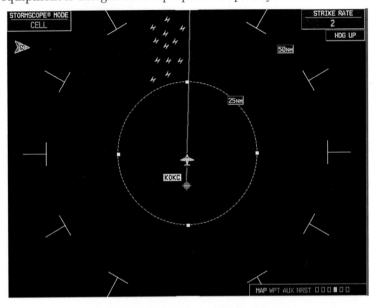

Figure 9-94. Lightning detection equipment provides many of the benefits of airborne radar at much lower cost, smaller size, and lower power consumption.

FLIGHT INFORMATION SERVICE-BROADCAST (FIS-B).

One advantage of equipping an aircraft with automatic dependent surveillance–broadcast (ADS-B) equipment prior to the 2020 deadline is the availability of **Flight Information Service-Broadcast (FIS-B)** to properly-equipped systems. [Figure 9-95]

FIS-B provides a number of broadcast weather and aeronautical information products that can include:

Figure 9-95. FIS-B provides free in-flight weather information over an ADS-B datalink.

- METARs
- PIREPs
- Winds and temperatures aloft
- Terminal aerodrome forecast (TAFs)
- NOTAMs
- AIRMETs
- SIGMETs and convective SIGMETs
- Special use airspace (SUA)
- Temporary flight restriction (TFRs)
- NEXRAD

You must use caution with regard to relying on in-flight weather products from FIS-B or XM satellite sources, especially those related to thunderstorms. The NTSB published a safety alert after investigating fatal accidents in which in-cockpit NEXRAD mosaic imagery was available to pilots operating near quickly-developing and fast-moving convective weather. In this safety alert, the NTSB warned that NEXRAD data can, in rare cases, be as much as 20 minutes older than the age indicated on the cockpit display. During that time delay, dramatic changes in the thunderstorm location and intensity can occur.

SUMMARY CHECKLIST

✓ You can obtain a preflight weather briefing from Flight Service 24 hours a day by calling the toll free number, 1-800-WX BRIEF. When you contact a weather briefer, give your aircraft number, your type of flight (VFR or IFR) and tell the briefer what weather information you have previously obtained.

✓ When you are planning a trip and have not obtained preliminary weather or a previous briefing, request a standard briefing.

✓ Request an abbreviated briefing when you need only one or two specific items or would like to update weather information from a previous briefing or other weather sources.

✓ An outlook briefing provides forecast information appropriate to your proposed flight to help you make an initial judgment about the feasibility of your flight.

✓ The telephone information briefing service (TIBS) provides a continuous recording of area and/or route meteorological briefings, airspace procedures, and special aviation-oriented announcements.

✓ Flight Service also offers a web portal (1800wxBrief.com), from which you can obtain an official FAA briefing by Internet. An advantage of using the web portal is that you can obtain graphic weather products customized to your route of flight.

✓ The Aviation Weather Center (AviationWeather.gov) provides pilots with direct Intenet access to Aviation Digital Data Service charts and other FAA-approved weather products from the National Weather Service.

✓ Hazardous in-flight weather advisory service (HIWAS) broadcasts, which include AIRMETs, SIGMETs, convective SIGMETs, and urgent PIREPs, are transmitted continuously over selected VORs.

✓ An unscheduled weather advisory issued by an ARTCC to alert pilots of existing or anticipated adverse weather conditions within the next two hours is called a center weather advisory (CWA).

✓ When flying below 18,000 feet MSL, you can contact the enroute flight advisory service (EFAS) on 122.0 MHz for real-time weather information, including any thunderstorm activity that could affect your route.

✓ Automated weather observation systems currently in use are the automated weather observing system (AWOS), the automated surface observing system (ASOS), and the automated weather sensor system (AWSS).

✓ You can obtain weather data from automated weather observation stations by tuning to discrete VHF frequencies or the voice portions a local navaids, or by calling the telephone number for the station.

✓ Airborne radar or lightning detection equipment usually can locate areas of hazardous weather ahead of your aircraft with greater reliability than ground-based radar.

✓ Flight Information Service-Broadcast (FIS-B) can display a wide variety of weather information during flight in ADS-B equipped aircraft.

KEY TERMS

Flight Service

Preflight Weather Briefing

Standard Briefing

Abbreviated Briefing

Outlook Briefing

Telephone Information Briefing Service (TIBS)

Aviation Digital Data Service (ADDS)

Aviation Weather Center (AWC)

Enroute Flight Advisory Service (EFAS)

Flight Watch

Hazardous In-Flight Weather Advisory Service (HIWAS)

Center Weather Advisory (CWA)

Automated Weather Observing System (AWOS)

Automated Surface Observing System (ASOS)

Automated Weather Sensor System (AWSS)

Airborne Weather Radar

Lightning Detection Equipment

Flight Information Service-Broadcast (FIS-B)

SECTION E ■ Sources of Weather Information

QUESTIONS

1. What information should you provide to a preflight weather briefer?

2. True/False. The telephone information briefing service (TIBS) replaces the need for an individual briefing from a Flight Service specialist.

3. Name two government sources from which to obtain weather products over the Internet that are approved for FAA preflight briefings.

4. What are two sources that you can use to obtain HIWAS frequencies?

5. When flying below 18,000 feet MSL, what frequency should you use to contact EFAS?

6. The most basic automated weather observation system provides only
   A. Wind direction and speed
   B. Altimeter setting
   C. Local time and favored runway

For questions 7 through 12, match the weather source with the appropriate description.

7. Standard briefing

8. Abbreviated briefing

9. Outlook briefing.

10. Pilot web portal

11. TIBS

12. EFAS

A. Internet access to Flight Services for FAA-approved weather briefings, weather maps, and filing of flight plans

B. Source of in-flight weather information

C. Obtained more than six hours before flight time to determine the feasibility of a proposed flight

D. Most comprehensive briefing available from an FSS briefer

E. Used to update previous weather information

F. Recorded weather information available by telephone from Flight Service.

13. What type of continuous weather broadcast provides weather information that is never more than one minute old?
   A. EFAS
   B. ASOS
   C. HIWAS

Refer to the IFR enroute chart to answer question 14.

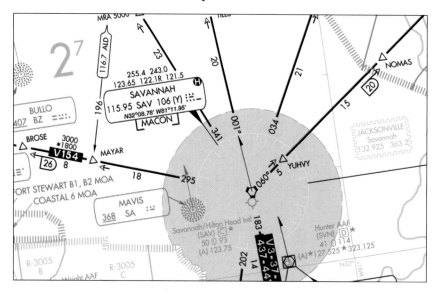

14. What type of weather information is available when monitoring Savannah VORTAC?
   A. Recorded information on expected sky cover, cloud tops, visibility, weather, and obstructions to vision in a route format
   B. Summarized SIGMETs, convective SIGMETs, AWWs, CWAs, AIRMETs, and urgent PIREPs
   C. ASOS broadcasts from nearby Savannah/Hilton Head International Airport.

15. What is the purpose of a Center Weather Advisory?
   A. To advise pilots of SIGMETs and AIRMETs so they can contact Flight Watch.
   B. To disseminate routine pilot reports so pilots do not need to leave the ATC frequency.
   C. To alert pilots of current or adverse weather conditions not covered by existing SIGMETs and AIRMETs.

CHAPTER 10

IFR Flight Considerations

Instrument/Commercial
Part III, Chapter 10 — IFR Flight Considerations

SECTION A
IFR Emergencies

No one likes to think about dealing with an emergency during instrument flight. However, proper planning and sound knowledge of emergency procedures can help you complete your flight safely if an emergency occurs.

Naturally, you should be thoroughly familiar with the pilot's operating handbook for the aircraft you fly. The POH outlines specific emergency procedures that apply to your particular aircraft. However, the POH cannot prepare you for every event that might occur. When you encounter an emergency that is not covered in the aircraft's POH, or in the regulations, you are expected to exercise good judgment in responding to the situation.

The *Aeronautical Information Manual* defines an emergency as a condition of distress or urgency. Pilots in **distress** are threatened by serious and/or imminent danger and require immediate assistance. Distress conditions can include in-flight fire, mechanical failures, or structural damage. An **urgency** situation, which is not immediately dangerous, requires prompt assistance to avoid a potentially catastrophic event. Any condition that adversely affects your flight, such as low fuel quantity or poor weather can result in an urgency condition that can develop into a distress situation if you do not manage the problem in a timely manner. If you become apprehensive about your safety for any reason, request assistance immediately.

Other situations associated with weather, such as inadvertent entry into a thunderstorm, hail, severe turbulence, or icing, are potential emergencies. Fuel starvation or inability to maintain the MEA are undeniable emergencies. If, after considering the particular circumstances of the flight, you feel a potentially dangerous or unsafe condition exists, declare an emergency. During the course of the emergency, if you are given priority handling by ATC, you may be required to submit a detailed report within 48 hours to the manager of that ATC facility, even though you violated no rule.

 ATC may request a detailed report of an emergency when priority assistance has been given, even though no rules have been violated.

DECLARING AN EMERGENCY

As pilot in command, you are directly responsible for the safety of your flight. Under the provisions of FAR 91.3, you are allowed to deviate from any rule in FAR Part 91 and from ATC instructions, to the extent required to meet an emergency. If you determine it is necessary to deviate from ATC instructions during an emergency, you must notify ATC as soon as possible and obtain an amended clearance.

To declare an emergency when operating in IFR conditions, contact ATC on the currently assigned frequency. If you receive no response, try calling the same facility on another available frequency. If the facility still does not respond, try to contact any other ATC facility that may be able to assist you. If you are unable to contact ATC on any of the normal frequencies, use the emergency frequency of 121.5 MHz.

In a distress situation, begin your initial call with the word **MAYDAY**, preferably repeated three times. Use **PAN-PAN** in the same manner in an urgency situation. Figure 10-1 provides an example of a distress or urgency message. You can tailor your transmission to fit prevailing conditions. For example, when in radar contact with an ATC facility, you need not include your aircraft's type, position, heading, or altitude, because the controller already has these facts.

INFORMATION	EXAMPLE
Distress or Urgency	"MAYDAY, MAYDAY, MAYDAY (or PAN-PAN, PAN-PAN, PAN-PAN),
Name of station addressed	Seattle Center,
Identification and type of aircraft	1114V Piper Arrow,
Nature of distress or urgency	severe icing,
Weather	IFR,
Your intentions and request	request immediate course reversal and lower altitude,
Present position and heading	JIMMY Intersection, heading 253°
Altitude or flight level	9,000.
Fuel remaining in hours and minutes	Estimate two hours fuel remaining,
Number of people aboard	five aboard,
Any other useful information	squawking 1146."

Figure 10-1. After repeating MAYDAY or PAN-PAN three times, provide information about your situation and the assistance that you require.

 During a flight in IFR conditions, do not hesitate to declare an emergency and obtain an amended clearance when you encounter a distress condition..

Another way to declare an emergency is to squawk **code 7700** on your transponder. This code triggers an alarm or a special indicator in radar facilities. However, if you are in radio contact with ATC, do not change your assigned transponder code from its current setting unless you are instructed to do so by that facility.

A **special emergency** is a condition of air piracy, or other hostile act by a person or persons aboard an aircraft, that threatens the safety of the aircraft or its passengers. Although these incidents rarely involve the average pilot, you should be aware of the recommended ATC procedures. In a special emergency, use the recommended distress or urgency procedures. When circumstances do not permit you to comply, transmit a message containing as much of the following information as possible on the frequency in use.

1. Name of the station addressed

2. Aircraft identification and present position

3. Nature of the special emergency condition and your intentions

If you are unable to provide the above information, alert ATC by transmitting the phrase, "*transponder seven five zero zero*" and/or squawking transponder **code 7500**. Either action means, "*I am being hijacked/forced to a new destination.*"

MALFUNCTION REPORTS

The loss of certain equipment during an IFR flight might have little significance to you. For example, if you are flying to a destination not served by an NDB, the loss of the ADF receiver might not cause you much concern. Regardless of your immediate need for that piece of equipment, you are required by regulations, while operating under IFR in controlled airspace, to report to ATC the loss of the ADF receiver. FAR 91.187 requires that you report the malfunction of any navigational, approach, or communication equipment.

When you make a **malfunction report**, you are expected to include the following information

1. Aircraft identification

2. Equipment affected

3. Degree to which the equipment failure will impair your ability to operate under IFR

4. Type of assistance desired from ATC

 FAR 91.187 requires that you report the malfunction of any navigational, approach, or communication equipment. For example, if a VOR receiver malfunctions while operating in controlled airspace under IFR in an airplane equipped with dual VOR receivers, immediately report the malfunction to ATC.

MINIMUM FUEL

If your remaining fuel is such that you can accept little or no delay, advise ATC that you have **minimum fuel**. This is not an emergency, but only an advisory that any undue delays could cause an emergency situation. If your remaining usable fuel supply indicates the need for traffic priority to ensure a safe landing, declare an emergency. When transmitting such a report, state the approximate number of minutes you can continue to fly with the fuel remaining.

 Declaring minimum fuel to ATC indicates an emergency situation is possible should any undue delay occur.

GYROSCOPIC INSTRUMENT FAILURE

Gyroscopic instruments that stop functioning in IFR conditions due to a vacuum or electrical system failure can result in a distress situation. This type of instrument failure can develop into an emergency because your ability to immediately and accurately comply with all ATC clearances will be limited. This is particularly true in circumstances when warning indications, such as a low-vacuum warning light or low-voltage warning light fail to provide adequate warning of an impending instrument system malfunction. If you are in IFR conditions and find that one of your gyroscopic instruments has failed, immediately switch to an alternate display, use your backup instruments or transition to partial-panel flying and notify ATC. Instrument failure provides little advance warning, so you need to maintain your proficiency in partial-panel attitude instrument flying.

Detecting a problem early is important in successfully handling a gyroscopic instrument failure. A good instrument cross-check is essential for discovering a problem quickly. Check the instrument system warning indicators occasionally as part of your instrument cross-check. If you suspect that a gyroscopic instrument has failed, verify the problem with related flight instruments. For example, you can confirm an attitude indicator failure by checking your airspeed indicator, vertical speed indicator, altimeter, turn coordinator, and heading indicator. [Figure 10-2]

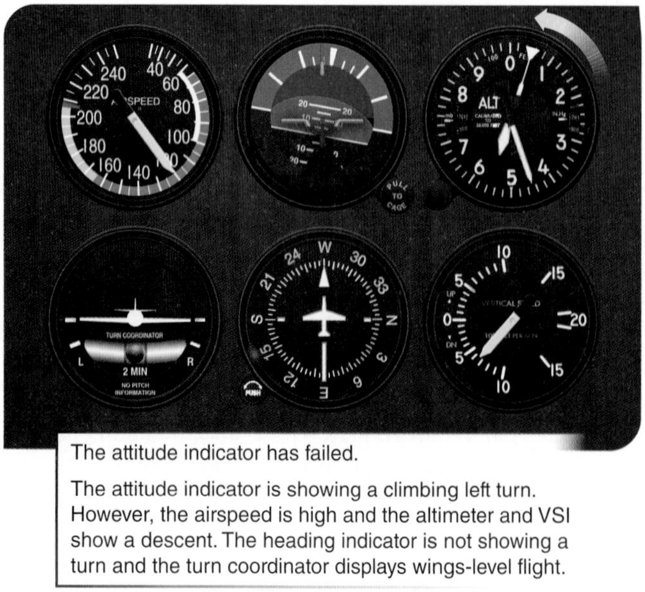

The attitude indicator has failed.

The attitude indicator is showing a climbing left turn. However, the airspeed is high and the altimeter and VSI show a descent. The heading indicator is not showing a turn and the turn coordinator displays wings-level flight.

Figure 10-2. With an effective instrument cross-check you will see a discrepancy between the failed attitude indicator and the supporting instruments.

After you determine that an instrument has failed, cover it so you are not distracted by the incorrect information it provides. Then contact ATC and make the appropriate malfunction report. Your highest priority during an instrument failure is to fly the airplane. If your airplane has an autopilot, you might be able to use it to keep the airplane level and on course. This depends on the nature of the failure and the configuration of the autopilot system. With the airplane under control, your next priorities are to navigate accurately and communicate your situation and intentions to ATC. Good partial-panel instrument flying procedures help you to maintain attitude control of your airplane. It is also important for you to use available ATC services like radar and no-gyro approaches to assist you in completing your flight safely. Emergency approach procedures available to you from ATC are discussed later in this section.

"BOTH FUEL CELLS WERE EMPTY..."

From the Files of the NTSB...

Aircraft: PA-32RT-300T

Location: Rogers, AR

Injuries: 1 Serious, 1 Minor

Narrative: According to witnesses and law enforcement personnel at the accident site, the pilot executed 3 missed approaches at the Rogers Municipal Airport while attempting to land with weather below published minimums. At 0734, the pilot reported to ATC that he was low on fuel. Two minutes later, the pilot reported that he was out of fuel. The airplane was last observed on radar descending through 1,500 feet and subsequently impacted trees approximately one mile northwest of the airport. Examination of the wreckage confirmed that both fuel cells were empty.

Had this pilot declared minimum fuel in a timely manner, ATC might have provided him the assistance he needed to complete his flight safely at an alternate airport. Waiting until just prior to fuel exhaustion can turn an urgent situation into a distress situation that can be unrecoverable.

COMMUNICATION FAILURE

Two-way radio communication failure procedures for IFR operations are outlined in FAR 91.185. Unless otherwise authorized by ATC, pilots operating under IFR are expected to comply with this regulation. Expanded procedures for communication failures are found in the *Aeronautical Information Manual*. In some cases, special lost communication procedures are established for certain IFR operations. [Figure 10-3]

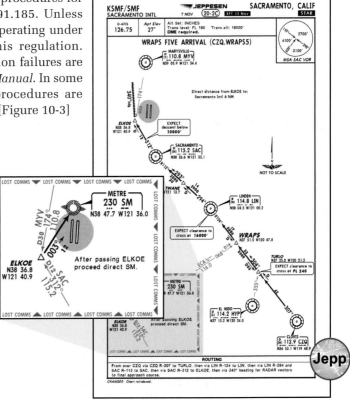

Figure 10-3. Specific lost communication procedures are sometimes included with charted procedures. If you lose communications while flying this STAR, comply with the lost communication procedures indicated on the chart.

ALERTING ATC

Use your transponder to alert ATC to a radio communication failure by squawking **code 7600**. [Figure 10-4] If only your transmitter is inoperative, listen for ATC instructions on any operational receiver, including your navigation receivers. It is possible ATC might try to contact you over a VOR, VORTAC, NDB, or localizer frequency. In addition to monitoring your navaid receivers, try to reestablish communications by contacting ATC on a previously assigned frequency, or calling Flight Service or Aeronautical Radio/Incorporated (ARINC).

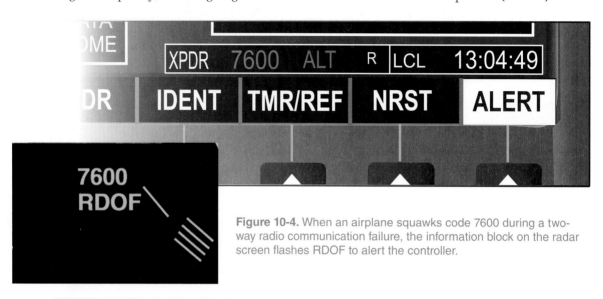

Figure 10-4. When an airplane squawks code 7600 during a two-way radio communication failure, the information block on the radar screen flashes RDOF to alert the controller.

 You are in IFR conditions and have two-way radio communication failure. If you do not exercise emergency authority, you should set your transponder code to 7600.

The primary objective of the regulations governing communication failures is to preclude extended IFR operations within the ATC system because these operations can adversely affect other users of the airspace. If your radio fails while operating on an IFR clearance but you are in VFR conditions, or if you encounter VFR conditions at any time after the failure, you should continue the flight under VFR conditions, if possible, and land as soon as practicable. Do not construe the requirement to land as soon as practicable to mean as soon as possible. Use your best judgment. You are not required to land at an unauthorized airport, at an airport that is not suitable for your aircraft, or to land only minutes short of your intended destination. However, if IFR conditions prevail, you must comply with procedures designated in the FARs to ensure aircraft separation.

 If you experience two-way radio communication failure when operating on an IFR clearance in VFR conditions, continue the flight under VFR if possible, and land as soon as practicable.

ROUTE

To continue your flight in IFR conditions after experiencing two-way radio communication failure, fly one of the following routes in the order shown. [Figure 10-5]

1. The route assigned by ATC in the last clearance you received

2. If being radar vectored, the direct route from the point of radio failure to the fix, route, or airway specified in the radar vector clearance

3. In the absence of an assigned route, the route ATC has advised you to expect in a further clearance

4. In the absence of an assigned or expected route, the route filed in your flight plan

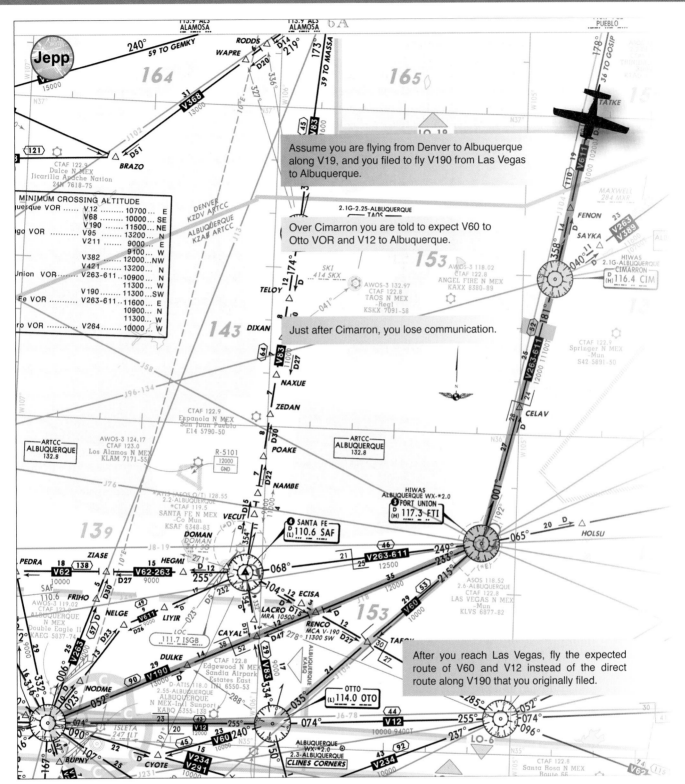

Figure 10-5. Here is an example of the route you should fly if you experience a communication failure when in IFR conditions.

ALTITUDE

It is also important for you to fly a specific altitude if you lose two-way radio communications. The altitude you fly after a communication failure can be found in FAR 91.185 and must be the highest of the following altitudes for each route segment flown.

- The altitude (or flight level) assigned in your last ATC clearance

- The minimum altitude (or flight level) for IFR operations

- The altitude (or flight level) that ATC has advised you to expect in a further clearance

In some cases, your assigned or expected altitude might not be as high as the MEA on the next route segment. In this situation, you normally begin a climb to the higher MEA when you reach the fix where the MEA rises. If the fix also has a published minimum crossing altitude (MCA), start your climb so you are at or above the MCA when you reach the fix. If the next succeeding route segment has a lower MEA, descend to the applicable altitude — either the last assigned altitude or the altitude expected in a further clearance — when you reach the fix where the MEA decreases. [Figure 10-6]

 If you have two-way radio communication failure in IFR conditions, fly the route specified in your clearance, and the highest of the following: the altitude assigned by ATC, told to expect by ATC, or the MEA. See figures 10-5 and 10-6.

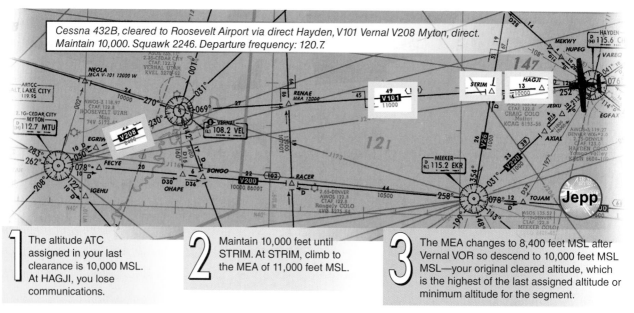

Cessna 432B, cleared to Roosevelt Airport via direct Hayden, V101 Vernal V208 Myton, direct. Maintain 10,000. Squawk 2246. Departure frequency: 120.7.

1 The altitude ATC assigned in your last clearance is 10,000 MSL. At HAGJI, you lose communications.

2 Maintain 10,000 feet until STRIM. At STRIM, climb to the MEA of 11,000 feet MSL.

3 The MEA changes to 8,400 feet MSL after Vernal VOR so descend to 10,000 feet MSL MSL—your original cleared altitude, which is the highest of the last assigned altitude or minimum altitude for the segment.

Figure 10-6. Follow these steps for maintaining the appropriate altitude if you lose communications on this route to Hayden Airport.

LEAVING THE CLEARANCE LIMIT

When the clearance limit specified in the ATC clearance you received prior to radio failure is also a point from which an approach begins, commence your descent and approach as close as possible to the expect further clearance (EFC) time. If you arrive at your clearance limit prior to the EFC time, you must hold at the clearance limit until that time has been reached. You may be required to adjust the holding pattern as necessary in order to begin the approach at the proper time. If ATC did not provide an EFC time, begin your descent and approach as close as possible to the ETA calculated from your filed or amended (with ATC) time enroute. In this case, it might still be necessary to hold at the clearance limit in order to begin the approach at the proper time if you arrive at the fix early.

Upon arrival at a destination with more than one instrument approach procedure, you may fly the approach of your choice. Similarly, if more than one initial approach fix is available for the approach you choose, you may select whichever fix is appropriate. ATC provides separation for your flight, regardless of the approach selected and the initial approach fix used.

When the clearance limit specified in your last clearance is not a fix from which an approach begins, leave the fix at the EFC time specified. After departing the fix and arriving at a point where an approach begins, commence your descent and complete the approach. If you have not received an EFC time, continue past the clearance limit to a point at which an approach begins. Then begin your descent and approach as close as possible to the ETA calculated from your filed or amended time enroute.

If you have an EFC time while holding at a holding fix that is not the approach fix and you experience two-way radio communication failure, depart the holding fix at the EFC time.

 While holding at a DME fix for an ILS approach, ATC advises you to expect clearance for the approach at 1015. At 1000 you experience two-way radio communication failure. In this case, you should immediately squawk 7600 and plan to begin your approach at 1015.

RADAR APPROACHES

In a distress situation, such as a loss of gyroscopic instruments, radar approach procedures might be available to assist you in completing your flight safely. These procedures require a ground-based radar facility and a functioning airborne radio transmitter and receiver. They allow the controller to provide horizontal, and in some cases vertical, course guidance during the approach. However, radar guidance during the approach does not waive the prescribed weather minimums for the airport or for the particular aircraft operator concerned. The three types of radar approaches that might be available are the airport surveillance radar approach (ASR), precision approach radar (PAR), and the no-gyro approach.

AIRPORT SURVEILLANCE RADAR APPROACH

In an **airport surveillance radar (ASR)** approach, the controller provides only azimuth navigational guidance. The ASR approach also is referred to as a **surveillance approach**. With this type of procedure, the controller assigns headings to fly to align your aircraft with the extended centerline of the landing runway. Before you begin the descent, the controller tells you the MDA. The controller advises when to start the descent to the MDA or, if appropriate, to an intermediate stepdown fix and then to the prescribed MDA.

During the approach, the controller will tell you the location of the missed approach point and, your position each mile from the runway or MAP while you are on final. At your request, the controller will give the recommended altitude at each mile on final. Normally, ATC provides navigation guidance until you reach the MAP. At the MAP, ATC terminates guidance and instructs you to execute a missed approach unless you have reported the runway environment in sight. Also, if at any time during the approach the controller considers that safe guidance for the remainder of the approach cannot be provided, guidance is terminated and you are instructed to execute a missed approach. When a surveillance approach ends in a circle-to-land maneuver, you tell the controller your aircraft approach category, and the controller provides the appropriate MDA.

The ASR approach is available only at airports where civil radar instrument approach minimums have been published. These minimums are published on separate pages in the FAA *Terminal Procedures Publication* (TPP) and on Jeppesen Radar Approach Charts. [Figure 10-7]

 In addition to headings, the information a radar controller provides without request during an ASR approach includes: when to commence descent to the MDA, the aircraft's position each mile on final from the runway, and arrival at the MAP.

 A surveillance approach may be used at airports for which civil radar instrument approach minimums have been published.

SECTION A ■ **IFR Emergencies**

SECTION A ■ IFR Emergencies

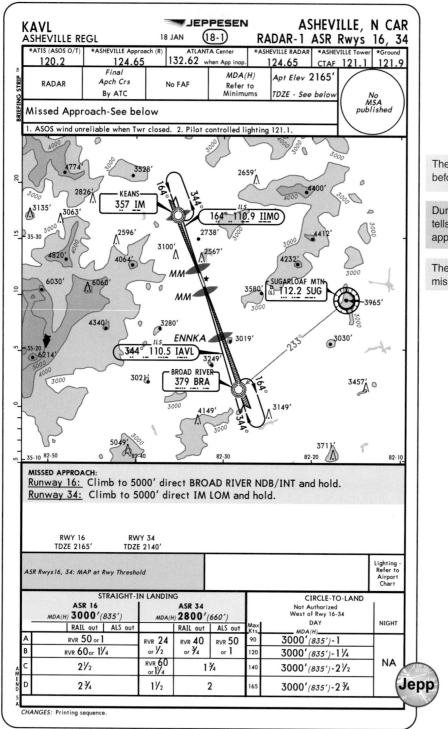

The controller will tell you the MDA before you begin your descent.

During the approach, the controller tells you the location of the missed approach point.

The controller also tells you the missed approach procedure.

Figure 10-7. The ASR approach is typically available as a backup procedure. Use it when you have lost the navigation equipment needed to fly the other instrument approaches available at the airport.

You've Seen One Emergency, You Haven't Seen Them All

Picture yourself flying a single-engine airplane enroute from Harbour Grace, Newfoundland, aiming for Paris, France. You have no co-pilot, no airways to follow, and no air traffic controllers to assist you. Now, imagine that you experience not one, but several emergencies with nothing but the depths of the Atlantic Ocean beneath you.

This is the same situation that Amelia Earhart faced in 1932 after she set out to fly solo across the Atlantic in a Lockheed Vega. Earhart's first crisis occurred when her altimeter failed, just a few hours after her departure. For the rest of the long flight, she had no indication of the Vega's altitude. Shortly after the altimeter failed, Earhart encountered a thunderstorm and wandered off course. About four hours into the flight, a bad weld caused the exhaust manifold seam to part and Earhart could see the glow of flames by looking through a gap under the rim of the cowling. During the night, Earhart faced increasing vibrations from the damaged manifold. As the flight progressed, the Vega began picking up ice in the clouds and then entered a spin. Earhart was able to recover just over the water with little altitude to spare. She tried to stay under the clouds, but ran into fog. Although Earhart finally found an altitude that allowed her to fly a safe distance from the water and stay clear of the icing conditions, her troubles continued.

Just prior to her transatlantic flight, Amelia Earhart poses on her Lockeed Vega.

About two hours from the coast of Ireland, Earhart turned on the reserve tank and discovered that the cabin fuel gauge was leaking. She became concerned that the fumes from the leaking fuel would be ignited by the flames from the exhaust system. At this point, Earhart decided not to continue as planned to Paris, but to land as soon as she could. The Lockheed Vega touched down in a pasture near Londonderry, Northern Ireland, after a flight which lasted almost 15 hours. As Earhart climbed out of the airplane, a surprised farmhand approached the Vega. *"Where am I?"* she called out. *"In Gallagher's pasture,"* was the reply.

PRECISION APPROACH RADAR

During an approach using **precision approach radar (PAR)** the controller provides precise navigational guidance in azimuth and elevation. The controller provides headings to fly to align your aircraft with the runway centerline and to keep you there during the approach. The controller advises you when you are about to intercept the glide slope, usually 10 to 30 seconds before it occurs, and tells you when to start your descent. The controller also reports your range to touchdown at least once each mile during the approach.

The controller provides course deviation and trend information to help you stay on the approach path. For instance, a controller may report that you are *"well above glide path, coming down rapidly."* This information enables you to adjust your airplane's flight path accordingly and keep you within the safety zone limits of the approach. Navigational guidance is provided by the controller down to the decision altitude. From the DA to the threshold, the controller provides advisory course guidance, and radar service is terminated upon completion of the approach.

SECTION A ■ IFR Emergencies

At an airport that has the proper equipment, you can use a PAR approach when you lose the navigation instruments needed to fly the other instrument approaches available at the airport. [Figure 10-8]

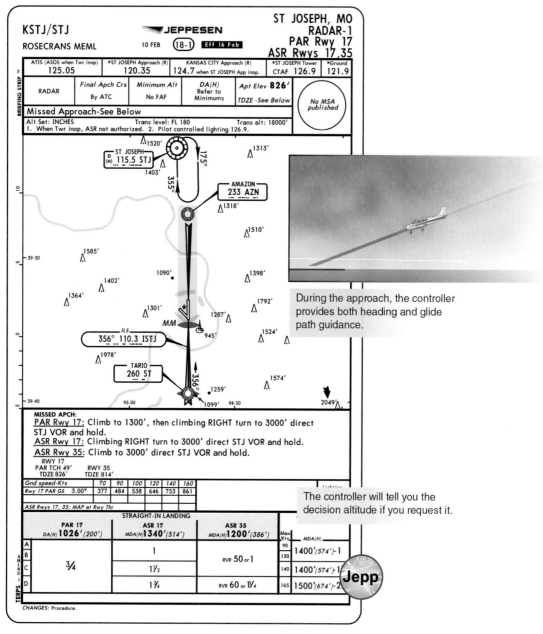

Figure 10-8. You can find the approach minimums for PAR approaches in the FAA TPP and on Jeppesen Radar Approach Charts.

NO-GYRO APPROACH

If your heading indicator becomes inoperative or inaccurate due to a gyroscopic instrument failure, advise ATC of the malfunction and request a **no-gyro vector** or **no-gyro approach**. During the approach, the controller guides you by telling you when to begin and stop your turns, saying *"turn right... stop turn,"* or *"turn left... stop turn."* The controller expects you to turn as soon as you receive the instructions. Make standard-rate turns until you have been turned onto final. After ATC tells you that you are on final approach, make all of your turns at half standard rate. [Figure 10-9]

FAA After being handed off to the final approach controller during a no-gyro surveillance or precision approach, the pilot should make all turns at half standard rate.

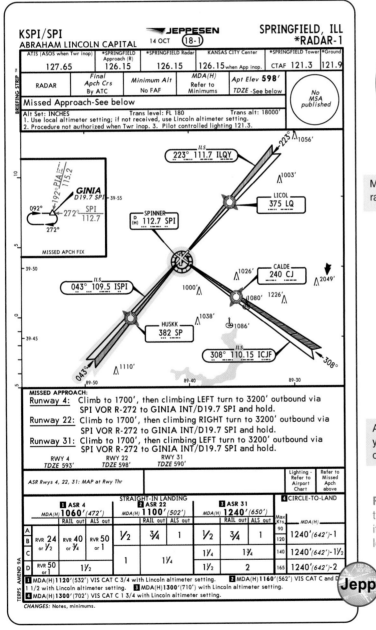

Make all of your turns at standard rate until you are on final approach

After the controller tells you that you are on final approach, make all of your turns at half standard rate.

Figure 10-9. During a no-gyro approach, the controller provides lateral guidance. If it is a PAR no-gyro approach, the controller also provides vertical guidance.

FAA Prior to being handed off the the final approach controller during a no-gyro approach, you should make all turns at standard rate unless otherwise advised.

SECTION A ■ IFR Emergencies

SUMMARY CHECKLIST

✓ The *Aeronautical Information Manual* defines an emergency as a condition of distress or urgency. Pilots in distress are threatened by serious and/or imminent danger and require immediate assistance. An urgency situation, such as low fuel quantity, requires timely but not immediate assistance.

✓ In an emergency, you may deviate from any rule in FAR Part 91 to the extent necessary to meet the emergency.

✓ The frequency of 121.5 MHz may be used to declare an emergency if you are unable to contact ATC on other frequencies.

✓ In a distress situation, begin your initial call with the word MAYDAY preferably repeated three times. Use PAN-PAN in the same manner in an urgency situation.

✓ Your transponder may be used to declare an emergency by squawking code 7700.

✓ A special emergency is a condition of air piracy and should be indicated by squawking code 7500 on your transponder.

✓ FAR Part 91 requires that you report the malfunction of any navigation, approach, or communications equipment while operating in controlled airspace under IFR. Include the aircraft ID, equipment affected, the degree to which the flight will be impaired by the failure, and any assistance you require from ATC in the malfunction report.

✓ If your remaining fuel quantity is such that you can accept little or no delay, alert ATC with a minimum fuel advisory.

✓ If the remaining usable fuel supply suggests the need for traffic priority to ensure a safe landing, declare an emergency due to low fuel and report fuel remaining in minutes.

✓ Gyroscopic instruments include the attitude indicator, heading indicator, and turn coordinator. These instruments are subject to vacuum and electrical system failures.

✓ During an instrument failure your first priority is to fly the airplane, navigate accurately, and then communicate with ATC.

✓ You can use your transponder to alert ATC to a radio communications failure by squawking code 7600.

✓ During a communication failure while operating under IFR, you are expected to follow the lost communication procedures specified in the regulations.

✓ During a communication failure in VFR conditions, remain in VFR conditions and land as soon as practicable.

✓ If you lose communication with ATC during your flight, you must fly the highest of the assigned altitude, MEA, or the altitude ATC has advised may be expected in a further clearance.

✓ If an approach is available at your clearance limit, begin the approach at the expect further clearance (EFC) time. If an approach is not available at your clearance limit, proceed from the clearance limit at your EFC to the point at which an approach begins.

✓ Radar approach procedures might be available to assist you during an emergency situation requiring an instrument approach.

✓ A radar instrument approach that provides only azimuth navigational guidance is referred to as an airport surveillance radar (ASR) approach.

✓ During a precision approach (PAR), the controller provides you with precise navigational guidance in azimuth and elevation as well as trend information to help you make the proper corrections while on the approach path.

✓ You may request a no-gyro approach if you have experienced a gyroscopic instrument failure. Controllers provide course guidance by with instructions such as *"turn right... stop turn"* to align you with the approach path. Make turns at standard rate until you have been turned onto final, then at half standard rate.

KEY TERMS

Distress	Code 7600
Urgency	Code 7700
MAYDAY	Airport Surveillance Radar (ASR)
PAN-PAN	Surveillance Approach
Malfunction Report	Precision Approach Radar (PAR)
Minimum Fuel	No-Gyro Vector
Special Emergency	No-Gyro Approach
Code 7500	

QUESTIONS

1. What phrase is used to begin a distress call to ATC?

2. Which transponder code is used during a special emergency?
   A. 7700
   B. 7600
   C. 7500

3. List the items you are expected to include in a malfunction report to ATC.

4. True/False. Declaring minimum fuel is an emergency.

5. True/False. If you are in IFR conditions and find that one of your gyroscopic instruments has failed, you should immediately transition to the partial panel technique of instrument flying.

6. What is the primary objective of the regulations governing communication failure during IFR operations?

7. You should fly the highest of three altitudes if you lose two-way radio communication in IFR conditions. What are those altitudes?

8. List the routes, in order of importance, you are expected to fly if you lose two-way radio communication in IFR conditions.

9. If, prior to a loss of two-way radio communication, you receive an EFC time from ATC for a holding fix from which an approach begins, and you arrive at that fix early, what should you do?

10. Two specific items are required in order to use a radar approach procedure. What are they?

11. List the three types of radar approach procedures that may be available for use during an emergency.

12. Which radar approach procedure provides course deviation and trend information?

13. True/False. After being turned onto final during a no-gyro approach, all turns should be made at standard rate.

SECTION B
IFR Single-Pilot Resource Management

The only thing that keeps a man out of a storm is his own decision not to enter it, his own hands turning the airplane back to clear air, his own skill taking him back to a safe landing. Flight remains the world of the individual, where he decides to accept responsibility for his action.

— Richard Bach, *A Gift of Wings*

When you fly in IFR conditions, without outside visual references, you face unique situations that you do not encounter during flights under VFR. **Single-pilot resources management (SRM)** is more complex in the IFR environment—you operate in a more challenging and structured environment in which you must precisely fly specific procedures and coordinate with ATC throughout your flight. [Figure 10-10]

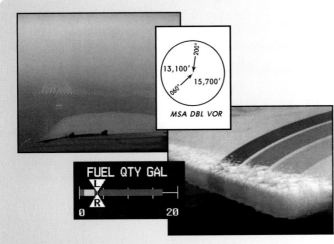

Consider what action you would take in each of these situations:

- You are on a weekend trip and scheduled to return to work for an important meeting. Although no PIREPs exist for icing, the forecast along your route indicates the potential for icing conditions. Your airplane has pitot heat, but no other deicing equipment.

- You are in IFR conditions on initial climb when your attitude indicator fails.

- An electrical system malfunction occurs while you are enroute in IFR conditions, 30 minutes from your destination.

- During your second ILS approach attempt, you see the approach lights at the decision altitude. As you descend, they disappear behind a patch of fog.

- After a lengthy hold, you begin an approach at your destination. At the missed approach point, you do not see the runway environment. You perform the missed approach and determine that you no longer have enough fuel to fly to your filed alternate.

- As you near your destination, ATC clears you for an immediate descent to the initial approach fix altitude. You are over an area of mountainous terrain, and following the clearance will cause you to descend below the minimum safe altitude for the area. The frequency is congested, and you are unable to contact the controller.

Figure 10-10. These scenarios illustrate the unique factors that affect decision making in the IFR environment.

IFR ACCIDENTS

When you fly under IFR, you are operating with one of the highest levels of safety available to general aviation, due to the amount of ATC support and control, and the training you must have to be instrument rated. However, accidents do occur. An understanding of accident causes in the IFR environment helps you better assess risk and avoid hazardous situations. Reviewing NTSB accident and incident reports can help you learn about faulty decision making and the relative safety of various IFR operations. Three common causes of accidents that involve IFR conditions are: attempted VFR flight into IFR conditions; controlled flight into terrain; and loss of control.

Continued flight under VFR flight into IFR conditions resulting in spatial disorientation is the most hazardous of accident scenarios. Typically over 70% of accidents attributed to attempts to fly under VFR into IFR conditions are fatal. Pilots with instrument ratings are not immune from this hazard and studies have shown that overconfidence in one's skill level can increase the risk of this accident type. Spatial disorientation leading to an accident can also occur on a flight under IFR due to lack of pilot instrument proficiency.

Controlled flight into terrain (CFIT) in the IFR environment is most often associated with instrument departure and approach procedures. Failure to follow safe takeoff and departure techniques, failure to fly a stabilized approach, and loss of situational awareness contribute to CFIT accidents.

Another cause of IFR accidents is loss of control in IFR conditions, sometimes brought on by flight into convective activity, and possibly compounded by spatial disorientation. A lack of awareness of wide-scale weather and failure to properly use onboard weather-detection equipment contributes to these accidents.

POOR JUDGMENT CHAIN

Typically, a sequence of contributing factors produces an accident, although at first glance it can appear to have only a single cause. The **poor judgment chain**, or error chain, describes this concept of contributing factors in a human-factors-related accident. Breaking one link in the chain by making a different decision is typically all that a pilot needs to do to avert a catastrophic outcome of a sequence of events. [Figure 10-11]

NTSB Report

The instrument-rated private pilot had 75 hours of simulated instrument time but only 10 hours of actual instrument flight time when he began a flight under VFR to Ogden, Utah.

While enroute in VFR conditions, the pilot contacted Cedar City Radio to determine the current conditions at Ogden. He was told that the weather at his destination was steadily deteriorating toward IFR conditions so he filed and activated an IFR flight plan.

As he neared his destination, but before being vectored to intercept the localizer for the ILS approach, the pilot was advised that the visibility was 1/4 mile less than the published approach minimums. Soon thereafter, a turbojet airplane attempting the same ILS approach reported conducting a missed approach and requested vectors to an airport with better visibility.

The pilot continued the approach but did not stabilize his airspeed or intercept the localizer after the airplane was inside the final approach fix. The pilot flew through the localizer twice and was at a point where the airplane would have been beyond the full-scale deflection of the CDI.

Although he failed to establish a stabilized approach or maintain the localizer course, he did not initiate a missed approach. He contacted the tower controller, who gave him an updated report of visibility that was 1/2 mile below the published approach minimums; however, the pilot elected to continue the approach. He descended below the decision altitude and impacted a power pole and trees about 1/2 mile from the end of the runway.

Figure 10-11. When you read accident reports, consider the actions that the pilots could have taken to break links in the poor judgment chain and maintain flight safety.

Aviation Safety Reporting System (ASRS) accounts illustrate some poor decisions, but also provide examples of effective decision making as pilots manage unexpected weather conditions, confusing ATC instructions, equipment malfunctions, and emergency situations. These reports also reveal how pilots broke a link in the poor judgment chain to prevent an accident or incident. Search the ASRS Database Online to explore situations specifically related to flight under IFR. [Figure 10-12}

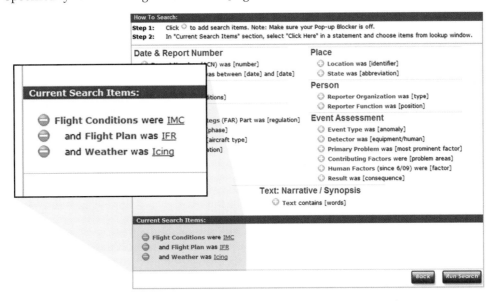

Figure 10-12. Customize your ASRS database search for specific flight conditions or events.

AERONAUTICAL DECISION MAKING

To gain experience in **aeronautical decision making (ADM)** in the IFR environment and to receive the greatest safety benefit from your instrument rating, file an IFR flight plan every time you fly cross country and close the flight plan only when a safe landing is assured. This practice familiarizes you with the IFR system and helps you maintain procedural proficiency. Operating on an IFR flight plan also provides an extra level of safety if weather conditions become marginal VFR or IFR. Accidents occur when instrument-rated pilots either fail to file IFR when conditions warrant, or cancel their IFR flight plans prematurely and continue flight into poor weather. [Figure 10-13]

Figure 10-13. By filing an IFR flight plan for each cross-country flight, you already have an IFR clearance, applicable charts, and a plan of action if weather deteriorates from VFR to marginal VFR or IFR conditions.

SECTION B ■ IFR Single-Pilot Resource Management

ADM PROCESS

Although you might not always be aware of it, you have been using the **ADM process** to manage your flights as you gain piloting experience. The ADM process helps you to determine and implement a course of action and to evaluate the outcome of that action in both routine and emergency situations. [Figure 10-14]

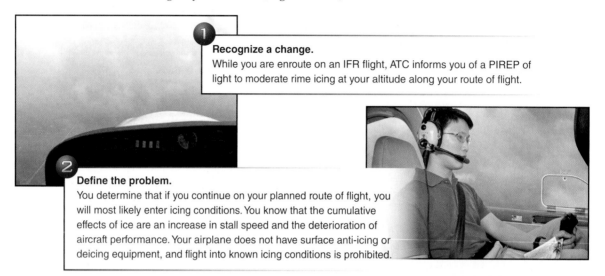

1 Recognize a change.
While you are enroute on an IFR flight, ATC informs you of a PIREP of light to moderate rime icing at your altitude along your route of flight.

2 Define the problem.
You determine that if you continue on your planned route of flight, you will most likely enter icing conditions. You know that the cumulative effects of ice are an increase in stall speed and the deterioration of aircraft performance. Your airplane does not have surface anti-icing or deicing equipment, and flight into known icing conditions is prohibited.

3 Choose a course of action.
You consult with ATC and Flight Service about the freezing level and reports of icing conditions in the area, and you check your remaining fuel. After considering your options, including continuing as planned to your destination, you determine that the best course of action to remain clear of icing is to alter your course and land at a nearby airport that is reporting marginal VFR conditions.

4 Implement your decision.
You ask ATC for an amended clearance to proceed direct to the diversion airport. When you are on your new course, you engage the autopilot and prepare for landing at your new destination by reviewing airport and approach information, programming the GPS, and setting appropriate navigation and communication frequencies.

5 Evaluate the outcome.
As you proceed to your destination, you monitor the enroute weather conditions for icing and check for any changes in the ceiling and visibility at the airport. You keep track of your position, monitor the fuel burn, stay alert for any ice accumulation on the wings, and ensure that you are prepared to fly the approach procedure.

Figure 10-14. This scenario, which is unique to the IFR environment, provides an example of how following the steps in the ADM process helps you make and implement effective decisions.

SELF ASSESSMENT

You are responsible for ensuring that the airplane is airworthy and safe for IFR flight, and through **self assessment**, that you are current and prepared to act as pilot in command in IFR conditions. Regulatory currency does not necessarily translate to proficiency in all IFR operations. Performing an approach at your destination with ceiling and visibility minimums at or just above minimums after a long cross-country flight in IFR conditions is a much greater challenge than flying a practice approach with a view limiting device and safety pilot at your local airport.

You must create a plan for maintaining your currency and proficiency. The best course of action is to frequently fly under IFR. However, if circumstances prevent you from flying for a period of time, maintain proficiency by practicing IFR procedures and approaches with a safety pilot on a regular basis. If significant time has lapsed since your last IFR flight, or you wish to increase your proficiency in actual conditions, schedule an instrument competency check with an experienced instructor. In many areas of the country, flight in IFR conditions is hard to acquire, and you might finish your training with little actual instrument time logged. Before you attempt flight as PIC in IFR conditions, make sure that you have flown in similar weather with an experienced instrument pilot or instrument instructor.

In addition to experience requirements, you must consider ceiling and visibility minimums for approach procedures prior to flight. The published minimums are established with the intent that the approach is flown by a proficient pilot at the controls of a familiar airplane. When you first receive your instrument rating, you should establish far more conservative minimums than the instrument approach procedures suggest. You can use the 5P Pilot and Plan checklists to list your personal minimums and limitations for both experience and weather conditions to help you make Go/No-Go decisions. [Figure 10-15]

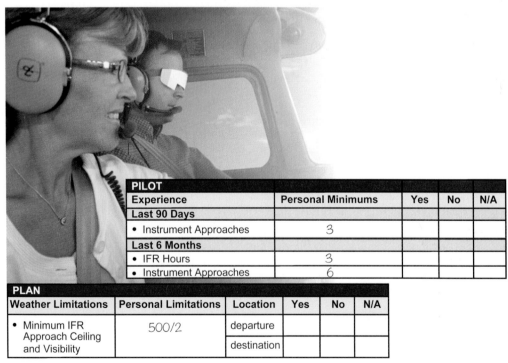

PILOT				
Experience	Personal Minimums	Yes	No	N/A
Last 90 Days				
• Instrument Approaches	3			
Last 6 Months				
• IFR Hours	3			
• Instrument Approaches	6			

PLAN					
Weather Limitations	Personal Limitations	Location	Yes	No	N/A
• Minimum IFR Approach Ceiling and Visibility	500/2	departure			
		destination			

Figure 10-15. Prior to a flight in IFR conditions, ensure you obtain the necessary experience to meet your personal minimums and limitations.

When the pilot in command is the only rated pilot in the cockpit, the operation is referred to as **single-pilot IFR**. Flying as sole pilot in IFR conditions presents one of the most demanding challenges as a pilot because of the high workload. This high workload can become extreme if you are required to manage an abnormal or emergency situation. Pilots working in the commercial environment who fly routinely in IFR conditions not only have more resources and training but are part of a crew sharing the workload. You might want to establish a personal limitation that requires another pilot on board when IFR conditions prevail. However, single-pilot IFR can be accomplished safely if you maintain strict standards for self assessment.

In addition to meeting or exceeding your personal minimums and limitations, you should be well-rested, organized, mentally sharp, and familiar with the route and approach procedures. You must also be proficient in operating all the equipment on the airplane, including programming and interpreting the avionics. In addition, consider establishing an autopilot as required equipment for this type of operation. [Figure 10-16]

SELF ASSESSMENT

REPORT

I started the procedure turn at the VOR where I started outbound course on a heading of 270° and after 1 minute began my parallel procedure turn by turning back to a heading of 30°...to intercept the 270 radial... I waited for the radial to come and it didn't so while trying to figure out what radial I was on, I accidently turned left to a heading of 330° and entered a restricted area. The controller notified me of this and I took action to turn back southwest toward the VOR... At this point I became disoriented and I lost about 1,000 feet of altitude...the controller contacted me and advised me to simply return to the airport and asked if I felt comfortable to perform an ILS approach... I then received vectors for the ILS approach into my home airport and then proceeded to land... While I'm an IFR-rated pilot and current, I do realize that I need more training before trying to perform these approaches alone in IMC. This was a valuable learning experience for me. It also has made me realize what my current limitations are in terms of IFR flying.

ANALYSIS

This pilot was instrument-rated and current but fully unprepared to fly single-pilot IFR. The serious errors that the pilot made during this flight easily could have led to an accident. Determining appropriate personal minimums based on experience level and sticking to these limitations might have prevented the pilot from attempting this flight without an experienced instrument-rated pilot or instructor on board.

Figure 10-16. This ASRS account illustrates how essential it is to perform self assessment and establish person minimums and limitations.

HAZARDOUS ATTITUDES

The five **hazardous attitudes** that you were introduced to in Chapter 1 require your consideration during each flight. Self-critiques can help you evaluate the reasons behind the choices you make as a pilot to determine which attitudes you are most likely to exhibit. To counteract a hazardous attitude you must recognize the hazardous thought and then state the corresponding antidote. [Figure 10-17]

ANTI-AUTHORITY

Don't tell me.

ATC says thunderstorms cells are reported ahead, and they're offering me vectors to divert, but i know what I'm doing.

Follow the rules. They are usually right.

ATC is trying to help; they have equipment that I don't so maybe they have a better handle on the situation.

INVULNERABILITY

It won't happen to me.

I have weather radar and a lighting detector on board — I'll be safe.

It could happen to me.

This equipment has important limitations to consider, and based on what ATC told me, I'll get into bad weather if I continue on this course.

MACHO

I can do it.

I'm tough. I can handle a little turbulence.

Taking chances is foolish.

There's severe turbulence inside a thunderstorm cell—I could damage the airplane or lose control.

IMPULSIVITY

Do it quickly.

I better try that break in the clouds before it closes up.

Not so fast. Think first.

Wait a minute – that hole isn't big enough for me to continue clear of the thunderstorms for another 50 miles to my destination.

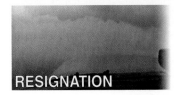

RESIGNATION

What's the use?

There's nothing I can do now. I'm going to fly into a thunderstorm.

I am not helpless. I can make a difference.

I can turn around and divert to another airport.

Figure 10-17. The pilot in this scenario displays each of the five hazardous attitudes that you need to avoid.

SECTION B ■ IFR Single-Pilot Resource Management

RISK MANAGEMENT

In addition to understanding the general risks associated with flying under IFR, you must perform effective **risk management** by identifying, assessing, and mitigating the risks that specifically apply to each flight. Use the **5P checklists** during flight planning to manage risks and make a Go or No-Go decision. Use the flight planning scenario introduced in Figure 10-18 to explore how to take these steps to use the 5P checklists to manage risk:

1. Identify risk factors by answering the question on each checklist.

2. Mitigate risks by modifying your plans if you answer No to any questions.

3. Make a Go or No-Go decision. If you cannot effectively mitigate all of the risks, make a No-Go decision.

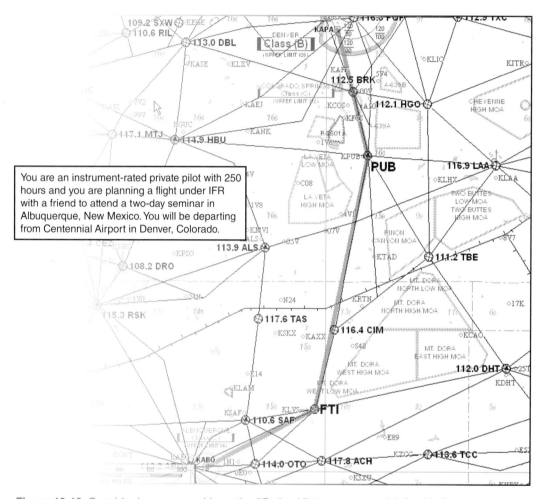

You are an instrument-rated private pilot with 250 hours and you are planning a flight under IFR with a friend to attend a two-day seminar in Albuquerque, New Mexico. You will be departing from Centennial Airport in Denver, Colorado.

Figure 10-18. Consider how you would use the 5P checklists to manage risk for this flight.

PILOT

When you first consider flying to Albuquerque, long before the day of the trip, you look at the 5P Pilot checklist to identify any necessary training and experience you need for the flight. Do you meet your personal minimums for recent instrument experience? Review the approach procedures that are available at Albuquerque and consider your airplane equipment. Do you feel comfortable with these procedures and setting up the navigation equipment? As your departure date gets closer and on the day of the flight, use the **I'M SAFE checklist** as part of the Pilot checklist to verify your fitness for flight. [Figure 10-19]

Pilot Risk — Experience
You have not met your personal minimums for instrument flight because you have not performed any instrument approaches in the last 90 days. During your instrument proficiency check, you logged two hours of simulated instrument time and performed three approaches, which means you need another hour of flight time and three more approaches to meet your personal minimums.

Risk Mitigation
To mitigate this risk, you increase your instrument proficiency and meet your personal minimums by completing IFR refresher training with an instructor before your trip.

Pilot Risk—Fitness
You felt pressure to meet a deadline prior to leaving on this trip and planned to work overtime earlier in the week to accomplish this goal.

Risk Mitigation
You discussed the situation with your boss and were able to obtain assistance to complete the project prior to your trip without working extra hours.

PILOT				
Summary of Training		Yes	No	N/A
Do I have a current flight review?		✔		
Am I current to carry passengers?		✔		
Have I had recent refresher training in this airplane?		✔		
Am I instrument-current?		✔		
Have I had recent mountain flying training or experience?		✔		
Experience	**Personal Minimums**	Yes	No	N/A
Hours in Specific Airplane	10	✔		
Last 90 Days				
• Hours	6	✔		
• Landings	6	✔		
• Instrument Approaches	3	✔	~~✔~~	
Last 6 Months				
• IFR Hours	3	✔	~~✔~~	
• Instrument Approaches	6	✔	~~✔~~	
• Night Hours	6	✔		
• Night Landings	6	✔		
• Strong Crosswind/Gusty Landings	2	✔		
• Mountain Flying Hours	1	✔		
Fitness — I'M SAFE		Yes	No	N/A
Illness — Am I healthy?		✔		
Medication — Am I free of prescription or over-the-counter drugs?		✔		
Stress — Am I free of pressure (job, financial matters, health problems, or family discord)?		✔		
Alcohol — Have I abstained from alcohol in the previous 24 hours?		✔		
Fatigue — Did I get at least seven hours of sleep?		✔		
Eating — Am I adequately nourished?		✔		
Emotion — Am I free of emotional upset?		✔		

Figure 10-19. Consider your recent instrument experience and your fitness for flight as you manage pilot risk.

PASSENGERS

Distractions your passengers cause can be a significant risk to flight safety, especially in the challenging IFR environment. Gather information about your passengers well ahead of the trip date. Ask passengers about their comfort and experience level in small airplanes and whether they are prone to motion sickness. Prepare them for possible delays or cancellation of the flight due to weather or other circumstances. Determine the experience level of any pilot that you are flying with. On the day of the flight, assess your passengers' fitness for flight again—ensure that they are feeling well and verify that they understand what the flight entails. Ensure your copilot is fit for flight as well. [Figure 10-20]

SECTION B ■ **IFR Single-Pilot Resource Management**

Passenger Risk — Flexibility
Your passenger is an experienced instrument pilot who can serve as a valuable resource, especially if the flight is in IFR conditions. However, he is concerned about missing the seminar due to weather or maintenance issues.

Risk Mitigation
To mitigate this risk, you discuss attending a similar seminar scheduled for later in the year if the proposed flight does not proceed as planned.

PASSENGERS			
Experience	Yes	No	N/A
Are my passengers comfortable flying? (spent time in small aircraft, certificated pilots, etc.)	✓		
Fitness	Yes	No	N/A
Are my passengers feeling well? (sickness, likely to experience airsickness, etc.)	✓		
Flexibility	Yes	No	N/A
Are my passengers flexible and well-informed about the changeable nature of flying? (arriving late, diverting to an alternate, etc.)	✓		

Figure 10-20. Before your flight, review the 5P Passengers checklist to help mitigate any problems that might arise.

PLANE

As you assess your airplane's status, you must consider some factors that are unique to flight under IFR. First, determine whether the airplane is airworthy. In addition to verifying that the airplane is not due for an annual or a 100-hour inspection, ensure that the VOR equipment check and the altimeter and static inspections required for IFR flight have been performed. Next, make sure the airplane meets the performance required for each phase of flight, including the climb gradients required for the IFR departure procedure and the ability to operate at or above the required MEA. Finally, confirm that the equipment required for IFR flight, including the navigation equipment necessary for the trip, is operational. [Figure 10-21]

Plane Risk — Airworthiness
The VOR equipment check was over 30 days old.

Risk Mitigation
You check the VOR equipment using the VOT at the airport and both displays are within the allowed tolerance.

PLANE			
Airworthiness	Yes	No	N/A
Are the aircraft inspections current and appropriate to the type of flight? (annual and 100-hour inspections, VOR check, etc.)	✓		
Have all prior maintenance issues been taken care of? (squawks resolved, inoperative equipment placarded, etc.)	✓		
Performance	Yes	No	N/A
Can the aircraft carry the planned load within weight and CG limits?	✓		
Is the aircraft performance (takeoff, climb, enroute, and landing) adequate for the available runways, density altitude, and terrain conditions?	✓		
Is the fuel capacity adequate for the proposed flight legs, including to an alternate airport if required?	✓		
Configuration	Yes	No	N/A
Is the required equipment on board and working for the type of flight? (lights for night flight, onboard oxygen, survival gear, etc.)	✓		

Figure 10-21. Consider the unique inspection, performance, and equipment requirements that apply to the IFR environment.

PROGRAMMING

The programming category is especially critical for IFR flight. As you gain experience, you might fly an increasing variety of airplanes with different avionics equipment. If you do not understand how to properly program and interpret the specific navigation and automation equipment onboard your airplane, you increase risk. Additional requirements must be met if you intend to use GPS equipment for navigation and approach procedures. You must refer to the AFM or AFM supplements to determine if the airplane's GPS equipment is approved for IFR and approach operations and whether it is WAAS-certified. In addition, for non-WAAS equipment, you must confirm that RAIM is available for the intended route and duration of the flight. [Figure 10-22]

Programming Risk
No significant risks are associated with programming for this flight. The avionics are working, the GPS databases are current, and you are proficient at operating the equipment. You plan to use GPS for enroute navigation—RAIM is available—and fly an ILS approach at your destination. The airplane is equipped with VOR equipment necessary to receive the VOR facilities on the route.

PROGRAMMING			
Avionics Airworthiness	**Yes**	**No**	**N/A**
Is the avionics equipment working properly? (squawks resolved, autopilot functional)	✔		
Are all databases current? (GPS navdata, terrain, etc.)	✔		
Avionics Operation	**Yes**	**No**	**N/A**
Are you proficient at operating the avionics equipment?	✔		
Avionics Configuration	**Yes**	**No**	**N/A**
Is the avionics configuration appropriate for the navigation required?	✔		
Is the GPS certified for IFR enroute and approach operations?	✔		
Is RAIM available (if applicable for the GPS equipment)?	✔		

Figure 10-22. To manage risk in the Programming category, verify that you are proficient in operating the avionics, the databases are current, and all the equipment is working.

PLAN

Your plan for the flight to Albuquerque includes a variety of risk factors. With the Plan checklist, you assess airport conditions, terrain, airspace, the external pressures of the mission, and weather. Flying in IFR conditions increases the risks associated with the plan. Make sure that no hazards exist, such as icing or embedded thunderstorms. Confirm that the minimums for the available approaches at the airport will enable you to land and determine whether an alternate airport is required. Ensure that the ceilings and visibilities meet or exceed your personal limitations and that you are comfortable flying the approach procedures.

Consider how the possibility of having to divert to the alternate would affect the mission. If a wide-spread weather system surrounds your destination, airports over a large geographical area could have similar low ceiling sand reduced visibilities—you might have difficulty finding a suitable alternate near your destination. When you select an alternate, consider your fuel capacity. Even if you meet the regulatory fuel requirements, would you have enough fuel to attempt the approach procedure more than once prior to diverting to your alternate? What if ATC requested that you hold for a period of time before performing the approach at your destination? [Figure 10-23]

SECTION B ■ **IFR Single-Pilot Resource Management**

Plan Risk — Airport Conditions
NOTAMs indicate that the localizer is out of service for Runway 3.

Risk Mitigation
The forecast wind of 15 knots at your destination is within your limitations, and it is expected to be aligned with Runway 8 with the operative ILS procedure. Two RNAV (GPS) approaches with minimums above the forecast ceiling and visibility are also available.

Plan Risk — Weather Minimums
The forecast ceiling and visibility for Albuquerque require you to file an alternate and are right at your personal minimums.

Risk Mitigation
Santa Fe's forecast indicates that it is a suitable alternate. Although the weather conditions are at your personal minimums, you feel confident flying an approach due to your recent IFR experience and the assistance of another pilot on board. In addition, conditions are not forecast to worsen and are expected to improve throughout the day.

PLAN					
Airport Conditions			Yes	No	N/A
Do NOTAMs indicate my flight can proceed as planned? (no runway or navaid closures, and so on)			✔		
Are services available at the airport during the appropriate time? (fuel, ATC, Unicom, etc.)			✔		
Terrain/Airspace			Yes	No	N/A
Does the airspace and terrain in the area allow me to fly my route as planned? (Check for mountainous terrain, and areas to avoid, such as TFRs, restricted or prohibited areas).			✔		
Mission			Yes	No	N/A
Do I have alternate plans to manage any commitments that exist at my destination? (reschedule meeting, airline reservations, etc.)			✔		
Did I tell the people whom I'm meeting at my destination that I might be late?			✔		
Do I have an overnight kit containing any necessary prescriptions and toiletries?			✔		
Weather		Location	Yes	No	N/A
Are the weather conditions acceptable? (no hazards such as thunderstorms, icing, turbulence, etc.)		departure	✔		
		enroute	✔		
		destination	✔		
Is there a suitable airport that meets the regulatory requirements for an alternate if the forecast at my destination requires an alternate airport?			✔		
Weather Limitations	**Personal Limitations**	**Location**	Yes	No	N/A
Are the weather conditions for my flight within my personal limitations?			✔		
• Minimum IFR Approach Ceiling and Visibility	*500/2*	departure	✔		
		destination	✔		
• Minimum Ceiling and Visibility (Day VFR)	*2000/10*	departure			✔
		enroute			✔
		destination			✔
• Minimum Ceiling and Visibility (Night VFR)	*5000/15*	departure			✔
		enroute			✔
		destination			✔
• Maximum Surface Wind Speed and Gusts	*15 G 20*	departure	✔		
		destination	✔		
• Maximum Direct Crosswind	*10*	departure	✔		
		destination	✔		

Figure 10-23. The Plan category includes identifying the mission's external pressures, assessing the weather conditions, and evaluating the destination airport, route, and alternate selection.

USING THE 5P CHECK IN FLIGHT

After making a Go decision, performing the preflight inspection, and starting the engine, you are ready to begin your flight to Albuquerque. During your flight, continue to manage risk by evaluating your situation using the **5P check**. Carefully monitoring weather conditions, including PIREPs for icing or lowering ceilings and visibilities, and keeping track of navigation system status are especially important tasks in IFR conditions. Use the 5P check at decision points that correspond to the phases of flight: before takeoff, initial cruise, enroute cruise, descent, and before approach and landing. [Figure 10-24]

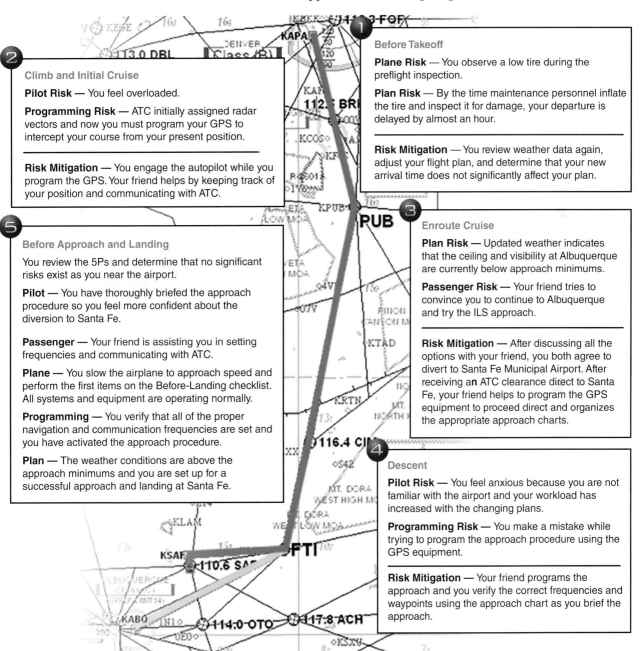

① Before Takeoff

Plane Risk — You observe a low tire during the preflight inspection.

Plan Risk — By the time maintenance personnel inflate the tire and inspect it for damage, your departure is delayed by almost an hour.

Risk Mitigation — You review weather data again, adjust your flight plan, and determine that your new arrival time does not significantly affect your plan.

② Climb and Initial Cruise

Pilot Risk — You feel overloaded.

Programming Risk — ATC initially assigned radar vectors and now you must program your GPS to intercept your course from your present position.

Risk Mitigation — You engage the autopilot while you program the GPS. Your friend helps by keeping track of your position and communicating with ATC.

③ Enroute Cruise

Plan Risk — Updated weather indicates that the ceiling and visibility at Albuquerque are currently below approach minimums.

Passenger Risk — Your friend tries to convince you to continue to Albuquerque and try the ILS approach.

Risk Mitigation — After discussing all the options with your friend, you both agree to divert to Santa Fe Municipal Airport. After receiving an ATC clearance direct to Santa Fe, your friend helps to program the GPS equipment to proceed direct and organizes the appropriate approach charts.

④ Descent

Pilot Risk — You feel anxious because you are not familiar with the airport and your workload has increased with the changing plans.

Programming Risk — You make a mistake while trying to program the approach procedure using the GPS equipment.

Risk Mitigation — Your friend programs the approach and you verify the correct frequencies and waypoints using the approach chart as you brief the approach.

⑤ Before Approach and Landing

You review the 5Ps and determine that no significant risks exist as you near the airport.

Pilot — You have thoroughly briefed the approach procedure so you feel more confident about the diversion to Santa Fe.

Passenger — Your friend is assisting you in setting frequencies and communicating with ATC.

Plane — You slow the airplane to approach speed and perform the first items on the Before-Landing checklist. All systems and equipment are operating normally.

Programming — You verify that all of the proper navigation and communication frequencies are set and you have activated the approach procedure.

Plan — The weather conditions are above the approach minimums and you are set up for a successful approach and landing at Santa Fe.

Figure 10-24. You must reevaluate each of the 5Ps during the flight to recognize any changes that have occurred that might increase your risk.

TASK MANAGEMENT

Effective **task management** means you are not fixating on one task to the exclusion of others. Planning and prioritizing are critical to managing the tasks associated with performing instrument procedures. The amount of tasks increases with flights under IFR compared to VFR flights. However, flights in the IFR environment are more structured and are coordinated with ATC so you have additional resources to aid in task management. Ensure that your resources, such as advanced avionics equipment, decrease your workload and do not become a distraction.

PLANNING AND PRIORITIZING

In addition to managing risk by using the 5Ps, you can increase flight safety by taking your preflight planning a few steps further. Rehearse your intended route of flight and determine if you are unsure about any segments of the flight. For example, you might have questions about obtaining a clearance at an airport without a control tower, performing a SID from a busy terminal area, or interpreting an item on an approach chart. Review the AIM or flight training content to refresh your memory regarding specific IFR operations, ask an experienced pilot about what to expect, and practice unfamiliar procedures using an aviation training device (ATD).

Follow the weather trends for several days before your flight to gain a more complete weather picture. For example, keep track of the movement and speed of frontal systems. Determine what change in forecast conditions would most adversely affect your flight, and plan for that change to occur. Determine how the weather might affect your fuel calculations and ensure that the forecast ceilings and visibilities are above the minimums of the available approach procedures at your destination. Consider your options if your airport only has nonprecision approaches available.

During a flight under IFR, you need to remain continually aware of what will happen next so you can prioritize the tasks you need to accomplish. Planning and prioritizing are especially important in periods of exceptionally high workload, such as during departure and approach in IFR conditions. Perform a departure briefing prior to takeoff and an approach briefing as soon as you know what approach to expect, preferably before you begin your descent. When workload is high, identify your most important tasks. Controlling the airplane is foremost, followed by staying aware of your position. Deal with equipment problems on an urgency basis. Obviously, emergencies such as an engine failure require your immediate attention. If a navigation source fails in the middle of the approach, such as the loss of the glide slope during an ILS, review your MDA and consider carefully whether to continue the approach or perform a missed approach.

RESOURCE USE

To benefit from many of the resources available to you as an instrument pilot, you must prepare for their use prior to your flight. In addition to obtaining a weather briefing, finalizing your flight planning, and performing the preflight inspection, you can accomplish several other tasks that will help you be better prepared to use your resources and reduce workload during flight. [Figure 10-25]

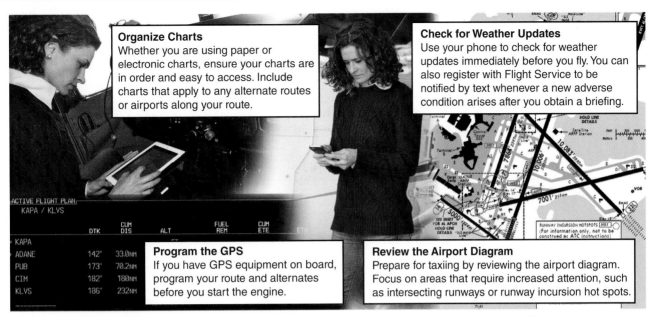

Organize Charts
Whether you are using paper or electronic charts, ensure your charts are in order and easy to access. Include charts that apply to any alternate routes or airports along your route.

Check for Weather Updates
Use your phone to check for weather updates immediately before you fly. You can also register with Flight Service to be notified by text whenever a new adverse condition arises after you obtain a briefing.

Program the GPS
If you have GPS equipment on board, program your route and alternates before you start the engine.

Review the Airport Diagram
Prepare for taxiing by reviewing the airport diagram. Focus on areas that require increased attention, such as intersecting runways or runway incursion hot spots.

Figure 10-25. Use these resources prior to flight to reduce head-down time during ground and flight operations.

Effective **cockpit management** is essential to IFR operations. Attempting to locate charts, checklists, and other supplies while flying in IFR conditions can lead you to lose situational awareness, become disoriented, and possibly lose control of the airplane. During preflight, ensure that all your resources for the flight are on board and accessible, secure items in the cockpit and cabin in case you encounter turbulence, and adjust your seat for best visibility and reach of the controls. You might use a tablet computer as a reference for electronic charts, as a performance calculator, or to review airport information. To ensure your tablet is ready for flight, create a preflight checklist that is customized for your specific apps and airplane. [Figure 10-26] During flight, it is critical that you know how to properly

Tablet Preflight

Battery — Ensure your battery is fully charged and backup battery packs or charging cables are available.

Apps — Run the apps you intend to use to verify that they start correctly and do not crash.

Databases — Verify that your databases are current and that the current chart coverage is saved for offline use.

Resources — Load your flight plan, routes, charts, airport information, performance data, and alternate resources. Ensure that they are organized and easy to access.

Wireless — Turn off wireless functions that you do not need.

Screen — Clean the screen and adjust the brightness.

Figure 10-26. If you intend to use a tablet during your flight, mitigate risk by preflighting your tablet to ensure it is airworthy and ready for the specific flight operations.

SECTION B ■ IFR Single-Pilot Resource Management

use internal resources, such as GPS equipment, multi-function displays, airborne weather radar, TAWS, traffic displays, and the autopilot. For example, accidents have occurred when professional flight crews have entered the wrong identifier into a flight management system. You must be thoroughly familiar with all equipment on board the airplane and have specific procedures to set up avionics and cross check programming. The head-down time you spend in the airplane figuring out a piece of equipment takes away from the time you spend monitoring the instruments and maintaining situational awareness. Use the autopilot as appropriate to ease your workload, but be sure you understand its limitations and how to operate it properly. [Figure 10-27]

Pilot's Operating Handbook

RESOURCE USE

REPORT

Pilot — *IFR clearance to CQX. In the clear at 3,000 feet, requested GPS approach to Runway 24. Cleared to the IAF, loaded and activated the approach on my GPS. Controllers very busy, entire area 600 feet to 700 feet overcast, tops 1,500 feet Controllers changed and we are now cleared to PPICE. Had difficulty loading page and in the confusion went off my heading. Controller called me on it... In reviewing my actions, I should have used the autopilot while sorting out the GPS loading and activation problem.*

ATC — *[Two] aircraft inbound to CQX... I instructed [the] low-wing, fixed-gear aircraft to proceed direct to PPICE. He said he would have to find it first, this surprised me as I would have thought the pilot would have the approach plate at the ready. ...I noticed the low-wing, fixed-gear aircraft heading northwest bound. I turned the air carrier right heading 140 and called traffic. ...We seem to be seeing more pilot deviations due to pilots not being completely in control of their aircraft due to unfamiliarity with the use of autopilot/flight management systems in small aircraft.*

ANALYSIS

In addition to be unable to properly use the GPS equipment, the pilot failed to use other resources, such as the autopilot, to manage workload in this situation. Head-down time and a failure to prioritize maintaining aircraft control caused a pilot deviation that could have had serious consequences. ATC based instructions on the assumption that the pilot would have and be able to use the necessary resources.

Figure 10-27. This ASRS account emphasizes the importance of understanding how to properly use resources, such as the GPS equipment.

In the IFR environment, ATC becomes your most vital external resource. In addition to routine IFR services, ATC can offer assistance in an abnormal or emergency situation. For example, a controller might provide vectors to an alternate airport or a radar approach in the event or navigation or gyroscopic equipment failure. You can coordinate with ATC to obtain an amended altitude or course clearance to avoid weather or icing conditions. ATC also provides information about facility and service outages, such as RAIM or WAAS.

CREW COORDINATION

Some of your flying as an instrument pilot requires you to share the cockpit. To maintain proficiency you might need to fly with a **safety pilot**, who is in charge of seeing and avoiding other aircraft and terrain while you practice instrument maneuvers with a view-limiting device. Anyone who holds a private pilot certificate, is rated in the airplane you are flying, and who has a current third-class medical certificate, can serve as your safety pilot. Pilots often take turns acting as safety pilot while the other flies by reference to the instruments.

In addition to acting as a safety pilot, another pilot on board during a flight under IFR can significantly increase your safety and decrease your workload if you effectively divide responsibilities. Obtain information about any copilots prior to each flight. Do they respect the FARs and aircraft limitations? Do they have more or less experience than you do in the airplane and in the area in which you will be flying? What are their motivations and expectations concerning the flight? Even when you fly with pilots whose habits you know well, you need to establish who will act as PIC, and who will be expected to perform what duties during the flight. This is also true when you fly with an instructor, such as during refresher training or an instrument proficiency check. [Figure 10-28]

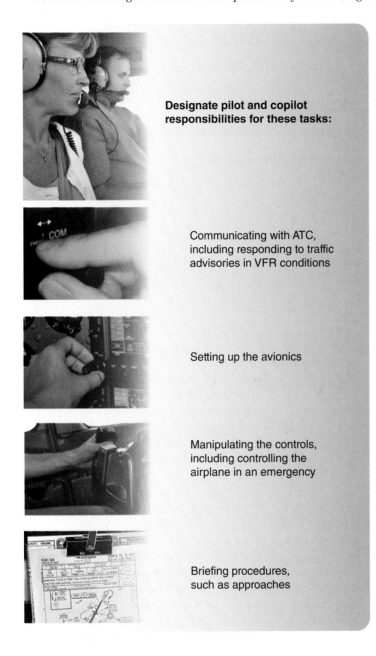

Designate pilot and copilot responsibilities for these tasks:

Communicating with ATC, including responding to traffic advisories in VFR conditions

Setting up the avionics

Manipulating the controls, including controlling the airplane in an emergency

Briefing procedures, such as approaches

Figure 10-28. Whether you are flying with an instructor or a pilot friend, you need to coordinate your efforts.

WORK OVERLOAD

At times during certain flights, the workload might outweigh your ability to stay ahead of the airplane. For example, when you fly an approach, you are particularly prone to work overload, especially if the approach involves multiple course changes, step-down fixes, and intermediate altitudes. Any additional workload, such as an equipment failure or an unusual request from ATC, could create a work overload situation. Maintain proficiency, not just currency, in flying a variety of procedures, review charts prior to your flight, and perform thorough briefings to help prevent work overload during approaches. During each phase of flight, there is a relationship between the amount of work and the ability to deal with workload effectively, which is referred to as the **margin of safety**. [Figure 10-29]

SECTION B ■ IFR Single-Pilot Resource Management

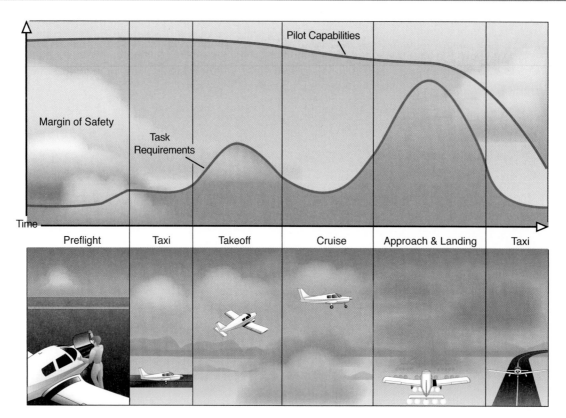

Figure 10-29. The margin of safety is the narrowest during the approach and landing phase of flight.

Recognizing work overload is an important component of managing workload. The first effect of high workload is that you are working harder but accomplishing less. As workload increases, your attention is not devoted to several tasks at one time, and you might begin to focus on one item. When you are task saturated, you have no awareness of input from various sources, so you might make decisions on incomplete information and the possibility of error increases. When you experience work overload, remain calm, stop, think, slow down, and prioritize. Consider the available resources to use to decrease your workload, such as the autopilot, a copilot, passenger, or ATC.

SITUATIONAL AWARENESS

The skills that enable you to know your location when you have no outside references are developed with your instrument training. Using these skills effectively is an important part of **situational awareness** when incorporated with knowledge of the airplane and systems, the weather affecting the flight, and ATC requirements. Situational awareness deteriorates when you experience problems with crew relationships, miscommunication, poor use of resources, and inadequate task management techniques.

Flying instrument procedures, such as SIDs, STARs, and approaches presents unique challenges because of the amount of information you must manage. Performing briefings prior to each procedure is essential to maintaining situational awareness. Review the chart and verbalize the primary elements of the procedure to your copilot or out loud to yourself. When you receive radar vectors, keep track of your location by monitoring the instruments or referring to a moving map display so you do not lose positional awareness. In addition, read back clearances, and when in doubt, verify instructions with ATC. Do not assume that controller silence after a readback is verification. Ask the controller for a verbal confirmation. [Figure 10-30]

SITUATIONAL AWARENESS

REPORT

We were cleared for the GPS 19 into FRG. ...I therefore gave what I thought was a thorough approach brief about 15 minutes out. We started getting vectors for the approach...we were told to go "direct PODAL, maintain 2000' till established, cleared for the GPS 19 approach. ...We manually plugged in PODAL and realized we were just coming up on it. The copilot was reading the approach plate and told me to turn left to a heading of 280 degrees for our base leg and descend to 1,500'. ...It wasn't until I reached 1,500' that he realized he had read the chart incorrectly and we should have still been at 2,000'. ...My problem started with me giving an inadequate approach brief. I should have briefed the full approach and stated that we should be ready and able to plug in the appropriate transition fix based on which side of the airport the TRACON was bringing us in on.

ANALYSIS

The crew performed an incomplete approach briefing and failed to keep track of the airplane's position relative to the IAF after receiving vectors. These errors caused the crew to enter the IAF without loading the entire approach procedure, and rush a descent without confirmation by both crew members of the correct procedure. An altitude deviation resulted from the loss of situational awareness by both crew members.

Figure 10-30. This ASRS account illustrates the challenge of maintaining situational awareness during approach procedures.

OBSTACLES TO SITUATIONAL AWARENESS

Falling into complacency because situations feel routine or because you rely too much on automation is an obstacle to maintaining situational awareness. To counteract complacency, continue to scan the flight instruments, and monitor the navigation displays and systems indications while using automation. Be prepared to hand-fly the airplane in case the autopilot malfunctions. Practice attitude instrument flying, holding, and instrument approaches by manually flying the airplane during frequent refresher training. Another way to prevent complacency is to follow **standard operating procedures (SOPs)** each time you fly. Even if the airplane is familiar and the situation is routine, establish and adhere to SOPs, such as using the 5P check, performing approach briefings, and following flow patterns to configure the airplane and avionics.

To maintain situational awareness you also must manage distractions. For example, consider these situations: you become so focused on correcting an altitude deviation that you drift off course toward high terrain or you forget to brief the approach procedure when ATC amends your clearance and gives you a vector to maintain separation from traffic. To manage distractions, avoid focusing on one task to the exclusion of others. Ensure that controlling the airplane is your priority and maintain proficiency in attitude instrument flying so you can perform other tasks easily. Maintain proficiency in instrument procedures to prepare for distractions, such as radio transmissions, in the busy IFR environment. Review charts and memorize pertinent information during low workload periods so you can avoid head-down time and focus on the instruments while flying approaches, holding patterns, and other procedures. [Figure 10-31]

SECTION B ■ **IFR Single-Pilot Resource Management**

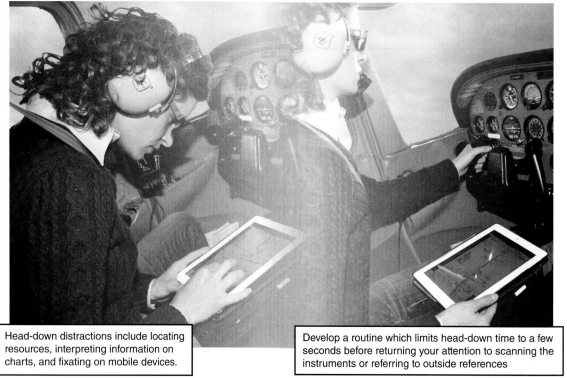

Head-down distractions include locating resources, interpreting information on charts, and fixating on mobile devices.

Develop a routine which limits head-down time to a few seconds before returning your attention to scanning the instruments or referring to outside references

Figure 10-31. To limit head-down time, train yourself to look up from a task every few seconds, even if the task is not complete.

Following the **sterile cockpit** procedure is another way to reduce distractions during critical phases of flight. Eliminate nonessential conversation with crew members or passengers during taxi, takeoff, landing, and all flight operations except cruise flight to avoid distractions that can cause you to lose situational awareness.

SITUATIONAL AWARENESS DURING GROUND OPERATIONS

In addition to keeping track of your status while in flight, you must maintain situational awareness during ground operations. The low visibility conditions and high workload that apply to the IFR environment increase the risk of a runway incursion. Plan for the airport surface movement portion of the flight just as you plan for other phases of flight. Prior to taxi, review the current airport diagram and check NOTAMs and ATIS for runway and taxiway closures, construction activity, and other airport-specific risks.

Just as you would for an approach procedure, brief taxi operations, including the taxi route, hold-short positions, crossing runways, and runway incursion hot spots before taxiing on departure and prior to initial descent on arrival. During taxi, maintain a sterile cockpit and view the airport diagram or low visibility taxi chart (if applicable). Cockpit equipment, such as a moving map display that shows your airplane's position on the airport, can help you maintain situational awareness during taxi. [Figure 10-32]

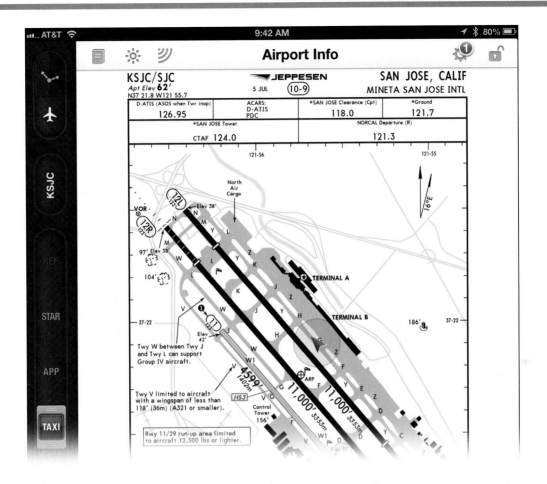

Figure 10-32. Using moving map technology, you can see the position of your airplane on the airport as you taxi.

Use a continuous-loop process to actively monitor and update your progress—know your airplane's present location and mentally calculate the next location on the route that requires increased attention, such as a turn onto another taxiway, an intersecting runway, or a hot spot. [Figure 10-33]

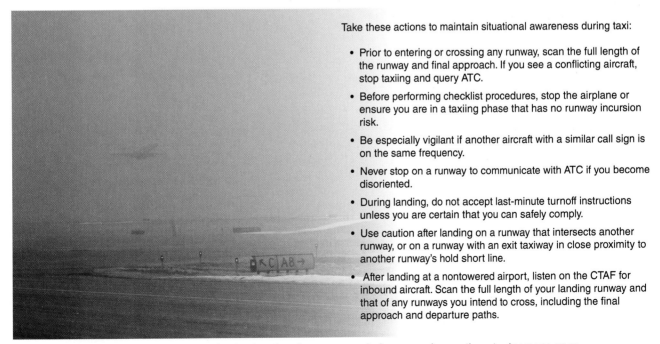

Take these actions to maintain situational awareness during taxi:

- Prior to entering or crossing any runway, scan the full length of the runway and final approach. If you see a conflicting aircraft, stop taxiing and query ATC.

- Before performing checklist procedures, stop the airplane or ensure you are in a taxiing phase that has no runway incursion risk.

- Be especially vigilant if another aircraft with a similar call sign is on the same frequency.

- Never stop on a runway to communicate with ATC if you become disoriented.

- During landing, do not accept last-minute turnoff instructions unless you are certain that you can safely comply.

- Use caution after landing on a runway that intersects another runway, or on a runway with an exit taxiway in close proximity to another runway's hold short line.

- After landing at a nontowered airport, listen on the CTAF for inbound aircraft. Scan the full length of your landing runway and that of any runways you intend to cross, including the final approach and departure paths.

Figure 10-33. You must maintain situational awareness during ground operations to decrease your risk of a runway incursion.

SECTION B ■ IFR Single-Pilot Resource Management

CONTROLLED FLIGHT INTO TERRAIN AWARENESS

Although, the risk of **controlled flight into terrain (CFIT)** exists for VFR flights at night or in reduced visibility, this risk primarily affects IFR operations. You will recall that CFIT

occurs when an aircraft is flown into terrain or water with no prior awareness on the part of the crew that the crash is imminent. You can avoid CFIT by increasing your **positional awareness**. A high level of positional awareness includes paying particular attention to your location relative to terrain and the minimum altitudes provided on IFR charts.

Installation of **terrain awareness and warning systems (TAWS)** by air carriers and professional flight departments have significantly reduced the number of CFIT-related accidents in the United States. TAWS equipment not only displays color-coded terrain data on a moving map but provides aural warnings and alert

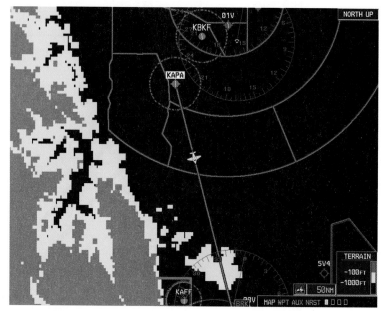

Figure 10-34. Moving map terrain displays provide a valuable resource for maintaining positional awareness in relation to surrounding terrain.

annunciations if the aircraft is close to terrain. All turbine-powered aircraft with six or more passenger seats must be equipped with TAWS and many general aviation aircraft are equipped with terrain proximity displays or TAWS. [Figure 10-34]

You can take specific actions to decrease your risk of CFIT during each phase of flight. During IFR departures, risk increases if no published departure procedures exist or if you are not fully prepared to fly the departure procedure. You must thoroughly review the charted departure procedure or the departure instructions provided by ATC, consider the surrounding terrain and obstacles, and brief the takeoff and departure. [Figure 10-35]

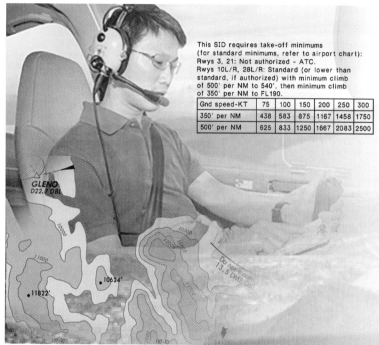

This SID requires take-off minimums (for standard minimums, refer to airport chart):
Rwys 3, 21: Not authorized - ATC.
Rwys 10L/R, 28L/R: Standard (or lower than standard, if authorized) with minimum climb of 500' per NM to 540', then minimum climb of 350' per NM to FL190.

Gnd speed-KT	75	100	150	200	250	300
350' per NM	438	583	875	1167	1458	1750
500' per NM	625	833	1250	1667	2083	2500

Initial Climb and Departure

- Review current charts with clear depictions of hazardous terrain and minimum safe altitudes.

- Ensure that your airplane performance meets any required climb gradients.

- Verify that ATC departure instructions provide adequate terrain clearance—do not assume that your assigned course and altitude ensures that you will clear the surrounding terrain and obstacles. If ATC gives a clearance that conflicts with your assessment of terrain criteria, question and, if necessary, refuse the clearance.

- Brief the takeoff and climb procedure prior to takeoff, including the outbound course, direction of the first turn, and any departure altitude crossing restrictions.

- During the takeoff briefing, set all communication and navigation frequencies and course selectors to eliminate distractions below 1,000 feet AGL.

- Brief the approach procedure in use at the departure airport in case you must return to the airport.

Figure 10-35. Take these actions to reduce the risk of CFIT during initial climb and departure under IFR.

To decrease your risk of CFIT during cruise flight, prior to departure, review the enroute chart to determine the minimum safe altitudes for the proposed flight. Consider your performance, especially when you plan to fly over high terrain. During flight, use VFR charts or a moving map to visualize the terrain you are flying over.

The final approach and landing phase of flight accounts for approximately 40 percent of CFIT accidents. Maintaining situational awareness and flying a stabilized approach is critical to preventing CFIT in IFR conditions. Proper briefings are also key to CFIT prevention. Always perform an approach overview and approach briefing when advised what procedure to expect. If you must fly a nonprecision approach, brief the procedure as a stabilized approach using a constant rate of descent. Brief the missed approach procedure with emphasis on the direction of the initial missed approach turn. In addition to briefings, there are many actions you can take to reduce the risk of CFIT during approach and landing. [Figure 10-36]

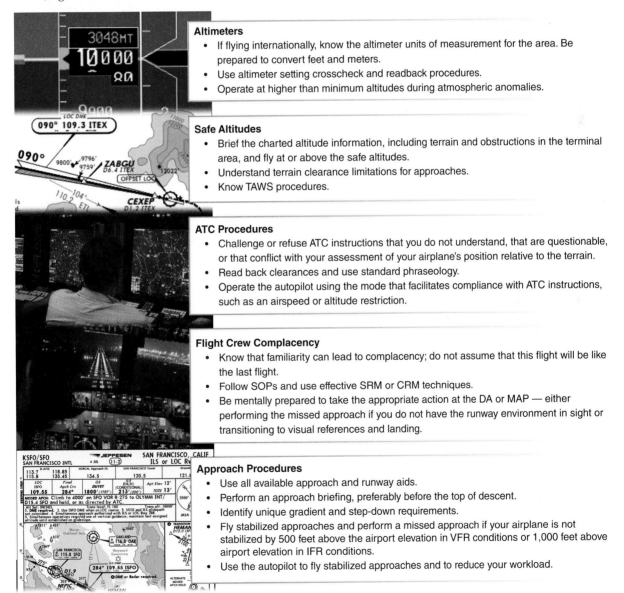

Altimeters
- If flying internationally, know the altimeter units of measurement for the area. Be prepared to convert feet and meters.
- Use altimeter setting crosscheck and readback procedures.
- Operate at higher than minimum altitudes during atmospheric anomalies.

Safe Altitudes
- Brief the charted altitude information, including terrain and obstructions in the terminal area, and fly at or above the safe altitudes.
- Understand terrain clearance limitations for approaches.
- Know TAWS procedures.

ATC Procedures
- Challenge or refuse ATC instructions that you do not understand, that are questionable, or that conflict with your assessment of your airplane's position relative to the terrain.
- Read back clearances and use standard phraseology.
- Operate the autopilot using the mode that facilitates compliance with ATC instructions, such as an airspeed or altitude restriction.

Flight Crew Complacency
- Know that familiarity can lead to complacency; do not assume that this flight will be like the last flight.
- Follow SOPs and use effective SRM or CRM techniques.
- Be mentally prepared to take the appropriate action at the DA or MAP — either performing the missed approach if you do not have the runway environment in sight or transitioning to visual references and landing.

Approach Procedures
- Use all available approach and runway aids.
- Perform an approach briefing, preferably before the top of descent.
- Identify unique gradient and step-down requirements.
- Fly stabilized approaches and perform a missed approach if your airplane is not stabilized by 500 feet above the airport elevation in VFR conditions or 1,000 feet above airport elevation in IFR conditions.
- Use the autopilot to fly stabilized approaches and to reduce your workload.

Figure 10-36. CFIT prevention actions for the approach and landing phase can be divided into five categories.

Many general aviation CFIT accidents occur because a pilot descended below the DA or MDA without the appropriate visual references, or failed to properly follow a missed approach procedure. You should not be tempted into continuing your descent below the DA or MDA if you have not met the necessary requirements, no matter how well you know the surrounding terrain, or how much you want to land. Prior to flight and during the approach briefing, double-check all approach minimums, and ensure that you are

SECTION B ■ IFR Single-Pilot Resource Management

following the correct procedure. Also, be aware that if a navigation or ground component is inoperable, you will need to comply with higher approach minimums than if the full system of instruments and navigation or visual aids were available. Before your flight, also note what obstructions or terrain are found in the airport vicinity. [Figure 10-37]

CONTROLLED FLIGHT INTO TERRAIN

REPORT

The pilot acquired a weather update that indicated that the weather at his destination was steadily deteriorating toward instrument meteorological conditions so he filed and activated an IFR flight plan. As he neared his destination, but before being vectored toward a localizer intercept for the ILS approach, the pilot was advised that the visibility was ¼ mile less than the published approach minimums. The pilot did not stabilize his airspeed or intercept the localizer when he was inside the FAF. The tower controller gave him an updated visibility report that was ½ mile below the published approach minimums; however, the pilot elected to continue the approach. As he did so, he descended below the decision altitude and impacted a power pole and trees about ½ mile from the end of the runway.

ANALYSIS

This report includes several factors that increase CFIT risk: minimums below the approach requirements, failure to stabilize the approach, and descent below the DA. In addition, the accident is a classic example of the poor judgment chain. The pilot continued the approach after first being advised that the visibility was below the published minimums; then after failing to intercept the localizer or establish a stabilized approach; and finally after a final report of deteriorating conditions.

Figure 10-37. This NTSB report illustrates the danger of descending below the DA or MDA without the required visual references in sight.

AUTOMATION MANAGEMENT

Equipment, such as digital displays, a GPS unit, a moving map, and an integrated autopilot can aid in decreasing workload and increasing situational awareness in the IFR environment. Your ability to successfully perform **automation management** determines whether your equipment provides a benefit or a distraction. If you over-rely on the avionics, you might be tempted to operate outside your personal or the environmental limits believing the equipment will compensate for any shortcomings you might have in flying instrument procedures. You must still maintain proficiency in hand-flying maneuvers and procedures to meet the requirements of the PTS.

 Risk is increased when a pilot believes advanced avionics enable operations closer to personal or environmental limits.

 The lighter workloads associated with glass (digital) flight instrumentation might lead to pilot complacency.

In a single-pilot environment, an autopilot system can greatly reduce workload and risk. However, you must carefully evaluate the risk of an inoperative autopilot, especially in IFR conditions. For example, consider the following situation. The ceiling and visibility are forecast to be close to minimums at your destination. You make a Go decision and plan to use the autopilot to fly a coupled approach. Would your assessment of the risk change if you knew that the autopilot was inoperative prior to flight? Even if the autopilot was working, would you be able to hand-fly the procedure if the autopilot failed in flight? You must carefully evaluate your skills and limitations to manage the risk associated with an inoperative autopilot.

INFORMATION MANAGEMENT

In addition to managing the autopilot, you must manage information. With the vast amount of information available on GPS equipment and multi-function displays, it is sometimes challenging to locate a specific piece of information. Memorizing the steps to obtain data is not enough—understanding the system and how the information is organized helps you remember procedures and solve problems. In addition to enroute flight planning, for flights under IFR, you must program and monitor procedures, such as SIDs, STARs and approaches.

Although, many of these tasks can be accomplished prior to flight and during low workload periods, at times you must modify programming to reflect changes in ATC clearances. For example, you must return to your original routing after receiving vectors; you are issued crossing restrictions as you descend to the terminal area; you are cleared to hold for traffic; or ATC changes your approach procedure. You must be able to effectively manage and prioritize the information flow to accomplish specific tasks. Knowing how to fly at each **equipment operating level** and understanding your limitations helps you manage both automation and information. [Figure 10-38]

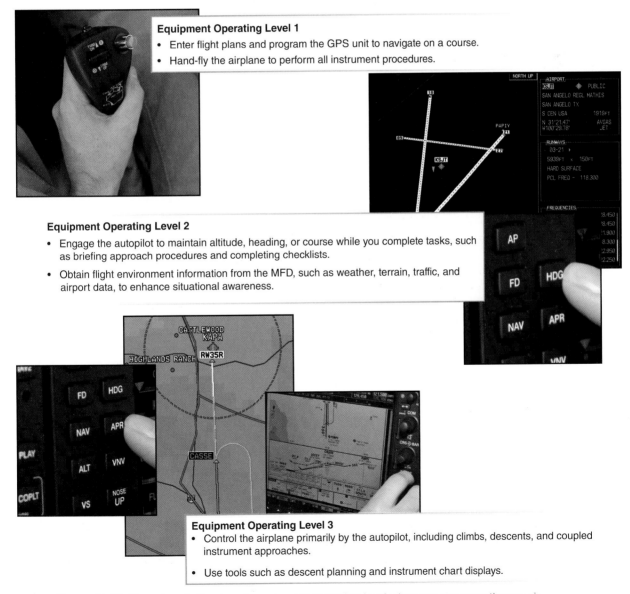

Equipment Operating Level 1
- Enter flight plans and program the GPS unit to navigate on a course.
- Hand-fly the airplane to perform all instrument procedures.

Equipment Operating Level 2
- Engage the autopilot to maintain altitude, heading, or course while you complete tasks, such as briefing approach procedures and completing checklists.
- Obtain flight environment information from the MFD, such as weather, terrain, traffic, and airport data, to enhance situational awareness.

Equipment Operating Level 3
- Control the airplane primarily by the autopilot, including climbs, descents, and coupled instrument approaches.
- Use tools such as descent planning and instrument chart displays.

Figure 10-38. Know how to fly at each equipment operating level when you are operating an airplane with an advanced avionics system.

SECTION B ■ **IFR Single-Pilot Resource Management**

To help you manage information, configure the PFD and MFD screens according to personal preference. For example, set the map orientation to "north up" or "track up," program the map scale settings for enroute versus terminal area operation, or configure the weather datalink to show echoes and METAR status flags on the map display. You can also tailor the information displayed to suit the needs of a specific flight. For example, use the terrain awareness page and display the nearest airports inset on the PFD for a flight under IFR near the mountains.

MAINTAINING SITUATIONAL AWARENESS WHILE USING AUTOMATION

Use automation only when it enhances your situational awareness. If you do not understand the equipment in your airplane, automation and flight management systems become distractions that only diminish your awareness of flight operations. Read and understand the manuals and supplements for any autoflight system including the autopilot and other onboard flight management systems. During flight planning, enter the planned route and legs, including headings and leg length, on a paper log so you can check your programming. For instrument approaches, verify that the waypoints are generally logical in location, in the correct order, and that their orientation to each other is as found on the approach chart. [Figure 10-39]

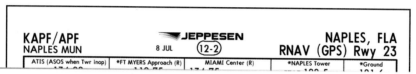

Take these actions to maintain situational awareness when using avionics and automation.
- Use verbal callouts when you arm the autopilot to change mode, course, or altitude.
- Verify all flight plan routing, waypoints, and approach fixes.
- Use all onboard navigation equipment, such as VOR indicators, to back up your GPS display and vice versa.
- Stay within your personal limitations for using avionics and autopilot features.

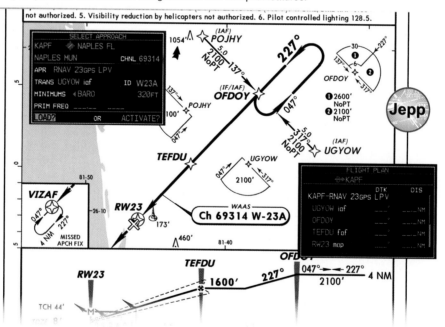

Figure 10-39. Effectively managing automation and information is key to maintaining situational awareness during flight operations.

AUTOMATION SURPRISE

An **automation surprise** can cause you to be momentarily confused about the state of the automation and, often, you have no immediate idea of what action to take to correct the situation. For example, when some autopilots are engaged in NAV (course tracking) mode, changing the HSI navigation source between GPS and localizer (LOC) or VOR disengages

NAV mode. The autopilot reverts to wings-level lateral mode until you reengage the NAV mode to track the desired navigation source. An automation surprise typically occurs in one of two ways:

- A change in the automation system is unexpected or uncommanded and is either recognized or unrecognized by you, such as an unexpected change in navigation mode.
- You command a change but the system does something unexpected, such as failing to capture an altitude. [Figure 10-40]

AUTOMATION MANAGEMENT

REPORT

...the crew loaded the SID for the JPOOL6 Departure from DAL in the FMS. The clearance given was "cleared to [destination] via JPOOL6 ACT As Filed, Climb 4000 Expect 6000, Departure Freq 124.3 [and a squawk]". The flight crew briefed the SID per the chart prior to takeoff from 31R. ...Upon takeoff climb, the autopilot was selected above 700 feet AGL and began a left turn to intercept a course to TTT VOR. Upon noticing the error, the captain disconnected the autopilot simultaneously while being queried by Departure Control about the clearance. Departure then issued a heading of 150 degrees which was complied with immediately.

Callback 1: The reporter advised he had programmed and flown the JPOOL SID on a number of previous occasions without problems. This was his first use since the latest chart and database revision. The crew had briefed the departure and were anticipating flying the initial charted headings "310 to 5.5 DME" thence "hdg 010." Instead TTT immediately became an active waypoint and when the autopilot was engaged it attempted to turn direct TTT.

ANALYSIS

This report emphasized the importance of performing briefings, monitoring equipment displays, and having the ability to hand-fly the airplane when an autopilot issue arises. Fortunately the crew was monitoring the instruments and noticed that the airplane was not navigating on the heading that they expected. They managed this automation surprise by disengaging the autopilot and hand-flying the airplane on a heading issued by ATC.

Figure 10-40. In this ASRS account, the crew experienced an automation surprise while flying a SID.

SECTION B ■ **IFR Single-Pilot Resource Management**

SUMMARY CHECKLIST

✓ Three common causes of accidents that involve IFR conditions are: attempted VFR flight into IFR conditions; controlled flight into terrain; and loss of control.

✓ The term poor judgment chain is used to describe the concept that a sequence of contributing factors produce most accidents rather than a single cause.

✓ File an IFR flight plan every time you fly cross country to increase your IFR experience and to provide and an extra level of safety.

✓ The ADM process helps you to determine and implement a course of action and to evaluate the outcome of that action in both routine and emergency situations.

✓ Based on your experience and abilities, establish personal ceiling and visibility minimums for approach procedures prior to flight.

✓ When the pilot in command is the only rated pilot in the cockpit, the operation is referred to as single-pilot IFR.

✓ Five hazardous attitudes that can interfere with your ability to make effective decisions are: anti-authority, impulsivity, invulnerability, macho, and resignation.

✓ To counteract a hazardous attitude you must recognize the hazardous thought and then state the corresponding antidote.

✓ Use the 5P checklists to identify, assess, and mitigate the risks that specifically apply to each flight to make a Go or No-Go decision.

✓ Use the I'M SAFE checklist to determine if illness, medication, stress, alcohol, fatigue, eating, and emotion are affecting your fitness for flight.

✓ During your flight, continue to manage risk by evaluating your situation using the 5P check at decision points that correspond to the phases of flight.

✓ Planning and prioritizing includes rehearsing your intended route of flight, determining the how the weather affects your fuel calculations and available approaches at your destination, performing briefings, and identifying important tasks.

✓ Prior to flight, organize charts, check for weather updates, program GPS equipment, and review the airport diagram to effectively use resources and reduce head-down time during ground and flight operations.

✓ Cockpit management includes ensuring that all your resources for the flight are on board and accessible, securing items in the cockpit and cabin in case you encounter turbulence, and adjusting your seat for best visibility and reach of the controls.

✓ Preflight your tablet to ensure it is airworthy and ready for specific flight operations.

✓ In addition to coordinating IFR traffic, ATC might provide vectors to an alternate airport, a radar approach, an amended altitude or course clearance, and information about facility and service outages.

✓ A safety pilot is in charge of seeing and avoiding other aircraft and terrain while you practice instrument maneuvers with a view-limiting device.

✓ Designate pilot and copilot responsibilities for communicating with ATC, setting up avionics, manipulating the controls, and briefing procedures.

✓ The relationship between the amount of work and the ability to deal with workload effectively is referred to as the margin of safety.

✓ To counteract complacency, scan the flight instruments and displays while using automation, be prepared to hand-fly the airplane, and follow standard operating procedures (SOPs).

✓ Follow the sterile cockpit procedure to eliminate nonessential conversation with crew members or passengers during taxi, takeoff, landing, and all flight operations except cruise flight.

✓ Brief taxi operations, including the taxi route, hold-short positions, crossing runways, and runway incursion hot spots before taxiing on departure and prior to initial descent on arrival.

✓ During taxi, maintain a sterile cockpit, view the airport diagram, low visibility taxi chart, or moving map display, and use a continuous-loop process to actively monitor and update your progress.

✓ A high level of positional awareness to avoid CFIT includes paying particular attention to your location relative to terrain and the minimum altitudes provided on IFR charts.

✓ Terrain awareness and warning systems (TAWS) display color-coded terrain data on a moving map and provide aural warnings and alert annunciations if the aircraft is close to terrain.

✓ To avoid CFIT on departure, thoroughly review the charted departure procedure or the departure instructions provided by ATC, consider the surrounding terrain and obstacles, and brief the takeoff and departure.

✓ To prevent CFIT on approach and landing, brief the approach and missed approach procedure and fly a stabilized approach.

✓ CFIT prevention actions for the approach and landing phase can be divided into five categories: altimeters, safe altitudes, ATC procedures, flight crew complacency, and approach procedures.

✓ Do not over-rely on automation and advanced avionics equipment. Maintain proficiency in hand-flying maneuvers and procedures to meet the requirements of the PTS.

✓ You must carefully evaluate your skills and limitations to manage the risk associated with an inoperative autopilot

✓ Knowing how to fly at each equipment operating level and understanding your limitations helps you manage both automation and information.

✓ To maintain situational awareness when using avionics and automation, use verbal callouts, verify routing and waypoints, use navigation equipment, to back up your GPS display, and stay within your personal limitations.

✓ An automation surprise causes you to be momentarily confused about the state of the automation.

KEY TERMS

Single-Pilot Resource Management (SRM)

Poor Judgment Chain

Aeronautical Decision Making (ADM)

ADM Process

Self Assessment

Single-Pilot IFR

Hazardous Attitudes

Risk Management

5P Checklists

I'M SAFE Checklist

5P Check

Task Management

Cockpit Management

Safety Pilot

Margin of Safety

Situational Awareness

Standard Operating Procedures (SOPs)

Sterile Cockpit

Controlled Flight Into Terrain (CFIT)

Positional Awareness

Terrain Awareness and Warning System (TAWS)

Automation Management

Equipment Operating Levels

Automation Surprise

SECTION B ■ IFR Single-Pilot Resource Management

QUESTIONS

1. What are three common causes of accidents that involve IFR conditions?

2. You are an hour into a cross-country in IFR conditions and you recognize a change—the low voltage light illuminates. What is the next step in the ADM process?
   A. Implement your decision. You ask ATC for instructions regarding the low voltage light.
   B. Choose a course of action. You consult the regulations to determine what actions to take to manage an electrical system failure.
   C. Define the problem. After failing to extinguish the low voltage light using the procedure outlined in the POH, you determine that the alternator has failed and you have limited battery power to supply the electrical equipment needed to complete the flight to your destination.

3. *So what if the Learjet ahead of me missed the approach twice and diverted to an alternate? I'm a good enough pilot to make it in.* What hazardous attitude is the pilot exhibiting?
   A. Macho
   B. Impulsivity
   C. Anti-authority

4. *Ice has already started to form on the wings. There's nothing I can do about it now.* What is the antidote to this hazardous attitude?
   A. Not so fast. Think first. — *There is not enough ice to worry about.*
   B. I can do it. — *I am going to continue the flight as planned.*
   C. I am not helpless. I can make a difference. — *I will request a change in altitude from ATC to get out of the conditions.*

5. Give specific examples of at least one risk factor in each of the 5P categories that you should consider during flight planning.

6. Select the true statement about using the 5P check in flight.
   A. Manage risk by using the 5P check in emergency situations only.
   B. Using the 5P check is not necessary in flight if you mitigated all risks during flight planning.
   C. Manage risk by using the 5P check at decision points that correspond to the phases of flight.

7. Provide an example of planning and prioritizing to manage tasks prior to or during a flight.

8. Give an example of effectively using resources prior to flight to reduce head-down time during ground and flight operations.

9. Which is an action that you can take to maintain situational awareness during flight?
   A. Follow standard operating procedures.
   B. Hand-fly the airplane every time you perform an instrument approach.
   C. Eliminate all communication with a copilot or passengers during every operation except cruise flight.

10. Which is an action that you can take to maintain situational awareness during ground operations?
    A. Perform your departure briefing during taxi to be prepared when you arrive at the takeoff runway.
    B. No matter what your position is on the airport, stop immediately to communicate with ATC if you become disoriented.
    C. Always know your airplane's present location and mentally calculate the next location in the route that requires increased attention.

11. Name at least three actions you can take to decrease your risk of CFIT during initial climb and departure.

12. Select the true statement regarding the actions to prevent CFIT during approach and landing.
    A. Follow an SOP that prohibits use of the autopilot during approach procedures.
    B. After passing the final approach fix, mentally commit to landing the airplane upon reaching the DA or MDA.
    C. Challenge or refuse ATC instructions that conflict with your assessment of your airplane's position relative to the terrain.

13. Select the true statement regarding automation and information management.
    A. Use verbal callouts and verify waypoints to maintain situational awareness while using automation.
    B. After you have mastered automation management skills, you do not need to hand-fly the airplane in the future.
    C. Perform all programming tasks prior to flight—do not risk becoming distracted by programming equipment during flight operations.

14. True/False. An automation surprise can be an unexpected or uncommanded change in the automation system either recognized or unrecognized by you.

SECTION C
IFR Flight Planning

Do not let yourself be forced into doing anything before you are ready. —Wilbur Wright

D ue to the complexity of IFR flight planning, Wilbur Wright's statement is sound advice. Although IFR flight planning is an extension of the VFR flight planning process, preparing for an IFR flight requires greater attention to detail. IFR flight planning emphasizes route selection, the collection of communication and navigation information, knowledge of charts and flight publications, and, above all, the gathering of timely and accurate weather information.

You are required by the regulations to perform numerous preflight actions and be familiar with a variety of information. During the IFR flight planning process, pay special attention to aircraft performance, current and forecast weather conditions, and planned alternatives. Use a risk assessment tool during flight planning, such as the 5P checklists covered in Section 10B, to identify and manage the risks associated with the flight.

To illustrate the IFR flight planning process, consider an IFR flight from Eppley Airfield in Omaha, Nebraska, to Rochester International Airport in Rochester, Minnesota. The flight will depart Eppley at 2000Z and should take approximately one hour and fifteen minutes to reach Rochester. You are flying a Cessna Turbo Skylane RG (TR182) with an HSI and VOR indicator, dual communication radios, Mode C transponder, and GPS equipment.

FLIGHT OVERVIEW

Before you start planning, take a preliminary look at factors that might prevent you from making the flight. This **flight overview** provides you with a rough idea of your ability to complete it. The preliminary overview enables you to make a **Go/No-Go decision** before you get very far into the flight planning process. If conditions look favorable during the overview, you can begin planning.

Initial factors to consider are weather, airplane performance and equipment, potential routes, and your instrument proficiency level. You can learn about the general weather patterns for your flight by watching The Weather Channel, the television news, reading the newspaper, contacting the National Weather Service for a long range forecast, or accessing online weather sites several days prior to the flight. Although these sources of weather information are quite good, they are not substitutes for a complete Flight Service weather briefing. [Figure 10-41]

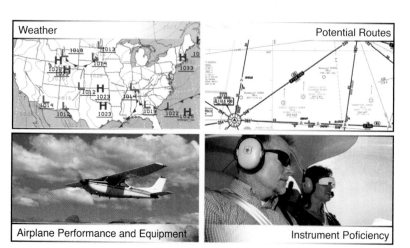

Weather

Potential Routes

Airplane Performance and Equipment

Instrument Poficiency

Figure 10-41. Consider these factors as you perform a preliminary overview of the flight.

When considering airplane performance and equipment, relate them to the airports of intended use and the terrain you will fly over. Familiarity with your airplane's performance gives you an idea of its capabilities relative to the demands of the planned flight. However, you need to calculate specific performance information like fuel consumption and takeoff and landing distances when planning the flight. Knowledge of the general route of flight and its terrain will enable you to determine whether additional equipment, such as supplemental oxygen, is needed. If your airplane is equipped with GPS, you might be able to make a direct flight instead of flying on airways.

Finally, consider your instrument flying proficiency. If the rest of the overview indicates the flight could be difficult to complete, you need to decide if your current skills are up to the task. If not, postpone the flight until conditions improve or until you have the chance to refresh your skills with an instructor's help.

FLIGHT PLANNING

Based on factors in the overview, including the TR182's performance and equipment, as well as the relatively flat terrain under your flight path, the flight from Omaha to Rochester looks like it can be completed. With a preliminary decision to go, you can plan the flight starting with the selection of your route. After you choose your route, you need to reference the flight publications applicable to the flight and gather detailed weather information in order to plan cruise performance and the use of alternate airports, if needed.

ROUTE

Several factors influence route selection, including the availability of route alternatives, aircraft performance considerations, and fuel economy. If a **preferred IFR route** is available, plan to fly it unless weather conditions or aircraft performance warrant a different route. Filing a preferred route results in fewer traffic delays and increased efficiency for departure, enroute, and arrival ATC service.

 Preferred IFR routes beginning with a fix indicate that departing aircraft will normally be routed to the fix via a standard instrument departure (SID), or radar vectors.

Official location identifiers are used in the preferred route description and intersections are spelled out. If a preferred route begins or ends with an airway number, it indicates that the airway overlies the airport and that flights normally are cleared directly on the airway. Preferred IFR routes beginning or ending with a fix indicate that aircraft may be routed to or from these fixes via a SID, radar vector, or STAR. Jeppesen publishes preferred routes for the low and high altitude environments with its charting services and preferred IFR routes are listed in the *Chart Supplement*. You can also search the preferred route online database at www.fly.faa.gov. [Figure 10-42]

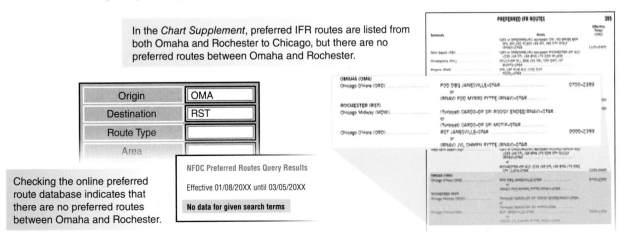

In the *Chart Supplement*, preferred IFR routes are listed from both Omaha and Rochester to Chicago, but there are no preferred routes between Omaha and Rochester.

Origin	OMA
Destination	RST
Route Type	
Area	

NFDC Preferred Routes Query Results

Effective 01/08/20XX until 03/05/20XX

No data for given search terms

Checking the online preferred route database indicates that there are no preferred routes between Omaha and Rochester.

Figure 10-42. Checking the preferred route database at www.fly.faa.gov indicates that there are no preferred routes between Omaha and Rochester.

SECTION C ■ IFR Flight Planning

When no preferred IFR route is available, review the enroute chart to select the most practical route for the flight. In all cases, check for applicable MEAs along the route. In some parts of the country, minimum enroute altitudes might be beyond your aircraft's climb capabilities or they might require the use of oxygen. If your airplane is equipped with an IFR-certified GPS, you might consider planning a direct route. Although the Turbo Skylane in this planning example does have GPS, this flight will be planned along airways between Omaha and Rochester. [Figure 10-43]

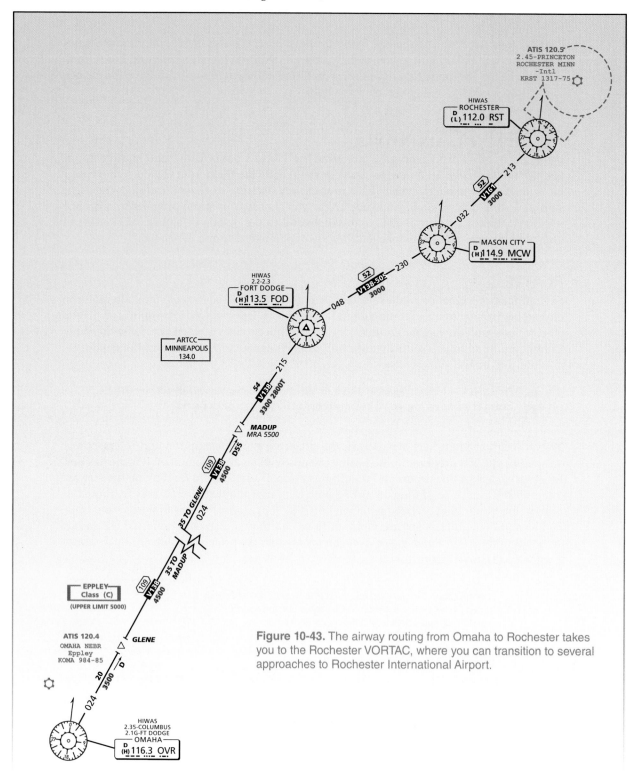

Figure 10-43. The airway routing from Omaha to Rochester takes you to the Rochester VORTAC, where you can transition to several approaches to Rochester International Airport.

After you select your route, you need to determine if Omaha and Rochester have published departure and arrival procedures. You can find out if departure and arrival procedures are published by reviewing either FAA or Jeppesen terminal charts for both airports. Because the flight originates in Omaha, check to see if Omaha has published standard instrument departure (SID) procedures. [Figure 10-44] You should also review the approach procedures into Eppley in case you have to return shortly after takeoff.

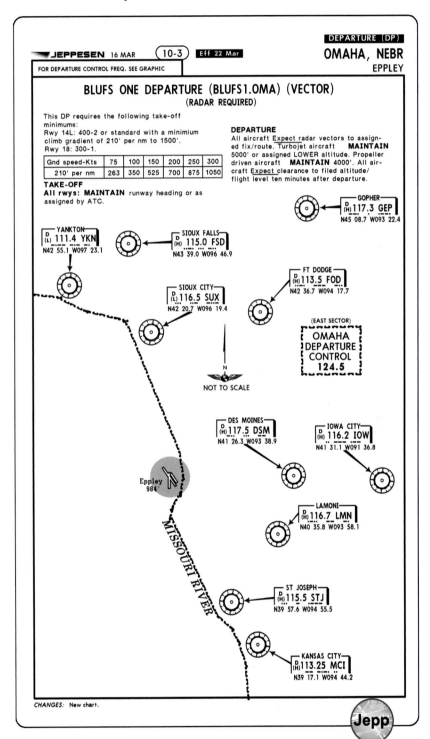

Figure 10-44. The BLUFS ONE Departure provides radar vectors to assigned fixes or routes for departing aircraft. For the flight to Rochester, you are vectored directly to V-138, which takes you to Fort Dodge and Mason City.

In the process of looking for SIDs and STARs, you find there are no published STAR procedures for Rochester. Therefore, you need to determine how to transition from the enroute to the approach segment of your flight. Reviewing the enroute charts as well as the approach charts at Rochester shows that many of the transition routes begin at the Rochester VORTAC, the final fix in your enroute segment. In addition, if you fly an RNAV (GPS) approach, you will fly direct to a waypoint to begin the approach. [Figure 10-45]

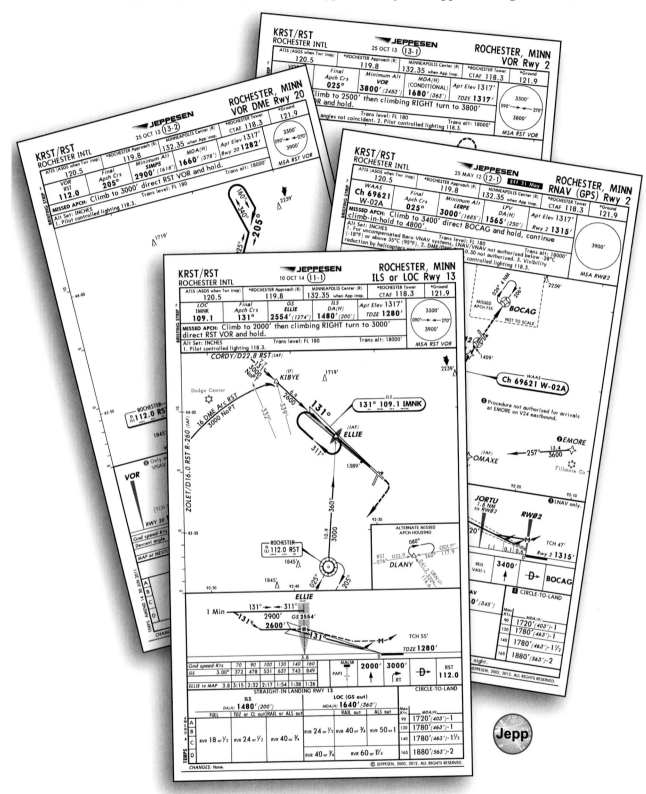

Figure 10-45. Your final enroute fix is the Rochester VORTAC. From there, you might be cleared for one of a number of approaches into KRST.

With your primary route selected, consider possible **alternate airports** in case of poor weather at Rochester. Each alternate should be far enough away to avoid adverse weather affecting your destination. In addition, your alternate should have adequate communications, weather reporting, and at least one instrument approach. Other factors being equal, the more approaches an alternate has, the better. Examine the approach minimums for airports in the area and compare them to the forecast weather at your ETA. Also be sure to note whether using the airport as an alternate in instrument conditions is authorized. If your alternate selection is limited, consider how an alternate that is far from your destination will affect your fuel requirements. For flight under IFR you must carry enough fuel to fly to the first airport of intended landing, then to the alternate airport, and then for 45 minutes at normal cruising speed. [Figure 10-46]

> **FAA** For flight under IFR you must carry enough fuel to fly to the first airport of intended landing, then to the alternate airport, and then for 45 minutes at normal cruising speed.

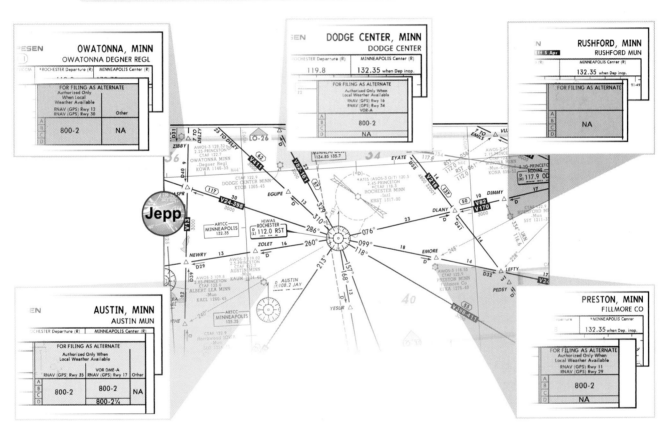

Figure 10-46. Some of the airports near Rochester cannot be filed as alternates, even though they have instrument approaches. Other airports have alternate minimums that require much better weather than the approaches at Rochester.

FLIGHT INFORMATION PUBLICATIONS

After choosing your route of flight you need to review the pertinent flight information publications. Navaid and lighting outages, runway closures, and limitations on instrument approach procedures can significantly affect your flight plan. NOTAMs are your best source of information regarding these factors. You can find **NOTAMs** online at www.faa.gov and NOTAMs are included in an online standard briefing from Flight Service. Jeppesen eletronic and paper chart services also provide NOTAMs. [Figure 10-47]

Navigation

OMA 06/037 Eppley Airfield, Omaha, NE (KOMA) Navigation ILS runway 14 right out of service Jun 08, 2015 1400Z to Sep 01, 2015 2359Z

Runways

RST 07/026 Rochester Municipal, Rochester, MN (KRST) Runway 2 runway end identifier light high intensity out of service Jul 22, 2015 1419Z to Dec 31, 2015 1800Z Estimated

FDC

FDC 5/3933 KZMP WI..ROUTE ZMP. V413 IRONWOOD (IWD) VORTAC, MI TO EAU CLAIRE (EAU) VORTAC, WI MEA 8000. 24 JUN 18:55 2015 UNTIL 21 DEC 18:55 2015 ESTIMATED. CREATED: 24 JUN 18:55 2015

FDC 5/3505 KOMA SID EPPLEY AIRFIELD, OMAHA, NE. BLUFS ONE DEPARTURE... CATTL ONE DEPARTURE... TAKE-OFF MINIMUMS: RWY 14L, 400-2 OR STANDARD WITH MINIMUM CLIMB OF 264 FEET PER NM TO 1500. ALL OTHER DATA REMAINS AS PUBLISHED. 13 JAN 21:35 2015 UNTIL 12 AUG 21:35 2015 ESTIMATED. CREATED: 13 JAN 21:35 2015

Figure 10-47. NOTAMs that could affect your flight range from navigation facility outages to changes to charted procedures. Shown here is a sample of some of the NOTAMs for a flight from Omaha to Rochester.

Review the Chart Supplement for specific information about your departure, destination, and alternate airports. Gathering data on runway lengths, fuel availability, lighting, hours of operation, and navigation, communication, and radar facilities helps you meet the requirements of FAR 91.103 concerning preflight action. Additionally, you are required to ensure that the airplane and its equipment meet FAR inspection requirements. If your airplane has GPS equipment and you plan on using it for navigation, you must ensure that it is IFR-certified. You will need to check the airplane flight manual supplement if you are not sure about the system in the airplane you are using.

 For a flight under IFR, you are required to have working navigation equipment appropriate to the ground facilities to be used.

In order to use VOR equipment for navigation under IFR, FAR 91.171 requires that it has been operationally checked within the preceding 30 days and found to be within acceptable limits. If your airplane's maintenance record indicates a VOR check is needed, you can use the information found in the VOR Receiver Check section of the Chart Supplement to locate a suitable checkpoint for the test. After completing the VOR receiver check, you must enter in the aircraft logbook or other record the date the test was done, its location, the bearing error of the receiver, and your signature.

The national airspace system changes continuously. To stay abreast of these changes and to review current IFR procedures, periodically consult the AIM. It provides information on items like navigation aids, lighting and airport markings, airspace, pilot/controller communication, emergency procedures, safety of flight, medical factors, and charts.

 It is your responsibility as pilot in command to make sure that the VOR check has been accomplished within the past 30 days, and the transponder has been checked within the past 24 calendar months. Transponder checks must be entered in aircraft logbooks. There also must be a written record of the VOR test, which includes the date, place, bearing error, and the signature of the person performing the test.

After you have chosen a route and consulted the appropriate publications, you can begin putting together your navigation log. List the routes, courses, distances, checkpoints, and necessary communication and navigation information as well as any additional information you feel is important. However, the bulk of your flight planning cannot be completed until you have collected updated weather information for your route of flight.

WEATHER CONSIDERATIONS

Lockheed Martin Flight Service (LMFS) provides most aviation weather briefings, and graphic weather products are delivered online to pilots' computers and mobile devices. Flight Service briefers are authorized to translate and interpret available National Weather Service (NWS) products and provide standard, abbreviated, and outlook briefings. By logging into the Pilot Portal, you can obtain a weather briefing, airport information, and NOTAMs. You can file and save favorite flight plans and aircraft data, as well as link to information such as GPS RAIM data and IFR terminal and enroute charts.

Begin gathering weather data several days before your flight so by the time you are ready to obtain a standard briefing from Flight Service, you already have some idea about the weather hazards along your route of flight and conditions at your destination. The weather products shown here for the flight from Omaha to Rochester illustrate the process of evaluating the weather for the flight. However, as new and improved weather products, are being developed, you can expect the appearance and functionality of these weather charts to vary significantly. Weather radar and satellite images of the region where you plan to fly can provide a quick idea of the current factors you need to pay attention to, as well as what you might expect to find in the forecast. [Figure 10-48]

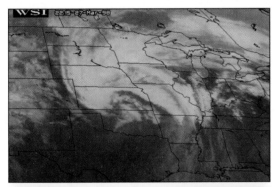

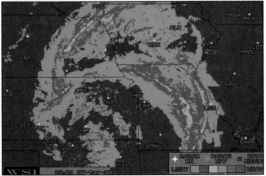

Figure 10-48. Radar and satellite images of the Nebraska, Iowa, and Minnesota region indicate a weather system with precipitation and cloud cover conditions throughout the area.

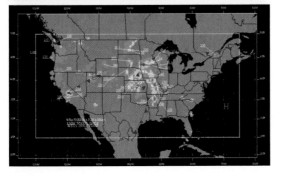

SECTION C ■ IFR Flight Planning

Along with the radar and satellite images, you can use a surface analysis chart to see greater detail. The surface analysis chart is useful for determining where fronts are located relative to your flight. With a front extending northeast along your route of flight, the surface analysis chart indicates you will be flying just ahead of the front during the trip. You also want to know how quickly and in what general direction the front is projected to move. A review of the 12-hour surface weather prog chart shows the proposed movement of the front and indicates the location of significant weather. [Figure 10-49]

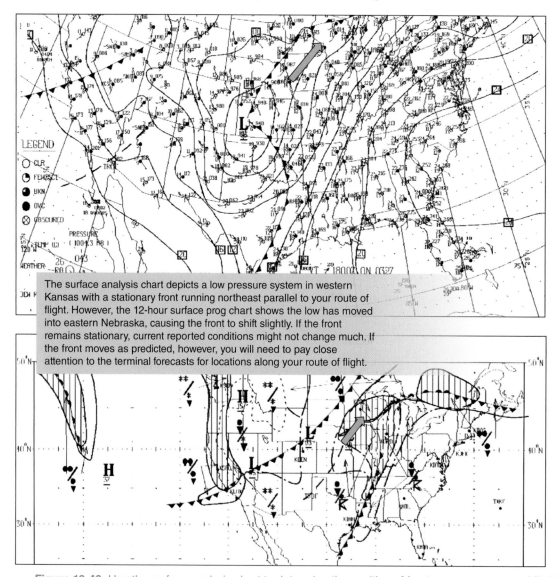

The surface analysis chart depicts a low pressure system in western Kansas with a stationary front running northeast parallel to your route of flight. However, the 12-hour surface prog chart shows the low has moved into eastern Nebraska, causing the front to shift slightly. If the front remains stationary, current reported conditions might not change much. If the front moves as predicted, however, you will need to pay close attention to the terminal forecasts for locations along your route of flight.

Figure 10-49. Use the surface analysis chart to determine the position of fronts near your route of flight.

The picture of the weather along your route of flight is starting to take shape. However, the radar plots, surface analysis, and surface prog charts only tell part of the story. For instance, the radar picture indicates you can expect precipitation between Omaha and Rochester, but it does not tell you whether you will be in IFR conditions the entire time. In this case, you might review a low-level significant weather prog chart to find out where areas of IFR, marginal VFR, and VFR conditions are expected to exist. The low-level significant weather prog chart can identify areas of forecast IFR and marginal VFR weather, turbulence, and the location of the freezing level. [Figure 10-50]

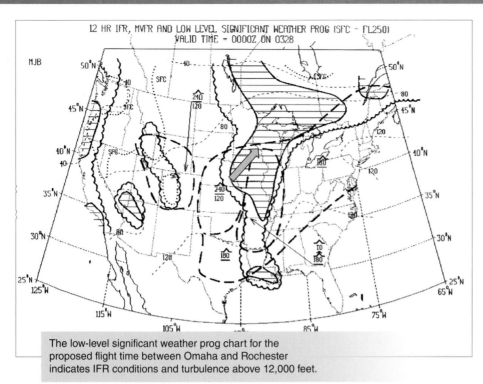

12 HR IFR, MVFR AND LOW LEVEL SIGNIFICANT WEATHER PROG (SFC - FL250)
VALID TIME = 0000Z ON 0328

Figure 10-50. Review the low-level significant weather prog chart to determine the locations of forecast IFR and marginal VFR weather, turbulence, and the freezing level.

The low-level significant weather prog chart for the proposed flight time between Omaha and Rochester indicates IFR conditions and turbulence above 12,000 feet.

For greater simplicity, you might want to reference the weather depiction chart. Although it does not provide information on frontal activity or the movement of pressure systems, it does provide a clear indication of the ceiling and visibility conditions of reporting points along your route. [Figure 10-51]

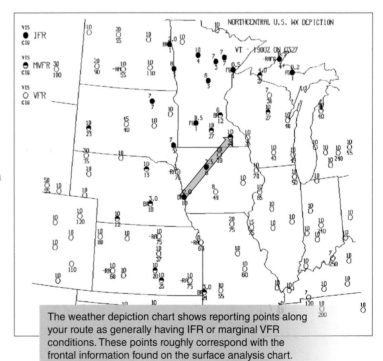

NORTHCENTRAL U.S. WX DEPICTION

VT - 1900Z ON 0327

Figure 10-51. The weather depiction chart indicates the ceiling and visibility conditions of reporting points.

The weather depiction chart shows reporting points along your route as generally having IFR or marginal VFR conditions. These points roughly correspond with the frontal information found on the surface analysis chart.

Both the low-level significant weather prog and weather depiction charts indicate that you will conduct the Omaha to Rochester flight primarily under IFR conditions. Because you will be flying in visible precipitation, you need to find out where the freezing level is along your route. The low-level significant weather prognostic chart can indicate to you whether or not to expect icing at your altitude during the trip. [Figure 10-52]

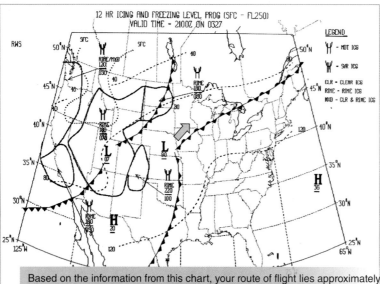

Figure 10-52. Knowing the freezing level helps you predict whether icing conditions are a risk for your flight.

Based on the information from this chart, your route of flight lies approximately halfway between the 8,000-foot and 12,000-foot freezing level lines depicted on the chart. Because you cannot determine exactly where the freezing level is for your route, check the pilot reports for icing conditions during your briefing.

The radar returns indicate some heavy precipitation near your route of flight, so you should check for convective activity in the area as well. The area forecast can provide you with much of the information you need to determine the location of severe weather. You can also use it to confirm or enhance information displayed on the graphic weather charts. [Figure 10-53]

Figure 10-53. Use the area forecast to confirm information that you obtained from graphic weather charts.

AREA FORECAST

271952
HI FA 271945 SYNOPSIS AND VFR CLDS/WX SYNOPSIS VALID UNTIL 281400
CLDS/WX VALID UNTIL 280800...OTLK VALID 280800-281400 ND SD NE KS
MN IA MO WI LM LS MI LH IL IN KY. SEE AIRMET SIERRA FOR IFR CONDS
AND MTN OBSCN. TS IMPLY SEV OR GTR TURB SEV ICE LLWS AND IFR
CONDS.   NON   MSL   HGTS   DENOTED   BY   AGL   OR   CIG...

MN NWRN/N CNTRL...AGL BKN-SCT015 TOPS TO 060. 02Z CIG BKN020. WDLY
SCT -SHRA. OTLK...MVFR CIG RA BR. SERN 1/4...CIG BKN030 TOPS TO
FL250. OCNL CIG OVC010 WITH WDLY SCT -TSRA. CB TOPS TO FL350. 00Z
CIG OVC010. SCT -SHRA/-TSRA. VIS 3-5SM BR. OTLK...IFR CIG RA BR.
IA WRN 1/3...CIG OVC020 TOPS TO FL250. SCT -SHRA/WDLY SCT -TSRA.
TS POSS SEV. CB TOPS TO FL350. 02Z CIG BKN030. WDLY SCT -SHRA.VIS
3-5SM BR. OTLK...MVFR CIG BR. ERN 2/3... CIG BKN030 OVC050 TOPS
TO FL250. SCT -SHRA/WDLY SCT -TSRA CNTRL 1/3 AFT 21Z AND ERN 1/3
AFT 23Z. TS POSS SEV. CB TOPS TO FL400. OTLK...MVFR CIG BR.

NE PNHDL...AGL SCT040 SCT100. LYRS OCNL BKN. 02Z CIG BKN100 TOPS
TO FL200. OTLK...VFR. ERN 1/2...CIG OVC015 TOPS TO FL250. VIS 3-
5SM -RA BR. WDLY SCT EMBD -TSRA. TS POSS SEV SERN NE. CB TOPS TO
FL400. 01Z CIG BKN025. WDLY SCT -SHRA/ISOL -TSRA. OTLK...MVFR CIG
BECMG VFR BY 10Z.

The VFR Clouds and Weather portions of the area forecast provide a general description of the conditions to be expected for your flight. It is important to note that ceilings might be as low as 1,500 feet when cloud tops extend to FL250 and beyond. Widely scattered thunderstorms are also possible in eastern Nebraska, Iowa, and southern Minnesota.

By now you should have a good idea of what the weather will be doing during your flight, but you still need to get specific information on the weather at your departure and destination airports as well as possible alternates near your flight path. For instance, the weather at your point of departure, (Omaha), and along your route (Fort Dodge, Mason City, Rochester) is reported as marginal VFR to IFR, which agrees with the weather depiction charts. At your estimated time of departure (2000Z), the weather at Omaha is forecast to be 2,500 feet overcast with four miles visibility in light rain and mist. This forecast is an important consideration because you need to know if it will be possible to return to Omaha if mechanical difficulties develop during departure. The forecast weather is well above the straight-in and circling minimums for all approaches into Omaha's Eppley Airfield, which means you should be able to return to the airport if necessary. [Figure 10-54]

> Except for temporary conditions, the Omaha forecast indicates that the ceiling and visibility are both expected to improve after 2100Z.

```
TAF

KOMA   271730Z 271818 15015G24KT 4SM -RA BR OVC 025
       FM 2100 17015G25KT 5SM -RA BR OVC 040
       TEMPO 2101 1SM +TSRA GR BR OVC 008CB
       FM 0100 22012KT P6SM BKN 025 OVC 040 PROB 40 0105 2SM -SHRA BKN 008
       FM 0600 28010KT P6SM BKN 030
       FM 0900 30006KT P6SM SCT 030 SCT 250
       FM 1500 12010KT P6SM SCT 035 SCT 100
```

Figure 10-54. Use the Omaha forecast to determine if you can return to the airport if necessary.

Next, check the forecast for Rochester. Remember, if the forecast weather at your destination from 1 hour prior to your arrival to 1 hour after your arrival is not expected to be 2,000 feet or higher and 3 miles or more, you must file an alternate. Pay close attention to the forecast weather at Rochester as well as airports in the area that may be used as alternates. The TAF for Rochester (KRST) during that time period does not indicate the need for an alternate. The forecast ceiling and visibility are only marginally better than the requirement for an alternate, so you would be wise to observe the forecasts at airports that may be used as alternates if the Rochester forecast proves to be inaccurate. [Figure 10-55]

Figure 10-55. The destination forecast is essential for determining whether an alternate is required.

> The Rochester forecast during your estimated time of arrival (2115Z) calls for visibility to be greater than 6 miles with a 3,500-foot ceiling. However, beyond that period the forecast shows the weather deteriorating. To be safe, check the forecasts for predicted conditions at airports in the area that might be suitable alternates if the weather at Rochester drops below minimums prior to your arrival.

```
TAF

KRST   271910Z 271918 20022G32KT P6SM BKN 035
       FM 0000 19018G25KT 3SM -TSR BR OVC 008CB
       FM 0600 21015KT 1SM -SHRA BR OVC 006
       FM 1500 28016G22KT 5SM BR OVC015
```

From previous chapters you know that an alternate should have one or more approaches and weather that is forecast to be above approach minimums. For instance, the forecast weather at an alternate at the estimated time of arrival must include a ceiling of at least 600 feet and 2 miles visibility if a precision approach is available, or 800 feet and 2 miles for nonprecision approaches, in order to be filed as an alternate. Of course, if you decide to divert to an alternate and fly the approach, the landing minimums for the approach being flown apply.

If you elect to proceed to your alternate, the landing minimums used at that airport should be the minimums specified for the approach procedure selected.

The alternate minimums that must be forecast at the ETA for an airport that has a precision approach procedure are a 600-foot ceiling and 2 miles visibility.

SECTION C ■ IFR Flight Planning

By reviewing your navigation charts, graphic weather charts, and radar and satellite images, you can determine quickly which airports in the vicinity might be VFR, or at least have better weather conditions than your destination. For instance, the radar images and surface analysis charts show VFR conditions to the west of Rochester. By checking the current and forecast conditions for airports west of Rochester, you find that Owatonna (KOWA) is above IFR minimums and conditions are forecast to improve as the weather system moves east. To the west of Owatonna, at Mankato (KMKT), current conditions are VFR and forecast to remain that way through the forecast period. By referring to terminal charts or the Chart Supplement, you determine that both Owatonna and Mankato have instrument approaches. As a result, both airports make suitable alternates if conditions at Rochester preclude you from landing there. [Figure 10-56]

```
TAF

KOWA 271740 171818 17013KT 4SM OVC 018
      FM 2100 17010KT P6SM BKN 020
      FM 0000 17011KT 5SM BKN 040
      FM 0400 16008KT 5SM SCT 060
      FM 1100 16008KT P6SM SCT 100


KMKT 271750 271818 18008KT P6SM SCT 050
      FM 0000 18010KT P6SM FEW 100
      FM 1000 17010KT P6SM SCT 250
      FM 1400 17006KT P6SM SCT 250
```

Figure 10-56. Review the TAFs for airports along your route to be aware of your options for an alternate airport.

The TAFs indicate that the further west you fly from Rochester, the better the conditions. This corresponds with the information gained from the radar and satellite images, as well as the surface analysis and 12-hour surface weather prog charts that indicate the weather system to be moving east.

FUEL EXHAUSTION AND PILOT CONFUSION

From the Files of the NTSB...

Aircraft: *Aronson Falco F8L*

Location: *Gainesville, FL*

Injuries: *2 Fatal*

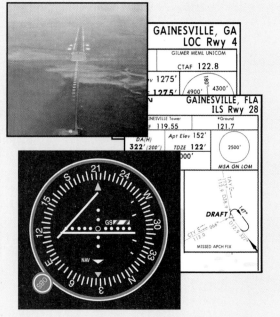

Narrative: *The pilot received a weather briefing and filed an IFR flight plan, then departed VFR. Except for a headwind, the first part of the flight was normal. In the vicinity of Macon, Georgia, the pilot requested and received an IFR clearance. Later, he elected to divert to the Gainesville Regional Airport and was vectored for an ILS approach. While diverting, he indicated some confusion concerning the approach plates. At first, he started using the Gainesville, Georgia plate, then he switched to the correct plate (Gainesville, FL). He had difficulty maintaining heading on the ILS and made a missed approach 2 miles east of the airport. He admitted having problems with the approach, declared a low fuel state and received vectors for another ILS. Again, he had difficulty maintaining heading control. On the second approach, the aircraft was observed to fly over the field and the pilot was cleared to land on any runway. However, the aircraft crashed on the approach end of Runway 6. There was evidence of little movement after impact and very little chordwise scraping of the prop. No fuel was found in the fuel tanks or fuel injector lines.*

In addition to improper in-flight planning, the NTSB declared that poor IFR procedures, inadequate fuel supply, and fuel exhaustion, were causative factors in this accident. Had the pilot been better prepared for a possible diversion to an alternate airport, he might have avoided the approach chart confusion and low fuel state that ultimately resulted in a fatal accident after missing two approaches.

With current and forecast weather in hand, your next step is to obtain the forecast winds aloft and any available pilot reports for the route of flight. In this case, the winds aloft through 12,000 feet for your route are 170° at 20 knots for the first half of the flight and 200° at 20 knots for the second half of the flight. Additionally, pilot reports indicate occasional light to moderate turbulence from 6,000 to 10,000 feet between Omaha and Fort Dodge, with light rime ice above 10,000 feet.

ALTITUDE SELECTION

Before you complete your planning, you must select a cruising altitude. With no significant terrain features between Omaha and Rochester, the highest MEA is 4,500 feet. Because ATC generally assigns altitudes that correspond with the hemispheric rule, the lowest altitude you should request for your easterly flight is 5,000 feet. You are not carrying oxygen for this trip, so the highest altitude you should request is 11,000 feet.

Next, consider the effects of winds aloft as well as turbulence and icing reports. From the winds and temperatures aloft forecast you know that the winds are from a southerly direction at 20 knots through 12,000 feet. Also, pilots have reported turbulence starting at 6,000 feet and light rime ice above 10,000 feet. Note that you might be able to avoid the turbulence and stay clear of the ice while enjoying a modest tailwind by choosing to fly at 5,000 feet. This altitude also ensures that you are above the MEA and in compliance with ATC's hemispheric rule. However, if you refer back to the significant weather prognostic charts you will see that at 5,000 feet you will probably be in IFR conditions. You can confirm this by looking at the current observations and forecast conditions for points along your route of flight. [Figure 10-57]

SECTION C ■ IFR Flight Planning

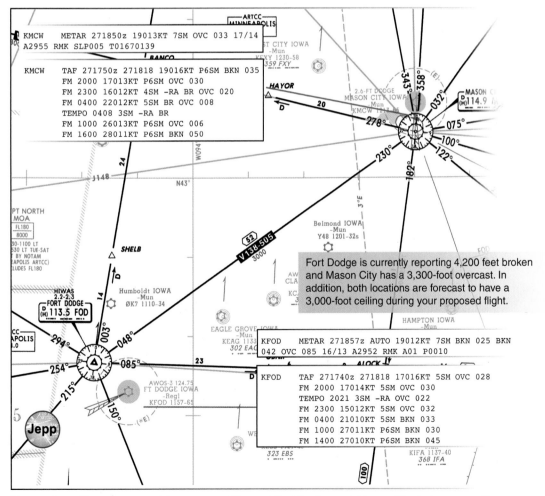

Figure 10-57. The current and forecast conditions at Fort Dodge and Mason City help you confirm weather along your route.

COMPLETING THE NAVIGATION LOG

With your weather briefing complete, you can make your Go/No-Go decision. Base your decision on the weather reports and forecasts you have gathered, as well as your airplane's capabilities. Also consider your personal limitations and level of proficiency. For this flight you will be below the reported turbulence and icing conditions but might be in IFR conditions while enroute. If you have to proceed to an alternate, there are at least two airports within an hour's flight time that are forecast to be above approach minimums or with VFR conditions. Based on this analysis, you decide the flight is within your capabilities and those of the aircraft. Your next step is to complete the navigation log. You might use a computer flight planning tool to fill out the nav log for your flight. [Figure 10-58]

KOMA Eppley	ATIS 120.4 / CLNC (PDC) 119.9 / DEP (IC) 120.1	TWR 132.1 / ARSA (IC) 120.1 / DEP 124.5	GND 121.9 / ARSA 124.5 / UNI 122.95	BLOCK OFF / TIME OFF

WAYPOINTS (FIXES)	ROUTE MEA/(MORA)	BEG ALT / END ALT	MC / MH	FUEL (Gal) LEG / REM	DIST (NM) LEG / REM	SPD (Kts) / TAS / EST GS	ETE / CUMM	ATA / ATE	WIND / OAT
KOMA Eppley N 41° 18.3' W 95° 53.7'	SID			87	221				
355TO N 41° 19.1' W 95° 53.7'	CLIMB — SID	981	355	0 + 1	1	103	00:00		170@20
	CLIMB — (4000)	1322	357	86	220	122	00:00		18°C
GLENE GLENE N 41° 27.1' W 95° 30.3'	CLIMB	1322	061	1	8	106	00:04		170@20
	CLIMB — (4000)	5000	071	85	212	109	00:05		14°C
	CRUISE	5000	061	1	11	155	00:04		170@20
	CRUISE — (4000)	5000	068	84	201	159	00:09		10°C
MADUP MADUP N 41° 56.4' W 95° 06.0'	CRUISE — V138	5000	027	3	35	155	00:12		170@20
	CRUISE — 4500	5000	032	81	166	170	00:21		10°C
FOD Fort Dodge N 42° 36.7' W 94° 17.7' 113.5	CRUISE — V138	5000	037	4	54	155	00:18		230@33
	CRUISE — 3900	5000	036	77	112	180	00:39		10°C
MCW Mason City N 43° 05.7' W 93° 19.8' 114.9	CRUISE — V138	5000	052	4	51	155	00:16		230@33
	CRUISE — 3000	5000	054	73	61	188	00:56		10°C
RST Rochester N 43° 47.0' W 92° 35.8' 112.0	CRUISE — V161	5000	035	3	38	155	00:12		230@33
	CRUISE — 3000	5000	032	70	23	187	01:08		10°C
	DESCNT — V161	5000	036	1	15	160	00:05		230@33
	DESCNT — 3000	2717	033	69	9	191	01:12		13°C
KRST Rochester ... N 43° 54.5' W 92° 30.0'	DESCNT	2717	027	1	9	156	00:03		230@33
	DESCNT — (3900)	1317	023	69	0	186	01:15		16°C
ROUTE TOTALS				18	221		01:15		

KRST Rochester Intl	ATIS 120.5 / GND 121.9 / UNI 122.95	ASOS 120.5 / APP (130°-309°) 119.8 / RADAR 119.6	TWR (CTAF PCL) 118.3 / APP (310°-129°) 119.2	TIME ON / BLOCK

Figure 10-58. When using a computer to automate a part of the planning process, you must use common sense, together with your navigation and dead reckoning skills, to verify that the results make sense.

Does the navigation log contain the waypoints you expect?

Does the magnetic course agree with the route on the enroute chart?

Does the magnetic heading make sense given the winds aloft?

Is the true airspeed (TAS) what you expect for this airplane for this flight?

Does the ground speed (GS) make sense given your TAS and the winds aloft?

Do the winds aloft shown on your navigation log agree with other weather information you have obtained?

Does the total distance agree with what you determine from the enroute chart?

Does the total flight time make sense given your total distance and ground speed?

What is the fuel consumption rate for this airplane at the planned altitude? Does the total fuel for the flight appear correct?

The navigation log is a convenient way for you to complete your preflight planning and organize your flight. It provides a concise textual description of your flight and allows you to monitor your progress in order to make adjustments if conditions change enroute. For example, if you start with 88 gallons of fuel, the fuel remaining should agree with the figures listed on the navigation log as you pass each checkpoint. Recording the time off and filling in the estimated time of arrival (ETA), actual time enroute (ATE), and actual time of arrival (ATA) boxes, helps alert you to any changes in winds aloft or in your airplane's performance.

 You can use a flight computer to compute time, speed, distance, wind, heading, and groundspeed. A personal computer or mobile device can automate this process, but you should verify that the results make sense.

FILING THE FLIGHT PLAN

After you complete the navigation log, transfer the appropriate information to your **IFR flight plan**. An important item to include on the IFR flight plan is the **aircraft equipment suffix** attached to the aircraft type in block 3. The suffixes and their meanings are found in the AIM. Because your airplane is equipped with GPS unit but does not have RVSM capability, use the suffix /G to indicate that you have a Mode C transponder and GNSS (global navigation satellite system) equipment. [Figure 10-59]

U.S. DEPARTMENT OF TRANSPORTATION FEDERAL AVIATION ADMINISTRATION	(FAA USE ONLY)	☐ PILOT BRIEFING ☐ VNR		TIME STARTED	SPECIALIST INITIALS
FLIGHT PLAN		☐ STOPOVER			

1. TYPE	2. AIRCRAFT IDENTIFICATION	3. AIRCRAFT TYPE/ SPECIAL EQUIPMENT	4. TRUE AIRSPEED	5. DEPARTURE POINT	6. DEPARTURE TIME		7. CRUISING ALTITUDE
					PROPOSED (Z)	ACTUAL (Z)	
VFR							
X IFR	3450B	TR182/G	155 KTS	KOMA	2000Z		5000
DVFR							

8. ROUTE OF FLIGHT

OMA4. OMA V138 KMCW V161 KRST

9. DESTINATION (Name of airport and city)	10 EST. TIME ENROUTE		11. REMARKS
	HOURS	MINUTES	
KRST	1	15	No SIDs/STARs

12. FUEL ON BOARD		13. ALTERNATE AIRPORT(S)	14. PILOT'S NAME, ADDRESS. TEL. NO. & AIRCRAFT HOME BASE	15. NUMBER ABOARD
HOURS	MINUTES		JOHN DOE 402-555-1111	
6	0	KOWA	1235 ZENIA WAY OMAHA, NE EPPLEY AIRFIELD	1
			17. DESTINATION CONTACT/TELEPHONE (OPTIONAL)	

16. COLOR OF AIRCRAFT	CIVIL AIRCRAFT PILOTS. FAR Part 91 requires you file an IFR flight plan to operate under instrument flight rules in controlled airspace. Failure to file could result in a civil penalty not to exceed $1,000 for each violation (Section 901 of the Federal Aviation Act of 1958, as amended). Filing of a VFR flight plan is recommended as a good operating practice. See also Part 99 for requirements concerning DVFR flight plans.
BLUE/WHITE	

Equipment determining the code to be entered in block 3 as a suffix to aircraft type on the flight plan form include DME, transponder, and RNAV.

If a flight has more than one leg at different altitudes, the altitude for the first leg should be entered in block 7 of an IFR flight plan.

The time entered in block 12 for an IFR flight should be based on the total usable fuel quantity on board the aircraft.

Put a note in block 11 if you do not plan to use SIDs or STARs.

Even if your flight does not require you to file an alternate airport, you may enter an alternate in block 13.

Figure 10-59. Make sure the flight plan form is filled out accurately before filing with Flight Service.

Use airport identifiers instead of the airport names to complete blocks 5, 9, and 13. Using the airport codes expedites the processing of your flight plan. If you do not know the correct code, list the name of the airport. For the route in block 8, use identifier codes for VORs, airways, waypoints, SIDs, and STARs.

 Fill out the blocks on the flight plan form accurately and completely with the information needed by Flight Service to process your flight plan. Be sure to include the correct aircraft equipment suffix, route, destination, and fuel available information on the form. See Figure 10-59.

 Selected equipment codes for aircraft with Mode C transponder and no RVSM capability:

/U—No DME

/A—DME

/I—RNAV, no GNSS

/G—GNSS

See the AIM for the complete list.

Enter your initial cruising altitude in block 7. If you want to change this altitude during the flight, you will need to direct your request to an ATC controller. Using the information from your navigation log you can compute the estimated time enroute to the point of your first intended landing. Enter this time in block 10 of the form. In block 12, record the total usable fuel on board expressed in hours and minutes.

 Use the point of first intended landing at your destination to compute the estimated time enroute on an IFR flight plan.

Remember to file your IFR flight plan at least 30 minutes prior to the listed departure time. This allows sufficient time for the flight plan to be processed.

CLOSING THE IFR FLIGHT PLAN

The requirement to close your flight plan is established in FAR 91.169. You can cancel an IFR flight plan anytime you are operating in VFR conditions below 18,000 feet MSL. However, if IFR conditions are again encountered, you must receive an IFR clearance before proceeding into those conditions. If your destination airport has an operating control tower, your IFR flight plan is automatically closed when you land.

If you are flying to an airport that does not have an operating control tower, you are responsible for closing your own IFR flight plan. You can do this after landing by by communicating directly with ATC or calling Flight Service by phone. According to the AIM, you also can cancel in VFR conditions while you are still airborne and able to communicate with ATC by radio. This is appropriate when air/ground communications with ATC are not possible at low altitudes. This saves you the time of canceling by phone, and releases the airspace to other aircraft.

 If your destination has IFR conditions and there is no operating control tower, you must close your flight plan by radio or by phone upon landing.

SUMMARY CHECKLIST

✓ A flight overview is a preliminary look at factors, such as weather, airplane performance and equipment, potential routes, and your instrument proficiency, that might prevent you from making the flight.

✓ Availability of preferred IFR routes, aircraft performance considerations, and fuel economy influences route selection.

✓ Check for published departure or arrival procedures relevant to your intended flight.

✓ If your alternate selection is limited, consider how an alternate that is far from your destination will affect your fuel requirements. You must carry enough fuel to fly to the first airport of intended landing, then to the alternate airport, and then for 45 minutes at normal cruising speed.

✓ Review NOTAMs for items like navaid and lighting outages or runway closures that can significantly affect your flight.

✓ Review the Chart Supplement for specific information about departure and arrival airports as well as possible alternate airports that are pertinent to your flight.

✓ Begin gathering weather data several days before your flight in order to obtain a general overview of weather patterns.

✓ Lockheed Martin Flight Service (LMFS) provides most aviation weather briefings, and graphic weather products are delivered online to pilots' computers and mobile devices. By logging into the Pilot Portal, you can obtain a weather briefing, airport information, and NOTAMs.

✓ If the weather at your intended destination is forecast to have a ceiling less than 2,000 feet or visibility less than 3 miles, you must file an alternate.

✓ A good alternate airport should be far enough away to be unaffected by weather at your destination, be equipped with appropriate communications and weather reporting capabilities, and have more than one approach.

✓ After you complete your weather briefing, you can make your Go/No-Go decision and begin planning the flight if conditions are favorable.

✓ The navigation log is a convenient way for you to complete your preflight planning, organize your flight, and provide you with a concise textual description of your flight.

✓ Before filing your flight plan, ensure you have all of the blocks in the flight plan form filled in correctly, including the aircraft equipment suffix in block 3.

✓ If you are flying to an airport that does not have an operating control tower, you are responsible for closing your own IFR flight plan by direct communications with ATC or by phone through Flight Service.

KEY TERMS

Flight Overview

Go/No-Go Decision

Preferred IFR Route

Alternate Airports

NOTAMs

Navigation Log

IFR Flight Plan

Aircraft Equipment Suffix

QUESTIONS

1. True/False. Factors to consider during your flight overview include airplane equipment and your instrument proficiency level.

2. Name at least two factors that influence your route selection.

3. Name at least three factors that you should consider when choosing an alternate airport.

4. What is the best source for information regarding navaid and lighting outages, runway closures, and limitations on instrument approach procedures?

5. True/False. It is not necessary to record the bearing error of the VOR receiver after conducting a required VOR receiver check.

6. To file an airport with a nonprecision approach as an alternate, what minimum weather requirements must it be forecast to have at your estimated time of arrival?

7. Name at least three factors that you should base your Go/No-Go decision on.

8. Which is an item that should be recorded on an IFR flight plan form?
   A. Aircraft type and equipment code
   B. Proposed altitude for the each leg of the flight
   C. Fuel remaining after reaching an alternate airport

9. How long prior to your departure time should you file an IFR flight plan?

10. Select the true statement about closing your IFR flight plan.
    A. ATC is responsible for closing for closing your flight plan.
    B. You may close your flight plan in IFR conditions after you are on final approach.
    C. You are responsible for closing your flight plan if the airport does not have an operating control tower.

Commercial Pilot Operations

I'm challenged to do a little bit better than yesterday . . . each time I fly.

— Robert A. "Bob" Hoover

PART IV

As you gain experience on your journey to becoming a commercial pilot you are likely to fly a variety of complex and high-performance airplanes. Chapter 11 introduces some of the advanced systems you will encounter as you transition to faster, more powerful airplanes. Aerodynamics and performance limitations in Chapter 12 will help you predict performance, control weight and balance, and define overall operating limitations for the airplanes you fly. Chapter 13 explores commercial flight considerations including emergency procedures and using single-pilot resource management principles in the commercial environment. Chapter 14 prepares you for the commercial pilot practical test by offering new insights when maneuvering an airplane near its maximum performance limits.

CHAPTER 11

Advanced Systems

Instrument/Commercial
Part IV, Chapter II—Advanced Systems

SECTION A ■ High Performance Powerplants

SECTION A
High Performance Powerplants

Most pilots look forward to the opportunity to fly larger, faster, and more powerful aircraft as they gain experience. The high performance powerplants installed in these aircraft often require different skills and operating procedures, and improper operation can cause serious damage to the engines and to other aircraft systems. Mastering these new skills is not difficult, but might require a shift in your thinking, from familiar habits, mental checklists, and rules of thumb to careful attention to written procedures and precise settings.

In the United States, pilots need to understand the difference between complex airplanes and high-performance airplanes. For pilot certification purposes, the FAA defines a complex airplane as one that has retractable landing gear, flaps, and a controllable pitch propeller. In many cases, airplanes with full-authority digital engine controls (FADEC) are considered to have a controllable-pitch propeller. A high-performance airplane has an engine of more than 200 horsepower. Most complex airplanes have more than 200 horsepower, but many do not, Likewise, many high-performance airplanes do not have retractable gear and flaps. [Figure 11-1]

| Complex, But Not High Performance | High Performance, But Not Complex | High Performance and Complex |

Courtesy of Piper Aircraft, Inc.   Courtesy of Cirrus Aircraft

Figure 11-1. Some airplanes are complex, some are high performance, and some are both complex and high performance.

 Applying carburetor heat enriches the fuel/air mixture, reducing engine power and decreasing aircraft performance.

CARBURETORS AND FUEL INJECTION

You might already be familiar with the two common methods of delivering fuel to the cylinders. The low cost and simplicity of carburetors make them a good choice for many aircraft, but **fuel injection systems** can offer significant advantages in efficiency and performance. You will probably operate both types of fuel system as you fly a variety of airplanes.

Engines with fuel injection are less susceptible to ice formation than those with traditional carburetors. Ice can form inside a carburetor due to the temperature drop caused by venturi effect and fuel vaporization. If you miss the indications of carburetor ice, the engine loses power and might even stop running. Using carburetor heat can help prevent icing, but because the warm air is less dense than cold air, the engine produces less power when carburetor heat is in use.

Compared to fuel injection systems, carburetors can be relatively inefficient because of their method of operation. When the air flowing through a carburetor venturi pulls liquid fuel out of a discharge nozzle, the fuel does not vaporize completely, but instead breaks up into irregular sized droplets that flow through the intake manifold to the engine's cylinders.

The size difference between the droplets causes some cylinders to receive more fuel than others, so it is seldom possible to set the mixture for peak performance in every cylinder. An excessively rich mixture in some cylinders can cause spark plug fouling and rough idle, and at higher RPM, engine power output suffers. In addition, as the fuel/air mixture flows through the intake manifold, it is warmed by heat from the engine, decreasing the density of the mixture and further reducing engine power.

Fuel injection addresses many of the problems of associated with carburetors. In addition to the reduced risk of induction system ice, a fuel injection system can provide greater efficiency, enhancing engine performance and safety. Fuel injection can reduce fuel consumption per unit of horsepower compared to the same engine with a carburetor, which means that an aircraft will often have increased range, endurance, and fuel economy. A fuel injected engine can often deliver more power for its weight than a carbureted engine. Increased combustion efficiency results in lower operating temperatures and less vibration.

FUEL INJECTION SYSTEM DESIGN AND OPERATION

Although fuel injection systems vary in design and operation, they all perform the same functions. They pressurize the fuel, meter it to provide a specific amount of engine power, and spray it directly into each cylinder intake port. Each cylinder receives the same quantity of fuel, making it possible to set the mixture precisely. As the fuel/air mixture vaporizes in the cylinder, it cools the combustion chamber, and injecting fuel at the cylinders rather than in the throttle area reduces the chances of ice forming in the induction system. [Figure 11-2]

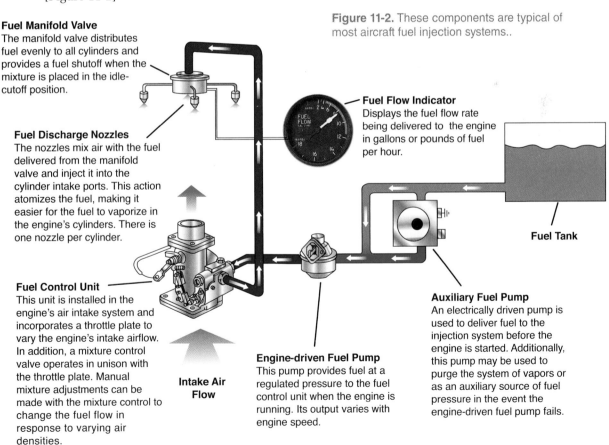

Fuel Manifold Valve
The manifold valve distributes fuel evenly to all cylinders and provides a fuel shutoff when the mixture is placed in the idle-cutoff position.

Fuel Discharge Nozzles
The nozzles mix air with the fuel delivered from the manifold valve and inject it into the cylinder intake ports. This action atomizes the fuel, making it easier for the fuel to vaporize in the engine's cylinders. There is one nozzle per cylinder.

Fuel Control Unit
This unit is installed in the engine's air intake system and incorporates a throttle plate to vary the engine's intake airflow. In addition, a mixture control valve operates in unison with the throttle plate. Manual mixture adjustments can be made with the mixture control to change the fuel flow in response to varying air densities.

Intake Air Flow

Figure 11-2. These components are typical of most aircraft fuel injection systems..

Fuel Flow Indicator
Displays the fuel flow rate being delivered to the engine in gallons or pounds of fuel per hour.

Fuel Tank

Auxiliary Fuel Pump
An electrically driven pump is used to deliver fuel to the injection system before the engine is started. Additionally, this pump may be used to purge the system of vapors or as an auxiliary source of fuel pressure in the event the engine-driven fuel pump fails.

Engine-driven Fuel Pump
This pump provides fuel at a regulated pressure to the fuel control unit when the engine is running. Its output varies with engine speed.

 A basic purpose for adjusting the mixture control at higher altitude is to decrease the fuel flow to the engine to compensate for the enrichening of the fuel/air mixture. Mixture enriching occurs if the fuel flow remains constant as the aircraft climbs into less dense air. If not corrected, spark plug fouling can occur at higher altitudes.

The fuel control unit is the heart of the system. It meters fuel to the engine according to the throttle position. The fuel control unit also has a mixture control, so that you can lean the mixture to compensate for the lower air density at higher altitudes. If you do not lean the mixture as your altitude increases, the mixture becomes richer. In addition to wasting fuel, an excessively rich mixture reduces power output, and can cause rough operation and spark plug fouling.

The venturi in a carburetor reduces air pressure to pull fuel into the engine, and many production airplanes fly safely using carbureted aircraft engines that were never equipped with fuel pumps. Fuel injection systems depend on fuel pumps to force fuel into the cylinders under pressure. Because fuel pressure is so important, fuel injection systems usually have two fuel pumps. If either pump fails, the other can provide fuel pressure for the engine. An engine-driven fuel pump operates whenever the engine is turning. The second fuel pump is often an electric pump, and might be called an **auxiliary fuel pump** or auxiliary boost pump. In many systems, the electric pump has two output levels. A low output level provides fuel under moderate pressure for priming and eliminating vapor bubbles in the fuel lines, and a higher level provides greater output to supply the engine with fuel if the engine-driven pump fails.

In some systems, running the electric pump at high output while the engine-driven pump is also operating can provide too much fuel pressure, causing rough engine operation or even engine stoppage. Although intended as a safety feature, many operational problems and accidents have been attributed to inappropriate use of the electric fuel pump. To avoid these problems, be sure to thoroughly review the electric fuel pump operating procedures for any fuel-injected aircraft that you fly. [Figure 11-3]

Figure 11-3. This split switch allows you to run the fuel pump at two output levels. Turning on the right side provides low output for normal operations, and turning on the left side provides high output for emergencies such as failure of the engine-driven pump.

The engine-driven fuel pump can also create special operating considerations. For instance, in some designs, the pump delivers more fuel to the metering unit than the engine needs. In this situation, the excess fuel usually flows back to a reservoir tank. The tank is often located in a low part of the aircraft where water and sediment tend to become trapped. If you neglect to check this tank by draining a sample of fuel during your preflight inspection, contaminants could build up and cause the engine to fail.

Another operating consideration involves the cooling effect of the fuel as it vaporizes inside the cylinder. This cools the cylinders, which is desirable during operation at a constant RPM, however, some manufacturers warn that suddenly injecting too much fuel into a hot cylinder could cause damage from shock cooling. Shock cooling might cause cylinder cracks due to the uneven contraction of metal. To reduce the chance of engine damage, make power changes slowly and enrich the mixture in small increments.

As you fly different fuel-injected aircraft, you might notice that some manufacturers measure fuel flow in pounds per hour instead of gallons per hour. Marking the **fuel flow indicator** in pounds per hour provides a more accurate indication of the energy available from the fuel. This is because the density of the fuel varies with temperature. As fuel temperature increases, there are fewer molecules in each gallon of fuel. Likewise, many aircraft also indicate fuel quantity in pounds. Measuring weight instead of volume gives a better indication of the amount of energy available in your fuel tanks. [Figure 11-4]

Figure 11-4. The fuel flow indicator displays the rate of fuel consumption, in gallons per hour, and might include fuel pressure indications measured in pounds per square inch. In addition, some indicators include range marks to allow for mixture adjustments in order to obtain the best economy or best power mixture for various power settings.

The fuel flow indicator actually measures fuel pressure. Because the fuel injection system contains calibrated orifices, the fuel flow rate can be derived from the pressure measurements. Some manufacturers display both fuel flow and pressure indications. Using the pressure to indicate fuel flow normally works very well, but if a fuel injector becomes plugged by dirt or debris, the pressure in the injection system increases, causing the indicator to show a higher-than-normal fuel flow rate. In response, you might be tempted to lean the mixture further in order to obtain the desired flow rate. Leaning the mixture too much can cause substantial engine damage or engine failure. Cross-checking the other engine instruments can help you to identify a clogged injector nozzle and take appropriate action.

OPERATING PROCEDURES

Operating procedures for fuel injection systems are a little different from those used with carbureted engines. Although injected engines have a reputation for being temperamental or difficult to operate, most problems result from not following the manufacturer's recommended procedures. The general guidelines that follow are typical of some common models of injected engines, but you should always refer to the pilot's operating handbook to determine the correct procedures for the specific aircraft you are flying.

STARTING

Starting a fuel-injected engine can be challenging until you gain some practice. You will usually use the electric (or auxiliary) fuel pump to prime the engine. Operating the pump sprays fuel directly into the intake ports of each cylinder. This not only provides a combustible mixture for starting, but also purges any vapors, or air pockets, from the injection system. If not eliminated, fuel vapors can prevent the injection system from functioning properly.

The most common starting problems are overpriming and underpriming. Operating the pump too long (overpriming) can "flood" the engine, making the mixture in the cylinders too rich to ignite. More severe overpriming can wet the sparkplugs with fuel, which prevents them from firing, or can wash the lubricating oil from the cylinder walls, which reduces compression.

On the other hand, if you do not operate the pump long enough (underpriming), there won't be enough fuel in the cylinders to start the engine. Either overpriming or underpriming can prevent the engine from starting.

When you are learning to operate a fuel injected engine, it might seem like you need at least three hands to manipulate the engine controls during starting. Although injected engines are equipped with conventional throttle and mixture controls, control operation during starting can be significantly different from carbureted engines. After some practice, these procedures will become routine.

SECTION A ■ High Performance Powerplants

NORMAL STARTS

When the engine is cool and the outside temperature is mild to warm, use the normal starting technique. The engine should only need a small amount of priming. The aircraft manufacturer normally prescribes a detailed sequence to follow in the starting checklist. Using the checklist is essential, but because of the need to perform the steps quickly, it is helpful to review all the steps before you prime and start the engine. [Figure 11-5]

STARTING ENGINE

1. Throttle—CLOSED

2. Propeller—HIGH RPM

3. Mixture—RICH

4. Propeller area—CLEAR

5. Master switch—ON

6. Beacon—ON

7. Electric fuel pump—ON

8. Throttle—ADVANCE to obtain 50-60 PPH fuel flow, then IDLE

9. Electric fuel pump—OFF

10. Ignition switch—START

11. Throttle—ADVANCE slowly

12. Ignition switch—RELEASE when engine starts

13. Oil pressure—CHECK

Figure 11-5. Starting procedures for fuel-injected engines vary between engine manufacturers and engine models. The procedures illustrated here show differences between the procedures for two widely used fuel-injected engines from different manufacturers.

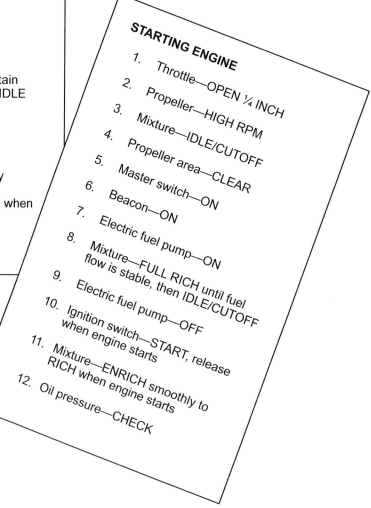

STARTING ENGINE

1. Throttle—OPEN ¼ INCH

2. Propeller—HIGH RPM

3. Mixture—IDLE/CUTOFF

4. Propeller area—CLEAR

5. Master switch—ON

6. Beacon—ON

7. Electric fuel pump—ON

8. Mixture—FULL RICH until fuel flow is stable, then IDLE/CUTOFF

9. Electric fuel pump—OFF

10. Ignition switch—START, release when engine starts

11. Mixture—ENRICH smoothly to RICH when engine starts

12. Oil pressure—CHECK

HOT STARTS

A fuel-injected engine tends to be more difficult to restart a few minutes after shutdown, particularly if it has been running for an extended period of time. With no cooling air flowing through the cowling, the residual heat in the engine can boil the fuel in the injection system's lines and components, and the resulting bubbles can cause **vapor lock**. The fuel injection components are designed to handle liquid fuel, not vapors, so the bubbles interfere with fuel metering and pumping. To start the engine, you must carefully follow the manufacturers instructions for hot starts.

After a hot engine is started, it might run erratically or quit if you turn off the electric fuel pump. This is because vapor bubbles can continue to form until the fuel system is cooled by airflow through the cowling and cooler fuel circulating through the lines and components. Running the auxiliary fuel pump can help maintain fuel flow until the fuel system cools and vapor bubbles are purged.

FLOODED STARTS

If the engine shows no sign of starting after cranking for about 30 seconds, stop cranking to prevent the starter from overheating. While allowing the starter motor to cool, you can check to see if fuel is dripping onto the ground from the intake manifold drain line. That fuel is a sure indication that the engine is flooded, but the engine could be flooded even if there is no fuel dripping. As with a curbureted engine, the objective of the flooded engine starting procedure is to purge the excess fuel from the cylinders until you obtain a combustible fuel/air ratio. [Figure 11-6]

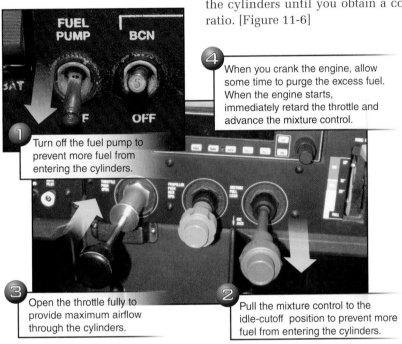

1 Turn off the fuel pump to prevent more fuel from entering the cylinders.

4 When you crank the engine, allow some time to purge the excess fuel. When the engine starts, immediately retard the throttle and advance the mixture control.

3 Open the throttle fully to provide maximum airflow through the cylinders.

2 Pull the mixture control to the idle-cutoff position to prevent more fuel from entering the cylinders.

Figure 11-6. A typical procedure for starting a flooded engine purges excess fuel while cranking.

AFTER-START PROCEDURES

After-start procedures for fuel-injected engines are similar to those used with carbureted engines. Below 3,000 feet MSL, ground operations are generally conducted with the mixture in the full-rich position. At higher elevation airports or higher density altitudes, lean the mixture according to the manufacturer's recommendations. Procedures for takeoff and climb might include leaning the mixture slightly to a specific range mark on the fuel flow indicator. Most high-performance airplanes have instruments to help you determine the optimum fuel/air mixture for cruise flight. With an understanding of the factors that affect your engine's operation, you can use these instruments to obtain the best performance from your aircraft.

ENGINE MONITORING

Aircraft with high performance engines typically have exhaust gas temperature and cylinder head temperature gauges to help you monitor engine performance and to adjust the fuel/air mixture to optimize engine efficiency, reliability, and safety. Older aircraft often have a single indicator for CHT and another for EGT, and it is common for only one cylinder to send data to the gauge. Other systems have probes on every cylinder, and allow you to monitor the temperature of each cylinder by turning a knob. Newer engine monitoring systems usually display EGT and CHT indications graphically, with vertical bar graphs to indicate the temperatures for every cylinder at the same time.

Leaning the mixture for cruise flight saves fuel and helps maintain the health of your engine. By making the final mixture adjustments using the hottest cylinder indications, you can be sure that all of the cylinders are receiving an adequate fuel/air supply. One cylinder running significantly hotter than the others usually indicate a problem, and you can help maintenance personnel to find the problem by telling them which cylinder is running hot. This might reduce the aircraft's down-time and maintenance costs.

EXHAUST GAS TEMPERATURE GAUGE

The **exhaust gas temperature gauge (EGT)**, as the name implies, measures the temperature of the exhaust gases leaving the combustion chamber. Generally, the exhaust temperature increases as you lean the mixture until the optimum fuel/air ratio is achieved. Further leaning causes the temperature to begin decreasing. By combining the high reliability of a fuel injection system with the accuracy of an EGT gauge, you can adjust the fuel/air mixture to obtain the engine's best performance. [Figure 11-7]

 The best power mixture is the fuel/air ratio that produces the most power for a given throttle setting.

 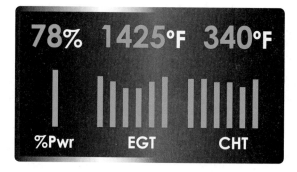

Figure 11-7. The gauge on the left shows the EGT in a single cylinder. The display on the right shows the relative EGT for each cylinder and the numeric temperature of the hottest cylinder.

The ideal mixture for combustion produces the highest EGT, or peak temperature. To find the peak temperature, you progressively lean the mixture until the EGT stops rising. This setting is called the **best economy mixture**, and produces the greatest fuel economy for the given cruise power setting. Flying at peak EGT gives the best fuel economy, but at the expense of a small reduction in horsepower, so you can expect to lose a few knots of true airspeed.

Most manufacturers recommend that you do not operate at peak EGT at power settings higher than 75%. At higher power settings, manufacturers recommend using a **best power mixture**. The best power mixture produces the greatest amount of power for a particular setting and generates less heat. To obtain best power, enrich the mixture to produce a cooler EGT reading. Manufacturers typically specify setting the mixture between 25°F and 125°F on the rich side of peak. Most engine manufacturers advise against operating on the lean side of peak EGT, but some engines have procedures that permit lean-of-peak operations to minimize fuel consumption on extended long range flights. These usually require precise power settings and careful monitoring of the engine instruments.

CYLINDER HEAD TEMPERATURE GAUGE

Cylinder head temperature gauges (CHTs) are common in both complex and high performance airplanes. If the airplane has cowl flaps, a CHT gauge is required equipment. Like the EGT gauge, a CHT gauge uses one or more thermocouple probes to sense temperature, but rather than measuring the temperature of exhaust leaving the engine, the CHT measures the temperature of the metal of the combustion chamber. Electronic displays might show EGT and CHT next to each other or superimpose one over the other. [Figure 11-8]

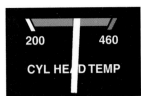

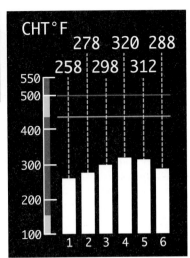

Figure 11-8. The CHT gauge in an older airplane (left) might show the temperature of a single cylinder. Newer systems (right) typically monitor all of the cylinders.

Engine temperatures can rise to high levels when cooling airflow through the cowling is insufficient, such as during extended ground operations or long, steep climbs. Two ways that you can control the CHT are by changing the mixture and by changing the flow of cooling air through the engine cowling. Enriching the mixture cools the engine by using fuel to carry excess heat away in the exhaust. You can increase the cooling airflow through the cowling by opening the cowl flaps or by climbing at a shallower angle.

ABNORMAL COMBUSTION

During normal combustion, the fuel/air mixture ignites and burns smoothly away from the spark plug, expanding so that maximum pressure pushes each piston at exactly the right time. For normal combustion, the mixture must be in the correct proportion and ignition must occur at the proper time. Unless both of these conditions are met, abnormal combustion can result. Detonation and preignition are two types of abnormal combustion. If not corrected, either can cause substantial engine damage or engine failure.

Detonation is the uncontrolled, explosive combustion of fuel, which can produce damaging pressures and temperatures inside the engine's cylinders. These explosions create abrupt pressure spikes that can act like hammer blows inside the cylinders, often melting or cracking the piston and other engine parts. Detonation usually causes high CHT and is most likely to occur when operating at high power settings. Common causes include using a lower fuel grade than specified by the manufacturer, operating with high manifold pressures combined with low RPM, or using too lean a mixture at high power settings. Even if you operate the engine correctly, mechanical problems can produce detonation. Detonation can also be initiated by higher-than-normal temperatures and pressures inside the cylinders. Watch the engine instruments for signs of detonation such as those listed above. If you suspect detonation, take immediate action to correct the problem by reducing the load on the engine and reducing engine temperature. [Figure 11-9]

Figure 11-9. This piston was damaged by detonation, which ultimately created a hole through the top.

Detonation might occur at high-power settings when the unburned fuel mixture charge in the cylinders is subjected to instantaneous combustion, instead of burning progressively and evenly. This condition can be caused by a mixture set too lean for the power setting.

SECTION A ■ **High Performance Powerplants**

You can help prevent detonation by following some basic guidelines. Always be sure the airplane is fueled with the correct grade of fuel. While on the ground, open the cowl flaps fully to provide maximum airflow through the cowling. During takeoff and initial climb, use a slightly rich fuel mixture, keep the cowl flaps open, and climb at a shallower angle to increase cooling airflow. Avoid extended climbs at high power. Monitor the engine instruments carefully to make precise power settings and to verify proper engine operation.

Preignition occurs when the fuel/air mixture ignites prior to the firing of the spark plug. Premature ignition is usually caused by a residual hot spot in the combustion chamber, often created by a small carbon deposit on a spark plug, a cracked spark plug insulator, or other damage in the cylinder that causes some part to stay hot enough to ignite the fuel/air charge. Preignition reduces engine power and produces high internal temperatures. Preignition can cause severe engine damage because the expanding gases exert excessive pressure on the piston while it is still moving toward the top of its compression stroke.

 The uncontrolled firing of the fuel/air charge in advance of normal ignition is known as pre-ignition.

The high temperatures caused by preignition can contribute to detonation, or detonation can lead to preignition. Because either condition causes high engine temperatures and reduced engine performance, it is often difficult to distinguish between the two. Operating the engine within the specified temperature, manifold pressure, and RPM limits reduces the probability of experiencing detonation or preignition.

INDUCTION ICING

Fuel injection systems are less likely than carbureted systems to develop internal icing, so there is no need for an induction air heater like those used for carburetor heat. However, **impact ice** can block the induction air filter or intake air scoop of either system. Impact icing forms when the airplane flies in visible moisture with the air temperature at or below freezing. Flying through super-cooled water droplets causes them to freeze on the airframe. As ice blocks the intake, the engine's performance decreases due to the reduced airflow. Most manufacturers provide an **alternate air source** that draws warmer, unfiltered air from inside the cowling to supply the engine intake. Depending on the aircraft design, the alternate air source might be automatic or manual. An automatic system usually has an alternate air door that is normally held closed by a spring. If the air filter becomes blocked, the reduced pressure within the intake pulls the alternate air door open to let warm air into the engine intake. A manual system allows you to check its operation during your preflight runup by observing an RPM drop when you switch to the alternate air source. [Figure 11-10]

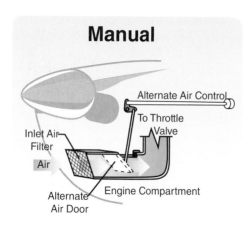

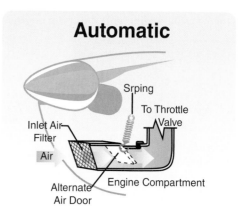

Figure 11-10. The alternate air system on a fuel-injected engine might be manual (left) or automatic (right).

TURBOCHARGING SYSTEMS

The amount of power that a normally-aspirated engine can produce decreases with altitude. Even though the engine draws in the same volume of air, at higher altitudes or higher temperatures, the lower-density air contains fewer air molecules for combustion. Compressing the intake air increases its density, enabling the engine to produce more power. Turbocharging compresses intake air before it enters the combustion chamber, providing a much higher manifold pressure than on a nonturbocharged engine. This higher manifold pressure allows you to climb higher and attain higher true airspeeds. You can often climb above adverse weather.

TURBOCHARGING PRINCIPLES

Turbocharging increases an engine's power by using energy that would otherwise be wasted. A turbocharger uses the flow of the engine's exhaust gases to drive a compressor that increases the density of the intake air. At the proper fuel/air ratio, the amount of power the engine develops is directly proportional to the mass of air pumped through it. Compressing the air increases its density, allowing more mass to flow through the engine.

A high performance airplane's power is typically measured by the amount of air pressure in the intake manifold. This pressure is referred to as the manifold absolute pressure (MAP). A manifold pressure gauge measures the MAP in the intake system in inches of mercury (Hg), and often includes colored range marks to indicate the engine's operating limits.

You can see how air density decreases with altitude on the manifold pressure gauge with the engine shut down. On a standard day at sea level, the manifold pressure gauge indicates the ambient absolute air pressure of 29.92 inches Hg. Because atmospheric pressure decreases approximately 1 inch Hg per 1,000 feet of altitude increase, the manifold pressure gauge indicates approximately 24.92 in. Hg. when sitting at an airport that is 5,000 feet above sea level with standard day conditions. You can also see the manifold pressure decrease as you climb at full throttle. [Figure 11-11]

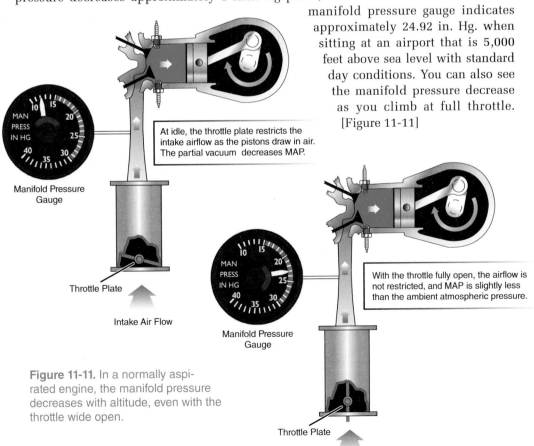

Manifold Pressure Gauge

At idle, the throttle plate restricts the intake airflow as the pistons draw in air. The partial vacuum decreases MAP.

Throttle Plate

Intake Air Flow

Manifold Pressure Gauge

With the throttle fully open, the airflow is not restricted, and MAP is slightly less than the ambient atmospheric pressure.

Throttle Plate

Intake Air Flow

Figure 11-11. In a normally aspirated engine, the manifold pressure decreases with altitude, even with the throttle wide open.

A practical measure of altitude performance is the **service ceiling**. The service ceiling is the maximum density altitude where the best rate-of-climb airspeed produces a 100 foot per minute climb at gross weight in a clean configuration with maximum continuous power. Engine power affects the service ceiling. Compressing the induction air increases engine power and increases the service ceiling. At altitudes below the service ceiling, the excess engine power can be used to increase airspeed.

A turbocharger has two main components—the turbine section and the compressor section. In the turbine section, the engine's exhaust gases drive a turbine wheel, which turns the impeller's drive shaft. The compressor section draws air into the compressor section, where the impeller compresses it to produce high pressure, high density air, which is delivered to the cylinders. [Figure 11-12]

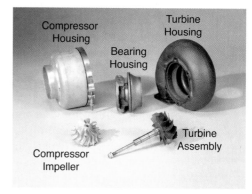

Forcing too much air into the cylinders can cause detonation and severe engine damage. A valve called a **wastegate** is usually installed to control the amount of boost by varying the amount of exhaust that flows through the turbine. When closed, the waste gate routes most of the exhaust gases through the turbine. When open, the wastegate allows the exhaust to bypass the turbine and flow directly out through the exhaust pipe. Some wastegates are manually controlled by the pilot, and others are automatically controlled.

Figure 11-12. Turbocharging increases engine power by using energy that would otherwise be wasted. Energy from the exhaust is captured by the turbine and used to compress engine intake air.

At relatively low altitudes, if all of the pressure of the exhaust is used to drive the turbine, the compressor provides too much intake air pressure. Using a manifold pressure that exceeds the engine's limitations is called **overboost**.

An open wastegate allows exhaust to flow directly out through the exhaust pipe to prevent overboost at lower altitudes. As the airplane climbs, an automatic wastegate gradually closes to maintain maximum manifold pressure without overboosting. [Figure 11-13]

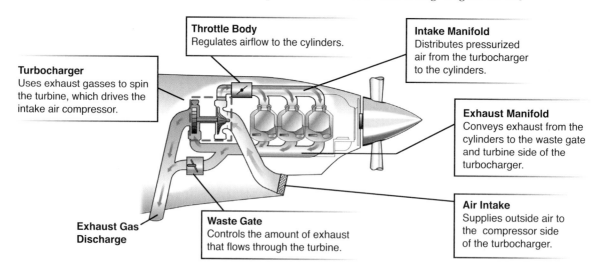

Figure 11-13. The waste gate regulates the flow of exhaust to the turbine to protect the engine from overboost.

Some turbocharged aircraft have an intercooler to increase the turbocharging system's efficiency. When air is compressed, its temperature rises, and hot air is less dense than cooler air. The intercooler reduces the temperature of the compressed air to increase its density. The intercooler works like a radiator. Cool outside air flows across tubes containing the hot intake air, removing heat. The resulting cooler intake air enables the engine to produce more power.

SYSTEM OPERATION

On engines with automatic wastegate controls, a pressure-sensing mechanism controls the position of the wastegate valve. On these systems, moving the throttle control automatically positions the wastegate to produce the desired MAP. On systems with manual control, you must closely monitor the manifold pressure gauge to determine when the desired MAP has been achieved. Airplanes that have been modified with aftermarket turbocharging systems often have manual wastegate systems. Follow the operating instructions carefully to avoid overboost. Although an automatic wastegate system is less likely to experience an overboost condition, it can still occur. For example, if you apply takeoff power when the engine oil temperature is below its normal operating range, the cold oil might not flow out of the wastegate actuator quickly enough to prevent an overboost. To help prevent overboosting, advance the throttle slowly and monitor the manifold pressure to keep it within operating limits. Some airplanes have annunciator lights to warn you when an overboost condition exists. If the annuciator illuminates, immediately retard the throttle to an allowable manifold pressure. [Figure 11-14]

Figure 11-14. An overboost annunciator light warns you to reduce the manifold pressure to an allowable level.

Here are some other considerations to keep in mind when flying a turbocharged airplane. A turbocharger typically operates at extremely high temperatures, and the turbine and impeller can spin at more than 80,000 RPM. This high rotational speed is possible because the turbine and impeller shaft is supported on pressure-oiled precision bearings. While the turbocharger is operating, these bearings must have a constant supply of engine oil to reduce the friction and carry away heat. For adequate lubrication, be sure the oil temperature is in the normal operating range before you apply high throttle settings. After a flight, let the engine idle for a few minutes before shutting it down to allow the turbine to slow down and the turbocharger to cool. If you shut down the engine when the turbine is still hot or spinning at high speed, the oil remaining in the bearing housing will boil, causing hard carbon deposits to form on the bearings and shaft. These deposits rapidly degrade the turbocharger's efficiency and reduce its service life.

To help monitor the temperature of the turbine, many installations include a turbine inlet temperature (TIT) gauge. If you use EGT to adjust the fuel/air mixture, be sure that the TIT stays within the manufacturer's specified limits. On many aircraft the mixture is set using the TIT instead of the EGT gauge.

HIGH ALTITUDE PERFORMANCE

As an airplane with an automatic wastegate climbs, the wastegate gradually closes to maintain the maximum allowable manifold pressure. After the wastegate closes fully, further increases in altitude cause the manifold pressure to decrease. This altitude is reported by the aircraft manufacturer in the POH, and is called the aircraft's **critical altitude**. If the manifold pressure begins decreasing before the aircraft reaches the critical altitude, you should have the engine and turbocharging system inspected by a qualified maintenance technician to determine why.

Above the critical altitude, airspeed changes affect manifold pressure. Ram air effect increases pressure in the induction system as airspeed increases. This increases air density to the turbocharger causing it to produce a higher manifold pressure. To obtain a desired manifold pressure, you need to allow for this effect when changing airspeed. For example, when you level off from a climb, set the manifold pressure to a value that is slightly less than desired, and allow it to increase to the desired value as the aircraft accelerates to cruise speed.

CONSTANT-SPEED PROPELLERS

A **constant-speed propeller** enables you to obtain the best combination of manifold pressure and RPM in different phases of flight to achieve a high rate of climb, increase cruise airspeed, or extend endurance by reducing fuel consumption. By using the optimum power settings to manage the load on the engine, you can increase the engine's efficiency, reliability, and service life. [Figure 11-15]

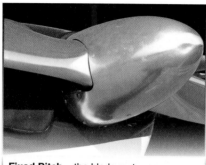
Fixed Pitch – the blade root merges smoothly into the propeller hub.

Constant Speed – the blade root is round, so it can rotate within the propeller hub..

Figure 11-15. A look at the blade root will help you to distinguish between a fixed pitch and a constant -speed propeller.

 Propeller efficiency is the ratio of thrust horsepower to brake horsepower.

PROPELLER PRINCIPLES

A propeller blade is an airfoil with its plane of rotation approximately perpendicular to the airplane's longitudinal axis. The blades of a propeller create an aerodynamic lifting force that is directed forward to produce thrust. Familiar airfoil terms like chord, camber, and angle of attack apply to a propeller blade cross section in the same way as for an airplane wing. Increasing either the angle of attack or the rotational velocity of the blade increases the amount of thrust it produces. Because the tips of the blades move so much faster through the air than the blade roots, the airfoil shape and its blade angle vary along the length of the blade. The root has a thick airfoil that is most efficient at low airspeeds, and it is placed at a high blade angle. The airfoil changes gradually from root to tip, and at the tip the airfoil is a thin, high-speed airfoil with a small blade angle. When you look along the length of a propeller blade from the tip, you can see how the blade becomes thicker toward the root, and the change in the blade angle causes the blade to look twisted. This increases propeller efficiency by allowing the blade to produce a more equal amount of thrust at every point along its length. Without these changes in airfoil shape and blade angle, much more thrust would be produced near the tips of the blades and very little near the roots, reducing thrust and increasing the bending loads on the blades.

Because the force a propeller produces is in the same direction as the airplane's direction of flight, the forward speed of the airplane causes a shift in the relative wind on the propeller blade. This causes the blade's angle of attack to decrease as the airplane's airspeed increases. [Figure 11-16]

SECTION A ■ **High Performance Powerplants**

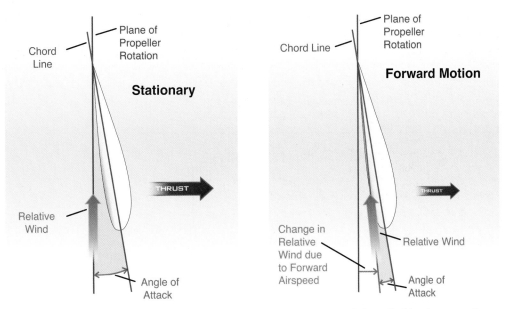

Figure 11-16. The faster the airplane moves forward, the more the relative wind for the propeller changes, reducing its angle of attack.

The angle between the chord line of the propeller blade and the relative wind is the **pitch angle**. Because the forward speed of the airplane reduces the pitch angle, a fixed-pitch propeller produces less thrust the faster the airplane goes.

A fixed-pitch propeller is most efficient only at one particular RPM and airspeed. A fixed pitch propeller can be made with a blade pitch that is ideal for steep climbs at relatively low airspeeds, or with a blade pitch that is most efficient at high cruising airspeeds, but not both. A propeller with blades pitched primarily for climb (a climb prop) will suffer reduced efficiency at high airspeeds, and a propeller with blades pitched for high airspeeds (a cruise prop) will have reduced efficiency during climbs.

CONSTANT-SPEED PROPELLER OPERATION

If you can change the blade angle in flight, you can enjoy the advantages of both a climb prop and and a cruise prop. A variable-pitch propeller can have a low blade angle for climb, and a high blade angle for cruise. [Figures 11-17 and 11-18]

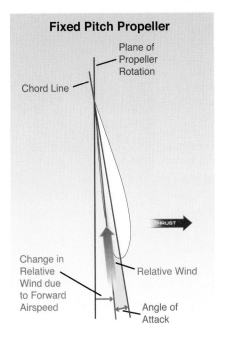

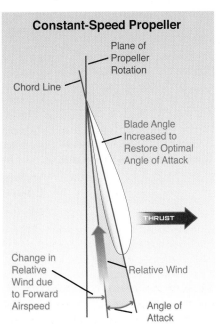

Figure 11-17. In contrast with the fixed pitch propeller, a constant-speed propeller can change the blade angle to the optimal angle of attack for the airspeed, producing more thrust.

SECTION A ■ **High Performance Powerplants**

FAA A fixed-pitch propeller is designed for best efficiency only at a given combination of airspeed and RPM.

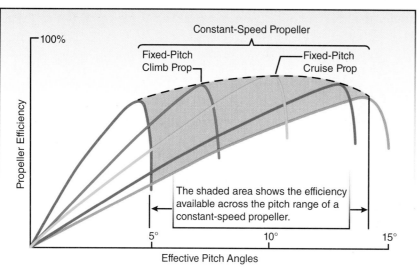

Figure 11-18. This graph contrasts the efficiency curves of fixed pitch propellers with the range available using a constant-speed propeller.

Many types of variable-pitch propeller systems have been developed over the years, including crank-operated mechanical systems and electric and hydraulically driven systems, but the constant-speed propeller has become the most widely used on modern high performance aircraft. Although all variable-pitch propellers can improve performance and efficiency by turning more of the engine's power into thrust in different phases of flight, constant-speed propellers offer the advantage of automatic RPM control. After you have set the RPM, a device called a governor automatically adjusts the blade angle to

FAA The reason for variations in geometric pitch (twisting) along a propeller blade is that it permits a relatively constant angle of attack along its length in cruising flight.

Q-Tipped Designs for Quieter Times

Propeller designs vary significantly on different types of aircraft. One design that will probably get your immediate attention is the Q-tip design. These propellers are manufactured by Hartzell Propeller, Inc. for installation on many different models of airplanes. This type of propeller has the tip of each blade bent back 90 degrees to help reduce noise.

Q-tips were originally designed to increase the distance of the blade tips from the fuselage on multi-engine airplanes. Bending the last inch of each blade backward reduced the cabin interior noise level and the propeller's production of thrust remained relatively unaffected. Since the Q-tip's original development in 1978, some single-engine airplanes have been modified with the design. In these situations, the Q-tip usually replaces a larger diameter propeller. The smaller diameter decreases the airflow speed at the blade tip, reducing propeller tip noise. As an additional benefit, the Q-tip's shorter blade length increases the blade-to-ground clearance. With a greater clearance, the blades tend to have less erosion and damage from ground debris.

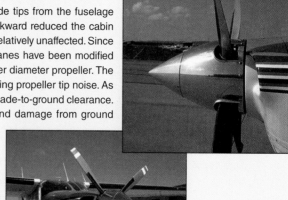

Other propeller models are being manufactured that increase efficiency as they reduce noise. One of the challenges is to develop propellers with enough diameter to use the engine's power effectively, but not so large that the blade tips approach the speed of sound. The blade tips of an 80-inch diameter propeller become transonic at about 2,900 RPM. If the airflow over the tip approaches the speed of sound, shock waves form that cause substantial losses in propeller efficiency and sharply increase noise levels.

maintain that RPM, even if you make a change in airspeed or flight attitude. For example, if you lower the nose for a descent without changing the engine controls, the increase in airspeed and the reduction in propeller load cause the governor to increase the blade angle to maintain the selected RPM. [Figure 11-19]

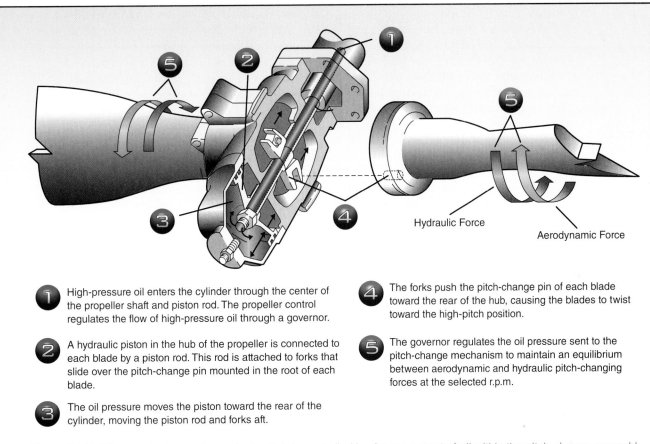

Hydraulic Force

Aerodynamic Force

1 High-pressure oil enters the cylinder through the center of the propeller shaft and piston rod. The propeller control regulates the flow of high-pressure oil through a governor.

2 A hydraulic piston in the hub of the propeller is connected to each blade by a piston rod. This rod is attached to forks that slide over the pitch-change pin mounted in the root of each blade.

3 The oil pressure moves the piston toward the rear of the cylinder, moving the piston rod and forks aft.

4 The forks push the pitch-change pin of each blade toward the rear of the hub, causing the blades to twist toward the high-pitch position.

5 The governor regulates the oil pressure sent to the pitch-change mechanism to maintain an equilibrium between aerodynamic and hydraulic pitch-changing forces at the selected r.p.m.

Figure 11-19. The constant-speed propeller's pitch is controlled by the movement of oil within the pitch-change assembly.

The range of possible blade angles for a constant-speed propeller is called the propeller's **governing range** and is defined by the limits of the blade's travel between high and low blade angle pitch stops. As long as the blade angle is within the governing range and not against either pitch stop, the governor can maintain a constant engine RPM. However, after the propeller blade reaches its pitch-stop limit, the RPM will vary as with a fixed pitch propeller, increasing or decreasing with changes in engine power, airspeed and propeller load. For example, as you prepare for landing, you set the propeller control for high RPM, and as you reduce power with the throttle, the RPM remains high until the blades reach their low pitch stops. Further power reduction causes the engine's RPM to decrease. Conversely, if you unload the engine and propeller by putting the airplane into a dive, the blade angle increases to maintain the selected RPM until the blades reach their high pitch stops, then the engine RPM begins increasing.

POWER CONTROLS

An airplane with a constant-speed propeller has separate controls for engine power and propeller RPM. The throttle controls engine power, which is indicated on the manifold pressure gauge. Propeller RPM is adjusted using the **propeller control** and is indicated on the tachometer. When used correctly, these controls can provide the most efficient combinations of power and RPM for a variety of flight conditions. For example, to develop maximum power during takeoff, move the throttle and propeller control full forward so the engine can produce its maximum RPM and maximum power. When leveling at your cruising altitude, you can use the throttle and propeller controls to reduce fuel consumption and optimize thrust.

The propeller control regulates the propeller's RPM. For takeoff, or to develop the maximum power and thrust, place the propeller control in the full forward position to provide a low blade angle and high RPM.

You can damage the engine if you do not operate the engine and propeller controls in the correct sequence. If the MAP is too high for the engine RPM, high internal pressures in the cylinders can lead to overheating and detonation. To avoid engine stress and possible damage, be sure that the manifold pressure is within allowable limits before you reduce the RPM with the propeller control. Conversely, when you increase power, be sure that the engine's RPM is high enough to handle the increased manifold pressure before you advance the throttle. For example, set the propeller control full forward before landing so that if you need to go around, you can apply full throttle without causing engine damage. In general, when reducing power, pull back the throttle before the propeller control; when increasing power, push the propeller control forward before increasing the throttle.

 When applying maximum power on an engine equipped with a constant-speed propeller, increase the RPM before increasing the manifold pressure to prevent undue stress on the engine. For the same reason, reduce the manifold pressure before decreasing the RPM when reducing engine power.

You can also damage the engine by making power changes too abruptly. When you move the throttle too quickly, heavy parts that are mounted on the engine crankshaft to damp out torsional vibration can shift out of place and begin hammering on their mountings. This is called detuning, and it can damage the magnetos, oil pump, and other engine parts. In extreme cases it can cause the crankshaft to break. You cannot detect detuning while it is happening, so it is important to avoid it in the first place.

Detuning of an engine crankshaft is a source of overstress that can be caused by rapid opening or closing of the throttle.

 ENVIRONMENTAL IMPACT AND PROPELLER NOISE

Aircraft noise is a significant issue at airports surrounded by highly populated residential developments as well as over National Parks, Wildlife Refuges, Wilderness Areas, and major tourist attractions. To be a good neighbor policy, you should be aware of these noise-sensitive areas and operate your aircraft in a manner that reduces its environmental impact. Many local airport authorities around the United States have developed noise abatement procedures. Follow these procedures to the extent possible within manufacturer and operational safety limits. In addition to avoiding noise sensitive areas, you can further reduce your aircraft's noise emissions by following some basic operating procedures.

Noise Sensitive Area Located Southeast of Runway 9/27

Noise studies show that some propeller-driven airplanes can produce a ground noise level as high as 88 decibels (dB) when flying over at 1,000 feet AGL. Noise levels in the range of 85 dB can cause hearing damage, and at lower noise levels, an overflying airplane can cause significant discomfort to a person on the ground. To reduce ground noise levels, avoid low altitude operations whenever possible. When low altitude flight is necessary, consider reducing the propeller RPM. For instance, after takeoff, decrease the propeller RPM as soon as safety permits. A reduction of as little as 100 RPM can significantly reduce the ground noise level.

SUMMARY CHECKLIST

✓ Fuel injection systems can increase engine efficiency by providing the same amount of fuel to every cylinder, which allows for more precise mixture control. This improves engine performance and reduces fuel waste. It also promotes safety by reducing the risk of induction system icing.

✓ Most operating difficulties of fuel-injected engines occur when pilots do not follow the manufacturer's recommended procedures.

✓ Proper use of the auxiliary fuel pump minimizes vapor lock problems.

✓ Preignition and detonation are the result of abnormal ignition and combustion. You can reduce or prevent them by using the correct fuel/air mixture and by monitoring the engine instruments to maintain the proper engine operating temperatures.

✓ EGT and CHT gauges provide you with a reliable and accurate method for adjusting the fuel/air mixture to obtain optimum engine performance.

✓ Fuel injection systems have an alternate air source that provides unfiltered, heated intake air to the engine if the main air source becomes obstructed.

✓ A turbocharger system produces increased intake air density. This allows the engine to develop more power and also provides a much higher service ceiling.

✓ When operating an aircraft with a turbocharger system, make slow throttle adjustments and monitor MAP and RPM carefully to prevent overboosting the engine. When flying an airplane with an with automatic wastegate system, be sure the engine's oil temperature is within normal limits before applying full throttle.

✓ Before shutting down an engine equipped with a turbocharger, let the engine idle for a few minutes to allow the turbocharger to slow down and cool off. Otherwise the turbocharger could be damaged and its life shortened.

✓ The critical altitude is the altitude at which the turbocharger wastegate is fully closed and the maximum allowable MAP is being maintained. With further increases in altitude, MAP will begin to decrease.

✓ When used correctly, a constant-speed propeller increases efficiency by optimizing the propeller pitch for the airspeed, engine RPM, and MAP.

✓ On a constant-speed propeller, the pilot sets a specific RPM and a governor changes the blade angle to maintain that RPM.

✓ Before increasing MAP or reducing RPM on an aircraft with a constant-speed propeller, be sure that the resulting MAP will not cause engine damage. To increase power on an engine with a constant-speed propeller, first use the propeller control to increase the RPM and then advance the throttle to increase MAP. To decrease power, first use the throttle to decrease the MAP and then use the propeller control to decrease the RPM.

SECTION A ■ **High Performance Powerplants**

KEY TERMS

Fuel Injection System

Auxiliary Fuel Pump

Fuel Flow Indicator

Vapor Lock

Exhaust Gas Temperature Gauge
(EGT)

Best Economy Mixture

Best Power Mixture

Cylinder Head Temperature Gauge
(CHT)

Detonation

Preignition

Impact Ice

Alternate Air Source

Turbocharging Manifold Absolute
Pressure (MAP)

Manifold Pressure Gauge

Service Ceiling

Overboost

Wastegate

Critical Altitude

Constant-Speed Propeller

Blade Angle

Pitch Angle

Governing Range

Propeller Control

QUESTIONS

1. Where is fuel injected into an engine that is equipped with a fuel injection system?

2. In most fuel-injected systems, if the engine-driven fuel pump fails, what can you do to restore fuel pressure and prevent total engine failure?

3. Why is a fuel flow indicator that measures flow rates in pounds per hour considered to be better than one that reads in gallons per hour?

4. True/False. Starting a fuel injected engine within a half hour after it has been shut down can be more difficult because residual engine heat causes the sparkplugs to become wet.

5. True/False. The best power mixture is obtained when the EGT is somewhat richer than its peak value, and is the condition that allows the engine to develop its maximum power for a given throttle setting.

6. What is the component that varies the flow of exhaust gases into the turbine of a turbocharger?

7. What happens if you climb above the critical altitude in a turbocharged airplane?
   A. High engine temperatures, detonation, and possible turbocharger damage
   B. Engine power steadily decreases as altitude increases
   C. The wastegate closes, allowing most of the exhaust to bypass the turbine

8. True/False. If the engine experiences a higher load and the constant-speed propeller is operating in its governing range, the propeller will automatically change its blade angles to a lower pitch.

9. Why is the propeller control placed in the high-RPM position before landing an airplane equipped with a constant-speed propeller?

10. When you decrease power on an engine equipped with a constant-speed propeller, what is the correct sequence for moving the engine controls?
    A. Reduce the RPM with the propeller control and then reduce the MAP using the throttle.
    B. Reduce the MAP with the propeller control and then reduce the RPM using the throttle.
    C. Reduce the MAP with the throttle and then reduce the RPM using the propeller control.

SECTION A ■ **High Performance Powerplants**

SECTION B
Environmental and Ice Control Systems

Many airplanes used in private and commercial service have the performance to climb above adverse weather into the flight levels, where higher cruising speeds are possible with less fuel consumption. However, at high altitudes, humans cannot breathe, and an airplane needs to be equipped with an oxygen or pressurization system. When these systems are available and functioning properly, you and your passengers will experience a safer and more comfortable flight environment. In addition to oxygen and pressurization systems, many airplanes have ice control systems to improve flight safety if you encounter icing conditions. Ice control systems increase time and options for maneuvering the aircraft out of hazardous icing conditions.

OXYGEN SYSTEMS

Oxygen systems for aviation vary in both their operation and their purpose. When unpressurized airplanes fly at high altitudes, pilots and passengers are required to use supplemental oxygen, while the oxygen systems in pressurized airplanes are primarily for emergency use. Continuous-flow oxygen systems are the simplest type, providing continuous delivery of oxygen to the user. Flight crewmembers of turboprop and jet airplanes commonly use diluter-demand and pressure-demand oxygen systems. These systems deliver oxygen more efficiently, incorporating more sophisticated oxygen masks and regulators that enable flight at higher altitudes than with a continuous-flow system. All of these systems can be built into an airplane and have similar storage and distribution components. [Figure 11-20]

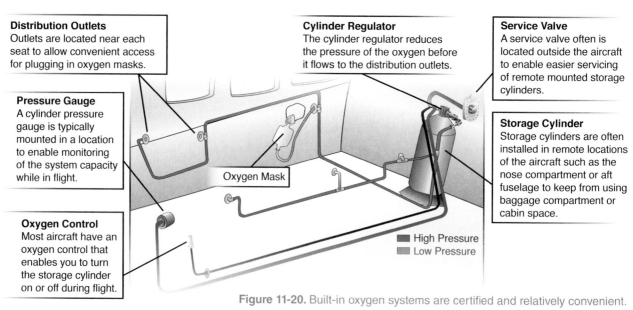

Distribution Outlets
Outlets are located near each seat to allow convenient access for plugging in oxygen masks.

Pressure Gauge
A cylinder pressure gauge is typically mounted in a location to enable monitoring of the system capacity while in flight.

Oxygen Control
Most aircraft have an oxygen control that enables you to turn the storage cylinder on or off during flight.

Cylinder Regulator
The cylinder regulator reduces the pressure of the oxygen before it flows to the distribution outlets.

Service Valve
A service valve often is located outside the aircraft to enable easier servicing of remote mounted storage cylinders.

Storage Cylinder
Storage cylinders are often installed in remote locations of the aircraft such as the nose compartment or aft fuselage to keep from using baggage compartment or cabin space.

Oxygen Mask

■ High Pressure
■ Low Pressure

Figure 11-20. Built-in oxygen systems are certified and relatively convenient.

CONTINUOUS FLOW

Continuous-flow systems provide adequate oxygen for flights up to 25,000 feet and are available in three styles: constant flow, adjustable flow, and altitude compensated. **Constant-flow** systems are used on many reciprocating-engine airplanes to provide continuous oxygen delivery at a constant flow rate. [Figure 11-21] A disadvantage of a constant-flow system is that at altitudes where people need less supplemental oxygen than the system supplies, a lot of oxygen is wasted.

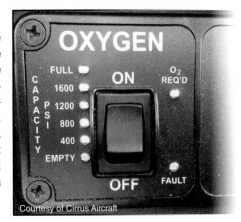

Courtesy of Cirrus Aircraft

Figure 11-21. With a constant-flow system you simply turn on a switch or valve.

Adjustable-flow systems enable pilots to vary oxygen delivery according to altitude and the pressure in the oxygen tank. These systems can have one main control for setting the altitude. Adjustable flow can also be achieved on a constant-flow system by using an adjustable flow meter in the tube to each individual oxygen mask or cannula that is plugged into the system. Each person can adjust their own oxygen flow to the correct altitude using their own flow valve. [Figure 11-22]

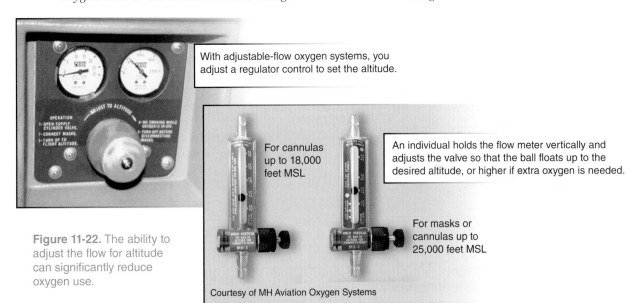

With adjustable-flow oxygen systems, you adjust a regulator control to set the altitude.

For cannulas up to 18,000 feet MSL

An individual holds the flow meter vertically and adjusts the valve so that the ball floats up to the desired altitude, or higher if extra oxygen is needed.

For masks or cannulas up to 25,000 feet MSL

Courtesy of MH Aviation Oxygen Systems

Figure 11-22. The ability to adjust the flow for altitude can significantly reduce oxygen use.

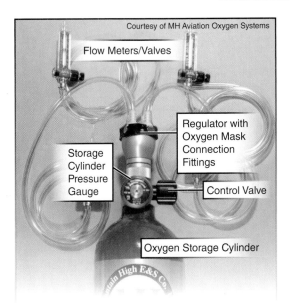

Courtesy of MH Aviation Oxygen Systems

Flow Meters/Valves

Regulator with Oxygen Mask Connection Fittings

Storage Cylinder Pressure Gauge

Control Valve

Oxygen Storage Cylinder

An **altitude-compensated** system is a further improvement of the adjustable-flow design. The system uses a barometric control regulator that automatically adjusts the rate of oxygen flow for the altitude. Because of its ease of use and efficiency, the altitude-compensated system is popular in high-performance airplanes.

In addition to built-in designs, a variety of portable oxygen systems are available. You can buy or rent a portable oxygen system when you are planning to fly at high altitude in an airplane that is not equipped with a built-in system. [Figure 11-23]

Figure 11-23. Portable oxygen systems use the same basic components as built-in systems, and have similar operating procedures.

SECTION B ■ **Environmental and Ice Control Systems**

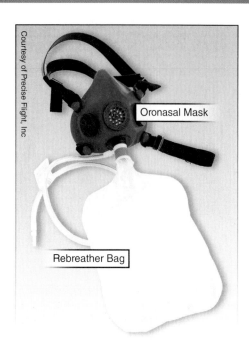

Courtesy of Precise Flight, Inc

Oronasal Mask

Rebreather Bag

CONTINUOUS-FLOW MASKS

The most common oxygen mask used with the continuous-flow system is an **oronasal rebreather** design. Oronasal simply means that the face mask covers both the nose and mouth, while rebreather refers to the fact that oxygen is diluted with a portion of exhaled air, and is then re-inhaled. Re-inhaling a diluted mixture wastes less oxygen and extends the duration of the oxygen supply. [Figure 11-24]

Figure 11-24. This oxygen mask uses a rebreather bag that is attached to the face mask and that fills with a mixture of oxygen diluted with exhaled air.

With adjustable-flow or altitude-compensated regulators, the amount of oxygen that flows into the rebreather bag is determined by the flow rate set on the regulator and the amount of atmospheric pressure surrounding the bag. At low altitude, the rebreather bag only partially inflates because the oxygen flow rate is low and the atmospheric pressure surrounding the bag is relatively high. Upon exhaling, a large percentage of exhaled air enters the bag and mixes with the oxygen. When the bag becomes fully inflated, any additional exhaled air exits the face mask through small holes or a check valve. Similarly, if the bag becomes completely deflated, cabin air enters the face mask through the small holes or another check valve when a person inhales. As altitude increases, the oxygen concentration in bag increases until the bag is full of 100% oxygen. At this point, all exhaled air is diverted out the mask and pure oxygen is inhaled.

Courtesy of Cirrus Aircraft

When a continuous-flow system is turned on, oxygen travels to the distribution outlet where a spring-loaded valve stops the flow until a mask is connected. Once connected, the valve allows oxygen to flow to the mask. [Figure 11-25]

Figure 11-25. Several types of oxygen valves are installed in built-in systems, depending on the age and manufacturer of the airplane. Make sure your connectors work with your airplane's system before flight.

Flow valves installed in the hose control enable you to monitor the flow of oxygen to the mask. These valves include a mechanism for indicating whether oxygen is flowing. [Figure 11-26]

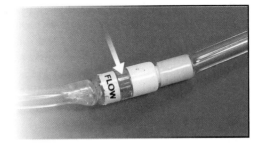
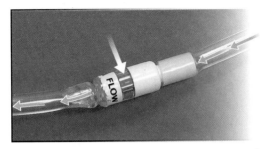

Figure 11-26. This flow valve indicates green when oxygen is flowing and red if oxygen flow stops.

NASAL CANNULA

For flight below 18,000 feet MSL, a **nasal cannula** is a popular alternative to an oronasal mask. Some of the advantages of a cannula are an unrestricted ability to eat, drink, and talk, as well as the ability to use a standard headset and microphone. [Figure 11-27] However, you should carry masks for aircraft occupants in case a head cold or nasal congestion prevents proper breathing through the nose. Above 18,000 feet, cannulas are not adequate—everyone should use a mask that provides an adequate seal to the face.

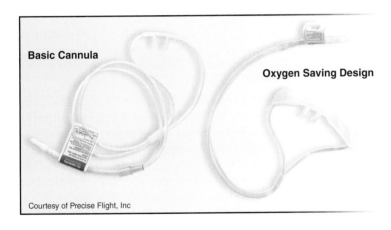

Basic Cannula

Oxygen Saving Design

Figure 11-27. A nasal canula does not hamper eating, drinking, or talking into a standard microphone.

Courtesy of Precise Flight, Inc

CONNECTING AND USING OXYGEN EQUIPMENT

Most masks and cannulas are easy to connect to an outlet. Simply push the connector into the outlet and turn it clockwise. Although the procedure is easy, passengers often are not familiar with the task. Before conducting a high-altitude flight, instruct your passengers on how to connect their masks. Turn on the oxygen system and let them try a few sample breaths. A couple of minutes spent instructing the passengers on the ground can prevent distractions during flight. If smoking is normally allowed in your aircraft, you must ensure that passengers know they may *not* smoke when the oxygen is turned on. Although oxygen itself does not burn, it dramatically accelerates combustion—a cigarette could become a little torch.

DILUTER DEMAND AND PRESSURE DEMAND

Most of the components of **diluter-demand** and **pressure-demand** oxygen systems are similar to those used with continuous-flow systems. Differences include a different style of oxygen mask, and the replacement of the distribution outlet with a special regulator unit. The style of mask used with either of these systems is a quick-donning design, which simply means you can put the mask on rapidly. When compared to an oronasal rebreather mask, a **quick-donning mask** provides a tighter seal around your nose and mouth, which improves oxygen delivery when you are flying at high altitude. Unlike a continuous-flow mask, the quick-donning mask does not use a rebreather bag for oxygen dilution. Instead, a valve in the regulator unit opens to allow cabin air into the mask to mix with oxygen when you are flying at an altitude that permits a diluted oxygen supply. As you climb, the flow through the valve progressively decreases. Above 28,000 feet the valve remains closed to provide 100% oxygen for inhalation. When supplying undiluted oxygen flow, the diluter-demand system is capable of supporting respiration up to 40,000 feet. At altitudes above 40,000 feet, even breathing 100% oxygen is not enough to provide adequate respiration because the atmospheric pressure is too low to support proper oxygen saturation into the bloodstream. For flight above 40,000 feet, the pressure-demand system is used to provide positive pressure oxygen, which is forced into your lungs when you inhale. Because the oxygen is delivered at a positive pressure, you need to receive special training to develop proper respiration techniques before using this system. These systems are used with quick-donning oxygen masks that can be put on and delivering oxygen within 5 seconds if the cabin air pressure suddenly drops. [Figure 11-28]

Figure 11-28. Quick-donning oxygen masks are required in some pressurized airplanes to provide emergency oxygen if depressurization occurs.

The regulator unit of a diluter-demand or pressure-demand oxygen system also uses a diaphragm-operated demand valve, which opens by the slight suction created during inhalation. When the demand valve is open, oxygen flows into the mask. When you begin to exhale, the valve closes, shutting off the flow of oxygen. The regulator unit also incorporates control switches that enable you to activate the oxygen system and to select different operating modes. One switch enables you to turn the dilution valve off to provide 100% oxygen each time you inhale, regardless of altitude. You might use this feature if you feel that the normal dilution mode is not providing an adequate supply of oxygen. Another switch enables you to select a continuous flow of oxygen for emergency purposes. For example, if smoke or fumes develop in the cabin, turning on that switch provides 100% oxygen flow to help prevent hazardous contaminates from entering the mask. The system includes a test switch that enables you to check the operation of the system before flight. To perform the check, breath into the oxygen mask while holding the switch in the test position. When the system is functioning properly, a flow indicator flashes each time you inhale. You can also monitor the flow indicator during normal operation to determine that oxygen is being delivered to the mask. [Figure 11-29]

Figure 11-29. This pressure-demand regulator can be set to provide 100-percent oxygen, or a normal diluted mixture based on altitude.

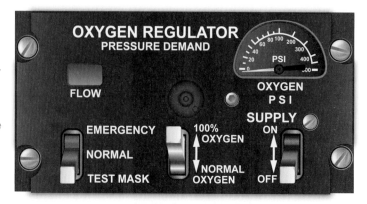

BRIEFING CARDS

As the pilot in command of an airplane, you are responsible for the safety and comfort of your passengers. One requirement of FAR Part 91 is that you must brief your passengers on the use of their safety belts and, if equipped, shoulder harnesses, and advise them to fasten them before takeoff or landing. However, there are many occasions that the passengers you fly with have little experience with other important aspects of your aircraft and the flight environment. As a courtesy, and to increase flight safety, you should take time to provide your passengers with a comprehensive preflight briefing. In addition, you also may want to consider providing your passengers with a briefing card similar to the one shown here.

Briefing cards often can be purchased from the manufacturer of your aircraft or you could make your own. This can be especially beneficial if your aircraft is equipped with amenities that the manufacturer does not cover in their briefing card design. If you decide to make your own, consider the information that commercial operators provide to their passengers. Some of these items include the following.

- If smoking is not allowed in your aircraft, it should have a *No Smoking* sign. Otherwise, if smoking is allowed, provide information regarding when and where your passengers can smoke in the aircraft.

- Illustrate and discuss the location and means of opening the passenger door and emergency exits.

- Provide information on the location of survival and emergency equipment including fire extinguishers and flotation devices, if applicable.

- If the flight will be conducted at high altitude, provide illustrations and instructions on the normal and emergency use of oxygen equipment.

- If your passengers have portable electronic devices such as cell phones, tablets or computers, discuss any restrictions regarding the use of these items during flight.

Other items that you may want to consider will vary with your aircraft. For example, if reclining passenger seats are installed, you should include information that explains how the seats are adjusted and when it is permissible to use the reclined position. You may even want to include some basic information on how to cope with certain physiological conditions such as sinus and ear blockages, air sickness, and anxiety. By taking a few minutes to discuss briefing card information with your passengers, you will help relieve anxiety that they may have with regard to the flight.

PULSE DEMAND

Initially developed for high-performance homebuilt aircraft, **pulse-demand** systems detect when the user begins to inhale and provide a measured amount of oxygen during each breath. They are typically portable systems with battery-operated electronic controls as shown in figure 11-30, but the FAA has also approved built-in systems for some airplanes.

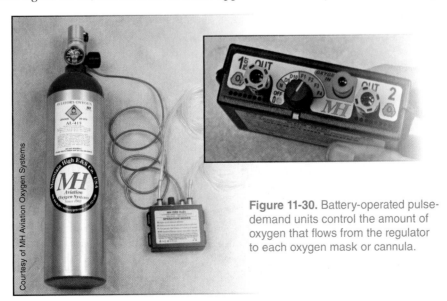

Courtesy of MH Aviation Oxygen Systems

Figure 11-30. Battery-operated pulse-demand units control the amount of oxygen that flows from the regulator to each oxygen mask or cannula.

SECTION B ■ **Environmental and Ice Control Systems**

Pulse-demand systems waste less oxygen than other systems, reducing the amount of oxygen needed by as much as 85 percent. In addition to stopping the flow of oxygen between breaths, they limit the amount of oxygen delivered in each breath, rather than allowing oxygen to flow throughout the inhalation. Most systems have a barometric sensor in the control unit that adjusts the amount of oxygen delivered during each breath, increasing the volume of each oxygen pulse as cabin pressure altitude increases. Like all oxygen systems, pulse-demand systems must be used in strict accordance with the manufacturer's instructions. Fatal accidents can occur when pulse-demand components are misused, or when they are improperly used in conjunction with built-in aircraft oxygen systems.

OXYGEN STORAGE

To transport and store oxygen, most civil aircraft use oxygen cylinders, available in various sizes. Most cylinders are made of steel or aluminum, but some newer airplanes use cylinders made from advanced composite materials to decrease weight. Cylinders are normally painted green with the words *Aviator's Breathing Oxygen* stenciled on the side, along with the normal servicing pressure. When the cylinder is part of a built-in system, it is securely mounted to the aircraft structure to prevent it from causing injuries in the event of a crash. If you are using a portable unit, make sure you secure the cylinder before flight. [Figure 11-31]

Figure 11-31. High-pressure cylinders provide safe oxygen storage, but must be properly secured.

Chemical oxygen generators are used in air carrier and other pressurized airplanes to provide emergency oxygen to passengers if the cabin loses pressure. FAR Part 91 requires you to have an oxygen supply of at least 10 minutes for each aircraft occupant when flying a pressurized airplane above FL250. Chemical oxygen generators meet this requirement using a solid chemical that produces gaseous oxygen suitable for breathing. Once started, the chemical process cannot be stopped, and continues until the chemical is fully consumed. To activate the system, the passenger pulls on the mask, which pulls a lanyard cord that triggers the mechanism to ignite the chemical.

OXYGEN SERVICING

A typical high-pressure oxygen cylinder is charged to a pressure of 1,800 to 1,850 pounds per square inch (psi) with a maximum pressure of approximately 2,200 psi. To prevent overpressure, cylinders are equipped with a pressure relief valve. When transporting a high-pressure cylinder, never leave it exposed to heat or direct sunlight for an extended time. Because oxygen expands when heated, the cylinder pressure could increase above maximum limits. Because compression of the oxygen increases its temperature when you fill a cylinder, the cylinder pressure gauge will indicate high immediately after servicing, and then decrease as the oxygen cools to ambient temperature. Be sure the cylinder has cooled before using an **oxygen duration chart** to compute the duration of your oxygen supply. In the example shown in figure 11-32, a cylinder that has a 1,600 psi pressure provides approximately 1¼ hours of oxygen for a pilot and 3 passengers.

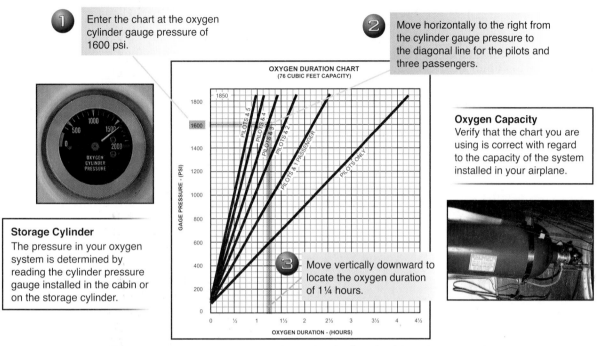

1 Enter the chart at the oxygen cylinder gauge pressure of 1600 psi.

2 Move horizontally to the right from the cylinder gauge pressure to the diagonal line for the pilots and three passengers.

Oxygen Capacity
Verify that the chart you are using is correct with regard to the capacity of the system installed in your airplane.

Storage Cylinder
The pressure in your oxygen system is determined by reading the cylinder pressure gauge installed in the cabin or on the storage cylinder.

3 Move vertically downward to locate the oxygen duration of 1¼ hours.

Figure 11-32. With an oxygen duration chart, you can determine the length of time that you and your passengers can remain at a given altitude.

Oxygen cylinders and their fittings must be kept clean of grease, oil, and hydraulic fluid. If flammable materials come in contact with high concentrations of oxygen, spontaneous combustion and a severe fire could occur. In addition, to prevent moisture from entering an oxygen cylinder, do not allow the tank pressure to deplete below 50 psi. Always fill the cylinders with aviator's breathing oxygen (ABO) or equivalent. That means the gas must be 99.5% pure oxygen with no more than 0.005 milligrams of water per liter. The *Chart Supplement* indicates which airports have oxygen system servicing. [Figure 11-33]

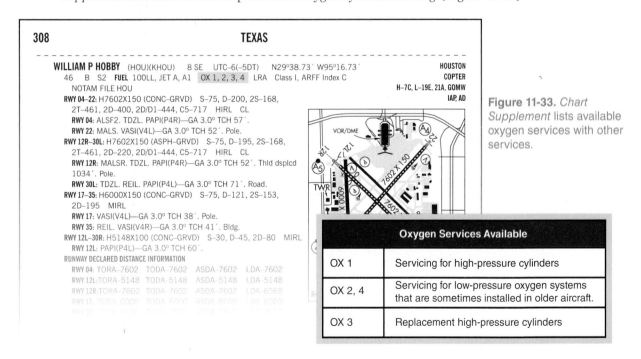

308   TEXAS

WILLIAM P HOBBY (HOU)(KHOU) 8 SE UTC-6(-5DT) N29°38.73´ W95°16.73´   HOUSTON
46   B S2 **FUEL** 100LL, JET A, A1   OX 1, 2, 3, 4   LRA   Class I, ARFF Index C   COPTER
  NOTAM FILE HOU   H–7C, L–19E, 21A, GOMW
  RWY 04–22: H7602X150 (CONC–GRVD)   S–75, D–200, 2S–168,   IAP, AD
    2T–461, 2D–400, 2D/D1–444, C5–717   HIRL   CL
    RWY 04: ALSF2. TDZL. PAPI(P4R)—GA 3.0° TCH 57´.
    RWY 22: MALS. VASI(V4L)—GA 3.0° TCH 52´. Pole.
  RWY 12R–30L: H7602X150 (ASPH–GRVD)   S–75, D–195, 2S–168,
    2T–461, 2D–220, 2D/D1–444, C5–717   HIRL   CL
    RWY 12R: MALSR. TDZL. PAPI(P4R)—GA 3.0° TCH 52´. Thld dsplcd
    1034´. Pole.
    RWY 30L: TDZL. REIL. PAPI(P4L)—GA 3.0° TCH 71´. Road.
  RWY 17–35: H6000X150 (CONC–GRVD)   S–75, D–121, 2S–153,
    2D–195   MIRL
    RWY 17: VASI(V4L)—GA 3.0° TCH 38´. Pole.
    RWY 35: REIL. VASI(V4R)—GA 3.0° TCH 41´. Bldg.
  RWY 12L–30R: H5148X100 (CONC–GRVD)   S–30, D–45, 2D–80   MIRL
    RWY 12L: PAPI(P4L)—GA 3.0° TCH 60´.
  RUNWAY DECLARED DISTANCE INFORMATION
    RWY 04: TORA–7602   TODA–7602   ASDA–7602   LDA–7602
    RWY 12L: TORA–5148   TODA–5148   ASDA–5148   LDA–5148
    RWY 12R: TORA–7602   TODA–7602   ASDA–7602   LDA–6568
    RWY 17: TORA–6000   TODA–6000   ASDA–6000   LDA–6000

Figure 11-33. *Chart Supplement* lists available oxygen services with other services.

Oxygen Services Available	
OX 1	Servicing for high-pressure cylinders
OX 2, 4	Servicing for low-pressure oxygen systems that are sometimes installed in older aircraft.
OX 3	Replacement high-pressure cylinders

CABIN PRESSURIZATION

Wearing an oxygen mask for extended periods of time can become uncomfortable and cause irritation. In addition, supplemental oxygen does not eliminate all the adverse physiological effects that can occur at high altitude. Decompression sickness and sinus or ear blockages are among some of the conditions that can cause severe pain or discomfort to you or your passengers. To mitigate these problems, many airplanes are equipped with a **cabin pressurization system**. A pressurized cabin is safer and more comfortable, making high-altitude flight possible without the need to wear an oxygen mask.

Before you act as the pilot in command of a pressurized airplane that is certified for operations above 25,000 feet MSL, FAR Part 61 requires that you obtain and log specific training. This training consists of ground and flight instruction that include high-altitude aerodynamics and meteorology, respiration, hypoxia, use of supplemental oxygen, and other physiological aspects of high-altitude flight.

PRESSURIZATION PRINCIPLES

Pressurization is accomplished by pumping air into an aircraft that is adequately sealed to limit the rate at which air escapes from the cabin. The air pressure increases to produce a cabin environment equivalent to that at a lower altitude. **Cabin pressure altitude** is a term that describes the equivalent altitude inside the cabin—it is the primary factor in the effectiveness of a pressurization system. Cabin altitude is limited by the strength of the airframe and its ability to withstand repeated pressurization and depressurization, as well as by the amount of compressed air the pressurization system can produce. **Cabin differential pressure** is the difference between the cabin air pressure and the outside air pressure.

Large transport category airplanes have maximum cabin differential pressures that are typically around 9.0 psid. However smaller general aviation airplanes can withstand maximum cabin differential pressure that are typically between 3.35 and 4.5 psid. So, as an example, if a pressurized single-engine airplane with a 3.7 psid is flying at FL240 (24,000 feet), the cabin pressure altitude would be 12,000 feet. [Figure 11-34]

Conditions
Pressure Altitude: 24,000 feet
Pressure Differential: 3.7 psid

STANDARD ATMOSPHERIC PRESSURE			
Altitude (ft)	Pressure (psi)	Altitude (ft)	Pressure (psi)
Sea Level	14.7	16,000	8.0
2,000	13.7	18,000	7.3
4,000	12.7	20,000	6.8
6,000	11.8	22,000	6.2
8,000	10.9	24,000	5.7
10,000	10.1	26,000	5.2
12,000	9.4	28,000	4.8
14,000	8.6	30,000	4.4

1. At 24,000 feet, the standard atmospheric pressure is 5.7 psi.

2. Add the cabin differential pressure: 5.7 psi + 3.7 psid = 9.4 psi

3. 9.4 psi corresponds to a cabin altitude of 12,000 feet.

Figure 11-34. With a standard atmospheric pressure chart, you can determine your cabin pressure altitude when you know the cabin differential pressure.

SECTION B ■ Environmental and Ice Control Systems

HOW LOW DO YOU NEED TO GO?

While it seems that a cabin pressure altitude close to sea-level would be desirable, most air carrier aircraft can only pressurize to a cabin altitude of about 8,000 feet when operating at their maximum altitude. Unfortunately, passengers on long flights at 8,000-foot cabin altitudes experience tiredness, jet lag, and other discomfort. Boeing sought to improve the passenger experience when designing the new 787 Dreamliner.

In addition to new lighting, increased humidity, and other comforts, a key design feature in helping passengers arrive at their destination feeling more refreshed and alert was reducing the cabin pressure altitude. But how low does the cabin altitude need to be? That is an important question because the airframe must be strengthened to hold higher pressure inside. So Boeing supported an Oklahoma State University study to determine what cabin altitude was necessary. After testing various persons in an altitude chamber, the researchers concluded that 6,000 feet would significantly increase passenger comfort on long-duration commercial flights. Lower altitudes did not provide much additional benefit. As a result, the Dreamliner was designed to operate at cabin pressure altitude of 6,000 feet.

Copyright Boeing

PRESSURIZATION COMPONENTS

On a pressurized airplane with a turbocharged reciprocating engine, pressurization air is provided by the compressor section of the turbocharger. As the compressor air is discharged, it enters a sonic venturi to limit the airflow and prevent too much air from being taken away from the engine. The airflow is limited by accelerating the air to a sonic speed as it flows through the venturi, which causes a shock wave to form. The shock wave acts as a barrier, preventing a portion of the compressor discharge air from flowing to the pressurization system.

From the sonic venturi, air enters a heat exchanger where it is heated or cooled to produce a comfortable temperature in the cabin. Because compressing the air increases its temperature, the air usually needs to be cooled. However, if additional cabin heat is needed when operating in the frigid flight levels, you can adjust a cabin heat valve to direct heated air through the heat exchanger from a shroud that surrounds the exhaust muffler.

From the heat exchanger, the pressurization air is distributed to the cabin through heating and ventilation outlets. To regulate the amount of air pressure in the cabin, an **outflow valve** opens and closes to allow the pressurized air to vent out of the cabin at a controlled rate. Another valve, the **safety/ dump valve**, vents the pressurized air overboard if the outflow valve fails. This valve is similar in design to the outflow valve, but is set to open at a higher cabin differential pressure—it opens automatically when the maximum cabin differential pressure is exceeded. [Figure 11-35]

CODE

BLUE – Ambient Air

RED – Compressor Discharge Air

ORANGE – Pressurization Air

BROWN – Pre-heated Ambient Air

GREEN – Conditioned Pressurization Air

Pressurized Cabin

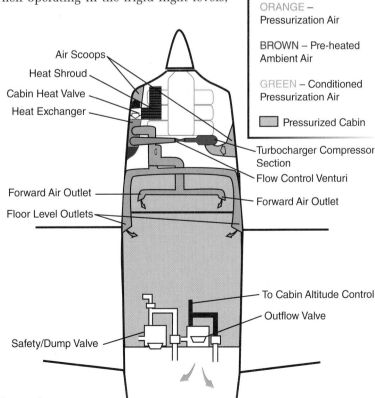

Figure 11-35. Although the components of pressurization systems vary between aircraft models, the principles of operation are similar.

PRESSURIZATION INSTRUMENTS

Pressurized airplanes are equipped with instruments to monitor the performance of the pressurization system. One of these instruments is a combined **cabin/differential pressure indicator**. This indicator works like an altimeter, except that the two hands indicate different pressures: one for cabin air pressure, and another for outside air pressure. By reading the indicator, you can determine either your cabin pressure altitude or the differential pressure between the cabin and outside air. Some systems also include a **cabin rate-of-climb indicator**. This instrument is referenced to the cabin air pressure and indicates the rate of pressure altitude change inside the cabin. [Figure 11-36]

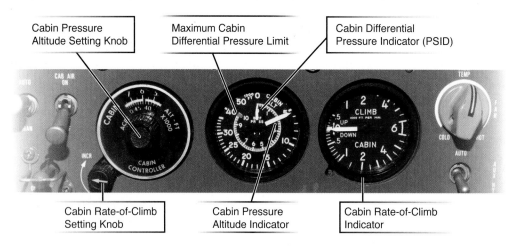

Figure 11-36. On this Learjet panel, the cabin pressure control knobs are next to the cabin/differential pressure indicator and the cabin rate-of-climb indicator.

PRESSURIZATION CONTROL

A basic system for controlling pressurization begins pressurizing the cabin when the airplane reaches a preset altitude. Although this altitude can vary with different manufacturers, 8,000 feet is commonly used. As the airplane ascends above the preset altitude, the outflow valve closes as needed to maintain the cabin pressure at that altitude as the airplane continues climbing. The cabin rate of climb drops to zero until the airplane reaches an altitude where the maximum cabin differential pressure occurs. Above this altitude, the pressurization system maintains the maximum cabin differential pressure, so the cabin pressure altitude has to climb as the airplane continues climbing. As a result, the cabin rate-of-climb indicator will show a climb rate that is slightly less than the airplane climb rate. The difference in the rate-of-climb values is because the air density inside the airplane is greater than the ambient air density. When the pressurization system is working to prevent the cabin differential pressure from exceeding maximum limits, it is operating in the **differential range**. On the other hand, when the system is operating at less than maximum differential and is able to maintain the cabin pressure altitude at the preset level, it is operating in the **isobaric range**.

A disadvantage of the basic system is that while flying below the altitude where pressurization begins, the cabin air pressure changes in response to climbs or descents. If the rate of altitude change is rapid, you and your passengers could experience physical discomfort such as sinus or ear blockage. Similarly, when the airplane is at an altitude that causes the pressurization system to operate in the differential range, rapid changes in altitude can produce physical discomfort. The second type of pressurization system alleviates these problems by using a **cabin pressure control**, which enables you to select the altitude where pressurization begins to operate. As an additional feature of most cabin pressure controls, you can also adjust the rate that the air pressure changes inside the cabin by varying the position of a rate control knob. By turning the knob, you can adjust the cabin rate of climb. To utilize the rate control, the pressurization system must be operating in the isobaric range. [Figure 11-37]

Figure 11-37. This King Air cabin pressure control, like the Learjet control shown in figure 11-34, enables you to set the desired cabin altitude and the cabin rate of climb or descent.

Cabin Pressure Altitude Selector Knob

Cabin Pressure Altitude Selector Scale

Aircraft Altitude Scale

Cabin Rate-of-Climb Adjustment Knob

To set the cabin pressure, adjust the pressure altitude selector to the desired cabin altitude, normally the lowest cabin altitude possible for your planned cruise altitude. On the system shown in figure 11-37, as you twist the selector knob, the outside scale shows the cabin pressure altitude and the inside scale shows the maximum airplane altitude possible within its differential pressure limitations. On the control shown in figure 11-38, the airplane altitude at maximum cabin differential pressure is shown in the window at the bottom. Rotating the adjustment knob moves both the indicator needle and the airplane altitude in the window. By observing the airplane altitude scale or window, you can determine the altitude where the pressurization system will begin operating in the differential range. If you climb above this altitude, the cabin altitude must increase—the pressurization system begins operating in the differential range. For best control and to avoid uncomfortable pressurization surges ("bumps"), keep the system operating in the isobaric range. To do this, set the cabin pressure control during your climb so that the airplane altitude scale indicates 500 feet higher than the altitude you are climbing to. Figure 11-38 shows how you could set the altitude control during a typical flight.

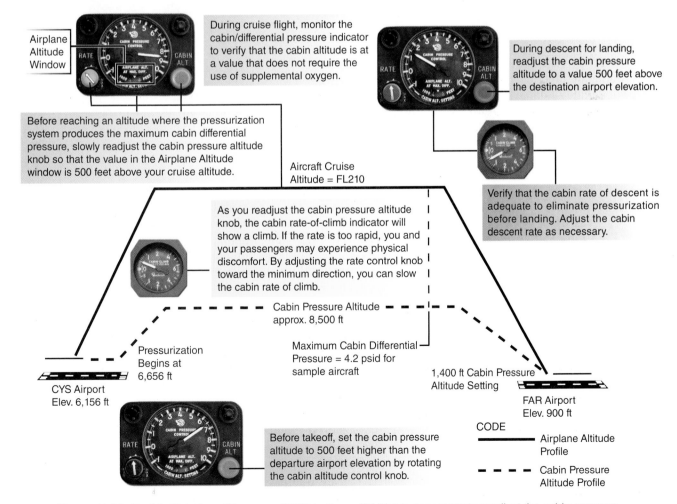

Figure 11-38. On this flight from Cheyenne (CYS) to Fargo (FAR) it is necessary to readjust the cabin pressure altitude during the climb to keep the system operating in the isobaric range.

SECTION B ■ Environmental and Ice Control Systems

The most compelling reason to operate the pressurization system in the isobaric range is so you can control the rate of cabin pressure change using the rate control. Make all cabin pressure control adjustments slowly, or extreme changes in cabin air pressure could occur, causing significant discomfort to you and your passengers.

Pressurization systems include a **dump valve** that can depressurize the cabin in an emergency. For example, you might need to depressurize to evacuate smoke from the cabin. Some dump valves remain open when the airplane is on the ground to prevent pressurization. Otherwise, the pressure could trap occupants inside the airplane by pushing against an exit door that opens inward. If the door opens outward, it could be blown open when the latch is released. This could injure someone inside the airplane, but it is an even bigger hazard for someone opening the door from the outside. [Figure 11-39]

Figure 11-39. On some aircraft, pulling a handle manually activates the dump valve. With other designs, this function is controlled by a switch.

PRESSURIZATION EMERGENCIES

Although cabin pressurization systems are highly reliable, malfunctions do occur with system components or aircraft structures. Of the malfunctions that can occur, **cabin decompression** is the most serious. Gradual decompression is hazardous because you might not be aware of the subtle change in cabin pressure. As the cabin altitude increases, your ability to detect the decompression is impaired by hypoxia. To alert the flight crew of loss of pressure, an annunciator light illuminates when the cabin pressure altitude exceeds a preset value—typically 10,000 feet or 12,500 feet. If the cabin altitude light illuminates, you should don an oxygen mask, turn on the oxygen system, and descend to a lower altitude if practical, especially if the oxygen supply is limited.

Rapid decompression is complete pressurization loss within 1 to 10 seconds, and an explosive decompression is complete pressurization loss in less than 1 second. Rapid and explosive decompressions are likely to occur when a large part of the cabin structure fails. Windshield, cabin window, and door failures are typical causes of rapid or explosive decompressions. To help prevent these hazards, pay close attention to cabin structural components before any pressurized flight. If cracks or crazing are apparent in the windshield or any cabin windows, have them inspected before attempting to fly with the cabin pressurized.

Pressurized airplanes have cabin doors that are designed to withstand high pressure. To maintain a sealed and structurally sound cabin, the doors are equipped with numerous locking pins. Most manufacturers provide viewing ports for you to determine that the door is securely closed. However, if you suspect that a door has come slightly ajar while the cabin is pressurized, do not attempt to close it in flight unless there are specific procedures to follow in the POH for the airplane. Because pressurized aircraft doors have special latches, the door should be closed and secured by an authorized flight crewmember. [Figure 11-40]

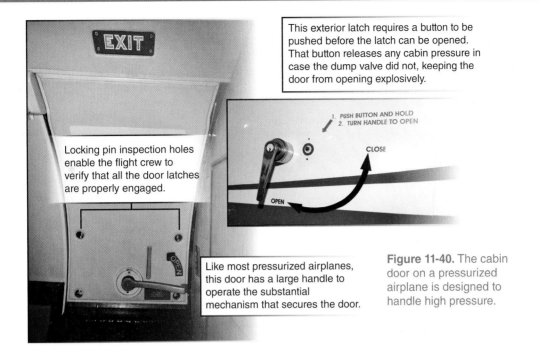

This exterior latch requires a button to be pushed before the latch can be opened. That button releases any cabin pressure in case the dump valve did not, keeping the door from opening explosively.

Locking pin inspection holes enable the flight crew to verify that all the door latches are properly engaged.

1. PUSH BUTTON AND HOLD
2. TURN HANDLE TO OPEN

CLOSE

OPEN

Like most pressurized airplanes, this door has a large handle to operate the substantial mechanism that secures the door.

Figure 11-40. The cabin door on a pressurized airplane is designed to handle high pressure.

Rapid or explosive cabin decompression is dramatic. In many cases, the cabin fills with fog because of immediate condensation of water vapor in the cabin. Anything that is not secured is sucked toward the cabin opening, resulting in flying dirt and debris. After the decompression, the cabin is extremely cold because most of the heated air is drawn out and the remaining air cools as it expands. Because the time of useful consciousness is very short, you must immediately don an oxygen mask and ensure that the oxygen system is operating. Start an emergency descent and declare an emergency. When you reach an altitude where oxygen is no longer required, proceed to the closest usable airport. A sudden cabin decompression at high altitude can cause altitude-induced decompression sickness (DCS). As a precaution, you and your passengers should seek medical attention from an aeromedical specialist, trained in DCS emergencies.

ICE CONTROL SYSTEMS

Ice control systems used on high performance or complex airplanes consist of a combination of **anti-icing** and **deicing** equipment. Anti-icing equipment prevents the formation of ice, while deicing equipment removes the ice after it has formed. Aircraft components that must be protected from ice accumulations include the leading edges of wing and tail surfaces, pitot and static source openings, fuel tank vents, stall warning sensors, windshields, and propeller blades. In addition, engines can require alternate sources of intake air or ice protected inlets, while ice detection lighting also is required to help you determine the extent of structural icing when flying at night. Even if your airplane is equipped with systems to protect some or all of these components, it still might not be certified to fly in icing conditions. To determine if your airplane is certified to operate in icing conditions, you should consult the FAA-approved POH for the airplane. However, even if certified, keep in mind that icing conditions pose significant hazards. Whenever you encounter ice, always seek out regions where meteorological conditions are less conducive to ice formation. To learn more about aircraft icing causes, effects, characteristics, and avoidance procedures, refer to Chapter 9, Section B — *Weather Hazards*. The aerodynamic effects of airframe ice are discussed in Chapter 12, Section A — *Advanced Aerodynamics*.

When operating in areas of precipitation or icing conditions, static discharge wicks help prevent static electricity from arcing between the airplane and the atmosphere. If static discharges are not controlled, radio interference can become so severe that communication and navigation signals are unusable. [Figure 11-41]

Figure 11-41. Static discharge wicks are particularly important when operating in precipitation and icing conditions.

AIRFOIL ICE CONTROL

To protect wing and tail surface leading edges from icing, most airplanes use pneumatic devices. On many reciprocating-engine and turboprop airplanes, **deicing boots** are pneumatically inflated to break the ice, allowing it to be carried away by the airstream. In another system, primarily used on turbine-powered airplanes, heated air is directed through ducting in the airfoil leading edge, to thermally prevent ice from forming. This system is often referred to as a **thermal anti-ice** system.

DEICING BOOTS

A high-pressure deicing boot is a fabric-reinforced rubber sheet that contains built-in inflation tubes. On reciprocating-engine airplanes, pneumatic pressure from engine-driven pumps inflates the tubes. The boots are installed in sections along each leading edge surface. On wings and horizontal stabilizers, corresponding sections on the left and right side of the airplane operate simultaneously to provide symmetrical airflow between both sides of the airplane. To limit the disruption of airflow over the surface, the inflation tubes within a boot might be alternately cycled by a sequencing timer. The cycling reduces the load on the pneumatic pumps.

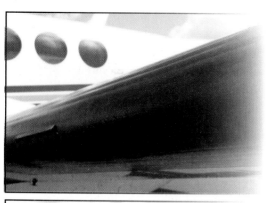

Deicing boots should be cleaned periodically with mild soap and water. Do not use abrasive equipment because deicing boots have a thin conductive coating to reduce static build-up. After cleaning, the boots can be coated with chemicals that help prevent ice adhesion, making them more effective. During preflight checks, inspect the boots for tears, holes, and secure attachment. [Figure 11-42]

Figure 11-42. Deicing boot shown before and during an inflation cycle.

The pneumatic pumps that power the deicing boots are often the same pumps that power the gyroscopic flight instruments. These pumps produce suction and positive-pressure air, which can be directed to the inflation tubes. When the boots are not in use, suction is applied to the inflation tubes, which holds the boot in the deflated position to maintain the contour of the leading edge. Switching on the boots sends positive-pressure air through the inflation tubes. The control usually has two positions, one for automatic cycling and the other for a single cycle. In the automatic position, a complete cycling of the boots is accomplished at timed intervals, whereas the single-cycle position only provides one complete cycle.

"Ice bridging," once a concern with pneumatic deicing boots, occurred when ice would form around the leading edge beyond the reach of the boots. The boots would expand into an air gap without breaking off this ice. [Figure 11-43] Past advice to counteract ice bridging was to wait until a layer of ice had formed on the wings before turning on the boots, so that the boots could effectively break off the ice. However, NTSB, NASA, and FAA studies have shown that ice bridging is not a problem on turbine-powered airplanes, and it rarely occurs on piston-engine airplanes. The NTSB's position is that the danger posed by even a small accumulation of ice far outweighs the risk of ice bridging. Generally, they recommend turning the boots on when first encountering icing conditions as long as the POH allows it.

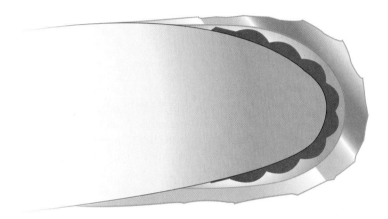

Figure 11-43. "Ice bridging" is when ice forms in a shape outside the reach of the boots.

Many deicing boot systems use the instrument system suction gauge and a pneumatic pressure gauge to indicate proper boot operation. These gauges have markings for the minimum and maximum operating limits for boot operation. When the boots are off, the suction gauge should indicate in the normal operating range. If suction is low, a boot section might have a leak, which prevents it from inflating properly. During boot cycling, the gauges fluctuate as each section inflates. While each section inflates, you should check the pressure gauge to verify that it indicates in the green, normal operating range.

Another type of indicator for deicing boots is annunciator lights. During boot operation, a red light illuminates until adequate pressure causes a cycling switch to actuate. When cycling occurs, a green light illuminates. If the red light remains on, the system is not operating properly and must be manually deactivated to deflate the boots.

THERMAL ANTI-ICE SYSTEMS

Thermal anti-ice systems heat the surfaces on airplanes to prevent ice formation. Hot air anti-ice systems are installed on some turbojet and turboprop airplanes. This is because a turbine engine has a ready source of hot air that can be used to heat airfoil leading edges. In this system, hot air is diverted ("bled") from one of the later stages of the compressor section of the engine and piped through ducts to the leading edges of the airfoils to be protected. [Figure 11-44] Engine inlets can also be protected with hot bleed air, or can be electrically heated.

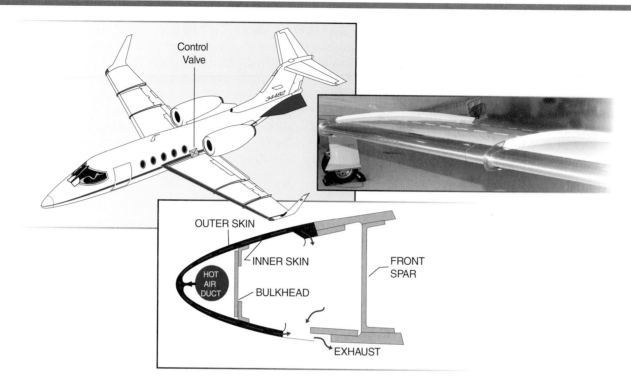

Figure 11-44. The leading edge of an airfoil that uses a thermal anti-ice system uses ducts and chambers that enable hot engine air to sufficiently heat the leading edge to prevent ice formation.

Another approach to thermal anti-ice and deicing uses a thin, electrically-heated graphite foil applied to leading edge surfaces combined with a non-stick film that conforms to the existing aircraft surfaces. The system uses electricity from the alternator to warm the leading edge of the protected airfoil. A non-stick coating helps ice to release from the area aft of the heated leading edge.

FLUID ANTI-ICE SYSTEMS

Before flight into icing conditions, ground personnel often spray liquid chemical solutions on airplanes to remove ice and to temporarily prevent new ice from forming. Applying similar liquids to airframe surfaces in flight can have comparable benefits. Such systems have been in use since the 1940s, and are usually either called TKS (for the British developers, Tecalemit, Kilfrost, and Sheepbridge-Stokes) or weeping wings, even though the systems typically protect tail surfaces, propellers, and windshields, as well as wings. Modern systems use leading edge panels that are either laser-drilled with thousands of small holes, or fitted with a fine stainless steel mesh. In operation, a pump forces a mixture of ethylene glycol, isopropyl alcohol, and water through the holes. This fluid runs back over the surface, forming a thin liquid film that prevents structural ice from forming.

The anti-icing fluid is stored in a reservoir that holds enough fluid to provide two or more hours of ice protection when flying in moderate icing conditions. When the system is combined with other ice control devices, many airplanes equipped with weeping wings are certified for flight into known icing conditions.

WINDSHIELD ICE CONTROL

Most aircraft are equipped with a defroster consisting of vents that direct heated air across the windshield on the inside of the cabin. Although this system is adequate for some operations, flight in icing conditions can cause ice to adhere to the outside of the windshield, restricting your visibility. To prevent ice formation, some **windshield anti-ice** systems use a flow of alcohol to coat a small section of the windshield. Although you can use these systems for ice removal, they should be used early enough when icing conditions are encountered to prevent ice from forming. The system is easy to operate, often using a switch that enables you to vary the flow rate of the alcohol. Before a flight with this type of windshield ice protection, check to make sure the reservoir is filled with the correct type of alcohol as recommended in the POH for your airplane.

Another effective way of protecting a windshield is by electrically heating it. Small wires or electrically conductive materials are embedded in the windshield or in a panel of glass installed over the exterior of the windshield. By passing electric current through the windshield or panel, sufficient heat is produced to prevent ice formation. When these systems are on, the high current flow can causes disturbances to the magnetic compass, introducing deviation errors as high as 40 degrees. You must also be careful to operate a heated windshield only during flight. If the heat is turned on during ground operations, the windshield could overheat and be seriously damaged. [Figure 11-45] This is true of most icing systems that generate heat—they must be operated only when the airflow from flight is available to cool them.

Figure 11-45. This anti-ice windshield panel developed bubbles between the window laminations because it was left on for an extended period of time while the aircraft was on the ground.

PROPELLER ICE CONTROL

Like windshields, propellers can be protected from ice by using alcohol or electric heating elements. With a **propeller anti-ice** system that uses alcohol, the spinner is equipped with discharge nozzles that are pointed toward each blade root. The alcohol is discharged from the nozzles, and centrifugal force causes the alcohol to flow down the leading edge of the blade to prevent ice formation. The inboard portions of each propeller blade can also have rubber boots attached to the leading edges that have grooves to direct the flow of alcohol. An electric propeller anti-ice system has rubber boots with wires embedded in them to heat the inboard portion of each blade. Electrically-heated propeller anti-ice boot sections are usually heated in a cycling fashion to prevent an excessive load on the electrical system. Check the system before flight by touching each boot section to determine if it is hot. During flight, you can refer to an ammeter that shows the amount of electrical current being supplied to the boots. [Figure 11-46]

Inboard Section   Outboard Section

Figure 11-46. Monitoring the current flowing to the propeller is a reliable way of verifying that the anti-icing system is working properly.

PROP ANTI-ICE AMMETER
When the system is operating, the prop ammeter will show in the normal operating range. As each boot section cycles, the ammeter will fluctuate.

PROP ANTI-ICE BOOT
The boot is divided into two sections: inboard and outboard. When the anti-ice is operating, the inboard section heats on each blade, and then cycles to the outboard section. If a boot fails to heat properly on one blade, unequal ice loading may result, causing severe vibration.

OTHER ICE CONTROL SYSTEMS

Other ice protection systems include heating of the pitot tube and static port openings, fuel vents, and stall warning sensors. These systems typically contain electric heating elements that can be checked during a preflight inspection by touching each component when the heat is on. Be careful, these devices can get very hot and burn your hand. Never wrap your hand around a pitot tube to check heating—instead, tap it with a moistened finger or use a rag to touch the tube lightly.

Even after you have conducted a thorough preflight inspection of each ice control system, you should check their operation in flight before encountering icing conditions. Because many of these systems are anti-ice devices, be sure to turn them on before entering icing conditions, as instructed in the POH. And if you encounter icing conditions, you should be looking for a different altitude or route. Although most small airplane ice control systems give you more time to get out of icing conditions, they cannot keep your airplane free of ice in moderate icing conditions for an extended time.

SUMMARY CHECKLIST

✓ Built-in and portable oxygen systems enable pilots and passengers to experience a safer and more comfortable flight environment while operating at high altitude.

✓ The types of oxygen systems used on aircraft are continuous-flow, diluter-demand, pressure-demand, and pulse demand systems.

✓ Constant-flow, adjustable-flow and altitude-compensated oxygen systems are all continuous-flow designs, and are capable of providing adequate respiration up to 25,000 feet.

✓ Oxygen masks that are used with continuous-flow oxygen systems are usually oronasal rebreather designs that dilute oxygen with a portion of exhaled air, to provide increased oxygen supply duration.

✓ Diluter-demand and pressure-demand oxygen systems only allow oxygen to flow when you inhale, and are capable of providing diluted or 100% oxygen.

✓ For flights as high as 40,000 feet, diluter-demand or pressure-demand oxygen systems are used. For flights above 40,000 feet, a pressure-demand system must be used.

✓ A pulse-demand system is an electronic oxygen controller that detects when a user begins to inhale and provides a measured amount of oxygen during each breath. The oxygen savings from these systems is dramatic, sometimes as high as 85 percent.

✓ Aviator's breathing oxygen is usually stored in a high-pressure cylinder that is serviced to between 1,800 to 1,850 psi and should never be allowed to decrease below 50 psi.

✓ A chemical oxygen generator provides an emergency oxygen supply, and is primarily used in pressurized airplanes in the event of a cabin decompression.

✓ To prevent a fire, never allow smoking or open flames near an oxygen system while it is in use. In addition, keep oxygen fittings free of grease, oil and hydraulic fluids.

✓ Pressurization systems increase the pressure inside an airplane to produce a lower cabin pressure altitude. In addition, some pressurization systems enable you to control the cabin "rate of climb" to maintain a comfortable environment.

✓ A basic pressurization system begins operating at a particular altitude, whereas a system with a cabin pressure control enables you to set the altitude where pressurization begins and, with most systems, control the cabin "rate of climb."

✓ When a pressurization system is operating at less-than-maximum differential pressure and is able to maintain the cabin pressure altitude at the preset level, it is considered to be operating in the isobaric range.

✓ When the maximum cabin differential pressure is reached, a cabin pressurization system operates in the differential range to avoid exceeding the maximum psid—the cabin altitude must increase if the airplane climbs higher.

✓ The pressurization instruments include the cabin rate-of-climb indicator and the cabin/differential pressure indicators.

✓ If a pressurized cabin decompresses, you must descend to an altitude where oxygen is not required. If the decompression is rapid or explosive, you should be checked by an aeromedical examiner for altitude-induced decompression sickness (DCS).

✓ Aircraft ice control systems provide more time for you to escape icing conditions. Even if an airplane is certified for flight into known icing conditions, you should try to avoid prolonged operations in icing conditions.

✓ Ice control systems are divided into deice and anti-ice systems. Deice systems remove ice after it has formed on an aircraft component, while anti-ice systems prevent ice from forming.

✓ Two major categories of ice control systems are pneumatic boots—which expand to break ice off airfoils; and thermal systems—which use bleed air or electricity to heat protected surfaces and prevent ice.

KEY TERMS

Oxygen Systems	Outflow Valve
Continuous Flow	Safety/Dump Valve
Constant Flow	Cabin/Differential Pressure Indicator
Adjustable Flow	Cabin Rate-of-Climb Indicator
Altitude Compensated	Differential Range
Oronasal Rebreather	Isobaric Range
Nasal Cannula	Cabin Pressure Control
Diluter Demand	Dump Valve
Pressure Demand	Cabin Decompression
Quick-Donning Mask	Ice Control Systems
Pulse Demand	Anti-Icing
Oxygen Cylinders	Deicing
Chemical Oxygen Generators	Deicing Boots
Oxygen Duration Chart	Thermal Anti-Ice
Cabin Pressurization System	Windshield Anti-Ice
Cabin Pressure Altitude	Propeller Anti-Ice
Cabin Differential Pressure	

SECTION B ■ Environmental and Ice Control Systems

QUESTIONS

1. Name the four basic types of oxygen systems.

2. True/False. An advantage of a pulse-demand system is that it uses less oxygen.

3. True/False. Nasal cannulas enable normal conversation, talking on the radio, and use of a normal headset up to FL250.

4. How do you determine if oxygen is flowing to an oronasal rebreather oxygen mask when used in a continuous-flow oxygen system?

5. To prevent moisture from entering a high-pressure oxygen supply cylinder, the cylinder pressure should not deplete below
   A. 15 psi.
   B. 50 psi.
   C. 100 psi.

6. If an outflow valve of a pressurization system fails in the closed position, what prevents the cabin pressure from exceeding the maximum cabin differential pressure?

7. To what altitude should you set a cabin pressure control on a pressurized airplane?
   A. The planned aircraft altitude
   B. The planned cabin cruising altitude
   C. The planned aircraft altitude plus 500 feet

8. What action should you first take if you experience a rapid cabin decompression in a pressurized airplane?
   A. Declare an emergency with ATC.
   B. Increase the pitch of the propellers.
   C. Don an oxygen mask and activate the oxygen system

9. True/False. On most airplanes, to prevent ice bridging, you should allow ice to accumulate on deicing boots before inflating them.

10. How can you determine that an electrically powered propeller anti-ice system is operating properly while in flight?

SECTION C
Retractable Landing Gear

Landing gear have a simple function: to absorb the load imposed during a landing, in order to protect the airplane's fuselage and preserve the comfort of those on board. You might not give much thought to the fixed gear on an airplane, except to ensure they are aligned with the runway upon touchdown. However, when you fly an airplane with retractable landing gear, you assume more responsibility in exchange for the additional speed and performance of the more complex design.

You will find certain differences when operating an airplane with retractable landing gear. In addition to faster cruise speeds, climb performance usually improves when the gear is raised after takeoff. Extending the gear during approach can help you slow down and descend easier, and lowering the gear during turbulence can help stabilize the airplane. Because there are numerous moving parts within the gear, you will need to preflight the system closely. You must always remember to lower the gear before landing and learn and practice the emergency procedures in case the gear will not extend or retract through normal means.

LANDING GEAR SYSTEMS

Most airplanes with retractable landing gear use a hydraulic system, an electric motor, or a combination of both to raise and lower the gear. Because systems differ, you should study your POH to learn about the system in your airplane.

The main gear retract either into the wings or into each side of the fuselage. The nose gear generally retracts into the forward fuselage, below the engine compartment. Gear doors are often installed to further streamline the fuselage after the gear has retracted.

ELECTRICAL GEAR SYSTEMS

The **electrical gear system** uses an electric motor that is mechanically connected to the landing gear. The motor is reversible so that it can both raise and lower the gear and drives a series of rods, levers, cables, and bellcranks that form what is essentially a motorized jack. If the system has gear doors, they are mechanically connected so that they open and close during the **gear cycle**. The gear cycle refers to the process that the gear goes through during extension and retraction. The electric motor moves the gear up or down and it continues to operate until the up or down limit switch on the motor's gearbox is tripped.

Like a fixed-gear system, retractable landing gear has struts, brakes, and other basic components. The drag struts help support the airplane's weight, while the shock strut provides cushioning during touchdown. [Figure 11-47]

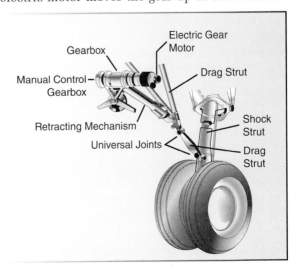

Figure 11-47. This diagram shows the main components of an electric retractable landing gear system.

SECTION C ■ Retractable Landing Gear

It's All About Having the Right Gear

Different airplanes require different types of landing gear to perform their particular jobs. While you may be familiar with the tricycle and conventional gear aircraft around your local airport, there are several other gear applications of which you may not be aware. Aircraft in remote areas use extra-large tires that can roll over rough terrain, while those that routinely land on snowfields may have skis installed. Seaplanes may either use pontoons or a keel for water landings, but amphibious types have wheels that either extend out of the pontoons or the fuselage for landings on hard-surfaced runways. If you fly a seaplane, neglecting to lower the gear for landing on pavement — or to raise the gear when landing on water — can have damaging consequences.

Copyright Corel.

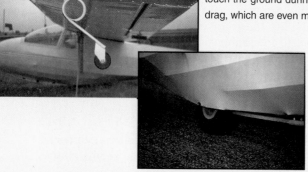

Gliders often have a single main gear, located on the bottom of the fuselage, and a small tailwheel. Because of this, crew are required to walk the wings so they do not touch the ground during takeoff. Having one fewer gear saves on weight and parasite drag, which are even more critical in gliders than in powered aircraft.

Large transport aircraft use multiple-wheel gear to distribute the weight of the aircraft over a larger surface area on the runway. Early landing gear experiments on transport aircraft tested extremely large, single wheels, and tracked gear, like the wheels on a tank, but found that the applications for those types of gear were more limited than for multiple-wheel gear.

HYDRAULIC GEAR SYSTEMS

Other airplanes utilize a **hydraulic gear system** to actuate the linkages that raise and lower the gear. When you move the gear switch to the retract position, hydraulic fluid, like that used in brake systems, is pressurized and directed into the gear-up line. The fluid flows through sequence valves and downlocks to the nose gear and main gear actuating cylinders. A similar process occurs during gear extension. The pump that pressurizes the fluid in the system can be either engine driven or electrically powered. If an electrically powered pump is used, the system is referred to as an **electrohydraulic system**. A hydraulic fluid reservoir contains any excess fluid. The reservoirs have dipsticks or other means to check the fluid level before flight. [Figure 11-48]

The hydraulic pump, regardless of its power source, is designed to operate within a specific pressure range. When a sensor detects excessive pressure, a relief valve within the pump opens and hydraulic fluid is routed back to the reservoir. A second type of relief valve prevents the excess pressure associated with thermal expansion. The hydraulic pressure is also regulated by limit switches on each of the landing gear that disengage the hydraulic pump after the landing gear has completed a gear cycle. Each gear has two switches, one for extension and one for retraction. These switches In case any of these switches fail, a backup valve relieves excess pressure in the system.

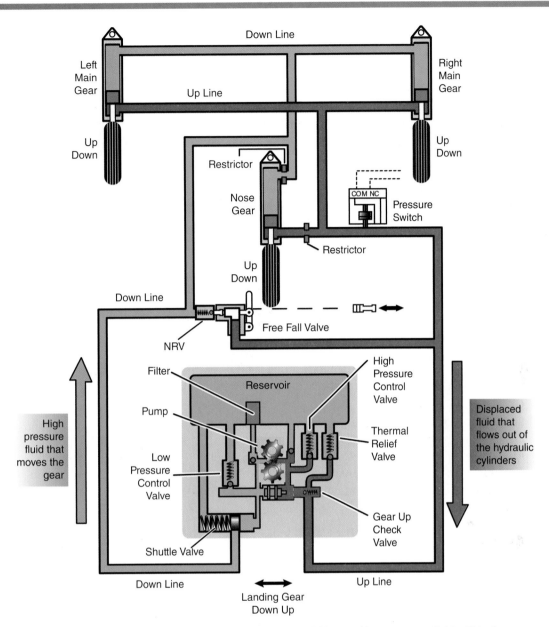

Figure 11-48. This diagram shows the movement of high and low pressure fluid within the hydraulic system that moves the landing gear. Some systems include additional cylinders that open and close landing gear doors.

GEAR SYSTEM SAFETY

Compared to fixed-gear systems, retractable landing gear has additional complexity and potential problems. For this reason, aircraft manufacturers have installed various devices on their airplanes that have retractable gear to enhance safety and ease of operation.

GEAR POSITION INDICATORS

In most airplanes, not all of the landing gear are visible from the cockpit. Therefore, one of several different types of **gear position indicators** is installed to help you keep track of where the gear is in the gear cycle. Position lights are one common type of indicator. Often, the grouping consists of one red or amber light and one or three green lights. The red or amber light is illuminated when the gear are in transit or unsafe for landing, and the green lights indicate when each gear is down and locked. Generally, the red light illuminates

Retractable Landing Gear ■ SECTION C

and then goes off after the gear is fully retracted or extended. These lights are often installed so that you can press on them to test for proper illumination. [Figure 11-49]

Figure 11-49. Before landing, ensure that all gear-down indicator lights are illuminated. This system allows swapping of bulbs if you suspect one of the bulbs is burnt out.

Other position indicators include miniature gear icons electrically placed by the movement of the actual gear, or an arrow indicator showing gear position, and some models have separate lights that illuminate solely when the gear is in transit. [Figure 11-50]

Figure 11-50. In addition to a horn, some airplanes have warning lights for unsafe landing gear conditions.

GEAR WARNING HORN

As a reminder to pilots, most airplanes with retractable gear have a **gear warning horn** that will sound when the airplane is configured for landing and the gear is not down and locked. Usually, the horn is linked to some combination of throttle setting, flap position, or airspeed indication. If the system detects that the gear is retracted when the airplane is at an airspeed, power setting, or flap setting that would be used for landing, the warning horn sounds. The horn generally sounds different than the stall warning horn, so that you know it is a gear warning.

SAFETY SWITCHES

Most retractable landing gear systems incorporate a switch that prevents the retraction of the gear when the airplane is on the ground. The **safety switch**, sometimes referred to as a **squat switch**, is usually installed on one of the main gear struts. When the strut is compressed, the switch disconnects the electrical circuit to the motor or mechanism that powers retraction. That way, if you move the gear switch in the cockpit to the UP position when weight is on the gear, such as during taxi, the gear does not retract and the gear warning horn sounds as an alert to the unsafe condition. If the gear switch remains in the UP position during takeoff, after the weight is off of the gear, the safety switch will release and the gear will retract. If the airplane does not have a positive rate of climb, it can settle back to the ground with the gear retracted. [Figure 11-51]

Figure 11-51. This safety (squat) switch is located on the left main gear.

AIRSPEED LIMITATIONS

Airspeed limits are established for gear operation in order to protect the gear components from becoming overstressed by air loads during flight. The airspeeds for gear retraction and extension can be different, because of the gear cycle sequence, and the relative strength of gear doors, struts, and other parts of the mechanism. Exceeding the landing gear speeds can cause structural damage. Although these speeds are usually not marked on the airspeed indicator, they are placarded, and published in the POH. The **maximum landing gear extended speed** (V_{LE}) is the maximum speed at which you can fly the airplane with the landing gear extended. The **maximum landing gear operating speed** (V_{LO}) is the highest speed at which you may operate the landing gear through its cycle. V_{LO} might be slower than V_{LE}, and this means that you will have to slow the airplane down to extend the gear, after which you could fly at a slightly faster speed. [Figure 11-52]

GEAR DOWN   129 KIAS (MAX)
GEAR UP   107 KIAS (MAX)
EXTENDED   129 KIAS (MAX)

Figure 11-52. Important landing gear speeds are posted on a placard in the cockpit.

DO BIRDS EVER LAND GEAR UP?

Every year, new and experienced pilots alike manage to inadvertently land aircraft with the gear retracted. Because pilots are not physically connected to the airframe, it is not intuitive to put the gear down before landing, as you would automatically extend your arms to brace a fall. You may wonder if birds and other animals that fly land on their feet by instinct, or if they have to learn to do so, as pilots do.

Just like airplanes, different species of flying creatures have "gear," or feet, that suit their environments. Belted kingfishers nest in burrows high on silt cliffs, and horned owls scavenge the nests that others leave behind. The hummingbird cannot walk — it must always use its wings to move, much like a helicopter on skids. Raptors such as the bald eagle have feet that serve double duty, being useful for snaring prey as well as landing. Bats land upside-down, which enables them to hang from cave ceilings and tree branches.

How much of an animal's ability to land safely is instinct, and how much is learned? If a bird landed simply on instinct, it would rarely suffer a bad landing. However, just as birds must learn to fly from watching their elders, so too must they perfect the skill of landing. There are moments when a young bird, struggling to touch down, obviously forgets to put its "gear" down, and the result is nearly as embarrassing as when a pilot does the same in an airplane. The albatross, for example, is notorious for never quite perfecting the landing process: it nearly always lands with a tumble across the water, but its awkwardness on land is offset by an incredible ability to soar.

You also must work to perfect your landing skills. To help you remember critical items such as extending the gear, you should always use a prelanding checklist. Also, if you fly in a crew, work with your fellow pilot as you run through the checklist. The coordination will help you ensure that you do not land someday with perfectly good gear still up in the wheel wells.

OPERATING PROCEDURES

You can prevent many potential gear system problems with a thorough preflight inspection of the landing gear. The wheel wells should be clear of obstructions, because foreign objects could damage the gear or cause it to jam inside the wells. Bent gear doors could be a sign of other problems with gear operation, and they could also become stuck during extension or retraction. Cracks, corrosion, or loose bolts in the linkage could lead to gear failure.

Because of the systems' complexity, some airplanes have airworthiness directives (ADs) related to the landing gear system. When you fly a particular airplane for the first time, make sure it is in compliance with any of these ADs. The POH or a maintenance technician familiar with the type of airplane should be able to tell you about specific items to look for.

You control the position of the landing gear through a switch in the cockpit. When you place the switch in the DOWN position, the gear extends and locks down. Conversely, when you move the switch to the UP position, the gear retracts and locks up inside the wells. On many airplanes, gear doors close to seal the gear from the airstream. The nosewheel steering linkage disengages from the nose gear, and the gear slides into a straightened position so that it fits into the wheel well.

As a general rule in a single-engine airplane, retract the gear after you no longer have usable runway left on which to land after takeoff. On a long runway, if an engine failure occurs with runway remaining, having the gear already down reduces the risk of landing gear up and damaging the airplane. After there is no more runway left to land on, having the gear up usually results in an increased climb rate or better glide in case of engine failure.

One risk with retractable landing gear airplanes is inadvertent gear retraction when attempting to retract the flaps. To reduce this risk, some gear switches have a detent over which you must lift the switch in order to raise the gear. The gear switch is normally shaped like a wheel, so that you can feel the difference from the flap switch, which is shaped like a flap. Although aircraft manufacturers have agreed on standardized positions for gear and flap switches, you must thoroughly familiarize yourself with your controls, especially on older aircraft that do not adhere to these standards. [Figure 11-53]

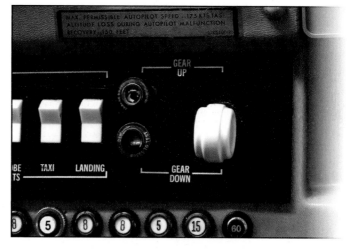

Figure 11-53. This gear switch is found on a Cessna 182RG and is typical of gear switches in many aircraft.

Avoid retracting the flaps while you are still rolling out after landing, unless you have a compelling need for maximum braking or if the POH requires it. When your attention is divided between taxiing, looking for traffic, and reconfiguring the airplane, the risk of accidentally reaching for the gear lever instead of the flap lever is higher than you might expect—and you cannot count on the squat switch to save you, especially when the wings are still producing some lift and the airplane is bouncing over bumps that could lighten the load on the main gear.

The gear takes several seconds to complete a cycle, so be sure to factor in this delay when deciding when to raise or lower the gear. The indicated airspeed decreases when the gear is extended and increases after the gear is retracted. You also will notice that the airplane pitches down when the gear is extended, so is often easier to extend the gear when you need to slow down and descend, if the gear speed limitations permit.

Circuit breakers protect electric landing gear circuitry from excessive loads. On some airplanes, one circuit breaker protects the landing gear circuit, while another protects the gear warning system. Other airplanes use a single breaker for the entire system. You can pull the gear pump breaker to keep the gear motor from overheating if a malfunction keeps it running after the landing gear has fully extended or retracted. Because of the heavy electrical load in a gear cycle, the circuit breakers should be one of the first items you check if the gear fails to operate. Avoid pulling a circuit breaker to silence the gear warning horn because this could lead to a gear-up landing.

During cold weather, slush and water can splash on to the gear linkages and freeze. Taxi slowly through snow, slush or water to prevent the gear from becoming wet, and avoid isolated areas of moisture on the ramp whenever possible. If the gear does become wet, cycle it several times after takeoff to keep the ice from freezing moveable parts in the system. If you are unable to retract the gear because of ice accumulation, leave it down, return to the airport, and have the gear deiced.

 Recycling the landing gear after takeoff from a slushy runway can help prevent the build-up of ice on the gear.

GEAR SYSTEM MALFUNCTIONS

Pay attention to the feedback that the landing gear system gives you when you move the lever to the DOWN position. Do you hear the motor run? Do you feel the airplane slow and pitch down from extra drag that should be there? Do you feel the "clunk" as the gear locks in position. Do you see the gear extended on airplanes on which it is visible? Some airplanes have mirrors installed on the wings or engine nacelles so that you can see the gear position from the cockpit. Even with all these signals, the position indicator lights are your primary means of determining whether the gear has extended correctly. A tower controller or other observer on the ground might be able to check for you if you are not sure the gear has extended properly.

If the position indicator lights do not illuminate after you move the gear lever, refer to the abnormal checklists before attempting an emergency gear extension. First the gear might be down, and one or more of the position indicator light bulbs might be burned out. Replace the suspect bulb with a working one and check it again. If you did not notice any other signs that the gear operated, check for a popped-out circuit breaker. If you find one, reset the breaker, make sure the gear lever is in the DOWN position and see if it extends. If it does not, or if the breaker pops again, follow your checklist for emergency gear extension.

EMERGENCY GEAR EXTENSION

When you establish that the gear has failed to extend, you should be ready to use whatever type of **emergency landing gear system** is available in the airplane. The most common kinds you will see are the hand crank, hand pump hydraulic, free fall, and carbon dioxide (CO_2) pressurized systems. These systems are designed for emergency gear *extension*—not retraction. Failure of gear to retract is not an emergency unless it retracts partially and cannot be extended again. On most light airplanes, with the gear stuck down and locked, you can either return to the airport or continue the flight to another airport where you can get it fixed, allowing extra time and fuel for flying with the landing gear extended.

Study the POH for the proper method and any precautions that apply to a particular emergency landing gear extension system. Normally, you will practice a manual gear extension with an instructor when obtaining a checkout for a complex airplane. However, with some airplanes, a mechanic must put the airplane on jacks to reset it after an emergency extension, and it is inadvisable to practice the procedure. After you practice an emergency gear extension, make sure that you stow the hand crank or pump properly—failure to do so could keep the landing gear from functioning normally.

A **hand crank system** is often found on airplanes with electric gear systems. The crank is employed to turn the gears that operate the actuators manually instead of through the electric motor. When you use this system, you will need to turn the crank a specific number of revolutions before the gear is fully extended. A good reason to practice this extension method in flight is that the position you must be in to turn the crank might be awkward, and the crank might be difficult to turn.

If you fly an airplane with a hydraulic system, you might use a **hydraulic hand pump system** to extend the gear when the primary pump fails. You supply the necessary hydraulic fluid pressure to the actuator cylinders by pumping a hand pump. With some systems, you need to put the gear switch in the DOWN position before operating the pump.

A **freefall system** is another method of gear extension used on airplanes that have hydraulic gear systems. A control lever is used to open a valve that releases the system pressure. Hydraulic pressure equalizes on both sides of the gear actuators and allows the landing gear to fall into position through the force of gravity and aerodynamic loads. On some airplanes, a spring assists in gear extension.

In the **carbon dioxide (CO_2) pressurized system**, compressed gas is used to apply the pressure to extend the gear if the hydraulic part of a gear system fails. When the CO_2 extension handle is pulled, pressure is released from a cylinder and directed through tubes to each landing gear actuator, which then extends the gear. Some CO_2 canisters might operate only once per flight, so consult your POH before extending the gear in this manner. You might need to be in a position where you can leave the gear down for the remainder of the flight. Other types of pressurized gas can be used in place of CO_2 for precharging the system. [Figure 11-54]

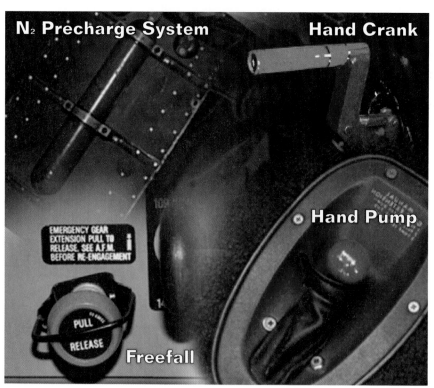

Figure 11-54. The procedures for emergency gear extension vary between airplanes. Preparing for a manual gear extension before you need to perform it in flight makes the operation safer and less of an actual emergency.

SUMMARY CHECKLIST

✓ Landing gear systems can be operated through a hydraulic system, an electrically driven motor, or a hybrid of the two methods.

✓ The electrical gear system consists of a reversible motor that drives a series of rods, levers, cables, and bellcranks that raise and lower the gear.

✓ The gear cycle refers to the process that the gear goes through during extension and retraction. The electric motor moves the gear up or down and it continues to operate until the up or down limit switch on the motor's gearbox is tripped.

✓ In a hydraulic gear system, hydraulic fluid flows under pressure through valves and downlocks to the gear actuating cylinders to raise and lower the gear.

✓ An electrohydraulic system utilizes an electric pump to pressurize a hydraulic system for gear extension and retraction.

✓ Gear position indicators enable you to determine the location of the gear in the gear cycle. Position lights are one common gear position indicator, and they consist of three green lights and one red light.

✓ As a reminder to pilots to lower the gear before landing, a gear warning horn sounds when the airplane is configured for landing with the gear unsafe.

✓ Most retractable landing gear systems incorporate a safety switch, or squat switch, to ensure that the gear does not retract when the airplane is sitting on the ground.

✓ Maximum landing gear extension speed (V_{LE}) is the fastest speed at which you can fly with the landing gear extended, and maximum landing gear operating speed (V_{LO}) is the highest speed at which you can safely operate the landing gear.

✓ Preflight the landing gear system before each flight, including a check for loose bolts, cracks and corrosion, and foreign objects in the wheel wells.

✓ The gear switch is often shaped differently from the flap switch to aid you in discriminating between the two.

✓ Besides the gear position indicators, a pitch change, a change in airspeed, and the sound of the gear mechanism enable you to determine if the gear is operating properly.

✓ One or more circuit breakers protect the landing gear system from electrical overloads.

✓ Recycling the landing gear after takeoff from a slushy runway can help prevent the build-up of ice on the landing gear.

✓ The position indicator lights are your primary means of determining gear position. If one or more fail to illuminate, check the bulbs and the circuit breakers before attempting to lower the gear manually.

✓ The four most common kinds of emergency gear extension systems are the hand crank, the hydraulic hand pump, the freefall, and the carbon dioxide (CO_2) pressurized systems. Check the POH to determine the proper method for operating the system on your airplane.

SECTION C ■ **Retractable Landing Gear**

KEY TERMS

Electrical Gear System

Gear Cycle

Hydraulic Gear System

Electrohydraulic System

Gear Position Indicators

Gear Warning Horn

Safety Switch (Squat Switch)

Maximum Landing Gear Extended Speed (V_{LE})

Maximum Landing Gear Operating Speed (V_{LO})

Emergency Landing Gear System

Hand Crank System

Hydraulic Hand Pump System

Freefall System

Carbon Dioxide (CO_2) Pressurized System

QUESTIONS

1. True/False. An illuminated red or amber indicator light generally means that the gear is down and locked and safe for landing.

2. What is the V-speed for the maximum speed you can fly with the landing gear extended?
    A. V_{LO}
    B. V_{LE}
    C. V_{S0}

3. How does the gear warning horn work?

4. Explain why, in addition to the possibility of a malfunction, a squat switch will not always prevent inadvertent gear retraction on the ground.

5. What should you do to prevent ice from building on the wheels after takeoff from a slushy runway?
    A. Recycle the gear.
    B. Leave the gear extended for 10 minutes after takeoff.
    C. Use the hand crank or hand pump to manually retract the gear.

6. Which of these are systems are used for emergency gear extension?
    A. Hand crank, hydraulic hand pump, and electrohydraulic system
    B. Hydraulic hand pump, freefall, and gear warning horn
    C. Hand crank, hydraulic hand pump, and carbon dioxide (CO_2) pressurized system

CHAPTER 12

Aerodynamics and Performance Limitations

Private Pilot
Part I, Chapter 3 — Aerodynamic Principles
Part IV, Chapter 8 — Predicting Performance
— Weight and Balance

SECTION A
Advanced Aerodynamics

Many of the concepts in this section will be familiar from your earlier training, but the basic ideas are expanded here to add depth and explain relationships that you might not have noticed before. To become a professional pilot, you need a more detailed knowledge of the forces that govern your flight.

The four fundamental flight maneuvers—straight-and-level flight, turns, climbs, and descents—are controlled by changing the balance between the four aerodynamic forces: lift, thrust, drag, and weight. As you know, opposing aerodynamic forces are balanced in straight-and-level flight. Lift balances weight, and thrust balances drag. The airplane is in a state of dynamic equilibrium, and there is no acceleration in any direction. A change in any one of the forces results in an acceleration until equilibrium is reestablished. These changes can occur even in seemingly straight and level flight. For instance, you might have noticed that your true airspeed increases slowly throughout a long flight when you maintain a constant altitude and power setting. This is a result of subtle changes in the four forces, The total weight of the airplane goes down as fuel is burned, resulting in an imbalance between lift and weight. To maintain your altitude, you gradually reduce the angle of attack, reducing the amount of lift the wings generate, and restoring the balance between lift and weight. The decrease in lift results in a reduction in induced drag, creating an imbalance between thrust and drag. The excess thrust accelerates the airplane until increasing parasite drag again equals thrust, and the airplane flies on at the higher airspeed.

The same principles apply in climbs and descents. If you create an imbalance between the forces, the airplane accelerates until it reaches a new equilibrium. The airplane only accelerates during the initial change in direction. After the climb or descent is established, the forces are again balanced, even though the flight path is now inclined. For example, to climb you increase the angle of attack, creating an excess of lift. If thrust remains constant, the increase in induced drag slows the airplane. This reduced airspeed decreases the amount of lift, bringing lift and weight back into balance. Because the thrust vector is now inclined upward, part of the thrust is now acting to lift the airplane, creating a component vector called the lift of thrust. In a stabilized descent, the thrust of weight becomes a factor. In both cases, upward and downward forces are balanced and forward and rearward forces are balanced. All forces are in equilibrium, as they are in straight-and-level flight. [Figure 12-1]

 The four fundamentals in maneuvering an aircraft are straight-and-level flight, turns, climbs, and descents.

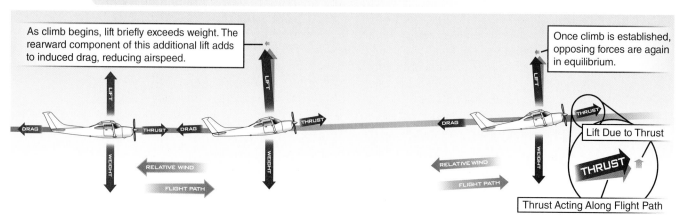

As climb begins, lift briefly exceeds weight. The rearward component of this additional lift adds to induced drag, reducing airspeed.

Once climb is established, opposing forces are again in equilibrium.

Lift Due to Thrust

Thrust Acting Along Flight Path

Figure 12-1. When you initiate a climb or descent, you momentarily create an imbalance in the four forces, which causes the airplane to accelerate until the forces reach equilibrium again. After the climb or descent is established, lift is equal to weight.

Opposing forces are equal in steady-state level flight.

LIFT

Formulated in the 17th century, Sir Isaac Newton's laws of motion are the foundation of classical mechanics. Two of his laws in particular are used to describe lift. Newton's second law of motion essentially says that a force results whenever a mass is accelerated. His third law states that for every action, there is an equal and opposite reaction. The wing causes the air moving past it to curve downward, creating a strong downwash behind the wing. As this mass of air is accelerated downward, the reaction force pushes the wing up. In level flight and in stable climbs and descents, this lift force is equal to the weight of the airplane. In other words, lift is simply the reaction that results from the action of forcing air downward.

Newton's laws describe what happens as air is accelerated downward, but what is the mechanism that causes the air to change direction? A flat plate could be used to deflect the air, but more efficient airfoils have been developed to maximize lift and minimize drag. In general, these airfoils are designed to smoothly and effectively bend the airmass in a curved path to create the downwash.

In normal flight, the air pressure on the bottom surface of the wing is somewhat greater than the pressure on the upper surface. When Newton's second law is applied to a fluid, such as air, the result is Bernoulli's equation. Bernoulli states that as the velocity of a fluid increases, its pressure decreases. The air pressure above a wing is reduced because the shape of the airfoil and the angle of attack cause air to flow faster over the upper surface of the wing. Likewise, air flowing along the lower surface of the wing slows down, causing its pressure to increase, and adding to lift. The net difference in pressure acting over the aerodynamic surfaces balances the weight of the airplane in straight-and-level flight. These pressure differences cause air to curve upward as it approaches the leading edge of the wing (upwash), and downward from the trailing edge as it leaves the wing.

 Lift results from relatively high pressure below the wing's surface and lower air pressure above the wing's surface.

Relative wind is directly opposite the flight path of the airplane. Three of the four forces, lift, drag, and thrust, are associated with the relative wind. Weight, of course, always acts toward the center of the earth. The angle between the chord line of the wing and the relative wind is the angle of attack. Lift generally acts perpendicular to the relative wind, regardless of the wing's angle of attack. Drag acts opposite the flight path, in the same direction as the relative wind. The angle of incidence is the small angle formed by the chord line and the longitudinal axis of the airplane. In most airplanes, the angle of incidence is fixed and cannot be changed by the pilot. The angle of incidence generally provides the proper angle of attack for level flight at cruising speed so that the longitudinal axis of the airplane can be aligned with the relative wind, helping to minimize drag. On many airplanes, the wings are built with less incidence at the tips than at the roots. Terms for this include washout and wing twist. By placing the wingtips at a lower angle of attack, the tips will remain unstalled after the wing roots have reached their critical angle of attack and stalled. This provides more stall warning to the pilot and better control during stall recovery. [Figure 12-2]

 Lift is defined as the force acting perpendicular to the relative wind. Drag acts parallel to the flight path, in the same direction as the relative wind.

SECTION A ■ **Advanced Aerodynamics**

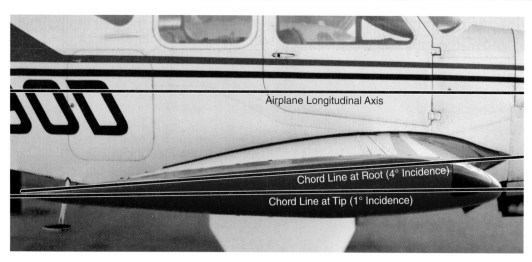

Airplane Longitudinal Axis

Chord Line at Root (4° Incidence)

Chord Line at Tip (1° Incidence)

Figure 12-2. You can see the subtle twist from root to tip in this Beechcraft wing.

SECTION A ■ Advanced Aerodynamics

LIFT EQUATION

As you would expect, for any wing there is a definite mathematical relationship between lift, angle of attack, airspeed, altitude, and the size of the wing. These factors correspond to the terms coefficient of lift, velocity, air density, and wing surface area in the lift equation, and their relationship is expressed in the accompanying formula.

In order to increase lift, you must increase one or more of the four factors on the other side of the equal sign. One way is to increase your airspeed. Lift is proportional to the square of the velocity, or airspeed, so doubling your airspeed quadruples the amount of lift, if the other factors remain the same. Likewise, if the other factors remain the

$$L = C_L V^2 \frac{\rho}{2} S$$

L = Lift

C_L = Coefficient of lift

V = Velocity

ρ = Air density

S = Wing surface area

For lift to increase, one or more of the four factors on the right side of the equal sign must increase.

same and the coefficient of lift increases, lift will also increase. The coefficient of lift goes up as the angle of attack increase, and will be discussed in more detail later. As air density increases, lift increases, but you will usually be more concerned with how lift is diminished by reductions in air density, for example, as you climb to higher altitudes or take off on a hot day. Air density varies with altitude, temperature, barometric pressure, and humidity. The remaining factor in the lift equation is wing area. Larger wings generate more lift, all other things being equal.

 If the angle of attack and other factors remain constant and airspeed is doubled, lift will be four times greater.

Another way of using the equation is to keep lift at the same value and notice how the factors on the other side of the equation affect each other. For example, to hold your altitude if you reduce the airspeed, one or more of the other three factors in the lift equation must increase. If you maintain your altitude (air density) and airplane configuration (wing area), the equation shows that you must increase the coefficient of lift, or angle of attack. Likewise, if you increase airspeed you will have to reduce the angle of attack to stay at the same altitude. You can see that for any particular amount of lift, there is a specific combination of angle of attack and airspeed. Similarly, because air density decreases with altitude, the airplane must fly with either a higher angle of attack or a higher speed to generate the same lift at a higher altitude.

 There is a corresponding indicated airspeed for every angle of attack to generate sufficient lift to maintain altitude.

 To generate the same amount of lift at a higher altitude, an airplane must be flown at either a higher angle of attack or a higher true airspeed.

CONTROLLING LIFT

Four ways are commonly used to control lift. Increasing airspeed generates more lift by causing more air molecules to act on the wing, and changing the angle of attack changes the coefficient of lift. The two other methods of controlling lift consist of changing the shape of the airfoil or varying the total area of the wing. Flaps and leading-edge devices are examples of how these methods are used in flight.

The most common method of controlling lift is to vary the angle of attack. Managing the angle of attack also allows you to control airspeed and drag to a certain extent. As you know, increasing the angle of attack causes the wing to generate more lift, but only up to a point. The coefficient of lift increases steadily until the airflow begins to separate near C_{Lmax} and then begins to drop as the wing stalls. As the airflow begins to separate, you can usually feel slight airframe buffeting. The buffeting becomes worse as the airflow separation progresses just before a stall. [Figure 12-3]

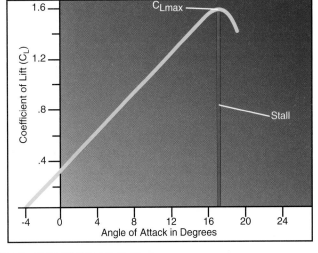

Figure 12-3. For a given airfoil, a stall always occurs at the same angle of attack regardless of weight, dynamic pressure, bank angle, or pitch attitude.

 The angle of attack directly controls the distribution of pressures acting on a wing. By changing the angle of attack, you can control the airplane's lift, airspeed, and drag.

The increase in lift also causes an increase in induced drag, which slows the airplane unless thrust is also increased. Flight at slow airspeeds demonstrates this relationship clearly. As your airspeed decreases, the angle of attack has to increase to maintain the lift necessary for level flight. The angle of attack, however, can be increased only until the wing reaches C_{Lmax}. At this point, you can no longer increase lift by increasing the angle of attack, and any further increase in angle of attack results in a loss of lift. In straight-and-level flight, you normally reach C_{Lmax} as the indicated airspeed approaches the published stall speed. Remember that stall speed is not a specific value. A wing can stall at a wide range of airspeeds, but it always stalls at the same angle of attack. Turbulence can cause abrupt changes in the direction of the relative wind and cause an increase in the stall speed. Stall speed also increases rapidly as G-loading increases during maneuvers such as steep turns. This is because the load factor multiplies the effective weight of the airplane, which must be balanced by a similar increase in lift from the wings, necessitating a higher angle of attack. High G-forces, such as those produced in violent or abrupt maneuvering, can cause a stall at speeds twice as high as the stall speed in level unaccelerated flight. Other factors such as weight, center of gravity location, configuration, and power can also affect stall speed, but the wing always stalls at the same angle of attack. Never attempt to stall an aircraft at a speed above the design maneuvering speed, because this can easily cause structural damage to the airframe.

 The angle of attack at which a wing stalls remains constant regardless of weight, dynamic pressure, bank angle, or pitch attitude.

You usually think of changing angle of attack by changing the pitch attitude with the elevator control, but you can also change the angle of attack without changing pitch. For example, if you reduce power and hold your pitch attitude, the airplane slows, the wing produces less lift due to the lower airspeed, weight momentarily exceeds lift and the airplane begins to descend, changing the relative wind direction, and thus increasing the angle of attack.

If you were to determine the change in pressure due to the airflow over each square inch of the wing, you would find that most places have decreased pressure, but some places have increased pressure. This pressure distribution pattern changes as you vary the angle of attack. Adding all of the pressure vectors for the entire wing surface, top and bottom, gives a large single vector representing the net lift of the entire airfoil. This vector can be called the center of lift, or center of pressure. On cambered wings, the center of pressure moves fore and aft in response to changes in the angle of attack. The location of the center of pressure is important in the discussion of stability later in this section. [Figure 12-4]

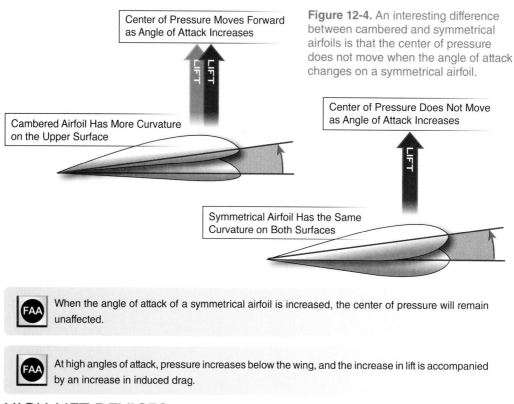

Center of Pressure Moves Forward as Angle of Attack Increases

Cambered Airfoil Has More Curvature on the Upper Surface

Center of Pressure Does Not Move as Angle of Attack Increases

Symmetrical Airfoil Has the Same Curvature on Both Surfaces

Figure 12-4. An interesting difference between cambered and symmetrical airfoils is that the center of pressure does not move when the angle of attack changes on a symmetrical airfoil.

FAA When the angle of attack of a symmetrical airfoil is increased, the center of pressure will remain unaffected.

FAA At high angles of attack, pressure increases below the wing, and the increase in lift is accompanied by an increase in induced drag.

HIGH-LIFT DEVICES

In addition to controlling lift with speed and angle of attack, you can change the camber and the area of the wing using trailing-edge flaps and leading-edge high-lift devices. Some of these devices also delay the separation of airflow and reduce the stall speed.

TRAILING-EDGE FLAPS

The most common high-lift device is the trailing-edge flap, which can produce a large increase in airfoil camber, increasing both lift and drag. Using flaps can add to your rate of descent without increasing airspeed. Consequently they are often used to make steeper landing approaches. Because flaps expand the coefficient of lift, they also decrease the stall speed. On the other hand, raising the flaps increases the stall speed—something you might want to remember before you raise them at low airspeeds or high angles of attack. You typically encounter four basic types of flaps on general aviation airplanes. [Figure 12-5]

FAA Flaps increase lift and reduce stall speed, allowing the wing to produce the same lift at a lower airspeed. Conversely, raising the flaps increases stall speed.

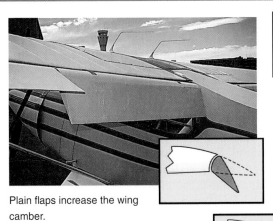

Plain flaps increase the wing camber.

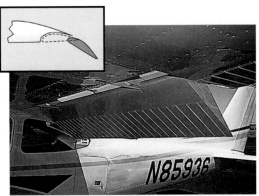

Fowler flaps increase camber, increase wing area, and help prevent airflow separation.

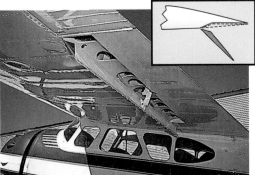

Split flaps also increase the wing camber.

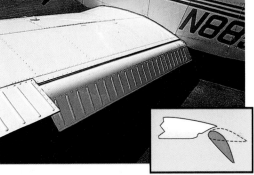

Slotted flaps increase camber and help prevent airflow separation.

Figure 12-5. Flaps increase lift (and drag) by increasing camber, which also increases the angle of attack. In some cases, flaps also enlarge the area of the wing.

As you can see, plain, split, and simple slotted flaps change the effective camber of the airfoil from a high speed, low drag configuration to a shape that is more effective at low speeds, but with a high penalty in additional drag. In addition, flaps with slots also allow some of the high pressure air blow the wing to flow to the upper surface, which increases lift by accelerating the air over the top of the wing, thus reducing the pressure there. Slotted flaps also improve flow over the trailing edge, delaying separation of the airstream and reducing the stall speed. Because of the way Fowler flaps are designed, they increase the area of the wings as they move down and back. Adding to the wing area also increases lift, while imposing less of a drag penalty. Some airplanes have Fowler flaps with multiple slots, further modifying the airfoil camber, wing area, and airflow. To increase the camber of the outer portions of the wings, some airplanes are equipped with ailerons that move simultaneously downward a few degrees as the flaps are extended to further increase lift at low speeds. The mechanism allows the "drooped" ailerons to function normally for roll control. Because of the aerodynamic stresses on the flaps and their support structure, the maximum operating speed with flaps extended is typically lower than the maximum cruising speed for a particular aircraft.

Because flaps increase lift and reduce the stall speed, many airplanes use them for takeoff as well as landing. Used properly, they can reduce ground roll and increase climb performance. In general, the first few degrees of flap extension provide the greatest lift benefit with the least penalty in drag, but the last few degrees of travel add relatively little lift and a great deal of drag. Permissible use of flaps on takeoff varies from airplane to airplane, so always comply with the limitations in the POH.

SECTION A ■ Advanced Aerodynamics

LEADING-EDGE DEVICES

The leading edges of the wings can also be modified in various ways to increase airfoil camber, add more wing area, or delay airflow separation at high angles of attack. The simplest leading-edge device is a fixed slot. When slots are incorporated into the wing structure near each wingtip, they serve a purpose similar to washout, allowing the airflow to remain attached over the outer portion of the wings after the roots have stalled. When the wing is at low angles of attack, relatively little air flows from the bottom of the leading edge through the opening, so slots do not cause a substantial change in the effectiveness of the airfoil. Slots are somewhat more effective than washout, because the entire wing can be placed at the most efficient angle of attack for a given flight situation. With washout, whenever the roots are at the ideal angle of attack, the tips are at a less efficient angle.

Slats are portions of the leading edge that are moved forward and down to create a path for air similar to a slot. On many types of aircraft they are deployed automatically by aerodynamic pressures. Other aircraft use electrical or hydraulic devices to extend them mechanically. The advantage of slats is that the wing is clean when they are retracted, yet the benefits of slots are available when needed. Most slats also increase the effective wing area, providing additional lift as well as delaying airflow separation. The main disadvantages are the weight, expense, and complexity of the mechanism.

Leading-edge flaps usually increase both wing camber and area. They are generally only found on jets, due to their expense, weight, and complexity, and because the airfoils of jets, which are optimized for high speeds, need them to create adequate lift at relatively low takeoff and landing speeds. [Figure 12-6]

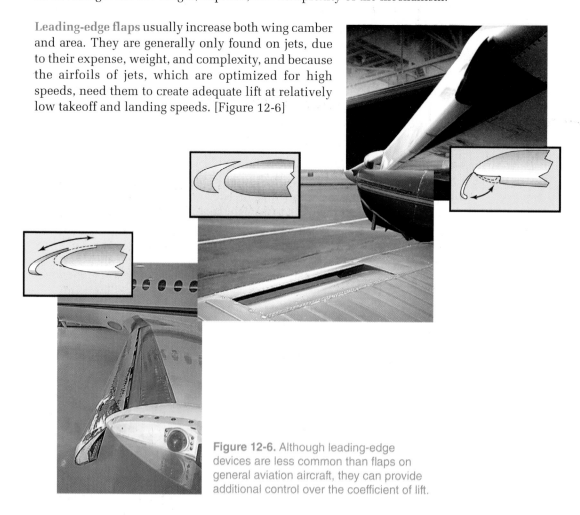

Figure 12-6. Although leading-edge devices are less common than flaps on general aviation aircraft, they can provide additional control over the coefficient of lift.

DRAG

Reducing the drag force means less thrust is required to fly at a given airspeed, so minimizing drag usually makes an airplane more efficient. Likewise, if drag is reduced, an airplane can go faster with the same thrust. Ordinarily, drag is separated into two types. Induced drag results from the production of lift by the wings, and decreases as the airplane goes faster. All other drag is classified as parasite drag, which increases as the square of the speed.

INDUCED DRAG

Whenever a wing is producing lift, drag is created as a by-product. The greater the angle of attack, the more drag is produced. At low speeds a wing must fly at a higher angle of attack to generate enough lift to support the airplane, and more high-pressure air from the lower surface comes around the wingtips, forming more powerful vortices, which are the primary cause of induced drag. The action of the vortices changes the local relative wind for the portion of the wing nearest the tip, which essentially reduces the angle of attack at the wingtips. At higher speeds, a lower angle of attack is sufficient to generate the necessary lift, so there are correspondingly less powerful wingtip vortices, and less induced drag. [Figure 12-7]

 Induced drag is a by-product of lift and is greatly affected by changes in airspeed.

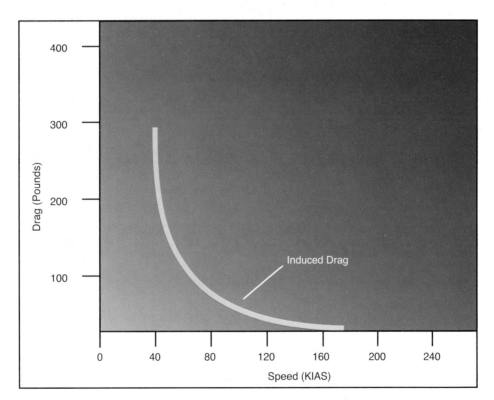

Figure 12-7. At low speeds, induced drag is at its maximum, and it diminishes as speed increases.

WING PLANFORM

The airfoil is only one characteristic of the wing's design. Planform is the term that describes the wing's outline as seen from above. Many factors influence the final shape of the planform, including the primary purpose of the airplane, the load factors and speeds anticipated, costs of construction and maintenance, maneuverability, stability, stall and spin characteristics, and whether or not the wings will house fuel tanks, high-lift devices, landing gear, etc. The wings can be tapered, the leading or trailing edges might be straight or curved, and wingtips can be square or rounded. There are advantages and disadvantages to each configuration, and many aircraft combine the features of multiple planforms to achieve the desired flight characteristics. [Figure 12-8]

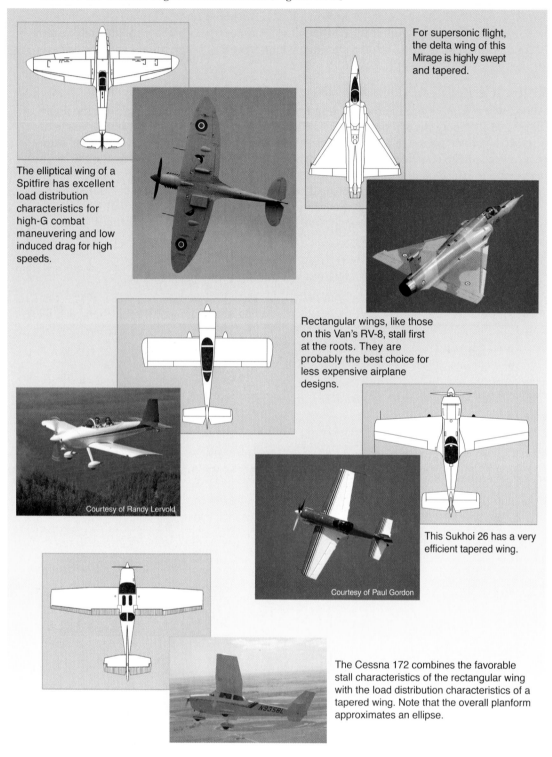

The elliptical wing of a Spitfire has excellent load distribution characteristics for high-G combat maneuvering and low induced drag for high speeds.

For supersonic flight, the delta wing of this Mirage is highly swept and tapered.

Rectangular wings, like those on this Van's RV-8, stall first at the roots. They are probably the best choice for less expensive airplane designs.

Courtesy of Randy Lervold

This Sukhoi 26 has a very efficient tapered wing.

Courtesy of Paul Gordon

The Cessna 172 combines the favorable stall characteristics of the rectangular wing with the load distribution characteristics of a tapered wing. Note that the overall planform approximates an ellipse.

Figure 12-8. Planforms are selected to take advantage of specific characteristics.

The ratio of the root chord to the tip chord is the **taper** of the wing. Rectangular wings have a taper ratio of one, and delta wings have a taper of zero. One of the first things the early aeronautical engineers realized is that the area of a wing nearest the fuselage does most of the lifting, but the wingtips provide relatively little lift. They learned that tapering the wing saved precious weight and distributed the load more efficiently. The downside was that each wing rib needed to be a different size, adding to the time and cost of production. Rectangular wings are simpler and more economical to produce and repair, because the ribs are the same size. Another benefit of the rectangular wing is that the wing roots tend to stall first, providing more warning to the pilot and more control during stall recovery. The planform that provides the best spanwise load distribution and the lowest induced drag, at least for subsonic airplanes, is an ellipse. The price for this efficiency is that the whole wing stalls at about the same time, which is undesirable compared to wings that stall progressively from root to tip. Elliptical wings also are among the most difficult, expensive and complex to build, so they are employed primarily on very efficient airplanes such as the Supermarine Spitfire and Culver Cadet.

> **FAA** Rectangular wings have a tendency to stall first at the wing root, with the stall progression toward the wingtip.

Dividing the wingspan by the average chord gives the **aspect ratio**. With some wing planforms, the average chord can be difficult to determine, so the formula of wingspan squared over area is often used, but the result is the same. Aspect ratio is especially important in reducing the amount of induced drag produced by a wing. In fact, doubling the aspect ratio cuts the induced drag coefficient in half. Increasing the wingspan while keeping the wing area the same results in smaller wingtips, which generate smaller wingtip vortices. The influence of these vortices on the local relative wind affects a smaller fraction of the wing surface, further reducing induced drag. Perhaps you have noticed that airplanes renowned for their efficiency, such as sailplanes, long-range transports, high altitude research airplanes, and human-powered airplanes all have high aspect ratios. On the other hand, airplanes that require extreme maneuverability and strength, like those designed for aerobatic competition or air combat maneuvering, generally have wings with a low aspect ratio. [Figure 12-9]

SECTION A ■ **Advanced Aerodynamics**

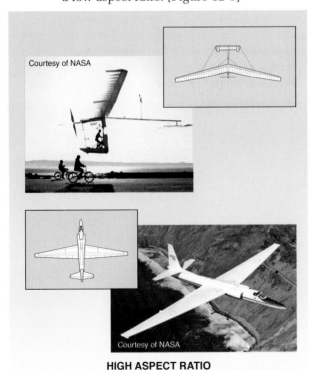

HIGH ASPECT RATIO

LOW ASPECT RATIO

Figure 12-9. A high aspect ratio decreases induced drag for efficient cruise flight.

Another element of wing planform is **sweep**. If a line connecting the 25% chord points of all the wing ribs is not perpendicular to the longitudinal axis of the airplane, the wing is said to be swept. [Figure 12-10] The sweep can be forward, but almost all swept wings angle back from root to tip. Most swept wing designs were developed to delay the onset of compressible airflow problems and control the shockwaves that form as an airplane flies near the speed of sound and beyond, but a number of relatively low-speed airplanes employ swept wings because of their contribution to lateral stability.

Figure 12-10. Forward swept wings provide many aerodynamic benefits, but require a more rigid structure to resist twisting loads.

D Winglets

Wing tip vortices cost airplanes a great deal in efficiency and performance, and over the years there have been many attempts to block or diffuse them. One of the most effective devices so far seems to be the winglet developed by Richard Whitcomb of NASA. These nearly vertical extensions on the wingtips are actually carefully designed, proportioned, and positioned airfoils with their camber toward the fuselage, and with span, taper, and aspect ratio optimized to provide maximum benefit at a specific speed and angle of attack. On most jets, this is the airplane's cruise speed, but some turboprops use winglets to improve lift and reduce drag at low speeds. The winglet combines many small factors to increase performance. Downwash from the trailing edge of the winglet blocks or counteracts the vortices, and even the vortex from the tip of the winglet is positioned to affect a portion of the main wingtip vortex. The leading edges of many winglets are actually toed out about 4°, but because of the relative wind induced by the wingtip vortex, the winglet is actually at a positive angle of attack, and part of the lift generated by the winglet acts in a forward direction, adding to thrust. Many winglets are canted outward around 15°, which adds to vertical lift and increases their aerodynamic efficiency while also contributing to dihedral effect. Depending on the application, performance improvements due to winglets can increase fuel efficiency at high speeds and altitudes by as much as 16 to 26%.

GROUND EFFECT

An interesting thing happens when an airplane flies within a distance from the ground (or water) surface equal to its own wingspan or less. The amount of induced drag decreases, due to changes in the upwash pattern ahead of the wing, and the downwash and wingtip vortices behind the wing. Induced drag is only about half of its usual value when the wing is at 10% of its span above the ground. **Ground effect** is greatest close to the surface and decreases rapidly with height, becoming negligible at an altitude equal to about one wingspan

With the reduction in induced drag, the amount of thrust necessary is also reduced, allowing the airplane to lift off at a lower-than-normal speed. It might feel as though you are getting something for nothing, but many pilots have gotten into trouble when using ground effect, either intentionally or unintentionally. If you try to climb out of ground effect at too low an airspeed, as normal induced drag values accumulate the airspeed can decrease, resulting in a stall. As an airplane climbs out of ground effect, more thrust is required. Because ground effect can allow an overloaded or improperly configured airplane to lift off, the pilot might believe the airplane will climb when it is only capable of flying in ground effect until it hits something.

Ground effect is also responsible for the floating effect you have probably encountered during the landing flare. Because the wing is able to create more lift at the same angle of attack in ground effect, the pitch angle might need to be reduced slightly to maintain a descent. Simultaneously, thrust will need to be reduced to continue slowing the airplane for landing. On a short field, ground effect could cause the airplane to float so far down the runway that insufficient room would remain to stop after touchdown. [Figure 12-11]

 An airplane leaving ground effect will experience an increase in induced drag and will require more thrust. If the same angle of attack is maintained, an airplane will have more lift and less induced drag when in ground effect, and, conversely, to generate the same lift within ground effect requires a lower angle of attack.

Figure 12-11. Flying close to the ground reduces upwash, downwash, and wingtip vortices, decreasing induced drag.

PARASITE DRAG

Although induced drag diminishes with speed, parasite drag increases. The rate of increase is proportional to the square of the airspeed, so doubling your speed quadruples parasite drag. [Figure 12-12] This kind of drag is easy to understand; it is the force you feel when you put your hand out the window of a moving car. Parasite drag can be subdivided into form drag, interference drag, and drag due to skin friction. **Form drag** is based on the shape of the airplane, how well it is streamlined, and how much frontal area it has. For example, an airplane with an abrupt, steep windshield will have more form drag than one with a shallow-angled, smooth-flowing windshield design, even if the frontal areas are identical. Likewise, if you had a small airplane with exactly the same overall shape as a larger airplane, the larger one would have more form drag because of its greater frontal area. Even the wing creates a certain amount of parasite drag. If you flew the wing at an angle of attack that produced zero lift, it would produce no induced drag. The form drag of the wing itself would still exist, however, and would increase with speed. Everything that sticks out into the airstream creates form drag: antennas, struts, landing gear, entry steps, door handles,

SECTION A ■ Advanced Aerodynamics

and so on. Streamlining is more important than you might think. A bracing wire with a round cross section has about ten times the drag of an equal-strength wire with a streamlined, teardrop-shaped cross section. Drag reduction is the sole aerodynamic purpose of retractable landing gear, and the drag of fixed gear can be reduced considerably by enclosing the gear legs in streamlined fairings and adding wheel pants around the tires.

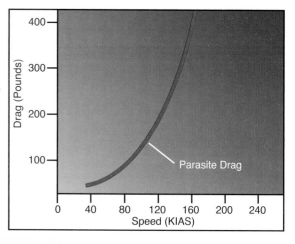

Figure 12-12. Parasite drag increases exponentially. Doubling your airspeed results in four times the parasite drag.

 Parasite drag increases in proportion to the square of the airspeed, thus doubling the airspeed quadruples parasite drag.

Interference drag is created when the airflow around one part of the airplane interacts with the airflow around an adjacent part. The greatest amount of interference drag usually occurs where the wing joins the fuselage of a low wing airplane, because air is traveling at a higher speed across the top of the wing than the air flowing along the fuselage. Many high performance low wing airplanes have large wing root fillets to smooth the transition and reduce interference drag. [Figure 12-13] On high wing airplanes, the high-speed air above the wings does not interfere as much with the air from around the fuselage, so they usually do not need fillets.

Skin friction drag is due to air molecules giving up some of their kinetic energy as they contact the skin surfaces of the airplane. Both the total wetted area of the airplane and the degree of smoothness or roughness of the skin surface affect this kind of parasite drag. Wetted area is a term for the total outer surface area of the airplane. As you might guess, it comes from marine engineering, in which drag on the hull of a ship is determined based on the part that is under water, or wetted.

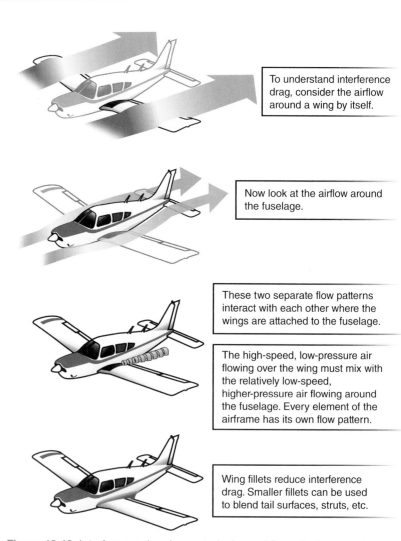

To understand interference drag, consider the airflow around a wing by itself.

Now look at the airflow around the fuselage.

These two separate flow patterns interact with each other where the wings are attached to the fuselage.

The high-speed, low-pressure air flowing over the wing must mix with the relatively low-speed, higher-pressure air flowing around the fuselage. Every element of the airframe has its own flow pattern.

Wing fillets reduce interference drag. Smaller fillets can be used to blend tail surfaces, struts, etc.

Figure 12-13. Interference drag is created where airflows that are moving at different speeds or in different directions mix and interact.

Add One of These to Your Airplane and Decrease Drag 75%

The National Advisory Committee for Aeronautics (NACA) was created in 1915 to "to supervise and direct the scientific study of the problems of flight, with a view to their practical solution." This government-sponsored research organization has solved many major aerodynamic problems over the years. One of their developments was the NACA cowl, which reduced airframe drag by about 75% on radial engine aircraft. It allowed higher speeds and better performance on a variety of airplanes, from fighters such as the Grumman F3F to private aircraft such as the Stinson Reliant. The NACA cowl is shown here on a Cessna 195.

In 1958, NACA became the National Aeronautics and Space Administration (NASA). Although primarily known for their extraordinary successes in space exploration, they continue to perform fundamental research in aerodynamics that benefits all sectors of aviation.

TOTAL DRAG

As you would expect, adding the induced drag to the parasite drag gives **total drag**. Because induced drag decreases as parasite drag increases, the curve for the sum of both types of drag usually looks something like figure 12-14.

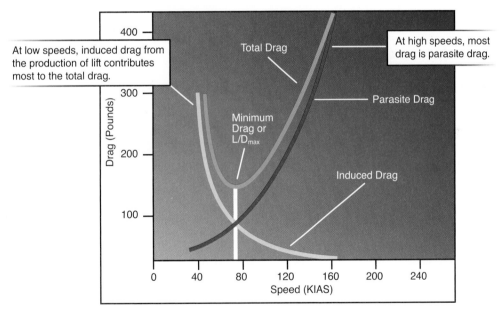

Figure 12-14. The point at which the total drag is lowest is L/D_{max}. This is also the power-off glide speed that provides maximum gliding distance.

 Total drag is lowest at the airspeed that produces the highest ratio of lift to drag (L/D_{max}). At airspeeds below L/D_{max}, total drag increases due to induced drag, and at speeds above L/D_{max}, total drag increases because of parasite drag. See figure 12-14.

SECTION A ■ **Advanced Aerodynamics**

The Eiffel Tower and the Dimples On Golf Balls

Almost everyone recognizes the Eiffel Tower, but did you know that it was used for aerodynamic research? Alexandre Gustave Eiffel was a pioneering aerodynamicist, and the tower was utilized in 1910 to measure the air resistance of flat plates. Monsieur Eiffel also formulated many of the basic techniques of wind tunnel testing, and did research on the aerodynamic characteristics of spheres. He came up with a drag coefficient for the sphere that was considerably different from the value found by some other researchers, but both values turned out to be correct. The difference is reconciled by taking into account the turbulent flow characteristics described by another aerodynamic pioneer, Osborne Reynolds. The Reynolds number is a dimensionless ratio that relates the viscosity of a fluid with velocity and distance. It helps to predict where a smooth, laminar flow will begin to transition to a turbulent flow as air flows over a surface. It is extremely important in many aspects of aircraft design, but also helps to explain why golf balls with dimples travel more than twice as far as smooth balls of identical size and weight.

Whenever anything moves through the air, the air molecules close to the surface of the object are slowed down by friction, creating a slower-moving boundary layer. At the front of an object, a ball for example, the boundary layer is smooth, and the air outside the boundary layer slips over with minimal drag. But farther back, the flow separates from the ball, creating large amounts of drag. It is relatively easy to separate the laminar flow, so it breaks away near the widest part of a smooth ball. If the ball has dimples, the laminar flow is broken up near the front of the ball, but the turbulence causes the airflow around the ball to resist separation, so that it sticks to the ball further back along the trailing side, thus reducing the diameter of the drag-producing wake. It seems contradictory to say that introducing turbulence to an airflow, which causes drag, could actually reduce drag, but the amount of drag caused by disrupting the laminar flow is relatively small compared with the drag of the larger wake of a smooth ball.

MAXIMUM RANGE

It stands to reason that the airspeed that produces the best power-off glide range would also be the most efficient in terms of fuel economy. If you fly at the airspeed for L/D_{max}, you will go the maximum possible distance for the amount of fuel you burn. Efficiency does not equate with speed, however. It is also important to remember that the airspeed for L/D_{max} varies with the weight of the airplane. The angle of attack for L/D_{max} does not vary significantly. Because weight determines the amount of lift that must be generated for level flight, the airspeed to produce that lift varies with weight.

The airspeed that gives the lowest total drag (L/D_{max}) will provide the best power-off glide range, as well as the greatest range. See figure 12-14. As aircraft weight decreases, the airspeed for L/D_{max} also decreases.

HIGH-DRAG DEVICES

Although engineers put a lot of effort into minimizing drag, they have also created devices solely to produce more drag. **Spoilers** are deployed from the upper surfaces of wings to spoil the smooth airflow, reducing lift and increasing drag. Spoilers are used for roll control on some aircraft, one of the advantages being the virtual elimination of adverse yaw. To turn right, for example, the spoiler on the right wing is raised, destroying some of the lift and creating more drag on the right. The right wing drops, and the airplane banks and yaws to the right. Deploying spoilers on both wings at the same time allows the aircraft to descend without gaining speed, and is the principle method of glide path control in many gliders and sailplanes. Spoilers are also deployed to help shorten ground roll after landing. By destroying lift, they transfer weight to the wheels, improving braking effectiveness. Dive bombers from the 1930s were equipped with dive brakes to permit extremely steep dives without unmanageable speed increases. During World War II, high performance airplanes were approaching the realm of transonic flight. At these airspeeds the effects of compressibility caused buffeting, difficulty in recovering from dives, and loss of control. Special dive recovery flaps were created for the fastest flighters, including the Lockheed P-38 Lightning and Republic P-47 Thunderbolt. These flaps, located on the bottom surfaces of the wings near the leading edge, assisted in the recovery from high-speed dives.

Propeller-driven airplanes have an automatic high-drag device whenever the throttle is retarded beyond the point at which zero thrust is produced. At less than zero thrust, energy from the airplane's forward motion is being used to turn the propeller and engine, creating a large amount of drag. This is why most multi-engine airplanes provide a means of feathering the propeller blades on an inoperative engine. The advent of jet aircraft in the 1950s increased the need for drag-producing devices for a couple of reasons. First, aerodynamically clean jet airframes just did not slow down quickly enough when thrust was reduced. Pilots who were accustomed to losing speed as soon as power was reduced had trouble adjusting to the slippery new jets. Also, the early jet engines took a relatively long time to go from idle to full thrust. If full thrust was needed for a go-around, for instance, several seconds could be lost waiting for the engine thrust to become effective. As a result, designers added drag-producing devices to manage airspeed so that pilots could maintain higher thrust settings during an approach. As jet engine technology progressed, spool-up time has improved, however, jet engines are still less responsive than reciprocating engines, and speed-retarding devices are useful. **Speed brakes** are found in many sizes, shapes, and locations on different airplanes, but they all have the same purpose — to increase drag and provide fairly rapid deceleration. [Figure 12-15]

SECTION A ■ **Advanced Aerodynamics**

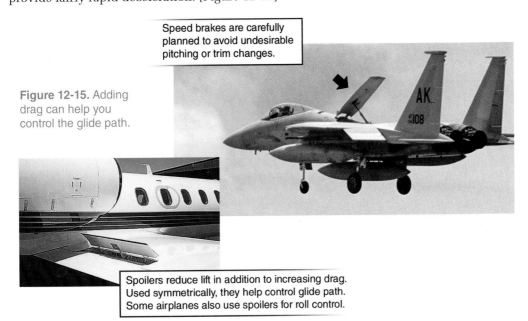

Speed brakes are carefully planned to avoid undesirable pitching or trim changes.

Figure 12-15. Adding drag can help you control the glide path.

Spoilers reduce lift in addition to increasing drag. Used symmetrically, they help control glide path. Some airplanes also use spoilers for roll control.

THRUST

Thrust is the force that opposes drag, and whenever there is more thrust than drag, the airplane accelerates along the flight path until the increasing drag restores the equilibrium. In conjunction with drag, thrust is the factor that limits the top speed of an airplane. Most airplanes use power generated by their engines to turn propellers, converting rotational energy into thrust. Jet engines produce thrust directly, through the expansion of burning gases. Interestingly, jets convert some of that thrust into rotational energy to turn their compressors and accessories.

The difference between thrust and power is fundamental to an understanding of aircraft performance. Thrust must equal drag in level flight. In other words, a pound of thrust must be present for each pound of drag at any airspeed. Parasite drag increases as the square of airspeed, so the thrust necessary for level flight at 150 knots will be four times the thrust needed at 75 knots, less whatever reduction there is in induced drag. On the other hand, power is the rate at which work is done, so it is tied directly to speed. It takes less power to do the same amount of work at a slower rate. If an airplane had the same amount of drag at low speed as at high speed, it would still take more power to fly at high speed, because the work of overcoming drag would be done at a faster rate. Of course, drag increases at any speed higher than L/D_{max}, so more thrust is required in addition to more power. When using our familiar units of pounds, knots, and horsepower, the power required for level flight is defined as thrust required times velocity over 325. (325 is simply a constant to convert horsepower in feet per second to knots.) If your airplane has 300 pounds of drag force at 100 knots, it requires 92.3 thrust horsepower to maintain level flight. At 125 knots, the drag force will be nearly 469 pounds, and about 180 thrust horsepower would be required. In this example, increasing speed by 25% requires a 95% increase in power to overcome a 53% increase in drag. [Figure 12-16]

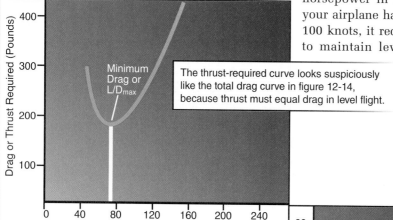

The thrust-required curve looks suspiciously like the total drag curve in figure 12-14, because thrust must equal drag in level flight.

The low point of the thrust-required curve defines L/D_{max}," but the lowest point on the power-required curve is at a significantly lower airspeed, and marks the minimum power required for level flight. Typically, the airspeed for minimum power required is 76% of the speed for L/D_{max}.

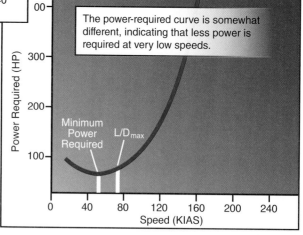

The power-required curve is somewhat different, indicating that less power is required at very low speeds.

Figure 12-16. In level flight, thrust required is always equal to total drag, but power required is related to the rate at which work is done.

PROPELLER EFFICIENCY

The propeller converts the engine power into thrust. In order to obtain maximum performance, the propeller must make this conversion as efficiently as possible. Because it is an airfoil, the propeller is subject to all the factors that affect airfoil efficiency, such as angle of attack and speed. There are additional factors that are unique to propellers because of their rotation. The shape of a propeller blade reflects many of the principles you reviewed in the lift discussion. It has a low speed airfoil at a high angle of attack near the root where the local speed is low, and a high-speed airfoil at a low angle of attack at the tip where speeds are much higher. It has a high aspect ratio to minimize induced drag, and most have an elliptical planform to distribute the load. Controllable-pitch propellers allow the pilot to vary the angle of attack of the blades. As with wings, high angles of attack create high induced drag, and that is why the engine slows down when you cycle the propeller during your runup. For takeoff, the blades must be in the low-pitch, high rpm setting to make maximum use of the engine's power. In cruise flight, the forward speed of the airplane changes the relative wind that the propeller blades encounter, reducing angle of attack. When you adjust the propeller pitch in cruise, you restore the blades to an angle of attack that provides a higher coefficient of lift, increasing the thrust provided. At peak efficiency, some propellers are able to convert 85% or more of the power produced by a reciprocating engine into thrust.

When the propeller's axis of rotation is different from the airplane's relative wind, the angle of attack of each blade changes continuously through each revolution. The angle of attack is at its minimum as the blade is ascending, and reaches its maximum as it descends on the other side. This varies the amount of lift, or thrust, produced by one side of the propeller disc compared to the other, and is most noticeable during climbs. [Figure 12-17]

The descending blade is at a higher angle of attack in a climb, so the right side of the propeller disc creates more thrust.

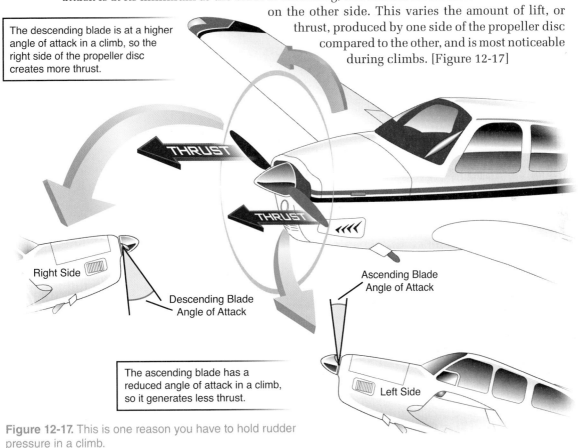

The ascending blade has a reduced angle of attack in a climb, so it generates less thrust.

Right Side

Descending Blade Angle of Attack

Ascending Blade Angle of Attack

Left Side

Figure 12-17. This is one reason you have to hold rudder pressure in a climb.

MAXIMUM LEVEL FLIGHT SPEED

There is an upper limit to how much thrust your engine and propeller can produce. When maximum thrust is produced, the airplane accelerates until the drag force is equal to the thrust. Power and thrust available vary with speed. [Figure 12-18]

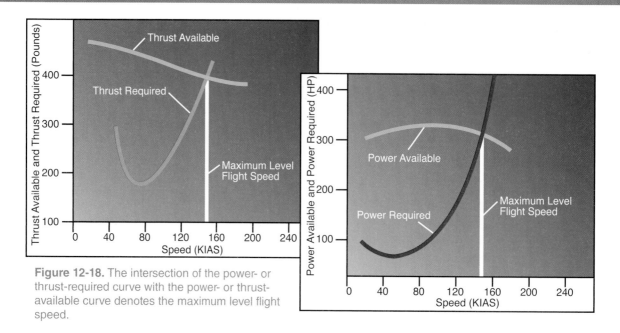

Figure 12-18. The intersection of the power- or thrust-required curve with the power- or thrust-available curve denotes the maximum level flight speed.

Richard T. Whitcomb

Many aircraft designers are associated with particular airplanes: Howard Hughes with the "Spruce Goose," Bill Lear with the Learjet, "Kelly" Johnson with most of Lockheed's advanced military projects, from the P-38 to the F-117, and Burt Rutan with innovative shapes like the Vari-Eze, Beech Starship, Voyager, and SpaceShipOne. But some engineers have had a profound influence on the aviation industry without ever designing an airplane or working for a manufacturer. Such a person was Richard T. Whitcomb.

Area rule

Courtesy of NASA Dryden Flight Research Center

Winglets

Supercritical Wing

Doctor Whitcomb was working for NACA, the predecessor of NASA, when Convair had a big problem with their new supersonic interceptor, the F-102 Delta Dagger. It could not exceed the speed of sound except in a dive. He had done some research a few years earlier on the way drag rises as an object nears the speed of sound. Although ridiculed at the time of publication, when his area rule was applied to the F-102, performance increased dramatically. Virtually every high-speed aircraft since has applied this principle. Later, he worked on developing the supercritical wing, an airfoil that helps to delay transonic drag rise. In the early 1970s, Dr. Whitcomb came up with the drag-reducing winglets seen on so many production aircraft today. Despite his achievements, Dr. Whitcomb lived humbly in the same apartment from 1943 until his death in 2009.

WEIGHT AND LOAD FACTOR

Weight is the only one of the four forces that does not depend on the flight path. Because weight is the force that results from the acceleration due to gravity, it always acts toward the center of the earth. The actual weight of the airplane in flight changes very gradually during flight as fuel is burned. However, the weight that the wings must actually support also depends on the load factor, and could be as much as several times the actual weight of the airplane.

LOAD FACTOR

The unit used to measure acceleration is the G, an abbreviation for gravity. Everything tries to accelerate toward the center of the earth. When you stand on the surface, that acceleration force is resisted by the force of the ground against the soles of your feet. You feel this as weight, even though you are not accelerating. The force of lift resists the force of gravity to keep an airplane in level flight, and the wings are bearing the weight of the airplane. In both cases, you experience an acceleration force of 1 times the force of gravity, or 1G. Even though we cannot change the force of gravity, whenever the airplane is changing speed or direction the magnitude of the acceleration can be measured in Gs. Although weight always acts straight down, acceleration forces, or G-forces, can be created in any direction. For example, in a 60° banked turn, the acceleration due to gravity added to the acceleration necessary to change the flight path results in a 2G force toward the bottom of the airplane. In this situation, the wings will have to generate twice as much lift as they would with the wings level in order to maintain the same altitude. The **load factor** is defined as the load the wings are supporting divided by the total weight of the airplane. With this in mind, you can understand why airplane structures are designed to withstand greater loads than normal flight is likely to produce. When an airplane is certified in the normal category, for example, each part of the structure is designed to do its job at 3.8 positive Gs and 1.52 negative Gs. Acrobatic-category airplanes are designed for higher load factors, and airliners for lower load factors.

 FAA Load factor is the ratio between the lift generated by the wings at any given time divided by the total weight of the airplane. The design load factor takes into account the effects of acceleration on the contents of the airplane.

G, I DIDN'T KNOW THAT!

Obviously, acceleration forces act on your body as well as on the aircraft structure. Some parts of your body are more affected than others. In positive G situations, you are being pushed down into your seat, and blood is pressed down into your legs and abdomen. This normally is not harmful, except that it reduces the blood available at the top of your body — your brain. Any reduction in the blood supply to your brain is bad news. Technically, this is stagnant hypoxia, and it can lead to GILOC, or G-Induced Loss of Consciousness. The onset of G-induced hypoxia usually brings tunnel vision as the light-sensitive rods in the retina stop supplying peripheral vision. This is quickly followed by gray-out as the remaining visual field begins to fade. At this point, sounds can also seem to fade away or become softer as hearing diminishes. Finally, blackout occurs. The onset of these symptoms might occur over a period of seconds, or might be nearly instantaneous, depending on the rate of G increase, the total acceleration, and the pilot's preparation and G tolerance. If the pilot reduces the acceleration forces at any stage before the blackout, full function returns almost instantly, and even blackouts might be momentary if Gs are reduced immediately. In World War II, dive-bomber pilots were instructed to tense their legs and abdomens and yell or grunt during pullouts from steep dives, in order to help prevent blood from sinking into their lower bodies. Most civilian aerobatic pilots use similar techniques. Modern military pilots use G suits, which fit tightly around legs and abdomen. Air bladders in the G suit are automatically inflated with compressed air during high-G maneuvers. Pressure breathing systems and whole-body G suits can help by forcing air into the lungs while squeezing the upper torso in addition to the lower body, thus helping the heart push blood into the head. These systems will probably remain too heavy and expensive for serious competition aerobatic pilots.

As with other types of flying, your physical condition for flight can have a major effect on your G tolerance. Besides the factors mentioned above, an aerobatic pilot's G tolerance also depends on proper hydration (drinking enough water), proper blood sugar levels, the oxygen-carrying capacity of the blood (no smoking), and other general fitness factors.

SECTION A ■ **Advanced Aerodynamics**

A heavily loaded airplane has a higher stall speed than the same airplane with a light load. This is because the heavily loaded airplane must use a higher angle of attack to generate the required lift at any given speed than when lightly loaded. Thus, it is closer to its stalling angle of attack, and will encounter C_{Lmax} at a higher airspeed. This is important to remember when flying a heavily loaded airplane at low airspeeds, because a bump, gust, or abrupt control movement could result in a stall. This property also means that at low speeds and/or high weights, abrupt use of the controls results in a stall instead of a structural overload. In this case, the stall acts as a safety valve, reducing the load factor prior to airframe damage.

At high speeds, the controls are more effective, and abrupt control movements can increase G loads so quickly that the structure could be damaged before the stalling angle of attack is reached. The maximum speed at which full or abrupt use of the controls will result in a stall rather than structural damage is the maneuvering speed (V_A). The maneuvering speed will vary with the airplane's total weight, because a lightly loaded airplane is easier to accelerate, and it will also have a larger margin between the angle of attack necessary for level flight and the stalling angle of attack. It takes less force, whether from an abrupt control movement or a from a gust or bump, to create a high-G situation, so the maneuvering speed is reduced. The maneuvering speed depicted on a cockpit placard is calculated for the maximum weight of the airplane, but some POHs include the V_A for other weights. The formulas used to calculate V_A are shown below.

$$V_A = V_S \sqrt{n_{limit}}$$

V_A = Maneuvering Speed (for this weight)

V_S = Stall Speed (for this weight)

n_{limit} = Limit Load Factor

$$V_{A_2} = V_A \sqrt{W_2 \div W_1}$$

V_{A_2} = Maneuvering Speed (at this weight)

V_A = Maneuvering Speed (at maximum weight)

W_2 = Actual Airplane Weight

W_1 = Maximum Weight

THE V-G DIAGRAM

Several of the factors that define an airplane's performance envelope can be combined in graphic formats. The V-g diagram is one example, relating velocity (V) to load factor (G). Each V-g diagram applies to one airplane type and the information is valid only for a specific weight, configuration, and altitude. V-g diagrams show the maximum amount of positive or negative lift the airplane is capable of generating at a given speed. They also show the safe load factor limits and the load factor, or number of Gs, the airplane can sustain at various speeds. Flying within the boundaries depicted by the diagram minimizes the risk of stalls, spins, and structural damage. [Figure 12-19]

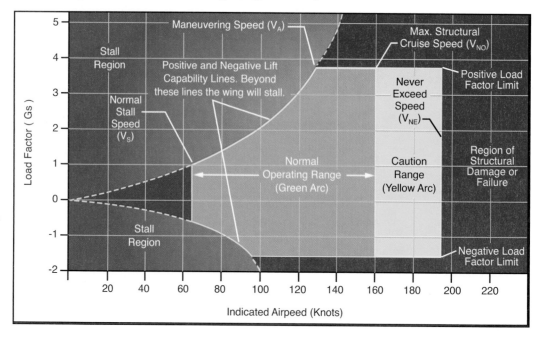

Figure 12-19. The horizontal scale indicates speed (V), and the vertical scale is load factor (G). The load factor limits shown are for a normal category airplane.

Major points of the V-g diagram include the curved lines representing positive and negative maximum lift capability. These lines portray the maximum amount of lift the airplane can generate at the specified speed. The intersection of these lines with the vertical speed lines indicates the maximum G-load capability at that speed. If you exceed the G-load limit at that speed, the airplane will stall. For example, at a speed of about 97 knots, this airplane will stall with a load factor of two Gs under the conditions represented. The horizontal positive and negative load factor limits represent the structural limitations of the airplane. Exceeding these values can cause structural damage.

Another important line on the V-g diagram is the normal stall speed, V_S. Note that at this speed, the airplane stalls at one positive G. This is the same speed shown by the lower limit of the green arc on the airspeed indicator. Above the one-G load factor, stalling speed increases. Any stall that occurs above the straight-and-level load of one G is an accelerated stall.

As discussed earlier, maneuvering speed (V_A) is the maximum speed at which you can use full and abrupt control movement without causing structural damage. V_A occurs at the point where the curved line representing maximum positive lift capability intersects the maximum positive load factor limit. At this speed, a load in excess of 3.8 Gs will result in a stall. Above this speed, G loads could cause structural damage before a stall occurs.

The vertical line at a speed of 160 is the maximum structural cruising speed (V_{NO}). Do not exceed this speed in rough air. The speed range from V_S to V_{NO} is the normal operating range and corresponds to the green arc on the airspeed indicator. The vertical line at a speed of about 195 represents the never-exceed speed, V_{NE}. This speed corresponds to the red line. If you fly faster than V_{NE}, there is a possibility of control surface flutter, airframe structural damage, or failure. The range from V_{NO} to V_{NE} is the caution range represented by the yellow arc on the airspeed indicator. Because turbulence and gusts are more likely to cause high load factors at higher speeds, use this speed range only in smooth air.

 V_{NO} is the maximum structural cruising speed during normal operations and V_{NE} is the never-exceed speed. Above V_{NE}, design limit load factors could be exceeded if gusts are encountered, causing structural damage or failure. See figure 12-19.

AIRFRAME ICING

When ice accumulates on airframe surfaces, it adversely affects all aspects of aircraft performance. Aerodynamic effects include changes in lift and drag due to the way that ice modifies the shapes of airframe components. As ice accumulates on airfoils such as wings, tail surfaces, and propeller blades, it alters the airfoil shape. Designers choose airfoil shapes carefully to provide specific flight characteristics, and any change in the airfoil modifies those characteristics, often in unpredictable ways. For example, ice buildup on the horizontal tail surface might cause that surface to stall at a higher airspeed, which could cause the airplane to pitch down suddenly and uncontrollably on final approach. Ice on propeller blades not only reduces thrust, but can also cause serious damage when it comes off. Chunks of ice thrown from propeller blades can damage adjacent areas of the wings and fuselage. If more ice is shed from one blade than the others, the imbalance causes extreme vibration that can damage the engine mounts.

Because ice increases total aircraft weight, the wing must fly at a higher angle of attack to create enough lift to maintain altitude. This is equivalent to increasing the load factor, which causes a corresponding increase in the stall speed. Combined with the change that ice produces in airfoil shape, the wing might not be able to generate sufficient lift for level flight even at speeds close to the stalling angle of attack.

Ice can affect your airplane in other subtle ways, too. It might cause changes in weight and balance that compromise stability. Runback icing can freeze control surfaces into place, making it difficult or impossible for you to use them to descend, turn, or climb. Ice accumulating on an antenna can cause the antenna to oscillate violently in the slipstream, possibly causing loss of the antenna or damage to the area where the antenna attaches to the airframe. These problems usually make it impossible to use the related transmitter or receiver, which can be especially serious during instrument flight.

See Chapter 9, Section B for information on icing processes and strategies for avoiding icing conditions. Chapter 11, Section B has information on the use and limitations of ice protection systems.

AIRCRAFT STABILITY

In unaccelerated flight, the airplane is in a state of equilibrium. Stability describes how the airplane reacts when that equilibrium is disturbed, either by control inputs, or by external factors such as gusts or bumps. A certain amount of stability is desirable, in most airplanes. It makes them easier to fly, especially on instruments or in turbulence, because the airplane tends to return to the trimmed attitude. It is possible to have too much stability, however. If the airplane is too resistant to changes in attitude, the pilot will have to use more effort to maneuver or change direction, so designers try to reconcile the need for stability with the contrasting needs for maneuverability and controllability. Although most aspects of stability are designed into the airplane, the pilot's actions can affect stability in several ways. [Figure 12-20]

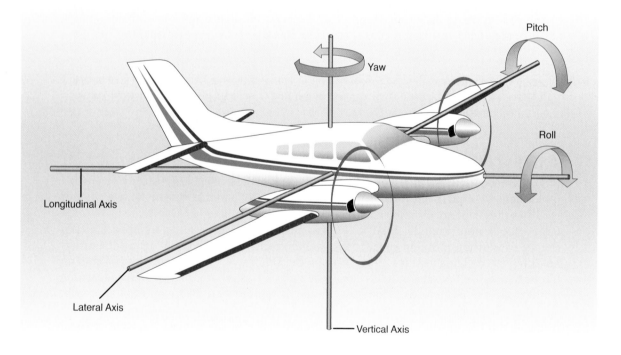

Figure 12-20. Stability characteristics can be described for each of the airplane's three axes of rotation.

STATIC STABILITY

Static stability is the most basic way of looking at stability. A system in equilibrium can only respond to a disturbance in one of three ways. If it initially tends to return toward equilibrium, it has positive static stability. If it initially tends to move away from equilibrium, it has negative static stability. If it does neither, it displays neutral static stability. [Figure 12-21]

 An airplane with positive static stability tends initially to return to equilibrium if disturbed. An airplane that remains in a new attitude without returning toward equilibrium or moving farther away from equilibrium displays neutral static stability. If an airplane tends initially to move away from equilibrium when disturbed, it has negative static stability.

POSITIVE	NEUTRAL	NEGATIVE
If disturbed, these systems tend to return to their former positions	If disturbed, these systems tend to remain in a new position	If disturbed, these systems move away from their former positions

Figure 12-21. You can find static stability characteristics all around you.

DYNAMIC STABILITY

Static stability refers to the initial response of a system to a disturbance, but **dynamic stability** describes how the system responds over time. What we will call dynamic stability is more correctly called damping, and refers to whether the disturbed system actually returns to equilibrium or not. The degree of stability can be gauged in terms of how quickly it returns to equilibrium. Again, the response can be described as positive, neutral, or negative.

Dynamic stability can be further divided into oscillatory and non-oscillatory modes. To see the difference, think of a smooth bowl with a marble at rest on the bottom. The system is in equilibrium. If you move the marble up the side of the bowl and let it go, you disturb the equilibrium. The marble rolls down the side and up the opposite side, then back across the bottom. After a series of oscillations, the marble comes to rest on the bottom again, showing positive static and oscillatory positive dynamic stability. If you do the same thing with a cotton ball in place of the marble, you see an example of non-oscillatory positive dynamic stability, as the cotton ball simply slides to the bottom without oscillations.

Negative dynamic stability, or instability, can also be oscillatory. As a top spins, it is held by gyroscopic forces in a stable state. These forces weaken as the top slows down, and a small wobble develops, which grows until the top loses all stability and falls over. In an aircraft with dynamic pitch instability, a small disturbance in equilibrium, if uncorrected by the pilot, can result in a series of pitch oscillations, each greater than the last, until structural failure or ground impact occurs. [Figure 12-22]

 Longitudinal dynamic instability is usually characterized by progressively steeper pitch oscillations.

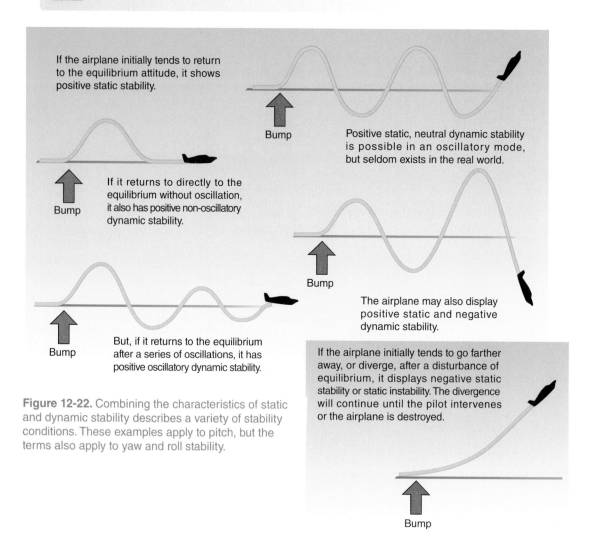

Figure 12-22. Combining the characteristics of static and dynamic stability describes a variety of stability conditions. These examples apply to pitch, but the terms also apply to yaw and roll stability.

LONGITUDINAL STABILITY

For an airplane to be stable in pitch, or longitudinally stable about the lateral axis, it must return to the trimmed pitch attitude if some force causes it to pitch up or down, whether the pitch change is caused by a bump, gust, or control input. Most training airplanes exhibit positive dynamic stability, or positive damping, in pitch.

FAA Longitudinal stability involves the motion of the airplane controlled by the elevators.

Longitudinal stability is achieved in most airplanes by locating the center of gravity slightly ahead of the center of lift of the wings, which makes the airplane tend to pitch down. This nose-heaviness is balanced in flight by a downward force generated by the horizontal tail. On many airplanes, the horizontal stabilizer and elevator form a cambered airfoil with the greater curvature on the bottom surface to create this **tail-down force**. Others use a symmetrical airfoil so that the left and right parts are interchangeable. On some airplanes, the stabilizer is installed with a slightly negative angle of incidence; on others, pitch trim is adjusted by changing the angle of the horizontal stabilizer. In cruising flight, the wings must generate somewhat more lift than the actual weight of the airplane to compensate for the negative lift of the tail-down force. [Figure 12-23]

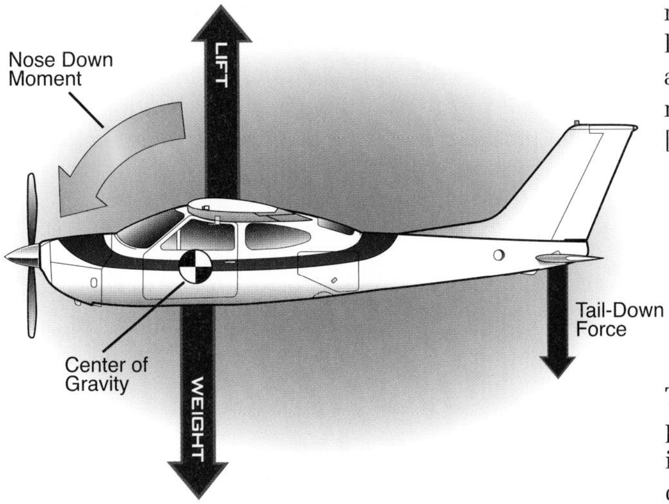

Nose Down Moment

LIFT

Tail-Down Force

Center of Gravity

WEIGHT

Figure 12-23. Tail-down force compensates for the nose-down moment that results from the center of gravity being located ahead of the center of lift.

Tail-down force contributes to pitch stability because of the way it changes in response to pitch disturbances. If a properly trimmed airplane is pitched up, the negative angle of attack of the stabilizer is reduced and increased drag causes a drop in airspeed, both of which reduce the tail-down force, allowing the airplane to pitch down. As the airplane then pitches down and accelerates, the increasing angle of attack and increasing airflow at the horizontal tail increase the tail-down force, raising the nose and causing the airspeed to decay again. After a series of progressively smaller oscillations, the airplane returns to level flight. [Figure 12-24]

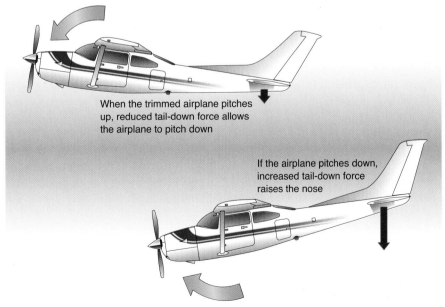

When the trimmed airplane pitches up, reduced tail-down force allows the airplane to pitch down

If the airplane pitches down, increased tail-down force raises the nose

Figure 12-24. The changing angle of attack and airflow over the tail varies the amount of tail-down force.

SECTION A ■ **Advanced Aerodynamics**

If the airplane is loaded with the center of gravity farther forward, you can see that the tail-down force must be increased to keep the airplane in trim. This adds to longitudinal stability, because the additional nose heaviness makes it more difficult to raise the nose, and the additional tail-down force makes it more difficult to pitch the nose down. Small disturbances are opposed by more powerful forces, so they tend to damp out more quickly. If the CG is too far forward, there might not be enough elevator authority to raise the nose, either for takeoff or to flare for landing. Conversely, as the CG is located further aft, the airplane becomes less stable in pitch. If the airplane is loaded so that the CG is actually behind the center of lift, the tail must exert an upward force to prevent the nose from pitching up. If a gust pitches the nose up in this situation, the reduction of airflow over the tail will allow the nose to pitch up further, a classic example of negative stability, or instability. Any disturbance of this precarious equilibrium will result in greater divergence from the trimmed condition. This is an extremely dangerous situation. The aft CG also makes it easier to stall or spin, there is more likelihood that a spin will go flat, and recovery might be impossible. If the CG coincides with the center of lift, control forces will be at their minimum, but the airplane will be difficult to fly, requiring constant attention and continuous control input even in calm air. In most airplanes, proper loading requires the CG to be forward of the center of lift.

TAIL STALLS

In normal flight, the horizontal tail creates lift in a downward direction, and, as discussed earlier, reducing this lift causes the airplane to pitch down. But, like any airfoil, the horizontal tail itself can also stall. If it stalls, the loss of tail-down force causes the airplane nose to drop suddenly.

Several factors can combine to create the conditions for a tail stall. The most common cause of tail stalls is icing. Some aircraft tend to accumulate ice more quickly on the horizontal tail than on the wings. The way ice changes the tail's airfoil shape might affect the tail's stall speed more than that of the wings, causing the tail to stall even though the wings are still generating lift.

Changes in power setting or in aircraft configuration (such as extending the flaps or landing gear) alter the airflow over the tail. This change in airflow can increase the tail's angle of attack. Combined with the reduction in airspeed for a landing, these factors make tail stalls most likely to occur at low altitude, during the turn from base to final or as flaps are extended on the final approach.

If the nose drops suddenly at low altitude, a pilot might assume that the wings have stalled and move the elevator control forward. If the tail has stalled, this action only forces the tail deeper into the stall, with catastrophic results. Even if the pilot recognizes the situation, adds full power, and applies back pressure to break the tail stall, the aircraft might not have sufficient altitude to recover; additionally, the act of raising the nose might cause the wings to stall.

Actions that can reduce the risk of tail stalls include avoiding icing conditions, using ice protection equipment as recommended in the POH, flying the approach at a higher airspeed, and making speed and configuration changes at altitudes that permit a recovery if a tail stall occurs.

LATERAL STABILITY

Stability around the longitudinal axis, or **lateral stability**, is the tendency of the airplane to return to a wings-level attitude following a roll deviation. Airplanes ordinarily have little resistance to roll inputs, and if you bank a few degrees in coordinated flight and let go of the controls, most airplanes show neutral static stability in roll. Most efforts to enhance lateral stability take advantage of the fact that when roll occurs accidentally, as the result of a bump or gust, it is almost always accompanied by a sideslip. Airplane designers use the forces and relative wind effects of the sideslip to return the airplane to a wings-level attitude, and still provide comfortable roll control forces for intentional turns. Wing dihedral and sweep are two methods of increasing lateral stability without adding to roll control forces.

Dihedral works because the relative wind during a sideslip increases the angle of attack on the lower, upwind wing while the higher wing experiences a reduced angle of attack. The difference in the lift produced tends to roll the airplane out of the slip, and the increase in induced drag on the lower wing helps to yaw the airplane into the relative wind. [Figure 12-25]

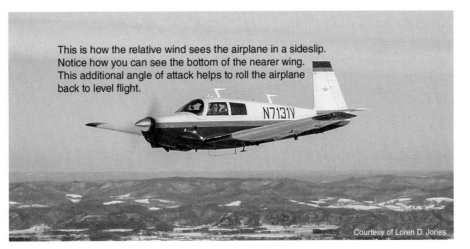

This is how the relative wind sees the airplane in a sideslip. Notice how you can see the bottom of the nearer wing. This additional angle of attack helps to roll the airplane back to level flight.

Courtesy of Loren D. Jones

Figure 12-25. Dihedral uses relative wind from the sideslip to create more lift on the upwind wing.

Walking around airport ramps, you might have noticed that low-wing airplanes generally have much more dihedral than high-wing types. The difference is due to the way the relative wind is influenced by the fuselage during a sideslip. In high-wing airplanes, the relative wind creates an upwash near the wing root at the leading edge of the upwind wing, and a slight downwash at the root of the downwind wing. This increases the local angle of attack on the upwind wing while decreasing it on the downwind wing, with the resulting difference in lift tending to roll the airplane out of the slip. The situation is reversed with a low-wing airplane; the sideslip creates a downwash for the upwind wing and an upwash for the downwind wing, which tends to increase the roll into the sideslip. Low-wing airplanes need to have a certain amount of dihedral to overcome the destabilizing effect of the fuselage, and an additional amount to provide lateral stability. [Figure 12-26]

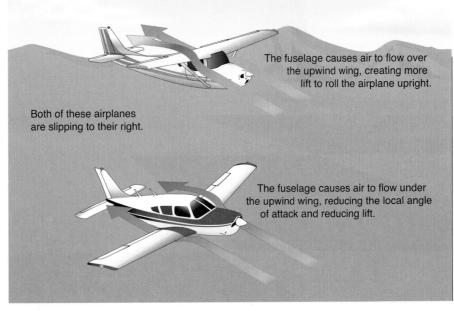

The fuselage causes air to flow over the upwind wing, creating more lift to roll the airplane upright.

Both of these airplanes are slipping to their right.

The fuselage causes air to flow under the upwind wing, reducing the local angle of attack and reducing lift.

Figure 12-26. Low-wing airplanes need more dihedral because of the way the fuselage influences airflow at the wing roots.

SECTION A ■ Advanced Aerodynamics

Long before swept wings became necessary to deal with the problems of drag rise and shockwaves at transonic speeds, designers used them to assist with lateral stability. Sweepback is especially useful when dihedral would be inappropriate, such as on an aerobatic airplane that needs lateral stability when inverted as well as when upright. [Figures 12-27 and 12-28]

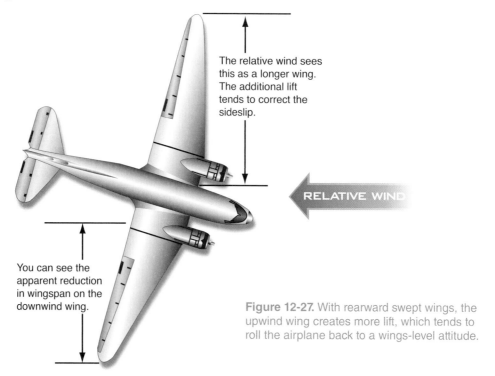

The relative wind sees this as a longer wing. The additional lift tends to correct the sideslip.

RELATIVE WIND

You can see the apparent reduction in wingspan on the downwind wing.

Figure 12-27. With rearward swept wings, the upwind wing creates more lift, which tends to roll the airplane back to a wings-level attitude.

Figure 12-28. Since the 1930s, aerobatic airplanes have used swept wings, without dihedral, to provide lateral stability in both upright and inverted flight.

Copyright Corel

Most airplanes have a moderate amount of lateral stability, because too much would make them difficult to control in turns, and would hamper crosswind takeoffs and landings. In fact, some airplanes are designed with negative dihedral to counteract some of the dihedral effect that results from their swept wings. [Figure 12-29]

Figure 12-29. These airplanes counteract unwanted lateral stability with negative dihedral.

DIRECTIONAL STABILITY

Stability in yaw, or resistance to undesired rotation around the vertical axis is called **directional stability**. The vertical tail and the sides of the fuselage contribute forces that help to keep the airplane's longitudinal axis aligned with the relative wind. Airplanes tend to weathervane into the relative wind due to the greater side area behind the center of gravity, plus the force created by the vertical stabilizer. Because most of the area of the vertical tail is above the longitudinal axis of the airplane, in a sideslip, this area also creates a small rolling force in addition to yaw, contributing somewhat to lateral stability. Uncoordinated yaw changes the angle of attack of the vertical stabilizer, creating a sideways force to restore the airplane's alignment with the relative wind. [Figure 12-30]

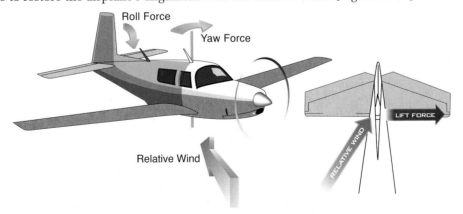

Figure 12-30. The area of the vertical surfaces behind the center of gravity contribute yaw and roll forces to provide directional stability.

INTERACTION OF LATERAL AND DIRECTIONAL STABILITY

Although the design factors that contribute to lateral and directional stability are carefully balanced to complement each other in flight, the complex manner in which they interact leaves many aircraft with a certain degree of instability in yaw and roll. Many of the design compromises are dictated by the wide speed range over which the aircraft must operate, for instance, the design elements that provide stability in a low speed configuration for takeoff and landing might lead to undesirable flight characteristics at high speed, and vice versa. Two of the most common problems are Dutch roll and spiral instability.

Dutch roll, or oscillatory lateral instability, is usually a consequence of too much dihedral effect, from the combination of actual dihedral, sweepback, a high wing configuration, relatively small vertical tail, and/or other factors. In Dutch roll, the airplane makes a continuous back-and-forth rolling and yawing motion with the roll out of phase with the yaw. Dutch roll is usually dynamically stable, that is, the oscillations tend to decrease in amplitude, but if the oscillation is weakly damped it could continue for a relatively long time, making it objectionable. In some airplanes, Dutch roll can be aggravated by the pilot's attempts to correct it, a form of pilot-induced oscillation. [Figure 12-31]

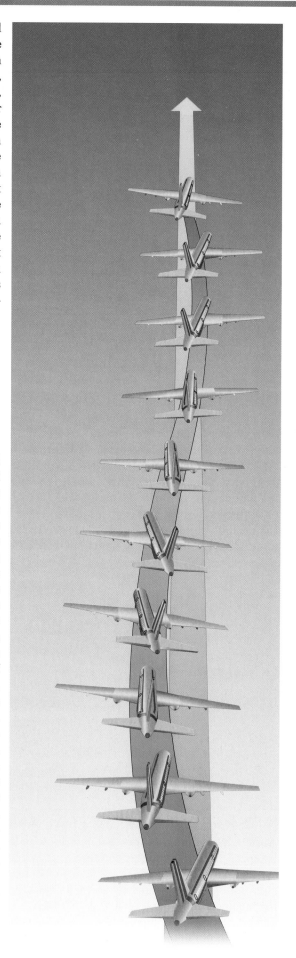

Figure 12-31. Dutch roll is a combined sequence of rolling/yawing oscillations, with the airplane always yawing away from the direction of bank.

If an airplane has strong directional stability relative to its lateral stability, it might display **spiral instability**. When a bump or gust produces a side slip in an airplane with spiral instability, its powerful directional stability tends to yaw the airplane back into alignment with the relative wind. As the outside wing travels faster it generates more lift, tending to roll the airplane in the direction of the yaw. This rolling force overcomes the comparatively weak dihedral effect, allowing the roll to progress. As the vertical component of lift decreases, the relative wind has an upward component, and as the airplane swings into alignment with the airstream, the nose begins to drop. This results in a gradually tightening spiral dive known as the graveyard spiral. Despite the name, which dates from the days when pilots attempted flight into IFR conditions without adequate instruments, spiral instability is generally considered less objectionable than Dutch roll. A certain degree of spiral instability is considered acceptable, so designers usually try to minimize Dutch roll by placing more emphasis on directional stability. [Figure 12-32]

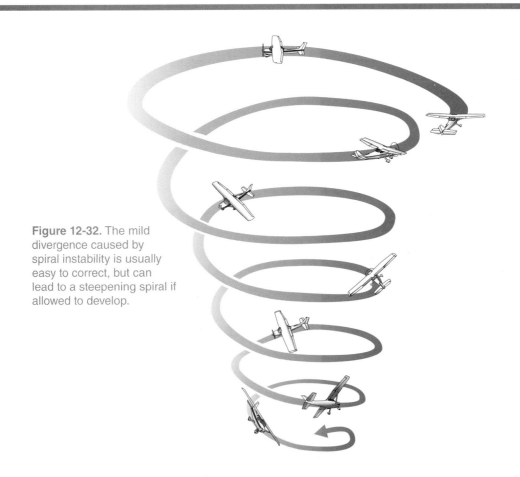

Figure 12-32. The mild divergence caused by spiral instability is usually easy to correct, but can lead to a steepening spiral if allowed to develop.

AERODYNAMICS AND FLIGHT MANEUVERS

Designers devote as much attention to an airplane's handling characteristics in maneuvering flight as they do to its stability. A great deal of an airplane's performance and appearance is dictated by the aerodynamic considerations of maneuvering flight.

STRAIGHT-AND-LEVEL FLIGHT

If you remain in straight-and-level flight, your maneuvering is limited to speeding up or slowing down. Maintaining straight-and-level flight while changing airspeed involves managing three of the four aerodynamic forces simultaneously. To reduce airspeed, you must create an excess of drag, usually by reducing thrust, although speed brakes, landing gear, or other devices are used in some circumstances. As the airplane slows, lift diminishes, so you increase the angle of attack to maintain altitude. When drag has dropped to a value that matches the new thrust level, equilibrium is restored. If you slow to a speed that requires an angle of attack near the stall, you might obtain more lift by changing the wing camber or area with flaps or other high-lift devices. Because these also increase drag, additional thrust will be required to maintain the desired airspeed. To increase airspeed, either thrust must be added, drag reduced, or both. As the speed increases, the angle of attack will need to be reduced to keep additional lift from causing the airplane to climb.

 To maintain altitude while airspeed is being reduced, the angle of attack must be increased.

CLIMBS

A climb is normally initiated by increasing the angle of attack, which momentarily increases lift. The additional induced drag slows the airplane, unless thrust is added, and the excess lift quickly returns to equilibrium. Whether thrust has been added or not, the thrust vector remains at a slight upward angle to the relative wind, and it is this vertical component of thrust that causes the airplane to climb. If you raise the nose without adjusting the power, you divert thrust from opposing drag and instead use it to create a difference between power required for level flight and power available, and it is this excess power that sustains a climb. The relationship between power and airspeed is easy to see on a graph. [Figure 12-33]

 Transitioning to a climb, angle of attack increases and lift momentarily increases.

SECTION A ■ **Advanced Aerodynamics**

The airspeed where the difference between thrust required and thrust available is greatest corresponds to the maximum angle of climb (V_X). Since engine-propeller combinations produce maximum thrust at low speeds, V_X is on the back side of the curve near the stall.

Figure 12-33. The difference between power required and power available determines the rate of climb, but the difference between thrust available and thrust required determines angle of climb.

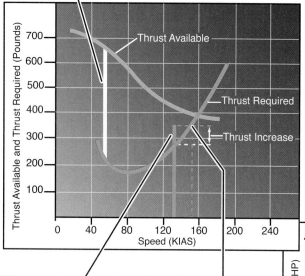

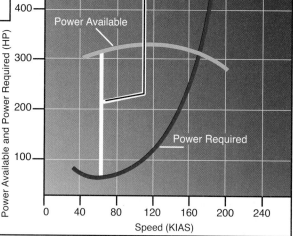

Where the power difference is greatest, there is maximum excess horsepower which can be used to increase altitude. This will be the airspeed that provides maximum rate of climb (V_Y). A faster or slower airspeed will reduce the amount of excess power and decrease the rate of climb.

If thrust is increased over the amount required for level flight at that airspeed, there will be an acceleration. If the same airspeed is maintained by raising the nose, lift will exceed weight for a few moments until equilibrium is restored and the airplane is established in a climb.

If the nose is held down to maintain level flight, the airspeed will increase until drag balances thrust at a higher point on the curve.

FACTORS AFFECTING CLIMB PERFORMANCE

Airspeed affects both the angle and rate of climb. At a given airplane weight, a specific airspeed is required for maximum performance. If your airspeed is faster or slower than best climb speed, climb performance will decrease. Generally, the larger the speed variation, the larger the performance variation. Weight also affects climb performance. If you change the weight of the airplane, you also change the drag and power required. As you increase weight, you reduce the maximum rate of climb and maximum angle of climb.

As you know, climb performance decreases with altitude. This is because more power and thrust are required, but the power and thrust available decrease with altitude. The airspeed necessary to obtain the maximum angle of climb increases with altitude, but the airspeed for the best rate of climb decreases. The point at which these two airspeeds converge is referred to as the airplane's **absolute ceiling**. When the best rate of climb is zero and the airplane cannot climb any higher, it has reached its absolute ceiling. Because the rate of climb deteriorates to nearly zero as the absolute ceiling is approached, a more practical value is commonly used. The **service ceiling** is the pressure altitude where the maximum rate of climb is 100 ft/min. For multi-engine airplanes, the service ceiling with one engine inoperative is the pressure altitude where the airplane can climb at 50 ft/min with one propeller feathered. These ceilings vary with temperature and aircraft weight.

GLIDES

If an engine fails, you will probably be interested in flying the airplane at the minimum glide angle so you can travel the maximum distance for the altitude you have available. As mentioned before, the best glide performance is at the maximum lift-to-drag ratio, or L/D_{max}. This occurs at a specific value of the lift coefficient and, therefore, at a specific angle of attack. [Figure 12-34]

FAA Approximate gliding distance can be found by multiplying your altitude AGL by the L/D ratio. Glide ratios for various angles of attack are obtained from an L/D graph. See figure 12-34.

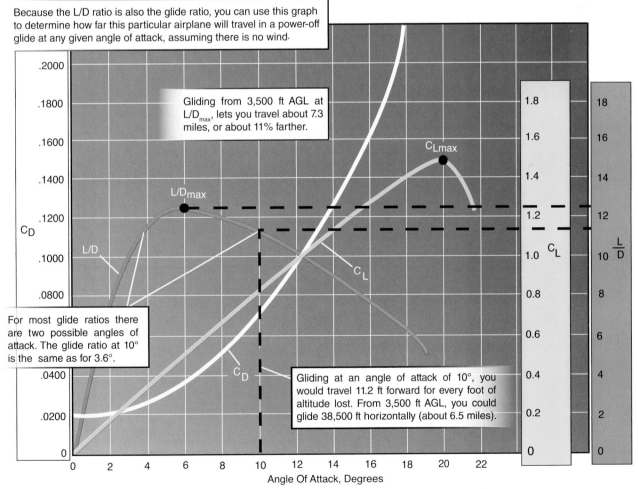

Because the L/D ratio is also the glide ratio, you can use this graph to determine how far this particular airplane will travel in a power-off glide at any given angle of attack, assuming there is no wind.

Gliding from 3,500 ft AGL at L/D_{max}, lets you travel about 7.3 miles, or about 11% farther.

For most glide ratios there are two possible angles of attack. The glide ratio at 10° is the same as for 3.6°.

Gliding at an angle of attack of 10°, you would travel 11.2 ft forward for every foot of altitude lost. From 3,500 ft AGL, you could glide 38,500 ft horizontally (about 6.5 miles).

Figure 12-34. This graph shows the curves for the coefficient of drag, C_D, and coefficient of lift, C_L, as well as the curve obtained by dividing lift by drag, L/D, for a specific airfoil at positive angles of attack.

SECTION A ■ Advanced Aerodynamics

TURNS

Newton's first law of motion says that an object in motion tends to remain in motion in a straight line unless acted on by some outside force. In order to turn an airplane, you provide that force through the flight controls, and this causes an acceleration. The acceleration continues for as long as you are preventing the airplane from following a straight line, that is, for as long as you are turning. When you roll the airplane into a bank, some of the lift of the wings is directed to the side, and it is this **horizontal component of lift** that causes the airplane to turn. Diverting a portion of lift to turn the airplane reduces the amount of lift available to support the weight of the airplane. In order to support the weight and prevent altitude loss, the wings must generate more lift than in straight flight. That is why you must increase the angle of attack by adding back pressure to maintain altitude while turning. [Figure 12-35]

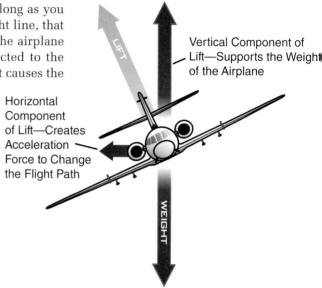

Vertical Component of Lift—Supports the Weight of the Airplane

Horizontal Component of Lift—Creates Acceleration Force to Change the Flight Path

Figure 12-35. In a bank, part of the lift acts vertically to support the weight of the airplane, and part of it acts horizontally to change the flight path.

FAA As the angle of bank is increased, the vertical component of lift decreases as more of the total lift is directed horizontally. To compensate for the loss of part of the vertical component of lift in a turn, you must increase the angle of attack by using elevator back pressure.

LOAD FACTOR IN TURNS

The increase in weight that you feel in a turn is due to the inertia of your own body as it tries to continue along a straight path rather than the curving flight path of the airplane. This is in accordance with Newton's second law of motion, which describes the relationships between force, acceleration, and mass. Briefly, a force acting on a certain mass will create a proportional acceleration. The more force you exert through the flight controls to change the airplane's path away from a straight line, the more acceleration you will feel. The lift of the wings exerts this force on every part of the airplane, increasing the load factor. A steeper bank means a greater horizontal component of lift, which corresponds to a higher load factor. Therefore, in a properly coordinated turn, the steeper the bank, the higher the flight load factor. [Figure 12-36]

② The stall speed increase is 19%, so the stall speed in the 45° bank is 1.19 x 62 = 74 KIAS.

① Suppose you are flying an airplane with a wings-level stall speed of 62 KIAS. To find the stall speed in a 45° banked turn, go up to the Stall Speed Increase curve.

Figure 12-36. The relationship between angle of bank, load factor, and stall speed is the same for all airplanes. You can use this graph to find the load factor in turns for any airplane, as well as the percentage the stall speed will increase.

Stall Speed Increase

Load Factor

Load Factor (Gs) / *Percent Increase In Stall Speed*

Bank Angle (Degrees)

③ To find the load factor, go up to the Load Factor curve and read across to the proper scale. The load factor at 45° is less than 1.5G.

The constant load factor generated in a coordinated, level turn does not depend on the rate or radius of turn, but on the bank angle. Load factor remains constant if there is no change in bank angle. At a bank angle of 60°, the load factor is 2Gs, which means that the wings are supporting twice the weight of the aircraft.

Load factor in turns increases at steeper bank angles, as does the stall speed. In a coordinated, level turn at a given bank angle, all airplanes will experience the same load factor and the same percentage of increase in stall speed over their wings-level stall speed.

RADIUS AND RATE OF TURN

Two variables determine the rate and radius of a turn. A steeper bank reduces turn radius and increases the rate of turn, but produce higher flight load factors. Reducing airspeed does the same thing, but without increasing the load factor. The radius of turn at any given bank angle varies directly with the square of the airspeed, that is, at twice the airspeed, the radius of the turn will be quadrupled, if the bank remains the same. The rate of turn also varies with airspeed, at any given bank angle, so slower airplanes require less time and area to complete a turn than faster airplanes at the same angle of bank. [Figure 12-37]

A specific angle of bank and true airspeed will produce the same rate and radius of turn regardless of weight, CG location, or airplane type. You can also see from this chart that increasing the velocity increases the turn radius and decreases the turn rate. The load factor on the airplane remains the same because you have not changed the angle of bank. To increase the rate and decrease the radius of a turn, you can steepen the bank and/or decrease your airspeed.

A given airspeed and bank angle will produce a specific rate and radius of turn in any airplane. In a coordinated, level turn, an increase in airspeed will increase the radius and decrease the rate of turn. Load factor is directly related to bank angle, so the load factor for a given bank angle is the same at any airspeed.

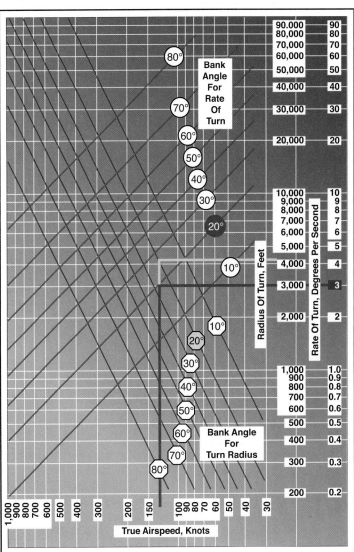

Figure 12-37. This graph will work for any airplane. The example shows that for a turn at 130 knots and a bank angle of 20°, the radius will be 4,200 feet and the rate of turn will be 3° per second.

SECTION A ■ Advanced Aerodynamics

COORDINATION IN TURNS

Before the first airplane flew, the Wright brothers experimented with control systems on their gliders. They found that they could turn by tilting the lift of the wings, which they accomplished by changing the camber on the outer portions of the wings. They used a system of wires and pulleys to twist the trailing edges of the wings down on one side and up on the other. The Wrights soon found that their gliders tended to yaw away from the direction of bank, due to the increase in induced drag on the side with the greater camber. Subsequently, they fitted a vertical rudder to assist them in keeping the aircraft aligned with the flight path, and most of the airplanes since have followed the same strategy for turning. In general, ailerons have replaced wing-warping as the method of changing the camber of the wingtips, so we refer to the tendency to yaw away from the bank as adverse aileron yaw, or simply **adverse yaw**. This effect is most noticeable at low airspeeds, when larger control movements are required for a given change in attitude, and the down-turned aileron creates proportionately more induced drag. Proper use of the rudder overcomes adverse yaw.

The ball in the inclinometer indicates whether your airplane is aligned with its flight path. If you do not use enough rudder for the bank angle, the airplane yaws to the outside of the turn, and the ball moves to the inside, indicating a slip. Conversely, using too much rudder for the amount of bank yaws the airplane to the inside of the turn, displacing the ball to the outside, indicating a skid. The same forces that cause the ball to move will try to shift your body sideways in the seat. This is one reason why maintaining coordinated flight without watching the ball is known as flying by the seat of your pants. Because slips increase drag, they are sometimes used to lose altitude without gaining speed. Some airplanes restrict intentional slips for aerodynamic or structural reasons. In addition, slipstream disturbances at the static ports might cause indicated airspeed errors during slips.

STALL AND SPIN AWARENESS

Most stall/spin accidents occur when the pilot is momentarily distracted from the primary task of flying the aircraft. Because of this, the FAA requires training that emphasizes recognition of situations that could lead to an unintentional stall and/or spin. An understanding of the aerodynamics of the stall and spin will help you avoid such situations, as well as improve your chances for a safe recovery if you enter an unintentional stall or spin.

STALLS

As you know, at any angle of attack beyond C_{Lmax}, the airflow can no longer follow the upper surface of the wing, and the flow separates. The wing loses lift, and the airplane accelerates downward because weight exceeds lift. Unless you reduce the angle of attack by movement of the yoke, the airplane will remain in the stalled condition, and might enter a spin. If the stall occurs near the ground or if the controls are incapable of reducing the angle of attack, recovery might not be possible.

CAUSES OF STALLS

The stall always occurs at the same angle of attack for any particular airfoil, regardless of weight, load factor, attitude, airspeed, or thrust. However, each of these factors does influence the stall speed. An airplane can stall at any airspeed, in any attitude, and at any power setting. The airflow separation is really a progressive event. It begins as the angle of attack approaches C_{Lmax}, and the rate of increase of the C_L begins to flatten out. As the angle of attack increases to C_{Lmax} and beyond, the separation increases, lift decreases, and drag increases. There are several ways a pilot can bring the airplane to the stalling angle of attack. Slowing the airplane compels you to increase the angle of attack to generate the required lift. Likewise, to compensate for the loss of part of the vertical component of lift in a turn, the angle of attack must be increased to maintain altitude. The load factor in a turn adds to the effective weight of the airplane, and whenever you increase the weight, either through flight load factors or by loading actual weight on board, the wings have to fly at a higher angle of attack at any given airspeed to generate a corresponding amount of lift. The location of the center of gravity also affects the load the wings must support, due to the effects of tail-down force. As the CG is moved forward, the tail-down force necessary for level flight increases. Each of these factors reduces the margin between a lift-producing angle of attack and the stalling angle of attack. If the wing is near C_{Lmax}, even a bump or gust can change the relative wind enough to produce a stall. Abrupt use of the flight controls can trigger a stall even when the airspeed is well above the published stall speed.

Total weight, load factor, power, and CG location affect stall speed.

Frost or ice on the wings can raise the stall speed in various ways. The weight of ice adds to the airplane's total weight, of course. Ice can also change the shape of the airfoil, either reducing the coefficient of lift or the stalling angle of attack, or both. Even a thin coating of ice or frost can trigger separation by disrupting the smooth flow of air. As mentioned in the discussion of stability, if the center of gravity is too far aft, the stall speed will decrease, but the controls might not have enough authority to reduce the angle of attack, making recovery impossible. The condition of the airplane itself can adversely affect its stall characteristics, for instance, if the airplane is poorly maintained, has damaged wing surfaces, or is improperly rigged.

TYPES OF STALLS

Stalls are usually classified according to whether the airplane is flying straight ahead or turning, and whether the power is on or off. You should be proficient in recognizing the most common stall situations as well as performing and recovering from the stalls associated with them. Normally, **power-on stalls** are associated with takeoff and climb configurations, and **power-off stalls** are most likely in an approach configuration. Consequently, power-on stalls are usually practiced with gear up and flaps at the takeoff setting, and power-off stalls with the gear and flaps down. Of course, stalls in either configuration can be done either straight ahead or turning. [Figure 12-38]

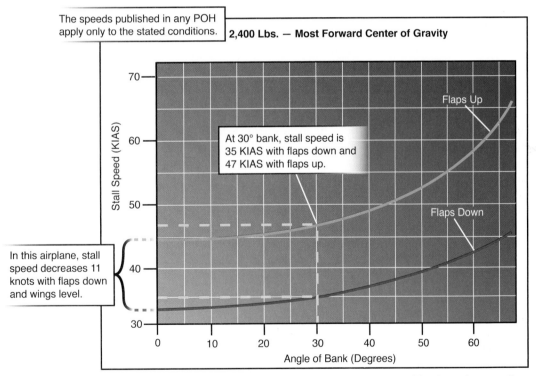

Figure 12-38. This graph shows the effect of flap position and bank angle on stall speed. This difference increases with the angle of bank.

Additional descriptive terms for stalls include accelerated, secondary, crossed-control, and elevator trim. Familiarity with these terms helps you to understand descriptions you might read in the aviation literature, press reports, or accident/incident analyses.

Accelerated stalls are caused by abrupt or excessive control movement. They commonly occur during maneuvers such as steep turns or rapid dive recoveries involving a high load factor or a sudden change in the flight path. Accelerated stalls are usually more violent

SECTION A ■ **Advanced Aerodynamics**

than unaccelerated stalls, and they are often unexpected because of the relatively high airspeed. Any time you are experiencing an increased flight load factor, that acceleration indicates that you have increased the angle of attack, and even though you might be well above the usual stall speed, you will be closer to the stalling angle of attack.

 Stalling speed is most affected by load factor. In any situation involving increased load factor, such as a rapid pullout from a dive, the stall speed increases.

If you pull up too quickly during recovery from a stall, you can trigger a **secondary stall**. This usually happens as a result of an attempt to hasten a stall recovery, either by increasing the angle of attack too quickly, or by not decreasing the angle of attack enough in the first place. Relax the back pressure and allow the airplane to regain flying speed. This might be extremely difficult if the primary stall occurred near the ground. In rare instances, too much forward pressure in a stall recovery could cause a negative G stall. This type of stall is used intentionally by aerobatic pilots to enter inverted spins or outside snap-rolls. Although very unlikely in visual conditions, a primary stall on instruments coupled with some spatial disorientation could lead you to make unusual control movements.

The **crossed-control stall** occurs when the flight controls are crossed, meaning that rudder pressure is being applied in one direction while ailerons are applied in the opposite direction. When combined with excessive back pressure, conditions are ripe for a crossed-control stall. The most likely time for this is during a poorly executed turn to final approach for a landing. In a typical crossed-control stall, excessive inside rudder is used to tighten the turn, along with opposite aileron to keep the bank from becoming too steep. If too much elevator back pressure is added, or if the aircraft becomes too slow due to the added drag of the skid, the nose might pitch down and the wing on the inside of the turn might suddenly drop. Often these stalls occur with little warning and insufficient altitude for recovery; however, a displaced ball in the inclinometer or a skidding-turn feeling can prompt you to coordinate the controls and go around if necessary.

An **elevator trim stall** is most likely to occur during a go-around from a landing approach. In this case, the airplane's trim is adjusted for the configuration and slow speed of the approach with considerable nose-up trim. As power is applied for the go-around, the normal tendency is for the nose to pitch up, and if positive pressure is not used to counteract the strong trim forces, the nose will continue to pitch up. In addition, because full power is required, the aircraft is subject to left-turning forces that can easily lead to an uncoordinated flight condition. Now you have the conditions that can cause a stall — a high angle of attack, uncoordinated flight, and decreasing airspeed.

STALL RECOGNITION AND RECOVERY
A major part of stall recognition is knowing the flight characteristics of the airplane you are flying. You must also maintain an awareness of the flight conditions that are conducive to stalls.

Most airplanes warn the pilot of an impending stall in a variety of ways. In general aviation airplanes there is usually a stall warning light or horn. This warning system is a simplified angle of attack indicator installed on the leading edge of the wing. On many airplanes it consists of a small mechanical switch attached to a vane that is activated by airflow as the wing approaches C_{Lmax}. Other systems use a reed-type horn similar to a party noisemaker connected to an opening in the wing. As the wing approaches C_{Lmax}, airflow on the wing creates suction that draws air through the horn. Most systems will trigger the stall warning horn and/or warning light about 5 to 10 knots above the stall speed. A disadvantage of this type of system is that it is attached to only one wing. It is conceivable that an uncoordinated or asymmetric stall on the other wing might not actuate the warning signal. The systems that require electricity are subject to blown fuses, open circuits, or electrical failures, and the reed systems are sometimes rendered inoperative by bugs or debris wedged in the horn or plumbing.

Most airplanes provide additional indications of an impending stall. As the airflow begins to separate from the wing, there is often a buffeting or shaking through the entire airframe. If the tail is within the turbulent wake from the wings, you might feel a trembling through the elevator or rudder controls. At low airspeeds, the controls often feel mushy, and you might notice the sound of air rushing along the fuselage fading away. As lift is diminishing, you might notice a sinking feeling. These preliminary indications serve as a warning for you to decrease the angle of attack and increase airspeed by adding power. Ideally, you should be able to detect the signs of an imminent stall and make appropriate corrections before it actually occurs. Recovery at the first indication is quite simple, but if you allow the stalled condition to progress, recovery becomes more difficult.

The first priority in recovery from a stall is to reduce the angle of attack with forward elevator to allow the wings to regain lift. This might consist of merely releasing back pressure, or you might have to firmly move the elevator control forward, depending on the aircraft design, severity of the stall, and other factors. Excessive forward movement of the control column, however, could impose a negative load on the wings and delay the stall recovery. The next step, which should be accomplished almost simultaneously, is to smoothly apply maximum power to increase the airspeed and to minimize the loss of altitude. As airspeed increases, adjust power to return the airplane to the desired flight condition. In most training situations, this is straight-and-level flight or a climb. During the recovery, coordinated use of the controls is especially important. Uncoordinated flight control inputs can aggravate a stall and result in a spin. You also must avoid exceeding the airspeed and RPM limits of the airplane.

SPINS

The spin is one of the most complex of all flight maneuvers. There are many aerodynamic and inertial factors that contribute to the spinning of an airplane. In spite of this, it is an easy maneuver to enter in most airplanes, and recovery is also easy in many general aviation airplanes. During an intentional spin in a typical aerobatic trainer, the ground seems to whirl around very fast and the nose might seem to be pointed straight down. It is difficult to believe that the airspeed is near stall speed, the nose is only down 45-60°, and each turn of the spin takes three or four seconds. Altitude loss can be 500-1,000 feet or more per turn, depending on the type of airplane. There are major differences between intentional spins performed by a well-trained pilot in a properly loaded airplane with no restrictions against spinning, and an accidental spin. The first can be enjoyable, the second deadly. [Figure 12-39]

For our purposes, a spin can be defined as an aggravated stall resulting in autorotation, which simply means that the rotation is stable and will continue due to aerodynamic forces if nothing intervenes. During the spin, the airplane descends in a helical, or corkscrew, path as the wings remain unequally stalled. Even though the

Figure 12-39. Because of the low G-forces and the relative ease of execution, the spin is usually the first maneuver taught to pilots learning aerobatics.

nose is usually well below the horizon, the angle of attack remains greater than the stalling angle of attack. This is usually due to the pilot holding back pressure, maintaining the high angle of attack and creating high drag, combined with the large upward component of the relative wind.

PRIMARY CAUSES

A stall must occur before a spin can take place, and all of the factors that affect stalls also affect spins. The principle difference that transforms a straight-ahead stall into a spin entry is that one wing stalls more than the other. This usually happens when there is an element of yaw as the stall breaks, and occurs most often when the airplane is in uncoordinated flight. A spin could also develop if forces on the airplane are unbalanced in other ways, for example, from yaw forces due to an engine failure on a multi-engined airplane, or if the CG is laterally displaced by an unbalanced fuel load. Stalling with crossed controls is a major cause of spins, and usually happens when either too much or not enough rudder is used for existing yawing forces. If an airplane stalls with crossed controls, it is likely to enter a spin. The spin rotation is usually in the direction of the rudder being applied, regardless of which wing is raised.

During an uncoordinated maneuver, the pitot/static instruments, especially the altimeter and airspeed indicator, could be unreliable due to the uneven distribution of air pressure over the fuselage. This error might lead you to believe that your airspeed is sufficient to maintain smooth airflow over the wing when, in fact, you are very close to stalling. Your only warnings of the stall might be aerodynamic buffeting and/or the stall warning horn.

Coordination of the flight controls is natural and easy under most conditions, but preoccupation with situations inside or outside the cockpit, maneuvering to avoid other aircraft, and maneuvering to clear obstacles during takeoffs, climbs, approaches, or landings have caused control problems for many pilots. Because of this, you will be required to learn how to recognize and cope with these distractions by practicing flight at slow airspeeds with realistic distractions in your training.

PHASES OF A SPIN

There are three phases in a complete spin maneuver. The **incipient spin** is the first phase, and exists from the time the airplane stalls and rotation starts until the spin is fully developed. A **fully developed spin** exists from the time the angular rotation rates, airspeed, and vertical descent rate are stabilized from one turn to the next. The third phase, **spin recovery**, begins when the anti-spin forces overcome the pro-spin forces.

If an airplane is near the stalling angle of attack, and if more lift is lost from one wing than from the other, that wing will drop more quickly than the other, creating a roll toward the wing with less lift. As this wing drops, its local relative wind will come more from below, further increasing the angle of attack for that wing. Likewise, as the airplane rolls around its center of gravity, the upper wing has a lower local angle of attack, and continues to develop some lift. This situation of unbalanced lift tends to increase as the airplane yaws toward the low wing, accelerating the higher outside wing while slowing the inner, lower wing still more. As with other stalls, the nose drops, and as inertial forces come into play, the spin usually stabilizes at a steady rate of rotation and descent.

It is crucial that you initiate recovery from an inadvertent spin as soon as possible, because many airplanes will not recover from a fully developed spin, and others continue for several turns before recovery control inputs become effective. The recovery from an incipient spin normally requires less altitude, and time, than the recovery from a fully developed spin. Keep in mind that although some characteristics of a spin are predictable, every airplane spins differently, and an individual airplane's spin characteristics vary depending on configuration, loading, and other factors.

How Many Ways to Spin?

The spin is perhaps the most basic of all aerobatic maneuvers. Although many early pilots were able to execute and recover from spins, it wasn't until after World War I that spin aerodynamics began to be explored in detail. The tailspin became a staple of barnstormers and stunt performers, and is still a crowd-pleaser at airshows today.

For competitive aerobatics, there is a catalog of standard aerobatic maneuvers, grouped according to the type of maneuver and assigned coefficients of difficulty (K) for judging purposes. It is named for its originator, the Spanish Count Ferdinand Aresti. There are 192 different spins listed, consisting of erect spins, inverted spins, flat spins, and inverted flat spins among others. Snap rolls are another family of maneuvers closely related to spins. In essence, a snap roll is an abrupt spin forced on the airplane at an airspeed well above the usual stall speed. The wings are unequally stalled, just as in a spin, but the stall is caused by quickly forcing the angle of attack past the critical angle of attack. Unlike spins, snap rolls can be performed horizontally or upward as well as downward. Just as spins can be erect or inverted, snap rolls can be inside or outside. If you add in all the various inside and outside snap rolls with all their possible entries and recoveries, the extended family of spins includes at least 840 different maneuvers, ranging in difficulty from the basic one-turn erect spin with right-side-up entry and recovery, with a K-factor of 10, to the 3 turn erect flat spin with inverted entry and inverted recovery with a K-factor of 74.

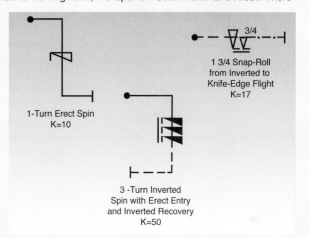

1-Turn Erect Spin
K=10

1 3/4 Snap-Roll from Inverted to Knife-Edge Flight
K=17

3 -Turn Inverted Spin with Erect Entry and Inverted Recovery
K=50

WEIGHT AND BALANCE

Both the total weight of the airplane and the distribution of weight influence the spin characteristics of the airplane. Higher weights generally mean slower initial spin rates, but as the spin progresses, spin rates can tend to increase. The higher angular momentum extends the time and altitude necessary for spin recovery in a heavily loaded airplane. The location of the center of gravity is even more significant, affecting the airplane's resistance to spins as well as all phases of the spin itself. Most airplanes are more stable with the CG near its forward limit. This increases control forces and makes it less likely that you will make large, abrupt control movements. It also means that when trimmed, the airplane will tend to return to level flight if you let go of the controls, but the stall speed will be higher with the CG forward. Because moving the CG aft decreases longitudinal stability and reduces pitch control forces in most airplanes, it tends to make the airplane easier to stall. After a spin is entered, an airplane with its CG farther aft tends to have a flatter spin attitude. If the CG is outside the limits of the CG envelope, or if power is not reduced promptly, the spin will be more likely to go flat. A flat spin is characterized by a near level pitch and roll attitude with the spin axis near the CG of the airplane. Although the altitude lost in each turn of a flat spin might be less than in a normal spin, the extreme yaw rates (often exceeding 400° per second) result in high descent rates. The relative wind in a flat spin is nearly straight up, keeping the wings at a high angle of attack. More importantly, the upward flow over the tail could render the elevators and rudder ineffective, making recovery impossible.

 Spin recovery might be difficult if the CG is too far aft and rotation is around the CG.

SPIN RECOVERY

The primary goal in recovery from a straight-ahead stall is to reduce the angle of attack to restore airflow over the wings, but spin recoveries have the additional goal of stopping the rotation. The complex aerodynamics of spins can dictate vastly different recovery procedures for different airplanes, so no universal spin recovery procedure can exist for all airplanes. The recommended recovery procedure for some airplanes is simply to reduce power to idle and let go of the controls, and others are so resistant to spins that they can be considered spin-proof. At the other extreme, the design of some airplanes is such that recovery from a developed spin requires definite control movements, precisely timed to coincide with certain points in the rotation, for several turns. You should be intimately familiar with the procedures in the POH for the aircraft you will be flying. The following is a general recovery procedure for erect spins, but it should not be applied arbitrarily without regard for the manufacturer's recommendations.

 In some airplanes, the displacement of the ball in spins depends on where the inclinometer is installed. If the inclinometer is on the left side of the cockpit, the ball will move to the left in both left and right spins.

- Move the throttle or throttles to idle. This minimizes the altitude loss and reduces the potential for a flat spin to develop in most airplanes. It also eliminates possible assymetric thrust in multi-engine airplanes. Engine torque and precession can increase the angle of attack or the rate of rotation in single-engine airplanes, aggravating the spin.

- Neutralize the ailerons. Aileron position is often a contributing factor to flat spins, or to high rotation rates in normal spins.

- Apply full rudder against the spin. Spin direction is most reliably determined from the turn coordinator. Do not use the ball in the inclinometer. Its indications are not reliable, and might be affected by its location within the cockpit. For example, in some airplanes, if the inclinometer is on the left side of the cockpit, the ball will move to the left in both left and right spins, and if installed on the right side of the cockpit, the ball will move to the right during a spin in either direction.

- Move the elevator control briskly to approximately the neutral position. Some aircraft merely require a relaxation of back pressure, but others require full forward elevator or stabilator pressure

- As rotation stops, indicating the stall has been broken, neutralize the rudder. If you maintain rudder pressure after rotation stops, you could enter a spin in the other direction.

- Recover from the resulting dive with gradual back elevator pressure. Pulling too hard could trigger a secondary stall, or worse, could exceed the flight load factor limits and damage the aircraft structure. Conversely, recovering too slowly from the dive could let the airplane exceed airspeed limits, especially in aerodynamically clean airplanes. Avoiding excessive speed buildup in the recovery is another reason for closing the throttle during spin recovery. Add power as you resume normal flight, being careful to observe power and RPM limits.

SUMMARY CHECKLIST

✓ Opposing forces are balanced in unaccelerated flight.

✓ The coefficient of lift increases with angle of attack, until the stalling angle of attack is reached.

✓ If all other factors remain constant, lift is proportional to the square of the speed.

✓ The four most common ways to increase lift are to increase angle of attack, increase airspeed, increase the camber of the wing, or increase the wing area.

✓ Modifying the camber of the wing with flaps and/or leading-edge devices can postpone airflow separation, resulting in lower stall speeds and greater coefficients of lift.

✓ Induced drag increases with angle of attack, and decreases with speed. Parasite drag increases in proportion to the square of the speed.

✓ A wing's planform affects induced drag, stall propagation, stability, maneuverability, and other characteristics.

✓ At a distance of less than one wingspan above the ground, induced drag diminishes, allowing the airplane to fly with less thrust. This phenomenon is called ground effect.

✓ Best glide angle is achieved at the speed at which the ratio of lift to drag is the greatest (L/D_{max}). This speed gives the greatest horizontal distance in a power-off glide, as well as maximum range with power.

✓ Maximum level flight speed is attained when maximum thrust is balanced by drag.

✓ Load factor is the ratio of lift being developed by the wings divided by the weight of the airplane.

✓ Stability characteristics can be described for each of the airplane's three axes of rotation.

✓ Static stability is determined by whether the airplane tends to return to equilibrium when disturbed, diverges farther from equilibrium, or maintains the same degree of displacement from equilibrium.

✓ Dynamic stability, or damping, describes how quickly the airplane reacts to its static stability, as well as whether it returns to equilibrium or not.

✓ The center of gravity is ordinarily located forward of the wings' center of lift. The resulting nose-down moment is normally balanced by the tail-down force created by the horizontal tail. This arrangement contributes to positive longitudinal stability, because pitch disturbances alter the tail-down force to return the airplane to balanced flight.

✓ In most airplanes, if the center of gravity is too far aft, the airplane will be unstable in pitch.

✓ Wing dihedral, sweepback, and mounting the wing on top of the fuselage are design factors that contribute to lateral stability.

✓ The vertical tail and the sides of the fuselage aft of the center of gravity tend to keep the fuselage aligned with the relative wind, contributing to directional stability.

✓ Too much lateral stability can lead to Dutch roll, but too much directional stability can lead to spiral instability. Spiral instability is considered less objectionable, so designers usually try to minimize Dutch roll at the expense of a little spiral instability.

✓ Climbs are a result of excess thrust. The maximum rate of climb (V_Y) occurs at the airspeed at which the difference between power available and power required is the greatest.

✓ The maximum angle of climb (V_X) is achieved at the airspeed at which the difference between thrust available and thrust required is the greatest.

✓ Higher aircraft weight reduces climb performance, glide ratio, and range.

✓ Load factor in coordinated, level turns is strictly a function of bank angle.

✓ Adverse yaw is caused by greater induced drag on the outside wing as an airplane rolls into a bank.

✓ Radius and rate of turn are influenced by airspeed and bank angle.

✓ Exceeding the stalling angle of attack (C_{Lmax}) will always result in a stall, regardless of weight, load factor, airspeed, or attitude.

✓ To spin, there must first be a stall. Prevent the stall and you prevent the spin.

✓ Spins occur when one wing stalls more fully than the other, and an autorotation develops.

✓ Spin recovery consists of breaking the stall by reducing angle of attack, stopping the rotation with rudder, and returning the airplane to normal flight.

KEY TERMS

Downwash	Longitudinal Stability
Relative Wind	Tail-Down Force
Angle Of Attack	Lateral Stability
Angle Of Incidence	Directional Stability
Slot	Dutch Roll
Slat	Spiral Instability
Leading-Edge Flaps	Absolute Ceiling
Taper	Service Ceiling
Aspect Ratio	Horizontal Component Of Lift
Sweep	Adverse Yaw
Ground Effect	Power-On Stalls
Form Drag	Power-Off Stalls
Interference Drag	Accelerated Stalls
Skin Friction Drag	Secondary Stall
Total Drag	Crossed-Control Stall
Spoilers	Elevator Trim Stall
Speed Brakes	Incipient Spin
Load Factor	Fully Developed Spin
Static Stability	Spin Recovery
Dynamic Stability	

QUESTIONS

1. True/False. The angle of attack at which a wing stalls varies depending on total aircraft weight, bank angle, load factor, and airspeed.

2. Wing slats deploy at high angles of attack, reducing the stall speed. The stall speed decreases because
   A. the chord line of the wings is reduced, decreasing the local angle of attack.
   B. the slats keep the airflow attached and increase the lifting area of the wings.
   C. the airflow through the slats increases the airspeed over the wings and reduces parasite drag.

3. True/False. Airplanes with a low aspect ratio have higher fuel efficiency because they have less induced drag.

4. True/False. There is an increase in lift when flying in ground effect that can allow an airplane to lift off even when it cannot climb, and which could cause a landing airplane to balloon or float before touchdown.

5. L/D_{max} is the airspeed that provides
   A. maximum range with or without power.
   B. maximum endurance and maximum rate of climb.
   C. maximum angle of climb and maximum level flight speed.

6. What term is used for the airspeed at which maximum thrust is balanced by drag in level flight?

7. Which of the four aerodynamic forces does not depend on the flight path or relative wind?

8. All other things being equal, why does increasing the weight of an airplane cause the stall speed to increase?

9. True/False. The flight load factor is the total load that the wings are supporting divided by the total weight of the airplane and its contents.

10. An airplane has positive static stability and negative dynamic stability in pitch. If it is trimmed for level flight and you disturb the equilibrium by pulling back and releasing the elevator control, how will the airplane respond after you release the controls?
    A. The airplane will continue to pitch up farther and farther without oscillating.
    B. There will be a series of increasing pitch oscillations, each steeper than the last.
    C. There will be a series of gradually decreasing pitch oscillations until the airplane is again in level flight.

11. True/False. An airplane with spiral instability has a tendency to steepen its bank and gradually nose down unless the pilot intervenes.

12. What is the term for the maximum altitude that an airplane is capable of climbing at 100 ft/min?

13. In a skidding right turn, what do you see in the inclinometer, and what should you do to coordinate the turn?
    A. The ball is to the left; add more left rudder.
    B. The ball is to the right; add more right rudder.
    C. The ball is to the right; steepen the bank with more aileron.

SECTION A ■ **Advanced Aerodynamics**

14. Using the adjacent chart, determine the stall speed for an airplane with a level-flight stalling speed of 42 KIAS when the airplane is in a coordinated turn at a bank angle of 55°.

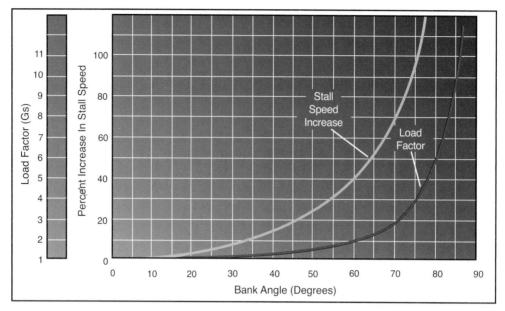

15. The radius of a coordinated turn can be decreased in two ways. What are they?

16. In most cases, stall recovery includes applying full power, but spin recovery procedures for most airplanes direct that the throttle be closed immediately. Why?

17. Why are flat spins considered more dangerous than other spins?

SECTION B
Predicting Performance

As you learn to fly aircraft with higher performance, you will discover that they are flown less by sight, sound, and feel, and more by the book and by the numbers. You have seen how aircraft behavior is governed by well-established physical laws and mathematical relationships. Now, you can use these concepts to predict the airplane's performance under different conditions, as well as to stay within operating limitations. The most frequently used performance information is usually provided in the POH in the form of tables and graphs.

FACTORS AFFECTING PERFORMANCE

Airplanes operate in an environment that is constantly changing, and several physical characteristics of the atmosphere influence aircraft performance. Temperature, pressure, humidity, and the movement of the air all have definite and foreseeable effects in every phase of flight, and runway conditions affect takeoff and landing performance. Although standard atmospheric conditions are the foundation for estimating airplane performance, airplanes are rarely flown in conditions that match the standard atmosphere. Some basic performance calculations will help you to take the differences between standard and existing conditions into account.

DENSITY ALTITUDE

The density of the air directly influences the performance of your airplane by altering the lift of the airframe as well as the ability of the engine to produce power. Both reciprocating and turbine engines produce less thrust as air density decreases and/or temperature increases, because these factors reduce the mass of the air passing through the engine. In propeller-driven airplanes, propeller efficiency is reduced when there are fewer air molecules to act upon. Jet thrust is the reaction force resulting from accelerating mass backward, so a reduction in the mass going into the engine reduces thrust if other factors remain the same. **Density altitude** is pressure altitude corrected for nonstandard temperature, and is equal to pressure altitude only when standard atmospheric conditions exist at that level. Because these specific conditions are uncommon, you should understand and be able to compute density altitude. Although the performance degradation due to increased density altitude occurs throughout the airplane's operating envelope, it is especially noticeable in takeoff and climb performance. You can find density altitude using either a flight computer or a density altitude chart. [Figure 12-40]

 As air temperature increases or air density decreases, engine performance decreases for both piston and gas turbine engines.

Most modern performance charts do not require you to compute density altitude. Instead, the computation is built into the performance chart itself. All you have to do is enter the chart with the correct pressure altitude and the temperature. Older charts, however, might require you to compute density altitude before entering them.

Water vapor also has an effect on density altitude. Humidity refers to the amount of water vapor in the atmosphere and is expressed as a percentage of the maximum amount of vapor the air can hold. This amount varies with air temperature. The warmer it is, the more water vapor the air can hold. When the air is saturated, it cannot hold any more water vapor at that temperature, and its humidity is 100 percent.

SECTION B ■ Predicting Performance

DENSITY ALTITUDE CHART

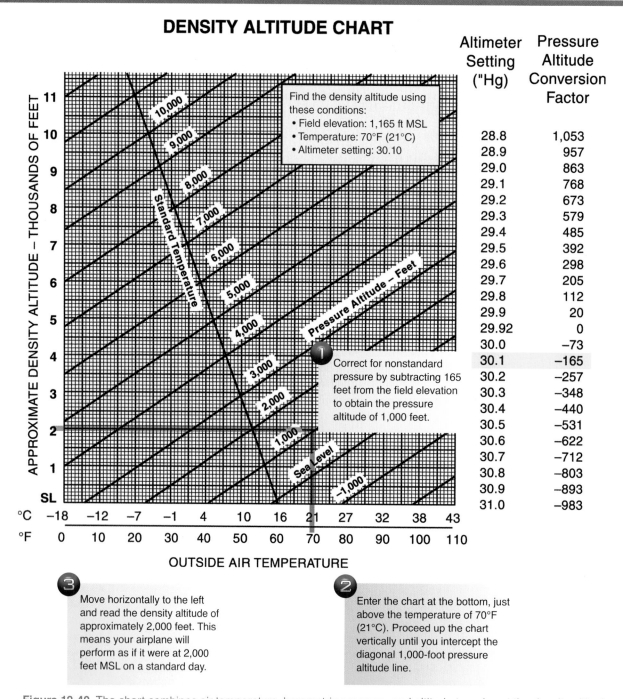

Find the density altitude using these conditions:
- Field elevation: 1,165 ft MSL
- Temperature: 70°F (21°C)
- Altimeter setting: 30.10

Altimeter Setting ("Hg)	Pressure Altitude Conversion Factor
28.8	1,053
28.9	957
29.0	863
29.1	768
29.2	673
29.3	579
29.4	485
29.5	392
29.6	298
29.7	205
29.8	112
29.9	20
29.92	0
30.0	−73
30.1	−165
30.2	−257
30.3	−348
30.4	−440
30.5	−531
30.6	−622
30.7	−712
30.8	−803
30.9	−893
31.0	−983

1 Correct for nonstandard pressure by subtracting 165 feet from the field elevation to obtain the pressure altitude of 1,000 feet.

3 Move horizontally to the left and read the density altitude of approximately 2,000 feet. This means your airplane will perform as if it were at 2,000 feet MSL on a standard day.

2 Enter the chart at the bottom, just above the temperature of 70°F (21°C). Proceed up the chart vertically until you intercept the diagonal 1,000-foot pressure altitude line.

Figure 12-40. The chart combines air temperature, barometric pressure, and altitude to arrive at the density altitude.

FAA Density altitude calculations are based on pressure altitude and air temperature. A flight computer or a density altitude chart may be used. See figure 12-40.

Although the effects of humidity are not shown on performance charts or included in density altitude computations, moist air does reduce airplane performance. Because water actually weighs less than dry air, any water vapor in the air reduces the total mass of the air entering the engine. This causes a small increase in density altitude. Conditions of very high humidity can reduce engine horsepower by as much as 7 percent, and the airplane's overall takeoff and climb performance by as much as 10 percent. Always provide yourself with an extra margin of safety by using longer runways and by expecting reduced takeoff and climb performance whenever it is hot and humid.

Records Ripe for Breaking

Getting the utmost performance out of an aircraft is a challenge that gives many pilots satisfaction. Perhaps you have thought of setting a speed, distance, or altitude record yourself. There are many aviation records that were set 30-60 years ago, so given the advances in engineering, materials and technology, it should be possible to advance some of these records today. To get your feet wet, you might take a crack at Francesco Agello's piston-engined seaplane speed record of 440.68 miles per hour (709.21 kph). He set this record on October 23, 1934 in a bright red Macchi-Castoldi MC-72. This racing floatplane had two 1,500 HP engines in tandem, driving fixed-pitch contra-rotating propellers.

Several of the speed records set in the 1950s and 1960s by Max Conrad, Sheila Scott, and Geraldine Mock still stand. These pilots did not use custom-built racing airplanes or converted fighters. They flew Cessnas and Pipers, similar to those you might use in your commercial training.

Want to build flight time? Perhaps you could try to beat the record for time aloft of 64 days, 22 hours, 19 minutes, and 5 seconds, set in a Cessna 172 from December 4, 1958 through February 7, 1959 by Robert Timm and John Cook over Nevada. You'd need to stay aloft for at least 1,558.3 hours, which would add about 779 hours to your logbook after you split it with your copilot.

You do not need a high-tech airplane to set a new record, just careful and thorough preflight preparation, accurate navigation, and precise flying skills. Good luck!

 Some performance tables are based on pressure/density altitude.

SURFACE WINDS

At Kitty Hawk, Wilbur and Orville Wright insisted on a measured wind of at least 11 miles per hour before they flew their airplane. A favorable surface wind can significantly shorten takeoff and landing distance. Because surface winds are not always aligned with your runway, you need to determine how much of the wind is acting down the runway and how much is acting across it. This is another instance of resolving a vector into its components.

The **headwind** or **tailwind component** of the wind vector affects the length of the ground run. Headwinds are less beneficial to takeoff distances than tailwinds are detrimental. For instance, in some airplanes a headwind of 10 knots reduces the takeoff distance by approximately 10 percent, but a tailwind of the same amount increases the takeoff distance by 40 percent. These differences vary between airplanes, and also depend on the pilot technique.

In your earlier training you learned that the **crosswind component** acts to push the airplane to the side, and must be compensated for to keep the airplane on the runway. Most airplanes have a maximum demonstrated crosswind component listed in the POH, although this is not an operating limitation. FARs require that all airplanes type-certificated since 1962 have safe ground handling characteristics in 90° crosswinds equal to 20 percent of V_{S0}. For example, if V_{S0} for an airplane is 65 knots, the manufacturer's **demonstrated crosswind component** is 13 knots. Your personal crosswind limit is based on your own skill level in taking off and landing safely in a particular airplane type.

You can easily compute headwind and crosswind components using a wind component chart. When you use the chart, remember that for takeoff or landing, surface wind is reported in magnetic direction, so it corresponds with the runway number. [Figure 12-41]

 Headwind and crosswind components can be found using the wind component chart. See figure 12-41.

SECTION B ■ **Predicting Performance**

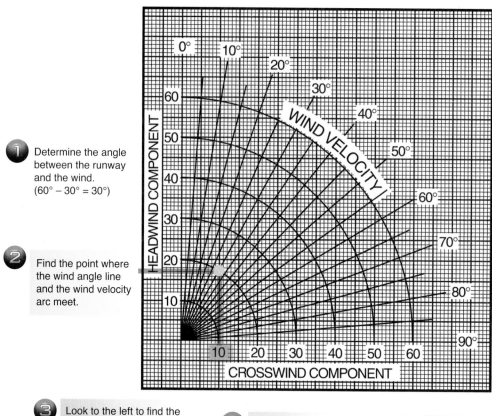

1 Determine the angle between the runway and the wind. (60° − 30° = 30°)

2 Find the point where the wind angle line and the wind velocity arc meet.

3 Look to the left to find the headwind component of 17 knots.

4 Find the crosswind component by following the vertical lines down to the bottom of the chart.

5 The crosswind component is 10 knots.

Figure 12-41. Determine the headwind and crosswind components for a takeoff on Runway 3, with winds from 060° at 20 knots.

JIMMY DOOLITTLE DISCUSSES DENSITY ALTITUDE

Aerial pioneer Jimmy Doolittle had a close encounter with the effects of density altitude during a tour in the 1930s.

"I had left the Hawk in China, so I had to borrow an aircraft to put on the show. This was almost my undoing at a field located at high altitude in the Dutch East Indies.

I borrowed a Hawk from the Dutch air force and went through my aerial routine. To conclude my act, I put the airplane into a power dive, intending to pull out as close to the ground as possible. When I started to pull out, the airplane didn't respond in the thin air as I had expected. It began to 'mush,' and the ground came up too fast. I managed to pull out, but only after my wheels hit the ground rather hard, though without damaging the Hawk. I had not calculated that the Hawk wouldn't perform in thin air as it would have at a lower altitude.

Several Dutch pilots who had seen the near accident congratulated me. The commander of the group said it was 'the most delicate piece of flying' he had ever seen. But I thought it was stupid flying and said so. He smiled and said, 'We knew; we wondered if you would lie about it.'"

That quote is from Doolittle's autobiography, *I Could Never Be So Lucky Again*. Part of maintaining situational awareness is to know what you can reasonably expect from your airplane under existing conditions.

WEIGHT

In order to maintain altitude during flight, lift must equal the effective weight of the airplane and its contents—an increase in weight requires a proportional increase in lift. During cruise, this additional lift is provided by flying at a higher angle of attack, but for takeoff, a heavily loaded airplane must accelerate to a higher speed to generate the required lift. The additional weight also reduces acceleration during the takeoff roll, adding to the total takeoff distance. After liftoff, the heavily loaded airplane climbs more slowly, and its service ceiling is lower. For an airplane to be safe and have adequate performance, it must be operated within weight and balance limitations. Procedures for computing weight and CG location are covered in the next section.

RUNWAY CONDITIONS

Most published takeoff and landing distances are based on a paved, level runway with a smooth, dry surface. However, many runways are *not* level. The gradient, or slope, of the runway is expressed as a percentage. For example, a gradient of 2 percent means the runway height changes 2 feet for each 100 feet of runway length. Positive gradients are uphill, and negative gradients are downhill. A positive gradient increases takeoff distance because the airplane must accelerate uphill. When landing uphill, a positive gradient is beneficial because it helps the airplane slow down and reduces the ground roll. A negative gradient has the opposite effects, shortening takeoff distance and lengthening the landing distance. Runways gradients of 0.3 percent or more are listed in the Chart Supplement. Many larger airplanes incorporate runway slope into their takeoff distance calculations.

 An uphill runway slope increases takeoff distance because the airplane accelerates more slowly.

The surface conditions of the runway affect both takeoff and landing distances. Rolling resistance from a rough or soft surface lengthens your takeoff roll, and the POH might include information to adjust takeoff distances for different runway surfaces. [Figure 12-42]

TAKEOFF DISTANCE
SHORT FIELD

This chart suggests an adjustment for takeoff from a grass runway, but grass runways can be very different. Takeoff distance from the wild turf at a back-country airstrip can be much longer than from the lawn-like grass at a well-groomed airport.

CONDITIONS:
Flaps 10°
2800 RPM, full throttle, mixture set per table prior to brake release
Cowl flaps open
Paved, dry, level runway
Zero wind

NOTES:
1. Short field technique.
2. Landing gear down until obstacles are cleared.
3. Decrease distances 10% for each 9 knots headwind. Increase distances 10% for each 2 knots tailwind (up to 10 knots).
4. For operation on a dry, grass runway, increase distances by 15% of the "ground roll" figure.

MIXTURE SETTINGS	
PRESS ALT.	PPH
S.L.	145
2000	139
4000	133
6000	127
8000	121

WEIGHT LBS	TAKEOFF SPEED KIAS		PRESSURE ALTITUDE FEET	0° C		10° C		20° C		30° C		40° C	
	LIFT OFF	AT 50 FEET		GROUND ROLL FEET	TOTAL FEET TO CLEAR 50-FOOT OBSTACLE	GROUND ROLL FEET	TOTAL FEET TO CLEAR 50-FOOT OBSTACLE	GROUND ROLL FEET	TOTAL FEET TO CLEAR 50-FOOT OBSTACLE	GROUND ROLL FEET	TOTAL FEET TO CLEAR 50-FOOT OBSTACLE	GROUND ROLL FEET	TOTAL FEET TO CLEAR 50-FOOT OBSTACLE

Figure 12-42. Be careful when you interpret and apply the information in performance charts.

During landing, **braking effectiveness** can be a major concern. A dry runway surface allows the brakes to dissipate the maximum amount of energy without skidding the tires, but when the runway is wet, the maximum coefficient of friction between the tires and runway can drop by 30-60 percent. The tires begin to break loose from the runway surface and slide at lower brake application forces, so you must apply the brakes more gently to maximize deceleration and maintain control. The lighter application of brakes means that energy is dissipated more slowly, increasing the length of the landing roll. Obviously, if the ground roll becomes too long, the airplane will run off the end of the runway. An ice-covered runway can reduce friction still more, but perhaps the worst situation is to lose braking effectiveness as a result of **hydroplaning**, which happens when a thin layer of water separates the tires from the runway. Hydroplaning reduces friction even more than smooth, clear ice. [Figure 12-43] When available, ATC furnishes pilots the quality of braking action received from pilots or airport management. The quality of braking action is described by the terms good, fair, poor, nil, or a combination of these terms. When braking action approaches nil, maintaining directional control might become impossible, and a strong crosswind could push the airplane off the side of the runway.

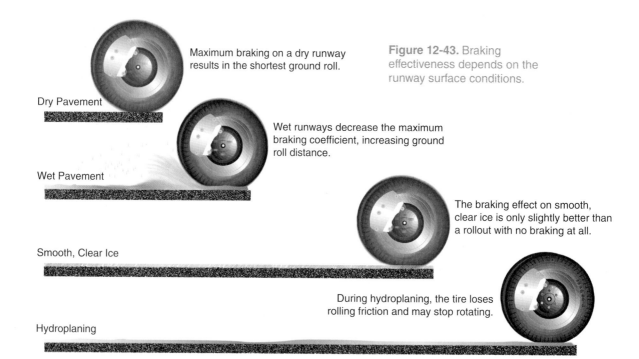

Maximum braking on a dry runway results in the shortest ground roll.

Figure 12-43. Braking effectiveness depends on the runway surface conditions.

Dry Pavement

Wet runways decrease the maximum braking coefficient, increasing ground roll distance.

Wet Pavement

The braking effect on smooth, clear ice is only slightly better than a rollout with no braking at all.

Smooth, Clear Ice

During hydroplaning, the tire loses rolling friction and may stop rotating.

Hydroplaning

Dynamic hydroplaning occurs when there is standing water or slush on the runway about one-tenth of an inch or more in depth. A wedge of water builds up, lifting the tires away from the runway surface. The speed of the airplane, the depth of the water, and the air pressure in the tires are some of the factors that affect dynamic hydroplaning. There is a simple rule of thumb you can use to estimate the minimum speed at which dynamic hydroplaning will occur. Take the square root of the tire pressure and multiply by 8.6 to obtain the hydroplaning groundspeed in knots. For example, with a tire pressure of 30 p.s.i., you could expect hydroplaning at about 47 knots. After hydroplaning has started, it can persist at lower speeds. Viscous hydroplaning can occur on just a thin film of water, not more than one-thousandth of an inch deep, if it covers a smooth surface. Reverted rubber hydroplaning is the result of a prolonged locked-wheel skid, in which reverted rubber acts as a seal between the tire and the runway. Entrapped water is heated to form steam, which supports the tire off the pavement. If you must use a runway where braking effectiveness is poor or nil, be sure the length is adequate and the surface wind is favorable.

THE PILOT'S OPERATING HANDBOOK

According to FARs, you can find your airplane's operating limitations in the approved airplane flight manual (AFM), approved manual materials, markings and placards, or any combination of these. For most airplanes manufactured in the U.S. after March 1, 1979, the **pilot's operating handbook (POH)** is the approved flight manual, and a page in the front of the handbook will contain a statement to that effect. Prior to that date, airplanes under 6,000 pounds were not required to have AFMs, but manufacturers usually provided similar information in Owner's Manuals or Information Manuals. Format and content in these manuals varied widely. Then, the General Aviation Manufacturers Association (GAMA) adopted a standardized format so that each POH provides the same information in the same order. The GAMA framework presents performance charts in a logical order, beginning with general information and flight planning calculations and progressing through takeoff, climb, cruise, descent, and landing. If you fly older airplanes, keep in mind that older manuals might not use the same conventions or units of measure as those in the newer, standardized style.

PERFORMANCE CHARTS

Performance charts are compiled from information gathered during actual flight tests. Because it is impractical to test the airplane under all the conditions portrayed on the performance charts, the engineers evaluate specific flight test results and mathematically derive the remaining data. In developing performance charts, manufacturers must make assumptions about the condition of the airplane. They assume the airplane is in good condition, and that the engine is developing its full rated power. It is prudent to keep in mind that the flight tests are performed by test pilots using average piloting techniques, and manufacturers often use the best results from many repetitions of each test. The performance numbers in the POH are achievable and reliable, but you should always consider your own proficiency, especially if you anticipate operating near the limits of the airplane's stated performance capabilities. If your flying skills are rusty or you have not flown for a long time, you are unlikely to be able to match the performance in the charts. Likewise, the charts were developed using factory-new airplanes, so you should consider the condition of your airplane and allow for an adequate margin of safety.

More sophisticated airplanes often have an assortment of criteria that must be considered when using performance charts. There could be optional flap settings, power settings, or correction factors for different runway conditions, so you must be careful to select the correct chart and pay attention to the conditions under which the chart is valid.

Remember that all performance charts in this section are samples and must never be used for a real airplane. For actual flight planning, you should refer only to the POH for the specific airplane you intend to fly. Performance data can vary significantly, even among airplanes of the same make and model. Although the general use of performance charts should be familiar to you, higher performance airplanes often have charts that employ more variables, more complex formats, or more conditions. This section reviews the use of some basic charts and also presents new material on higher performance equipment.

Tables provide information for a limited list of conditions, and if the conditions for your flight are not listed, you will need to interpolate to find your performance values. Interpolation is the estimation of an unknown value between two known values. For instance, if the performance table only provides information for 2,000 and 4,000 feet, and you need to find a value for an altitude of 3,000 feet, you can find the midpoint between the values provided to estimate the value for 3,000 feet. Similarly, you can use simple proportions to estimate other intermediate values. If information is given for 20°C and 30°C, you can estimate the performance at 28°C by adding 80% of the difference to the value for 20°C.

SECTION B ■ Predicting Performance

Takeoff Ground Roll: Zero

The use of rocket engines to shorten takeoff distances was pioneered in 1941. The concept was first tested using an Ercoupe, a low-wing, two-place light airplane that is still a familiar sight at airports around the country. The success of the Ercoupe experiments led to extensive military use of this technique to assist heavily-loaded airplanes in taking off from limited space. Many bombers, transports, and patrol airplanes were equipped to use a refined version of the system, usually called JATO, for jet-assisted takeoff, or RATO, for rocket-assisted takeoff.

As rocket technology developed through the 1950s, it became possible to use a single, large rocket engine to launch a fully armed fighter from a flatbed trailer and accelerate it to flying speed in a few seconds. The spent rocket was then jettisoned. Although tested successfully, the zero-length launch was never used operationally.

Courtesy USAF Museum

TAKEOFF CHARTS

Takeoff charts usually incorporate compensation for pressure altitude, outside air temperature, airplane weight, and headwind or tailwind component. Some manuals include separate charts for normal and obstacle takeoff distances, two- or three-bladed propellers, various flap settings, or specific pilot techniques, such as short field or maximum effort. To review, start by looking over the sample problem in figure 12-44.

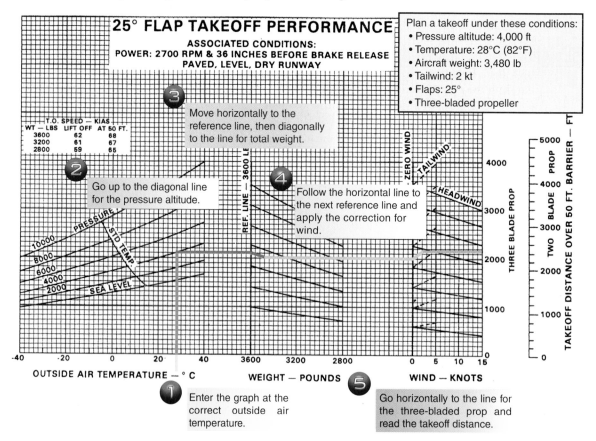

Figure 12-44. This chart provides adjustments for five separate variables.

To estimate takeoff ground roll and distance to clear 50 feet, use the takeoff distance charts. See figure 12-44.

The manuals for larger airplanes often include charts to help you determine additional takeoff and climb performance values. One example is the climb gradient chart, which can be useful when you plan takeoffs over obstacles or terrain in the first few miles after liftoff. [Figure 12-45]

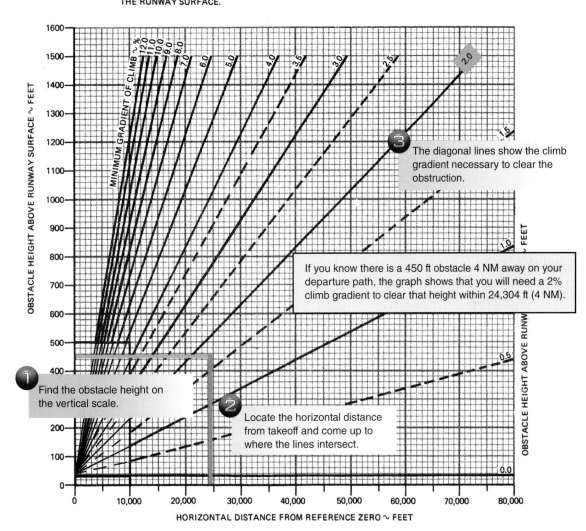

Figure 12-45. Use a graph like this to find the climb gradient necessary to reach a given altitude at a particular distance from takeoff.

CLIMB PERFORMANCE CHARTS

In manuals that follow the GAMA format, you will ordinarily find at least two different climb performance charts. One type shows the maximum rate of climb for various combinations of air temperature, pressure altitude, airplane weight, and airspeed. Another chart depicts the time, fuel, and distance required to climb from one altitude to another based on temperature, airplane weight, and the altitudes concerned.

SECTION B ■ **Predicting Performance**

The maximum rate-of-climb chart is commonly based on the best rate-of-climb airspeed (V_Y) for the airplane at different weights and altitudes. As you climb higher, the indicated airspeed for V_Y decreases. Some manuals offer two rate-of-climb charts, one for takeoff power, the other for maximum continuous power. Climbing at takeoff power can be hard on the engine in many high-performance airplanes. It is important to thoroughly understand the consequences of operating your engine at high power settings for extended periods, especially at climb airspeeds when cooling airflow is reduced. The POH and engine operating handbook provide the appropriate information. [Figure 12-46]

 Temperature, pressure altitude, and total airplane weight are used on charts to estimate maximum rate of climb. See figure 12-46.

SECTION B ■ Predicting Performance

RATE OF CLIMB

MAXIMUM

 4 Remember to comply with the specified conditions when you depart.

CONDITIONS:
Flaps UP
Gear UP
2800 RPM
Full throttle
Mixture set per table
Cowl flaps open

MIXTURE SETTINGS	
PRESS ALT.	PPH
S.L.	138
4000	126
8000	114
12,000	102

Find the maximum rate of climb under these conditions:
• Weight: 3,500 lb
• Air temperature: 20°C
• Pressure altitude: 5,000 ft

 2 Find the column for the air temperature.

 1 Begin by finding the section of the table for the appropriate airplane weight.

WEIGHT LBS	PRESSURE ALTITUDE FEET	CLIMB SPEED KIAS	RATE OF CLIMB - FPM			
			-20°C	0°C	20°C	40°C
3800	S. L.	97	1115	1020	925	830
	2000	95	995	900	810	720
	4000	94	870	785	700	615
	6000	93	750	670	585	505
	8000	91	635	555	475	395
	10,000	90	520	440	365	- - -
	12,000	89	405	330	255	- - -
3500	S. L.	95	1255	1160	1060	960
	2000	94	1125	1035	940	845
	4000	93	1000	910	820	730
	6000	91	870	785	705	620
	8000	90	745	665	585	505
	10,000	89	625	550	470	- - -
	12,000	87	505	430	355	- - -
3200	S. L.	94	1415	1315	1215	1110
	2000	92	1275	1185	1085	990
	4000	91	1140	1050	960	865
	6000	90	1010	920	835	750
	8000	88	875	795	710	630
	10,000	87	745	670	590	- - -
	12,000	86	620	545	470	- - -

3 Interpolate between the values for the pressure altitudes closest to your takeoff pressure altitude.
820 - 705 = 115
(115 ÷ 2) + 705 = 762.5

Figure 12-46. For many solutions, you need to interpolate between the values. This table also provides fuel flow settings for various pressure altitudes.

Using the time, fuel, and distance to climb chart is a two-step process. First, find the values for your cruising altitude, then find and subtract the values for your takeoff altitude. The difference is the time, fuel, and distance to climb from the takeoff elevation to the cruising altitude. Use the same procedure if you need to make an enroute climb from one altitude to another. You can only expect to achieve the published values by adhering to the conditions set forth in the chart, which means precise airspeed control as well as compliance with the configuration and power settings stipulated in the chart notes. Winds will affect the distance required for the climb. Many manuals provide separate charts for different climb speeds. For example, one chart is provided for maximum rate-of-climb data, and another chart supplies information for a normal climb that uses a lower power setting.

The normal climb reduces stress on the engine, provides better engine cooling, and gives you better visibility over the nose. Your passengers will appreciate the lower noise level in the cabin, and there will be less noise on the ground as you fly over. Unless there is some reason to climb at the maximum rate, such as terrain or obstructions in your departure path, you will usually prefer to use the normal climb. [Figure 12-47]

 1 Verify that you have the proper chart and that the specified conditions are met.

TIME, FUEL, AND DISTANCE TO CLIMB

NORMAL CLIMB -108 KIAS

CONDITIONS:
Flaps up
Gear up
2500 RPM
30 In. Hg.
140 PPH fuel flow
Cowl flaps open
Standard temperature

 6 Add 15 lb for engine start, taxi, and takeoff.

Fuel: 58.8 + 15 = 73.8 lb

NOTES:
1. Add 15 pounds of fuel for engine start, taxi and takeoff allowances.
2. Increase time, fuel and distance by 10% for each 8° above standard temperature.
3. Distances shown are based on zero wind.

 5 Add 20% to adjust for the higher-than-standard temperature.

Time: 21 X 1.2 = 25.2 min
Fuel: 49 X 1.2 = 58.8 lb
Distance: 46 X 1.2 = 55.2 NM

Compute the time, fuel and distance required for a normal climb under these conditions:
- Weight: 3,800 lb
- Airport pressure altitude: 4,000 ft
- Cruising altitude: FL200
- Temperature: 16°C above standard

2 Read the time fuel and distance to climb to 20,000 ft at a weight of 3,800 lb.

3 Find the time, fuel and distance to be subtracted for departing an airport at a pressure altitude of 4,000 ft.

WEIGHT LB	PRESSURE ALTITUDE FEET	RATE OF CLIMB FT/M	FROM SEA LEVEL		
			TIME MINUTES	FUEL USED POUNDS	DISTANCE NM
4200	S. L.	740	0	0	0
	4000	720	6	12	10
	8000	700	11	25	21
	12000	630	17	38	34
	16000	565	23	54	48
	20000	470	31	71	66
	24000	340	40	92	91
3800	S.L.	880	0	0	0
	4000	860	4	10	8
	8000	820	9	21	18
	12,000	770	14	33	28
	16,000	700	19	45	40
	20,000	600	25	59	54
	24,000	465	33	76	73

4 Subtract the values for the takeoff altitude from the values for the cruise altitude.

Time: 25 - 4 = 21
Fuel: 59 - 10 = 49
Distance: 54 - 8 = 46

Figure 12-47. Determine the time, fuel, and distance to climb by finding the numbers for your cruising altitude and then subtracting the numbers for your starting altitude. Remember to adjust for nonstandard temperature and add the fuel allowance for start, taxi, and takeoff.

 Climb performance charts usually provide information on time, fuel, and distance required to climb from one altitude to another. Remember to subtract the values for the starting altitude. See figure 12-47.

SECTION B ■ **Predicting Performance**

Because the service ceiling is the altitude where the maximum rate of climb is 100 ft/min, you can often use a maximum rate-of-climb chart to determine the service ceiling for different airplane weights or outside air temperatures. Start with the 100 ft/min rate-of-climb, and work back through the chart to the pressure altitude. [Figure 12-48]

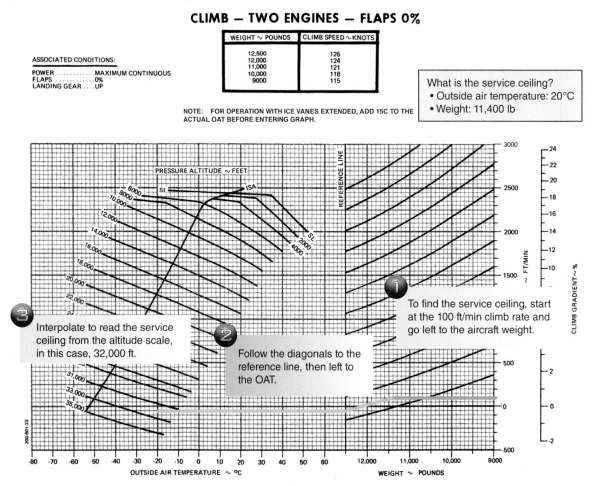

CLIMB — TWO ENGINES — FLAPS 0%

WEIGHT ~ POUNDS	CLIMB SPEED ~ KNOTS
12,500	125
12,000	124
11,000	121
10,000	118
9000	115

ASSOCIATED CONDITIONS:

POWER ....MAXIMUM CONTINUOUS
FLAPS 0%
LANDING GEAR ....UP

NOTE: FOR OPERATION WITH ICE VANES EXTENDED, ADD 15C TO THE ACTUAL OAT BEFORE ENTERING GRAPH.

What is the service ceiling?
• Outside air temperature: 20°C
• Weight: 11,400 lb

③ Interpolate to read the service ceiling from the altitude scale, in this case, 32,000 ft.

② Follow the diagonals to the reference line, then left to the OAT.

① To find the service ceiling, start at the 100 ft/min climb rate and go left to the aircraft weight.

Figure 12-48. You can use a climb chart to determine the service ceiling at different airplane weights and air temperatures.

CRUISE PERFORMANCE CHARTS

The performance of the airplane in cruise depends on many variables. You have direct control over some of them, such as manifold pressure, propeller RPM, and fuel flow settings. You can also exercise indirect control over some of the other variables, for instance, selecting an altitude that provides favorable winds or temperatures. You need a thorough understanding of the effects of each variable on the airplane's overall performance, so you can decide on the best combination for each particular flight. If you increase power to add a couple of knots to your airspeed, will you cut into your fuel reserve? Do the performance penalties of flying the airplane at a lower power setting with a heavy fuel load cancel out the time savings of skipping a fuel stop? The cruise performance charts contain the information you need to answer questions like these. Besides the elements in the performance charts, you also will want to consider less tangible factors, such as the stress on the engine. The effects of high operating temperatures, high manifold pressures, excessively lean mixture settings, and other harsh operating procedures can increase maintenance costs and, in some cases, compromise engine reliability.

As you know, if you maintain the same power settings, you can generally expect higher true airspeeds at higher altitudes. This is due to the reduction in drag as air density decreases. Going faster and farther while using fuel at the same rate is an attractive idea, however, the lower airspeed and high power setting during a long climb can offset the benefit of a high cruising altitude. Always remember to consider the wind direction at altitude, because even a few degrees of wind correction angle or a few knots of headwind can reduce your groundspeed significantly, and winds are typically stronger the higher you fly.

The mixture must be adjusted to compensate for the reduced air density at higher altitudes. Two popular methods of setting the mixture involve using an exhaust gas temperature (EGT) gauge or a fuel flow meter. Always follow the manufacturer's recommendations for leaning, both to avoid possible engine damage and to obtain the fuel consumption values that you determined in your preflight planning. A seemingly minor difference in mixture setting could result in a higher fuel flow rate, or in a lower true airspeed. Either situation could lead to fuel quantity problems on a long flight. Some performance charts distinguish between the mixture settings for best power and best economy. The best economy mixture is a leaner setting that results in lower fuel consumption and higher engine temperatures. Cruise performance charts can be used to determine the true airspeed expected under a particular set of conditions. [Figure 12-49]

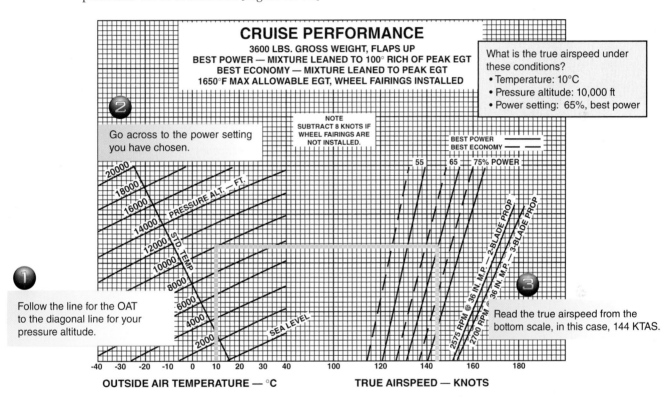

Figure 12-49. The cruise performance chart can help you to understand the effects of altitude and mixture setting on your airspeed.

Range is the distance an airplane can travel with a given amount of fuel, and **endurance** is the length of time the airplane can remain in the air. The range and endurance charts in the POH help you to estimate how far you can go and how long you can remain aloft at various cruise power settings. In most cross-country situations, range is more desirable than endurance, because you will want to maximize the distance traveled per pound of fuel. Endurance might be more important in a holding pattern, or in circumstances where you do not want to arrive at a certain point before a specific time. Examples could include a clearance limit, a landing slot assignment, or when the weather is improving at your destination. Most charts include allowances for normal climb and descent, as well as for fuel reserves. [Figure 12-50] After obtaining a preliminary range from the chart, you must still adjust the result for the effects of any headwind or tailwind.

If you maintain the same engine horsepower, lower temperatures generally reduce your true airspeed and range. Higher temperatures have the opposite effect. Outside air temperatures on cruise charts might include International Standard Atmosphere (ISA) values, as well as colder and warmer temperatures. For instance, categories might specify ISA−20°C, standard day ISA, and ISA+20°C. Both Celsius and Fahrenheit values could be

SECTION B ■ Predicting Performance

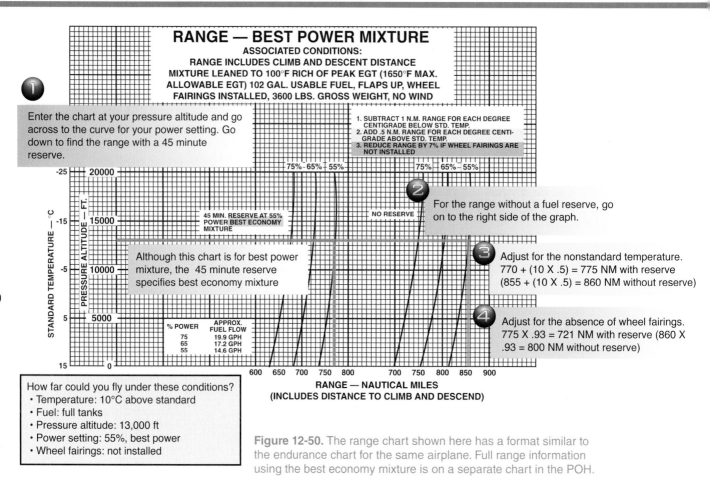

1 Enter the chart at your pressure altitude and go across to the curve for your power setting. Go down to find the range with a 45 minute reserve.

1. SUBTRACT 1 N.M. RANGE FOR EACH DEGREE CENTIGRADE BELOW STD. TEMP.
2. ADD .5 N.M. RANGE FOR EACH DEGREE CENTIGRADE ABOVE STD. TEMP.
3. REDUCE RANGE BY 7% IF WHEEL FAIRINGS ARE NOT INSTALLED

RANGE — BEST POWER MIXTURE
ASSOCIATED CONDITIONS:
RANGE INCLUDES CLIMB AND DESCENT DISTANCE
MIXTURE LEANED TO 100°F RICH OF PEAK EGT (1650°F MAX. ALLOWABLE EGT) 102 GAL. USABLE FUEL, FLAPS UP, WHEEL FAIRINGS INSTALLED, 3600 LBS. GROSS WEIGHT, NO WIND

45 MIN. RESERVE AT 55% POWER BEST ECONOMY MIXTURE

NO RESERVE

Although this chart is for best power mixture, the 45 minute reserve specifies best economy mixture

% POWER	APPROX. FUEL FLOW
75	19.9 GPH
65	17.2 GPH
55	14.6 GPH

2 For the range without a fuel reserve, go on to the right side of the graph.

3 Adjust for the nonstandard temperature. 770 + (10 X .5) = 775 NM with reserve (855 + (10 X .5) = 860 NM without reserve)

4 Adjust for the absence of wheel fairings. 775 X .93 = 721 NM with reserve (860 X .93 = 800 NM without reserve)

RANGE — NAUTICAL MILES
(INCLUDES DISTANCE TO CLIMB AND DESCEND)

How far could you fly under these conditions?
- Temperature: 10°C above standard
- Fuel: full tanks
- Pressure altitude: 13,000 ft
- Power setting: 55%, best power
- Wheel fairings: not installed

Figure 12-50. The range chart shown here has a format similar to the endurance chart for the same airplane. Full range information using the best economy mixture is on a separate chart in the POH.

Endurance: Several Months

An airplane similar to this one should be capable of what the designers call semi-perpetual flight. Operating at altitudes up to 97,000 feet, the Helios converted sunlight into electricity to power its 14 electric motors. During the day, electricity was used to break water down into hydrogen and oxygen, which were recombined in fuel cells to provide power at night. The crewless flying wing will had a longer wingspan than a 747, yet weighed only 2,048 pounds. The Pathfinder, pictured here, is essentially a smaller version of the Helios. It flew to 71,530 feet on solar power in 1997.

There are many possible uses for such airplanes. High altitude scientific research, reconnaissance, communications relay, environmental monitoring, and earth-resource applications are a few likely prospects.

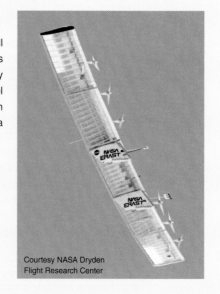

Courtesy NASA Dryden Flight Research Center

included. In addition, temperature figures for some manufacturers might be adjusted for frictional heating of the temperature probe at higher speeds.

 Range, endurance, fuel consumption, true airspeed, and other cruise information can be obtained from cruise performance charts. See figures 12-49 and 12-50.

As discussed in the preceding section, an airplane will realize its maximum range at the airspeed with the greatest ratio of lift to drag (L/D_{max}). Maximum endurance is achieved when using the minimum power necessary to maintain level flight. [Figure 12-51].

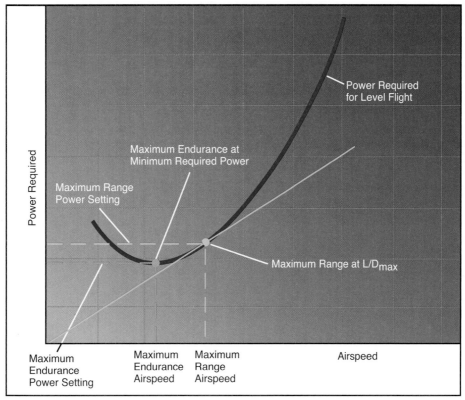

Figure 12-51. On the power- required graph, the maximum endurance power setting is at the lowest point of the curve. A line from the origin of the graph is tangent to the curve at maximum range (L/D_{max}).

The speeds for maximum range and endurance do provide high levels of efficiency, but they are slow compared to normal cruise speeds. Bear in mind that most cruise performance charts do not include range or endurance information for less than 45 percent power, which is far more power than the minimum required for level flight. As previously noted, the airspeed for maximum range is the same as the best glide speed, and the airspeed for maximum endurance is usually about 76 percent of the best glide speed. In many general aviation airplanes, these speeds are very close to the stall speed.

DESCENT CHARTS

Some manufacturers supply charts to help you plan your descent. For a given airspeed and configuration, you can use them to predict the time, fuel, and distance to descend from your cruising altitude to your destination. As with other performance charts, be sure to comply with the conditions specified in the chart. [Figure 12-52]

SECTION B ■ **Predicting Performance**

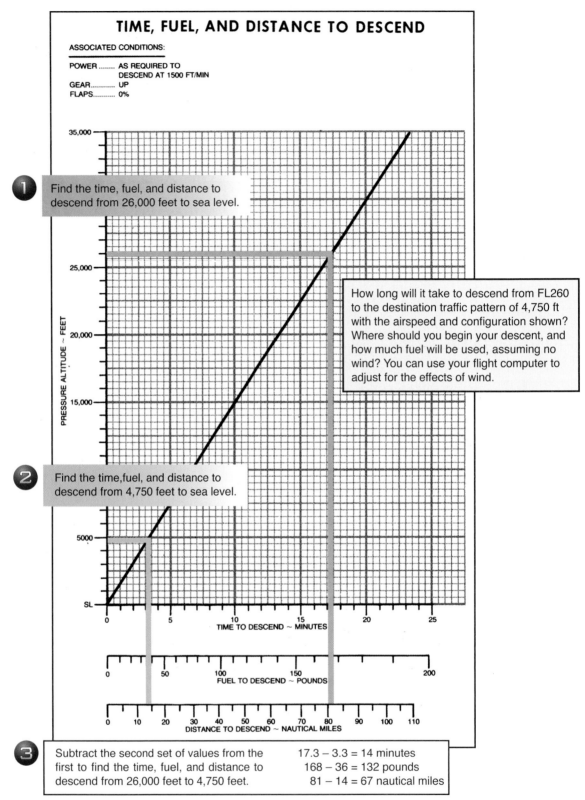

TIME, FUEL, AND DISTANCE TO DESCEND

ASSOCIATED CONDITIONS:

POWER .... AS REQUIRED TO
                 DESCEND AT 1500 FT/MIN
GEAR............ UP
FLAPS........... 0%

1 Find the time, fuel, and distance to descend from 26,000 feet to sea level.

How long will it take to descend from FL260 to the destination traffic pattern of 4,750 ft with the airspeed and configuration shown? Where should you begin your descent, and how much fuel will be used, assuming no wind? You can use your flight computer to adjust for the effects of wind.

2 Find the time, fuel, and distance to descend from 4,750 feet to sea level.

3 Subtract the second set of values from the first to find the time, fuel, and distance to descend from 26,000 feet to 4,750 feet.

17.3 − 3.3 = 14 minutes
168 − 36 = 132 pounds
81 − 14 = 67 nautical miles

Figure 12-52. Your descent is an important part of cross-country planning, especially in a high-performance airplane. After finding the distance you need for descent, use your flight computer to adjust for the effects of wind.

LANDING DISTANCE CHARTS

In many respects, landing distance charts are similar to takeoff distance charts. They normally include compensations for temperature, altitude, airplane weight, and headwind or tailwind component, and most provide the landing distance from a height of 50 feet as well as the length of the ground roll itself. Manufacturers sometimes incorporate other variables into landing charts, such as the configuration of flaps, touchdown speed, use of reverse propeller pitch or reverse thrust, or the amount of runway slope. Separate charts might be supplied for short field or obstacle clearance landing techniques. As with the other charts, be sure to take your own abilities and proficiency into account, and always leave yourself an adequate safety margin. [Figure 12-53]

FAA Use landing charts to estimate landing distances and runway requirements. See figure 12-53.

> What is the ground roll and minimum landing distance over a 50-foot obstacle under these conditions?
> • Pressure altitude: 3,000 ft
> • Temperature: 30°C
> • Wind: 10 kt headwind

LANDING DISTANCE
SHORT FIELD

CONDITIONS:
Flaps 40°
Power off
Maximum braking after touchdown
Paved, dry, level runway
Zero wind

 1 Verify that you will match the conditions on the chart, including landing technique (short field), flap setting, landing weight, and runway conditions.

 2 Find the row and column for your pressure altitude and air temperature.

NOTES:
1. Short field technique.
2. Decrease distances 10% for each 10 knots headwind. Increase distances 10% for each 2.5 knots tailwind (up to 10 knots).
3. For operation on a dry, grass runway, increase distances by 15% of the "ground roll" figure.

WEIGHT LBS	AIR-SPEED AT 50 FEET KIAS	PRESSURE ALTITUDE FEET	0° C		10° C		20° C		30° C		40° C	
			GROUND ROLL FEET	TOTAL FEET TO CLEAR 50-FOOT OBSTACLE	GROUND ROLL FEET	TOTAL FEET TO CLEAR 50-FOOT OBSTACLE	GROUND ROLL FEET	TOTAL FEET TO CLEAR 50-FOOT OBSTACLE	GROUND ROLL FEET	TOTAL FEET TO CLEAR 50-FOOT OBSTACLE	GROUND ROLL FEET	TOTAL FEET TO CLEAR 50-FOOT OBSTACLE
3800	70	S. L.	730	1445	750	1480	780	1520	805	1560	830	1600
		1000	755	1480	780	1520	810	1560	835	1605	860	1645
		2000	780	1520	810	1565	840	1605	870	1650	895	1695
		3000	810	1565	840	1610	870	1660	900	1705	930	1750
		4000	840	1615	870	1660	900	1715	930	1750	965	1800
		5000	870	1665	905	1710	935	1755	965	1805	1000	1855
		6000	905	1715	940	1765	980	1810	1005	1860	1035	1910
		7000	940	1770	975	1815	1015	1865	1045	1920	1075	1970
		8000	975	1820	1010	1870	1050	1925	1085	1980	1120	2035

 3 Read the ground roll and the distance over a 50 foot obstacle. Interpolate for intermediate values as needed.

 4 Apply any necessary correction factors. In this example, subtract 10% for the 10 knots headwind.

900 - 90 = 810 feet ground roll
1,705 - 170 = 1,535 feet over 50 foot obstacle

Figure 12-53. Charts like this assume good piloting technique. Allow an additional margin if your skill might be rusty.

GLIDE DISTANCE

These charts show how far your airplane will glide at the best glide airspeed (L/D_{max}), provided there is no wind. Some manufacturers place this chart in the Performance section and others place it in the Emergency Procedures section. The simplest chart shows maximum glide distance based on height above the terrain. The chart also shows the appropriate airspeed, and provides information on the configuration to be used. The glide ratio also might be included, expressed as a distance in nautical miles per thousand feet of altitude. [Figure 12-54]

SECTION B ■ Predicting Performance

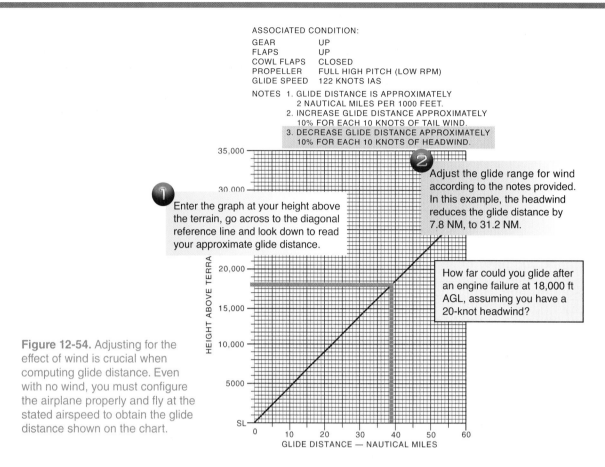

ASSOCIATED CONDITION:
GEAR   UP
FLAPS   UP
COWL FLAPS   CLOSED
PROPELLER   FULL HIGH PITCH (LOW RPM)
GLIDE SPEED   122 KNOTS IAS

NOTES 1. GLIDE DISTANCE IS APPROXIMATELY
          2 NAUTICAL MILES PER 1000 FEET.
       2. INCREASE GLIDE DISTANCE APPROXIMATELY
          10% FOR EACH 10 KNOTS OF TAIL WIND.
       3. DECREASE GLIDE DISTANCE APPROXIMATELY
          10% FOR EACH 10 KNOTS OF HEADWIND.

1 Enter the graph at your height above the terrain, go across to the diagonal reference line and look down to read your approximate glide distance.

2 Adjust the glide range for wind according to the notes provided. In this example, the headwind reduces the glide distance by 7.8 NM, to 31.2 NM.

How far could you glide after an engine failure at 18,000 ft AGL, assuming you have a 20-knot headwind?

Figure 12-54. Adjusting for the effect of wind is crucial when computing glide distance. Even with no wind, you must configure the airplane properly and fly at the stated airspeed to obtain the glide distance shown on the chart.

More detailed charts incorporate air temperature and pressure altitude, and are similar in use to the time-to-climb charts. Begin by calculating the glide range from your current density altitude to sea level, and then subtract the distance that would be covered from the height of the terrain to sea level. [Figure 12-55]

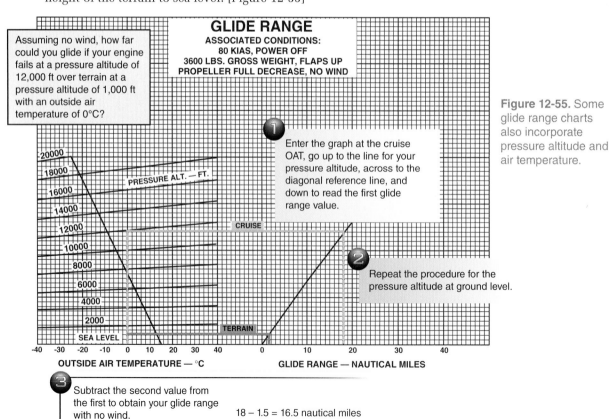

GLIDE RANGE
ASSOCIATED CONDITIONS:
80 KIAS, POWER OFF
3600 LBS. GROSS WEIGHT, FLAPS UP
PROPELLER FULL DECREASE, NO WIND

Assuming no wind, how far could you glide if your engine fails at a pressure altitude of 12,000 ft over terrain at a pressure altitude of 1,000 ft with an outside air temperature of 0°C?

1 Enter the graph at the cruise OAT, go up to the line for your pressure altitude, across to the diagonal reference line, and down to read the first glide range value.

2 Repeat the procedure for the pressure altitude at ground level.

3 Subtract the second value from the first to obtain your glide range with no wind.

18 – 1.5 = 16.5 nautical miles

Figure 12-55. Some glide range charts also incorporate pressure altitude and air temperature.

STALL SPEEDS

As discussed in the previous section, stall speed varies with factors such as weight, CG location, configuration, and bank angle. Because of the change in stall speed due to weight, many airplane flight manuals specify a higher approach speed when the airplane is heavily loaded. With power on, most airplanes stall at a lower airspeed because of the airflow over the wings induced by the propeller. Manufacturers provide charts to help you estimate the stall speed for various conditions. [Figure 12-56]

 Stall speed charts present the stall speeds that can be expected in various configurations and at different bank angles. See figure 12-56.

STALL SPEEDS

To use these tables, find the row for the appropriate flap setting and look across to the angle of bank. Interpolate to find stall speeds for intermediate CG locations. For example, if the CG is halfway between the limits, the stall speed with 40° of flaps and a bank angle of 45° is 60 KIAS.

 Find the stall speed at the most rearward CG for the conditions in question.

MOST REARWARD CENTER OF GRAVITY

WEIGHT LBS	FLAP SETTING	ANGLE OF BANK							
		0°		30°		45°		60°	
		KIAS	KCAS	KIAS	KCAS	KIAS	KCAS	KIAS	KCAS
3850	Up	64	65	69	70	76	77	91	92
	10°	62	64	67	69	74	76	88	91
	40°	46	56	49	60	55	67	65	79

 Find the corresponding stall speed for the forward CG limit.

MOST FORWARD CENTER OF GRAVITY

WEIGHT LBS	FLAP SETTING	ANGLE OF BANK							
		0°		30°		45°		60°	
		KIAS	KCAS	KIAS	KCAS	KIAS	KCAS	KIAS	KCAS
3850	Up	68	69	73	74	81	82	96	98
	10°	67	68	72	73	80	81	95	96
	40°	55	61	59	66	65	73	78	86

 Interpolate to find the stall speed for a midrange CG under those conditions.
65 − 55 = 10
10 ÷ 2 = 5
55 + 5 = 60 KIAS

Figure 12-56. Stall speed changes depending on the location of the CG. A forward CG increases the stall speed because the wings must fly at a higher angle of attack to compensate for the tail-down force that contributes to stability.

SECTION B ■ **Predicting Performance**

SUMMARY CHECKLIST

✓ Atmospheric properties such as temperature, pressure, and humidity have predictable effects on airplane performance.

✓ Density altitude affects all aspects of airplane performance, but the effects are most noticeable during takeoff and climb.

✓ Your own proficiency must be taken into account when using performance charts.

✓ Headwind and crosswind components can be determined by using a wind component chart.

✓ Demonstrated crosswind capability must be at least 20 percent of V_{S0}.

✓ Increasing the weight of your airplane increases takeoff and landing distances.

✓ Wet or icy runways decrease braking effectiveness and increase landing distances. Braking effectiveness is reported as good, fair, poor, or nil, or some combination of these terms.

✓ Hydroplaning is when the tires are separated from the runway surface by a thin layer of water. Hydroplaning not only increases stopping distances, it can also lead to complete loss of airplane control.

✓ Operating limitations are contained in the approved flight manual (AFM), approved manual materials, markings and placards, or any combination of these. For most modern airplanes, the pilot's operating handbook (POH) is the approved flight manual.

✓ Even small tailwind components can increase takeoff or landing distances significantly. A tailwind increases your takeoff or landing distance much more than the same headwind reduces it. Climb and descent gradients are similarly affected.

✓ Range is the distance the airplane can travel on a given amount of fuel. Endurance is the amount of time an airplane can remain airborne on a given amount of fuel. The airspeeds for maximum range and endurance usually are near the airplane's stall speed.

✓ Because of the change in stall speed, airplanes are usually flown at a higher approach speed when they are heavily loaded.

KEY TERMS

Density Altitude	Braking Effectiveness
Headwind Component	Hydroplaning
Tailwind Component	Pilot's Operating Handbook (POH)
Crosswind Component	Range
Demonstrated Crosswind Component	Endurance

QUESTIONS

1. If the stall speed of your airplane in its landing configuration (V_{S0}) is 55 knots, what is the minimum demonstrated crosswind component?

2. True/False. All other factors being equal, an increase in density altitude causes your airplane's engine to produce more horsepower.

3. With very high relative humidity, how much of a reduction in engine output can be expected?
   A. 7 percent
   B. 12 percent
   C. 18 percent

Use the accompanying takeoff distance chart to answer questions 4 and 5.

TAKEOFF DISTANCE
SHORT FIELD

CONDITIONS:
Flaps 15°
2750 RPM, 37 In. Hg., and fuel flow set at 210 PPH prior to brake release
Paved, dry, level runway
Cowl flaps open
Zero wind

NOTES:
1. Short field technique.
2. Decrease distances 10% for each 10 knots headwind. Increase distances by 10% for each 2 knots (up to 10 knots) for a tailwind.
3. For operation on a dry, grass runway, increase distances by 15% of the "ground roll" figure.

| WEIGHT LBS | TAKEOFF SPEED KIAS | | PRESSURE ALTITUDE FEET | 0° C | | 10° C | | 20° C | | 30° C | | 40° C | |
	LIFT OFF	AT 50 FEET		GROUND ROLL FEET	TOTAL FEET TO CLEAR 50-FOOT OBSTACLE	GROUND ROLL FEET	TOTAL FEET TO CLEAR 50-FOOT OBSTACLE	GROUND ROLL FEET	TOTAL FEET TO CLEAR 50-FOOT OBSTACLE	GROUND ROLL FEET	TOTAL FEET TO CLEAR 50-FOOT OBSTACLE	GROUND ROLL FEET	TOTAL FEET TO CLEAR 50-FOOT OBSTACLE
4100	68	74	S. L.	1115	1845	1215	2015	1325	2210	1450	2425	1580	2675
			1000	1185	1945	1290	2125	1410	2330	1535	2565	1680	2830
			2000	1255	2055	1370	2250	1495	2465	1635	2715	1785	2995
			3000	1335	2170	1460	2380	1595	2610	1740	2875	1905	3180
			4000	1420	2295	1555	2520	1695	2770	1855	3050	2030	3380
			5000	1515	2430	1655	2670	1810	2935	1980	3240	2165	3590
			6000	1615	2580	1765	2830	1930	3120	2110	3445	2310	3825
			7000	1725	2735	1885	3005	2060	3315	2255	3665	2470	4080
			8000	1840	2910	2015	3200	2205	3530	2410	3905	2645	4355

4. What is the minimum distance to take off and climb to an altitude of 50 feet, if the pressure altitude is 5,500 feet, the air temperature is 30°C, the total aircraft weight is 4,100 pounds, and you have a 10 knot headwind?

5. What is the minimum ground roll for takeoff from a dry, grass runway at a pressure altitude of 3,000 feet and an air temperature of 25°C, with a 5 knot tailwind? The takeoff weight is 4,100 pounds.

6. True/False. If you drained 120 pounds of fuel from the airplane in question 5, the takeoff roll would be shorter.

Use the accompanying climb performance charts to answer questions 7, 8, and 9.

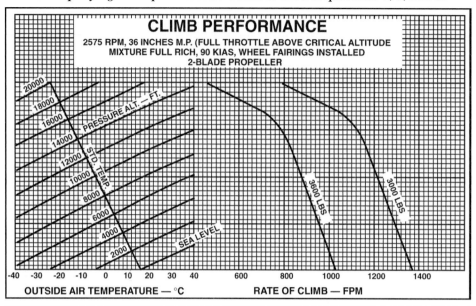

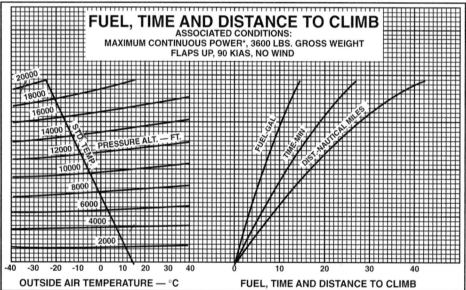

7.   What is the maximum rate of climb for a pressure altitude of 4,000 feet, an air temperature of 10°C, and an aircraft weight of 3,600 pounds?
     A.   1,010 ft/min.
     B.   1,110 ft/min.
     C.   1,190 ft/min.

8.   How much fuel would be required for a normal climb from an airport at a pressure altitude of 2,000 feet to a pressure altitude of 14,000 feet? The air temperature at ground level is 25°C, the temperature at 14,000 feet is −5°C, and the airplane weight is 3,600 pounds.
     A.   7 gallons
     B.   8 gallons
     C.   9 gallons

9.   How much time would it take to climb from a pressure altitude of 4,000 feet (temperature 15°C) to an altitude of 20,000 feet (temperature −30°C)? The airplane weight is 3,600 pounds.
     A.   21 minutes
     B.   26 minutes
     C.   27 minutes

SECTION B ■ Predicting Performance

Use the accompanying cruise performance chart to answer questions 10 and 11.

CRUISE PERFORMANCE

CONDITIONS:
4400 pounds
Cowl flaps closed
Best economy mixture setting

NOTE
Some of the power settings listed might not be obtainable, but are provided to aid interpolation.

RPM	MP	CRUISE PERFORMANCE--Pressure Altitude 18,000 ft								
		20°C BELOW STANDARD TEMP -41°C			STANDARD TEMP -21°C			20° ABOVE STANDARD TEMP -1°C		
		% BHP	KTAS	PPH	% BHP	KTAS	PPH	% BHP	KTAS	PPH
2500	30	81	198	118	77	198	111	72	197	104
	28	76	193	110	72	193	104	67	192	98
	26	70	186	102	66	186	96	62	184	91
	24	64	179	93	60	178	89	56	175	86
	22	57	170	86	54	168	83	50	164	80
2400	31.5	81	198	117	77	198	111	72	197	104
	30	77	194	112	73	194	105	68	193	99
	28	72	188	104	68	188	99	64	187	93
	26	66	182	96	62	181	91	59	179	87
	24	60	174	89	57	173	85	53	169	82
2300	33	81	197	116	76	197	110	71	196	103
	31	76	192	110	71	192	103	67	191	97
	29	70	187	102	66	186	97	62	185	91
	27	65	181	95	61	180	90	58	177	86
	25	60	173	88	56	172	84	53	168	80
2200	34.5	79	196	115	75	196	108	70	195	102
	33	76	193	110	72	192	104	67	192	98
	31	71	188	104	67	187	98	63	186	92
	29	66	182	97	63	181	91	59	179	87
	27	61	176	90	58	174	86	54	171	82
	25	56	168	83	53	165	80	49	161	76
2100	34.5	75	191	108	70	191	102	66	190	96
	33	72	188	104	68	188	98	63	186	92
	31	67	183	98	63	182	92	59	180	87
	29	62	177	91	59	176	87	55	173	83
	27	57	170	85	54	168	81	51	164	77
	25	52	161	79	49	158	75	46	153	72

10. What is the rate of fuel consumption in cruise at a pressure altitude of 18,000 feet, with a manifold pressure of 28 inches, a propeller RPM of 2,400, and an air temperature of −31°C? The airplane weight is 4,400 pounds.
    A. 99 pounds per hour
    B. 101.5 pounds per hour
    C. 188 pounds per hour

11. What is the true airspeed under the conditions specified in question 10?

SECTION B ▪ Predicting Performance

12. True/False. A runway gradient of more than 0.3 percent is listed in the airport information in the Chart Supplement.

Use the accompanying landing distance chart to answer questions 13 and 14.

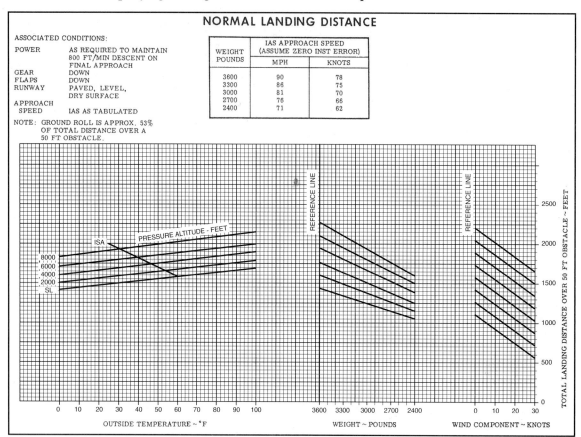

NORMAL LANDING DISTANCE

ASSOCIATED CONDITIONS:

POWER   AS REQUIRED TO MAINTAIN
               800 FT/MIN DESCENT ON
               FINAL APPROACH
GEAR   DOWN
FLAPS   DOWN
RUNWAY   PAVED, LEVEL,
               DRY SURFACE
APPROACH
SPEED   IAS AS TABULATED

NOTE: GROUND ROLL IS APPROX. 53%
      OF TOTAL DISTANCE OVER A
      50 FT OBSTACLE.

WEIGHT POUNDS	IAS APPROACH SPEED (ASSUME ZERO INST ERROR)	
	MPH	KNOTS
3600	90	78
3300	86	75
3000	81	70
2700	76	66
2400	71	62

13. For a weight of 2,800 pounds, what indicated approach speed should you use?

14. Determine the ground roll distance for this airplane at an air temperature of 42°F, a pressure altitude of 6,000 feet, an airplane weight of 3,100 pounds, and a headwind component of 6 knots?
    A. 800 feet
    B. 1,400 feet
    C. 1,600 feet

SECTION C
Controlling Weight and Balance

As a private pilot, you became aware of the importance of weight and balance control and learned how to determine the loading conditions of an airplane using a variety of methods. Although concepts and techniques for performing weight and balance computations are similar for commercial flights, last minute load changes might require you to quickly amend your original loading computations. In addition, you will probably fly larger airplanes that have a greater variety of loading options than the airplanes you have been flying. To conduct safe and efficient flights, you should thoroughly understand the effects of various weight and balance conditions, as well as the terminology and techniques provided by manufacturers for weight and balance control.

WEIGHT AND BALANCE LIMITATIONS

As discussed earlier, the weight and distribution of items carried in an airplane has a tremendous effect on aerodynamic stability and control, as well as overall performance. One of your responsibilities as pilot in command is to confirm that the loading conditions of your airplane are within allowable limits before beginning a flight. These limits are established by the aircraft manufacturer and have been demonstrated to the FAA to meet airworthiness certification standards. When loaded within these limits, and under normal operating conditions, the airplane will be stable and controllable throughout the flight envelope. In addition, the performance values obtained from the POH will enable you to plan your flight with sufficient accuracy to help ensure safety. On the other hand, if you fly an improperly loaded airplane, safety and performance will be compromised in many ways. [Figure 12-58]

EFFECTS OF EXCESSIVE AIRPLANE WEIGHT
— Higher takeoff speed and longer takeoff run.
— Reduced rate and angle of climb.
— Lower maximum altitude.
— Shorter range and endurance.
— Reduced cruising speed and maneuverability.
— Higher stalling speeds.
— Higher landing speed and longer landing roll.

Figure 12-58. Overloading an airplane adversely affects performance.

MAXIMUM WEIGHT LIMITS

As you know, you must maintain the total, or gross, weight of an airplane at or below maximum limits for safe operations. These weight limits are established to maintain the structural integrity of the airframe up to the limit load factors. For low-powered airplanes, the maximum weight limit is specified as **maximum weight**, maximum certificated weight, or maximum gross weight. For other airplanes, the manufacturer designates maximum weight limits for various stages of flight and ground operations. [Figure 12-59]

MAXIMUM BAGGAGE
200 LBS.
NO HEAVY OBJECTS
ON HAT SHELF

Figure 12-59. Weight limits for specific areas in the airplane such as baggage or cargo compartments are typically placarded to indicate the limitations. These weight limits help prevent damage to the airframe structure from high G-loads.

SECTION C ■ Controlling Weight and Balance

Many high-performance airplanes have a **maximum ramp weight**, which is the maximum amount the airplane can weigh while on the ramp or during taxi. This weight limit is higher than the maximum weight allowed for takeoff to provide an allowance for the amount of fuel used from engine start until takeoff. Another term for the same limitation is maximum taxi weight. Manufacturers might also specify a different **maximum weight for takeoff** and a **maximum landing weight**. For these limitations, the manufacturer has determined that the total weight of the airplane permitted for flight might cause structural load limits to be exceeded during takeoff or landing. When maximum takeoff and landing weights are designated, the amount of fuel consumed during flight must be adequate to reduce the total weight of the airplane to the maximum landing weight before touchdown. For smaller airplanes, the difference between these weight limits is usually only a few pounds. If an emergency requires you to land immediately after takeoff, these airplanes have adequate structural strength for a safe landing. However, you should advise maintenance personnel of the overweight landing occurrence, because the manufacturer generally requires special inspections to check for any damage caused by the landing. Along with landing weight considerations, you must also verify that your airplane weight is within the strength capacity of runways that you plan to use. Runway weight capacities are listed in the *Chart Supplement*, according to the type of landing gear on the airplane. [Figure 12-60]

```
BISMARCK MUNI    (BIS)    3 SE    UTC−6(−5DT)    N46°46.44' W100°44.87'          TWIN CITIES
   1677    B    S4    FUEL  100LL, JET A    OX 1, 2    ARFF Index B               H−1D, L−10E
   RWY 13−31: H8794X150 (ASPH−PFC)    S−117, D−153, DT−252    HIRL                     IAP
     RWY 13: MALS. VASI(V4L)—GA 3.0° TCH 54'. Pole.        RWY 31: MALSR.
   RWY 03−21: H5107X75 (ASPH)    S−30, D−45    MIRL
     RWY 03: PAPI(P4L)—GA 3.0° TCH 20'.        RWY 21: PAPI(P4L)—GA 3.0° TCH 20'. Pole.
   RWY 17−35: H4009X100 (ASPH)    S−12.5, D−30    MIRL    0.7% up N
     RWY 35: Pole.
```

Runway 13-31 at Bismarck Municipal can support 153,000 pounds when the airplane has dual-wheel landing gear.

Other landing gear configuration types shown here include:
S—Single-wheel and
DT—Dual-tandem.

Figure 12-60. You can find runway weight capacities in the *Chart Supplement*, which indicates weight limits according to the type of landing gear on the airplane.

Weight — Before You Land

To prevent structural damage, it is important to verify that an airplane is at or below its maximum landing weight before touchdown. An example of the effects of landing a heavy airplane occurred when Scott Crossfield had to make an emergency landing with the North American X-15 rocket plane. As a result of an engine explosion and fire, Mr. Crossfield had to abort the flight and attempt to land with a heavy fuel load. Although the airplane design was adequate to handle the extra weight, as the nose gear touched down, the X-15 broke into two pieces at about the midsection. Later, it was discovered that a flaw in the nose gear design prevented it from absorbing the landing shock. When the nose gear touched down, nearly the entire nose gear landing load was transferred into the airframe structure. When the nose gear design was corrected, the airplane was repaired and used in further research into the effects of high speed, high altitude flight.

Courtesy of NASA Dryden Flight Research Center

Maximum weight values might be established to prevent structural damage, but might also be imposed to meet various performance requirements. For example, when operating on a short runway, the maximum takeoff and landing weights might need to be reduced to provide adequate performance for the available runway length. Other performance considerations include the effects of density altitude, wind, and the mechanical condition of the airplane during takeoff and landing. For a multi-engine airplane to meet minimum climb performance requirements if an engine fails, the maximum takeoff weight might need to be limited. Maximum weights established for performance reasons are commonly referred to as operational weight restrictions. If the maximum weight is limited for structural load considerations, it is generally referred to as a design weight limit. You can find operational weight restrictions in the POH. [Figure 12-61]

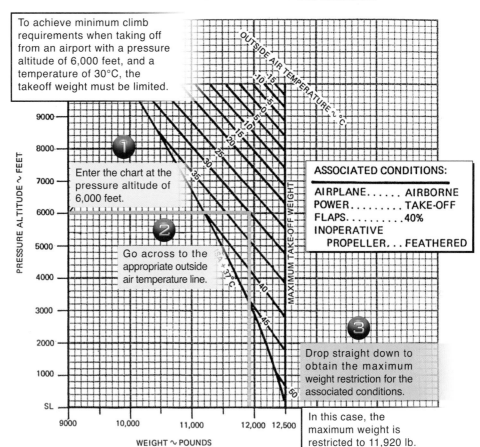

TAKE-OFF WEIGHT — FLAPS 40%
TO MEET FAR 25 TAKE-OFF CLIMB REQUIREMENTS

To achieve minimum climb requirements when taking off from an airport with a pressure altitude of 6,000 feet, and a temperature of 30°C, the takeoff weight must be limited.

Enter the chart at the pressure altitude of 6,000 feet.

Go across to the appropriate outside air temperature line.

ASSOCIATED CONDITIONS:

AIRPLANE...... AIRBORNE
POWER......... TAKE-OFF
FLAPS..........40%
INOPERATIVE
   PROPELLER...FEATHERED

Drop straight down to obtain the maximum weight restriction for the associated conditions.

In this case, the maximum weight is restricted to 11,920 lb.

Figure 12-61. This chart provides maximum takeoff weight restrictions based on pressure altitude and air temperature for a twin-engine turboprop airplane.

Some airplanes also have a **maximum zero fuel weight** limit, which is the maximum amount the airplane can weigh without usable fuel. This limit essentially establishes the maximum weight that can be carried in the fuselage. The wings of an airplane can support only a limited load before structural damage or failure occurs. In larger airplanes, the distribution of the load along the wingspan is often critically important, and you need to limit the weight of passengers and baggage even when the airplane is below its maximum takeoff weight. In airplanes that have a maximum zero-fuel weight, the structure is designed to support a specific amount of the useful load in the fuselage, and the rest as fuel. The weight of fuel in the wings safely spreads the additional load spanwise to the outer wing panels. If too much weight is concentrated in the fuselage, flight loads from maneuvering or turbulence could cause structural damage or failure. To determine zero fuel weight, you simply subtract the weight of the usable fuel on board the airplane from the total weight. If the zero fuel weight is greater than the maximum zero fuel weight limit, you must reduce the load in the fuselage. [Figure 12-62]

Figure 12-62. When weight is properly distributed between the fuselage and wings, the wings' maximum load limits will not be exceeded, provided you operate in normal flight conditions.

Fuselage Weight

CENTER OF GRAVITY LIMITS

Although it is important to stay within weight limits, you must also keep the **center of gravity** (CG) within the allowable range. The manufacturer establishes the CG range by designating the forward and aft CG limits, expressed as distances from the **reference datum**. The reference datum, as you recall, is an imaginary vertical plane from which longitudinal measurements are made. Given normal flight conditions, if you load your airplane within the CG range, the longitudinal stability and control of the airplane will be satisfactory. However, loading the airplane beyond the CG limits affects control and stability.

To understand the effects of CG position, think about the basic aerodynamic forces acting on the airplane. When the wings produce lift, the force is considered to act through a region called the center of pressure. To increase longitudinal stability and improve stall characteristics, the center of gravity is usually located ahead of the center of pressure. If The relative position of the CG and the center of pressure cause the nose to tend to pitch down. A **moment**, as you recall, is the product of weight, which is a force, times a distance or arm. Although this nose-down pitching moment is a desirable design characteristic, it creates an unbalanced force. To provide balance, the tail produces a downward force to counteract the nose-down tendency. Loading can place the CG at different distances from the center of pressure, so the tail-down force changes with the CG position. The relationship between the CG location and tail-down force affects performance and flight characteristics.

FORWARD CG EFFECTS

Longitudinal stability increases as the CG moves toward the forward CG limit. With the CG at the forward limit, the airplane is more stable because of the balance between the CG and the tail-down force. If the nose pitches downward, the angle of attack on the tail increases to create a greater tail-down force, which causes the nose to rise. On the other hand, if the nose pitches upward, the angle of attack on the tail decreases, resulting in a reduction in tail-down force, causing the nose to drop. However, as the airplane becomes more stable, its controllability decreases. Because the tail is exerting a greater force to maintain the stability of the airplane, it takes more effort for you to move the horizontal control surface, and the surface must deflect further to cause a pitch change. If the CG is located ahead of the forward CG limit, at low airspeed full deflection of the control surface might not exert enough force to sufficiently raise the nose. This could be a problem during landing because you might not be able to raise the nose to flare, and the nosewheel might strike the runway before the main gear, causing damage.

A forward CG also affects efficiency, because tail-down force adds to the apparent weight of the airplane. To generate the additional lift required to support that weight, you fly the airplane at a higher angle of attack. The additional lift creates more induced drag, causing small reductions in takeoff and climb performance, cruise speed, range, ceiling, and fuel efficiency. The higher angle of attack brings the wing closer to its stalling angle of attack, so there is less margin when operating at low airspeeds. [Figure 12-63]

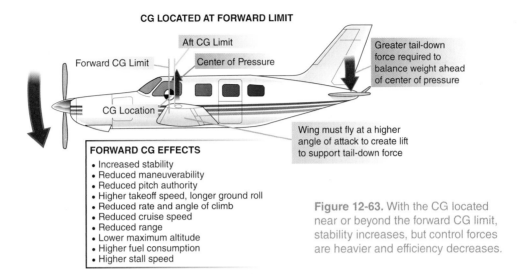

CG LOCATED AT FORWARD LIMIT

Aft CG Limit

Forward CG Limit

Center of Pressure

CG Location

Greater tail-down force required to balance weight ahead of center of pressure

Wing must fly at a higher angle of attack to create lift to support tail-down force

FORWARD CG EFFECTS
- Increased stability
- Reduced maneuverability
- Reduced pitch authority
- Higher takeoff speed, longer ground roll
- Reduced rate and angle of climb
- Reduced cruise speed
- Reduced range
- Lower maximum altitude
- Higher fuel consumption
- Higher stall speed

Figure 12-63. With the CG located near or beyond the forward CG limit, stability increases, but control forces are heavier and efficiency decreases.

AFT CG EFFECTS

When the CG of an airplane is located at the aft limit, the amount of tail-down force required decreases because the CG is located closer to the center of pressure. This causes the horizontal control surface to become more effective. However, with the increased control responsiveness, it might be possible for you to over-control the airplane. In addition, the airplane tends to pitch up more easily due to the aft CG position, which could cause an inadvertent stall. If the CG is located behind the aft limit, it might be difficult or impossible to recover from a stall. Spins also are more dangerous with an aft CG, since the spin will tend to be flat, making recovery difficult or impossible. However, when the CG is located at the aft limit, there is a slight increase in TAS and fuel efficiency due to the reduction of the tail-down force. If the CG is located near or aft of the center of pressure, the airplane is likely to be unstable in pitch. [Figure 12-64]

 When an airplane is loaded with the CG near the aft limit, it tends to become unstable about the lateral axis.

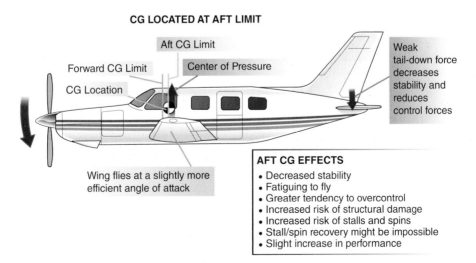

CG LOCATED AT AFT LIMIT

Aft CG Limit

Forward CG Limit

Center of Pressure

CG Location

Weak tail-down force decreases stability and reduces control forces

Wing flies at a slightly more efficient angle of attack

AFT CG EFFECTS
- Decreased stability
- Fatiguing to fly
- Greater tendency to overcontrol
- Increased risk of structural damage
- Increased risk of stalls and spins
- Stall/spin recovery might be impossible
- Slight increase in performance

Figure 12-64. A CG that is located aft of limits creates greater hazards than a CG located beyond forward limits. For the safest condition, fly with the CG located near the center of the CG range.

SECTION C ■ Controlling Weight and Balance

Loading the Big Rigs

The CG location in transport airplanes is usually expressed in terms of the percentage of mean aerodynamic chord (% MAC). As you know, a chord is the distance from the leading edge to the trailing edge of the wing, and on a tapered wing this distance varies from root to tip. The mean aerodynamic chord is the chord drawn through the geometric center of the planform of one wing. [Figure A] It is a convenient reference for weight and balance as well as aerodynamic purposes. The leading edge of the mean aerodynamic chord (LEMAC) is 0% MAC, and the trailing edge (TEMAC) is 100% MAC. The CG range typically falls between 15% MAC and 37% MAC.

Because transport airplanes have a relatively large CG range, control pressures can vary significantly even when the airplane is loaded within the approved CG envelope. To help compensate, the pitch trim is adjusted on the ground before takeoff according to the computed CG location. With the CG located toward the forward limit, more nose-up trim is set than when the CG is toward the aft limit. The longitudinal trim on most large airplanes is controlled by changing the angle of the horizontal stabilizer [Figure B], but at least one type of airplane moves the whole empennage.

B

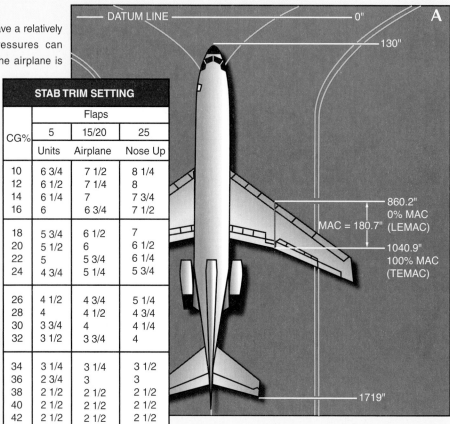

A

DATUM LINE — 0"
130"
860.2"
0% MAC
(LEMAC)
MAC = 180.7"
1040.9"
100% MAC
(TEMAC)
1719"

STAB TRIM SETTING			
	Flaps		
CG%	5	15/20	25
	Units	Airplane	Nose Up
10	6 3/4	7 1/2	8 1/4
12	6 1/2	7 1/4	8
14	6 1/4	7	7 3/4
16	6	6 3/4	7 1/2
18	5 3/4	6 1/2	7
20	5 1/2	6	6 1/2
22	5	5 3/4	6 1/4
24	4 3/4	5 1/4	5 3/4
26	4 1/2	4 3/4	5 1/4
28	4	4 1/2	4 3/4
30	3 3/4	4	4 1/4
32	3 1/2	3 3/4	4
34	3 1/4	3 1/4	3 1/2
36	2 3/4	3	3
38	2 1/2	2 1/2	2 1/2
40	2 1/2	2 1/2	2 1/2
42	2 1/2	2 1/2	2 1/2

LATERAL CG EFFECTS

It is generally easier to maintain lateral weight and balance control because of the symmetry between the left and right side of the airplane. The CG can shift laterally if fuel is unevenly distributed between left and right fuel tanks, or if baggage weight is not distributed evenly between wing lockers. This causes wing heaviness. You can use the ailerons to raise the heavy wing, but by deflecting the ailerons, you increase drag, which causes a reduction in cruise speed, range, and endurance. To prevent the lateral imbalance, use fuel from left and right side fuel tanks simultaneously or alternate between the tanks at regular intervals.

WEIGHT AND BALANCE DOCUMENTS

To determine the weight and balance limitations and loading conditions of an airplane, you need to be familiar with various weight and balance documents. These include the **weight and balance report** and **equipment list**. A weight and balance report is initially prepared by the manufacturer and is maintained by the airplane owner or operator. To meet airworthiness requirements, the report must be in the airplane anytime it is flown. Equipment lists are generally considered to be part of a weight and balance report, and are used to inventory the weight and location of standard and optional equipment installed in the airplane.

WEIGHT AND BALANCE REPORT

A weight and balance report is required for all airplanes, and can appear in a variety of formats. For airplanes that are required to have a POH, the report is kept in the handbook. For these

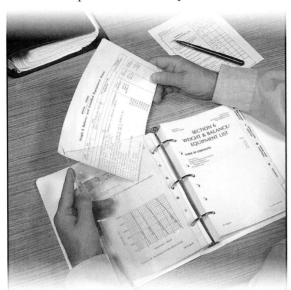

airplanes, the POH contains charts, graphs, or tables for determining loading conditions. The POH usually includes sample problems to demonstrate how to perform weight and balance computations. Remember that the sample problems provide weight and balance values for a hypothetical airplane. Do not use these values for performing actual load computations. [Figure 12-65]

Figure 12-65. For airplanes requiring a POH, the weight and balance report for that specific airplane is usually located in the weight and balance section of the handbook.

For airplanes not requiring a POH, the manufacturer compiles the weight and balance report into a single document. The report usually provides information similar to the weight and balance section of a POH. For some older airplanes, the weight configurations of items that will produce acceptable flight conditions are detailed in loading schedules. These schedules could be displayed inside the airplane as placards, and others contained in the weight and balance report. Regardless of the format, you must make sure that the weight and balance information is appropriate and current for your airplane.

The weight and balance report includes the empty weight and **empty weight center of gravity** position of the airplane. Depending on the certification requirements in effect when the airplane was manufactured, the empty weight might be referred to as a **basic empty weight**, or a **licensed empty weight**. Airplanes manufactured after March 1, 1979 use the term basic empty weight. This weight includes the standard airplane, optional equipment, unusable fuel, and full operating fluids including full engine oil. For older airplanes, the term licensed empty weight is used, which is similar to basic empty weight, except that engine oil is not included. For these airplanes, you must remember to include the weight of the oil when you perform weight and balance computations. Engine oil weighs 7.5 pounds per gallon, or 1.875 pounds per quart. [Figure 12-66]

Figure 12-66. To determine the empty weight and empty weight center of gravity location, maintenance personnel actually weigh an airplane by placing it on scales or other weighing devices. Airplanes used for commercial operations are weighed at specific intervals to maintain accurate weight and balance records.

 The empty weight of an airplane includes unusable fuel, hydraulic fluid, and undrainable oil, or, in some aircraft, all of the oil.

The weight and balance report includes maximum ramp, takeoff and landing weights, or the maximum weight only, as previously discussed. The report also indicates the **useful load** of the airplane, which includes usable fuel, pilot and crew, passengers, baggage or cargo, and engine oil if it is not already included in the empty weight. If the airplane has a maximum zero fuel weight limit, it is in the report as well.

EQUIPMENT LIST

An equipment list provides an inventory of the weight and location of standard and optional equipment installed in the airplane. The list often includes equipment that is available from the manufacturer, but not be installed in your airplane. Installed equipment is marked with a check mark or an X. When a POH is required, the equipment list is usually in the weight and balance section of the handbook. On airplanes that do not require a POH, the equipment list is included in the weight and balance report. The list includes permanently installed components such as radio equipment and flight instruments, as well as some removable items such as the POH, portable fire extinguisher, and tow bar. You can refer to the equipment list to determine if an item is part of the empty weight. [Figure 12-67]

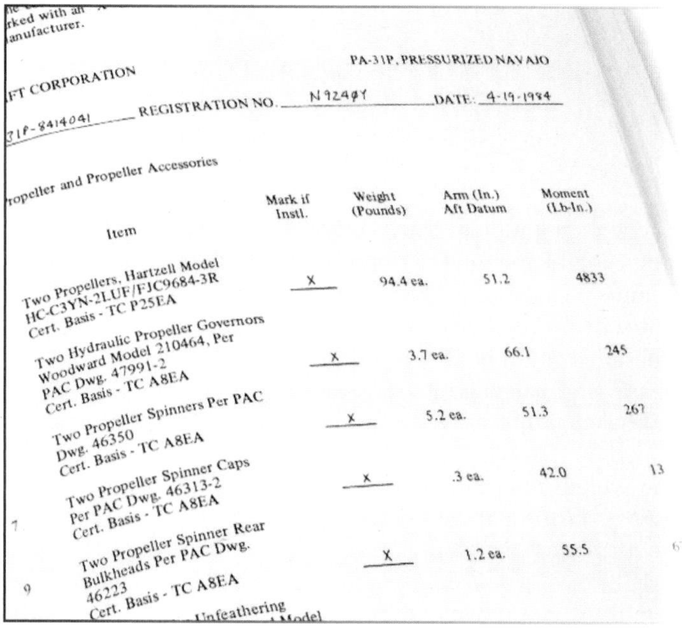

rked with an
anufacturer.

PA-31P, PRESSURIZED NAVAJO

FT CORPORATION

31P-8414041 REGISTRATION NO. N9240Y DATE: 4-19-1984

ropeller and Propeller Accessories

Item	Mark if Instl.	Weight (Pounds)	Arm (In.) Aft Datum	Moment (Lb-In.)
Two Propellers, Hartzell Model HC-C3YN-2LUF/FJC9684-3R Cert. Basis - TC P25EA	X	94.4 ea.	51.2	4833
Two Hydraulic Propeller Governors Woodward Model 210464, Per PAC Dwg. 47991-2 Cert. Basis - TC A8EA	X	3.7 ea.	66.1	245
Two Propeller Spinners Per PAC Dwg. 46350 Cert. Basis - TC A8EA	X	5.2 ea.	51.3	267
Two Propeller Spinner Caps Per PAC Dwg. 46313-2 Cert. Basis - TC A8EA	X	.3 ea.	42.0	13
Two Propeller Spinner Rear Bulkheads Per PAC Dwg. 46223 Cert. Basis - TC A8EA	X	1.2 ea.	55.5	67

Figure 12-67. Equipment installed in a specific airplane is marked on the equipment list in the POH.

When the installation or removal of equipment alters an airplane, the technician or agency conducting the alteration must revise the equipment list to reflect the change. In addition, the weight and balance report is also revised to reflect changes to the empty weight, empty weight CG, and useful load. When equipment is added to an airplane, the empty weight increases, which decreases the useful load.

FAA: When using weight information given in a typical aircraft owner's manual, the actual useful load of the aircraft might be lower than that shown in the manual because of the installation of additional equipment.

WEIGHT AND BALANCE COMPUTATIONS

You must perform weight and balance computations to verify that both total weight and CG location are within allowable limits. To compute total weight, you merely add the weight of useful load items to the empty weight. To determine the location of the CG, you must compute the total moment, then divide the total moment by the total weight.

MOMENT COMPUTATIONS

To determine the effects of useful load items on balance conditions, you must calculate the moment that each item produces. You can think of the moment as a torque or twisting force that is applied about a fulcrum. Moment is usually expressed in pound-inches. To find a moment value, multiply the weight of an item by its arm. For weight and balance purposes, an **arm** is the horizontal distance in inches that an item is located away from the reference datum. Some POHs express arms as fuselage stations (abbreviated F.S. or sta.), which are simply distances from the reference datum. For ease of computation, some cargo aircraft designate zones within the airplane, identified by the location of seams in floor panels or by placards along the cabin wall. [Figure 12-68]

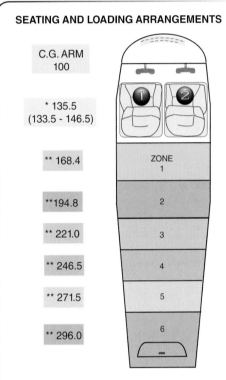

SEATING AND LOADING ARRANGEMENTS

C.G. ARM
100

* 135.5
(133.5 - 146.5)

** 168.4

**194.8

** 221.0

** 246.5

** 271.5

** 296.0

ZONE
1
2
3
4
5
6

2-PLACE SEATING

* Pilot or front passenger center of gravity on adjustable seats positioned for an average occupant with the seat locking pin at station 145.0. Numbers in parentheses indicate forward and aft limits of occupant center of gravity range.

** Cargo or baggage area center of gravity in zones 0 thru 6.

Figure 12-68. Some airplanes are divided into zones to make moment calculations easier. In this diagram, the arm for each zone is listed on the left.

 When the reference datum is located at or ahead of the nose, the moment index will always be positive when items are loaded in the airplane.

Because the product of the weight and arm can result in relatively large numbers, most manufacturers use **moment indexes**. To simplify computations the actual moment value is divided by a standard reduction factor. For example, when the manufacturer uses a reduction factor of 1,000 in weight and balance tables and graphs, a moment of 130,000 pound-inches has a moment index of 130. To designate the position of an item as being ahead of or behind the reference datum, the arms are assigned positive or negative values. Items located ahead of the reference datum have negative values, and items located aft have positive values. To eliminate negative numbers in the arithmetic, some manufacturers locate the reference datum on the nose or at some point ahead of the airplane so that all arm values are positive. If the reference datum is located where there is significant weight in front of the datum, for example, at the firewall or the wing leading edge, the weight and balance calculations can have positive or negative moments. To avoid errors, pay attention to positive and negative values in your computations. [Figure 12-69]

(–) Arms   **(+) Arms**

CG

Reference
Datum

Weight added (+) x Arm ahead of datum (–) = (–) Moment
Weight removed (–) x Arm ahead of datum (–) = (+) Moment

Weight added (+) x Arm aft of datum (+) = (+) Moment
Weight removed (–) x Arm aft of datum (+) = (–) Moment

Figure 12-69. Moment can be positive or negative depending on whether the weight is forward or aft of the reference datum.

DETERMINING CENTER OF GRAVITY POSITION

After you determine the moment of each item, you can locate the CG by adding up the weight of the items, totaling the moments, and dividing total moment by total weight. The result is the CG position in inches from the datum. [Figure 12-70]

> **FAA** To compute the combined CG of assorted weights, find the moment of each item by multiplying the item weights by the arm. To find the CG location, divide the total moment by the total weight.

Given:

Weight A—175 pounds at 135 inches aft of datum
Weight B—135 pounds at 115 inches aft of datum
Weight C—75 pounds at 85 inches aft of datum

Find the CG location of the combined weights.

Solution:

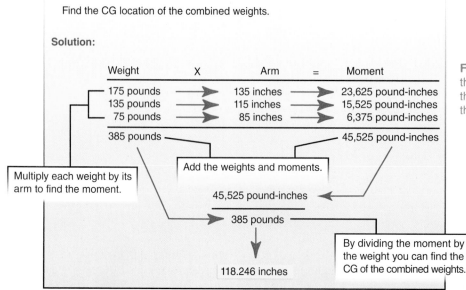

Weight	X	Arm	=	Moment
175 pounds	→	135 inches	→	23,625 pound-inches
135 pounds	→	115 inches	→	15,525 pound-inches
75 pounds	→	85 inches	→	6,375 pound-inches
385 pounds				45,525 pound-inches

Add the weights and moments.

Multiply each weight by its arm to find the moment.

45,525 pound-inches

385 pounds

By dividing the moment by the weight you can find the CG of the combined weights.

118.246 inches

Figure 12-70. To find the CG location, divide the total moment by the total weight.

WEIGHT AND BALANCE CONDITION CHECKS

Manufacturers provide various methods for determining weight and balance conditions, including the computation, table, and graph methods. From your previous flying experience, you are probably familiar with each of these methods. However, as you fly larger and more complex airplanes, you will face more complex loading computations. To help you understand some of them, the following examples use airplanes you might find in typical general aviation commercial operations.

Many manufacturers provide a chart in the POH to help you determine if the loading is acceptable. The formats of the charts differ from airplane to airplane. Some compare weight and moment, and others compare weight and CG location. [Figure 12-71]

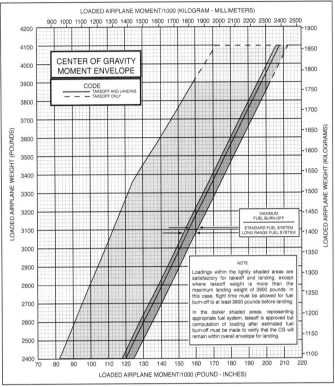

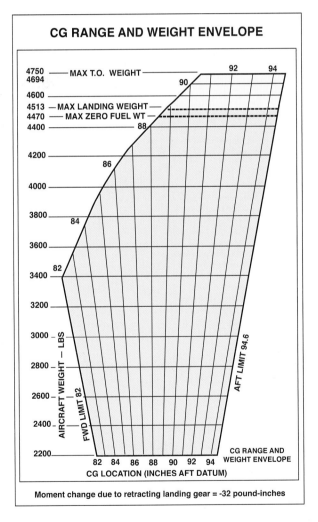

Moment change due to retracting landing gear = -32 pound-inches

Figure 12-71. Charts differ in both format and application. The left chart uses weight and **CG location**, and the right chart uses weight and **moment**.

COMPUTATION METHOD

The computation method can be used with any airplane. The first step is to locate the empty weight and empty CG position in the weight and balance report. In most cases, the report also includes the empty moment of the airplane. List them on a note pad or a copy of the weight and balance loading form supplied in the POH. Next, list the weight of each item of the useful load. To convert aviation gasoline from gallons to pounds, you can use either the standard six pounds per gallon or the weight specified by the manufacturer. Using a standard loading form for the airplane enables you to perform an organized and complete weight and balance condition check. [Figure 12-72]

SECTION C ■ Controlling Weight and Balance

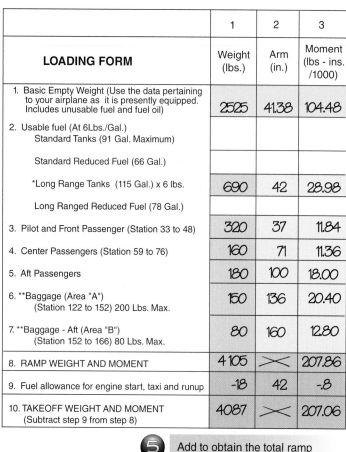

LOADING FORM	1 Weight (lbs.)	2 Arm (in.)	3 Moment (lbs - ins. /1000)
1. Basic Empty Weight (Use the data pertaining to your airplane as it is presently equipped. Includes unusable fuel and fuel oil)	2525	41.38	104.48
2. Usable fuel (At 6Lbs./Gal.) Standard Tanks (91 Gal. Maximum)			
Standard Reduced Fuel (66 Gal.)			
*Long Range Tanks (115 Gal.) x 6 lbs.	690	42	28.98
Long Ranged Reduced Fuel (78 Gal.)			
3. Pilot and Front Passenger (Station 33 to 48)	320	37	11.84
4. Center Passengers (Station 59 to 76)	160	71	11.36
5. Aft Passengers	180	100	18.00
6. **Baggage (Area "A") (Station 122 to 152) 200 Lbs. Max.	150	136	20.40
7. **Baggage - Aft (Area "B") (Station 152 to 166) 80 Lbs. Max.	80	160	12.80
8. RAMP WEIGHT AND MOMENT	4105	✕	207.86
9. Fuel allowance for engine start, taxi and runup	-18	42	-.8
10. TAKEOFF WEIGHT AND MOMENT (Subtract step 9 from step 8)	4087	✕	207.06

① Begin by entering the weight, arm, and moment of the empty airplane from the weight and balance report.

② Record the weight of each item of useful load.

③ Use the loading diagram to find the moment arm for each item.

④ Multiply the weight by the arm to obtain the moment for each item.

⑤ Add to obtain the total ramp weight and moment.

⑥ Subtract to obtain the takeoff weight and moment.

Figure 12-72. To provide a convenient method of locating arm distances for the loading form, some manufacturers provide loading arrangement charts like the one on the right.

LOADING ARRANGEMENTS

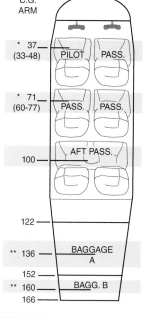

* Pilot or passenger center of gravity on adjustable seats positioned for average occupant. Numbers in parentheses indicate forward and aft limits of occupant center of gravity range.

** Baggage area center of gravity.

NOTES:

1. The usable fuel C.G. arm is located at station 43.0 (standard fuel tanks) and 42.0 (long-range tanks)

2. The aft baggage wall (approximate station 166 can be used as a convenient interior reference point for determining the location of baggage area fuselage station.

After you enter weight and moment values on the loading form, add the weights to determine the total weight of the airplane and then add the moments to find the total moment. Before continuing, check to make sure that the total weight does not exceed the maximum ramp weight limit specified by the manufacturer. The ramp weight limit might be shown on the loading form, or you might find it in the limitations section of the POH. The loading form in figure 12-72 indicates that the manufacturer has determined that 18 pounds of fuel are typically used for engine start, runup, and taxi. You can deduct this fuel weight and moment from the total weight and moment to determine the airplane's weight and balance condition for takeoff. After you make these adjustments, you can use a CG moment envelope chart to determine if the adjusted weight and moment values are within allowable limits. These charts depict the forward and aft CG limits, maximum weight values, and notes regarding special loading considerations. [Figure 12-73]

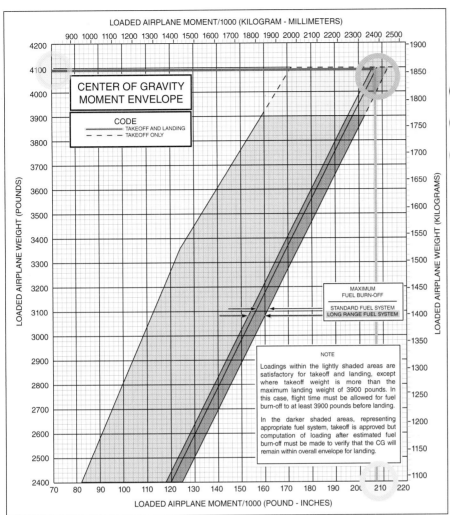

 Locate the moment/1000

 Locate the takeoff weight.

 If the takeoff CG is within the the darker shaded area, you must also compute the CG at landing. See Figure 12-74.

Using the numbers from Figure 12-72, determine if the takeoff weight and moment are within limits.

In this example, the airplane has the long range fuel system, so the wider part of the darker area applies.

Figure 12-73. This chart shows that the loading conditions of the sample airplane are within limits, but fall within the darker shaded area, which indicates that you need to comply with a note on the chart.

SECTION C ■ Controlling Weight and Balance

To determine if the CG of the airplane in the example will remain within limits, you need to compute how much fuel will be used during flight. Normally this will include the amount used for takeoff, climb, and cruise. For example, assume that the sample airplane uses all but 45 minutes of fuel during flight. If the airplane burns 13 gallons per hour (gal/h) during cruise, you can divide 13 gal/h by 60 minutes for a fuel consumption rate of .217 gallons per minute. By multiplying .217 g.p.m. by 45 minutes, you find that the fuel remaining in the airplane will be approximately 9.75 gallons. By multiplying 9.75 gallons by 6 pounds per gallon, you can see that there will be 58.5 pounds of fuel remaining in the airplane upon landing. Because the airplane originally contained 690 pounds of fuel, the weight of the airplane will decrease by 631.5 pounds (690 pounds − 58.5 pounds). To determine the effects on the CG, follow the example in figure 12-74.

SECTION C ■ Controlling Weight and Balance

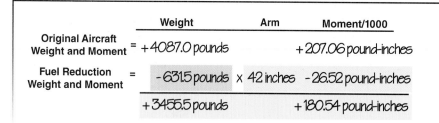

	Weight	Arm	Moment/1000
Original Aircraft Weight and Moment =	+4087.0 pounds		+207.06 pound-inches
Fuel Reduction Weight and Moment =	-631.5 pounds	× 42 inches	-26.52 pound-inches
	+3455.5 pounds		+180.54 pound-inches

 To determine the landing weight and moment, begin by computing the weight of fuel you will use in flight.

 Multiply the weight by the fuel arm to find the moment of the fuel used. Divide the moment by 1,000 for the moment index.

 Subtract to obtain the landing weight and moment index.

 Locate the landing weight on the moment envelope graph.

Locate the landing moment index.

The intersection falls outside the envelope, so you must reposition items in the airplane to keep the CG within limits until landing.

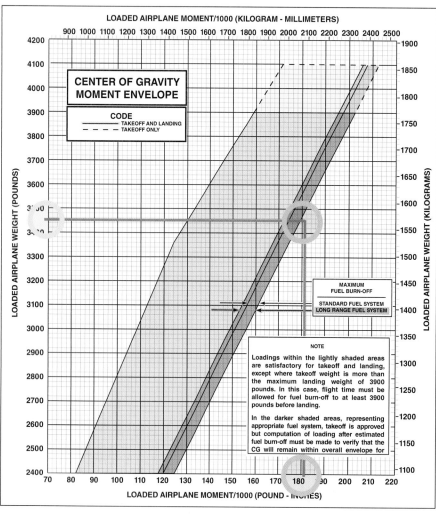

Figure 12-74. Because the first weight and balance solution fell in the shaded part of the envelope, you must perform a second computation to determine if the airplane will remain within the CG envelope until landing.

FAA To determine the effects of fuel consumption on weight and balance, calculate the weight of fuel consumed for the specified period of time. After the weight has been determined, deduct it from the original fuel weight and recompute the weight and balance for the airplane.

When the CG position falls outside of allowable limits, you can correct the condition by repositioning items to different locations. When possible, it is more practical to move a heavy item because you only need to reposition it a short distance. To help determine the amount of weight that must be moved, you can use the weight shift formula. Examples of weight shift computations are provided later in this section, and one provides a solution to the out of balance condition of this airplane.

GRAPH METHOD

To reduce the arithmetic during weight and balance condition checks, some manufacturers provide graphs to find the moment index for each item of useful load. Using the loading graph is easier, but generally less precise, than multiplying each weight by its respective arm. [Figure 12-75]

LOADING FORM		
	Weight (Lbs.)	Moment Index (In-Lbs./1000)
Basic Empty Weight	3212	284.26
Pilot and Front Passenger	350	30.00
Passengers (Center Seats) (Forward Facing)	275	32.50
Passengers (Center Seats) (Aft Facing) (Optional)		
Passengers (Rear Seats)	300	47.50
Passenger (Jump Seat) (Optional)		
Baggage (Forward) (100 Lbs. Max.)	100	2.5
Baggage (Aft) (100 Lbs. Max.)		
Zero Fuel Weight (4470 Lbs. Max - Std) (See equipment list.)	4237	396.76
Fuel (93 Gal. Max.) - Std. (123 Gal. Max.) - Opt.	480	45.00
Ramp Weight (4773 Lbs. Max.)	4717	441.76
Fuel Allowance for Start, Taxi, Runup	-23	.22
Takeoff Weight (4750 lbs. Max.)	4694	441.54

In this case, the weight of the airplane without fuel is less than the maximum zero-fuel weight. If the weight exceeds the maximum zero-fuel weight, you need to reduce the passenger or baggage weight.

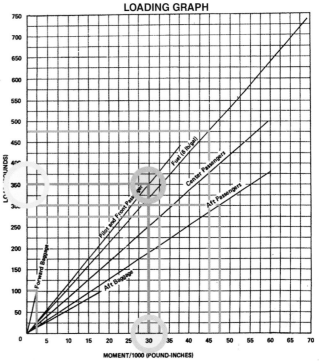

LOADING GRAPH

Figure 12-75. A loading graph makes it simple to find moment values.

 To find the moment index for the front seat occupants, start by locating the weight.

 Move horizontally to the diagonal line for Pilot and Front Seat Passenger.

 Drop vertically to find the moment index. Repeat for each item of the useful load.

 To perform weight and balance condition checks you can use a loading graph to find the moment of all useful load items. After the total weight and total moment are computed, determine if the moment and weight are within allowable limits by using a center of gravity envelope graph.

SECTION C ■ Controlling Weight and Balance

Refer to the appropriate chart to see if the combination of weight and CG fall within the allowable envelope. [Figure 12-76]

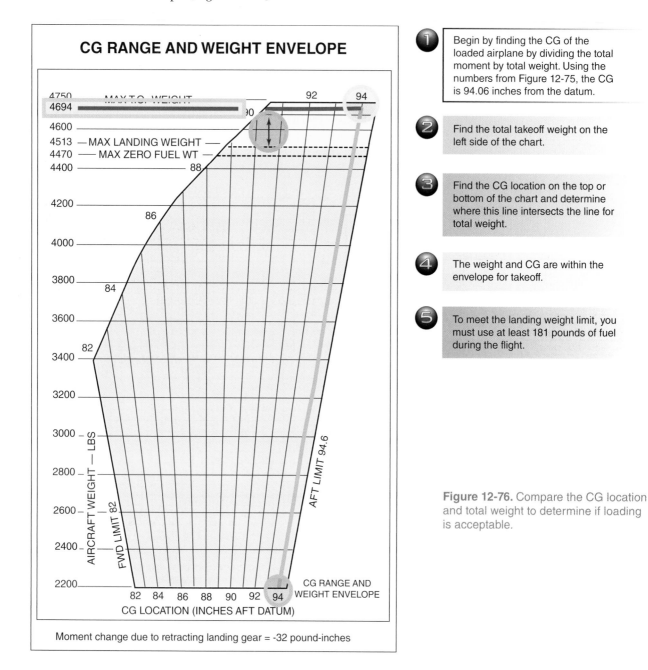

CG RANGE AND WEIGHT ENVELOPE

1. Begin by finding the CG of the loaded airplane by dividing the total moment by total weight. Using the numbers from Figure 12-75, the CG is 94.06 inches from the datum.

2. Find the total takeoff weight on the left side of the chart.

3. Find the CG location on the top or bottom of the chart and determine where this line intersects the line for total weight.

4. The weight and CG are within the envelope for takeoff.

5. To meet the landing weight limit, you must use at least 181 pounds of fuel during the flight.

Figure 12-76. Compare the CG location and total weight to determine if loading is acceptable.

Moment change due to retracting landing gear = -32 pound-inches

TABLE METHOD

Many manufacturers of larger airplanes supply tables to simplify weight and balance computations by tabulating the moments of useful load items at various weights and fuselage station locations. Because large airplanes often have a variety of possible cabin configurations, you need to first determine which tables to use. The manufacturer provides cabin configuration diagrams to illustrate various positions of the cabin furnishings. Identify the diagram that matches your airplane's configuration, and use the appropriate tables for weight and balance computations. Use a loading form to list the weights, arms, and moments of the useful load items carried in the airplane. For large airplanes, these loading forms might include additional weight considerations such as **payload** and **basic operating weight**. Payload can be thought of as potential revenue generating items such as passengers and baggage or cargo. Basic operating weight includes the airplane and crew, but without fuel and payload items. [Figure12-77]

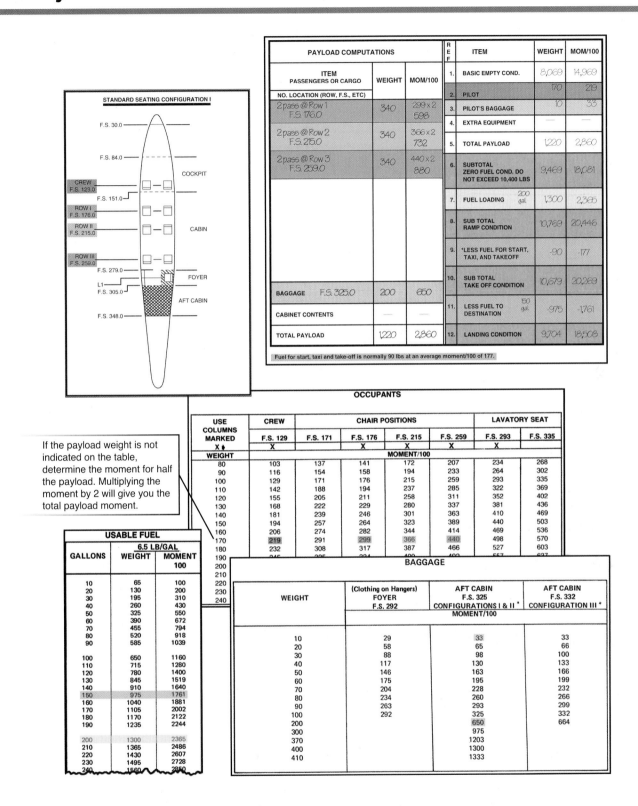

Figure 12-77. After you locate the cabin configuration diagram that matches the airplane you are flying, use it to determine the moments to enter on the loading form.

After you determine the total weight and total moment of the airplane, you can refer to a moment limit versus weight table to determine if the airplane is loaded within allowable CG limits. [Figure 12-78]

SECTION C ■ Controlling Weight and Balance

MOMENT LIMITS VS. WEIGHT

WEIGHT	MINIMUM MOMENT/100	MAXIMUM MOMENT/100	
9900	17919	19444	
9950	18010	19542	
10000	18100	19640	
10050	18190	19738	
10150	18372	19935	
10200	18462	20033	
10250	18552	20131	
10300	18643	20229	
10350	18734	20327	
10400	18824	20426	
10450	18914	20524	
10500	19005	20622	
10550	19096	20720	
10600	19186	20818	
10650	19276	20917	
10700	19367	21015	
10750	19458	21113	
10800	19548	21211	
10850	19638	21309	

MAX ZERO FUEL WEIGHT (row at 10400)

Figure 12-78. Locate the total weight of the airplane, then determine whether the moment is within the acceptable range of moments.

By interpolating between the weight values, you can determine that the takeoff moment of 20,269 pound-inches /100 is within allowable limit.

WEIGHT SHIFT COMPUTATION

During weight and balance computations, you might find that either the weight of the airplane or its CG location is beyond acceptable limits. As you add up the weight, you can see if the weight exceeds one of the maximum weight limits. If the weight is acceptable but the CG is outside the CG range, you might be able to rearrange the load to bring the CG within limits. Use the weight shift formula to solve weight shift problems.

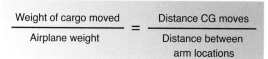

$$\frac{\text{Weight of cargo moved}}{\text{Airplane weight}} = \frac{\text{Distance CG moves}}{\text{Distance between arm locations}}$$

Performing a few sample weight shift problems gives you practice in applying this formula. [Figures 12-79 and 12-80]

You have a loaded airplane weight of 3,200 pounds with a CG location of 45.6 inches. If you move a 120 lb box from Cargo Area B to Cargo Area A, how far will the CG move? Start by placing the known values into the weight shift equation.

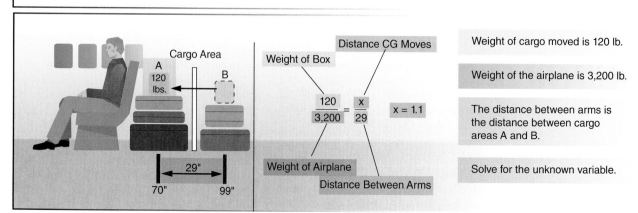

Weight of cargo moved is 120 lb.

Weight of the airplane is 3,200 lb.

The distance between arms is the distance between cargo areas A and B.

Solve for the unknown variable.

Figure 12-79. The weight shift formula can help you to correct an unacceptable loading situation.

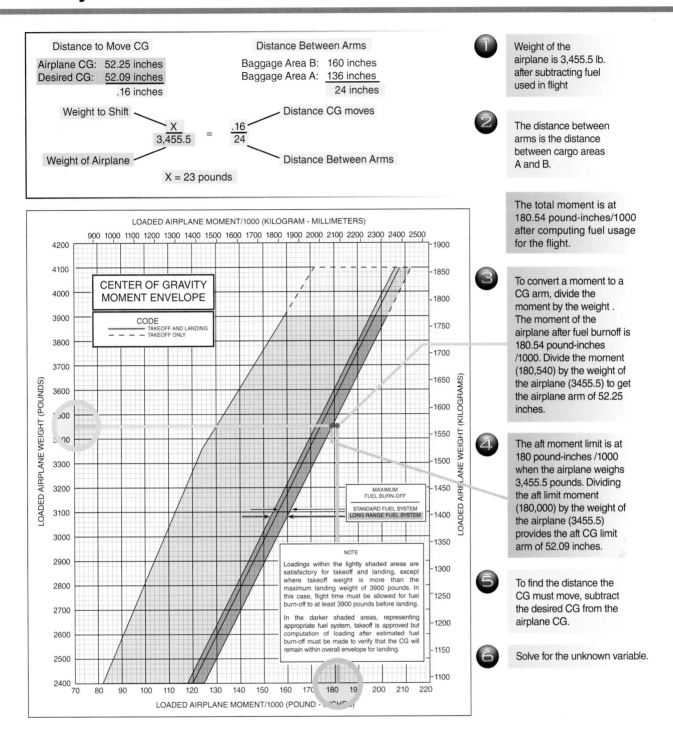

Distance to Move CG

Airplane CG: 52.25 inches
Desired CG: 52.09 inches
                .16 inches

Distance Between Arms

Baggage Area B: 160 inches
Baggage Area A: 136 inches
                  24 inches

Weight to Shift ─┐   ┌─ Distance CG moves

$$\frac{X}{3,455.5} = \frac{.16}{24}$$

Weight of Airplane ─┘   └─ Distance Between Arms

X = 23 pounds

① Weight of the airplane is 3,455.5 lb. after subtracting fuel used in flight

② The distance between arms is the distance between cargo areas A and B.

The total moment is at 180.54 pound-inches/1000 after computing fuel usage for the flight.

③ To convert a moment to a CG arm, divide the moment by the weight . The moment of the airplane after fuel burnoff is 180.54 pound-inches /1000. Divide the moment (180,540) by the weight of the airplane (3455.5) to get the airplane arm of 52.25 inches.

④ The aft moment limit is at 180 pound-inches /1000 when the airplane weighs 3,455.5 pounds. Dividing the aft limit moment (180,000) by the weight of the airplane (3455.5) provides the aft CG limit arm of 52.09 inches.

⑤ To find the distance the CG must move, subtract the desired CG from the airplane CG.

⑥ Solve for the unknown variable.

SECTION C ■ Controlling Weight and Balance

Figure 12-80. In Figure 12-74, the CG would exceed the aft limits as fuel was consumed during the flight. Use the weight shift formula to see if moving some baggage before takeoff will keep the CG within limits throughout the flight.

 The weight shift formula can be used to calculate the amount of weight that must be moved a specific distance or to determine the distance a specific weight would need to move to bring the CG within approved limits.

JUST SAY NO

After landing on a soft beach near a fishing camp, the pilot of the Cessna 207 was approached by eleven people that needed to be flown into a nearby town to purchase supplies. The pilot permitted all eleven people to board his airplane, which was only certified to carry seven occupants. The airplane was unable to become airborne when attempting takeoff from the soft sand, and it collided with a boat that was moored on the beach. Fortunately, none of the occupants was seriously injured, primarily because they were packed so tightly in the airplane.

The pilot was trying to satisfy his employer, an air charter operator, and accommodate the passengers. If he had refused to carry the extra passengers, this accident probably would not have occurred. But when feeling the pressure to please passengers, he allowed himself to compromise safety, which resulted in an accident.

When you are employed as a professional pilot, you will likely face situations in which you are asked to fly an airplane when you know conditions are not safe or legal. Part of a professional pilot's responsibility is being able to respond with both empathy and firmness to people who try to pressure you into compromising situations. Although you might feel that you have the ability to stand your ground, sometimes you will have to make difficult decisions. Thinking about the possible consequences of your actions can help you to make these decisions. If

Courtesy of Dr. Alvin J. Lagger — Aviation Safety Consultant

you compromise safety and an incident or accident occurs, you will be held responsible and accountable. Remember, it is an agonizing ordeal to look back at your past decisions and wish that you had only said no.

SUMMARY CHECKLIST

✓ Both the amount and distribution of weight significantly affect airplane stability, control, and efficiency.

✓ An airplane might have a single maximum weight limit or multiple maximum weight limits for various stages of ground and flight operations.

✓ Maximum weight limits might be required for structural or performance considerations.

✓ An airplane loaded near the forward CG limit becomes more stable, but less controllable in flight, and an airplane loaded near the aft limit is less stable, and more sensitive to control input.

✓ Weight and balance reports and equipment lists contain essential information for weight and balance control and must be kept current by the airplane owner or operator.

✓ Weight and balance condition checks can be accomplished by the computation, graph, or table methods.

✓ When the CG of an airplane is outside of allowable limits, you can use the weight shift formula to determine how much weight to move or the distance that a given weight must be moved to bring the CG within allowable limits.

KEY TERMS

Maximum Weight

Maximum Ramp Weight

Maximum Takeoff Weight

Maximum Landing Weight

Maximum Zero Fuel Weight

Center of Gravity

Reference Datum

Moment

Weight and Balance Report

Equipment List

Empty Weight Center of Gravity

Basic Empty Weight

Licensed Empty Weight

Useful Load

Arm

Moment Index

Payload

Basic Operating Weight

QUESTIONS

1. Which of the following weight limits represents the heaviest total weight value?
    A. Maximum ramp weight
    B. Maximum takeoff weight
    C. Maximum landing weight

2. Which of the following terms is used to describe the weight of an airplane without fuel or payload items?
    A. Useful load
    B. Basic operating weight
    C. Maximum zero fuel weight

3. Which of the following flight characteristics would you expect when the CG of an airplane is near the aft limit?
    A. The stability of the airplane increases and the elevator control becomes less effective.
    B. The airplane becomes less stable and the elevator control becomes less effective.
    C. The elevator control becomes more effective and stability decreases.

4. True/False. Loading an airplane near the aft CG limit produces a higher true airspeed than when loaded with the CG located near the forward limit.

5. The total weight of an airplane is 3,100 pounds and the total moment index is 310 pound-inches /1000. Where is the CG located in inches aft of the datum?
    A. +10 inches
    B. +100 inches
    C. +1,000 inches

6. Using the accompanying loading graph, what would be the CG of the total combined weight of the following items?

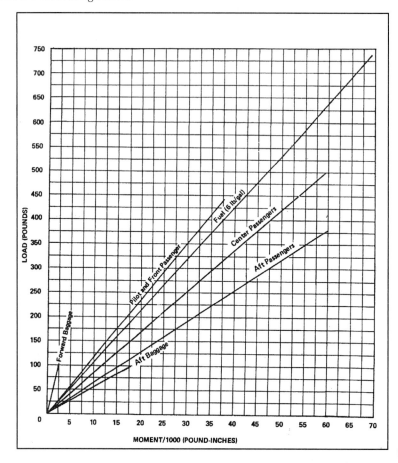

Pilot and front passenger	350 pounds	30,000
Center seat passengers	300 pounds	35,000
Usable fuel	80 gallons	80 x 6 = 480 45,000
Aft baggage	50 pounds	3000

1180 lbs

A. Approximately +101.27 inches aft of the reference datum
B. Approximately +156.38 inches aft of the reference datum
C. Approximately +105.13 inches aft of the reference datum

7. Use the item information from question number 6 and the CG range and weight graph shown here to determine if an airplane is loaded within the CG envelope. Assume the airplane has an empty weight of 3,200 pounds with an empty weight moment index of 2,842.6 pound-inches /100.   4380

    A. The CG falls within the envelope and is safe for flight.
    B. The CG falls in the envelope, but exceeds the maximum zero fuel weight.
    C. The CG falls inside the envelope but the fuel burn-off in flight must be sufficient to reduce the total weight to below the maximum landing weight.

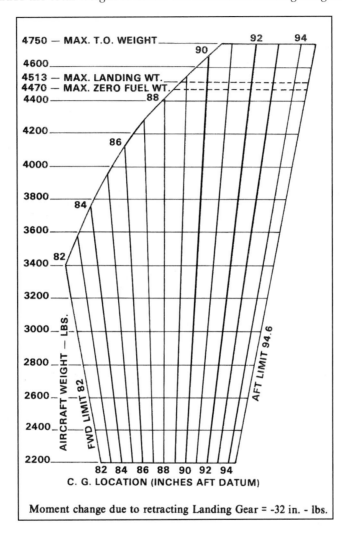

SECTION C ■ Controlling Weight and Balance

8. An airplane is loaded with 100 gallons of fuel at station +38 inches, which causes the airplane to have a total weight of 3,500 pounds and a CG located at +42 inches. If the airplane burns 12.6 gallons per hour, where will the CG be located after 3 hours and 20 minutes of flight? Assume the fuel weighs 6 pounds per gallon.

    A. +42.83 inches aft of datum
    B. +42.31 inches aft of datum
    C. +42.05 inches aft of datum

CHAPTER 13

Commercial Flight
Considerations

Private Pilot Maneuvers
Volume I — Emergency Landing Procedures

SECTION A
Emergency Procedures

Although modern aircraft are extremely reliable, the possibility of emergencies in flight due to mechanical failure, fuel problems, or pilot error has not been eliminated. Problems resulting from these factors are not common, but they are frequent enough that you should be aware of them and know how to handle them if they occur. The following discussion emphasizes VFR emergencies; you also can refer to Chapter 10, Section A — IFR Emergencies.

Unfortunately, not all in-flight emergencies allow you sufficient time to reference your pilot's operating handbook or checklist. In fact, some emergencies might not be addressed in the POH at all. Therefore, when you fly, you need to be prepared for distress situations by knowing the emergency procedures for your airplane and by using good judgment in responding to the situation. To assist you, the FAA provides some general guidelines for dealing with various emergencies. Although you should follow the specific procedures recommended by your airplane's manufacturer, the general emergency procedures discussed in this section can help provide a foundation for understanding the steps to follow for specific emergency situations when you must act quickly.

An FAA study has shown that power loss is a major contributing factor in general aviation accidents. Power loss accidents have a variety of causes. Examples include operating powerplants beyond normal limits, poor maintenance, failure of engine parts or system components, and most often, fuel starvation due to pilot error or other factors. Unexpected power loss coupled with inadequate pilot response can easily result in an accident. A well-prepared and competent pilot can usually deal with an emergency situation in a manner resulting in a safe outcome for the flight. The most important thing to remember in any emergency situation is to fly the airplane.

EMERGENCY DESCENT

An **emergency descent** is used to achieve the fastest practical rate of vertical descent to reach a safe altitude or landing during an emergency situation. You might need to perform this maneuver due to an uncontrollable fire, a sudden loss of cabin pressurization, or any other situation demanding an immediate and rapid loss of altitude. Your objective is to descend as quickly as possible without exceeding the airspeed limitations of the airplane.

Establish an emergency descent using the configuration and airspeed recommended by the manufacturer. Reduce the power to idle, and if your airplane is equipped with a controllable propeller, set the prop control to low pitch (high RPM). This setting allows the propeller to act as an aerodynamic brake to help prevent excessive airspeed. Extend the landing gear and flaps as recommended by the manufacturer. The drag produced by extending the landing gear and flaps increases the descent rate without increasing the airspeed. Roll into a bank angle of approximately 30 to 45 degrees in order to establish and maintain a positive load factor on the airplane. Doing so will help you remain within the safe operating limits of the airplane, and also enables you to stay over, and closely observe, a potential landing area. [Figure 13-1]

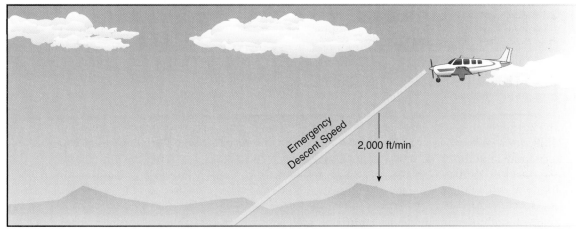

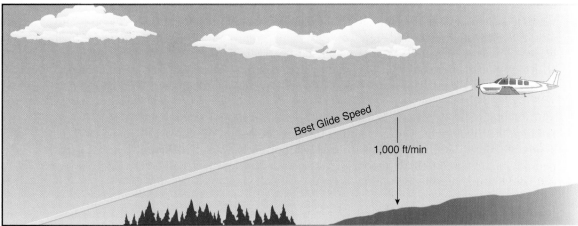

Figure 13-1. Flying at an airspeed greater than best glide speed but within the airplane's limitations and extending the landing gear and flaps (if recommended by the manufacturer) create a steep descent angle that results in a quick loss of altitude.

At no time should you allow the airplane's airspeed to rise above the never exceed speed (V_{NE}), the maximum gear extended speed (V_{LE}), or the maximum flap extended speed (V_{FE}) depending on the airplane configuration. If the descent is conducted in turbulent conditions, you also should comply with the recommended maneuvering speed (V_A) limitations. These procedures should be continued until a safe altitude has been reached or until you begin the emergency approach and landing if necessary. In airplanes with piston engines, avoid prolonged practice emergency descents to prevent the excessive cooling of engine cylinders.

 EMERGENCY PARALYSIS

The NTSB has identified several factors that diminish a pilot's ability to deal with emergency landings.

1. Pilots can be reluctant to accept the emergency situation, paralyzed with the thought that the aircraft will be on the ground in a short time regardless of what they do. As a result, they delay action, fail to maintain flying speed, or attempt desperate measures at the expense of aircraft control.

2. There might be a desire on the part of the pilot to save the aircraft rather than sacrificing it to save the occupants. Such a desire can cause pilots to stretch a glide or make abrupt maneuvers at low altitude resulting in accidents.

3. The fear of injury can cause pilots to panic, inhibiting their ability to properly carry out emergency procedures resulting in the situation they wanted to avoid most.

EMERGENCY APPROACH AND LANDING

Your own fear of injury or of damage to the airplane can interfere with your ability to act decisively when you are faced with an emergency involving a forced landing. Records show, however, that survival rates favor those pilots who maintain their composure and know how to apply the recommended procedures and techniques that have been developed throughout the years.

The key to dealing with these fears is to fly the airplane. Concentrate on maintaining your glide speed, adhering to the checklists, and managing resources, and this will help you keep your mind off what might happen and allow you to continue flying the airplane. If you practice simulated emergency procedures enough, you will be more confident in your ability to deal with an emergency approach and landing.

Before practicing an emergency approach and landing during training, clear the area below and ensure that you are over favorable terrain in the event an actual emergency landing becomes necessary. Normally, in training, when all the prescribed procedures and airspeeds are established and stabilized, the maneuver should be terminated. You must begin recovery at an altitude high enough to ensure a safe return to level flight. In airplanes with piston engines, avoid a prolonged descent to prevent the excessive cooling of engine cylinders. Apply carburetor heat as recommended by the manufacturer, if applicable.

Many factors are important in successfully performing an emergency approach and landing, the first of which is the landing field. A competent pilot normally is on alert for a suitable forced landing site. Ideally, the best option is an established airport, or hard-packed, long, smooth field with no high obstacles on the approach end and situated so you can land directly into the wind.

Because these ideal conditions rarely present themselves, you must select the next best field available. Cultivated fields are generally satisfactory because they will be fairly level. Plowed fields can be acceptable as long as you land parallel to the furrows. If the field appears to be soft or snow covered, you might even consider a gear up landing, if your airplane has retractable gear. Otherwise, you should ensure that the nose wheel is not allowed to sink in and cause the airplane to nose over.

Field size and wind direction are also important factors to consider in selecting an emergency landing site. Wind direction and speed will affect your airplane's gliding distance over the ground, the track along the ground during the approach, the groundspeed at which the airplane touches down, and the distance required for deceleration after the landing. These factors will be important in selecting your landing field. However, do not allow yourself to be locked into landing directly into the wind. For instance, limited options in an emergency might dictate making a downwind landing to clear obstacles or because the best field might be too far upwind to reach. Furthermore, the field you select should also be wide enough to allow you to extend the base leg before turning final in the event you have misjudged your airspeed or altitude. [Figure 13-2]

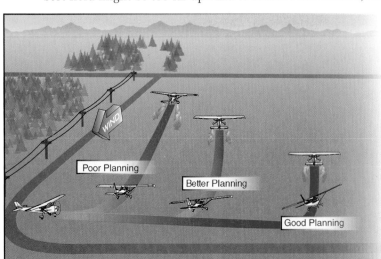

Figure 13-2. A wide field provides the opportunity to adjust your approach without making extreme maneuvers at low altitude.

In most cases, the altitude you have is the primary controlling factor in the successful accomplishment of a forced landing. The lower you are when a power loss occurs, the fewer your options. Should an engine failure happen prior to reaching a safe maneuvering altitude, your choice of actions will be limited to flying straight ahead or making shallow turns to avoid objects in your immediate path.

When a forced landing appears imminent, regardless of your altitude, the main priority is to complete a safe landing in the best field available. This involves getting the airplane on the ground in as near a normal landing attitude as possible without striking obstructions. Large, abrupt turns near the ground in an attempt to avoid a poor landing area makes attitude control difficult. If you can fly the airplane all the way to the ground and make a relatively normal landing, you increase the chances of completing the procedure without catastrophic consequences to you and your passengers.

Performing a safe approach and landing begins with airspeed control. For each particular airplane, the manufacturer recommends an airspeed and configuration that will provide the **maximum glide distance**. The **best glide speed**, found in the pilot's operating handbook, will determine the distance you can glide and consequently the number of landing areas available to you. In some airplanes, the best glide speed can change as gross weight changes. Of course, any deviation from best glide speed can negatively affect your ability to reach a suitable landing site. [Figure 13-3]

Figure 13-3. Any deviation from best glide speed reduces the distance you can glide and can cause you to land short of a safe touchdown point.

Crash Course

"The success of an emergency landing under adverse conditions is as much a matter of the mind as it is of skill!" —Mick Wilson, former Manager, FAA Aviation Safety Program, Denver Flight Standards District Office

Mick Wilson developed a Safety Seminar and text entitled How to Crash an Airplane (and Survive!). His presentation includes numerous insights into basic crash safety concepts including the following observations concerning post-impact deceleration of groundspeed.

The overall severity of a deceleration process is governed by groundspeed and the stopping distance of the aircraft. For instance, doubling the groundspeed means quadrupling the total destructive energy at impact. This is why it is so important to reduce your landing speed to the lowest possible while still maintaining aircraft control.

Very little stopping distance is required if the speed can be dissipated evenly over the available distance. Assume an aircraft is exposed to deceleration forces equaling 9 times the force of gravity, the standard to which general aviation aircraft are certified. The stopping distance required while traveling at 50 mph is 9.4 feet. At 100 mph, the stopping distance is 37.6 feet, or four times the stopping distance required when traveling at 50 mph. While these are not distances you would prefer for a normal landing, it is nice to know just how little space is needed to successfully decelerate an airplane during an emergency landing.

Understanding the need for a firm but uniform deceleration process in very poor terrain provides you more landing options. As a result, you can select touchdown conditions that, while not ideal, can reduce the peak deceleration of the airplane and increase your chances of walking away from the landing. Courtesy of Mick Wilson, www.crashandsurvive.com

To achieve best glide speed, retract the landing gear and flaps to eliminate unwanted drag. Unlike emergency descent procedures in which your focus is on a quick and controlled loss of altitude, your objective during an emergency approach is to remain airborne long enough to set up a safe landing. As a result, it is necessary to eliminate as much drag as possible. However, during a power loss immediately after takeoff or at a low altitude, keep the gear and flaps extended to prepare for touchdown. Adjust your airplane's pitch attitude to obtain best glide speed, and trim to maintain that pitch attitude.

After you have established the proper pitch attitude and airspeed, complete the appropriate emergency checklist in the POH for the particular airplane. Perform critical tasks from memory and then refer to the checklist, if you have time, to ensure you have completed each task. Many emergency checklists indicate memory items in bold or underlined text and tasks to secure the engine might appear on a separate emergency/forced landing checklist. [Figure 13-4]

Engine Failure In Flight

Emergency Procedures

If the engine fails at altitude, pitch as necessary to establish best glide speed. While gliding toward a suitable landing area, attempt to identify the cause of the failure and correct it.

1. Best Glide Speed .... ESTABLISH
2. Mixture .... FULL RICH
3. Fuel Selector .... SWITCH TANKS
4. Fuel Pump .... BOOST
5. Alternate Induction Air .... ON
6. Ignition Switch .... CHECK, BOTH
7. If engine does not start, proceed to Engine Airstart or Forced Landing checklist, as required.

Figure 13-4. This checklist underlines critical items that you perform from memory if your engine fails.

180 DEGREES OF TROUBLE

From the files of the NTSB...

Aircraft: *Piper PA-18*

Injuries: *1 Minor*

Narrative: *The airplane departed a restricted landing area runway for a local flight. Shortly after departing, the airplane's engine stopped running at 300 feet above the ground. The pilot performed a 180 degree turn toward the departure runway. During the turn, the airplane stalled and subsequently collided with the ground. The airplane was destroyed by a post impact fire.*

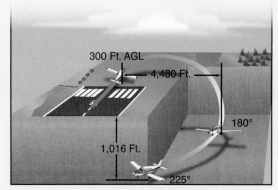

The desire to turn back to an airport if the engine fails shortly after takeoff can be quite powerful. Unfortunately, giving in to the desire can have disastrous consequences considering the glide performance of airplanes during turns. That is why it is usually best to continue straight ahead, utilizing small heading changes, to keep the airplane under control in order to complete an emergency landing as safely as possible.

To emphasize the danger in these situations, assume you have just taken off from your local airport and climbed to 300 feet AGL when the engine fails. After a four-second reaction time, you decide to turn back to the runway. If you turn at a standard rate, it will take a minute to turn 180°. At a glide speed of 65 knots, the radius of the turn is 2,100 feet, so at the completion of the turn, you are now 4,200 feet to one side of the runway. You must turn another 45° to head the airplane toward the runway. By now, your total change of direction equals 225° equating to 75 seconds plus the four-second reaction time. If the average light airplane in a no-power gliding turn descends at approximately 1,000 feet per minute, you will have descended 1,316 feet —1,016 feet below the runway!

To perform a successful landing, you must set up the approach correctly. The FAA recommends using any combination of normal gliding maneuvers from wings level to spirals to arrive at a point from which a normal landing can be made. This point, or **key position**, is a convenient point at which you judge whether the glide will safely terminate at the desired spot. The key position is normally abeam your intended touchdown point or on the base leg. Follow the recommended flap and gear extension procedures in the POH and add full flaps only when you know you can reach the touchdown point. From the key position, any miscalculations about the glide angle can be corrected with the use of flaps, slipping, or moving the touchdown point if feasible. [Figure 13-5]

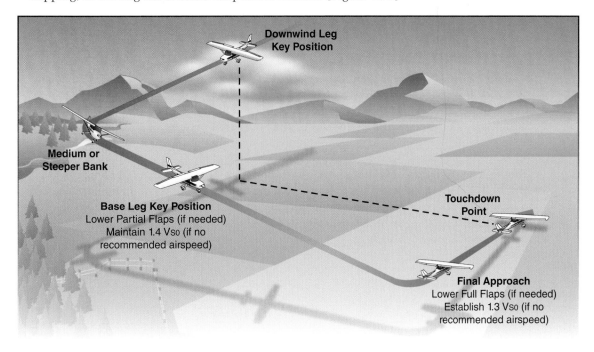

Figure 13-5. Key positions on downwind or base allow you to judge your gliding distance in the same manner you would during a normal traffic pattern.

SYSTEMS AND EQUIPMENT MALFUNCTIONS

There are some emergency conditions that do not appear in checklists or in your airplane's POH. Although these situations are not specifically addressed, the FAA provides some general recommendations for dealing with them. The procedures are not intended to be used in lieu of the particular recommendations that might be provided by a manufacturer, but rather in their absence.

IN-FLIGHT FIRE

If you experience a fire while in flight, follow the checklist procedures specified in the POH for your airplane and declare an emergency by radio. The checklist might address only one type of in-flight fire or it might include procedures for different types of fires ranging from cabin and electrical fires to engine fires. In any event, follow the appropriate procedure for the situation. In addition, a general recommendation can be of benefit to you during such an emergency. Should the fire and flames be visible outside the cabin during the emergency descent, attempt to slip away from the fire as much as possible. For example, if the fire is observed on the left side of the airplane, slip to the right. This can move the fire away from the cabin.

PARTIAL POWER LOSS

It is possible that during a flight you might experience a partial loss of engine power. Two options might be available to you, depending on the degree of power loss and the airplane's resulting decrease in performance. You might be able to continue the flight in a reduced power condition as long as you are able to hold altitude or climb. In this situation, maintain an airspeed that will provide the best airplane performance available. In most cases, the **best performance airspeed** will be approximately the best glide speed. However, it is also possible the engine will not continue to run in this condition and a forced landing will still need to be made. With an engine problem, you should continually monitor your engine instruments and update your choice of landing options.

Alternatively, your airplane's performance with partial power might not be sufficient to maintain altitude. In this case, a forced landing is imminent. Consequently, you will need to declare an emergency with ATC and begin the emergency approach and landing procedures specified in your airplane's checklist.

DOOR OPENING IN FLIGHT

A cabin or baggage compartment door opening in flight can be a disconcerting event. Although a door generally will not open very far, the sudden noise can be startling. Regardless of the noise and confusion, it is important to maintain control of the airplane, particularly during departure. Accidents have occurred on takeoff because pilots have stopped flying the airplane to concentrate on closing cabin or baggage doors.

Although an open door does not normally compromise airplane control, it is possible that control will become more difficult. If such a condition should occur it might be necessary to increase airspeed in all phases of flight, including the approach, in order to ensure that you can control the airplane. After you have adequate airplane control, land as soon as practical and secure the door.

ASYMMETRICAL FLAP EXTENSION

An unexpected rolling motion during flap extension can be due to an asymmetrical or split flap condition. If one flap extends while the other remains in place, a differential in lift across the wing is the cause of the rolling motion. A split flap condition can be hazardous, particularly in the traffic pattern or during a turn at low altitude. [Figure 13-6]

Figure 13-6. Extending the flaps during a turn can result in a dangerous situation should an asymmetrical flap extension occur.

If the unexpected rolling motion occurs during flap extension, immediately return the flap control to the up, or the previous position, while maintaining control of the airplane. Should you be in the approach phase of the traffic pattern when an asymmetrical extension occurs, perform a go-around and adjust your airspeed for approach and landing.

SECTION A ■ Emergency Procedures

EMERGENCY EQUIPMENT AND SURVIVAL GEAR

You may carry a survival kit for years and not need it. But when you do need it, you need it badly and the biggest survival kit is none too big. — Private Pilot's Survival Manual by Frank Kingston Smith

Regulations only require you to carry flotation gear and a signaling device during certain overwater commercial operations. However, it is highly recommended that you include several other basic survival items in the event of an emergency. A survival kit should be able to provide you with sustenance, shelter, medical care and a means to summon help without a great deal of effort or improvisation on your part. That is why a minimally equipped survival kit should be avoided. You can tailor the contents of your **survival kit** to the conditions of the flight. Any complete survival kit should contain a basic core of survival supplies around which you can assemble the additional items that are appropriate to the terrain and weather you would have to deal with in an emergency.

When making decisions about the emergency gear to take with you, consider the terrain you will be flying over, the climate or season during which the flight will be made, and what type of emergency communication equipment you might need. For instance, an emergency landing in mountainous terrain in December requires different survival gear than a ditching in the ocean in August. Some general items you might consider as the basis on which to build a survival kit for all flight operations include: a comprehensive first aid kit and field medical guide, flashlight, supply of water, knife, matches, shelter, and a signaling device.

Survive to Fly

A wide variety of survival kits are available commercially. They can range in price up to several hundred dollars for larger kits designed to support 4 or 5 people. However, you can put together your own survival kit tailored to meet your specific flying needs.

Keeping in mind weight considerations, you might begin with the basics. Your kit should include items covering the important survival factors like water, shelter and protection, food, first aid, signals, and personal or miscellaneous supplies.

This commercially available survival kit is designed to sustain 4 to 6 people in an emergency. You might opt to purchase a kit like this, or you might elect to build your own kit.

There are many sources of information that have been published to help you determine what items are appropriate for your kit. In addition, survival courses can be available locally, particularly in mountainous parts of the western United States.

SUMMARY CHECKLIST

✓ You need to be prepared for emergency situations by knowing the procedures for your airplane.

✓ An emergency descent is used to achieve the fastest practical rate of vertical descent to reach a safe altitude or landing during an emergency situation, such as an uncontrollable fire or a sudden loss of cabin pressurization.

✓ NTSB records indicate accident survival rates favor pilots who maintain their composure and know how to apply the recommended procedures and techniques.

✓ Limited options during an emergency might dictate making a downwind landing.

✓ When you experience a power loss, altitude is usually the primary controlling factor in the successful accomplishment of a forced landing.

✓ The FAA recommends using any combination of normal gliding maneuvers from wings level to spirals to arrive at a point from which a normal landing can be made.

✓ Should fire be visible outside the cabin during an in-flight fire, attempt to slip away from the fire.

✓ If you experience a partial power loss, continue the flight in a reduced power condition if the airplane can maintain altitude or perform a forced landing if the airplane's performance is insufficient to maintain altitude,

✓ If a door opens in flight, maintain control of the airplane and land as soon as practical to secure the door.

✓ An unexpected rolling motion during flap extension can be due to an asymmetrical or split flap condition. Immediately return the flap control to the up, or the previous position, while maintaining control of the airplane.

✓ Some general items you might consider for a survival kit include, a first aid kit, flashlight, container of water, knife, matches, and a signaling device.

KEY TERMS

Emergency Descent   Key Position

Maximum Glide Distance   Best Performance Airspeed

Best Glide Speed   Survival Kit

SECTION A ■ **Emergency Procedures**

QUESTIONS

1. During an emergency descent, what airspeed limitations should you observe?

2. True/False. The most important thing to remember in any emergency situation is to fly the airplane.

3. Why should the emergency landing field you select be wide instead of narrow?

4. In most cases, what is the primary controlling factor in the successful accomplishment of a forced landing?
   A. Wind
   B. Altitude
   C. Airspeed

5. True/False. Airspeeds below best glide increase the number of landing options available to you.

6. True/False. An open baggage door normally compromises airplane control.

7. An unexpected split flap extension will be most dangerous during which phase of flight?
   A. Climb
   B. Cruise
   C. Turns at low altitude

8. True/False. It is prudent to consider the type of terrain you will be flying over when selecting items for your emergency survival kit.

9. True/False. FAA regulations require flotation gear and a signalling device to be carried on board during all overwater operations.

SECTION B
Commercial Pilot SRM

The thing we call luck is merely professionalism and attention to detail, it's your awareness of everything that is going on around you, it's how well you know and understand your airplane and your own limitations. Luck is the sum total of your abilities as an aviator.

— Stephen Coonts, *The Intruders*

No matter what your reasons are for pursuing a commercial pilot certificate, the additional knowledge you acquire during commercial training will make you a more competent pilot. The advanced skills and experience that you gain will hone your decision-making abilities and enhance your flight safety. This section explores **single-pilot resource management (SRM)** concepts from the perspective of a pilot flying for a commercial operation; however, the skills involved are essential for all pilots. Because commercial operations are often conducted under IFR, if you have already received your instrument rating and you are obtaining your commercial certificate separately, review Chapter 10, Section B — IFR Single-Pilot Resource Management.

COMMERCIAL OPERATIONS

As a commercial pilot, decision making can be complex as you balance public perceptions of aviation, your company's schedule, and your desire to conduct safe flight operations. Previously, your motivation to fly safely was based on your own personal expectations. Now, you have passengers and company personnel to consider when you make choices regarding each flight. Relying on flying for your income could also impair your ability to make sound decisions if you are not careful.

Your priority as pilot in command is to stay focused on the continuous safety of the flight. You might need to make the sometimes difficult and unpopular choice to cancel a flight or divert to an alternate. You assume this responsibility when you contract to work for a commercial operator, so you should fully research these concerns before you accept a position with a particular company. A conscientious employer considers these issues as a part of doing business. You should never make an in-flight decision based on whether it will affect your career. [Figure 13-7]

Figure 13-7. When you work as a pilot for a small company, you have a lot of direct contact with your customers. You might serve as baggage handler, fuel technician, and flight attendant, as well as pilot in command.

The Airmail Pilot's Oath of Office

Some of the first commercial pilots were those who flew the mail, and they were entrusted with a very serious mission — to get the mail through regardless of the weather. Below is the oath that airmail pilots swore to uphold when assuming the job. Would you commit to the same contract?

"I hereby make application for position of pilot in the Air Mail Service and hereby agree, if appointed, to fly whenever called upon and in whatever Air Mail plane that I may be directed by the superintendent of the division to which I am assigned, or his representative on the field, and in the event of my refusal to fly, such refusal shall constitute my resignation from the service, which you are hereby authorized to accept. If appointed, I pledge myself to serve the Air Mail Service of the Post Office Department for a period of one year, and to carry out its orders implicitly, unless separated for cause or in accordance with the foregoing agreement…"

CREW RESOURCE MANAGEMENT

Crew resource management (CRM) training has been a major factor in the marked increase in the safety of commercial operations. The SRM skills that you learn during instrument and commercial training will help you transition to the CRM training environment when you become employed as a professional pilot. A typical CRM program includes classes that provide background in group dynamics, the nature of human error, and the elements of people working with machines. Flight crews might be asked to review NTSB and ASRS reports that highlight the importance of crew coordination.

CRM training also involves the use of flight simulators and aviation training devices during **line-oriented flight training (LOFT)**. Scenarios explore a crew's ability to manage routine flights and handle complex problems, such as severe weather situations or mechanical failures that require more than simply following a procedures checklist. A

LOFT session normally involves a complete flight, including filling out the necessary paperwork and performing crew briefings, while an instructor directs the session and analyzes the crew's behavior. A post-simulation debriefing follows, in which the crew and instructor view video recordings of the simulator session. You can follow the example of LOFT to prepare for flying in a crew environment by practicing in-flight scenarios with other pilots in an aviation training device or simulator. [Figure 13-8]

Figure 13-8. LOFT examines a flight crew's ability to work together to manage tasks, mitigate risk, and make effective decisions.

AERONAUTICAL DECISION MAKING

As pilot in command of an airplane in a commercial operation, you are remain the final authority as to the safe conduct of each flight. However, you share some decisions with management and crew as to where, how, and when each flight occurs. You are typically required to refer to a **flight operations manual (FOM)** that outlines company procedures regarding such items as crew member duties and responsibilities, enroute flight, navigation and communication, weight limitations, emergencies, operating in hazardous weather, and obtaining aircraft maintenance. The FOM also includes the **operations specifications (Ops Specs)**, which are the conditions under which your company must operate in order to retain approval from the FAA. Ops Specs include information regarding authorized areas of operations, aircraft, crew complements, and types of operations (IFR, VFR, day, night).

 Aeronautical decision making is a systematic approach to the mental process used by pilots to consistently determine the best course of action for a given set of circumstances.

ADM PROCESS

When you are employed as a pilot, you might feel that **aeronautical decision making (ADM)** is easier because many choices are made for you and you have applied the ADM process many times as pilot in command. With experience, you become more adept at making effective choices and managing the risks associated with each flight. However, you have many more factors to consider as you make decisions in the commercial environment. Performing each step in the **ADM process** is critical to making sound in-flight judgments. [Figure 13-9]

1 Recognize a change.

The forecast was for VFR conditions along your route of flight; however, as you near a point of interest, you notice a cloud layer obscuring terrain.

2 Define the problem.

You must remain VFR according to your company's operations specifications, ensure flight safety, and please your passengers to the extent possible. You contact Flight Watch and are informed that the visibility is restricted in the area you normally overfly. An updated weather briefing indicates that the marginal weather is isolated and widespread VFR conditions are still forecast to prevail.

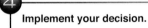

| Type of Aircraft | | Type of Operation | | |
Make/Model/Series	Class of Operation	En Route Flight Rule	Day/Night Conditions	Flight Attendant Cargo On
C-U206F	SEL	VFR	DAY	NONE
BE-90-E90	MEL	IFR/VFR	DAY/NIGHT	NONE
BE-200-200	MEL	IFR/VFR	DAY/NIGHT	NONE

3 Choose a course of action.

Instead of discontinuing the flight and returning to the airport, you decide to divert to another scenic area with VFR conditions.

4 Implement your decision.

You request current weather for another area nearby that you know has a stunning waterfall as a point of interest. After determining that VFR conditions prevail at your new destination, you plot a course and amend your flight plan. You inform your passengers of the alternate routing and continue the flight.

5 Evaluate the outcome.

You pay close attention to the weather conditions and PIREPs in the area. Because one of your passengers is unhappy about the change in plans, you agree to fly over the original site if the weather clears soon. If the conditions do not improve, you may be able to offer a refund or discounted flight.

Figure 13-9. As a pilot flying for a scenic charter operation, you must maintain flight safety as well as balance the demands of your employer and passengers.

The acronym DECIDE is used by the FAA to describe the basic steps in the decision-making process.

    1. Detect the fact that a change has occurred.

    2. Estimate a need to counter or react to the change.

    3. Choose a desirable outcome for the success of the flight.

    4. Identify actions that could successfully control the change.

    5. Do the necessary action to adapt to the change.

    6. Evaluate the effect of the action.

SELF ASSESSMENT

You are used to establishing your own personal minimums and limitations through **self assessment** and determining a plan for maintaining your currency and proficiency. As a professional pilot employed by a commercial operator, the company's Ops Specs provide the restrictions under which you must operate. For example, the Ops Specs might limit the types of approaches that you are authorized to perform or specify ceiling and visibility minimums that are higher then those published for the approach.

In some cases, flight crew qualifications are the limiting factor for the minimums on an instrument approach. For example, you are not allowed to fly some procedures, such as CAT II and III approach procedures, unless you have received specific training and the airplane is equipped and authorized to conduct these approaches. Part 121 and 135 regulations also require increased approach minimums for pilots who have limited experience in the airplane.

Although you might not have as much responsibility for determining your minimums and scheduling training, your assessment of your fitness for flight is critical as a professional pilot. The I'M SAFE checklist is still an effective way to consider the factors that affect your fitness prior to flight. In addition, you must be aware of dangerous tendencies, referred to as **operational pitfalls**, that can develop as you gain experience. As you face pressure from your company to complete a flight as planned, please passengers, and meet schedules, you must be on the alert for these pitfalls and be prepared to counteract them. Performing self-critiques after each flight is one way to help you recognize if you have any of these tendencies. [Figure 13-10]

 You must recognize and eliminate any dangerous tendencies that could affect your flight safety. The FAA has identified 12 of these tendencies that are referred to as operational pitfalls.

Operational Pitfall	Description
Peer Pressure	Allowing the opinions of coworkers or other pilots to prevent you from evaluating a situation objectively.
Mind-Set	Inability to recognize and cope with changes in a given situation.
Get-There-Itis	Fixating on the original goal or destination, combined with disregarding any alternative course of action.
Duck-Under Syndrome	Succumbing to the temptation to make it into an airport by descending below minimums on an instrument approach. Also applies to VFR pilots who attempt to land under a cloud layer that is lower than VFR minimums.
Scud Running	Trying to maintain visual contact with the terrain at low altitudes when instrument conditions are present.
Continuing VFR Flight into Instrument Conditions	Flying into deteriorating weather by a non-instrument-qualified pilot, entering instrument conditions—resulting in controlled flight into terrain (CFIT) or spatial disorientation and loss of control.
Getting Behind the Aircraft	Becoming reactive instead of proactive, losing the ability to anticipate the next events and being constantly surprised by what happens next. A result of poor workload management.
Loss of Situational Awareness	Losing track of the aircraft's geographical location or becoming unable to recognize other deteriorating circumstances; a consequence of getting behind the aircraft.
Operating Without Adequate Fuel Reserves	Allowing overconfidence, lack of flight planning, or a disregard for regulations to undermine your judgment regarding fuel. Also can occur when encountering unexpected headwinds or delays during flight without recalculating the flight plan.
Descent Below the Minimum Enroute Altitude	Ducking under by a pilot flying IFR.
Flying Outside the Envelope	Overestimating your aircraft's performance or your own flying skills.
Neglect of Flight Planning, Preflight Inspections, and Checklists	Relying on memory, regular flying skills, and familiar routes by an experienced pilot with resulting neglect of established procedures and published checklists.

Figure 13-10. The FAA has identified 12 operational pitfalls that can endanger pilots who become complacent with experience.

HAZARDOUS ATTITUDES

Even as you gain experience, you are not immune from **hazardous attitudes**. In fact, you might be overconfident in your abilities so you have an increased risk of exhibiting attitudes such as macho and invulnerability. You also must be alert for hazardous attitudes exhibited by a copilot. Perform a self-analysis after each flight. Did you show any signs of a hazardous attitude even during routine situations? Which hazardous attitude do you have the greatest tendency to exhibit under pressure? Do not hesitate to ask copilots or instructors of their impression of your actions. In this way, you can be better prepared to recognize and manage the effects of a hazardous attitude when you face a critical challenge during a flight. [Figure 13-11]

 Five hazardous attitudes that can interfere with the ability to make effective decisions are: anti-authority, impulsivity, invulnerability, macho, and resignation.

 Recognition of hazardous thoughts is the first step toward neutralizing them. To effectively counteract a hazardous attitude, redirect the attitude so that correct action can be taken. After recognizing a thought as hazardous, label it as hazardous, then state the corresponding antidote.

SECTION B ■ Commercial Pilot SRM

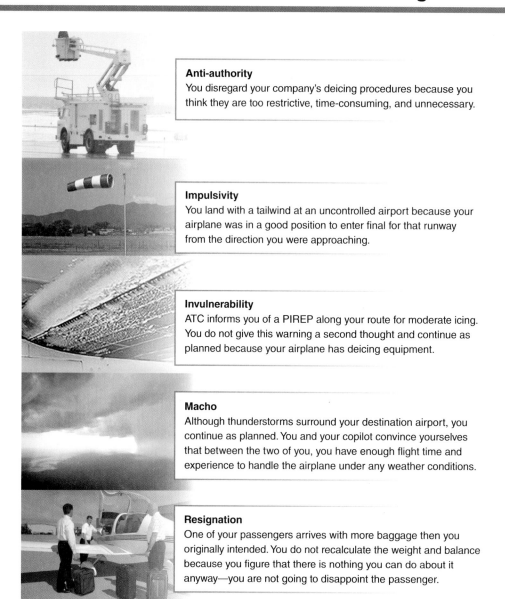

Anti-authority
You disregard your company's deicing procedures because you think they are too restrictive, time-consuming, and unnecessary.

Impulsivity
You land with a tailwind at an uncontrolled airport because your airplane was in a good position to enter final for that runway from the direction you were approaching.

Invulnerability
ATC informs you of a PIREP along your route for moderate icing. You do not give this warning a second thought and continue as planned because your airplane has deicing equipment.

Macho
Although thunderstorms surround your destination airport, you continue as planned. You and your copilot convince yourselves that between the two of you, you have enough flight time and experience to handle the airplane under any weather conditions.

Resignation
One of your passengers arrives with more baggage then you originally intended. You do not recalculate the weight and balance because you figure that there is nothing you can do about it anyway—you are not going to disappoint the passenger.

Figure 13-11. You might be displaying a hazardous attitude if you take these types of actions in similar situations.

RISK MANAGEMENT

You might have been using a tool such as the 5Ps prior to and during flights for **risk management**. You can review a flight planning and in-flight scenario using the 5Ps in Chapter 10, Section B – *IFR Single-Pilot Resource Management.* As a professional pilot, your company might provide you with a risk management checklist to use prior to flight and SOPs might dictate crew actions to take during flight to evaluate and mitigate risk.

In the commercial environment, you will encounter some risk factors that are specific to your operation or that require additional consideration. For example, the pilot risk factor of fatigue due to workload, sleep loss, and circadian disruption is a particular problem due to the unique schedules of commercial pilots. Although you are familiar with many of the risks associated with passengers, the demands of paying customers place more pressure on you to complete flights as planned. If you work for a large commercial operation, company ground personnel perform many of your preflight tasks, so you must be careful to identify and mitigate risks associated with aircraft performance and limitations. [Figure 13-12]

Pilot
Although FAR Parts 121 and 135 list specific flight time limitations and rest requirements for flight crews, you must assume joint responsibility with your company for ensuring that you are not fatigued and are fit for duty.

Passengers
As a professional pilot with paying passengers, you must meet the challenge of balancing the needs of your passengers with maintaining flight safety.

Plane
To ensure the airplane is airworthy, your responsibilities as a professional pilot could include tasks such as confirming specialized equipment is onboard, arranging deicing services, stocking drinks and snacks, and verifying performance data provided by ground personnel.

Programming
Because a flight management system (FMS) provides information for continuous automatic navigation, guidance, and aircraft performance management, you must be vigilant about making the proper inputs and verifying the correct data is displayed.

Copyright Boeing

Plan
If you have reservations regarding the success of the flight, do not allow yourself to be pressured by management or passengers to take off or continue a flight as planned. State your position clearly, and provide evidence, such as weather reports, ATC recordings, or maintenance records.

Figure 13-12. Consider how these risk factors in the 5P categories apply to commercial operations.

Risk also stems from external pressures that exist in commercial operations. Often the purpose of the flight influences a decision. For example, turbulence that would cause you to cancel a sightseeing flight might be an acceptable risk on a flight to deliver an organ for transplant. Time-related risks that you must manage as a professional pilot include: the need of a company agent or ground personnel to open a gate for another aircraft; insistence from ATC to expedite taxi for takeoff or to meet a restriction in clearance time; the pressure to keep on schedule when delays have occurred due to maintenance or weather; or the inclination to hurry to avoid exceeding duty-time regulations. [Figure 13-13]

RISK MANAGEMENT

REPORT

The airplane was taking off on the first flight of the day and had accelerated normally during the short field takeoff roll. During entry into the initial climb, the airplane suddenly rolled into an uncommanded left bank and entered an uncontrolled descent. The left wingtip struck terrain. Photos taken five minutes after the accident show that the leading edges and tops of the wings and horizontal tail surfaces were covered in rough frost.

REPORT

We agreed that the taxi time needed to taxi from the de-ice pad to the end of the runway would probably take 10 to 12 minutes and this would easily exceed the 5 minute limitation in the section under "OPERATIONAL RESTRICTIONS"…However, pressure was put on the pilots that it was the stance of "the company" that we try to taxi out, de-ice, and depart.

ANALYSIS

To ensure a safe flight, the pilots in these situations needed to assess and mitigate two primary risks: one associated with the plane— ice and frost on the wings, and the other with the plan—pressure to depart to complete a commercial operation. The first report involved a charter crew flying a Cessna 206 who did not properly manage risk, including pilot risk of the tendency toward get-there-itis. The airline crew involved in the second scenario worked together to assess the risk and agreed that they would not be able to complete deicing in a safe manner although they felt company pressure to depart.

Figure 13-13. An NTSB report and an ASRS account illustrates the importance of risk management in the commercial environment.

TASK MANAGEMENT

As a professional pilot, you typically perform **task management** as part of a crew. Your company's SOPs designate each crew member's responsibilities. Effective cockpit communication is critical to successful task management—in two-pilot crew operations, each person is responsible for completing specific tasks, and you both need to be informed of the other's actions. In most crew operations, the **pilot flying (PF)** is in charge of manipulating the controls, while **pilot monitoring (PM)** is responsible for such tasks as monitoring the flight progress, communication with ATC, and navigation.

PLANNING AND PRIORITIZING

If you work for a large commercial operation, your responsibility might shift from performing the actual flight planning to supervising and verifying that the information given to you is timely and correct. Do not become complacent because many of your preflight tasks are performed by dispatchers. After reviewing all the flight data, rehearse the flight, and prepare for any contingencies that might arise.

In contrast, when you work for a smaller company, you might have many more preflight responsibilities than you had as a private pilot. For example, in addition to the normal required preflight duties, you could also be responsible for preparing a flight manifest, which includes items such as the number of passengers, the origin and destination of the flight, the registration number of the airplane, and weight and balance information.

Regardless of the type of company, you typically arrive an hour prior before the scheduled departure to prepare for the flight. In order to complete all of your duties within the hour, you must plan ahead to establish priorities and a logical sequence to accomplish tasks so you are not rushed and do not forget items. You might accomplish some tasks prior to arriving at the airport. [Figure 13-14]

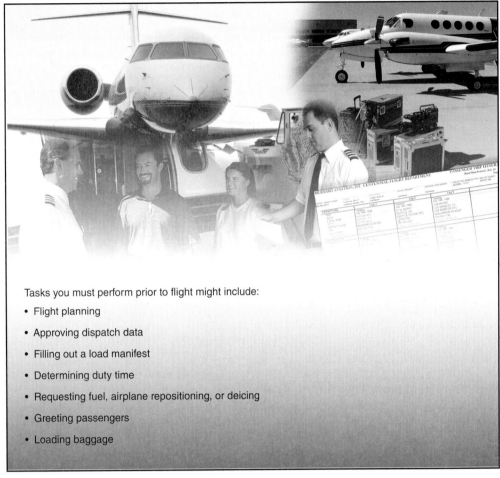

Tasks you must perform prior to flight might include:

- Flight planning
- Approving dispatch data
- Filling out a load manifest
- Determining duty time
- Requesting fuel, airplane repositioning, or deicing
- Greeting passengers
- Loading baggage

Figure 13-14. Planning and prioritizing are essential to accomplish the many tasks required to prepare for the flight after you arrive at the airport.

During flight, one way to plan for high workload periods and to ensure that both crew members are prepared to perform the necessary tasks is to perform briefings. Before takeoff, review the proposed departure routing, either given by ATC or through published procedures. Note any required climb gradients and obstructions or terrain that might be a factor on initial climb. As you near the destination, brief the arrival and approach procedures.

As you fly larger, more complex airplanes in the commercial environment, performing an operational briefing is essential. You are required to comply with specific airplane performance limitations that govern approach and landing so you must determine your airplane's performance under specific conditions and in a particular configuration. You must also gather information about the airport and runway to make effective decisions about the approach procedure you intend to fly and your airplane's capabilities. You should review and brief all this information as you prepare to fly the approach.

RESOURCE USE

The amount of resources available to you most likely will multiply when you work as a professional pilot and the efficiency of the flight depends on your ability to effectively use these resources. Depending upon the type of operations your company conducts, you might have more advanced aircraft equipment, additional crew members in the cockpit or cabin, and more personnel on the ground to support each flight, such as dispatchers, maintenance technicians, baggage handlers, and gate personnel. Though these people are there so that you can focus on flying the airplane, you still are responsible as PIC to check all weather, route, and airport information concerning the flight, as well as ensure the airplane is airworthy.

A thorough understanding of the systems and operation of all equipment on board the aircraft is critical to flight safety. A number of systems are considered vital to safe commercial operations, and their use is required during certain stages of flight under FAR Parts 121, 125, or 135. For example, the use of an autopilot is required for certain aircraft to be operated under IFR with a single pilot, as stated in FAR 135.105.

Company procedures dictate how specific equipment is set up and other equipment is left to pilot technique. In general, the techniques used by pilots at a specific company are similar. For example, after the anticipated approach and runway have been selected, you use information gathered from ATIS, dispatch (if available), ATC, the specific chart for the approach selected, and any other available resources to set up each side of the cockpit. The number of items that you set ahead of time depends on the level of automation and the avionics available. You might set airspeed bugs based on performance calculations, the altimeter bug to DA or MDA, the go-around thrust/power setting, and the navigation and communication radios. You also follow checklist procedures to set up aircraft-specific items, such as the autopilot modes, pressurization system, fuel system, seat belt signs, and anti-icing/deicing equipment. [Figure 13-15]

Figure 13-15. The pilot monitoring (PM) usually programs the GPS navigation equipment or FMS for the approach and the pilot flying (PF) verifies the information.

An **electronic flight bag (EFB)** is another valuable cockpit resource. EFBs can be mobile devices, units that are mounted and connected to the airplane, or permanently installed in the aircraft panel. You can use EFB features during flight planning and during each phase of flight. EFBs display flight plans, routes, checklists, flight operations manuals, regulations, minimum equipment lists (MELs), moving map and weather displays, approach charts, airport diagrams, logbooks, and operating procedures. You can also use the EFB to calculate aircraft performance and accomplish many tasks traditionally handled by a dispatcher. [Figure 13-16]

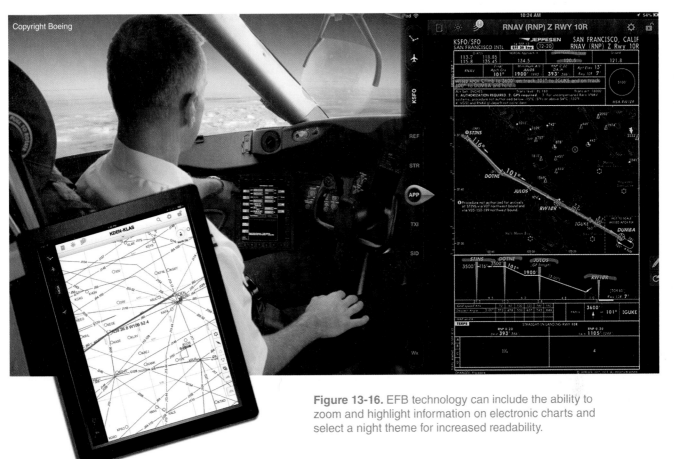

Figure 13-16. EFB technology can include the ability to zoom and highlight information on electronic charts and select a night theme for increased readability.

Research that separated crews flying simulators into higher and lower performing groups for comparison found that the ability to use resources to gather and interpret information is key to effective decision making. The higher performing crews engaged in more information gathering, monitoring, and planning. These crews requested significantly more data, such as weather conditions, from ATC. In addition, to allow more time for making decisions and accomplishing necessary tasks, higher performance crews requested ATC assistance in the form of radar vectors and clearances for holding or long final approaches. [Figure 13-17]

Pilot's Operating Handbook

RESOURCE USE

REPORT

During cruise, we got a #1 engine overheat light ... then it went out. [Later], the light came back on, followed by a fire loop fault light. We got clearance to divert to the nearest airport. While completing the emergency checklists, we got a #1 engine fire light and bell. We declared an emergency and fired both extinguisher bottles. We landed without further problems. The fire trucks reported no evidence of smoke or fire, and [later] the mechanics confirmed a short-circuit in the #1 engine fire detection system. I had the copilot fly while I got hold of company. We had a jumpseat pilot ... who made an announcement to the passengers, after which he handled ATC communications. I completed checklists, kept an eye on aircraft position, and talked to the lead flight attendant. CRM can take full credit for the uneventful completion of this flight.

ANALYSIS

Through the effective use of resources, this crew was able to successfully manage their workload during an emergency situation. Each crewmember performed specific tasks and the help of a jumpseat pilot was enlisted. By declaring an emergency and requesting an amended clearance, the crew was able to utilize ATC as a valuable resource. Extensive knowledge of the aircraft's systems and the efficient use of checklists proved essential. Additional resources on the ground included an emergency crew and aviation maintenance technicians.

Figure 13-17. As you study this report, consider how the crew used planning, prioritizing, and available resources to manage tasks during an emergency.

CREW COORDINATION

Your first experience in the crew environment normally is as the first officer, or second in command. Although the captain has the final authority as pilot in command, your experience and skill are a vital part of the cockpit resources. In certain situations, you might have information that the captain does not possess that is essential to flight safety. You should voice your opinions in a respectful yet confident manner, and express your concern regarding any practices you deem unsafe. Depending on the procedures specified by your employer, you should expect to fly the airplane roughly 50% of the time that you are in the cockpit so you can maintain proficiency and gain the experience necessary to eventually act as PIC.

When you make the transition to the left seat, you should provide leadership and exercise authority in a manner that encourages and supports an open exchange of opinions. Because it is your responsibility to provide direction for the other crew members, you must be assertive in your actions. However, you must be careful to avoid a domineering attitude. By allocating duties, as well as soliciting and accepting feedback from crew members, you will facilitate a professional and effective working environment.

Strict adherence to established procedures and consistent use of checklists are among the most important factors in the successful reduction of accidents and incidents in commercial crew operations. Proper checklist use is a core task management skill. Most flight crews use the **challenge-response method** when performing checklist items. This procedure requires one pilot to read the checklist item out loud, while the other crew member completes the task and repeats the instruction verbally. Because both crew members are directly involved in the checklist process, the chance that a mistake or omission will occur is reduced. [Figure 13-18]

"Flaps . . ."   ". . . set for approach."

Figure 13-18. The challenge-response method enhances communication as both crew members are involved in completing important checklist items.

SITUATIONAL AWARENESS

Although having a second pilot generally increases your overall **situational awareness**, issues unique to being part of a two-pilot crew can detract from your knowledge of the position and state of the aircraft. For example, you might have trouble maintaining an awareness of operations that are not under your direct control. If you are not responsible for communicating with ATC, you might not be immediately aware of a radio problem. You need to ensure that you maintain an awareness of the entire flight situation by eliciting information from other crew members and keep the other pilot informed of the status of operations for which you are responsible. Typically, the PF monitors and controls the aircraft, regardless of the level of automation employed and the PM monitors the aircraft and the actions of the PF.

OBSTACLES TO SITUATIONAL AWARENESS

Complacency is a particular risk for professional pilots. Extensive experience in the same type of airplane, flying a consistent scheduled route, and relying heavily on automation can lead to complacency. One way to prevent complacency is to follow **standard operating procedures (SOPs)** each time you fly. SOPs specifically dictate what procedures the crew should follow in a wide variety of situations. SOPs include crew member responsibilities and procedures for every phase of flight. In addition, SOPs include items such as procedures for determining required runway lengths and airport restrictions, as well as airplane and avionics configurations and flight deck flow patterns for specific flight operations. [Figure 13-19]

SOPs typically include procedures that apply to:

- Flight plans/dispatch procedures/takeoff and landing calculations
- Boarding passengers and cargo
- Maintenance procedures
- Flight phases: taxiing, takeoff, climb, cruise, descent, approach, landing
- Use of checklists
- Communications and briefings
- Flight deck discipline
- Use of automation
- Altitude awareness
- Position reports and PIREPs
- Emergency procedures
- Wind shear avoidance

Figure 13-19. Your company's SOPs will most likely cover topics ranging from the use of automation to flying a stabilized approach.

Following the sterile cockpit procedure is another way to reduce distractions during critical phases of flight. Part 121 and 135 regulations specifically prohibit crew members from performing nonessential duties or activities while the aircraft is involved in taxi, takeoff, landing, and all other flight operations conducted below 10,000 feet MSL, except cruise flight. Whether you are part of a commercial crew or flying with friends, adhering to sterile cockpit rules, helps you prevent runway incursions, CFIT, and altitude and course deviations during taxi, takeoff, and departure. To ensure all crew members are reminded of this requirement, brief the sterile cockpit rule prior to engine start or taxi. [Figure 13-20]

During all ground operations involving taxi, takeoff and landing, and all other flight operations conducted below 10,000 feet, except during cruise flight:

- Do not perform any duties, such as ordering galley supplies, confirming passenger connections, promoting the air carrier, pointing out sights of interest, and filling out company records during a critical phase of flight except those duties required for the safe operation of the aircraft.

- Do not engage in or permit any activity, such as eating meals, engaging in nonessential conversations and communications, and reading publications not related to the flight during a critical phase of flight that could distract any flight crew member from the performance of his or her duties or which could interfere in any way with the proper conduct of those duties.

Copyright Boeing

Figure 13-20. Regulations for commercial operations are very specific regarding maintaining a sterile cockpit.

SITUATIONAL AWARENESS DURING GROUND OPERATIONS

A key to maintaining situational awareness on the ground and preventing runway incursions is adhering to SOPs for taxiing. SOPs should increase flight crew situational awareness without increasing workload during taxi. Effective SOPs cover seven major categories: planning, situational awareness, written taxi instructions, flight crew verbal communication, ATC/pilot communication, taxi, and exterior aircraft lighting. {Figure 13-21]

Categories of SOPs to increase situational awareness during ground operations include:

- **Planning** — Brief taxi operations before taxi on departure and prior to initial descent on arrival.
- **Situational awareness** — Use a continuous loop process to actively monitor and update your progress during taxi.
- **Written taxi instructions** — Write down complex taxi instructions as a reference for reading back the instructions to ATC and to confirm the taxi route and any restrictions.
- **Flight crew verbal communication** — Confirm that you understand all ATC instructions to the other crew member so you have a chance to discover and correct any misunderstandings.
- **ATC/pilot communication** —Use standard phraseology and read back clearances.
- **Taxi** —Complete all pre-taxi checklist items and enter all navigation data prior to taxi. During taxi, use the airport diagram and confirm the correct taxiway or runway with the heading indicator.
- **Exterior aircraft lighting** — Use various combinations of exterior lights to convey your location and intent to other pilots, ATC, and ground personnel.

Figure 13-21. The FAA recommends that companies create SOPs for crews to follow that increase situational awareness during ground operations.

Brief the taxi route, hold-short positions, crossing runways, and runway incursion hot spots. In addition to these items, when flying as part of a crew, your pre-taxi briefing should include when and where to perform aircraft checklists and company communication, a reminder to turn off cell phones and devices, and SOPs, such as maintaining a sterile cockpit and displaying the airport diagram or low visibility taxi chart.

Contact ATC to resolve any persistent disagreement or uncertainty among crew members about any taxi clearance. When it is necessary to stop monitoring any ATC frequency to prepare for takeoff or landing, tell the other flight crew member when you stop and when you resume monitoring the ATC frequency. During taxi, one crew member can be responsible for monitoring the airplane's position on a moving map display. For example, EFB applications include a display of your position on an airport chart or a database that dynamically renders maps of an airport's runways, taxiways, and structures. [Figure 13-22]

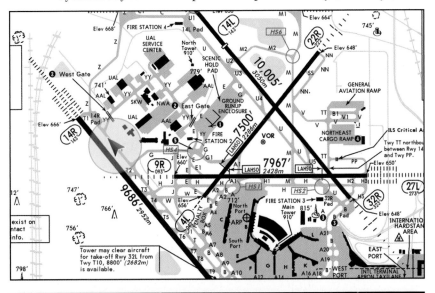

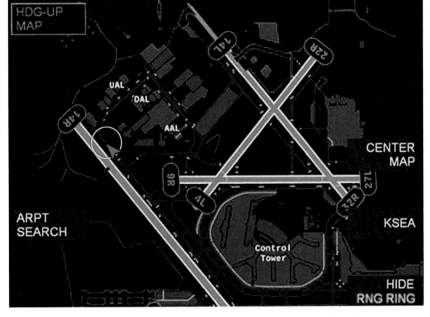

Figure 13-22. Both of these EFB applications help you identify and anticipate the airplane's location on the surface to aid in situational awareness.

As a professional pilot, you might use standard taxi routes at high density airports with scheduled airline service, or charted low visibility taxi procedures. These published procedures provide details on the route to a specific runway for enhanced situational awareness. Regardless of the taxi route, use a continuous loop process to actively monitor and update your progress during taxi—know the airplane's present location and mentally calculate the next location on the route that requires increased attention, such as a turn onto another taxiway, an intersecting runway, or a hot spot. [Figure 13-23]

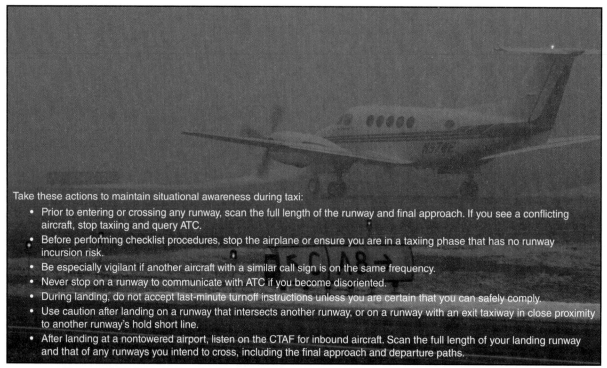

Take these actions to maintain situational awareness during taxi:
- Prior to entering or crossing any runway, scan the full length of the runway and final approach. If you see a conflicting aircraft, stop taxiing and query ATC.
- Before performing checklist procedures, stop the airplane or ensure you are in a taxiing phase that has no runway incursion risk.
- Be especially vigilant if another aircraft with a similar call sign is on the same frequency.
- Never stop on a runway to communicate with ATC if you become disoriented.
- During landing, do not accept last-minute turnoff instructions unless you are certain that you can safely comply.
- Use caution after landing on a runway that intersects another runway, or on a runway with an exit taxiway in close proximity to another runway's hold short line.
- After landing at a nontowered airport, listen on the CTAF for inbound aircraft. Scan the full length of your landing runway and that of any runways you intend to cross, including the final approach and departure paths.

Figure 13-23. You must maintain situational awareness during ground operations to decrease your risk of a runway incursion.

CONTROLLED FLIGHT INTO TERRAIN

Your company's type of operation, SOPs, and safety culture are all factors that affect your risk of **controlled flight into terrain (CFIT)** as a professional pilot. The Flight Safety Foundation designed a CFIT risk assessment safety tool—the CFIT Checklist—as part of an international program to reduce CFIT accidents. You can download the checklist from the Flight Safety Foundation website. [Figure 13-24]

Part I: CFIT Risk Assessment

Section 1—Destination CFIT Risk Factors   Value

Airport and Approach Control Capabilities:

ATC approach radar with MSAWS 0   _____
ATC minimum radar vectoring charts.. 0   _____
ATC radar only... −10   _____
ATC radar coverage limited by terrain masking............................... −15   _____
No radar coverage available (out of service/not installed)................. −30   _____
No ATC service.. −30   _____

Expected A
Airport lo
ILS ....
VOR/DM
Nonprecis
to the airp
NDB ......
Visual nig

Runway Lig
Complete

① Record the values assigned to the risk factors that apply to a specific flight or flight segment.

Part II: CFIT Risk-Reduction Factors

Section 1—Company Culture   Value

Corporate/company management:

Places safety before schedule 20
CEO signs off on flight operations manual 20
Maintains a centralized safety function... 20
Fosters reporting of all CFIT incidents without threat of discipline 20
Fosters communication of hazards to others 15
Requires standards for IFR currency and CRM training.................... 15
Places no negative connotation on a diversion or missed approach.... 20

115–120 points   Tops in company culture

② Record the values for the risk reduction factors in four sections—Company Culture, Flight Standards, Hazard Awareness and Training, and Aircraft Equipment—that apply to your company.

Part III: Your CFIT Risk

Part I CFIT Risk Factors Total (−) _____ + Part II CFIT Risk-Reduction Factors Tota
= CFIT Risk Score (+) _____

③ Add the totals from Part 1 and Part II to determine your CFIT Risk Score. A negative CFIT Risk Score indicates a significant threat.

Figure 13-24. You can use the CFIT Checklist to evaluate the risk of CFIT for specific flight operations and to enhance your awareness of CFIT risk factors.

In addition to calculating risk for a specific flight, the CFIT Checklist is a valuable resource for identifying general factors that affect CFIT risk. Your risk increases at airports that do not have radar or approach control capability or if you are flying a nonprecision approach to a runway with a limited lighting system. Other factors to consider when assessing CFIT risk are your company's type of operation and the crew configuration. For example, the risk for a two-person crew flying scheduled trips is less than a single-pilot freight operation.

Risk is reduced when your company culture values safety, you follow SOPs, you receive hazard awareness training, and your aircraft is equipped with a **terrain awareness and warning system (TAWS)**. TAWS equipment displays color-coded terrain data on a moving map and provides aural warnings and alert annunciations if the aircraft is close to terrain. All turbine-powered aircraft with six or more passenger seats (not including the pilot and copilot) must be equipped with TAWS. [Figure 13-25]

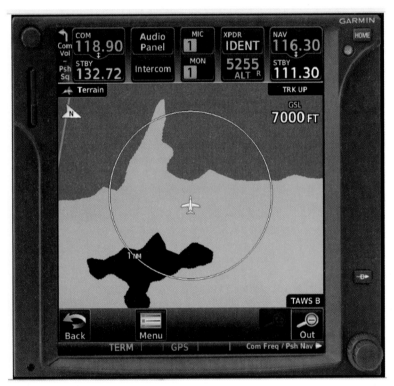

Figure 13-25. Installation of TAWS by air carriers and professional flight departments has significantly reduced the number of CFIT-related accidents in the United States.

You can take specific actions to decrease your risk of CFIT during each phase of flight. For initial climb and departure, thoroughly review and brief the charted departure procedure or the departure instructions provided by ATC. Verify that ATC instructions provide adequate terrain clearance—do not assume that your assigned course and altitude ensures that you clear the surrounding terrain. Ensure that your airplane can meet any required climb gradients. Also brief the approach procedure in use at the departure airport in case you must return to the airport. Prior to takeoff, set all communication and navigation frequencies and course selectors to eliminate distractions below 1,000 feet AGL.

To decrease your risk of CFIT during cruise flight, prior to departure review the enroute chart to determine the minimum safe altitudes for the proposed flight. Consider your performance, especially when you plan to fly over high terrain. During flight, use VFR charts or a moving map to visualize the terrain you are flying over.

During the final approach and landing phase of flight, performing proper approach briefings and flying a stabilized approach are critical to preventing CFIT. If you must fly a nonprecision approach, brief the procedure as a stabilized approach using a constant rate of descent. Brief the missed approach procedure with emphasis on the direction of the initial missed approach turn. In addition to briefings, you can take actions to reduce the risk of CFIT during approach and landing that apply to altimeters, safe altitudes, ATC procedures, flight crew complacency, and approach procedures. [Figure 13-26]

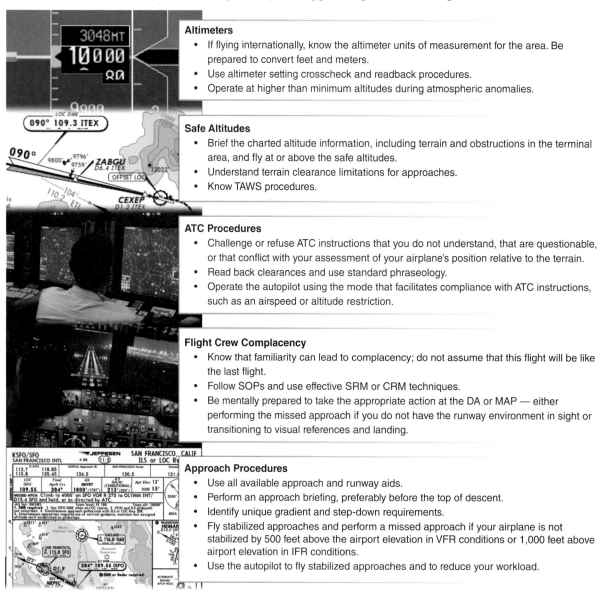

Altimeters
- If flying internationally, know the altimeter units of measurement for the area. Be prepared to convert feet and meters.
- Use altimeter setting crosscheck and readback procedures.
- Operate at higher than minimum altitudes during atmospheric anomalies.

Safe Altitudes
- Brief the charted altitude information, including terrain and obstructions in the terminal area, and fly at or above the safe altitudes.
- Understand terrain clearance limitations for approaches.
- Know TAWS procedures.

ATC Procedures
- Challenge or refuse ATC instructions that you do not understand, that are questionable, or that conflict with your assessment of your airplane's position relative to the terrain.
- Read back clearances and use standard phraseology.
- Operate the autopilot using the mode that facilitates compliance with ATC instructions, such as an airspeed or altitude restriction.

Flight Crew Complacency
- Know that familiarity can lead to complacency; do not assume that this flight will be like the last flight.
- Follow SOPs and use effective SRM or CRM techniques.
- Be mentally prepared to take the appropriate action at the DA or MAP — either performing the missed approach if you do not have the runway environment in sight or transitioning to visual references and landing.

Approach Procedures
- Use all available approach and runway aids.
- Perform an approach briefing, preferably before the top of descent.
- Identify unique gradient and step-down requirements.
- Fly stabilized approaches and perform a missed approach if your airplane is not stabilized by 500 feet above the airport elevation in VFR conditions or 1,000 feet above airport elevation in IFR conditions.
- Use the autopilot to fly stabilized approaches and to reduce your workload.

Figure 13-26. CFIT prevention actions for the approach and landing phase can be divided into five categories.

Because CFIT is always the final link in an accident chain, all the SRM skills, including risk, task, and automation management, aeronautical decision making, and maintaining situational awareness apply to preventing a CFIT accident. In crewed cockpits, the presence of a second pilot generally decreases the risk of a CFIT accident. However, the copilot can also be a distraction unless the crew has been trained to work well together and is following good CRM techniques. [Figure 13-27]

CONTROLLED FLIGHT INTO TERRAIN

REPORT

On June 8, 1992, a Beechcraft C99 scheduled passenger flight crashed while maneuvering to land at the Anniston Metropolitan Airport in Anniston, Alabama. The NTSB determined that this CFIT accident occurred when the flight crew experienced a loss of situational awareness. When cleared for the ILS approach to Runway 5 at Anniston, the flight crew turned the airplane north away from the airport in the mistaken belief that the airplane was south of the airport. The flight crew did not fly outbound or execute the procedure turn which was required by the IAP. The C99 intercepted the back course localizer signal for the ILS approach, and the flight crew tried to fly the approach at an excessive airspeed about 2,000 feet above the specified altitude for crossing the FAF. The airplane continued a controlled descent until it impacted terrain.

0848:10
ATC: *. . . and a eight sixty one, proceed direct Bogga maintain four thousand 'til Bogga, cleared localizer run- er ILS runway five approach.*
F/O: *Direct, direct to Bogga four thousand and cleared for the ILS runway five. Eight sixty one. Thank you.*
Captain: *Ask him distance from . . .*
F/O: *From Bogga?*
Captain: *That's okay, I'll just . . .*
F/O: *We're ah . . . minus six point one. We're five miles from Bogga.*
F/O: *Go ahead and slow on up.*
F/O: *There you go keep the shiny side up.*
Captain: *Ah.*
F/O: *There you go. Should have moved your heading bug. Here you go I'll get you set in here.*
Captain: *Okay let's go approach flaps.*
F/O: *Speed checks coming now.*
F/O: *Didn't realize that you're going to get this much on your first day did ya.*
Captain: *Well it's all kind of ganged up here on me a little fast.*

0851:34
F/O: *Okay watch your airspeed. One fifteen on the airspeed.*
F/O: *We're inside — through twenty-two we can continue our descent on down. We're way high.*
Captain: *Okay, is the glide slope working?*
F/O: *Nope I'm not gettin' any.*
F/O: *So with no glide slope, we're down to eleven hundred.*
Captain: *You got your frequency in there?*
F/O: *Five hundred — one eleven five, double check, yup.*
Captain: *What's our missed approach point now?*
F/O: *Missed approach at the middle marker ah . . .*
F/O: *Eleven hundred but we need to add a hundred so twelve hundred.*
F/O: *Comin' up . . .*

0852:25 - *Sound of impact*

ANALYSIS

The NTSB determined that one of the causes of this accident was the failure of the flight crew to use approved instrument flight procedures, which resulted in a loss of situational awareness and terrain clearance. The crew's failure to effectively manage their cockpit duties in part stemmed from the pairing of an inadequately prepared captain with a relatively inexperienced first officer. In addition, crew coordination suffered due to a role reversal on the part of the captain and first officer.

Figure 13-27. A review of the details of this accident and an excerpt from its transcript reveals how important the skills that apply to SRM and CRM are to maintaining situational awareness.

AUTOMATION MANAGEMENT

As you continue to gain experience and operate airplanes with more advanced automation and navigation systems, you will likely find yourself using the autopilot for most of your flying. As a professional pilot flying a large airplane in a commercial operation, you typically use the autopilot for most of the flight and hand-fly the airplane only during takeoffs and landings. Many computer systems can fly the airplanes more precisely and efficiently than a human pilot can and certain instrument procedures require the use of a flight director system, head-up display (HUD), autopilot or even autoland capability. These procedures typically require Ops Specs approval and specialized flight crew training to effectively manage the automation. [Figure 13-28]

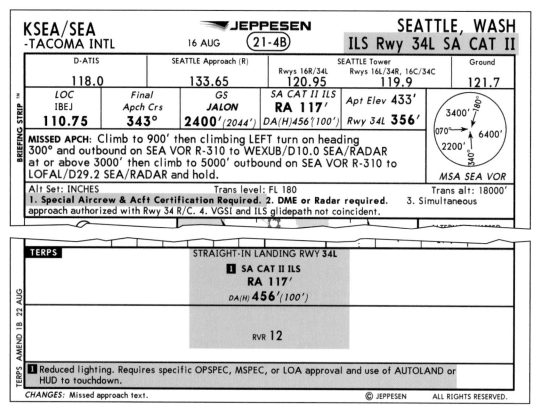

Figure 13-28. In addition to other requirements, This special authorization CAT II approach requires the use of an autoland or head-up display to touchdown.

Effective **automation management** requires training to not only command, recognize, and monitor the various modes of flight but to gain a thorough understanding of how the autopilot interacts with other systems. You also must learn the proper action if the equipment fails or does something unexpected. And, you must be proficient in "stick and rudder" skills so you are able to hand-fly the airplane if necessary.

INFORMATION MANAGEMENT

You might transition to airplanes that are equipped with **flight management systems (FMS)** and automation systems that control both the airplane's lateral navigation (autoflight) and vertical navigation and airspeed (autothrust). An FMS is a flight computer system that uses a large database to allow routes to be pre-programmed and fed into the system by means of a data loader. The FMS is constantly updated with respect to position accuracy by reference to conventional navigation aids, inertial reference system technology, or GPS. The sophisticated program and its associated database ensure that the most appropriate navigation aids or inputs are automatically selected during the information update cycle.

In addition to enroute flight planning, for flights under IFR, you must program and monitor procedures, such as SIDs, STARs and approaches. Although, many of these tasks can be accomplished prior to flight and during low workload periods, at times you must be able modify programming to reflect changes in ATC clearances. To maintain situational awareness, it is critical that the crew member programming the FMS or GPS equipment verifies the inputs with the other pilot. [Figure 13-29]

Use Equipment Operating Levels
Be able to use automation and avionics equipment at different levels. Be able to precisely control the airplane and manage information whether you are hand-flying or performed a coupled approach.

Copyright Boeing

Verify Programming
After the PM programs the GPS navigation equipment or FM, the PF must verify the information.

Perform Callouts
Verbalize your actions when changing a mode, programming equipment, or setting up a display to verify to yourself and inform the other crew member.

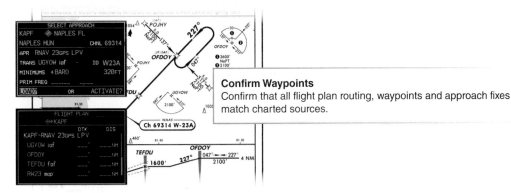

Confirm Waypoints
Confirm that all flight plan routing, waypoints and approach fixes match charted sources.

Know the Mode of Operation
Know at all times which modes are engaged and which modes are armed to engage. Verify that armed functions, such as navigation tracking or altitude capture, engage at the appropriate time.

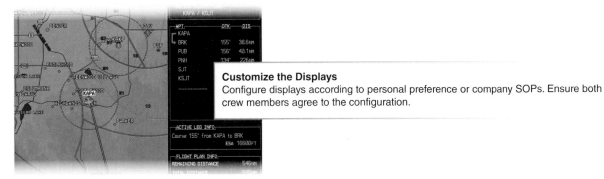

Customize the Displays
Configure displays according to personal preference or company SOPs. Ensure both crew members agree to the configuration.

Figure 13-29. Take these actions to effectively manage both automation and information during commercial operations.

AUTOMATION SURPRISE

An **automation surprise** can cause you to be momentarily confused about the state of the automation and, often, you have no immediate idea of what action to take to correct the situation. An automation surprise typically occurs in one of two ways:

- A change in the automation system is unexpected or uncommanded and is either recognized or unrecognized by you, such as an unexpected change in navigation mode.
- You command a change but the system does something unexpected, such as failing to capture an altitude. [Figure 13-30]

AUTOMATION MANAGEMENT

REPORT

On July 6, 2013, a Boeing 777-200ER, operating as Asiana Airlines flight 214, was on approach to Runway 28L when it struck a seawall at San Francisco International Airport. The flight was vectored for a visual approach to Runway 28L and intercepted the final approach course about 14 nautical miles from the threshold at an altitude slightly above the desired 3° glide path. After the flight crew accepted an ATC instruction to maintain 180 knots to 5 nautical miles from the runway, the flight crew mismanaged the descent, causing the airplane to be well above the desired 3° glide path when it reached the 5 nautical mile point. In an attempt to capture the desired glide path, the pilot flying (PF) selected an autopilot mode that instead caused the autoflight system to initiate a climb because the airplane was below the selected altitude. The PF disconnected the autopilot and moved the thrust levers to idle, which caused the autothrottle to change to the HOLD mode, a mode in which the autothrottle does not control airspeed. The PF then pitched the airplane down and increased the descent rate. Neither the PF, the pilot monitoring (PM), nor the observer noted the change in autothrottle mode to HOLD.

As the airplane reached 500 feet above airport elevation, the point at which Asiana's procedures dictated that the approach must be stabilized, the PAPI would have shown that the airplane was slightly above the desired glide path and that the decreasing airspeed was at the proper approach speed of 137 knots. However, the thrust levers were still at idle, and the descent rate was about 1,200 ft/min, well above the descent rate of about 700 ft/min needed to maintain the desired glide path; two indications that the approach was not stabilized. The flight crew should have initiated a go-around, but they did not do so. As the approach continued, the PAPI displayed three and then four red lights as the airplane continued to descend below the desired glide path. The decreasing trend in airspeed continued, and at about 200 feet, the flight crew became aware of the low airspeed and low glide path conditions but did not initiate a go-around until the airplane was below 100 feet, at which point the airplane did not have the performance capability to accomplish a go-around.

ANALYSIS

The flight crew mismanaged the airplane's descent during the visual approach because they were used to relying on automation and did not adequately monitor the approach airspeed. The PF unintentionally deactivated automatic airspeed control and the crew did not adequately monitor the approach airspeed. They also did not follow SOPs that dictated that they must initiate a go-around at 500 feet if the approach was not stabilized. The crew did not effectively communicate and coordinate their actions regarding the use of the autothrottle and autopilot systems. In addition, the PF was not prepared or adequately trained to fly a visual approach and the PM did not properly supervise the situation. Finally, fatigue degraded the crew's performance.

Figure 13-30. The crew involved in this accident did not properly monitor their automation and were not proficient at flying the airplane manually.

SUMMARY CHECKLIST

✓ A typical crew resource management (CRM) training program includes classes that provide background in group dynamics, the nature of human error, and the elements of people working with machines.

✓ Line-oriented flight training (LOFT) scenarios conducted in fight simulators explore a crew's ability to manage routine flights and handle complex problems.

✓ A flight operations manual (FOM) outlines company procedures regarding such items such as crew member duties and responsibilities, enroute flight, navigation and communication, weight limitations, emergencies, operating in hazardous weather, and obtaining aircraft maintenance.

✓ Operations specifications (Ops Specs) are included in the FOM and cover the conditions under which your company must operate to retain approval from the FAA.

✓ With experience, you become more adept at making effective choices and managing the risks associated with each flight by following the steps in the ADM process.

✓ The I'M SAFE checklist is an effective way to consider the factors that affect your fitness prior to flight in the commercial environment.

✓ As you face pressure from your company to complete a flight as planned, please passengers, and meet schedules, you must be on the alert for operational pitfalls and be prepared to counteract them.

✓ Five hazardous attitudes that can interfere with your ability to make effective decisions are: anti-authority, impulsivity, invulnerability, macho, and resignation.

✓ Use a tool such as the 5Ps prior to and during flights to manage risk. As a professional pilot, your company might provide you with a risk management checklist and SOPs might dictate actions to take during flight to manage risk.

✓ In most crew operations, the pilot flying (PF) is in charge of manipulating the controls, while pilot monitoring (PM) is responsible for such tasks as monitoring the flight progress, communication with ATC, and navigation.

✓ If you work for a large commercial operation, your responsibility might shift from performing the actual flight planning to supervising and verifying that the information given to you is timely and correct.

✓ To complete all of your responsibilities to prepare for a flight, you must plan ahead to establish priorities and a logical sequence to accomplish tasks.

✓ To plan for high workload periods and to ensure that both crew members are prepared to perform the necessary tasks, perform briefings prior to departure, arrival, and approach.

✓ An operational briefing includes aircraft performance and configuration data and information about the airport and runway so you can make effective decisions about the approach procedure you intend to fly and your aircraft's capabilities.

✓ Company procedures dictate how specific equipment is set up and other equipment is left to pilot technique.

✓ A electronic flight bag (EFB) can display items, such as flight plans, checklists, FOMs, approach charts, and aircraft performance data.

✓ The challenge-response method requires one pilot to read the checklist item out loud, while the other crew member completes the task and repeats the instruction verbally.

✓ To maintain situational awareness in a crew environment, elicit information from other crew members and keep the other pilot informed of the status of operations for which you are responsible.

✓ Standard operating procedures (SOPs) help prevent complacency by specifically dictating the procedures the crew should follow in a wide variety of situations.

✓ Follow the sterile cockpit procedure by eliminating nonessential duties or activities while the aircraft is involved in taxi, takeoff, landing, and all other flight operations conducted below 10,000 feet MSL, except cruise flight.

✓ Effective SOPs for preventing runway incursions cover seven major categories: planning, situational awareness, written taxi instructions, flight crew verbal communication, ATC/pilot communication, taxi, and exterior aircraft lighting.

✓ Use a continuous loop process to actively monitor and update your progress while you taxi.

✓ The Flight Safety Foundation designed a CFIT risk assessment safety tool—the CFIT Checklist—as part of an international program to reduce CFIT accidents.

✓ Terrain awareness and warning system (TAWS) equipment displays color-coded terrain data on a moving map and provides aural warnings and alert annunciations if the aircraft is close to terrain.

✓ To avoid CFIT on departure, thoroughly review the charted departure procedure or the departure instructions provided by ATC, consider the surrounding terrain and obstacles, and brief the takeoff and departure.

✓ To prevent CFIT on approach and landing, brief the approach and missed approach procedure and fly a stabilized approach.

✓ CFIT prevention actions for the approach and landing phase can be divided into five categories: altimeters, safe altitudes, ATC procedures, flight crew complacency, and approach procedures.

✓ Effective automation management requires training to not only command, recognize, and monitor the various modes of flight but to gain a thorough understanding of how the autopilot interacts with other systems.

✓ Automation management requires you to learn the proper action if the equipment fails or does something unexpected and to be able to the hand-fly the airplane if necessary.

✓ A flight management system (FMS) is a flight computer system that uses a large database to enable routes to be pre-programmed and constantly updated with respect to position accuracy by reference to conventional navigation aids, inertial reference system technology, or GPS.

✓ To effectively manage both automation and information: use equipment operating levels, verify programming, perform callouts, confirm waypoints, know the mode of operation, and customize displays.

✓ An automation surprise causes you to be momentarily confused about the state of the automation.

KEY TERMS

Single-Pilot Resource Management (SRM)

Crew Resource Management (CRM)

Line-Oriented Flight Training (LOFT)

Aeronautical Decision Making (ADM)

Flight Operations Manual (FOM)

Operations Specifications (Ops Specs)

Aeronautical Decision Making (ADM)

ADM Process

Self Assessment

Operational Pitfalls

Hazardous Attitudes

Risk Management

Task Management

Pilot Flying (PF)

Pilot Monitoring (PM)

Electronic Flight Bag (EFB)

Challenge-Response Method

Situational Awareness

Standard Operating Procedures (SOPs)

Sterile Cockpit

Controlled Flight Into Terrain (CFIT)

Terrain Awareness and Warning System (TAWS)

Automation Management

Flight Management System (FMS)

Automation Surprise

QUESTIONS

1. Select the true statement about CRM training.
   A. CRM instruction focuses primarily on managing emergency situations.
   B. LOFT sessions use scenarios to explore a crew's ability to manage routine flights and handle complex problems.
   C. A typical CRM program involves pilots practicing maneuvers and procedures in the airplane with instructors providing evaluations of hand-flying skills.

2. True/False. When you fly for a commercial operation, your employer is responsible for making all Go/No-Go decisions.

3. After managing an equipment malfunction, you and your copilot make and implement the decision to divert to a nearby airport. You receive vectors from ATC. What is the next step in the ADM process?

4. Name at least three operational pitfalls that can endanger pilots who become complacent with experience.

5. You disregard your company's SOPs for coordinating with your copilot because you feel that many of the callouts and verification procedures are unnecessary. What hazardous attitude are you exhibiting?
   A. Impulsivity
   B. Resignation
   C. Anti-authority

6. Give an example of at least one risk factor in each of the 5P categories that is specific to the commercial environment.

7. Select the true statement regarding task management in the commercial environment.
    A. SOPs typically state specific crew member responsibilities for the PF and the PM.
    B. You have the same duties as a professional pilot that you do as a private pilot.
    C. The PM normally performs checklist tasks and informs the PF when the procedure is complete.

8. True/False. The challenge-response method requires one pilot to read the checklist item out loud, while the other crew member completes the task and repeats the instruction verbally.

9. Name at least two actions that you can take to maintain situational awareness during flight operations.

10. Name at least three actions that you can take to maintain situational awareness during taxi.

11. What is the CFIT Checklist?
    A. A in-flight tool to evaluate CFIT risk at decision points that correspond to the phases of flight.
    B. A tool for determining the CFIT risk for a specific flight and a resource for identifying general factors that affect CFIT risk
    C. A self-critique checklist to determine if you exhibited any hazardous attitudes during a flight that might increase your risk of CFIT in the future.

12. Name at least three actions you can take to decrease your risk of CFIT during approach and landing.

13. Select the true statement regarding automation and information management.
    A. As a professional pilot, you do not need to maintain skills in hand-flying the airplane.
    B. An automation surprise occurs when the PM disengages the autopilot and does not inform the PF.
    C. To maintain situational awareness, the crew member programming equipment must verify the inputs with the other pilot.

CHAPTER 14

Commercial Maneuvers

SECTION A
Accelerated Stalls

As with all stalls, the accelerated stall is the result of exceeding the critical angle of attack. During flight, the wing's angle of attack is determined by several factors, including the airspeed, the airplane's gross weight, and the load factors imposed by maneuvering. At the same gross weight, airplane configuration, and power setting, a given airplane consistently stalls at the same indicated airspeed if no acceleration is involved. However, the airplane stalls at a higher indicated airspeed when excessive maneuvering loads are imposed by steep turns, pull-ups, or other abrupt changes in its attitude. This type of stall is called an accelerated stall.

Accelerated stalls tend to be more rapid, or severe, than unaccelerated stalls. Because the wing stalls at a higher-than-normal airspeed and at a lower-than-anticipated pitch attitude, you could be surprised by an accelerated stall if you do not receive training to recognize this type of stall. Failure to take immediate steps toward recovery when an accelerated stall occurs can result in a complete loss of flight control and a power-on spin.

You will practice recovering from an accelerated stall by inducing a stall in a 45° bank. Do not perform accelerated stalls in any airplane that is prohibited from such maneuvers by its type certification restrictions, the airplane flight manual, or pilot's operating handbook. As with all training maneuvers, you must be aware of other traffic in the area. Before you start the maneuver, make clearing turns to ensure the practice area is free of conflicting traffic. Start at an altitude that enables you to perform and recover from the stall no lower than 3,000 feet AGL.

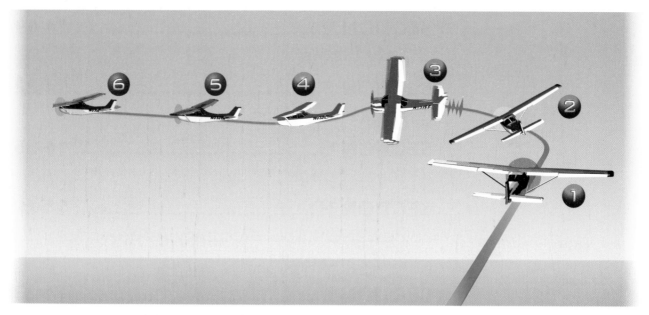

1 Upon completion of your clearing turns, select a reference point on the horizon and note your heading and altitude. Reduce power and increase elevator back pressure to establish straight-and-level flight at an airspeed below V_A, 20 knots above unaccelerated stall speed or the manufacturer's recommended airspeed.

You must maintain an airspeed below V_A so you do not exceed the airplane's limit load factor. In addition, because of the lower G-load limitations in a flaps-down configuration, never practice accelerated stalls with the flaps extended.

Roll into a level turn at a 45° angle of bank while gradually increasing back pressure to maintain altitude.

 After you have established the bank, increase back pressure steadily and firmly to induce the stall.

Induce the stall at an airspeed below V_A and within 20 knots of the unaccelerated stall speed. You must observe these speed restrictions to prevent exceeding the load limit of the airplane.

Maintain coordinated turning flight to ensure that both wings stall simultaneously. If the airplane is slipping toward the inside of the turn when the stall occurs, it tends to roll rapidly toward the outside of the turn at the onset of the stall because the outside wing stalls before the inside wing. If the airplane is skidding toward the outside of the turn, it has a tendency to roll to the inside of the turn because the inside wing stalls first.

 At the onset of the stall (buffeting), recover immediately by releasing elevator back pressure and increasing power. Level the wings using coordinated aileron and rudder pressure.

Recognize when the stall is imminent promptly act to prevent a completely stalled condition. You must avoid a prolonged stall, excessive airspeed, excessive loss of altitude, or a spin.

 Return to the original altitude and heading.

Be careful not to induce a secondary stall if you are climbing to regain lost altitude.

 Establish straight-and-level, coordinated flight at an appropriate airspeed. If in cruise flight, set the power for a cruise airspeed and trim to relieve control pressure.

FAA ACCELERATED STALLS

To meet the PTS requirements, you must:

- Exhibit satisfactory knowledge of the elements related to accelerated (power on or power off) stalls.
- Select an entry altitude that allows the task to be completed no lower than 3,000 feet AGL.
- Establish the airplane in a steady flight condition with the airspeed below V_A, 20 knots above unaccelerated stall speed or the manufacturer's recommendations.
- Transition smoothly from the cruise attitude to the angle of bank of approximately 45° that will induce a stall.
- Maintain coordinated turning flight while increasing elevator back pressure steadily and firmly to induce the stall.
- Recognize and recover promptly at the "onset" (buffeting) stall condition.
- Return to the altitude, heading, and airspeed specified by the examiner.

SECTION A ■ Accelerated Stalls

QUESTIONS

1. Define accelerated stall.

2. What is true about the airplane configuration for practicing accelerated stalls?
   A. Establish a bank angle greater than 45° to induce the stall.
   B. Extend the flaps to stabilize the airplane and decrease the severity of the stall.
   C. Establish an airspeed below V_A, 20 knots above unaccelerated stall speed or the manufacturer's recommended airspeed prior to entering the bank and inducing the stall.

3. Why is important to maintain coordinated flight throughout the stall and recovery?

4. True/False. Recover from the accelerated stall only after a full stall occurs.

SECTION B
Maximum Performance Takeoffs and Landings

During flight training, you typically learn to fly at airports with relatively long, paved runways. However, not all airports have long runways and many have runways made of dirt, grass, or sod. It is important that you learn how to perform short-field and soft-field takeoffs, climbs, approaches, and landings. These maneuvers, also referred to as maximum performance takeoffs and landings, are designed to allow you to operate safely into and out of unimproved airports.

SOFT-FIELD TAKEOFF AND CLIMB

A soft field can be defined as any runway that measurably retards acceleration during the takeoff roll. The objective of the soft-field takeoff is to transfer the weight of the airplane from the landing gear to the wings as quickly and smoothly as possible to eliminate the drag caused by surfaces such as tall grass, soft dirt, or snow. Takeoffs and climbs from soft fields require special procedures, as well as knowledge of your airplane's performance characteristics including, best angle-of-climb speed (V_X) and best rate-of-climb speed (V_Y). When using the FAA-approved flight manual or POH performance data, keep in mind that the figures, such as takeoff distance, apply to an airplane in good operating condition, and they are valid only for the listed conditions.

You actually begin the soft-field procedure during the taxi phase. If the taxi area surface is soft, use full back pressure to maintain full-up elevator (or stabilator) deflection with a slight amount of power to keep the airplane moving. This technique transfers some of the airplane's weight from the nosewheel to the main wheels, resulting in lower power requirements and greater ease in taxiing.

1. Complete the before-takeoff check on a paved or firm surface area, if practical. This helps to avoid propeller damage and the possibility of the airplane becoming stuck.

   - Set the flap position as recommended by the manufacturer.
   - Clear the approach and departure areas and the traffic pattern prior to taxiing onto the runway. After obtaining a clearance (at an airport with a control tower) or self announcing your intentions (at a non-towered airport), taxi into position for takeoff without stopping.

Use full elevator back pressure to reduce the amount of weight on the nosewheel as you align the airplane with the center of the runway. While still rolling, smoothly add takeoff power and check the engine instruments as the engine reaches full power. As you increase speed and the elevator (or stabilator) becomes more effective, reduce back pressure slightly but continue to apply sufficient back pressure to raise the nosewheel from the soft surface.

Remember that nosewheel steering (if applicable) is ineffective when the nosewheel is clear of the runway. However, rudder control is sufficient to maintain directional control due to the increasing air flow.

If you do not release some back pressure while accelerating during the takeoff roll, the airplane can assume an extremely nose-high attitude that can cause the tail skid to come in contact with the surface.

 As the airplane lifts from the runway surface, reduce back pressure to achieve a level flight attitude.

If you do not release some back pressure while accelerating during the takeoff roll, the airplane can assume an extremely nose-high attitude that can cause the tail skid to come in contact with the surface.

 Allow the airplane to accelerate in level flight, within ground effect, to V_X or V_Y (as required) before starting a climb.

As the airspeed increases, lift increases and more of the aircraft's weight is transferred to the wings. This causes the airplane to become airborne at an airspeed slower than safe climb speed. The airplane is now flying in ground effect.

 Establish the climb attitude maintaining V_Y. After the airplane is climbing at a positive rate, retract the landing gear and raise the flaps. Then, trim to relieve control pressures.

On a rough surface the airplane may skip or bounce into the air before its full weight can be supported aerodynamically. Therefore, it is important to hold the pitch attitude as constant as possible (an important application of slow flight). If you permit the nose to lower after a bounce, the nosewheel can strike the ground. On the other hand, sharply increasing the pitch attitude after a bounce can cause the airplane to stall. If obstacles are in the departure path, accelerate to V_X before climbing out of ground effect. If no obstacles are in the departure path, accelerate to V_Y and then begin to climb.

SOFT-FIELD TAKEOFF AND CLIMB

To meet the PTS requirements, you must:

- Utilize procedures before taxiing onto the runway to ensure runway incursion avoidance. Verify the ATC clearance and that no aircraft are on final before entering the runway, and ensure that the aircraft is on the correct takeoff runway.
- Exhibit satisfactory knowledge of the elements related to a soft-field takeoff and climb.
- Position the flight controls for existing conditions and maximize lift as quickly as possible.
- Clear the area; taxi onto the takeoff surface at a speed consistent with safety without stopping while advancing the throttle smoothly to takeoff power.
- Establish and maintain a pitch attitude that transfers the weight of the airplane from the wheels to the wings as rapidly as possible.
- Rotate and lift off at the lowest possible airspeed and remain in ground effect while accelerating to V_X or V_Y, as appropriate.
- Establish a pitch attitude for V_X or V_Y, as appropriate, and maintain selected airspeed ±5 knots, during the climb.
- Retract the landing gear, if appropriate, and flaps after clearing any obstacles, or as recommended by the manufacturer.
- Maintain takeoff power and V_X or $V_{Y\ +/-5\ knots}$ to a safe maneuvering altitude.
- Maintain directional control and proper wind-drift correction throughout the takeoff and climb.
- Complete the appropriate checklist.

SECTION B ▪ **Maximum Performance Takeoffs and Landings**

SOFT-FIELD APPROACH AND LANDING

The objective of a soft-field landing is to ease the weight of the airplane from the wings to the main landing gear as gently and slowly as possible, while keeping the nosewheel off the soft surface during most of the landing roll. If executed properly, this technique prevents the nosewheel from sinking into the soft surface and reduces the possibility of an abrupt stop or possible damage to the airplane during the landing roll. Consult your airplane's POH for the appropriate speeds and specific procedures for performing soft-field landings. In the absence of a manufacturer's recommended approach speed, use 1.3 times the stalling speed in the landing configuration (1.3 V_{S0}). In addition a gust factor adjustment to the approach speed might be applicable.

APPROACH

① Ensure that you have completed the before-landing checklist and that the approach and landing areas are clear. Lower the landing gear and extend approach flaps.

② Extend the flaps to an intermediate setting (if applicable), while progressively reducing the airspeed. Use trim to relieve control pressures.

③ Unless obstacles are in the approach path, maintain the same descent angle on final as you would during a normal approach. Maintain the recommended approach speed and extend final flaps.

LANDING

 Hold the airplane one to two feet above the surface as long as possible to dissipate forward speed. Maintain that attitude with power and slowly continue the descent until the airplane touches down at the lowest possible airspeed with the airplane in a nose-high attitude.

> When you maintain power during the landing flare and touchdown, the slipstream flow over the empennage increases the effectiveness of the elevator (or stabilator). The amount of power required during the landing flare and touchdown varies with the weight and density altitude.

 Touch down in a nose-high attitude at the slowest possible airspeed. Maintain elevator back pressure to hold the nosewheel off the surface as long as practical. As the airspeed decreases on the roll-out, smoothly and gently lower the nosewheel to the surface.

> Adding a small amount of power after touchdown will help you to ease the nosewheel down, under control.

 Increase the power slightly, if necessary, to keep the aircraft moving and prevent it from stopping suddenly on the soft surface. Avoid using the brakes because braking can cause the nosewheel to dig into the soft surface and cause damage to the landing gear. The soft surface should provide sufficient braking action to slow the aircraft.

FAA **SOFT-FIELD APPROACH AND LANDING**

To meet the PTS requirements, you must:

- Exhibit satisfactory knowledge of the elements related to a soft-field approach and landing.
- Consider the wind conditions, landing surface, and obstructions, and select the most suitable touchdown area.
- Establish the recommended approach and landing configuration and airspeed; adjust pitch attitude and power as required.
- Maintain a stabilized approach and the manufacturer's recommended airspeed, or in its absence, not more than 1.3 V_{SO}, ±5 knots, with wind gust factor applied.
- Make smooth, timely, and correct control application during the roundout and touchdown.
- Touch down softly with no drift and with the airplane's longitudinal axis aligned with the runway/landing path.
- Maintain crosswind correction and directional control throughout the approach and landing sequence.
- Maintain proper position of the flight controls and sufficient speed to taxi on the soft surface.
- Utilize after-landing runway incursion avoidance procedures.
- Complete the appropriate checklist.

SECTION B ■ Maximum Performance Takeoffs and Landings

SHORT-FIELD TAKEOFF AND MAXIMUM PERFORMANCE CLIMB

You normally perform short-field takeoff and maximum performance climb procedures when the usable runway length is short, or when the runway available for takeoff is restricted by obstructions, such as trees, powerlines, or buildings, at the departure end. During short-field practice sessions, it is usually assumed that you are departing from a short runway and that you must clear an obstacle which is 50 feet in height. To accomplish successful short-field takeoffs and climbs, you must be familiar with the best angle-of-climb speed (V_X) and the best rate-of-climb speed (V_Y) for your airplane. Many manufacturers also specify a best obstacle clearance speed. You should consult your airplane's POH for the appropriate speeds and specific procedures for performing short-field takeoffs.

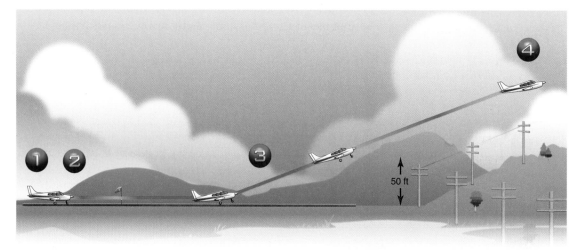

1   Complete the before-takeoff check. Ensure that the runway, as well as the approach and departure paths are clear of other aircraft. After obtaining a clearance (at an airport with a control tower) or self announcing your intentions (at a non-towered airport), taxi into position at the beginning of the runway so as to allow maximum utilization of the available runway, and align the airplane on the runway centerline.

2   Set the flaps as recommended by the manufacturer. The appropriate flap setting varies between airplanes. While holding the brakes, smoothly add takeoff power and then release the brakes to begin the takeoff roll.

> Holding the brakes until you achieve full power enables you to determine that the engine is functioning properly before you take off from a field where power availability is critical and distance to abort a takeoff is limited.

3   Allow the airplane to accelerate with its full weight on the main wheels by maintaining the elevator (or stabilator) in a neutral position. Smoothly and firmly apply elevator back pressure to lift off at the recommended airspeed. Because the airplane accelerates quickly after lift off, you might need to apply additional back pressure to establish and maintain V_X (or best obstacle clearance speed).

> Avoid raising the nose prior to the recommended liftoff speed. A premature nose-high attitude increases drag and results in a longer takeoff roll. If you attempt to lift the airplane off the runway prematurely, or to climb too steeply, the airplane might settle back to the runway. In addition, the airplane might stall or impact the obstacle. Deviating from the recommended climb speed, by as little as five knots, can result in a significant reduction in climb performance in some airplanes.

④ Once you have cleared the obstacle and reached a safe altitude, lower the nose and accelerate to V_Y. Retract the landing gear and then retract the flaps (if applicable). If no obstacles are present during training, you should maintain V_X until you are at least 50 feet above the runway surface. Trim to relieve control pressures.

 ## SHORT-FIELD TAKEOFF AND MAXIMUM PERFORMANCE CLIMB

To meet the PTS requirements, you must:

- Utilize procedures before taxiing onto the runway to ensure runway incursion avoidance. Verify the ATC clearance and that no aircraft are on final before entering the runway, and ensure that the aircraft is on the correct takeoff runway.
- Exhibit satisfactory knowledge of the elements related to a short-field takeoff and maximum performance climb.
- Position the flight controls for the existing wind conditions and set the flaps as recommended.
- Clear the area; taxi into the takeoff position for maximum utilization of the available takeoff area and align the airplane on the runway center.
- Apply brakes, if appropriate, while smoothly advancing the throttle to takeoff power.
- Rotate and lift off at the recommended airspeed and accelerate to the recommended obstacle clearance speed or V_X.
- Establish a pitch attitude that maintains the recommended obstacle clearance speed, or V_X, +5/–0 knots, until the obstacle is cleared or the airplane is 50 feet above the surface.
- After clearing the obstacle, establish the pitch attitude for V_Y, accelerate to V_Y and maintain V_Y, ±5 knots, during the climb.
- Retract the landing gear, if appropriate, and flaps after clearing any obstacles or as recommended by the manufacturer.
- Maintain takeoff power and V_Y ±5 knots, to a safe maneuvering altitude.
- Maintain directional control and proper wind-drift correction throughout the takeoff and climb.
- Complete the appropriate checklist.

SHORT-FIELD APPROACH AND LANDING

A short-field landing is necessary when you have a relatively short landing area or when you must fly an approach over obstacles that limit the available landing area. A short-field landing consists of a steep approach over an obstacle, using power and flaps (normally full flaps). A minimum landing speed is desired with a touchdown point as close to the threshold as possible. During short-field landing practice, assume you are making the approach and landing over a 50-foot obstacle. You should consult your airplane's POH for the appropriate speeds and specific procedures for performing short-field landings. In the absence of a manufacturer's recommended speed use 1.3 times the stalling speed in the landing configuration (1.3 V_{S0}). In gusty conditions, an increase in airspeed of no more than one-half the gust factor should be added.

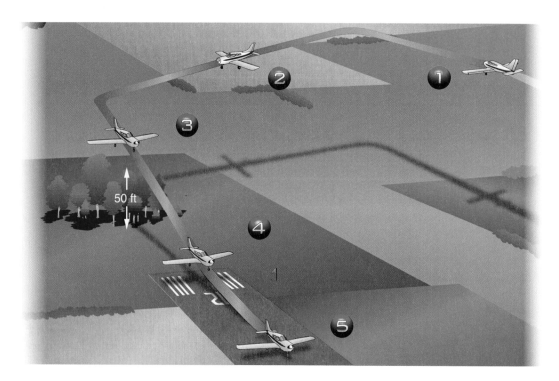

APPROACH

1   Ensure that you have completed the before-landing checklist and that the approach and landing area is clear. Lower the landing gear and extend approach flaps.

2   Extend the flaps to an intermediate setting (if applicable), while progressively reducing the airspeed. Use trim to relieve control pressures.

3   Begin the final approach at least 500 feet higher than the touchdown area. Maintain the recommended approach speed and extend the final flaps.

> The descent angle for the short-field approach is steeper than the angle for a normal approach. This enables you to clear an obstacle located near the approach end of the runway. Extending full flaps enables a steeper descent angle without an increase in airspeed, which results in a decrease in the distance required to bring the airplane to a full stop.

LANDING

 As you begin the flare, reduce power smoothly to idle and allow the airplane to touch down in a full-stall condition. Because you fly the short-field approach at a steep descent angle and close to the airplane's stalling speed, you must judge the initiation of the flare accurately to avoid flying into the ground or stalling prematurely and sinking rapidly.

Reducing power too rapidly can result in an immediate increase in the rate of descent and a hard landing. On the other hand, the airplane should touch down with little or no float. An excessive amount of airspeed can result in a touchdown too far beyond the runway threshold and a roll-out that exceeds the available landing area. As your training progresses, your goal will be to touch down beyond and within 100 feet of a point specified by your instructor.

 When the airplane is firmly on the runway, lower the nose, retract the flaps (if recommended) and apply the brakes, as necessary to further shorten the roll-out.

In nosewheel-type airplanes, holding the landing pitch attitude, as long as elevator authority remains effective, provides aerodynamic braking by the wings. Some manufacturers recommend retraction of flaps on the landing roll. This transfers more weight to the main gear and enhances braking.

 ## SHORT-FIELD APPROACH AND LANDING

To meet the PTS requirements, you must:

- Exhibit satisfactory knowledge of the elements related to a short-field approach and landing.
- Consider the wind conditions, landing surface, and obstructions, and select the most suitable touchdown point.
- Establish the recommended approach and landing configuration and airspeed; adjust power and pitch attitude.
- Maintain a stabilized approach and recommended approach airspeed, or in its absence not more than 1.3 V_{S0}, ±5 knots, with wind gust factor applied, .
- Make smooth, timely, and correct control application during the roundout and touchdown.
- Touch down smoothly at minimum control airspeed.
- Touch down at or within 100 feet beyond a specified point, with no side drift, with minimum float, and with the longitudinal axis aligned with and over the runway center.
- Maintain the crosswind correction and directional control throughout the approach and landing sequence.
- Apply brakes, as necessary, to stop in the shortest distance consistent with safety.
- Utilize after-landing runway incursion avoidance procedures.
- Complete the appropriate checklists.

QUESTIONS

1. True/False. The soft-field takeoff procedure begins during the taxi phase.

2. During a soft-field takeoff, liftoff normally occurs at a speed below the safe climb speed. What action should you take before starting a climb?

3. What is the correct procedure for the roll-out after a soft-field landing?
    A. Maintain power at idle and apply heavy braking.
    B. Hold forward elevator pressure and avoid braking.
    C. Maintain elevator back pressure and increase power slightly, if necessary.

4. True/False. During a soft-field landing, you should lower the nosewheel to the surface as quickly as possible after touchdown.

5. Why should you hold the brakes until you achieve full power prior to beginning a short-field takeoff?

6. During short-field takeoff practice sessions, it is assumed that you must clear an obstacle that is how many feet high?

7. True/False. While performing a short-field landing, you should reduce power to idle in the flare and allow the airplane to touch down in a full-stall condition.

8. Is the descent angle for a short-field approach steeper, shallower, or the same as that flown for a normal approach and landing?

SECTION C
Steep Turns

Steep turns are level, high-performance turning maneuvers normally performed as a series of 360° turns in opposite directions with a bank angle of approximately 50°, ±5°. The objective of the maneuver is to help develop the ability to accurately control an aircraft near its maximum performance limits. Performing steep turns also increases your knowledge of the associated performance factors, including load factor, angle-of-bank limitations, effect on stall speed, power required, and the overbanking tendency.

The actual turning performance of an airplane is limited by the amount of power the engine is developing, load limit (structural strength), and aerodynamic design. As you increase the bank angle, you eventually approach maximum performance or the load limit. In most light airplanes, the maximum bank angle you can maintain with full power is 50° to 60°. If you exceed the maximum performance limit while maintaining your airspeed at or below the airplane's design maneuvering speed (V_A), the airplane will either stall or will lose altitude. With airspeed above V_A, it is possible to exceed the load limit.

As is the case with all training maneuvers, you must be aware of other traffic in the area. Before you start the maneuver, make clearing turns to ensure the practice area is free of conflicting traffic.

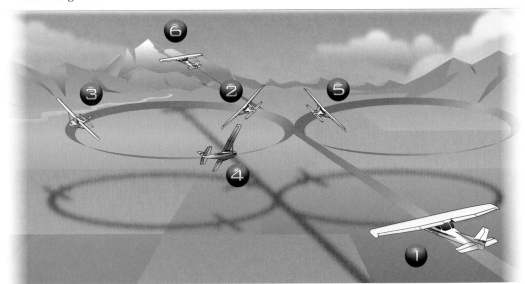

① Upon completion of your clearing turns, select a reference point on the horizon and note your heading and altitude.

② Roll into a 50° angle-of-bank turn at or below V_A. During roll-in, smoothly add power and slowly increase elevator back pressure to maintain altitude. Maintain coordinated flight and trim to relieve control pressures.

As you enter the turn, establish the bank at a moderate rate. If you roll the airplane too rapidly, you might have difficulty establishing the pitch attitude necessary to maintain altitude. Do not apply too much back pressure while initially entering the turn or you will gain altitude. However, as you become established in the turn, greater back pressure will be needed to maintain altitude.

Maintain your angle of bank and altitude. Confirm your attitude by referring to both the natural horizon and attitude indicator. Use your altimeter and vertical speed indicator to determine if changes in pitch are required.

> If you are losing altitude in the turn, slightly decrease the angle of bank first, then increase back pressure to raise the nose. After you regain the altitude, roll back to the desired angle of bank.

 Anticipate the change in direction of the turn by leading the roll-out heading by one-half the bank angle, approximately 25°. Roll out on the entry heading and briskly roll into a 50° banked turn in the opposite direction.

> During steep turns, you encounter an overbanking tendency that is less apparent in right turns than it is in left turns. This is because torque and P-factor tend to roll the aircraft to the left and work against the overbanking tendency during a right turn. Generally, you need more rudder and aileron pressure during the roll-out than you needed during the roll-in. This is because the control pressures exerted during the roll-out must overcome the airplane's overbanking tendency.

 After the initial roll-in to the turn, confirm your attitude by referring to both the natural horizon and attitude indicator. Use your altimeter and vertical speed indicator to determine if changes in pitch are necessary. Anticipate the roll-out by leading the roll-out heading by approximately 25°.

 Roll out on the entry heading and altitude. Decrease back pressure and reduce power to maintain altitude and airspeed. Trim to relieve control pressures.

 STEEP TURNS

To meet the PTS requirements, you must:

- Exhibit satisfactory knowledge of the elements related to steep turns.
- Establish the manufacturer's recommended airspeed, or if one is not stated, a safe airspeed not to exceed V_A.
- Roll into a coordinated 360° steep turn with at least a 50° bank, followed by a 360° steep turn in the opposite direction.
- Divide your attention between airplane control and orientation.
- Maintain the entry altitude, ±100 feet; airspeed, ±10 knots; bank, ±5°; and roll out on the entry heading, ±10°.

QUESTIONS

1. What is the first thing you should do if you begin to lose altitude during a steep turn?

2. Why is overbanking tendency less apparent in right turns than it is in left turns?
    A. Torque and P-factor tend to roll the aircraft to the right and work against the overbanking tendency during a left turn.
    B. Torque and P-factor tend to roll the aircraft to the left and work against the overbanking tendency during a right turn.
    C. There is no difference between left and right turns; overbanking occurs because the angle of bank has exceeded the limits of the airplane.

3. True/False. The entry speed for a steep turn should be above V_A.

4. How many degrees should you lead your desired heading when you initiate the recovery from a steep turn?

SECTION D
Chandelles

Achandelle can be described as a maximum performance 180° climbing turn. It involves continual changes in pitch, bank, airspeed, and control pressures. During the maneuver, the airspeed gradually decreases from the entry speed to a few knots above stall speed at the completion of the 180° turn. Because you use full power (in airplanes with a fixed-pitch propeller) throughout the chandelle, you must control airspeed by adjusting the pitch attitude of the airplane. Maintaining the proper pitch attitude is a key element of this maneuver. Due to variables, such as atmospheric density and airplane performance, altitude gain is not a criterion for successfully completing a chandelle. However, the airplane should gain as much altitude as possible for the given bank angle and power setting without stalling. The objective of the maneuver is to help you develop good coordination habits and refine the use of airplane controls at varying airspeeds and flight attitudes.

As is the case with all training maneuvers, you must be aware of other traffic in the area. Before you start the maneuver, make clearing turns to ensure the practice area is free of conflicting traffic. Start at an altitude recommended by the aircraft manufacturer or 1,500 feet AGL, whichever is higher.

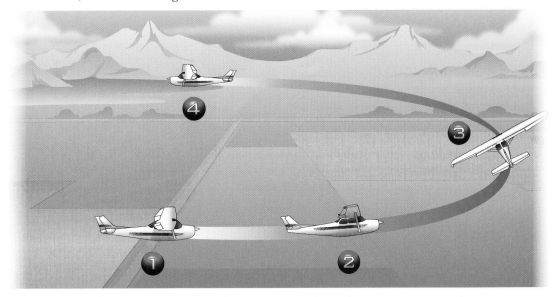

 Before entering the maneuver, configure the airplane in straight-and-level flight with the landing gear and flaps up, using the entry airspeed recommended in the pilot's operating handbook or maneuvering speed (V_A), whichever is slower.

Although the prevailing wind has little or no effect on the chandelle, begin the maneuver by turning into the wind to help you remain within the practice area. Select a prominent feature on the ground to help maintain orientation.

2 Establish a coordinated turn not to exceed 30° of bank. Then, simultaneously apply back elevator pressure to begin a climb and smoothly apply full power. If your airplane has a constant speed propeller, increase the RPM to the climb or takeoff setting, then advance the throttle to the climb setting.

Throughout the first 90° of the turn, the bank angle of 30° should remain the same. However, pitch attitude should gradually increase, reaching its maximum at the 90° point.

Begin a gradual reduction of bank angle, while maintaining a constant pitch attitude.

During the second 90° of turn, time the roll-out rate so you reach wings level at the 180° point. As airspeed decreases you normally need more elevator back pressure to maintain a constant pitch attitude. You will also notice that the left-turning tendency caused by P-factor and propeller slipstream is more prevalent, and you need to apply right rudder pressure to coordinate both right and left turns.

 Reduce the pitch attitude to resume a level flight attitude, allowing your airplane to accelerate while maintaining a constant altitude.

In a chandelle to the right, the aileron on the right wing is lowered slightly during the roll-out. This causes more drag on the right wing and tends to make the airplane yaw slightly to the right. At the same time, the left-turning tendency is pulling the nose to the left. As a result, aileron drag and the left-turning tendency counteract each other, and very little left rudder pressure is required. Actually, releasing some of the right rudder pressure, which you used to correct for left-turning tendencies, normally has the same effect as using left rudder pressure. In contrast, when you roll out from a chandelle to the left, two turning forces are pulling the nose of the airplane to the left. In this case, you need a significant amount of right rudder pressure.

 CHANDELLES

To meet the PTS requirements, you must:

- Exhibit satisfactory knowledge of the elements related to chandelles.
- Select an altitude that allows the maneuver to be performed no lower than 1,500 feet AGL.
- Establish the recommended entry configuration, power, and airspeed.
- Establish the angle of bank at approximately 30°.
- Simultaneously apply power and pitch to maintain a smooth, coordinated climbing turn to the 90°point with a constant bank.
- Begin a coordinated constant rate roll-out from the 90° point to the 180° point maintaining power and a constant pitch attitude.
- Complete the roll-out at the 180° point, ±10°, just above a stall airspeed, and maintain that airspeed, momentarily avoiding a stall.
- Resume straight-and-level flight with minimum loss of altitude.

QUESTIONS

1. What is the maximum wind limit for practicing chandelles?
   A. 5 to 10 knots
   B. 15 to 20 knot surface wind
   C. Wind is not a factor when practicing chandelles

2. True/False. During the second 90° of the turn, you should always maintain the highest angle of bank and continue to increase the pitch angle.

3. What factor counteracts left-turning tendency in a chandelle to the right?

4. What maximum angle of bank should you use during a chandelle?
   A. 10°
   B. 20°
   C. 30°

SECTION E
Lazy Eights

The lazy eight is basically two 180° turns in opposite directions, with each turn including a climb and a descent. It is called a lazy eight because the longitudinal axis of the airplane appears to scribe a flight pattern about the horizon that resembles a figure eight lying on its side. Throughout the maneuver, airspeed, altitude, bank angle, and pitch attitude, as well as control pressures, are constantly changing. Because of these constant changes, you cannot fly the lazy eight mechanically or automatically. The lazy eight requires a high degree of piloting skill and a sound understanding of the associated performance factors. The objective of this maneuver is to develop and improve your coordination, orientation, planning, division of attention, and ability to maintain precise aircraft control. A good way to visualize the lazy eight is to break each 180° turn into segments.

As is the case with all training maneuvers, you must be aware of other traffic in the area. Before you start the maneuver, make clearing turns to ensure the practice area is free of conflicting traffic. Start at an altitude recommended by the aircraft manufacturer or 1,500 feet AGL, whichever is higher. Because you will be changing heading and altitude continually, be particularly careful to maintain vigilance throughout the maneuver. While scanning the area, look for visual reference points that you can use for orientation. You should also try to determine the direction of the wind and an entry reference point on the horizon, which will enable you to make turns into the wind. Additional reference points at 45°, 90°, and 135° are also useful.

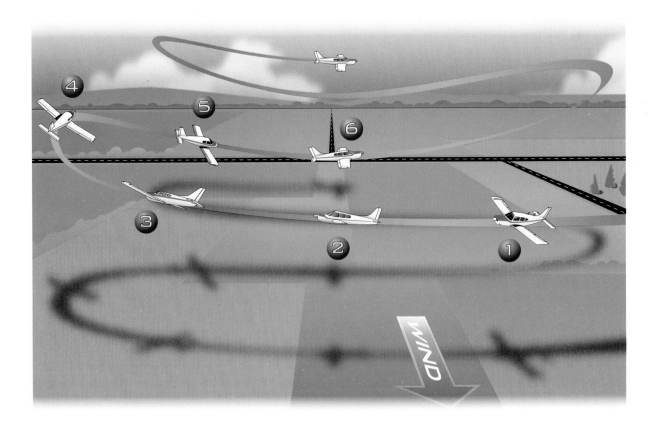

SECTION E ■ **Lazy Eights**

1 Align your flight path with your initial reference point and establish straight-and-level flight at the recommended airspeed.

2 Begin a gradual climbing turn toward the 45° point, increasing pitch attitude while you slowly increase the angle of bank.

> It is important to remember that as airspeed decreases, your rate of turn at a given angle of bank increases. If you allow the rate of turn to become too rapid, you will reach the 45° point of the turn before the maximum pitch has been attained.

3 As you pass through the 45° point of the turn, your pitch attitude should be at its maximum and your bank angle should be about 15°. From 45° to the 90° point you should begin to decrease your pitch attitude to the horizon and continue to increase the angle of bank.

> You might need to apply a slight amount of opposite aileron pressure to prevent the angle of bank from progressing beyond the maximum. To control yaw associated with the left-turning tendencies, apply right rudder pressure. To prevent yaw from decreasing the rate of turn, use more right rudder pressure during a climbing turn to the right than in a turn to the left. In a left turn, torque contributes to the turn so less right rudder pressure is necessary.

4 At 90°, you should be in a level flight attitude, at the maximum angle of bank (approximately 30°), and your airspeed should be about 5 to 10 knots above the stall speed. Then, slowly begin to roll out of the 30° bank and gradually lower the nose for the descending turn as you allow the airspeed to increase.

> Because the angle of bank is decreasing during the roll-out, the vertical component of lift increases. As the wings return to a level attitude, lift will continue to increase, so reduce the elevator back pressure to avoid leveling off too soon.

5 When you reach the 135° reference point, the nose of the airplane should be at its lowest pitch attitude. Continue a gradual roll-out and allow the airspeed to continue to increase, so that you are in a level flight attitude at your entry altitude and airspeed as you reach 180° of turn.

> As the airspeed increases you can gradually relax rudder and aileron pressure.

6 At this point you should immediately begin a climbing turn in the opposite direction toward the selected reference point to complete the second half of the lazy eight in the same manner as the first half.

> One of the key factors in making symmetrical turns is proper airspeed control. Because the power is set before you begin the maneuver, you control airspeed by varying the pitch attitude. During the first 90° of turn, which is the climbing segment, the airspeed should decrease from the entry speed to slightly above the stall speed at the 90° point. This will occur only if you constantly adjust your pitch attitude throughout the maneuver. You should pass through a level-flight pitch attitude at the 90° point, then gradually establish a nose-low pitch attitude that allows your airplane to accelerate to the entry speed after 180° of turn.

LAZY EIGHTS

To meet the PTS requirements, you must:

- Exhibit satisfactory knowledge of the elements related to lazy eights.
- Select an altitude that allows the task to be performed no lower than 1,500 feet AGL.
- Establish the recommended entry configuration, power, and airspeed.
- Maintain coordinated flight throughout the maneuver.
- Achieve throughout the maneuver —
  a. approximately 30° bank at the steepest point.
  b. constant change of pitch and roll rate.
  c. altitude tolerance at 180° points, ±100 feet, from the entry altitude.
  d. airspeed tolerance at the 180° point, ±10 knots, from the entry airspeed.
  e. heading tolerance at the 180° point, ±10°.
- Continue the maneuver through the number of symmetrical loops specified and resume straight-and-level flight.

SECTION E ■ Lazy Eights

QUESTIONS

1. What is the possible cause for reaching the 45° point before the airplane attains the maximum pitch angle?

2. At the 90° point your airspeed should be
    A. At or above stall speed.
    B. 5 knots to 10 knots above stall speed.
    C. 10 knots to 20 knots above stall speed.

3. True/False. From the 90° reference point to the 135° reference point, you should increase elevator back pressure until level flight is achieved.

4. What is the key to keeping both sides of a lazy eight symmetrical?

SECTION F
Eights-on-Pylons

Eights-on-pylons involve flying a figure eight around two points, or pylons, on the ground. In this maneuver, you fly the airplane at an altitude and airspeed that enables you to hold a line-of-sight reference point (usually near the wingtip) on the pylon. This reference point should appear to pivot about the pylon. A complete maneuver consists of a turn in one direction around the first pylon, followed by a turn in the opposite direction around the second pylon. The objective of eights-on-pylons is to refine your ability to control the airplane at traffic pattern altitude over a varied ground track while dividing your attention between instrument indications and visual cues outside the airplane. To accomplish this you should choose a reference point on, or near, the wingtip so your line of sight through the reference point is parallel to the lateral axis of the airplane. It is important to remember that the reference varies considerably on different airplanes. It might be above the wingtip on a low-wing aircraft, below the wingtip on a high-wing aircraft, and ahead of the wingtip on a tapered-wing airplane.

Line of Sight

Lateral Axis

Because you perform this maneuver at a relatively low altitude, select pylons that are in an open area and are not near hills or obstructions. Obstruction-induced turbulence, as well as updrafts and downdrafts caused by uneven terrain, increase the difficulty of the maneuver. Select pylons with approximately the same elevation to avoid the added burden of adjusting altitude for variations in terrain. The pylons also should be in a line that is perpendicular to the wind, and they should be spaced to provide three to five seconds of straight-and-level flight between the turns. Carefully select pylons that will be visible, clear of obstructions, and properly oriented in relation to the prevailing wind. The pylons you select should be in a location that enables a safe emergency landing.

As is the case with all training maneuvers, you must be aware of other traffic in the area. Before you start the maneuver, make clearing turns to ensure the practice area is free of conflicting traffic. Because you are continually changing direction you should keep a lookout for other aircraft throughout the maneuver.

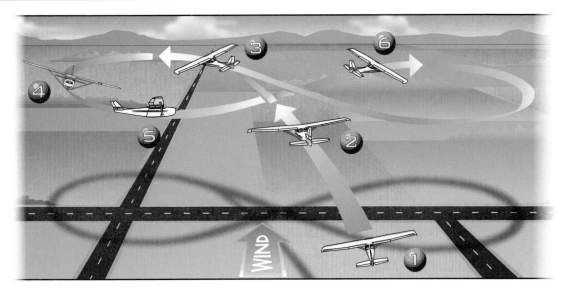

1 Adjust the power to the recommended entry airspeed. As you approach the pylons, the entry altitude you select should be close to the estimated pivotal altitude.

You can estimate your pivotal altitude by using a simple formula: $V^2 \div 11.3$, where V is the relative velocity to the pylon in knots (true airspeed in no-wind conditions, groundspeed with wind). As an example, if your groundspeed is 100 knots, your estimated pivotal altitude is approximately 885 feet $(100)^2 = 10,000 \div 11.3 =$ 885. Because you seldom know the exact TAS, groundspeed, and elevation, use your estimate as a starting point and determine your actual pivotal altitude by experimenting while flying the maneuver.

2 Begin by flying diagonally crosswind between the pylons to a point downwind from the first pylon so that you can make the first turn into the wind.

With a downwind entry, the airplane has the highest groundspeed and the highest pivotal altitude. As groundspeed decreases so does pivotal altitude.

3 Maintain straight-and-level flight until you are approximately abeam the first pylon, then roll into a 30° to 40° angle of bank.

As you proceed around the pylon, if your line-of-sight reference point moves forward of the pylons, your pivotal altitude is too low and you need to climb. Likewise, if your reference point moves aft of the pylon, decrease your pivotal altitude. Normally, when flying into the wind, your groundspeed decreases; therefore, you need to descend. Remember, pivotal altitude increases as groundspeed increases and decreases as groundspeed decreases.

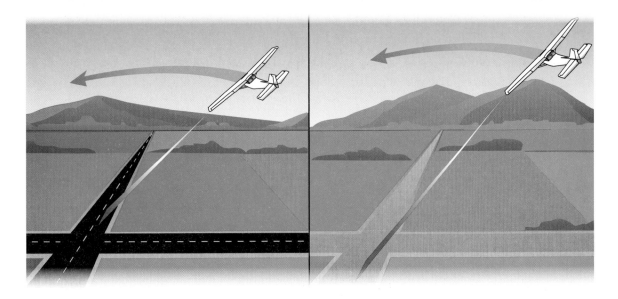

Gradually decrease your pivotal altitude and slightly reduce your angle of bank as you turn directly into the wind.

A descent has a two-fold effect on pivotal altitude. First, it provides the correction needed to hold the pylon, and second, the descent increases groundspeed. The reverse is true for climbs. Use altitude changes, rather than rudder pressure, to hold the reference point on the pylon. Maintain coordinated flight throughout the maneuver.

 Begin the roll-out to straight-and-level flight as you complete the first turn. Maintain straight-and-level flight for 3 to 5 seconds and crab into the wind, as necessary, to correct for wind drift.

Without proper wind drift correction you might fly too close to the pylon to enter the second turn and maintain a bank angle between 30° to 40°.

 Initiate a turn in the opposite direction when the pylon is aligned with the wing reference point.

Repeat the same steps in the opposite direction around the second pylon. Keep in mind that your line-of-sight reference point might look different on the opposite wing.

 EIGHTS-ON-PYLONS

To meet the PTS requirements, you must:

- Exhibit satisfactory knowledge of the elements related to eights-on-pylons.
- Determine the approximate pivotal altitude.
- Select suitable pylons that permit straight and level flight between the pylons.
- Enter the maneuver at the appropriate altitude and airspeed and at a bank angle of approximately 30° to 40° at the steepest point.
- Apply the necessary corrections so that the line-of-sight reference line remains on the pylon.
- Divide attention between accurate coordinated airplane control and outside visual references.
- Hold the pylon using appropriate pivotal altitude avoiding slips and skids.

QUESTIONS

1. What is your approximate pivotal altitude if your groundspeed is 120 knots?

2. Why should you begin eights-on-pylons with a downwind entry?

3. True/False. You should use altitude changes, rather than rudder pressure, to hold the reference point on the pylon.

4. You should select pylons that provide a suitable emergency landing area and allow for
   A. an immediate turn for the next pylon.
   B. 1 or 2 seconds of straight-and-level flight between the pylons
   C. 3 to 5 seconds of straight-and-level flight between the pylons.

SECTION G
Steep Spirals

Asteep spiral is a maximum performance maneuver that requires you to combine a steep-spiraling descent with the basic elements of turns about a point. The maneuver is invaluable for teaching you coordination, planning, orientation, aircraft control, corrections for wind effect, and division of attention. Like other performance maneuvers for commercial pilot certification, a steep spiral is rarely performed during routine flight operations. It does, however, provide you with practical skills that you can use when you must perform a no-power descent within a tight radius due to surrounding terrain or clouds.

The maneuver consists of a minimum of three, uniform-radius, 360° turns around a ground reference point. To maintain a constant radius, you vary the bank angle to adjust for wind effect. At the steepest part, you should achieve a bank angle of approximately 50°, but never greater than 60° of bank. For increased practical application, after rolling out of the spiral, you can add a downwind, base, and final approach pattern to simulate an approach to an emergency landing.

As with all training maneuvers, you must be aware of other traffic in the area. Before beginning the maneuver, make clearing turns to ensure you are clear of conflicting traffic. You must also verify that you have sufficient altitude to complete three, idle-power spirals, and ensure a recovery by 1,000 feet AGL. Do not descend below 1,000 feet AGL unless a suitable emergency landing is assured, should one become necessary. The entry altitude that you use varies with your aircraft's glide performance and the prevailing conditions such as thermal activity, density altitude, and surrounding terrain. Typically, this starting altitude is no lower than 4,000 feet AGL.

1. When you are established at the correct entry altitude, perform your clearing turns. Remember that you will be descending rapidly, so clear the area above, below, and around your aircraft.

2. Select a suitable ground reference point that is distinct and easily seen.

Select a ground reference point that is located in a sparsely populated area, with surrounding terrain that would permit an emergency landing should one become necessary.

3. After choosing the reference point, position the airplane so it will pass within 1/4 mile of the point on the downwind side.

By entering the spiral on the downwind side, you roll into the steepest part of the bank at the beginning of the maneuver. This helps you establish the radius to use throughout the spiral. Remember, however, that the distance you need to be away from the point varies, depending on the airspeed and bank angle that you use.

4. As you approach the reference point, configure the airplane with the landing gear and flaps up, carburetor heat on (if necessary), and auxiliary fuel pump on (as required). Adjust power and pitch to obtain the proper entry airspeed recommended by the airplane manufacturer, or if one is not prescribed, use a speed that is at or below maneuvering speed (V_A).

Performing the steep spiral at the airspeed required by the manufacturer or maneuvering speed reduces the risk of exceeding structural load limits during the maneuver, yet provides enough airflow to provide positive control feel. Although the loads induced during the spiral are slight, if improperly performed at an airspeed that is too high, you can quickly exceed load limits. Excessive loads can be imposed if you pull back too abruptly on the flight controls. This can occur if you attempt to arrest an excessive, or runaway, airspeed by increasing elevator back pressure without decreasing the bank angle.

5 After you are abeam the reference point, reduce the power to idle, lower the pitch to maintain the desired airspeed, adjust trim to relieve back pressure as necessary, and roll into a 50° – 60° angle of bank, 60° being the maximum allowable bank angle for the maneuver. Continually divide your attention between the ground reference point and the instruments to ensure you are maintaining your ground track as well as your airspeed and altitude.

As you continue toward the upwind side of the spiral turn, gradually reduce the angle of bank to compensate for the effects of the wind.

Airspeed control is critical throughout the maneuver to help maintain the desired radius around the ground reference point. Remember, the faster the airspeed, the greater your groundspeed and radius of turn. To aid in maintaining a constant airspeed, trim to relieve elevator back pressure as you enter the spiral. Keep in mind that while in the spiral, you must constantly adjust back pressure to compensate for varying bank angles, but if you practice with the same initial trim setting, you can develop a consistent feel for the amount of back pressure to use.

 Once on the upwind side of the turn, you are at the shallowest bank angle of the spiral turn, and you are exerting the least amount of elevator back pressure. Your bank angle and back pressure slowly increases as you continue a turn toward the downwind side of the spiral.

 As you approach the original entry point, briefly advance the throttle to clear the engine and then return it to idle.

You should clear the engine to verify that it continues to operate smoothly for recovery from the maneuver. Periodically adding power also helps prevent excessive engine cooling and spark plug fouling that can occur when operating at idle for long periods of time. You might want to develop the habit of clearing the engine with each subsequent revolution. This helps you confirm when you have completed each 360° circuit of the spiral.

Once you have completed three complete rotations, roll out within 10° of the entry heading. Although it is not specified in the PTS, your flight instructor or designated examiner might ask you to perform a steep spiral and, upon roll out, immediately perform a simulated emergency approach and landing. Typically, upon roll-out of the spiral, you would be established on the downwind leg, ready to make a turn to base and then final for the emergency landing.

Practice steep spirals with both left and right turns. Typically, you learn left-spirals first since you can see the reference point throughout the maneuver. You should be proficient in performing the maneuver in either direction.

FAA STEEP SPIRALS

To meet the PTS requirements, you must:

- Exhibit satisfactory knowledge of the elements related to a steep spiral.
- Select an altitude sufficient to continue through a series of at least three 360° turns.
- Select a suitable ground reference point.
- Apply wind-drift correction to track a constant radius circle around the selected reference point with a bank not to exceed 60° at the steepest point in the turn.
- Divide attention between airplane control and ground track, while maintaining coordinated flight.
- Maintain the specified airspeed, ±10 knots, and roll out toward an object or specified heading ±10°.

QUESTIONS

1. What is the maximum bank angle for a steep spiral?
    A. 50°
    B. 55°
    C. 60°

2. True/False. The bank angle is the steepest when on the upwind side of the reference point.

3. Why is it important to maintain an airspeed at or below maneuvering speed (V_A)?

4. The elevator back pressure you must use:
    A. increases as you turn to the upwind side of the turn.
    B. increases as you turn to the downwind side of the turn.
    C. decreases as you turn to the downwind side of the turn.

SECTION H
Power-Off 180° Accuracy Approaches and Landings

Power-off accuracy approaches are approaches and landings made by gliding, with the engine idling, through a specific pattern to a touchdown beyond and within 200 feet of a designated line or mark on the runway. The objective is to impart the judgment and procedures necessary for accurately flying the airplane, without power, to a safe landing.

The ability to estimate the distance an airplane will glide to a landing is the real basis of all power-off accuracy approaches and landings. This largely determines the amount of maneuvering that may be done from a given altitude. In addition to the ability to estimate distance, it requires the ability to maintain the proper glide while maneuvering the airplane.

The objective of a good approach is to descend at an angle that permits the airplane to reach the desired landing area, and at an airspeed that results in minimum floating just before touchdown. To accomplish this, it is essential that you accurately control both the descent angle and the airspeed.

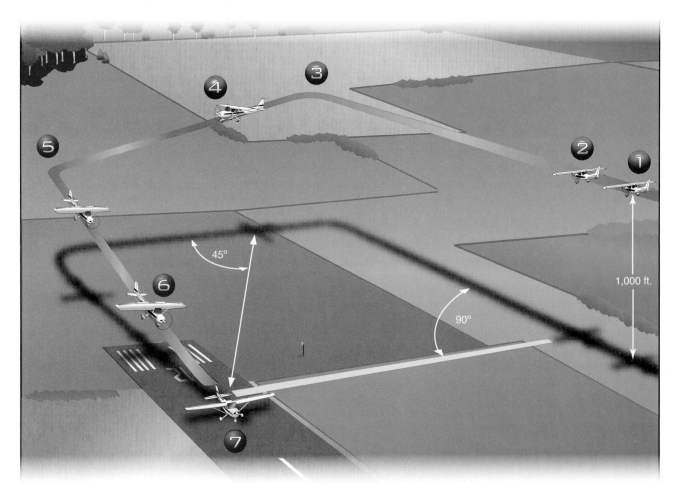

Your instructor might introduce you to the 90° power-off accuracy approach before moving to the more challenging 180° approach. The 360° power-off accuracy approach is an advanced maneuver and will develop your power-off approach skills to a higher level.

 Begin the maneuver by entering a normal traffic pattern. You can determine the strength and direction of the wind by the amount of crab required to maintain the proper ground track on the legs of the traffic pattern. When on the downwind leg of the traffic pattern your altitude should be no higher than 1,000 feet AGL. Perform your before-landing checklist and visually clear the final approach path and landing runway. Extend the landing gear at this point if your airplane is so equipped. Select the point on the runway at which you intend to land.

When you are picking your intended point of landing, choose a spot that is easily identifiable such as the thousand-foot markings or runway numbers.

 Upon reaching the downwind key position, which is directly abeam the point of intended landing, reduce the power to idle. Decrease your airspeed to the manufacturer's recommended glide speed while maintaining altitude. In the absence of a recommended glide speed, use 1.4 V_{S0}.

You must trim for the proper airspeed to maintain the recommended glide, or 1.4 V_{S0}. The pitch controls the airspeed, so the more you trim the less control pressure you have to apply to maintain the glide angle.

 Make the turn to the base leg of the traffic pattern at a point that is appropriate for the existing wind conditions and your glide angle. You should use the base leg to dissipate or conserve altitude as necessary.

Techniques to conserve altitude:	Techniques to dissipate altitude:
• Shorten downwind leg.	• Extend downwind leg.
• Round your turns.	• Square or extend your turns.
• Remain coordinated.	• Perform a slip.
• Extend flaps later.	• Extend flaps earlier.
• Minimize turns.	• Perform S turns.

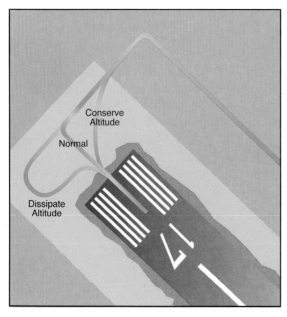

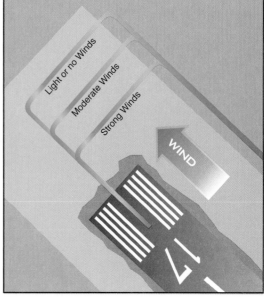

6 At the base leg key position, 45° from the intended point on landing, reassess your altitude, wind speed and direction. Determine if you need to dissipate or conserve altitude.

If your instructor had you start with 90º power-off accuracy approaches, you will find that the 180º approach is identical from the 45º base leg key point to landing.

7 Time your turn to the final approach course so as to roll out on the runway center-line just as you would in a normal traffic pattern. Clear the final approach path for traffic prior to beginning the turn.

Rounding your turn to final can help conserve altitude if your find yourself low on base leg. Similarly, squaring, or even extending the base leg can help dissipate altitude, if necessary.

8 On the final approach, lower the flaps or enter a slip if necessary to increase your descent angle without increasing your airspeed. Your goal is to descend at an angle that enables you to reach your intended point of landing at an airspeed that results in little or no float just prior to touchdown.

Should you find yourself in a position where you might undershoot, never try to stretch the glide or retract the flaps to reach the desired landing spot. Raising the flaps reduces both lift and drag and increases the stall speed. If you are slipping to increase the descent angle and determine you might undershoot the landing point, simply return to coordinated flight to increase lift and reduce drag, which might enable you to reach your landing spot.

9 Land with little or no float on or past but within 200 feet of the intended landing point. While your goal is to make the intended landing point, do not fixate on making your landing on that particular spot. A good, safe landing is far more important.

Critique your performance of the 180° approach and landing. You might need to alter your flight path or change your glide angle to compensate for various wind and weather conditions and airplane configurations. By reviewing your approach and landing, you can gain a better understanding of the power-off characteristics of your airplane.

 POWER-OFF 180° ACCURACY APPROACH AND LANDING

To meet the PTS requirements, you must:
- Exhibit satisfactory knowledge of the elements related to a power-off 180° accuracy approach and landing.
- Consider the wind conditions, landing surface, obstructions, and select an appropriate touchdown point.
- Position airplane on the downwind leg, parallel to the landing runway, and not more than 1,000 feet AGL.
- Complete final airplane configuration.
- Touch down in a normal landing attitude at or within 200 feet beyond the specified touchdown point.
- Complete the appropriate checklist.

SECTION H ■ **Power-Off 180° Accuracy Approaches and Landings**

QUESTIONS

1.   What is the key position?

2.   What is the purpose of power-off accuracy approaches?

3.   True/False. You should retract flaps on final approach to reduce drag and extend the glide.

4.   Entering a slip will cause
     A.   an increase in drag and an increase in lift.
     B.   an increase in drag and a decrease in lift.
     C.   a decrease in drag and an increase in lift.

SECTION I
Emergency Descent

An emergency descent is a maneuver for descending as rapidly as possible to a lower altitude or to a position to set up an emergency or precautionary landing. You might need to perform this maneuver if you experience an uncontrollable fire, smoke in the cockpit, a sudden loss of cabin pressurization, or any other situation that demands an immediate rapid descent.

The objective is to descend as soon and as rapidly as possible, within the structural limitations of the airplane. Perform emergency descents as recommended by the POH, observing recommended aircraft configurations, power settings, and airspeeds. Do not allow the airplane to exceed the never-exceed speed (V_{NE}), maximum landing gear extended speed (V_{LE}), maximum flap extended speed (V_{FE}), or maneuvering speed (V_A), as applicable.

When performing an emergency descent, make a radio call to alert ATC and other aircraft of your intentions. Configure the airplane, within the POH guidelines, to descend as rapidly as possible

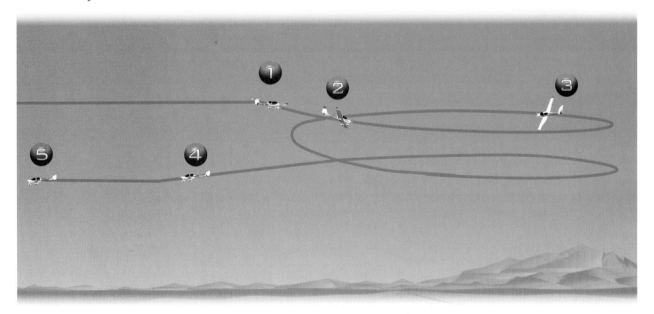

 Configure the airplane to descend.
- Reduce the power to idle.
- Place the propeller control (if equipped) to the low-pitch/high-rpm position.
- Extend the landing gear and flaps, as recommended by the POH.

> A bank angle of approximately 30° to 45° will maintain a positive load factor on the airplane.

2 Establish a descending turn. Bank approximately 30° to 45° to:
- Scan for other traffic below.
- Look for a possible emergency landing area.
- Increase the rate of descent.

SECTION I ■ Emergency Descent

 Maintain the bank angle and maximum allowable airspeed:

- V_{NE} for a clean aircraft, with no structural damage, in smooth air.

- V_A for a clean aircraft, with no structural damage, in turbulent air.

- V_{FE} or V_{LE} whichever is more restrictive and applicable to your POH recommended aircraft configuration.

④ Complete the appropriate emergency descent checklist.

⑤ Return to straight-and-level flight. Roll out of the bank. Level off the airplane by gradually raising the nose approximately 100 feet prior to the desired leveloff altitude.

Generally, a 10% lead is sufficient for leveloff. For example, 10% of a 1,000 ft/min descent would yield a 100-foot lead for leveloff.

⑥ Return to cruise flight or prepare for landing.

- To return to cruise flight, adjust power and mixture to the cruise setting and trim to relieve control pressures.

- To prepare for landing, head toward an appropriate site, configure the airplane for landing and maintain approach airspeed.

During training, you should terminate the procedure when the descent is stabilized and the Emergency Descent checklist is complete. In airplanes with piston engines, avoid prolonged practice of emergency descents to prevent excessive cooling of the engine cylinders.

 Emergency Descent

To meet the PTS requirements, you must:

- Exhibit satisfactory knowledge of the elements related to an emergency descent.
- Recognize situations, such as depressurization, cockpit smoke, and/or fire that require an emergency descent.
- Establish the appropriate airspeed, ±10 knots, and configuration for the emergency descent.
- Exhibit orientation, division of attention, and proper planning.
- Maintain positive load factors during the maneuver.
- Maintain appropriate airspeed, +0/–10 knots, and levels off at a specified altitude, ±100 feet.
- Complete the appropriate checklist.

QUESTIONS

1. What are two situations that might require you to make an emergency descent?

2. What is the purpose of banking the airplane during an emergency descent?

3. True/False. You should begin to level off at least 1,000 feet above the intended leveloff altitude.

4. What are the maximum airspeeds at which you should perform an emergency descent (based on flight conditions and airplane configuration)?

APPENDIX A

Answers

NOTE: There are no questions for CHAPTER 1 — Building Professional Experience.

CHAPTER 2

SECTION A

1. B

2. The gyroscopic flight instruments are the attitude indicator, heading indicator, and turn coordinator. The two principles are rigidity in space and precession.

3. Attitude indicator

4. True

5. The turn coordinator is electrically powered, while the attitude indicator and heading indicator are vacuum powered. If either the electrical or vacuum system fails, you still have bank information.

6. 14°

7. B

8. B

9. C

10. A

11. A

12. 307°

13. Airspeed indicator, altimeter, and vertical speed indicator.

14. B

15. A

16. D

17. Indicated altitude is higher than true altitude when the temperature is lower than standard, resulting in less terrain and obstruction clearance during cold weather operations.

18. To provide attitude, heading, rate of turn, and slip/skid information, integrated flight displays use an attitude and heading reference system (AHRS). The AHRS uses inertial sensors such as electronic gyroscopes and accelerometers to determine the aircraft's attitude relative to the horizon. An electronic magnetometer provides magnetic heading data.

19. C

20. The end of the trend vector shows what the airplane's heading will be in six seconds if the turn continues at the same rate. Index marks 18 degrees either side of center on the turn-rate indicator provide a reference for standard-rate turns.

21. A

22. C

23. C

24. The integrated flight display is configured so that the functions of the PFD can be transferred to the MFD screen, and vice versa. If the PFD screen turns black, the PFD display should automatically switch to the MFD in reversionary mode. In the event that the PFD does not appear on the MFD, most systems enable you to manually switch to reversionary mode.

25. False

SECTION B

1. The three common instrument cross-check errors are:

   - Fixation is applying your full concentration on a single instrument and excluding all others

   - Omission is excluding one or more pertinent instruments from your scan.

   - Emphasis is relying on an instrument that you readily understand, even when it provides inadequate information, instead of relying on a combination of instruments.

2. You can easily adjust the attitude with gentle pressure on the controls if the airplane is properly trimmed. If you are constantly holding control pressure, you cannot apply the precise pressures needed for controlled changes in attitude. An improperly trimmed airplane increases tension, interrupts your cross-check, and can result in abrupt or erratic control.

3. The two methods of attitude instrument flying are:

   - Control and performance — This method divides the instruments into three groups: control, performance, and navigation. The control and performance method is based on the idea that if you accurately establish a specific attitude and power setting using the control instruments, the airplane will perform as expected. The performance instruments indicate how the aircraft responds to changes in attitude and power.

- Primary and supporting — This method divides the panel into pitch instruments, bank instruments, and power instruments and further classifies instruments as being primary or supporting depending on the maneuver you are performing and whether you are establishing or maintaining an attitude. Use the primary instruments to provide the most essential information. Supporting instruments reinforce the indications on the primary instruments to help you meet the desired performance.

4. C

5. B

6. B

7. Standard-rate turn—bank control:

- Establishing: primary—attitude indicator; supporting—turn rate indicator/turn coordinator, HSI/heading indicator

- Maintaining: primary—turn rate indicator/turn coordinator; supporting—attitude indicator

8. B

9. Attitude indicator

10. Vertical speed indicator (VSI)

11. True

12. Common errors that apply to maintaining altitude during attitude instrument flying are:

- Error—not correcting for pitch deviations during roll-out from a turn; solution—do not fixate on the heading indicator.

- Error—consistent loss of altitude during turn entries; solution—during turn entry, apply back pressure to compensate for the loss of vertical lift.

- Error—consistent gain in altitude when rolling out from a turn; solution—relax back pressure during roll-out. If you added nose-up trim during the turn, use some forward pressure until you can trim for level flight.

- Error—chasing the vertical speed indications; solution—use a proper cross-check of other pitch instruments, such as the altimeter and attitude indicator. Remember that the VSI has a lag in its indications.

- Error—applying excessive pitch corrections for the altimeter deviation; solution—do not rush the pitch correction. If you aggressively apply a large correction, you are more likely to aggravate the existing error.

- Error—failure to maintain established pitch corrections; solution—continue to maintain your scan after making a correction and be sure to trim off any control pressures.

13. A

14. B

15. The correct sequence to recover from a nose-low unusual attitude is to reduce power, level the wings, and raise the nose to place the aircraft symbol on the horizon line of the attitude indicator.

SECTION C

1. B

2. An HSI always provides proper sensing when tuned to a VOR because the CDI is mounted on a compass card which automatically rotates to the correct heading.

3. False

4. 7°; 1.75 nautical miles

5.

A. 3

B. 4

C. 1

D. 2

6. False

7. 130 nautical miles; 18,000 feet to 45,000 feet

8. True

9. 4°

10. False

11. Required navigation performance (RNP) is a set of standards that apply to both airspace and navigation equipment. The use of RNP in conjunction with RNAV provides greater flexibility in procedure and airspace design, as well as making it more effective for ATC to offer direct routing.

12. B

13. A flight management system (FMS) automates the tasks of managing the onboard navigation equipment. An FMS acts as the input/output device for navigational data from navaids, such as VOR/DME and localizer facilities, and from GPS or INS equipment.

14. A

15. C

16. True

17. B

18. C

19. When you program a departure, arrival, approach, or other route, the receiver senses when the airplane passes a waypoint and automatically cycles to the next waypoint.

20. True

21. A

22. B

23. C

24. The 45° index marks on the heading indicator make it easy to see when you have established the correct intercept heading; similar index marks on the ADF show when you have intercepted the bearing.

25. C

26. A

27. C

CHAPTER 3

SECTION A

1. D

2. A

3. E

4. C

5. B

6. False

7. C

8. C

9. G

10. F

11. A

12. Green, Red

13. 3,000 feet

14. It might indicate that ground visibility is less than three miles and/or the ceiling is less than 1,000 feet.

15. A

16. B

17. B

18. The base of Class A airspace is 18,000 feet MSL and extends up to and including FL600.

19. G

20. E

21. F

22. A

23. B

24. C

25. D

26. 200 knots

27. False

28. 6:00 AM — 11:00 PM (0600 —2300) local time

29. MALSR (medium intensity approach light system with runway alignment indicator lights)

30. 234 feet

31. Denver Center

32. 111.5, I-LBF

33. B

34. NOTAM(D) information is disseminated for all navigational facilities which are part of the U.S. airspace system, all public use airports, seaplane bases, and heliports listed in the Chart Supplement. FDC NOTAMs, issued by the National Flight Data Center, contain regulatory information such as temporary flight restrictions or amendments to instrument approach procedures and other current aeronautical charts.

SECTION B

1. ARTCCs provide these services to IFR flights:

   • Separation from IFR traffic

   • IFR clearances

   • Processing of IFR flight plans

   • Reports of VFR traffic that might affect the flight, if workload permits

   • Information regarding convective activity, including vectors if requested

   • Hazardous weather reports

   • Terrain or obstruction alerts

   • Aircraft conflict alerts

   • Emergency assistance

2. C

3. 30 minutes

4. Regulations state that you may not act as pilot in command of a flight conducted under IFR unless you hold an instrument rating and meet the recency of experience requirements for instrument flight as specified under FAR Part 61. In addition, your aircraft must meet the equipment and inspection requirements of FAR Part 91. If weather conditions are below VFR minimums, you must file an IFR flight plan and obtain an IFR clearance before departing from within, or prior to entering controlled airspace.

5. A

6. ATC issues a terrain or obstruction alert when your Mode C altitude readout indicates your flight is

below the published minimum safe altitude for that area.

7. ATC issues an aircraft conflict alert when the controller determines that the minimum separation between an aircraft being controlled and another aircraft could be compromised

8. Clearance delivery

9. C

10. F

11. D

12. A

13. E

14. B

15. C

16. C

17. C

SECTION C

1. Controlled

2. A

3. C

4. True

5. True

6. A

7. A

8. D

9. E

10. H

11. B

12. G

13. C

14. F

15. False

16. False

17. B

18. A

19. B

20. Flight Service

21. A

22. True

23. *". . . cleared to the Cheyenne Airport as filed. Climb and maintain 8,000. Departure Control frequency is 120.9. Squawk 5417."*

24. 37R C DAL A DR BYP○ ↓M120 RP150 DP BYP○ HDG 210 RV RWY31R ILS FAP CRS LDG RWY31R

CHAPTER 4

SECTION A

1. B

2. B

3. 275°

4. B

5. 124.35 MHz

6. B

7. 8,500 feet MSL

8. C

9. C

10. C

SECTION B

1. False

2. Departure airport, procedure name, computer code, restrictions, communications frequencies, initial departure instructions, departure route, transition route, navaid and fix information, lost communication procedures, and minimum climb gradient.

3. False

4. B

5. 550 feet per minute

6. 030°

7. At or below 9,000 feet MSL

8. C

9. At POAKE Intersection

10. True

11. The FAA prints textual obstacle departure procedures in the front of each Terminal Procedures Publication.

12. True

13. False

14. C

15. You are responsible for your own terrain/obstruction clearance until you reach the minimum altitude for IFR operations in the area.

CHAPTER 5

SECTION A

1. False
2. D
3. A
4. E
5. B
6. C
7. B
8. True
9. C
10. C
11. False
12. False
13. B
14. C
15. False
16. C

SECTION B

1. A
2. Return to the previous frequency and ask for an alternate frequency.
3. No
4. False
5. True
6. If radar contact has been lost or radar service terminated, the FARs require you to provide ATC with position reports over compulsory reporting points. In addition, you should report the final approach fix inbound on a nonprecision approach and when you leave the outer marker inbound on a precision approach. A report also is necessary when it becomes apparent that an estimated time, that you previously submitted to ATC, will be in error in excess of 3 minutes.
7. A

8. "Minneapolis Center, Aztec 3490R, Dickinson, 30, 9,000, ULLIN 45, Bismarck next."
9. 17,000 feet MSL
10. Tango routes are published routes that enable RNAV-equipped aircraft to more efficiently fly around or through busy terminal areas without needing radar vectors from ATC.
11. False
12. True
13. True

SECTION C

1. True
2. C
3. 200 KIAS
4. C
5. A
6. B
7. B
8. C
9. True

CHAPTER 6

SECTION A

1. At WISKE Intersection.
2. C
3. 7000 feet MSL
4. CTW.WISKE3
5. 6,000 feet MSL
6. 120.87
7. True

SECTION B

1. You should obtain weather information as early as practical.
2. A descend via clearance authorizes you to follow the altitudes published on the STAR procedure. Descent is at your discretion; however you must adhere to the minimum crossing altitudes and airspeed restrictions printed on the chart.
3. False
4. 24 nautical miles ahead of FREDY Intersection

5. B

CHAPTER 7

SECTION A

1. Initial, intermediate, final, and missed approach

2. B

3. C

4. A

5. B

6. C

7. 108.3 MHz, 255°

8. True

9. C

10. The missed approach icons represent the initial pilot actions in the event of a missed approach. They provide symbolic information about the initial up and out maneuvers. You must always refer to the missed approach instructions in the heading section, plan view, and profile view for complete information about the missed approach procedure.

11. ³/₄ mile

12. C

13. G

14. A

15. B

16. F

17. D

18. E

19. 120.15 MHz

20. B

21. 111.1 MHz, 310°

22. B

23. B

24. B

25. C

26. A

27. B

28. 3:20

29. 1,160 feet MSL with ENTRA, 1,520 feet MSL without ENTRA

30. C

31. False

SECTION B

1. A

2. C

3. Straight-in landing minimums normally are used when the final approach course is positioned within 30° of the runway and a minimum of maneuvering is required to align the airplane with the runway. If the final approach course is not properly aligned, or if it is desirable to land on a different runway, a circling approach may be executed and circle-to-land minimums apply. In contrast to a straight-in landing, the controller terminology, *"cleared for straight-in approach . . ."* means that you should not perform any published procedure to reverse your course, but does not reference landing minimums. A straight-in approach may be initiated from a fix closely aligned with the final approach course, may commence from the completion of a DME arc, or you may receive vectors to the final approach course.

4. 140°, 2,000 feet MSL

5. B

6. A

7. C

8. MDA – 880 feet MSL; visibility – 1 statute mile

9. 200 knots IAS

10. A

11. No

12. C

13. B

14. False

15. C

16. ATC can initiate a visual approach if the reported ceiling is at least 1,000 feet AGL and visibility is at least 3 statute miles. ATC can issue a clearance for a contact approach only upon your request when the reported ground visibility at the airport is 1 statute mile or greater. During a visual approach, you must have the airport or preceding aircraft in sight. If you report the preceding aircraft in sight, you are responsible for maintaining separation from that aircraft and avoiding the associated wake turbulence. When executing a contact approach you are responsible for your own obstruction clearance, but ATC provides separation from other IFR or special VFR traffic. Separation from normal VFR traffic is not provided.

CHAPTER 8

SECTION A

1. C

2. B

3. B

4. A

5. A

6. B

7. C

8. B

9. B

10. A

11. B

SECTION B

1. C

2. C

3.

  A. 1

  B. 5, 10

  C. 4, 7

  D. 2, 8

  E. 3, 6, 9

4.

  A. 3, 4

  B. 5

  C. 1

  D. 2, 6

  E. 2, 6

5. 710 feet to the right of the localizer centerline and 140 feet above the glide slope

6. Power

7. C

8. A

9. B

10. C

11. B

12. Climb to 2,000 feet MSL and then perform a climbing right turn to 3,000 feet MSL to intercept the 263° radial outbound from IRW VOR. Track this course to JESKE intersection which is at 12.0 DME from IRW and enter the hold.

13. The MDA is 1,640 feet MSL if you can identify COTOX or 1,800 feet MSL without COTOX. The MAP is 1.8 DME from IOKC or 3:28 from IVEYI at a groundspeed of 90 knots.

14. C

15. A

16. An LDA has a course width of between 3° and 6°. The width of an SDF course is either 6° or 12°.

SECTION C

1. Icons on the plan view indicate minimum altitudes that you must maintain within a 30 nautical mile boundary as you arrive from the enroute structure to a specific initial approach fix; there is no published MSA; the Basic T approach segment is optimum from the enroute to the terminal environment.

2. A

3. Refer to the airplane flight manual (AFM) or AFM supplement.

4. B

5. A

6. C

7. B

8. E

9. D

10. A

11. C

12. B

13. A

14. C

15. A

16. C

17. B

18. At the DA of 6,397 feet MSL, begin a climb to 10,300 feet MSL. Take the GPS receiver out of suspend mode and proceed to IVUCI. At IVUCI, turn left to a course of 287° to SENSE and enter the hold. Continue to climb in the hold to 10,300 feet MSL.

19. C

CHAPTER 9

SECTION A

1. The troposphere. The change of temperature lapse rate at the tropopause acts like a lid to trap water vapor and associated weather.

2. B

3. C

4. C

5. E

6. A

7. B

8. I

9. G

10. D

11. C

12. H

13. A, C, E

14. False

15. False

16. B

17. C

18. C

19. C

SECTION B

1. Unstable air, some type of lifting action, and a relatively high moisture content

2. A

3. B

4. C

5. A

6. B

7. True

8. B

9. Slow to the airspeed recommended for rough air, such as maneuvering or penetration speed, try to maintain a level flight attitude, and accept variations in airspeed and altitude.

10. B

11. After

12. False

13. C

14. B

15. A

16. In humid climates where the bases of convective clouds tend to be low, microbursts are associated with a visible rainshaft. In drier climates, the higher thunderstorm cloud bases result in the evaporation of the rainshaft. The only visible indications under these conditions may be virga at the cloud base and a dust ring on the ground.

17. B

18. B

19. A

20. C

21. True

22. False

23. B

24. B

SECTION C

1. C

2. B

3. A

4. The actual temperature is 6.7°C and the dewpoint is 6.1°C

5. 1008.6 (hPa)

6. True

7. TEMPO indicates a temporary forecast when wind, visibility, weather, or sky conditions are expected to last less than an hour.

8. A

9. The forecast winds will be 200° true at 8 knots with visibility greater than 6 statute miles, cloud bases are 1,200 feet broken, 3,000 feet overcast. Conditions are forecast to temporarily change to 2 statute miles visibility in light rain and overcast skies with a ceiling 800 feet AGL.

10. C

11. False

12. A

13. True

14. 1,500 feet to 2,500 feet overcast with occasional ceilings of overcast conditions below 2,000 feet, visibility is expected to be below 5 miles in light rain and light snow.

15. A

16. Winds are forecast to be from 250° true at 110 knots; temperature at that altitude is forecast to be -15°C.

17. True

18. A

19. B

SECTION D

1. B

2. IFR conditions with ceilings less than 1,000 feet and/or visibility less than 3 miles

3. The visible satellite weather picture generally is used to determine the presence of clouds as well as the cloud shape and texture. An infrared photo, on the other hand, depicts the heat radiation emitted by various cloud tops and the earth's surface. For this

reason, the infrared picture can be used to determine cloud height. Usually, cold temperatures show up as light gray or white, with high clouds appearing the whitest.

4. Moderate turbulence from the surface to 10,000 feet MSL

5. A

6. The wind is from the northwest at 25 knots.

7. False

8. B

9. 1015.7mb (hPa)

10. It indicates an automated observation.

11. A

12. A

13. True

14. A

15. The height of the precipitation in that cell is 25,000 feet MSL.

16. NE indicates there were no echoes detected by the radar, and NA indicates that no report was received from the radar site.

17. B

18. B

19. C

20. B

21. Moderate turbulence from 10,000 feet to FL200 in the area over Montana, Wyoming, Colorado, and New Mexico enclosed by the dashed line.

22. The height of the tropopause is 34,000 feet MSL.

23. B

24. True

25. The forecast is for moderate clear air turbulence from below FL240 up to FL370.

26. C

SECTION E

1. When you request a briefing, identify yourself as a pilot, whether you plan to fly VFR or IFR, your aircraft number or your name, aircraft type, departure airport, route of flight, destination, flight altitude(s), estimated time of departure, and estimated time enroute.

2. False.

3. Aviation Weather Center (AviationWeather.gov) and Flight Service web portal (1800WxBrief.com)

4. Alerts broadcast on ARTCC frequencies, notations on VFR and IFR charts, and notes on VOR listings in the *Chart Supplement*

5. 122.0 MHz

6. B

7. D

8. E

9. C

10. A

11. F

12. B

13. B

14. B

15. C

CHAPTER 10

SECTION A

1. MAYDAY

2. C

3. Aircraft identification, equipment affected, degree to which the equipment impairs your IFR operations, and type of assistance desired from ATC

4. False

5. True

6. To preclude extended IFR operations by these aircraft within the ATC system because they can adversely affect other users of the airspace.

7. You should fly at the highest of the following altitudes: the altitude assigned in your last ATC clearance, the minimum altitude for IFR operations, or the altitude ATC has advised you to expect in a further clearance.

8. You should fly one of the following routes in the order given: the route assigned by ATC in your last clearance; if being radar vectored, the direct route from the point of radio failure to the fix route, or airway specified in the radar vector clearance; in the absence of an assigned route, the route ATC has advised you to expect in a further clearance; or the route filed in your flight plan.

9. Hold until the EFC time, then begin the approach.

10. Ground-based radar facility and a functioning airborne radio transmitter and receiver

11. Surveillance approach (ASR), precision approach radar (PAR), and no-gyro approach.

12. Precision approach radar (PAR)

13. False

14. True

SECTION B

1. Attempted VFR flight into IFR conditions; controlled flight into terrain; loss of control

2. C

3. A

4. C

5. The examples should include risk factors associated with these categories:
   - Pilot—training, experience, fitness
   - Passengers—experience, fitness, flexibility
   - Plane—airworthiness, performance, configuration
   - Programming—avionics airworthiness, operation, and configuration
   - Plan—airport conditions, terrain, airspace, mission, weather

6. C

7. Planning and prioritizing includes: rehearsing your intended route of flight; determining how the weather affects your fuel calculations and available approaches at your destination; performing briefings; and identifying important tasks.

8. Some actions that you can take prior to flight to effectively use resources and reduce head-down time during ground and flight operations include: organizing charts; checking for weather updates; programming GPS equipment; reviewing the airport diagram; and preflighting your tablet.

9. A

10. C

11. You can take these actions to decrease your risk of CFIT during initial climb and departure:
    - Review current charts with clear depictions of hazardous terrain and minimum safe altitudes.
    - Ensure that your airplane performance meets any required climb gradients.
    - Verify that ATC departure instructions provide adequate terrain clearance.
    - Brief the takeoff and climb procedure prior to takeoff.
    - During the takeoff briefing, set all communication and navigation frequencies and course selectors.
    - Brief the approach procedure in use at the departure airport in case you must return to the airport.

12. C

13. A

SECTION C

1. True

2. The availability of route alternatives, aircraft performance considerations, and fuel economy

3. Approaches available at the alternate, aircraft equipment required for the available approaches, alternate minimums, forecast weather at your ETA, distance from your primary destination, fuel requirements

4. NOTAMs

5. False

6. 800 foot ceiling and 2 miles visibility

7. Weather reports and forecasts, the airplane's capabilities, your personal limitations, and your level of proficiency

8. A

9. At least 30 minutes

10. C

CHAPTER 11

SECTION A

1. Fuel is injected into each cylinder's intake port.

2. You should place the electric (auxiliary) boost pump switch in the high output position.

3. Measuring the weight of the fuel instead of its volume gives a better indication of the fuel's available energy.

4. False

5. True

6. Waste gate

7. B

8. True

9. To prevent engine damage and provide maximum power if a go-around becomes necessary.

10. C

SECTION B

1. Continuous-flow, diluter-demand, pressure-demand, and pulse demand.

2. True

3. False

4. Check the inline flow indicator; some types indicate green and in others, a ball floats up in the tube.

5. B

6. A safety valve will open when the maximum cabin differential pressure is reached.

7. C

8. C

9. False

10. Check the propeller anti-ice electrical ammeter for proper indication.

SECTION C

1. False

2. B

3. When the throttle is reduced below a certain value, the flaps are extended, or the airspeed falls below a preset limit, the gear warning horn sounds to warn you that the gear is in an unsafe position for landing.

4. The safety switch, or squat switch, inhibits gear operation when the weight of the airplane is pushing down on the landing gear strut. If the switch is accidentally moved while the airplane is sitting on the ramp, it sounds a warning to return the gear lever to the DOWN position. However, during takeoff or landing rolls, when the wings are producing lift, the squat switch can close and allow gear retraction.

5. A

6. C

CHAPTER 12

SECTION A

1. False

2. B

3. False

4. True

5. A

6. Maximum level flight speed

7. Weight

8. Additional lift is required to support a higher weight. The wing must fly at a higher angle of attack to generate the additional lift, so it reaches the stalling angle of attack at a higher airspeed.

9. True

10. B

11. True

12. Service ceiling

13. A

14. 55 KIAS

15. Increase the angle of bank and/or reduce airspeed

16. Close the throttle to minimize altitude loss during recovery. In addition, engine rotation may cause the spin rate to increase, and thrust may cause the spin to go flat. If the spin is in a multi-engine airplane, asymmetrical thrust could aggravate the spin.

17. Because the relative wind in a flat spin is nearly straight up, the wings remain in a high angle of attack or stalled condition. In addition, the upward flow over the tail may render the elevators and rudder ineffective, making recovery impossible.

SECTION B

1. 11 knots

2. False

3. A

4. 3,008 feet

5. 2,397 feet

6. True

7. B

8. B

9. A

10. B

11. 188 knots

12. True

13. Approximately 78 mph or 67 knots

14. A

SECTION C

1. A

2. B

3. C

4. True

5. B

6. A

7. A

8. B

CHAPTER 13

SECTION A

1. V_{NE}, V_{LE}, V_{FE}

2. True

3. To enable you to make adjustments for wind and obstacles during the approach without using extreme maneuvers at low altitude.

4. B

5. False

6. False

7. C

8. True

9. False

SECTION B

1. B

2. False

3. Evaluate the outcome. — Keep track of the situation to ensure that your decision is producing the desired outcome. Monitor the aircraft instruments and systems, including the equipment that malfunctioned. Maintain positional awareness and obtain updates on enroute and destination weather conditions.

4. Operational pitfalls include:
   - Peer pressure
   - Mind-set
   - Get-there-it is
   - Duck-under syndrome
   - Scud running
   - Continuing VFR flight into instrument conditions
   - Getting behind the aircraft
   - Loss of situational awareness
   - Operating without adequate fuel reserves
   - Descent below the minimum enroute altitude
   - Flying outside the envelope
   - Neglect of flight planning, preflight inspections, and checklists

5. C

6. The examples should include risk factors associated with these categories:
   - Pilot—training, experience, fitness
   - Passengers—experience, fitness, flexibility
   - Plane—airworthiness, performance, configuration
   - Programming—avionics airworthiness, operation, and configuration
   - Plan—airport conditions, terrain, airspace, mission, weather

7. A

8. True

9. Actions that you can take to maintain situational awareness during flight operations include: eliciting information from other crew members; keeping the other pilot informed of the status of operations; adhering to SOPs; and following the sterile cockpit procedure.

10. Actions to maintain situational awareness during taxi include:
    - Prior to entering or crossing any runway, scan the full length of the runway and final approach. If you see a conflicting aircraft, stop taxiing and query ATC.
    - Before performing checklist procedures, stop the airplane or ensure you are in a taxiing phase that has no runway incursion risk.
    - Be especially vigilant if another aircraft with a similar call sign is on the same frequency.
    - Never stop on a runway to communicate with ATC if you become disoriented.
    - During landing, do not accept last-minute turnoff instructions unless you are certain that you can safely comply.
    - Use caution after landing on a runway that intersects another runway, or on a runway with an exit taxiway in close proximity to another runway's hold short line.
    - After landing at a nontowered airport, listen on the CTAF for inbound aircraft. Scan the full length of your landing runway and that of any runways you intend to cross, including the final approach and departure paths.

11. B

12. Examples of actions you can take to decrease your risk of CFIT during approach and landing should be drawn from five categories: altimeters, safe altitudes, ATC procedures, flight crew complacency, and approach procedures.

13. C

CHAPTER 14

SECTION A

1. An accelerated stall occurs when the airplane stalls at a higher indicated airspeed because excessive maneuvering loads are imposed by steep turns, pull-ups, or other abrupt changes in its flight path.

2. C

3. False

4. Maintain coordinated turning flight to ensure that both wings stall simultaneously. If the airplane is slipping toward the inside of the turn when the stall occurs, it tends to roll rapidly toward the outside of the turn as the nose pitches down because the outside wing stalls before the inside wing. If the airplane is skidding toward the outside of the turn, it has a tendency to roll to the inside of the turn because the inside wing stalls first.

SECTION B

1. True
2. Accelerate to V_X or V_Y and then begin to climb.
3. C
4. False
5. Holding the brakes until you achieve full power enables you to determine that the engine is functioning properly before you take off from a field where power availability is critical and distance to abort a takeoff is limited.
6. 50 feet
7. True
8. Steeper
9.

SECTION C

1. Slightly decrease the angle of bank first, then increase back pressure on the yoke to raise the nose. Once you regain your desired altitude, roll back to the desired angle of bank.
2. B
3. False
4. 25°

SECTION D

1. C
2. False
3. In a chandelle to the right, the aileron on the right wing is lowered slightly during the roll-out. This causes more drag on the right wing and tends to make the airplane yaw slightly to the right counteracting some of the left turning tendency.
4. C

SECTION E

1. A possible cause is an airspeed which is too slow causing the rate of turn to increase at a given bank angle.

2. B
3. False
4. One of the key factors in making symmetrical turns is proper airspeed control.

SECTION F

1. 960 feet
2. A downwind entry results in the highest groundspeed and the highest pivotal altitude at the start of the maneuver.
3. True
4. C

SECTION G

1. C
2. False
3. Using an airspeed above maneuvering speed (V_A) can impose excessive loads on the aircraft and exceed the structural load limits of the aircraft.
4. B

SECTION H

1. The point on the downwind leg abeam the landing spot where the power is reduced to idle.
2. To develop an understanding of the power-off characteristics of your aircraft.
3. False
4. B

SECTION I

1. Uncontrollable fire, smoke in the cockpit, a sudden loss of cabin pressurization, or any other situation that demands an immediate rapid descent
2. To scan for traffic below, to look for an emergency landing area, and to maintain a positive load factor on the airplane.
3. False
4. The maximum airspeed at which should perform an emergency descent is:
   - V_{NE} for a clean aircraft, with no structural damage, in smooth air.
   - V_A for a clean aircraft, with no structural damage, in turbulent air.
   - V_{FE} or V_{LE} whichever is more restrictive and applicable to your POH recommended aircraft configuration.

APPENDIX A ■ Answers

APPENDIX B

ABBREVIATIONS

A

AC — advisory circular

AC — convective outlook

ACARS — aircraft communication addressing and reporting system

ACAS — Adverse Conditions Alerting Service

AD — airworthiness directive

ADDS — Aviation Digital Data Service

ADF — automatic direction finder

ADIZ — air defense identification zone

ADM — aeronautical decision making

ADS-B — automatic dependent surveillance–broadcast

AFM — aircraft flight manual

AFSS — automated flight service station

AGL — above ground level

AHRS — attitude and heading reference system

AIM — *Aeronautical Information Manual*

AIREP — PIREP from ACARS system

AIRMET — airman's meteorological information

ALS — approach light system

ALSF — ALS with sequenced flashers

AM — amplitude modulation

AME — aviation medical examiner

APC — approach control

APV — approach with vertical guidance

AR — authorization required

ARINC — Aeronautical Radio, Incorporated

ARP — airport reference point

ARSR — air route surveillance radar

ARTCC — air route traffic control center

ARTS — automated radar terminal system

ASOS — automated surface observing system

ASR — airport surveillance radar

ATA — actual time of arrival

ATC — air traffic control

ATCRBS — ATC radar beacon system

ATD — along track distance

ATD — aviation training device

ATE — actual time enroute

ATIS — automatic terminal information service

ATP — airline transport pilot

ATS — air traffic service

AWC — Aviation Weather Center

AWOS — automated weather observing system

AWSS — automated weather sensor system

AWW — alert severe weather watch

B

BC — back course

BCN — beacon

BHP — brake horsepower

BRG — bearing

C

CAS — calibrated airspeed

CAT — clear air turbulence

CCFP — Collaborative Convective Forecast Product

CDI — course deviation indicator

CFI — certificated flight instructor

CFIT — controlled flight into terrain

CFR — Code of Federal Regulations

CG — center of gravity

CH — course heading

CHT — cylinder head temperature

CL — center of lift

C_L — coefficient of lift

CLC — course-line computer

C_{Lmax} — maximum coefficient of lift

CLNC — clearance

CLNC DEL — clearance delivery

CNF — computer navigation fix

CO — carbon monoxide

CO_2 — carbon dioxide

COP — changeover point

CRM — crew resource management

CTAF — common traffic advisory frequency

CVFP — charted visual flight procedures

CWA — center weather advisory

D

DA — density altitude

DA — decision altitude

DA(H) — decision altitude (height)

DALR — dry adiabatic lapse rate

DCS — decompression sickness

DP — instrument departure procedures

DPC — departure control

DGPS — differential global positioning system

DH — decision height

DME — distance measuring equipment

DOD — Department of Defense

DUATS — direct user access terminal system

DVFR — defense visual flight rules

E

EAS — equivalent airspeed

EFAS — enroute flight advisory service

EFB — electronic flight bag

EFC — expect further clearance

EFVS — enhanced flight vision system

EGT — exhaust gas temperature

ETA — estimated time of arrival

ETD — estimated time of departure

ETE — estimated time enroute

F

ft/min — feet per minute

FA — area forecast

FAA — Federal Aviation Administration

FAC — final approach course

FAF — final approach fix

FAP — final approach point

FARs — Federal Aviation Regulations

FAWP — final approach waypoint

FBO — fixed base operator

FD — winds and temperatures aloft forecast

FDC — Flight Data Center

FIS-B — flight information service-broadcast

FL — flight level

FLIP — flight information publication

FMS — flight management system

FSDO — Flight Standards District Office

FSS — flight service station

G

G — gravity; unit of measure for acceleration

GBAS — ground-based augmentation system

GCA — ground controlled approach

GCO — ground communication outlet

GLONASS — global navigation satellite system

GNSS — global navigation satellite system

g.p.h. — gallons per hour

gal/h — gallons per hour

GPS — global positioning system

GPWS — ground proximity warning system

H

HAA — height above airport

HAT — height above touchdown

HATh — height above threshold

HDG — heading

HF — high frequency

HIRLs — high intensity runway lights

HIWAS — hazardous in-flight weather advisory service

HMR — hazardous materials regulations

hPa — hectoPascals

HSI — horizontal situation indicator

HVOR — high altitude VOR

Hz — Hertz

I

IAF — initial approach fix

IAP — instrument approach procedure

IAS — indicated airspeed

ICAO — International Civil Aviation Organization

IF — intermediate fix

IFR — instrument flight rules

ILS — instrument landing system

IM — inner marker

IMC — instrument meteorological conditions

in Hg — inches of mercury

INS — inertial navigation system

IR — infrared

ISA — International Standard Atmosphere

IVSI — instantaneous vertical speed indicator

K

kg — kilogram

KCAS — knots calibrated airspeed

kHz — kilohertz

KIAS — knots indicated airspeed

km — kilometer

KTAS — knots true airspeed

Kts — knots

kw — kilowatt

kwh — kilowatt hour

L

L/MF — low/medium frequency

LAA — local airport advisory

LAHSO — land and hold short operation

Lb — pound(s)

LDA — localizer-type directional aid

L/D — lift/drag ratio

L/D$_{max}$ — maximum lift/drag ratio

LEMAC — leading edge mean aerodynamic chord

LI — lifted index

LIRLs — low intensity runway lights

LLT — low level turbulence

LLWAS — low level windshear alert system

LMM — locator middle marker

LNAV — lateral navigation

LOC — localizer

LOFT — line-oriented flight training

LOM — outer compass locator

LORAN — long range navigation

LP — localizer performance

LPV — localizer performance with vertical guidance

LVOR — low altitude VOR

M

M — Mach

MAA — maximum authorized altitude

MAC — mean aerodynamic chord

MALS — medium intensity approach light system

MALSF — MALS with sequenced flashers

MALSR — MALS with RAIL

MAHWP — missed approach holding waypoint

MAP — missed approach point

MAP — manifold absolute pressure

MAWP — missed approach waypoint

mb — millibar

MB — magnetic bearing

MC — magnetic course

MCA — minimum crossing altitude

MDA — minimum descent altitude

MDA(H) — minimum descent altitude (height)

MDH — minimum descent height

MEA — minimum enroute altitude

METAR — aviation routine weather report

MFD — multifunction display

MH — magnetic heading

MHA — minimum holding altitude

MHz — megahertz

MIA — minimum IFR altitude

MIRLs — medium intensity runway lights

MLS — microwave landing system

MM — middle marker

MOA — military operations area

MOCA — minimum obstruction clearance altitude

MORA — minimum off-route altitude

MPH — miles per hour

MRA — minimum reception altitude

MSA — minimum safe altitude

MSAW — minimum safe altitude warning

MSL — mean sea level

MTI — moving target indicator

MTR — military training route

MVA — minimum vectoring altitude

MVFR — marginal VFR

N

NA — not authorized

NACG — National Aeronautical Charting Group

NAR — North American Route (also refers to North Atlantic Route)

NAS — national airspace system

NASA — National Aeronautics and Space Administration

NAVAID — Navigation aid

NCAR — National Center for Atmospheric Research

NCWF — National Convective Weather Forecast

NDB — nondirectional radio beacon

n.m. — nautical miles

NM — nautical miles

NMC — National Meteorological Center

NOAA — National Oceanic and Atmospheric Administration

NoPT — no procedure turn

NORDO — no radio

NOTAM — Notices to Airmen

NPA — nonprecision approach

NSA — national security area

NSF — National Science Foundation

NTSB — National Transportation Safety Board

NTZ — no transgression zone

NWS — National Weather Service

O

OAT — outside air temperature

OBS — omnibearing selector

ODP — obstacle departure procedure

OM — outer marker

OPD — optimized profile descent

OROCA — off-route obstruction clearance altitude

OTS — out of service

P

PA — precision approach

PAPI — precision approach path indicator

PAR — precision approach radar

PAVE — Pilot, Aircraft, enVironment, External pressures

PCATD — personal computer-based aviation training device

PCL — pilot-controlled lighting

PF — pilot flying

PFD — primary flight display

PIC — pilot in command

PIREP — pilot weather report

PM — pilot monitoring

POH — pilot's operating handbook

PPS — precise positioning service

PRM — precision runway monitor

psi — pounds per square inch

psid — pounds per square inch differential

PT — procedure turn

PTS — practical test standards

PVASI — pulsating visual approach slope indicator

R

r.p.m. — revolutions per minute

RPM — revolutions per minute

RA — resolution advisory

RAF — Research Aviation Facility

RAIL — runway alignment indicator lights

RAIM — receiver autonomous integrity monitoring

RB — relative bearing

RCC — rescue coordination center

RCLS — runway centerline light system

RCO — remote communication outlet

REIL — runway end identifier lights

RMI — radio magnetic indicator

RMK — remarks

RNAV — area navigation

RNP — required navigation performance

RRL — runway remaining lights

RVR — runway visual range

RVSM — reduced vertical separation minimum

RVV — runway visibility value

S

SALR — saturated adiabatic lapse rate

SALS — short approach light system

SAR — search and rescue

SD — radar weather report

SDF — simplified directional facility

SFL — sequenced flashing lights

SIAP — standard instrument approach procedure

SID — standard instrument departure

SIGMET — significant meteorological information

SLP — sea level pressure

s.m. — statute miles

SM — statute miles

SPECI — non-routine (special) aviation weather report

SPS — standard positioning service

SRM — single-pilot resource management

SSALS — simplified SALS

SSALSF — SALS with SFL

SSALSR — SALS with RAIL

SSV — standard service volume

STAR — standard terminal arrival route

SVFR — special visual flight rules

T

TA — traffic advisory

TAA — terminal arrival area

TACAN — tactical air navigation

TAF — terminal aerodrome forecast

TAS — true airspeed

TC — true course

TCAD — traffic alert and collision avoidance device

TCAS — traffic alert and collision avoidance system

TCH — threshold crossing height

TCU — towering cumulonimbus

TDWR — terminal Doppler weather radar

TDZE — touchdown zone elevation

TDZL — touchdown zone lighting

TEC — tower enroute control

TEMAC — trailing edge mean aerodynamic chord

TERPS — U.S. Standard for Terminal Instrument Procedures

TH — true heading

TIBS — telephone information briefing service

TIT — turbine inlet temperature

TRSA — terminal radar service area

TSO — technical standard order

TVOR — terminal VOR

TWEB — transcribed weather broadcast

U

UA — pilot report

UCAR — University Corporation for Atmospheric Research

UHF — ultra high frequency

UNICOM — aeronautical advisory station

UTC — Coordinated Universal Time (Zulu time)

UUA — urgent pilot report

V

V_1 — takeoff decision speed

V_2 — takeoff safety speed

V_A — design maneuvering speed

VAFTAD — volcanic ash forecast transport and dispersion chart

VASI — visual approach slope indicator

VDP — visual descent point

V_{FE} — maximum flap extended speed

VFR — visual flight rules

VHF — very high frequency

V_{LE} — maximum landing gear extended speed

V_{LO} — maximum landing gear operating speed

VMC — visual meteorological conditions

V_{NE} — never-exceed speed

V_{NO} — maximum structural cruising speed

VOR — VHF omnirange station

VOR/DME — collocated VOR and DME

VORTAC — collocated VOR and TACAN

VOT — VOR test facility

V_R — rotation speed

VSI — vertical speed indicator

V_{S0} — stalling speed or minimum steady flight speed in the landing configuration

V_{S1} — stalling speed or minimum steady flight speed obtained in a specified configuration

V_X — best angle of climb speed

V_Y — best rate of climb speed

W

WA — AIRMET

WAAS — wide area augmentation system

WAC — world aeronautical chart

WCA — wind correction angle

WFO — Weather Forecast Office

WH — hurricane advisory

WPT — waypoint

WS — SIGMET

WSP — weather systems processor

WST — Convective SIGMET

WW — severe weather watch bulletin

WX — weather

Z

Z — Zulu time (UTC)

INDEX